# Oxford
# Pocket
# School
# Thesaurus

Editor: Robert Allen

OXFORD
UNIVERSITY PRESS

# OXFORD
UNIVERSITY PRESS

Great Clarendon Street, Oxford OX2 6DP

Oxford University Press is a department of the University of Oxford.
It furthers the University's objective of excellence in research, scholarship,
and education by publishing worldwide in

Oxford New York

Auckland Cape Town Dar es Salaam Hong Kong Karachi
Kuala Lumpur Madrid Melbourne Mexico City Nairobi New Delhi
Shanghai Taipei Toronto

with offices in

Argentina Austria Brazil Chile Czech Republic France Greece
Guatemala Hungary Italy Japan Poland Portugal Singapore
South Korea Switzerland Thailand Turkey Ukraine Vietnam

Oxford is a registered trade mark of Oxford University Press
in the UK and in certain other countries

© Copyright Oxford University Press 2007

Based on *Oxford School Thesaurus* 2002

First published 2005
This edition 2007

Database right Oxford University Press (maker)

British Library cataloguing in Publication Data available

ISBN 978-0-19-911539-6

10 9 8 7 6 5 4 3 2 1

Typeset in OUP Argo and OUP Swift

Printed in Italy by Rotolito Lombarda

Do you have a query about words, their origin, meaning, use,
spelling, pronunciation, or any other aspect of the English language?
Visit our website at www.askoxford.com where you will be able to
find answers to your language queries.

# Contents

# Preface

This new edition of a popular and widely used thesaurus has been rewritten from scratch, making it virtually a new book. It is intended to be a companion to the *Oxford Pocket School Dictionary*, and is suitable for use by students at upper primary and secondary levels. The emphasis is on language production and vocabulary building: the choice of headwords, the range of alternative words given, and the other information contained in the entries are all organized on the assumption that users will want to progress from what they already know in the language to what is less familiar but more appropriate, more precise, more imaginative, or more colourful, or all of these things.

There are two aspects to the way a thesaurus is organized: the way the entries are listed, and the organization of the synonyms and other information within the entries. The earliest thesauruses, including the famous one of Peter Mark Roget published in 1852, were totally thematic: that is, the entries were organized by themes (such as *health*, *thinking*, and *food*) and not as an alphabetical list of words. Some thesauruses still do this, but they are generally found to be difficult to use because if you are looking up a particular word you have to know which heading it appears under: so the book needs an index, and every time you look up a word you have to look in two places!

In this thesaurus, the main headwords – the words you look up – are arranged alphabetically so that you can find a particular word easily, but within each entry the alternative words (synonyms) are ordered by meanings, with those that are most useful – and closest in meaning to the headword – coming first. For example, in an alphabetical arrangement of synonyms (which is how some thesauruses are organized), the first synonyms typically given for *afraid* are *aghast* and *agitated*; although these sometimes work as substitutes for *afraid*, the most useful are *frightened* and *scared*, and then perhaps *terrified* and *alarmed* and other more powerful words. This is therefore the order in which you will find these words in this thesaurus: *frightened*, *scared*, *terrified*, *alarmed*, *fearful*, and so on.

Every meaning of a headword is illustrated by an example of its use in context. These examples are mostly based on actual usage, so that they are as natural as possible and do not appear forced and artificial. Many of the synonyms can be substituted for the headword in these examples, sometimes with some changes to the grammar of the sentence: many but not all, because a list based on total substitutability would be too limiting. This point is explained further in the following section.

There are two kinds of specially highlighted entries. The first kind is devoted to 'overused' words, very common words for which users often want to find more interesting alternatives, such as *big*, *bit*, *go*, *good*, and *nice*. We have also included a number of panels of language families, which list associated words that are not synonyms of the headword but related to it in various ways, such as the parts of the body (at the entry for *body*) and words to do with the weather (at the entry for *weather*). These lists are organized thematically, and will provide useful material for project work on particular topics.

Robert Allen

# How a thesaurus can help you

The purpose of a thesaurus is not to explain the meanings of words like a dictionary but to give you alternatives to the words you already know and use. There are all sorts of reasons why you might need to find a different word: perhaps the word you have in mind does not sound exactly right or have quite the right meaning, or it is one that is used so often that it has lost its force: for example, *nice*. A thesaurus gives you many other words to choose from: *pleasant, agreeable, enjoyable, likeable, friendly,* and so on.

## Why there are synonyms

Synonyms are words that have the same meaning, such as *close* and *shut*, and *begin, start,* and *commence*. In many cases this has happened because of the way English has developed over many centuries. The origins of the language we use today lie in older languages: Old English, the language of the Anglo- Saxons, Old Norse, the language of the Vikings who settled in parts of England in the ninth and tenth centuries, and – after the Norman Conquest in 1066 – French, or the form of it used by the Norman invaders. French is based largely on earlier Latin vocabulary, and that is why English contains such a large number of words that are related to words in Latin: all the words ending in - *tion*, for example, such as *accusation, deception,* and *position*.

These different origins of our vocabulary explain why we sometimes have more than one word for the same thing. For example, *close* is a Middle English (thirteenth century) word that comes from Old French, whereas *shut* is an older Anglo- Saxon word. Because French was the language of government in England after the Norman Conquest, some of the words taken from French belong to the world of administration and officialdom and sound stuffy or pretentious in ordinary use, for example, *commence* instead of *begin*, and *purchase* instead of *buy*.

## The special 'feel' words can have

Some synonyms mean the same as other words but have a different effect or 'feel' and make a different impression on the people who hear or read them. An important role a thesaurus can have is to provide you with more vivid or 'powerful' words. For example, *kill* is a general word whereas *slay* is mostly found in stories and dramas, and *little* is a much more affectionate and intimate word than its more neutral synonym *small* (compare *a little child* and *a small child*). Many words are loosely described as synonyms although their meanings are close rather than identical, and they are not always used in identical ways (e.g. *entreat* and *implore*, *leave* and *depart*).

## Synonyms that behave differently

The words *danger* and *risk* have close meanings, and can be substituted for each other in some sentences. You can say, for example, *There was a danger of the roof collapsing* or *There was a risk of the roof collapsing.* But you talk about something being *in danger* but *at risk*, so that although the two words are synonyms the way they are used with other words differs. The three words *accuse*, *blame*, and *charge* are all related in meaning, but you accuse someone *of* doing wrong, blame them *for* it, and charge them *with* it: the three linking words *of*, *for*, and *with* are all different. If you look at the entry for *accuse*, you will see that these three words are included in the list of synonyms, making it clear that the 'complementation' (as it is called) differs.

Other synonyms are more restricted in use than the words they might replace. For example, *enquire* and *request* are given as synonyms of *ask*, but their effect is more formal and you cannot always use them at all even for the same general meaning:

> *The headteacher asked the mayor if he would give the prizes.*
> *The headteacher requested the mayor if he would give the prizes.*
> *The headteacher requested the mayor to give the prizes.*

The second of these is ungrammatical, and the third, with its grammar corrected, does not convey the meaning of the original wording. It is important to take note of any labels in the dictionary entries (such as *formal*, *informal*, and *archaic*) that tell you about the words and how suitable they are in a particular piece of speaking or writing. If a particular synonym is more informal in use than the headword, this is stated: for example, in the entry for *deficient*, the alternative word *duff* is marked as 'more informal' because, unlike *deficient*, which is a fairly formal word, *duff* would typically be used only in informal conversation.

## Synonyms for describing words

Synonyms are most useful as more exact or descriptive alternatives for very generalized words. The following sentences all contain the adjective *nice*, which is one of the most overworked words in English:

> *He wished her a nice time in Paris.*
> *We are hoping tomorrow will be a nice day.*
> *Frank always seems such a nice man.*

In ordinary conversation *nice* will often be quite adequate in these sentences, but in more continuous speaking and writing it is useful to find alternatives to avoid repeating the same word too often. Anyone hearing or reading the word *nice* over and over again will become tired of it. Instead of *nice* in the three sentences you can say:

> *He wished her an enjoyable* (or *agreeable* or *pleasant*) *time in Paris.*
> *We are hoping tomorrow will be a fine* (or *sunny* or *warm* or *pleasant*) *day.*

Notice that *pleasant* is possible in all three sentences. It is often an improvement on *nice* but because it too is so versatile it is liable to be overused just as *nice* is.

There are some idiomatic uses in which *nice* cannot be replaced word for-word:

> *The house looked nice and tidy again.*
> *Go and have a nice little sleep.*

## Synonyms for action words

Verbs (words expressing action) are another kind of word that can have useful synonyms, for example movement words like *go* and *walk*. Often you will want to use a more colourful or powerful word such as *stroll, ramble, saunter, march, hike, tramp,* or *trek,* all of which are given in the thesaurus entry for *walk.*

## Euphemisms

Some words have synonyms that are really euphemisms, or ways of saying something unpleasant in a more pleasant way, such as *pass away* or *perish* for *die.* You need to be careful when you use synonyms of this type as the effect can sometimes be artificial and coy.

## Synonyms for overused words

In this thesaurus you will find that some entries, about fifty in all, have been specially highlighted as 'overused words': *big, bit, go, good, nice, lovely, put,* and so on. These are all words with very general meanings that can be useful for saying what you want to say, but very often you will want to find more interesting or colourful alternatives, as we saw with *nice* in the section on 'describing words' above. These are the entries that you are likely to use most often, and they are specially highlighted in this book with a wide range of examples and alternative words for you to choose from.

## Special words ('hyponyms')

Other synonyms are not really equivalents at all but are special kinds of a more general word. These words are sometimes called *hyponyms* (from *hypo-* meaning 'down' – i.e. one level of meaning 'down' – instead of *syn-* meaning 'with' or 'sharing'). There is no synonym for the word *bed* (in its furniture meaning): words like *berth, bunk, divan, futon,* and so on are not alternatives for the word *bed* but types of bed, and you can only use them when you mean that particular type (and even then you will be changing the emphasis). There is no synonym for *sing*: words like *chant, croon,* and *warble* mean particular kinds of singing but not singing in general.

## Antonyms

Antonyms are words that are opposite in meaning, such as *open* and *close, rich* and *poor, give* and *take.* There are few genuine antonyms in language, because few words allow opposite meaning (even *give* and *take* are only approximately opposite, and in some contexts are not opposite at all). Some words do not have any genuine antonyms, for example concrete nouns such as *cat* and *floor.*

Many descriptive adjectives form antonyms by adding *un-* (or sometimes *in-* or *im-* ) at the beginning, e.g. *unattractive, unaware, unbelievable, ineffective, unfair, unimportant, impossible,* and *unworthy.* Verbs can also form opposites in this way, e.g. *unblock, uncover, unfold,* and *unload.*

Some words that we might expect from their form to be opposites are not. For example, *shameful* and *shameless* mean practically the same. *Indifferent* is not the opposite of *different* but means 'not very good', and *invaluable* means 'having a value that cannot be measured', i.e. 'extremely valuable'; it is not the opposite of *valuable*, which is *valueless*.

## Choosing the right words

Whenever you use this thesaurus, make sure you choose words that suit the context you are writing for, and are neither too formal for everyday use nor too informal or casual for more serious writing. If you are unsure about an alternative, check it in a dictionary, which will give you more information about its meaning and use than is possible in a thesaurus.

The display page given below gives you the main features of this thesaurus and shows how the information is organized.

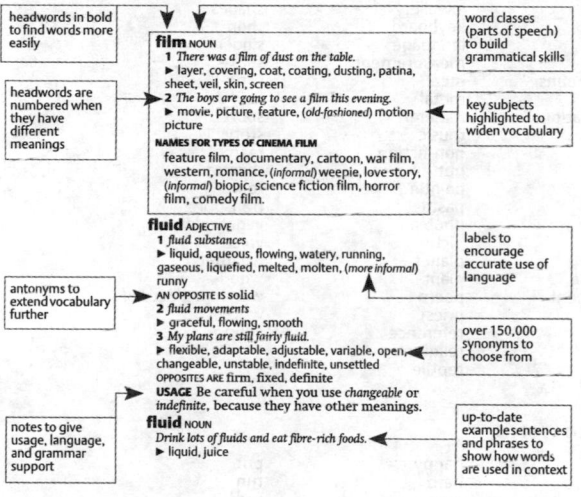

| headwords in bold to find words more easily | | word classes (parts of speech) to build grammatical skills |
| --- | --- | --- |

**film** NOUN
**1** *There was a film of dust on the table.*
▶ layer, covering, coat, coating, dusting, patina, sheet, veil, skin, screen
**2** *The boys are going to see a film this evening.*
▶ movie, picture, feature, (*old-fashioned*) motion picture

**NAMES FOR TYPES OF CINEMA FILM**
feature film, documentary, cartoon, war film, western, romance, (*informal*) weepie, love story, (*informal*) biopic, science fiction film, horror film, comedy film.

| headwords are numbered when they have different meanings | | key subjects highlighted to widen vocabulary |
| --- | --- | --- |

**fluid** ADJECTIVE
**1** *fluid substances*
▶ liquid, aqueous, flowing, watery, running, gaseous, liquefied, melted, molten, (*more informal*) runny
AN OPPOSITE IS solid
**2** *fluid movements*
▶ graceful, flowing, smooth
**3** *My plans are still fairly fluid.*
▶ flexible, adaptable, adjustable, variable, open, changeable, unstable, indefinite, unsettled
OPPOSITES ARE firm, fixed, definite
**USAGE** Be careful when you use *changeable* or *indefinite*, because they have other meanings.

| antonyms to extend vocabulary further | | labels to encourage accurate use of language |
| --- | --- | --- |

| | | over 150,000 synonyms to choose from |
| --- | --- | --- |

**fluid** NOUN
*Drink lots of fluids and eat fibre-rich foods.*
▶ liquid, juice

| notes to give usage, language, and grammar support | | up-to-date example sentences and phrases to show how words are used in context |
| --- | --- | --- |

# List of panels

## Topic panels

acid
animal
anniversary
bird
body
bone
cereal
cheese
chemical elements
clothes
coat
coast
coffee
collective nouns
colour
communication
computer
crockery
crime
dance
dinosaur
disaster
doctor
dwelling
engineering
entertainment
family
festival
fiction
fish

film
food
fruit
game
gem
government
habitat
herb
insect
jewellery
keyboard
language
measurement
meal
metal
mineral
music
non-fiction
nut
painting
pasta
phobia
picture
planet
plant
poem
priest
reference
religion
reptile

restaurant
road
rock
rodent
room
ruler
sacred, texts
sail
science
shapes
shop
singer
snake
song
sound
sport
story
team
theatre
tool
transport
vegetable
voice
weather
wood
worship, places of
writer
young

## Overused words

all right
bad
big
bit
cry
eat
end
fat
get
go
good
great

happy
hard
hit
laugh
like
little
look
lovely
move
new
nice
old

put
run
sad
say
short
small
strong
thin
very
walk

# Aa

**aback** ADVERB
**taken aback** *Mrs Diggory looked taken aback for a moment.*
▶ surprised, shocked, astonished, startled, disconcerted, nonplussed, dumbfounded

**abandon** VERB
**1** *The children had been abandoned in the war*
▶ desert, leave behind, leave stranded, strand, forsake, leave in the lurch, maroon, wash your hands of
**2** *The car was abandoned near the motorway.*
▶ leave, (more informal) dump, (more informal) ditch
**3** *The entire project had to be abandoned.*
▶ cancel, drop, discontinue, (more informal) give up, (more informal) scrap, (very informal) ditch
**4** *The company abandoned its claims to the money*
▶ drop, give up, renounce, waive, (more formal) relinquish

**abbreviate** VERB
*The medium is known as a digital video disc, usually abbreviated to DVD.*
▶ shorten, reduce, abridge

**abduct** VERB
*The woman had been abducted by two men and held for several days.*
▶ kidnap, seize, carry off, capture

**abhorrent** ADJECTIVE
*Racial abuse is abhorrent to most people.*
▶ hateful, loathsome, detested (by), detestable, repugnant, repellent, obnoxious, odious, offensive, horrifying, repulsive, revolting, abominable, disgusting, distasteful, execrable, horrible, horrid, nauseating

**abide** VERB
**1** *I cannot abide grown men walking around in trainers.*
▶ bear, stand, endure, tolerate, (more informal) stomach, (more informal) put up with
**2** **abide by** *The company expects its employees to abide by its rules.*
▶ obey, observe, follow, accept, keep to, carry out, conform to, stick to, adhere to, act in accordance with, stand by, submit to

**ability** NOUN
**1** *An unexpected inheritance gave him the ability to travel the world.*
▶ power, resources, capability, capacity, means, opportunity, potential, wherewithal
**2** *Jane's new employers had received good reports of her ability.*
▶ capability, competence, aptitude, expertise, proficiency, (more informal) know-how
**3** *You have the ability to do well in life.*
▶ capacity, talent, intelligence, skill, aptitude, flair
**4** *He has many unusual abilities.*
▶ talent, skill, accomplishment, gift, qualification

**able** ADJECTIVE
**1** *a group of the most able students*
▶ talented, accomplished, proficient, efficient, gifted, capable, clever, skilled, competent, intelligent, effective
AN OPPOSITE IS incompetent
**2** **able to** *Are you able to come?*
▶ allowed to, free to, prepared to, in a position to, (more informal) up to (coming)

**abnormal** ADJECTIVE
**1** *The tests produced some abnormal results.*
▶ unusual, untypical, uncommon, extraordinary, exceptional, unrepresentative, aberrant, anomalous, freak
**2** *He was surprised by her abnormal beliefs and behaviour.*
▶ strange, peculiar, odd, weird, curious, eccentric, wayward, perverse, erratic, queer, bizarre
AN OPPOSITE IS normal

**abnormality** NOUN
**1** *The study gave evidence of some abnormality.*
▶ strangeness, peculiarity, irregularity, oddity, oddness, aberration, anomaly, deviation, eccentricity, idiosyncrasy, waywardness, singularity
**2** *The baby was born with several abnormalities.*
▶ deformity, malformation

**abolish** VERB
*a decision to abolish the community charge*
▶ end, cancel, put an end to, (more informal) get rid of, (more informal) do away with, (technical) abrogate, annul, repeal, remove, rescind, revoke, quash, suppress, terminate, eliminate, eradicate, overturn, withdraw
AN OPPOSITE IS create

**abominable** ADJECTIVE
*The revolt was suppressed with abominable cruelty.*
▶ atrocious, appalling, detestable, hateful, odious, vile, obnoxious, brutal, dreadful, abhorrent, diabolical, disgusting, repellent, horrifying
AN OPPOSITE IS humane

**abort** VERB
**1** *The treatment caused the foetus to abort.*
▶ miscarry
**2** *The pilot had reached a speed at which the take-off could not be aborted.*
▶ terminate, cancel, discontinue, stop, end, halt, call off

**abortion** NOUN
*She decided against an abortion.*
▶ termination (of pregnancy)

**abortive** ADJECTIVE
*There had been several abortive attempts to assassinate the president.*
▶ failed, vain, unsuccessful, fruitless, futile, ineffective, ineffectual, useless, pointless, unproductive
AN OPPOSITE IS successful

**about-turn** NOUN

*The change in policy amounted to a complete about-turn.*
▶ reversal, U-turn, volte face, change of direction, change of course, change of mind, sea change

**abrasive** ADJECTIVE

*Charles had a manner that some thought abrasive.*
▶ harsh, curt, brusque, caustic, acerbic, abrupt, grating, biting, vitriolic, rough, insensitive
OPPOSITES ARE kind, gentle

**abridge** VERB

*The editor may want to abridge letters for publication.*
▶ shorten, reduce, cut, truncate, edit, trim, condense, abbreviate
OPPOSITES ARE expand, lengthen

**abridged** ADJECTIVE

*For the exam you can read an abridged version of the novel.*
▶ shortened, reduced, cut, cut down, condensed, edited, censored, (more informal) potted

**abridgement** NOUN

*In 1676 he published an abridgement of the Book of Martyrs.*
▶ short version, condensation, summary, synopsis, digest, precis

**abrupt** ADJECTIVE

1 *She gave a cry and came to an abrupt halt.*
▶ sudden, hurried, unexpected, quick, hasty, rapid, swift, precipitate, unforeseen, unpredicted
2 *Beyond the cliff edge they could see an abrupt drop.*
▶ sheer, sharp, steep, precipitous
AN OPPOSITE IS gradual
3 *He had a decidedly abrupt manner.*
▶ blunt, harsh, curt, terse, gruff, rude, offhand, brusque, insensitive, outspoken, plain-spoken
OPPOSITES ARE polite, courteous

**absent** ADJECTIVE

1 *The man had been absent from work all week.*
▶ away, off, missing, (more informal) skiving
AN OPPOSITE IS present
2 *Her eyes had an absent look.*
▶ distracted, dreamy, far-away, absorbed, inattentive, preoccupied absent-minded
OPPOSITES ARE attentive, alert

**absent-minded** ADJECTIVE

*Stephen looked absent-minded as he hurried off.*
▶ forgetful, distracted, preoccupied, inattentive, absorbed, scatterbrained
OPPOSITES ARE attentive, alert

**absolute** ADJECTIVE

1 *The house was an absolute mess.*
▶ complete, total, utter, sheer, perfect, downright, unmitigated
2 *The venture had been an absolute success.*
▶ complete, total, outright, categorical, out-and-out, unqualified
3 *Speak only the absolute truth.*
▶ definite, positive, categorical, undoubted, unquestioned

4 *The country had known only absolute rulers.*
▶ autocratic, despotic, dictatorial, tyrannical, omnipotent, sovereign, totalitarian, unrestricted, undemocratic

**absolutely** ADVERB

*You are absolutely right.*
▶ completely, totally, utterly, perfectly, quite, unquestionably, unreservedly

**absorb** VERB

1 *Wood absorbs wetness and expands.*
▶ soak up, suck up, assimilate, take in
AN OPPOSITE IS emit
2 *It is difficult to absorb so much information at once.*
▶ assimilate, take in, soak up, digest, comprehend
3 *Getting through the day absorbed all her energies.*
▶ consume, drain, exhaust, use up, take up, swallow up
4 *Special buffers absorb the impact.*
▶ cushion, deaden, soften, reduce, lessen
5 *The children were absorbed by their game.*
▶ preoccupy, engross, captivate, occupy, enthral, fascinate, interest, involve, rivet

**absorbent** ADJECTIVE

*Line the cage with a good layer of absorbent paper.*
▶ porous, spongy, absorptive, permeable
AN OPPOSITE IS impervious

**abstain** VERB

**abstain from** *They agreed to abstain from violent action for the time being.*
▶ go without, give up, forgo, refrain from, eschew, avoid, reject, renounce, deny yourself, desist from
AN OPPOSITE IS indulge (yourself)

**abstemious** ADJECTIVE

*They lead an abstemious life.*
▶ frugal, temperate, austere, ascetic, restrained, sparing, puritanical, strict, spartan, sober
AN OPPOSITE IS self-indulgent

**abstract** ADJECTIVE

1 *Abstract concepts are hard to define.*
▶ theoretical, conceptual, hypothetical, academic, notional, metaphysical, philosophical, intangible, intellectual, indefinite
AN OPPOSITE IS concrete
2 *The pieces are stitched together to form a large abstract design.*
▶ symbolic, non-pictorial, non-representational
AN OPPOSITE IS representational

**abstract** NOUN

*An abstract of the lecture was circulated in advance.*
▶ summary, precis, résumé, outline

**abstruse** ADJECTIVE

*He had spent a lifetime poring over abstruse codes.*
▶ obscure, cryptic, complex, difficult, hard, puzzling, incomprehensible, perplexing, mysterious, unfathomable
AN OPPOSITE IS obvious

**absurd** ADJECTIVE

It was an absurd suggestion.
▶ ridiculous, preposterous, ludicrous, unreasonable, nonsensical, incredible, irrational, senseless, insane, mad, anomalous, silly, stupid, illogical, incongruous, meaningless, paradoxical, untenable, laughable, (more informal) crazy, (more informal) daft, (more informal) barmy, (more informal) zany
OPPOSITES ARE reasonable, sensible

**abundant** ADJECTIVE

Luckily, there was an abundant supply of things to do.
▶ plentiful, copious, ample, liberal, profuse, generous, lavish, rich, bountiful, prolific, inexhaustible
OPPOSITES ARE scarce, sparse

**abuse** NOUN

1 The action amounted to a serious abuse of authority.
▶ misuse, misapplication
2 No society can tolerate the abuse of children.
▶ maltreatment, mistreatment, ill-treatment, misuse, (sexual) assault, molestation
3 A group of mothers yelled abuse.
▶ insults, invective, obscenities, curses, slanders

**abuse** VERB

1 Players on both sides were abusing the referee.
▶ insult, be rude to, curse, swear at, call someone names, malign, revile, defame, slander
2 He was accused of abusing children.
▶ mistreat, maltreat, ill-treat, (sexually) assault, molest, interfere with, batter, harm, hurt
3 The judge had abused his authority in his directions to the jury.
▶ misuse, misapply, exploit

**abusive** ADJECTIVE

He was thrown out of the hall for yelling abusive remarks.
▶ insulting, derogatory, rude, offensive, opprobrious, pejorative, defamatory, disparaging, scathing, hurtful, impolite, libellous, obscene, scurrilous, slanderous, vituperative
OPPOSITES ARE friendly, polite

**abysmal** ADJECTIVE

1 The service was abysmal.
▶ poor, very bad, awful, appalling, dreadful, disgraceful, terrible, worthless
2 the abysmal ignorance of science in Britain
▶ profound, extreme, utter, complete, deep, unfathomable, immeasurable, incalculable, infinite

**abyss** NOUN

There is still a deep abyss to be crossed.
▶ chasm, pit, void, gulf, crater, fissure, gap, hole, opening, rift

**academic** ADJECTIVE

1 She had spent her entire life in an academic environment.
▶ educational, scholastic, scholarly, pedagogical

2 They are academic historians and not writers for the popular market.
▶ scholarly, studious, learned, intellectual, erudite, educated, cultured, bookish, clever, highbrow, intelligent, well-read, (more informal) brainy
3 The point is of more than academic interest.
▶ theoretical, notional, conceptual, conjectural, hypothetical, speculative
AN OPPOSITE IS practical

**academic** NOUN

a group of visiting academics
▶ scholar, intellectual, professor, lecturer, thinker, (more informal) egghead, (more informal) highbrow

**academy** NOUN

The students of the academy were involved in a project to catalogue the papers.
▶ college, educational institution, training establishment, conservatory, conservatoire, university, institute

**accede** VERB

accede to He acceded to all her demands.
▶ agree to, consent to, accept, grant, comply with, concur with

**accelerate** VERB

1 The vehicle accelerated sharply.
▶ go faster, speed up, pick up speed, quicken speed
OPPOSITES ARE decelerate, slow down
2 The oil-producing countries have agreed to accelerate production.
▶ increase, step up, stimulate, expedite, promote, spur on

**accent** NOUN

1 She spoke with a distinct Welsh accent.
▶ pronunciation, intonation, inflection, tone, cadence, enunciation
2 There is an accent on the first syllable.
▶ stress, emphasis, accentuation, force
3 The accent is on economy.
▶ emphasis, stress

**accept** VERB

1 I decided to accept the offer.
▶ receive, take, get, welcome, (more informal) jump at
2 The council does not accept responsibility
▶ admit, acknowledge, bear, assume, undertake
3 Reluctantly, he had to accept the decision.
▶ agree to, go along with, accede to, acquiesce in, defer to, comply with, consent to, concur with, abide by, acknowledge, be reconciled to, recognize, resign yourself to, submit to, yield to
AN OPPOSITE IS reject

**acceptable** ADJECTIVE

1 The agreement was acceptable to the majority.
▶ welcome, agreeable, appreciated, gratifying, pleasant, pleasing, worthwhile
2 The courses fell below an acceptable standard.
▶ adequate, satisfactory, reasonable, tolerable, admissible, appropriate, passable, suitable
AN OPPOSITE IS unacceptable

## acceptance NOUN

**1** *The plan found wide acceptance.*
▶ approval, consent, acquiescence, agreement, welcome
AN OPPOSITE IS **refusal**

**2** *Their acceptance of the explanation came as some relief.*
▶ belief (in), confidence (in)

## accepted ADJECTIVE

*These artists question accepted notions of taste and beauty.*
▶ recognized, acknowledged, agreed, undisputed, indisputable, standard, unquestioned, undeniable
AN OPPOSITE IS **controversial**

## access NOUN

**1** *The away fans could not gain access to that end of the stadium.*
▶ entry, admission, admittance, right of entry

**2** *The building has no access at the front.*
▶ entrance, entry, way in, approach

## accessible ADJECTIVE

**1** *The library has been made accessible for wheelchairs.*
▶ reachable, within reach, at hand, available, convenient, (more informal) get-at-able, (more informal) handy
AN OPPOSITE IS **inaccessible**

**2** *Ministers want to be more accessible.*
▶ approachable, available, informal, welcoming

## accessory NOUN

**1** *Accessories include a remote control.*
▶ attachment, fitting, extra, addition, appendage, extension

**2** *He might be charged with being an accessory to the crime.*
▶ accomplice, associate, collaborator (in)

## accident NOUN

**1** *He died in an accident while working on his boat.*
▶ misfortune, mishap, disaster, calamity, catastrophe, misadventure

**2** *She had witnessed a traffic accident.*
▶ collision, smash, (more informal) pile-up

**3** *It was pure accident that we met that day.*
▶ chance, luck, coincidence, fate, a fluke

**by accident** *I found it by accident.*
▶ by chance, accidentally, fortuitously, unwittingly, coincidentally

## accidental ADJECTIVE

*Make sure you avoid accidental erasure of the tape.*
▶ unintentional, chance, coincidental, fortuitous, inadvertent, unintended, adventitious, arbitrary, casual, lucky, random
AN OPPOSITE IS **intentional**

## accidentally ADVERB

*We met accidentally.*
▶ by accident, by chance, fortuitously, unintentionally, unwittingly
AN OPPOSITE IS **intentionally**

## acclaim VERB

*The film has been widely acclaimed in the press.*
▶ praise, applaud, commend, cheer, congratulate, celebrate

## acclimatize VERB

*They soon became acclimatized to their new surroundings.*
▶ accustom, adjust, familiarize

## accolade NOUN

*He received the accolade of a knighthood.*
▶ praise, honour, tribute, recognition, admiration, acclamation, plaudits

## accommodate VERB

**1** *We will do our best to accommodate your wishes.*
▶ serve, help, aid, assist, supply, oblige, provide

**2** *The lodge accommodates nine residents.*
▶ house, lodge, provide for, cater for, shelter, board, take in, hold, (more informal) put up

## accommodating ADJECTIVE

*The local tourist office is very accommodating*
▶ helpful, obliging, cooperative, considerate

## accommodation NOUN

*The cost includes three days' accommodation in Bruges.*
▶ board, lodging, shelter, housing, rooms

## accompany VERB

**1** *She regularly accompanied groups of her students.*
▶ go with, escort, travel with, attend, follow, chaperon, look after, partner, (more informal) tag along with

**2** *A note accompanied the flowers.*
▶ go with, occur with, coincide with, be present with, coexist with, complement, belong with, supplement

## accomplice NOUN

*An accomplice stood at the door on lookout.*
▶ associate, partner, accessory, abetter, confederate, collaborator, co-conspirator

## accomplish VERB

*Brady believes his side can accomplish the awesome task.*
▶ achieve, fulfil, succeed in, realize, complete, conclude, bring off, carry out, discharge, attain, effect, execute, finish, perform

## accomplished ADJECTIVE

*Diana is an accomplished pianist.*
▶ expert, talented, able, skilled, gifted, capable, clever, competent, proficient

## accomplishment NOUN

*This was quite an accomplishment and she was duly rewarded.*
▶ achievement, attainment, ability, talent, skill, gift

## accord VERB

**accord with** *The theory accords with all the known facts.*
▶ correspond to, agree with, concur with, be compatible with, (more informal) square with

**accost** VERB
*A police officer accosted me in the street.*
▶ stop, approach, detain, waylay, apprehend

**account** NOUN
1 *Write down a full account of what you saw.*
▶ description, report, statement, record, explanation, narrative, version, commentary, (more informal) write-up
2 *An account for the work has come in the post.*
▶ invoice, statement, bill
3 *The damage done to the vehicles is of little account.*
▶ importance, significance, consequence, concern, moment, interest, worth, value, use
**on account of** *They stayed indoors on account of the bad weather.*
▶ because of, in view of, owing to, due to, as a result of, as a consequence of, considering

**account** VERB
**account for** *It is difficult to account for such a sudden change in their attitude.*
▶ explain, justify, clarify, elucidate, answer for, give reasons for, excuse, make excuses for, rationalize, vindicate

**accountable** ADJECTIVE
*The Minister is accountable to Parliament*
▶ responsible, answerable, subject, liable

**accrue** VERB
*The honour that is supposed to accrue from being unpaid.*
▶ result, follow, ensue, arise, stem, spring, emanate, be produced

**accumulate** VERB
1 *He accumulated information from different sources.*
▶ gather, collect, amass, assemble, bring together, heap up, mass, pile up, hoard, store up, (more informal) stash away
AN OPPOSITE IS disperse
2 *Leaves tend to accumulate in the gullies.*
▶ build up, increase, multiply, grow, accrue
AN OPPOSITE IS decrease

**accumulation** NOUN
*The book is an accumulation of work by many scholars.*
▶ collection, build-up, mass, store, supply, heap, pile, hoard, stock, conglomeration

**accuracy** NOUN
*Can we trust the accuracy of these figures?*
▶ precision, correctness, exactness, validity, reliability

**accurate** ADJECTIVE
1 *It was an accurate account of what had happened.*
▶ faithful, factual, authentic, true, truthful, close, exact, precise, reliable
2 *She took accurate notes during the meeting.*
▶ exact, precise, correct, careful, faultless, errorless, error-free, meticulous, minute, perfect, scrupulous
3 *His aim was steady and accurate.*
▶ certain, unerring, sure, (more informal) spot-on
AN OPPOSITE IS inaccurate

**accursed** ADJECTIVE
*She was determined to leave the accursed house that very night.*
▶ hateful, loathsome, detestable, damnable, damned, diabolical, evil
AN OPPOSITE IS holy

**accusation** NOUN
*There had been several accusations of cheating.*
▶ allegation, charge, complaint, indictment, alleged offence

**accuse** VERB
1 *accuse of The men were accused of disorderly behaviour.*
▶ charge with, blame for, put on trial for, take to court for, indict for
2 *accuse of The banks are accused of creating confusion among customers.*
▶ blame for, hold responsible for, criticize for condemn for, denounce for
AN OPPOSITE IS defend

**accustomed** ADJECTIVE
*Wars remove whole populations from their accustomed ways of life.*
▶ normal, customary, familiar, habitual, established, usual, common, conventional, traditional, ordinary, regular, routine, set
**become** or **get accustomed to** *The family soon became accustomed to life in the country.*
▶ get used to, adapt to, adjust to, acclimatize to, become conditioned to, become inured to, familiarize yourself with, (more informal) feel at home in

**ache** NOUN
*A nagging stomach ache spoiled the evening.*
▶ pain, pang, soreness, hurt, discomfort, twinge

**ache** VERB
*His tooth was beginning to ache.*
▶ hurt, smart, be painful, be sore, throb, sting

**achieve** VERB
1 *Students who achieve their goals will be promised jobs.*
▶ succeed in, accomplish, fulfil, complete, carry out, attain, manage, bring about, bring off
2 *They worked hard to achieve success.*
▶ acquire, win, gain, earn, get, obtain, procure, reach, score

**achievement** NOUN
1 *They are proud of their achievement.*
▶ accomplishment, attainment, success, deed, exploit
2 *We hoped for the achievement of all our aims.*
▶ attainment, realization, accomplishment, fulfilment, reaching, gaining, winning, conclusion

**acid** NOUN
**TYPES OF ACID**

monobasic acid, dibasic acid, tribasic acid, amino acid, carbolic acid, fatty acid, Lewis acid, mineral acid, nucleic acid, organic acid.

**A**

## acid ADJECTIVE

**1** *The fruit had an acid taste.*
▶ sour, sharp, bitter, tart, tangy, vinegary
AN OPPOSITE IS sweet

**2** *They had to put up with acid comments from their supervisors.*
▶ sharp, sarcastic, scathing, caustic, acerbic, cutting, bitter, spiteful, vicious, abrasive

## acknowledge VERB

**1** *They acknowledged their obligation to their predecessors.*
▶ admit, concede, accept, grant, recognize, allow
AN OPPOSITE IS deny

**2** *No one has acknowledged my letter.*
▶ answer, reply to, respond to, react to, notice

**3** *She acknowledged him with a nod.*
▶ greet, salute, hail, recognize, respond to, (more informal) say hallo to

## acknowledgement NOUN

**1** *There was an acknowledgement of a need for action.*
▶ admission, acceptance, agreement, realization, concession

**2** *Tom gave a smile of acknowledgement.*
▶ greeting, recognition, welcome, (more formal) salutation

## acquaint VERB

**be acquainted with** *Lorna is acquainted with several European languages.*
▶ be familiar with, be conversant with, be versed in, be informed about
AN OPPOSITE IS be ignorant of

## acquaintance NOUN

*Philip was just a business acquaintance.*
▶ associate, colleague, contact

## acquiesce VERB

**acquiesce in** *We found it difficult to acquiesce in such a foolish scheme.*
▶ consent to, agree to, allow, permit, concur with, cooperate with, (more informal) go along with, (more informal) okay

## acquire VERB

*His father had acquired some shares in a freight company.*
▶ obtain, get, receive, come by, gain, appropriate

## acquisition NOUN

*There will be a display of the museum's new acquisitions.*
▶ accession, addition, purchase, (more informal) buy, gain, possession

## acquisitive ADJECTIVE

*You are acquisitive, like a magpie.*
▶ hoarding, possessive, avaricious, grasping, mercenary

## acquit VERB

*The jury acquitted all three of the accused.*
▶ absolve, clear, exonerate, find innocent, find not guilty, free, discharge, excuse, (more informal) let off

**acquit yourself** *The youngsters acquitted themselves with distinction.*
▶ perform, conduct yourself, behave, act, operate, work

## acrid ADJECTIVE

*People were choking on the acrid fumes.*
▶ pungent, sharp, bitter, caustic, harsh, unpleasant

## acrimonious ADJECTIVE

*The meetings were acrimonious and badly managed.*
▶ bitter, hostile, abusive, peevish, acerbic, caustic, angry, petulant, bad-tempered, ill-tempered, ill-natured, venomous, biting, sharp
AN OPPOSITE IS peaceable

## acrobat NOUN

*An acrobat performed a back somersault.*
▶ gymnast, tumbler, contortionist

## act NOUN

**1** *It needed an act of great courage.*
▶ deed, feat, action, exploit, undertaking, effort, enterprise, operation, proceeding

**2** *The next act will be a juggler.*
▶ item, turn, performance, routine, sketch

**put on an act**
▶ pretend, dissemble, play a part

## act VERB

**1** *Jim was beginning to act strangely.*
▶ behave, conduct yourself

**2** *The large table also acted as a work area. The medicine will soon begin to act.*
▶ function, operate, serve, work, take effect, have an effect

**3** *He has always wanted to act the role of a villain.*
▶ play, portray, appear (as), perform, represent, assume the character of, characterize, enact, impersonate

**4** *It was obvious that they were only acting.*
▶ pretend, sham, fake, pose, (more informal) kid

## acting ADJECTIVE

*Henry will be acting captain.*
▶ deputy, interim, temporary, substitute, stand-by, provisional, stopgap

## action NOUN

**1** *It was a decisive action and very effective.*
▶ act, deed, step, feat, exploit, endeavour, enterprise, proceeding, effort, measure, performance, process, undertaking

**2** *Write a story with plenty of action.*
▶ activity, drama, excitement, vitality, movement, energy, livellness, vigour

**3** *The action of the play is set in medieval France.*
▶ story, plot, events, happenings, incidents

**4** *The clock has a mechanical action.*
▶ working, works, mechanism, functioning, operation

A B C D E F G H I J K L M N O P Q R S T U V W X Y Z

5 *McLeish led his troops into action.*
▶ battle, engagement

**activate** VERB
*The smaller button activates the reboot function.*
▶ operate, start, initiate, mobilize, actuate, trigger off, set in motion

**active** ADJECTIVE
1 *They were having an active time.*
▶ busy, lively, eventful, energetic, vivacious
OPPOSITES ARE inactive, uneventful
2 *She is very active for her age.*
▶ energetic, agile, sprightly, lively, spry, frisky, (*more informal*) on the go, (*more informal*) full of beans
OPPOSITES ARE inactive, lethargic
3 *Yvonne is an active member of the society.*
▶ diligent, hard-working, dedicated, enthusiastic, assiduous, industrious, committed, devoted, staunch, zealous
OPPOSITES ARE inactive, unenthusiastic
4 *Part of the old factory was still active.*
▶ functional, functioning, operative, working, in operation
OPPOSITES ARE inactive, defunct

**activity** NOUN
1 *At weekends the house is always a scene of great activity.*
▶ liveliness, action, commotion, bustle, life, hustle, animation, movement, excitement, hurly-burly, industry, stir
2 *Marketing is an activity in which all staff can be involved.*
▶ job, task, venture, enterprise, undertaking, project, scheme
3 *She enjoyed many leisure activities.*
▶ interest, pursuit, hobby, pastime, occupation

**actor** NOUN
*He was the actor who played James Bond.*
▶ player, performer, stage performer, artist, (*female*) actress, (*female*) artiste

**actual** ADJECTIVE
*Have you seen the actual damage done?*
▶ real, true, physical, genuine, definite, certain, concrete
OPPOSITES ARE imaginary, supposed, notional, non-existent

**acute** ADJECTIVE
1 *The pain was acute.*
▶ sharp, severe, stabbing, burning, intense, piercing, fierce
AN OPPOSITE IS mild
2 *There is an acute shortage of teachers.*
▶ severe, drastic, extreme, serious, dire, grave
AN OPPOSITE IS continual
3 *He was suffering from an acute illness.*
▶ critical, sudden
4 *Jenna has an acute mind.*
▶ sharp, keen, astute, shrewd, penetrating, perceptive, quick, discerning
OPPOSITES ARE dull, stupid

**adamant** ADJECTIVE
*They were adamant that we should come.*
▶ determined, insistent, resolved, resolute
AN OPPOSITE IS hesitant

**adapt** VERB
1 **adapt to** *The children have adapted well to their new surroundings.*
▶ adjust to, acclimatize yourself to, get used to, reconcile yourself to
2 *The vans are all adapted to carry dangerous substances.*
▶ modify, alter, convert, change, rearrange, reorganize, reconstruct, customize, tailor, prepare, transform
3 *The story has been adapted for television.*
▶ edit, modify, prepare, alter

**adaptable** ADJECTIVE
1 *The tool is adaptable to many tasks.*
▶ adjustable, versatile, convertible
2 *Michael is always willing and very adaptable.*
▶ flexible, versatile, resilient, amenable

**add** VERB
1 *Add all the numbers in the first column*
▶ add up, count, count up, calculate, total, find the sum of, work out, (*more informal*) tot up
OPPOSITES ARE deduct, subtract
2 *A conservatory was added in the 1930s.*
▶ build on, attach, add on, integrate, join, (*more informal*) tack on
OPPOSITES ARE remove, demolish
3 **add to** *Our shouts only added to the confusion.*
▶ increase, intensify, amplify, augment, enlarge, supplement

**add up**
1 *It was time to add up the scores.*
▶ count, count up, calculate, total, find the sum of, work out, (*more informal*) tot up
2 (*more informal*) *The story didn't add up.*
▶ make sense, be convincing, be reasonable, (*more informal*) hold water, (*more informal*) ring true
**add up to** *The costs added up to many thousands.*
▶ total, amount to, come to, make

**addict** NOUN
1 *a drug addict*
▶ abuser, (*more informal*) user, (*more informal*) dope fiend, (*more informal*) junkie
2 *a football addict*
▶ enthusiast, devotee

**addiction** NOUN
*An addiction to crisps was putting cellulite on her thighs.*
▶ dependence, compulsion, craving, fixation, habit, obsession

**addition** NOUN
1 *I'm not very good at addition.*
▶ adding, adding up, counting, calculating, totalling
2 *The porch is a nineteenth-century addition.*
▶ supplement, appendage, extension, attachment, afterthought, (*more informal*) add-on

**A**

**additional** ADJECTIVE

*The railways need additional resources.*
▶ extra, added, further, supplementary, increased, more, new, other, spare

**address** NOUN

**1** *They live at a smart address in town.*
▶ residence, location, locality, home, abode

**2** *The president gave a short address to the press.*
▶ speech, talk, discourse, lecture, monologue, (*more formal*) oration, (*more formal*) disquisition

**address** VERB

*A man came up and addressed me.*
▶ greet, hail, salute, speak to, talk to, accost, approach, engage in conversation, (*more informal*) buttonhole

**address yourself to** (*formal*) *Let us address ourselves to the task in hand.*
▶ concentrate on, devote yourself to, apply yourself to, attend to, engage in, focus on, settle down to, get involved in, tackle, undertake

**adept** ADJECTIVE

*Becoming an adept interviewer is an invaluable skill.*
▶ skilled, skilful, expert, accomplished, proficient, talented, gifted, competent, deft

**adequate** ADJECTIVE

**1** *The work must be of an adequate standard.*
▶ satisfactory, acceptable, sufficient, suitable, tolerable, competent, fair, good enough, passable, presentable, respectable
AN OPPOSITE IS inadequate

**2** *The hospital lacks adequate resources.*
▶ sufficient, enough, suitable, appropriate

**adhere** VERB

**1** *A piece of fluff adhered to his collar.*
▶ stick, cling, be fixed, be fastened

**2** *adhere to We must adhere to our principles.*
▶ maintain, observe, follow, respect, stick to, abide by, stand by, comply with

**adherent** NOUN

*an adherent of a single currency*
▶ supporter, follower, advocate, defender, upholder, devotee, enthusiast, (*more informal*) fan

**adhesive** ADJECTIVE

*a substance with adhesive properties*
▶ sticky, tacky, gluey

**adhesive** NOUN

*Fix the handle with some adhesive.*
▶ glue, paste, gum, cement, (*more informal*) sticky stuff

**adjacent** ADJECTIVE

*adjacent to the area adjacent to the fire station*
▶ adjoining, bordering, abutting, neighbouring, alongside, touching, next to, close by, nextdoor to, (*more formal*) contiguous with

**adjoin** VERB

*The house adjoins an old warehouse.*
▶ be next to, abut, border on, connect with, link up with, be next door to, touch, (*more formal*) be contiguous with

**adjourn** VERB

*The meeting was adjourned for a week.*
▶ suspend, break off, discontinue, defer, dissolve, postpone, interrupt, put off

**adjournment** NOUN

*The reason for the adjournment of the meeting will become clear in time.*
▶ suspension, postponement, putting off, break (in), pause (in), interruption, discontinuation, deferment

**adjust** VERB

**1** *You need to adjust the picture.*
▶ modify, alter, regulate, rectify, tune, vary, change, balance, amend, arrange, position, put right

**2** *adjust to The workforce have had to adjust to new procedures.*
▶ adapt to, acclimatize yourself to, accommodate yourself to, familiarize yourself with, get used to, reconcile yourself to, harmonize yourself with

**adjustable** ADJECTIVE

*The driver has an adjustable seat.*
▶ modifiable, adaptable, variable, alterable, changeable, flexible, movable
AN OPPOSITE IS fixed

**ad-lib** ADJECTIVE

*The chairperson made a few ad-lib remarks.*
▶ impromptu, extempore, improvised, spontaneous, unplanned, unprepared, unrehearsed, made-up, (*more informal*) off the cuff, (*more informal*) off the top of your head

**ad-lib** VERB

*She ad-libbed a large part of her speech.*
▶ improvise, extemporize, make it up, (*more informal*) play it by ear

**administer** VERB

**1** *The director administers an organization of two hundred people.*
▶ regulate, run, manage, direct, preside over, conduct the affairs of, control, supervise, govern, head, lead, look after, command, organize, oversee

**2** *A nurse administered medicines throughout the ward.*
▶ dispense, hand out, deal out, give, provide, supply, apply, distribute, dole out, measure out, mete out (a punishment)

**admirable** ADJECTIVE

*Their aims are admirable but will be difficult to achieve.*
▶ laudable, praiseworthy, worthy, fine, commendable, creditable, estimable, excellent, pleasing, exemplary, honourable, wonderful, marvellous, enjoyable, likeable
AN OPPOSITE IS deplorable

**admiration** NOUN

*Their achievement won much admiration.*
▶ esteem, acclaim, commendation, high regard, honour, praise, respect, appreciation, approval
AN OPPOSITE IS contempt

**admire** VERB

1 *Jill is much admired for her efficiency.*
▶ applaud, approve of, respect, praise, revere, esteem, value, look up to, marvel at, think highly of, (*more formal*) laud
AN OPPOSITE IS despise
2 *Come and admire the view.*
▶ enjoy, appreciate, be delighted by

**admirer** NOUN

*He is a great admirer of Napoleon.*
▶ fan, devotee, supporter, adherent, enthusiast

**admissible** ADJECTIVE

*The court ruled that a claim for damages is admissible.*
▶ allowable, permissible, permitted, acceptable, tolerable, legitimate, justifiable
AN OPPOSITE IS inadmissible

**admission** NOUN

1 *Admission to the gallery is free.*
▶ entrance, entry, admittance, access
2 *The statement sounded like an admission of guilt.*
▶ confession, declaration, acknowledgement, profession, revelation, affirmation, avowal, acceptance
AN OPPOSITE IS denial

**admit** VERB

1 *Some of the people were not admitted to the house.*
▶ let in, allow in, grant access, receive, take in
AN OPPOSITE IS exclude
2 *She admitted she had been to the house that morning.*
▶ acknowledge, concede, confess, reveal, declare, disclose, divulge, agree, grant, accept, allow, own up, profess, recognize
AN OPPOSITE IS deny

**adolescence** NOUN

*The problems are the normal ones of adolescence and will pass in time.*
▶ puberty, teens, youth, boyhood, girlhood, growing up

**adolescent** ADJECTIVE

*Two adolescent girls were standing arm in arm.*
▶ teenage, boyish, girlish, youthful, juvenile, immature, puerile
**USAGE** These words, and especially the last three, are often used in a way that disapproves of young people's behaviour.

**adolescent** NOUN

*The highest sugar consumers are male adolescents.*
▶ teenager, youth, juvenile, minor, youngster

**adopt** VERB

1 *The blue shirt was adopted as the official uniform in the 1930s. He asked them to adopt a more professional approach.*
▶ take up, choose, support, follow, accept, approve, back, embrace, espouse, endorse, (*more informal*) go for
2 *She already knew that she had been adopted.*
▶ foster, take in

**adorable** ADJECTIVE

*What an adorable little cat!*
▶ lovable, delightful, charming, appealing, enchanting

**adore** VERB

1 *Neil obviously still adores you.*
▶ love, be fond of, dote on, idolize, worship, cherish, admire, glorify, revere, venerate, (*more informal*) think the world of
2 *We all adore shopping.*
▶ love, like
OPPOSITES ARE hate, detest

**adorn** VERB

*The room was adorned with tapestries.*
▶ decorate, embellish, enhance, beautify, furnish, trim

**adornment** NOUN

*The room was stark and without adornment.*
▶ embellishment, decoration, enhancement

**adult** ADJECTIVE

*a medical problem associated with adult males*
▶ grown-up, of age, fully grown, full-grown, developed, mature
AN OPPOSITE IS immature

**adulterate** VERB

*The brewery was accused of adulterating its beer.*
▶ contaminate, pollute, taint, dilute, thin down, water down, weaken, (*more informal*) doctor

**advance** NOUN

*There has been a considerable advance in cancer treatments.*
▶ progress, development, improvement, headway, step, stride

**advance** VERB

1 *The column of soldiers began to advance.*
▶ move forward, go forward, proceed, press ahead, press on, progress, approach, come near, gain ground, forge ahead, make headway, make progress, (*more informal*) make strides, (*more informal*) push on
AN OPPOSITE IS retreat
2 *Computer technology has advanced in the last few years.*
▶ develop, evolve, improve, increase, grow, thrive
AN OPPOSITE IS regress
3 *Good qualifications will advance your career.*
▶ benefit, boost, further, promote, foster, assist, expedite, facilitate, accelerate
AN OPPOSITE IS hinder
4 *The Bank has agreed to advance the money.*
▶ lend, loan, pay in advance, provide, supply
5 *He advanced some interesting ideas.*
▶ present, propose, submit, suggest, adduce, cite, furnish, give

**advanced** ADJECTIVE

**1** *Advanced techniques have solved many of these problems.*
► progressive, leading, modern, sophisticated, up-to-date, forward, latest
AN OPPOSITE IS obsolete

**2** *Their ideas were very advanced for the time.*
► forward-looking, innovative, pioneering, progressive, revolutionary, trend-setting, leading, futuristic, avant-garde, new, novel, original
AN OPPOSITE IS old-fashioned

**3** *a course in advanced mathematics*
► higher, complex, complicated, difficult, hard
AN OPPOSITE IS elementary

**4** *Jamie appears quite advanced for his age.*
► mature, grown-up, sophisticated, well-developed

**advantage** NOUN

*There is an advantage in having a bank account.*
► benefit, asset, help, assistance, aid, blessing, convenience, boon, favour, gain, use, service

**take advantage of** *His friends all took advantage of him.*
► exploit, make use of, utilize, profit by, manipulate

**advantageous** ADJECTIVE

*An element of surprise can be advantageous.*
► beneficial, helpful, useful, fruitful, worthwhile, favourable, profitable, valuable

**advent** NOUN

*the advent of the personal computer*
► arrival, appearance, emergence, coming

**adventure** NOUN

**1** *His adventures had already turned him into a local hero.*
► exploit, escapade, venture, enterprise, undertaking, deed, feat

**2** *They travelled the world together in search of adventure.*
► excitement, danger, interesting times, fun, stimulation

**adventurous** ADJECTIVE

**1** *an adventurous child*
► daring, enterprising, bold, venturesome, heroic, intrepid, valiant

**2** *an adventurous time*
► eventful, exciting, challenging, dangerous, perilous, risky
AN OPPOSITE IS unadventurous

**adverse** ADJECTIVE

**1** *The request brought an adverse response.*
► hostile, unfriendly, unfavourable, critical, antagonistic, negative, uncomplimentary, derogatory, disapproving, censorious

**2** *The treatment can produce adverse side effects.*
► harmful, unfavourable, disadvantageous, unfortunate, inauspicious, uncongenial, unpropitious, contrary
AN OPPOSITE IS favourable

**adversity** NOUN

*Peter showed he was stable in adversity.*
► misfortune, bad luck, hardship, difficulty, affliction, tribulation, suffering, sorrow, misery, hard times

**advertise** VERB

*The job will be advertised in national newspapers.*
► publicize, promote, make known, market, announce, broadcast, display, flaunt, show off, (more informal) push, (more informal) spotlight, (more informal) tout, (more informal) plug

**advertisement** NOUN

**1** *There are far more advertisements on television now.*
► commercial, (more informal) ad, (more informal) advert

**2** *Let's put an advertisement in the local newsagent.*
► announcement, notice, (more informal) ad, (more informal) advert

**3** *There are advertisements all along the main road.*
► hoarding, placard

**advice** NOUN

*I could do with some advice.*
► guidance, counselling, counsel, directions, suggestions, recommendations, tips, pointers

**advisable** ADJECTIVE

*It is advisable to arrive early.*
► wise, sensible, prudent, desirable, a good idea, recommended
AN OPPOSITE IS inadvisable

**advise** VERB

**1** *He advised her to go to the police.*
► recommend, counsel, instruct, encourage, admonish, caution, warn, (more formal) enjoin, (more formal) exhort

**2** *The doctor advised a period of rest.*
► suggest, prescribe, urge, advocate

**3** *Visitors are advised that the house will close at six o'clock.*
► inform, notify, warn

**adviser** NOUN

*a personal adviser to the Queen*
► counsellor, consultant, counsel, confidant

**advocate** NOUN

**1** *an advocate of political and economic reform*
► supporter, champion, exponent, proponent, upholder

**2** *a legal advocate*
► lawyer, barrister, counsel

**advocate** VERB

*They advocated sweeping changes.*
► recommend, prescribe, advise

**affair** NOUN

**1** *The meeting was an odd affair.*
► incident, event, happening, episode, occurrence, circumstance, occasion, (more informal) business

**2** *She suspected her husband was having an affair.*
► relationship, love affair, romance, (more informal) fling

**3 affairs** *They need to put their financial affairs in order.*
▶ business, activities, concerns, transactions, operations, undertakings, interests, matters

**affect** VERB
**1** *Alcohol affects women and men differently.*
▶ have an effect on, have an impact on, influence, impinge on, modify, act on, alter, attack, change, transform, (*more informal*) hit
**2** *The sad news affected all of us.*
▶ upset, disturb, trouble, concern, move, perturb, sadden, distress, agitate, grieve, impress, stir, touch
**3** *The man affects a Glasgow accent.*
▶ assume, feign, put on

**affectation** NOUN
*His accent is an affectation.*
▶ pretence, mannerism, sham, insincerity

**affected** ADJECTIVE
*He assumed an affected voice, as though coming from God.*
▶ artificial, sham, insincere, pretentious, assumed, (*more informal*) put on

**affection** NOUN
*The friends show obvious affection for one another.*
▶ fondness, friendship, friendliness, attachment, devotion, tenderness, warmth, feeling, liking, love, (*more informal*) soft spot
AN OPPOSITE IS hatred

**affectionate** ADJECTIVE
*an affectionate smile*
▶ fond, loving, devoted, tender, friendly, kind, kind-hearted, warm-hearted, sympathetic

**affiliate** VERB
*a political group affiliated to an international organization.*
▶ associate (with), join, ally, connect (with), federate, unite

**affirm** VERB
*The government affirmed their intention to reduce taxation.*
▶ declare, confirm, assert, pronounce

**affirmative** ADJECTIVE
*The answer was affirmative.*
▶ positive, agreeing, consenting, assenting, concurring, confirming
AN OPPOSITE IS negative

**afflict** VERB
*The family has been afflicted by illness.*
▶ trouble, bother, torment, beset, burden, strike, distress, oppress, harass, vex, plague

**affliction** NOUN
*He bore his affliction with great dignity.*
▶ suffering, distress, misfortune, hardship, misery, torment, ordeal, pain, trouble, tribulation, adversity

**affluence** NOUN
*In recent years the country has shown signs of greater affluence.*
▶ wealth, prosperity, opulence, fortune, richness

**affluent** ADJECTIVE
*The more affluent houses had compost heaps in their large gardens.*
▶ prosperous, rich, well-off, wealthy, opulent, (*more informal*) flush
OPPOSITES ARE poor, impoverished

**afford** VERB
**1** *We can't afford a holiday this year.*
▶ have enough money for, pay for, manage
**2** *The area affords many beautiful walks.*
▶ provide, offer, present, furnish, give, render, produce

**afraid** ADJECTIVE
**1** *The younger children were afraid of the dark.*
▶ frightened, scared, terrified, alarmed (at, by), fearful, intimidated (by), anxious, nervous
OPPOSITES ARE unafraid, bold, confident
**2** *I'm afraid all the food has gone.*
▶ sorry, regretful, unhappy
**3** *Don't be afraid to ask.*
▶ reluctant, hesitant, shy, slow, chary (of)

**aftermath** NOUN
*There were several important tasks awaiting him in the aftermath of his election victory.*
▶ consequences, repercussions, results, effects, outcome

**age** NOUN
**1** *The grandparents were showing signs of age.*
▶ old age, senility, elderliness, decrepitude, dotage, decline
AN OPPOSITE IS youth
**2** *The Elizabethan age*
▶ era, period, epoch, days, generation, time, years
**3** *(more informal) It's an age since you were last here. We've had to wait for ages.*
▶ lifetime, long time, aeon

**age** VERB
**1** *Frank had aged in the last few years.*
▶ decline, degenerate, grow older, fade
**2** *A good wine needs to age.*
▶ mature, mellow, ripen, develop, grow older

**aged** ADJECTIVE
*an aged relative*
▶ elderly, old, senile

**agency** NOUN
*a recruitment agency*
▶ office, business, department, service, bureau

**agenda** NOUN
*The meeting had no fixed agenda.*
▶ list of items, schedule, plan, programme, timetable

**agent** NOUN
*When she became a writer she needed an agent.*
▶ representative, mediator, intermediary, broker, delegate, emissary, go-between, middleman, negotiator, trustee

# aggravate VERB

1 *The delays only aggravated the situation.*
▶ worsen, exacerbate, increase, intensify, magnify, add to, make more serious, make worse, augment, compound, heighten, inflame, exaggerate
AN OPPOSITE IS alleviate

2 (*informal*) *Their flippant remarks aggravated us.*
▶ annoy, irritate, bother, exasperate, incense, vex, irk, anger, nettle, provoke, trouble, (*more informal*) needle, (*more informal*) peeve

# aggravation NOUN

*It's not worth all the aggravation.*
▶ bother, annoyance, nuisance, trouble, hassle, irritation, difficulty

# aggression NOUN

*an act of aggression*
▶ hostility, aggressiveness, provocation, militancy, violence

# aggressive ADJECTIVE

*Lily was in one of her aggressive moods.*
▶ hostile, provocative, pugnacious, antagonistic, militant, belligerent, bellicose, argumentative, quarrelsome, attacking, violent, warlike, assertive, bullying, (*more informal*) pushy, (*more informal*) macho
AN OPPOSITE IS friendly

# aggrieved ADJECTIVE

*He sounded aggrieved and astonished.*
▶ offended, indignant, resentful, wronged, distressed, discontented, piqued, riled

# aghast ADJECTIVE

*They were aghast at the news.*
▶ horrified, appalled, shocked, dismayed, astounded, astonished, amazed

# agile ADJECTIVE

*The child was as agile as a monkey.*
▶ nimble, lithe, spry, deft, graceful, fleet, adroit, sprightly, supple, lively, acrobatic, active, limber, lissom, mobile, quick-moving, swift
OPPOSITES ARE clumsy, slow

# agitate VERB

1 *A special device agitates the clothes.*
▶ stir, disturb, shake, ruffle, stimulate, beat, churn, convulse, toss

2 *Her remark seemed to agitate her guest.*
▶ upset, alarm, rouse, unsettle, disquiet, disturb, excite, worry, confuse, trouble, disconcert, fluster, perturb, stir up
AN OPPOSITE IS calm

# agitated ADJECTIVE

*She became agitated when they did not appear.*
▶ upset, unsettled, anxious, confused, disturbed, ruffled, edgy, excited, distraught, flustered, nervous, restive, restless, fidgety, feverish, (*more informal*) in a tizzy
OPPOSITES ARE calm, relaxed

# agonize VERB

*We agonized for hours over the decision.*
▶ worry, fret, fuss, struggle, labour, suffer, wrestle, be anxious

# agonizing ADJECTIVE

*an agonizing pain*
▶ excruciating, acute, intense, severe, extreme, piercing, painful

# agony NOUN

*The victims died in agony.*
▶ pain, torment, torture, suffering, anguish, distress, suffering

# agree VERB

1 *I'll have a word with your father, and I'm sure he'll agree.*
▶ approve, consent, be willing
2 *You must agree to take six books in the first year of membership.*
▶ be willing, consent, undertake, promise
3 *I think we all agree on the action needed.*
▶ concur, be unanimous, be united, (*more informal*) see eye to eye
4 *No two versions of the story seem to agree.*
▶ match, accord, correspond, tally, coincide, conform, harmonize, fit
OPPOSITES ARE disagree, conflict
**agree on** *We should agree on a price.*
▶ fix, settle, decide on, choose
**agree to** *He agreed to their requests.*
▶ accept, consent to, acquiesce in, accede to, assent to, grant, allow
**agree with** *I don't agree with the decision to go to war.*
▶ support, advocate, defend, argue for, (*more informal*) back

# agreeable ADJECTIVE

*I spent an agreeable day with their family.*
▶ pleasant, likeable, pleasing, delightful, congenial, appealing
OPPOSITES ARE disagreeable, unpleasant

# agreement NOUN

1 *There's a large measure of agreement between them.*
▶ accord, concord, concurrence, unanimity, consensus, harmony, unity, affinity, similarity, sympathy, conformity, consistency, correspondence
AN OPPOSITE IS disagreement
2 *The two sides reached an agreement.*
▶ settlement, deal, compact, accord, pact, understanding, pledge, arrangement

# aid NOUN

*The project was largely financed from foreign aid.*
▶ help, support, assistance, relief, favour, patronage

# aid VERB

1 *an agreement to aid the poorest countries*
▶ help, assist, support, sustain, relieve, subsidize
2 *These measures will aid the process.*
▶ encourage, support, promote, facilitate, expedite

**aim** NOUN

*Our aim is to win the championship.*
▶ ambition, goal, objective, object, aspiration, plan, purpose, intention, target, wish, end, dream, hope, desire, design

**aim** VERB

1 *He aimed a gun at her.*
▶ point, direct, level, train, focus

2 *We aim to meet our targets in full next year.*
▶ intend, aspire, resolve, want, wish, seek, plan, strive, try, endeavour, attempt

**aimless** ADJECTIVE

*an aimless existence*
▶ pointless, purposeless, undirected, haphazard, random, meaningless, senseless, fruitless

**air** NOUN

1 *the air around us*
▶ sky, atmosphere, ether, heavens, airspace

2 *Open the window and let some air in.*
▶ breeze, draught, breath of air, oxygen, waft, wind

3 *She showed an air of defiance.*
▶ appearance, look, aura, manner, impression, bearing, aspect, ambience, character, demeanour, effect, feeling

**air** VERB

1 *You will need to air the room.*
▶ ventilate, aerate, freshen

2 *an opportunity to air your opinions*
▶ express, voice, utter, disclose, divulge, vent, declare, make known

**airy** ADJECTIVE

1 *The room was light and airy.*
▶ fresh, well ventilated, spacious, roomy, breezy
OPPOSITES ARE stuffy, airless, close, oppressive

2 *He looked at them with an airy confidence.*
▶ cheerful, cheery, light-hearted, nonchalant, lively
OPPOSITES ARE serious, solemn

**aisle** NOUN

*The cinema had several aisles.*
▶ gangway, passage, passageway, corridor, lane

**alarm** NOUN

1 *The woman looked round in alarm.*
▶ fear, fright, panic, terror, trepidation, apprehension, consternation, dismay, anxiety, distress, nervousness, uneasiness

2 *Suddenly the alarm sounded.*
▶ signal, alarm signal, warning signal, distress signal, siren

**alarm** VERB

*The news had alarmed us*
▶ frighten, scare, startle, unnerve, agitate, shock, disturb, fluster, surprise, terrify, upset, daunt, dismay, distress, panic, (*more informal*) put the wind up
AN OPPOSITE IS reassure

**alcohol** NOUN

*I don't touch alcohol.*
▶ liquor, drink, strong drink, (*more informal*) booze

**alcoholic** ADJECTIVE

*Certain religions may prohibit alcoholic drink.*
▶ intoxicating, distilled, fermented, brewed, potent, (*more informal*) hard, (*more informal*) strong

**alcove** NOUN

*There was an alcove with several rows of shelves.*
▶ recess, niche, bay, nook, opening

**alert** ADJECTIVE

1 *We need to stay alert driving in the dark.*
▶ attentive, vigilant, watchful, aware, circumspect, wide awake, on the lookout, on the ball, on your guard, (*more informal*) on the qui vive
AN OPPOSITE IS inattentive

2 *mentally alert*
▶ sharp, quick-witted, alive, active, acute

**alert** VERB

*We alerted them to the problem.*
▶ warn (of), notify (of), tip off (about), inform (about)

**alias** NOUN

*Jack was not his real name, only an alias.*
▶ pseudonym, false name, assumed name, (*said of a writer*) pen name, (*said of an actor*) stage name

**alibi** NOUN

*She has a cast-iron alibi for that evening.*
▶ excuse, pretext, story, defence, explanation

**alien** ADJECTIVE

1 *an alien landscape*
▶ strange, unfamiliar, outlandish, exotic, foreign, remote

2 *alien beings*
▶ foreign, extra-terrestrial, remote

**alien** NOUN

*illegal aliens*
▶ foreigner, immigrant, stranger, outsider

**alienate** VERB

*She managed to alienate all her friends.*
▶ antagonize, estrange, drive away, turn away, isolate, distance

**alight** ADJECTIVE

*The house was well and truly alight.*
▶ on fire, ablaze, burning, blazing, in flames, ignited, lit up

**alight** VERB

1 *Three passengers alighted from the train.*
▶ get off, get down, descend, disembark, dismount

2 *The bird alighted on a branch.*
▶ land, settle, perch, come to rest, touch down, come down

## align VERB

1 *The shelves are aligned in rows.*
▶ place in line, arrange in line, line up, straighten up
2 *He aligns himself with the workers.*
▶ associate, affiliate, side, sympathize, agree, ally, cooperate, join

## alike ADJECTIVE

*All the houses looked alike.*
▶ similar, identical, indistinguishable, the same, uniform, comparable, interchangeable

## alive ADJECTIVE

1 *She was last seen alive a week ago.*
▶ living, live, breathing, animate, existing
AN OPPOSITE IS dead

2 *Many of the old customs of the country are kept alive.*
▶ active, in existence, current, functioning, flourishing, surviving
OPPOSITES ARE obsolete, inactive

3 *The company is alive to recent developments.*
▶ alert, sensitive, aware (of), conscious (of), apprised (of), cognizant (of)

## allay VERB

*The report had a decisive effect in allaying public fears.*
▶ reduce, lessen, alleviate, assuage, alleviate, relieve, calm, ease, quell
OPPOSITES ARE increase, stimulate

## allegation NOUN

*There were the usual allegations of police brutality.*
▶ accusation, charge, claim, assertion, declaration, statement, testimony

## allege VERB

*She alleged that he had attacked her.*
▶ assert, affirm, maintain, claim, contend, declare, insist, state

## allegiance NOUN

*an oath of allegiance to the king*
▶ loyalty, fidelity, obedience, devotion, duty, faithfulness, (*historical*) fealty

## allergic ADJECTIVE

1 *If you are allergic to foods, you'll know what these are.*
▶ sensitive
2 (*more informal*) *I think I must be allergic to hard work.*
▶ averse, opposed, hostile, resistant, disinclined, antagonistic, unsympathetic, antipathetic

## alleviate VERB

*Medicines can help alleviate the pain.*
▶ ease, relieve, calm, soothe, diminish, reduce, lessen, dull, assuage, moderate
AN OPPOSITE IS aggravate

## alliance NOUN

1 *a political alliance*
▶ association, confederation, federation, compact, league, bloc, treaty, pact
2 *a business alliance*
▶ partnership, relationship, consortium, affiliation

## allocate VERB

*Funds are allocated to each project.*
▶ allot, assign, apportion, grant, award, distribute, set aside (for), allow, dispense, give out, share out

## allot VERB

*An extra three billion pounds were allotted to transport.*
▶ allocate, assign, apportion, grant, award, distribute, set aside (for), allow, dispense, give out, share out

## allow VERB

1 *Smoking is only allowed in certain parts of the hotel.*
▶ permit, approve, authorize, tolerate, bear, (*more informal*) put up with
AN OPPOSITE IS forbid

2 *The teacher allowed him to go home..*
▶ permit, let, authorize, give permission, enable

3 *We need to allow more time for the journey.*
▶ provide, set aside, grant, allot, allocate, give

4 *I will allow that you are right about that.*
▶ admit, concede, acknowledge, agree, grant, accept

## allowance NOUN

1 *A weekly allowance is provided for each prisoner.*
▶ allocation, portion, measure, quota, ration, share, amount

2 *He received an allowance from his father.*
▶ remittance, payment, pocket money, subsistence, annuity, grant, stipend, pension

3 *The shop will offer you an allowance for your old appliance.*
▶ discount, rebate, reduction, deduction

**make allowances for** *You have to make allowances for possible delays on the journey.*
▶ take into account, consider, bear in mind, keep in mind, remember, have regard for

## alloy NOUN

*an alloy of two metals*
▶ blend, combination, composite, compound, amalgam, fusion, mixture

---

**all right** ADJECTIVE This word is often overused.
Here are some alternatives:
1 *She seemed all right.*
▶ well, unhurt, unharmed, uninjured, in good health, safe, secure
2 *The food's all right, though not very exciting.*
▶ satisfactory, acceptable, adequate, reasonable, tolerable, passable
OPPOSITES ARE unsatisfactory, unacceptable

---

## allude VERB

**allude to** *Several speakers alluded to the problem.*
▶ refer to, hint at, make an allusion to, mention, touch on, speak of, suggest

# allure VERB
*allured by the smell of food*
▶ attract, entice, lure, tempt, coax, draw

# alluring ADJECTIVE
*She wore a stunning dress and an alluring perfume.*
▶ attractive, enticing, appealing, tempting, beguiling, seductive

# allusion NOUN
*The 'twins' are an allusion to the legendary founders of Rome, Romulus and Remus.*
▶ reference, mention (of), hint (of), suggestion (of), intimation (of)

# ally NOUN
*a political ally*
▶ associate, colleague, collaborator, partner, companion, confederate, supporter, friend, helper, accomplice, helpmate
AN OPPOSITE IS enemy

# ally VERB
*Bruce again allied himself with the English.*
▶ unite, join, band together, join forces, side, team up, form an alliance, make common cause

# almighty ADJECTIVE
**1** *Almighty God*
▶ all-powerful, omnipotent, supreme, pre-eminent
**2** *an almighty explosion*
▶ huge, enormous, tremendous, mighty, overpowering, overwhelming, big

# almost ADVERB
*The riders had almost reached her  He was earning almost a million a year by now  I was almost tempted to ask why they had come.*
▶ nearly, not quite, practically, virtually, about, just about, all but, around, as good as, approximately

# alone ADJECTIVE
**1** *The man was alone in the house at the time.*
▶ on your own, by yourself, solitary, single, unaccompanied, apart, separate, solo
**2** *She said she often felt very alone.*
▶ lonely, isolated, lonesome, solitary, friendless, forlorn, desolate

# aloof ADJECTIVE
*Michele seemed aloof and oddly tense.*
▶ distant, remote, haughty, supercilious, forbidding, cold, unfriendly, reserved, standoffish, austere, scornful, unsympathetic, unforthcoming, inaccessible, detached
OPPOSITES ARE friendly, approachable

# aloud ADVERB
*Madge read the letter aloud.*
▶ out loud, audibly, clearly, distinctly, plainly, loudly
AN OPPOSITE IS silently

# also ADVERB
*His married sister also lives nearby.*
▶ too, additionally, in addition, as well, besides, furthermore, moreover

# alter VERB
*The text of the speech had been altered to take account of the recent events.*
▶ change, adjust, modify, vary, adapt, convert, transform, amend, re-form

# alteration NOUN
*After a few alterations the typescript was ready for publication.*
▶ change, modification, variation, adaptation, adjustment, amendment, reorganization, transformation

# alternate VERB
*In a democratic system political parties alternate in office.*
▶ take turns, interchange, act alternately, swap round, replace each other, rotate

# alternative NOUN
*There is no alternative.*
▶ choice, option, other possibility, substitute, replacement

# altitude NOUN
*an altitude of 35,000 feet*
▶ height, elevation

# altogether ADVERB
*We are not altogether satisfied.*
▶ completely, entirely, fully, wholly, totally, perfectly, absolutely, quite, thoroughly, utterly

# always ADVERB
**1** *You are always late.*
▶ every time, constantly, repeatedly, habitually, invariably, regularly
**2** *He is always complaining.*
▶ forever, constantly, incessantly, endlessly
**3** *I will always remember you.*
▶ for ever, permanently, perpetually, evermore

# amalgamate VERB
*The two departments amalgamated.  We amalgamated the two departments.*
▶ combine, merge, integrate, unite, join together, consolidate, fuse, link up

# amass VERB
*The family amassed a huge art collection.*
▶ gather, collect, accumulate, assemble, hoard

# amateur ADJECTIVE
*The band was made up entirely of amateur musicians.*
▶ unpaid, unqualified, untrained, inexperienced
AN OPPOSITE IS professional

# amateur NOUN
*The players were all amateurs.*
▶ non-professional, layman, layperson, enthusiast, devotee, dabbler
AN OPPOSITE IS professional

# amateurish ADJECTIVE
*There are some very poor amateurish productions around.*
▶ unskilful, incompetent, inept, inexpert, crude, bumbling, amateur
AN OPPOSITE IS skilled

a b c d e f g h i j k l m n o p q r s t u v w x y z

## amaze VERB

*It always amazes me how dirty the place is.*
▶ astonish, astound, surprise, stagger, startle, disconcert, dumbfound, shock, flabbergast, perplex, stun, stupefy, bewilder, confound

## amazed ADJECTIVE

*The girl stood there looking amazed.*
▶ astonished, astounded, surprised, staggered, startled, disconcerted, dumbfounded, speechless, shocked, flabbergasted, perplexed, stunned, stupefied, bewildered, (*more informal*) thunderstruck

## amazing ADJECTIVE

*an amazing sight*
▶ astonishing, astounding, extraordinary, remarkable, staggering, startling, stunning, breathtaking, fantastic, wonderful, magnificent, phenomenal, incredible
AN OPPOSITE IS unimpressive

## ambiguous ADJECTIVE

*The replies were ambiguous and misleading.*
▶ confusing, obscure, enigmatic, ambivalent, uncertain, unclear, equivocal, indefinite, indeterminate, puzzling, vague, woolly
AN OPPOSITE IS definite

## ambition NOUN

**1** *young people with a lot of ambition*
▶ drive, enthusiasm, enterprise, self-assertion, zeal, (*more informal*) push
**2** *Her ambition is to become a model.*
▶ aim, dream, hope, goal, aspiration, objective, object, target, wish, desire, ideal, intention

## ambitious ADJECTIVE

**1** *an ambitious politician*
▶ aspiring, assertive, determined, enthusiastic, (*more informal*) go-ahead, (*more informal*) pushy
AN OPPOSITE IS apathetic.
**2** *ambitious ideas*
▶ grand, grandiose, large-scale, big, far-reaching, unrealistic
OPPOSITES ARE modest, realistic

## ambivalent ADJECTIVE

*an ambivalent attitude towards the new technology*
▶ equivocal, uncertain, hesitant, fluctuating, contradictory, inconsistent, vacillating, wavering, ambiguous, confused, muddled

## amble VERB

*He ambled up the road to the local post office.*
▶ stroll, saunter, ramble, wander, meander, drift, dawdle

## ambush NOUN

*The fighters set up an ambush.*
▶ surprise attack, trap, snare, ambuscade

## ambush VERB

*The gang specialized in ambushing unsuspecting passers-by.*
▶ waylay, pounce on, surprise, swoop on, trap, entrap, ensnare, intercept, attack

## amenable ADJECTIVE

*an amenable child*
▶ compliant, accommodating, agreeable, biddable, responsive, acquiescent, manageable
OPPOSITES ARE obstinate, stubborn

## amend VERB

*Some parts of the law need amending.*
▶ alter, revise, modify, change, rectify, adapt, adjust, put right, reform, remedy, correct, improve

## amends NOUN

**make amends to** *It's not too late to make amends to them for the trouble you caused.*
▶ recompense, compensate, make it up to

## amenity NOUN

*an old house with few amenities*
▶ facility, service, benefit, provision

## amiable ADJECTIVE

*an amiable old fellow*
▶ friendly, amicable, agreeable, affable, likeable, pleasant, congenial

## ammunition NOUN

**1** *The house was full of ammunition.*
▶ bullets, cartridges, shells, bombs, missiles, shrapnel
**2** *The blunder provided ammunition for the opposition.*
▶ evidence, arguments, material, information

## amnesty NOUN

*The new government granted an amnesty.*
▶ pardon, reprieve, release, discharge, dispensation, indulgence

## amok, amuck ADVERB

**run amok** *Some of the animals had broken loose and run amok.*
▶ go berserk, go on the rampage, run riot, go out of control, go crazy

## amoral ADJECTIVE

*Guy was greedy, amoral, and obsessed with power.*
▶ unprincipled, loose, lax, unethical
AN OPPOSITE IS moral.

## amorous ADJECTIVE

*Her employer had made amorous advances.*
▶ sexual, romantic, lustful, erotic, carnal, passionate, impassioned
OPPOSITES ARE unloving, frigid

## amorphous ADJECTIVE

*an amorphous mass of cells*
▶ shapeless, formless, indeterminate, nebulous, unformed

## amount NOUN

**1** *He wrote out a cheque for the whole amount.*
▶ quantity, sum, total, lot, whole
**2** *The program needs a large amount of computer memory.*
▶ quantity, volume, bulk, lot, mass, expanse, extent, measure, supply

## amount VERB

**amount to** *The cost amounted to several thousands.*
▶ add up to, come to, total, aggregate, be equivalent to, equal, make

## ample ADJECTIVE

1 *an ample supply of books and magazines*
▶ plentiful, abundant, copious, lavish, generous, liberal, rich
AN OPPOSITE IS meagre

2 *ample space for several cars*
▶ enough, adequate, sufficient, plenty of
OPPOSITES ARE inadequate, insufficient

## amplify VERB

1 *A good acoustic will amplify the sound.*
▶ louden, magnify, boost, intensify, heighten, increase, make louder, raise the volume of
AN OPPOSITE IS decrease

2 *The following notes amplify the position.*
▶ expand, enlarge on, elaborate on, develop, supplement, augment, add to, flesh out, broaden
AN OPPOSITE IS condense

## amputate VERB

*The injured leg had to be amputated.*
▶ cut off, sever, chop off, remove, truncate, separate

## amuse VERB

*Their comments amused him.*
▶ entertain, delight, divert, enliven, gladden, cheer up, make laugh, raise a smile, *(more informal)* tickle
**amuse yourself** *He amused himself by writing postcards.*
▶ occupy yourself, pass the time, engage yourself, interest yourself, immerse yourself (in)

## amusement NOUN

1 *We read the article with amusement.*
▶ mirth, hilarity, delight, merriment, enjoyment, laughter

2 *A theme park with a wide range of amusements for all the family.*
▶ entertainment, activity, leisure activity, recreation, diversion, interest, delight, distraction, enjoyment, game, hobby, pastime, sport

## amusing ADJECTIVE

*an amusing story*
▶ entertaining, enjoyable, witty, funny, diverting, pleasing

## anaemic ADJECTIVE

*Her complexion looked anaemic.*
▶ colourless, bloodless, pale, pallid, pasty, sallow, sickly, insipid, wan, weak, feeble, frail

## analogy NOUN

*There is an analogy between the human brain and a computer.*
▶ similarity, parallel, resemblance, comparison, likeness, correspondence, correlation

## analyse VERB

1 *You need to analyse your motives.*
▶ examine, evaluate, review, scrutinize, consider, study, interpret, investigate

2 *The substance can be analysed by several methods.*
▶ break down, resolve, separate, separate out, dissect

## analysis NOUN

*An analysis of the unemployment figures.*
▶ examination, breakdown, evaluation, study, scrutiny, research (into), enquiry (into), interpretation, investigation, test

## analytical ADJECTIVE

*an analytical approach to the problem*
▶ systematic, logical, methodical, rational, critical, rigorous, searching, inquiring, investigative, penetrating, questioning
AN OPPOSITE IS unsystematic

## anarchist NOUN

*a trashy novel about spies and anarchists*
▶ rebel, revolutionary, agitator, terrorist

## anarchy NOUN

*The country is threatened with anarchy.*
▶ lawlessness, disorder, bedlam, disorganization, insurrection, chaos, confusion, misgovernment, misrule, mutiny, pandemonium, riot

## ancestor NOUN

*We can trace our ancestors back to the Stuarts.*
▶ forebear, forefather, antecedent, predecessor, progenitor
AN OPPOSITE IS descendant
RELATED ADJECTIVE atavistic

## ancestry NOUN

*The family has a Spanish ancestry.*
▶ lineage, origin, pedigree, roots, stock, parentage, ancestors, forebears

## anchor VERB

1 *Several ships had anchored in the harbour.*
▶ berth, moor, tie up, make fast

2 *The lid was anchored to the sides with screws.*
▶ fasten, attach, fix

## ancient ADJECTIVE

1 *the ancient buildings at Pompeii*
▶ old, historic, early, classical

2 *ancient civilizations*
▶ early, old, historic, prehistoric (= before the time of written records), archaic, bygone
AN OPPOSITE IS modern

## anecdote NOUN

*an anecdote about an elopement*
▶ story, tale, narrative, reminiscence, *(more informal)* yarn

## angel NOUN

1 *a depiction of angels with wings and beautiful faces*
▶ archangel, divine messenger, cherub, seraph

2 *She was an absolute angel during my illness.*
▶ dear, darling, treasure, gem, *(more informal)* brick

## angelic ADJECTIVE

**1** *angelic beings*
► heavenly, celestial, divine, ethereal

**2** *an angelic expression*
► beautiful, lovely, heavenly, enchanting

**3** *angelic behaviour*
► innocent, virtuous, exemplary, pure, saintly, pious, unworldly
AN OPPOSITE IS devilish.

## anger NOUN

*Anger surged through him.*
► annoyance, irritation, crossness, exasperation, displeasure, fury, rage, indignation, temper, vexation, bitterness, hostility, outrage, resentment, passion, pique, (*more formal*) rancour, (*literary*) wrath, (*literary*) ire

## anger VERB

*Their rudeness angered all of us.*
► enrage, annoy, irritate, infuriate, exasperate, incense, vex, madden, aggravate, antagonize, displease, incite, inflame, make angry, (*more informal*) needle, (*more informal*) rile, (*more informal*) bug, (*more informal*) rub up the wrong way
OPPOSITES ARE pacify, placate, appease

## angle NOUN

**1** *a cupboard built into the angle of the two walls*
► corner, intersection, recess

**2** *We need to look at the problem from another angle.*
► perspective, point of view, standpoint, viewpoint, position, slant, approach, outlook

## angle VERB

*Angle the light towards the ceiling.*
► slant, turn, direct, point, tilt, twist, bend

## angry ADJECTIVE

*John looked angry and started to shout.  She gave us all an angry look.*
► annoyed, enraged, angered, cross, displeased, furious, irritated, irate, infuriated, incensed, indignant, outraged
OPPOSITES ARE pleased, calm

**become angry** *Eventually the witch became angry.*
► lose your temper, go into a rage, fly into a rage, flare up, (*more informal*) see red, (*more informal*) fly off the handle, (*more informal*) hit the roof, (*more informal*) go off the deep end, (*very informal*) freak out, (*very informal*) go ballistic

## anguish NOUN

*a cry of anguish*
► agony, pain, distress, torment, torture, sorrow, suffering, anxiety, grief, misery, tribulation, heartache, (*literary*) woe

## anguished ADJECTIVE

*an anguished look*
► agonized, distressed, tormented, tortured, despairing, wretched, heart-broken

## animal NOUN

**1** *Like many animals they hibernate in winter.*
► living being, creature, beast, being, brute

**2** *animals*
► wildlife

**WORDS FOR TYPES OF ANIMAL**

**vertebrates** (animals with skeleton and backbone): mammals (warm-blooded, have hair or fur, feed young on milk, e.g. humans, elephants, rats, mice, horses, cattle, deer, whales); birds (warm-blooded, have feathers and wings, e.g. sparrows, larks, thrushes, ostriches); reptiles (cold-blooded, have scaly skin, most lay eggs, e.g. snakes, lizards, crocodiles, tortoises, turtles); amphibians (cold-blooded, have thin, moist skin, young breathe with gills, adults breathe with lungs, lay eggs with tadpole or larval stage, e.g. frogs, toads and newts); fish (cold-blooded, have scaly skin, breathe with gills, most lay eggs, e.g. salmon, plaice, shark, catfish);.

**invertebrates** (animals with no backbone): arthropods (segmented bodies, hard external skeleton, jointed legs, e.g. spiders, insects, crabs, lobsters); echinoderms (spiny skin, sucker feet with a five-rayed body, e.g. starfish, sea urchin); molluscs (soft body, most with shells, e.g. snails, slugs, octopuses, squid); worms (flatworms, roundworms, segmented worms); jellyfish (body with an opening surrounded by tentacles); sponges (body like a bag with only one opening).

## animal ADJECTIVE

**1** *animal passions*
► carnal, bodily, physical, sensual
AN OPPOSITE IS spiritual

**2** *animal behaviour*
► bestial, brutish, inhuman, savage, wild, coarse, crude

## animate ADJECTIVE

*an animate being*
► live, living, alive, breathing, conscious, feeling, sentient
AN OPPOSITE IS inanimate

## animate VERB

*A feeling of excitement animated the whole team.*
► invigorate, enliven, vitalize, revitalize, energize, stimulate, hearten, activate, revive, liven up, excite, encourage, exhilarate, fire, inspire, arouse, rejuvenate, galvanize, (*more informal*) buck up, (*more informal*) pep up, (*more informal*) give a buzz

## animated ADJECTIVE

*There was a sound of animated conversation in the next room.*
► lively, spirited, excited, enthusiastic, exuberant,

heated, vivacious, high-spirited, passionate, impassioned
OPPOSITES ARE lethargic, lifeless

## animation NOUN

*They arrived full of animation and determination.*
▶ liveliness, energy, vitality, spirit, enthusiasm, excitement, activity
OPPOSITES ARE lethargy, inertia

## animosity NOUN

*There was a strong animosity between the two brothers.*
▶ hostility, ill-feeling, antagonism, enmity, acrimony, antipathy, rancour, bitterness, hate, hatred, loathing, venom
OPPOSITES ARE goodwill, rapport, friendship

## annex VERB

*The king annexed further territory during each campaign.*
▶ occupy, seize, appropriate, usurp, acquire, conquer, take over

## annexe NOUN

*the hospital annexe*
▶ extension, wing, addition, attached building

## annihilate VERB

*The army set about annihilating the whole population.*
▶ destroy, wipe out, eliminate, eradicate, exterminate, extinguish, obliterate, slaughter, raze, abolish, erase, liquidate, *(more formal)* extirpate, *(more informal)* kill off

---

### anniversary NOUN

**SPECIAL ANNIVERSARIES**

centenary (100 years), sesquicentenary (150 years), bicentenary (200 years), tercentenary (300 years), quatercentenary (400 years), quincentenary (500 years), sexcentenary (600 years), septcentenary (700 years), octocentenary (800 years), millenary (1,000 years).
**USAGE** The names for anniversaries from 300 years to 900 years are not often used in ordinary writing. It is more normal to write, e.g., 'the four-hundredth anniversary'. There is no word in ordinary use for a nine-hundredth anniversary. Note that the fifth name in the list is spelt *quater-* (from Latin *quater* = four times) and not *quarter-*.

**SPECIAL WEDDING ANNIVERSARIES ARE**

paper (first), wood (fifth), tin (tenth), crystal (fifteenth), china (twentieth), silver (twenty-fifth), pearl (thirtieth), coral (thirty-fifth), ruby (fortieth), sapphire (forty-fifth), golden (fiftieth), emerald (fifty-fifth), diamond (sixtieth), platinum (seventieth).

---

## announce VERB

**1** *The government will announce its plans next week.*
▶ make public, make known, declare, reveal, disclose, divulge, publish, publicize, broadcast, advertise
OPPOSITES ARE conceal, suppress
**2** *The presenter announced the next act.*
▶ introduce, present

## announcement NOUN

**1** *There will be an announcement from the Palace this afternoon.*
▶ statement, declaration, communiqué, pronouncement, proclamation, bulletin, dispatch
**2** *We are still waiting for an announcement of the decision.*
▶ declaration, notification, intimation, disclosure

## announcer NOUN

*The announcer gave details of the programme changes.*
▶ presenter, anchorman, anchorwoman, newscaster, newsreader, broadcaster, commentator, compère, master of ceremonies

## annoy VERB

*The comments had clearly annoyed her.*
▶ irritate, displease, anger, infuriate, enrage, exasperate, incense, vex, madden, aggravate, nettle, antagonize, inflame, make angry, *(more informal)* needle, *(more informal)* rile, *(more informal)* bug, *(more informal)* rub up the wrong way
OPPOSITES ARE please, gratify

## annoyance NOUN

**1** *Much to her annoyance, Mike had taken the car.*
▶ irritation, indignation, displeasure, exasperation, pique, chagrin, vexation
**2** *The animals in the road proved quite an annoyance.*
▶ irritant, irritation, nuisance, bother, worry, *(more informal)* aggravation

## annoyed ADJECTIVE

*His mother was beginning to look annoyed.*
▶ irritated, angry, cross, displeased, vexed, peeved, infuriated, incensed, enraged, *(more informal)* miffed, *(more informal)* put out
AN OPPOSITE IS pleased

## annoying ADJECTIVE

*His mouth curled into an annoying smile.*
▶ irritating, infuriating, exasperating, maddening, irksome, bothersome, tiresome
OPPOSITES ARE pleasant, agreeable

## anonymous ADJECTIVE

**1** *The author was anonymous.*
▶ unnamed, nameless, incognito, unacknowledged, unidentified, unknown, unspecified, *(literary)* unsung
**2** *an anonymous letter*
▶ unattributed, unsigned
**3** *an anonymous way of writing*
▶ impersonal, nondescript, characterless, faceless, unremarkable

**A**

**answer** NOUN

**1** *Our letter brought a quick answer.*
▶ reply, response, reaction, acknowledgement, riposte

**2** *The answer to the question was far from clear.*
▶ solution, explanation

**3** *Violence is no answer.*
▶ solution, remedy, way out

**4** *his answer to the charge*
▶ defence, plea, vindication

**answer** VERB

**1** *Please answer my question. Will nobody answer me?*
▶ reply to, respond to, acknowledge, give an answer to, react to

**2** *"I'm not feeling well," she answered.*
▶ rejoin, reply, respond, retort, return

**3** *A good encyclopedia will answer your problem.*
▶ resolve, solve, explain

**4** *The accused could answer all but one of the charges.*
▶ refute, rebut, defend yourself against

**5** *We have enough money to answer our present needs.*
▶ satisfy, serve, fulfil, meet, correspond to, echo, fit, match up to, suffice, suit

**6** *The police have arrested a man answering the description.*
▶ match, fit, correspond to, conform to

**answer someone back** *It was unwise to answer back in those days, however provoked you felt.*
▶ talk back to, be impertinent to, be cheeky to, contradict, (*more informal*) cheek

**answerable** ADJECTIVE

*Ministers are answerable to Parliament.*
▶ responsible, accountable, subject

**antagonism** NOUN

*She was pleased, despite her antagonism to him.*
▶ hostility, ill-feeling, animosity, enmity, acrimony, antipathy, rancour, bitterness, hate, hatred, loathing, venom
OPPOSITES ARE goodwill, rapport, friendship

**antagonist** NOUN

*Old friends and old antagonists came across one another again.*
▶ opponent, adversary, enemy, rival, competitor, contender

**antagonistic** ADJECTIVE

*The march threatened to attract an antagonistic rival mob.*
▶ hostile, opposed, ill-disposed, antipathetic

**antagonize** VERB

*They seem to be trying to antagonize us.*
▶ alienate, provoke, make an enemy of, offend, anger, annoy, embitter, estrange, irritate, upset
OPPOSITES ARE pacify, placate

**anthem** NOUN

*The choir sang an anthem.*
▶ hymn, song, song of praise, chorale, paean, psalm, canticle, chant

**anthology** NOUN

*an anthology of short stories*
▶ collection, selection, treasury, compilation, compendium, miscellany, digest

**anticipate** VERB

**1** *It was impossible to anticipate all the possible moves.*
▶ forestall, pre-empt, intercept, prevent

**2** *I anticipate that the result will be a draw.*
▶ expect, foresee, predict, forecast, foretell, hope

**anticlimax** NOUN

*After all the excitement, the journey proved to be rather an anticlimax.*
▶ let-down, comedown, disappointment

**antics** NOUN

*He was reminded of his childhood antics.*
▶ foolery, tricks, capers, buffoonery, tomfoolery, clowning, escapades, fooling, pranks, (*more informal*) larking about, (*more informal*) skylarking

**antidote** NOUN

*The poison has no known antidote.*
▶ antitoxin, cure, remedy, neutralizing agent

**antipathy** NOUN

*He expressed his antipathy to institutions of any kind.*
▶ hostility, ill-feeling, animosity, enmity, acrimony, antagonism, rancour, bitterness, hate, hatred, loathing, venom
OPPOSITES ARE fondness, goodwill, liking

**antiquated** ADJECTIVE

*Their ideas seem antiquated these days.* *an antiquated typewriter*
▶ old-fashioned, out-dated, outmoded, out-of-date, obsolete, ancient, antediluvian, antique, archaic, dated, anachronistic, old, passé, (*more informal*) past it, (*more informal*) prehistoric, primitive, quaint, (*humorous*) superannuated, unfashionable
OPPOSITES ARE up to date, modern, current, new

**antique** ADJECTIVE

*Amanda has an eye for good antique furniture.*
▶ old, ancient, antiquarian, antiquated, historic, old-fashioned, traditional, veteran (car), vintage (car)
OPPOSITES ARE modern, new

**antique** NOUN

*a sale of antiques*
▶ collector's item, curio, curiosity, rarity

**antiquity** NOUN

**1** *The place had been a harbour in antiquity.*
▶ ancient times, the ancient past, past times

**2** *a site of great antiquity*
▶ age, oldness, elderliness

**antiseptic** ADJECTIVE

**1** *an antiseptic dressing*
▶ aseptic, germfree, disinfected, medicated, sanitized, sterile, sterilized, hygienic, clean, unpolluted

**2** *antiseptic cream*
▶ disinfectant, germicidal, sterilizing

## antisocial ADJECTIVE

*Most people show some signs of antisocial behaviour.*
▶ asocial, unsociable, unacceptable, objectionable, undisciplined, offensive, disorderly, disruptive, obnoxious, uncooperative, unfriendly, troublesome, unruly, alienated, anarchic, disagreeable, nasty, rebellious, rude
OPPOSITES ARE friendly, sociable

## anxiety NOUN

1 *anxiety about money*
▶ concern, apprehension, unease, worry, disquiet, foreboding, nervousness, tension, distress, doubt, dread, fear, fretfulness, misgiving, qualm, scruple, strain, stress, uncertainty
AN OPPOSITE IS calmness

2 *She showed a strong anxiety to please.*
▶ eagerness, enthusiasm, desire, keenness, impatience, willingness
OPPOSITES ARE reluctance, unwillingness

## anxious ADJECTIVE

1 *Anxious relatives were waiting for further news. Everyone is anxious about the next few weeks.*
▶ worried, concerned, nervous, apprehensive, fearful, uneasy, troubled, distressed, agitated, tense, restless
AN OPPOSITE IS calm

2 *She always seems anxious to please.*
▶ eager, keen, enthusiastic, willing, impatient
**be anxious** *He was anxious about his work.*
▶ worry, fret

## apart ADVERB

*Their parents are now living apart.*
▶ separately, independently, on your own
**apart from** *Everyone came apart from him.*
▶ except (for), but for, aside from, besides, excepting, excluding

## apartment NOUN

*an apartment in the centre of town*
▶ flat, set of rooms

## apathetic ADJECTIVE

*They seem apathetic about the whole idea.*
▶ uninterested (in), indifferent (to), unconcerned, unenthusiastic, uncommitted, unfeeling, uninvolved, unmotivated (by)
OPPOSITES ARE enthusiastic, eager, keen (on)

## apathy NOUN

*At the general election the voters showed more than usual apathy.*
▶ indifference, coolness, lack of interest, unconcern, lassitude, lethargy, listlessness, passivity, inertia, inactivity
AN OPPOSITE IS enthusiasm

## aperture NOUN

*There was a strange window-like aperture in one wall.*
▶ opening, hole, gap, slit, vent, fissure, (technical) orifice

## apex NOUN

1 *Two poles cross at the apex of the tent.*
▶ tip, top, peak, summit, pinnacle, crest, crown, head, point, vertex
OPPOSITES ARE bottom, base

2 *Her career had reached its apex.*
▶ climax, acme, pinnacle, peak, high point, culmination, height, zenith, apogee, consummation, crowning moment
OPPOSITES ARE nadir, low point

## apologetic ADJECTIVE

*They don't sound too apologetic considering it was their fault.*
▶ regretful, repentant, sorry, contrite, penitent, remorseful, rueful
OPPOSITES ARE unrepentant, defiant

## apologize VERB

*He apologized for his mistake.*
▶ say sorry, express regret, ask for forgiveness, be penitent, make an apology, repent

## apology NOUN

*We all owe you an apology.*
▶ expression of regret, acknowledgement, confession, explanation, justification, defence, excuse, plea

## apostle NOUN

*a Christian apostle*
▶ evangelist, proselytizer, preacher, teacher
**the Apostles**
▶ Christ's disciples, Christ's followers

## appal VERB

*The level of violence appals most people.*
▶ horrify, shock, alarm, outrage, dismay, scandalize, repel, offend, disgust, sicken, revolt

## appalling ADJECTIVE

1 *Their attitude was appalling in its callousness.*
▶ horrifying, horrific, shocking, outrageous, revolting, repellent, repulsive, terrifying, terrible, dreadful, awful, unnerving, sickening, nauseating, horrible

2 *an appalling piece of work*
▶ dreadful, awful, terrible, atrocious, abysmal

## apparatus NOUN

1 *an apparatus for processing sea water*
▶ device, appliance, gadget, instrument, machine, mechanism, system, tool, (usually disapproving) contraption, (more informal) setup

2 *Laboratory apparatus can be extremely expensive.*
▶ equipment, implements, materials, machinery, (more informal) tackle, (more informal) gear

## apparent ADJECTIVE

*There was no apparent motive for the crime. A sense of relief was all too apparent.*
▶ evident, discernible, ostensible, perceptible, recognizable, noticeable, observable, obvious, clear, manifest, conspicuous, detectable, overt, patent, visible, self-explanatory
OPPOSITES ARE obscure, hidden, concealed

a b c d e f g h i j k l m n o p q r s t u v w x y z

# apparently ADVERB
*Apparently satisfied, the man leaned back.*
▶ seemingly, evidently, ostensibly

# apparition NOUN
*The white apparition turned out to be a dead swan.*
▶ ghost, spectre, phantom, hallucination, illusion, manifestation, phantasm, presence, shade, spirit, chimera, vision, wraith, (*more informal*) spook

# appeal NOUN
**1** *The radio station broadcast an appeal for calm.*
▶ call, request, cry, entreaty, petition, supplication, prayer
**2** *Packaging is an important part of a product's appeal.*
▶ attraction, attractiveness, charm, allure, charisma, seductiveness, (*more informal*) pull

# appeal VERB
**1 appeal for** *Detectives are appealing for information about the incident.*
▶ call for, cry out for, beg for, plead for, ask earnestly for, request, solicit
**2 appeal to** *Hoskins said that at first the film role didn't appeal to him.*
▶ attract, interest, please, entice, tempt

# appealing ADJECTIVE
*The prospect of a whole day with Jemima was rather appealing.*
▶ attractive, agreeable, engaging, captivating, charming, delightful, lovely, enchanting
OPPOSITES ARE unappealing, disagreeable

# appear VERB
**1** *A large building appeared in the distance.*
▶ come into view, come into sight, be seen, arise, loom up
OPPOSITES ARE disappear, vanish
**2** *By lunchtime the twins still hadn't appeared.*
▶ arrive, come, make an appearance, put in an appearance, (*more informal*) show your face, (*more informal*) show up, (*more informal*) turn up
**3** *A few problems have appeared since we last met.*
▶ emerge, arise, develop, come to light, materialize, occur, (*more informal*) crop up, (*more informal*) turn up
**4** *The road did not appear to lead anywhere.*
▶ seem, look, turn out
**5** *Jake's sister was appearing in the school play for the first time.*
▶ perform, take part, act

# appearance NOUN
**1** *His scruffy appearance took us by surprise.*
▶ look, looks, aspect, bearing, demeanour, impression
**2** *an appearance of friendliness*
▶ semblance, air, pretence, illusion, facade, guise, veneer

# appease VERB
*The gift was an attempt to appease him.*
▶ placate, calm, win over, assuage, mollify, pacify, conciliate, propitiate, reconcile, soothe, quiet, (*more informal*) sweeten
AN OPPOSITE IS anger

# appendix NOUN
*an appendix to a book*
▶ addendum, supplement, addition, annexe, postscript, rider

# appetite NOUN
**1** *A long walk will sharpen our appetites.*
▶ hunger, need for food, taste buds
**2** *Her appetite for information was phenomenal.*
▶ craving, longing, yearning, eagerness, hankering (after), desire, passion, thirst, relish, zest, demand

# appetizing ADJECTIVE
*The woman brought in a large appetizing meal.*
▶ tasty, delicious, inviting, palatable, (*more informal*) mouth-watering

# applaud VERB
**1** *The audience applauded loudly.*
▶ clap, cheer, give an ovation, acclaim, show your approval, (*more informal*) bring the house down
OPPOSITES ARE boo, hiss
**2** *They were watching and applauding the youngsters' efforts.*
▶ acclaim, commend, praise, salute, congratulate, compliment, eulogize, extol, (*more formal*) laud
AN OPPOSITE IS criticize

# applause NOUN
**1** *There was a great round of applause when the dance ended.*
▶ clapping, cheering, acclamation, (an) ovation, plaudits, approval
**2** *The author wins universal applause from his followers.*
▶ praise, acclaim, approval, acclamation, plaudits, accolades, admiration

# appliance NOUN
*There's no reason why you shouldn't use individual heating appliances.*
▶ device, apparatus, gadget, instrument, machine, mechanism, system, tool, (*usually disapproving*) contraption, (*more informal*) setup

# applicable ADJECTIVE
*The law is not applicable in all cases.*
▶ appropriate, relevant, pertinent, apposite, germane

# applicant NOUN
*The best applicant was a female graduate with fresh ideas.*
▶ candidate, contender, interviewee, competitor, entrant, participant, aspirant

# application NOUN
**1** *an application for a grant*
▶ request, appeal, claim
**2** *the application of new solutions to old problems*
▶ implementation, employment, use, exercise
**3** *A degree is a sign that you have the application needed to hold down a job.*
▶ diligence, conscientiousness, industry, dedication, commitment, perseverance, endurance, stamina

# apply VERB

1 *Apply antiseptic cream to the cut.*
▶ administer, bring into contact, lay on, put on, spread

2 *Contestants will need to apply all their skill and experience.*
▶ employ, exercise, use, utilize, bring into use, implement, practise

**apply for** *More than a hundred people have applied for the job.*
▶ put in an application for, seek, request, (more informal) put in for

**apply to** *The rules only apply to England and Wales.*
▶ be relevant to, pertain to, refer to, relate to, appertain to, concern, affect, involve

**apply yourself**
▶ concentrate, exert yourself, be diligent, be assiduous, be industrious, work hard, make an effort, persevere, (more informal) buckle down

# appoint VERB

*Amanda had been appointed store manager.*
▶ name, nominate, designate, choose (to be), engage (as), take on (as), install (as)

# appointment NOUN

1 *June had to rush to keep her five o'clock appointment.*
▶ engagement, assignation, arrangement, consultation, session, date, fixture, meeting, rendezvous, (in poetry) tryst

2 *the appointment of new members of staff*
▶ nomination, selection, choice, choosing, commissioning, election, naming

3 *Frank held an appointment at the University.*
▶ position, post, job, situation, office, place

# appraisal NOUN

*The article is an honest appraisal of the problems.*
▶ assessment, evaluation, estimation, valuation, review, rating, consideration, appreciation

# appraise VERB

*They stood back to appraise the work they had done.*
▶ assess, evaluate, estimate, review, consider, (more informal) size up

# appreciable ADJECTIVE

*an appreciable sum of money*
▶ considerable, substantial, significant, sizeable, large, (more informal) tidy

# appreciate VERB

1 *I'd appreciate any help you can give me.*
▶ be grateful for, value, welcome, prize, regard highly, esteem
OPPOSITES ARE think little of, despise, disparage

2 *We appreciate good music.*
▶ enjoy, value, cherish, respect, treasure, like, think highly of
OPPOSITES ARE despise, dislike

3 *I appreciate that you cannot stay long.*
▶ recognize, realize, understand, acknowledge, comprehend, know, apprehend, see
OPPOSITES ARE be unaware of, disregard

4 *Most properties in the area have appreciated in value.*
▶ increase, gain, rise, go up, grow, improve, build up, escalate, mount, soar, strengthen
OPPOSITES ARE depreciate, decrease, fall, go down, weaken

# appreciation NOUN

1 *They showed their appreciation by taking us out to dinner.*
▶ gratitude, indebtedness, thanks, obligation, thankfulness

2 *an appreciation of good literature*
▶ enjoyment, understanding

# appreciative ADJECTIVE

*We are appreciative of all your efforts.*
▶ grateful (for), thankful (for), indebted (for)
OPPOSITES ARE unappreciative, ungrateful

# apprehension NOUN

*A run of bad luck left him with great apprehension about the future.*
▶ anxiety, concern, unease, worry, disquiet, foreboding, nervousness, tension, distress, doubt, dread, fear, fretfulness, misgiving, uncertainty

# apprehensive ADJECTIVE

*Polly was apprehensive about going back up on deck.*
▶ anxious, worried, concerned, nervous, fearful, uneasy, troubled, distressed, agitated, tense, restless

# apprentice NOUN

*James joined his uncle's engineering firm as an apprentice.*
▶ trainee, learner, novice, beginner, probationer, pupil, starter, (humorous) tiro

# apprise VERB

*He promised to apprise them fully of any developments.*
▶ inform, notify, advise, enlighten (about), keep posted (about), update (on)

# approach NOUN

1 *Flowers in the park announced the approach of spring.*
▶ arrival, coming, advance, appearance, nearing, imminence, advent
OPPOSITES ARE retreat, departure

2 *The most beautiful approach to the city is from the south.*
▶ access, passage, road, way in, entry, entrance, drive

3 *His approach was to try out new ideas on other people.*
▶ method, procedure, technique, way, system, course, manner, means, style, mode

4 *We need an international approach to problems such as global warming.*
▶ attitude, perspective, policy (for, regarding), outlook (on), point of view (on), viewpoint (on)

5 *I made an informal approach to the bank manager*
▶ appeal, application, invitation, offer, overture, proposal, proposition

# A

## approach VERB

1 *A grinning dark-haired youth approached them, holding out his hand.*
▶ move towards, proceed towards, come towards, go towards, come near, draw near, advance on, bear down on, near

2 *The committee approached its task with determination.*
▶ set about, tackle, embark on, make a start on, begin, undertake, get down to

3 *Should we approach the bank manager about a loan?*
▶ contact , speak to, sound out, appeal to

4 *The likely cost was now approaching several millions.*
▶ border on, get near, get close to, verge on, approximate, (*more informal*) get on for

## approachable ADJECTIVE

*She looked younger and more approachable.*
▶ friendly, welcoming, well-disposed, congenial, cordial, agreeable, pleasant, obliging, communicative, accessible, affable, informal, kind, open, sociable, sympathetic, (*more informal*) unstuffy, (*more informal*) matey
OPPOSITES ARE aloof, formal

## appropriate ADJECTIVE

1 *This isn't an appropriate time to ask questions.*
▶ suitable, fitting, proper, apt

2 *The form should be completed with any appropriate comments.*
▶ relevant, apposite, pertinent, applicable, germane
OPPOSITES ARE inappropriate, irrelevant

## approval NOUN

1 *Jane looked at them with approval.*
▶ favour, approbation, admiration, support, appreciation, commendation, acclaim, acclamation, applause, respect, regard, esteem, liking
OPPOSITES ARE disapproval, disfavour

2 *Congress had given final approval to the bill in October.*
▶ consent, assent, support, agreement, endorsement, acceptance, authorization, acquiescence, (*more informal*) blessing, (*more informal*) (the) go-ahead, (*more informal*) (the) green light, (*more informal*) OK, (*more informal*) thumbs up
OPPOSITES ARE refusal, veto

## approve VERB

1 *Some members are thought to have approved the plan.*
▶ support, accept, agree to, assent to, consent to, acquiesce in, accede to, endorse, back, subscribe to, authorize
OPPOSITES ARE refuse, veto

2 **approve of** *Some parents and teachers still do not approve of the use of calculators.*
▶ welcome, favour, endorse, advocate, support, hold with, countenance, tolerate, recommend, (*more informal*) go along with
OPPOSITES ARE disapprove of, condemn, reject

## approximate ADJECTIVE

*All measurements are approximate.*
▶ rough, estimated, close, inexact, near
AN OPPOSITE IS exact

## approximately ADVERB

*Homework should last approximately an hour.*
▶ roughly, about, round about, around, more or less, nearly, in the region of, in the order of, approaching, (*more informal*) something like, (*more informal*) ... or so, (*more informal*) ... or thereabouts, (*much more informal*) pushing, (*literary*) nigh on

## apt ADJECTIVE

1 *He tried to think of an apt reply.*
▶ appropriate, suitable, fitting, proper

2 *The old man is apt to fall asleep in the evening.*
▶ inclined, liable, prone, likely

## aptitude NOUN

*an aptitude for dancing*
▶ talent, gift, flair, ability, genius, faculty, capacity

## arable ADJECTIVE

*arable land*
▶ cultivated, cultivable, cultivatable, productive
AN OPPOSITE IS infertile

## arbitrary ADJECTIVE

1 *Decisions can appear arbitrary without all the information.*
▶ random, irrational, indiscriminate, capricious, unreasonable, unpredictable, whimsical, wilful, casual, chance, fanciful, illogical, subjective
OPPOSITES ARE methodical, rational

2 *the exercise of arbitrary power*
▶ autocratic, despotic, dictatorial, absolute, unrestrained, high-handed, oppressive, repressive, imperious, summary, tyrannical, tyrannous

## arbitrate VERB

*The ambassador offered to arbitrate in the dispute.*
▶ adjudicate, judge, intercede, mediate, negotiate, pass judgement, referee, umpire, settle, make peace, decide the outcome

## arbitration NOUN

*The county court will automatically refer the matter to arbitration.*
▶ mediation, negotiation, conciliation, adjudication, judgement, settlement

## arbitrator NOUN

*An independent arbitrator will review all the facts of the case.*
▶ adjudicator, mediator, arbiter, intermediary, judge, go-between, negotiator, ombudsman, peacemaker, referee, umpire, (*more informal*) troubleshooter

## arch NOUN

*The entrance consists of a high stone arch.*
▶ archway, arc, bridge, vault, curve

## arch VERB

*The cat arched its back*
▶ curve, arc, bend, bow

**archaic** ADJECTIVE

1 *archaic Greek sculpture*
▶ ancient, old, primitive
2 *He arrived in a top hat and morning coat, already a somewhat achaic form of working dress.*
▶ old-fashioned, antiquated, outmoded, obsolete

**architect** NOUN

*Ictinus, architect of the Parthenon*
▶ builder, master builder, designer, planner

**archives** NOUN

*Bernard said he would go to the archives and read the files for himself.*
▶ records, annals, chronicles, documents, libraries, papers

**ardent** ADJECTIVE

*ardent admirers of good music*
▶ passionate, avid, fervent, zealous, eager, keen, enthusiastic

**ardour** NOUN

*She spoke about her travels with all the ardour of youth.*
▶ fervour, eagerness, intensity, enthusiasm, excitement, passion, vigour, energy, spirit, keenness, zeal, warmth

**arduous** ADJECTIVE

*an arduous journey over the hills*
▶ exhausting, tiring, punishing, onerous, demanding, daunting, rigorous, tough
OPPOSITES ARE easy, effortless

**area** NOUN

1 *They came to an open area of land.*
▶ expanse, extent, stretch, patch, tract, sector, sheet, space, surface, width, breadth
2 *More money is needed for deprived urban areas.*
▶ district, region, sector, locality, neighbourhood, precinct, vicinity, zone, environment, environs, province, territory
3 *an area of study*
▶ field, domain, sphere, subject

**arena** NOUN

1 *A new sports arena will be built in time for the games.*
▶ stadium, ground, park, pitch, field, playing area, ring, rink, amphitheatre
2 *She wanted to be more active in the political arena.*
▶ scene, sphere, domain, realm

**arguable** ADJECTIVE

*It is arguable that the official figures exaggerate the unemployment problem.*
▶ possible, conceivable, tenable, credible, defensible

**argue** VERB

1 *The children do seem to argue a lot.*
▶ quarrel, squabble, wrangle, bicker, row
2 *The group argued late into the night.*
▶ deliberate, discuss, debate, dispute
3 *Some people argue that all ownership is theft.*
▶ contend, maintain, postulate, assert, claim, submit, suggest, reason, insist, show, demonstrate, prove

**argument** NOUN

1 *A fierce argument followed.*
▶ quarrel, disagreement, squabble, row, wrangle, altercation, difference, dispute, dissension, clash, controversy, feud, fight, remonstration, expostulation, (*more informal*) set-to
2 *a long argument about politics*
▶ discussion, debate, consultation, deliberation
3 *No convincing argument has been offered.*
▶ case, line of reasoning, demonstration, hypothesis, defence, gist, idea, summary, synopsis, view
4 *the principal argument of the book*
▶ thesis, contention, theme, topic, plot

**argumentative** ADJECTIVE

*He could be difficult and argumentative at times.*
▶ quarrelsome, combative, contentious, disputatious, truculent, aggressive

**arid** ADJECTIVE

*an arid landscape*
▶ barren, parched, desert, dry, waste, waterless, infertile, lifeless, sterile, torrid, unproductive
OPPOSITES ARE fertile, lush

**arise** VERB

1 *If any problems arise go and see your doctor.*
▶ emerge, develop, appear, come to light, materialize, occur, (*more informal*) crop up, (*more informal*) turn up
2 *The misunderstanding arose from poor communications.*
▶ result, originate, stem, derive, spring, follow, ensue, proceed
3 (*more formal*) *The animal arose and began to walk.*
▶ rise, stand up, get up, spring up, jump up, get to your feet

**aristocrat** NOUN

*an aristocrat from an old family*
▶ noble, nobleman, noblewoman, lord, lady, peer, peeress, patrician, grandee, titled person, (*more informal*) toff, (*more informal*) nob

**aristocratic** ADJECTIVE

*a member of an aristocratic family*
▶ noble, upper-class, high-born, titled, patrician, blue-blooded, lordly, princely, royal, courtly, élite, thoroughbred

**arm** NOUN

*the political arm of the movement*
▶ branch, section, division, wing, offshoot

**arm** VERB

*The woman had gone downstairs, armed with an empty bottle.*
▶ equip, provide, protect, supply, fortify, furnish

**A**

**armada** NOUN

*an armada of heavily-armed warships*
▶ fleet, flotilla, navy, squadron, task force

**armistice** NOUN

*Fighting ended with an armistice.*
▶ ceasefire, suspension of hostilities, cessation of hostilities, truce, agreement, peace, treaty, peace treaty

**armour** NOUN

1 *a knight in armour*
▶ chain mail, mail

2 *an animal's armour*
▶ protective covering, sheathing, shield, protection

**armoury** NOUN

*an armoury of weapons*
▶ arsenal, arms depot, depot, ordnance depot, magazine, stockpile, ammunition dump

**army** NOUN

1 *The king raised an army of ten thousand foot soldiers.*
▶ armed force, fighting force, force, militia, horde
RELATED ADJECTIVE military

2 *An army of tourists*
▶ crowd, swarm, throng, horde, stream, mass, herd, host, multitude

**aroma** NOUN

*an aroma of fresh coffee*
▶ smell, fragrance, odour, bouquet, perfume, scent, (*more informal*) whiff

**arouse** VERB

*The proposals aroused strong public hostility.*
▶ rouse, cause, kindle, prompt, provoke, instigate, spark off, stimulate, stir up, (*more informal*) whip up
AN OPPOSITE IS allay

**arrange** VERB

1 *It was time to arrange the seating for dinner.*
▶ organize, set out, lay out, sort out, put in order, plan, fix, order, spread out, dispose

2 *We hope to arrange an outing for next week.*
▶ organize, fix, fix up, plan, set up, make arrangements for, devise, schedule, contrive, coordinate, manage, prepare, see to, settle

3 *Ravel arranged the music for an orchestra.*
▶ adapt, score, set, harmonize, orchestrate

**arrangement** NOUN

1 *They've changed the arrangement of the furniture.*
▶ positioning, layout, placing, planning, spacing, disposition, distribution, organization, setting out, alignment, display, grouping, design

2 *an arrangement to share the costs*
▶ agreement, understanding, settlement, compact, contract, deal, pact, scheme, terms

3 *a musical arrangement*
▶ adaptation, setting, harmonization, orchestration, version

**array** NOUN

*a gleaming array of vintage cars*
▶ arrangement, display, presentation, show, exhibition, parade, collection, muster, (*more informal*) line-up

**array** VERB

1 *A picnic was arrayed on rugs on the ground.*
▶ arrange, lay out, spread out, display, assemble

2 *We were arrayed in our best clothes.*
▶ dress, attire, clothe, deck out, adorn, fit out, garb, robe, wrap, decorate, (*more informal*) get up, (*more informal*) rig out

**arrest** VERB

1 *Police arrested him for shoplifting.*
▶ apprehend, detain, take into custody, take in, (*more informal*) book, (*more informal*) pull in, (*more informal*) pick up, (*more informal*) nick, (*more informal*) nab

2 *Recent measures have arrested the spread of disease.*
▶ check, stop, end, halt, prevent, retard, slow, stem, impede, slow down, block, inhibit, interrupt, delay, hinder, obstruct

**arrival** NOUN

1 *A crowd awaited the Queen's arrival.*
▶ coming, appearance, approach, entrance, homecoming, landing, return, touchdown

2 *Pretty girls greeted the new arrivals.*
▶ comer, caller, newcomer, visitor

**arrive** VERB

1 *Guests started to arrive at around six o'clock.*
▶ come, come along, appear, enter, present yourself, (*more informal*) turn up, (*more informal*) roll up, (*more informal*) show up

2 (*informal*) *When they got the invitation they knew they had arrived.*
▶ succeed, be successful, reach the top, break through, (*more informal*) make it

**arrive at** VERB *We arrived at the bus station.*
▶ reach, come to, get to, (*more informal*) make

**arrogance** NOUN

*His arrogance took her breath away.*
▶ haughtiness, conceit, self-importance, high-handedness, condescension, disdain, insolence

**arrogant** ADJECTIVE

*He was proud, and had an arrogant manner.*
▶ haughty, conceited, self-important, high-handed, lordly, overbearing, boastful, scornful, condescending, supercilious, superior, bumptious, disdainful, cavalier, imperious, insolent, pompous, presumptuous, proud, snobbish, vain, (*more informal*) hoity-toity, (*more informal*) cocky, (*more informal*) high and mighty, (*more informal*) stuck-up
AN OPPOSITE IS modest

**arsenal** NOUN

*Both countries have arsenals of nuclear weapons.*
▶ armoury, arms depot, depot, ordnance depot, magazine, stockpile, ammunition dump

**art** NOUN

1 *She had done an art course.*
▶ fine art, painting, sculpture, drawing, artistry, artwork, craft, craftsmanship, draughtsmanship
2 *the art of writing*
▶ skill, craft, talent, technique, aptitude, gift, knack, expertise, facility, knack, proficiency, trick, cleverness, dexterity

**article** NOUN

1 *various household articles*
▶ object, item, thing, commodity, product, (*in plural*) goods
2 *I read an article on the subject.*
▶ essay, report, paper, study, feature, review, account, piece

**articulate** ADJECTIVE

*a most articulate speaker*
▶ eloquent, fluent, lucid, expressive, intelligible, clear, coherent, comprehensible, distinct
OPPOSITES ARE inarticulate, unintelligible

**articulate** VERB

*It is not easy to articulate your feelings.*
▶ express, voice, state, speak, say, communicate, utter, declare, set forth, pronounce

**artificial** ADJECTIVE

1 *artificial light  artificial trees*
▶ synthetic, imitation, simulated, unnatural, man-made, manufactured, false, fake, substitute
AN OPPOSITE IS natural
2 *an artificial smile*
▶ false, spurious, affected, fake, feigned, assumed, pretended, bogus, contrived, counterfeit, factitious, pseudo, sham, simulated, unreal, (*more informal*) phoney, (*more informal*) put on
AN OPPOSITE IS genuine

**artist** NOUN

1 *The artist used a wide range of colour.*
▶ painter, sculptor, craftsman, craftswoman, designer
2 *a music-hall artist*
▶ performer

**artistic** ADJECTIVE

*Desktop publishing requires artistic skills.  The designs looked very artistic.*
▶ creative, imaginative, aesthetic, decorative, ornamental, tasteful, stylish, elegant, beautiful, attractive, cultured
OPPOSITES ARE crude, ugly

**ascend** VERB

1 *He ascended the stairs.*
▶ climb, climb up, go up, come up, mount, move up, scale
2 *The little plane began slowly to ascend.*
▶ rise, soar, take off, lift off, fly up

3 *An unmade road ascends to the church.*
▶ climb, slope up
AN OPPOSITE IS descend

**ascent** NOUN

*A gradual ascent made the walk more arduous.*
▶ rise, slope, gradient, hill, incline, climb, elevation, ramp
AN OPPOSITE IS descent

**ascertain** VERB

*The police had to ascertain whether Darren had actually entered the room.*
▶ find out, establish, confirm, determine, discover, learn, make certain, make sure, settle, verify, identify

**ascribe** VERB

*The inquest ascribed his death to natural causes.*
▶ attribute, assign, put down, blame (on), connect (with), associate (with)

**ash** NOUN

*Ash from a fire lay in the hearth.*
▶ cinders, clinker, embers, burnt remains

**ashamed** ADJECTIVE

1 *She was ashamed of her outburst of bad temper.*
▶ sorry (for), apologetic (about), remorseful (about), contrite (about), repentant (about), shamefaced (about), abashed (about), penitent (about), embarrassed (about), distressed (about), upset (about), conscience-stricken (about), discomfited (about), mortified (about), red-faced (about), chastened (about), rueful (about)
OPPOSITES ARE unrepentant, unabashed
2 *He seemed too ashamed to admit his mistake.*
▶ reticent, reluctant, loath, unwilling, bashful, shy, diffident, hesitant, embarrassed, modest, prudish, self-conscious, sheepish
OPPOSITES ARE proud, shameless

**ask** VERB

1 *I'll ask him what he means.*
▶ enquire, (*of somebody*), quiz (somebody about)
2 *They want to ask a few questions.*
▶ pose, put, raise, submit
3 *Ask them to fetch help.*
▶ entreat, request, implore, beg, solicit, exhort, urge, plead with, (*literary*) beseech, (*literary*) enjoin
4 *We could ask them to dinner.*
▶ invite, summon, (*more formal*) request the pleasure of the company of

**ask for** *Don't hesitate to ask for anything you need.*
▶ request, demand, seek
**ask for** *The remarks were asking for trouble.*
▶ look for, provoke, invite, attract, court, incite, tempt, cause, encourage, generate, (*more informal*) stir up

**asleep** ADJECTIVE

*The girls were asleep in bed.*
▶ sleeping, slumbering, dozing, napping, (*more informal*) out like a light, (*more informal*) dead to the world

# A

**aspect** NOUN

1 *The article describes every aspect of life in deprived areas.*
▶ feature, facet, characteristic, side, angle, respect, particular, circumstance, detail, standpoint

2 *Dark stone gave the facade a grim aspect.*
▶ appearance, look, air

3 *The house has a southern aspect*
▶ outlook, view, prospect, exposure, orientation, direction, position, situation

**aspersions** NOUN

**cast aspersions on** *The remarks are not intended to cast any aspersions on your honesty.*
▶ criticize, disparage, denigrate, belittle, vilify, deprecate, poor scorn on, decry, condemn, malign, discredit, stigmatize, denounce

**aspiration** NOUN

*Giotto, the artist who Matisse said was the peak of his aspiration.*
▶ ambition, hope, desire, wish, longing, purpose, aim, goal, target, objective, object, dream

**aspire** VERB

**aspire to** *They aspired to be back in the city to which they belonged. We can aspire to a higher and fuller life.*
▶ aim to or for, wish to or for, want, yearn to or for, strive (after), seek (to), long to or for, desire to, crave to or for, dream of, hope to or for, pursue, set your sights on, have ambitions to or for

**aspiring** ADJECTIVE

*aspiring young writers*
▶ would-be, intending, aspirant, budding, hopeful, eager, potential

**assault** VERB

*He was prosecuted for assaulting a police officer.*
▶ attack , hit, strike, set upon, beat up, fall on, molest, *(more informal)* rough up

**assault** NOUN

*an assault on the enemy position*
▶ attack , onslaught, strike, offensive, raid, foray, sortie, charge

**assemble** VERB

1 *A crowd began to assemble.*
▶ gather, congregate, come together, collect, converge, convene, crowd together, rally, rally round, meet, flock together, join up, swarm, muster, throng round, accumulate

2 *We assembled our belongings in the hall. The general assembled his forces.*
▶ gather, collect together, bring together, amass, convene, get together, round up, marshal, mobilize, muster, pile up, rally
OPPOSITES ARE disperse, scatter

3 *Few cars are now assembled in Britain.*
▶ build, construct, manufacture, produce, put together, erect, fabricate, fit together, make, piece together
AN OPPOSITE IS dismantle

**assembly** NOUN

1 *a political assembly   an assembly of bishops*
▶ gathering, meeting, congress, convocation, assemblage, council, synod (church)

2 *An assembly of spectators waited at the gates.*
▶ crowd , gathering, throng, rally, meeting, *(literary)* multitude

3 *The special glue is used in the assembly of model aircraft.*
▶ construction, building, making, putting together, manufacture, erection (of buildings)

**assent** NOUN

*Parents need to give their assent to attendance on field trips.*
▶ agreement, approval, consent, permission, authorization, blessing, *(more informal)* go-ahead
AN OPPOSITE IS refusal

**assert** VERB

1 *She asserted that multinational companies should not be blamed for damage to the environment.*
▶ declare, maintain, contend, submit, insist, argue, proclaim, profess, claim, emphasize, affirm, allege, protest, state, stress

2 *It is not always easy for people to assert their rights.*
▶ insist on, claim, stand up for, make use of, uphold

**assert yourself** *Some of the newer committee members began to assert themselves at meetings.*
▶ be assertive, behave confidently, be resolute, make yourself felt, exert your influence, make demands, persist, stand firm, *(more informal)* stick to your guns

**assertive** ADJECTIVE

*You will need to be assertive in this job.*
▶ forceful, determined, resolute, confident, decisive, firm, assured, self-assured, authoritative, strong-willed, bold, positive, aggressive, domineering, strong, *(usually disapproving)* pushy
OPPOSITES ARE submissive, reticent, retiring

**assess** VERB

1 *The hospital used a scanner to assess the extent of their head injuries.*
▶ evaluate, gauge, judge, determine, review, reckon, estimate, appraise, calculate, work out, value

2 *All pupils are assessed and graded at the end of their first term.*
▶ rate, judge, appraise, check, review

**asset** NOUN

1 *A good sense of humour can be an asset.*
▶ benefit, advantage, blessing, boon, strength, virtue, help, aid, support, good, *(more informal)* plus, *(more informal)* godsend

2 **assets** *The family's assets were reckoned at over two million dollars.*
▶ capital, resources, possessions, reserves, property, estate, funds, goods, holdings, means, money, savings, securities, wealth, *(more informal)* worldly goods

## assign VERB

1 *Tasks are assigned on the basis of experience.*
▶ allocate, distribute, allot, apportion, dispense, give out, hand over, share out
2 *Kathryn was told she would be assigned to the case.*
▶ appoint, consign, delegate, designate, nominate, put down, choose (for), select (for)

## assignment NOUN

1 *I have a difficult assignment to finish.*
▶ task, piece of work, exercise, project, job, duty
2 *the assignment of responsibilities*
▶ allocation, issuing, granting

## assist VERB

*Could you assist us for a while?*
▶ help, aid, support, give a hand to, lend a (helping) hand to, oblige
OPPOSITES ARE hinder, impede

## assistance NOUN

*They said they would not need any assistance.*
▶ help, support, aid, encouragement, reinforcement, backing, collaboration, cooperation, contribution, patronage, sponsorship, subsidy
AN OPPOSITE IS hindrance

## assistant NOUN

*The team leader has three assistants.*
▶ helper, subordinate, supporter, associate, deputy, colleague, underling, junior, ancillary, collaborator

## associate VERB

1 *Stephen had been associating with dropouts and oddballs.*
▶ mix, keep company, go about, consort, socialize, fraternize, mingle, (more informal) hang about
AN OPPOSITE IS dissociate
2 *Patience was not a quality I associated at all with him.*
▶ connect, link, identify, equate, relate (to)

## association NOUN

1 *They enjoyed several years of friendly association.*
▶ relationship, connection, link, bond, ties, friendship, attachment, union
2 *an association of sports clubs*
▶ organization, confederation, federation, coalition, society, league, partnership, alliance, syndicate, group

## assorted ADJECTIVE

*a collection of assorted objects*
▶ miscellaneous, mixed, different, sundry, varied, various, differing, diverse, diversified, heterogeneous, manifold, motley, multifarious, several, (old-fashioned) divers

## assortment NOUN

*an assortment of dog-eared paperbacks*
▶ mixture, selection, collection, variety, array, miscellany, choice, diversity, medley, mélange

## assume VERB

1 *I assumed the book was a gift.*
▶ presume, suppose, infer, deduce, take for granted, surmise, conjecture, reckon, imagine, come to the conclusion, guess, suspect, believe, imagine, deduce, expect, think, understand, (more informal) have a hunch
2 *The children should be encouraged to assume responsibilities.*
▶ take on, undertake, accept, embrace
3 *To play the part she had to assume a Scottish accent.*
▶ adopt, put on, feign, acquire

## assumed ADJECTIVE

*She writes under an assumed name.*
▶ false, fictitious, invented, adopted, made-up, bogus, fake, spurious

## assumption NOUN

*The assumption is that prices will stay the same.*
▶ supposition, presumption, conjecture, expectation, belief, guess, hypothesis, premise, surmise, theory

## assurance NOUN

*She had an air of complete assurance.*
▶ confidence, composure, self-confidence, poise, aplomb, level-headedness, self-possession, self-reliance

## assure VERB

1 *He assured me he would arrive in time.*
▶ promise, reassure, convince, persuade, satisfy
2 *The win assured them a place in the finals.*
▶ ensure, secure, guarantee, make certain, confirm, establish

## assured ADJECTIVE

*an assured manner*
▶ confident, self-confident, self-assured, positive, assertive, composed, collected, calm, level-headed

## astonish VERB

*We were astonished at how much the place had changed.*
▶ amaze, astound, surprise, stagger, startle, disconcert, dumbfound, shock, flabbergast, perplex, stun, stupefy, bewilder

## astonishing ADJECTIVE

*The results were astonishing.*
▶ amazing, astounding, staggering, extraordinary, startling, stunning, breathtaking, fantastic, wonderful, phenomenal, incredible

## astound VERB

*His arrogance astounded her.*
▶ astonish, amaze, surprise, stagger, startle, disconcert, dumbfound, shock, flabbergast, perplex, stun, stupefy, bewilder

## astounding ADJECTIVE

*an astounding statement*
▶ amazing, astonishing, staggering, extraordinary, startling, stunning, breathtaking, fantastic, wonderful, phenomenal, incredible

## astray ADVERB

*Several missiles had gone astray and hit civilian targets.*
▶ off course, adrift, amiss, awry, lost, wide of the mark

**astute** ADJECTIVE

*an astute manager   some astute remarks*
▶ shrewd, sharp, acute, canny, prudent, clever, intelligent, quick-witted, perceptive, discerning, crafty, wily
AN OPPOSITE IS stupid

**asylum** NOUN

*Spain refused to hand over four men who had sought asylum in their embassy.*
▶ haven, shelter, refuge, retreat, safety, sanctuary

**athletic** ADJECTIVE

*an athletic physique*
▶ muscular, fit, well-built, powerful, strong, sturdy, acrobatic, active, energetic, robust, sinewy, vigorous, wiry, (*more informal*) sporty, (*more informal*) strapping
OPPOSITES ARE frail, weak

**atmosphere** NOUN

1 *Harmful gases are escaping into the atmosphere.*
▶ air, sky, ether, (*literary*) heavens
2 *the warm cosy atmosphere of the kitchen*
▶ ambience, aura, environment, surroundings, quality, character, climate, mood, feeling, (*more informal*) vibes

**atom** NOUN

*There is not an atom of truth in the story.*
▶ scrap, speck, spot, trace, morsel, bit, crumb, grain, iota, jot, molecule, particle

**atrocious** ADJECTIVE

*They were guilty of atrocious brutality.*
▶ abominable, appalling, brutal, vicious, detestable, hateful, odious, vile, obnoxious, dreadful, abhorrent, diabolical, disgusting, repellent, horrifying
AN OPPOSITE IS humane

**atrocity** NOUN

*Further atrocities have been reported.*
▶ outrage, enormity, cruelty, act of brutality

**attach** VERB

1 *The brackets are attached to the wall with a pair of small screws.*
▶ fix, fasten, secure, affix, join, link, stick, bond, couple, anchor, connect, tie, add, append
OPPOSITES ARE detach, remove
2 *We attach great importance to punctuality.*
▶ attribute, ascribe, assign, apply, put (on), place (on), associate (with), impute

**attached** ADJECTIVE

*attached to The sisters seem very attached to each other.*
▶ fond of, close to, devoted to, dear to, affectionate to or towards, friendly to or towards, loving to or towards, loyal to or towards, warm to or towards

**attack** NOUN

1 *An attack on the enemy was planned for the next day.*
▶ assault, onslaught, strike, offensive, raid, charge, ambush, foray, sortie, rush, blitz, bombardment, broadside, cannonade, counter-attack

2 *Their attack on her honesty upset her very much.*
▶ criticism (of), tirade (against), outburst (against), vilification (of), abuse (of), censure (of), denunciation (of), diatribe (against), revilement (of), invective (against)
3 *an attack of coughing*
▶ fit, bout, spasm, convulsion, outbreak, paroxysm, seizure, stroke, (*more informal*) turn

**attack** VERB

1 *We attack the enemy position at dawn.*
▶ charge, bombard, assault, ambush, raid, rush, descend on, storm, strike at, (*more informal*) blast, (*more informal*) pitch into, (*more informal*) wade into
2 *A bunch of youths attacked him in the street on his way home.*
▶ assault, mob, mug, pounce on, ambush, set about, set on, jump on, (*more informal*) beat up, (*more informal*) do over, (*more informal*) lay into
3 *The clergy regularly attack government policy.*
▶ criticize, find fault with, censure, denounce, condemn, impugn, vilify, inveigh against, malign, round on, snipe at
AN OPPOSITE IS defend
4 *We need to attack the problem of poverty.*
▶ confront, address, focus on, attend to, apply yourself to, deal with, (*more informal*) have a go at

**attacker** NOUN

1 *The little force fought bravely against its attackers.*
▶ aggressor, assailant, invader, opponent, raider, enemy
2 *The attacker ran off empty-handed.*
▶ assailant, mugger, aggressor, intruder, rapist
3 *The journal agreed to publish a defence against her attackers.*
▶ critic, detractor, persecutor, opponent, enemy

**attain** VERB

*He did not attain this honour until the reign of Queen Victoria.*
▶ achieve, accomplish, obtain, gain, win, earn, get, acquire, secure, reach, (*more informal*) clinch, (*more informal*) carry off, (*more informal*) pull off

**attainment** NOUN

*many exceptional attainments*
▶ achievement, accomplishment, success, deed, exploit

**attempt** NOUN

*a brave attempt*
▶ try, effort, endeavour, venture, (*more informal*) shot

**attempt** VERB

1 *We attempted to visit all three sites in one day.*
▶ try, endeavour, aim, aspire, strive, undertake, set out, make an effort or every effort, do your best, do your utmost, venture, seek, (*more informal*) have a go (at), (*more informal*) have a stab (at), (*more informal*) bend over backwards
2 *Candidates should attempt three questions.*
▶ undertake, try, choose, answer

## attend VERB

**1** *Frances had to attend an interview the following week.*
▶ go to or for, present yourself at, appear at, be present at

**2** *The bride was attended by two bridesmaids.*
▶ escort, assist, accompany, chaperon, follow, guard, usher, wait on

**3** **attend to** *A nurse attended to the injured.*
▶ look after, care for, tend, treat, help, deal with, (*more formal*) minister to

**4** **attend to** *Frank said he would attend to the details of the trip.*
▶ deal with, take care of, look after, see to, manage, organize, make arrangements for, take responsibility for

**5** **attend to** *Please attend to what I say.*
▶ listen to, pay attention to, heed, mark, mind, concentrate on, follow carefully, hear, note, notice, observe, think about

## attendant NOUN

*The Queen had three attendants.*
▶ assistant, aide, retainer, companion, escort, equerry, servant, bodyguard

## attention NOUN

*Please give the matter your full attention.*
▶ concentration, observation, regard, consideration, scrutiny, notice, thought, concern, care, diligence, heed, recognition

## attentive ADJECTIVE

**1** *Julian was standing silent and attentive in the shadows.*
▶ alert, vigilant, watchful, aware, circumspect, wide awake, on the lookout, on the ball, on your guard, (*more informal*) on the qui vive

**2** *Helen was patient and attentive, holding my hand to calm me.*
▶ thoughtful, considerate, kind, caring, understanding, tender, devoted

## attitude NOUN

*a positive, joyful attitude*
▶ outlook, approach, air, manner, demeanour, disposition, inclination, position, bearing, frame of mind, mien, mood, posture, stance, behaviour

## attract VERB

**1** *The recent lecture attracted a good turnout.*
▶ draw, bring, bring in, produce, cause, generate

**2** *They were attracted by the beauty of the place.*
▶ enchant, entrance, excite, captivate, lure, entice, allure, tempt, charm, fascinate, beguile, bewitch
AN OPPOSITE IS repel

## attractive ADJECTIVE

**1** *an attractive young woman*
▶ good-looking, nice-looking, pretty, striking, fetching, beautiful, gorgeous, lovely, charming, engaging, appealing, delightful, glamorous, stunning
AN OPPOSITE IS repulsive

**2** *an attractive offer*
▶ appealing, agreeable, tempting, interesting, difficult to resist or refuse

## attribute VERB

*A cool head is not the first quality I would attribute to the colonel.*
▶ ascribe, associate (with), connect (with), assign, put down, blame (on)

## audacious ADJECTIVE

*an audacious decision*
▶ bold, daring, brave, courageous, adventurous, enterprising

## audacity NOUN

**1** *His sheer audacity was enough to carry the day.*
▶ bravery, daring, boldness, courage, enterprise

**2** (*usually disapproving*) *Then they had the audacity to ask for money.*
▶ effrontery, cheek, nerve, boldness, temerity, impertinence, impudence, insolence, presumptuousness, shamelessness, (*more informal*) sauce

## audible ADJECTIVE

*Her words were hardly audible above the noise of the traffic.*
▶ perceptible, discernible, recognizable, clear, distinct, detectable, high, loud, noisy, strong
AN OPPOSITE IS inaudible

## audience NOUN

*There was a more lively audience on the Saturday.*
▶ spectators, onlookers, crowd, gathering, turnout, (*television*) viewers, (*radio*) listeners

## audit NOUN

*an audit of the company's accounts*
▶ inspection, examination, scrutiny, investigation, vetting, survey, study, analysis

## auditorium NOUN

*It was difficult to see the performers from the back of the packed auditorium.*
▶ theatre, concert hall, hall, assembly room

## auspicious ADJECTIVE

*an auspicious day for a picnic*
▶ favourable, hopeful, positive, promising, propitious

## austere ADJECTIVE

**1** *Their lives tended to be short and austere.*
▶ severe, sober, frugal, strict, spartan, restrained, abstemious, ascetic, temperate, simple, chaste
OPPOSITES ARE indulgent, elaborate

**2** *She seemed austere but had a great deal of charm, once you got to know her.*
▶ stern, severe, strict, grave, solemn, forbidding, dour, formal, remote, distant, aloof
AN OPPOSITE IS genial

**3** *Dark windows gave the house an austere appearance.*
▶ stark, grim, bleak, forbidding
OPPOSITES ARE bright, ornate

a
b
c
d
e
f
g
h
i
j
k
l
m
n
o
p
q
r
s
t
u
v
w
x
y
z

## authentic ADJECTIVE

**1** *an authentic painting by Rembrandt*
▶ actual, bona fide, certain, genuine, legitimate, original, real, true, valid
AN OPPOSITE IS fake

**2** *an authentic story*
▶ accurate, authoritative, dependable, factual, honest, reliable, truthful, veracious
AN OPPOSITE IS false

## authenticate VERB

*The claim has still to be authenticated.*
▶ validate, substantiate, verify, corroborate, confirm, certify, support, back up

## author NOUN

**1** *modern American authors*
▶ writer, novelist, dramatist, composer, creator, playwright, poet, scriptwriter

**2** *the author of the plan*
▶ originator, creator, initiator, instigator, architect, producer, begetter, designer, inventor

## authoritarian ADJECTIVE

*an authoritarian regime*
▶ dictatorial, autocratic, tyrannical, despotic, oppressive, harsh, disciplinarian

## authoritative ADJECTIVE

**1** *an authoritative edition of the text*
▶ definitive, authorized, classic, standard

**2** *an authoritative source of information*
▶ reliable, dependable, sound, authentic, trustworthy

## authority NOUN

**1** *The salesperson does not always have the authority to deal with a complaint.*
▶ authorization, power, right, prerogative, consent, licence, mandate, permission

**2** *I was convinced that she would never accept a challenge to her authority.*
▶ power, sovereignty, control, jurisdiction, domination, supremacy, charge, command, force, influence, might, prerogative, right, sway, weight

**3** *He is the world's foremost authority on the subject.*
▶ expert, specialist, pundit, boffin, connoisseur (of)

**the authorities** *The matter was reported to the authorities.*
▶ officials, officialdom, government, management, administration, people in charge, (more informal) the powers that be

## authorize VERB

*The government has authorized a further billion pounds of spending on health.*
▶ approve, permit, allow, agree to, enable, sanction, back, accede to, consent to, (more informal) OK, ratify, (more informal) rubber-stamp, (more informal) give the go-ahead for

## autobiography NOUN

*She began her autobiography in middle age.*
▶ memoirs, reminiscences, life history

## autocrat NOUN

*The new king acted like an autocrat.*
▶ despot, dictator, tyrant, absolute ruler

## autocratic ADJECTIVE

*an autocratic ruler*
▶ dictatorial, authoritarian, tyrannical, despotic, oppressive, harsh, disciplinarian

## automatic ADJECTIVE

**1** *His reaction was automatic.*
▶ instinctive, spontaneous, involuntary, unconscious, reflex, unthinking, unintentional, natural, mechanical, habitual, impulsive

**2** *automatic windows*
▶ mechanical, automated, computerized, programmed, robotic, self-regulating, unmanned

## autonomous ADJECTIVE

*an autonomous nation*
▶ independent, self-governing, sovereign, free, self-ruling, self-determining
AN OPPOSITE IS subject

## auxiliary ADJECTIVE

*an auxiliary power supply*
▶ supplementary, additional, ancillary, reserve, secondary, spare, subsidiary, emergency, extra, (more informal) back-up

## available ADJECTIVE

*Camping facilities will be available on site.*
▶ obtainable, accessible, procurable, ready, at or on or to hand, to be had, usable, disposable
AN OPPOSITE IS unavailable

## avenge VERB

*We shall avenge their deaths a thousand times.*
▶ take revenge for, take vengeance for, punish, exact punishment for, exact retribution for, repay, (more informal) get your own back for

## avenue NOUN

*The house was separated from the field by an avenue of trees.*
▶ row, broadway, boulevard, thoroughfare, road

## average ADJECTIVE

**1** *Few of us have any idea how much water we use on an average day.*
▶ typical, normal, ordinary, usual, regular, standard

**2** *He is only an average golfer.*
▶ mediocre, undistinguished, unremarkable, indifferent, unexceptional, run-of-the-mill, second-rate, passable, tolerable, mainstream
OPPOSITES ARE exceptional, outstanding

**3** *The average summer temperature is 18 degrees.*
▶ mean, medial, standard

## average NOUN

*Prices of new cars will rise by an average of 3 per cent.*
▶ mean, median, mid-point

## averse ADJECTIVE

averse to *She is not averse to bribery.*
► opposed to, against, hostile to, resistant to, antagonistic to or towards, unfavourably disposed to or towards
AN OPPOSITE IS keen (on)

## aversion NOUN

*He had an obvious aversion to work of any kind.*
► opposition, hostility, loathing (of), distaste (for), disgust (for), revulsion (for or towards), repugnance (for or towards), abhorrence (of)

## avert VERB

1 *The outbreak of war helped avert a financial crisis.*
► prevent, avoid, forestall, (*more informal*) nip in the bud
2 *She was sitting still with her head partly averted.*
► turn away, turn aside
3 *It was difficult to avert the blow.*
► deflect, avoid, parry, stave off

## avid ADJECTIVE

*avid fans of the movies*
► keen, eager, enthusiastic, ardent, passionate, fervent, devoted, dedicated, zealous
OPPOSITES ARE uninterested, apathetic

## avoid VERB

1 *I try to avoid arguments.*
► refrain from, stay clear of, steer clear of, eschew, circumvent
OPPOSITES ARE seek, confront
2 *You cannot avoid responsibility for the decision.*
► evade, escape, dodge, shirk, sidestep, (*more informal*) get out of, (*more informal*) duck
AN OPPOSITE IS face up to
3 *She had to swerve to avoid a collision.*
► prevent, avert, circumvent
4 *There was a woman at the party he was anxious to avoid.*
► ignore, shun, keep away from, hide from, stay clear of, steer clear of
AN OPPOSITE IS seek out
5 *Women should avoid alcohol during pregnancy.*
► refrain from, desist from, abstain from, eschew
AN OPPOSITE IS indulge in

## await VERB

*Relatives of the victims continued to await news.*
► wait for, hope for, expect, look out for, be ready for, lie in wait for

## awake ADJECTIVE

*They are often not awake until ten or eleven.  She felt too awake to go back to sleep again.*
► conscious, alert, sleepless, wakeful, wide awake, lively, restless
AN OPPOSITE IS asleep

## awake VERB

1 *The alarm awoke her at six.*
► wake (up), waken, awaken, rouse, arouse
2 *James awoke with a start.*
► wake (up), waken, awaken, stir, come to

3 *The accident awoke old fears about passenger safety.*
► awaken, waken, rouse, arouse, stir up, revive, stimulate, trigger, bring back

**USAGE** The normal word to use for the main meanings is *wake* or *wake up*. There are three other words, *awake*, *awaken*, and *waken*, but you cannot use *up* with any of these. All four words can be transitive (i.e. can take an object, as in the first example in this entry) or intransitive (i.e. can have no object, as in the second example). *Awaken* and *waken* are rather more formal or literary in effect than *awake* and *wake*.

## awaken VERB

1 *The noise outside awakened us.  We awakened early.*
► wake (up), waken, awake, stir, come to
2 *The incident awakened strong feelings in her.*
► awake, waken, rouse, arouse, stir up, revive, stimulate, trigger, bring back

## award NOUN

1 *By his third year he had won three awards.*
► prize, trophy, decoration, medal
2 *an award of £5,000*
► payment, grant, subsidy, subvention, bursary
3 *the award of an honour*
► granting, bestowal, conferment, conferral

## award VERB

1 *MPs plan to award themselves a four-per-cent pay rise.  Referee Hart did not even award a free kick.*
► grant, give, present, accord, allot, assign
2 *The college awarded her a scholarship.*
► grant, present, (*more formal*) endow, (*more formal*) confer, (*more formal*) bestow

**USAGE** If you use *present* or *endow*, you say *The college presented* (or *endowed*) *her with a scholarship.* If you use *bestow* or *confer*, you say *They bestowed* (or *conferred*) *a scholarship on her.* These words are much more formal in effect and are mainly used in official language.

## aware ADJECTIVE

aware of *The children were aware of the dangers.*
► conscious of, acquainted with, alive to, appreciative of, mindful of, informed about, knowledgeable about, sensitive to, familiar with, attentive to, conversant with, heedful of, observant of, responsive to
OPPOSITES ARE unaware, ignorant, insensitive (to)

## awe NOUN

*He regarded her with awe.*
► wonder, wonderment, amazement, admiration, astonishment, respect, reverence, veneration, dread, fear, terror

## awe-inspiring ADJECTIVE

*The stained-glass windows were awe-inspiring in gold and blue.*
► awesome, breathtaking, dramatic, stunning, stupendous, spectacular, astonishing, grand, imposing, impressive, magnificent, amazing,

marvellous, overwhelming, wonderful, fearsome, (*poetic*) wondrous
OPPOSITES ARE insignificant, unimpressive

**awful** ADJECTIVE

**1** *awful weather*
► bad, terrible, dreadful, atrocious, appalling, frightful, poor, (*more informal*) lousy
OPPOSITES ARE wonderful, lovely

**2** *an awful smell*
► unpleasant, disgusting, nasty, dreadful, terrible, horrible, horrid, foul, frightful, obnoxious
OPPOSITES ARE pleasant, lovely

**3** *awful news  an awful illness*
► grave, serious, bad, terrible, dreadful
AN OPPOSITE IS excellent

**4** *I felt awful for losing my temper.*
► guilty, remorseful, regretful, ashamed, sorry

**awkward** ADJECTIVE

**1** *The case was an awkward object to carry.*
► cumbersome, bulky, unmanageable, unwieldy, inconvenient
AN OPPOSITE IS convenient

**2** *He ran with awkward movements.*
► clumsy, ungainly, inept, inexpert, unskilful, uncoordinated, graceless, blundering, bungling, gauche, gawky, ham-fisted, maladroit
OPPOSITES ARE skilful, dexterous, adroit

**3** *This is an awkward situation to be in.*
► difficult, troublesome, trying, vexatious, vexing, annoying, perplexing
AN OPPOSITE IS straightforward

**4** *There was an awkward pause in the conversation.*
► embarrassing, uncomfortable, uneasy, delicate, tricky, unwelcome
AN OPPOSITE IS comfortable

**5** *He thought she was being extremely awkward.*
► unreasonable, unhelpful, uncooperative, stubborn, obstinate, perverse, tiresome, exasperating, wayward, (*more informal*) bloody-minded, (*more informal*) bolshie
OPPOSITES ARE cooperative, obliging, amenable

**axe** NOUN

*Daniel was walking towards the tree carrying a large axe.*
► hatchet, chopper, cleaver, battleaxe, tomahawk

**axe** VERB

*The company will axe thousands of jobs.*
► terminate, discontinue, eliminate, cut, cancel, drop, get rid of, remove, withdraw

**axis** NOUN

*The earth spins on its axis once a day.*
► centre line, central line, pivot

**axle** NOUN

*Something had broken the car's back axle.*
► rod, shaft, spindle

# Bb

**baby** NOUN

**1** *The woman was holding a baby.*
► babe, infant, toddler, child

**2** *a baby car*
► miniature, mini, small-scale, midget, diminutive

**babyish** ADJECTIVE

*Older children are usually told that it is babyish to cry.*
► childish, juvenile, puerile, immature, infantile
AN OPPOSITE IS mature

**back** NOUN

**1** *a person's back*
► spine, backbone, spinal column
RELATED ADJECTIVE dorsal (upper side of an animal), lumbar (lower back)

**2** *the back of the vehicle*
► end, rear, tail-end
AN OPPOSITE IS front

**3** *the back of the building*
► rear, rear side
OPPOSITES ARE front, facade

**4** *the back of the ship*
► stern
OPPOSITES ARE front, bow

**5** *the back of an envelope*
► reverse, verso
AN OPPOSITE IS front

**6** *the back of an animal*
► rear, tail, hindquarters, posterior
AN OPPOSITE IS front

**back** ADJECTIVE

**1** *the back door*
► rear
AN OPPOSITE IS front

**2** *an animal's back legs*
► rear, hind, hindmost
AN OPPOSITE IS front

**3** *the back row of the hall*
► end, rearmost
AN OPPOSITE IS front

**4** *a bird's back feathers  the back fin of a fish*
► (*technical*) dorsal

**5** *back issues of a journal*
► past, previous
OPPOSITES ARE forthcoming, future

**back** VERB

**1** *He decided to back his van into the space.  The car backed slowly up the drive.*
► reverse, go backwards, move back

**2** *We would like them to back our plan.*
► support, endorse, approve of, stand behind, sponsor, patronize

**3** *He backed a horse at 3-1.*
► bet on, place a bet on, put money on

**back down** *The government has had to back down on tax increases.*
► withdraw, concede, yield, give way, retreat,

change your mind, (*more informal*) do a U-turn
**back out of** *Mr James wanted to back out of the deal.*
► withdraw from, give up, pull out of

## backbone NOUN

1 *She has an injured backbone.*
► spine, spinal column, vertebrae
RELATED ADJECTIVE spinal

2 *The backbone of a good team is a good manager.*
► mainstay, foundation, cornerstone, chief support

3 *Drivers need to have some backbone to sustain pole position.*
► courage, nerve, spirit, mettle, determination, strength of character, firmness of purpose

## backfire VERB

*The plan backfired.*
► miscarry, misfire, fail, flop, rebound

## background NOUN

1 *You can see a steeple in the background.*
► distance, (on the) horizon
AN OPPOSITE IS foreground

2 *the background to the war*
► circumstances (of), context (of), history, (*informal*) lead-up

3 *students from different backgrounds*
► environment, social circumstances, breeding, culture, (*formal*) milieu, tradition, upbringing

## backing NOUN

1 *We need the backing of the unions.*
► support, agreement, endorsement, assistance, encouragement, help

2 *financial backing*
► support, funding, patronage, subsidy, sponsorship

3 *a musical backing*
► accompaniment, orchestration, scoring

## backlash NOUN

*The announcement provoked a violent backlash.*
► reaction, response, repercussion, retaliation

## backlog NOUN

*a backlog of work*
► arrears, accumulation, mountain

## backward ADJECTIVE

1 *a backward movement*
► reverse, rearward, regressive, retrograde, retrogressive
AN OPPOSITE IS forward

2 *Don't be backward if you need to ask for help.*
► reticent, bashful, coy, diffident, shy, timid, unforthcoming, hesitant, inhibited, afraid, modest, reluctant, reserved, self-effacing
AN OPPOSITE IS confident

3 *The decision was a backward step.*
► retrograde, regressive, negative

4 *a backward learner*
► subnormal, (*offensive*) retarded

## bad ADJECTIVE This word is often overused. Here are some alternatives:

1 *bad work*
► poor, inferior, substandard, second-rate, unsatisfactory, inadequate, deficient, awful, terrible, dreadful, (*more informal*) shoddy, (*more informal*) ropy
OPPOSITES ARE excellent, outstanding, good

2 *a bad driver*
► incompetent, poor, awful, terrible, dreadful

3 *a bad effect*
► harmful, damaging, detrimental, injurious, undesirable
OPPOSITES ARE beneficial, good

4 *leading a bad life*
► wicked, sinful, immoral, depraved, degenerate, dissolute
OPPOSITES ARE virtuous, good

5 *a bad child*
► naughty, badly behaved, disobedient, mischievous
OPPOSITES ARE well behaved, good

6 *bad language*
► vulgar, crude, foul, coarse, indecent, offensive, profane, blasphemous

7 *bad news*
► unpleasant, disagreeable, unwelcome
OPPOSITES ARE good, welcome

8 *a bad time to buy a house*
► unsuitable, inappropriate, difficult, unfavourable, unfortunate, inauspicious
OPPOSITES ARE favourable, suitable, good

9 *a bad accident  a bad toothache*
► serious, severe, acute, grave, critical
OPPOSITES ARE minor, slight

10 *the meat is bad*
► rotten, off, putrid, decomposing, decomposed, mouldy, contaminated, sour (milk), rancid (butter)
AN OPPOSITE IS fresh

11 *feeling bad*
► unwell, ill, sick
OPPOSITES ARE well, healthy

12 *a bad leg*
► injured, wounded, diseased

13 *I felt bad after losing my temper.*
► guilty, remorseful, ashamed, conscience-stricken
OPPOSITES ARE proud, unrepentant

## badge NOUN

*a police officer's badge*
► identification, insignia, shield, emblem, sign

## badger VERB

*Stop badgering me.*
► harass, bother, pester, annoy

## bad-tempered ADJECTIVE

*She was a thoroughly selfish, bad-tempered little girl.*
► irritable, irascible, grumpy, testy, grouchy, touchy, crotchety, cantankerous, peevish, fractious,

cross, (*more informal*) stroppy, (*more informal*) shirty
OPPOSITES ARE good- tempered, good- humoured,
affable

**baffle** VERB

*Her answer baffled him.*
► perplex, bewilder, puzzle, mystify, confuse,
bemuse, disconcert, confound, fox, (*more informal*)
flummox, (*more informal*) floor

**baffling** ADJECTIVE

*a baffling response*
► puzzling, bewildering, perplexing, confusing,
mystifying, mysterious, inexplicable, inscrutable,
insoluble, unfathomable, extraordinary, frustrating
OPPOSITES ARE clear, straightforward,
comprehensible

**bag** NOUN

1 *I'll put these things in a bag.*
► container, carrier bag, carrier
2 *We'd better go and pack our bags*
► case, suitcase
3 *She always carried a bag.*
► handbag, shoulder bag
4 *The walkers had bags on their backs.*
► backpack, rucksack

**bag** VERB

1 *You need to get there early and bag a good seat.*
► secure, obtain, reserve, acquire, get
2 *He bagged four pheasants.*
► catch, shoot, kill, capture

**baggage** NOUN

*She put her baggage in and climbed aboard.*
► luggage, bags, cases, suitcases, trunks,
belongings, paraphernalia, (*informal*) gear, (*informal*)
stuff

**baggy** ADJECTIVE

*baggy trousers*
► loose, loose-fitting, roomy

**bait** NOUN

*The offer was meant to be a bait.*
► enticement, inducement, lure, bribe, allurement,
attraction

**bait** VERB

*The boys wouldn't stop baiting her.*
► tease, torment, annoy, goad, persecute, pester,
provoke, hound, jeer at, (*more informal*) needle

**bake** VERB

*The hot sun was baking the earth.*
► scorch, burn, parch, sear

**balance** NOUN

1 *You can weigh the fruit in the balance.*
► scales, weighing machine
2 *It is easy to stumble and lose your balance.*
► equilibrium, stability, equipoise, poise, steadiness
3 *a balance between fairness and firmness*
► parity, correspondence, symmetry, evenness,
equality, equivalence

4 *a sense of personal balance*
► composure, self-assurance, equanimity,
self-possession
5 *The balance of the payment is due in July.*
► remainder, difference, rest, residue
**on balance** *On balance it is a good scheme.*
► overall, all in all, by and large

**balance** VERB

1 *If I carry one bag in each hand, they balance each
other*
► counteract, counterbalance, neutralize, offset,
equalize, match, stabilize, steady
2 *He tried to eat by balancing a plate on his knee.*
► support, keep, keep balanced, steady
3 *You have to balance the advantages and
disadvantages*
► weigh, weigh up, compare, assess, appraise,
consider, estimate

**balanced** ADJECTIVE

1 *a balanced view of the issues*
► fair, objective, impartial, equitable, even-handed,
impartial, disinterested
OPPOSITES ARE partial, biased
2 *a balanced individual*
► level-headed, equable, sensible, sane, stable,
practical
OPPOSITES ARE unbalanced, neurotic
3 *a balanced diet*
► mixed, varied, well-planned, healthy
OPPOSITES ARE unbalanced, unhealthy

**bald** ADJECTIVE

1 *a bald man*
► bald-headed, hairless, (*euphemistic*) thin on top
2 *bald tyres*
► bare, smooth
3 *a bald statement*
► plain, direct, forthright, plain, simple, stark,
straightforward, unadorned, uncompromising

**bale** NOUN

*huge bales of firewood*
► bundle, pack, pack, load, parcel, truss, bunch

**ball** NOUN

1 *a ball of string The little animal curled itself into a
ball.*
► sphere, globe, globule, orb, shot, spheroid
2 *a ball of food*
► pellet, globule, slug
3 *a fancy-dress ball*
► dance, party, disco, social

**balloon** NOUN

*across the ocean in a balloon*
► hot-air balloon, airship, dirigible

**balloon** VERB

*The curtains ballooned out into the room.*
► billow, blow, puff, swell, bulge

**ballot** NOUN

*a ballot for the party leadership*
► election, vote, poll, plebiscite, referendum

## ban NOUN

*a ban on smoking*
► embargo, prohibition, bar, moratorium, veto

## ban VERB

*The government wants to ban some blood sports.*
► prohibit, forbid, bar, disallow, proscribe, suppress, make illegal, stop, restrict
OPPOSITES ARE permit, allow

## banal ADJECTIVE

*a banal image of the perfect married couple*
► trite, hackneyed, commonplace, stereotypical, stock, humdrum, clichéd, dull, unimaginative, tired, boring, tedious, (*more informal*) corny
OPPOSITES ARE original, interesting

## band NOUN

**1** *red with a blue band along the top*
► strip, stripe, streak, belt, line, loop, ribbon, ring
**2** *a band of followers*
► troop, body, company, group, gang, horde, party, association, clique, club, crew, flock, herd, society
**3** *A band was playing.*
► orchestra, ensemble, group

## band VERB

**band together** *The village banded together to repel their attackers.*
► gather, group, unite, cooperate, join together, work together, fight together, collaborate

## bandage NOUN

*The nurse put a bandage on his wound.*
► dressing, plaster, gauze, lint

## bandit NOUN

*The camp was attacked by bandits.*
► robber, brigand, thief, outlaw, desperado, gangster, gunman, marauder, highwayman, pirate, hijacker

## bandy ADJECTIVE

*All ducks are bandy. They waddle.*
► bow-legged, bandy-legged, bowed

## bandy VERB

**bandy about** *Several prices are being bandied about.*
► put about, discuss, circulate, spread about or around, pass about or around, exchange, interchange, swap, toss about or around

## bane NOUN

*Tight deadlines continue to be the bane of journalists' lives.*
► ruin, curse, death, misfortune

## bang NOUN

**1** *He had got a bang on the head.*
► blow, hit, smack, knock, thump, rap, clout, punch, whack, cuff, bump, collision, slam, stroke, (*more informal*) wallop
**2** *Suddenly there was a loud bang.*
► blast, report, boom, crack, thud, thump, explosion, clap, crash, pop

## bang VERB

*He banged the table with his fist.*
► hit, thump, strike, whack, (*more informal*) bash, (*more informal*) clout

## banish VERB

**1** *The authorities banished him as a traitor.*
► exile, expel, deport, send away, eject, evict, expatriate, outlaw, ship away, transport
**2** *Her look banished any remaining fears.*
► dispel, remove, dismiss, disperse, allay, scatter, dissipate, drive away or out

## bank NOUN

**1** *a grassy bank*
► slope, rise, incline, earthwork, embankment, mound, ridge, dike, rampart
**2** *the bank of the lake*
► edge, border, margin, shore, side, brink
**3** *a steep bank on the curve*
► camber, gradient, incline, slope, tilt, ramp, rise, (*formal*) declivity
**4** *a bank of dials and switches*
► array, row, panel, tier, console, collection, series, display, file, group, line
**5** *a blood bank*
► store, reserve, stock, supply, fund, depository

## bank VERB

**1** *The little plane banked to the left.*
► tilt, lean, slant, pitch, tip, incline, cant, heel, list, slope
**2** *Bank the cheque immediately.*
► deposit, pay in

## bankrupt ADJECTIVE

**1** *The business was soon bankrupt.*
► insolvent, failed, ruined, in liquidation, (*more informal*) bust
AN OPPOSITE IS solvent
**2** *By the end of the day Ken was bankrupt.*
► broke, penniless, destitute, (*more formal*) impecunious, (*more informal*) skint
OPPOSITES ARE wealthy, flush

## banner NOUN

*A banner was flying from a tall building.*
► flag, pennant, pennon, standard, streamer, ensign, colours (*plural*)

## banquet NOUN

*The conference ended with a sumptuous banquet.*
► feast, dinner, (*literary*) repast, (*more informal*) blowout

## banter NOUN

*good-humoured banter*
► joking, jesting, repartee, badinage, raillery, ribbing, jocularity, teasing, word play, chaffing, pleasantry

## bar NOUN

**1** *an iron bar*
► rod, pole, stake, shaft, batten, stick, strut, beam, girder, rail, railing

## bar

2 *a bar of chocolate  a bar of soap*
► block, slab, cake, tablet, chunk, wedge, piece, hunk, ingot, lump, nugget
3 *a bar to progress*
► obstacle, barrier, obstruction, hindrance, impediment, block, hurdle, check, deterrent, barricade
4 *eating and drinking at bars*
► pub, public house, saloon, cafe, tavern

## bar VERB

1 *The people were barred from entering the country.*
► ban, prohibit, forbid, exclude, debar, forbid to enter, prevent from entering, keep out
2 *An angry crowd barred the way.*
► block, obstruct, hinder, impede, check, halt, prevent, stop, thwart

## barbarian NOUN

*attacked by barbarians*
► savage, vandal, brute, ruffian, hooligan, heathen, hun, philistine

## barbaric ADJECTIVE

*a barbaric attack*
► barbarous, brutal, cruel, cold-blooded, inhuman, primitive, savage, uncivilized, wild
OPPOSITES ARE civilized, humane

## bare ADJECTIVE

1 *bare flesh*
► naked, unclothed, uncovered, nude, stark-naked, exposed, stripped, unclad, undressed, bald
OPPOSITES ARE clothed, covered
2 *a bare landscape*
► barren, bleak, desolate, exposed, featureless, treeless, stark, empty, open, windswept
OPPOSITES ARE lush, fertile
3 *bare trees*
► leafless, defoliated
AN OPPOSITE IS leafy
4 *a bare room*
► empty, unfurnished, vacant, cleared, plain, simple, austere
5 *a bare wall*
► blank, clean, uncovered, unadorned, undecorated, unmarked, stripped
6 *the bare facts*
► straightforward, plain, simple, basic, pure, essential, fundamental, hard, bald, literal, unadorned, unambiguous, unembellished, unconcealed, undisguised
7 *the bare necessities*
► basic, essential, minimum, mere, just adequate, just sufficient

## bare VERB

*She bared her arm for the injection.*
► uncover, expose, unclothe, strip

## barefaced ADJECTIVE

*a barefaced lie*
► shameless, flagrant, blatant, glaring, undisguised, patent

## bargain NOUN

1 *The government has made a bargain with the other parties.*
► agreement, deal, understanding, arrangement, pact, pledge, compact, contract, negotiation, promise, settlement, transaction, treaty
2 *a bargain at £12.99*
► good buy, good value, (*more informal*) snip, (*more informal*) steal
**into the bargain** *They were half an hour late into the bargain.*
► in addition, furthermore, as well, besides, moreover, what is more

## bargain VERB

*The union is trying to bargain with the employers.*
► negotiate, do a deal, barter, discuss terms, hold talks, argue, haggle
**bargain on** or **for** *The crush at the doors was something I hadn't bargained for.*
► expect, foresee, imagine, plan for, allow for, reckon on, anticipate, be prepared for, contemplate, consider

## bark VERB

1 *The dog barked.*
► woof, yap, yelp
2 *The sergeant barked an order.*
► shout, snap, growl, snarl

## bark NOUN

*the dog's bark*
► woof, yap, yelp

## barmy ADJECTIVE

(*informal*) *You must be barmy.  a barmy idea*
► mad, crazy, foolish

## barn NOUN

*The farm vehicles were kept in a barn.*
► shed, outbuilding

## barrage NOUN

1 *a barrage across a river*
► dam, barrier, embankment, wall
2 *a barrage of gunfire*
► bombardment, salvo, battery, cannonade, fusillade, storm, volley, assault, attack, onslaught
3 *a barrage of criticism*
► stream, deluge, flood, onslaught, torrent, shower, mass

## barrel NOUN

*a barrel of beer*
► cask, butt, keg, tub, tun, drum, canister, hogshead, water-butt

## barren ADJECTIVE

1 *barren desert*
► infertile, lifeless, arid, parched, desert, dry, waste, waterless, sterile, torrid, unproductive
OPPOSITES ARE fertile, lush
2 *a barren woman*
► infertile, sterile, childless, sterilized
AN OPPOSITE IS fertile

**barricade** NOUN

*barricades across the road*
► barrier, obstruction, obstacle, blockade, bulwark, fence, palisade, stockade

**barrier** NOUN

1 *Police put up barriers to keep out the crowd.*
► barricade, fence, obstacle, obstruction, railing, fencing, wall, bar, hurdle
2 *a barrier to progress*
► obstacle, hindrance, impediment, check, drawback, handicap, limitation, restriction, stumbling block

**barter** VERB

1 *You can barter with the shopkeepers for souvenirs.*
► bargain, haggle, negotiate, deal
2 *The peasants were able to barter any surplus food for equipment.*
► trade, exchange, swap, traffic

**base** ADJECTIVE

*base motives*
► immoral, dishonourable, depraved, low, evil, shameful, sordid, vile, wicked

**base** NOUN

1 *the base of the tower*
► foot, bottom, foundation, pedestal
2 *The hut was used as a base for the expedition.*
► headquarters, centre, station, camp, depot, post

**base** VERB

1 *The company is based in Paris.*
► locate, establish, set up, station
2 *Base your story on events in the news.*
► build, construct, establish, found, ground

**basement** NOUN

*They stored old papers in the basement.*
► cellar, crypt, vault

**bash** VERB

*She could hardly avoid bashing him in the stomach.*
► hit, strike, knock, smack, clout, (*more informal*) biff
**bash into** *The car bashed into a lamp post.*
► collide with, crash into, run into, bang into, bump into

**bashful** ADJECTIVE

*Men tend to be bashful about their feelings.*
► shy, coy, reserved, diffident, embarrassed, inhibited, modest, self-conscious, hesitant, timid, reserved, retiring
OPPOSITES ARE assertive, forward, bold, confident

**basic** ADJECTIVE

1 *You must first learn the basic principles of the subject.*
► fundamental, chief, main, key, crucial, principal, central, primary, elementary
AN OPPOSITE IS secondary
2 *Washing facilities at the camp are very basic.*
► plain, simple, crude, modest, stark, sparse, spartan, unsophisticated
OPPOSITES ARE elaborate, sophisticated

**basin** NOUN

*She poured some water into the basin.*
► bowl, dish, sink, stoup

**basis** NOUN

*The accusations had no factual basis.*
► foundation, justification, support, rationale, base

**bask** VERB

*basking in the sunshine*
► laze, relax, lounge, wallow, sunbathe, bathe
**bask in** *basking in the glory of their success*
► revel in, wallow in, delight in, glory in, relish, enjoy

**basket** NOUN

*a basket of fruit*
► hamper, pannier, creel, punnet, trug

**bass** ADJECTIVE

*a bass note*
► low, deep, bottom

**batch** NOUN

*a batch of cakes*
► consignment, group, quantity, assortment, lot, set

**bath** NOUN

*I'm going to have a bath.*
► wash, douche, jacuzzi, sauna, shower, (*more informal*) soak

**bathe** VERB

1 *Holidaymakers were bathing in the sea.*
► swim, paddle, plunge, splash about, (*more informal*) take a dip
2 *The wound must be carefully bathed.*
► cleanse, clean, wash, rinse, immerse, moisten, soak, steep, swill

**batter** VERB

1 *Someone battered on the door.*
► pound, beat, knock
2 *Winds were battering the waterfront.*
► pound, buffet, lash, pummel
3 *He was battered into submission.*
► beat, pummel, thump

**battered** ADJECTIVE

*help for battered wives*
► beaten, abused, assaulted, maltreated, victimized

**battle** NOUN

1 *The battle took place a few miles north of the city.*
► fight, engagement, action, clash, encounter, conflict
2 *a legal battle for ownership of the club*
► conflict, struggle, dispute
3 *a battle to save the library from closure*
► campaign, crusade

**battle** VERB

*They battled to control the fire.*
► fight, struggle, strive

**baulk** VERB

**baulk at** *Some farmers baulk at using pesticides.*
► resist, (*more formal*) eschew, be reluctant to

## bawdy ADJECTIVE
bawdy stories
► rude, indecent, crude, ribald, naughty, improper, risqué, lewd, vulgar, obscene

## bawl VERB
1 The child sat on its bed bawling.
► cry, sob, weep, blubber
2 'Get out,' she bawled.
► yell, shout, roar, bellow, shriek, scream

## bay NOUN
1 a large bay on the coast
► cove, inlet, gulf, bight
2 a loading bay
► recess, alcove, booth, compartment, niche, nook, opening

## bazaar NOUN
the church bazaar
► sale, fair, fete, jumble sale, car boot sale, bring-and-buy, market, auction

## be VERB
1 There was a young family next door.
► exist, live
2 After he'd been there a while he ordered a drink.
► remain, stay, wait, linger, (more informal) hang on
3 The next performance of the play will be tomorrow.
► take place, occur, happen, come about

## beach NOUN
a picnic on the beach
► shore, sand, sands, seashore, coast, (poetic) strand

## beacon NOUN
a beacon on the hill
► flare, signal, bonfire, beam

## bead NOUN
beads of sweat
► drop, droplet, globule, blob, drip, pearl

## beaker NOUN
a beaker of water
► mug, tumbler, goblet, cup, glass, jar, tankard

## beam NOUN
1 a house with wooden beams
► timber, joist, girder, spar, bar, plank, post, rafter, support, stanchion, boom
2 a beam of light
► ray, shaft, gleam, stream

## beam VERB
1 Satellites beam radio waves to rooftop aerials.
► broadcast, transmit, direct, emit, radiate, send out, aim
2 Daphne beamed happily.
► smile, grin
OPPOSITES ARE glower, frown

## bear VERB
1 The rope would no longer bear his weight.
► support, carry, hold, sustain, prop up, take
2 The document bore a signature.
► display, possess, show, exhibit, have

3 The postman arrived, bearing a large parcel.
► carry, bring, convey, transport, deliver, fetch, move, take, transfer
4 I cannot bear pain. We found the noise hard to bear.
► put up with, endure, tolerate, stand, stomach, abide, accept, cope with, live with, suffer, sustain, undergo, brook
5 The woman bore a child.
► give birth to, produce, mother, bring forth
**bear down on** A huge vehicle was bearing down on them.
► approach, advance on, close in on
**bear out** The report bears out what I was saying.
► confirm, endorse, corroborate

## bearable ADJECTIVE
The pain was only just bearable.
► tolerable, endurable, acceptable

## bearing NOUN
1 The Baroness had a regal bearing.
► demeanour, air, manner, look, appearance, behaviour, presence, carriage, deportment, mien, poise, posture, style
2 The discovery could have some bearing on the mystery.
► connection (with), relevance (to), significance (for), import (for), pertinence (to), reference (to), relationship (with)

## bearings PLURAL NOUN
When it got dark we began to lose our bearings.
► sense of direction, orientation, whereabouts, position, situation, way

## beast NOUN
1 the roars of wild beasts
► animal , creature, brute
2 Her husband was a beast.
► brute, monster, fiend, demon
RELATED ADJECTIVE bestial

## beastly ADJECTIVE
Derek had been beastly to them.
► unkind, cruel, mean, nasty, horrible, spiteful

## beat NOUN
1 music with a strong beat
► rhythm, pulse, throb, accent, stress
2 a policeman's beat
► circuit, rounds, route, itinerary, journey, path, way

## beat VERB
1 The man was beating a dog with a stick.
► hit, strike, thrash, whip, attack, assault, (more informal) wallop, (more informal) whack
2 Molly was beating eggs for her omelette.
► whip, agitate, blend, froth up, mix, stir
3 His heart was beating faster.
► pound, pulsate, race, thump, flutter, palpitate
4 William of Normandy beat the English at the Battle of Hastings. The visitors beat the home team decisively.

▶ defeat, overcome, conquer, vanquish, subdue, crush, overpower, overwhelm, rout, trounce, win against, get the better of, (more informal) thrash

**beat about the bush** Let's not beat about the bush.
▶ prevaricate, vacillate, hedge, (more informal) flannel

**beat up** They went into town and got beaten up.
▶ assault, attack

**beautiful** ADJECTIVE
a beautiful young woman  a beautiful garden
▶ attractive, pretty, good-looking, nice-looking, lovely, glamorous, gorgeous, stunning
AN OPPOSITE IS ugly

**beauty** NOUN
the beauty of the scene
▶ attractiveness, prettiness, loveliness, charm, allure, magnificence, radiance, splendour, appeal, glamour, glory, grace, handsomeness
AN OPPOSITE IS ugliness
RELATED ADJECTIVE aesthetic

**beaver** VERB
**beaver away** She beavered away at her homework.
▶ work hard, toil, labour, slave

**because** CONJUNCTION
**because of** He missed most of the season because of injury.
▶ on account of, owing to, due to, as a result of, as a consequence of, in view of

**beckon** VERB
She beckoned him to go over to her.
▶ signal, gesture, motion, gesticulate, invite

**become** VERB
1 Caterpillars become butterflies.
▶ grow into, turn into, change into, develop into
2 The family soon became rich.
▶ grow, come to be, turn
3 She wants to become the second woman prime minister.
▶ be appointed, be elected, be chosen, be made
4 Dark colours become you.
▶ suit, flatter, befit, grace, set off, enhance, harmonize with

**becoming** ADJECTIVE
The dress is very becoming.
▶ attractive, elegant, fetching, pretty, comely

**bed** NOUN
1 A cat lay on the bed.
▶ divan, bunk, couch
2 a flower bed
▶ plot, patch, area
3 the bed of a river
▶ bottom, floor, course
4 posts set in a bed of concrete
▶ base, foundation, support, setting

**bedraggled** ADJECTIVE
The heavy rain had left him looking bedraggled.
▶ dishevelled, unkempt, untidy, sodden, messy, scruffy, dirty, soiled, stained, wet
OPPOSITES ARE neat, clean, spruce

**bee** NOUN
Bees hovered round the flowers.
▶ drone, worker, bumblebee, honeybee, queen
**a bee in your bonnet** He had a bee in his bonnet about queues.
▶ obsession, preoccupation, fixation, compulsion, (more informal) hang-up

**beefy** ADJECTIVE
A beefy man sat at the bar.
▶ muscular, brawny, burly, hefty, stocky, fat, portly

**befitting** ADJECTIVE
Wear clothes befitting the occasion.
▶ suitable for, appropriate to, fitting

**before** ADVERB
She had called the day before.
▶ earlier, in advance, previously, sooner

**befriend** VERB
He had tried to befriend the new boy.
▶ make friends with, get to know, look after, stand by, help, support, take under your wing

**beg** VERB
1 A man on the pavement was begging.
▶ ask for money, solicit money, (more informal) cadge, (more informal) scrounge
2 Do we have to beg for a favour?
▶ plead, entreat, implore, ask, beseech, crave, importune, petition, pray, request, (formal) supplicate

**beggar** NOUN
He always gave money to beggars he met in the street.
▶ tramp, vagrant, destitute person, down-and-out, homeless person, (more formal) mendicant, pauper, poor person

**begin** VERB
1 We will begin work tomorrow.
▶ start, embark on, set about, get down to, (more formal) commence
AN OPPOSITE IS finish
2 The interviewer began with a few quick questions.
▶ start, start off, open, lead off, get going
AN OPPOSITE IS conclude
3 Where did the rumour begin?
▶ start, originate, spring up, emerge, (more formal) commence
AN OPPOSITE IS end
RELATED ADJECTIVE incipient

**beginner** NOUN
The course is for beginners.
▶ novice, initiate, learner, starter, new recruit, trainee, apprentice, tiro

## beginning NOUN

**1** *the beginning of a new era*
▶ birth, dawn, start, starting point, inception, establishment, origin, onset, emergence

**2** *She had been opposed to the idea from the beginning*
▶ outset, start

**3** *the beginning of the story*
▶ opening, start, prelude

## begrudge VERB

*Kate didn't seem to begrudge Harry all his wealth.*
▶ resent, grudge, mind, object to, be bitter about, covet, envy, be jealous of, be envious of

## behave VERB

*The children worked hard and behaved well.*
▶ conduct yourself, act, react, respond, run, acquit yourself

**behave yourself** *Try to behave yourself.*
▶ be good, act correctly, be on your best behaviour

## behaviour NOUN

*Their behaviour was disgusting.*
▶ conduct, manners, attitude, demeanour, deportment, bearing

## behead VERB

*The king was beheaded.*
▶ decapitate, execute, guillotine

## being NOUN

**1** *She loves him with all her being.*
▶ existence, soul, spirit, essence, actuality, life, living, reality, solidity, substance

**2** *a mortal being*
▶ person, creature, individual, animal, entity

## belated ADJECTIVE

*belated birthday greetings*
▶ late, tardy, overdue
OPPOSITES ARE timely, opportune

## belch VERB

**1** *Laurence belched behind his hand.*
▶ burp, emit wind

**2** *The vehicle was belching black smoke.*
▶ emit, give out, discharge, send out, smoke, spew out, erupt, fume, gush

## belief NOUN

**1** *She had a strong belief that he was innocent.*
▶ conviction, confidence, opinion, certainty, credence, sureness
OPPOSITES ARE disbelief, doubt

**2** *a belief in the benefits of a good diet*
▶ trust, reliance (on), credence

**3** *religious belief*
▶ faith, ideology, principle, creed, dogma
AN OPPOSITE IS scepticism

## believe VERB

**1** *I find that hard to believe.*
▶ accept, be certain about, be convinced by, regard as true, (*more informal*) swallow
AN OPPOSITE IS disbelieve
RELATED ADJECTIVE credible

**2** *I believe several people have cheated.*
▶ think, consider, maintain, conclude, be of the opinion, think it likely, feel, imagine, judge, suppose, take it for granted

## believer NOUN

*a religious believer*
▶ devotee, disciple, follower, adherent, fanatic, proselyte, supporter, upholder, zealot
OPPOSITES ARE sceptic, agnostic, atheist

## belittle VERB

*There is a tendency to belittle or ignore old people.*
▶ ridicule, dismiss, decry, undervalue, run down, disparage, criticize, denigrate, depreciate, (*more informal*) rubbish

## bell NOUN

*I can hear the bell.*
▶ chime, gong, alarm, carillon, knell, peal, signal

## belligerent ADJECTIVE

**1** *She stared in a belligerent manner.*
▶ aggressive, hostile, antagonistic, confrontational, argumentative, quarrelsome, militant, combative, provocative, contentious, pugnacious

**2** *a belligerent nation*
▶ warlike, bellicose, militant, militaristic, violent
AN OPPOSITE IS peaceable

## bellow VERB

*He bellowed something in her ear.*
▶ shout, yell, bawl, roar, boom, shriek

## belly NOUN

*He stood scratching his belly.*
▶ stomach, abdomen, middle, (*usually disapproving*) paunch, (*more informal*) tummy, (*much more informal*) tum

## belong VERB

**1 belong to** *The house belongs to his mother.*
▶ be owned by, be the property of

**2 belong to** *I belong to a sports club.*
▶ be a member of, be affiliated with, be connected with

**3** *They felt they did not belong there.*
▶ feel welcome, have a place, be at home

**4** *The book belongs on the top shelf.*
▶ be located, have a place, go

## belongings NOUN

*Remember to take all your belongings with you.*
▶ possessions, property, personal effects, (*more informal*) stuff

## beloved ADJECTIVE

*her beloved father*
▶ dear, dearest, darling, loved, much loved, cherished

## belt NOUN

**1** *a raincoat tied with a belt*
▶ girdle, sash, strap, waistband, (*of a man's evening suit*) cummerbund

**2** *a spindle driven by a belt*
▶ band, loop, circle

43

**3** *a belt of woodland*
► strip, stretch, area, tract, zone, region, district, line, swathe

**belt** VERB

**belt along** (*informal*) *They all belted along to the bus station.*
► hurry, rush, speed

**bemused** ADJECTIVE
*She sat there with a bemused expression.*
► bewildered, confused, distracted, puzzled, muddled, baffled, perplexed

**bench** NOUN
*The children sat in a row on a bench.*
► pew, long seat, form, stall

**bend** NOUN
*We came to a bend in the road.*
► curve, turn, angle, corner, twist, zigzag

**bend** VERB
**1** *You can bend the pipe round the tank.*
► curve, curl, angle, turn
**2** *The road bends ahead.*
► curve, turn, veer, deviate, twist
**bend down** *He bent down to pick up the piece of paper.*
► stoop, bow, crouch, duck, kneel, lean

**benefactor** NOUN
*An anonymous benefactor paid for my trip*
► patron, supporter, backer, donor, promoter, sponsor, philanthropist, well-wisher

**beneficial** ADJECTIVE
*A good diet is beneficial to health.*
► good (for), advantageous, favourable, useful, valuable, helpful, salutary, wholesome
AN OPPOSITE IS harmful

**benefit** NOUN
**1** *the benefits of a healthy diet*
► advantage, reward, strength, blessing, convenience, gain, asset, service
AN OPPOSITE IS disadvantage
**2** *We are doing it for your benefit.*
► good, sake, interest, welfare, advantage
**3** *the unemployed who are on benefit*
► social security, welfare, assistance, allowance, income support

**benefit** VERB
*The tax cuts will benefit those on a low income.*
► help, advantage, assist, aid, advance, be beneficial to, do good to, profit, serve
AN OPPOSITE IS hinder

**benevolence** NOUN
*The hospital is dependent on the benevolence of local businesses.*
► kindness, generosity, goodness, goodwill, consideration, charity, magnanimity

**benevolent** ADJECTIVE
*She smiled a benevolent smile.*
► kind, generous, helpful, caring, benign, friendly, magnanimous, sympathetic, considerate, philanthropic
AN OPPOSITE IS unkind

**benign** ADJECTIVE
**1** *a benign smile*
► friendly, kind, benevolent
**2** *a benign influence*
► favourable, beneficial, advantageous, propitious

**bent** ADJECTIVE
**1** *a bent nail*
► crooked, twisted, misshapen, angled, buckled, distorted, folded, looped, warped
AN OPPOSITE IS straight
**2** *a man with a bent back*
► crooked, hunched, arched, bowed, curved
**3** (*informal*) *bent politicians*
► corrupt, criminal, dishonest, fraudulent, immoral, untrustworthy, wicked
AN OPPOSITE IS honest

**bequeath** VERB
*He bequeathed his estate to his grandchildren.*
► will, leave, settle (on), endow, hand down, pass on

**bequest** NOUN
*She received a bequest under her aunt's will.*
► legacy, inheritance, settlement, endowment, gift

**bereavement** NOUN
*a bereavement in the family*
► death, loss, deprivation

**bereft** ADJECTIVE
**bereft of** *bereft of intelligence*
► lacking, deprived of, wanting, destitute of, devoid of, robbed of, in need of

**berserk** ADJECTIVE
**go berserk** *reports of a man who went berserk in the street and was hit by a car*
► go crazy, go mad, become demented, become frantic, become hysterical, go out of your mind, rave, become deranged, run amok, (*more informal*) freak out

**berth** NOUN
*a berth for a ship*
► mooring, anchorage, quay, dock, wharf
**give a wide berth to** *After that she gave Gerald a wide berth.*
► avoid, shun, keep away from, steer clear of

**berth** VERB
*The ship berthed at Hull.*
► dock, moor, tie up, drop anchor, land

**beseech** VERB
*She beseeched him to stay.*
► beg, implore, entreat, ask

## besiege VERB

1 *Alexander besieged the city for two years.*
▶ lay siege to, blockade, surround, encircle, confine, beleaguer, (*old use*) invest

2 *She spent a whole day besieged by reporters outside her London home.*
▶ surround, mob, plague, harass, pester, overwhelm

## best ADJECTIVE

1 *one of the best bookshops in London*
▶ foremost, leading, top, finest, pre-eminent, supreme, premier, optimum, outstanding, unsurpassed, unequalled, unrivalled
AN OPPOSITE IS worst

2 *Do whatever you think best.*
▶ most suitable, most appropriate, most fitting, most sensible

## bestow VERB

*The college bestowed a scholarship on her.*
▶ award, confer, endow, (*less formal*) present, (*less formal*) give

**USAGE** If you use *award*, you say *The college awarded her a scholarship*. This is a much less formal and more ordinary word. If you use *present* or *endow*, you say *The college presented (or endowed) her with a scholarship*. If you use *confer*, you say *The college conferred a scholarship on her.*

## bet NOUN

1 *a £10 bet*
▶ gamble, wager, (*informal*) punt

2 *My bet is they won't come.*
▶ opinion, forecast, prediction, feeling, hunch

## bet VERB

1 *She bet all her savings and won.*
▶ wager, gamble, stake, risk

2 (*informal*) *I bet I'm right.*
▶ (*less informal*) be sure, (*less informal*) be confident, (*less informal*) be convinced, (*less informal*) expect

## betray VERB

1 *We trusted him and he betrayed us.*
▶ let down, break your promise to, be unfaithful to, double-cross, deceive

2 *They were betrayed to the authorities.*
▶ inform on, denounce

3 *Please don't betray my secret. He found it hard not to betray his feelings.*
▶ reveal, give away, manifest, show, indicate, disclose, divulge, expose, let out, let slip, tell

## betrothed ADJECTIVE

*His elder son was betrothed to Mark's sister.*
▶ engaged, pledged

## better ADJECTIVE

1 *We are looking for better facilities.*
▶ superior, finer, preferable

2 *Are you feeling better?*
▶ healthier, fitter, stronger, recovered, (*more informal*) on the mend

## better VERB

*The idea cannot be bettered.*
▶ improve on, surpass, outdo

## beware VERB

1 *There are landmines in the fields so beware.*
▶ watch out, look out, be careful, take care, be on the lookout, be on the alert

2 *Beware of the dog.*
▶ watch out for, mind, avoid, steer clear of

## bewilder VERB

*His remarks had bewildered her.*
▶ puzzle, perplex, baffle, mystify, confuse, bemuse, disconcert, confound, (*more informal*) flummox, (*more informal*) floor

## bewildered ADJECTIVE

*Harry looked quite bewildered.*
▶ puzzled, perplexed, baffled, mystified, confused, bemused, disconcerted, (*more informal*) flummoxed

## bewitch VERB

*We were bewitched by the beauty of the place.*
▶ captivate, charm, enchant, entrance, enthral, delight, mesmerize
AN OPPOSITE IS repel

## bewitching ADJECTIVE

*a bewitching sight*
▶ captivating, charming, enchanting, entrancing, enthralling, attractive

## bias NOUN

*The management was accused of bias.*
▶ prejudice, partiality, discrimination, unfairness, injustice, partisanship, favouritism, bigotry, intolerance, chauvinism, racism, sexism

## biased ADJECTIVE

*a biased attitude The judge was clearly biased.*
▶ prejudiced, partial, one-sided, partisan, subjective, bigoted, chauvinistic, racist, sexist
OPPOSITES ARE unbiased, impartial

## bicker VERB

*I don't want to stand here all day bickering about it.*
▶ quarrel, squabble, wrangle, argue, scrap, row

## bid NOUN

1 *a bid of £5,000*
▶ offer, tender, proposal, price, proposition

2 *a bid to discover the truth*
▶ attempt, effort, endeavour, try (at), (*informal*) go (at), (*informal*) crack (at)

## bid VERB

*A buyer bid a record price at the auction.*
▶ offer, make an offer of, put in a bid of, tender, proffer, propose

## biff VERB

*He had biffed her by mistake.*
▶ hit, strike, knock, smack, bash, clout

**big** ADJECTIVE This word is often overused. Here are some alternatives:

**1** *a big house* *The bill was very big.*
▶ large, great, huge, enormous, colossal, immense

**2** *a big difference*
▶ significant, important, substantial, considerable, sizeable

**3** *big ideas*
▶ ambitious, grand, grandiose, far-reaching

**4** *That was big of you.*
▶ generous, considerate, magnanimous, kind, gracious

**bigoted** ADJECTIVE

*He disliked people who held such bigoted views.*
▶ prejudiced, biased, partial, intolerant, narrow-minded

**USAGE** Note that *bigoted* is a much stronger word than the alternatives given here.

**bilious** ADJECTIVE

*He woke up feeling bilious.*
▶ sick, nauseous, liverish, queasy, ill

**bill** NOUN

**1** *The bill came to over a thousand pounds.*
▶ account, invoice, statement, list of charges

**2** *a bill advertising a sale*
▶ poster, notice, advertisement, placard, sheet, leaflet, broadsheet, circular, handout, bulletin

**3** *a bill in parliament*
▶ draft law, proposed law

**billow** VERB

**1** *Her dress billowed out in the wind.*
▶ balloon, blow, puff, swell, bulge

**2** *Smoke billowed from the chimney.*
▶ pour, swirl, spiral

**bin** NOUN

*a row of storage bins*
▶ container, canister, receptacle, drum

**bind** VERB

**1** *I'll bind the two pieces with string.*
▶ fasten, tie, secure, attach, clamp, stick, connect, join, lash, link, rope, strap, truss, hitch

**2** *A nurse bound their wounds.*
▶ bandage, dress, cover, wrap, swathe

**3** *They were bound by a solemn oath not to reveal their secret.*
▶ oblige, require, compel, constrain, force, necessitate

**4** *Their sufferings had bound them together.*
▶ unite, join, draw, hold

**binding** ADJECTIVE

*a binding agreement*
▶ irrevocable, obligatory, mandatory, compulsory, permanent

AN OPPOSITE IS informal

**biography** NOUN

*He read biographies of his great heroes.*
▶ life-story, life, memoirs, recollections, autobiography (= a biography written by its subject)

**bird** NOUN

**WORDS FOR TYPES OF BIRD**

**passerine (perching) birds:** sparrow, thrush, blackbird, robin, starling, bluetit, linnet, chaffinch, greenfinch, swallow, wren, martin, jay, swift, skylark, crow, raven, magpie, jackdaw, jay, pigeon, dove, nightingale, woodpecker.

**waterbirds:** duck, goose, swan, grebe, heron, flamingo, stork, pelican, kingfisher, mallard, moorhen, coot, dipper, crane.

**sea birds:** gull, guillemot, tern, albatross, gannet, cormorant, shag, auk, penguin, puffin.

**owls and birds of prey:** eagle, hawk, falcon, kite, merlin, kestrel, buzzard, osprey, vulture, condor, tawny owl, barn owl, little owl, eagle owl, snowy owl.

**game birds:** pheasant, grouse, partridge, quail, gamebird.

**flightless or running birds:** emu, ostrich, rhea, kiwi, cassowary, penguin.

**cage birds:** canary, budgerigar ((informal) budgie), lovebird, parrot, parakeet, cockatoo, cockatiel, myna bird, macaw, toucan.

**domesticated birds:** chicken, hen, turkey, duck, goose, guinea fowl.

**birth** NOUN

**1** *the birth of a child*
▶ delivery, childbirth, (technical) parturition
RELATED ADJECTIVE natal

**2** *of noble birth*
▶ ancestry, descent, origin, parentage, lineage, pedigree, breeding, background, blood, extraction, family, genealogy, line, race, stock, strain

**3** *the birth of socialism*
▶ beginning, origin, emergence, advent, dawn

**bit** NOUN This word is often overused. Here are some alternatives:

*a bit of chocolate* *a bit of stone*
▶ piece, portion, chunk, lump, hunk, fragment, morsel, particle, slice

**a bit** *That was a bit hard.*
▶ rather, fairly, slightly, somewhat, a little, (more informal) pretty

**a bit of** *a bit of a shame*
▶ rather

**bit by bit** *Bit by bit she began to understand.*
▶ gradually, slowly, little by little

**bitchy** ADJECTIVE

(informal) *bitchy remarks*
▶ spiteful, vindictive, malicious, backbiting, nasty, mean

**bite** NOUN
1 *a bite on the arm*
► nip, sting, pinch, wound
2 *a bite to eat*
► mouthful, snack, morsel, bit, nibble, piece, taste

**bite** VERB
1 *He bit a chunk out of an apple.*
► munch, nibble, chew, crunch, gnaw, nip, champ, (*formal*) masticate
2 *She had been bitten by an insect.*
► sting, pierce
3 *Tax increases will begin to bite in the new tax year.*
► take effect, have an effect, take hold
4 **bite into** *Acid starts to bite into the metal.*
► eat into, corrode, erode, wear away

**biting** ADJECTIVE
1 *a biting wind*
► bitterly cold, bitter, freezing, icy, raw, piercing, perishing, arctic
2 *a biting remark*
► caustic, harsh, cutting, incisive, bitter, penetrating, stinging, hurtful, cruel, sharp

**bitter** ADJECTIVE
1 *a bitter taste*
► sour, sharp, acid, acrid, tart, harsh
OPPOSITES ARE mild, sweet
2 *The decision was seen as a bitter disappointment.*
► cruel, distressing, painful, unpleasant
3 *bitter remarks*
► harsh, cutting, caustic, incisive, biting, penetrating, stinging, hurtful, cruel, sharp
4 *She felt bitter about what had happened.*
► resentful, embittered, cynical, aggrieved, disgruntled
5 *a bitter quarrel*
► acrimonious, rancorous, angry, vitriolic
6 *a bitter wind*
► biting, freezing, icy, raw, piercing, perishing, bitterly cold, arctic
AN OPPOSITE IS gentle

**bizarre** ADJECTIVE
*a bizarre story of survival in wartime*
► strange, weird, odd, extraordinary, eccentric, peculiar, curious, queer, unusual, grotesque
AN OPPOSITE IS ordinary

**black** ADJECTIVE
1 *black ink*
► jet-black, coal-black
2 *a black night*
► dark, unlit, moonless, starless, gloomy
3 *hands black from mending the mower*
► filthy, dirty, grimy, grubby, soiled
AN OPPOSITE IS spotless
4 *in a black mood*
► melancholy, miserable, glum, wretched, unhappy, despondent

**black** VERB
*I blacked my shoes.*
► blacken, polish

**blacken** VERB
*She decided to blacken her hair.*
► darken, make black

**blackmail** NOUN
*He was always vulnerable to blackmail.*
► extortion, intimidation

**blame** NOUN
1 *They were cleared of all blame.*
► responsibility, guilt, liability, culpability
2 *Who got the blame for it?*
► criticism, censure, condemnation, (*more informal*) rap

**blame** VERB
*The report blamed the driver for the accident.*
► hold responsible, hold accountable, condemn, censure, criticize, reprove, reprimand, accuse (of), charge (with)
AN OPPOSITE IS excuse

**blameless** ADJECTIVE
*a blameless life*
► innocent, guiltless, faultless, exemplary, irreproachable, upright, virtuous, unblemished
OPPOSITES ARE blameworthy, guilty

**bland** ADJECTIVE
1 *a bland taste*
► insipid, uninteresting, dull, weak, nondescript, watery, mild, boring, flat
OPPOSITES ARE sharp, strong
2 *a bland personality  bland remarks*
► dull, tedious, uninteresting, unexciting, monotonous, drab, dreary, feeble, vapid, weak, (*informal*) wishy-washy
OPPOSITES ARE interesting, stimulating

**blank** ADJECTIVE
1 *a blank page*
► empty, unused, unfilled, clear, bare, void, unmarked
AN OPPOSITE IS used
2 *a blank look*
► expressionless, featureless, impassive, vacant, deadpan, inscrutable, unresponsive
AN OPPOSITE IS expressive

**blanket** NOUN
*a blanket of fog*
► covering, layer, film, shroud, cloak, mantle, mask, sheet, cover

**blare** VERB
*Sirens were blaring.*
► blast, resound, screech, shriek

**blasé** ADJECTIVE
*He had become blasé about the dangers.*
► nonchalant, indifferent, unconcerned, apathetic

**blaspheme** VERB
*How dare you blaspheme before your own father!*
► curse, swear, profane

**blasphemous** ADJECTIVE
*blasphemous language*
► sacrilegious, profane, irreverent, irreligious, godless, impious, ungodly, disrespectful
AN OPPOSITE IS reverent

**blast** NOUN
1 *a blast of cold air*
► gust, rush, blow, draught, squall
2 *Hundreds were injured in the blast.*
► explosion, discharge, shock

**blast** VERB
1 *A series of missiles blasted the building*
► blow up, bomb, demolish, raze
2 *radios blasting out rock music*
► blare, boom, roar, thunder, bellow

**blatant** ADJECTIVE
*a blatant lie*
► flagrant, brazen, barefaced, glaring, shameless, unconcealed
AN OPPOSITE IS inconspicuous

**blaze** NOUN
1 *It took firefighters all night to control the blaze.*
► fire, flames
2 *a blaze of light*
► burst, flash, gleam, streak, beam, glitter

**blaze** VERB
1 *The fire began to blaze.*
► burn, flare up, be alight
2 *Lights blazed from the top floor.*
► shine, beam, flare, flash, gleam, glitter

**bleach** VERB
*The blinds were bleached in the sun.*
► turn white, whiten, fade, blanch

**bleak** ADJECTIVE
*a bleak landscape*
► bare, barren, desolate, exposed, featureless, treeless, stark, empty, open, windswept

**bleary** ADJECTIVE
*bleary eyes   bleary vision*
► blurred, blurry, unfocused, clouded, cloudy, fogged, foggy, hazy, murky
AN OPPOSITE IS clear

**bleed** VERB
*The wound began to bleed.*
► lose blood, haemorrhage, weep, seep

**blemish** NOUN
*a beautiful rose bloom without a single blemish.*
► imperfection, flaw, fault, defect, spot, mark, stain, speck, taint

**blend** NOUN
*a blend of several ingredients*
► mixture, mix, combination, mingling, amalgam, fusion, synthesis

**blend** VERB
1 *Blend the ingredients carefully.*
► mix, combine, mingle, merge, stir together, beat, fold in, integrate, whip, whisk

2 *The colours blend well.*
► harmonize, match, fit

**bless** VERB
*The couple were blessed with a child.*
► favour, grace, endow

**blessed** ADJECTIVE
*a blessed place*
► holy, sacred, sanctified, adored, divine, hallowed, revered

**blessing** NOUN
1 *The priest gave a blessing*
► benediction, grace, prayer
2 *The manager gave the scheme his blessing.*
► approval, backing, support, consent, approbation, leave, permission
AN OPPOSITE IS disapproval
3 *Central heating is a blessing in the winter*
► benefit, advantage, asset, boon, comfort, convenience, godsend, help
AN OPPOSITE IS affliction

**blight** NOUN
1 *potato blight*
► disease, rot, decay, (more formal) infestation
2 *the blight of traffic noise*
► affliction, curse, plague, menace, nuisance, tribulation, trial, misfortune
AN OPPOSITE IS blessing

**blight** VERB
*Their lives were blighted by troublesome neighbours.*
► ruin, wreck, spoil, afflict, shatter, disrupt

**blind** ADJECTIVE
1 *She had been blind from birth.*
► sightless, unsighted, visually impaired, partially sighted, unseeing
2 *blind to all dangers*
► oblivious, imperceptive, heedless (of), unaware (of), inattentive, indifferent, insensible, insensitive, ignorant (of), blinkered (from)
OPPOSITES ARE aware, perceptive
3 *showing a blind acceptance of criticism*
► uncritical, reckless, impulsive, indiscriminate, unreasoning, mindless
4 *a blind corner*
► concealed, hidden, obscure, obstructed

**blind** NOUN
*She pulled down a blind.*
► screen, shade, cover, curtain, shutter

**blind** VERB
1 *The light blinded her for a few moments.*
► dazzle
2 *They are trying to blind us all with science.*
► confuse, deceive, overawe, intimidate, disconcert, unsettle, (more informal) put off

**blink** VERB
*A light on the control panel began to blink.*
► flash, wink, flicker, twinkle, flutter, gleam, glimmer

**B**

**bliss** NOUN
*a life of bliss*
▶ joy, delight, pleasure, rapture, ecstasy, euphoria, felicity, gladness, happiness, heaven, paradise
AN OPPOSITE IS misery

**blissful** ADJECTIVE
*They spent a blissful week together.*
▶ ecstatic, joyful, rapturous, euphoric, elated, happy
AN OPPOSITE IS miserable

**blizzard** NOUN
*They were kept indoors by blizzards.*
▶ snowstorm, squall

**bloated** ADJECTIVE
*a bloated stomach*
▶ swollen, dilated, distended, enlarged, inflated
OPPOSITES ARE shrunken, shrivelled

**blob** NOUN
*a blob of ice cream*
▶ drop, droplet, globule, lump

**bloc** NOUN
*the former communist bloc*
▶ alliance, association, federation, union

**block** NOUN
1 *a block of chocolate  a block of stone*
▶ chunk, hunk, slab, bar, brick, cake, lump, mass, piece
2 *The pipe had a block in it.*
▶ blockage, obstruction, stoppage
3 *Lack of funds proved a block to progress.*
▶ barrier, hindrance, impediment, obstacle

**block** VERB
1 *(informal) The drain was blocked with leaves*
▶ bung up, choke, clog, close, congest, constrict, dam, fill, jam, obstruct, plug, stop up
2 *A parked van was blocking access to the house.*
▶ obstruct, bar, impede, inhibit, restrict, limit
3 *The scheme was blocked by the directors.*
▶ stop, prevent, halt, thwart

**blockade** NOUN
*a blockade of the city*
▶ siege, encirclement, investment

**blockage** NOUN
*The drain has a blockage.*
▶ obstruction, stoppage, block, constriction, jam, obstacle, resistance, barrier, bottleneck, congestion

**bloke** NOUN
*(informal) He's a funny bloke, isn't he?*
▶ chap, fellow, guy, man, boy, individual

**blond, blonde** ADJECTIVE
*blond hair*
▶ fair, flaxen, golden, light, yellow, bleached

**blood** NOUN
*a person of noble blood*
▶ ancestry, descent, origin, parentage, lineage, pedigree, breeding, background, birth, extraction, family, genealogy, line, race, stock, strain

**bloodcurdling** ADJECTIVE
*a bloodcurdling scream*
▶ terrifying, frightening, horrifying, fearful, spine-chilling, hair-raising

**bloodshed** NOUN
*The government were anxious to avoid further bloodshed.*
▶ killing, slaughter, carnage, butchery, violence

**bloodthirsty** ADJECTIVE
*bloodthirsty attackers*
▶ brutal, murderous, cruel, barbaric, savage, vicious, violent, warlike, bloody, ferocious, fierce

**bloody** ADJECTIVE
1 *a bloody wound*
▶ bleeding, bloodstained, raw, gaping
2 *a bloody battle*
▶ fierce, gory, bloodthirsty, violent

**bloom** NOUN
1 *rose blooms*
▶ blossom, flower, bud
2 *the bloom of youth*
▶ prime, peak, glow, flush, acme

**bloom** VERB
1 *The roses have all bloomed now.*
▶ blossom, flower, open
AN OPPOSITE IS fade
2 *The children had bloomed in the country air.*
▶ flourish, thrive, prosper, blossom, develop

**blossom** NOUN
*apple blossom*
▶ blooms, buds, florets, flowers

**blossom** VERB
1 *The trees have started to blossom.*
▶ bloom, flower, open
AN OPPOSITE IS fade
2 *The scheme can blossom with the right support.*
▶ flourish, thrive, prosper, bloom, develop

**blot** NOUN
1 *a blot of ink*
▶ spot, blotch, mark, smear, smudge, stain, splodge, blob
2 *a blot on the landscape*
▶ eyesore, blemish, defect, fault, flaw

**blot** VERB
*Ink blotted the page.*
▶ smudge, mark, spoil, spot, stain, bespatter, mar

**blot out** *A tall building blotted out the view*
▶ conceal, hide, mask, obliterate, obscure, cover, delete, eclipse, erase, expunge, rub out, wipe out, cancel

**blotch** NOUN
*The walls had damp blotches down them.*
▶ patch, smudge, speck, speckle, blot, mark

**blotchy** ADJECTIVE
*a blotchy skin*
▶ spotty, spotted, blemished, marked, patchy, smudged, uneven

## blow NOUN

**1** *a blow on the head*
▶ knock, bang, hit, thump, smack

**2** *The news was a terrible blow.*
▶ shock, surprise, reverse, setback, upset, disappointment, calamity, disaster

## blow VERB

**1** *The storm blew the ship on the rocks.*
▶ drive, sweep, force, blast, fling, whisk

**2** *Leaves were blowing across the drive.*
▶ drift, flutter, whirl, stream

**blow out** *The heater blows out hot air.*
▶ puff out, blast out, exhale, breathe, fan, waft

**blow up**

**1** *I'll blow up the tyres.*
▶ inflate, pump up, fill, dilate, expand
OPPOSITES ARE let down, deflate

**2** *The photograph can be blown up.*
▶ enlarge

**3** *A bomb blew up the building.*
▶ bomb, blast, detonate, dynamite, explode

**4** (*informal*) *When he heard what we had done he blew up.*
▶ grow angry, lose your temper, rage

## blue ADJECTIVE

**1** *a pretty blue colour*
▶ sky-blue, turquoise, ultramarine, aquamarine, azure, cerulean, cobalt, indigo, navy, sapphire

**2** *a blue movie*
▶ indecent, coarse, obscene, salacious, risqué

**3** (*informal*) *Jake was feeling blue that day.*
▶ sad, depressed, dejected

## blueprint NOUN

**1** *blueprints of the new aircraft*
▶ design, plan, drawing, draft, outline, pattern, layout, prototype

**2** *a blueprint for political reform*
▶ model, plan, scheme, framework, basis, pattern, guide, proposal

## blues NOUN

**the blues** *I woke up with the blues just like you did.*
▶ depression, sadness, melancholy, dejection, despondency, low spirits, misery, gloom

## bluff NOUN

*The offer is regarded as a crude bluff.*
▶ deception, subterfuge, sham, pretence, fake, fraud, ruse, artifice, trick

## bluff VERB

**1** *We think they must be bluffing us.*
▶ deceive, delude, mislead, hoodwink, trick

**2** *I am sure they are only bluffing.*
▶ pretend, sham, put on an act, lie, (*more informal*) kid

## blunder NOUN

*Harry shook his head at his own blunder.*
▶ mistake, error, gaffe, slip, faux pas, (*more informal*) howler, (*much more informal*) cock-up

## blunder VERB

*The security officer had blundered by letting the men into the building.*
▶ make a mistake, bungle, err, be in error, misjudge, miscalculate, slip up, (*more informal*) put your foot in it, (*more informal*) goof, (*much more informal*) screw up, (*much more informal*) cock up

## blunt ADJECTIVE

**1** *a blunt knife*
▶ dull, rounded, thick, unpointed, unsharpened
AN OPPOSITE IS sharp

**2** *a blunt reply*
▶ abrupt, harsh, curt, terse, gruff, rude, offhand, brusque, insensitive, outspoken, plain-spoken
OPPOSITES ARE polite, tactful

## blunt VERB

*A series of snacks blunted my appetite.*
▶ dull, reduce, dampen, take the edge off, weaken
OPPOSITES ARE sharpen, intensify

## blur VERB

*The steam had blurred her glasses.*
▶ cloud, fog, mask, obscure, befog, blear, dim, smear

## blurred ADJECTIVE

*When he lifted his head everything looked blurred.*
▶ indistinct, blurry, bleary, fuzzy, hazy, misty

## blurt VERB

**blurt out** *She had blurted out the first thing that came into her head.*
▶ come out with, exclaim, cry out, disclose, divulge, let out, let slip, reveal

## blush VERB

*She blushed as he kissed her hand.*
▶ go red, flush, glow, colour

## blustery ADJECTIVE

*a wet blustery day*
▶ gusty, squally, windy

## board NOUN

**1** *a wooden board*
▶ plank, panel, beam, length of timber, lath

**2** *the board of directors*
▶ committee, council, panel

## board VERB

**1** *Passengers may now board the aircraft.*
▶ get on, go on board, enter, embark, ascend

**2** *His wife boarded students in a spare room.*
▶ accommodate, house, lodge, put up, billet, quarter

## boast VERB

*His mother had been boasting about how clever he was.*
▶ brag, crow, bluster, swank, show off, gloat, sing someone's praises, (*more informal*) talk big

## boastful ADJECTIVE

(*informal*) *He was constantly boastful of all his achievements.*
▶ bragging, conceited, big-headed, bumptious,

proud, puffed up, swaggering, swollen-headed,
vain, egotistical, (*informal*) cocky, (*informal*) swanky
AN OPPOSITE IS modest

**boat** NOUN
*boats in the little harbour*
► craft, vessel, ship

**bob** VERB
*Little boats were bobbing in the water.*
► bounce, move up and down, dance, toss about,
skip about, oscillate

**bob up** *A woman at the back bobbed up to ask a
question.*
► jump up, leap up, spring up, rise (up), appear

**bode** VERB
*This incident did not bode well for his future as a film
director.*
► augur, promise, signal, forebode, herald, portend

**bodily** ADJECTIVE
*bodily contact*
► physical, corporeal

---

**body** NOUN
**1** *the human body*
► frame, figure, form, physique, shape, anatomy,
being, build
RELATED ADJECTIVES corporal, somatic
**2** *a blow to the body*
► trunk, torso
**3** *a body floating in the river*
► corpse, cadaver, carcass, mortal remains, (*more
informal*) stiff
**4** *the managing body*
► committee, company, association, corporation,
society, band
**5** *a large body of evidence*
► quantity, collection, volume, mass,
accumulation, agglomeration, corpus

**WORDS FOR PARTS OF THE BODY**
**the skin**: skin, pores.
**the head**: head, scalp, face; jaw, chin, cheek,
eye, ear, forehead, nose, nostril; mouth, lip,
tooth, tongue, gum; neck, throat.
**the limbs**: limb; arm, elbow, funny bone, wrist,
hand, finger, fingernail, thumb, knuckle; leg,
foot, toe, toenail, ankle, heel, shin, calf, thigh,
knee, kneecap, hip.
**the torso**: torso, trunk; buttocks, bottom; waist,
abdomen, belly, chest, navel, breast, nipple,
shoulder, shoulder blade.
**main internal parts**: skeleton, backbone,
vertebra, spine, spinal cord, bone; blood,
artery, vein, capillary, gland, marrow, muscle,
nerve, ovary, oviduct; adrenals, saliva;
hormones; brain, tonsils, adenoids, windpipe;
heart, lung, liver, appendix, bladder, bowels,
colon, gall bladder, gullet, gut, intestines,
kidney, pancreas, pelvis, penis, stomach, testis,
uterus or womb; rectum, anus. ►►

---

**bodily systems**: blood system, digestive
system, endocrine system (hormone
production), excretory system, nervous
system, reproductive system, respiratory
system (breathing), skeletal system (bones and
muscles).

---

**bodyguard** NOUN
*He could not travel anywhere without a bodyguard.*
► guard, minder, protector

**boffin** NOUN
*the boffins who invented radar*
► expert, specialist, scientist

**bog** NOUN
*The ground became wetter, and eventually they were on
the edge of a bog.*
► marsh, marshland, swamp, mire, morass, fen,
quicksands, mudflats, quagmire

**bogged down** *bogged down with all the work*
► encumbered, hindered, impeded, slowed down,
in difficulties, stuck, sunk

**bogus** ADJECTIVE
*The man had given a bogus address.*
► fake, false, spurious, fraudulent, counterfeit,
pretended

**bogy** NOUN
*bogies and other beings of the night*
► evil spirit, ghost, spectre, phantom

**boil** NOUN
*a boil on the skin*
► swelling, pustule, pimple, abscess, blister, spot,
tumour

**boil** VERB
**1** *Boil the potatoes in water.*
► bring to boiling point, bring to the boil, cook, heat,
simmer
**2** *The water was beginning to boil.*
► bubble, effervesce, foam, seethe, steam
**3** *She was boiling with anger.*
► seethe, be angry, lose your temper, go into a rage,
fly into a rage, flare up, (*more informal*) see red

**boisterous** ADJECTIVE
*a boisterous beach game*
► lively, spirited, animated, exuberant, rough,
rowdy
OPPOSITES ARE restrained, calm

**bold** ADJECTIVE
**1** *a bold move  a bold traveller*
► brave, courageous, daring, adventurous,
audacious, confident, dauntless, enterprising,
fearless, forceful, gallant, heroic, intrepid,
self-confident, valiant, valorous, venturesome, (*more
informal*) plucky
AN OPPOSITE IS cowardly

**2** *bold remarks*
▶ brazen, forward, cheeky, brash, impertinent, impudent, insolent, presumptuous, fresh, pert, rude, saucy, shameless, unashamed
OPPOSITES ARE polite, reticent

**3** *a bold pattern   bold colours*
▶ striking, strong, bright, clear, conspicuous, eye-catching, prominent, pronounced, showy, vivid
AN OPPOSITE IS inconspicuous

**boldness** NOUN
*Their boldness took everyone by surprise.*
▶ bravery, daring, audacity

**bolt** NOUN
**1** *The door bolt was stuck.*
▶ catch, bar, latch, lock, fastening
**2** *Put a nut on the bolt.*
▶ pin, rivet, rod, screw
**a bolt from the blue**
▶ shock, surprise, (*more informal*) bombshell

**bolt** VERB
**1** *We'd better bolt the door.*
▶ fasten, latch, lock, secure, bar
**2** *She bolted from the room.*
▶ dash, dart, flee, fly, rush, hurry, sprint, run, escape
**3** *He was in such a rush he had to bolt his food.*
▶ gobble, gulp, wolf, guzzle, stuff, scoff down

**bomb** NOUN
*The building was destroyed by bombs.*
▶ explosive, missile

**bomb** VERB
*The city was bombed for days on end.*
▶ bombard, drop bombs on, shell

**bombard** VERB
**1** *Offshore ships bombarded the city all night.*
▶ shell, pound, blast, strafe, assault, attack, beset, bomb, fire at, pelt, shoot at, assail
**2** *The speaker was bombarded with questions.*
▶ overwhelm, inundate, swamp, flood, deluge, pester, plague

**bombardment** NOUN
*The city was practically demolished by the bombardment.*
▶ barrage, blast, shelling, attack, cannonade, discharge, fusillade, hail, salvo, volley

**bond** NOUN
**1** *There was a close bond between the two brothers.*
▶ attachment, connection, tie, link, relationship, affinity, unity, affiliation
**2** *By running away he had broken his bond*
▶ promise, pledge, word, agreement, compact, contract, covenant, guarantee
**3** *bonds The prisoner struggled to undo his bonds.*
▶ chains, fetters, manacles, shackles, restraints, fastenings

**bond** VERB
*The fitting is bonded to the wall with strong glue.*
▶ stick, fix, attach, fasten

**bondage** NOUN
*The slaves were released from years of bondage.*
▶ slavery, servitude, enslavement, subjection, captivity, imprisonment, incarceration

---

**bone** NOUN
**THE BONES OF THE HUMAN BODY INCLUDE**
**in the head:** cranium (skull), mandible (jaw), orbit (eye socket), maxilla (upper jaw), mandible (lower jaw).

**in the upper body and trunk:** scapula (shoulderblade), clavicle (collarbone), ribs, sternum (breastbone), thoracic vertebrae (supporting the ribs), lumbar vertebrae (in the lower back), sacrum (at the base of the spine), coccyx, pelvis (or pelvic girdle, consisting of ilium, pubis, and ischium).

**in the arms:** humerus (in the upper arm), radius (on the side where the thumb is), ulna (on the side where the little finger is), carpus (wrist bones, consisting of carpals), metacarpus (hand bones, consisting of metacarpals), phalanx (plural phalanges), bones of the fingers.

**in the legs:** femur (thighbone), patella (kneebone), tibia (shinbone), fibula, tarsus (ankle, consisting of tarsal bones), metatarsus (foot, consisting of metatarsals), phalanx (plural phalanges), bones of the toes.

---

**bonny** ADJECTIVE
*a bonny baby*
▶ beautiful, attractive, pretty, sweet, cute

**bonus** NOUN
**1** *no Christmas bonus this year*
▶ extra payment, handout, reward
**2** *A meal out was an unexpected bonus.*
▶ benefit, extra, addition, advantage, (*informal*) plus

**bony** ADJECTIVE
*a bony figure*
▶ thin, angular, gawky, lanky, gaunt, emaciated, gangling, lean, scraggy, scrawny, skinny
AN OPPOSITE IS plump

**book** NOUN
*a book to read and enjoy*
▶ volume, tome, publication, tract, booklet

**book** VERB
**1** *On his way to the hospital he was booked for speeding.*
▶ arrest, take your name, write down details
**2** *We booked tickets for the concert.*
▶ reserve, order, arrange for, prearrange, buy
**3** *Will you book a disco for the party?*
▶ engage, organize, sign up, arrange

**booklet** NOUN
*a booklet of travel advice*
▶ pamphlet, brochure, leaflet, paperback

**boom** NOUN
**1** *Suddenly there was the boom of the one o'clock gun.*
▶ bang, reverberation, roar, sound, blast

B

**boom**

2 *a boom in trade*
▶ upturn, upsurge, upswing, boost, growth, improvement, expansion, increase, spurt
AN OPPOSITE IS slump

**boom** VERB

1 *The guns began to boom.*
▶ rumble, thunder, crash, reverberate, resound, echo

2 *Business is booming.*
▶ thrive, prosper, flourish, do well, (*more informal*) pick up
OPPOSITES ARE decline, slump

**boon** NOUN

*Cheap travel is such a boon.*
▶ benefit, blessing, help, asset, advantage, (*more informal*) piece of luck

**boost** NOUN

1 *a boost to morale*
▶ impetus, stimulus, lift, uplift, (*more informal*) shot in the arm

2 *a boost in sales*
▶ increase, expansion, growth, improvement, boom, upturn, upsurge, upswing, spurt
OPPOSITES ARE decrease, decline

**boost** VERB

*The award boosted everyone's morale.*
▶ raise, uplift, heighten, stimulate, bolster, increase, enhance
OPPOSITES ARE depress, hinder

**boot** NOUN

*He had lost his left boot in the mud.*
▶ gumboot, wellington, (*more informal*) welly

**booth** NOUN

*a telephone booth   a voting booth*
▶ cubicle, kiosk, stall, compartment, enclosure, carrel, hut, stand

**booty** NOUN

*The gang arranged to meet and divide the booty.*
▶ loot, plunder, haul, pillage, spoils

**booze** NOUN

*Lunch had to include lots of booze* (*informal*).
▶ alcohol, drink, alcoholic drink, liquor, spirits

**booze** VERB

*They had been boozing all night* (*informal*).
▶ drink, have a drink, indulge, imbibe, (*also informal*) tipple

**border** NOUN

1 *the border of a tablecloth   the border of a lake*
▶ edge, margin, perimeter, fringe, verge

2 *the border between Italy and Slovenia*
▶ frontier, boundary, borderline

**border** VERB

*border on* *The park borders a housing estate.*
▶ skirt, adjoin, be adjacent to, be alongside, abut on, join, share a border with, touch

**borderline** ADJECTIVE

*a borderline case*
▶ marginal, indeterminate, uncertain, ambivalent

**bore** VERB

1 *You need to bore a hole in the wall.*
▶ drill, punch, cut, pierce, sink

2 *Long films tend to bore him.*
▶ weary, tire, (*more informal*) turn off
OPPOSITES ARE interest, entertain

**bore** NOUN

*What a bore to have to wait another hour.*
▶ nuisance, bother, annoyance, (*more informal*) drag, (*more informal*) pain, (*more informal*) pest

**boring** ADJECTIVE

*What a boring book.   The work turned out to be very boring.*
▶ tedious, dull, monotonous, dreary, humdrum, routine, uninteresting, unexciting, insipid, vapid, jejune
OPPOSITES ARE interesting, stimulating

**born** ADJECTIVE

*a born comic*
▶ natural, untaught, instinctive, genuine

**borrow** VERB

*I need to borrow a pen.*
▶ loan, have use of, obtain, acquire, (*more informal*) cadge, (*more informal*) scrounge
AN OPPOSITE IS lend

**bosom** NOUN

1 *The dress was cut high over her bosom.*
▶ bust, chest, breasts

2 *The family took her into its bosom.*
▶ care, protection, shelter

**boss** NOUN

(*informal*) *The boss would be away all that week.*
▶ head, chief, manager, leader

**boss** VERB

*You have no right to boss me about like this.*
▶ order, dictate to, push around, lord it over, bully, domineer

**bossy** ADJECTIVE

*Why do you treat us in such a bossy manner?*
▶ domineering, officious, overbearing, high-handed, imperious, dictatorial, authoritarian, autocratic, aggressive, bullying, despotic, lordly, oppressive, peremptory, tyrannical
AN OPPOSITE IS submissive

**botch** VERB

*They managed to botch the next job as well.*
▶ bungle, make a mess of, mismanage, mishandle, do badly, spoil, mess up, (*more informal*) screw up
AN OPPOSITE IS succeed in

**bother** NOUN

1 *There was some bother at the disco.*
▶ disorder, trouble, disturbance, difficulty, fuss, (*more informal*) hassle, (*more informal*) aggro

**2** *It was a bother to keep the food hot.*
► nuisance, annoyance, irritation, inconvenience, palaver, pest, trouble, worry, trial, job

**bother** VERB

**1** *We found a quiet spot where no one would be able to bother us.*
► disturb, trouble, pester, molest, annoy, vex, worry, concern, dismay, exasperate, harass, (*informal*) hassle, inconvenience, irk, irritate, nag, plague, upset

**2** *The accident was too minor to bother about.*
► concern yourself, be concerned, be worried, care, mind

**bottle** NOUN

**1** *a bottle of wine water in bottles*
► flask, carafe, decanter, flagon, jar, pitcher

**2** (*informal*) *She had bottle to stand up to him, they had to admit.*
► courage, nerve, pluck, spirit, mettle, daring, audacity, boldness, bravery

**bottle** VERB

**bottle up** *He had bottled up his problems for too long.*
► suppress, repress, hold in, keep in, stifle

**bottleneck** NOUN

*There was a bottleneck ahead at the old bridge.*
► blockage, hold-up, traffic jam, tailback

**bottom** ADJECTIVE

**1** *the bottom rung of a ladder*
► deepest, lowest
AN OPPOSITE IS top

**2** *bottom marks*
► least, minimum
AN OPPOSITE IS top

**bottom** NOUN

**1** *the bottom of the stairs*
► foot, base
AN OPPOSITE IS top

**2** *the bottom of the wall*
► foot, base, foundation
AN OPPOSITE IS top

**3** *the bottom of the car*
► underside, underneath
AN OPPOSITE IS topside

**4** *the bottom of the sea*
► bed, depths, floor
AN OPPOSITE IS surface

**5** *They were at the bottom of their fortunes*
► lowest point, nadir
AN OPPOSITE IS peak

**6** *It is very hard to get to the bottom of the problem.*
► origin, root, source, heart, essence, grounds

**7** *She said she had a tattoo on her bottom.*
► buttocks, rear, rump, seat, (*more informal*) behind, (*more informal*) backside, (*more informal*) bum, (*humorous*) sit-upon, (*formal or humorous*) posterior

**bottomless** ADJECTIVE

*a bottomless pit*
► deep, profound, fathomless, boundless, immeasurable

**bounce** VERB

*The ball hit the ground and bounced up.*
► rebound, spring up, bob up, bound, leap up, recoil, ricochet

**bounce** NOUN

*She was exhausted and had lost much of her bounce.*
► vitality, energy, vigour, liveliness, vivacity, verve, exuberance

**bound** ADJECTIVE

**1** *Our friends are bound to help.*
► certain, sure, very likely, liable, obliged, destined, fated

**2** *bound by an oath*
► obligated, committed, obliged, duty-bound, pledged, compelled

**3** *His wrists and ankles were bound with rope.*
► tied, tied up, shackled, fettered, secured, trussed up, strapped

**4** *bound for* *a train bound for the north*
► going to, heading for, making for, off to, travelling towards

**bound** VERB

*A dog bounded across the lawn.*
► leap, jump, skip, spring, bounce, gambol, bob, caper, frisk

**boundary** NOUN

**1** *A wire fence marks the boundary.*
► border, frontier, borderline, dividing line

**2** *the boundary of the estate*
► bounds, confines, circumference, perimeter, extremity, outer edge, fringe, limit, margin

**boundless** ADJECTIVE

*The boys seemed to have boundless energy.*
► unlimited, limitless, unbounded, untold, endless, immeasurable, incalculable, inexhaustible, infinite, unflagging, vast
AN OPPOSITE IS limited

**bouquet** NOUN

**1** *a bouquet of flowers*
► bunch, spray, posy, sprig, nosegay, corsage, garland

**2** *The white wine had a sweet bouquet.*
► aroma, fragrance, nose, scent

**bourgeois** ADJECTIVE

*a bourgeois family*
► middle-class, suburban, conventional, traditional, conservative

**bout** NOUN

**1** *a bout of coughing*
► attack, fit, spasm, outburst, burst, convulsion

**2** *a boxing bout*
► contest, match, round, fight, encounter, engagement, struggle, combat, competition

**bow** VERB (rhymes with *cow*)
1 *The man bowed his head.*
▸ incline, lower, bend
2 *In the end they had to bow to pressure.*
▸ yield, succumb, submit, surrender, give way, give in

**bow** NOUN (rhymes with *cow*)
*the bow of a ship*
▸ front, prow, fore-end

**bow** NOUN (rhymes with *no*)
*She tied the ribbon into a neat bow.*
▸ loop, knot

**bowl** NOUN
*a bowl of soup*
▸ dish, basin, tureen, vessel

**bowl** VERB
*He bowled three fast balls in a row.*
▸ throw, toss, fling, hurl, pitch, lob

**box** NOUN
*a box of coloured pencils*
▸ carton, pack, packet, case, casket, chest

**boy** NOUN
*He had loved reading as a boy.*
▸ lad, youngster, (*more informal*) kid, (*more informal*) nipper

**boycott** NOUN
*a boycott of imported goods*
▸ ban, bar, embargo, moratorium, prohibition, blacklist

**boycott** VERB
*Palestinian leaders threatened to boycott the talks.*
▸ shun, spurn, avoid, stay away from, ignore, cold-shoulder

**boyish** ADJECTIVE
*He had a boyish sense of fun.*
▸ youthful, childlike, young, (*disapproving*) childish, (*disapproving*) puerile
OPPOSITES ARE manly, mature, adult

**bracing** ADJECTIVE
*The sea air is very bracing.*
▸ invigorating, stimulating, refreshing, exhilarating, fortifying
AN OPPOSITE IS debilitating

**bracket** NOUN
*The shelf is fixed to the wall with a pair of brackets.*
▸ support, prop

**brag** VERB
*He was bragging about all the friends he had (informal).*
▸ boast, crow, bluster, swank, show off, gloat, sing someone's praises, (*more informal*) talk big

**brain** NOUN
1 *You need brains to succeed in this job.*
▸ intelligence, intellect, sense, common sense, understanding, a good mind, a good head, (*informal*) grey matter, (*informal*) nous

2 *the brains of the family*
▸ intellectual, clever one, clever person, mastermind, (*more informal*) egghead
RELATED ADJECTIVE cerebral

**brainwash** VERB
*He likes to brainwash people into thinking they need help.*
▸ indoctrinate, condition, re-educate

**brainy** ADJECTIVE
*a brainy child*
▸ intelligent, clever, bright, gifted, brilliant, intellectual, highbrow, (*more informal*) smart
OPPOSITES ARE stupid, unintelligent

**brake** VERB
*She saw a child step out and braked quickly.*
▸ slow down, reduce speed, put on the brakes, (*more formal*) decelerate
AN OPPOSITE IS accelerate

**branch** NOUN
1 *a branch of a tree*
▸ bough, limb, arm, offshoot, sprig
2 *the executive branch of government*
▸ department, section, division, subdivision, wing, part
3 *The firm has closed several overseas branches.*
▸ office, bureau, agency

**branch** VERB
*The road branches ahead.*
▸ divide, fork

**branch out** *She wanted to branch out into another career.*
▸ diversify, develop, expand, extend, enlarge, broaden out

**brand** NOUN
*a new brand of margarine*
▸ make, kind, type, variety, brand-name, trademark, label, line, sort

**brand** VERB
1 *The cattle are branded with hot irons.*
▸ mark, stamp, burn, identify, label, scar
2 *The men are all branded as troublemakers.*
▸ stigmatize, vilify, censure, denounce, discredit, disgrace, taint, give (someone) the reputation of

**brandish** VERB
*a woman brandishing an umbrella*
▸ flourish, wield, flaunt, wave

**brash** ADJECTIVE
*a group of brash youths*
▸ brazen, forward, insolent, (*more informal*) cocky
OPPOSITES ARE meek, shy

**bravado** NOUN
*With great bravado, she attacked her pile of work.*
▸ boldness, swagger, bluster, bombast, show, pretence

**brave** ADJECTIVE

*He was a good fighter and a brave man. They put up a brave fight.*
► courageous, valiant, daring, audacious, spirited, intrepid, plucky, adventurous, fearless
AN OPPOSITE IS cowardly

**bravery** NOUN

*Everyone praised their bravery.*
► courage, audacity, boldness, daring, nerve, gallantry, determination, fearlessness, fortitude, heroism, (more informal) bottle, (more informal) grit, (more informal) guts, (more informal) pluck, (much more informal) spunk
AN OPPOSITE IS cowardice

**brawl** NOUN

*The argument rapidly grew into a drunken brawl.*
► fight, affray, melee, wrangle, altercation, fracas, clash, fray, scrap, scuffle, tussle, (informal) punch-up, (more informal) set-to, (more informal) bust-up

**brawl** VERB

*grown men brawling in the street*
► fight, scuffle, scrap, tussle, wrestle, exchange blows

**brawny** ADJECTIVE

*a brawny wrestler*
► muscular, sinewy, athletic, burly, beefy, strong
OPPOSITES ARE puny, scrawny

**brazen** ADJECTIVE

*a brazen lie*
► blatant, barefaced, flagrant, shameless, unashamed, unabashed, audacious, cheeky, defiant, impertinent, impudent, insolent, rude
OPPOSITES ARE modest, shamefaced

**breach** NOUN

1 *a breach of the rules*
► breaking, infringement, violation, contravention, offence (against), transgression
2 *a breach between the king and his chancellor*
► rift, break, split, difference, disagreement, drifting apart, estrangement, quarrel, separation, alienation
3 *a breach in the sea wall*
► break, split, fissure, gap, crack, fracture, rupture, aperture, chasm, hole, opening

**bread** NOUN

*She was responsible for keeping a roof over their heads and bread in their mouths.*
► food, nourishment, sustenance, subsistence

**break** NOUN

1 *a break in a pipe*
► breach, split, fissure, gap, crack, fracture, rupture, aperture, chasm, hole, opening
2 *a break in work*
► pause, respite, rest, breathing space, intermission, interval, hiatus, interlude, (informal) let-up, (informal) breather
3 *He had listened to thirty new songs without a break.*
► interruption, disruption, halt, stop, lapse, suspension

**break** VERB

1 *The cup fell to the floor and broke.*
► shatter, smash, crack, split, fragment, splinter, (more informal) bust
2 *He broke the bar into three pieces.*
► split, cut, divide, sever, (more informal) bust
OPPOSITES ARE repair, mend
3 *It would be unwise to break the law.*
► contravene, violate, disobey, flout, infringe
OPPOSITES ARE obey, respect, abide by
4 *Let's break for lunch.*
► pause, stop, take a break, (more informal) knock off
5 *She was determined to break the power of the unions.*
► subdue, tame, defeat, crush, smash, suppress, undermine

**break down**

1 *The car broke down near the border.*
► stop working, go wrong, (more informal) pack up, (more informal) conk out
2 *Negotiations broke down without an agreement.*
► fail, collapse, fall through, come to nothing

**break in**

1 *His mother then broke in with a question about the arrangements.*
► interrupt, butt in, intrude
2 *Thieves had broken in during the night.*
► commit burglary, force your way in, make a raid

**break off** *It was hard to break off before finishing the chapter.*
► discontinue, pause, stop

**break out of** *Several prisoners were able to break out of the detention centre.*
► escape from, abscond from, break loose from

**break up**

1 *A dump where they break up old cars.*
► demolish, dismantle, take apart
2 *The meeting broke up after several hours.*
► adjourn, finish, end, come to an end, (more formal) terminate
3 *The crowd began to break up.*
► disperse, scatter, disband, go their separate ways
4 *Jane and her boyfriend had recently broken up.*
► separate, split up, stop living together, get divorced

**breakdown** NOUN

1 *The system has experienced a complete breakdown.*
► malfunction, failure, collapse
2 *A breakdown in the peace talks*
► failure, collapse
3 *a breakdown of the figures*
► analysis, classification, itemization

**break-in** NOUN

*a break-in at the bank*
► burglary, robbery, theft, raid

**breakneck** ADJECTIVE

*driving at breakneck speed*
► headlong, dangerous, reckless, fast, hasty, suicidal

## breakthrough NOUN
*a breakthrough in the search for a cure*
▶ advance, leap forward, discovery, development, revolution, progress, find, improvement, innovation, invention, success

## breakwater NOUN
*A breakwater sheltered them from the wind.*
▶ sea wall, embankment, sea-defence, jetty, mole, pier, groyne

## breast NOUN
*a woman's breast*
▶ bosom(s), bust, chest, front
RELATED ADJECTIVE mammary

## breath NOUN
**1** *Take a deep breath.*
▶ gulp of air, (*technical*) inhalation
**2** *a breath of wind*
▶ puff, waft, whiff, whisper, breeze, sigh

## breathe VERB
**1** *It is lovely to breathe fresh air again.*
▶ inhale, exhale, respire, puff, pant
**2** *Try not to breathe a word of what happened.*
▶ speak, whisper, hint, let out

## breathless ADJECTIVE
*They arrived breathless and red in the face.*
▶ out of breath, gasping, panting, puffing, tired out, wheezy, exhausted

## breathtaking ADJECTIVE
*The view was breathtaking.*
▶ spectacular, magnificent, stunning, amazing, astonishing, astounding, staggering, startling, fantastic, wonderful, phenomenal
AN OPPOSITE IS unimpressive

## breed NOUN
**1** *a rare breed of dog*
▶ variety, type, kind, sort, strain, family, pedigree
**2** *a new breed of writer*
▶ type, kind, sort, class, variety, genre, order

## breed VERB
**1** *Rabbits have a reputation for breeding rapidly.*
▶ reproduce, produce young, bear young, multiply, procreate, increase
**2** *Familiarity breeds contempt*
▶ produce, cause, create, arouse, engender, foster, cultivate, develop, generate, induce, nourish, nurture, occasion

## breeze NOUN
*A slight breeze made the tall grass tremble.*
▶ gentle wind, breath of air, puff of air, flurry

## breezy ADJECTIVE
**1** *a breezy afternoon*
▶ windy, blowy, fresh, brisk, airy, draughty
OPPOSITES ARE still, windless
**2** *She walked in with a breezy air.*
▶ cheerful, jaunty, lively, bright, animated, carefree, light-hearted
OPPOSITES ARE sombre, serious

## brevity NOUN
*Everyone who had to read it welcomed the brevity of the report.*
▶ conciseness, shortness, succinctness, economy, briefness, compression, incisiveness, pithiness, terseness, crispness, curtness
OPPOSITES ARE verbosity, long- windedness

## brew NOUN
*a strong brew made with fruit juices*
▶ mixture, blend, concoction, compound, infusion, potion, preparation, punch, drink, liquor

## brew VERB
**1** *Southerners just can't brew good beer.*
▶ ferment, make
**2** *Christopher and Francis disappeared to brew coffee.*
▶ make, prepare, heat
**3** *Someone is brewing mischief for us.*
▶ plot, stir up, foment, threaten, concoct, contrive, hatch, plan, prepare, scheme, (*more informal*) cook up
**4** *Trouble is brewing.*
▶ develop, loom, build up, threaten, gather

## bribe NOUN
*He was accused of accepting bribes.*
▶ inducement, enticement, incentive, (*more informal*) sweetener, (*more informal*) backhander, (*more informal*) carrot

## bribe VERB
*They had tried to bribe an official.*
▶ offer a bribe to, buy off, pay off, corrupt, entice, influence, pervert, (*more formal*) suborn

## bric-à-brac NOUN
*an old shop full of enticing bric-à-brac.*
▶ ornaments, odds and ends, oddments, trinkets, curios, antiques, baubles, knick-knacks

## brick NOUN
*an outhouse made of bricks*
▶ block, building block, breeze-block

## bridge NOUN
*a bridge over the river*
▶ viaduct, aqueduct (carrying water), arch, crossing, span, way over

## bridge VERB
*A footpath bridged the motorway.*
▶ span, cross, straddle, traverse, go over, extend across, reach across

## brief ADJECTIVE
**1** *a brief visit*
▶ short, cursory, fleeting, passing, quick, hasty, limited, little, momentary, sharp, short-lived, temporary, transient
OPPOSITES ARE long, prolonged
**2** *a brief account of the incident*
▶ short, concise, succinct, pithy, crisp, incisive, compact, condensed, curt, terse, thumbnail
OPPOSITES ARE wordy, verbose, lengthy

## brief NOUN

1 *Here is a detailed brief for the assignment.*
▶ (set of) instructions, (set of) orders, (set of) directions, (set of) guidelines, set of information, outline, plan

2 *a barrister's brief*
▶ case, defence, argument, dossier, summary

## brief VERB

*Staff will be briefed about the changes.*
▶ inform, advise, direct, instruct, prime, apprise of, give the facts, guide, prepare, (more informal) fill in, (more informal) put in the picture

## briefly ADVERB

*He paused briefly.*
▶ for a moment, for a few moments, momentarily, temporarily

## briefs PLURAL NOUN

*He stood in the doorway in nothing but briefs.*
▶ underpants, pants, knickers, panties, shorts, trunks

## brigade NOUN

*a brigade of infantry*
▶ unit, contingent, division

## brigand NOUN

*The travellers were robbed by brigands.*
▶ bandit, robber, thief, outlaw, desperado, gangster, gunman, marauder, highwayman, footpad, pirate, hijacker

## bright ADJECTIVE

1 *bright colours  bright sunshine*
▶ shining, luminous, brilliant, vivid, radiant, dazzling, glaring, blazing, sparkling, twinkling
OPPOSITES ARE dark, dull

2 *a bright morning*
▶ sunny, fine, fair, clear, cloudless
OPPOSITES ARE dull, cloudy

3 *a bright manner*
▶ cheerful, jaunty, lively, breezy, animated
AN OPPOSITE IS subdued

4 *a bright student*
▶ clever, intelligent, gifted, sharp, quick, quick-witted, smart, brilliant
OPPOSITES ARE dull, stupid, unintelligent

## brighten VERB

*The weather brightened*
▶ become sunny, become bright, clear up, lighten
AN OPPOSITE IS darken

**brighten up** *Some pictures will brighten the place up.*
▶ cheer up, smarten up, embellish, enhance, enliven, gladden, illuminate, light up, revitalize
AN OPPOSITE IS darken

## brilliant ADJECTIVE

1 *brilliant light*
▶ blazing, bright, dazzling, glaring, gleaming, glittering, glorious, resplendent, scintillating, shining, showy, sparkling, splendid, vivid
AN OPPOSITE IS dull

2 *a brilliant student*
▶ clever, intelligent, outstanding, gifted, sharp, quick, quick-witted, smart, bright
OPPOSITES ARE dull, stupid

3 (informal) *a brilliant game*
▶ excellent, marvellous, wonderful, superb, exceptional

## brim NOUN

*full to the brim*
▶ top, rim, edge, limit, lip, brink, circumference, margin, perimeter, periphery

## bring VERB

1 *She brought me a mug of tea.*
▶ fetch, carry, convey, bear, deliver, take, transfer, transport

2 *Bring your friends into the garden.*
▶ escort, accompany, conduct, guide, lead, usher

3 *Their success brought a great deal of attention.*
▶ draw, attract, produce, cause, engender, generate

**bring about** *The new manager brought about many changes.*
▶ cause, effect, achieve, create, engineer, manage

**bring in**
1 *The appeal brought in a huge response.*
▶ result in, lead to, realize, yield, earn, gross

2 *The company is bringing in a new product.*
▶ introduce, initiate, start, make available

**bring off** *It was a difficult play to bring off.*
▶ achieve, accomplish, be successful in, do successfully, succeed in

**bring on** *The shock brought on his asthma.*
▶ cause, give rise to, induce, trigger, lead to, precipitate, provoke, aggravate

**bring out**
1 *The publishers are to bring out a new edition.*
▶ publish, release, issue, produce, print

2 *The description brings out the comical side of the story.*
▶ emphasize, accentuate, underline, highlight, stress, dwell on, feature, make obvious, point up, show clearly, spotlight

**bring up**
1 *As a young child she was brought up in Poland.*
▶ raise, rear, educate, care for, look after, nurture, teach, train

2 *The baby brought up his dinner.*
▶ vomit, sick up

3 *There's a small matter I want to bring up.*
▶ mention, raise, broach, touch on, refer to

## brink NOUN

1 *The children stood at the brink staring into the water.*
▶ edge, verge, margin, bank, brim, border

2 *We were on the brink of a major discovery.*
▶ verge, point, threshold, start

## brisk ADJECTIVE

1 *walking at a brisk pace*
▶ quick, rapid, fast, lively, energetic, speedy, swift, hurried
OPPOSITES ARE leisurely, slow

**2** *brisk exercise*
► vigorous, energetic, bracing, refreshing

**3** *The hotel was doing a brisk trade.*
► busy, bustling, lively, hectic, good
OPPOSITES ARE quiet, slack

**bristle** NOUN
*John rubbed a hand over his bristles.*
► stubble, facial hair, whisker, prickle, spine, wire

**bristle** VERB
**1** *She bristled at his remarks.*
► become angry, get angry, be infuriated, be irritated

**2** *The roofs bristled with antennae.*
► abound (in), teem, be crowded, be packed

**bristly** ADJECTIVE
*His skin felt bristly.*
► hairy, whiskery, scratchy, prickly, rough, coarse

**brittle** ADJECTIVE
*brittle bones*
► breakable, fragile, frail, delicate, splintery, crackly
OPPOSITES ARE flexible, resilient

**broach** VERB
*I was reluctant to broach the subject again.*
► introduce, mention, bring up, touch on, refer to

**broad** ADJECTIVE
**1** *They were walking along a broad path.*
► wide, large, big, ample, capacious, expansive, extensive, great, large, open, roomy, spacious, sweeping, vast
OPPOSITES ARE narrow, small

**2** *a broad sweep of countryside*
► wide, spacious, ample, extensive, vast, rolling

**3** *the broad outline of the story*
► general, rough, vague, loose, imprecise, indefinite, inexact, undetailed
OPPOSITES ARE detailed, precise

**4** *She had broad tastes in music*
► comprehensive, eclectic, catholic, wide-ranging, all-embracing, encyclopaedic, universal
OPPOSITES ARE restricted, limited, narrow

**5** *broad humour*
► coarse, earthy, racy, ribald, indecent, vulgar, indelicate, bawdy, suggestive, improper, impure, (more informal) blue

**6** *a broad local accent*
► pronounced, strong, marked, noticeable

**7** *You'll need to drop a broad hint.*
► clear, direct, obvious, unmistakable

**broadcast** NOUN
*a radio broadcast*
► transmission, relay, programme

**broadcast** VERB
**1** *The concert was broadcast worldwide on television.*
► transmit, relay, send out, televise, show, (more informal) screen, (more informal) air

**2** *This is sensitive information and should not be broadcast too widely.*
► report, publicize, circulate, spread, make known, make public, proclaim, advertise, announce, (more formal) disseminate, (more formal) promulgate

**broadcaster** NOUN
*a well-known writer and broadcaster*
► presenter, announcer, linkman, newsreader, commentator, compère, anchorman, anchorwoman, disc jockey, DJ, entertainer

**broaden** VERB
*You need to broaden your interests*
► expand, extend, develop, increase, open up, spread, widen, branch out (into something), diversify, enlarge, build up

**broad-minded** ADJECTIVE
*Their language would offend the most broad-minded of people.*
► liberal, tolerant, enlightened, permissive, forbearing, open-minded, unbiased, receptive
OPPOSITES ARE narrow-minded, intolerant

**broadside** NOUN
*The artillery fired broadsides.*
► salvo, volley, barrage, bombardment

**brochure** NOUN
*a travel brochure*
► leaflet, prospectus, pamphlet, booklet, circular, folder, handbill, broadsheet, catalogue

**broke** ADJECTIVE
(informal) *He reached home completely broke.*
► impoverished, penniless, poor, insolvent, destitute, ruined

**broken** ADJECTIVE
**1** *A waitress was picking up the broken plates.*
► smashed, shattered, cracked, split
OPPOSITES ARE whole, unbroken

**2** *The television is broken.*
► faulty, defective, out of order, not working, (more formal) inoperative
OPPOSITES ARE working, fixed

**3** *The failure of the company left him a broken man.*
► defeated, crushed, beaten, overwhelmed

**4** *a broken marriage*
► failed, ended

**5** *a few hours of broken sleep*
► interrupted, disturbed, disrupted, fitful, troubled
OPPOSITES ARE continuous, uninterrupted

**broken-down** ADJECTIVE
*a few broken-down cars by the side of the road*
► dilapidated, worn-out, out-of-order, ruined

**broken-hearted** ADJECTIVE
*The little girl was broken-hearted at the loss of her doll.*
► heartbroken, inconsolable, devastated, grief-stricken, desolate, despairing
AN OPPOSITE IS happy

**broker** NOUN
*a city broker*
► dealer, agent, intermediary

**brooch** NOUN
*Louise was wearing a little opal brooch.*
▶ clasp, breastpin, clip, badge

**brood** NOUN
1 *a mother hen and her brood*
▶ young, offspring, clutch, family
2 *Felicity was the eldest of a large brood.*
▶ family, household

**brood** VERB
1 *A hen was brooding her eggs.*
▶ hatch, incubate, sit on
2 *It's a mistake to brood over past mistakes.*
▶ dwell (on), agonize, muse (on), ponder, reflect (on), think (about), sulk (about), fret, meditate (on), mope, mull over

**brook** NOUN
*a babbling brook*
▶ stream, beck, burn, channel, rivulet, (*poetic*) rill

**brother** NOUN
*Freddie was Margaret's brother.*
▶ sibling
RELATED ADJECTIVE fraternal

**brow** NOUN
*the brow of the hill*
▶ peak, crest, summit, crown, top
OPPOSITES ARE foot, bottom

**browbeat** VERB
*They had tried to browbeat him into changing his story.*
▶ bully, intimidate, badger, coerce, pressurize, harass

**brown** ADJECTIVE
1 *brown hair*
▶ brunette, auburn, bronze, chestnut, chocolate-coloured
2 *a brown coat*
▶ fawn, beige, buff, tan, tawny, biscuit, terracotta, dun, khaki, ochre, russet, sepia, umber

**browned off** ADJECTIVE
(*informal*) *He was feeling tired and browned off.*
▶ fed up, dispirited, depressed, peeved, disgruntled, disheartened

**browse** VERB
1 *I was browsing in a book*
▶ flick through, leaf through, look through, scan, skim, thumb through, dip in, (*more formal*) peruse
2 *Cattle browsed in a field.*
▶ graze, pasture, crop grass, feed, eat

**bruise** NOUN
*He had a bruise on his leg.*
▶ swelling, bump, contusion, lesion, discoloration

**bruise** VERB
*The blow bruised her arm.*
▶ mark, discolour, injure, hurt

**brunt** NOUN
*His wife bore the brunt of his temper tantrums.*
▶ force, impact, impetus, thrust, effect, shock, burden

**brush** NOUN
1 *Use a brush to sweep up.*
▶ broom, besom
2 *a brush with the law*
▶ clash, encounter, altercation, quarrel, wrangle

**brush** VERB
*Wait while I brush my hair.*
▶ tidy, comb, groom
**brush aside** *The minister tried to brush aside the objections.*
▶ discount, dismiss, disregard, ignore, shrug off, put aside, (*more informal*) pooh-pooh
**brush off** *He was trying to be friendly but they brushed him off.*
▶ spurn, rebuff, snub, cold-shoulder, reject, disregard, ignore, slight
**brush up** *Are you going to brush up your French?*
▶ revise, improve, read up, go over, refresh your memory of, relearn, study, (*more informal*) swot up

**brush-off** NOUN
(*informal*) *Be careful you don't get another brush-off.*
▶ rejection, snub, rebuff, dismissal

**brusque** ADJECTIVE
*The reply seemed a shade brusque.*
▶ curt, abrupt, blunt, terse, discourteous, tactless
OPPOSITES ARE polite, courteous

**brutal** ADJECTIVE
*a brutal attack*
▶ savage, cruel, vicious, fierce, ferocious, barbaric, callous, heartless, cold-blooded, pitiless, ruthless, merciless, vile, sadistic, brutish
OPPOSITES ARE gentle, humane

**brutality** NOUN
*The crime was committed with staggering brutality.*
▶ savagery, cruelty, viciousness, ferocity, barbarity, callousness, heartlessness, cold-bloodedness, ruthlessness
AN OPPOSITE IS gentleness

**brutalize** VERB
*Life in the trenches brutalized many soldiers.*
▶ dehumanize, desensitize, harden, toughen, degrade

**brute** NOUN
*He began behaving like the brute he was.*
▶ beast, animal, monster, fiend, demon

**brute** ADJECTIVE
*brute force*
▶ physical, crude, rough, unthinking

**bubble** NOUN
1 *bubbles rising to the ceiling*
▶ globule, ball, blister, hollow, (*more formal*) vesicle
2 *bubbles soap bubbles*
▶ foam, froth, lather, suds
3 *bubbles bubbles of champagne*
▶ effervescence, fizz

**bubble** VERB
*The water was bubbling.*
▶ boil, gurgle, seethe, sparkle

**bubbly** ADJECTIVE

**1** *a bubbly drink*
► fizzy, carbonated, foaming, seething, sparkling, effervescent
OPPOSITES ARE still, flat

**2** *a bubbly personality*
► vivacious, animated, spirited, vibrant, lively
AN OPPOSITE IS dull

**buccaneer** NOUN

*a crew of daring buccaneers*
► adventurer, brigand, corsair, bandit, marauder, pirate, privateer, robber

**buck** VERB

*The horse began to buck.*
► jump, leap, prance, bound, jerk, spring

**buck up** (*informal*)

**1** *We'll have to buck up if we're going to catch the train.*
► hurry, speed up, get a move on

**2** *She did her best to buck me up but I still felt miserable.*
► cheer up, encourage, rally, hearten, enliven, inspire, make cheerful, please, revitalize, revive

**bucket** NOUN

*a bucket of water*
► pail, can, tub, pitcher

**buckle** NOUN

*a belt buckle*
► clasp, clip, fastener, fastening, hasp, catch

**buckle** VERB

**1** *He quickly buckled his coat.*
► fasten, do up, clasp, hook up, secure, clip

**2** *The bridge began to buckle under the weight.*
► bend, warp, twist, crumple, distort, fold, bulge, collapse, contort, curve, dent

**bud** NOUN

*the buds of flowers*
► shoot, sprout, floret

**bud** VERB

*The trees are budding early.*
► shoot, sprout, form buds

**budding** ADJECTIVE

*a budding young singer*
► promising, aspiring, developing, (*informal*) hopeful, inexperienced, intending, new, potential, (*more informal*) would-be
OPPOSITES ARE established, experienced

**budge** VERB

**1** *The window was stuck and wouldn't budge.*
► give way, move, shift, change position

**2** *The solution is a compromise but no one will budge.*
► change your mind, give way, yield, compromise, influence, move, persuade, propel, push, remove, shift, sway

**3** *They are much too stubborn and won't be budged.*
► persuade, influence, sway, induce, cajole

**budget** NOUN

*The hospital had not spent all its budget for the year.*
► allowance, allocation of funds, quota, estimate, resources, funds, means

**budget** VERB

*We will need to budget five thousand pounds for computers next year.*
► allocate, assign, earmark, put aside, designate

**buffer** NOUN

*a buffer against inflation*
► cushion, safeguard, shield, protection

**buffet** NOUN

*We went to the buffet for a snack.*
► cafeteria, counter, snack bar, café, refreshment room, bar

**buffet** VERB

*The sea front was buffeted by the wind and spray.*
► batter, pound, lash, dash

**buffoon** NOUN

*She thought her cousin was a complete buffoon.*
► fool, idiot, clown, ass, dolt, blockhead, (*more informal*) prat, (*more informal*) halfwit, (*more informal*) chump

**bug** NOUN

**1** *The plants were covered in tiny bugs.*
► insect, pest, mite

**2** *a stomach bug*
► illness, disease, upset, ailment, complaint, disorder

**3** *The computer software developed a bug.*
► fault, error, defect, flaw, (*more informal*) gremlin

**bug** VERB

**1** *The telephone had been bugged.*
► intercept, tap, interfere with, listen in to

**2** (*informal*) *Her constant whining was bugging me.*
► annoy, irritate, anger, infuriate, needle, rile

**build** VERB

*There are plans to build a new apartment block on the site.*
► construct, erect, raise, put up, set up, assemble, fabricate
OPPOSITES ARE demolish, destroy

**build up**

**1** *He has built up a thriving business.*
► establish, develop, create, enlarge, expand, raise, accumulate, amass, assemble, begin, bring together, collect

**2** *Traffic is building up in the city centre.*
► increase, intensify, escalate, grow, mount up, strengthen, rise, augment

**build** NOUN

*a man of slim build*
► physique, form, frame, body

**building** NOUN

*a large grim building with few windows*
► structure, construction, premises, erection, establishment, place, piece of architecture, (*more formal*) edifice, (*more informal*) pile

**build-up** NOUN

*a steady military build-up on the border*
► increase, growth, escalation, expansion, development, accumulation, proliferation

# bulge

**bulge** NOUN

*There was a strange bulge at the bottom of the bed.*
▶ bump, swelling, protuberance, hump, lump, projection, (*more formal*) protrusion

**bulge** VERB

*The sheets bulged in the breeze.*
▶ swell, billow, puff out, balloon out, dilate, distend, expand, belly, enlarge, project, protrude, stick out

**bulk** NOUN

**1** *The sheer bulk of the containers was staggering.*
▶ size, volume, dimensions, proportions, extent, magnitude, mass, substance, amplitude, body, immensity, largeness
**2** *We did the bulk of the work ourselves*
▶ most, best part, greater part, preponderance, majority

**bulky** ADJECTIVE

*a bulky parcel*
▶ sizeable, large, substantial, cumbersome, unwieldy, massive, immense, enormous
OPPOSITES ARE small, compact, manageable

**bulletin** NOUN

**1** *a television news bulletin*
▶ report, statement, announcement, communication, communiqué, dispatch, message, newsflash, notice, proclamation
**2** *The club's monthly bulletin*
▶ newsletter, news-sheet, gazette

**bully** NOUN

*the well-known school bullies*
▶ tormentor, persecutor, oppressor, thug, tough, (*more informal*) heavy

**bully** VERB

*Some of the other children used to bully him.*
▶ persecute, torment, intimidate, oppress, tyrannnize, (*more informal*) push around

**bump** NOUN

**1** *The man fell on the floor with a bump.*
▶ thud, thump, smack, crash, bang, blow, collision, hit, knock, smash
**2** *When he got up he had a bump on the head.*
▶ swelling, lump, bulge, (*technical*) contusion, protuberance

**bump** VERB

**1** *Chris bumped his head while snorkelling.*
▶ hit, strike, knock, bang
**2** *bump into A lorry had bumped into a parked car.*
▶ collide with, run into, crash into, bang into, smash into, knock into, knock, hit, ram, slam, strike
**3** *We were bumping up and down on the rough road.*
▶ bounce, shake, jerk, jolt
**bump off** (*informal*) *He became president by bumping off all his rivals .*
▶ kill, murder, assassinate, eliminate

**bumper** ADJECTIVE

*a bumper harvest*
▶ abundant, plentiful, bountiful, copious, ample

**bumpy** ADJECTIVE

**1** *a bumpy ride*
▶ bouncy, rough, jerky, jolting, lurching
**2** *a bumpy surface*
▶ uneven, rough, irregular, pitted, knobbly, lumpy
OPPOSITES ARE even, smooth

**bunch** NOUN

**1** *a bunch of carrots   a bunch of keys*
▶ bundle, cluster, clump, collection, heap, batch, set, lot, number, quantity
**2** *a bunch of flowers*
▶ bouquet, posy, spray, garland
**3** *a friendly bunch of people*
▶ group, set, circle, band, (*more informal*) gang, (*more informal*) crowd

**bunch** VERB

*The friends had bunched together in a corner.*
▶ gather, assemble, cluster, huddle, collect, congregate, crowd, flock, group, herd
AN OPPOSITE IS scatter

**bundle** NOUN

*a bundle of papers*
▶ bunch, sheaf, carton, collection, pack, package, packet, parcel, bag, bale

**bundle** VERB

**1** *He quickly bundled up the remaining papers.*
▶ tie, bind, wrap, bale, truss, fasten, pack, roll
**2** *The kidnappers bundled their victim into the back of the car.*
▶ hustle, jostle, shove, sweep

**bung** VERB

*You'd better bung that in the bin.*
▶ throw, chuck, toss, stick, put

**bungle** VERB

*Two prisoners bungled an escape bid after running either side of a lamp post while handcuffed.*
▶ mishandle, mismanage, botch, ruin, spoil, fluff, muff, mess up, make a mess of, (*more informal*) make a hash of, (*much more informal*) cock up, (*much more informal*) screw up
OPPOSITES ARE succeed in, bring off

**bunk** NOUN

**do a bunk** (*informal*) *He tried to do a bunk while the guard was preoccupied.*
▶ escape, make off, run off, skive off, play truant

**buoy** VERB

**buoy up** *Her spirits were buoyed up by knowing her father was in the audience*
▶ cheer, brighten, lift, raise, support, invigorate, hearten, comfort

**buoyant** ADJECTIVE

**1** *a buoyant material*
▶ floating, light
**2** *in a buoyant mood*
▶ cheerful, happy, cheery, carefree, light-hearted, lively, optimistic, animated, sunny
OPPOSITES ARE depressed, pessimistic

**burden** NOUN

1 *donkeys carrying heavy burdens*
▶ load, weight, encumbrance, pack, bundle, cargo
2 *a large financial burden*
▶ responsibility, obligation, liability, duty, onus, charge, affliction, anxiety, worry, care, handicap, problem, millstone

**burden** VERB

*For years she was burdened by family worries.*
▶ afflict, oppress, bother, beset, torment, distress, strain, tax, trouble, worry, encumber, hamper, handicap, load (with), (*informal*) lumber (with), (*informal*) saddle (with)

**bureau** NOUN

*an information bureau*
▶ agency, office, service, department, organization, counter

**bureaucracy** NOUN

*hampered by regulations and bureaucracy*
▶ administration, government, officialdom, paperwork, (*more informal*) red tape

**burglar** NOUN

*Burglars stole jewellery worth thousands of pounds.*
▶ housebreaker, robber, thief, intruder

**burglary** NOUN

*Barry had been convicted of burglary.*
▶ housebreaking, breaking and entering, robbery, theft, forcible entry, larceny, pilfering, stealing, thieving, break-in

**burgle** VERB

*The house had been burgled several times before.*
▶ break into, steal from, thieve from

**burial** NOUN

*a burial service*
▶ burying, entombment, funeral, interment, obsequies

**burly** ADJECTIVE

*a burly figure*
▶ hefty, beefy, sturdy, well-built, strapping, brawny, hulking, muscular, powerful, stocky, stout, athletic, big, heavy
OPPOSITES ARE slight, thin

**burn** VERB

1 *The bonfire burned all day*
▶ be alight, be on fire, be ablaze, flare, blaze, flicker, glow, smoke, smoulder
2 *An incinerator will burn anything.*
▶ ignite, kindle, incinerate, cremate, consume
3 *The heat began to burn our skin.*
▶ scald, scorch, blister, brand, toast, char, sear, singe, sting

**burning** ADJECTIVE

1 *a burning building*
▶ blazing, flaming, glowing, ablaze, afire, alight, incandescent, lit up, on fire, raging, smouldering
2 *a burning pain*
▶ scalding, searing, acute, stinging, biting

3 *a burning desire*
▶ intense, extreme, fervent, passionate, eager, ardent, profound, consuming
4 *a burning question*
▶ urgent, crucial, vital, essential, pressing, important, pertinent, relevant

**burrow** VERB

*A rabbit could burrow under the fence.*
▶ tunnel, excavate, dig, mine, delve

**burst** VERB

1 *The impact caused a tyre to burst.*
▶ rupture, split open
2 *Water burst through the hole.*
▶ gush, surge, stream, pour, spurt, cascade
3 *A man suddenly burst into the room.*
▶ rush, run, charge, plunge, shove your way

**bury** VERB

1 *The dog buried its bone in the ground.*
▶ hide, conceal, cover, sink, embed
AN OPPOSITE IS uncover
2 *The dead are buried in the local cemetery.*
▶ inter, lay to rest, entomb
3 *She buried herself in her work.*
▶ absorb, engross, engage, occupy, immerse

**bush** NOUN

*The ball was caught up in a bush.*
▶ shrub, hedge, thicket, undergrowth

**bushy** ADJECTIVE

*a bushy beard*
▶ thick, shaggy, fuzzy, rough, bristling, bristly, dense, hairy, tangled, thick-growing, untidy

**business** NOUN

1 *It proved to be quite a tricky business.*
▶ matter, affair, issue, problem, point, question, concern
2 *What sort of business do you want to go into?*
▶ work, job, occupation, employment, career, line of work, profession, pursuit, trade, vocation, calling, craft, industry
3 *The new supermarket has taken a lot of business from the local shops.*
▶ trade, trading, buying and selling, selling, merchandising, transactions, commerce, dealings, industry, marketing
4 *He wants to run his own business.*
▶ firm, company, establishment, enterprise, organization, concern, venture, corporation, practice, (*more informal*) outfit, (*more informal*) set-up

**businesslike** ADJECTIVE

*The office was run in a businesslike way.*
▶ efficient, professional, competent, methodical, well organized, systematic, practical, pragmatic, orderly

**businessman, businesswoman** NOUN

*a shrewd businesswoman*
▶ entrepreneur, executive, industrialist, dealer, financier, manager, merchant, trader, tycoon, magnate

**bust** NOUN
*a woman's bust*
► bosom, chest, breast, breasts

**bust** VERB
*Be careful with that or you'll bust it.*
► break, snap, crack, split, burst

**bustle** NOUN
*The air terminal was full of bustle*
► activity, hustle, commotion, stir, excitement, flurry, fuss, haste, hurly-burly, hurry, movement, restlessness, scurry, agitation

**bustle** VERB
*People were bustling about looking for their friends.*
► rush, dash, scurry, scamper, scuttle, hurry, hustle, dart, fuss, move busily, scramble, whirl, hasten, (*more informal*) tear

**busy** ADJECTIVE
1 *Are you very busy at work?*
► active, occupied, hard-pressed, (*more informal*) rushed off your feet
AN OPPOSITE IS idle
2 *She's a very busy person.*
► active, energetic, diligent, industrious
OPPOSITES ARE lazy, idle
3 *The manager is busy at the moment but can see you this afternoon.*
► engaged, unavailable, occupied, (*more informal*) tied up
AN OPPOSITE IS free
4 *Her mother leads a busy life.*
► active, hectic, lively, strenuous, demanding, exacting
5 *The committee members are busy organizing the next conference.*
► occupied (with), working (at), engaged (in), hard at work (on), wrapped up (in)
6 *The shopping malls were busy all day.*
► crowded, hectic, lively, teeming, bustling, swarming, thronging, frantic, full of people
AN OPPOSITE IS quiet

**busybody** NOUN
*Pry was an inquisitive busybody.*
► meddler, interferer, gossip, scandalmonger, snooper, eavesdropper, (*more informal*) nosy parker, (*more informal*) gawper

**butch** ADJECTIVE
(*informal*) *a butch builder*
► masculine, manly, virile
OPPOSITES ARE effeminate, feminine

**butt** NOUN
1 *the butt of a rifle*
► stock, shaft, shank, handle, hilt, haft
2 *a water butt*
► barrel, cask, keg, vat
3 *a cigarette butt*
► stub, end, stump, remnant, (*more informal*) fag end
4 *the butt of a joke*
► target, victim, object, subject, mark

**butt** VERB
*He butted her playfully with his head.*
► hit, ram, bump, knock, jab, prod, poke
**butt in** *Nick didn't want to butt in, so he waited patiently.*
► interrupt, break in, cut in, (*more informal*) chip in

**buttocks** NOUN
*He knelt with his heels against his buttocks.*
► bottom, behind, backside, rear, rump, seat, haunches, hindquarters, (*more informal*) arse, (*informal*) bum, (*usually humorous*) posterior

**buttonhole** VERB
*I'll try to buttonhole him after the meeting.*
► catch, accost, intercept, waylay, (*more informal*) get hold of, (*more informal*) nab

**buttress** NOUN
*a stone buttress*
► support, brace, stay, prop, pier, reinforcement

**buy** VERB
1 *I will buy the drinks.*
► get, pay for, obtain, acquire, (*more formal*) purchase
AN OPPOSITE IS sell
2 *a man who could not be bought*
► bribe, buy off, suborn, corrupt

**buy** NOUN
*A well looked-after used car can be a good buy.*
► acquisition, deal, bargain, (*more formal*) purchase

**buyer** NOUN
*Typical buyers of this product are younger women.*
► customer, shopper, consumer, (*more informal*) purchaser
AN OPPOSITE IS seller

**bypass** NOUN
*proposals for a new bypass round the town*
► ring road, relief road

**bypass** VERB
1 *To speed things up we can bypass the usual checking process.*
► ignore, omit, avoid, circumvent, sidestep, neglect, find a way round, get out of, go round, dodge, evade
2 *The road bypasses the viaduct.*
► go round, go past, pass round, avoid, make a detour round

**by-product** NOUN
*Temporary deafness was a by-product of her illness.*
► side effect, consequence, repercussion, result, complement, corollary, (*more informal*) knock-on effect, (*more informal*) spin-off (from), (*more informal*) fallout (from)

**bystander** NOUN
*The man had assaulted a bystander and smashed windows.*
► onlooker, passer-by, observer, spectator, watcher, witness, eyewitness

# Cc

**cab** NOUN
*the driver's cab*
► compartment, cabin

**cabaret** NOUN
*a cabaret at a nightclub in town*
► floor show, revue, entertainment

**cabin** NOUN
1 *a cabin by the river*
► hut, lodge, chalet, shack, shanty, shed, shelter
2 *a cabin on the lower deck*
► berth, compartment, sleeping quarters
3 *the driver's cabin*
► cab, compartment

**cabinet** NOUN
*a glass-fronted cabinet for china*
► cupboard, dresser, closet, chest

**cable** NOUN
1 *The ship was moored by means of thick cables.*
► rope, cord, hawser, line, chain, mooring
2 *Watch out for the power cable.*
► wire, lead, line

**cache** NOUN
*a cache of weapons  a cache of gold*
► hoard, store, stock, stockpile, depot, dump, repository, storehouse, supply

**cadet** NOUN
*a naval cadet*
► recruit, trainee, beginner, learner

**cadge** VERB
*Can we cadge a lift to the station?*
► beg, scrounge, sponge, hitch

**cafe** NOUN
*We could have a snack at a local cafe.*
► snack bar, cafeteria, coffee bar, coffee shop, tea shop, buffet, canteen, bistro

**cage** NOUN
*an animal's cage*
► enclosure, pen, pound, coop, hutch
**USAGE** A large cage for birds is called an *aviary*.

**cagey** ADJECTIVE
*He was being very cagey about what he had been up to.*
► secretive, guarded, cautious, tight-lipped, reticent, evasive, wary, chary
OPPOSITES ARE open, frank

**cajole** VERB
**cajole into** *Tania had been cajoled into giving the party at her house.*
► coax into, talk into, wheedle into, persuade to, beguile into, entice into

**cake** NOUN
1 *There are cakes for tea today.*
► bun, gateau

2 *a cake of soap*
► bar, tablet, block, lump, piece, slab

**cake** VERB
*Finn's shoes were caked with mud.*
► cover, coat, clog, encrust

**calamity** NOUN
*Disobedience will bring calamity on the nation.*
► disaster, catastrophe, tragedy, misfortune, affliction, blow, cataclysm, tribulation, mishap

**calculate** VERB
*Interest on the loan is calculated monthly.*
► work out, compute, reckon, assess, count, determine, add up

**calculated** ADJECTIVE
*a calculated risk*
► deliberate, intentional, planned, premeditated, conscious, considered, purposive

**calculating** ADJECTIVE
*Cohen looked around and nodded his head in a calculating manner.*
► cunning, crafty, sly, devious, wily, scheming, shrewd

**calibre** NOUN
*People of this calibre are not something you come across every day.*
► quality, ability, distinction, excellence, capacity, standard, talent, stature, character

**call** VERB
1 *'Come here!' she called.*
► cry, cry out, shout, yell, exclaim
2 *I'll call you this evening.*
► phone, telephone, ring, ring up, give someone a call
3 *What did they call him?*
► baptize, christen, dub, name
4 *Why did you call your cat Albert?*
► name
5 *His mother said she would call him early next morning.*
► wake, wake up, waken, awaken, get someone up, arouse, rouse
6 *The headteacher called me to her office.*
► summon, invite, order
7 *We'd better call the doctor.*
► send for, fetch, summon, ask to come
8 *We need to call a meeting.*
► convene, organize, gather
9 *Harriet's mother called the next day.*
► visit, pay a visit, (more informal) drop in, (more informal) drop by

**call for**
1 *The assignment calls for careful planning.*
► require, need, demand, necessitate, make necessary, involve, entail, warrant
2 *Shall we call for you about six o'clock?*
► fetch, pick up, come for, collect

**call off** *The barbecue was called off because of bad weather.*

## call

► cancel, abandon, postpone, adjourn, discontinue, drop, end, halt

**USAGE** You use *cancel* if you mean calling off for good, and *postpone* if you mean calling off until a later date. You often use *abandon* to refer to things that have been started but cannot be completed.

**call on** *I might call on my friends this afternoon.*
► visit, go and see, (*more informal*) drop in on, (*more informal*) look up

## call NOUN

1 *a call for help*
► cry, exclamation, shout, yell, scream

2 *a call for strike action*
► appeal, plea, summons, demand, request

3 *He decided to pay a call on his old father.*
► visit, stop

4 *There's little call for caviar here.*
► demand, market, need

5 *There's no call for that kind of talk.*
► need, necessity, occasion, reason, justification, excuse

## calling NOUN

*He thought that the law was the right calling.*
► profession, career, line of work, occupation, vocation, business, employment, walk of life, job, trade, work

## callous ADJECTIVE

*a callous remark*
► heartless, hard-hearted, unfeeling, uncaring, indifferent, insensitive, cruel, brutal, ruthless
OPPOSITES ARE kind, considerate

## calm ADJECTIVE

1 *a calm sunny day*
► still, tranquil, quiet, peaceful, balmy
OPPOSITES ARE stormy, windy

2 *The sea was calm.*
► smooth, tranquil, still, flat, waveless

3 *He remained calm despite the difficulties.*
► composed, collected, cool, poised, dispassionate, unperturbed, imperturbable, unruffled, unflustered, unbothered, untroubled, unemotional, (*more informal*) unflappable, (*more informal*) laid-back
OPPOSITES ARE anxious, upset, excited

4 *a calm temperament*
► serene, placid, phlegmatic, tranquil, relaxed

## calm NOUN

1 *the calm of a summer afternoon*
► tranquillity, calmness, quietness, stillness, peace, quiet, quietude
AN OPPOSITE IS storm

2 *I had to admire her calm.*
► composure, calmness, self-possession, equanimity

## calm VERB

*He was so upset it was impossible to calm him.*
► soothe, placate, quieten, mollify, pacify, settle down, sober down, tranquillize, appease, compose, control, cool down, lull
OPPOSITES ARE agitate, upset

## camouflage NOUN

1 *The foliage made good camouflage.*
► disguise, concealment, cover, screen, veil, blind, cloak, front, guise, mask

2 *an animal's camouflage*
► protective colouring

3 *Their friendly manner was only camouflage.*
► facade, front, disguise, mask, pretence

## camouflage VERB

*The vehicle was camouflaged with branches from the trees.*
► disguise, hide, mask, conceal, cover up, obscure, screen

## camp NOUN

*an army camp*
► encampment, camping ground, campsite, base

## campaign NOUN

1 *a military campaign*
► operation, offensive, action, engagement, advance, battle, push

2 *a campaign to save the environment*
► crusade, movement, drive, effort, struggle, fight, push

## campaign VERB

*He began campaigning for the Wildlife Trust.*
► crusade, fight, work, agitate

## can NOUN

*a can of orange juice*
► tin, canister, jar

## canal NOUN

*There is a path by the canal.*
► channel, watercourse, waterway

## cancel VERB

1 *The family had to cancel their holiday.*
► call off, abandon, drop, end, (*more informal*) axe

2 *They agreed to cancel the debt.*
► revoke, annul, nullify, rescind, erase, expunge, set aside, withdraw

**cancel out** *One small mistake could cancel out all our hard work.*
► counterbalance, neutralize, wipe out, offset, outweigh, make up for, compensate for

## cancer NOUN

1 *The problem was diagnosed as cancer*
► malignant growth, tumour, melanoma, lymphoma
RELATED ADJECTIVE carcinogenic

2 *Violent crime is a cancer in our society.*
► evil, blight, scourge, plague, pestilence, poison

**candid** ADJECTIVE
*a candid reply*
▶ frank, honest, open, sincere, straightforward, blunt, truthful, outspoken, forthright, unequivocal
OPPOSITES ARE insincere, guarded, devious

**candidate** NOUN
**1** *a candidate for a job*
▶ applicant, contender, aspirant
**2** *a candidate in an exam*
▶ entrant, examinee

**candour** NOUN
*He gave his opinion with complete candour.*
▶ frankness, honesty, openness, sincerity, directness, forthrightness, bluntness

**canny** ADJECTIVE
*a canny businessman*
▶ shrewd, astute, sharp, acute, perceptive, clever, prudent
**USAGE** *Canny* is a generally favourable word. Other words that are less favourable, because they imply a kind of dishonesty, are *cunning*, *crafty*, and *wily*..

**canopy** NOUN
*The caravan has a canopy at the side.*
▶ awning, shade, cover, covering

**cantankerous** ADJECTIVE
*The heat had made him especially cantankerous.*
▶ bad-tempered, irritable, irascible, grumpy, testy, grouchy, touchy, crotchety, peevish, fractious, cross, (more informal) stroppy, (more informal) shirty
OPPOSITES ARE good-tempered, good-humoured, affable

**canteen** NOUN
*Let's have a quick lunch in the canteen.*
▶ snack bar, cafeteria, cafe, coffee bar, coffee shop, tea shop, buffet, bistro

**canvass** VERB
*They are canvassing for the green party.*
▶ campaign, electioneer, seek votes

**canyon** NOUN
*The army moved through a deep canyon.*
▶ gorge, ravine, defile

**cap** VERB
*The mountains were capped with snow.*
▶ cover , top, crown, blanket

**capable** ADJECTIVE
*a capable young woman*
▶ competent, able, accomplished, proficient, efficient, talented, gifted, clever, skilled, intelligent, effective
AN OPPOSITE IS incompetent
**be capable of** *He's capable of doing any of these tasks.*
▶ have the ability (to do), be competent (to do), be adept (at doing), be equal (to doing)
AN OPPOSITE IS incapable of

**capacity** NOUN
**1** *The tank's capacity is 30 litres.*
▶ size, volume, magnitude, extent, space

**2** *You need the capacity to motivate yourself.*
▶ ability, power, potential, capability, competence, aptitude, faculty, skill, talent
**3** *He acted in his capacity as commander-in-chief of the army.*
▶ position, function, role, office

**cape** NOUN
**1** *She was wearing a waterproof cape.*
▶ cloak, mantle, shawl, wrap, stole
**2** *The ship rounded the cape at dawn.*
▶ headland, promontory, head, point, foreland

**caper** VERB
*The children capered about the room.*
▶ skip, bound, dance, leap, cavort, jump, spring, bounce, gambol, bob, frisk

**capital** ADJECTIVE
**1** *a capital city*
▶ chief, principal, leading, main, first, foremost
**2** *in capital letters*
▶ upper-case, large, big, block

**capital** NOUN
**1** *Rome is the capital of Italy.*
▶ chief city, first city, seat of government, centre of government
**2** *In three years he had enough capital to start his own business.*
▶ funds, finance, money, cash, assets, savings, means, wherewithal

**capitalize** VERB
**capitalize on** *The opposition capitalized on the government's mistakes.*
▶ exploit, take advantage of, profit from, make capital out of

**capitulate** VERB
*The enemy capitulated after a siege of ten months.*
▶ surrender, give in, submit, succumb, admit defeat, yield, (more informal) throw in the towel
OPPOSITES ARE resist, hold out

**capricious** ADJECTIVE
*the capricious nature of the financial markets*
▶ changeable, erratic, unstable, variable, volatile, uncertain, unpredictable, inconstant, unreliable, fickle, wayward
OPPOSITES ARE predictable, steady

**capsize** VERB
*Some of the boats capsized.*
▶ overturn, tip over, turn over, turn upside down, flip over, keel over, (more informal) turn turtle

**capsule** NOUN
**1** *The medicine is taken in the form of capsules.*
▶ pill, tablet, lozenge
**2** *a space capsule*
▶ module, craft, pod

**captain** NOUN
**1** *the captain of the winning team*
▶ leader, chief player, head, boss
**2** *the ship's captain*
▶ commander, master, officer in charge, skipper

**caption** NOUN

3 *a captain of industry*
▶ magnate, mogul, tycoon, mandarin, baron

**caption** NOUN

*The poster needed a caption.*
▶ title, legend, heading, label, description, explanation, headline, (*technical*) superscription

**captivate** VERB

*The beauty of the scene captivates all visitors.*
▶ charm, enchant, delight, entrance, enthral, fascinate, bewitch, beguile, engross, excite, mesmerize
OPPOSITES ARE repel, disgust

**captivating** ADJECTIVE

*a captivating young woman*
▶ charming, enchanting, entrancing, delightful, enthralling, bewitching, beguiling

**captive** ADJECTIVE

1 *captive animals*
▶ confined, caged, captured, incarcerated, chained, detained, enslaved, ensnared, fettered, gaoled, imprisoned, jailed, restricted, secure, taken prisoner
2 *The men had been held captive for several weeks.*
▶ locked up, imprisoned, jailed, detained, under lock and key
AN OPPOSITE IS free

**captive** NOUN

*The captives all wore handcuffs.*
▶ prisoner, convict, detainee, inmate, internee, hostage

**captivity** NOUN

*Years of captivity had ruined his health.*
▶ imprisonment, confinement, internment, incarceration, detention, custody
AN OPPOSITE IS freedom

**capture** VERB

1 *He was captured boarding a ship for France.*
▶ catch, arrest, apprehend, seize, take prisoner, take into custody, (*more informal*) nab, (*more informal*) pull in, (*much more informal*) nick
2 *The building was captured by stormtroopers.*
▶ occupy, take, seize, secure

**car** NOUN

*A lot of the students arrived in cars.*
▶ motor car, automobile, motor, vehicle

**carcass** NOUN

1 *an animal's carcass*
▶ cadaver, corpse, body, meat, remains
2 *the rusting carcass of an old car*
▶ hulk, shell, remains, skeleton, framework, structure

**card** NOUN

1 *a piece of stiff card*
▶ cardboard, pasteboard, board
2 *Let's play cards.*
▶ card game, game of cards

**USAGE** *Card* is often short for *playing card*, *greetings* (or *birthday* or *Christmas*) *card*, and *credit card*.

**on the cards** (*informal*) *A marriage was always on the cards.*
▶ possible, a possibility, likely, a likelihood, probable, a probability, in the offing
AN OPPOSITE IS out of the question

**cardboard** NOUN

*a cardboard cutout*
▶ card, pasteboard

**care** NOUN

1 *We need to proceed with care.*
▶ caution, carefulness, vigilance, watchfulness, awareness, prudence, circumspection, concentration, attention, concern, diligence, heed
AN OPPOSITE IS carelessness
2 *The job needs to be done with great care.*
▶ discretion, thought, attention, thoroughness, meticulousness, concentration
3 *You need to escape from all your cares.*
▶ worry, anxiety, trouble, concern, burden, problem, difficulty, hardship, responsibility, sorrow, stress, tribulation, vexation, woe
AN OPPOSITE IS joy
4 *She left the baby in the care of a minder.*
▶ charge, safe keeping, keeping, custody, control, supervision, protection

**care** VERB

1 **care about** *She obviously cares about her staff.*
▶ interest yourself in, concern yourself about, mind about, bother about, worry about, be troubled by
2 **care for** *The hospice cares for sick children.*
▶ look after, take care of, tend, attend to, provide for, nurse, supervise, watch over, (*more informal*) keep an eye on
3 **care for** *He cares for his grandchildren.*
▶ love, be fond of, adore, cherish, hold dear, dote on, think the world of
4 **care for** *I don't really care for those biscuits.*
▶ like, fancy, feel like, be keen on, enjoy, want

**career** NOUN

*a career in teaching*
▶ profession, occupation, job, calling, position

**career** VERB

*The shopping trolley careered down the slope.*
▶ rush, hurtle, shoot, speed, dash, zoom

**carefree** ADJECTIVE

1 *a carefree young girl*
▶ unworried, untroubled, cheerful, cheery, light-hearted, easy-going, casual, relaxed, (*more informal*) laid-back
OPPOSITES ARE anxious, tense
2 *a carefree time*
▶ relaxing, restful, trouble-free, untroubled, peaceful, quiet
OPPOSITES ARE hectic, nerve-wracking

**careful** ADJECTIVE

**1** *Be careful walking through the park at night.*
► alert, vigilant, heedful, attentive, watchful
AN OPPOSITE IS careless

**2** *You must be careful with your spending.*
► prudent, cautious, circumspect, economical, thrifty, canny
OPPOSITES ARE careless, extravagant, reckless

**3** *Such a long journey needs careful planning*
► detailed, thorough, meticulous, conscientious, scrupulous

**4** *She's a very careful driver.*
► attentive, diligent, conscientious
OPPOSITES ARE careless, inattentive

**careless** ADJECTIVE

**1** *a careless driver   careless remarks*
► inattentive, thoughtless, inconsiderate, negligent, absent-minded, heedless, irresponsible, reckless
OPPOSITES ARE careful, attentive

**2** *There is no excuse for careless work.*
► slipshod, shoddy, slapdash, slovenly, inaccurate, scrappy, incorrect
OPPOSITES ARE careful, accurate

**3** *She has always been rather careless about money.*
► extravagant, reckless
OPPOSITES ARE careful, prudent

**carelessness** NOUN

*The accident was caused by carelessness.*
► inattention, inattentiveness, absent-mindedness, negligence, recklessness, irresponsibility, slovenliness, thoughtlessness, untidiness, haste, (*more informal*) sloppiness
OPPOSITES ARE care, carefulness

**caress** NOUN

*She longed for his gentle caress.*
► embrace, touch, stroke, cuddle, hug, kiss, pat

**caress** VERB

*He caressed her lovingly.*
► stroke, embrace, hug, cuddle, touch, fondle, kiss, pet, rub against, smooth

**caretaker** NOUN

*the caretaker at the village hall*
► janitor, warden, custodian, attendant, keeper, porter, custodian, superintendent, watchman

**careworn** ADJECTIVE

*a face that was old and careworn*
► haggard, drawn, weary , anxious, worried, strained, harassed

**cargo** NOUN

*a ship's cargo*
► freight, load, haul, payload, consignment, merchandise, shipment, goods

**caricature** NOUN

*He drew a clever caricature of the President.*
► cartoon, parody, satire, lampoon, travesty, (*more informal*) send-up, (*more informal*) take-off

**caricature** VERB

*She caricatured the movements of a ballerina.*
► parody, mimic, imitate, lampoon, mock, ridicule, satirize, burlesque, make fun of, exaggerate, (*more informal*) send up, (*more informal*) take off

**caring** ADJECTIVE

*a caring employer*
► kind, kind-hearted, considerate, thoughtful, concerned

**carnage** NOUN

*the carnage of the battlefield*
► slaughter, massacre, bloodshed, bloodbath, butchery

**carnival** NOUN

*the town's annual carnival*
► festival, gala, jamboree, fiesta, fete, fair, celebration, revelry

**carp** VERB

*Journalists always find something to carp about.*
► complain, grumble, grouse

**carriage** NOUN

*a railway carriage*
► coach, wagon

**carry** VERB

**1** *We will have to carry our own luggage.*
► convey, take, transfer, bring, fetch, haul, lift, manhandle, move, remove, shoulder, (*more informal*) lug

**2** *The channel ships carry passengers and freight.*
► transport, convey, handle, ferry, ship

**3** *Telegraph wires carry signals.*
► communicate, relay, transmit

**4** *The bridge would not bear the weight of a large vehicle.*
► support, bear, hold up

**5** *The job carries many responsibilities.*
► demand, entail, involve, require, lead to, result in

**carry on**

**1** *We carried on for as long as we could.*
► persevere, persist, continue, go on, keep on, last, remain, stay, (*informal*) stick it out

**2** *She has been carrying on her own business for several years.*
► run, engage in, maintain, manage, operate, administer

**3** (*informal*) *Tell them to stop carrying on like that!*
► misbehave, behave badly, cause trouble
**carry out** *They were just carrying out orders.*
► obey, follow, discharge, implement, execute, finish, perform, complete

**cart** NOUN

*The fruit was taken to the barns in carts.*
► barrow, wheelbarrow, handcart, trolley, truck

**cart** VERB

(*informal*) *The books were too bulky to cart around.*
► carry, move, take, haul, (*informal*) lug

**carton** NOUN
*a carton of ice cream*
▶ box, packet, pack, case, container

**cartoon** NOUN
1 *The story is in the form of a cartoon.*
▶ comic strip, drawing, caricature, sketch
2 *a film cartoon*
▶ animation
3 *a political cartoon*
▶ caricature, parody, lampoon

**cartridge** NOUN
1 *a film cartridge   a tape cartridge*
▶ cassette, canister, capsule, cylinder, tube, case
2 *a cartridge for a rifle*
▶ magazine, round, shell

**carve** VERB
1 *It was time to carve the meat.*
▶ cut, slice, chop
2 *a tool for carving wood*
▶ chisel, hew, sculpt, fashion, form, shape

**carving** NOUN
*ancient rock carvings*
▶ sculpture, figure, statue, effigy

**cascade** NOUN
*cascades of water down the rock face*
▶ torrent, shower, fall, waterfall, cataract

**case** NOUN
1 *She hurriedly threw a few clothes into a case.*
▶ suitcase, bag, travel bag, trunk
2 *The books were still in their packing cases.*
▶ box, chest, canister, carton, crate, container
3 *The videotape was spilling out of its case.*
▶ shell, cartridge, cassette, container, capsule, cover
4 *The china was kept in a handsome display case.*
▶ cabinet, cupboard, showcase, sideboard
5 *a classic case of misunderstanding*
▶ instance, example, occurrence, occasion, manifestation, illustration
6 *If that's the case we'll have to think of an another way.*
▶ situation, position, state of affairs, event, circumstances
7 *Police from several forces are involved in the case.*
▶ investigation, inquiry
8 *The lawyers agreed it was a difficult case.*
▶ lawsuit, action, legal action, suit, trial

**cash** NOUN
*a purse full of cash*
▶ money, notes, banknotes, coins, change, ready money

**cash** VERB
*I need to cash a cheque.*
▶ exchange, change, get money for, get cash for
**cash in on** *I don't like to cash in on your bad luck.*
▶ take advantage of, profit by, exploit

**cashier** NOUN
*Take your payment to one of the cashiers.*
▶ teller, clerk, checkout, banker, treasurer

**casing** NOUN
*The hard disk has its own protective casing.*
▶ case, shell, cover, sheath, housing, sleeve

**cask** NOUN
*a cask of wine*
▶ barrel, keg, butt, vat, tun, hogshead, firkin

**casket** NOUN
*a casket of jewels*
▶ case, box, chest

**cast** VERB
1 *He cast a coin into the fountain.*
▶ throw, toss, fling, flip, sling, (*more informal*) chuck, hurl
2 *The statue is cast entirely in bronze.*
▶ mould, form, shape, model, sculpture
**cast down** *They all felt cast down at the news.*
▶ dejected, depressed, saddened, upset, disheartened

**castle** NOUN
*The castle was heavily fortified.*
▶ fort, fortress, citadel, palace, stronghold, tower, château

**casual** ADJECTIVE
1 *a casual encounter with an old friend*
▶ chance, unexpected, unforeseen, unintentional, unplanned, fortuitous, accidental, random
OPPOSITES ARE deliberate, intentional
2 *a casual remark*
▶ offhand, spontaneous, impromptu, unconsidered, random
OPPOSITES ARE committed, enthusiastic
3 *a casual acquaintance*
▶ slight, vague
OPPOSITES ARE close, intimate
4 *a casual approach to life*
▶ relaxed, nonchalant, lackadaisical, indifferent, carefree, easy-going, offhand, apathetic, flippant, (*more informal*) laid-back
OPPOSITES ARE concerned, serious
5 *He gave her a casual glance.*
▶ cursory, fleeting, passing, hasty, quick, perfunctory
OPPOSITES ARE thorough, careful
6 *casual clothes*
▶ informal
AN OPPOSITE IS formal

**casualty** NOUN
*The bombing led to many casualties.*
▶ death, fatality, injury, loss, victim, (*in plural*) dead and wounded

**cat** NOUN
*People thought he was odd for talking to his cat.*
▶ tom, tomcat, tabby, kitten, (*more informal*) moggy, (*more informal*) pussy
RELATED ADJECTIVE feline

**catalogue** NOUN
1 *a library catalogue*
▶ inventory, list, record, register, directory, index, roll, schedule, table

**catalogue** NOUN

2 *a catalogue of mistakes*
▶ series, sequence, string, long list

**catalogue** VERB

*It will take a long time to catalogue the whole collection.*
▶ index, make an inventory of, record, archive, classify, list, register, log, file

**catastrophe** NOUN

*The floods were a catastrophe for the area.*
▶ calamity, tragedy, misfortune, mishap, affliction, cataclysm, blow

**catch** VERB

1 *Josh caught the ball.*
▶ seize, grab, take hold of, grip, clutch, intercept
2 *They hadn't managed to catch any fish.*
▶ hook, net, land, trap
3 *Do you think they will catch the thief?*
▶ capture, arrest, apprehend
4 *We have a train to catch.*
▶ board, be in time for, get to, reach
5 *He caught a rare virus on a business trip.*
▶ contract, be infected with, develop, get, go down with, become sick with, become ill with
6 *She caught them in the act.*
▶ discover, detect, find, find out, surprise, expose
7 *A trip to Paris caught their fancy.*
▶ capture, attract, appeal to, seize, win, absorb, engross
8 *I didn't catch what you said.*
▶ hear, perceive, discern, make out, recognize
**catch up** *If we hurry we can catch them up.*
▶ reach, overtake, draw level with

**catch** NOUN

1 *The fishermen returned with their catch over their shoulders.*
▶ haul, net, bag, booty, prize
2 *The price is so good there must be a catch.*
▶ snag, disadvantage, difficulty, drawback, obstacle, problem, trap, trick
3 *He tried to slip the catch on the window.*
▶ latch, lock, fastener, fastening, bolt, clasp

**catching** ADJECTIVE

*Fortunately the disease is not catching.*
▶ infectious, contagious, communicable, transmittable, spreading

**catchy** ADJECTIVE

*a catchy tune*
▶ memorable, tuneful, haunting, attractive, popular, singable

**categorical** ADJECTIVE

*a categorical assurance*
▶ absolute, unqualified, unconditional, unequivocal, unreserved, outright, complete, definite, express

**category** NOUN

*There is a maximum penalty for each category of offence. Non-fiction books fall into several categories.*
▶ class, type, classification, kind, sort, division, group, grade, heading

**cater** VERB

1 **cater for** *The hotel will cater for vegetarians.*
▶ provide for, make arrangements for, supply, feed, cook for
2 **cater for** *A simple barrow will cater for most of your gardening needs.*
▶ serve, satisfy, answer, provide for, cope with, take care of

**catholic** ADJECTIVE

*Their taste in reading is very catholic.*
▶ broad, wide, wide-ranging, varied, diverse, eclectic, comprehensive, broad-based, all-embracing, general, universal, cosmopolitan, liberal

**cattle** PLURAL NOUN

*The farmers need land for grazing their cattle.*
▶ livestock, cows, bulls, bullocks, calves, heifers, oxen
RELATED ADJECTIVE bovine

**catty** ADJECTIVE

*(informal) a catty remark*
▶ spiteful, malicious, mean, nasty, unkind, hurtful, snide, vindictive, cruel

**cause** NOUN

1 *Police are still trying to find the cause of the explosion.*
▶ source, origin, root, basis, reason (for), beginning, genesis, grounds, motivation, motive, occasion, spring, stimulus
2 *The older boys were the cause of much of the trouble.*
▶ initiator, instigator, originator, producer, agent
3 *There is no cause for alarm.*
▶ reason, grounds, justification, call, need, necessity, occasion, excuse, pretext
4 *a worthy cause*
▶ purpose, object, end, aim, ideal, undertaking, enterprise

**cause** VERB

1 *The bad weather has caused many delays.*
▶ bring about, result in, give rise to, lead to, produce, generate, create, precipitate, induce, entail, stimulate
2 *Poor health caused him to give up work.*
▶ force, compel, lead, encourage, induce, make

**caustic** ADJECTIVE

1 *a caustic substance*
▶ corrosive, acid, astringent, burning
2 *caustic remarks*
▶ sharp, sarcastic, scathing, hurtful, acid, acerbic, cutting, bitter, spiteful, vicious, abrasive

**caution** NOUN

1 *Drivers were advised to proceed with extreme caution.*
▶ care, alertness, attentiveness, carefulness, wariness, watchfulness, vigilance, restraint, discretion, circumspection, heed, heedfulness, prudence
AN OPPOSITE IS recklessness
2 *A first offender is usually let off with a caution.*
▶ reprimand, warning, admonition

# caution VERB

**1** *Everyone was cautioned about the dangers of the place.*
▶ warn, advise, alert (to)
**2** *The offenders were all cautioned.*
▶ reprimand, give a warning (to), admonish, censure, reprehend

# cautious ADJECTIVE

**1** *He was a cautious man and avoided risks.*
▶ careful, attentive, vigilant, circumspect, heedful, alert, prudent, scrupulous, watchful
OPPOSITES ARE careless, reckless
**2** *Their response was cautious.*
▶ guarded, discreet, wary, chary, tactful
OPPOSITES ARE forthright, impetuous

# cave NOUN

*There are caves at the foot of the cliffs.*
▶ cavern, grotto, hollow, cavity, underground chamber, den, hole, pothole

# cave VERB

**1 cave in** *The roof caved in*
▶ collapse, fall in, give way, disintegrate, crumble
**2 cave in** *The government refused to cave in to the protesters' demands.*
▶ yield, surrender, comply (with)

# cavernous ADJECTIVE

*a cavernous space*
▶ vast, huge, large, spacious, immense, capacious, voluminous, gaping

# cavity NOUN

*a secret cavity in the wall*
▶ space, chamber, hollow, hole, pit, cave, crater, dent

# cavort VERB

*The children cavorted about the room.*
▶ skip, bound, dance, leap, caper, jump, spring, bounce, gambol, bob, frisk

# cease VERB

*Hostilities will cease at midnight. Both armies have ceased military activity.*
▶ end, stop, finish, halt, come or bring to an end, conclude, terminate
AN OPPOSITE IS commence

# ceasefire NOUN

*A ceasefire had been in force for three months.*
▶ armistice, suspension of hostilities, cessation of hostilities, truce, agreement, peace, treaty, peace treaty

# ceaseless ADJECTIVE

*ceaseless activity*
▶ continuous, continual, constant, incessant, endless, unceasing, interminable, non-stop
OPPOSITES ARE temporary, intermittent

# cede VERB

*The treaty required both countries to cede territory won during the fighting.*
▶ relinquish, surrender, yield, concede, renounce, hand over

# celebrate VERB

**1** *They celebrated with a bottle of champagne.*
▶ enjoy yourself, have fun, have a good time, make merry
**2** *The couple celebrate their golden wedding this week.*
▶ commemorate, observe, mark, recognize, honour, remember, keep

# celebrated ADJECTIVE

*a celebrated writer and broadcaster*
▶ acclaimed, admired, famous, well-known, prominent, revered, renowned, distinguished, honoured, eminent, exalted, illustrious, notable, noted
OPPOSITES ARE unknown, obscure

# celebration NOUN

**1** *a birthday celebration*
▶ party, function, festivity, (more informal) binge
**2** *a cause for celebration*
▶ festivities, jollification, merrymaking, enjoying yourself, partying

# celebrity NOUN

**1** *a team made up of celebrities*
▶ star, famous person, public figure, dignitary, idol, personality, luminary
**2** *The group seemed to be enjoying their celebrity.*
▶ fame, stardom, prominence, popularity, glory, reputation, renown

# celestial ADJECTIVE

**1** *celestial bodies*
▶ heavenly, extraterrestrial, stellar, universal, cosmic, galactic, interplanetary, interstellar, starry
**2** *celestial music*
▶ heavenly, divine, sublime, ethereal, blissful, angelic, godlike

# celibacy NOUN

*priests who had taken a vow of celibacy*
▶ chastity, virginity, self-denial, abstinence, purity, bachelorhood, spinsterhood

# celibate ADJECTIVE

*a celibate life*
▶ chaste, single, unmarried, unwedded, pure, virgin

# cell NOUN

**1** *a prison cell*
▶ room, cubicle, chamber, compartment, enclosure, unit
**2** *cells of a honeycomb*
▶ compartment, cavity, chamber, hollow, section
**3** *a terrorist cell*
▶ unit, group, faction, caucus, section, arm, wing

# cellar NOUN

*Old bottles are kept in the cellar.*
▶ basement, crypt, vault

# cemetery NOUN

*Mourners will want to visit the cemetery.*
▶ graveyard, burial ground, churchyard, necropolis (= ancient cemetery)

a b c d e f g h i j k l m n o p q r s t u v w x y z

**censor** VERB
*Parts of the film had to be censored.*
▶ cut, edit, expurgate

**censure** NOUN
*Her voice had a note of censure.*
▶ criticism, disapproval, reproach, rebuke, condemnation, reproof

**censure** VERB
*The authorities censured people who had not voted.*
▶ criticize, reprimand, condemn, rebuke, reproach

**central** ADJECTIVE
**1** *the central chamber of the temple*
▶ innermost, inner, interior, middle, focal
**2** *the central issues*
▶ chief, key, main, essential, pivotal, primary, principal, vital, fundamental, crucial, major, overriding, important
AN OPPOSITE IS peripheral

**centralize** VERB
*The processes will be centralized in a business centre.*
▶ concentrate, unify, amalgamate, bring together, rationalize, streamline
OPPOSITES ARE devolve, disperse

**centre** NOUN
**1** *the centre of a circle*
▶ middle, mid-point, heart, core, eye, bullseye
**2** *the centre of the city*
▶ middle, heart, nucleus

**cereal** NOUN
*farmers who prefer cereal production to livestock*
▶ corn, grain

**CEREALS INCLUDE**
barley, corn, maize, millet, oats, rice, rye, sorghum, sweetcorn, wheat.

**ceremonial** ADJECTIVE
*a ceremonial occasion*
▶ formal, official, stately, solemn, ritual, ritualistic
OPPOSITES ARE informal, unofficial

**ceremony** NOUN
**1** *a wedding ceremony*
▶ rite, ritual, service, observance, celebration
**2** *a grand occasion with all due ceremony*
▶ formality, pomp, protocol, propriety, ritual, solemnity

**certain** ADJECTIVE
**1** *I was certain they did it.*
▶ sure, confident, positive, convinced, assured, satisfied
OPPOSITES ARE uncertain (whether), doubtful (whether)
**2** *It is certain that there will be reprisals.*
▶ definite, undeniable, indubitable, unquestionable, clear, plain, evident, obvious, conclusive
OPPOSITES ARE uncertain (whether), doubtful
**3** *She faced certain failure.*
▶ inevitable, assured, inescapable, unavoidable

**4** *They are certain to win.*
▶ sure, bound, assured (of winning)
AN OPPOSITE IS unlikely
**5** *A certain person has been here.*
▶ particular, specific, definite, unnamed, individual

**certainly** ADVERB
*It was certainly a beautiful building.*
▶ undoubtedly, unquestionably, surely, undeniably, definitely, without question, without doubt

**certainty** NOUN
**1** *The answers may never be known with certainty.*
▶ assurance, assuredness, confidence, conviction, certitude
OPPOSITES ARE uncertainty, doubt
**2** *A high-scoring match seemed a certainty.*
▶ inevitability, certain fact, foregone conclusion, matter of course, necessity, (more informal) sure thing
AN OPPOSITE IS impossibility

**certificate** NOUN
*a certificate of airworthiness*
▶ guarantee, document, permit, certification, diploma, award, licence, authorization, warrant, proof

**certify** VERB
*You have to sign the form to certify that the information is true.*
▶ verify, guarantee, confirm, affirm, testify, warrant, declare, demonstrate

**chain** NOUN
**1** *The prisoners were held in chains.*
▶ fetters, shackles, bonds, irons, manacles, coupling, handcuffs, links
**2** *a chain of events*
▶ series, sequence, succession, string, course, train, progression
**3** *a chain of supermarkets*
▶ group, firm, series

**chain** VERB
*The bicycle was chained to a fence.*
▶ tie, fasten, secure, hitch, tether, manacle, fetter

**chairman, chairwoman** NOUN
*the chairman of a committee*
▶ chairperson, chair, president, convener, organizer, director, speaker

**challenge** VERB
**1** *The woman had challenged an intruder.*
▶ accost, confront, take on
**2** *It was a job that would challenge their abilities.*
▶ test, tax, try, stretch
**3** *He challenged one of the men to a duel.*
▶ dare, summon, invite, defy, provoke
**4** *We will have to challenge the decision.*
▶ dispute, oppose, object to, protest against, query, question, disagree with, argue against, dissent from

**challenge** NOUN
**1** *Will you accept the challenge?*
▶ dare, summons

2 *Coping with the extra work proved quite a challenge.*
▶ trial, task, undertaking, problem, difficulty
3 *a challenge to the party leadership*
▶ opposition, confrontation (with), dispute (with)

**challenging** ADJECTIVE
*a challenging task*
▶ demanding, testing, taxing, exacting, stimulating
OPPOSITES ARE easy, undemanding

**chamber** NOUN
1 *a debating chamber*
▶ room, hall
2 *the chambers of the heart*
▶ compartment, cavity, cell, space

**champion** NOUN
1 *the world champion*
▶ title-holder, victor, conqueror, winner
2 *a champion of reform*
▶ supporter, advocate, defender, upholder, patron, backer, guardian, protector

**champion** VERB
*a charity championing the rights of asylum-seekers*
▶ support, promote, uphold, defend, campaign for, fight for, stand up for, advance, espouse, protect

**championship** NOUN
*a golf championship*
▶ competition, contest, tournament

**chance** ADJECTIVE
*a chance discovery*
▶ accidental, fortuitous, coincidental, casual, incidental, unintentional, unforeseen, random
OPPOSITES ARE intentional, planned

**chance** NOUN
1 *There is a slight chance of snow.*
▶ possibility, likelihood, probability, prospect, risk, danger
2 *Give them a chance to answer.*
▶ opportunity, time, turn, occasion
3 *We were taking an awful chance.*
▶ risk, gamble
**by chance** *I found the earring by chance.*
▶ by accident, accidentally, fortuitously, inadvertently, unwittingly

**chance** VERB
1 *I chanced to be passing at that moment.*
▶ happen
2 *Shall we chance another look?*
▶ risk, venture, hazard, try

**chancy** ADJECTIVE
*(informal) It was chancy taking a shortcut across the meadow in the dark.*
▶ risky, dangerous, hazardous, unsafe, precarious, insecure, tricky, uncertain, unpredictable, (more informal) dicey
OPPOSITES ARE safe, predictable

**change** NOUN
1 *a change of plan*
▶ alteration, modification, variation, revision, amendment (to), replacement (for)

2 *We'd like a change.*
▶ diversion, novelty, innovation, variety
3 *I've got no change for the bus.*
▶ coins, small change, loose change

**change** VERB
1 *These events have changed the world for ever.*
▶ alter, make different, transform, modify, reshape, refashion, reorder
2 *Things have changed a lot since we were last here.*
▶ alter, become different, develop, fluctuate, (more informal) move on
3 *I need to change my library book.*
▶ exchange, swap, substitute, switch, replace

**changeable** ADJECTIVE
*The weather is very changeable.*
▶ variable, unsettled, unpredictable, unreliable, temperamental, volatile

**channel** NOUN
1 *a water channel*
▶ duct, conduit, gully, gutter, furrow, flume
2 *a channel of communication*
▶ medium, avenue, means, route, path, way
3 *a television channel (informal)*
▶ station, waveband, wavelength

**channel** VERB
*It would be wiser to channel your energies into something new.*
▶ direct, guide, devote (to), put

**chaos** NOUN
*When we arrived on the scene there was total chaos.*
▶ confusion, disorder, mayhem, muddle, bedlam, pandemonium, anarchy, disorganization, lawlessness, shambles, tumult
AN OPPOSITE IS order

**chaotic** ADJECTIVE
1 *A good party is a chaotic jumble of noise and movement.*
▶ disorderly, confused, disorganized, disordered, topsy-turvy, uncontrolled, muddled, tumultuous
OPPOSITES ARE organized, orderly
2 *The country was in a chaotic state for years.*
▶ anarchic, lawless, unruly, uncontrolled
AN OPPOSITE IS orderly

**chap** NOUN
*Some chap gave it to me (informal).*
▶ man, boy, individual, bloke

**chapter** NOUN
1 *a chapter of a book*
▶ section, part, division
2 *a new chapter in the nation's history*
▶ stage, phase, period, era, epoch

**char** VERB
*The heat has charred the woodwork.*
▶ scorch, sear, singe, blacken, brown, burn, carbonize

## character NOUN

**1** *Jane has a forceful character.*
▶ personality, temperament, nature, temper

**2** *The trees and parks add a special character to the town.*
▶ distinctiveness, individuality, uniqueness, stamp, feature

**3** *He was acquitted without a stain on his character.*
▶ reputation, name, standing, stature, position

**4** (*informal*) *The new doctor is a charming character.*
▶ person, individual, being, sort, type, fellow, (*more informal*) bloke, (*more informal*) chap

**5** (*informal*) *Her father is something of a character.*
▶ eccentric, oddity, (*more informal*) oddball, (*more informal*) case

**6** *a woman of character*
▶ integrity, honour, quality

**7** *She has played several characters in the same play.*
▶ part, role

**8** *The sign was printed in Greek characters.*
▶ letter, figure, symbol

## characteristic ADJECTIVE

*He spoke with his characteristic eloquence.*
▶ typical, distinctive, usual, normal, particular, singular, special, individual, peculiar, recognizable, specific, unique, distinguishing, essential, idiosyncratic

## characteristic NOUN

*The building has some interesting characteristics.*
▶ feature, peculiarity, trait, attribute, distinguishing feature, property, aspect, hallmark, idiosyncrasy

## characterize VERB

**1** *The film characterizes the king as a cruel dictator.*
▶ portray, depict, represent, describe, categorize, delineate, draw, present

**2** *The period after the War was characterized by great social hardship.*
▶ distinguish, mark, identify, set apart, brand, differentiate, individualize, recognize, typify

## charade NOUN

*The presidential elections had been a shameless charade.*
▶ farce, pantomime, fabrication, pretence, sham, mockery, deception, masquerade

## charge NOUN

**1** *Our charges will increase from next April.*
▶ fee, price, cost, tariff

**2** *The children were left in their sister's charge.*
▶ care, protection, custody, keeping, surveillance, command, control, responsibility, safe-keeping, trust

**3** *The company's directors face criminal charges.*
▶ accusation, allegation, indictment, imputation

**4** *The infantry suffered heavy casualties in the charge.*
▶ assault, attack, onslaught, offensive, rush, sortie, raid

**in charge of** *He was in charge of the factory during his father's absence.*
▶ responsible for, in control of, managing, running, looking after

## charge VERB

**1** *What do they charge for a coffee?*
▶ ask for, ask in payment, make you pay, exact, levy, require

**2** *They charged him with producing a video of the event.*
▶ entrust, burden, saddle, tax, empower

**3** *The witness was later charged with perjury.*
▶ accuse (of), prosecute (for), indict (for), put on trial (for)

**4** *The mounted cavalry charged the enemy line.*
▶ attack, storm, rush, assault, assail, fall on, set on

## charitable ADJECTIVE

**1** *a charitable activity*
▶ philanthropic, humanitarian, benevolent

**2** *a charitable attitude*
▶ generous, magnanimous, friendly, liberal, benign, considerate, compassionate, understanding, broad-minded

## charity NOUN

**1** *Show some charity towards those in need.*
▶ goodwill, generosity, consideration, kindness, sympathy, compassion, fellow feeling
AN OPPOSITE IS selfishness

**2** *The church depends on the charity of parishioners.*
▶ financial assistance, generosity, donations, contributions, subsidies, patronage

## charm NOUN

**1** *As he relaxed, his charm and humour returned.*
▶ attractiveness, appeal, allure, lure, charisma, desirability, fascination, enchantment

**2** *magical charms*
▶ spell, incantation

**3** *a lucky charm*
▶ trinket, talisman, amulet, mascot, idol

## charm VERB

*He charmed everyone with his stories.*
▶ delight, please, captivate, bewitch, enchant, entrance, enthral, mesmerize
OPPOSITES ARE repel, disgust

## charming ADJECTIVE

*My mother tells me that I was a charming baby.*
▶ delightful, attractive, pleasant, pleasing, endearing, alluring, disarming, likeable

## chart NOUN

**1** *a flow chart*
▶ diagram, graph, plan, table

**2** *a weather chart*
▶ map

## charter NOUN

*The company was granted a royal charter*
▶ privilege, right, permit, licence, authority, authorization, franchise, contract

## charter VERB

*We can charter an aircraft over the mountains.*
▶ hire, lease, rent, commission, employ, engage

## chary ADJECTIVE

*She was chary about lending him any more money.*
▶ wary, cautious, doubtful, dubious, careful, hesitant, guarded
AN OPPOSITE IS heedless

## chase VERB

*The farmer chased the intruders across a field.*
▶ pursue, run after, track, trail, drive, follow, hound, hunt

**chase around** *I've been chasing around all morning trying to finish my work.*
▶ rush, hurry, bustle, scamper

## chasm NOUN

*Below the bridge was a deep chasm*
▶ crevasse, ravine, opening, abyss, canyon, gorge, void, drop, fissure, gap, gulf, hollow, rift, pit, hole

## chaste ADJECTIVE

*leading a chaste life*
▶ pure, virtuous, virginal, celibate, innocent
AN OPPOSITE IS immoral

## chastise VERB

*He was chastised for his rudeness.*
▶ punish, discipline, beat, scold, reprimand, admonish, upbraid

## chastity NOUN

*a life of chastity*
▶ celibacy, purity, virginity, innocence, virtue, abstinence

## chat VERB

*We spent hours chatting about nothing in particular.*
▶ talk, gossip, chatter, (more informal) jabber, (more informal) babble

**chat up** (informal) *He tried to chat Jenny up in the bus queue.*
▶ flirt with, make up to, make advances to

## chat NOUN

*I needed to have a chat with her.*
▶ talk, conversation, chatter, (more informal) natter, (more informal) chinwag

## chatter VERB

*Some of the people stayed chattering at one end of the room.*
▶ talk, gossip, chat, (more informal) jabber, (more informal) babble

## chatty ADJECTIVE

(informal) *She seemed to be in a chatty mood.*
▶ talkative, communicative, effusive, expansive, open, friendly

## chauvinism NOUN

1 *His devotion to his country amounted to chauvinism.*
▶ jingoism, excessive patriotism, nationalism
2 *The management were accused of chauvinism.*
▶ sexism, discrimination, prejudice, bigotry

## cheap ADJECTIVE

1 *a cheap edition of Shakespeare's works*
▶ inexpensive, economical, low-priced, affordable, reasonable
2 *racks of cheap digital watches*
▶ inferior, second-rate, shoddy, vulgar, tawdry, (more informal) tatty, (more informal) tacky
3 *cheap tabloid journalism*
▶ mean, despicable, low, contemptible, tasteless
4 *They made us feel cheap.*
▶ ashamed, embarrassed, humiliated, degraded

## cheapen VERB

*They cheapened themselves with their boastful talk.*
▶ demean, belittle, discredit, disgrace, diminish

## cheat VERB

*Some dealers are cheating their customers.*
▶ swindle, defraud, deceive, exploit, hoodwink, short-change, dupe, (more informal) con, (more informal) rip off

## cheat NOUN

1 *He called his brother a cheat.*
▶ swindler, deceiver, fraud, charlatan, impostor, (more informal) phoney
2 *The scheme was really a bit of a cheat.*
▶ deception, deceit, fraud, pretence, hoax, trick, (more informal) racket, (more informal) fiddle

## check VERB

1 *Police were checking vehicles at roadblocks.*
▶ examine, inspect, test, look over, scrutinize, scan, investigate
2 *I'll check the answers against this list.*
▶ verify, confirm, test, compare
3 *He checked an impulse to look round.*
▶ resist, control, suppress, restrain, curb, repress, stifle
4 *Extensive flooding checked their progress.*
▶ hinder, obstruct, hamper, impede, restrict, inhibit, frustrate

## check NOUN

1 *There will be an official check of documents at the border.*
▶ inspection, examination, scrutiny, perusal, investigation
2 *a check on the abuse of power*
▶ curb, restraint, control

## check-up NOUN

*The car goes for a check-up next week.*
▶ check, inspection, examination, overhaul

## cheek NOUN

*He had the cheek to tell me to leave* (informal).
▶ audacity, effrontery, nerve, temerity, impertinence, impudence, insolence, presumptuousness, shamelessness, (more informal) sauce

## cheeky ADJECTIVE

*A cheeky boy from down the road called after him.*
▶ impudent, impertinent, insolent, impolite, disrespectful, brazen, audacious, forward, pert

## cheer VERB

1 *We'll be there to cheer our team.*
▶ applaud, acclaim, clap, shout

2 *The good news cheered them a great deal.*
▶ comfort, console, gladden, delight, encourage, uplift, exhilarate, make cheerful, please, solace
AN OPPOSITE IS sadden

**cheer up** *As I reached home I began to cheer up.*
▶ take heart, become more cheerful, perk up, brighten, rally, revive

## cheer NOUN

*The spectators gave her a cheer.*
▶ hurrah, cry of approval, shout of approval, ovation, acclamation, applause, encouragement

## cheerful ADJECTIVE

*They arrived looking cheerful. It was a cheerful occasion.*
▶ happy, jolly, glad, joyful, joyous, lively, elated, animated, contented, buoyant, good-humoured, light-hearted, chirpy
OPPOSITES ARE sad, dejected

## cheerless ADJECTIVE

*The town was a nondescript cheerless place.*
▶ dreary, dull, gloomy, bleak, dismal, grim, sombre, dingy, drab, stark, desolate
AN OPPOSITE IS cheerful

## cheery ADJECTIVE

*She answered the phone with a cheery 'Good morning'.*
▶ cheerful, jolly, merry, spirited, jaunty, carefree, happy, sunny, joyful, joyous

## cheese NOUN

### KINDS OF CHEESE

**USAGE** Many cheeses are named after the place where they were first developed: this is true of most English cheeses and some others, eg Camembert (in Normandy, North-West France), Edam (In the Netherlands), and Parmesan (from Parma in northern Italy). Some cheeses are also produced in countries other than the country of origin; for example, a kind of Brie is also made in Britain. Some names are trademarks: for example, Boursin and Cambozola.

**British cheeses**: Caerphilly, Cheddar, Cheshire, Colby, Cotswold, crowdie (Scottish), Derby, Double Gloucester, Ilchester, Iancashire, Leicester, Red Leicester, sage Derby, Stilton, Wensleydale, Wiltshire, Windsor, Windsor Red.

**Dutch cheeses**: Edam, Gouda.

**French cheeses**: Beaufort, blue brie, Boursin, Brie, Camembert, Cantal, Chaumes, chèvre (goat's-milk cheese), fromage blanc (= 'white cheese'), fromage frais (= 'fresh cheese'), Gervais, Neufchâtel, Port Salut, Roquefort. ▶▶

**German cheeses**: Cambozola (a cross between Camembert and Gorgonzola), Tilsit.

**Italian cheeses**: Bel Paese (="fair country'), Dolcelatte (= 'sweet milk'), fontina, Gorgonzola, mascarpone, mozzarella, Parmesan, pecorino (= sheep's-milk cheese), provolone, ricotta (= 'cooked again'), taleggio.

**Swiss cheeses**: Emmental, Gruyère.

**Other European cheeses**: feta (Greece, made from sheep's or goat's milk), Limbourger (Belgium).

**other types of cheese**: cottage cheese, cream cheese, curd cheese, quark (low-fat curd cheese).

## chemical elements NOUN

### WORDS FOR CHEMICAL ELEMENTS

115 chemical elements have been discovered, but only 90 occur naturally. Elements can be sorted into metals, non-metals and semi-metals. Over three-quarters of all the most important are listed below.

**metals**: lithium(Li), beryllium (Be), sodium (Na), magnesium (Mg), aluminium (Al), potassium (K), calcium (Ca), scandium (Sc), titanium (Ti), vanadium (V), chromium (Cr), manganese (Mn), iron (Fe), cobalt (Co), nickel (Ni), copper (Cu), zinc (Zn), gallium (Ga), strontium (Sr), zirconium (Zr), molybdenum (Mo), silver (Ag), cadmium (Cd), tin (Sn), barium (Ba), tungsten (W), platinum (Pt), gold (Au), mercury (Hg), lead (Pb), bismuth (Bi), uranium (U).

**non-metals**: hydrogen (H), helium (He), carbon (C), nitrogen (N), oxygen (O), fluorine (F), neon (Ne), phosophorus (P), sulphur (S), chlorine (Cl), argon (Ar), bromine (Br), krypton (Kr), iodine (I), xenon (Xe), radon (Rn).

**semi-metals or metalloids**: boron (B), silicon (Si), germanium (Ge), arsenic (As), selenium (Se), antimony (Sb), tellurium (Tb), polonium (Po), astatine (At).

## cherish VERB

1 *His friends all cherished him.*
▶ adore, love, be devoted to, be fond of, hold dear, care for, foster, keep safe, look after, nourish, nurse, protect

2 *I shall cherish this gift all my life.*
▶ treasure, value, prize

## chest NOUN

1 *The ball hit him in the chest.*
▶ breast, ribcage
RELATED ADJECTIVE pectoral

2 *a large chest of tools*
▶ case, crate, box, casket, coffer, strongbox, trunk

## chew VERB

*Claire was chewing a piece of bread.*
▶ eat, munch, nibble, champ, bite, crunch, gnaw, (*more formal*) masticate

## chewy ADJECTIVE

*The meat was very chewy.*
▶ tough, gristly, leathery, rubbery
AN OPPOSITE IS tender

## chic ADJECTIVE

*a woman in a chic outfit*
▶ stylish, elegant, fashionable, smart, modish
OPPOSITES ARE unfashionable, drab, dowdy

## chief ADJECTIVE

1 *Money was the chief problem.*
▶ main, principal, primary, prime, most important, overriding, foremost, fundamental, key, crucial, central, paramount, predominant, basic, essential

2 *the chief cook*
▶ head, senior, principal, leading

## chief NOUN

*He is the chief of a merchant bank.*
▶ head, principal, president, chairman, chief executive

## chiefly ADVERB

*Dogs were chiefly to blame for the damage.*
▶ mainly, mostly, primarily, principally, predominantly, especially, essentially

## child NOUN

1 *She was only a child when I last saw her.*
▶ youngster, girl (or boy), baby, infant, little one, (*more informal*) kid, (*more informal*) nipper, (*more informal*) tot
RELATED ADJECTIVE juvenile

2 *She is the child of Greek parents.*
▶ offspring, progeny, daughter (or son), descendant, heir, issue

## childhood NOUN

*He has suffered from the illness from childhood.*
▶ infancy, youth, boyhood (or girlhood), adolescence, teens

## childish ADJECTIVE

*It was childish of him to say that.*
▶ immature, babyish, puerile, infantile, juvenile, silly, foolish
AN OPPOSITE IS mature

**USAGE** Note that *childish* is normally an unfavourable word, whereas *childlike* is favourable or neutral in tone.

## childlike ADJECTIVE

*a world of childlike simplicity*
▶ innocent, naive, artless, guileless, ingenuous, trusting
OPPOSITES ARE artful, disingenuous

## chill NOUN

1 *We felt a distinct chill in the air.*
▶ coldness, chilliness, coolness, crispness, rawness, bite, nip

2 *She decided to stay at home because of her chill.*
▶ cold, flu

## chill VERB

*The drinks need to be chilled.*
▶ cool, refrigerate, ice, freeze, make cold
AN OPPOSITE IS warm

## chilly ADJECTIVE

1 *a chilly evening in March*
▶ cold, crisp, sharp, fresh, cool, frosty, icy, raw, (*more informal*) nippy, (*more informal*) parky
AN OPPOSITE IS warm

2 *You may get a chilly reception.*
▶ unfriendly, cool, lukewarm, unwelcoming, frigid, hostile, unsympathetic, reserved, aloof, (*informal*) standoffish
OPPOSITES ARE warm, friendly, enthusiastic

## chime VERB

*The church bells began to chime.*
▶ sound, strike, ring, peal, toll

## china NOUN

*Put out the best china.*
▶ porcelain, crockery, cups and saucers, earthenware

## chink NOUN

1 *a chink in the clouds   a chink in the wall*
▶ opening, gap, hole, space, crack, split, fissure

2 *the chink of glasses*
▶ clink, tinkle, ring

## chip NOUN

1 *a chip of wood*
▶ fragment, piece, bit, sliver, splinter, slice, flake, fleck, scrap, shaving

2 *The cup had a chip in it.*
▶ crack, nick, flaw, scratch, gash, notch, snick

## chip VERB

*Someone had chipped the teapot.*
▶ crack, nick, scratch, splinter, notch, damage

## chirp VERB

*Birds chirped in the trees.*
▶ cheep, tweet, chirrup, twitter, sing

## chirpy ADJECTIVE

*She came in with a chirpy grin.*
▶ cheerful, happy, jolly, glad, joyful, joyous, lively, elated

## chivalrous ADJECTIVE

*He treated everyone in the same chivalrous manner.*
▶ gallant, courteous, polite, honorable, considerate, gracious, thoughtful
OPPOSITES ARE dishonourable, rude

## chivalry NOUN

*Where is your sense of chivalry Roger?*
▶ gallantry, courtesy, politeness, consideration, graciousness, thoughtfulness

a b **c** d e f g h i j k l m n o p q r s t u v w x y z

**choice** NOUN

**1** *We have no other choice now.*
► option, alternative, possibility, answer
**2** *the viewers' choice of programmes*
► selection, choosing, preference, election
**3** *Write in with your choice.*
► decision, selection, vote, nomination
**4** *a wide choice of good food*
► range, variety, selection, array, assortment, display

**choice** ADJECTIVE

*choice vegetables*
► fine, superior, first-class, first-rate, excellent, prime, select

**choir** NOUN

*Her mother sang in a local choir.*
► chorus, choral group, choral society, vocal ensemble

**choke** VERB

**1** *The dust was nearly choking them.*
► suffocate, asphyxiate, smother, stifle
**2** *There was a danger of the necklace choking her to death.*
► strangle, throttle, suffocate, asphyxiate
**3** *Oliver choked and had to be thumped on the back.*
► gag, gasp, retch, suffocate
**4** *The motorways are constantly choked with traffic.*
► clog, congest, constrict, block, obstruct
**choke back** *Sandra choked back the tears as she tried to answer.*
► stifle, suppress, fight back, hold back

**choose** VERB

**1** *We chose a quiet spot by the river.*
► pick, pick out, select, opt for, plump for, go for, settle on, fix on, decide on
**2** *Mark chose to go in first.*
► decide, elect, make up your mind, determine, prefer, resolve, see fit

**choosy** ADJECTIVE

*choosy about food*
► fussy, finicky, particular, fastidious, picky

**chop** VERB

**1** *He was in the yard chopping wood.*
► cut, hew
**2** *Chop the vegetables into small chunks.*
► cut up, slice, split, dice
**chop down** *The tree should be chopped down.*
► cut down, fell
**chop off** *His arm had been chopped off in an accident.*
► sever, amputate, detach, lop off

**chopper** NOUN

*He cut up the logs with a chopper.*
► axe, cleaver

**choppy** ADJECTIVE

*a choppy sea*
► rough, turbulent, stormy, heavy
OPPOSITES ARE calm, smooth

**chore** NOUN

*I spent the day cooking and doing household chores.*
► task, job, duty, burden, errand

**chorus** NOUN

**1** *The chorus sang well.*
► choir, choral group, choral society, vocal ensemble
**2** *Everyone can join in the choruses.*
► refrain, response

**christen** VERB

**1** *The church in which Tania was christened.*
► baptize, name
**2** *His friends christened him 'The King'*
► name, dub, style, designate

**chronic** ADJECTIVE

**1** *a chronic illness*
► persistent, long-standing, lifelong, lingering, incurable
OPPOSITES ARE acute, temporary
**2** *chronic food shortages*
► constant, persistent, continuous, continual

**chronicle** NOUN

*a chronicle of events in the region*
► record, account, history, annals, diary, journal, narrative, story

**chronological** ADJECTIVE

*chronological order*
► consecutive, sequential

**chubby** ADJECTIVE

*a chubby little baby*
► plump, tubby, podgy, round, dumpy, portly, rotund, stout, buxom

**chuck** VERB

*(informal) I'll chuck the letter in the bin.*
► throw, toss, fling, hurl, dump, sling
**chuck out** *There are a lot of old clothes to chuck out.*
► throw away, discard, dispose of, reject, scrap

**chuckle** VERB

*Andrew chuckled as he left the room.*
► chortle, snigger, giggle, laugh

**chunk** NOUN

*little chunks of cheese on a plate   a chunk of wood*
► lump, hunk, block, wedge, piece, portion, slab

**chunky** ADJECTIVE

*a chunky lad of twenty*
► stocky, sturdy, burly, bulky, beefy, dumpy

**churlish** ADJECTIVE

*It seems churlish to complain.*
► rude, boorish, discourteous, ill-mannered, ungracious, impolite

**churn** VERB

**churn up** *The propellers churned up the water.*
► agitate, stir up, disturb
**churn out** *When he was young he churned out poem after poem.*
► produce, turn out

**circle** NOUN

**1** *The children stood in a circle*
► ring, round
RELATED ADJECTIVE circular

**2** *He has a new circle of friends.*
► group, set, band, body, company, society, association, gang, party

**circle** VERB

**1** *The birds circled over his head.*
► wheel, fly round, spiral

**2** *Satellites circle the earth.*
► orbit, go round, circumnavigate, revolve round

**3** *The grass was circled by trees.*
► surround, enclose, encircle, ring, skirt, girdle, hem in

**circuit** NOUN

**1** *two circuits of the playing field*
► lap, turn, round, revolution

**2** *a racing circuit*
► track, course

**circuitous** ADJECTIVE

*a circuitous route*
► roundabout, indirect, meandering, winding, rambling, tortuous
OPPOSITES ARE direct, straight

**circular** ADJECTIVE

*a circular window*
► round, disc-shaped, ring-shaped
**USAGE** You can also use *oval* and *elliptical* to describe a shape that is nearly circular but slightly flattened.

**circular** NOUN

*an advertising circular*
► advertisement, leaflet, letter, notice, pamphlet

**circulate** VERB

*We circulated a notice about our sale*
► send round, distribute, issue, publicize, publish, spread about, disseminate

**circulation** NOUN

**1** *air circulation*
► flow, motion, movement, course

**2** *the circulation of information*
► dissemination, distribution, spread, transmission, broadcasting

**3** *a newspaper's circulation*
► distribution, readership, sales figures

**circumference** NOUN

*the circumference of the field*
► circuit, perimeter, border, boundary, edge, periphery, rim, limit, margin, outline, outside

**circumstances** PLURAL NOUN

**1** *the right economic circumstances*
► situation, conditions, state of affairs, factors, position, background

**2** *The police wanted to know all the circumstances.*
► facts, details, particulars, incidents, events

**citadel** NOUN

*A river passes the citadel walls.*
► fortress, stronghold, bastion, castle, keep, tower, fortification, acropolis

**cite** VERB

**1** *You should cite the passage in full.*
► quote, reproduce

**2** *She cited the decisions reached in previous cases.*
► refer to, name, quote, mention, adduce, specify, advance, invoke, (more informal) bring up

**citizen** NOUN

**1** *a British citizen*
► subject, national, taxpayer, voter
RELATED ADJECTIVES civic, civil, civilian

**2** *the citizens of Glasgow*
► inhabitants, resident, native, townsperson, householder

**city** NOUN

*a large city north of the river*
► town, metropolis, conurbation
RELATED ADJECTIVES civic, urban

**civil** ADJECTIVE

**1** *I know you don't like her but try to be civil.*
► polite, respectful, well-mannered, courteous, considerate, affable, civilized, refined, obliging
OPPOSITES ARE impolite, rude

**2** *a civil wedding*
► secular, non-religious

**3** *civil rights*
► social, state, communal, national, public

**4** *civil politics*
► domestic, home, internal, national, local

**civilization** NOUN

**1** *ancient civilizations*
► culture, society, people

**2** *advances in civilization*
► human development, human achievements, human attainments, enlightenment

**civilized** ADJECTIVE

**1** *a civilized nation*
► advanced, developed, enlightened, cultured, refined
AN OPPOSITE IS uncivilized

**2** *civilized behaviour*
► polite, orderly

**claim** VERB

**1** *You can claim a refund at the office.*
► ask for, request, demand, collect, require, take

**2** *He claimed the witness had been lying.*
► allege, maintain, contend, assert, avow, protest, insist

**claim** NOUN

**1** *a claim for damages   an insurance claim*
► application, demand, request

**2** *Their claim is hardly credible.*
► assertion, allegation, contention, declaration

**clairvoyant** ADJECTIVE

*I didn't know about it and I'm not clairvoyant.*
► psychic, telepathic, prophetic, extrasensory, oracular

**clairvoyant** NOUN

*The woman claimed she was a clairvoyant.*
► psychic, fortune teller, prophet, oracle, seer, sibyl, soothsayer

**clamber** VERB

*It was dangerous clambering over the rocks.*
► scramble, crawl, climb, move awkwardly

**clammy** ADJECTIVE

1 *They sat waiting with clammy hands for an hour and a half.*
► moist, sticky, sweaty, damp

2 *The atmosphere was cold and clammy.*
► dank, humid, damp, moist, muggy, slimy, sticky

**clamp** VERB

*Each shelf is clamped to three brackets.*
► fasten, fix, secure, attach, clip

**clamp down on** *a plan to clamp down on illegal parking*
► reduce, suppress, end, stop, eradicate, get tough on, crack down on

**clan** NOUN

*a Scottish clan*
► family, house, tribe, dynasty

**clap** NOUN

1 *a clap of thunder*
► crash, crack, boom, bang, thunderclap

2 *a clap on the shoulder*
► slap, thump, smack, blow

**clap** VERB

1 *The audience clapped her performance.*
► applaud, cheer, acclaim

2 *Someone clapped me on the shoulder.*
► slap, hit, pat, smack

**claptrap** NOUN

*(informal) He was speaking claptrap.*
► nonsense, rubbish, gibberish, drivel, (informal) poppycock

**clarify** VERB

*To clarify matters, let us ask some basic questions.*
► explain, throw light on, elucidate, make clear, gloss, illuminate, define
AN OPPOSITE IS confuse

**clarity** NOUN

*She explained the problem with great clarity.*
► clearness, lucidity, transparency, intelligibility, simplicity, precision, coherence

**clash** NOUN

1 *There was a metallic clash as the two vehicles came together.*
► crash, striking, bang

2 *Clashes followed between students and riot police.*
► fight, conflict, hostilities, collision

3 *a clash between the president and his secretary of state*
► disagreement, altercation, argument, quarrel, exchange

**clash** VERB

1 *The cymbals clashed.*
► crash, strike, resound, bang

2 *The violence began outside a chip shop, when rival gangs clashed.*
► disagree, conflict, quarrel, wrangle, fight

3 *The interview clashes with my holiday.*
► coincide, conflict, come at the same time (as)

**clasp** NOUN

1 *The bracelet needs a strong clasp.*
► fastener, fastening, catch, hook, buckle, clip, hasp, pin

2 *His clasp loosened a bit, but he didn't let her go.*
► hold, grasp, grip, embrace, squeeze, hug, cuddle

**clasp** VERB

1 *John clasped the woman in his arms.*
► hug, hold, embrace, squeeze, cling to, clutch, enfold, grasp, grip

2 *Before leaving she clasped his hand for a few moments.*
► grasp, hold, grip, clutch

**class** NOUN

1 *Our hotel is quite good for its class.*
► category, grade, classification, group, section, division, status

2 *a new class of medicine*
► type, kind, sort, genre, species, genus

3 *discrimination on the basis of social class*
► status, standing, position, station, caste, grouping

4 *a history class*
► form, set, group, stream

**class** VERB

*Her performance was classed as a distinction.*
► classify, categorize, group, grade, designate, rank, label

**classic** ADJECTIVE

1 *the classic book on the subject  classic works of literature*
► definitive, outstanding, established, best, ideal, time-honoured, abiding, enduring

2 *a classic example of how a good idea has gone wrong*
► typical, characteristic, quintessential, archetypal, perfect

**classic** NOUN
*The film has good points but is certainly not a classic.*
► masterpiece, masterwork, model

**classical** ADJECTIVE
1 *classical civilizations*
► ancient, Greek and Roman
2 *a classical style*
► traditional, simple, pure, restrained, elegant, well-proportioned
3 *classical music   classical ballet*
► traditional, established, harmonious, highbrow
AN OPPOSITE IS modern

**classification** NOUN
*the classification of volcanoes into active, dormant, and extinct   a system of classification*
► categorization, division, grading, ordering, organization, codification, taxonomy

**classify** VERB
*We can classify the plants according to the shape of their leaves.*
► categorize, class, group, organize, grade, sort, catalogue, order

**classy** ADJECTIVE
*a classy outfit*
► stylish, elegant, smart, chic, sophisticated, fashionable, high-class, (more informal) posh, (more informal) snazzy

**clatter** VERB
*Something in the engine began to clatter.*
► rattle, clank, clunk

**clause** NOUN
*There is an extra clause in the new contract.*
► section, article, condition, provision, proviso, subsection, paragraph, item, part, passage

**claw** NOUN
1 *a bird's claws*
► talon, nail
2 *a crab's claw*
► pincer, nipper

**claw** VERB
*One soldier lifted his arm and clawed at her face.*
► scratch, scrabble, scrape, tear

**clean** ADJECTIVE
1 *She went in to put on clean clothes.*
► washed, cleaned, laundered, pristine
2 *Keep the wound clean.*
► sterile, sterilized, healthy, uncontaminated
3 *Write your details on a clean sheet of paper.*
► blank, unused, empty, plain, fresh, bare
4 *The air is clean in the mountains.*
► pure, clear, fresh, untainted
5 *The family all led a clean life.*
► virtuous, honest, moral, decent, respectable, exemplary, blameless, upright, pure, innocent
6 *We hope for a clean fight.*
► fair, honest, sporting
7 *Make a clean cut with a sharp knife.*
► smooth, neat, tidy, straight, accurate
8 *I decided to make a clean break with the place.*
► complete, total, thorough, decisive, final

**clean** VERB
1 *I'll go and clean the car.*
► wash, sponge, hose down, shampoo, polish
2 *We'll have to clean the bathroom floor.*
► wash, wipe, sponge, scrub, sweep, mop, swab
3 *Put out the clothes you want to be cleaned.*
► launder, dry-clean
4 *The whole room needs cleaning.*
► dust, brush, spruce up
5 *Make sure you clean the wound.*
► cleanse, wash, bathe, disinfect, sanitize, purify

**clear** ADJECTIVE
1 *clear instructions*
► plain, understandable, easy, direct, logical
2 *It was clear we would have to wait.   a clear case of discrimination*
► evident, obvious, plain, apparent, patent, blatant, glaring, manifest
3 *a pool of clear water*
► transparent, translucent, crystalline
4 *a clear blue sky*
► bright, cloudless, unclouded, sunny, fair, fine
5 *a clear complexion*
► fresh, unblemished
6 *a clear voice*
► pure, distinct
7 *The motorway was clear again by the afternoon.*
► open, unobstructed, unblocked, unrestricted, passable
8 *a clear conscience*
► untroubled, undisturbed, easy, calm, guiltless, blameless
9 *a clear month's notice*
► full, whole, entire, complete, total

**clear** VERB
1 *The weather seemed to be clearing.*
► brighten, become brighter, turn fine, lighten
OPPOSITES ARE darken, get worse
2 *Rain will slowly clear from the south.*
► disappear, fade out, dwindle, disperse, recede, diminish, peter out, wear off, dry out
3 *We should clear the backlog of work by Friday.*
► complete, eliminate, deal with, get rid of
4 *a special tool for clearing drains*
► unblock, unclog, free, loosen
AN OPPOSITE IS block
5 *I have cleared most of the weeds.*
► tidy, remove, get rid of, eliminate, disentangle
6 *Staff were told to clear the building immediately.*
► evacuate, empty, leave
7 *The ball cleared the bar easily.*
► go over, pass over, go above

8 *The appeal judges are expected to clear him this week.*
▶ acquit, exonerate, free
AN OPPOSITE IS condemn

## clear up

1 *I'll stay here and clear up the mess.*
▶ tidy (up), clean (up)

2 *I'm glad we've cleared up the misunderstanding.*
▶ resolve, explain, straighten out, get to the bottom of

## clear-cut ADJECTIVE

*It is not always easy to make a clear-cut distinction between the two ideas.*
▶ definite, clear, precise, hard and fast, distinct, well defined

## clearing NOUN

*a clearing in the forest*
▶ opening, space, gap, glade

## clearly ADVERB

1 *Clearly we will need to make some changes.*
▶ obviously, evidently, surely, plainly, undoubtedly, patently

2 *It is important to write clearly.*
▶ legibly, distinctly, intelligibly

## clench VERB

1 *She clenched her hands to stop them shaking.*
▶ squeeze (tightly), press (together)

2 *He looked ridiculous, clenching a rose in his teeth.*
▶ hold, clasp, grasp, grip

## clergyman, clergywoman NOUN

*an elderly clergyman in a cassock*
▶ cleric, churchman, churchwoman, man or woman of God, minister, priest, vicar, pastor, parson, chaplain

**USAGE** Special ranks of clerics include *canon, curate, deacon, dean, rector.*

## clerical ADJECTIVE

1 *There is a good deal of clerical work involved.*
▶ administrative, secretarial, office

2 *To his surprise, she wore a clerical collar.*
▶ ecclesiastical, pastoral

## clerk NOUN

*One of the clerks turned up for work with a black eye.*
▶ office worker, clerical worker, office assistant, filing clerk, administrator
RELATED ADJECTIVE clerical

## clever ADJECTIVE

*a clever young student   It was clever of you to work that out.*
▶ intelligent, bright, gifted, brilliant, intellectual, talented, capable, (*more informal*) smart

## cleverness NOUN

*They made you marvel at their cleverness.*
▶ intelligence, ability, talent, sharpness, shrewdness, (*more informal*) brains
AN OPPOSITE IS stupidity

## cliché NOUN

*The speech was a string of clichés*
▶ platitude, commonplace, familiar phrase, hackneyed expression, banality, well-worn phrase

## client NOUN

*a salesman with about a hundred clients to deal with*
▶ customer, buyer, patron, purchaser, user, consumer

## cliff NOUN

*Tiny figures at the top of the cliff*
▶ rock face, bluff, crag, escarpment, precipice

## climate NOUN

1 *countries with a temperate climate*
▶ weather, weather conditions, weather pattern

2 *a changed political climate*
▶ atmosphere, mood, spirit, ambience, temper, trend, environment, feeling

## climax NOUN

*The appointment marked the climax of her career.*
▶ peak, summit, acme, zenith, highlight, high point, head
AN OPPOSITE IS nadir

## climb VERB

1 *She climbed the stairs.*
▶ ascend, go up, mount, move up, scale, clamber up

2 *The plane climbed to 30,000 feet.*
▶ rise, ascend, fly up, soar

3 *The road climbs steeply into the hills.*
▶ rise, ascend, slope up

4 *They climbed the mountain in three days.*
▶ conquer, reach the top of

**climb down** *The Government has had to climb down on the issue.*
▶ give way, back down, yield, retreat, capitulate

## climb NOUN

*a steep climb*
▶ ascent, clamber
AN OPPOSITE IS descent

## clinch VERB

*eager to clinch a deal*
▶ conclude, agree, settle, sign, close, ratify, confirm, decide, make certain of, shake hands on, verify

## cling VERB

1 **cling to** *Climbing plants cling to the walls.*
▶ adhere to, fasten on, stick to

2 **cling to** *Charles took her hand and clung to it.*
▶ clasp, clutch, embrace, grasp, hug

3 **cling to** *I still cling to the hope that I'm mistaken.*
▶ adhere to, stand by, abide by, have faith in, cherish

## clinic NOUN

*an appointment at the local clinic*
▶ health centre, infirmary, medical centre, surgery

## clinical ADJECTIVE

*Her attitude seemed surprisingly clinical.*
▶ detached, unemotional, uninvolved, impersonal, dispassionate, aloof, distant

a
b
c
d
e
f
g
h
i
j
k
l
m
n
o
p
q
r
s
t
u
v
w
x
y
z

## clip NOUN

**1** *He undid the clip and opened the case.*
► fastener, clasp, catch, hook

**2** *a clip from a film*
► excerpt, extract, section, fragment

## clip VERB

**1** *It's my job to clip the hedge.*
► cut, trim, snip, prune, crop

**2** *Clip the coupon and send it to the address below.*
► cut out, remove, detach, tear out

**3** *He clipped him on the head and made him yell.*
► slap, smack, hit, cuff

## clique NOUN

*a clique of London journalists*
► circle, group, set, coterie, crowd

## cloak NOUN

**1** *She threw her cloak over her shoulder.*
► cape, wrap, mantle, coat, cope, robe

**2** *a cloak of secrecy*
► screen, mask, shield, cover, veneer

## clog VERB

*Wet leaves had clogged the drains.*
► block, bung up, stop up, obstruct, choke

## close ADJECTIVE

**1** *close to A large proportion of the world's population lives close to rivers.*
► near, near to, adjacent to, alongside, not far from, in the vicinity of, within reach of

**2** *close to He seemed to be close to tears as he told the story.*
► near to, on the verge of, on the brink of, on the point of

**3** *The house is fairly close.*
► near, nearby

**4** *At last an agreement seemed close.*
► imminent, impending, at hand

**5** *It was a very close contest.*
► even, level, evenly matched, evenly balanced, hard-fought

**6** *The aircraft were flying in a close formation.*
► tight, dense, concentrated, compact

**7** *They are close friends.*
► intimate, dear, devoted, loving, constant

**8** *The problem needs our close attention.*
► careful, thorough, fixed, concentrated, keen, intense

**9** *The weather has become somewhat close.*
► humid, muggy, stuffy, airless, heavy, sticky, clammy, oppressive

## close VERB

**1** *Come in and close the door.*
► shut, lock, secure, fasten, bolt

**2** *The road was closed at the far end.*
► block off, cordon off, bar, barricade, obstruct

**3** *The chairman closed the meeting at this point.*
► conclude, end, finish, stop, terminate, discontinue, wind up, complete

**4** *The hole had been closed with a wad of paper.*
► fill, stop, seal, plug, bung

**5** *a plan to close the gap between rich and poor*
► narrow, reduce, lessen, shorten, fill, make smaller

## close NOUN

*At the close of polling, the votes are collected in a central area.*
► end, finish, completion, conclusion, cessation, termination

## clot NOUN

**1** *a clot of blood (formal)*
► lump, mass, (in an artery or vein) embolism, thrombosis

**2** *I felt a real clot. (informal)*
► fool, idiot

## clot VERB

*a substance to make the blood clot*
► coagulate, congeal, set, thicken, solidify, stiffen

## cloth NOUN

*a length of cloth*
► fabric, material, textile

## clothe VERB

**1** *Despite the war she was able to clothe herself well.*
► dress, fit out, attire

**2** *be clothed in He was clothed in a long striped garment.*
► be dressed in, be attired in, wear

---

## clothes PLURAL NOUN

*She wore lovely clothes, beautifully made from fine materials.*
► clothing, garments, attire, garb, dress, (more informal) gear, wardrobe, outfit
RELATED ADJECTIVE sartorial

### NAMES FOR TYPES OF CLOTHES

**outdoor coats:** coat, overcoat, raincoat, mackintosh, (informal)mac, duffel coat, trench coat, cape.

**casual coats:** anorak, cagoule, bomber jacket, windcheater, blouson, Barbour jacket, combat jacket, donkey jacket, fleece, wrap, parka, poncho, reefer, safari jacket, shell jacket.

**other outdoor clothes:** gloves, scarf, muffler.

**men's clothes:** jacket, blazer, trousers, suit, slacks, jeans, shorts; kilt; shirt, T-shirt, sweatshirt; jersey, jumper, cardigan, waistcoat; underpants, jeans, briefs, boxer shorts, vest; socks; tie, cravat.

**women's clothes:** dress, suit, blouse, T-shirt, sweatshirt; skirt, miniskirt, sarong; shorts; jersey, jumper; bra, underpants, knickers, panties, petticoat, slip; stockings, tights, pantihose, leggings, leg warmers.

**shoes:** shoe, boot, bootee, court shoe, brogue, sandal, pump, espadrille, flip-flop, moccasin, mule, slip-on, slipper, sneaker, trainer, plimsoll, gymshoe; galosh, wellington, wader, gumboot.

## cloud NOUN

1 *Visibility was affected by cloud.*
▶ haze, vapour, mist
2 *a cloud of steam*
▶ mass, billow, haze, mist, puff

## cloud VERB

1 *A light haze clouded the view.*
▶ obscure, shade, hide, conceal, shroud, mist, dim
2 *Anger clouded their judgement.*
▶ confuse, obscure, blur, muddle, obfuscate

## cloudy ADJECTIVE

1 *a cloudy sky*
▶ overcast, dull, grey, gloomy, hazy, leaden
OPPOSITES ARE clear, bright
2 *The water went cloudy.*
▶ hazy, milky, murky, muddy
AN OPPOSITE IS clear

## clout VERB

*His mother clouted him on the ear.*
▶ hit, slap, thump, bash, box, smack, cuff, strike

## clout NOUN

*She threatened him with another clout on the ear.*
▶ slap, smack, thump, bash

## clown NOUN

*They regarded him as the clown of the group.*
▶ joker, jester, comedian, comic, fool, funny man or woman, buffoon

## club NOUN

1 *He had been hit with a heavy club.*
▶ cosh, cudgel, bat, bludgeon, truncheon, baton, stick
2 *She belonged to a local book club.*
▶ society, association, circle, group, union, organization, league, set

## club VERB

*The man had been clubbed almost to death.*
▶ beat, batter, cosh, cudgel, hit, strike, (*more informal*) clobber

## clue NOUN

1 *Give me a clue what it's all about.*
▶ hint, indication, sign, pointer, inkling, tip, idea, pointer, suggestion, key
2 *Police are looking for clues in the immediate area of the crime.*
▶ piece of evidence, lead, evidence
**not have a clue** *I didn't have a clue what to do next* (*informal*).
▶ have no idea, be baffled, be completely stuck, be at a loss, (*more informal*) not have the faintest idea

## clump NOUN

1 *a clump of trees*
▶ cluster, group, mass, thicket, bunch, bundle, collection
2 *a clump of grass*
▶ tuft, bundle, bunch
3 *a clump of earth*
▶ lump, clod, mass

## clumsy ADJECTIVE

1 *She was clumsy and spilt most of the milk.*
▶ inept, bungling, bumbling, blundering, fumbling, uncoordinated, unskilful
OPPOSITES ARE careful, adroit
2 *His movements looked clumsy.*
▶ awkward, ungainly, graceless, ungraceful, gawky, gangling, fumbling
OPPOSITES ARE graceful, elegant

## cluster NOUN

1 *a cluster of buildings*
▶ group, bunch, collection
2 *a cluster of people*
▶ crowd, group, gathering, body, throng, assembly

## clutch VERB

*They were all clutching beer mugs.*
▶ grip, grasp, clasp, hold

## clutches PLURAL NOUN

*At last he was free from their clutches.*
▶ power, control, grasp, clasp, grip, hold, possession

## clutter NOUN

*It's difficult to work with all this clutter around.*
▶ mess, muddle, confusion, untidiness, disorder, jumble, junk, litter, lumber, mix-up, odds and ends, rubbish

## clutter VERB

*Bits of broken machinery cluttered the yard.*
▶ litter, fill, cover, bestrew, mess up

## coach NOUN

1 *The coach takes the motorway.*
▶ bus, motor coach
2 *a horse-drawn coach*
▶ carriage, hansom, hackney, trap
3 *a railway coach*
▶ carriage, wagon, van
4 *a sports coach*
▶ trainer, instructor, teacher

## coach VERB

*Michael coached her to an international standard.*
▶ train, instruct, tutor, teach, prepare

## coagulate VERB

*The warm blood coagulates.*
▶ clot, congeal, cake, set, thicken, solidify, stiffen

## coalition NOUN

*a coalition from the three main political parties*
▶ combination, alliance, union, partnership

## coarse ADJECTIVE

1 *coarse sand   coarse cloth*
▶ rough, unrefined, unprocessed, lumpy, gritty
OPPOSITES ARE fine, soft
2 *coarse language*
▶ crude, vulgar, offensive, bawdy, lewd, foul, dirty, smutty, indecent, indelicate, improper, obscene, ribald
OPPOSITES ARE refined, polite

**coast** NOUN

*a house by the coast*
▶ seaside, seashore, sea, shore, beach, coastline, seaboard

**WORDS FOR COASTAL FEATURES**

**geographical features:** bay, beach, cliff, coral reef, current, delta, estuary, fjord, harbour, headland, island, mudbank, port, reef, sandbank, sand-dune, salt marsh, sea cave, shingle ridge, rock pool, stack, strand, strandline, tide, tideline, wave.

**structures for coastal protection:** breakwater, groyne, sea-wall.

**coast** VERB

*The little car coasted down the slope.*
▶ freewheel, cruise, taxi, drift, glide, sail

**coat** NOUN

1 *Put on a coat if you go out.*
▶ overcoat, jacket
2 *the coat of an animal*
▶ fur, hair, hide, pelt, skin, fleece
3 *a coat of paint*
▶ layer, coating, covering, veneer

**KINDS OF COAT**

**long outdoor coats:** overcoat, raincoat, mackintosh, (informal) mac, duffel coat, trench coat, cape.

**casual outdoor coats:** anorak, cagoule, bomber jacket, windcheater, blouson, Barbour jacket, combat jacket, donkey jacket, fleece, wrap, parka, poncho, reefer, safari jacket, shell jacket.

**coat** VERB

*Coat the surface with varnish.*
▶ cover, paint, glaze, varnish, laminate, smear

**coating** NOUN

*a thick coating of paint*
▶ layer, covering, coat, veneer

**coax** VERB

*It was impossible to coax them back home.*
▶ persuade, tempt, cajole, allure, entice, induce, wheedle, beguile, inveigle, woo

**cobble** VERB

*He had two days to cobble together a report.*
▶ improvise, contrive, scribble, knock up, put together

**cocky** ADJECTIVE

*He had a cocky look on his face.*
▶ arrogant, presumptuous, vain, conceited, self-important, bumptious, superior, disdainful, (more informal) pushy
AN OPPOSITE IS modest

**code** NOUN

1 *a code of conduct    a social code*
▶ system, set of rules, set of principles
2 *The message was written in code.*
▶ cipher, secret language

**coerce** VERB

*He was coerced into signing an agreement.*
▶ pressure, pressurize, force (to), compel (to), constrain (to), bully, browbeat, intimidate

**coercion** NOUN

*Some form of coercion is needed to get them to start work.*
▶ compulsion, pressure, force, constraint, intimidation, duress, harassment

**coffee** NOUN

**KINDS OF COFFEE**

cappuccino (milky with froth), cafe au lait (with milk), cafe noir (black, ie without milk), decaffeinated coffee, espresso (strong black Italian coffee), filter coffee, latte (frothy milk mixed with espresso), mocha (fine coffee with added chocolate), Gaelic coffee (with cream and whisky), Greek coffee (strong black coffee with grounds at the bottom), instant coffee, percolated coffee, Irish coffee (kind of Gaelic coffee), Turkish coffee (like Greek coffee).

**coherent** ADJECTIVE

*a coherent argument*
▶ logical, reasonable, rational, lucid, clear, sound, cogent, compelling, persuasive
OPPOSITES ARE incoherent, illogical

**coil** NOUN

*coils of rope*
▶ loop, twist, ring, spiral, roll, turn

**coil** VERB

*He coiled her hair round his finger.*
▶ curl, wind, twine, loop, roll

**coin** NOUN

1 *a pile of silver coins*
▶ piece, bit
2 *large quantities of coin*
▶ change, loose change, small change, coppers, silver

**coin** VERB

1 *The city began to coin silver money at this time.*
▶ mint, make, mould, stamp
RELATED ADJECTIVE numismatic
2 *A Czech writer coined the word 'robot'*
▶ invent, devise, make up, create, originate, think up, conceive

**coincide** VERB

**1** *It was a nuisance that the two programmes coincided.*
► come together, occur simultaneously, happen at the same time, overlap, clash

**2 coincide with** *His life coincides with the decline of the Empire.*
► clash, coexist, fall together, happen together, synchronize

**3** *Your interests and ours do not always coincide.*
► correspond, tally, agree, match, accord, harmonize

**coincidence** NOUN

*The resemblance was just coincidence.*
► accident, chance, fluke, luck, providence

**coincidental** ADJECTIVE

*Any resemblance is purely coincidental.*
► accidental, fortuitous, by chance, unintentional

**cold** ADJECTIVE

**1** *a cold day   cold weather*
► chilly, cool, fresh, freezing, icy, raw, bitter, biting, perishing, wintry, (*more informal*) nippy, (*more informal*) parky
AN OPPOSITE IS hot

**2** *I was feeling cold.*
► chilly, chilled, shivery, freezing, frozen
AN OPPOSITE IS hot

**3** *a cold reception*
► unfriendly, unsympathetic, unwelcoming, cool, frosty, lukewarm, forbidding, indifferent, unenthusiastic
OPPOSITES ARE warm, friendly

**cold** NOUN

*We all feel the cold in winter.*
► coldness, chill, chilliness

**cold-blooded** ADJECTIVE

*cold-blooded murder*
► cruel, brutal, savage, barbaric, callous, inhuman, pitiless, merciless, sadistic
AN OPPOSITE IS humane

**collaborate** VERB

**1** *Several companies have collaborated to develop a new vaccine.*
► cooperate, combine, unite, work together, join forces, team up

**2** *Several villagers were accused of collaborating with the enemy.*
► conspire, fraternize, collude, consort, cooperate

**collaboration** NOUN

**1** *The work was done in collaboration with a British firm.*
► association, cooperation, partnership, combination, alliance, tandem

**2** *collaboration with the enemy*
► collusion, connivance, conspiring

**collaborator** NOUN

**1** *She wrote the book with the help of a collaborator*
► associate, colleague, partner, co-worker, co-author

**2** *After the war he was accused of being a collaborator.*
► traitor, fraternizer, colluder, defector, fifth-columnist, quisling

**collapse** VERB

**1** *Part of the floor collapsed.*
► fall in, cave in, fall down, give way, crumble, crumple, tumble down, buckle, disintegrate

**2** *People were collapsing in the heat.*
► faint, pass out, lose consciousness, black out, keel over, (*more informal*) flake out

**3** *Harriet collapsed exhausted in her chair.*
► fall, sink, slump

**4** *The banking system was about to collapse.*
► fail, break down, founder, come to grief

**collapse** NOUN

**1** *the collapse of part of the floor*
► cave-in, disintegration, subsidence

**2** *the collapse of peace talks*
► breakdown, failure, foundering

**colleague** NOUN

*It is important to get on with your colleagues.*
► workmate, fellow worker, co-worker, teammate, associate

**collect** VERB

**1** *He collected data from over fifty countries.*
► accumulate, gather, assemble, amass, accrue, bring together

**2** *The squirrels scurried round collecting nuts.*
► gather, heap, hoard, lay up, pile up, put by, reserve, save, scrape together, stockpile, store
AN OPPOSITE IS scatter

**3** *People collected to watch the fireworks.*
► assemble, gather, come together, congregate, crowd round, convene, converge, flock, group, muster
AN OPPOSITE IS disperse

**4** *We are collecting money for charity.*
► raise, appeal for, ask for, seek, solicit

**5** *I must collect the children from school.*
► fetch, get, meet, go and get, bring, call for
OPPOSITES ARE take, drop off

**collection** NOUN

**1** *a collection of strange objects*
► assortment, accumulation, hoard, array, cluster, conglomeration, heap, mass, pile, supply, stock, set, stack

**2** *a collection of people outside the ground*
► group, crowd, gathering, band, accumulation

**3** *a collection of poems*
► anthology, selection, compilation, treasury, miscellany

**collective** ADJECTIVE

*collective action to bring about change*
► combined, concerted, united, unified, joint, corporate, common, group, shared, composite, cooperative, democratic
AN OPPOSITE IS individual

---

### collective nouns PLURAL NOUN

**COLLECTIVE NAMES FOR GROUPS OF BIRDS AND ANIMALS**

**general words:** brood or clutch (of chickens), flock (of birds and sheep), flight (of birds flying), drove (of cattle), herd (of cows and other cattle, and large animals such as elephants and giraffes), gaggle (of geese on the ground), litter (of young born in large numbers, such as puppies, kittens, fox cubs, and pigs), pack (animals that hunt in a group, such as hounds and wolves), pride (of lions), school (of sea mammals such as dolphins and whales), shoal (of fish), swarm (of densely flying insects, e.g. bees and locusts), team (of horses and other draught animals), troop (of monkeys).

**USAGE** There are many other names that come from collections made by antiquarian writers in the 18th and 19th centuries, for example an *exaltation of larks* and a *bloat of hippopotamuses*. These are all fanciful names that are not used in normal writing. Some names have special meanings, e.g. a swarm of bees is not just a group of bees but a dense mass of bees flying to make a new colony.

---

**college** NOUN

*a college of art*
► school, academy, institute, conservatory

**collide** VERB

**1 collide with** *A van collided head on with the stolen vehicle.*
► crash into, smash into, hit, strike
**2** *The two vehicles collided head on.*
► crash, hit each other, run into each other, meet

**collision** NOUN

*a collision on the motorway*
► crash, accident, smash, pile-up

**colloquial** ADJECTIVE

*colloquial language*
► informal, conversational, everyday, casual, vernacular
AN OPPOSITE IS formal

**collude** VERB

*Officials colluded with the smugglers at the border.*
► conspire, connive, collaborate, plot, scheme, intrigue

**collusion** NOUN

*collusion between officials and the smugglers*
► conspiracy, connivance, collaboration, complicity, intrigue, scheming

---

**colonist** NOUN

*the first European colonists in North America*
► settler, colonizer, pioneer, immigrant, newcomer

**colonize** VERB

*Settlers colonized the southern part of the country.*
► settle in, found a colony in, move into, occupy, people, populate

**colony** NOUN

**1** *Britain's former colonies in the region*
► territory, possession, dependency, dominion, protectorate, province, settlement, outpost
**2** *the British colony in New York*
► population, community

**colossal** ADJECTIVE

*A colossal building*
► huge, massive, enormous, gigantic, immense, vast, giant, towering, mammoth, monumental, elephantine
AN OPPOSITE IS tiny

---

### colour NOUN

**1** *You can choose from over thirty beautiful colours.*
► hue, shade, tint, tone, tinge, pigment, tincture, colouring
**2** *The exercise put some colour back in her cheeks.*
► bloom, redness, pinkness, glow, rosiness, ruddiness
**3 colours** *the team's new colours*
► strip, kit, uniform, livery, outfit
**4 colours** *the regimental colours*
► banner, ensign, flag, standard

**NAMES OF COLOURS**

The colours are listed in an order that goes from pale (or bright) to dark (or deep). Many colours are named after things of the same colour, including flowers and fruits (eg *cherry* and *rose*), gems and precious stones (eg *emerald* and *ruby*), minerals (eg *coral*), and wines (eg *burgundy* and *claret*).

**reds:** cerise, pink, magnolia (creamy-pink), vermilion, scarlet, cherry, orange (yellowish-red), pink rose (warm pink), peach (pinkish-orange), flame (bright orange-red), plum (purplish-red), fuchsia (purplish-red), crimson, cardinal (deep scarlet), claret (deep purplish-red), ruby, burgundy, copper (brownish-red), auburn (brownish-red), rust (brownish-red), sepia (brownish-red), maroon (brownish-red), magenta (reddish-mauve), puce (purplish-brown), purple (bluish-red).

**yellows:** cream (whitish-yellow), primrose, lemon, canary, straw, saffron, amber (honey-yellow), gold, topaz, sand (pale brownish-yellow), cinnamon (brownish-yellow), ochre (brownish-yellow), bronze (brownish-yellow), mustard (brownish-yellow).

►►

**blues**: azure, sky blue, aquamarine (greenish-blue), jade (greenish-blue), turquoise (greenish-blue), cyan (greenish-blue), sapphire, lavender (pale bluish-mauve), lilac (pale pinkish-violet), slate (greyish-blue), cerulean, cobalt, royal blue, Oxford blue, Prussian blue, navy, indigo, violet (bluish-purple), gentian (bluish-purple).

**greens**: emerald, chartreuse, pea green, viridian (bluish-green), sea green (bluish-green), sap green (yellowish-green), bottle green, sage (greyish-green), olive (greyish-green).

**browns**: biscuit, fawn, sable, taupe (brownish-grey), sludge, burnt ochre (yellowish-brown), sienna (yellowish-brown), tawny (yellowish-brown), umber (yellowish-brown), chocolate.

**greys and blacks**: silver, charcoal, ebony, pitch, jet.

**whites**: ivory, off-white (greyish-white), pearl (greyish-white).

## colour VERB

1 *Why not colour it blue?*
▶ paint, tint, tinge, dye, stain, shade, colourwash
2 *Her face began to colour.*
▶ blush, flush, redden, go red
OPPOSITES ARE fade, go pale
3 *The experience had coloured his judgement.*
▶ influence, affect, prejudice, sway, impinge on, slant, bias, distort, pervert

## colourful ADJECTIVE

1 *a colourful bunch of flowers*
▶ brilliant, bright, showy, radiant, vibrant, gaudy, iridescent, multicoloured, psychedelic
OPPOSITES ARE colourless, dull
2 *a colourful account of the incident*
▶ graphic, vivid, dramatic, picturesque, animated, exciting, stimulating, striking, florid, picturesque, rich
OPPOSITES ARE dull, plain
3 *music and colourful dancing*
▶ lively, flamboyant, glamorous, energetic, dashing, vigorous, flashy
AN OPPOSITE IS restrained

## colourless ADJECTIVE

1 *a bottle of colourless liquid*
▶ transparent, uncoloured, neutral, watery
2 *a colourless complexion*
▶ pale, pallid, wan, anaemic, sickly
3 *a colourless personality*
▶ dull, uninteresting, unexciting, boring, tedious, insipid, dismal, drab, characterless, dreary, vapid, lacklustre, monotonous
AN OPPOSITE IS colourful

## column NOUN

1 *The temple stood on massive columns.*
▶ pillar, support, pilaster, post, upright

2 *His sister writes a column in the local newspaper.*
▶ article, report, feature, review, editorial
3 *a column of figures*
▶ list, line, string
4 *The troops advanced in three columns.*
▶ line, row, rank

## comb VERB

1 *He looked for a mirror to comb his hair.*
▶ groom, tidy, neaten, arrange, smarten up, smooth out, untangle
2 *Police combed the house and garden for signs of a struggle.*
▶ search, scour, explore, rake, ransack, hunt, sweep

## combat NOUN

*Many men were killed in the combat that followed.*
▶ action, battle, fight, fighting, hostilities, warfare, engagement, encounter, armed conflict, contest, clash

## combat VERB

*new measures to combat crime*
▶ fight, battle against, tackle, contest, counter, contend against, stand up to, strive against, struggle against, withstand, face up to, grapple with, oppose, resist

## combination NOUN

1 *a combination of luck and good judgement*
▶ blend, mixture, amalgamation, fusion, synthesis
2 *The evidence was considered in combination with other factors.*
▶ conjunction, association

## combine VERB

1 *His father combines a social visit with a trip to the laundry.*
▶ merge, amalgamate, join (to)
2 *Several drivers combined to get everyone home.*
▶ cooperate, collaborate, join forces, pool resources, come together, get together, link up, unite

## come VERB

1 *Our friends came last night.*
▶ arrive, appear, visit, (*more informal*) turn up
2 *Spring came early this year.*
▶ occur, happen
3 *come to Eventually they came to a river.*
▶ reach, arrive at, get to, come across, happen on, approach, near
4 *come to The shirt came to his knees.*
▶ reach, extend to
**come about**
▶ happen, occur, (*more formal*) come to pass
**come across** *I came across an old friend.*
▶ find, encounter, discover, chance upon, meet, (*more informal*) bump into
**come apart** *One of my shoes came apart.*
▶ disintegrate, fall to pieces, break up
**come clean** *You'd better come clean before they find out.*
▶ confess, own up
**come out with** *Goodness knows what he'll come out with next.*

**comeback**

▶ say, let out, utter, disclose
**come round** *It took nearly an hour for her to come round after the operation.*
▶ recover, wake, awake
**to come up** *Something has come up and she has had to leave.*
▶ arise, occur, happen, crop up
**to come upon** *He came upon a little hut in the wood.*
▶ find, discover, (*more informal*) bump into

**comeback** NOUN
*The band has achieved an amazing comeback.*
▶ recovery, revival, resurgence, rally, upturn

**comedian** NOUN
*a well-known television comedian*
▶ comic, entertainer, humorist, wit, jester, buffoon, clown, fool, joker, wag

**comedown** NOUN
*His new job was a bit of a comedown.*
▶ anticlimax, humiliation, let-down, disappointment

**comedy** NOUN
*The show contained a great deal of comedy.*
▶ humour, farce, wit, jesting, facetiousness, clowning, satire, slapstick, fun, joking, buffoonery, hilarity

**comfort** NOUN
1 *They like to live in comfort.*
▶ ease, tranquillity, luxury, opulence, prosperity, relaxation, well-being
OPPOSITES ARE discomfort, hardship
2 *We tried to offer the unfortunate woman some words of comfort.*
▶ consolation, sympathy, condolence, commiseration, encouragement, moral support, reassurance, solace, succour, support, aid, help
OPPOSITES ARE misery, grief

**comfort** VERB
*Her sister tried to comfort her.*
▶ console, soothe, cheer, assuage, hearten, encourage, reassure, solace, sympathize with

**comfortable** ADJECTIVE
1 *a comfortable chair a comfortable house*
▶ snug, cosy, relaxing, convenient, pleasant, easy, enjoyable, roomy, plush, soft, well furnished, warm, (*more informal*) comfy
AN OPPOSITE IS uncomfortable
2 *comfortable shoes*
▶ well-fitting, well-made, snug
3 *a comfortable lifestyle*
▶ prosperous, affluent, pleasant, well-off, luxurious, agreeable

**comic** ADJECTIVE
*The effect of the speech was almost comic.*
▶ comical, humorous, funny, amusing, entertaining, diverting, laughable, facetious, hilarious, absurd, ridiculous, ludicrous

**comic** NOUN
1 *The show included a rather feeble comic.*
▶ comedian, entertainer, jester, clown, humorist
2 *A girl was buying a comic to read on the train.*
▶ magazine, cartoon paper

**command** NOUN
1 *Officers shouted commands.*
▶ order, instruction, directive, direction, requirement
2 *He has twenty men under his command.*
▶ authority, control, direction, charge, leadership, supervision, jurisdiction
3 *She has a good command of French and German.*
▶ knowledge, mastery, grasp, understanding, comprehension, grip, fluency (in)

**command** VERB
1 *He commanded his men to advance.*
▶ order, instruct, direct, tell, call on, require, bid
2 *Meredith commands a squadron.*
▶ be in charge of, be in command of, have charge of, lead, head, manage, supervise, rule, control, govern

**commandeer** VERB
*The army commandeered all vehicles in the area.*
▶ seize, appropriate, requisition, impound, sequester, take over, take possession of, confiscate

**commander** NOUN
*Army commanders were discouraged from getting involved in politics.*
▶ chief, leader, officer, general, head, captain, commanding officer

**commemorate** VERB
*The ceremony commemorated those who died in war.*
▶ celebrate, honour, salute, remember, be a memorial to, be a reminder of, pay respects to, pay tribute to

**commence** VERB
1 *Work will commence in the spring.*
▶ begin, start, get under way
2 *He has now commenced his contract with an Italian club.*
▶ begin, start, inaugurate, launch, open, get under way

**commend** VERB
1 *The committee commended her for a thorough and useful report.*
▶ praise, compliment, congratulate, applaud, salute, acclaim
AN OPPOSITE IS criticize
2 *They have done well and I commend them unreservedly.*
▶ recommend, endorse, support, vouch for

**comment** NOUN
1 *I have had some very positive comments about it.*
▶ remark, opinion, criticism, observation, reference, statement, mention
2 *He added a few comments at the end of the paper.*
▶ note, annotation, footnote, gloss
3 *The news caused a lot of comment in the press.*
▶ discussion, debate, interest, consideration

# comment

**comment** VERB

**comment on** *The article commented on the problems of travel in the area.*
▶ mention, discuss, refer to, allude to, remark on, touch on, speak about

**commentary** NOUN

1 *a commentary on the test match*
▶ description, report, narration, account

2 *The second part contains a commentary on the text.*
▶ analysis, criticism, critique, explanation, review, interpretation, treatise, discourse, elucidation, notes

**commentator** NOUN

*a radio commentator*
▶ announcer, reporter, narrator, broadcaster, journalist

**commerce** NOUN

*Settlers came to Gaul for the sake of commerce.*
▶ trade, trading, buying and selling, business, dealing, traffic, (old-fashioned) merchandising

**commercial** ADJECTIVE

1 *The ships were built for commercial use.*
▶ trading, trade, business, economic, financial, mercantile

2 *She turned to writing as a commercial venture.*
▶ business, monetary, financial, profitable, profit-making, viable, lucrative

**commercial** NOUN

*The drama was ruined by so many breaks for commercials.*
▶ advertisement, promotion, (more informal) ad, (more informal) advert

**commercialized** ADJECTIVE

*Christmas has become so commercialized.*
▶ commercial, mercenary, profit-orientated, materialistic

**commiserate** VERB

**commiserate with** *We commiserated with the victims.*
▶ sympathize with, express sympathy for, console, feel for, comfort

**commission** NOUN

*a commission to paint the family's portraits*
▶ assignment, appointment, contract, order, mandate, charge, instruction, project, undertaking, task

**commission** VERB

*They went on to commission him to build a palace for the queen.*
▶ appoint, engage, contract, recruit, employ, hire, retain, delegate, select, nominate

**commit** VERB

1 *He swore he had not committed any crime.*
▶ carry out, be guilty of, be responsible for, perform, perpetrate, do, effect, enact, execute, (more informal) pull off

2 *The child was committed to her care.*
▶ entrust, consign, hand over, give over, turn over, deliver, deposit

**commit yourself to** *Students often have to commit themselves to long leases on lodgings.*
▶ undertake, pledge, guarantee, promise, contract

**commitment** NOUN

1 *The contract included a commitment to complete the work by the end of the year.*
▶ promise, pledge, undertaking, guarantee, assurance, liability, duty

2 *The team felt a commitment to continue the search.*
▶ determination, resolution, obligation, responsibility, dedication, devotion

3 *There are only a few commitments this week.*
▶ engagement, duty, appointment

**committed** ADJECTIVE

*a committed member of the group*
▶ dedicated, active, devoted, keen, staunch, loyal, faithful, devout, enthusiastic, diligent, resolute, ardent, earnest, fervent
AN OPPOSITE IS apathetic

**committee** NOUN

*A committee will be set up to supervise the project.*
▶ board, panel, council, supervisory body, advisory group, task force

**common** ADJECTIVE

1 *This is a common question. Accidents are quite common on this stretch of road.*
▶ frequent, regular, usual, normal, habitual, customary, familiar, standard, typical, routine, everyday

2 *Her parents had thought some of her friends were too common for her.*
▶ inferior, low-class, ill-bred, vulgar, coarse, crude

3 *There is a common belief in these superstitions.*
▶ widespread, general, popular, universal, prevalent, conventional, established, accepted

4 *working for the common good*
▶ collective, communal, public, shared, joint

**common** NOUN

*Local children play ball games on the common.*
▶ heath, park

**commonplace** ADJECTIVE

1 *a commonplace occurrence*
▶ common, regular, normal, typical, familiar, routine, standard, everyday, unremarkable
AN OPPOSITE IS unusual

2 *a commonplace style of writing*
▶ ordinary, plain, simple, unremarkable, undistinguished, average, indifferent, humdrum, pedestrian, prosaic
OPPOSITES ARE remarkable, original

**commonsense** ADJECTIVE

*a commonsense approach to life*
▶ sensible, practical, level-headed, down-to-earth, pragmatic, no-nonsense, realistic, sane, sound
OPPOSITES ARE unreasonable, unrealistic

**commotion** NOUN

*She was distracted by the commotion across the street.*
► disturbance, uproar, racket, tumult, hullabaloo, hubbub, rumpus, fracas, furore, upheaval, agitation, excitement

**communal** ADJECTIVE

*communal washing facilities*
► collective, shared, joint, common, public, general, mutual, open
AN OPPOSITE IS private

**commune** NOUN

*She lived for several years in a commune in Chicago.*
► community, collective, settlement, colony, fellowship, kibbutz

**communicate** VERB

1 *Somebody has to communicate the bad news to her.*
► convey, announce, report, reveal, declare, disclose, impart, pass on, relate

**USAGE** You can also say *Somebody has to tell her the bad news,* or *Somebody has to inform her of the bad news,* or *Somebody has to acquaint her with the bad news.*

2 **communicate with** *Parents and teachers need to communicate with one another regularly.*
► speak to, talk to, make contact with, liaise with

3 **communicate with** *Each bedroom communicates with its own bathroom.*
► connect with, adjoin, lead to

4 *It is possible to communicate the disease through ordinary contact.*
► transmit, pass on, infect someone with, spread, transfer, give

**communication** NOUN

1 *She received an official communication from the tax office.*
► message, letter, correspondence, advice
2 *There has been little communication between them for several years.*
► contact, dealings, association, relations, correspondence, intercourse
3 *The newsletters are used for the communication of information.*
► transmission, imparting, disclosure, dissemination, reporting, passing on

NAMES FOR TYPES OF COMMUNICATION

**spoken communication:** conversation, dialogue, message, rumour, gossip, phone conversation; broadcasting, radio, television; advertising.

**written communication:** letter, correspondence, postcard, note, memo (in offices), cable.

**official communication:** announcement, statement, notice, bulletin, dispatch, memorandum, proclamation; newsflash. ►►

**electronic communication:** email, network, Internet, fax, text messages.
**the mass media:** newspapers, journalism, the press, magazine, television, films.

**communicative** ADJECTIVE

*They are always friendly and communicative.*
► forthcoming, outgoing, informative, candid, uninhibited, frank, open, sociable, talkative
OPPOSITES ARE uncommunicative, secretive

**community** NOUN

1 *He had the interests of the community in mind.*
► population, populace, society, people, residents, inhabitants, local people, general public

2 *a small farming community in the Borders*
► district, region, locality, neighbourhood

3 *a community of gay men*
► group, colony, commune, coterie, band, society

**commute** VERB

1 *The death sentence will be commuted to life imprisonment.*
► reduce, lessen, cut , lighten, remit, moderate, adjust

2 *Her husband commutes to the city every day.*
► travel, journey, shuttle

**compact** ADJECTIVE

1 *a compact machine that will fit in a small suitcase*
► small, little, petite, portable

2 *a compact encyclopedia*
► concise, succinct, condensed, brief

**compact** NOUN

*the government's compact with the unions*
► agreement, pact, accord, deal, bargain, arrangement, understanding

**companion** NOUN

*He turned to speak to his companions.*
► friend, associate, comrade, colleague, partner, mate, escort

**company** NOUN

1 *I miss her company.*
► companionship, fellowship, society, presence, friendship

2 *We are expecting company tomorrow evening.*
► visitors, guests, callers

3 *He works for an insurance company.*
► firm, business, corporation, establishment, concern, enterprise, office, bureau

4 *a performance by the local theatre company*
► group, troupe, society, ensemble, association

5 *a company of friends*
► group, circle, community, band, gang, gathering

**comparable** ADJECTIVE
*Customers will look elsewhere for better service at comparable prices. Interest rates are not comparable to those in the rest of Europe.*
▶ similar, equivalent, corresponding, proportionate, commensurate (with), analogous, parallel, compatible (with), equal, related
AN OPPOSITE IS dissimilar

**comparative** ADJECTIVE
*He would have to leave the comparative comfort he had enjoyed up to now.*
▶ relative

**compare** VERB
1 *We have to compare this year's results with last year's.*
▶ check (against), contrast, correlate, juxtapose, set side by side, weigh, draw parallels between, make connections between, match, relate
2 *You can't compare the book to the video.*
▶ liken, equate, draw a parallel between (*the book and the video*), regard (*the book*) as the same as (*the video*)
**compare with** *Our achievements hardly compare with yours.*
▶ match, equal, compete with, emulate, rival, vie with

**comparison** NOUN
1 *There is no comparison between the two versions of the story.*
▶ resemblance, likeness, similarity, correspondence, parallel, correlation, equivalence, analogy
2 *The conclusions are based on a comparison of Hackney and Westminster.*
▶ analysis, collation, correlation, juxtaposition, contrast

**compartment** NOUN
1 *He then discovered that the case had a secret compartment.*
▶ section, space, pocket, cavity, recess
2 *The shed has a small compartment at the back for tools.*
▶ alcove, space, niche, cubby-hole, chamber, division

**compassion** NOUN
*She felt for him the compassion of an elder sister.*
▶ sympathy, pity, concern, understanding, commiseration, tenderness, warmth, fellow feeling, mercy
OPPOSITES ARE indifference, heartlessness

**compatible** ADJECTIVE
1 *The couple were never compatible.*
▶ well suited, well matched, harmonious, like-minded, suitable
2 *The injuries are not compatible with its having been an accident.*
▶ consistent, reconcilable, consonant, accordant, congruent, matching
AN OPPOSITE IS incompatible

**compel** VERB
1 *The court could compel him to give evidence.*
▶ force, oblige, coerce, constrain, order, pressure, pressurize
2 **be compelled to** *In the end Jem was compelled to admit the truth.*
▶ have to, be obliged to, be bound to, have no choice but to

**compelling** ADJECTIVE
*a compelling argument*
▶ forceful, convincing, cogent, persuasive, powerful, irresistible

**compensate** VERB
1 *If you have lost money you will be compensated for it.*
▶ recompense, repay, reimburse, pay back, remunerate
2 **compensate for** *Nothing can compensate for such a dreadful loss.*
▶ make up for, make amends for, balance, offset, counteract, cancel out, neutralize, redress, atone for

**compensation** NOUN
1 *You will receive compensation for any loss.*
▶ reparation, recompense, reimbursement, repayment, restitution, amends
2 *The balmy evenings were some compensation for the unpleasantness of the day.*
▶ consolation, recompense, comfort

**compère** NOUN
*the compere of a TV programme*
▶ host, presenter, anchorman, anchorwoman, anchorperson, announcer, Master of Ceremonies, MC

**compete** VERB
1 *The boys were competing in a five-a-side tournament.*
▶ take part, participate, perform, enter, go in for
2 *You will have to compete with children over twice your age.*
▶ contend, vie
3 **compete with** *No one can compete with him when he's on good form.*
▶ match, rival, compare with, equal, challenge, emulate, keep up with

**competent** ADJECTIVE
1 *a competent builder*
▶ capable, proficient, accomplished, qualified, able, skilful, efficient, adept
AN OPPOSITE IS incompetent
2 *a competent performance*
▶ adequate, satisfactory, acceptable, decent, reasonable

**competition** NOUN
1 *We face some fierce competition this year.*
▶ opposition, rivalry, contention, struggle, contest
2 *Lisa came third in the competition.*
▶ contest, match, tournament, game, championship, race

**competitive** ADJECTIVE

**1** *a competitive sport*
▶ combative, contentious, aggressive, antagonistic

**2** *a competitive player*
▶ ambitious, aggressive, combative

**3** *Banking is a highly competitive business.*
▶ ruthless, aggressive, contentious, fierce, cut-throat

**4** *top quality at competitive prices*
▶ reasonable, moderate, affordable, keen, economical
OPPOSITES ARE exorbitant, uncompetitive

**competitor** NOUN

**1** *Every competitor has to take a blood test.*
▶ candidate, contestant, entrant, participant, contender

**2** *We have to improve on our business competitors*
▶ rival, challenger, adversary, opponent

**compile** VERB

*An editor is needed to compile a new encyclopedia.*
▶ assemble, put together, edit, organize, compose, gather together, collect together

**complacent** ADJECTIVE

*We are doing a good job but we must not be complacent.*
▶ smug, self-satisfied, overconfident, oversatisfied, pleased with yourself, self-congratulatory, self-righteous, unconcerned, contented, untroubled
AN OPPOSITE IS dissatisfied

**complain** VERB

**1** *We'll wait till we get home before complaining.*
▶ protest, make a complaint, grumble

**2 complain about** *The neighbours complained about the noise.*
▶ protest about, grumble about, make a fuss about, object to, carp about, find fault with, criticize, condemn, (more informal) whinge about, (more informal) go on about

**complaint** NOUN

**1** *After a series of complaints about his behaviour he was sent back to England.*
▶ protest, objection (to), criticism (of), accusation, grumble, censure, fault-finding, (more informal) gripe

**2** *Supporters have little cause for complaint.*
▶ grievance, dissatisfaction, disapproval, criticism, grumbling, fuss

**3** *Her breathing difficulty was due to a lung complaint.*
▶ disorder, disease, illness, infection, sickness, upset, affliction, ailment, indisposition, malady, malaise

**complement** NOUN

*The ship was carrying its full complement of passengers.*
▶ capacity, quota, amount, total, allowance, aggregate
**USAGE** Do not confuse *complement* with *compliment*.

**complement** VERB

*The restaurant's wine list complements its good food perfectly.*
▶ accompany, complete, go with, round off, enhance, make complete, make perfect
**USAGE** Do not confuse *complement* with *compliment*.

**complete** ADJECTIVE

**1** *The complete report will be published tomorrow.*
▶ whole, full, entire, unabridged, unedited, unexpurgated, total, unabbreviated
AN OPPOSITE IS incomplete

**2** *The exercise is now complete.*
▶ completed, finished, concluded, ended, accomplished, achieved
AN OPPOSITE IS incomplete

**3** *He was acting like a complete fool.*
▶ absolute, utter, out-and-out, thorough, thoroughgoing, outright
OPPOSITES ARE qualified, partial

**4** *The story was complete rubbish.*
▶ utter, absolute, downright, sheer, pure, total, unqualified, unmitigated

**complete** VERB

**1** *She will complete her training in two years.*
▶ finish, end, conclude, terminate, finalize, fulfil, round off, accomplish, achieve, carry out, clinch, close, do, perfect, perform, (informal) wind up

**2** *Please complete the application form attached.*
▶ fill in, fill out, fill up, answer

**completely** ADVERB

*He was completely honest about what had happened.*
▶ totally, absolutely, utterly, entirely, perfectly, quite

**completion** NOUN

*the completion of the project*
▶ finish, conclusion, realization, achievement, fulfilment

**complex** ADJECTIVE

*a complex subject*
▶ complicated, intricate, involved, elaborate, convoluted, tortuous, tangled, diverse, manifold
OPPOSITES ARE simple, straightforward

**complexion** NOUN

**1** *a young girl with a pale complexion*
▶ colouring, colour, appearance, skin, skin colour

**2** *The latest revelation put a new complexion on things.*
▶ perspective, angle, slant

**3** *political views of different complexions*
▶ type, kind, sort, nature, character

**complicate** VERB

*His odd attitude complicated his relationships.*
▶ make more difficult, confuse, muddle, tangle, mix up
AN OPPOSITE IS simplify

**complicated** ADJECTIVE

*a complicated story   a complicated set of rules*
▶ complex, intricate, involved, elaborate, convoluted, tortuous, tangled, diverse, manifold
OPPOSITES ARE simple, straightforward

**complication** NOUN

**1** *Patients can leave hospital after three days if no complications occur.*
▶ problem, setback, repercussion, difficulty, drawback, snag, complexity, ramification
**2** *the complication of modern city life*
▶ intricacy, complexity, confusion

**complicity** NOUN

*their complicity in the crime*
▶ collusion, collaboration, connivance, involvement

**compliment** NOUN

*She blushed at the unexpected compliment.*
▶ praise, flattery, tribute, accolade, approval, eulogy, (*more informal*) pat on the back
AN OPPOSITE IS insult
**USAGE** Do not confuse *compliment* with *complement. Flattery* usually means insincere praise.

**compliment** VERB

*He complimented her on the performance.*
▶ praise, applaud, commend, congratulate, flatter
OPPOSITES ARE criticize, insult
**USAGE** See the note at the previous entry.

**complimentary** ADJECTIVE

**1** *The comments were all complimentary.*
▶ appreciative, approving, favourable, congratulatory, laudatory, admiring, commendatory, eulogistic, flattering, fulsome, generous, rapturous, supportive
OPPOSITES ARE critical, insulting
**2** *You get a complimentary lunch on the day of arrival.*
▶ free, gratis, courtesy

**comply** VERB

**comply with** *He was anxious to comply with their wishes.*
▶ abide by, accede to, observe, obey, follow, fulfil, acquiesce in, submit to, yield to, agree to, assent to, conform to, consent to, defer to, fall in with, perform, satisfy
OPPOSITES ARE ignore, defy

**component** NOUN

*a store full of components for computers*
▶ part, piece, bit, constituent part, spare part, unit, element, ingredient, item, (*more informal*) spare

**compose** VERB

**1** *The village was composed of small huts*
▶ build, compile, constitute, construct, fashion, form, frame, make, put together
**2** *That year he composed mainly film music.   She sat down to compose a letter.*
▶ write, create, arrange, devise, imagine, make up, produce

**compose yourself** *He began to tremble and tried to compose himself.*
▶ calm down, control yourself, settle down, pull yourself together

**be composed of** *The government was composed of individuals rather than parties.*
▶ consist of, comprise, contain, embody, incorporate, involve, comprehend, embrace, include

**composed** ADJECTIVE

*She looked stunning that day and very composed.*
▶ calm, confident, self-controlled, placid, relaxed, at ease, unruffled

**composition** NOUN

**1** *the composition of the new team*
▶ structure, make-up, formation, constitution, content, establishment, formulation
**2** *the composition of a group of poems*
▶ writing, creation, devising, production
**3** *a musical composition*
▶ piece, work, (*technical*) opus

**composure** NOUN

*She acted with great composure.*
▶ self-control, dignity, calmness, coolness, tranquillity, (*more informal*) cool

**compound** NOUN

**1** *a chemical compound*
▶ amalgam, synthesis, alloy, blend, mixture, composite, composition, fusion
**2** *a compound of energy and enthusiasm*
▶ combination, blend, mixture, synthesis
**3** *a compound for animals*
▶ enclosure, pen, run

**compound** VERB

*The bad weather compounded our difficulties.*
▶ aggravate, exacerbate, intensify, increase, worsen, complicate

**comprehend** VERB

*I tried to comprehend what he was saying.*
▶ understand, grasp, conceive, fathom, make sense of, appreciate, conceive, discern, fathom, follow, perceive

**comprehensible** ADJECTIVE

*The explanation was thorough and comprehensible.*
▶ understandable, intelligible, clear, straightforward, lucid, meaningful
AN OPPOSITE IS incomprehensible

**comprehension** NOUN

*She spoke in a dialect that was beyond my comprehension.*
▶ understanding, grasp, knowledge, perception

**comprehensive** ADJECTIVE

*a comprehensive account of the topic*
▶ inclusive, complete, full, broad, exhaustive, compendious, wide-ranging, detailed, extensive, all-embracing, thorough, total, universal, encyclopedic
OPPOSITES ARE selective, partial

## compress VERB

1 *The activities can be compressed into an eight-hour day.*
▶ squeeze, press, squash, jam

2 *The text has been compressed into a mere ten pages.*
▶ condense, abridge, shorten, cut, summarize

## comprise VERB

*The building comprises several apartments.*
▶ consist of, contain, be composed of, include, incorporate, embody, embrace, involve

## compromise NOUN

*Eventually the two sides reached a compromise.*
▶ understanding, accommodation, settlement, agreement, middle course, middle way

## compromise VERB

1 *In the end we had to compromise.*
▶ make concessions, meet halfway, strike a balance, concede a point, negotiate, settle

2 *The scandal has severely compromised his reputation.*
▶ undermine, discredit, jeopardize, weaken, prejudice, risk, dishonour, imperil

## compromising ADJECTIVE

*Before he left he tore up the compromising letter.*
▶ embarrassing, damaging, scandalous, discreditable, dishonourable, improper

## compulsion NOUN

1 *There is no compulsion to go.*
▶ obligation, necessity, constraint, pressure

2 *She felt a strong compulsion to tell the whole story.*
▶ urge, impulse, desire, longing, obsession

## compulsive ADJECTIVE

1 *He felt a compulsive urge to jump out.*
▶ irresistible, uncontrollable, overpowering, overwhelming, besetting, compelling, driving, involuntary, powerful

2 *Not all fat people are compulsive over-eaters.*
▶ habitual, obsessive, addicted, persistent, incorrigible, incurable

## compulsory ADJECTIVE

*Each exam paper has one compulsory question. Carrying an identity card is now compulsory.*
▶ obligatory, mandatory, binding, required, stipulated, unavoidable, de rigueur, imperative, imposed, incumbent, inescapable, official
AN OPPOSITE IS optional

## compunction NOUN

*He had no compunction about lying.*
▶ scruples, misgivings, qualms, guilt feelings, conscience

## compute VERB

*Interest is computed daily.*
▶ calculate, reckon, work out, assess, add up, total, count, estimate, evaluate, measure

## computer NOUN

**WORDS ASSOCIATED WITH COMPUTERS**

**types of computer:** mainframe, personal computer (PC), laptop, notebook, palmtop, workstation, word processor.

**parts of a computer:** hardware, system, network, server, terminal; disk drive or hard disk, central processing unit (CPU), motherboard, memory, buffer (temporary memory), cache (extra memory for high-speed retrieval), clipboard (temporary storage area for copied or cut data), floppy disk, CD-ROM, CD-ROM drive, sound card, graphics card; monitor or visual display unit (VDU), desktop, speaker; keyboard, mouse, cursor, icon; modem; bus (set of conductors), parallel port, USB (universal serial bus) port, gateway.

**peripherals:** printer, scanner.

**software and documents:** program, BIOS (Basic Input-Ouput System), firmware (software permanently installed), code (program instructions), application (piece of software for a particular purpose), applet (small application within a larger program), file, directory (group of files), data, database, spreadsheet, record, batch (group of records processed together), bit (unit of information), byte (group of units), hyperlink, hypertext; screen saver.

**processes:** boot (starting up), data processing, saving, autosave, back-up, bookmark, Boolean operator; click, double-click, drag, cut-and-paste, download (file from system or network), import, export, exit (leave a program or system); zip (compressing files), unzip.

**Internet and emailing:** service provider (ISP), browser (for displaying Internet websites), website, cookie (data sent by an Internet server to a browser); email, attachment; online, offline.

**problems:** crash (complete failure of system), freeze (sudden locking of computer screen), bug (error in a program), virus (harmful code).

## comrade NOUN

*The officers went back up the slope to their comrades.*
▶ companion, associate, colleague, friend, partner, mate, escort

## con NOUN

*The offer proved to be just a con.*
▶ trick, cheat, swindle, deception, fraud

## con VERB

*They conned the couple out of their life savings.*
▶ trick, cheat, swindle, dupe, deceive, inveigle, hoodwink, (*more informal*) bamboozle

## conceal VERB

1 *She concealed the device in her camera A mass of cloud concealed the sun.*
▶ hide, cover up, disguise, secrete, blot out, mask,

a b c d e f g h i j k l m n o p q r s t u v w x y z

obscure, screen, veil, bury, cloak, envelop, camouflage
OPPOSITES ARE reveal, expose, uncover
2 *He could barely conceal his frustration.*
▶ hide, suppress, keep secret, hush up, keep dark, keep quiet
AN OPPOSITE IS reveal

**concealed** ADJECTIVE
*The house stood behind a concealed entrance.*
▶ hidden, invisible, camouflaged, disguised, secret, cloaked, furtive, unobtrusive
OPPOSITES ARE obvious, visible

**concede** VERB
1 *I conceded that I might have been wrong.*
▶ admit, acknowledge, accept, grant, agree, recognize, allow, confess
AN OPPOSITE IS deny
2 *The country conceded some of the territory to its neighbour.*
▶ surrender, yield, give up, relinquish, cede, hand over, submit

**conceit** NOUN
*She said it without conceit, simply as a fact.*
▶ vanity, arrogance, pride, boastfulness

**conceited** ADJECTIVE
*Without sounding conceited, I think we offer the best service.*
▶ vain, boastful, immodest, arrogant, haughty, self-satisfied, proud, complacent, (more informal) cocky
AN OPPOSITE IS modest

**conceivable** ADJECTIVE
*There is no conceivable reason for agreeing.*
▶ imaginable, credible, believable, possible

**conceive** VERB
1 *She was unable to conceive.*
▶ get pregnant, become pregnant, have a baby
2 *The plan was conceived after the war.*
▶ think up, devise, originate, create, form, formulate, invent, design
3 *It is hard to conceive what it must have been like for them.*
▶ imagine, envisage, visualize, picture, appreciate, comprehend, apprehend, grasp

**concentrate** VERB
1 **concentrate on** *Sharon was concentrating on the video.*
▶ pay attention to, keep your mind on, put your mind to, apply yourself to, focus on, be engrossed in, be absorbed in, attend to, think about
2 *Troops concentrated on the border.*
▶ gather, mass, collect, congregate, converge, crowd, accumulate
AN OPPOSITE IS disperse
3 *We need to concentrate our efforts on improving public services.*
▶ focus, direct (to), aim (at), intensify
OPPOSITES ARE reduce, dilute

**concentrated** ADJECTIVE
1 *concentrated fruit juice*
▶ condensed, undiluted, reduced, rich, dense, strong, evaporated
AN OPPOSITE IS diluted
2 *making concentrated efforts*
▶ intense, strenuous, intensive, concerted, vigorous, committed, thorough, hard, (more informal) all-out
AN OPPOSITE IS half-hearted

**concentration** NOUN
1 *The work calls for long periods of concentration.*
▶ attention, application
AN OPPOSITE IS inattention
2 *the concentration of power in the hands of a few companies*
▶ accumulation, consolidation, centralization, collection, compression, focusing

**concept** NOUN
*It's not an easy concept to grasp.*
▶ idea, notion, principle, theory, thought, hypothesis, image, conception

**conception** NOUN
1 *They have no conception of how difficult life can be in the country.*
▶ understanding, knowledge, comprehension, appreciation, perception, inkling, grasp, idea
2 *The proposal took three months from conception to implementation.*
▶ creation, origination, inception, genesis, formulation

**concern** NOUN
1 *concern for others*
▶ regard, consideration, thought, care, attention (to), interest (in)
2 *It's no concern of ours.*
▶ affair, business, matter, responsibility, problem
3 *a cause for great concern*
▶ anxiety, worry, disquiet, unease, distress, apprehension
4 *a publishing concern*
▶ company, firm, business, enterprise, establishment, organization, corporation

**concern** VERB
1 *What I have to say concerns everyone.*
▶ affect, involve, apply to, refer to, relate to, be relevant to, be important to, interest, matter to, (more formal) pertain to
2 *The book concerns various aspects of the subject.*
▶ deal with, be about, treat, describe, review, relate to
3 *Her news concerned us deeply.*
▶ worry, disturb, upset, trouble, distress, bother

**concerned** ADJECTIVE
1 *His parents looked concerned.*
▶ worried, anxious, troubled, bothered, disturbed, distressed, fearful, upset
AN OPPOSITE IS unconcerned

**2** *If you want more information, talk to the people concerned.*
► connected, interested, involved, relevant

**concerning** PREPOSITION
*the part of the treaty concerning boundaries*
► about, relating to, regarding, relevant to, dealing with, germane to, involving, with reference to, with regard to

**concert** NOUN
*a concert at the town hall*
► recital, musical performance, show, production, session

**concerted** ADJECTIVE
**1** *a concerted effort to deal with the financial crisis*
► intense, strenuous, intensive, concentrated, vigorous, committed, thorough, hard, (*more informal*) all-out
**2** *We have to take concerted action.*
► joint, collective, cooperative, collaborative, united, combined, mutual, shared

**concession** NOUN
*You get a concession if you are a student or pensioner.*
► reduction, discount, allowance
**make a concession** *The management refuses to make any concessions over pay.*
► compromise, give way, concede a point

**concise** ADJECTIVE
*a concise account of events in the war*
► brief, succinct, compact, short, condensed, concentrated, compressed, abridged, abbreviated, pithy, terse
OPPOSITES ARE lengthy, diffuse

**conclude** VERB
**1** *Hostilities concluded at midnight.*
► finish, end, stop, cease, terminate, be over, come to a close, be brought to an end
OPPOSITES ARE start, commence
**2** *The jury concluded that the witness had been lying.*
► infer, deduce, decide, gather, judge, suppose, think, reckon, surmise, assume
**3** *an attempt to conclude a treaty*
► negotiate, agree, come to terms on, arrange, effect, bring about, broker

**conclusion** NOUN
**1** *A few gentle jokes formed the conclusion of her speech.*
► end, finish, close, completion, termination, culmination, finale, rounding-off, peroration
**2** *The court's original conclusion in the case has been proved correct.*
► deduction, decision, judgement, verdict, opinion, interpretation, inference, resolution, belief, conjecture, assumption, presumption, surmise

**conclusive** ADJECTIVE
*It will be difficult to provide conclusive proof.*
► decisive, definitive, definite, indisputable, incontrovertible, irrefutable, unequivocal, unambiguous, unarguable, convincing, persuasive, unanswerable
AN OPPOSITE IS inconclusive

**concoct** VERB
*She didn't have much time to concoct her story.*
► make up, think up, invent, fabricate, contrive, formulate, prepare, devise, create, develop, (*more informal*) cook up

**concrete** ADJECTIVE
**1** *concrete objects*
► solid, physical, material, palpable, substantial, tactile, touchable, visible
**2** *The case lacks concrete evidence. The proposals are not yet concrete.*
► firm, solid, objective, tangible, material, physical, factual, real, actual, definite, existing
OPPOSITES ARE abstract, theoretical

**condemn** VERB
**1** *He condemned all forms of violence.*
► deplore, denounce, castigate, criticize, censure
OPPOSITES ARE commend, approve of
**2** *The committee condemned them for their behaviour.*
► criticize, censure, denounce, reprehend, deprecate, disparage, berate, revile
**3** *After a lengthy trial the court finally condemned them.*
► convict, find guilty, sentence, pass judgement, prove guilty, punish, judge
AN OPPOSITE IS acquit

**condensation** NOUN
*The windows were misty with condensation.*
► moisture, steam, water-drops

**condense** VERB
**1** *She condensed the ten episodes into a single hour-long drama.*
► shorten, reduce, abridge, compress, cut, contract, telescope, summarize
AN OPPOSITE IS expand
**2** *The liquid is slowly condensed.*
► distil, reduce, concentrate, solidify, thicken
AN OPPOSITE IS dilute

**condescend** VERB
*Eventually an official condescended to see us.*
► deign, consent, see fit, vouchsafe, stoop, lower yourself

**condescending** ADJECTIVE
*She narrowed her eyes at us in a condescending manner.*
► superior, supercilious, disdainful, patronizing, haughty, imperious, lofty, (*more informal*) snooty

**condition** NOUN
**1** *Check that your vehicle is in good condition.*
► order, state, shape, (*more informal*) trim, (*more informal*) nick
**USAGE** If you use *state* you have to say *in a good state.*
**2** *She was told she had a medical condition.*
► disorder, illness, disease, complaint, ailment, infirmity
**3** *There are some conditions attached to membership.*
► requirement, proviso, terms, qualification, restriction, stipulation, limitation, obligation

## conditional ADJECTIVE

*The offer of a place was a conditional one.*
▶ provisional, qualified, dependent, limited, restricted
AN OPPOSITE IS unconditional

## condom NOUN

*Stay with one partner, or use a condom every time.*
▶ sheath, contraceptive, (more informal) French letter, (more informal) johnny

## condone VERB

*We cannot condone this sort of behaviour.*
▶ tolerate, endorse, disregard, overlook, pardon, forgive, ignore, allow, connive at, excuse, let someone off
OPPOSITES ARE condemn, punish

## conducive ADJECTIVE

*The noise in the room was not conducive to concentration.*
▶ advantageous, beneficial, encouraging, favourable, helpful, supportive (of)

## conduct NOUN

1 *good conduct*
▶ behaviour, demeanour, attitude, bearing, manner, ways, actions
2 *the conduct of the nation's affairs*
▶ management, direction, handling, organization, running, supervision, administration, control, discharge

## conduct VERB

1 *Visitors are conducted round the building in small groups.*
▶ escort, guide, accompany, take, usher, lead, convey, shepherd
2 *The group conducted a survey into children's eating habits.*
▶ organize, administer, coordinate, carry out, manage, direct, run, handle, preside over
**conduct yourself** *He conducted himself in a typically high-handed manner.*
▶ behave, act, carry on, acquit yourself

## confer VERB

1 *The King conferred a knighthood on him.*
▶ bestow, award, accord, give, grant, honour with, invest
**USAGE** Note that with all the alternatives apart from *bestow*, you say (for example) *The King awarded him a knighthood.* If you use *bestow* you follow the same pattern as for *confer.*
2 *He asked for a pause to confer with his colleagues.*
▶ consult, discuss things, have a discussion, communicate, deliberate

## conference NOUN

1 *an international conference on the environment.*
▶ congress, convention, meeting, symposium, summit
2 *They gathered round the table for a conference.*
▶ discussion, consultation, deliberation, exchange of views, talks

## confess VERB

1 *Several of the suspects later confessed.*
▶ admit guilt, plead guilty, own up, accept blame, (more informal) come clean
2 *She confessed that she had broken the man's window.*
▶ own up, admit, acknowledge, concede
3 *I confess I agree with all they have said.*
▶ admit, concede, grant, allow

## confession NOUN

*The interrogators failed to get a confession out of him.*
▶ admission of guilt, acknowledgement of guilt, declaration, disclosure, profession, revelation

## confide VERB

1 *He confided his fears to his wife.*
▶ reveal, disclose, divulge, admit, declare
2 **confide in** *He is not easy to confide in.*
▶ unburden yourself to, tell all to, trust in

## confidence NOUN

1 *We can face the future with confidence. She shows a lot of confidence.*
▶ optimism, assurance, positiveness, conviction, certainty, credence, faith, hope, reliance, trust
OPPOSITES ARE doubt, diffidence
**have confidence in** *They have confidence in your abilities.*
▶ trust , believe, be sure of

## confident ADJECTIVE

1 *We are confident that the money can be found.*
▶ optimistic, hopeful, sure, certain, convinced, sanguine, positive, trusting
AN OPPOSITE IS doubtful
2 *She lifted her head in a confident gesture.*
▶ self-assured, self-confident, assertive, assured, self-possessed, self-reliant, positive, bold, composed, definite, fearless, secure, unafraid
AN OPPOSITE IS diffident

## confidential ADJECTIVE

1 *All conversations are strictly confidential.*
▶ secret, top secret, private, personal, classified, restricted, suppressed, intimate, (more informal) hush-hush, (more informal) off the record
2 *a confidential secretary*
▶ personal, private, trusted

## confine VERB

1 *She confined her writing to poems and short stories.*
▶ restrict, limit, keep
2 *During the winter months the animals are confined in a small field near the buildings. He was confined in the Tower to await his trial.*
▶ enclose, imprison, keep, shut, close, fence, box, cage, incarcerate, intern, isolate

## confinement NOUN

1 *a period of confinement*
▶ imprisonment, incarceration, detention, internment, custody, captivity, restraint
OPPOSITES ARE freedom, liberty
2 *She was admitted to hospital for her confinement.*
▶ labour, delivery, childbirth

**confines** PLURAL NOUN
*the confines of the park*
▶ limits, boundaries, bounds, perimeter, edge, extremities

**confirm** VERB
1 *What happened next day confirmed her suspicions about the place.*
▶ support, corroborate, bear out, back up, upheld, validate, approve, give credence to, substantiate
OPPOSITES ARE contradict, disprove
2 *The hotel will need a deposit to confirm the booking (informal)*
▶ verify, guarantee, clinch, endorse, validate, ratify, formalize, make legal, make official
AN OPPOSITE IS cancel
3 *I confirm that I will be arriving on Saturday.*
▶ affirm, assert, assure you, give an assurance

**confirmation** NOUN
1 *The DNA evidence provided confirmation of his guilt.*
▶ proof, corroboration, verification, testimony, substantiation
2 *Confirmation of the appointment will follow shortly.*
▶ ratification, endorsement, approval, validation, formalization

**confiscate** VERB
*The police confiscated his passport.*
▶ seize, take possession of, impound, appropriate, remove, sequester, take away
OPPOSITES ARE return, restore

**conflict** NOUN
1 *conflict between management and workers*
▶ dispute, disagreement, discord, contention, confrontation, dissension, antagonism, hostility, friction, strife, clash
AN OPPOSITE IS harmony
2 *a military conflict*
▶ war, struggle, confrontation, contest, clash, campaign, encounter, engagement, action, battle, combat, feud, fight, quarrel, skirmish, warfare

**conflict** VERB
*This fact conflicts with statements made back in September.*
▶ clash, disagree, differ (from), be incompatible, be inconsistent, be at variance, be at odds
OPPOSITES ARE support, agree with

**conform** VERB
1 *I conform because I think it gives a good impression.*
▶ comply, acquiesce, follow convention, fit in, obey the rules, play by the rules, keep in step
OPPOSITES ARE rebel, disobey, differ
2 *conform to You have to conform to strict rules of etiquette.*
▶ comply with, follow, obey, abide by, accept, accede to, fit in with, uphold, fulfil
3 *conform to Our experiences do not always conform to our beliefs.*
▶ match, fit, suit, correspond to, agree with, tally with, harmonize with, accord with, compare with, square with

**conformity** NOUN
*There is a lot of conformity among young people.*
▶ conventionality, orthodoxy, uniformity, compliance, obedience, submission
OPPOSITES ARE eccentricity, rebellion

**confound** VERB
*Their successes confounded all the critics.*
▶ astonish, astound, amaze, surprise, stagger, startle, disconcert, dumbfound, shock, flabbergast, perplex, stun, stupefy, bewilder

**confront** VERB
1 *He confronted an intruder in the hallway.*
▶ challenge, accost, approach, stand up to, take on, tackle, defy, face, meet, oppose, withstand, argue with, brave
AN OPPOSITE IS avoid
2 *He realized he had to confront his problems and sort himself out.*
▶ tackle, face up to, address, deal with, cope with

**confrontation** NOUN
*a serious confrontation with the authorities*
▶ conflict, dispute, disagreement, discord, contention, dissension, antagonism, hostility, friction, strife, clash

**confuse** VERB
1 *All these comments only confuse the issue.*
▶ complicate, muddle, obscure, cloud, obfuscate
2 *Too much detail will confuse us.*
▶ bewilder, perplex, baffle, puzzle, mystify, bemuse, disconcert, confound, (more informal) flummox, (more informal) floor

**confused** ADJECTIVE
1 *The children were very confused about what was happening.*
▶ bewildered, perplexed, baffled, puzzled, mystified, bemused, disconcerted, confounded, (more informal) flummoxed
AN OPPOSITE IS clear
2 *Her clothes lay in a confused pile on the floor.*
▶ untidy, disorderly, disorganized, muddled, jumbled
OPPOSITES ARE tidy, organized
3 *confused accounts of the incident*
▶ vague, muddled, unclear, indistinct
AN OPPOSITE IS clear

**confusion** NOUN
1 *a lot of confusion about which system to buy*
▶ uncertainty, indecision, misunderstanding, hesitation, doubt, ignorance
2 *People were wandering about in confusion.*
▶ bewilderment, perplexity, bafflement, mystification, shock
3 *The kitchen was in a terrible state of confusion.*
▶ disorder, disorganization, untidiness, clutter, chaos, mayhem, disarray, muddle, jumble, mess, shambles

**congeal** VERB
*Blood had congealed around the wound.*
▶ clot, coagulate, thicken, harden, set, solidify

**congested** ADJECTIVE

*More traffic will be forced on to already congested roads.*

▶ crowded, overcrowded, clogged, packed, full, teeming, swarming, stuffed

AN OPPOSITE IS clear

**congratulate** VERB

*I must congratulate Freda on her success.*

▶ praise, compliment, commend, applaud, acclaim

**congratulations** PLURAL NOUN

**1** *We sent our congratulations on their wedding.*

▶ compliments, good wishes, greetings, felicitations

**2** *You all deserve warm congratulations on the success of the enterprise.*

▶ praise, commendation, applause

**congregate** VERB

*A large crowd had congregated in the town square.*

▶ gather, assemble, come together, collect, converge, convene, crowd together, rally, rally round, meet, flock together, join up, swarm, muster, throng round, accumulate

**conjure** VERB

*The magician seemed to conjure eggs from behind people's ears.*

▶ magic, charm, rouse, summon, raise

**conjure up** *Her words conjured up a vision of a beautiful landscape.*

▶ produce, evoke, recall, bring to mind, call to mind, summon up, stir up

**connect** VERB

**1** *The speakers are connected to a powerful amplifier.*

▶ link, attach, couple, join, fasten

AN OPPOSITE IS disconnect.

**2** *Police believe the two crimes could be connected.*

▶ associate, link, relate, couple, compare, tie up, bracket together, put together

AN OPPOSITE IS dissociate

**connection** NOUN

*There is a connection between money and power.*

▶ relationship, link, association, correlation, correspondence, bond, affinity, coherence, contact, interrelationship, join, unity, *(more informal)* tie-up

AN OPPOSITE IS distinction

**connoisseur** NOUN

*a connoisseur of good food*

▶ expert (on), good judge, authority (on), specialist (in), epicure, gourmet, pundit

**conquer** VERB

**1** *Napoleon's attempt to conquer Europe.*

▶ seize, capture, overrun, occupy, invade, take possession of, subjugate, take, win, annex, subject

**2** *William of Normandy conquered the English at the Battle of Hastings.*

▶ defeat, beat, overcome, conquer, vanquish, subdue, crush, overpower, rout

**3** *With a great effort she conquered her fears.*

▶ overcome, suppress, master, control, curb, surmount, prevail over

**conqueror** NOUN

*He entered the capital of Bengal as a conqueror.*

▶ victor, subjugator, defeater, winner, champion, master

**conquest** NOUN

*Alexander's conquest of the Persian Empire*

▶ defeat, subjection, subjugation, capture, invasion, occupation, annexation, appropriation, overthrow, triumph (over), victory (over), *(more informal)* takeover

**conscience** NOUN

**1** *His conscience forced him to admit the truth in the end.*

▶ moral sense, principles, morals, ethics, standards

**2** *Large organizations have no conscience about getting rid of people.*

▶ scruples, compunction, misgivings, qualms, reservations

**conscientious** ADJECTIVE

*a conscientious worker*

▶ hard-working, diligent, industrious, painstaking, thorough, meticulous, punctilious, accurate, attentive, dedicated, rigorous, careful, dutiful, unflagging, assiduous, scrupulous

OPPOSITES ARE careless, irresponsible, lazy

**conscious** ADJECTIVE

**1** *Despite the blow to his head, he remained conscious.*

▶ awake, aware, alert, compos mentis, sensible

AN OPPOSITE IS unconscious

**2** *It was a conscious attempt to deceive us.*

▶ deliberate, intended, intentional, calculated, knowing, planned, premeditated, studied, wilful

AN OPPOSITE IS accidental

**consecrate** VERB

*The Bishop had come to consecrate the new cathedral.*

▶ sanctify, dedicate, bless, devote, beatify, make sacred

**consecrated** ADJECTIVE

*A churchyard is consecrated ground.*

▶ holy, sacred, sanctified, blessed, hallowed

**consecutive** ADJECTIVE

*Interest rates have remained unchanged for six consecutive months.*

▶ continuous, successive, uninterrupted, running *(six months running)*, in succession *(six months in succession)*, in a row *(six months in a row)*

**consent** VERB

**1** *In the end she consented to do something about it.*

▶ agree, be willing, undertake

OPPOSITES ARE refuse, decline

**2** *consent to* *He said the girl had consented to his advances.*

▶ agree to, allow, approve, concede, grant, authorize, permit, comply with

OPPOSITES ARE refuse, forbid

## consent NOUN

*The authorities refused their consent.*
▶ agreement, assent, permission, authorization, approval, backing, endorsement, (*more informal*) go-ahead

## consequence NOUN

**1** *Cooling of the stratosphere was seen as a consequence of the greenhouse effect.*
▶ result, effect, outcome, aftermath, by-product, corollary, repercussion, sequel, side-effect, upshot
**2** *These small losses are of little consequence*
▶ importance, significance, account, concern, moment, note, value, weight

## consequent ADJECTIVE

*We hope the consequent effects are not too serious.*
▶ resulting, resultant, ensuing, consequential, subsequent, following

## conservation NOUN

*the conservation of energy and resources*
▶ preservation, protection, safeguarding, saving, careful management, economy, maintenance, upkeep
AN OPPOSITE IS destruction

## conservative ADJECTIVE

**1** *conservative ideas his conservative father*
▶ traditional, conventional, orthodox, reactionary, old-fashioned, die-hard, hidebound, moderate, narrow-minded, sober, unadventurous
OPPOSITES ARE progressive, radical
**2** *the conservative section of the party*
▶ right-wing, right-of-centre, reactionary, traditionalist, Tory
OPPOSITES ARE radical, socialist
**3** *Fifty pounds is a conservative estimate.*
▶ cautious, moderate, reasonable, understated, unexaggerated
AN OPPOSITE IS extreme

## conservative NOUN

*a political conservative*
▶ conformist, reactionary, right-winger, Tory, traditionalist, diehard

## conservatory NOUN

*The family were sitting in the conservatory.*
▶ summer house, glasshouse, greenhouse, hothouse

## conserve VERB

*It is important to conserve energy.*
▶ save, preserve, protect, sustain, maintain, safeguard, be economical with, use sparingly, keep, look after, store up
OPPOSITES ARE waste, squander

## consider VERB

**1** *Donna paused to consider the possibilities.*
▶ think about, contemplate, ponder, reflect on, weigh up, mull over, cogitate, deliberate, muse, meditate on, discuss, examine, ruminate, study, (*informal*) turn over

**2** *I consider it a privilege.*
▶ regard (as), deem, count, think, judge, reckon, believe (to be)

## considerable ADJECTIVE

*There was a considerable amount of traffic on the road. He had inherited a considerable sum from his grandparents.*
▶ substantial, sizeable, appreciable, significant, reasonable, respectable, tolerable, worthwhile, large, comfortable, noteworthy, noticeable, perceptible
AN OPPOSITE IS negligible

## considerate ADJECTIVE

*We are encouraged to be polite, modest, and considerate to others.*
▶ kind, thoughtful, attentive, helpful, caring, obliging, generous, sensitive, accommodating
OPPOSITES ARE inconsiderate, selfish

## consideration NOUN

*The matter needs careful consideration.*
▶ thought, attention, deliberation, reflection, examination, contemplation, meditation, scrutiny, review

## consign VERB

**1** *May we consign this to your care?*
▶ commit, assign, entrust, hand over, deliver, devote, give, pass on
**2** *The packet was consigned by an international carrier.*
▶ send, dispatch, transmit, convey, ship, transfer

## consignment NOUN

*another consignment of goods*
▶ shipment, delivery, load, batch, cargo, shipload, lorryload

## consist VERB

**consist of** *Audiences consist of very different types of people.*
▶ be composed of, comprise, be made of, include, contain, incorporate, involve

## consistency NOUN

**1** *The pudding had an odd consistency.*
▶ thickness, density, firmness, viscosity
**2** *The figures show a remarkable consistency.*
▶ uniformity, regularity, stability, steadiness, constancy, evenness

## consistent ADJECTIVE

**1** *a consistent pattern of behaviour*
▶ steady, uniform, stable, regular, even, constant, unchanging, unvarying, dependable, reliable, predictable, unfailing
**2** *The theory is consistent with recent research.*
▶ compatible, in accordance, in agreement, in harmony
AN OPPOSITE IS inconsistent

## consolation NOUN

*I tried to offer her some consolation for her loss.*
▶ comfort, solace, sympathy, commiseration, compassion, reassurance, support, succour, encouragement, cheer, ease, help, relief

**console** VERB

*His friends tried to console him.*
▶ comfort, solace, hearten, encourage, relieve, soothe, sympathize with, calm, cheer

**consolidate** VERB

1 *attempts to consolidate their reputation in Europe*
▶ strengthen, reinforce, fortify, enhance, stabilize, make secure, make strong
AN OPPOSITE IS weaken

2 *All the resources need to be consolidated.*
▶ amalgamate, combine, integrate, merge, unify, bring together, fuse

**consort** VERB

*consort with consorting with the opposition*
▶ associate, socialize with, have dealings with, befriend, fraternize with, keep company with, mix with, be friends with, be seen with

**conspicuous** ADJECTIVE

1 *Her bright clothes made her conspicuous.*
▶ prominent, distinct, clearly visible, easily seen, noticeable, apparent, perceptible
AN OPPOSITE IS inconspicuous

2 *The infantry showed conspicuous bravery that day.*
▶ obvious, manifest, evident, outstanding, exceptional, marked, pronounced, unmistakable

**conspiracy** NOUN

*They were involved in a conspiracy to kill the king.*
▶ plot, scheme, intrigue, machination, plan, stratagem

**conspirator** NOUN

*Three of the conspirators were executed.*
▶ plotter, schemer, intriguer, traitor

**conspire** VERB

*They twice conspired to overthrow the dictatorship.*
▶ plot, scheme, intrigue, plan, collude, connive, collaborate, consort, be in league

**constant** ADJECTIVE

1 *the constant hum of traffic on the bypass*
▶ continuous, continual, persistent, ceaseless, incessant, endless, unending
OPPOSITES ARE changeable, irregular

2 *The wheel should turn at a constant speed*
▶ steady, regular, stable, uniform, even, invariable, fixed

3 *She proved to be a constant friend.*
▶ faithful, loyal, devoted, staunch, true, firm, dependable, reliable, dedicated
OPPOSITES ARE fickle, unreliable

**constantly** ADVERB

*The train times are constantly changing.*
▶ always, continually, repeatedly, all the time, forever

**constitute** VERB

1 *Their attitude constitutes a form of discrimination.*
▶ amount to, be equivalent to, be tantamount to, compose, comprise, form, make up

2 *A Scottish Parliament was constituted in 1999.*
▶ establish, set up, inaugurate, create, found, appoint

**constrain** VERB

1 *He felt constrained to write an account of the whole affair.*
▶ compel, force, oblige, coerce, order, pressure, pressurize

2 *Financial dependence constrained women's freedom.*
▶ restrict, limit, restrain, impede, frustrate, curtail, hinder, hamper

**constraint** NOUN

*Political constraints prevented him from speaking his mind.*
▶ restriction, restraint, limitation, inhibition, control, hindrance, check

**constrict** VERB

*Excessive fat constricts the arteries.*
▶ narrow, tighten, compress, contract, shrink, squeeze

**constriction** NOUN

*He felt a constriction in his throat.*
▶ tightening, tightness, narrowing, pressure, stricture

**construct** VERB

1 *The local council wants to construct a new bridge over the railway line.*
▶ build, erect, put up, set up, assemble

2 *We must construct a new form of society.*
▶ create, devise, develop, formulate, fashion, design, invent

**construction** NOUN

1 *In 1858 the construction of the present chapel was put in hand.*
▶ building, erection, assembly, creation, establishment, putting-up, setting-up, erecting

2 *The new building was a mainly timber construction.*
▶ building, edifice, erection, structure, framework

**constructive** ADJECTIVE

*The talks proved to be helpful and constructive.*
▶ positive, useful, worthwhile, beneficial, advantageous, creative, helpful, practical, valuable
AN OPPOSITE IS destructive

**consult** VERB

1 *He wanted to consult the workforce before introducing any changes.*
▶ speak to, confer with, refer to, seek advice from, debate with, discuss matters with, exchange views with

2 *Consult your doctor before attempting these exercises.*
▶ see, ask, get advice from, refer to

3 *He consulted a list pinned to the wall.*
▶ refer to, turn to, look something up in

**consume** VERB

1 *A lot of food and drink was consumed that day.*
▶ eat, drink, devour, digest, swallow, feast on, (*more informal*) gobble up

A B C D E F G H I J K L M N O P Q R S T U V W X Y Z

**2** *The factory consumes thousands of tons of fuel each year.*
▶ use, use up, utilize, expend, absorb, swallow up, deplete, drain, eat into, employ, exhaust

**3** *Fire consumed a row of buildings.*
▶ destroy, demolish, devastate, wipe out, annihilate, wreck, ravage, ruin

**4** *George was consumed by guilt.*
▶ overcome, overwhelm, preoccupy, obsess, absorb

**consumer** NOUN
*Consumers want good value above all.*
▶ customer, purchaser, shopper, buyer, user, end-user, client

**contact** NOUN
**1** *He had been avoiding physical contact with her all day.*
▶ touch, touching, proximity

**2** *Contact between Europe and Africa can be traced back hundreds of years.*
▶ communication, connection, association

**3** *Make sure all electrical contacts are secure.*
▶ connection, join

**4** *I will ask one of my contacts in Italy.*
▶ associate, connection, acquaintance, liaison

**contact** VERB
*I'll contact them when I have more information.*
▶ notify, communicate with, get in touch with, get hold of, approach, correspond with, call, call on, phone, ring, speak to, talk to, (more informal) drop a line to

**contagious** ADJECTIVE
*a contagious disease*
▶ infectious, communicable, catching, spreading, transmittable, transmissible
AN OPPOSITE IS non-infectious

**contain** VERB
**1** *The box contained bottles of red wine.*
▶ hold, accommodate

**2** *The atlas contains photographs taken from space.*
▶ include, incorporate, comprise, consist of, be composed of

**3** *You will have to contain your impatience.*
▶ restrain, curb, suppress, control, hold back, keep back, repress, check, stifle, limit

**container** NOUN
*a watertight container*
▶ receptacle, vessel, holder, repository, canister, case

**contaminate** VERB
*Farming contaminates watercourses every day.*
▶ pollute, adulterate, defile, infect, poison, foul, soil, taint
AN OPPOSITE IS purify

**contemplate** VERB
**1** *He contemplated her over his glasses.*
▶ look at, view, observe, regard, survey, watch, eye, gaze at, stare at, (in literature) behold

**2** *She could not even contemplate what might happen.*
▶ think about, consider, cogitate, deliberate, examine, mull over, plan, reflect on, study, work out

**3** *He contemplated leaving.*
▶ consider, think about, envisage, have in mind, intend (to), propose

**4** *She sat quietly and contemplated (informal).*
▶ ponder, reflect, ruminate, think, meditate, muse

**contemporary** ADJECTIVE
**1** *The historical information comes from contemporary accounts.*
▶ contemporaneous, concurrent, synchronous, coinciding, simultaneous, coexistent, of the time

**2** *a concert of contemporary music*
▶ modern, current, present-day, recent, fashionable, the latest, newest

**contempt** NOUN
*She had nothing but contempt for them.*
▶ disgust, scorn, disdain, loathing, abhorrence, derision, disparagement, detestation, dislike, disrespect, hatred, ridicule
AN OPPOSITE IS admiration

**feel** or **show contempt for** *He showed contempt for their extreme views.*
▶ despise, spurn, revile, detest

**contemptible** ADJECTIVE
*a contemptible insult*
▶ despicable, shameful, disgraceful, detestable, hateful, deplorable, ignominious, loathsome, odious, mean, vile, low, cheap
AN OPPOSITE IS admirable

**contemptuous** ADJECTIVE
*a contemptuous tone of voice*
▶ scornful, disdainful, scathing, disrespectful, insulting, derisive, dismissive, supercilious, condescending, insolent, haughty, mocking, withering, arrogant
AN OPPOSITE IS admiring

**be contemptuous of**
▶ denigrate, disparage, revile, malign, belittle, decry, impugn, abuse

**contend** VERB
**1** *political parties contending for power*
▶ compete, struggle, vie, strive, fight, grapple, oppose one another, rival one another, contest, dispute

**2** *She contended that she had been given bad advice.*
▶ claim, declare, maintain, aver, hold, assert, allege, argue, affirm, plead

**3** *contend with* *They have a lot to contend with.*
▶ cope with, deal with, put up with, sort out, manage, organize

**content** ADJECTIVE
*He seems content now that he's got his way.*
▶ happy, contented, satisfied, pleased, gratified, glad, cheerful, smug

**content** NOUN

**1** *The article is admired more for its content than its style*
▶ subject matter, subject, theme, substance, argument, message

**2** *Butter has a high fat content.*
▶ element, ingredient, substance

**3** *She smiled with content.*
▶ happiness, contentment, satisfaction, pleasure

**content** VERB

*The answer seemed to content him.*
▶ satisfy, please, placate, appease, pacify, soothe

**contented** ADJECTIVE

*a contented feeling*
▶ happy, content, satisfied, pleased, gratified, glad, cheerful, smug
OPPOSITES ARE discontented, dissatisfied

**contention** NOUN

*Her contention is that the action would be illegal.*
▶ argument, claim, opinion, view, assertion, submission, belief, position

**contentious** ADJECTIVE

**1** *a contentious issue*
▶ controversial, debatable, disputed, disputable, vexed

**2** *a contentious group of people*
▶ quarrelsome, argumentative, disputatious, difficult

**contentment** NOUN

*They achieved contentment in the country.*
▶ happiness, well-being, comfort, pleasure, content, contentedness, gratification, satisfaction, peace of mind, tranquillity, ease, fulfilment, relaxation, serenity
OPPOSITES ARE dissatisfaction, unhappiness

**contest** NOUN

**1** *a song contest   a boxing contest*
▶ competition, tournament, match, bout, encounter, fight, battle, dispute

**2** *a contest for the leadership*
▶ struggle, challenge, confrontation, duel

**contest** VERB

**1** *Seven candidates will contest the election.*
▶ enter, compete in, take part in, participate in, contend in, fight in, (informal) make a bid for, strive for, struggle for, take up the challenge of, vie for

**2** *They decided to contest the decision.*
▶ oppose, challenge, dispute, object to, argue against, take issue with, query, refute, resist, debate, doubt, question

**contestant** NOUN

*The winner beat fifteen other contestants.*
▶ competitor, candidate, contender, participant, entrant, player

**context** NOUN

*The events have to be put in their historical context.*
▶ background, circumstances, surroundings, framework, situation, ambience, frame of reference, milieu, position

**contingency** NOUN

*The arrangement needs to provide for all contingencies*
▶ eventuality, circumstance, event, incident, occurrence, accident

**continual** ADJECTIVE

*She needed continual reassurance.   The service is affected by continual breakdowns.*
▶ constant, repeated, frequent, regular, perpetual, ceaseless, incessant, persistent
OPPOSITES ARE occasional, sporadic

**continuation** NOUN

**1** *He returned to the clinic for the continuation of his treatment.*
▶ resumption, maintenance, continuing, continuance, carrying on, extension, prolongation

**2** *the continuation of a story*
▶ sequel, supplement, addition, appendix, postscript

**continue** VERB

**1** *Police continued the search until dark.*
▶ carry on, maintain, keep up, keep going, persevere with, proceed with, prolong, pursue, (more informal) stick at

**2** *Shall we continue after lunch?*
▶ resume, restart, begin again, recommence

**3** *Talks continued all week.*
▶ last, carry on, go on, endure, persist, keep on, linger, live on, remain, stay, survive

**continuous** ADJECTIVE

*three days of continuous rain*
▶ uninterrupted, unbroken, constant, steady, ceaseless, endless, incessant, persistent, non-stop
OPPOSITES ARE intermittent, sporadic

**contorted** ADJECTIVE

*lengths of contorted metal*
▶ twisted, misshapen, buckled, deformed, distorted, screwed up

**contour** NOUN

*the contours of the distant hills*
▶ outline, form, profile, shape, line, silhouette, curve, relief

**contract** NOUN

*A contract is legally binding.*
▶ agreement, settlement, covenant, compact, commitment, deal, bond, pact, concordat, bargain, indenture, lease, treaty, understanding, undertaking

**contract** VERB

**1** *The glass contracts as it cools.   Labour markets contracted in this area.*
▶ shrink, lessen, diminish, reduce, become smaller, condense, shrivel, decrease, dwindle, wither, close

# contraction

up, draw together, fall away, narrow, slim down, thin
out
OPPOSITES ARE expand, enlarge

**2** *The company contracted to build an extension to the
house.*
▶ sign an agreement, undertake, covenant, make a
deal, promise, agree, arrange

**3** *The woman might have contracted smallpox.*
▶ develop, catch, get, become infected by, be taken
ill with

## contraction NOUN
**1** *a contraction of overseas markets*
▶ shrinking, shrivelling, diminution, decline,
decrease

**2** *"Goodbye" is a contraction of "God be with you".*
▶ abbreviation, diminutive, short form, shortened
form

## contradict VERB
**1** *I didn't like to contradict him but I really didn't agree.*
▶ disagree with, challenge, oppose, speak against,
impugn

**2** *The new evidence contradicts earlier conclusions.*
▶ conflict with, be at odds with, be inconsistent
with, run counter to, challenge, disprove

**3** *The statement was later contradicted by the Prime
Minister*
▶ deny, repudiate, rebut, dispute, counter
AN OPPOSITE IS confirm

## contradictory ADJECTIVE
*The two points of view are completely contradictory.*
▶ opposite, opposed, conflicting, contrary,
incompatible, inconsistent, irreconcilable, different,
discrepant, antithetical
OPPOSITES ARE consistent, compatible

## contraption NOUN
*Above his head was a contraption consisting of springs
and wires.*
▶ device, contrivance, gadget, apparatus,
mechanism, invention, machine

## contrary ADJECTIVE
**1** (with the stress on *con-*) *Others may take the
contrary view.*
▶ opposite, opposing, opposed, contradictory,
conflicting, contrasting, reverse, converse, different,
other
AN OPPOSITE IS similar

**2** (with the stress on *-trary*, pronounced like *Mary*) *a
contrary child*
▶ perverse, awkward, difficult, uncooperative,
obstinate, unhelpful, tiresome, disobedient,
vexatious, (*more informal*) bolshie, (*more informal*)
stroppy
AN OPPOSITE IS cooperative

**3 contrary to** *The result was contrary to all
expectations.*
▶ in conflict with, at odds with, at variance with,
counter to

# control

## contrast NOUN
*a noticeable contrast between what they say and what
they do*
▶ difference, dissimilarity, disparity, variance,
divergence, contradiction, opposition
AN OPPOSITE IS similarity

## contrast VERB
**1** *People contrast the two brothers.*
▶ differentiate, distinguish, make distinctions
between, discriminate between, compare

**2 contrast with** *Her fair hair contrasted with her dark
dress.*
▶ set off, complement, clash with

## contrasting ADJECTIVE
*contrasting colours  contrasting opinions*
▶ complementary, conflicting, different, opposing,
opposite
AN OPPOSITE IS similar

## contribute VERB
**1** *Employers have to contribute a set amount to the
fund.*
▶ give, subscribe, donate, provide, put up, supply,
add, grant, bestow

**2 contribute to** *The weather contributed to the success
of the occasion.*
▶ play a part in, add to, be a factor in, have a hand in,
make for, enhance, help, reinforce, support,
encourage

## contribution NOUN
*All income comes from charitable contributions.*
▶ donation, benefaction, payment, gift,
subscription, allowance, endowment, grant,
offering, sponsorship, (*more informal*) handout

## contributor NOUN
**1** *The charity has acquired several new contributors.*
▶ donor, benefactor, subscriber, supporter, patron,
sponsor, giver, backer, helper

**2** *a regular contributor to the magazine*
▶ writer, columnist, correspondent, freelance,
journalist, reporter

## contrivance NOUN
*The blinds were opened by a strange contrivance at the
side.*
▶ device, contraption, gadget, apparatus,
mechanism, invention, machine

## contrived ADJECTIVE
*He looked at her with a contrived smile.*
▶ affected, artificial, studied, unnatural, strained,
forced

## control NOUN
**1** *this theme of giving back control over civic affairs to
the local people*
▶ jurisdiction, administration, management,
regulation, authority, charge, power, government,
supervision, command, direction, oversight,
organization, guidance, influence

a b **c** d e f g h i j k l m n o p q r s t u v w x y z

**2** *He needs to exercise a little more control and not lose his temper so much.*
▶ restraint, self-control, self-command, self-possession, composure

**3** *Some of the controls were difficult to reach.*
▶ switch, knob, button, lever, handle, dial

**gain control of** *The Portuguese had gained control of the Indian Ocean a century earlier.*
▶ take over, dominate, usurp, win, annex, seize, steal

**control** VERB
**1** *You have to be able to control all the resources.*
▶ be in charge of, manage, administer, have authority over, supervise, govern, oversee, run, operate, look after

**2** *He found it hard to control his temper.*
▶ restrain, check, contain, curb, confine, keep in check, master, repress, subdue, suppress

**controversial** ADJECTIVE
*He wrote a controversial article on the death penalty.*
▶ contentious, controvertible, debatable, disputable, questionable, doubtful, polemical, problematical, arguable
OPPOSITES ARE uncontroversial, straightforward

**controversy** NOUN
*There is controversy over new road-building plans.*
▶ disagreement, dispute, contention, altercation, dissension, debate, argument, issue, polemic, quarrel, war of words, wrangle

**convalesce** VERB
*She needed several weeks to convalesce after her illness.*
▶ recuperate, recover, get better, get well, regain strength, improve, make progress, mend

**convene** VERB
**1** *The chairman convened a meeting*
▶ call, summon, assemble, bring together, (more formal) convoke

**2** *The committee convened at two o'clock.*
▶ assemble, meet, gather, come together

**convenient** ADJECTIVE
**1** *He asked when it would be convenient to interview her.*
▶ suitable, appropriate, opportune, fitting, agreeable, neat, timely, usable
OPPOSITES ARE inconvenient, awkward

**2** *Fast foods are often the most convenient option.*
▶ practical, handy, useful, helpful, labour-saving

**3** *There is a regular bus service and convenient shops.*
▶ nearby, accessible, handy, at hand, available

**4 convenient for** *The house was so convenient for London.*
▶ accessible to, within easy reach of, well situated for, handy for
AN OPPOSITE IS inconvenient

**convention** NOUN
**1** *All these social conventions can become tedious.*
▶ custom, practice, tradition, rule, protocol, canon, formality, matter of form, matter of etiquette

**2** *American-style political conventions*
▶ conference, meeting, congress, assembly, symposium

**3** *a convention signed by all the countries of the area*
▶ agreement, treaty, accord, compact, understanding

**conventional** ADJECTIVE
**1** *He was willing to follow conventional ideas.*
▶ orthodox, established, traditional, customary, prevalent, mainstream, commonplace, routine, unoriginal, hackneyed
OPPOSITES ARE unconventional, unorthodox

**2** *Kevin was a conventional man.*
▶ conservative, hidebound, traditional, traditionalist, conformist, formal, correct, proper, bourgeois, stereotyped, unadventurous, unimaginative, unoriginal, (more informal) stuffy, (more informal) fuddy-duddy
OPPOSITES ARE unconventional, radical

**3** *A conventional telephone can be a lot less fiddly than many mobiles.*
▶ standard, normal, regular, traditional, ordinary

**converge** VERB
*The light rays converge to form a sharp image.*
▶ merge, combine, meet, join, come together, coincide
OPPOSITES ARE separate, diverge

**conversation** NOUN
*The rest of the conversation was in French.*
▶ discussion, talk, discourse, dialogue, exchange, consultation, (more informal) chat

**converse** NOUN (with the stress on con-)
*The converse is true.*
▶ opposite, reverse, contrary, antithesis, obverse

**converse** VERB (with the stress on -verse)
*They conversed for hours about the old days.*
▶ talk, speak, chat, discourse, chatter, gossip

**conversion** NOUN
**1** *the conversion of waste into forms of energy*
▶ change, changing, turning, transformation

**2** *The house has had a loft conversion.*
▶ adaptation, alteration, renovation, reconstruction, rebuilding, modification

**3** *a religious conversion*
▶ rebirth, regeneration, reformation, change of heart

**convert** VERB
**1** *We plan to convert the loft into a workroom. Most of her novels have now been converted into films.*
▶ adapt, change, turn, rebuild, reconstruct, renovate, modify, reorganize

**2** *a device for converting digital data into audio signals*
▶ turn, change, transform, translate

**convey** VERB
**1** *A shuttle service conveys passengers form the city to the suburbs.*
▶ transport, carry, take, transfer, deliver, bring, fetch, move

2 *The dancer's movements can convey a variety of meanings.*
► communicate, signify, indicate, impart, disclose, relate, imply, mean, reveal, put across, get across

**convict** NOUN (with the stress on con-)
*He looked like a convict in his striped pyjamas.*
► prisoner, criminal, condemned person

**convict** VERB (with the stress on -vict)
*A jury had earlier convicted Duncan of assault.*
► condemn, declare guilty, find guilty
OPPOSITES ARE acquit, clear

**conviction** NOUN
1 *He spoke with complete conviction.*
► confidence, assurance, certainty, sureness, positiveness, firmness
AN OPPOSITE IS uncertainty
2 *She has keenly felt political convictions.*
► belief, opinion, view, principle, persuasion, creed, faith, tenet

**convince** VERB
*It will be difficult to convince them. She tried to convince herself that nobody would have heard her.*
► persuade, assure, prove to, reassure, satisfy, sway, win over, bring round

**convincing** ADJECTIVE
1 *a convincing argument*
► strong, powerful, conclusive, cogent, decisive, compelling, definite, persuasive, unambiguous, unarguable, unequivocal
AN OPPOSITE IS inconclusive
2 *a convincing victory*
► decisive, conclusive, resounding, emphatic, impressive

**convoy** NOUN
*a convoy of ships*
► group, fleet, armada, procession

**convulsion** NOUN
1 *The convulsions stopped and Charles lay back exhausted.*
► fit, seizure, spasm, attack, paroxysm
2 *seismic convulsions a political convulsion*
► upheaval, disturbance, tremor, turbulence, eruption, outburst

**convulsive** ADJECTIVE
*convulsive movements*
► spasmodic, jerky, shaking, uncontrolled, uncoordinated, violent, (more informal) twitchy

**cook** NOUN
*the hotel's new cook*
► chef

**cook** VERB
*She cooked them both a romantic dinner.*
► prepare, make, get, put together, (more informal) fix
RELATED ADJECTIVE culinary
**cook something up** *He cooked up an idea for getting her to go with him.*
► concoct, devise, contrive, plot, scheme

**cool** ADJECTIVE
1 *the cool air of early morning*
► fresh, bracing, crisp, brisk, chilly, chilled, (more informal) nippy
OPPOSITES ARE warm, balmy
2 *We got a cool response.*
► unfriendly, chilly, lukewarm, unwelcoming, frigid, hostile, unsympathetic, reserved, aloof, (informal) standoffish
OPPOSITES ARE warm, friendly, enthusiastic
3 *He was determined to keep cool in the crisis.*
► calm, composed, collected, clear-headed, self-controlled, self-possessed, unflustered, unruffled
4 (informal) *She seems to think she's so cool.*
► fashionable, trendy, stylish, sophisticated, chic
5 (informal) *It's a cool song.*
► good, excellent, super, superb

**cool** NOUN
*He finally lost his cool and started shouting.*
► composure, self-control, self-possession, calm, calmness

**cool** VERB
1 *He threw open the shutters to cool the room.*
► chill, make cooler, lower the temperature of
2 *Cool the mixture in the fridge for about an hour.*
► chill, refrigerate, make cold
3 *Their enthusiasm had begun to cool. Recent events had cooled their enthusiasm.*
► lessen, reduce, moderate, dampen, diminish, abate, take the edge off or lose its edge

**cooped up** ADJECTIVE
*She doesn't like being cooped up at home all day.*
► confined, shut in, shut up, caged, trapped, locked up, imprisoned, incarcerated

**cooperate** VERB
1 *Several police forces cooperated in the operation.*
► collaborate, combine, unite, work together, join forces, team up
2 **cooperate with** *He absolutely refused to cooperate with them.*
► assist, help, support, work with

**cooperation** NOUN
1 *wise cooperation between management and workers*
► collaboration, coordination, joint action, teamwork, unity, mutual support
OPPOSITES ARE conflict, rivalry
2 *She thanked them all for their cooperation.*
► assistance, help, helpfulness, support, backing

**cooperative** ADJECTIVE
1 *The staff were pleasant and cooperative.*
► helpful, obliging, accommodating, supportive, constructive, willing, keen
AN OPPOSITE IS uncooperative
2 *The project was achieved by a cooperative effort*
► joint, combined, collective, concerted, coordinated, corporate, shared, communal
AN OPPOSITE IS individual

a b c d e f g h i j k l m n o p q r s t u v w x y z

**coordinate** VERB
*A committee will coordinate all the sporting activities.*
▶ harmonize, organize, bring together, synchronize, systematize

**cope** VERB
1 *She is too old now to cope by herself.*
▶ manage, survive, carry on, get by, fend for yourself, make do
2 **cope with** *We found so many problems at once difficult to cope with.*
▶ deal with, handle, manage, contend with, endure, tolerate

**copious** ADJECTIVE
*They sat listening and writing copious notes. a long breakfast of croissants and copious coffee*
▶ plenty of, abundant, plentiful, extensive, substantial, profuse, lavish, generous, ample, numerous, full
OPPOSITES ARE sparse, meagre

**copy** NOUN
1 *Keep a copy of your letter.*
▶ duplicate, photocopy, Xerox, facsimile, transcript, clone, double, pattern, print, representation, tracing
2 *The painting is only a copy.*
▶ reproduction, replica, imitation, likeness, model, fake, forgery, twin
AN OPPOSITE IS original
**USAGE** You use *fake* or *forgery* when you mean a copy that is intended to deceive people.

**copy** VERB
1 *Copy the passage from the book.*
▶ write out, reproduce, make a copy of, duplicate, repeat
2 *He copied several drawings by Hogarth.*
▶ reproduce, make a copy of, forge, fake, plagiarize, counterfeit, crib, follow
**USAGE** You use *fake* or *forge* or *counterfeit* when you mean make a copy that is intended to deceive people.
3 *A lot of musicians have tried to copy their sound.*
▶ imitate, mimic, reproduce, emulate, ape, impersonate, parrot, poach

**cord** NOUN
*I tightened the cord on the hood of my jacket.*
▶ string, thread, strap, tape, rope, strand, cable

**cordial** ADJECTIVE
*a cordial greeting*
▶ friendly, warm, genial, amiable, affectionate, fond, good-natured, heartfelt, enthusiastic

**core** NOUN
1 *the earth's core*
▶ centre, nucleus, heart, middle, inside
2 *the core of the problem*
▶ heart, essence, crux, nub, central issue, kernel, (more informal) nitty-gritty

**core** ADJECTIVE
*the core issue*
▶ central, key, chief, basic, fundamental, principal, crucial, vital

**cork** NOUN
*Ken pulled the corks from all the bottles.*
▶ stopper, plug, bung

**corn** NOUN
*a field of corn*
▶ grain, cereal, cereal crop, wheat, barley

**corner** NOUN
1 *Turn left at the corner.*
▶ bend, curve, turning
2 *Three women sat in a corner of the room.*
▶ nook, niche, recess, alcove
3 *Stuart felt he was in a bit of a corner.*
▶ predicament, plight, quandary, dilemma, awkward situation, mess, (more informal) spot, (more informal) scrape, (more informal) stew
**round the corner** *The shops are round the corner.*
▶ nearby, close at hand, not far away, within reach

**corner** VERB
*The animal had cornered its prey.*
▶ trap, shut in, bring to bay, run to ground, capture, catch

**corny** ADJECTIVE
*corny jokes*
▶ hackneyed, banal, stereotyped, stale, feeble, tired

**corporation** NOUN
1 *a business corporation*
▶ company, firm, organization, concern, enterprise
2 *a city corporation*
▶ council, town council, local authority

**corpse** NOUN
*Police found the corpse under the floorboards.*
▶ body, dead body, remains, cadaver, carcass, skeleton

**correct** ADJECTIVE
1 *What is the correct time? Not all the information proved correct.*
▶ right, accurate, exact, true, precise, genuine, authentic, reliable, factual, faithful, faultless, flawless, strict
OPPOSITES ARE inaccurate, wrong
2 *She wanted to know the correct course of action.*
▶ right, proper, appropriate, fitting, suitable, acceptable, just
OPPOSITES ARE inappropriate, wrong
3 *correct behaviour*
▶ proper, decent, well-mannered, tactful, unexceptionable

**correct** VERB
1 *Please correct your mistakes.*
▶ rectify, put right, make good, amend, remedy, cure, redress, adjust, alter, repair, right
2 *Your work will be corrected within two days.*
▶ mark, assess, evaluate, appraise
3 *She corrected him for his lateness.*
▶ scold, admonish, rebuke, chastise, punish

## correction NOUN

*the correction of errors*
▶ rectification, righting, putting right, resolution, adjustment, amendment

## correspond VERB

**1** *correspond to The translator must choose words that correspond to the sense of the original.*
▶ match, fit, conform to, accord with, agree with, be consistent with, parallel, concur with, harmonize with, square with, tally with, convey

**2** *Emma and I corresponded for many years.*
▶ communicate, exchange letters, write to each other

## correspondence NOUN

**1** *a collection of the composer's published correspondence*
▶ letters, communications, memoranda, notes

**2** *There is some correspondence between the two ideas.*
▶ correlation, similarity, resemblance, comparability, agreement

## corresponding ADJECTIVE

*Climate change brings a corresponding change in average temperature.*
▶ matching, equivalent, commensurate, related, analogous, appropriate, complementary, parallel

## corroborate VERB

*The witness corroborated his story.*
▶ confirm, support, endorse, verify, back up, reinforce

## corrode VERB

**1** *Damp conditions will corrode the metal.*
▶ rust, tarnish, erode, consume, wear away, eat away, oxidize, rot

**2** *Iron corrodes rapidly in damp conditions.*
▶ rust, tarnish, deteriorate, perish, disintegrate, crumble

## corrugated ADJECTIVE

*a corrugated surface*
▶ ridged, ribbed, fluted, grooved, furrowed, wrinkled, crinkled, (*more informal*) crinkly

## corrupt ADJECTIVE

**1** *The government is accused of being corrupt and incompetent.*
▶ dishonest, dishonourable, unprincipled, unscrupulous, untrustworthy, underhand, disreputable, discreditable, bribable, unsound, false, (*more informal*) bent
OPPOSITES ARE honest, reputable

**2** *They were involved in some form of corrupt practice.*
▶ dishonest, crooked, criminal, fraudulent, unethical

**3** *Some people say society is getting more corrupt.*
▶ sinful, immoral, decadent, degenerate, depraved, dissolute, debauched, rotten, wicked, evil, iniquitous, low, perverted, profligate, venal
AN OPPOSITE IS moral

## corrupt VERB

**1** *Some firms even try to corrupt local officials.*
▶ bribe, suborn, buy off, pay off, influence, (*more informal*) fix

**2** *Pornography corrupts the innocent.*
▶ pervert, deprave, debauch, lead astray, make corrupt, contaminate, degrade, tempt, seduce

## corruption NOUN

**1** *He was found guilty of treason, espionage, and corruption.*
▶ dishonesty, deception, misconduct, bribery, fraud
AN OPPOSITE IS honesty

**2** *all kinds of moral corruption*
▶ sin, immorality, degradation, depravity, degeneracy, impurity
OPPOSITES ARE morality, purity

## cosmetic ADJECTIVE

*The improvements were largely cosmetic*
▶ superficial, surface, external, decorative, insubstantial
OPPOSITES ARE fundamental, substantial

## cosmetics NOUN

*I had all the cosmetics a woman could want, and I liked to dress up.*
▶ make-up, beauty products, face paint, toiletries

## cosmic ADJECTIVE

*a musical work of cosmic proportions*
▶ vast, huge, immense, boundless, endless, infinite, limitless, universal

## cosmopolitan ADJECTIVE

**1** *a large city with a cosmopolitan atmosphere*
▶ international, multicultural, sophisticated
AN OPPOSITE IS provincial

**2** *cosmopolitan attitudes*
▶ worldly, well-travelled, sophisticated, urbane, liberal

## cost NOUN

**1** *The cost of a ticket has increased.*
▶ price, charge (for), expense, amount, payment (for), levy (on), tariff (on), outlay (on), expenditure (on), rate (for), value, fare, figure

**2** *The cost in human lives is too great.*
▶ sacrifice, loss, penalty, price, suffering

## cost VERB

**1** *Each item on this shelf costs a pound.*
▶ be priced at, sell for, go for, come to, fetch, realize, (*more informal*) set you back

**2** *We must cost your proposals before we take them any further.*
▶ price, put a price on, value, estimate the cost of

## costly ADJECTIVE

*The five-star service is very costly.*
▶ expensive, dear, overpriced, exorbitant, (*more informal*) pricey

## costume NOUN

*a prize for the best costume*
▶ outfit, dress, ensemble, clothing, suit, attire, (*informal*) get-up

## cosy ADJECTIVE
*They lived in a cosy little house.*
► snug, comfortable, warm, homely, restful, secure, intimate, reassuring, relaxing, soft, *(more informal)* comfy
AN OPPOSITE IS uncomfortable

## cottage NOUN
*a cottage in the country*
► little house, bungalow, cabin, chalet, *(mainly Scottish)* bothy

## couch NOUN
*a cat sat next to her on the couch.*
► sofa, settee, chesterfield, ottoman, divan

## council NOUN
**1** *The council is responsible for maintaining the roads.*
► local authority, legislature, corporation, assembly
**2** *a meeting of the society's administrative council*
► board, committee, commission, panel

## counsel NOUN
*We look to her for wise counsel.*
► advice, guidance, direction, instruction, suggestions

## counsel VERB
*She is good at counselling her staff.*
► advise, guide, give help to, discuss matters with

## counsellor NOUN
*A trained counsellor will help you.*
► adviser, consultant, therapist

## count VERB
**1** *He was counting the number of cars parked along the street.*
► add up, total, calculate, work out, reckon, check, *(more informal)* tot up
**2** *It's important for people to feel that they count.*
► matter, be important, have significance, signify
**3** **count on** *You can count on my support*
► rely on, depend on, bank on, be sure of, trust, believe in, expect, have faith in

## count NOUN
**1** *There were over a hundred members at the last count.*
► calculation, reckoning, counting, tally, poll, census
**2** *a high calorie count*
► total, sum, amount, tally, number

## counter NOUN
**1** *He had left his glasses on the counter.*
► worktop, work surface, work table
**2** *You play the game with counters.*
► token, disc, piece

## counteract VERB
*new laws to counteract terrorism*
► prevent, resist, oppose, curb, forestall, fight against, act against, work against, thwart, frustrate, foil, reduce, neutralize, withstand

## counterbalance VERB
*High interest rates counterbalance the high level of risk.*
► compensate for, make up for, offset, balance, equalize, even out, counteract

## counterfeit ADJECTIVE
*a counterfeit £20 note*
► forged, fake, imitation, bogus, sham, copied, *(more informal)* phoney
AN OPPOSITE IS genuine

## counterfeit VERB
**1** *The notes had been counterfeited.*
► copy, fake, forge
**2** *His brother managed to counterfeit his signature.*
► forge, fake, copy, reproduce, falsify, imitate, simulate

## counterpart NOUN
*Heads of department were to meet their counterparts from neighbouring schools.*
► equivalent, opposite number, peer, equal

## countless ADJECTIVE
*They have to make countless decisions every day.*
► innumerable, untold, myriad, numerous, numberless, unnumbered, endless, immeasurable, incalculable, infinite, many, measureless, limitless
AN OPPOSITE IS few

## country NOUN
**1** *a country of warlike people*
► nation, land, state, territory, realm
**2** *They could return to their own country at last.*
► homeland, home, native land, native soil, mother country, country of origin, birthplace
**3** *The prime minister would appeal to the country in an election.*
► people, nation, public, populace, population, community
**4** *You drive through lovely open country.*
► terrain, landscape, countryside, scenery, surroundings, environment
RELATED ADJECTIVE rural

## couple NOUN
**1** *A couple were dancing on the balcony.*
► pair, twosome, partners, duo, husband and wife
**2** *Let me know if you see him in the next couple of days.*
► few, two or three
**USAGE** You can also say *in the next day or so.*

## couple VERB
*A second locomotive is coupled to the train at Crewe.*
► connect, attach, join, link, fasten, hitch, yoke, unite (with), combine (with), pair

## coupon NOUN
**1** *The offer includes money-saving coupons.*
► voucher, token, ticket, certificate
**2** *For more information fill in the coupon below.*
► form, tear-off slip, slip

## courage NOUN
*It needs courage to argue with them.*
► bravery, audacity, boldness, daring, nerve, pluck, gallantry, determination, fearlessness, fortitude, heroism, *(more informal)* bottle, *(more informal)* grit, *(more informal)* guts, *(much more informal)* spunk
AN OPPOSITE IS cowardice

**courageous** ADJECTIVE
*It was a courageous attempt against all the odds.*
▶ brave, valiant, daring, audacious, spirited, intrepid, plucky, adventurous, fearless
AN OPPOSITE IS cowardly

**courier** NOUN
1 *A courier brought a package.*
▶ messenger, carrier, dispatch rider, runner
2 *She worked as a courier for a travel firm.*
▶ representative, guide, tour guide

**course** NOUN
1 *a beginner's course in German*
▶ programme of study, course of study, educational programme, classes, lessons, studies
2 *The aircraft had changed its course again.*
▶ direction, route, way, tack, path, flight path, bearing, itinerary
3 *an event that changed the course of history*
▶ progress, progression, development, advance, evolution, flow, unfolding, future
4 *the best course to adopt*
▶ plan, plan of action, procedure, approach, method, programme, policy
5 *They had only just started the main course.*
▶ dish, part of a meal, menu item
6 *six laps of the course*
▶ track, circuit, ground, stadium

**court** NOUN
1 *The court acquitted them all.*
▶ lawcourt, court of law, bench, tribunal
2 *entertainment for the Queen's court*
▶ entourage, followers, royal household, establishment
3 *a court for ball games*
▶ enclosure, playing area, ground, field

**courteous** ADJECTIVE
*The staff are always helpful and courteous.*
▶ polite, civil, obliging, considerate, respectful, well-mannered, affable, civilized, refined

**courtesy** NOUN
*Everyone is entitled to the same level of courtesy.*
▶ politeness, consideration, civility, respect, attention

**courtyard** NOUN
*People gathered in a courtyard behind the house.*
▶ yard, quadrangle, (more informal) quad, court, enclosure, forecourt, patio

**cover** NOUN
1 *The computer screen has its own plastic cover.*
▶ covering, envelope, wrapper, case
2 *Lift the cover and look inside.*
▶ lid, top, cap
3 *The book has a blue cover.*
▶ jacket, dust jacket, dust cover, wrapper
4 *a thick cover of snow*
▶ covering, layer, coat, coating, blanket, carpet, cloak, overlay
5 *The trees provide some sort of cover.*
▶ shelter, protection, refuge, shield, haven, defence

6 *The business is a cover for spying activities.*
▶ front, facade, pretext, disguise, screen

**cover** VERB
1 *She covered her knees with a blanket.*
▶ envelop, enclose, protect, overlay
**USAGE** You can also say *She put (or placed) a blanket over her knees.*.
2 *The car was covered in mud.*
▶ coat, cake, encrust, plaster, smother, spread
3 *The book covers most of the main topics.*
▶ deal with, treat, consider, include, contain, comprise, encompass, embrace, provide for, incorporate
4 *The money should cover most of our needs.*
▶ cater for, be enough for, meet, suffice for, pay for

**covering** NOUN
*a light covering of snow*
▶ cover, layer, coat, coating, blanket, carpet, cloak, overlay

**cover-up** NOUN
*The fraud had taken years to be discovered because of a massive cover-up at high level.*
▶ concealment, deception, suppression, disguise, pretence

**covet** VERB
*Claudia looked longingly at the smoky-blue suit she coveted.*
▶ desire, long for, crave, yearn for, hanker after, dream of, (more informal) fancy

**coward** NOUN
(informal) *He accused them of being cheats and cowards.*
▶ weakling, faint-heart, (more informal) chicken, (more informal) wimp
AN OPPOSITE IS hero

**cowardice** NOUN
*Her husband had been executed for cowardice.*
▶ cowardliness, faint-heartedness, spinelessness, timorousness, timidity
OPPOSITES ARE bravery, courage

**cowardly** ADJECTIVE
*The thieves ran off, showing how cowardly they are. The decision was feeble and cowardly.*
▶ faint-hearted, lily-livered, spineless, craven, weak, timid, pusillanimous, (more informal) gutless, (more informal) yellow
OPPOSITES ARE brave, courageous

**cowed** ADJECTIVE
*The regime ruled over a cowed people.*
▶ frightened, scared, subdued, overawed, browbeaten, disheartened, daunted, unnerved

**cower** VERB
*The children cowered in fear.*
▶ cringe, shrink, crouch, recoil, flinch, quail, pull back, back away, grovel, hide, shiver, skulk

**coy** ADJECTIVE

*Don't be coy: come and be introduced*
► shy, bashful, reserved, diffident, embarrassed, inhibited, self-conscious, hesitant, timid, reserved, retiring
OPPOSITES ARE assertive, forward, bold

**crack** NOUN

**1** *a plate with a crack in it*
► break, crack, chink, split, fracture, fissure, gap
**2** *a crack on the head*
► blow, bang, knock, smack, hit, punch, (*more informal*) bash
**3** *the crack of a rifle   a crack of thunder*
► bang, report, crash, explosion, burst, snap, pop
**4** *a cheap crack*
► joke, jest, quip, wisecrack, gibe, dig, (*more informal*) gag
**5** *have a crack at it*
► try, attempt, (*more informal*) go, (*more informal*) shot, (*more informal*) stab

**crack** VERB

**1** *She dropped a cup and cracked it.*
► break, split, shatter, splinter, chip, fracture
**2** *Guns cracked in the distance.*
► burst, bang, go bang, explode, thump, boom, pop, crackle, crash
**3** *She cracked him round the head.*
► strike, smack, thump, slap, hit, (*more informal*) bash, (*more informal*) whack
**4** *The problem proved hard to crack.*
► solve, resolve, work out, puzzle out, fathom, decipher, break
**5** *A suspect finally cracked and confessed.*
► break down, give in, give way, collapse, yield
**crack down on** *a drive to crack down on street crime*
► reduce, suppress, end, stop, eradicate, get tough on, clamp down on

**crack up**

**1** *I'm so anxious I could be cracking up (informal).*
► break down, have a breakdown, lose control, go to pieces, go mad, go crazy
**2** *The remark made everyone want to crack up.*
► burst out laughing, roar with laughter, laugh uncontrollably

**crackle** VERB

*The fire began to crackle.*
► sizzle, fizzle, crack, fizz, hiss, sputter

**cradle** NOUN

*a baby's cradle*
► cot, crib, bed

**cradle** VERB

*She cradled a mug of tea in her hands.*
► hold, support, nurse, tend, protect

**craft** NOUN

**1** *the traditional craft of hand weaving*
► handicraft, trade, business, pursuit, activity, occupation, profession, work, job
**2** *Pete demonstrated the blacksmith's craft*
► skill, art, technique, expertise, mastery, talent, ability

**3** *The harbour was teeming with river craft.*
► vessels, ships, boats

**craftsman** NOUN

*Passers-by could watch the craftsmen at work.*
► artisan, artist, craftsperson, master

**craftsmanship** NOUN

*an age when craftsmanship in building reached a peak*
► skill, technique, expertise, workmanship, artistry, ability, dexterity, handiwork, (*more informal*) know-how

**crafty** ADJECTIVE

*That's a crafty way of avoiding the problem.*
► cunning, clever, shrewd, ingenious, wily, artful, canny

**crag** NOUN

*a high crag overlooking the bay*
► cliff, bluff, ridge, rock, precipice

**craggy** ADJECTIVE

*a craggy cliff*
► rocky, rough, rugged, jagged, steep

**cram** VERB

**1** *They were busy cramming burgers into their mouths. The shelves were crammed with books.*
► stuff, force, press, squeeze, jam, pack, overfill
**2** *I'll never know how we managed to cram into such a tiny car.*
► crowd, crush, squeeze, pack
**3** *Many of the students are still cramming for tomorrow's exam.*
► study hard, (*more informal*) swot, (*more informal*) mug up

**cramped** ADJECTIVE

*It was hard to sleep in the cramped quarters of the submarine.*
► restricted, confined, poky, constricted, narrow, tight, uncomfortable
AN OPPOSITE IS roomy

**crash** NOUN

**1** *There was a loud crash in the kitchen.*
► bang, smash, clash, clatter, clang, racket, thump, thud, boom
**2** *She had been injured in a car crash.*
► accident, collision, smash, bump, pile-up, derailment, disaster, impact, knock, wreck
**3** *a stock-market crash*
► collapse, failure, depression, fall, ruin

**crash** VERB

**1 crash into** *The car crashed into a tree.*
► hit, strike, smash into, collide with, bump into, knock into, lurch into, pitch into
**2** *The company had crashed in the recession.*
► fail, collapse, fold up, go under, founder, become bankrupt
**3** *Parts of the roof crashed to the ground.*
► collapse, fall, plunge, topple, hurtle

**crass** ADJECTIVE
*It had been a crass thing to do, and he apologized for it.*
► stupid, foolish, blundering, insensitive, mindless, witless

**crate** NOUN
*Three crates of books stood by the door.*
► case, packing case, box, carton, tea chest

**crater** NOUN
*Volcanic peaks tower above deep craters.*
► pit, hole, chasm, hollow, cavity, opening, abyss

**crave** VERB
*The chapel might provide the privacy she craved.*
► long for, yearn for, hunger for, dream of, hanker after, desire, seek

**craving** NOUN
*the body's natural craving for food*
► longing, desire, hankering, hunger, thirst, appetite

**crawl** VERB
1 *He escaped by crawling out of the back of the house.*
► creep, edge, inch, slither, clamber
2 *(informal) You can get their support without having to crawl to them all the time.*
► grovel, pander, kowtow, fawn (over), be obsequious, *(more informal)* suck up
**be crawling with** *The place is crawling with visitors in the summer months.*
► be full of, be overrun by, be teeming with, be packed with, be crowded with

**craze** NOUN
*the latest craze to sweep the country*
► fad, trend, vogue, fashion, rage, mania, diversion, enthusiasm, infatuation, novelty, obsession, passion, pastime

**crazy** ADJECTIVE
1 *It was crazy to expect them to agree.*
► absurd, ridiculous, ludicrous, preposterous, foolish, idiotic, stupid, foolhardy, unwise, *(more informal)* barmy
2 *She was going crazy with all the work.*
► mad, insane, out of your mind, off your head, unbalanced, demented, deranged
3 *The whole family are crazy about golf.*
► mad, passionate, keen (on), devoted (to), smitten (with), taken (with), *(more informal)* potty

**creak** VERB
*The door began to creak.*
► squeak, grate, groan, scrape, grind, rasp

**cream** NOUN
1 *Rub in some skin cream.*
► lotion, ointment, rub, salve, moisturizer
2 *the cream of the country's jockeys*
► pick, elite, choice, finest, best
AN OPPOSITE IS dregs

**creamy** ADJECTIVE
*The powder makes a creamy paste when mixed with water.*
► smooth, thick, rich, velvety, milky, oily

**crease** NOUN
*The cloth was full of creases and would have to be ironed.*
► wrinkle, crinkle, pucker, fold, furrow, groove, line, pleat, ridge, ruck, tuck, corrugation

**crease** VERB
*I tried not to crease my clothes.*
► crumple, crinkle, wrinkle, pucker, crush, crimp, rumple, ruck, fold, furrow, pleat, ridge

**create** VERB
1 *A new work had to be created from scratch.*
► produce, make, generate, develop, compose, devise, design
2 *His father had created the business fifty years before.*
► set up, start, begin, found, establish, institute, initiate
3 *The appointment created a lot of resentment.*
► cause, bring about, lead to, engender, prompt, produce, result in, give rise to

**creation** NOUN
1 *the creation of a modern industrial society*
► making, formation, foundation, fashioning, establishment, institution, conception, birth, development, origination, production
OPPOSITES ARE disintegration, destruction
2 *The decor was entirely her creation.*
► work, effort, conception, invention, design, devising, achievement, handiwork, brainchild, product, work of art

**creative** ADJECTIVE
*Students need to be creative in their thinking.*
► imaginative, inventive, expressive, resourceful, original, productive, fertile, artistic, positive, ingenious, clever, inspired, talented, visionary
AN OPPOSITE IS destructive

**creator** NOUN
1 *the creator of many good novels*
► writer, author, producer, composer, designer, deviser, initiator, inventor, maker, manufacturer, parent
2 *the creators of the Assyrian Empire*
► architect, builder, originator, begetter

**creature** NOUN
1 *Whales are the largest living creatures.*
► animal, living thing, beast, being, brute
2 *The poor creature had been out in the rain all night.*
► fellow, individual, person, wretch, beggar, chap

**credentials** NOUN
1 *A police officer checked the driver's credentials.*
► documents, papers, identity papers, authorization, permit, licence, proof of identity, passport, warrant
2 *Her credentials for the job were impeccable.*
► qualifications, references, accreditation

**credibility** NOUN
*The details give credibility to the story.*
► plausibility, conviction, integrity, believability, reliability, probability, trustworthiness

**credible** ADJECTIVE
*The man was unable to give any credible explanation for his presence there.*
▸ believable, plausible, reasonable, tenable, conceivable, possible, convincing, imaginable, likely, persuasive
AN OPPOSITE IS incredible

**credit** NOUN
1 *Gary helped him with his chemistry and deserves a lot of the credit for the good grades he got.*
▸ praise, acclaim, approval, recognition, acknowledgement, commendation, distinction, prestige, merit, esteem, fame, glory, honour, (*more informal*) kudos, reputation, status
AN OPPOSITE IS dishonour
2 *Kate had better taste than she'd been given credit for.*
▸ recognition, acknowledgement, approval

**credit** VERB
1 *It is difficult to credit such an unlikely story*
▸ accept, believe, subscribe to, trust, have confidence in, have faith in, rely on, depend on, count on, endorse, reckon on, (*more informal*) swallow, (*informal*) buy
AN OPPOSITE IS disbelieve
2 *The idea is credited to Aristotle.*
▸ attribute to, ascribe to, assign to, attach to, associate (with)

**creditable** ADJECTIVE
*The team were on good form and put on a creditable performance.*
▸ commendable, laudable, respectable, estimable, admirable, praiseworthy, worthy, excellent, good, honourable, meritorious, well thought of
AN OPPOSITE IS unworthy

**creed** NOUN
1 *All are welcome regardless of race or creed.*
▸ faith, religion, beliefs, persuasion, convictions
2 *a belief in the religion's creed*
▸ doctrine, dogma, principles, tenets, system of belief

**creek** NOUN
*There used to be a toll bridge crossing the creek.*
▸ inlet, estuary, arm of the sea, bay

**creep** VERB
1 *She watched him creep under the table.*
▸ crawl, slither, slink, wriggle, worm your way, writhe, edge, inch, move slowly
2 *Gilly packed a suitcase and crept down the stairs.*
▸ slip, sneak, steal, move quietly, tiptoe

**creepy** ADJECTIVE
*The place gave her creepy feelings.*
▸ frightening, eerie, spooky, scary, weird, sinister, uncanny, unearthly, macabre, ominous
AN OPPOSITE IS pleasant

**crest** NOUN
1 *a bird with a bright crest*
▸ plume, tuft, comb
2 *We reached the crest of the hill.*
▸ peak, crown, brow, ridge, summit, top, apex
3 *the royal crest*
▸ insignia, regalia, emblem, badge, seal, sign, symbol

**crew** NOUN
1 *a ship's crew*
▸ company, complement, sailors, seamen
2 *a road-mending crew*
▸ team, gang, unit, party, squad

**crime** NOUN
1 *The report shows a decrease in street crime.*
▸ lawbreaking, lawlessness, delinquency, wrongdoing, transgression, misconduct, dishonesty, illegality
2 *Blackmail is a serious crime.*
▸ offence, misdeed, misdemeanour, transgression, illegal act, unlawful act, (*more informal*) racket, (*old use*) felony

**NAMES FOR TYPES OF CRIME**
These are names in general use, and not all of them are legal terms.

**crimes involving killing**: homicide, murder (intentional killing), manslaughter (unintentional killing), assassination (killing of a prominent figure).

**crimes involving stealing**: theft, robbery, burglary, mugging, pilfering; handling stolen goods.

**other violent crimes against people**: assault, rape (sexual assault), grievous bodily harm ((*informal*) GBH), actual bodily harm (less serious than grievous); battery; kidnapping, abduction, hijacking, piracy, terrorism.

**violent crimes against property**: sabotage, vandalism, arson (setting fire to property), criminal damage; drink-driving, joy-riding, being drunk and disorderly.

**other, usually non-violent, crimes against the state or against individuals**: treason; fraud, forgery, counterfeiting, corruption, embezzlement, extortion, blackmail, bribery, smuggling, drug-peddling; perjury (lying on oath).

**criminal** NOUN
*His friends were criminals, working with the smugglers.*
▸ lawbreaker, offender, villain, wrongdoer, delinquent, miscreant, convict, culprit, (*more informal*) crook

**criminal** ADJECTIVE
*Hardship can never justify criminal behaviour.*
▸ illegal, unlawful, illicit, dishonest, corrupt, nefarious, (*more informal*) crooked, (*more informal*) bent
OPPOSITES ARE legal, honest

**cringe** VERB
1 *The old man cringed, his hands shaking.*
▸ cower, shrink back, draw back, recoil, flinch, shy away, quail, tremble, crouch, quiver, dodge, duck, grovel

2 *I cringe when I hear those songs these days.*
► wince, blench, squirm, blush

**cripple** VERB

1 *The car hit her, crippling her for life.*
► disable, incapacitate, maim, injure, lame, damage, paralyse

2 *Industry was crippled by a series of strikes.*
► ruin, destroy, crush, paralyse, scupper, bring to a standstill, put out of action, spoil

**crippled** ADJECTIVE

1 *His crippled right leg is bent back at the knee.*
► disabled, deformed, lame, incapacitated, physically impaired, injured, maimed, paralysed, handicapped, hurt, invalid, mutilated

2 *Witnesses watched the crippled car being winched on to the Relay tender.*
► immobilized, damaged, incapacitated, out of action, sabotaged, useless

**crisis** NOUN

1 *Events in Europe were reaching a crisis.*
► climax, critical point, turning point, moment of truth

2 *The following year there was another economic crisis.*
► emergency, predicament, problem, danger, difficulty

**crisp** ADJECTIVE

1 *crisp biscuits*
► crunchy, crispy, brittle, crackly, fragile, crumbly
AN OPPOSITE IS soft

2 *a crisp morning in November*
► fresh, brisk, bracing, exhilarating, refreshing

3 *a crisp style of writing*
► terse, incisive, pithy, succinct, sparing, laconic

**criterion** NOUN

*The main criterion of good training is to reach the government's official standard.*
► basis, yardstick, measure, benchmark, point of reference, justification, principle, gauge

**critic** NOUN

1 *the most famous music critic of the time*
► commentator, reviewer, authority, expert, pundit, judge, analyst

2 *a major critic of government policy*
► detractor, attacker

**critical** ADJECTIVE

1 *a critical assessment of the available literature*
► analytical, objective, evaluative, discerning, perceptive

2 *He is highly critical of American foreign policy.*
► disapproving, censorious, derogatory (about), disparaging (about), scathing (about), uncomplimentary (about)
OPPOSITES ARE appreciative, complimentary (about)

3 *He only escaped death by moving his head at the critical moment.*
► crucial, vital, decisive, essential, all-important

4 *She was taken to hospital where her condition is described as critical.*
► serious, grave, dangerous, precarious
AN OPPOSITE IS safe

**criticism** NOUN

1 *The management have come in for a lot of criticism.*
► disapproval, blame, censure, disparagement, fault-finding, reproach, stricture, tirade, verbal attack, (more informal) flak

2 *Their work will be submitted for criticism.*
► evaluation, assessment, appraisal, analysis, judgement, appreciation

**criticize** VERB

1 *Police criticized motorists for using mobile phones while driving.*
► condemn, censure, find fault with, denounce, blame, castigate, disparage, denigrate, deprecate, (more informal) knock, (more informal) slam, (more informal) pan
AN OPPOSITE IS praise

2 *a review criticizing the work of four modern poets*
► appraise, assess, evaluate, analyse, judge, review

---

**crockery** NOUN

*The table had been laid and the crockery brought out.*
► dishes, plates, tableware, china, crocks, earthenware, porcelain, pottery, ceramics

TYPES OF CROCKERY

**things for eating off:** dinner service, tea set; plate, side plate, dinner plate, dessert plate.

**things for eating out of:** bowl, cereal bowl, soup bowl, salad bowl, sugar bowl.

**things for drinking from:** cup (and saucer), teacup, coffee cup, mug, beaker.

**containers:** jug, milk jug, pot, teapot, coffee pot, percolator, cafetière; dish, butter dish, tureen, gravy boat, cruet.

---

**crook** NOUN

1 *His head was lying in the crook of her arm.*
► bend, curve, angle

2 *She accused them of being crooks.*
► criminal, lawbreaker, villain, wrongdoer

**crooked** ADJECTIVE

1 *The picture looks slightly crooked.*
► askew, awry, lopsided, offcentre, slanting, angled, (more informal) skew-whiff

2 *The garden was a maze of crooked paths.*
► winding, twisting, tortuous, twisty, zigzag

3 *She put a crooked finger to her lips*
► bent, misshapen, deformed, bowed, curved, curving

4 *Several officials were probably crooked.*
► criminal, dishonest, corrupt, nefarious, (more informal) bent

**crop** NOUN

*My crop of Brussels sprouts are ready to eat.*
► harvest, yield, produce, gathering

**crop** VERB

1 *Sheep cropped grass in the fields.*
▶ graze on, browse on, eat, nibble, bite off
2 *She had to crop her long blonde hair.*
▶ cut short, cut, clip, trim, snip, shear

**crop up** *The same names keep cropping up over the years.*
▶ occur, arise, appear, come up, turn up, emerge, spring up, happen

**cross** ADJECTIVE

*Dad got cross and said I was setting a bad example.*
▶ angry, annoyed, testy, tetchy, vexed, irate, bad-tempered, cantankerous, crotchety, ill-tempered, irascible, irritable, peevish, short-tempered, (*more informal*) grumpy
AN OPPOSITE IS good-humoured

**cross** NOUN

1 *a difficult cross to bear*
▶ burden, problem, difficulty, misfortune, trial, tribulation, trouble, worry, grief, sorrow, affliction
2 *a cross between a yak and a cow*
▶ hybrid, cross-breed, amalgam (of), blend (of), combination (of), half-way house, mixture (of)

**cross** VERB

1 *The roads cross north of the town.*
▶ intersect, intertwine, meet
2 *There is only one place you can cross the river.*
▶ go across, pass over, ford, traverse
3 *It's better not to cross the common in the dark.*
▶ go across, walk across, traverse
4 *A stone bridge crossed the stream.*
▶ span, bridge, arch, go across, extend across, pass across
5 *He blew up if anyone crossed him.*
▶ oppose, annoy, defy, argue with, obstruct, thwart

**cross out** *He crossed out part of the sentence and rewrote it.*
▶ delete, strike out, erase, cancel

**crossroads** NOUN

*A large van was waiting at the crossroads.*
▶ junction, intersection, interchange

**crouch** VERB

*The boys crouched behind a large tree.*
▶ squat, kneel, stoop, bend, bob down, bow down, cower, cringe, duck, hunch, huddle

**crowd** NOUN

1 *The crowd dispersed quickly.*
▶ throng, multitude, mob, masses, horde, gathering, company, rabble, crush
2 *a large crowd at the ground*
▶ gate, attendance, audience, spectators

**crowd** VERB

1 *Some of them had crowded round a drinks machine.*
▶ gather, collect, cluster, congregate, huddle, muster, mass, swarm, surge
2 *The guests were crowding into the dining room.*
▶ stream, push, pile, pack, squeeze, swarm, flock, surge, jostle

**crowded** ADJECTIVE

*It was hard to find a space on the crowded beach.*
▶ packed, congested, overcrowded, swarming, teeming, thronging, cramped, full, busy, jammed, jostling, overflowing
OPPOSITES ARE empty, deserted

**crown** NOUN

1 *The Queen was wearing her crown.*
▶ coronet, diadem, tiara
2 *He paused at the crown of the hill*
▶ brow, crest, top, summit, peak, ridge, head, apex

**crown** VERB

1 *William was crowned in Westminster Abbey on Christmas Day.*
▶ install, enthrone, anoint
2 *He crowned his career with a diplomatic post in America.*
▶ cap, round off, top off, complete, conclude, consummate, fulfil, finish off, perfect

**crucial** ADJECTIVE

1 *Police investigation plays a crucial role in the criminal process.*
▶ major, central, pivotal, decisive, critical, important, momentous, serious
OPPOSITES ARE minor, unimportant
2 *Secrecy is crucial in this matter.*
▶ paramount, essential, vital, critical, indispensable

**crude** ADJECTIVE

1 *increased production of crude oil*
▶ unrefined, unpurified, unprocessed, natural, raw
AN OPPOSITE IS refined
2 *a crude method of counting votes*
▶ primitive, simple, basic, rudimentary, rough, makeshift, improvised, homespun, clumsy, unrefined, amateurish, awkward, inelegant, inept
OPPOSITES ARE sophisticated, advanced
3 *He went in for a very crude type of humour.*
▶ coarse, indecent, vulgar, bawdy, lewd, offensive, obscene

**USAGE** Obscene is a very strong word and often implies an intention to offend or corrupt people.

**cruel** ADJECTIVE

1 *Their opponents were huge cruel men. Hunting is widely regarded as a cruel sport.*
▶ brutal, savage, vicious, fierce, ferocious, barbaric, callous, heartless, cold-blooded, pitiless, ruthless, merciless, vile, sadistic, brutish
OPPOSITES ARE gentle, humane, kind, compassionate
2 *Her father's sudden death was a cruel blow.*
▶ severe, harsh, bitter, grim, painful
OPPOSITES ARE mild, gentle

**cruelty** NOUN

*The rebellion was put down with great cruelty.*
▶ brutality, savagery, viciousness, ferocity, barbarity, callousness, heartlessness, cold-bloodedness, ruthlessness

**cruise** NOUN

*a sea cruise*
▶ voyage, journey, trip, sail

**cruise** VERB

*The family decided to cruise in the Mediterranean.*
▶ sail, voyage, travel, journey, take a cruise

**crumb** NOUN

*crumbs of bread  a small crumb of comfort*
▶ fragment, grain, morsel, scrap, bit, speck, particle, shred

**crumble** VERB

**1** *The damaged buildings were beginning to crumble.*
▶ disintegrate, break up, collapse, fall apart, fall down, decay, decompose, deteriorate
**2** *He crumbled the soil into a fine powder.*
▶ crush, grind, pound, powder, pulverize, break into pieces, fragment

**crumbly** ADJECTIVE

*crumbly cake*
▶ powdery, friable, granular
AN OPPOSITE IS solid

**crumple** VERB

*It's hard not to crumple your clothes in such a tiny car.*
▶ crease, crush, crinkle, wrinkle, squash

**crunch** VERB

**1** *She sat there crunching biscuits.*
▶ munch, chomp, champ, masticate, devour
**2** *He was fed up with getting his head crunched in rugger matches.*
▶ crush, pound, pulverize, grind, smash

**crunch** NOUN

*(informal) The crunch came when all the men returned from the war.*
▶ critical time, moment of truth, crisis, crux, decision time

**crusade** NOUN

*a crusade against street crime*
▶ campaign, movement, drive, effort, struggle, fight, push

**crush** VERB

**1** *He nearly crushed his arm in the lift doors.*
▶ squash, squeeze, mangle, crunch, scrunch, compress, mash, break, bruise, grind
**2** *She was afraid she would crush her dress.*
▶ crease, crumple, crinkle, wrinkle, squash
**3** *The army crushed the rebellion in a short time.*
▶ suppress, subdue, quell, quash, put down, defeat, vanquish, overcome

**crush** NOUN

*There was quite a crush by the doors.*
▶ crowd, throng, congestion, jam, press, multitude, mob

**crust** NOUN

*The paint left in the pot had formed a hard crust.*
▶ covering, skin, surface, shell, exterior, outside

**crusty** ADJECTIVE

**1** *a meal of dry crusty bread and cheese*
▶ crisp, crispy, brittle, crunchy
**2** *He seems so crusty these days.*
▶ irritable, grumpy, gruff, grouchy, tetchy, testy, bad-tempered, irascible, fractious

**crux** NOUN

*Here lay the crux of the matter.*
▶ essence, nub, heart, core, kernel, central point, crucial issue, main issue

---

**cry** VERB This word is often overused. Here are some alternatives:

**1** *Debbie looked upset and about to cry.*
▶ weep, shed tears, sob, howl, whimper, snivel, blubber, bawl, wail
USAGE The last six synonyms are unfriendly or disapproving, and sob means to cry uncontrollably and unattractively. *Weep* and *shed tears* are more neutral in tone, although *weep* is more literary.
**2** *'Come on!' cried Sam.*
▶ call, yell, exclaim, shout, shriek, scream, bawl
**cry off** *The game was cancelled when three players cried off.*
▶ withdraw, back out, cancel, excuse yourself
**cry out** *Somebody was crying out in the darkness.*
▶ call out, yell, scream, screech, shout, shriek

---

**cry** NOUN

**1** *a cry of pain*
▶ call, shout, yell, shriek, scream, screech, roar, bellow
**2** *a cry for help*
▶ appeal, plea, entreaty

**cryptic** ADJECTIVE

*a cryptic note about a ransom*
▶ mysterious, obscure, puzzling, enigmatic, unclear, perplexing, unintelligible, coded, veiled, secret
OPPOSITES ARE clear, straightforward

**cuddle** VERB

*So far he had only kissed and cuddled her.*
▶ hug, caress, embrace, hold, clasp, pet, fondle, huddle against, snuggle against

**cue** NOUN

*A quick glance was her cue to speak.*
▶ signal, sign, prompt, hint, reminder

**cuff** VERB

*She cuffed him round the head.*
▶ hit, box, smack, thump, biff, clout, strike

**culminate** VERB

**culminate in** *The campaign culminated in a massive demonstration in central London.*
▶ build up to, lead up to, come to a climax with, rise to a peak with, reach a finale with, conclude with, end with, finish with, terminate with, close with

**culmination** NOUN

*These events marked the culmination of a two-month festival.*

▶ climax, pinnacle, high point, peak, height, conclusion, crowning moment

**culprit** NOUN

*New evidence showed that he was not the culprit after all.*

▶ guilty party, person responsible, offender, criminal, wrongdoer, miscreant, transgressor

**cult** NOUN

1 *a cult that worshipped the moon*
▶ sect, religious group, denomination
2 *The sport had become a cult in parts of the country.*
▶ craze, fashion, trend, vogue, enthusiasm

**cultivate** VERB

1 *Peasants cultivated the land.*
▶ farm, till, dig, work, plough
2 *They were helped with cultivating food crops.*
▶ grow, raise, rear, sow, plant, tend, produce
3 *We need to cultivate a better attitude to work.*
▶ develop, foster, nurture, encourage, promote, pursue, try to achieve, cherish, further, improve

**cultural** ADJECTIVE

*a country's cultural heritage*
▶ artistic, intellectual, aesthetic, educational, elevating, enlightening, improving

**culture** NOUN

1 *modern popular culture*
▶ civilization, society, intellectual activity, arts, traditions, customs, education, learning
2 *a person of culture*
▶ intellectual awareness, achievement, enlightenment, education, discernment, good taste

**cultured** ADJECTIVE

*a pleasant, cultured man*
▶ cultivated, educated, well-educated, well-read, enlightened, civilized, erudite, artistic, refined, urbane, highbrow, knowledgeable, scholarly
AN OPPOSITE IS ignorant

**cumbersome** ADJECTIVE

*The suitcases were cumbersome rather than heavy.*
▶ unwieldy, awkward, bulky, clumsy, hefty, burdensome

**cunning** ADJECTIVE

1 *a cunning plan*
▶ crafty, wily, artful, sly, devious, knowing, guileful, disingenuous, machiavellian
OPPOSITES ARE ingenuous, guileless
2 *The crime was solved by cunning detective work.*
▶ skilful, clever, shrewd, astute, adroit, subtle, ingenious

**cunning** NOUN

*The defence counsel will need quite a bit of cunning.*
▶ guile, craftiness, artfulness, shrewdness, astuteness, adroitness, deviousness

**cup** NOUN

1 *They were drinking tea from pretty cups.*
▶ teacup, coffee cup, mug, tankard
2 *a silver cup for the winner*
▶ trophy, award, prize

**cupboard** NOUN

*The tools and nails were kept in a cupboard.*
▶ cabinet, closet, locker, dresser, (for clothes) wardrobe, (for food) larder

**curb** VERB

*He tried to curb his temper.*
▶ restrain, suppress, control, contain, check, hold back, stifle
AN OPPOSITE IS release

**curdle** VERB

*The milk began to curdle.*
▶ coagulate, congeal, clot, thicken, turn, turn sour, go lumpy, go sour

**cure** VERB

1 *A long period of rest will cure his ailment.*
▶ heal, remedy, treat, alleviate, counteract, ease, help, palliate, relieve
OPPOSITES ARE aggravate, worsen
2 *The fault may be difficult to cure.*
▶ correct, rectify, mend, repair, put right, solve, (more informal) fix

**cure** NOUN

1 *a cure for cancer*
▶ remedy, treatment, antidote, medicine, prescription, restorative, panacea, palliative, therapy
2 *Her unexpected cure amazed the doctors*
▶ recovery, healing, restoration to health

**curiosity** NOUN

1 *I found it hard to contain my curiosity.*
▶ inquisitiveness, interest, nosiness, prying, meddling, snooping
**USAGE** The last four synonyms are unfavourable in tone, whereas the first two are neutral.
2 *He had an elephant's head displayed as a curiosity in his house.*
▶ novelty, oddity, curio, rarity, collector's item

**curious** ADJECTIVE

1 *I was curious about the reason for this unexpected visit.*
▶ inquisitive, intrigued, interested, puzzled, eager to know, agog
OPPOSITES ARE incurious, unconcerned, indifferent.
2 *He walked off with a curious jerking motion.*
▶ strange, odd, peculiar, queer, funny, bizarre, unusual, extraordinary, eccentric
AN OPPOSITE IS normal

**curl** NOUN

1 *Her hair was a mass of curls.*
▶ ringlet, wave, coil, loop, kink
2 *a pattern with repeated curls*
▶ loop, spiral, swirl, twist, bend, circle, curve, scroll, turn

3 *There was a curl of smoke in the distance.*
► spiral, coil, swirl, twirl, whorl, corkscrew

**curl** VERB
1 *Smoke curled from the tall chimney.*
► coil, spiral, twirl, swirl, furl
2 *The path curls round old tree trunks.*
► wind, twist, curve, meander, snake, writhe, zigzag
3 *Sarah curled an arm round his waist.*
► wind, twine, entwine, wrap, twist
4 *a treatment to curl the hair*
► crimp, wave, frizz, perm

**curly** ADJECTIVE
*thick curly hair*
► wavy, curled, curling, crinkly, kinky, frizzy, fuzzy, crimped, permed
AN OPPOSITE IS straight

**currency** NOUN
1 *The euro simplifies the business of getting foreign currency.*
► money, legal tender, coinage, cash, coins, banknotes
2 *This view of the matter has gained currency in the last few years.*
► acceptance, popularity, circulation, prevalence
**USAGE** You can also say ... *has become more widespread* or ... *has become more prevalent.*

**current** ADJECTIVE
1 *keeping abreast of current events*
► modern, contemporary, present-day, topical
AN OPPOSITE IS past
2 *The opinion is still current.*
► common, prevalent, prevailing, widespread, popular, accepted
AN OPPOSITE IS obsolete
3 *a current driving licence*
► valid, usable, up to date
OPPOSITES ARE out of date, expired
4 *the current administration in the White House*
► present, incumbent, existing, extant, reigning
OPPOSITES ARE past, former

**current** NOUN
1 *a current of air*
► stream, flow, draught, jet, course
2 *The girls were in danger from the strong currents.*
► tide, undertow, drift

**curriculum** NOUN
*the school curriculum*
► syllabus, programme of study, course

**curse** NOUN
1 *John caught his finger in the door and let out a curse.*
► swear word, oath, expletive, profanity, obscenity, blasphemy, exclamation
2 *The witch had put a curse on them.*
► malediction, imprecation, jinx
3 *the curse of unemployment*
► affliction, blight, scourge, plague, bane, misfortune, torment, evil

**curse** VERB
*I listened to him cursing and shouting.*
► swear, utter profanities, blaspheme, damn, fulminate
**be cursed with** *The family was cursed for years with sickness and poverty.*
► be afflicted with, be blighted with, be plagued with, be troubled by, be burdened with

**cursory** ADJECTIVE
*a cursory read of the newspaper*
► brief, perfunctory, superficial, desultory, hasty, hurried, quick, fleeting, casual
OPPOSITES ARE thorough, intensive

**curt** ADJECTIVE
*Carl dismissed the idea with a curt grunt.*
► abrupt, blunt, harsh, terse, gruff, rude, offhand, brusque, insensitive, outspoken, plain-spoken
OPPOSITES ARE polite, courteous

**curtail** VERB
1 *Bad weather forced them to curtail their holiday.*
► shorten, break off, truncate, cut
AN OPPOSITE IS extend
2 *economic measures needed to curtail public spending*
► reduce, decrease, limit, cut back, restrict, restrain, control

**curtain** NOUN
*Clive closed the curtains.*
► drape, drapery, hanging, blind, screen

**curve** NOUN
1 *a series of curves in the road*
► bend, turn, twist, loop
2 *a tall window with a curve at the top*
► arch, arc, bow, crescent

**curve** VERB
*The river curved to the west.*
► bend, twist, wind, loop, snake, turn, swerve

**curved** ADJECTIVE
1 *a tall building with a curved roof*
► arched, bowed, rounded, humped, crescent, vaulted, convex, bent
OPPOSITES ARE flat, straight
2 *The road was narrow and curved.*
► twisty, twisted, sinuous, meandering, serpentine, sweeping
AN OPPOSITE IS straight

**cushion** NOUN
1 *She put a cushion behind her and leaned back.*
► pillow, bolster, headrest, hassock, pad, beanbag
2 *a cushion against inflation*
► protection, buffer, shield, defence

**cushion** VERB
*Buffers would cushion the impact of a collision.*
► absorb, soften, deaden, lessen, reduce, mitigate, muffle

**cushy** ADJECTIVE
*(informal) a cushy job*
► easy, undemanding, comfortable, secure, *(informal)* jammy

a b c d e f g h i j k l m n o p q r s t u v w x y z

## custody NOUN

**1** *Sean had given custody of the baby to her brother.*
▶ care, guardianship, charge, protection, safe-keeping, keeping, possession

**2** *He had died when still in police custody.*
▶ detention, captivity, confinement, imprisonment, incarceration, (on) remand

## custom NOUN

**1** *local customs dating back to the thirteenth century*
▶ tradition, practice, usage, institution, convention, procedure, observance, form, habit, way, etiquette, manner, formality, routine

**2** *It is our custom to visit relatives at the weekends.*
▶ practice, habit, routine, way, rule, policy, wont

**3** *The shop offers discounts to attract custom*
▶ business, trade, customers, buyers, patronage, support

## customary ADJECTIVE

**1** *It is customary to stand during the playing of the anthem. the customary rules of behaviour*
▶ traditional, normal, usual, common, conventional, established, expected, general, ordinary, popular, prevailing, routine, fashionable
AN OPPOSITE IS unusual

**2** *Dr Ali fell once again into his customary silence.*
▶ usual, accustomed, regular, wonted, habitual, typical

## customer NOUN

*The business is trying to attract younger customers.*
▶ shopper, buyer, purchaser, client, consumer, patron
AN OPPOSITE IS seller

## cut NOUN

**1** *He had a cut on his hand.*
▶ gash, wound, injury, nick, incision, scratch, graze
**USAGE** *Scratch* and *graze* do not normally involve breaking of the skin and escape of blood.

**2** *She had to accept a small cut in pay.*
▶ reduction, decrease, lowering (of), lessening (of)

**3** *The leader of the gang demanded a higher cut.*
▶ share, portion, slice, (*more informal*) whack

## cut VERB

**1** *He had cut his finger with a kitchen knife.*
▶ gash, pierce, wound, injure, slash, nick, incise, scratch, graze
**USAGE** *Scratch* and *graze* do not normally involve breaking of the skin and escape of blood.

**2** *Cut the vegetables into small pieces.*
▶ slice, chop, dice, cube, divide, pare

**3** *She was going to have her hair cut. It will soon be time to start cutting the grass again.*
▶ trim, clip, crop, mow

**4** *The supermarkets have cut prices on a wide range of goods.*
▶ reduce, lower, lessen, (*more informal*) slash

**5** *Parts of the story were cut to make the film version.*
▶ omit, remove, delete, excise, take out, edit out

**6** *You will have to cut your essay by about a third.*
▶ shorten, abridge, condense, reduce, precis, truncate

**7** *The remarks were spiteful and cut her deeply.*
▶ hurt, offend, upset, wound

## cut down

**1** *Men are cutting the trees down.*
▶ fell, hew, lop

**2** *I'm trying to cut down some of these expenses.*
▶ reduce, decrease, lower, lessen

**cut in** *Tessa cut in with a remark that made everyone laugh.*
▶ interrupt, butt in, break in, interject, intervene, intrude

## cut off

**1** *The blade nearly cut off her finger.*
▶ sever, chop off, amputate, hack off, remove

**2** *The Gas Board threatened to cut off the supply.*
▶ disconnect, discontinue, interrupt, suspend
OPPOSITES ARE restore, reconnect

**3** *Storms cut off the village for several days.*
▶ isolate, separate, seclude

**4** *Her family had cut her off without a penny.*
▶ disinherit, disown, reject, repudiate, cast aside

**cut out** *The report mentioned several ways in which we could cut out inefficiencies.*
▶ remove, eliminate, excise, get rid of

**cut up** *Cut up the meat into small cubes.*
▶ chop, slice, dice, carve

## cutback NOUN

*cutbacks in spending*
▶ reduction, cut, decrease, saving, economy, limit (to)

## cute ADJECTIVE

*When I was young I had a cute little collie dog.*
▶ appealing, lovely, delightful, attractive, pretty, endearing, adorable, engaging

## cutting ADJECTIVE

*They had to endure some cutting remarks about their lifestyle.*
▶ hurtful, scathing, caustic, sharp, sarcastic, acid, acerbic, bitter, spiteful, vicious, abrasive

## cutting NOUN

*a newspaper cutting*
▶ clipping, snippet, extract, excerpt

## cycle NOUN

*a cycle of growth and decline lasting 75 years*
▶ pattern, sequence, round, circle, series, era, period, revolution, rotation

## cyclical ADJECTIVE

*cyclical changes in the climate*
▶ recurring, recurrent, periodic, repeated, seasonal

## cylinder NOUN

*The paper is rolled up to form a cylinder.*
▶ column, tube, drum, reel, spool

## cynic NOUN

*Only a cynic would think her dishonest.*
▶ sceptic, doubter, pessimist, doom merchant
OPPOSITES ARE optimist, idealist

**cynical** ADJECTIVE

*I may be unduly cynical in thinking they are only in it for the money.*
▶ sceptical, distrustful, suspicious, disbelieving, pessimistic, negative, doubting, questioning
AN OPPOSITE IS optimistic

**cynicism** NOUN

*The touch of cynicism in his voice struck a sour note.*
▶ scepticism, doubt, disbelief, suspicion, incredulity, pessimism

**cyst** NOUN

*If a cyst forms in the eye, it will need to be removed.*
▶ growth, abscess, blister, (technical) vesicle

# Dd

**dab** VERB

*He dabbed paint on the scratch.*
▶ pat, daub, touch, apply (to)

**dabble** VERB

1 *The children dabbled their feet in the water.*
▶ dip, paddle, splash, wet
2 **dabble in** *She began to dabble in astrology.*
▶ toy with, dip into, tinker with, trifle with

**daft** ADJECTIVE

*a daft idea*
▶ silly, stupid, absurd, foolish, crazy, unwise, idiotic

**daily** ADJECTIVE

*a daily occurrence*
▶ everyday, day-to-day, regular

**dainty** ADJECTIVE

1 *a dainty lace handkerchief*
▶ delicate, elegant, exquisite, neat, charming, fine, graceful, pretty
OPPOSITES ARE clumsy, crude
2 *a dainty eater*
▶ fastidious, choosy, fussy, finicky, discriminating, careful
AN OPPOSITE IS gross

**dally** VERB

*There's not enough time to dally.*
▶ dawdle, delay, linger, loiter, waste time, idle, loaf, play about, procrastinate, (more informal) hang about, (informal) dilly-dally, (literary) tarry

**dam** NOUN

*The dam could burst after such heavy rain.*
▶ barrier, barrage, embankment, bank, dike, wall, weir

**dam** VERB

*The river has been dammed to form a lake.*
▶ block, obstruct, barricade, check, hold back, restrict, stem, stop

**damage** NOUN

*Fortunately the thieves caused little damage.*
▶ harm, injury, destruction, devastation, havoc, hurt, mutilation

**damage** VERB

*High winds damaged properties along the sea front.*
▶ harm hurt, injure, spoil, wreck, blemish, disfigure, deface, mutilate

**damn** VERB

1 *The voices damned him to hell.*
▶ curse, put a curse on, (more formal) execrate
2 *They had been damned for something that was not their fault.*
▶ condemn, censure, blame, abuse, revile, criticize, denounce, castigate, reprove

**damnation** NOUN

*condemned to eternal damnation*
▶ doom, perdition, condemnation, hell, ruin
AN OPPOSITE IS salvation

**damp** ADJECTIVE

1 *Someone had applied a damp cloth to her head.*
▶ moist, dampened, moistened, wet, wetted, soggy
2 *The air was damp and cold.*
▶ wet, drizzly, muggy, humid

**dampen** VERB

1 *Dampen a soft cloth.*
▶ moisten, wet, damp
2 *Nothing could dampen their enthusiasm now.*
▶ lessen, diminish, deaden, dull, stifle, muffle, restrain, smother, discourage, dishearten

---

**dance** NOUN

*My grandparents first met at a dance.*
▶ ball, disco, (more informal) hop
RELATED ADJECTIVE choreographic
RELATED NOUN choreography

**NAMES FOR TYPES OF DANCE**

**main styles of dance:** ballet, ballroom dancing, country dancing, barn dancing, folk dance, formation dancing, line dancing, lap dancing, old-time dancing, rock and roll, tap dance.

**some dances from around the world:** waltz, veleta, quickstep, foxtrot, two-step, beguine, tango, rumba, mambo, samba, bossa nova, paso doble, fandango, flamenco, bolero, charleston, cha-cha, tarantella, black bottom, cakewalk, can-can, clog dance, tap dance, jig, morris dance, rigadoon, turkey trot, Highland fling, bhangra, lambada, belly dance, Bharata Natyan, Kathak, Capoeira, Noh dance-drama, Mapouka, kabuki, skank, meringue, hula.

**group dances:** ecossaise, eightsome reel, strathspey, hokey-cokey, Paul Jones, line dancing, quadrille, reel, roundelay, conga, roundelay, square dance, strip the willow. ▶▶

---

**old dances (often also a piece of music in the same time):** waltz, minuet, polonaise, gavotte, allemande, bourrée, galop, chaconne, courante, galliard, gigue, hornpipe, mazurka, passepied, pavane, polka, sarabande, siciliano.
**modern dances:** bop, body-popping, boogaloo, boogie, break-dancing, disco, jive, salsa, shake, shimmy, shuffle, skank, stomp, twist.

**dance** VERB

*Children danced around playfully.*
▶ caper, cavort, frisk, frolic, skip, prance, leap, gambol, hop, jig, jump

**danger** NOUN

1 *There is a danger of flooding on low ground.*
▶ risk, threat, chance, probability, possibility, likelihood, prospect, liability

2 *The contamination could become a danger to public health.*
▶ threat, hazard, menace, risk

3 *There was a real sense of danger about the place.*
▶ insecurity, vulnerability, uncertainty, precariousness

4 *Their very lives were in danger.*
▶ peril, jeopardy, (at) risk
AN OPPOSITE IS safety

**dangerous** ADJECTIVE

1 *Building at such a height can be dangerous work.*
▶ hazardous, perilous, risky, unsafe, precarious, insecure, tricky

2 *He was charged with dangerous driving.*
▶ reckless, careless

3 *a dangerous criminal*
▶ ruthless, violent, vicious, desperate

**dangle** VERB

1 *There were curtains dangling above my head.*
▶ hang, droop, swing, flap, sway, trail, be suspended, wave about

2 *She dangled the keys in his face.*
▶ wave, swing, brandish, flourish, hold

**dank** ADJECTIVE

*the dank basement*
▶ damp, musty, chilly, clammy, moist, unaired

**dare** VERB

1 *No one dared to say anything.*
▶ have the courage, be brave enough, take the risk (of), take a chance, venture

2 *She dared him to jump.*
▶ challenge, defy, provoke, goad, taunt

**daring** ADJECTIVE

*a daring attack*
▶ bold, brave, courageous, adventurous, audacious, intrepid, gallant, confident, dauntless, enterprising, heroic, valiant, (more informal) plucky
AN OPPOSITE IS timid

**daring** NOUN

*a feat of great daring*
▶ audacity, boldness, bravery, courage, enterprise

**dark** ADJECTIVE

1 *a dark room*
▶ dim, dingy, dull, gloomy, unlit, unilluminated, shadowy
OPPOSITES ARE light, bright

2 *a dark night*
▶ black, pitch-black, starless, moonless, unlit, unilluminated
OPPOSITES ARE light, bright

3 *a dark colour*
▶ deep, strong, heavy
OPPOSITES ARE pale, light

4 *a dark secret*
▶ mysterious, enigmatic, hidden, obscure, impenetrable, cryptic

5 *dark thoughts*
▶ pessimistic, gloomy, sinister, sombre, grim, dismal, bleak, cheerless, fatalistic
AN OPPOSITE IS optimistic

**dark** NOUN

*afraid of the dark*
▶ darkness, blackness, gloom, night, night-time
AN OPPOSITE IS light

**darken** VERB

1 *The sky darkened.*
▶ become dark, become overcast, cloud over
OPPOSITES ARE lighten, brighten

2 *These fears darkened his life for many years.*
▶ overshadow, shadow, blacken, threaten, dim, make gloomy
OPPOSITES ARE lighten, brighten

**darling** ADJECTIVE

*his darling wife*
▶ dear, dearest, beloved, adored, cherished, treasured

**darling** ADJECTIVE

*his darling wife*
▶ dear, dearest, beloved, adored, cherished, treasured

**darling** NOUN

1 *Jane had always been his darling.*
▶ beloved, loved one, love, sweetheart, dear, dearest

2 *the darling of the gods*
▶ favourite, pet, idol

**dart** VERB

*Children were darting about everywhere.*
▶ dash, rush, hurtle, leap, shoot, spring, bound, flit, fly, move suddenly, (more informal) whiz, (more informal) zip

**dart** NOUN

*a poisoned dart*
▶ bolt, arrow, shaft, missile

**dash** NOUN
*They made a dash for the door.*
▶ rush, bolt, leap, sprint, spurt, race, run, chase

**dash** VERB
**1** *We dashed home as soon as we could.*
▶ rush, race, bolt, tear, hasten, hurry, speed, shoot, run, sprint, chase, dart, fly, hasten, (*informal*) zoom
**2** *He dashed the plate against the wall.*
▶ smash, crash, hurl, strike, throw, knock

**dashing** ADJECTIVE
*a dashing captain in the Scots Guards*
▶ handsome, debonair, stylish, elegant, flamboyant, lively

**data** NOUN
*a group collecting data on teenage pregnancies*
▶ information, details, particulars, facts and figures, statistics, evidence, material

**date** NOUN
**1** *coins and pottery from a very early date*
▶ time, age, era, period
**2** *She was in danger of missing her date with Paul.*
▶ meeting, appointment, rendezvous, engagement, assignation, fixture
**3** *Mary was his date for the evening.*
▶ partner, escort, girlfriend (or boyfriend)

**dated** ADJECTIVE
*The design looks rather dated.*
▶ old-fashioned, outdated, archaic, obsolete, antiquated, (*more informal*) out of the ark

**daub** VERB
*The walls of the house were daubed with graffiti.*
▶ smear, plaster, cover, bedaub, spatter, smother

**daunt** VERB
*It's a situation that would daunt much tougher people than me.*
▶ intimidate, alarm, deter, discourage, unnerve, frighten, overawe, put off, dismay, dishearten, dispirit, depress
AN OPPOSITE IS encourage

**daunting** ADJECTIVE
*They had set themselves the daunting task of writing two thousand words a day.*
▶ arduous, difficult, onerous, tough

**dauntless** ADJECTIVE
*a spirited and dauntless young woman*
▶ fearless, resolute, determined, courageous, brave, intrepid, plucky, gritty

**dawdle** VERB
*Ruth dawdled back through the wood, reluctant to return.*
▶ linger, dally, take your time, delay, idle, (*more informal*) dilly-dally
AN OPPOSITE IS hurry

**dawn** NOUN
**1** *We got up at dawn.*
▶ daybreak, sunrise, break of day, first light, (*more informal*) first thing
AN OPPOSITE IS dusk

**2** *the dawn of modern civilization*
▶ beginning, start, birth, origin, genesis, advent, emergence

**day** NOUN
**1** *He looked after Lucy during the day while I was at work.*
▶ daytime, daylight
AN OPPOSITE IS night
**2** *The girls are required to plan their own day.*
▶ working day, working time, work time, period of work
**3** *He was the leading musician of the day.*
▶ age, period, time, era, epoch

**daydream** NOUN
*She tried to shake off her daydreams.*
▶ reverie, fantasy, trance, fancy, dream, vision, imagining, absent-mindedness, meditation, musing, illusion, pipe dream

**daydream** VERB
*He went out, leaving me to dress and daydream.*
▶ fantasize, dream, muse, meditate, be lost in thought, imagine

**daylight** NOUN
*Until eight o'clock there is no daylight in our room.*
▶ sunlight, light of day, natural light

**daze** VERB
**1** *The fall dazed him for a few minutes.*
▶ stun, stupefy, shock
**2** *She was dazed by the news.*
▶ astound, amaze, astonish, startle, dumbfound, bewilder, stagger

**dazzle** VERB
**1** *The sunlight burst through the window and dazzled him.*
▶ daze, blind
**2** *The beauty of the place dazzled her.*
▶ overpower, overwhelm, overawe, impress, amaze, astonish

**dead** ADJECTIVE
**1** *Both her parents were dead.*
▶ deceased, departed, passed on, gone
OPPOSITES ARE alive, living
**2** *There was a dead animal on the road.*
▶ lifeless, killed, inanimate
**3** *Latin is a dead language.*
▶ extinct, obsolete, defunct, disused, died out
AN OPPOSITE IS existing
**4** *My feet were dead with cold.*
▶ numb, deadened, insensitive, paralysed, without feeling
AN OPPOSITE IS sensitive
**5** *The battery was dead.*
▶ flat, unresponsive, defunct, inoperative, not working, burnt out, used up, useless, worn out
AN OPPOSITE IS operational
**6** *When Sheila picked up the phone again the line was dead.*
▶ not working, inoperative, out of order, unresponsive

**7** *The place is dead on a Friday night.*
▶ lifeless, dreary, uninteresting, boring, dull, moribund, slow
OPPOSITES ARE lively, exciting

**8** *(informal) He felt dead by the time he got home.*
▶ exhausted, worn out, drained, tired

**9** *He is the dead image of his brother.*
▶ exact, absolute, perfect, complete, utter, downright

**dead** ADVERB
*The road ahead was dead straight.*
▶ completely, absolutely, perfectly, utterly

**deaden** VERB
**1** *Mufflers deaden the noise.*
▶ muffle, soften, mute, damp, reduce, quieten, smother, stifle, suppress, weaken, cushion, lessen, check, hush
OPPOSITES ARE amplify, sharpen

**2** *A local anaesthetic will deaden the pain.*
▶ numb, stifle, dull, blunt, suppress, alleviate, soothe, desensitize, anaesthetize
OPPOSITES ARE intensify, aggravate

**deadline** NOUN
*a new deadline for withdrawing troops*
▶ time limit, target date, latest time

**deadlock** NOUN
*The talks had reached deadlock*
▶ stalemate, impasse, standstill, stand-off
AN OPPOSITE IS breakthrough

**deadly** ADJECTIVE
**1** *a deadly poison*
▶ lethal, noxious, harmful, mortal, dangerous
AN OPPOSITE IS harmless

**2** *a deadly disease*
▶ terminal, fatal, life-threatening, destructive
AN OPPOSITE IS mild

**3** *(informal) The party turned out to be deadly.*
▶ dull, boring, dreary, tedious, unexciting, uninteresting
OPPOSITES ARE lively, exciting

**4** *He fired an arrow with a deadly aim.*
▶ unerring, unfailing, true, perfect

**deaf** ADJECTIVE
**1** *By this time he was deaf and nearly blind.*
▶ hard of hearing

**2** *deaf to They were deaf to all our pleas.*
▶ indifferent to, unmoved by, heedless of, oblivious to, unconcerned with

**deafening** ADJECTIVE
*a deafening roar*
▶ loud, noisy, piercing, ear-splitting, booming, thunderous, overpowering

**deal** NOUN
**1** *He was good at business deals and not much more.*
▶ agreement, arrangement, negotiation, transaction, settlement, contract, bargain, understanding

**2** *Shoppers should look around for the best deal.*
▶ buy, bargain, transaction

**a good deal** or **a great deal** *We have already achieved a great deal.*
▶ a lot, much, plenty, a large amount, a large quantity

**deal** VERB
**1** *She dealt the cards for another round.*
▶ give out, distribute, share out, dispense, apportion, allot, assign, divide, (informal) dole out

**2** *The man dealt him a blow on the head*
▶ deliver, inflict, give, administer, apply, mete out

**3** *He deals in stocks and shares.*
▶ trade, do business, buy and sell, traffic

**4** *deal with a difficult issue to deal with*
▶ handle, manage, tackle, cope with, attend to, come to grips with, resolve, control, consider, grapple with, look after, see to, sort out, take action on

**5** *deal with The book deals with several important topics.*
▶ be concerned with, treat, cover, tackle, explain

**dealer** NOUN
*an antique dealer  a dealer in second-hand cars*
▶ trader, supplier, merchant, wholesaler, retailer, merchandiser, shopkeeper, stockist, tradesman

**dear** ADJECTIVE
**1** *They soon became dear friends.*
▶ beloved, close, intimate, lovable, loved, valued, darling
AN OPPOSITE IS hated

**2** *Fruit is dear at this time of year.*
▶ expensive, costly, high-priced, overpriced, exorbitant, (more informal) pricey
AN OPPOSITE IS cheap

**dear** NOUN
*Everyone agrees he's a dear.*
▶ darling, lovable person, treasure, pet

**dearly** ADVERB
*She loved Simon dearly.*
▶ deeply, intensely, profoundly, fondly, tenderly, very much, a great deal

**death** NOUN
**1** *Charles phoned to tell her of her uncle's death.*
▶ dying, passing, passing away, end
RELATED ADJECTIVE mortal

**2** *The disaster caused many deaths*
▶ casualty, fatality
RELATED ADJECTIVE fatal

**3** *The news meant the death of all their dreams.*
▶ end, ending, finish, collapse, ruin, destruction, termination, cessation

**put to death** *The king put all the conspirators to death.*
▶ execute, kill, have killed

**debase** VERB
*We debase art by praising such trashy work.*
▶ degrade, demean, devalue, cheapen, sully, discredit, defile, dishonour, vulgarize, lower the tone of, pollute

**debatable** ADJECTIVE
*It is debatable whether the public wants this sort of sensationalism.*
▶ arguable, questionable, disputable, doubtful, dubious, a moot point, open to doubt, open to question, contentious, controversial, controvertible, problematical, uncertain
AN OPPOSITE IS indisputable

**debate** NOUN
*a debate about personal freedom*
▶ discussion, argument, exchange of views, controversy, deliberation, contention, dialogue, dispute, (more formal) dialectic, (more formal) disputation

**debate** VERB
**1** *Parliament will debate schemes for reducing traffic in cities.*
▶ discuss, consider, deliberate, confer about, exchange views on, dispute, argue, weigh up
**2** *I am debating whether to get in touch with them.*
▶ consider, think over, ponder, deliberate, contemplate, reflect, (more informal) mull over

**debris** NOUN
**1** *There was debris all around from the collapsed buildings.*
▶ rubbish, rubble, ruins, remains, wreckage
**2** *Use rubber gloves to clean out debris from the gutters.*
▶ waste, remains, detritus, refuse, litter, bits, dregs, scraps

**debt** NOUN
**1** *The state is encouraging students to build up large debts.*
▶ money owed, arrears, financial obligation, financial commitment, bill
**2** *I owe you a great debt for your kindness*
▶ duty, indebtedness, obligation
**in debt** *By the end of the year he was heavily in debt.*
▶ owing money, in arrears, insolvent
**in someone's debt** *I shall be forever in your debt.*
▶ grateful to, indebted to, obliged to, beholden to

**debtor** NOUN
*Debtors who fail to pay their hotel bill are not usually sent to prison any more.*
▶ bankrupt, defaulter

**debut** NOUN
*The new car has made its debut in Birmingham.*
▶ first appearance, launch, entrance, inauguration, initiation, introduction

**decadent** ADJECTIVE
*a decadent society*
▶ immoral, dissolute, degenerate, dissipated, corrupt, depraved, declining
AN OPPOSITE IS moral

**decay** VERB
**1** *The skulls were in good condition but the bones had decayed.*
▶ decompose, rot, putrefy, go bad, waste away, perish, deteriorate, degrade, disintegrate
**2** *Inner cities had been allowed to decay.*
▶ decline, deteriorate, degenerate, crumble, corrode, disintegrate, wither, fall apart, go downhill

**decay** NOUN
**1** *Today I found a dead blackbird in an advanced state of decay.*
▶ decomposition, rotting, festering, putrefaction
**2** *Television is often blamed for the so-called decay in social values.*
▶ deterioration, decline, degradation, collapse, fall, disintegration

**deceit** NOUN
*They achieved much by lies and deceit.*
▶ deception, duplicity, trickery, pretence, cheating, misrepresentation, fraud, guile, subterfuge, artifice, ruse
OPPOSITES ARE honesty, openness

**deceitful** ADJECTIVE
*George got used to the fact that I was deceitful and irresponsible.*
▶ dishonest, untruthful, insincere, untrustworthy, deceptive, duplicitous, underhand, false, fraudulent, (more informal) two-faced

**deceive** VERB
*It had not been too difficult to deceive him.*
▶ trick, fool, mislead, hoodwink, delude, dupe, cheat, swindle, (more informal) take in

**decelerate** VERB
*I get a whine from the gearbox every time I decelerate in fourth gear.*
▶ slow down, go slower, reduce speed, lose speed, decrease speed, brake
AN OPPOSITE IS accelerate

**decency** NOUN
*She said she had been brought up to respect honesty and decency.*
▶ good behaviour, propriety, respectability, courtesy, correctness, morality

**decent** ADJECTIVE
**1** *Mum always said it wasn't decent to watch people undress.*
▶ proper, respectable, appropriate, suitable, fitting, seemly, becoming, nice, modest, decorous, tasteful
AN OPPOSITE IS indecent
**2** *Apart from that, he seemed a decent enough bloke.*
▶ obliging, courteous, honest, trustworthy, reliable, dependable, upright, polite, honourable
**3** *It was her first decent meal of the day.*
▶ good, satisfactory, nice, pleasant, agreeable
AN OPPOSITE IS unsatisfactory

# D

## deception NOUN

*For a spy, I'm not very good at deception.*
▶ deceit, duplicity, trickery, pretence, cheating, misrepresentation, fraud, guile, subterfuge, artifice, ruse
OPPOSITES ARE honesty, openness

## deceptive ADJECTIVE

1 *Similarities can be deceptive.*
▶ misleading, illusory, false, unreliable, delusive, fallacious, fraudulent, insincere, specious, spurious, treacherous
AN OPPOSITE IS genuine

2 *deceptive practices*
▶ dishonest, deceitful, fraudulent, underhand, duplicitous, sham, bogus
AN OPPOSITE IS honest

## decide VERB

1 *He decided to become a journalist.*
▶ resolve, determine, make up your mind, choose, reach a decision, opt, plan, aim

2 *We don't have enough evidence to decide the issue.*
▶ determine, judge, adjudicate on, make a judgement on, pronounce on

## decipher VERB

*It was hard to decipher the writing.*
▶ decode, unscramble, interpret, make sense of, read, understand, construe, (*more informal*) crack, (*more informal*) make out

## decision NOUN

1 *the jury's decision on damages*
▶ verdict, finding, ruling, conclusion, judgement, pronouncement, adjudication

2 *The King agreed with this decision.*
▶ resolution, conclusion, outcome, result, recommendation, resolve, determination

## decisive ADJECTIVE

1 *The car's faster speed proved to be a decisive advantage.*
▶ conclusive, definite, significant, crucial, critical, positive, deciding, determining, convincing, final, influential
OPPOSITES ARE inconclusive, insignificant

2 *His decisive no-nonsense manner had given him quite a reputation. They showed themselves capable of decisive action.*
▶ resolute, determined, firm, strong-willed, strong-minded, forceful, forthright, unhesitating, incisive, decided, definite
OPPOSITES ARE indecisive, hesitant

## declaration NOUN

1 *a joint declaration by the four heads of state*
▶ announcement, proclamation, notification, promulgation, edict, manifesto

2 *a declaration of trust in the government*
▶ affirmation, assertion, acknowledgement, profession, confirmation, pledge, avowal

## declare VERB

1 *Both sides declared their intentions.*
▶ announce, proclaim, express, voice, affirm, reveal, divulge

2 *He declared that he was ready to do a deal.*
▶ assert, insist, maintain, announce, aver, state, claim, certify, vow, avow

## decline NOUN

1 *a decline in profits*
▶ reduction, decrease, drop, fall, downturn, falling off, recession, slump, diminution (of), loss (of), failing (of)

2 *a decline in their fortunes*
▶ deterioration, degeneration, worsening (of)

## decline VERB

1 *He declined all our invitations.*
▶ refuse, reject, dismiss, turn down, pass up, forgo
AN OPPOSITE IS accept

2 *After the accident her health declined.*
▶ worsen, deteriorate, weaken, degenerate, flag, die away, fail, fall off, sink, wane, wilt
AN OPPOSITE IS improve

3 *Profits have declined for the third year in succession.*
▶ decrease, diminish, be reduced, lessen, go down, drop away, dwindle, ebb

## decode VERB

(*informal*) *The messages were quickly decoded.*
▶ decipher, unscramble, interpret, make sense of, understand, construe, solve, read, (*more informal*) crack, (*more informal*) make out, (*more informal*) figure out
OPPOSITES ARE code, encode

## decompose VERB

*The severed hand was already decomposing.*
▶ decay, rot, putrefy, go bad, waste away, perish, deteriorate, degrade, disintegrate

## decor NOUN

*The decor is tasteful and includes many fine paintings.*
▶ decoration, design, interior design, style, colour scheme, furnishing

## decorate VERB

1 *a nursery chair decorated with little rabbits*
▶ adorn, ornament, embellish, trim, beautify, enhance

2 *We will decorate the house before moving in.*
▶ paint, renovate, smarten up, refurbish, redecorate, paper, wallpaper, (*more informal*) do up

3 *He was decorated for bravery at the end of the war.*
▶ honour, reward, give a medal to, mention in dispatches

## decoration NOUN

1 *a tall ceiling with elaborate decoration*
▶ ornamentation, adornment, embellishment, trimmings, filigree, tracery, frill, scroll

2 *a decoration for bravery*
▶ award, badge, medal, ribbon, star, (*more informal*) gong

**decorative** ADJECTIVE
*a decorative mirror in a frame*
▶ ornamental, ornate, fancy, adorning, embellishing, enhancing, elaborate, non-functional
AN OPPOSITE IS functional

**decorous** ADJECTIVE
*decorous behaviour*
▶ proper, seemly, decent, becoming, correct, suitable, tasteful, respectable
AN OPPOSITE IS unbecoming

**decorum** NOUN
*He treated the occasion with respect and decorum.*
▶ propriety, decency, dignity, seemliness, politeness, respectability, good taste, good manners, gravity, modesty

**decoy** NOUN
*They set up a decoy to distract our attention.*
▶ lure, bait, trap, enticement

**decoy** VERB
*His enemies had decoyed him to another part of the country.*
▶ lure, entice, induce, inveigle, ensnare, seduce, tempt, bait, draw, lead

**decrease** NOUN
*a decrease in crime levels*
▶ reduction, decline, lessening (of), falling off, drop, downturn
AN OPPOSITE IS increase

**decrease** VERB
1 *We need to decrease our costs.*
▶ reduce, lessen, lower, cut, cut down, curtail
AN OPPOSITE IS increase
2 *The aircraft's speed was rapidly decreasing.*
▶ diminish, lessen, reduce, fall off, dwindle
AN OPPOSITE IS increase

**decree** NOUN
*a presidential decree banning all protest meetings*
▶ order, edict, command, mandate, proclamation, dictum, enactment

**decree** VERB
*The law decreed that Sunday should be a day of rest.*
▶ order, command, declare, prescribe, ordain, proclaim, pronounce, direct, rule, decide, determine, dictate

**decrepit** ADJECTIVE
1 *He lived in a decrepit old cottage.*
▶ dilapidated, battered, ramshackle, tumbledown, worn out, broken down, derelict
2 *a decrepit old woman*
▶ feeble, frail, weak, infirm

**decry** VERB
*She decried the quality of commercial broadcasting.*
▶ denounce, condemn, criticize, censure, deplore, damn, rail against

**dedicate** VERB
1 *The church is dedicated to St Peter.*
▶ consecrate, sanctify, hallow, set apart

2 *He dedicated the book to his father's memory*
▶ inscribe, address
3 *We need to dedicate a whole week to the task.*
▶ devote, commit, assign, allot, allocate

**dedicated** ADJECTIVE
1 *a dedicated musician*
▶ devoted, committed, keen, staunch, steadfast, fervent, loyal, enthusiastic, zealous, wholehearted, single-minded, faithful
2 *a dedicated computer terminal*
▶ customized, specific, exclusive

**dedication** NOUN
1 *She appreciated all his hard work and dedication.*
▶ devotion, commitment, allegiance, faithfulness, loyalty, adherence, single-mindedness
2 *The book bore a dedication to his wife.*
▶ inscription

**deduce** VERB
*He deduced that she must be a good cook.*
▶ conclude, come to the conclusion, reason, work out, gather, infer, surmise, glean

**deduct** VERB
*(informal) The cost of the breakage will be deducted from his allowance.*
▶ subtract, knock off, take away, debit (to)
OPPOSITES ARE add (to), credit (to)

**deduction** NOUN
USAGE from the verb *deduct*.
1 *Income is subject to the deduction of tax.*
▶ subtraction, taking away, taking off, removal, stoppage
USAGE from the verb *deduce*.
2 *Her deduction was quite correct.*
▶ conclusion, inference, reasoning

**deed** NOUN
1 *a heroic deed*
▶ act, action, feat, exploit, endeavour, enterprise, achievement, adventure, effort, performance, undertaking
2 *The Bank will keep the deeds of the property.*
▶ title (to), papers, records, contract, documents

**deem** VERB
*the changes they deem desirable*
▶ regard as, consider, judge, view as, believe to be, reckon as

**deep** ADJECTIVE
1 *The well is deep.*
▶ bottomless, fathomless, cavernous, yawning
AN OPPOSITE IS shallow
2 *a deep disappointment*
▶ intense, profound, extreme, serious
3 *a deep mystery*
▶ obscure, secret, mysterious, unfathomable, fathomless, arcane
4 *deep affection*
▶ intense, heartfelt, fervent, ardent, deep-seated
5 *a deep thinker*
▶ wise, intelligent, profound, perceptive, learned, discerning

a b c d e f g h i j k l m n o p q r s t u v w x y z

**6** *They were deep in conversation.*
▶ rapt, absorbed, engrossed, immersed, preoccupied, riveted
**7** *a deep sound*
▶ low, low-pitched, bass, resonant, booming
**8** *a deep colour*
▶ dark, rich, vivid, strong, intense

**deepen** VERB
**1** *Their love had deepened over the years.*
▶ increase, intensify, grow, grow stronger
**2** *The hole had been deepened.*
▶ dig out, make deeper, hollow, scoop out

**deep-seated** ADJECTIVE
*He had a deep-seated fear of flying.*
▶ profound, intense, fundamental, ingrained, deep, deep-rooted
OPPOSITES ARE superficial, temporary

**deface** VERB
*Graffiti had defaced the monument.*
▶ disfigure, spoil, mar, injure, mutilate, vandalize, damage

**defamatory** ADJECTIVE
*The remarks are defamatory.*
▶ insulting, abusive, slanderous, libellous, disparaging, derogatory, malicious

**default** NOUN
*a large number of defaults on loans*
▶ non-payment, failure to pay, neglect, deficiency, lapse, (more informal) welshing

**defeat** NOUN
**1** *the defeat of Napoleon at Waterloo*
▶ conquest, subjugation, overthrow, beating, victory (over)
**2** *The home side faced defeat.*
▶ failure, loss, setback, humiliation, disappointment, reverse, trouncing
AN OPPOSITE IS victory

**defeat** VERB
**1** *The French army defeated the enemy in a long engagement.*
▶ overcome, beat, conquer, overpower, subdue, vanquish, subjugate, quell, rout
**2** *The complexity of the task defeated them.*
▶ confound, baffle, frustrate, fox, (more informal) flummox

**defect** NOUN (with the stress on *de-*)
*The machinery showed several defects.*
▶ fault, flaw, imperfection, deficiency, weakness, failing, inadequacy, blemish, error, (more informal) bug

**defect** VERB (with the stress on *-fect*)
*MPs might defect to other parties.*
▶ desert, go over, change sides, revolt

**defective** ADJECTIVE
*The car's brakes were defective.*
▶ faulty, out of order, deficient, broken, malfunctioning, inoperative

**defence** NOUN
**1** *Several friends spoke in defence of his actions.*
▶ support, vindication, justification, endorsement
**2** *a defence against attack*
▶ protection, resistance (to), shield, deterrent, barricade, bulwark

**defenceless** ADJECTIVE
*defenceless victims*
▶ helpless, vulnerable, powerless, impotent, unprotected, exposed
AN OPPOSITE IS protected

**defend** VERB
**1** *An air squadron helped to defend the country against enemy attack.*
▶ protect, guard, safeguard, secure, shield, shelter, screen, cover
**2** *He found it hard to defend his actions.*
▶ justify, vindicate, make a case for

**defendant** NOUN
*The defendant stood in the dock.*
▶ accused, prisoner, appellant, offender

**defensive** ADJECTIVE
**1** *The aircraft formed a defensive circle.*
▶ defending, protective, protecting, guarding
AN OPPOSITE IS aggressive
**2** *Her attitude seemed nervous and defensive.*
▶ wary, watchful, cautious, apologetic, self-justifying
AN OPPOSITE IS assertive

**defer** VERB
**1** *She had decided to defer unpacking to the following day.*
▶ postpone, put off, delay, adjourn, hold over, suspend, (more informal) shelve
**2** *defer to He agreed to defer to his parents' wishes.*
▶ yield to, submit to, respect, accede to, give way to, agree to, surrender to

**defiance** NOUN
*Her dark eyes were ablaze with defiance.*
▶ opposition, confrontation, resistance, challenge, audacity, bravado, contempt

**defiant** ADJECTIVE
*He remained defiant in spite of the threats.*
▶ obstinate, determined, intransigent, resistant, confrontational, recalcitrant, unyielding
OPPOSITES ARE cooperative, apologetic

**deficiency** NOUN
*a vitamin deficiency*
▶ insufficiency, shortage, inadequacy, lack, deficit, shortfall

**deficient** ADJECTIVE
**1** *a diet deficient in vitamins*
▶ lacking, wanting, defective, inadequate, insufficient
OPPOSITES ARE adequate, excessive

**deficit**

2 *deficient leadership*
▶ defective, flawed, faulty, unsound, imperfect, inadequate, (*more informal*) duff
AN OPPOSITE IS perfect

**deficit** NOUN
*a deficit in the budget*
▶ loss, shortfall, deficiency, lack
AN OPPOSITE IS surplus

**define** VERB
1 *We can define evidence as information about whether a particular thing is true or not.*
▶ explain, interpret, clarify, formulate, give the meaning of
2 *The fence defines the boundary of the estate.*
▶ mark, mark out, indicate, set, determine, demarcate, outline

**definite** ADJECTIVE
1 *She came to some definite conclusions.*
▶ clear, clear-cut, explicit, express, precise, established, fixed, concrete, plain, hard
AN OPPOSITE IS indefinite
2 *There are definite signs of improvement.*
▶ distinct, clear, plain, discernible, obvious, perceptible, noticeable, positive, unmistakable, marked, pronounced, apparent
AN OPPOSITE IS imperceptible

**definitely** ADVERB
*She definitely hadn't been there before.*
▶ certainly, positively, surely, unquestionably, beyond doubt, assuredly, for certain, indubitably, doubtless, without doubt, without fail

**definition** NOUN
1 *It is hard to write a good definition of 'left' and 'right'.*
▶ explanation, description, elucidation, interpretation, meaning
2 *The photograph lacked definition.*
▶ clarity, clearness, sharpness, precision, focus

**definitive** ADJECTIVE
1 *the definitive film guide*
▶ authoritative, standard, classic, recognized, accepted, official, ultimate, complete, reliable
2 *a definitive reply*
▶ decisive, conclusive, categorical, final
AN OPPOSITE IS provisional

**deflate** VERB
1 *Someone had deflated two of the tyres.*
▶ let down, let the air out of, flatten
AN OPPOSITE IS inflate.
2 *The news deflated him.*
▶ subdue, humble, humiliate, dishearten, dispirit, dismay, chasten, mortify
OPPOSITES ARE encourage, boost

**deflect** VERB
*He managed to deflect the blow.*
▶ divert, turn aside, parry, fend off, intercept, avert, head off, prevent, ward off

**deformed** ADJECTIVE
*He was so deformed the gods took pity on him.*
▶ misshapen, contorted, crippled, crooked, distorted, disfigured, twisted, malformed, maimed, bent, warped, mutilated, buckled, mangled, defaced, gnarled, grotesque, ugly

**deformity** NOUN
*His strange position gave the impression of a deformity.*
▶ malformation, misshapenness, disfigurement, defect, abnormality, irregularity

**defraud** VERB
*He was defrauding the state by making false tax claims.*
▶ swindle, cheat, dupe, (*more informal*) con, (*more informal*) diddle, (*more informal*) fleece, (*more informal*) rip off

**deft** ADJECTIVE
*He tipped back his glass with a deft movement of his arm.*
▶ adroit, skilful, adept, neat, agile, expert, delicate, dexterous, nimble, (*more informal*) nifty
OPPOSITES ARE clumsy, awkward

**defunct** ADJECTIVE
*a defunct coal mine*
▶ disused, obsolete, unused, inoperative, extinct, discontinued

**defy** VERB
1 *He was arrested for defying a court order to hand over the property.*
▶ disobey, refuse to obey, flout, disregard, violate, contravene, infringe, breach, resist
AN OPPOSITE IS obey
2 *She defied Robin to admit the truth.*
▶ challenge, dare
3 *The situation defied all attempts at rational explanation.*
▶ elude, escape, defeat, frustrate, thwart, resist

**degenerate** ADJECTIVE
*degenerate behaviour*
▶ immoral, corrupt, decadent, depraved, dissolute, debauched

**degrading** ADJECTIVE
*Asking for money can be a degrading experience.*
▶ humiliating, demeaning, shaming, mortifying, embarrassing, ignominious, undignified
OPPOSITES ARE uplifting, ennobling

**degree** NOUN
*The work involves a high degree of trust.*
▶ level, order, measure, extent, range, stage, intensity, standard
**to some degree** *The risk will still be present to some degree.*
▶ partly, to some extent, up to a point

**deify** VERB
*The emperor was deified on his death.*
▶ treat as a god, make a god, idolize, venerate, worship

**deign** VERB

*She practised all the things she would say to him when he deigned to contact her.*
▶ condescend, see fit, consent, descend, stoop

**deity** NOUN

*statues of deities*
▶ god, goddess, divinity, demigod, idol, immortal

**dejected** ADJECTIVE

*Lisa was looking dejected.*
▶ downcast, depressed, despondent, dispirited, disheartened, downhearted, unhappy, fed up, sad, down, glum, melancholy, miserable, cast down
OPPOSITES ARE cheerful, happy

**delay** NOUN

1 *Traffic is subject to long delays.*
▶ hold-up, wait, waiting period, stoppage, obstruction
2 *A delay in the proceedings followed.*
▶ deferment, postponement, suspension

**delay** VERB

1 *Heavy traffic delayed many of the guests.*
▶ detain, hold up, make late, hamper, impede
2 *We might have to delay the start of the game.*
▶ postpone, put off, defer, suspend, adjourn, hold over
OPPOSITES ARE advance, bring forward
3 *There is no time to delay.*
▶ linger, dally, take your time, (*more formal*) procrastinate, (*more informal*) drag your feet, (*more informal*) hang about

**delegate** NOUN

*trade-union delegates*
▶ representative, agent, envoy, legate, messenger, spokesperson, ambassador

**delegate** VERB

1 *The council delegated a member to speak to the press.*
▶ appoint, authorize, commission, nominate, designate, empower, mandate
2 *She delegates routine tasks to an assistant.*
▶ assign, entrust, pass on, hand over, devolve, consign

**delegation** NOUN

*There was a delegation from Nigeria.*
▶ deputation, commission, legation, delegacy, mission, representative group, contingent

**delete** VERB

*One paragraph was deleted from the article.*
▶ remove, cut out, take out, erase, expunge, cross out

**deliberate** ADJECTIVE

1 *The disaster may have been an accident rather than deliberate sabotage.*
▶ intentional, calculated, conscious, planned, culpable, premeditated, wilful
OPPOSITES ARE unplanned, accidental, fortuitous

2 *She could hear the slow deliberate footsteps.*
▶ careful, measured, steady, cautious, unhurried, considered, methodical
AN OPPOSITE IS hasty

**deliberate** VERB

*They deliberated for a long time about what to do.*
▶ reflect, consider, think, debate, ponder, cogitate, meditate

**deliberation** NOUN

1 *After some deliberation, he agreed.*
▶ consideration, thought, reflection, contemplation, discussion, consultation
2 *She went to the door with deliberation.*
▶ care, caution, circumspection
AN OPPOSITE IS haste

**delicacy** NOUN

1 *lacework of great delicacy*
▶ fineness, exquisiteness, daintiness, fragility, intricacy, precision, accuracy, care
2 *It was an unpleasant matter that called for some delicacy.*
▶ sensitivity, subtlety, tact, discrimination, finesse
3 *Several plates of delicacies were brought in.*
▶ titbit, rarity, speciality, treat

**delicate** ADJECTIVE

1 *The tablecloths were made of beautiful, delicate fabrics.*
▶ fine, exquisite, elegant, intricate, graceful, flimsy, fragile
OPPOSITES ARE coarse, crude
2 *He awoke feeling somewhat delicate, after his night on the town.*
▶ unwell, sickly, ill, unfit, poorly, frail, weak
OPPOSITES ARE healthy, fit, robust
3 *The old clock had a delicate mechanism.*
▶ precise, intricate, accurate, exact
4 *a delicate shade of blue*
▶ subtle, muted, soft, pale, gentle, pastel, subdued
5 *Angie made a tiny, delicate gesture with her hand.*
▶ gentle, deft, adroit, neat, skilful
6 *The next issue to come up was delicate, to put it mildly.*
▶ difficult, tricky, sensitive, awkward, embarrassing, problematical
7 *The matter called for delicate handling.*
▶ sensitive, careful, discriminating
8 *It would not be easy to cater for their delicate taste in food.*
▶ fastidious, discriminating, fussy, (*more informal*) choosy, (*more informal*) pernickety, (*more informal*) faddy, (*more informal*) picky

**delicious** ADJECTIVE

1 *You can have a delicious meal at the local pub.*
▶ tasty, appetizing, palatable, delectable, enjoyable, luscious, succulent, choice, savoury, (*more informal*) mouth-watering, (*more informal*) scrumptious, (*more informal*) yummy
OPPOSITES ARE unpleasant, uneatable

**2** *a delicious feeling of contentment*
► delightful, exquisite, lovely, pleasurable, heavenly, glorious

## delight NOUN

*Florence laughed with delight.*
► pleasure, happiness, joy, enjoyment, bliss, rapture, ecstasy

## delight VERB

**1** *She delighted her father by singing for him.*
► please, charm, thrill, gratify, enchant, captivate, enthral, entrance, amuse, (*more informal*) bowl over
OPPOSITES ARE displease, disgust
**2 delight in** *Fran delighted in the flowers he gave her.*
► relish, enjoy, love, savour, revel in
OPPOSITES ARE hate, dislike, loathe

## delighted VERB

*He was delighted to see that Jenny had arrived.*
► pleased, happy, glad, thrilled, overjoyed, gratified, excited, ecstatic
OPPOSITES ARE dismayed, disappointed

## delightful ADJECTIVE

*He told Julie how delightful it had been to meet her.*
► pleasant, lovely, enjoyable, pleasing, pleasurable, gratifying, satisfying, marvellous, wonderful

## delinquency NOUN

*attacking the root causes of delinquency*
► crime, wrongdoing, criminality, lawbreaking, misconduct, misbehaviour

## delinquent ADJECTIVE

*She was quite good with delinquent adolescents.*
► lawless, lawbreaking, errant, unruly, offending, criminal, unmanageable, uncontrollable

## delinquent NOUN

*It was not fair to label them delinquents.*
► offender, lawbreaker, wrongdoer, young offender, criminal, hooligan, hoodlum, miscreant, (*informal*) tearaway

## delirious ADJECTIVE

**1** *The illness made Luke delirious for days on end.*
► demented, raving, incoherent, hysterical, irrational, feverish, frenzied
**2** *She was delirious with joy.*
► ecstatic, elated, thrilled, beside yourself, exultant, wild

## deliver VERB

**1** *The books will be delivered to your address within the next week.*
► send, convey, transport, bring, supply, take, dispatch
**2** *The court delivered its verdict.*
► utter, give, make, read, announce, declare, pronounce, speak
**3** *He delivered a powerful blow to the back of the head.*
► administer, deal, launch, aim, strike, hit
**4** *The hostages were all delivered from their captors.*
► rescue, save, set free, liberate, release, redeem, ransom

## delivery NOUN

**1** *There is a daily delivery of fresh vegetables.*
► consignment, batch, shipment, distribution
**2** *The delivery of the message was timed at 3.30.*
► dispatch, transmission, conveyance

## delude VERB

*You are deluding yourself if you think that.*
► deceive, mislead, fool, take in, hoodwink, beguile, bamboozle, trick

## deluge NOUN

*The deluge left many homes under water.*
► downpour, rainstorm, inundation, flood, rainfall, spate

## deluge VERB

*Callers deluged the help lines all day.*
► overwhelm, swamp, engulf, flood, inundate, drown, submerge

## delusion NOUN

*The idea that he might win was a delusion.*
► fantasy, misconception, misapprehension, deception, dream, hallucination, illusion, mirage, mistake

## delve VERB

*He delved in his coat pocket.*
► burrow, rummage, probe, search, explore, dig, investigate

## demand NOUN

**1** *She refused to give way to their demands.*
► request, requirement, claim, ultimatum, stipulation, insistence
**2** *There is much less demand for hardback books.*
► call, market, need, necessity

## demand VERB

**1** *The workers demanded a 10% pay rise.*
► call for, ask for, claim, want, insist on, require, request, expect
**2** *'Where are they?' he demanded.*
► ask, enquire, challenge, question

## demanding ADJECTIVE

**1** *a demanding child*
► insistent, trying, tiresome, importunate, nagging
**2** *a demanding task*
► difficult, challenging, testing, exacting, taxing, hard, tough, onerous, arduous, formidable

## demeaning ADJECTIVE

*He found the job unpleasant and demeaning.*
► degrading, humiliating, shaming, mortifying, embarrassing, ignominious, undignified
OPPOSITES ARE uplifting, ennobling

## demeanour NOUN

*an anxious and nervous demeanour*
► attitude, bearing, manner, disposition

## demented ADJECTIVE

*A severely demented person might not be able to respond at all.*
► mad, deranged, delirious, insane, crazy

**demise** — **dent**

**demise** NOUN
*the demise of the Assyrian Empire*
▶ downfall, collapse, end, disappearance, failure

**democratic** ADJECTIVE
*a democratic government*
▶ elected, elective, popular, representative, chosen, popular, egalitarian
AN OPPOSITE IS undemocratic

**demolish** VERB
*The explosion demolished a row of houses.*
▶ destroy, wreck, flatten, level, knock down, tear down, break down, obliterate, reduce to ruins
OPPOSITES ARE construct, assemble

**demolition** NOUN
*The houses face demolition.*
▶ destruction, dismantling, levelling, pulling down, flattening, clearance

**demon** NOUN
*demons from hell*
▶ devil, fiend, spirit, goblin, imp

**demonstrable** ADJECTIVE
*a demonstrable connection between the two crimes*
▶ verifiable, provable, incontrovertible, irrefutable, clear, evident, palpable, certain, positive, undeniable

**demonstrate** VERB
**1** *The evidence demonstrates a major change in the role of women.*
▶ show, indicate, establish, display, exhibit, point to, prove, substantiate, verify, exemplify, illustrate, manifest, represent
**2** *People demonstrated in the streets.*
▶ protest, rally, hold a rally, lobby, march, parade, picket

**demonstration** NOUN
**1** *a demonstration of skill and creativity*
▶ display, exhibition, manifestation, indication, revelation, expression, presentation, embodiment
**2** (*informal*) *a demonstration against the war.*
▶ protest, demo, rally, march, parade, sit-in, vigil

**demonstrative** ADJECTIVE
*a demonstrative person*
▶ affectionate, expressive, emotional, effusive, open, uninhibited, unreserved, unrestrained, fulsome, loving
OPPOSITES ARE reserved, inhibited

**demoralize** VERB
*Poor pay demoralized the staff.*
▶ discourage, dishearten, depress, deject, dispirit, disconcert

**demote** VERB
*Some of the less successful managers were demoted.*
▶ downgrade, reduce, put down, lower in rank
AN OPPOSITE IS promote

**demur** VERB
*Her husband demurred, despite wanting to support her.*
▶ object, raise objections, disagree, dissent, protest

**demure** ADJECTIVE
*She was sitting demure, her hands in her lap.*
▶ modest, reserved, bashful, unassuming, diffident, reticent, prim, shy, sober, strait-laced
OPPOSITES ARE brazen, forward

**den** NOUN
*He worked all evening in his den upstairs.*
▶ study, retreat, sanctum, hideaway, hideout, lair, sanctuary, private place, secret place

**denial** NOUN
**1** *Reports of a threatened strike met with a firm denial.*
▶ contradiction, renunciation, repudiation, disavowal, dismissal, abnegation, disclaimer, negation, rejection
AN OPPOSITE IS admission
**2** *the denial of rights to certain minorities*
▶ refusal, withholding, withdrawal, veto

**denigrate** VERB
*Do not denigrate our city so quickly.*
▶ belittle, disparage, revile, malign, vilify, deprecate, defame, (*more informal*) run down
AN OPPOSITE IS praise

**denomination** NOUN
**1** *a Christian denomination*
▶ religion, religious group, church, sect, communion, persuasion, creed, cult
**2** *coins of several denominations*
▶ unit, value, category, designation, class, size, type

**denote** VERB
*A snort from the corner denoted disagreement.*
▶ indicate, mean , express, signify, stand for, represent, symbolize, be the sign for

**denounce** VERB
*He denounced them for their dishonesty.*
▶ condemn, censure, find fault with, criticize, blame, castigate, disparage, denigrate, deprecate, (*more informal*) knock, (*more informal*) slam, (*more informal*) pan

**dense** ADJECTIVE
**1** *a dense crowd   dense undergrowth*
▶ thick, closely packed, tightly packed, impenetrable, massed
AN OPPOSITE IS sparse
**2** *dense smoke*
▶ thick, heavy, concentrated
OPPOSITES ARE thin, light
**3** *too dense to understand the point*
▶ stupid, foolish, crass, dull, slow, slow-witted, unintelligent
OPPOSITES ARE clever, intelligent

**dent** NOUN
*There were several small dents in the side of the vehicle.*
▶ indentation, dint, dimple, dip, concavity, depression, hollow, pit

**dent** VERB
**1** *He dropped the saucepan and dented it.*
▶ make a dent in, push in, knock in, buckle, depress

2 *Nothing much could dent her confidence.*
▶ diminish, reduce, impair, damage, harm, affect

**deny** VERB
1 *The story was denied by the Prime Minister's office. The accused denied all the charges.*
▶ contradict, repudiate, rebut, reject, dismiss, contest, oppose, refute
**USAGE** Note that *refute* means 'to disprove by using arguments'.
2 *The authorities have denied them their basic rights.*
▶ refuse, forbid, withhold

**depart** VERB
1 *The officials departed after lunch.*
▶ leave, go, go away, go off, withdraw, make off, retire, quit, (*old-fashioned*) take your leave, (*old-fashioned*) decamp
AN OPPOSITE IS arrive
2 *At this point the speaker departed from his notes.*
▶ deviate, digress, differ, diverge, drift
AN OPPOSITE IS stick to

**department** NOUN
1 *He works in a government department.*
▶ division, section, sector, unit, branch, subdivision, office, bureau, agency, ministry
2 (*informal*) *I'm afraid travel arrangements are not my department.*
▶ domain, responsibility, business, affair, concern, field, area, sphere, line, province, function, job, specialism, (*more informal*) pigeon, (*more informal*) baby

**departure** NOUN
1 *Our departure has been delayed by half an hour.*
▶ leaving, setting off, going, exit, withdrawal, disappearance, embarkation, escape, exodus, retirement, retreat
AN OPPOSITE IS arrival
2 *The book represents a departure from the author's familiar style.*
▶ change, change of direction, deviation, digression, shift, variation, innovation, branching out

**depend** VERB
1 *depend on Choice of university can depend a lot on expected exam grades.*
▶ be dependent on, hinge on, hang on, rest on, revolve around
2 *depend on I shall depend on you to help me.*
▶ rely on, count on, need, bank on, trust

**dependable** ADJECTIVE
*She looked at Roland: so strong and dependable.*
▶ reliable, trustworthy, faithful, true, loyal, constant, unswerving, sensible, responsible, conscientious, sound, steady, unfailing
AN OPPOSITE IS unreliable

**dependence** NOUN
1 *Trevor was determined to reduce his dependence on his family.*
▶ reliance, need (for), trust (in), confidence (in)

2 *a rise in drug dependence*
▶ addiction, dependency, reliance, craving, abuse

**dependent** ADJECTIVE
1 **dependent on** *A lot is dependent on their decision.*
▶ conditional on, contingent on, connected with, controlled by, determined by, liable to, relative to, subject to, vulnerable to
AN OPPOSITE IS independent
2 **dependent on** *Prisoners remain dependent on what visitors bring for them.*
▶ reliant on, supported by, sustained by, needful of
3 **dependent on** *Some of these people are dependent on drugs.*
▶ addicted to, reliant on, enslaved by, (*more informal*) hooked on

**depict** VERB
1 *The painting depicts a village in winter.*
▶ show, portray, represent, picture, illustrate, reproduce, delineate, describe, draw, narrate, outline, paint, sketch
2 *The author depicts his own childhood in the story.*
▶ describe, relate, narrate, recount, present, record, outline, delineate, portray, characterize

**deplete** VERB
*Local wars have depleted the food supply.*
▶ exhaust, use up, consume, expend, reduce, decrease, lessen, drain, cut
OPPOSITES ARE increase, augment, boost

**deplorable** ADJECTIVE
1 *Their behaviour had been deplorable.*
▶ disgraceful, shameful, inexcusable, unforgivable, disreputable, lamentable, shocking, blameworthy, discreditable, reprehensible, scandalous, unfortunate, unworthy
OPPOSITES ARE admirable, praiseworthy
2 *The troops lived in deplorable conditions.*
▶ lamentable, regrettable, awful, wretched, terrible, miserable, atrocious

**deplore** VERB
1 *We deplore all forms of violence.*
▶ condemn, disapprove of, denounce, abhor, decry, deprecate
2 *He deplored the past difficulties and promised a brighter future.*
▶ regret, lament, bemoan, express regret for

**deploy** VERB
1 *The government deployed troops to prevent demonstrations.*
▶ position, station, post, install, establish, bring into action
2 *You will need to deploy all your personal and social skills.*
▶ use, make use of, utilize, employ, exploit, take advantage of

**deport** VERB
*Illegal immigrants were deported.*
▶ expel, banish, exile, expatriate, transport, extradite

**depose** VERB

*A military coup deposed the government.*
▶ overthrow, overturn, bring down, oust, get rid of, remove, displace, (*more informal*) topple
AN OPPOSITE IS enthrone

**deposit** NOUN

**1** *You will need to pay a deposit to clinch the booking.*
▶ down payment, advance payment, part payment, security, retainer, first payment
**2** *a thick deposit of mud*
▶ layer, covering, coating, accumulation, sediment, silt, sludge, dregs, lees, precipitate
**3** *a deposit at the bottom of the bottle*
▶ sediment, accumulation, dregs, silt

**deposit** VERB

**1** (*informal*) *She deposited a pile of papers on the desk.*
▶ put down, set down, lay down, place, leave, (*more informal*) dump, (*more informal*) stick, (*more informal*) plonk, (*more informal*) park
**2** *The money is deposited each Friday.*
▶ pay in, bank, lodge, save
**3** *The flood water deposited layers of mud.*
▶ precipitate, wash up

**depot** NOUN

**1** *a military depot*
▶ store, storehouse, base, cache, depository, arsenal, dump, hoard
**2** *a bus depot*
▶ garage, station, terminus, headquarters

**depraved** ADJECTIVE

*a depraved person    depraved behaviour*
▶ corrupt, decadent, degenerate, dissolute, sinful, immoral, debauched, rotten, wicked, evil, iniquitous, low, perverted, profligate, venal
AN OPPOSITE IS moral

**deprecate** VERB

*I had always rather deprecated such flashy good looks.*
▶ disapprove of, deplore, frown on, condemn, censure, abhor, dislike

**depreciate** VERB

*The value of property is not likely to depreciate.*
▶ drop, fall, become less, lessen, lower, reduce, decrease, go down, deflate, slump, weaken
AN OPPOSITE IS appreciate

**depress** VERB

**1** *The latest news depressed everyone.*
▶ sadden, deject, dishearten, dispirit, upset, discourage, grieve, lower the spirits of, oppress, make sad
AN OPPOSITE IS cheer

**2** *Aid tends to depress local markets.*
▶ undermine, weaken, impair, inhibit, check, make less active, slow down, bring down, push down, deflate
AN OPPOSITE IS boost

**depressed** ADJECTIVE

*Sam looked tired and depressed.*
▶ dejected, downcast, despondent, dispirited, disheartened, downhearted, disconsolate, unhappy, sad, down, glum, melancholy, miserable, cast down
OPPOSITES ARE cheerful, happy

**depressing** ADJECTIVE

**1** *Tuesday was a cold, depressing day.*
▶ gloomy, bleak, dreary, dismal, grim, drab, sombre, dingy, cheerless
**2** *He tried to get rid of all such depressing thoughts.*
▶ dispiriting, disheartening, upsetting, distressing, melancholy, painful, morbid

**depression** NOUN

**1** *A sudden feeling of depression took hold of him.*
▶ sadness, dejection, melancholy, sorrow, despondency, unhappiness, low spirits, glumness, desolation, despair, pessimism, (*more informal*) blues, (*more informal*) dumps
AN OPPOSITE IS cheerfulness
**2** *an economic depression*
▶ recession, slump, decline, downturn, slowdown, stagnation, hard times
AN OPPOSITE IS boom
**3** *a meteorological depression*
▶ area of low pressure, cyclone, low
AN OPPOSITE IS anticyclone
**4** *The wheel hit a depression in the ground.*
▶ hollow, indentation, dent, cavity, hole, pothole, dip, dimple, concavity
OPPOSITES ARE bump, protuberance

**deprive** VERB

**deprive of** *The war deprived her of her income.*
▶ deny, dispossess of, rob of, divest of, strip of, take away, starve of, refuse, prevent from having

**deprived** ADJECTIVE

*deprived sections of society*
▶ disadvantaged, underprivileged, needy, poor, badly off, destitute

**depth** NOUN

**1** *They tried to measure the depth of the water.*
▶ deepness, distance to the bottom, vertical extent, drop
**2** *The orchestra's playing showed a great depth of feeling.*
▶ extent, degree, range, breadth, scope

**deputation** NOUN

*A deputation arrived from the King of Spain.*
▶ delegation, commission, legation, mission, delegacy, group of envoys, embassy

**depute** VERB

*He was deputed to continue the negotiations.*
▶ appoint, designate, nominate, assign, commission, authorize, empower

**deputize** VERB

**deputize for** *His job is to deputize for the manager.*
▶ stand in for, act as deputy for, cover for, represent, substitute for, take over from, take the place of, do the job of, replace, understudy

**USAGE** Note that *understudy* is normally used about an actor who takes the place of the main actor when they are ill or indisposed.

## deputy NOUN
*During her absence her duties are done by a deputy.*
▶ second in command, number two, substitute, assistant, stand-in, representative, understudy
**USAGE** Note that *understudy* normally means an actor who takes the place of the main actor when they are ill or indisposed.

## deranged ADJECTIVE
*The jury found that he had been in a deranged state of mind.*
▶ insane, mad, disordered, demented, unbalanced, unstable, disturbed, crazed, confused, distraught

## derelict ADJECTIVE
*The car passed a row of derelict buildings*
▶ dilapidated, ramshackle, run down, tumbledown, ruined, deserted, abandoned, neglected, broken down, decrepit

## deride VERB
*Critics derided the film when it originally appeared.*
▶ ridicule, mock, jeer at, scoff at, poke fun at, laugh at, pillory, denigrate, dismiss, (*more informal*) pooh-pooh

## derision NOUN
*Their excuses were met with derision.*
▶ scorn, ridicule, disdain, mockery, contempt, vilification, disparagement, denigration, dismissal

## derisive ADJECTIVE
*Robyn gave a short, derisive laugh.*
▶ mocking, scornful, ridiculing, disdainful, dismissive, contemptuous

## derisory ADJECTIVE
*The house was sold for a derisory sum.*
▶ laughable, ridiculous, inadequate, trifling, paltry, pitiful

## derivation NOUN
1 *the derivation of the word 'posh'*
▶ origin, etymology, root, provenance, source
2 *a family of noble derivation*
▶ ancestry, origin, genealogy, descent, provenance

## derivative ADJECTIVE
*The theme of the story is very derivative.*
▶ unoriginal, imitative, uninspired, plagiaristic, second-hand

## derive VERB
1 *She derived some comfort from the fact that she knew the truth.*
▶ gain, receive, obtain, draw, acquire, get
2 *The family's wealth derives from oil.*
▶ originate (in), stem, arise, spring, flow, emanate
3 **be derived from** *The word 'yacht' is derived from Dutch.*
▶ come from, originate in, stem from, descend from

## derogatory ADJECTIVE
*derogatory remarks*
▶ uncomplimentary, disparaging, depreciatory, insulting, offensive, defamatory

## descend VERB
1 *The little plane descended towards the runway.*
▶ come down, go down, drop, subside, fall, move down, sink, dive, plummet
OPPOSITES ARE ascend, climb
2 *The road descends to a small village.*
▶ slope, dip, drop, fall, incline, slant
AN OPPOSITE IS ascend
3 **be descended from** *We are descended from an Italian family.*
▶ come from, originate in, spring from, stem from
4 **descend from** *He watched her descend from the train.*
▶ get off, alight from, disembark from, dismount from
5 **descend on** *A coach party descended on the local pub.*
▶ engulf, overwhelm, invade
6 **descend to** *In the end they descended to trickery.*
▶ condescend to, stoop to, lower yourself to, resort to, be reduced to, go as far as

## descendants PLURAL NOUN
*descendants of J S Bach*
▶ line, lineage, heirs, family, successors, offspring, progeny, children, issue, posterity
AN OPPOSITE IS ancestors

## descent NOUN
1 *the descent into Dentdale from Newby Head*
▶ way down, drop, incline, dip, declivity, slant, slope, fall
AN OPPOSITE IS ascent
2 *a person of British descent*
▶ ancestry, parentage, origin, lineage, extraction, heredity, blood, pedigree, genealogy, background, derivation, family, stock, strain

## describe VERB
1 *A witness described the incident in detail.*
▶ report, narrate, relate, set out, explain, recount
2 **describe as** *I would never describe him as 'charming'*
▶ call, speak of, refer to, classify, categorize, characterize as, portray, present, represent
3 *The pencil described a circle.*
▶ draw, mark out, trace

## description NOUN
1 *She launched into a detailed description of her day.*
▶ account, explanation, report, narration, commentary (on)
2 *The room was crammed with furniture of every description.*
▶ sort, kind, variety, type, category, class, order

## descriptive ADJECTIVE
*an exercise using descriptive language*
▶ expressive, graphic, colourful, detailed, pictorial, vivid, striking, explanatory, illustrative

**desert** NOUN (with the stress on *des-*)
*lost in the desert*
► wasteland, wilderness, waste, wilds

**desert** ADJECTIVE (with the stress on *des-*)
1 *desert conditions*
► arid, dry, waterless, parched, barren, infertile, sterile, uncultivated, wild
AN OPPOSITE IS fertile
2 *a desert island*
► uninhabited, solitary, lonely, desolate, isolated, lonely, unfrequented
AN OPPOSITE IS inhabited

**desert** VERB (with the stress on *-sert*)
1 *Her husband had deserted her.*
► abandon, leave, strand, forsake, give up, jilt, renounce, betray, (*more informal*) dump, (*more informal*) walk out on, (*more informal*) leave in the lurch
2 *He had decided to desert the party and join the opposition.*
► renounce, abandon, leave, quit, disavow, forsake, (*more informal*) have done with
3 *Soldiers were deserting in large numbers.*
► abscond, defect, decamp, make off, go absent, turn tail, run away

**deserted** ADJECTIVE
1 *a deserted village*
► uninhabited, empty, unoccupied, evacuated, neglected, desolate, vacant
2 *a deserted wife*
► abandoned, stranded, forsaken, jilted, cast off, betrayed

**deserter** NOUN
*a deserter from the army*
► absconder, runaway, turncoat, absentee, fugitive, renegade, traitor, defector

**deserve** VERB
1 *You deserve a holiday.*
► be entitled to, be worthy of, have earned, have a right to, be good enough for
2 *The work deserves the highest praise.*
► merit, justify, warrant, rate

**deserving** ADJECTIVE
*hardworking and deserving people*
► worthy, laudable, admirable, praiseworthy, meritorious, commendable, creditable, good, worth supporting
AN OPPOSITE IS unworthy

**design** NOUN
1 *a design for the new building*
► plan, blueprint, drawing, outline, pattern, prototype, sketch, draft, model
2 *furniture of a fresh bright design*
► pattern, style, form, composition, arrangement, configuration
3 *His design was to travel and enjoy life.*
► intention, ambition, aim, aspiration, goal, object, objective, purpose, end, scheme

**design** VERB
1 *Wren designed several London churches.*
► plan, draw plans of, map out, outline, draw, sketch
2 *an engineer who designed a new kind of aero engine*
► create, invent, develop, devise, originate, conceive, think up

**designate** VERB
*He has designated me his representative.*
► appoint, nominate, delegate (to be), name, identify

**designation** NOUN
1 *She has the designation 'matron'.*
► title, name, label, description, epithet
2 *the designation of this land as an area of outstanding natural beauty*
► classification, specification, selection, choice

**designer** NOUN
*a designer of women's fashions*
► creator, deviser, inventor, originator

**desirable** ADJECTIVE
1 *a very desirable woman*
► attractive, beautiful, alluring, appealing, (*more informal*) sexy
2 *It would be desirable for them to express their support.*
► advantageous, advisable, helpful, beneficial, worthwhile, preferable, sensible, prudent

**desire** NOUN
1 *Ed has always had a desire to travel.*
► wish, longing, yearning, craving, inclination, eagerness, enthusiasm, impulse, appetite (for), (*more informal*) yen
2 *Her eyes glowed with desire.*
► lust, passion, ardour, lasciviousness, libido, love

**desire** VERB
1 *We all desire peace.*
► want, wish for, yearn for, long for, covet, crave, need, hanker after, hunger for, thirst for, pine for, ache for, fancy, like, prefer, (*informal*) set your heart on, (*informal*) itch for, (*informal*) have a yen for
2 *Paris desired Helen of Troy.*
► be attracted to, be captivated by, be infatuated by, (*more informal*) have a crush on

**desolate** ADJECTIVE
1 *They reached a desolate spot near the coast.*
► deserted, uninhabited, abandoned, barren, bare, bleak, gloomy, dismal, dreary, godforsaken
2 *Feeling desolate, she asked him to forgive her.*
► miserable, sad, unhappy, forlorn, depressed, dejected, downcast, despondent, disconsolate
AN OPPOSITE IS cheerful

**despair** NOUN
*Stephen was in a state of despair.*
► hopelessness, desperation, despondency, anguish, pessimism, melancholy, gloom, misery, wretchedness, dejection, depression
AN OPPOSITE IS hope

## despair VERB

*At times like this you can easily despair.*
▸ lose hope, give up hope, lose heart, be demoralized
AN OPPOSITE IS hope

## desperate ADJECTIVE

**1** *He tried not to listen to the desperate cries outside.*
▸ despairing, hopeless, anguished, inconsolable, distraught, distressed, miserable, wretched

**2** *There was a desperate shortage of food.*
▸ acute, critical, severe, serious, grave, dire, urgent

**3** *a band of desperate criminals*
▸ violent, wild, dangerous, reckless, impetuous

## desperation NOUN

**1** *In desperation, she decided to go back to London to find him.*
▸ despair, hopelessness, anguish, despondency, distress

**2** *The robbery seemed like an act of desperation.*
▸ recklessness, rashness, impetuosity, foolhardiness, frenzy

## despicable ADJECTIVE

*guilty of despicable crimes*
▸ contemptible, loathsome, hateful, vile, shameful, detestable, abhorrent

## despise VERB

*She despised the methods he used in business.*
▸ scorn, disdain, look down on, deride, condemn, deplore, revile, detest, loathe, feel contempt for
AN OPPOSITE IS admire

## despondent ADJECTIVE

*Perhaps he was feeling despondent about his exam results.*
▸ disheartened, dejected, depressed, downhearted, downcast, gloomy, upset, down, miserable, sad

## despot NOUN

*the brutal methods used by despots to keep power*
▸ tyrant, dictator, autocrat, oppressor, (*more informal*) Big Brother

## despotic ADJECTIVE

*They disliked any form of despotic rule.*
▸ dictatorial, autocratic, authoritarian, oppressive, brutal, cruel, harsh, repressive, tyrannical

## despotism NOUN

*the despotism of some ancient rulers*
▸ tyranny, dictatorship, authoritarianism, oppression, repression, brutality

## destination NOUN

*At last their destination was in sight.*
▸ journey's end, stopping place, objective, goal, purpose, target, terminus

## destined ADJECTIVE

**1** *The universe might be destined to go on expanding for ever.*
▸ fated, doomed, bound, certain

**2** *the destined outcome*
▸ predetermined, preordained, predestined, unavoidable, inescapable, inevitable, intended, ordained

**3** *a cargo of cement destined for a factory at Tima*
▸ heading, headed, bound, en route, scheduled, consigned (to)

## destiny NOUN

**1** *Destiny had intervened to help them.*
▸ fate, fortune, chance, luck, providence, karma

**2** *He seemed once more in control of his destiny.*
▸ future, fortune, fate, lot

## destitute ADJECTIVE

*He had left her destitute with two children to care for.*
▸ penniless, impoverished, poverty-stricken, impecunious, homeless, indigent, deprived, down and out, insolvent, needy, poor, (*informal*) skint
AN OPPOSITE IS wealthy

## destroy VERB

**1** *A bomb had destroyed the building.*
▸ demolish, ruin, wreck, obliterate, devastate, shatter, blow up

**2** *Disease destroyed all hopes of an economic recovery.*
▸ wreck, ruin, spoil, obliterate, disrupt, upset, put an end to, frustrate, thwart, undermine
OPPOSITES ARE raise, revive

**3** *Their intention was to destroy the enemy.*
▸ kill, slaughter, annihilate, slay, eradicate

## destruction NOUN

**1** *Fires caused widespread destruction.*
▸ devastation, damage, demolition, ruination, havoc

**2** *Much wildlife faces destruction. the destruction of all their hopes*
▸ annihilation, obliteration, elimination, extinction, extermination

## destructive ADJECTIVE

**1** *a destructive storm*
▸ devastating, damaging, ruinous, catastrophic, violent, ravaging

**2** *destructive criticism*
▸ hostile, antagonistic, vicious, negative, fierce, disparaging
AN OPPOSITE IS constructive

## detach VERB

*You can detach the printing head for cleaning.*
▸ remove, unfasten, disconnect, take off, separate, disengage, unfix, free
AN OPPOSITE IS attach

## detached ADJECTIVE

**1** *detached houses set back from the road*
▸ free-standing, separate, unconnected

**2** *Her face expressed detached amusement.*
▸ dispassionate, disinterested, impartial, aloof, distant, objective
AN OPPOSITE IS committed

a b c **d** e f g h i j k l m n o p q r s t u v w x y z

## detachment NOUN

**1** *He regarded the matter with detachment.*
▶ dispassion, objectivity, disinterest, impartiality, neutrality, unconcern, aloofness, remoteness

**2** *a detachment of soldiers*
▶ unit, squad, force, troop, corps, brigade, task force

## detail NOUN

**1** *The copy of the painting was accurate in every detail.*
▶ feature, particular, aspect, characteristic, circumstance, respect, item, point, factor, specific, fact, ingredient
**USAGE** You can also use **minutiae**, which is a Latin plural word meaning 'details'.

**2** *She has an eye for detail.*
▶ precision, exactness, accuracy, rigour, thoroughness

**in detail** *They commented on the proposals in detail.*
▶ in depth, thoroughly, closely, methodically, minutely, meticulously, point by point, item by item

## detail VERB

**1** *An appendix details the sources used in the book.*
▶ describe, list, present, explain, recount, spell out
**2** *The head boy was detailed to look after the visitors.*
▶ appoint, assign, delegate, commission, nominate, chosen

## detailed ADJECTIVE

*a detailed description of the scene*
▶ precise, exact, comprehensive, complete, elaborate, exhaustive, minute, intricate, specific
OPPOSITES ARE general, summary

## detain VERB

**1** *The authorities wanted to detain them for questioning.*
▶ hold, arrest, apprehend, hold in custody, confine, restrain, intern, imprison, gaol, capture
AN OPPOSITE IS release
**2** *Something must have detained them.*
▶ delay, hold up, impede, hinder, keep, check, prevent, keep waiting, retard, slow, stop, waylay

## detect VERB

**1** *We detected slight patches of rust.*
▶ notice, become aware of, perceive, discern, make out, recognize, identify, spot
**2** *The crime was detected with the help of DNA evidence.*
▶ discover, uncover, expose, reveal, unearth, find out, root out, unmask, track down

## detective NOUN

*Detectives were quickly on the scene.*
▶ investigator, police officer, CID officer, (*more informal*) sleuth, (*more informal*) private eye

## detention NOUN

*She had spent two months in police detention.*
▶ custody, imprisonment, confinement, internment, (under) arrest

## deter VERB

**1** *It was mainly the expense that deterred them.*
▶ discourage, put off, inhibit, dissuade, intimidate, prevent, exclude
AN OPPOSITE IS encourage
**2** *measures to deter crime*
▶ prevent, stop, check, put a stop to, reduce, discourage, counteract

## deteriorate VERB

**1** *His health deteriorated rapidly after his wife's death.*
▶ worsen, weaken, decline, lapse, fail, fade, fall off, get worse, relapse, slip, collapse, depreciate, (*more informal*) go downhill
AN OPPOSITE IS improve
**2** *These materials deteriorate if they are not stored correctly.*
▶ decay, degenerate, disintegrate, decompose, crumble

## determination NOUN

**1** (*informal*) *His determination to win grew daily stronger.*
▶ resolution, resolve, will, strength of will, intentness
**2** *You will need a lot of determination.*
▶ resolve, firmness of purpose, tenacity, persistence, dedication, drive

## determine VERB

**1** *It can be difficult to determine the sex of pandas.*
▶ find out, discover, ascertain, decide, establish, identify, verify
**2** *Certain chromosomes determine the sex of an embryo.*
▶ control, regulate, decide, direct, dictate, govern, influence, affect

## determined ADJECTIVE

**1** *He is determined he will have his way.*
▶ adamant, resolute, insistent, convinced, bent (on having), resolved (to have), intent (on having)
AN OPPOSITE IS doubtful
**2** *a determined young woman*
▶ resolute, purposeful, strong-willed, single-minded, strong-minded, steadfast, tenacious, dogged
AN OPPOSITE IS irresolute

## deterrent NOUN

*Penalties need to serve as a deterrent to those tempted to offend.*
▶ discouragement, disincentive, impediment, warning, caution, brake, check, curb, obstacle, restraint, threat, (*more informal*) turn-off
AN OPPOSITE IS encouragement

## detest VERB

*I detest that kind of talk.*
▶ hate, abhor, loathe, despise, dislike, deplore, recoil from

## detestable ADJECTIVE

*She needed to get away from that detestable man.*
▶ hateful, loathsome, horrible, abhorrent, repellent

# detour NOUN

*a detour of five miles*
▶ deviation, diversion, roundabout route, indirect route

# detract VERB

**detract from** *These criticisms do not detract from the overall quality of the performance.*
▶ reduce, diminish, take away from, minimize, affect

# devastate VERB

1 *Storms have devastated the region.*
▶ destroy, damage severely, ravage, demolish, flatten, ruin, wreck, lay waste, level, overwhelm, raze
2 *He was clearly devastated by the news.*
▶ shatter, shock, dismay, stun, distress, overwhelm, upset

# develop VERB

1 *Our plans have developed rapidly in the last few weeks.*
▶ progress, advance, evolve, grow, flourish, get better, improve, mature, thrive, move on
AN OPPOSITE IS regress
2 *An argument developed.*
▶ arise, ensue, result, emerge, start, begin, erupt, come about, (*informal*) blow up
3 *The company wants to develop its overseas business.*
▶ expand, extend, diversify, build up, enlarge, increase, swell
4 *Children develop their reading skills at this age.*
▶ evolve, expand, advance, cultivate, acquire
5 *Let's see if we can develop these ideas.*
▶ amplify, augment, elaborate, enlarge on
6 *People were developing the disease at an early age.*
▶ contract, catch, get, succumb to, be infected with, come down with

# development NOUN

1 *the development of a national road network*
▶ evolution, growth, advance, furtherance, expansion, spread, enlargement, promotion, improvement
2 *The Cabinet met to discuss recent developments in the Middle East.*
▶ event, happening, occurrence, outcome, result, change, incident
3 *The land has been set aside for industrial development*
▶ exploitation, building, conversion, use

# deviate VERB

*politicians who deviate from the party policy*
▶ diverge, depart, digress, drift, stray, wander, turn aside, differ, part, veer, vary, err

# deviation NOUN

*Any deviation from the normal routine caused chaos.*
▶ departure, divergence, digression, variation, variance, deflection, alteration, fluctuation, change, shift, disparity

# device NOUN

1 *a device for converting digital data into audio signals*
▶ implement, apparatus, appliance, contraption, contrivance, tool, utensil, gadget, instrument, invention, machine
2 *a device to avoid prosecution*
▶ ploy, tactic, plan, ruse, scheme, stratagem, manoeuvre, contrivance, trick, stunt, expedient, wile, gambit, gimmick, (*more informal*) dodge
3 *a shield with a device showing the family arms*
▶ emblem, symbol, motif, badge, crest, insignia, seal, figure, logo

# devil NOUN

1 *a sermon on the Devil and his works*
▶ Satan, Lucifer, the Evil One, the Prince of Darkness, the Adversary
2 *a painting with green-skinned devils holding tridents*
▶ demon, fiend, imp, spirit
3 *The poor devil looked frozen and soaked through.*
▶ wretch, fellow, soul
4 *cheeky young devils*
▶ rascal, rogue, monkey, scamp

# devilish ADJECTIVE

*a devilish laugh*
▶ diabolical, diabolic, fiendish, wicked, hellish, infernal, satanic, demoniac, demoniacal, evil
AN OPPOSITE IS angelic

# devious ADJECTIVE

1 *a devious route round the hills*
▶ circuitous, indirect, winding, rambling, meandering, tortuous, roundabout, erratic, deviating, wandering, crooked
AN OPPOSITE IS direct
2 *devious methods   a devious person*
▶ underhand, deceitful, dishonest, scheming, calculating, cunning, treacherous, evasive, insincere, misleading, sly, sneaky, wily
AN OPPOSITE IS straightforward

# devise VERB

*Devise a history project that includes role play.*
▶ conceive, think up, think out, work out, invent, make up, plan, form, prepare, design, concoct, contrive, scheme, formulate, imagine, plot

# devote VERB

*He claimed he wanted to devote more time to his family.*
▶ set aside, dedicate, assign, allot, commit, give yourself

# devoted ADJECTIVE

*a devoted wife and mother*
▶ loyal, faithful, dedicated, staunch, fond, loving, caring, committed, devout, steadfast, true

# devotee NOUN

*devotees of rock music*
▶ enthusiast, fan, addict, aficionado, admirer, (*more informal*) buff, (*more informal*) freak

# devotion NOUN

1 *her devotion to her family*
▶ loyalty, dedication, commitment, faithfulness, staunchness, steadfastness, fondness (for)

**A**
**B**
**C**
**D**
**E**
**F**
**G**
**H**
**I**
**J**
**K**
**L**
**M**
**N**
**O**
**P**
**Q**
**R**
**S**
**T**
**U**
**V**
**W**
**X**
**Y**
**Z**

2 *a life of religious devotion*
▶ piety, spirituality, devoutness, holiness, sanctity

**devour** VERB
1 *She watched him as he devoured his meal.*
▶ eat, consume, guzzle, gobble, wolf down, bolt down, (*more informal*) scoff, (*more informal*) demolish
2 *Flames devoured the barn.*
▶ destroy, consume, engulf, envelop, demolish, ravage, wreck, dispatch

**devout** ADJECTIVE
*a devout Muslim*
▶ pious, devoted, dedicated, reverent, faithful, dutiful, true

**dexterity** NOUN
*The job needs patience and dexterity.*
▶ skill, deftness, adroitness, expertise, proficiency

**dexterous** ADJECTIVE
*a dexterous flick of the wrist*
▶ adroit, deft, skilful, adept, neat, agile, expert, delicate, nimble, (*more informal*) nifty
OPPOSITES ARE clumsy, awkward

**diabolical** ADJECTIVE
1 *The soldiers showed diabolical cruelty.*
▶ outrageous, appalling, atrocious, wicked, vile, shocking, fiendish, devilish
2 (*informal*) *The standard of driving was diabolical.*
▶ dreadful, awful, frightful, terrible, poor, bad

**diagnose** VERB
*The consultant diagnosed a tumour.*
▶ identify, detect, recognize, spot, determine, isolate, distinguish, find, pinpoint

**diagnosis** NOUN
*The original diagnosis proved to be incorrect.*
▶ identification, explanation, pronouncement, opinion, verdict, analysis, conclusion, interpretation

**diagonal** ADJECTIVE
*She drew a diagonal line across the page.*
▶ oblique, slanting, crosswise, angled

**diagram** NOUN
*a diagram showing the workings of the digestive system*
▶ chart, plan, drawing, outline, representation, sketch, schematic representation, figure, table, flowchart, graph, illustration, picture

**dial** NOUN
*the control panel was a mass of dials*
▶ pointer, instrument, clock, display

**dial** VERB
*He seized the phone and dialled the police.*
▶ phone, telephone, call, ring

**dialect** NOUN
*The local dialect was hard to understand.*
▶ vernacular, language, speech, patois, accent, brogue, idiom

**dialogue** NOUN
*A concentrated dialogue is needed to resolve the dispute.*
▶ conversation, discussion, exchange, series of talks, communication, discourse, conference

**diary** NOUN
1 *She kept a diary from the age of ten.*
▶ journal, chronicle, daily record, log
2 *Put the date in your diary.*
▶ appointment book, engagement book, organizer, personal organizer

**dicey** ADJECTIVE
(*informal*) *Crossing the bridge can be dicey in high winds.*
▶ risky, chancy, dangerous, hazardous, unsafe, precarious, insecure, tricky, uncertain, unpredictable
AN OPPOSITE IS safe

**dictate** VERB
1 *He dictated a letter to his secretary.*
▶ read out, say aloud, recite, utter
2 *She wasn't going to let him dictate how she wore her hair.*
▶ prescribe, lay down, direct, order, ordain, impose, command, decree, enforce, give orders about, make the rules about, (*informal*) lay down the law about

**dictate to** *He does rather tend to dictate to his friends.*
▶ order about, boss, tyrannize, bully, domineer, lord it over, (*more informal*) push around, (*more informal*) walk all over

**dictator** NOUN
*what I would do if I were dictator for a day*
▶ tyrant, despot, autocrat, oppressor, (*more informal*) Big Brother

**dictatorial** ADJECTIVE
*a dictatorial regime*
▶ autocratic, authoritarian, (*informal*) bossy, despotic, totalitarian, tyrannical, domineering, oppressive, absolute, intolerant, overbearing, repressive, undemocratic
AN OPPOSITE IS democratic

**dictatorship** NOUN
*The army imposed a dictatorship in the 1960s.*
▶ autocracy, totalitarian state, despotism, tyranny

**diction** NOUN
1 *unclear diction*
▶ enunciation, articulation, speech, elocution, intonation
2 *poetic diction*
▶ phraseology, choice of words, phrasing, expression, vocabulary

**dictionary** NOUN
*a word that was not in their dictionary*
▶ lexicon, glossary, vocabulary, wordbook, wordfinder, thesaurus

**dictum** NOUN
1 *Kipling's dictum that 'never the twain shall meet'*
▶ saying, maxim, proverb, epigram, precept
2 *an official dictum*
▶ pronouncement, proclamation, ruling, direction, decree, edict, fiat

**die** VERB

**1** *He was sixteen when his father died.*
▶ pass away, pass on, lose your life, meet your end, breathe your last, expire, (*more formal*) decease, (*more informal*) snuff it, (*more informal*) bite the dust, (*more informal*) kick the bucket

**2** *Hopes are dying of a peaceful settlement*
▶ fade, dwindle, sink, disappear, vanish, wither, melt away, dissolve

**3** *The engine spluttered and died.*
▶ fail, cut out, stall

**diehard** ADJECTIVE

*a group of diehard socialists*
▶ reactionary, intransigent, hardline, fanatical

**diet** NOUN

**1** *You need a healthy diet.*
▶ nutrition, nourishment, nutriment, food, fare

**2** *His doctor put him on a diet.*
▶ dietary regime, regimen, abstinence, fast

**diet** VERB

*She had been dieting for several months.*
▶ follow a diet, slim, watch your weight, reduce weight, fast

**differ** VERB

**1** *Opinions on the matter differed.*
▶ vary, diverge, be different

**2** *Our beliefs differ from those of other religious groups.*
▶ diverge, vary, deviate, be different, contrast (with)
AN OPPOSITE IS conform (to)

**3** *The ministers differed about what to do next.*
▶ disagree, argue, dispute, dissent, clash, conflict, be at odds, oppose each other, contradict each other, fall out, quarrel
AN OPPOSITE IS agree

**difference** NOUN

*There is a big difference in their ages.*
▶ dissimilarity, divergence, contrast, disparity, discrepancy, distinction, diversity, gap, variety, inconsistency, incompatibility, differential, differentiation, incongruity
AN OPPOSITE IS similarity

**difference of opinion** *The brothers were trying to resolve their difference of opinion.*
▶ disagreement, misunderstanding, dispute, argument, clash, conflict, controversy, debate, disharmony, dissent, quarrel, strife, tiff, wrangle

**different** ADJECTIVE

**1** *There were many different answers to the question.*
▶ dissimilar, unlike, unalike, diverging, divergent, varying, deviating, opposed, inconsistent, incompatible, contradictory, contrary, clashing
OPPOSITES ARE identical, similar

**2** *Everything about the house looked different.*
▶ changed, altered, transformed, strange, unfamiliar
AN OPPOSITE IS unchanging

**3** *We want to try something different.*
▶ unusual, unorthodox, uncommon, new, fresh, original, unconventional, unique, abnormal, extraordinary, irregular
AN OPPOSITE IS conventional

**4** *Every person's fingerprint is different.*
▶ distinct, unique, distinctive, individual, special, peculiar, personal, particular, specific
OPPOSITES ARE identical, indistinguishable

**differentiate** VERB

*It was hard to differentiate fact from fiction.*
▶ distinguish, tell apart, tell the difference between, discriminate between

**difficult** ADJECTIVE

**1** *a difficult problem*
▶ complicated, complex, hard, intricate, involved, intractable, abstruse, obscure, advanced, perplexing, problematical, baffling, deep, enigmatic, (*more informal*) thorny, (*more informal*) tricky
OPPOSITES ARE easy, straightforward

**2** *a difficult climb   a difficult task*
▶ hard, arduous, laborious, demanding, strenuous, tough, formidable, wearisome, burdensome, exacting, challenging
OPPOSITES ARE easy, light

**3** *difficult neighbours   a difficult child*
▶ unmanageable, troublesome, trying, tiresome, uncooperative, intractable, unruly, unhelpful, perverse
OPPOSITES ARE manageable, tractable, accommodating

**difficulty** NOUN

**1** *They found themselves in some difficulty.*
▶ trouble, distress, hardship, adversity, need, predicament, embarrassment, (*more informal*) fix, (*more informal*) mess

**2** *The cost of the holiday might be a difficulty.*
▶ problem, complication, snag, obstacle, hindrance, stumbling block, hurdle, pitfall, (*more informal*) headache, (*more informal*) hiccup

**diffidence** NOUN

*She replied with some diffidence.*
▶ reserve, shyness, bashfulness, timidity, modesty, humility, hesitancy, uncertainty, unassertiveness, self-consciousness

**diffident** ADJECTIVE

*a diffident smile*
▶ shy, coy, reserved, bashful, sheepish, inhibited, embarrassed, modest, self-conscious, hesitant, timid, reserved, retiring
OPPOSITES ARE assertive, forward, bold, confident

**diffuse** VERB

*The sound was diffused by specially designed reflectors.*
▶ spread, disperse, scatter, distribute, disseminate, dissipate
OPPOSITES ARE concentrate, collect

**dig** VERB

1 *The little dog was digging a hole in the garden.*
▶ burrow, excavate, scoop, tunnel, gouge out, hollow out, mine, quarry, delve
2 *Dinah dug him in the ribs.*
▶ poke, prod, jab, nudge, shove

**dig up**

1 *The police dug up the remains.*
▶ disinter, extricate, exhume
2 *Can you dig up some more information?*
▶ uncover, find out, discover

**digest** VERB

1 *The food is stodgy and difficult to digest.*
▶ absorb, assimilate, process, dissolve, break down
2 *There is a lot of information to digest.*
▶ take in, consider, absorb, ponder, study, understand

**digest** NOUN

*a digest of the latest research*
▶ summary, synopsis, outline, precis

**digit** NOUN

1 *Add up the digits*
▶ numeral, figure, number, integer
2 *We tried to bring the blood back to our frozen digits.*
▶ finger, toe, extremity

**dignified** ADJECTIVE

*Dr McNab combined an air of authority with a calm and dignified manner.*
▶ stately, solemn, noble, majestic, imposing, distinguished, honourable, becoming, august, proper, grand, grave, decorous, sedate
AN OPPOSITE IS undignified

**dignify** VERB

*Customs that are dignified with the name of laws.*
▶ honour, distinguish, exalt, graced, adorn

**dignitary** NOUN

*The occasion was attended by numerous foreign dignitaries.*
▶ majesty, grandee, worthy, important person, (*more informal*) bigwig, (*more informal*) big shot

**dignity** NOUN

1 *They accepted their misfortune with great dignity.*
▶ calmness, decorum, gravity, propriety, self-respect, eminence
2 *the dignity of a state occasion*
▶ majesty, grandeur, formality, solemnity, stateliness, magnificence, glory, greatness, honour, importance, nobility, pride, respectability, seriousness

**digress** VERB

*We have digressed from our main theme.*
▶ diverge, deviate, stray, wander, depart, go off at a tangent, ramble, veer

**digs** NOUN

*My father paid for my digs in Paddington.*
▶ lodgings, room(s), accommodation, living quarters, bedsit, flat, (*more informal*) place, (*more informal*) pad

**dilapidated** ADJECTIVE

*a row of dilapidated Victorian houses*
▶ run-down, ramshackle, decrepit, tumbledown, rickety, derelict, broken down, crumbling, neglected, ruined, decayed, tottering, uncared for
OPPOSITES ARE smart, well-maintained

**dilemma** NOUN

(*informal*) *The need to earn money while still studying placed him in a dilemma.*
▶ quandary, difficulty, predicament, awkward situation, (*more informal*) catch-22

**diligent** ADJECTIVE

*She had been diligent about her piano lessons.*
▶ conscientious, industrious, hard-working, painstaking, thorough, meticulous, punctilious, accurate, attentive, dedicated, rigorous, careful, dutiful, unflagging, assiduous, scrupulous
OPPOSITES ARE careless, irresponsible, lazy

**dilute** VERB

*a glass of wine diluted with water*
▶ weaken, thin, water down, mix, adulterate, make less concentrated, reduce the strength of
AN OPPOSITE IS concentrate

**dim** ADJECTIVE

1 *dim shapes in the distance   dim memories of their childhood*
▶ vague, indistinct, shadowy, unclear, fuzzy, blurred
OPPOSITES ARE distinct, clear
2 *a dim room*
▶ dark, sombre, dingy, gloomy, murky, dismal
AN OPPOSITE IS bright
3 (*informal*) *You probably think I'm awfully dim.*
▶ stupid, dense, obtuse, (*more informal*) thick

**dim** VERB

1 *The sky slowly dimmed*
▶ grow dark, darken, blacken, dull, cloud over
2 *He insisted on dimming the lights.*
▶ turn down, fade, lower, dip, shade, obscure
OPPOSITES ARE turn up, brighten

**dimension** NOUN

*dimensions a palace of huge dimensions*
▶ proportions, magnitude, size, scale, capacity, extent, scope

## diminish VERB

**1** *His angry feelings diminished in time.*
► decrease, reduce, lessen, decline, subside, wane, become less, depreciate, dwindle, peter out, shrink, shrivel, contract
AN OPPOSITE IS increase

**2** *We must not diminish their achievement.*
► belittle, disparage, demean, minimize, undervalue, devalue
OPPOSITES ARE exaggerate, magnify

## diminutive ADJECTIVE

*a woman leading a diminutive poodle*
► tiny, miniature, minuscule, minute, midget, undersized, dwarf, pygmy, small

## dimple NOUN

*Her smile produced an instant dimple in each cheek.*
► hollow, dip, depression, dint, cleft

## din NOUN

*It was hard to hear anything above the din.*
► uproar, racket, rumpus, commotion, hubbub, clamour, tumult, hullabaloo, noise, outcry, pandemonium, row, shouting

## dine VERB

*We will be dining at eight o'clock.*
► have dinner, eat, feed, feast

## dingy ADJECTIVE

*The front door opened on to a dingy hallway.*
► gloomy, dismal, dim, dreary, sombre, dark, drab, dull, murky
OPPOSITES ARE bright, cheerful

## dinosaur NOUN

**WORDS FOR TYPES OF DINOSAUR**
**large dinosaurs:** Allosaurus, Ankylosaurus, Brachiosaurus, Brontosaurus, Diplodocus, Iguanodon, Ornithomimus, Parasaurolophus, Spinosaurus, Stegosaurus, Styracosaurus, Trachodon, Triceratops, Tyrannosaurus.
**smaller dinosaurs:** Archaeopteryx, Coleophysis, Dimetrodon, Dromaeosaurus, Elasmosaurus, Proceratops, Saltopus.
**sea-dwelling dinosaurs:** Elasmosaurus, Ichthyosaurus.
**flying dinosaurs:** Archaeopteryx, Pteranadon, Rhamphorhynchus.

## dip NOUN

**1** *We reached a dip in the ground.*
► slope, incline, depression, declivity, dent, hollow, fall, hole, concavity

**2** *There will be a dip in sales after Christmas.*
► decrease, fall, decline, downturn, falling off

**3** *He likes a quick dip in the river.*
► bathe, swim, dive, plunge, splash, paddle

## dip VERB

**1** *She dipped her hand in the water.*
► immerse, lower, plunge, submerge, douse, dunk, drop, duck

**2** *The path dips towards the village.*
► descend, slope down, go down, subside, dive, slump

**3** *He would just smile and dip his head a little.*
► lower, drop

## diplomacy NOUN

**1** *They gave up the war and tried diplomacy.*
► negotiation, discussion, consultation, dialogue, statesmanship, statecraft

**2** *Her answer combined honesty and diplomacy.*
► tact, tactfulness, sensitivity, politeness, discretion, delicacy

## diplomat NOUN

**1** *An Iranian diplomat has been ordered to leave London.*
► envoy, official, ambassador, consul

**2** *Ever the diplomat, he offered them his help.*
► mediator, conciliator, peacemaker, tactful person

## diplomatic ADJECTIVE

*He tried to be diplomatic but the news was not good.*
► tactful, sensitive, considerate, discreet, subtle, polite, understanding, politic, careful, delicate, judicious, prudent, thoughtful
OPPOSITES ARE tactless, outspoken

## dire ADJECTIVE

**1** *The economy was in a dire state*
► terrible, dreadful, awful, appalling, disastrous, catastrophic

**2** *a dire warning*
► ominous, portentous, dreadful, gloomy, grim

**3** *in dire need of help*
► urgent, desperate, pressing, sore, serious, grave

## direct ADJECTIVE

**1** *Travel by the direct route.*
► straight, undeviating, shortest, quickest, nonstop, unswerving
AN OPPOSITE IS indirect

**2** *We want a direct answer.*
► straightforward, honest, frank, candid, unequivocal, sincere, blunt
AN OPPOSITE IS evasive

**3** *The sisters are direct opposites in character.*
► absolute, exact, complete, diametrical, downright, thorough, utter, head-on, (*informal*) out-and-out

## direct VERB

**1** *Earlier in her career she directed a child-growth project.*
► manage, run, administer, be in charge of, be responsible for, control, preside over, lead, organize

**2** *An official directed them to the meeting room.*
► show the way, tell the way, indicate the way, give directions to, guide, point, route

**3** *The books are mainly directed at teenagers.*
► target, aim, point, design (for), orient (towards)

4 *The judge directed the jury to return a verdict of not guilty.*
▶ instruct, order, tell, require, advise, charge, bid, enjoin

**direction** NOUN
1 *She left an hour later and went off in another direction.*
▶ route, way, course, line, bearing, orientation
2 **directions** *The nursing staff receive regular directions on new medicines.*
▶ instructions, guidelines, guidance, indications, briefing, plans, orders

**directive** NOUN
*an EU directive on pollution*
▶ ruling, instruction, order, regulation, direction, law

**directly** ADVERB
1 *She will join us directly.*
▶ immediately, at once, instantly, right away, straight away, in a moment, forthwith, presently
2 *You can fly directly from here to Montreal.*
▶ straight, immediately, by a direct route

**director** NOUN
*the directors of the main London museums*
▶ head, chief, manager, administrator, principal, (*more informal*) boss

**directory** NOUN
*a business directory*
▶ register, index, list, listing, catalogue

**dirt** NOUN
1 *The area in front of the house was covered in dirt.*
▶ grime, filth, muck, refuse, rubbish, garbage, dust, slime, sludge, mess, mire, pollution
2 *Chickens were scratching about in the dirt.*
▶ earth, soil, mud, loam, clay

**dirty** ADJECTIVE
1 *a dirty room   dirty clothes*
▶ filthy, grimy, grubby, soiled, stained, mucky, dingy, unwashed, squalid
AN OPPOSITE IS clean
2 *dirty water*
▶ impure, muddy, murky, polluted, untreated, cloudy
AN OPPOSITE IS pure
3 *dirty tricks*
▶ corrupt, dishonest, illegal, mean, treacherous, unfair, ungentlemanly, unsporting, (*more informal*) low-down
OPPOSITES ARE honest, sporting
4 *a dirty joke*
▶ rude, indecent, obscene, coarse, crude, smutty, suggestive, improper, risqué, offensive, vulgar
AN OPPOSITE IS clean
5 *a dirty look*
▶ angry, hostile, resentful, peeved, black

**dirty** VERB
*Try not to dirty the towels.*
▶ soil, stain, mess up, spoil, taint, tarnish
AN OPPOSITE IS clean

**disability** NOUN
*A disability can make the most routine tasks extremely difficult.*
▶ handicap, incapacity, infirmity, disablement, impairment, affliction, complaint, abnormality, weakness

**disable** VERB
1 *The injury disabled her for several months.*
▶ incapacitate, injure, immobilize, cripple, debilitate, enfeeble, handicap, impair, lame, maim, paralyse, weaken, (*informal*) hamstring
2 *The army succeeded in disabling the device.*
▶ incapacitate, put out of action, deactivate, disarm, make useless, stop working
OPPOSITES ARE restore, repair

**disabled** ADJECTIVE
*The house caters well for disabled visitors.*
▶ handicapped, physically handicapped, physically impaired, incapacitated, immobilized, bedridden, crippled, deformed, lame, paralysed
AN OPPOSITE IS able-bodied

**disadvantage** NOUN
*Heavy traffic is a major disadvantage of road travel.*
▶ drawback, snag, downside, inconvenience, weakness, nuisance, handicap, hardship, liability, privation, trouble, hindrance, impediment, (*more informal*) minus

**disadvantaged** ADJECTIVE
*schools in disadvantaged areas*
▶ deprived, underprivileged, depressed, impoverished, needy

**disadvantageous** ADJECTIVE
*in a disadvantageous position*
▶ unfavourable, inauspicious, unfortunate, unlucky, bad

**disagree** VERB
1 *We constantly disagree.*
▶ dissent, differ, argue, conflict, clash, fall out, quarrel, squabble, wrangle, bicker
AN OPPOSITE IS agree
2 **disagree with** *She disagrees with everything he says.*
▶ oppose, contradict, counter, argue with, dissent from, object to, take issue with, be at variance with, deviate from
3 **disagree with** *Onions disagree with me*
▶ make ill, make unwell, upset

## disagreeable ADJECTIVE

*a disagreeable taste   a disagreeable person*
▶ unpleasant, nasty, horrible, horrid, offensive,
repugnant, revolting, repellent

## disagreement NOUN

**1** *The two brothers had a disagreement.*
▶ argument, altercation, clash, quarrel, dispute,
contretemps, misunderstanding, squabble,
wrangle, (*more informal*) tiff, (*more informal*) barney
AN OPPOSITE IS agreement

**2** *There is some disagreement between the two versions
of the story.*
▶ difference, disparity, variance, dissimilarity,
discrepancy, incompatibility, divergence

## disappear VERB

**1** *The crowd rapidly disappeared.*
▶ vanish, disperse, recede, clear, evaporate, fade,
melt away, wane, dissolve, dwindle, cease to exist,
ebb
**2** *She disappeared round a corner.*
▶ go, pass, withdraw, run away, walk away, depart,
retire, escape, flee, fly
AN OPPOSITE IS appear
**3** *a way of life that has almost disappeared*
▶ die out, become extinct, vanish, perish
OPPOSITES ARE emerge, appear

## disappoint VERB

**1** *We will try not to disappoint you.*
▶ let down, fail, dissatisfy, disillusion, disenchant,
dishearten
AN OPPOSITE IS satisfy
**2** *In the end their hopes were disappointed.*
▶ thwart, frustrate, dash, defeat, foil

## disappointed ADJECTIVE

*I was disappointed when you didn't come.*
▶ saddened, unhappy, upset, let down, dissatisfied,
dejected, despondent, downcast, downhearted,
crestfallen, discontented, disenchanted,
disgruntled, disillusioned, frustrated
OPPOSITES ARE dissatisfied, contented

## disappointment NOUN

**1** *She could not hide her feeling of disappointment.*
▶ regret, sorrow, sadness, displeasure,
dissatisfaction, disapproval, dismay,
disillusionment, discontent
**2** *The exam result had been a disappointment*
▶ let-down, setback, misfortune, blow, anticlimax

## disapproval NOUN

*Her face clearly showed her disapproval.*
▶ dislike, displeasure, dissatisfaction, criticism,
anger, disapprobation, disfavour, dissent, reproach,
hostility, censure, condemnation, reprimand
AN OPPOSITE IS approval

## disapprove VERB

**disapprove of** *They disapprove of gambling*
▶ dislike, condemn, deplore, deprecate, object to,
frown on, look askance at, be displeased by, take
exception to, reject, criticize, denounce, censure,
disparage, make unwelcome, regret, (*more informal*)
take a dim view of
AN OPPOSITE IS approve of

## disapproving ADJECTIVE

(*informal*) *a disapproving glance*
▶ reproachful, critical, censorious, deprecatory,
disparaging, slighting, unfavourable, unfriendly
AN OPPOSITE IS approving

## disarray NOUN

*The room was by now in some disarray.   The opposition
parties were in disarray.*
▶ disorder, confusion, chaos, mess, muddle

## disaster NOUN

**1** *the world's worst air disaster*
▶ catastrophe, calamity, tragedy, misfortune,
mishap, affliction, cataclysm, blow
**2** (*informal*) *It would be a complete disaster for him if
she came back.*
▶ failure, fiasco, catastrophe, setback, reversal
AN OPPOSITE IS success

**SOME TYPES OF NATURAL DISASTER**

earthquake, volcanic eruption, avalanche,
hurricane, tornado, landslide, mudslide, flood;
tidal wave, tsunami, seaquake; famine.

## disastrous ADJECTIVE

*a disastrous fire   a disastrous choice*
▶ catastrophic, calamitous, cataclysmic,
devastating, ruinous, terrible, tragic, crippling,
destructive, dire, dreadful, fatal, bad
OPPOSITES ARE fortunate, successful

## disband VERB

*The team disbanded once the work was done.*
▶ break up, disperse, scatter, separate, part
company, go your own way

## disbelief NOUN

*He looked at her in disbelief*
▶ incredulity, distrust, scepticism, doubt, mistrust,
suspicion
OPPOSITES ARE belief, credence

## disbelieve VERB

*He disbelieved everything we said.*
▶ doubt, mistrust, reject, suspect, discount,
discredit, have no faith in, be sceptical of
AN OPPOSITE IS believe

## disbelieving ADJECTIVE

*Her manner was disbelieving.*
▶ incredulous, mistrustful, distrustful, sceptical

a b c **d** e f g h i j k l m n o p q r s t u v w x y z

**disc** NOUN

**1** *the disc of the sun*
► circle, round, ring
**2** *a new disc from the same band*
► CD, compact disc, record, album, single

**discard** VERB

*I decided to discard some old clothes.*
► get rid of, dispose of, dispense with, throw away, cast off, reject, eliminate, jettison, scrap, shed, dump, (*more informal*) chuck away, (*more informal*) ditch

**discern** VERB

*We discerned a tower in the distance.*
► perceive, spot, make out, pick out, detect, recognize, distinguish, become aware of

**discernible** ADJECTIVE

*His face was clearly discernible to her all the time.*
► visible, perceptible, observable, noticeable, distinct, manifest, conspicuous

**discerning** ADJECTIVE

*a discerning critic*
► discriminating, perceptive, refined, judicious, cultivated, enlightened, perspicacious

**discharge** VERB

**1** *Factories along the river were discharging thick smoke.*
► emit, give out, pour out, give off, exude, belch, release, secrete, produce, send out, eject, expel
**2** *He discharged the gun by accident.*
► fire, shoot, detonate, let off, explode
**3** *Three employees were discharged on the same day.*
► dismiss, fire, make redundant, remove, sack, throw out
**4** *The authorities discharged him from prison on a Sunday.*
► release, liberate, free, allow to leave, dismiss, excuse

**discharge** NOUN

**1** *discharge from prison*
► release, liberation
**2** *the discharge of a duty*
► accomplishment, execution, completion, fulfilment, achievement

**disciple** NOUN

*a disciple of Aristotle*
► follower, pupil, adherent, devotee, student, supporter, acolyte, admirer, apostle

**disciplinarian** NOUN

*a strict disciplinarian*
► taskmaster, authoritarian, autocrat, martinet, despot
AN OPPOSITE IS libertarian

**discipline** NOUN

**1** *Good financial discipline is important.*
► control, regulation, order, authority, orderliness, management, self-control, strictness, system, training, obedience
**2** *Their mother had been responsible for administering discipline.*
► punishment, chastisement, correction
**3** *Sociology is a fairly new discipline.*
► field of study, field, branch of knowledge speciality

**discipline** VERB

**1** *Families have different ways of disciplining their children.*
► train, control, instruct, educate, restrain, break in, drill
**2** *Several staff have been disciplined.*
► punish, reprimand, reprove, penalize, chasten, chastise

**disciplined** ADJECTIVE

*a disciplined workforce*
► orderly, well-trained, well-behaved
AN OPPOSITE IS undisciplined

**disclaim** VERB

*The company disclaimed all responsibility for the pollution.*
► deny, reject, renounce, repudiate, disown, forswear
OPPOSITES ARE acknowledge, accept, admit

**disclose** VERB

*This information should not be disclosed to anyone outside this room.*
► divulge, reveal, communicate, make known, pass on

**discolour** VERB

*Spilt liquid had discoloured the paintwork.*
► stain, mark, tarnish, tinge, fade, bleach

**discomfort** NOUN

*Her arm felt numb but she managed to hide the discomfort.*
► pain, soreness, ache, irritation, distress, hardship
AN OPPOSITE IS comfort

**disconcerting** ADJECTIVE

*He answered all the questions with disconcerting honesty.*
► unsettling, unnerving, offputting, confusing, disturbing, perplexing, upsetting, worrying
AN OPPOSITE IS reassuring

**disconnect** VERB

**1** *The power company had disconnected the supply.*
► cut off, break off, stop
OPPOSITES ARE reconnect, restore
**2** *The engine was disconnected at Crewe.*
► uncouple, detach, disengage, decouple, separate
OPPOSITES ARE attach, connect
**3** *Televisions should be disconnected at night.*
► unplug, deactivate
OPPOSITES ARE connect, plug in

# disconnected ADJECTIVE
*a disconnected argument*
▶ incoherent, disjointed, garbled, confused, disorganized, rambling, uncoordinated
OPPOSITES ARE coherent, logical

# discontent NOUN
*Soon their grumblings became open discontent.*
▶ dissatisfaction, unease, disquiet, disgruntlement, unhappiness

# discontented ADJECTIVE
*He felt discontented with his lot in life.*
▶ dissatisfied, unhappy, aggrieved, resentful, disgruntled, disaffected, (*more informal*) fed up, (*more informal*) browned off

# discontinue VERB
*The ferry to the island will be discontinued next year.*
▶ stop, end, finish, cease, break off, terminate, suspend, abandon, cancel, bring to an end

# discord NOUN
*Families can so often become a source of discord.*
▶ strife, conflict, friction, disagreement, dissension, disunity, argument, hostility
AN OPPOSITE IS agreement

# discordant ADJECTIVE
*discordant sounds*
▶ unharmonious, dissonant, jarring, cacophonous
AN OPPOSITE IS harmonious

# discount NOUN
*a £5 discount on the sticker price*
▶ reduction, deduction, concession, cut, allowance, rebate, (*more informal*) markdown

# discount VERB
*We discounted all these rumours.*
▶ disregard, reject, disbelieve, overlook, ignore

# discourage VERB
**1** *The audience was discouraged from asking questions.*
▶ deter, dissuade, restrain, prevent, hinder, put off, warn off
**2** *Her cool response discouraged them.*
▶ dishearten, dispirit, demoralize, disappoint, dismay, depress, unnerve, intimidate

# discouragement NOUN
*Strong police presence is a discouragement to crime.*
▶ deterrent, disincentive, constraint, hindrance, impediment, restraint, obstacle, setback, (*informal*) damper (on)
AN OPPOSITE IS encouragement

# discouraging ADJECTIVE
*The latest news is discouraging.*
▶ depressing, dispiriting, disheartening, demoralizing, disappointing, daunting

# discourse NOUN (with the stress on *dis-*)
**1** *They continued their discourse well into the night.*
▶ conversation, disquisition, literature, speech
**2** *a discourse on semantics*
▶ dissertation, essay, treatise, monograph, thesis, paper

# discourse VERB (with the stress on -*course*)
*He likes to discourse on his favourite topics.*
▶ speak, hold forth, expatiate, pontificate

# discourteous ADJECTIVE
*It would be discourteous to refuse.*
▶ rude, impolite, bad-mannered, ill-mannered, disrespectful, uncivil, churlish, ungracious, boorish

# discourtesy NOUN
*He had committed the grave discourtesy of not turning up for the speech.*
▶ rudeness, bad manners, ill manners, disrespect, incivility, churlishness

# discover VERB
**1** *The children had discovered a secret door at the bottom of the garden.*
▶ find, locate, come across, uncover, chance on, stumble on
**2** *We discovered that he had been lying.*
▶ find out, learn, realize, come to know, come to realize, work out, perceive
**3** *Faraday discovered electricity.*
▶ originate, develop, pioneer, invent
**USAGE** Note that *discover* and *invent* do not mean quite the same: you discover something natural that was always there (e.g. electricity), and you invent something new that did not exist before (e.g. television).

# discovery NOUN
**1** *a major new discovery*
▶ invention, innovation, revelation, breakthrough, disclosure, exploration, (*more informal*) find
**2** *the discovery of the body*
▶ finding, location, locating, detection, uncovering, unearthing

# discredit VERB
**1** *His enemies are looking for information that might discredit him.*
▶ disparage, defame, disgrace, smear, slander, dishonour, ruin the reputation of, slur, vilify
**2** *The new evidence discredits the witness's story.*
▶ disprove, prove false, invalidate, challenge, refute, raise doubts about, (*more informal*) explode, (*more informal*) show up

# discredit NOUN
*The arms sales brought discredit on the government.*
▶ disgrace, dishonour, disrepute, shame, ignominy, censure, blame

# discreet ADJECTIVE
**USAGE** Do not confuse this word with *discrete*, which means 'distinct' or 'separate'.
*I made a few discreet enquiries.*
▶ careful, circumspect, cautious, guarded, wary, tactful, judicious, prudent, considerate, delicate, diplomatic, sensitive, thoughtful, polite, politic
OPPOSITES ARE indiscreet, rash

# discrepancy NOUN
*There is a discrepancy between the two versions of the story.*
▶ inconsistency, difference, disparity, variance,

**discrete** ADJECTIVE

**USAGE** Do not confuse this word with *discreet*, which means 'careful' or 'cautious'.
*teaching the course in discrete units*
▶ distinct, separate, individual, detached

**discretion** NOUN

1 *The police conducted their enquiries with discretion.*
▶ diplomacy, tact, sensitivity, good sense, judgement, maturity, prudence, responsibility, wisdom
AN OPPOSITE IS indiscretion

2 *Payment of interest is at the Bank's discretion.*
▶ choice, option, judgement, will, wish, preference

**discriminate** VERB

1 *It is hard to discriminate between the two theories.*
▶ differentiate, distinguish, make a distinction, tell the difference

2 *Some employment practices still discriminate against women.*
▶ be biased, be prejudiced, show discrimination, be intolerant (towards)

**discriminating** ADJECTIVE

*a discriminating art collector*
▶ discerning, perceptive, astute, judicious, fastidious, critical, particular, selective, (*more informal*) choosy
AN OPPOSITE IS undiscriminating

**discrimination** NOUN

1 *She shows discrimination in her choice of music*
▶ discernment, good taste, insight, judgement, perceptiveness, refinement, selectivity, subtlety, taste

2 *victims of discrimination*
▶ prejudice, bias, bigotry, intolerance, chauvinism, favouritism, male chauvinism, racism, sexism, unfairness
AN OPPOSITE IS impartiality

**discuss** VERB

*It was good to discuss other people's problems.*
▶ debate, consider, talk about, confer about, consult about, deliberate, examine, deal with

**discussion** NOUN

*a lively discussion about funding universities*
▶ debate, deliberation, conference, dialogue, consultation, conversation, argument, discourse, consideration, examination, exchange of views, symposium, talk

**disease** NOUN

*suffering from a disease   a country afflicted by disease*
▶ illness, sickness, bad health, ailment, malady, disorder, infirmity
RELATED ADJECTIVE morbid

**diseased** ADJECTIVE

*poor and diseased villagers*
▶ ill, sick, unhealthy, unwell, ailing, infected
AN OPPOSITE IS healthy

**disentangle** VERB

1 *The cord had a knot that was difficult to disentangle.*
▶ untangle, undo, untie, untwist, sort out, straighten, unknot, unravel
AN OPPOSITE IS entangle

2 *She disentangled his hand from her twisted clothing.*
▶ free, release, extricate, extract, remove, disengage, liberate, separate
AN OPPOSITE IS enmesh

**disfigure** VERB

*A new motorway will disfigure the landscape.*
▶ mar, scar, deface, deform, mutilate, spoil, damage
OPPOSITES ARE enhance, beautify

**disgrace** NOUN

1 *the public disgrace of being prosecuted for shoplifting*
▶ dishonour, shame, humiliation, ignominy, degradation, slur, stain, stigma, discredit, embarrassment, opprobrium, scandal
AN OPPOSITE IS honour

2 (*informal*) *The local facilities for children were a disgrace.*
▶ outrage, scandal, affront, insult
OPPOSITES ARE credit, asset

**disgrace** VERB

*He very nearly disgraced his friends by reciting an improper poem.*
▶ shame, bring shame on, defame, humiliate, scandalize

**disgraceful** ADJECTIVE

*Their behaviour had been disgraceful.*
▶ shameful, deplorable, shocking, dreadful, despicable, dishonourable, reprehensible, appalling, bad

**disgruntled** ADJECTIVE

*complaints from disgruntled customers*
▶ dissatisfied, discontented, aggrieved, resentful, disappointed, unhappy, indignant, angry

**disguise** NOUN

*She looked quite convincing in her nun's disguise.*
▶ costume, outfit, impersonation, camouflage, concealment, pretence, cloak, cover, fancy dress, make-up, front, mask, (*more informal*) get-up

**disguise** VERB

1 *Her long sleeves disguised her burns.*
▶ hide, conceal, cover, mask, screen, shroud, veil, camouflage, dress up, make inconspicuous

2 *He made no attempt to disguise his anger.*
▶ hide, conceal, cover up, gloss over, misrepresent

3 *disguise yourself as I changed my identity and disguised myself as one of the locals.*
▶ dress up as, impersonate, pretend to be, pose as, counterfeit, imitate, mimic, (*more informal*) take off

## disgust NOUN

*She turned and looked in disgust at the body on the back seat.*

▶ revulsion, repugnance, repulsion, abhorrence, distaste, aversion, antipathy, contempt, loathing, detestation, nausea, dislike, hatred

OPPOSITES ARE liking, relish

## disgust VERB

*The hospital food disgusted me.*

▶ revolt, nauseate, offend, appal, repel, sicken, be distasteful to, displease, horrify, outrage, put off, shock, (*more informal*) turn your stomach

OPPOSITES ARE please, appeal to

## disgusting ADJECTIVE

*The smell was disgusting. They showed disgusting bigotry.*

▶ revolting, nauseating, offensive, sickening, loathsome, repugnant, repulsive, unpleasant

OPPOSITES ARE pleasant, appealing, attractive

## dish NOUN

**1** *He tipped the pasta into a dish.*

▶ plate, bowl, platter

**2** *a nutritious vegetarian dish*

▶ food, recipe

## dish VERB

**dish out** *The children helped by dishing out piles of books.*

▶ distribute, give out, hand round, deal out, issue

**dish up** *Shirley was busy dishing up burgers and hot dogs.*

▶ serve, serve up, provide, dispense

## dishearten VERB

*The result disheartened them so much they almost gave up.*

▶ discourage, dispirit, dismay, depress, disappoint, deter, put off, sadden

OPPOSITES ARE hearten, encourage

## dishevelled ADJECTIVE

*She ran a hand through her dishevelled hair*

▶ untidy, bedraggled, disordered, unkempt, scruffy, disarranged, tangled, ruffled, rumpled, slovenly, tousled, uncombed, messy

OPPOSITES ARE neat, tidy

## dishonest ADJECTIVE

*Their solicitor proved to be dishonest. a dishonest statement*

▶ deceitful, untruthful, lying, fraudulent, false, double-dealing, cheating, swindling, corrupt, underhand, untrustworthy, (*more informal*) crooked

OPPOSITES ARE honest, truthful

## dishonesty NOUN

*a charge of dishonesty against former colleagues*

▶ corruption, fraud, fraudulence, cheating, deceit, deception, deviousness, lying, falsity, falsehood, (*more informal*) crookedness, (*more informal*) shadiness

AN OPPOSITE IS honesty

## dishonour NOUN

*I have no wish to bring dishonour on you or your family.*

▶ disgrace, shame, discredit, degradation, humiliation, ignominy, stigma, opprobrium, indignity

OPPOSITES ARE honour, credit

## dishonourable ADJECTIVE

*It would be dishonourable to refuse to pay.*

▶ disgraceful, shameful, discreditable, ignominious, contemptible, reprehensible

## dishy ADJECTIVE

*Judging by the photograph, the author's dishy, too.*

▶ attractive, good-looking, charming, sexy, appealing

## disillusioned ADJECTIVE

*They soon became disillusioned by the reality of wedded bliss.*

▶ disappointed, disenchanted, disabused, let down, discouraged

AN OPPOSITE IS enthusiastic

## disinclined ADJECTIVE

*He held Madeleine's hand, which she seemed disinclined to remove.*

▶ reluctant, unwilling, loath, hesitant, resistant (to moving), averse (to moving)

## disinfect VERB

*An aromatic plant is used to disinfect houses where malaria is present.*

▶ sterilize, sanitize, clean, cleanse, purify, fumigate

OPPOSITES ARE infect, contaminate

## disinfectant NOUN

*She wiped the surface down with disinfectant.*

▶ antiseptic, sterilizer, germicide, carbolic, cleaner

## disintegrate VERB

*The aircraft caught fire and disintegrated in the air.*

▶ break up, fall apart, fall to pieces, explode, come apart, decompose

## disinterested ADJECTIVE

*Her advice would always be disinterested.*

▶ impartial, neutral, unbiased, unprejudiced, dispassionate, open-minded, even-handed

AN OPPOSITE IS biased

**USAGE** Note that *disinterested* means 'impartial' and does not mean the same as *uninterested*.

## disjointed ADJECTIVE

*She turned her disjointed thoughts over in her mind.*

▶ disconnected, incoherent, confused, disordered, unconnected, disorganized, jumbled, rambling, fitful, erratic

AN OPPOSITE IS coherent

## dislike VERB

*She dislikes me because I won't do what she says.*

▶ not like, detest, hate, object to, abhor, disapprove of, despise

AN OPPOSITE IS like

## dislike NOUN
He had a fear and dislike of big cities.
▶ aversion (to), distaste (for), antagonism (to), antipathy (to), contempt (for), disgust (for), revulsion (from), detestation, disapproval, hatred, loathing
AN OPPOSITE IS liking

## dislocate VERB
He had dislocated his left shoulder in a Rugby game.
▶ put out of joint, disjoint, displace, disengage, (more informal) put out

## dislodge VERB
Several stones had been dislodged, causing a hazard to passers-by.
▶ displace, disarrange, dislocate, disturb, misplace, move, shift, remove, knock out of place, knock out of position

## disloyal ADJECTIVE
His colleagues criticized him for being disloyal in his comments.
▶ unfaithful, faithless, treacherous, subversive, seditious, dissident, false, traitorous
OPPOSITES ARE loyal, faithful

## disloyalty NOUN
She felt a sense of guilt, of disloyalty.
▶ unfaithfulness, infidelity, betrayal, duplicity, faithlessness, falseness, inconstancy, perfidy, treachery, treason, double-dealing
AN OPPOSITE IS loyalty

## dismal ADJECTIVE
1 She led them into a dismal little room.
▶ gloomy, dingy, dim, dreary, sombre, dark, drab, dull, murky
OPPOSITES ARE bright, cheerful
2 (informal) a row of dismal performances
▶ dreadful, awful, terrible, feeble, disgraceful
3 We looked at the dismal faces around us.
▶ glum, gloomy, sad, miserable, melancholy, sombre, forlorn, despondent, downcast, sorrowful, mournful, woeful

## dismantle VERB
Before they left, the soldiers dismantled the row of huts.
▶ take apart, take to pieces, take down, knock down, break up, demolish, strip down
OPPOSITES ARE assemble, build

## dismay NOUN
Laura gave a yelp of dismay as she caught sight of the time on her watch.
▶ alarm, shock, surprise, consternation, concern, distress, apprehension, agitation, trepidation, fright, horror

## dismay VERB
You should not be dismayed by these comments.
▶ alarm, daunt, horrify, shock, appal, discourage, dishearten, dispirit, distress, deject, depress, devastate, disappoint, unnerve, frighten, scare
AN OPPOSITE IS encourage

## dismember VERB
Thugs slaughtered and dismembered a pet goat.
▶ cut up, disjoint, divide, remove the limbs of

## dismiss VERB
1 Elaine dismissed her husband with a wave of her hand.
▶ send away, discharge, free, let go, release
2 (informal) Three employees were dismissed on the spot.
▶ give someone notice, discharge, lay off, (more informal) sack, (more informal) fire
3 She had dismissed Nina's allegations as rubbish.
▶ reject, discount, disregard, set aside, repudiate, discard, spurn, drop, get rid of, give up, shelve, wave aside, (more informal) pooh-pooh
4 He tried to dismiss these thoughts from his mind.
▶ banish, dispel, remove, reject, shrug off

## disobedience NOUN
They were punished for their disobedience.
▶ insubordination, naughtiness, misbehaviour, bad behaviour, misconduct, unruliness, rebelliousness, wilfulness

## disobedient ADJECTIVE
The children had been disobedient and demanding.
▶ naughty, badly behaved, insubordinate, troublesome, disorderly, disruptive, fractious, rebellious, unruly, wayward, intractable, obstreperous, wilful, contrary
AN OPPOSITE IS obedient

## disobey VERB
1 The Queen was angry that so many people had disobeyed her orders.
▶ defy, flout, rebel against, contravene, disregard, ignore, infringe, break, resist, transgress, violate
2 Remember never to disobey.
▶ be disobedient, rebel, revolt
AN OPPOSITE IS obey

## disorder NOUN
1 They were arrested for acts of public disorder.
▶ disturbance, unrest, agitation, disruption, upheaval, tumult, insurrection, rebellion
OPPOSITES ARE order, peace
2 The house is in total disorder.
▶ untidiness, disarray, disorganization, confusion, chaos, a mess, a muddle, a shambles
OPPOSITES ARE order, tidiness

## disorderly ADJECTIVE
1 behaving in a disorderly manner
▶ unruly, rowdy, rebellious, disruptive, undisciplined, disobedient, boisterous, rough, wild
OPPOSITES ARE orderly, disciplined
2 a disorderly arrangement
▶ untidy, disorganized, messy, muddled, confused, chaotic
OPPOSITES ARE orderly, tidy

## disorganized ADJECTIVE
1 The room looked completely disorganized.
▶ untidy, disorderly, messy, muddled, confused, chaotic
OPPOSITES ARE neat, systematic

**disown**

2 *I was accused of being careless and disorganized.*
▶ unmethodical, slapdash, slovenly, absent-minded, scatterbrained, inefficient

**disown** VERB

*Her family disowned her when she married Jem.*
▶ reject, renounce, repudiate, cast off, abandon, end relations with

**disparaging** ADJECTIVE

*make disparaging remarks*
▶ derogatory, depreciatory, insulting, abusive, uncomplimentary

**dispassionate** ADJECTIVE

*a dispassionate assessment of the situation*
▶ objective, impartial, detached, neutral, unemotional, calm, cool, impersonal, level-headed
OPPOSITES ARE emotional, biased

**dispatch** NOUN

*A messenger brought dispatches.*
▶ bulletin, communiqué, letter, message, report

**dispatch** VERB

1 *Reminders will be dispatched next week.*
▶ send, post, transmit, consign, convey, forward
2 *In the film the good guy has to dispatch a host of vicious villains.*
▶ kill, put an end to, put to death, dispose of, finish off

**dispel** VERB

*It was a feeling that he found difficult to dispel.*
▶ banish, eliminate, dismiss, get rid of, drive away

**dispense** VERB

1 *Waiters were there to dispense drinks.*
▶ distribute, give out, pass round, mete out, provide, allocate, allot, apportion, deal out, dole out, share
2 *The local chemist dispenses medicines.*
▶ supply, prepare, make up
3 **dispense with** *We can dispense with the formalities.*
▶ waive, disregard, ignore, forgo, do without, pass over, drop, omit, cancel, dispose of, get rid of

**disperse** VERB

1 *Troops arrived to disperse the demonstrators.*
▶ break up, split up, separate, scatter, drive away, send away, disband, dispel, dismiss
OPPOSITES ARE assemble, collect
2 *The crowd dispersed quickly.*
▶ break up, split up, disband, separate, scatter, dissolve, disappear, vanish, melt away
OPPOSITES ARE collect, gather, assemble
3 *Birds disperse the seed.*
▶ scatter, spread, disseminate, distribute, strew
AN OPPOSITE IS centralize

**dispirited** ADJECTIVE

*He felt tired and dispirited.*
▶ disheartened, depressed, dejected, downcast, despondent, downhearted, disconsolate, unhappy, sad, down, glum, melancholy, miserable, cast down
OPPOSITES ARE cheerful, happy

**displace** VERB

1 *The gales have displaced many roof tiles.*
▶ dislodge, disarrange, dislocate, disturb, misplace, move, shift, remove, knock out of place, knock out of position
2 *The recent land reforms have displaced thousands of people.*
▶ force out, drive out, eject, expel, oust, remove, supplant

**display** NOUN

*an air display a display of horsemanship*
▶ exhibition, demonstration, show, spectacle, pageant, presentation, parade

**display** VERB

1 *A room will be built to display the marbles.*
▶ exhibit, show, put on show, present
2 *He displayed a good knowledge of the subject.*
▶ show, reveal, demonstrate, manifest, flaunt, produce, betray, air, evince

**displease** VERB

*The decision clearly displeased him.*
▶ annoy, irritate, infuriate, incense, anger, enrage, vex, exasperate, madden, aggravate, antagonize, inflame, make angry, (more informal) needle, (more informal) rile, (more informal) bug, (more informal) rub up the wrong way

**disposable** ADJECTIVE

1 *a large disposable income*
▶ available, usable, accessible, spendable
2 *disposable plates*
▶ expendable, replaceable, single-use, (more informal) throwaway

**disposal** NOUN

1 *the disposal of troops for battle*
▶ arrangement, disposition, order, grouping, mustering
2 *the disposal of radioactive waste*
▶ removal, elimination, discarding, destruction, riddance

**dispose** VERB

1 *A general disposes his troops for battle*
▶ arrange, array, group, place, position, set out
2 **dispose of** *Equipment was needed to dispose of soiled nappies.*
▶ deal with, get rid of, destroy, discard, jettison, scrap, sell, throw away, dump
**be disposed to** *Brian was not disposed to question this idea.*
▶ be inclined to, be ready to, be willing to, be liable to, be likely to

**disposition** NOUN

1 *the disposition of the armed forces*
▶ arrangement, disposal, order, grouping, mustering
2 *a nervous disposition*
▶ temperament, character, nature, humour, inclination, tendency, leaning, make-up, constitution

**disproportionate** ADJECTIVE

*Small tasks can take up a disproportionate amount of time.*
▶ undue, uneven, unequal, unreasonable, inordinate, excessive, unbalanced
OPPOSITES ARE proportional, reasonable

**disprove** VERB

*New evidence has disproved the original verdicts.*
▶ invalidate, refute, overturn, confute, contradict, controvert, discredit, negate, rebut, expose, (*more informal*) explode
OPPOSITES ARE prove, confirm

**dispute** NOUN

*a matter of great dispute*
▶ debate, discussion, controversy, contention, argument, disagreement, conflict, dissension

**dispute** VERB

**1** *We disputed with them deep into the night.*
▶ debate, argue, contend, exchange views, quarrel
**2** *No one can dispute their claim.*
▶ challenge, contest, question, oppose, deny, doubt, contradict, controvert, impugn, argue against, quarrel with
AN OPPOSITE IS accept

**disqualify** VERB

*He was disqualified from driving for a year.*
▶ ban, bar, debar, prohibit, forbid (to drive), preclude

**disquiet** NOUN

*The decision caused a lot of public disquiet.*
▶ unease, concern, worry, distress, anxiety, alarm, anguish

**disregard** VERB

*Anne tried to disregard the noise.*
▶ ignore, take no notice of, pay no attention to, discount, overlook, pass over, make light of, brush aside
AN OPPOSITE IS heed

**disrepair** NOUN

*The house is in a serious state of disrepair.*
▶ dilapidation, deterioration, decay, neglect, collapse, bad condition, ruin, shabbiness
AN OPPOSITE IS good repair

**disreputable** ADJECTIVE

**1** *disreputable minicab drivers without proper licences*
▶ dishonest, suspect, dubious, discreditable, dishonourable, notorious, corrupt, (*more informal*) sleazy, (*more informal*) shady
AN OPPOSITE IS reputable
**2** *His bare feet and stubbly chin gave him a disreputable appearance.*
▶ scruffy, shabby, unkempt, dishevelled, bedraggled, raffish, unconventional
AN OPPOSITE IS respectable

**disrespectful** ADJECTIVE

*He was often disrespectful towards his elders.*
▶ rude, discourteous, impertinent, impolite, insolent, impudent, cheeky
OPPOSITES ARE respectful, polite

**disrupt** VERB

*A strike of air-traffic controllers has disrupted holiday travel.*
▶ interrupt, break up, dislocate, disturb, upset, interfere with, throw into disorder, break the routine of

**disruptive** ADJECTIVE

*Disruptive behaviour often leads to considerable stress.*
▶ unruly, troublesome, rowdy, undisciplined, disorderly, rebellious, misbehaving, errant

**dissatisfaction** NOUN

*There is widespread dissatisfaction with the quality of service.*
▶ discontent, discontentment, disappointment, disquiet, disgruntlement, frustration, annoyance, irritation, unhappiness, displeasure, anger, exasperation, chagrin, dismay, regret
AN OPPOSITE IS satisfaction

**dissatisfied** ADJECTIVE

*They were clearly dissatisfied with our answer.*
▶ discontented, disappointed, unsatisfied, unhappy, disgruntled, displeased, aggrieved (by), disaffected (by), frustrated (by), (*more informal*) fed up, unfulfilled
OPPOSITES ARE satisfied, contented

**dissect** VERB

**1** *He had to dissect his dumpling with the edge of his fork.*
▶ cut up, take apart, dismember
**2** *The argument was dissected and the various aspects considered.*
▶ analyse, split up, examine, inspect, investigate, study, scrutinize, sift, probe

**dissension** NOUN

*The tax cuts were an attempt to head off possible dissension.*
▶ disagreement, dissent, discord, dispute, conflict, contention, strife, friction, argument

**dissent** NOUN

*The military government would not tolerate dissent or criticism.*
▶ disagreement, objection, protest, insubordination, argument, disapproval

**dissent** VERB

**dissent from** *I do not dissent from the ideas you propose.*
▶ disagree with, differ from, demur from, diverge from, dispute, object to, take issue with, quibble with

**disservice** NOUN

*You have done a disservice to the African people.*
▶ unkindness, wrong, injustice, disfavour, bad turn, mischief, harm, injury, damage, offence
AN OPPOSITE IS favour

**dissident** NOUN

*dissidents who had been imprisoned by the regime*
▶ protester, dissenter, agitator, rebel, nonconformist, (*more informal*) refusenik
AN OPPOSITE IS conformist

**dissimilar** ADJECTIVE

**1** *a wide range of dissimilar tasks*
▶ different, differing, diverse, distinct, unrelated, varying, unlike, disparate, heterogeneous
**2 dissimilar to** *This catfish shows a parental care not dissimilar to that of the cuckoo.*
▶ unlike, different from or to, unrelated to
AN OPPOSITE IS similar

**dissipate** VERB

**1** *Her good humour soon dissipated.*
▶ disappear, vanish, evaporate, dissolve, subside, disperse
OPPOSITES ARE grow, develop
**2** *He went on to dissipate his entire fortune.*
▶ waste, squander, fritter, fritter away, misspend, consume, burn up, drain, exhaust
OPPOSITES ARE save, preserve

**dissociate** VERB

*We decided to dissociate ourselves from the more extravagant claims being made.*
▶ break away, back away, detach, distance, separate, cut off, divorce, isolate
AN OPPOSITE IS associate

**dissolve** VERB

**1** *The acids dissolve in water.*
▶ liquefy, become liquid, diffuse, disperse, melt, deliquesce, disappear, disintegrate
**2** *Dissolve salts in the water to keep it pure.*
▶ liquefy, melt, disintegrate, disperse
**3** *His anger began to dissolve.*
▶ disappear, vanish, evaporate, dissipate, subside, disperse
OPPOSITES ARE grow, develop
**4** *The Assembly was dissolved after the revolution.*
▶ disband, terminate, abolish, close down, suspend, break up, dismiss, end, bring to an end, cancel, (*more informal*) wind up

**dissuade** VERB

**dissuade from** *He dissuaded his colleagues from taking strike action.*
▶ discourage from, prevent from, deter from, divert from, disincline (to take), talk out of, urge against, advise against, persuade not (to take)
AN OPPOSITE IS persuade (to)

**distance** NOUN

**1** *the distance between the two vehicles*
▶ space, interval, gap, extent, length, range, reach, separation

**2** *She keeps her distance.*
▶ aloofness, reserve, detachment, reticence, coolness, remoteness, coldness
AN OPPOSITE IS closeness

**in the distance** *a church spire visible in the distance*
▶ far away, far off, in the background, on the horizon, yonder

**distance** VERB

**distance yourself** *The President had to distance himself from these men.*
▶ withdraw, detach yourself, dissociate yourself, separate yourself, remove yourself, keep your distance, keep at arm's length, set yourself apart, keep away, stay away
OPPOSITES ARE involve yourself (with), become close (to)

**distant** ADJECTIVE

**1** *distant countries*
▶ far-off, faraway, remote, outlying, isolated
AN OPPOSITE IS close
**2** *a distant memory*
▶ vague, dim, faint, indistinct, obscure, indefinite
**3** *a distant manner*
▶ aloof, detached, impersonal, reserved, reticent, unfriendly, withdrawn, cool
OPPOSITES ARE friendly, warm

**distaste** NOUN

**1** *George looked with distaste at the man sitting opposite.*
▶ disgust, revulsion, abhorrence, repugnance, disdain, disfavour, dislike
**2** *a distaste for politics*
▶ dislike (of), aversion (to), repugnance (for), disapproval (of)

**distasteful** ADJECTIVE

*The day was hot and their work distasteful.*
▶ unpleasant, disagreeable, offensive, repulsive, objectionable, unappealing, unpalatable, repugnant, abhorrent, unsavoury

**distinct** ADJECTIVE

**1** *four distinct categories*
▶ discrete, separate, individual, detached
OPPOSITES ARE indistinct, fuzzy
**2** *a distinct improvement*
▶ clear, definite, marked, sharp, decided, unmistakable, obvious, plain

**distinction** NOUN

**1** *There is a clear distinction between politicians and the rest of us.*
▶ difference, contrast, dissimilarity, divergence, variance, variation, differentiation, discrimination, distinctiveness
AN OPPOSITE IS similarity
**2** *a writer of distinction*
▶ importance, significance, note, consequence, account, greatness, renown, celebrity, eminence, fame, reputation, repute, prestige, honour
AN OPPOSITE IS mediocrity

**3** *treating people without distinction of race, age, creed, or sex*
▶ differentiation, discrimination (between)

**4** *He served with distinction in the war.*
▶ honour, credit, merit, courage, valour

**distinctive** ADJECTIVE
*This duck has a distinctive white neck.*
▶ distinguishing, characteristic, typical, individual, peculiar, unique, special, singular, different, original, idiosyncratic, unusual

**distinguish** VERB
**1** *the capacity to distinguish between good and bad in literature*
▶ differentiate, discriminate, decide, tell the difference, pick out (good and bad), determine (what is good and bad)

**2** *We could distinguish a line of trees in the darkness.*
▶ make out, identify, discern, perceive, recognize, observe, notice, glimpse

**distinguished** ADJECTIVE
*a distinguished statesman*
▶ eminent, famous, prominent, well known, celebrated, acclaimed, renowned, illustrious, famed, notable, noteworthy, esteemed, respected, honoured, outstanding

**distort** VERB
**1** *His face was distorted with pain.*
▶ twist, contort, warp, deform, misshape, bend, wrench

**2** *That explanation distorts the truth.*
▶ twist, misrepresent, pervert, slant, falsify, misstate, garble, put a slant on, (*more informal*) put a spin on

**distorted** ADJECTIVE
*a distorted version of the events*
▶ twisted, slanted, misrepresented, perverted, coloured, false, biased, one-sided, prejudiced, inaccurate

**distract** VERB
**1** *A noise across the street distracted him.*
▶ divert, sidetrack, disturb

**2** *Helen appeared to be distracted by the back of the cereal packet.*
▶ puzzle, bewilder, disconcert, confuse, perplex, trouble, worry

**distraction** NOUN
**1** *the distractions of life in a big city*
▶ amusement, entertainment, diversion, pleasure, recreation, enjoyment, fun, interest, pastime

**2** *The baby's crying drove her to distraction.*
▶ frenzy, distress, insanity, madness, delirium

**distraught** ADJECTIVE
*The poor woman looked distraught.*
▶ upset, overwrought, distressed, distracted, agitated, frantic, (*more informal*) beside yourself

**distress** NOUN
**1** *She put her hand over her mouth to hide her distress.*
▶ anguish, suffering, misery, torment, discomfort, wretchedness, unhappiness, disquiet, despair, desolation, agony, grief
OPPOSITES ARE happiness, comfort

**2** *the distress of extreme poverty*
▶ hardship, adversity, tribulation, destitution, privation, trial
AN OPPOSITE IS prosperity

**distress** VERB
*I was distressed by the fact that everyone seemed to turn against him.*
▶ upset, perturb, disturb, trouble, bother, worry, sadden, afflict, torment
OPPOSITES ARE comfort, soothe

**distribute** VERB
**1** *They spent the day distributing pamphlets.*
▶ circulate, issue, spread, disperse, hand out, make available

**2** *The house was sold and the money distributed among his heirs.*
▶ share out, divide up, apportion, allocate

**3** *The seed should be distributed evenly.*
▶ scatter, spread, disperse, strew, disseminate, arrange

**district** NOUN
*the shopping district of the town*
▶ area, region, quarter, locality, zone, neighbourhood, sector, vicinity, part

**distrust** VERB
*On the whole the public distrusts politicians.*
▶ mistrust, suspect, be suspicious of, be sceptical about, have misgivings about, have qualms about, be wary of, disbelieve, doubt, question
AN OPPOSITE IS trust

**distrustful** ADJECTIVE
*He was distrustful of the people who were most trying to help him.*
▶ suspicious, mistrustful, unsure, sceptical (about), doubtful (about), cautious (about)

**disturb** VERB
**1** *He crept into the house quietly so as not to disturb his sleeping parents.*
▶ bother, annoy, interrupt, intrude on, disrupt, upset, alarm, wake

**2** *Try not to disturb the books and papers.*
▶ muddle, mix up, disarrange, disorganize, confuse

**disturbance** NOUN
*People were injured in violent disturbances in the capital.*
▶ commotion, uproar, racket, tumult, hullabaloo, hubbub, rumpus, fracas, furore, upheaval, agitation, excitement

**disused** ADJECTIVE
*An unexploded bomb was found in a disused cellar.*
▶ abandoned, neglected, obsolete, unused, unoccupied, discontinued, idle, discarded
AN OPPOSITE IS operational

**ditch** NOUN

*Some sheep had fallen into a ditch and had to be rescued.*
▶ trench, channel, gully, watercourse, conduit, dike, drain, gutter, moat

**ditch** VERB

*(informal) We will have to ditch that idea.*
▶ abandon, drop, scrap, jettison, throw out, shelve, discard, forget, *(more informal)* dump, *(more informal)* pull the plug on

**dither** VERB

*He dithered over which suit to wear that day.*
▶ hesitate, waver, be in two minds, vacillate, *(more informal)* shilly-shally

**dive** VERB

*1 A young girl dived into the water.*
▶ plunge, leap, jump, drop
*2 The hawk dived rapidly towards its prey.*
▶ swoop, plunge, plummet, descend, nose-dive, drop, pitch

**diverge** VERB

*1 The roads diverged at this point.*
▶ separate, divide, part, split, branch, deviate, fork
OPPOSITES ARE converge, come together, join
*2 Clearly our opinions diverge.*
▶ differ, disagree, clash, be different
OPPOSITES ARE agree, coincide

**diverse** ADJECTIVE

*information from diverse sources*
▶ various, varying, different, sundry, assorted, miscellaneous, mixed, distinct, *(more formal)* manifold

**diversify** VERB

*The company wishes to diversify into producing hang gliders.*
▶ expand, branch out, spread out

**diversion** NOUN

*1 a traffic diversion*
▶ detour, deviation, alternative route
*2 a large city with plenty of diversions*
▶ entertainment, amusement, recreation, relaxation, distraction, pastime, game, hobby, play, sport

**diversity** NOUN

*a great diversity of fruit and vegetables*
▶ variety, assortment, miscellany, mixture, range, array, multiplicity
OPPOSITES ARE uniformity, similarity

**divert** VERB

*1 The plane was diverted to another airport.*
▶ redirect, reroute, deflect, turn aside, switch
*2 We tried to divert them with funny stories.*
▶ amuse, entertain, distract, occupy, interest, cheer up, delight, keep happy, recreate, regale

**divide** VERB

*1 The river divides north of the city. We divided into two groups*
▶ separate, diverge, split, split in two, fork, branch
AN OPPOSITE IS converge
*2 We divided the food between us*
▶ share out, allocate, allot, apportion, distribute, pass round
*3 We divide the eggs according to size.*
▶ sort, classify, grade, group, arrange, organize, categorize, sort out, separate, subdivide
AN OPPOSITE IS combine

**divine** ADJECTIVE

*1 divine worship*
▶ holy, sacred, religious
*2 a divine being*
▶ supernatural, godlike, superhuman, heavenly, spiritual, immortal, deific

**divinity** NOUN

*1 a statue of the divinity*
▶ deity, god, goddess, divine being
*2 arguments about Christ's divinity*
▶ godhead, divine nature
*3 She wanted to study divinity.*
▶ theology, religion, religious studies

**division** NOUN

*1 divisions in modern society*
▶ split, disunity, rupture, breach, disunion, schism, disagreement, conflict
*2 the division of Germany after the war*
▶ dividing, splitting, partitioning, separation
*3 the overseas division of the company*
▶ department, branch, arm, sector, office, bureau, subsidiary
*4 the division of the spoils*
▶ distribution, dividing up, sharing out, allocation, apportionment, allotment

**divorce** NOUN

*One in three marriages ends in divorce.*
▶ separation, annulment, *(more informal)* break-up, *(more informal)* split-up

**divorce** VERB

*Her parents divorced last year.*
▶ separate, end a marriage, *(more informal)* split up

**divulge** VERB

*The article did not divulge the whereabouts of the individuals.*
▶ disclose, reveal, communicate, make known, pass on

**dizzy** ADJECTIVE

*All that leaping about made her feel dizzy.*
▶ giddy, faint, shaky, wobbly, light-headed, *(more informal)* woozy

**do** VERB

*1 I have a lot of work to do.*
▶ carry out, undertake, perform, achieve, fulfil, complete, discharge

**2** *You can do as you please.*
▶ behave, act, conduct yourself
**3** *If there's no tea, a glass of water will do.*
▶ suffice, satisfy, serve, be enough, be adequate
**4** *Shall I do the lunch now?*
▶ prepare, make, get ready, fix, organize, provide
**5** *She went upstairs to do her hair.*
▶ arrange, groom, style, brush, comb, wash, fix
**6** *He will be doing languages at university.*
▶ study, read, learn, take a course in
**7** *She has been doing very well in the new job.*
▶ get on, progress, succeed

**do away with**
**1** *We want to do away with outdated practices.*
▶ abolish, get rid of, discontinue, put an end to, dispense with, terminate, suppress
**2** *I was afraid his enemies might want to do away with him.*
▶ kill, murder, put to death, assassinate, eliminate, exterminate

**do up**
**1** *He stopped to do up his laces.*
▶ tie, fasten, secure
**2** *They have bought an old farmhouse to do up.*
▶ renovate, restore, refurbish, decorate, revamp, (*more informal*) make over

**do without**
*I cannot do without my eight hours' sleep.*
▶ forgo, dispense with, give up, renounce, abstain from

**docile** ADJECTIVE
*Hannah has a docile nature.*
▶ gentle, compliant, meek, mild, obedient, amenable, cooperative, submissive, deferential

**dock** NOUN
*The boat was moored at the end of the dock.*
▶ harbour, quay, wharf, jetty, landing stage, marina, dockyard, boatyard, waterfront

**dock** VERB
**1** *The ship docked the next morning.*
▶ moor, berth, tie up, put in, anchor, drop anchor
**2** *The dog's tail had been docked.*
▶ cut short, cut off, crop, shorten
**3** *The company will dock your wages for any misdemeanour.*
▶ reduce, cut, lessen, decrease

**doctor** NOUN
*Jane is unwell and should see a doctor.*
▶ GP, physician, medical officer, consultant, (*more informal*) medic
RELATED ADJECTIVE medical

**TYPES OF DOCTOR**

**doctors who treat types of patient: general practitioner (GP:** local doctor consulted first**), geriatrician (**for treatment of old people**), gynaecologist (**for treatment of women and girls**), obstetrician (**for treatment of diseases to do with childbirth**), paediatrician (**for treatment of children**).**

**doctors who treat parts of the body: brain surgeon, cardiologist (**for heart diseases**), chiropractor (**for treatment of the joints**), chiropodist (**for treatment of the feet**), dentist (**for treatment of the teeth**), dermatologist (**for skin diseases**), gastroenterologist (**for stomach and intestine diseases**), haematologist (**for blood disorders**), heart surgeon, immunologist (**studies immunity**), laryngologist (**for treatment of the air passage to the lungs**), nephrologist (**for treatment of the kidneys**), neurologist (**for treatment of the nervous system**), oculist (**for treatment of the eyes**), oncologist (**for the treatment of tumours**), ophthalmologist (**for disorders of the eyes**), orthodontist (**for disorders of the teeth and jaws**), orthopaedist (**for disorders of the bones and muscles**), periodontist (**for treatment of the gums and other parts supporting the teeth**), plastic surgeon (**repairs and rebuilds body tissue**), podiatrist (**for treatment of the feet**), rheumatologist (**for treatment of the joints and ligaments**), trichologist (**for treatment of the hair and scalp**), urologist (**for treatment of the bladder and urinary system**).**

**other names: anaesthetist (**gives anaesthetics**), clinician (**any doctor who treats patients as distinct from doing research**), consultant (**senior specialist in a hospital**), embryologist (**studies embryos**), epidemiologist (**studies spread of diseases**), pathologist (**studies the causes and effects of diseases**), radiologist (**gives X-rays**), radiotherapist (**treats diseases by using radiation**), registrar (**hospital doctor of middle rank**), surgeon (**performs operations**).**

**doctrine** NOUN
*Christian doctrine*
▶ belief, creed, dogma, teaching, tenet, principle, conviction, orthodoxy, set of beliefs

**document** NOUN
*a legal document*
▶ paper, certificate, contract, deed, record, charter, (*technical*) instrument

**dodge** NOUN
*a clever dodge*
▶ ruse, ploy, trick, device, scheme, tactic, manoeuvre, stratagem, (*informal*) wheeze

**dodge** VERB
**1** *He flicked his head to one side as if dodging a blow.*
▶ avoid, duck, fend off, evade, move out of the way of, swerve away from, turn away from, veer away from
**2** *The Minister may try to dodge the issue.*
▶ avoid, evade, shun, equivocate over, get out of, fudge, sidestep, (*more informal*) duck
**3** *He managed to dodge between parked cars.*
▶ dart, dive, duck, leap, swerve, jump

**dodgy** ADJECTIVE

**1** (*informal*) *Avoid dodgy travel agents at all costs.*
▶ dishonest, suspect, unreliable, underhand
**2** (*informal*) *He took out a dodgy-looking sausage sandwich.*
▶ suspicious, suspect, dubious, unappealing, inferior, nasty

**dog** NOUN

*She was walking her dog along the beach.*
▶ hound, mongrel, pedigree, pup, puppy, whelp, bitch, dingo

**dogged** ADJECTIVE

*She was found again by the dogged efforts of her father.*
▶ determined, persistent, resolute, persevering, tenacious, steadfast, single-minded, unflagging, relentless

**dogma** NOUN

*religious dogma*
▶ belief, creed, doctrine, teaching, tenet, principle, conviction, orthodoxy, set of beliefs

**dogmatic** ADJECTIVE

*He was far too dogmatic to argue with.*
▶ opinionated, doctrinaire, assertive, peremptory, insistent, arrogant, categorical, overbearing
AN OPPOSITE IS open-minded

**dole** NOUN

(*informal*) *He lived on the dole for three years.*
▶ unemployment benefit, state benefit, benefit, social security, income support

**dole** VERB

**dole out** *Mum started doling out cornflakes.*
▶ distribute, give out, share out, hand round, dish up, issue

**domain** NOUN

**1** *the king's domain*
▶ realm, kingdom, empire, dominion, territory, country
**2** *the domain of science education*
▶ field, sphere, area, concern, speciality, department

**domestic** ADJECTIVE

**1** *fuel for domestic use*
▶ household, home, family, private
AN OPPOSITE IS public
**2** *goods for the domestic market*
▶ national, inland, internal, local, state
AN OPPOSITE IS foreign
**3** *a domestic type of person*
▶ home-loving, homely, domesticated

**domesticated** ADJECTIVE

*domesticated animals*
▶ tame, tamed, domestic, house-trained, trained
AN OPPOSITE IS wild

**dominant** ADJECTIVE

**1** *She was the dominant member of the partnership.*
▶ leading, primary, prime, main, principal, foremost, uppermost, prominent, pre-eminent

**2** *The leader plays a dominant role.*
▶ controlling, leading, authoritative, powerful, influential, assertive
**3** *the dominant feature of the landscape*
▶ conspicuous, prominent, imposing

**dominate** VERB

*London no longer dominates the British arts scene.*
▶ control, monopolize, govern, rule, direct, overshadow, predominate in

**domineering** ADJECTIVE

*He had a domineering mother.*
▶ overbearing, authoritarian, autocratic, tyrannical, dictatorial, despotic, oppressive, harsh, strict

**dominion** NOUN

**1** *a British dominion*
▶ dependency, territory, colony, protectorate
**2** *The Persians wished to extend their dominion to the Greek mainland.*
▶ power, authority, control, mastery, hegemony, overlordship, sovereignty, suzerainty, supremacy, ascendancy

**donate** VERB

*He agreed to donate his fee to charity.*
▶ give, present, contribute, subscribe

**donation** NOUN

*The organization depends on voluntary donations.*
▶ gift, contribution, subscription, benefaction

**donor** NOUN

*a large gift from an anonymous donor*
▶ benefactor, contributor, philanthropist, provider, sponsor, giver
AN OPPOSITE IS recipient

**doom** NOUN

*There was a feeling of doom about the place.*
▶ ruin, downfall, catastrophe, destruction, disaster

**doomed** ADJECTIVE

*The project seemed doomed from the start.*
▶ ill-fated, ill-omened, condemned, damned, fated, cursed, jinxed, hopeless, hapless

**doomsday** NOUN

*He kept bomb-making equipment for a doomsday scenario.*
▶ apocalypse, end of the world, judgement day

**door** NOUN

*She walked out through the door.*
▶ doorway, entrance, exit

**dope** NOUN

**1** (*informal*) *smuggling dope*
▶ drugs, narcotics, cannabis, heroin
**2** (*informal*) *He must have looked a real dope.*
▶ fool, idiot, dolt, dinwit, nincompoop

**dopey** ADJECTIVE

*He grew dopey and fell asleep.*
▶ dazed, groggy, befuddled, drowsy

## dormant ADJECTIVE

**1** *The animals remain dominant until the next rainy season.*
▶ asleep, sleeping, hibernating, comatose, resting
AN OPPOSITE IS awake

**2** *The volcano has been dormant for centuries.*
▶ inactive, passive, inert, latent, quiescent, quiet
AN OPPOSITE IS active

## dose NOUN

*a dose of cough mixture*
▶ measure, prescribed amount, dosage, portion, quantity

## dot NOUN

*The picture consists of tiny dots.*
▶ spot, speck, point, mark, particle

## dot VERB

*Small houses dot the landscape.*
▶ sprinkle, scatter, fleck, punctuate, pepper

## dote VERB

**dote on** *She doted on the boy for years.*
▶ adore, love, be fond of, idolize, worship, cherish

## double ADJECTIVE

*double yellow lines on the road*
▶ dual, twin, duplicate, matched, matching, twofold, duple
AN OPPOSITE IS single

## double NOUN

*It was either you or your double.*
▶ lookalike, clone, replica, spitting image

## double VERB

*We must double our efforts.*
▶ increase, multiply, magnify, enlarge, repeat
**double back** *He doubled back, crossed the bridge, and reached home.*
▶ turn back, backtrack, retrace your steps, return
**double up** *She doubled up with pain.*
▶ collapse, crumple up, fold over, fold up, bend over

## double-cross VERB

*He was double-crossing his friends.*
▶ cheat, betray, deceive, defraud, (more informal) two-time

## doubt NOUN

**1** *There was some doubt about the identity of the father.*
▶ uncertainty, hesitation, confusion, difficulty

**2** *I was plagued by doubt.*
▶ indecision, uncertainty, misgiving, lack of confidence, distrust, mistrust, suspicion, reservation, qualm

## doubt VERB

**1** *I doubt whether they will be there.*
▶ question, think it unlikely

**2** *I do not doubt their motives.*
▶ disbelieve, distrust, question, query, suspect

## doubtful ADJECTIVE

**1** *At first I was doubtful about taking him with me. The woman sounded doubtful.*
▶ hesitant, uncertain, unsure, undecided, dubious, irresolute, ambivalent, wavering, tentative, sceptical, in two minds
OPPOSITES ARE confident, assured

**2** *It was doubtful whether the witness would back him up.*
▶ dubious, uncertain, questionable, debatable, in doubt, open to question
AN OPPOSITE IS certain

**3** *We are very doubtful of the conclusions they reached.*
▶ suspicious, distrustful, mistrustful, cautious, wary, uneasy (about), sceptical, unsure
OPPOSITES ARE confident, trusting

**4** *The chances of success are fairly doubtful.*
▶ unlikely, improbable, uncertain, dubious, remote
OPPOSITES ARE probable, likely

## doubtless ADVERB

*They will doubtless forget all about it.*
▶ undoubtedly, without doubt, indubitably, certainly, surely, probably, presumably, of course, most likely

## dowdy ADJECTIVE

*a woman in a dowdy black dress*
▶ drab, shabby, unattractive, dull, dingy, dreary, old-fashioned, inelegant, frumpy, (more informal) tatty
OPPOSITES ARE smart, colourful, fashionable

## down ADJECTIVE

*He felt down all day.*
▶ depressed, dejected, sad, unhappy, miserable, downcast, despondent, dispirited, disheartened, disconsolate, glum, melancholy, cast down
OPPOSITES ARE cheerful, happy

## down and out ADJECTIVE

*down and out in the streets of a big city*
▶ destitute, homeless, penniless, vagrant, living rough
OPPOSITES ARE prosperous, affluent, well-off

## downcast ADJECTIVE

*Their mother often looked downcast.*
▶ dejected, depressed, despondent, dispirited, disheartened, downhearted, unhappy, sad, down, glum, melancholy, miserable, cast down
OPPOSITES ARE cheerful, happy

## downfall NOUN

*the downfall of the military regime*
▶ ruin, undoing, fall, overthrow, collapse, failure, debacle

## downgrade VERB

*The consulate in Moscow has been downgraded.*
▶ demote, lower in status, reduce in importance
OPPOSITES ARE upgrade, promote

## downhearted ADJECTIVE

*Steve tried not to look too downhearted.*
▶ dejected, depressed, despondent, dispirited, disheartened, downcast, unhappy, sad, down, glum, melancholy, miserable, cast down
OPPOSITES ARE cheerful, happy

## downpour NOUN
*On the way home we were caught in a downpour.*
▶ rainstorm, cloudburst, deluge

## downright ADJECTIVE
*They were telling half-truths and downright lies.*
▶ utter, absolute, total, complete, out-and-out, outright, positive, categorical, sheer, unmitigated

## downtrodden ADJECTIVE
*a country downtrodden during years of dictatorship*
▶ oppressed, subjugated, repressed, tyrannized, subdued, crushed, ground down, abused

## downturn NOUN
*a downturn in the family's fortunes*
▶ decline, reversal (of), failure (of), collapse (of), foundering (of)

## downward ADJECTIVE
*Take the downward path. a downward trend in prices*
▶ descending, downhill, falling, sloping, going down
AN OPPOSITE IS upward

## doze VERB
*He began to doze by the fire.*
▶ sleep lightly, nap, catnap, drowse, (more informal) snooze, (more informal) have a snooze, (more informal) have forty winks

## doze NOUN
*She needed a short doze before her guests arrived.*
▶ nap, catnap, light sleep, siesta, (more informal) snooze, (more informal) forty winks

## drab ADJECTIVE
*The room had a few pieces of drab furniture.*
▶ dowdy, shabby, dreary, dingy, dull, shabby, sombre, lacklustre, unattractive, uninteresting, (more informal) tatty
OPPOSITES ARE bright, colourful

## draconian ADJECTIVE
*the country's draconian security measures*
▶ harsh, severe, strict, stringent, drastic, swingeing, punitive, authoritarian

## draft NOUN
**USAGE** Do not confuse this word with *draught*.
**1** *a draft of a speech*
▶ outline, sketch, abstract, first version, rough version, plan
**2** *a bank draft*
▶ cheque, order, banker's order, money order

## draft VERB
**USAGE** Do not confuse this word with *draught*.
**1** *He went off to draft his letter.*
▶ plan, prepare, sketch out, outline, compose, work out, write a draft of
**2** *Lawrence had been drafted into the army.*
▶ conscript

## drag VERB
**1** *She dragged another chair over to the table.*
▶ pull, draw, haul, heave, (more informal) yank
AN OPPOSITE IS push

**2** *Time began to drag.*
▶ become tedious, crawl, go slowly, move slowly, pass slowly
OPPOSITES ARE fly, pass quickly

## drag NOUN
(informal) *Working six days a week can become a drag.*
▶ bore, nuisance, bother, pest, annoyance, trial, (informal) pain in the neck

## drain NOUN
*The drain had become clogged with leaves.*
▶ channel, conduit, culvert, pipe, drainpipe, outlet, duct, gutter, sewer, watercourse

## drain VERB
**1** *There is a tap to drain water from the tank.*
▶ draw off, empty, remove, bleed, clear, take off
**2** *Lisa drained the cocoa from her mug.*
▶ empty, drink up, quaff, gulp, swallow, finish off, polish off
**3** *The water drains through into the river.*
▶ seep, leak out, ooze, strain, trickle
**4** *The colour had drained from her face.*
▶ fade, vanish, disappear, wane, evaporate
**5** *The expense drained all my funds.*
▶ exhaust, consume, deplete, use up, sap, spend

## drama NOUN
**1** *Ruth is studying drama.*
▶ acting, dramatics, dramatic art, the theatre, the stage, stagecraft
**2** *Hardly a day goes by without some family drama or other.*
▶ scene, incident, excitement, spectacle, crisis, commotion, disturbance, fracas

## dramatic ADJECTIVE
**1** *a dramatic production*
▶ theatrical, stage
**2** *a dramatic rescue at sea*
▶ exciting, striking, thrilling, stirring
OPPOSITES ARE unexciting, routine
**3** *a dramatic change in the weather*
▶ substantial, significant, marked, pronounced
AN OPPOSITE IS insignificant

## dramatize VERB
**1** *The novel has been dramatized for television.*
▶ adapt, make into a play, rewrite
**2** *He tends to dramatize small difficulties.*
▶ exaggerate, overplay, overstate, overdo, make too much of

## drape VERB
*She draped a cloth over the table.*
▶ wrap, hang, drop, fold, arrange, swathe

## drastic ADJECTIVE
*drastic measures to reduce pollution*
▶ extreme, harsh, severe, radical, rigorous, draconian, desperate, dire

## draught NOUN
**USAGE** Do not confuse this word with *draft*.
**1** *The draught made her shiver.*
▶ current of air, puff, wind, breeze

a b c d e f g h i j k l m n o p q r s t u v w x y z

**draw**

2 *He took another draught of his beer.*
► drink, gulp, swallow, mouthful, (*more informal*) swig

**draw** NOUN
*She won a prize in the office draw.*
► raffle, lottery

**draw** VERB
1 *Neil drew a shape on his beer mat.*
► sketch, depict, trace, outline, mark out, pencil, map out, (*more formal*) delineate
2 *The secretary drew another chair up to the desk.*
► pull, drag, haul, heave, (*more informal*) yank
3 *His aunt went over to draw the curtains.*
► close, shut, pull together, open, part
**USAGE** Note that *draw* can mean either 'close' or 'open' when referring to curtains.
4 *By Saturday the show was drawing huge audiences.*
► attract, bring in, win, entice, allure, persuade
5 *That is the conclusion I drew.*
► reach, arrive at, deduce, infer
6 *The teams drew after extra time.*
► tie, be even, be equal
**draw out** *We could draw out the conversation for hours.*
► prolong, extend, protract, stretch, lengthen
**draw up**
1 *The lawyers will draw up a contract.*
► formulate, compose, prepare, write, draft
2 *A car drew up outside the house.*
► stop, pull up, come to a halt, come to a standstill

**drawback** NOUN
*The weather was rather a drawback.*
► disadvantage, snag, hitch, nuisance, weakness, (*more informal*) fly in the ointment
OPPOSITES ARE advantage, benefit

**drawing** NOUN
*She made drawings of the children.*
► sketch, picture, illustration, study, portrayal, design, outline

**dread** VERB
*He dreaded the telephone call that might take her away from him.*
► fear, be afraid of, shrink from, be anxious about, worry about

**dread** NOUN
*With a mounting feeling of dread I went to answer the door.*
► fear, trepidation, apprehension, foreboding, anxiety

**dreadful** ADJECTIVE
1 *a dreadful accident  a dreadful mistake*
► terrible, frightful, horrible, awful, fearful, ghastly, hideous, shocking, frightening, terrifying
2 *a dreadful person*
► unpleasant, disagreeable, nasty, awful, deplorable

**dream** NOUN
1 *I had a dream about lizards.*
► fantasy, nightmare, delusion, vision, hallucination, illusion, reverie, trance

2 *She was walking around in a dream.*
► daydream, reverie, trance, daze
3 *It had always been his dream to run a country pub.*
► ambition, wish, desire, yearning, aspiration, pipedream, daydream, ideal

**dream** VERB
1 *She dreamed she was on a journey.*
► have a dream, imagine, fantasize, fancy
2 *I have always dreamt of playing for England.*
► long (to play), yearn (to play), hanker (after), fantasize (about)
**dream up** *There's not much time to dream up an excuse.*
► invent, devise, think up, concoct, contrive, work out

**dreary** ADJECTIVE
1 *a dreary story*
► dull, uninteresting, drab, tedious, boring, monotonous, unexciting
OPPOSITES ARE exciting, interesting
2 *dreary countryside*
► gloomy, dismal, bleak, drab, sombre, murky

**dregs** NOUN
1 *dregs at the bottom of a bottle*
► sediment, deposit, grounds, lees, remains
2 *the dregs of society*
► rabble, riff-raff, outcasts, scum

**drench** VERB
*Rain drenched the countryside.*
► soak, saturate, douse, inundate, flood, swamp, submerge

**dress** NOUN
1 *Guests must wear formal dress*
► clothes, clothing, costume, attire, apparel, garb, garments, ensemble, outfit, (*more informal*) gear
RELATED ADJECTIVE sartorial
2 *She wore a beautiful red dress.*
► frock, gown, robe, shift
**USAGE** A *robe* is usually a long dress, and a *shift* is usually a short one.

**dress** VERB
1 *She had to dress her disabled husband.*
► clothe, provide clothes for, put clothes on
AN OPPOSITE IS undress
2 *He dressed quickly and left the house.*
► put on clothes, get dressed
3 *A nurse dressed the wound.*
► bandage, put a dressing on, bind up, tend, treat, attend to

**dribble** VERB
1 *A dog lay in the hearth dribbling.*
► drool, slaver, slobber, salivate
2 *Water dribbled from the end of the hose.*
► trickle, seep, drip, ooze, flow, leak, run

**drift** NOUN
1 *a drift of deep snow*
► pile, heap, bank, mass, mound, ridge, accumulation

**drift**
2 *the drift of the story*
▶ gist, essence, core, substance, thrust, import, tenor, purport

**drift** VERB
1 *The boat began to drift downstream*
▶ be carried, be borne, float, stray, coast, move slowly
2 *People drifted out into the gardens.*
▶ wander, ramble, stray, meander, move casually, dawdle, potter
3 *The snow had drifted across the road.*
▶ pile up, bank up, heap up, accumulate, gather, form drifts

**drill** NOUN
1 *three months of military drill*
▶ training, instruction, discipline, exercise, practice
2 *Everyone knows the drill.*
▶ routine, procedure, system

**drill** VERB
1 *He filed the edges and drilled a series of holes.*
▶ bore, make a hole, pierce, penetrate
2 *A sergeant was drilling the new recruits.*
▶ train, instruct, coach, teach, exercise

**drink** NOUN
1 *She had another drink of her coffee.*
▶ sip, swallow, gulp, swill, (*more informal*) swig
2 *In the end he turned to drink.*
▶ alcohol, liquour, alcoholic drink, strong drink, (*more informal*) booze

**drink** VERB
1 *She drank her tea.*
▶ swallow, sip, gulp down, quaff, swill
2 *an upright citizen who never drank.*
▶ take alcohol, indulge, (*more informal*) tipple, (*more informal*) booze

**drip** NOUN
1 *You could hear the drips from the blocked gutters.*
▶ drop, dribble, splash, plop, trickle
2 (*informal*) *He thought he must have seemed a complete drip.*
▶ weakling, idiot, (*informal*) ninny, (*informal*) wimp, (*informal*) weed, (*informal*) wally

**drip** VERB
*Water was dripping on the floor.*
▶ drop, plop, splash, dribble, leak, drizzle, fall in drips, sprinkle, trickle

**drive** NOUN
1 *a short drive into town*
▶ trip, run, ride, excursion, journey, outing, jaunt
2 *a young woman with plenty of drive*
▶ motivation, ambition, initiative, enterprise, determination, enthusiasm, energy, keenness, persistence, zeal, (*more informal*) push
3 *a drive to recruit blood donors*
▶ campaign, crusade, effort, appeal

**drive** VERB
1 *I'll drive them to the station.*
▶ take, transport, ferry, carry

2 *Can you drive a tractor?*
▶ operate, control, manage, handle
3 *She drives everywhere.*
▶ go by car, travel by car, (*old-fashioned*) motor
4 *Most teachers drove their students very hard.*
▶ work, push, urge, drive
5 *Poverty drove them to crime.*
▶ force, compel, urge, push
6 *He drove a nail into the wall.*
▶ hammer, bang, ram
7 **drive at** *What was he driving at?*
▶ imply, suggest, intimate, insinuate, allude to, refer to, hint at, (*more informal*) get at

**droop** VERB
*The flowers began to droop.*
▶ wither, wilt, flop, sag, slump, go limp, hang, bend, dangle, fall

**drop** NOUN
1 *a drop of water*
▶ droplet, drip, globule, bead, bubble
2 *It needs a drop of glue.*
▶ dash, spot, dab, trace, pinch, small amount
3 *a drop of 100 metres*
▶ descent, fall, dive, plunge
4 *She walked to the edge of the cliff and peered at the drop below her.*
▶ precipice, chasm, gorge, abyss, slope
5 *a drop in prices*
▶ reduction, decrease, cut, falling off, downturn, slump
AN OPPOSITE IS rise

**drop** VERB
1 *A maid had dropped a tray in the hallway.*
▶ let fall, let go of
2 *They all dropped to their knees.*
▶ sink, fall, go down
3 *The union decided to drop some of its claims.*
▶ abandon, give up, relinquish, discontinue
4 *She dropped many of her friends after leaving university.*
▶ desert, abandon, renounce, give up, disown, reject, discard
5 *Many outlets have dropped their prices.*
▶ reduce, lower, cut
6 *He was dropped from the team.*
▶ exclude, leave out (of), discard, expel
7 *The aeroplane dropped a thousand feet.*
▶ descend, fall, plunge, plummet, dive, nosedive, sink

**drown** VERB
1 *He fell into the water and nearly drowned*
▶ submerge, sink, go under
2 *Noises from the street drowned our conversation.*
▶ overwhelm, overpower, drown out, engulf, make inaudible, silence

**drowsy** ADJECTIVE
*We became drowsy in the heat.*
▶ sleepy, dozy, lethargic, somnolent, (*more informal*) snoozy

**drudge** NOUN
*Sometimes he felt he was no more than a drudge.*
▶ menial, servant, hack, (*more informal*) dogsbody, (*more informal*) lackey

**drudgery** NOUN
*She disliked drudgery and tried to make the work interesting.*
▶ hard work, hard labour, tedium, (*more informal*) donkey work

**drug** NOUN
1 *Her doctor prescribed a new drug.*
▶ medicine, medication, medicament, remedy, potion
2 *under the influence of drugs*
▶ narcotic, hallucinogen, stimulant, (*more informal*) dope, (*more informal*) junk

**drug** VERB
*The victim seems to have been drugged before being driven off.*
▶ anaesthetize, knock out, stupefy, (*more informal*) dope

**drum** NOUN
*a drum of oil*
▶ barrel, canister, cask, butt, keg, tub, tun

**drunk** ADJECTIVE
*The men got drunk and waved bottles around.*
▶ intoxicated, inebriated, tipsy, drunken, under the influence, (*more informal*) plastered, (*more informal*) tight, (*more informal*) sloshed

**dry** ADJECTIVE
1 *Ahead lay miles of dry desert.*
▶ arid, parched, barren, waterless, desiccated, scorched, torrid
2 *a dry story*
▶ dull, tedious, boring, dreary, monotonous
3 *dry humour*
▶ droll, ironic, wry, sardonic, subtle

**dry** VERB
*It wasn't easy drying clothes in such a wet climate.*
▶ get dry, make dry

**dual** ADJECTIVE
*The tool has a dual purpose.*
▶ double, twofold, twin, combined

**dubious** ADJECTIVE
1 *I was dubious about the idea.*
▶ doubtful, hesitant, uncertain, unsure, undecided, irresolute, ambivalent, wavering, tentative, sceptical, in two minds
OPPOSITES ARE confident, assured
2 *a dubious excuse*
▶ suspect, suspicious, untrustworthy, unreliable, (*more informal*) fishy, (*more informal*) shady

**duck** VERB
1 *The boys ducked behind a bush.*
▶ crouch, stoop, bob down
2 *I ducked to avoid an overhanging branch*
▶ dodge, sidestep, bend, swerve, bob down

3 *They ducked him in the river.*
▶ dip, immerse, plunge, submerge, lower

**dud** ADJECTIVE
*The light bulb was dud.*
▶ faulty, defective, useless

**dud** NOUN
*Some of the fireworks were duds.*
▶ failure, flop, disappointment

**due** ADJECTIVE
1 *Your subscription is due this week.*
▶ owing, owed, payable, outstanding
2 *She drove with due care.*
▶ proper, rightful, fitting, appropriate, necessary, suitable, adequate
3 *the respect due to an eminent statesman*
▶ deserved (by), merited (by), earned (by), fitting, appropriate, suitable (for)

**due to**
1 *Death was due to a heart attack.*
▶ caused by, the result of, attributable to
2 *The game was cancelled due to bad weather.*
▶ owing to, because of, on account of, as a consequence of, as a result of, in view of, thanks to

**due** NOUN
*We must give them their due.*
▶ deserts, entitlement, rightful treatment, rights, merits, reward

**duel** NOUN
*The Count was killed in a duel.*
▶ single combat, fight, encounter, affair of honour

**dull** ADJECTIVE
1 *dull colours*
▶ drab, dreary, sombre, dark, lacklustre
AN OPPOSITE IS bright
2 *a dull winter morning*
▶ gloomy, overcast, dark, dim, dismal, bleak, murky, sunless
OPPOSITES ARE sunny, bright
3 *The report makes dull reading.*
▶ boring, tedious, uninteresting, unexciting, monotonous, tiresome, insipid
OPPOSITES ARE interesting, exciting
4 *a dull pupil*
▶ stupid, slow, unintelligent, dim, slow-witted, dense
OPPOSITES ARE clever, bright

**dumb** ADJECTIVE
1 *He kept dumb while the others argued.*
▶ mute, silent, speechless, tongue-tied, unable to speak
2 *He's not as dumb as he makes out.*
▶ stupid, unintelligent, foolish, slow-witted, dull, dim

**dumbfounded** ADJECTIVE
*I gazed back at him, dumbfounded.*
▶ astonished, astounded, amazed, surprised, staggered, startled, nonplussed, disconcerted,

speechless, shocked, flabbergasted, perplexed, stunned, stupefied, bewildered, (*more informal*) thunderstruck

**dummy** NOUN
1 *The gun was only a dummy.*
▶ imitation, fake, sham, substitute, toy, copy, model, counterfeit
2 *a ventriloquist's dummy*
▶ doll, puppet, manikin, figure

**dummy** ADJECTIVE
*a dummy attack*
▶ simulated, pretended, trial, mock, practice, bogus, (*more informal*) pretend

**dump** NOUN
1 *We've a lot to take to the dump.*
▶ tip, refuse dump, rubbish heap, junk yard
2 *an ammunition dump*
▶ cache, depot, hoard, store

**dump** VERB
1 *Worn-out cars had been dumped at the side of the road.*
▶ dispose of, discard, get rid of, jettison, reject, scrap, (*more informal*) ditch
2 (*informal*) *She dumped her shopping by the door.*
▶ put down, set down, throw down, deposit, drop, tip, place, unload, (*more informal*) park

**duplicate** ADJECTIVE
*The manager opened his room with a duplicate key.*
▶ matching, identical, twin, second, alternative, copied, corresponding

**duplicate** NOUN
*The document in the file is a duplicate.*
▶ copy, facsimile, photocopy, carbon copy, reproduction, replica

**duplicate** VERB
*The documents have been duplicated.*
▶ copy, photocopy, print, reproduce

**durable** ADJECTIVE
1 *a coat made of durable material*
▶ hard-wearing, tough, strong, sturdy, stout, substantial
2 *a durable peace settlement*
▶ lasting, enduring, abiding, stable, secure

**duress** NOUN
*The statement was obtained by duress.*
▶ force, coercion, intimidation, constraint, pressure, threats

**dusk** NOUN
*It was only four o'clock and already dusk.*
▶ twilight, evening, sundown, sunset, gloaming, gloom
AN OPPOSITE IS dawn

**dust** NOUN
*The surfaces were covered in dust.*
▶ dirt, grime, grit, filth, smut, particles, powder

**dusty** ADJECTIVE
1 *The tables were dusty.*
▶ dirty, filthy, grubby
2 *a light dusty substance*
▶ powdery, chalky, crumbly, granular, sandy

**dutiful** ADJECTIVE
*His dutiful parents were there waiting for him.*
▶ devoted, conscientious, responsible, dedicated, faithful, attentive, scrupulous, obedient
OPPOSITES ARE irresponsible, remiss

**duty** NOUN
1 *He felt a strong sense of duty.*
▶ responsibility, loyalty, obligation, allegiance, faithfulness, obedience, service
2 *One of his duties was to make the afternoon tea.*
▶ job, role, task, assignment, function, (*more informal*) chore
3 *an increased duty on cigarettes*
▶ tax, levy, tariff, excise, toll, dues

**dwarf** ADJECTIVE
*a dwarf cactus*
▶ miniature, small, little, undersized, diminutive

**dwarf** NOUN
*The little dwarf sat on the floor, directing operations.*
▶ person of restricted growth, midget, pygmy
**USAGE** *Person of restricted growth* is the least offensive of these terms.

**dwarf** VERB
*The tower blocks dwarf the old cathedral.*
▶ dominate, tower over, overshadow

**dwell** VERB
**dwell in** *Hermits used to dwell in these caves.*
▶ inhabit, live in, populate, lodge in, (*more formal*) reside in

---

**dwelling** NOUN
*Several dwellings have disappeared from the village.*
▶ house, residence, home

**TYPES OF DWELLING**

**town and city houses:** house, bungalow (on one floor), mansion (large and grand), town house (usually in a terrace), detached house (completely separate), semi-detached house (or semi, joined to another house on one side), terraced house (joined to others houses on both sides).

**houses in the country:** country house (large), grange (large country house with farm buildings), manor (large house with a lot of land), villa (usually in the country with its own grounds), farmhouse, cottage (small), dacha (Russian-style house in the country).

**special houses:** palace (for royalty and heads of state), parsonage (for clergy), rectory (for clergy), vicarage (for clergy).. ▶▶

**small houses**: hut, cabin, chalet, hovel (small and unpleasant), lodge (small house on a country estate, often at the entrance), mud hut, prefab (small temporary house), shack, igloo, caravan, tent, tepee.

**homes in parts of buildings**: flat, apartment, flatlet (small flat), penthouse (large apartment at the top of a building), maisonette (second floor flat with front door on ground level), studio flat (having one large main room), bed-sitting room (or bedsit, in one room).

**buildings for a short stay**: hotel, guest house, hostel, motel; gîte (holiday house in France).

**dwindle** VERB
*After the war the population dwindled.*
▶ decrease, decline, diminish, shrink, contract, peter out, wane, fall off, die out

**dye** NOUN
*a yellow dye*
▶ colouring, colourant, pigment, stain, tint, tinge

**dye** VERB
*She dyed the curtains to match the new paint.*
▶ colour, tint, stain, pigment, colour-wash

**dynamic** ADJECTIVE
*The country needs dynamic leadership.*
▶ energetic, vigorous, forceful, spirited, positive, effective, bold, vital, active

**dynasty** NOUN
*The ruling dynasty went back to medieval times.*
▶ family, house, line, bloodline, succession, regime

# Ee

**eager** ADJECTIVE
**1** *It was good to see smiling, eager faces.*
▶ keen, enthusiastic, avid, fervent, zealous
OPPOSITES ARE apathetic, unenthusiastic
**2** *They were eager to find a seat near the front.*
▶ keen, anxious, determined
**3** *The young ones are eager for more adventure.*
▶ longing, yearning, intent (on)

**eagerness** NOUN
*Her eyes shone with eagerness.*
▶ enthusiasm, keenness, fervour, ardour, earnestness, excitement, intentness, longing, passion
OPPOSITES ARE apathy, indifference

**ear** NOUN
*He had the ear of the President.*
▶ attention, heed, notice, consideration, regard
RELATED ADJECTIVE aural

**early** ADJECTIVE
**1** *early symptoms of the disease*
▶ initial, first, advance, preliminary, forward
AN OPPOSITE IS late
**2** *early civilizations*
▶ ancient, primitive, prehistoric
**USAGE** Note that *prehistoric* means 'before the time of written records'. *Primitive* means 'early in history', but can also mean 'not advanced, simple', and so it is not always a good choice for the meaning shown here. .

**earn** VERB
**1** *She earns a six-figure salary.*
▶ receive, be paid, make, (*more informal*) bring in, (*more informal*) take home
**2** *They have all earned our gratitude.*
▶ deserve, merit, warrant, justify, be worthy of, gain, secure, obtain
OPPOSITES ARE lose, forfeit

**earnest** ADJECTIVE
**1** *an earnest attempt to help*
▶ committed, determined, resolute, conscientious, devoted, diligent, purposeful, eager, industrious, involved
OPPOSITES ARE casual, flippant
**2** *He was an earnest, church-going man.*
▶ serious, serious-minded, thoughtful, solemn, grave, sober, staid, humourless
OPPOSITES ARE casual, half-hearted

**earnings** NOUN
*He looked for ways to supplement his earnings.*
▶ income, pay, salary, wages, remuneration

**earth** NOUN
**1** *life on earth*
▶ this world, the planet, the globe
RELATED ADJECTIVE terrestrial
**2** *The fork turned the soft earth.*
▶ soil, topsoil, loam, clay, sod, ground, humus, land

**earthly** ADJECTIVE
**USAGE** Do not confuse this word with *earthy*.
*our earthly environment*
▶ terrestrial, material, physical, mundane, human, materialistic, secular, temporal
AN OPPOSITE IS spiritual

**earthquake** NOUN
*The town had been damaged by earthquakes.*
▶ tremor, convulsion, shock, (*more informal*) quake, upheaval
RELATED ADJECTIVE seismic

**earthy** ADJECTIVE
**USAGE** Do not confuse this word with *earthly*.
*an earthy sense of humour*
▶ rude, crude, coarse, vulgar, bawdy, indelicate, racy, smutty

**ease** NOUN
**1** *Most people can recognize road symbols with ease.*
▶ effortlessness, straightforwardness, no trouble, no problem, facility, simplicity
AN OPPOSITE IS difficulty

**2** *Notice the ease with which he completed the task.*
▶ skill, dexterity, facility, naturalness, deftness, mastery, cleverness

**3** *a life of ease*
▶ affluence, comfort, contentment, enjoyment, relaxation, luxury, leisure, wealth, prosperity
AN OPPOSITE IS stress

**ease** VERB

**1** *The medicine will ease the pain.*
▶ relieve, alleviate, mitigate, soothe, assuage, allay, lessen, deaden, dull, calm, lighten, moderate, quell, comfort
OPPOSITES ARE aggravate, worsen

**2** *measures taken to ease the tension*
▶ reduce, relax, decrease, slacken, take off
AN OPPOSITE IS increase

**3** *He eased the stopper out of the bottle.*
▶ guide, slide, slip, edge, inch, manœuvre, move gradually

**ease off** *The rain eased off*
▶ abate, subside, let up, slacken off, die out, lessen

**easily** ADVERB

**1** *She is easily the brightest student of her year.*
▶ by far, without doubt, undoubtedly, indubitably, indisputably, undeniably, definitely, certainly, patently

**2** *In the end I managed the work easily.*
▶ effortlessly, comfortably, with ease, simply, straightforwardly, with no difficulty

**easy** ADJECTIVE

**1** *an easy task*
▶ straightforward, undemanding, effortless, light, pleasant, painless, (*more informal*) cushy
OPPOSITES ARE difficult, heavy

**2** *easy instructions to follow*
▶ simple, straightforward, elementary, clear, uncomplicated, understandable, plain, user-friendly, foolproof, manageable
OPPOSITES ARE complicated, difficult

**3** *an easy manner*
▶ relaxed, easy-going, affable, natural, friendly, tolerant, informal, open, docile, amenable, accommodating, undemanding, (*more informal*) laid-back
OPPOSITES ARE difficult, intolerant

**4** *I long for an easy life.*
▶ comfortable, carefree, untroubled, leisurely, peaceful, restful, serene, relaxed, contented, cosy, tranquil
AN OPPOSITE IS stressful

**easy-going** ADJECTIVE

*Despite his easy-going nature he was extraordinarily energetic.*
▶ relaxed, easy, affable, natural, friendly, tolerant, informal, open, docile, amenable, accommodating, undemanding, (*more informal*) laid-back

**eat** VERB This word is often overused. Here are some alternatives:

**1** *The condemned man ate a hearty breakfast.*
▶ consume, devour, swallow, (*more informal*) put away, (*more informal*) tuck into, (*more informal*) scoff, (*more informal*) polish off, (*more informal*) get stuck into
RELATED ADJECTIVE edible

**2** *Where shall we eat tonight?*
▶ have a meal, have dinner, dine, (*more informal*) feed

**3** *eat into* *Rust was eating into the bodywork.*
▶ corrode, erode, wear away, wear through, rot, decay

**eatable** ADJECTIVE

*The food is a little overcooked, but still eatable.*
▶ palatable, wholesome, edible, fit to eat, safe to eat, digestible
OPPOSITES ARE uneatable, inedible

**USAGE** Note that *edible* does not mean quite the same as *eatable*. You say that something is *edible* when you mean it is suitable as food and is not (for example) poisonous, whereas you use *eatable* about food that is good enough to eat and not (for example) burnt or undercooked.

**eavesdrop** VERB

**eavesdrop on** *He tried as hard as he could to eavesdrop on the conversation in the next room.*
▶ listen in on, overhear, monitor, spy on, snoop on, intrude on

**ebb** VERB

**1** *The tide ebbed late in the morning.*
▶ go out, recede, fall back, flow back, retreat
AN OPPOSITE IS come in

**2** *Her strength was beginning to ebb.*
▶ dwindle, decline, fade, wane, diminish, disappear, vanish, weaken
OPPOSITES ARE increase, revive

**eccentric** ADJECTIVE

*His eccentric behaviour was worrying.*
▶ unconventional, abnormal, irregular, odd, strange, peculiar, weird, bizarre, extraordinary, idiosyncratic, capricious, quirky, erratic
OPPOSITES ARE ordinary, conventional

**eccentric** NOUN

*She too had a reputation as an eccentric.*
▶ individualist, nonconformist, oddity, (*more informal*) oddball, (*more informal*) weirdo, (*more informal*) crackpot

**echo** NOUN

*The mountains are full of strange echoes.*
▶ reverberation, reiteration, reflection of sound

**echo** VERB

**1** *The slightest sound echoes across the hall. The words echoed in Isabel's head.*
▶ reverberate, resound, ring, resonate

**eclipse**

2 *These thoughts were echoed by another speaker.*
► repeat, reiterate, reproduce, say again, ape, copy, imitate, mimic

**eclipse** VERB
1 *The sun is eclipsed by the moon.*
► blot out, block out, obscure, veil, cloud, cover, shade, darken, extinguish
2 *This achievement eclipsed all previous attempts.*
► overshadow, outshine, surpass, excel, outdo, put into the shade, dim

**eclipse** NOUN
1 *a lunar eclipse on 6 August*
► darkening, obscuration, blotting out, shading
2 *the eclipse of the ancient empires*
► decline, fall, deterioration, degeneration, sinking

**economic** ADJECTIVE
**USAGE** The main meanings of *economic* are 'to do with economics or use of money' (the first meaning below) and 'providing good value or profit' (the second meaning below). If you mean 'careful in using money' you should use *economical* or its synonyms.
1 *an outline of the government's economic policies*
► financial, monetary, commercial, fiscal, budgetary, business, money-making, trading
2 *The railway line was closed because it was no longer economic.*
► profitable, lucrative, fruitful, productive

**economical** ADJECTIVE
**USAGE** See the note at the entry for *economic*.
1 *It may be more economical to use an alternative form of fuel.*
► inexpensive, cost-effective, reasonable
OPPOSITES ARE wasteful, extravagant
2 *She is very economical with what money she has.*
► thrifty, careful, prudent, provident, sensible, canny
AN OPPOSITE IS expensive

**economize** VERB
*One way of economizing is to grow your own vegetables.*
► save, save money, cut back, cut costs, cut expenditure, spend less, (*more informal*) tighten your belt
AN OPPOSITE IS be extravagant

**economy** NOUN
1 *You can enjoy life and still exercise economy.*
► thrift, frugality, prudence, parsimony, providence
AN OPPOSITE IS wastefulness
2 *To avoid debt we had to make some economies.*
► saving, cut
3 *the country's economy*
► financial system, wealth, budget

**ecstasy** NOUN
*He ran out in ecstasy, doing cartwheels across the grass.*
► rapture, bliss, joy, delight, elation, euphoria, exultation

**ecstatic** ADJECTIVE
*They were ecstatic as they returned with the good news.*
► elated, rapturous, exultant, euphoric, enraptured, joyful, overjoyed, blissful, delirious, gleeful, happy, (*more informal*) over the moon, (*more informal*) on top of the world

**eddy** NOUN
*There were small eddies near the river bank.*
► swirl, whirl, whirlpool, vortex

**eddy** VERB
*The water eddied around the rocks.*
► swirl, whirl, seethe

**edge** NOUN
1 *We sat by the edge of the lake.*
► border, bank, fringe, extremity, verge, perimeter
2 *They now have the edge over their competitors.*
► advantage, upper hand, superiority
3 *Her excitement gave an edge to her voice.*
► sharpness, pointedness, pungency, asperity, bite

**edge** VERB
1 *a dress edged with lace*
► trim, decorate, finish, fringe, border
2 *She edged closer to the table.*
► creep, inch, slink, steal, sidle, move stealthily

**edgy** ADJECTIVE
*The thought of what was coming made her edgy.*
► tense, nervous, anxious, on edge, apprehensive, uneasy, ill at ease, twitchy, nervy

**edible** ADJECTIVE
**USAGE** See the note at the entry for *eatable*.
*The decorations on the tree were all edible.*
► fit to eat, safe to eat, eatable, wholesome
AN OPPOSITE IS inedible

**edict** NOUN
*a royal edict*
► decree, order, command, mandate, proclamation, dictum, enactment

**edifice** NOUN
*a huge edifice outlined against the sky*
► building, structure, construction, erection, development, property

**edit** VERB
1 *She mentioned that she had edited the school magazine.*
► direct, manage, be the editor of, be in charge of, supervise
2 *You need to edit the text to make it clearer.*
► revise, improve, adapt, modify, rework

**edition** NOUN
1 *the Christmas edition of the magazine*
► issue, number
2 *a first edition of a book*
► printing, publication, impression, version

**educate** VERB
*They hired a tutor to educate the children at home.*
► teach, tutor, instruct, coach, train, drill, cultivate, school

## educated ADJECTIVE

an educated woman named Fiona
► learned, knowledgeable, cultivated, cultured, well-read, informed, refined, enlightened, civilized, erudite, literate, numerate, sophisticated
AN OPPOSITE IS uneducated

## education NOUN

He had received a first-class education.
► schooling, training, teaching, instruction, tuition, coaching, curriculum, enlightenment, guidance

## eerie ADJECTIVE

an eerie silence
► weird, strange, uncanny, sinister, frightening, (more informal) spooky, (more informal) creepy, (more informal) scary

## effect NOUN

1 The effect of all these announcements was to confuse everyone.
► result, consequence, upshot, outcome, conclusion
2 Sandy and I were feeling the effect of our long day.
► consequence, repercussion, result, influence, aftermath
3 The violence of those years had a profound effect on people.
► impression, impact
4 The drug was losing its effect.
► effectiveness, efficacy, power, potency
**in effect** He was now in effect a figurehead with little real power.
► in fact, effectively, really, actually, in truth, to all intents and purposes
**take effect** The change takes effect next April.
► come into force, be effective, become operative, become valid, be implemented
AN OPPOSITE IS lapse

## effect VERB

**USAGE** Do not confuse this word, which means 'to achieve or bring about', with affect, which means 'to cause a change in'.
We need to effect a compromise.
► achieve, accomplish, bring about, carry out, initiate, make, put into effect, cause, create, execute, implement

## effective ADJECTIVE

1 There is no effective alternative.
► useful, workable, successful, fruitful, productive, worthwhile, potent, powerful, effectual, efficient, real, strong, (more formal) efficacious
AN OPPOSITE IS ineffective
2 The government still lacks an effective opposition.
► capable, competent, able, proficient, useful
3 He produced several effective arguments.
► convincing, cogent, persuasive, compelling, telling, striking, meaningful
OPPOSITES ARE weak, unconvincing
4 The changes will be effective from midnight.
► operative, in force, valid
OPPOSITES ARE inoperative, invalid

## effeminate ADJECTIVE

His speech and manner were somewhat effeminate.
► womanish, girlish, effete, unmanly, camp, (more informal, disapproving) pansy, (more informal, disapproving) sissy
AN OPPOSITE IS manly

## effervescent ADJECTIVE

effervescent drinks
► sparkling, carbonated, fizzy, bubbling, bubbly, foaming

## efficiency NOUN

1 These measures can increase the efficiency of the business.
► productivity, cost-effectiveness
2 She was praised for her efficiency.
► competence, proficiency, ability, capability, good organization, expertise

## efficient ADJECTIVE

1 The housekeeping was extremely efficient.
► methodical, systematic, well-organized, cost-effective
AN OPPOSITE IS inefficient
2 She was lucky to have found such an efficient young assistant.
► capable, competent, proficient, able, well-organized, businesslike

## effort NOUN

1 We will make an effort to complete the task in time.
► attempt, endeavour, try, (more informal) shot, (more informal) stab
2 It took considerable effort to get the boiler working again.
► exertion, energy, trouble, force, application, pains
3 It was a tremendous team effort.
► achievement, accomplishment, performance, feat, undertaking, success

## effortless ADJECTIVE

She showed the effortless fluency of an experienced speaker.
► easy, simple, undemanding, painless, trouble-free, smooth

## effrontery NOUN

(usually disapproving) He had the effrontery to offer his story to the papers.
► cheek, audacity, nerve, boldness, temerity, impudence, impertinence, insolence, presumptuousness, shamelessness, (more informal) sauce

## effusive ADJECTIVE

He spoke with effusive politeness.
► unrestrained, extravagant, fulsome, lavish, demonstrative

## egg VERB

**egg on** One of the group was egging the others on.
► urge, goad, drive, provoke, incite, encourage

**egotistic, egotistical** ADJECTIVE
*an egotistic attitude to life*
► self-centred, egocentric, egomaniacal, conceited, self-interested, self-absorbed

**ejaculate** VERB
*'No!' he ejaculated, startled.*
► exclaim, shout, yell, cry out, call out, scream

**eject** VERB
1 *Two heavy bouncers arrived to eject him from the club.*
► expel, throw out, evict, remove, dismiss, (*more informal*) kick out
2 *A tall chimney was ejecting black smoke.*
► emit, discharge, send out, pour out, spew out, give off, belch, disgorge

**elaborate** ADJECTIVE
1 *elaborate schemes to raise money*
► complicated, complex, intricate, detailed, extensive, well worked out, involved
AN OPPOSITE IS simple
2 *elaborate wood carvings*
► ornate, decorative, ornamental, intricate, fancy, baroque, rococo, showy
OPPOSITES ARE simple, plain

**elaborate** VERB
**elaborate on** *He would not elaborate on his news until he had washed.*
► expand on, enlarge on, add to, give details of, amplify, develop, supplement, expatiate on, fill out
AN OPPOSITE IS simplify

**elapse** VERB
*Several years elapsed before we returned to the house in Corfu.*
► pass, go by, slip by, lapse

**elastic** ADJECTIVE
1 *An elastic cord is tied to an ankle.*
► flexible, plastic, pliable, pliant, rubbery, bendy, ductile, yielding, (*more informal*) bouncy, (*more informal*) springy, (*more informal*) stretchy
AN OPPOSITE IS rigid
2 *The arrangements can be made more elastic if you wish.*
► flexible, adaptable, adjustable, variable, accommodating
OPPOSITES ARE rigid, fixed

**elated** ADJECTIVE
*Her huge win left her feeling elated.*
► thrilled, exhilarated, ecstatic, exultant, delighted, euphoric, overjoyed, (*more informal*) over the moon, (*more informal*) on top of the world

**elbow** VERB
*She tried to elbow him out of her way.*
► push, force, shoulder, muscle

**elderly** ADJECTIVE
*the increase in the number of elderly people*
► aged, ageing, old, senile

**elect** VERB
*The Party elects a leader every four years.*
► choose, select, vote for, pick, adopt, appoint, decide on, name, nominate

**election** NOUN
1 *the election of a president*
► selection, choosing, ballot (for), poll (for), vote (for)
2 *She became an MP in the 1997 election.*
► poll, vote, ballot
RELATED NOUN psephology

**electric** ADJECTIVE
*The atmosphere in the room was electric.*
► electrifying, exciting, dramatic, thrilling, tense, charged

**electrifying** ADJECTIVE
*an electrifying performance*
► thrilling, exciting, astounding, hair-raising, stimulating, amazing, astonishing, electric

**elegant** ADJECTIVE
1 *Fire destroyed an elegant building in the Old Town.*
► handsome, stylish, graceful, gracious, smart, tasteful
AN OPPOSITE IS inelegant
2 *A tall elegant woman walked in.*
► graceful, fashionable, beautiful, chic, smart
3 *an elegant solution to an awkward problem*
► neat, ingenious, clever, deft, effective

**element** NOUN
1 *That is only one element of the situation.*
► component, factor, part, ingredient, constituent, piece, strand, aspect
2 *There is an element of truth in the story.*
► trace, hint, touch, suspicion, smattering, soupçon
3 *James was in his element messing about with old cars.*
► environment, domain, habitat, sphere
**the elements** *We could brave the elements in our cagoules.*
► the weather, the wind and rain

**elementary** ADJECTIVE
1 *an elementary maths course*
► basic, rudimentary, fundamental, introductory, primary
AN OPPOSITE IS advanced
2 *The answer to the question is elementary.*
► simple, easy, straightforward, uncomplicated

**elevated** ADJECTIVE
1 *an elevated roadway*
► raised, overhead, high
2 *elevated discussions*
► grand, dignified, noble, superior, exalted, lofty

**elicit** VERB
*The police were unable to elicit any more information.*
► obtain, extract, bring out, draw out, derive, evoke

**eligible** ADJECTIVE
be eligible for *You would be eligible for tax relief on donations.*
▶ be entitled to, qualify for, be allowed, be permitted
AN OPPOSITE IS ineligible

**eliminate** VERB
1 *We can eliminate sabotage as a cause of the accident.*
▶ exclude, discount, disregard, remove
2 *The junta went on to eliminate many of their opponents.*
▶ get rid of, do away with, eradicate, exterminate, kill, murder, stamp out

**elite** NOUN
1 *Higher wages are earned by an elite of urban craftsmen.*
▶ the best, the cream, the flower
2 *the social elite*
▶ aristocracy, nobility, gentry, establishment

**elocution** NOUN
*lessons in elocution*
▶ diction, pronunciation, articulation, delivery

**eloquence** NOUN
*She spoke with great eloquence.*
▶ expressiveness, fluency, articulacy, sensitivity

**eloquent** ADJECTIVE
*After dinner he made an eloquent speech.*
▶ expressive, articulate, fluent, moving, stirring, forceful, potent, persuasive, powerful, unfaltering
AN OPPOSITE IS inarticulate

**elude** VERB
*For many years they managed to elude justice.*
▶ escape, avoid, evade, circumvent, dodge, shake off, foil, get away from

**elusive** ADJECTIVE
1 *Despite his phone calls she continued to be elusive for several days.*
▶ evasive, hard to find, difficult to track down, shifty
2 *The play's meaning is elusive*
▶ obscure, subtle, indefinable, intangible, ambiguous, difficult

**emaciated** ADJECTIVE
*Her hair had turned grey and she grew pale and emaciated.*
▶ thin, skeletal, bony, haggard, wasted, attenuated

**emanate** VERB
*The leak emanated from a government department.*
▶ originate, stem, arise, proceed, spring, derive, emerge, issue

**embargo** NOUN
*There is an embargo on weapon supplies to the area.*
▶ ban, bar, prohibition, moratorium, proscription, restriction

**embark** VERB
1 *Passengers may embark from eight o'clock this evening.*
▶ board, go aboard, go on board
OPPOSITES ARE disembark, land

2 embark on *He was ready to embark on a career in medicine.*
▶ begin, start, enter on, commence, undertake, take up, set about

**embarrass** VERB
*He gazed at her until he realized he was embarrassing her.*
▶ make (someone) uncomfortable, make (someone) feel embarrassed, disconcert, distress, upset, shame, mortify, fluster, nonplus, humiliate

**embarrassed** ADJECTIVE
*Geoff's outspoken remarks left him feeling embarrassed.*
▶ awkward, self-conscious, disconcerted, uncomfortable, abashed, mortified, ashamed, confused, distressed, flustered, nonplussed, humiliated, shamed, upset, (*more informal*) red in the face

**embarrassing** ADJECTIVE
*She was afraid of making an embarrassing mistake.*
▶ awkward, humiliating, shaming, shameful, disconcerting, distressing, mortifying, upsetting

**embarrassment** NOUN
*Jane tried to hide her embarrassment.*
▶ awkwardness, self-consciousness, discomfort, unease, mortification, humiliation, distress

**embassy** NOUN
*the American embassy*
▶ consulate, legation, mission

**embezzle** VERB
*He admitted embezzling thousands of pounds from the company.*
▶ steal, misappropriate, pilfer, take fraudulently, appropriate

**embezzlement** NOUN
*They were found guilty of embezzlement.*
▶ fraud, theft, stealing, misappropriation, appropriation

**embittered** ADJECTIVE
*He was left tired and embittered by the experience.*
▶ bitter, disillusioned, disaffected, resentful, envious, sour

**emblem** NOUN
*America's national emblem, the bald eagle*
▶ symbol, sign, token, mark, insignia, badge, crest, device, image, regalia, seal

**embody** VERB
1 *a spiritual fellowship embodying everything that is true and good*
▶ embrace, include, incorporate, contain, assimilate, take in
2 *They embody everything associated with the culture of the sixties.*
▶ personify, represent, exemplify, symbolize, epitomize, encapsulate, stand for

**embrace** VERB
1 *The old man got up and embraced his son.*
▶ hug, clasp, hold, cuddle, grasp, squeeze

**embryonic** *(continued)*

2 *Imelda could not embrace the idea of life without a husband.*
▶ accept, espouse, welcome, take on, receive
3 *The county embraces the best part of two national parks.*
▶ comprise, embody, include, incorporate, bring together, contain, assimilate, take in

**embryonic** ADJECTIVE
*An urban community existed there in embryonic form.*
▶ rudimentary, undeveloped, unformed, early, immature, incipient, incomplete

**emend** VERB
*The text was published in an emended version.*
▶ alter, edit, modify, correct, revise, rewrite

**emerge** VERB
1 *A cyclist emerged from the entrance.*
▶ come out, appear, come into view, issue, emanate
AN OPPOSITE IS disappear
2 *Another version of the story later emerged.*
▶ become known, become evident, be revealed, come to light, surface, unfold, (*more informal*) crop up

**emergency** NOUN
*She offered a helping hand in an emergency.*
▶ crisis, danger, difficulty, predicament, urgent situation, extremity, (*more informal*) tight spot

**eminent** ADJECTIVE
*an eminent scientist and scholar*
▶ distinguished, famous, prominent, well known, celebrated, acclaimed, renowned, illustrious, famed, notable, noteworthy, esteemed, respected, honoured, outstanding

**emission** NOUN
*carbon dioxide emissions*
▶ discharge, release, issue, outpouring, emanation

**emit** VERB
*Vehicle exhausts emit hydrocarbons.*
▶ discharge, release, give off, give out, pour out, radiate

**emotion** NOUN
*He spoke with a voice full of emotion.*
▶ feeling, passion, sentiment, intensity, warmth, agitation, excitement, fervour
AN OPPOSITE IS indifference

**emotional** ADJECTIVE
1 *an emotional tribute*
▶ poignant, passionate, impassioned, intense, moving, touching, warm-hearted
2 *an emotional woman*
▶ passionate, demonstrative, fervent, sensitive, temperamental, excitable, romantic

**emotive** ADJECTIVE
*Hunting is an emotive issue.*
▶ sensitive, inflammatory, controversial, contentious, delicate

**emphasis** NOUN
*This year there is a special emphasis given to creative writing.*
▶ importance, significance, prominence, priority, urgency, weight, stress, attention

**emphasize** VERB
*The spokesman emphasized the need to remain calm.*
▶ stress, underline, focus on, highlight, point up, draw attention to, play up, make a point of
OPPOSITES ARE understate, play down

**emphatic** ADJECTIVE
*an emphatic refusal*
▶ absolute, firm, forceful, vehement, vigorous, definite, unequivocal, direct, positive, energetic, out-and-out

**empire** NOUN
*the Babylonian Empire*
▶ kingdom, realm, domain, dominion, territory
RELATED ADJECTIVE imperial

**employ** VERB
1 *The business employs over a hundred people.*
▶ engage, hire, pay, take on, retain, use the services of, give work to, have on the payroll
2 *This medical practice employs the most modern techniques.*
▶ use, utilize, apply

**employee** NOUN
*He was an employee of his own brother's bank.*
▶ worker, member of staff, member of the workforce

**employees** *measures to improve working conditions for the employees*
▶ staff, workforce

**employer** NOUN
1 *His employer was younger than he was.*
▶ boss, manager, manageress, proprietor, chief executive, head
2 *The Health Service is the country's largest employer.*
▶ business, management, company, organization

**employment** NOUN
*She found employment as a bank clerk.*
▶ work, a job, a post, a position, a situation, a livelihood

**empower** VERB
*The edict empowered local governors to arrest suspects.*
▶ authorize, entitle, permit, allow, enable, sanction, warrant

**empty** ADJECTIVE
1 *The house had been empty for years.*
▶ vacant, unoccupied, uninhabited, abandoned, deserted
2 *Without him her life felt empty.*
▶ aimless, futile, worthless, purposeless, unimportant, hollow
3 *These warnings were not just empty threats.*
▶ vain, idle, meaningless, ineffectual

**empty** VERB

1 *No one had troubled to empty the washing machine.*
▶ unload, unpack, clear
OPPOSITES ARE fill, load

2 *He emptied the glass for a second time.*
▶ drain, exhaust, drink up
AN OPPOSITE IS fill

**enable** VERB

1 *The new law will enable individuals to own shares in these companies.*
▶ authorize, permit, allow, qualify, empower, equip, aid, assist

2 *Wells took time off work to enable him to train twice a day.*
▶ allow, permit, let, help, make it possible for, provide the means for
AN OPPOSITE IS prevent

**enamoured** ADJECTIVE

enamoured of *She was jealous because the prince was clearly enamoured of her sister and not her.*
▶ in love with, infatuated with, fond of, keen on, taken with, smitten with, captivated by, (more informal) crazy about, (more informal) nuts about

**enchant** VERB

*The scenery never ceased to enchant me.*
▶ delight, please, captivate, bewitch, charm, entrance, enthral, mesmerize
OPPOSITES ARE repel, disgust

**enclose** VERB

1 *A tall fence enclosed the garden.*
▶ surround, circle, encircle, bound, border, skirt, encompass, shut in, fence in, confine, contain

2 *Please enclose payment with your order.*
▶ include, insert, put in

**enclosed** ADJECTIVE

*an enclosed area*
▶ confined, fenced, walled, shut in, contained, surrounded, encircled, limited, restricted
AN OPPOSITE IS open

**enclosure** NOUN

1 *Dogs drove the animals into the enclosure.*
▶ pen, compound, fold, paddock, stockade, corral

2 *an enclosure in an envelope*
▶ contents, inclusion, insertion

**encompass** VERB

*The talks encompass a wide range of subjects.*
▶ include, embrace, cover, incorporate, comprise, deal with

**encounter** VERB

1 *One day, they encountered a beautiful blonde on the beach.*
▶ meet, run into, come across, chance on, (more informal) bump into

2 *You may encounter a few problems.*
▶ experience, be faced with, come up against, suffer, undergo

**encounter** NOUN

1 *an encounter with a wizard*
▶ meeting, rendezvous

2 *an encounter with the enemy*
▶ battle, clash, fight , conflict, confrontation, struggle, collision

**encourage** VERB

1 *The cries of support encouraged the players.*
▶ hearten, cheer, inspire, buoy up, uplift, motivate, stimulate, animate, invigorate, spur, rally, reassure

2 *The government is keen to encourage small businesses.*
▶ support, promote, endorse, stimulate, aid, advance, assist, aid, foster, strengthen

3 *Clever marketing encourages sales.*
▶ promote, increase, boost, generate, foster, further, be conducive to, be an incentive to, engender, help, induce

4 *Her mother encouraged her to take up medicine.*
▶ persuade, prompt, urge, invite
AN OPPOSITE IS discourage

**encouragement** NOUN

*All they need is a little encouragement.*
▶ reassurance, support, inspiration, stimulation, cheering up

**encouraging** ADJECTIVE

*The first results were very encouraging.*
▶ reassuring, heartening, promising, favourable, gratifying, hopeful, auspicious, cheering, comforting, optimistic

**encroach** VERB

encroach on *I did not want to encroach on their privacy.*
▶ intrude on, trespass on, impinge on, invade, violate, enter on

---

**end** VERB This word is often overused. Here are some alternatives:

1 *The programme ends at midnight. The bus route ends at this point.*
▶ finish, conclude, terminate, come to an end, close
OPPOSITES ARE start, begin

2 *He wanted to end his relationship with Greta.*
▶ break off, stop, halt, discontinue, wind up
OPPOSITES ARE maintain, continue

3 *The government plans to end the benefit next year.*
▶ abolish, terminate, finish, extinguish, put an end to

---

**endanger** VERB

*She could not be moved any distance without endangering her life.*
▶ risk, jeopardize, imperil, threaten, put at risk, expose to risk
AN OPPOSITE IS protect

**endearing** ADJECTIVE
*She has the endearing habit of kissing you on both cheeks.*
▶ charming, appealing, attractive, enchanting, engaging, lovable, winning, disarming
AN OPPOSITE IS unappealing

**endeavour** VERB
*We will endeavour to answer these questions later.*
▶ attempt, try, venture, undertake, strive, set out

**endeavour** NOUN
*The company will support them in their endeavour.*
▶ attempt, venture, effort, striving

**ending** NOUN
*The story has an exciting ending.*
▶ end, conclusion, finish, close, resolution, completion, climax, denouement

**endless** ADJECTIVE
1 *an endless source of good ideas*
▶ boundless, infinite, unlimited, unbounded
2 *He sipped endless cups of strong coffee.*
▶ ceaseless, countless, innumerable, constant, perpetual, interminable, eternal

**endorse** VERB
*We entirely endorse the conclusions reached.*
▶ approve, support, back, uphold, confirm, subscribe to, agree with, condone

**endurance** NOUN
1 *The race is a test of endurance*
▶ stamina, staying power, fortitude, perseverance, determination, tenacity, resoluteness, resolution, strength, (*more informal*) grit, (*more informal*) bottle
2 *Such suffering is beyond anyone's endurance.*
▶ toleration, tolerance, bearing, sufferance, forbearance

**endure** VERB
1 *The pain is greater than anyone could endure.*
▶ tolerate, bear, withstand, suffer, cope with, undergo, submit to
2 *Their love will endure for ever.*
▶ last, survive, abide, persist, prevail, continue, remain, stay

**enduring** ADJECTIVE
*an enduring friendship*
▶ lasting, persisting, abiding, continuing, durable, steadfast, constant

**enemy** NOUN
*The country faces a new and more dangerous enemy.*
▶ foe, adversary, opponent, antagonist, opposition
OPPOSITES ARE friend, ally

**energetic** ADJECTIVE
1 *an energetic young person*
▶ dynamic, active, lively, spirited, animated, enthusiastic, indefatigable, tireless, unflagging
OPPOSITES ARE inactive, lethargic, lazy
2 *energetic exercises*
▶ strenuous, vigorous, rigorous, arduous, brisk

3 *an energetic sales promotion*
▶ forceful, vigorous, aggressive, determined, powerful
OPPOSITES ARE feeble, half-hearted

**energy** NOUN
1 *She felt full of energy.*
▶ vitality, vigour, drive, liveliness, spirit, verve, zest, zeal, exuberance, strength, (*more informal*) zip
AN OPPOSITE IS lethargy
2 *new and cleaner sources of energy*
▶ power, fuel

**enforce** VERB
*There was no one left to enforce the laws.*
▶ apply, impose, administer, implement, execute, carry out, put into effect

**engage** VERB
1 **engage in** *She is always eager to engage in conversation.*
▶ participate in, take part in, become involved in, go in for, enter into, share in
2 *They decided to engage a nanny for the younger children.*
▶ employ, hire, recruit, take on, appoint, retain
3 *These activities do not always engage the imagination very well.*
▶ occupy, absorb, engross, attract, interest, capture, captivate, grip
4 *The infantry engaged the enemy early the next day.*
▶ fight, do battle, clash with, encounter, enter into battle with
5 *The lowest gear did not engage properly.*
▶ connect, mesh, interlock

**engaged** ADJECTIVE
1 *an engaged couple*
▶ betrothed, affianced, attached
2 *He was engaged in his work.*
▶ occupied, busy, engrossed, absorbed, immersed, preoccupied

**engagement** NOUN
1 *They have broken off their engagement.*
▶ betrothal, promise to marry
2 *He had a business engagement that afternoon.*
▶ appointment, arrangement, commitment, obligation, meeting, date
3 *A series of military engagements followed.*
▶ battle, conflict, encounter, fight, clash, skirmish, offensive

**engaging** ADJECTIVE
*an engaging little girl*
▶ charming, attractive, appealing, delightful, lovely, pleasing, likeable, lovable

**engender** VERB
*Modern art engenders a lot of argument.*
▶ generate, cause, produce, rouse, provoke, give rise to, be the cause of, result in

**engine** NOUN
1 *a car engine*
▶ motor, power unit, mechanism

**2** *a railway engine*
▶ locomotive

**engineer** NOUN
*the engineer's drawings*
▶ designer, planner, inventor, architect

**engineer** VERB
*Near the election the government will engineer an economic boom.*
▶ devise, create, bring about, produce, contrive, plan, construct, manage

---

**engineering** NOUN
**BRANCHES OF ENGINEERING**

aerodynamics, aeronautical engineering, agricultural engineering, astronautics, automotive engineering, chemical engineering, civil engineering, electrical engineering, environmental engineering, fluid dynamics, geotechnics, hydraulics, mechanical engineering, mining engineering, naval engineering, nuclear engineering, production engineering, structural engineering.

---

**engrave** VERB
*The watch is engraved with a dedication on the back.*
▶ inscribe, etch, print, mark, cut

**engraving** NOUN
*an engraving of the two younger children*
▶ etching, print, impression, woodcut, carving

**engrossed** ADJECTIVE
*Fran was engrossed in her book.*
▶ absorbed, immersed, involved, interested, engaged, preoccupied (by), gripped (by), captivated (by), occupied (by), enthralled (by), fascinated (by), riveted (by)

**enhance** VERB
*These successes enhanced his reputation.*
▶ improve, further, increase, heighten, reinforce, boost, intensify, strengthen, build up

**enigma** NOUN
*We never did solve the enigma of the missing passenger.*
▶ puzzle, mystery, riddle, problem, conundrum, paradox

**enigmatic** ADJECTIVE
*an enigmatic smile*
▶ mysterious, puzzling, perplexing, strange, obscure, impenetrable
AN OPPOSITE IS straightforward

**enjoy** VERB
**1** *We all enjoy our outings. She enjoyed playing the piano.*
▶ like, love, appreciate, be keen on, be pleased by, take pleasure from or in, delight in, indulge in, rejoice in, relish, revel in, savour
OPPOSITES ARE dislike, hate
**2** *Visitors enjoy many privileges.*
▶ benefit from, have the benefit of, have the advantage of, experience, use

**3** *enjoy yourself*
▶ have fun, have a good time, celebrate, (*informal*) have a ball, (*informal*) let your hair down

**enjoyable** ADJECTIVE
*You can have a good meal in enjoyable surroundings.*
▶ agreeable, pleasant, delightful, gratifying, likeable, satisfying, delicious, pleasurable, rewarding, entertaining, amusing
OPPOSITES ARE unpleasant, disagreeable

**enlarge** VERB
**1** *The new emperor sought to enlarge his territory to the east.*
▶ increase, expand, augment, develop, add to, stretch
**2** *enlarge on He didn't want to enlarge on his remarks.*
▶ elaborate on, expand on, amplify, develop, broaden, supplement, flesh out

**enlighten** VERB
*If you really don't know perhaps we should enlighten you.*
▶ inform, illuminate, advise, explain to, update, notify

**enlightened** ADJECTIVE
*an enlightened attitude to funding the arts*
▶ informed, educated, liberal, sophisticated, knowledgeable, civilized, cultivated, refined, open-minded

**enlist** VERB
**1** *Arafat enlisted thousands of young people in his army.*
▶ recruit, enrol, conscript, engage, muster
**2** *enlist in The brothers enlisted in the Royal Engineers.*
▶ enrol in, sign up for, join, enter, join up for, volunteer (for)
**3** *In Paris, he enlisted the aid of an influential American physician.*
▶ obtain, secure, procure, engage, win

**enliven** VERB
*A little humour often helps to enliven a dull subject.*
▶ liven up, brighten up, make more interesting, animate, enhance, improve

**enmity** NOUN
*people who live in a state of enmity with one another*
▶ hostility, antagonism, animosity, strife, opposition (towards), antipathy (towards), acrimony (towards)
AN OPPOSITE IS friendship

**enormity** NOUN
**1** *the enormities of the Nazi years*
▶ atrocity, outrage, horror, crime, abomination, wickedness
**2** *the enormity of the task*
▶ immensity, hugeness, magnitude, vastness, seriousness, enormousness

**USAGE** Note that *enormity* is not correct when the reference is simply to physical size, e.g. *the enormity of the building*. It's better to say *the huge size of the building* or use one of the synonyms given above. .

**enormous** ADJECTIVE
*An enormous insect crept across the floor.*
▶ huge, gigantic, immense, massive, colossal, (*more informal*) whopping, (*more informal*) ginormous

**enough** ADJECTIVE
*Do you have enough food? £10 will not be enough.*
▶ sufficient, adequate, ample, as much (food) as you need

**enquire** VERB
*She enquired about times of the trains home.*
▶ ask, make enquiries, seek information, want to know
**USAGE** Note that *inquire* is normally used in the meaning 'to make an official investigation', as in *a committee appointed to inquire into the incident.*

**enquiry** NOUN
*routine telephone enquiries*
▶ query, question
**USAGE** Note that *inquiry* is normally used in the meaning 'official investigation', as in *The opposition called for a public inquiry into the incident.*

**enrage** VERB
*Such a casual attitude enraged her.*
▶ anger, annoy, irritate, infuriate, exasperate, incense, vex, madden, aggravate, antagonize, displease, incite, inflame, make angry, (*more informal*) needle, (*more informal*) rile, (*more informal*) bug, (*more informal*) rub up the wrong way
OPPOSITES ARE pacify, placate

**enrol** VERB
*enrol in You can enrol in your course any evening this week.*
▶ register for, sign up for, join

**enslave** VERB
*The invading armies enslaved the population.*
▶ make slaves of, subjugate, suppress, disenfranchise, dominate, subject, take away the rights of
OPPOSITES ARE liberate, emancipate

**ensue** VERB
*A fierce argument ensued.*
▶ follow, result, develop, arise, occur, come about

**ensure** VERB
**USAGE** Note that *ensure* means 'to make sure' whereas *insure* means 'to take out insurance'.
*A mild sedative ensured a good night's sleep.*
▶ guarantee, make sure, secure, confirm, make certain

**entail** VERB
*Travel home entailed a five-hour drive.*
▶ involve, necessitate, require, call for, demand, occasion

**entangle** VERB
*By switching hands she entangled the dog's lead in her shopping bags.*
▶ tangle, twist, catch, intertwine, mix up, knot

**enter** VERB
**1** *Soldiers entered the building.*
▶ go in or into, come in or into, gain access to, set foot in, pass into
AN OPPOSITE IS leave
**2** *While the sign is up please do not enter.*
▶ go in, come in
AN OPPOSITE IS leave
**3** *A bullet had entered his chest.*
▶ penetrate, pierce, puncture, perforate, make a hole in
**4** *That year the Americans entered the war.*
▶ join, take part in, participate in
**5** *I'm going to enter a competition.*
▶ go in for, become a contestant in, enrol for
**6** *Please enter your details on the form.*
▶ record, register, note, write down

**enterprise** NOUN
**1** *a dangerous enterprise*
▶ undertaking, endeavour, venture, pursuit, operation, project, adventure, business, effort
**2** *a charitable enterprise*
▶ organization, business, establishment, company, firm
**3** *Success in the job calls for considerable enterprise.*
▶ initiative, resourcefulness, resource, adventurousness, spirit, drive, determination, imagination

**enterprising** ADJECTIVE
*An enterprising buyer can get quite a bargain at this time of year.*
▶ adventurous, resourceful, daring, bold, enthusiastic, energetic, imaginative, inventive, creative
AN OPPOSITE IS unadventurous

**entertain** VERB
**1** *He told stories to entertain his children.*
▶ amuse, divert, delight, gladden, cheer up, make laugh, raise a smile, (*more informal*) tickle
**2** *We will be entertaining friends this Christmas.*
▶ receive, play host to, cater for, welcome
**3** *She refused to entertain the idea.*
▶ consider, contemplate, countenance, accept, agree to

**entertainer** NOUN
*a television entertainer*
▶ performer, artiste, artist

**entertaining** ADJECTIVE
*an entertaining story*
▶ amusing, enjoyable, witty, funny, diverting, pleasing

## entertainment NOUN

*The holiday includes free evening entertainment.*
▶ amusement, diversion, enjoyment, recreation, pastime, play, fun, pleasure, sport, distraction

**TYPES OF ENTERTAINMENT**

**home entertainment**: television, video, home cinema, CD, minidisc, DVD, radio, hi-fi, computer games, board games.

**public entertainment**: theatre, cinema or film, concert hall, opera, pantomime, musical, variety show, music hall, revue, cabaret, nightclub, casino, circus, waxworks, puppet show; dance, disco, ceilidh, karaoke, magic show, ice-skating show, street entertainment.

**outdoor entertainment**: firework show, air show, fair, funfair, gymkhana, rodeo, zoo; son et lumière (at a historic building), tattoo, laser-light show, carnival, pageant, fete, barbecue, festival.

## enthralling ADJECTIVE

*They watched an enthralling series of singles matches.*
▶ exciting, fascinating, engrossing, captivating, dazzling

## enthusiasm NOUN

**1** *They will take on their new role with enthusiasm. He has a new-found enthusiasm for the game.*
▶ eagerness, excitement, keenness, ardour, relish, commitment, zeal, zest, fervour, ambition, drive, panache, spirit, verve
AN OPPOSITE IS apathy

**2** *Their latest enthusiasm is swimming.*
▶ interest, pursuit, pastime, diversion, hobby, passion, craze, (*informal*) fad

## enthusiast NOUN

*an amateur radio enthusiast*
▶ devotee, fan, fanatic, aficionado, follower, lover, (*more informal*) buff

## enthusiastic ADJECTIVE

*The visitors got an enthusiastic reception a group of enthusiastic supporters*
▶ eager, keen, ardent, fervent, devoted, passionate, wholehearted
OPPOSITES ARE unenthusiastic, apathetic

## entice VERB

*A friend of mine enticed me to go to a club with him.*
▶ persuade, tempt, lure (into going), induce, coax

## entire ADJECTIVE

**1** *He spent his entire life on the island.*
▶ whole, complete, total, full

**2** *The arch of one of the gates is entire.*
▶ intact, complete, undamaged

## entirely ADVERB

*I entirely agree with you.*
▶ completely, absolutely, fully, totally, utterly, thoroughly

## entitle VERB

**1** *entitle to The voucher entitles you to free entrance to the gallery.*
▶ qualify for, authorize to, allow, permit, warrant

**2** *The story is entitled 'A Day in the Life of My Dog'*
▶ call, name, title, designate

## entitlement NOUN

*their entitlement to the money*
▶ right, title, claim, ownership (of)

## entity NOUN

*a separate entity*
▶ being, thing, body, organism

## entrance NOUN

**1** *The main entrance to the building is round the corner.*
▶ entry, way in, access, door, doorway, gateway, approach

**2** *At the entrance of the hosts a silence fell on the room.*
▶ entry, appearance, arrival, approach, coming in, going in, (*more formal*) ingress

**3** *Several people were refused entrance.*
▶ admission, admittance, entry, access

## entrant NOUN

*There are over a hundred entrants in the competition.*
▶ candidate, competitor, contender, contestant, entry, participant, player

## entreaty NOUN

*She ignored their entreaties.*
▶ plea, appeal, pleading, exhortation

## entrust VERB

**1** *She entrusted her brother with the task.*
▶ charge, give responsibility for, put in charge of, trust, (*more informal*) saddle

**2** *She entrusted the task to her brother.*
▶ assign, allocate, commit, delegate, confer (on), turn over

## entry NOUN

**1** *The entry to the grounds was closed.*
▶ entrance, way in, access, door, doorway, gateway, approach

**2** *They were allowed entry on production of a passport.*
▶ admission, admittance, entrance, access

**3** *the entry in the diary*
▶ item, record, statement, note, insertion

**4** *an entry in a competition*
▶ candidate, competitor, contender, contestant, entrant, participant, player

## envelop VERB

*A poison gas enveloped the place.*
▶ cover, surround, enfold, blanket, enwrap, engulf, cloak, cocoon

## envelope NOUN

*He put the money in an envelope*
▶ wrapper, wrapping, cover, sleeve

## enviable ADJECTIVE

*She has the enviable job of entertaining celebrities.*
▶ attractive, desirable, favourable

**envious** ADJECTIVE

*He was envious of his brother's success.*
► jealous, resentful, grudging, begrudging, bitter (about), covetous, dissatisfied, (*more informal*) green with envy (about or over)

**environment** NOUN

1 *a natural environment for wild birds*
► habitat, location, setting, surroundings, conditions, situation, milieu, territory
2 **the environment** *industrial activities that threaten the environment*
► the natural world, the earth, the planet, the world we live in

**envisage** NOUN

1 *It is hard to envisage what might happen.*
► imagine, visualize, picture, contemplate
2 *We envisage many changes.*
► foresee, predict, expect, intend, propose

**envoy** NOUN

*an envoy from Spain*
► ambassador, representative, delegate, agent, intermediary

**envy** NOUN

*He could not help feeling envy at her good luck.*
► jealousy, bitterness, resentment, covetousness, cupidity, dissatisfaction, ill-will

**envy** VERB

*He envied her success.*
► be jealous of, be envious of, begrudge, grudge, resent

**epidemic** NOUN

*a measles epidemic*
► outbreak, plague, upsurge

**episode** NOUN

1 *a happy episode in my life*
► incident, event, occurrence, happening, occasion, circumstance
2 *the final episode of the series*
► instalment, part, section, programme

**epitome** NOUN

*He was the epitome of an English gentleman.*
► personification, embodiment, essence, quintessence, representation, model, type

**equal** ADJECTIVE

1 *a row of houses of equal size*
► identical, similar, uniform, the same, like, corresponding, comparable, commensurate
OPPOSITES ARE unequal, different, varying
2 *an equal contest*
► even, balanced, level, evenly matched
OPPOSITES ARE unequal, uneven
3 **equal to** *We thought he was equal to the task.*
► capable of, fit for, adequate for, good enough for, suitable for, suited for
AN OPPOSITE IS incapable of

**equal** NOUN

*They treated him as their equal.*
► peer, equivalent, counterpart, fellow

**equal** VERB

1 *Her performance almost equalled the world record.*
► match, reach, be as good as, compete with, rival
2 *Three and ten equals thirteen.*
► total, amount to

**equality** NOUN

1 *an equality of supply and demand*
► evenness, similarity, balance (between), parity, uniformity, correspondence, identity
2 *equality before the law*
► fairness, justice, equal rights, impartiality

**equalize** VERB

1 *The law equalizes pay for men and women.*
► balance, make equal, level, match, even up, (*more informal*) square
2 *Celtic equalized after ten minutes.*
► level the score, draw level

**equate** VERB

*She would not equate good looks with lack of brains.*
► identify, compare, juxtapose, liken, match, parallel

**equip** VERB

1 *Each seat is equipped with a set of headphones.*
► provide, supply, furnish, fit, fit up
2 *qualifications that will equip you for your careers*
► qualify, prepare

**equipment** NOUN

*equipment needed to record the concert*
► apparatus, appliances, tools, gear

**equivalent** ADJECTIVE

*a degree or an equivalent qualification*
► comparable, similar, identical, corresponding

**era** NOUN

*a new era of peace*
► age, period, epoch

**eradicate** VERBS

*progress in eradicating malnutrition among the aged*
► eliminate, suppress, weed out, remove, abolish

**erase** VERB

*They erased a sentence that might cause offence.*
► delete, remove, rub out

**erect** ADJECTIVE

*an erect posture*
► upright, rigid, stiff

**erect** VERB

*They will erect a walkway to join the two buildings*
► build, construct, assemble, put up

**erection** NOUN

*the erection of houses*
► construction, building, assembly

**erode** VERB

*Rainwater has eroded the soil.*
► wear away, wear down, eat away, corrode

**erotic** ADJECTIVE
*erotic art*
▶ sensual, sexual, amatory, carnal, titillating, (*disapproving*) pornographic, (*disapproving*) salacious, (*disapproving*) lewd, (*disapproving*) suggestive

**err** VERB
1 *The authorities had erred in not making the information known.*
▶ be wrong, make a mistake, misjudge, miscalculate, blunder, slip up
2 *They were punished if they erred.*
▶ misbehave, do wrong, be bad, be naughty, disobey, transgress

**errand** NOUN
*They did errands for their parents.*
▶ task, job, duty, assignment, commission, mission

**erratic** ADJECTIVE
*It is hard to explain such erratic behaviour.*
▶ changeable, unpredictable, inconstant, irregular, unstable, variable
OPPOSITES ARE consistent, stable

**erroneous** ADJECTIVE
*The argument was based on an erroneous conclusion.*
▶ incorrect, inaccurate, mistaken, false, wrong, invalid, unsound, untrue, faulty, flawed

**error** NOUN
*The report contained many factual errors.*
▶ mistake, inaccuracy, slip, blunder, fault, flaw, miscalculation

**erupt** VERB
1 *Lava continued to erupt from the volcano.*
▶ spew, spout, spurt, gush, issue, pour out, shoot out, belch, be discharged, be emitted, be expelled
2 *Violence erupted on the streets of the city.*
▶ break out, flare up

**eruption** NOUN
1 *an eruption of Vesuvius   an eruption of violence*
▶ outbreak, outburst, discharge, burst, explosion
2 *a skin eruption*
▶ rash, inflammation

**escalate** VERB
*The dispute might escalate into an all-out war.*
▶ grow, develop, build up, heighten, intensify, accelerate

**escalation** NOUN
*an escalation of the conflict*
▶ intensification, heightening, aggravation, worsening, enlargement, deterioration

**escapade** NOUN
*a dangerous escapade*
▶ adventure, exploit, prank, caper, mischief, romp, antic, spree, fling, scrape, stunt, (*more informal*) lark

**escape** NOUN
1 *an escape from prison*
▶ breakout, getaway, absconding, bolt, flight, flit, retreat, running away
2 *an escape of gas*
▶ leak, leakage, emission, seepage, discharge

3 *an escape from life's troubles*
▶ distraction, diversion, relief, avoidance, relaxation

**escape** VERB
1 *They must have had help to escape.*
▶ get away, break free, break out, break loose, run away, abscond, make a break for it
2 *Oil was escaping from a crack in the hull.*
▶ leak, seep, ooze, discharge, drain, pour out, run out
3 *The passengers all escaped serious injury.  We managed to escape a lot of the work.*
▶ avoid, evade, elude, dodge, miss

**escapism** NOUN
*People need escapism in these difficult times.*
▶ fantasy, pretence, unreality, wishful thinking, romance, reverie

**escort** NOUN
1 *The police provided an escort.*
▶ guard, guide, bodyguard, convoy
2 *a royal escort*
▶ attendant, entourage, train, retinue

**escort** VERB
*A representative will escort you to your seat.*
▶ accompany, conduct, guide, lead, take, show, usher

**especially** ADVERB
1 *Property is especially expensive in the central area of the city.*
▶ particularly, exceptionally, extremely, peculiarly, extraordinarily, remarkably, uncommonly
2 *Patients, especially those with head injuries, become disoriented.*
▶ chiefly, mainly, principally, particularly, in particular, above all, primarily

**essay** NOUN
*I have to write an essay by the end of the week.*
▶ article, piece of writing, composition, assignment, study

**essence** NOUN
1 *The essence of good detective work is patience.*
▶ nature, substance, quintessence, core, kernel, basis, crux, essential part
2 *Add a little vanilla essence.*
▶ extract, concentrate

**essential** ADJECTIVE
*The leaflet provides essential travel information.*
▶ necessary, basic, vital, important, indispensable, crucial, fundamental, principal, key, primary, requisite, indispensable, main
AN OPPOSITE IS inessential

**establish** VERB
1 *The new evidence established their guilt.*
▶ prove, demonstrate, substantiate, confirm, indicate, affirm, verify, certify, authenticate
2 *The Bank aims to establish branches throughout the world.*
▶ set up, install, found, initiate, institute, organize, inaugurate, create, base

A B C D **E** F G H I J K L M N O P Q R S T U V W X Y Z

**established** ADJECTIVE

*an established practice*

► accepted, confirmed, orthodox, traditional, customary, prevailing, well-known, well-tried, familiar, entrenched, long-standing, routine

**establishment** NOUN

1 *the establishment of a new republic*

► creation, institution, introduction, constitution, formation, foundation, inauguration, inception, composition

2 *an old publishing establishment*

► business, concern, enterprise, venture, undertaking, company

**estate** NOUN

1 *The family lived in a housing estate*

► development, area, land

2 *Her grandfather had left an estate worth several millions.*

► assets, possessions, wealth, property, belongings, holdings

**esteem** NOUN

*She was held in high esteem by all her friends.*

► respect, admiration, favour, honour, regard, opinion, acclaim, estimation, credit, reverence, veneration

**estimate** NOUN

1 *Our estimate of the situation is fairly dire.*

► assessment, appraisal, evaluation, estimation, judgement, opinion, view

2 *The painter will let us have an estimate.*

► price, quotation, reckoning, specification, valuation, calculation

**estimate** VERB

*The agents estimated the selling price of the house at over a million pounds.*

► reckon, consider, assess, evaluate, calculate, gauge, work out

**estimation** NOUN

*The builders had done a good job in my estimation.*

► judgement, opinion, view, assessment, consideration, reckoning, estimate, evaluation, appraisal, appreciation, calculation

**estranged** VERB

*the rift between her and her estranged husband*

► separated, alienated, disaffected, divided, antagonized, divorced

AN OPPOSITE IS reconciled

**estuary** NOUN

*a river estuary*

► mouth, delta, creek, fjord, inlet, (*Scottish*) firth

**eternal** ADJECTIVE

1 *eternal happiness*

► everlasting, never-ending, unending, undying, enduring, abiding, timeless, infinite

OPPOSITES ARE transient, ephemeral

2 *I'm tired of your eternal complaining.*

► constant, continual, interminable, ceaseless, unceasing, incessant, everlasting, never-ending, perpetual, persistent, unremitting

OPPOSITES ARE occasional, intermittent

**eternity** NOUN

1 *the eternity after death*

► afterlife, eternal life, infinity, perpetuity, immortality

2 *an eternity* (*informal*) *We waited an eternity for a train.*

► ages, hours, a long time, for ever

**ethical** ADJECTIVE

*It would not be ethical to increase the cost of health care.*

► morally correct, proper, just, right, principled, fitting, appropriate

**ethics** NOUN

*the ethics of medical research*

► morality, moral code, morals, principles, propriety, standards, values, ideals, rights and wrongs

**ethnic** ADJECTIVE

1 *people with different ethnic backgrounds*

► cultural, national, indigenous, genetic, tribal, racial

2 *men and women in ethnic dress*

► local, traditional, national, folk

**ethos** NOUN

*The head teacher helps determine the ethos of a school.*

► spirit, character, atmosphere, climate, mood

**etiquette** NOUN

*He showed an easy charm that made up for any lack of etiquette.*

► protocol, manners, courtesy, civility, politeness, decorum, ceremony, good manners, correct behaviour

**euphoria** NOUN

*It was hard not to get caught up in the euphoria of victory.*

► elation, joy, happiness, exhilaration, jubilation, ecstasy, thrill

**evacuate** VERB

1 *It is essential to evacuate everybody from the building.*

► remove, clear, move out, send away

2 *Police decided to evacuate the area.*

► vacate, leave, quit, relinquish, withdraw from, abandon, decamp from, desert, empty

**evacuation** NOUN

1 *the evacuation of buildings*

► clearance, vacation, abandonment

2 *the evacuation of civilians*

► removal, clearance, eviction

**evade** VERB

1 *Charlie was clearly guilty of evading his responsibilities.*

► avoid, shirk, shun, dodge, duck, sidestep, steer clear of, turn your back on

AN OPPOSITE IS accept

**2** *They did all they could to evade capture.*
► avoid, elude, escape, escape from, fend off, circumvent

**evaluate** VERB
*A panel of doctors will evaluate the treatment.*
► assess, value, gauge, appraise, rate, calculate

**evaluation** NOUN
*The results need proper evaluation.*
► assessment, appraisal, valuation, analysis, estimation, reckoning

**evaporate** VERB
**1** *The water quickly evaporates.*
► disperse, dry up, vaporize
AN OPPOSITE IS condense
**2** *With this news all their hopes evaporated.*
► disappear, fade, vanish, melt away, come to an end, dissolve, dissipate
AN OPPOSITE IS materialize

**evasive** ADJECTIVE
*Lydia was evasive, not having a good answer ready.*
► prevaricating, elusive, equivocal, equivocating, ambiguous, devious, misleading, unforthcoming, disingenuous, non-committal, uninformative
AN OPPOSITE IS straightforward

**even** ADJECTIVE
**1** *an even surface*
► flat, smooth, level, flush, true, unbroken
AN OPPOSITE IS rough
**2** *an even temperament*
► calm, stable, equable, even-tempered, placid, composed, serene, steady
OPPOSITES ARE moody, excitable
**3** *the even ticking of the clock*
► steady, regular, constant, uniform, unvarying
AN OPPOSITE IS irregular
**4** *The scores were even.*
► level, equal, identical, balanced, the same
AN OPPOSITE IS unequal

**even** VERB
**even out** *I tried to even out the wrinkled carpet.*
► smooth, straighten, flatten, level
**even up** *Another point will even up the scores*
► level, balance, equalize, (*more informal*) square

**evening** NOUN
*It was evening when we reached home.*
► dusk, sunset, sundown, nightfall, twilight, (*poetic*) eventide, (*poetic*) gloaming

**event** NOUN
**1** *an annual event*
► occurrence, happening, occasion, affair, episode, experience, activity, function, business, circumstance, contingency, eventuality, incident, chance
**2** *a sporting event*
► game, match, competition, tournament
**in the event** *In the event, the plan was abandoned.*
► as it turned out, as it happened, in the end, in actual fact, as a result, as a consequence

**even-tempered** ADJECTIVE
*Sam was an even-tempered chap and took it well.*
► calm, stable, equable, placid, composed, serene
OPPOSITES ARE excitable, moody

**eventful** ADJECTIVE
*It had been a long and eventful week.*
► busy, lively, active, full, action-packed, remarkable, noteworthy, momentous
OPPOSITES ARE routine, uneventful, dull

**eventual** ADJECTIVE
*We will have to wait for the eventual verdict.*
► final, ultimate, ensuing, resulting, prospective, future

**eventually** ADVERB
*Eventually they agreed.*
► in the end, by and by, finally, at length

**everlasting** ADJECTIVE
*The gift would be an everlasting reminder of her evening.*
► eternal, never-ending, unending, undying, enduring, abiding, timeless, infinite
OPPOSITES ARE transient, ephemeral

**everyday** ADJECTIVE
*Road accidents were an everyday occurrence.*
► commonplace, common, frequent, ordinary, regular, familiar

**everyone** NOUN
*She was afraid everyone would know by now.*
► everybody, the whole world, every person, one and all, (*more informal*) every Tom, Dick, and Harry

**everywhere** ADVERB
*He looked everywhere for his keys.*
► all over, in every place, far and wide, high and low

**evict** VERB
*If they didn't pay their rent that week they would be evicted.*
► expel, eject, throw out, remove, (*more informal*) kick out, (*more informal*) give (someone) the boot

**evidence** NOUN
**1** *evidence of life on other planets*
► confirmation, verification, proof, corroboration, substantiation, authentication
**2** *Her evidence helped convict all four of them.*
► testimony, statement, information

**evident** ADJECTIVE
*It was evident that he didn't like her.*
► obvious, apparent, clear, plain, noticeable, observable, transparent, discernible
AN OPPOSITE IS unclear

**evil** ADJECTIVE
**1** *an evil act the most evil person he had met*
► wicked, bad, wrong, sinful, vile, immoral, depraved
OPPOSITES ARE good, virtuous

A B C D **E** F G H I J K L M N O P Q R S T U V W X Y Z

**evil**

2 *An evil smell came from the drains.*
▶ nasty, foul, noxious, unpleasant, offensive, unspeakable, vile, pestilential, poisonous, troublesome
AN OPPOSITE IS pleasant
3 *an evil influence*
▶ harmful, hurtful, pernicious, destructive, deadly, poisonous

**evil** NOUN
1 *a crime of the utmost evil*
▶ wickedness, wrong, sinfulness, depravity, immorality, vileness, vice, iniquity
2 *a great social evil*
▶ catastrophe, affliction, disaster, enormity, calamity, curse, misfortune

**evoke** VERB
*The scene evoked memories of her childhood.*
▶ arouse, stir up, summon up, bring to mind, call to mind, call up, raise, stimulate, inspire, awaken, conjure up, elicit, excite, kindle, produce, provoke, suggest

**evolution** NOUN
*the evolution of scientific methods*
▶ development, emergence, growth, improvement, maturing, progress, unfolding

**evolve** VERB
*The plan evolved from quite a simple idea.*
▶ develop, grow, derive, progress, mature, emerge, expand

**exact** ADJECTIVE
1 *Stacey likes to be exact in her work.*
▶ careful, precise, accurate, meticulous, methodical, painstaking, rigorous
2 *These are the exact measurements of the room.*
▶ precise, accurate, correct, definite
3 *Is this an exact copy?*
▶ identical, faithful, close

**exacting** ADJECTIVE
*an exacting task*
▶ demanding, taxing, tough, difficult, laborious, strenuous

**exactly** ADVERB
1 *She looks exactly like her mother at that age.*
▶ precisely, entirely, absolutely, completely, totally, utterly, every inch
2 *Describe the scene exactly.*
▶ accurately, precisely, faithfully, in detail

**exaggerate** VERB
*The press reports exaggerated the scale of the fire.*
▶ overstate, over-emphasize, overestimate, overstress, overdo, inflate, magnify, make too much of, amplify, enlarge, maximize, (more informal) play up
OPPOSITES ARE understate, underestimate

**examination** NOUN
1 *the annual examination of the accounts*
▶ inspection, scrutiny, study, scanning, analysis, appraisal

2 *a written examination in history*
▶ exam, test, paper
3 *a medical examination*
▶ check-up, check, inspection, review

**examine** VERB
1 *The Fraud Squad will examine the company accounts for the last ten years.*
▶ inspect, scrutinize, study, investigate, check, analyse, review, scan, probe
2 *Students are examined at the end of each year.*
▶ test, assess, appraise
3 *The defence counsel will examine the witness tomorrow.*
▶ cross-examine, interrogate, cross-question

**example** NOUN
1 *a fine example of a Tudor building*
▶ specimen, sample, case, exemplar, illustration, instance, occurrence
2 *We ought to follow their example.*
▶ precedent, model, pattern, ideal, standard
3 *They were convicted as an example to others.*
▶ warning, lesson, deterrent, caution

**exasperate** VERB
*This stupid behaviour exasperated us.*
▶ infuriate, incense, anger, annoy, irritate, enrage, vex, (more informal) rile

**excavate** VERB
1 *Moles had excavated tunnels under the grass.*
▶ dig, bore, burrow, hollow out
2 *A coin hoard was excavated from the ancient site.*
▶ unearth, dig up, uncover, discover, reveal

**exceed** VERB
1 *Total luggage weight must not exceed 300 kilos.*
▶ be more than, be greater than, go over
2 *Police stopped her for exceeding the speed limit.*
▶ break, go beyond, go faster than
3 *The amount exceeded all our expectations.*
▶ surpass, beat, outstrip, better, outdo, excel, pass, top

**exceedingly** ADVERB
*an exceedingly good meal*
▶ extremely, exceptionally, especially, supremely, outstandingly, immensely, amazingly, unusually, extraordinarily, tremendously, really, very

**excel** VERB
1 *One choir excelled all the others and was invited back for next year.*
▶ surpass, outdo, outclass, outstrip, do better than, beat, exceed
2 *He excels at most things he turns his hand to.*
▶ shine, do well, be good, stand out, be outstanding

**excellent** ADJECTIVE
*an excellent idea  The book is excellent.*
▶ outstanding, very good, first-class, first-rate, superlative, superb, remarkable, exceptional, splendid, wonderful, marvellous, tremendous

## except PREPOSITION

*The restaurant is open every evening except Monday.*
► excluding, except for, apart from, other than, besides

## exception NOUN

*Most countries are represented, although there are a few exceptions.*
► abnormality, irregularity, oddity, peculiarity, deviation, anomaly, departure, eccentricity, special case, freak, quirk, rarity

**take exception to** *She takes exception to people smoking in the house.*
► object to, disapprove of, complain about, demur at, resent, be offended by

## exceptional ADJECTIVE

**1** *a woman of exceptional ability*
► outstanding, excellent, very good, first-class, first-rate, superlative, superb, remarkable
**2** *exceptional weather patterns*
► unusual, abnormal, untypical, extraordinary, strange, irregular, peculiar, freakish

## excerpt NOUN

*(formal) We read excerpts from his new book.*
► extract, passage, selection, section, portion, quotation, snippet

## excess NOUN

**1** *an excess of vitamin E*
► surplus, surfeit, superfluity, oversufficiency, superabundance, abundance, glut
OPPOSITES ARE scarcity, deficit
**2** *a lifestyle characterized by excess*
► extravagance, overindulgence, intemperance, lavishness, prodigality

## excessive ADJECTIVE

**1** *excessive drinking*
► immoderate, inordinate, extreme, extravagant, disproportionate, superfluous
**2** *The cost proved excessive.*
► unreasonable, exorbitant, inordinate, (more informal) steep

## exchange NOUN

**1** *The two sides agreed to an exchange of prisoners.*
► switch, interchange, replacement, substitution, (informal) swap
**2** *This misunderstanding led to a series of bitter exchanges.*
► argument, altercation, recrimination, war of words
**3** *Archaeological evidence points to an exchange of goods between the two areas.*
► trade, traffic, barter, dealing

## exchange VERB

**1** *The players exchanged shirts at the end of the game.*
► swap, change, switch, interchange
**2** *I exchanged my old bike for a smart new one.*
► swap, barter, trade, substitute

## excitable ADJECTIVE

*She was afraid to tell him everything as he could be so excitable.*
► emotional, volatile, temperamental, sensitive, highly strung, nervous, irascible, jumpy

## excite VERB

*The prospect of a day out excited them.*
► thrill, exhilarate, elate, enliven, stimulate
AN OPPOSITE IS bore

## excited ADJECTIVE

*The children were becoming excited.*
► animated, stimulated, worked up, boisterous, lively, elated, restless, overwrought, vivacious

## excitement NOUN

**1** *They could hardly conceal their excitement.*
► enthusiasm, exhilaration, agitation, elation, eagerness, stimulation
**2** *There will be a lot of excitement at the party this afternoon.*
► commotion, activity, adventure

## exciting ADJECTIVE

*an exciting story*
► thrilling, stirring, exhilarating, rousing, stimulating, invigorating, enthralling, gripping, dramatic, sensational
OPPOSITES ARE dull, unexciting

## exclaim VERB

*He exclaimed that he had never been there.*
► cry, cry out, call, yell, shout, shriek, scream

## exclamation NOUN

*With an exclamation of horror she rushed upstairs.*
► cry, yell, call, shout, shriek, interjection, (old-fashioned) ejaculation

## exclude VERB

**1** *They were anxious to exclude the inevitable gatecrashers from the house.*
► keep out, deny access to, ban, disallow, prevent, prohibit, deter, debar, reject
**2** *He excluded his own name from the list.*
► omit, leave out, miss out, fail to include, rule out
**3** *These figures exclude any allowance for inflation.*
► omit, be exclusive of, not include

## exclusive ADJECTIVE

**1** *The room is for your exclusive use.*
► sole, unique, private, unshared, undivided, unrestricted
**2** *one of London's most exclusive clubs*
► select, elite, fashionable, restrictive, private, premier, (more informal) classy, (more informal) posh

## excursion NOUN

*an excursion to Brighton*
► trip, outing, jaunt, journey, expedition, day out, drive, run

## excuse NOUN

**1** *He trotted out the usual feeble excuses.*
► defence, pretext, explanation, alibi, plea, reason

**A B** (letters down left margin)

**excuse**

2 *There is no excuse for what you did.*
► justification, vindication

**excuse** VERB

1 *We cannot excuse bad behaviour.*
► justify, defend, condone, tolerate, overlook, ignore, sanction, mitigate

2 *She found it hard to excuse them this time.*
► forgive, pardon, absolve

**execute** VERB

1 *The manoeuvre is particularly hard to execute in heavy traffic.*
► carry out, implement, perform, complete, accomplish, achieve, do, effect

2 *The State no longer executes convicted murderers.*
► put to death, apply the death penalty to, hang, behead, electrocute

**execution** NOUN

1 *the execution of the plan*
► implementation, carrying out, performance, accomplishment, achievement, prosecution

2 *a sentence of execution*
► capital punishment, the death penalty, hanging, beheading, electrocution

**executive** NOUN

*a meeting of company executives*
► manager, director, chief, principal

**executive** ADJECTIVE

*executive powers*
► administrative, decision-making, managerial, supervisory

**exemplary** ADJECTIVE

*Their exemplary behaviour impressed everyone.*
► ideal, perfect, impeccable, exceptional, model, admirable, faultless, flawless

**exemplify** VERB

*The case exemplifies many of today's problems.*
► typify, epitomize, symbolize, demonstrate

**exempt** ADJECTIVE

*Students should be exempt from health charges*
► excused, excepted, absolved, immune, excluded, released, free, let off, spared
AN OPPOSITE IS liable (to)

**exempt** VERB

*We hope they will exempt him from jury service.*
► excuse, release, free, let (someone) off

**exercise** NOUN

1 *Regular exercise will keep you fit.*
► physical activity, working out, exertion, training

2 *the exercise of authority*
► use, application, practice

3 *exercises army exercises*
► operations, manoeuvres

**exercise** VERB

1 *She exercises every day.*
► work out, do exercises, keep fit

2 *Please exercise a little patience.*
► use, have, employ, apply

3 *The problem continues to exercise us.*
► trouble, worry, bother, make anxious

**exert** VERB

1 *She exerts a considerable influence on the children.*
► exercise, wield, bring to bear, apply

2 *exert yourself He exerted himself to get the job done on time.*
► strive, endeavour, try hard, make an effort, go to some trouble

**exertion** NOUN

*They were all panting from the exertion.*
► effort, strain, toil

**exhale** VERB

*He exhaled a misty cold breath.*
► breathe out, puff out, blow out

**exhaust** VERB

1 *We exhausted the fuel supply after only a week.*
► use up, consume, drain, empty, deplete, dry up, finish off, go through, spend, sap, void

2 *Her day out had exhausted her.*
► tire out, wear out, fatigue, weary, tax, strain

**exhaust** NOUN

*a vehicle exhaust*
► emission, discharge, fumes, gases, smoke

**exhausted** ADJECTIVE

1 *They went to bed exhausted that night.*
► tired out, worn out, weary, fatigued, shattered, (*more informal*) dead tired, (*more informal*) played out, (*more informal*) washed out

2 *exhausted money reserves*
► depleted, used up, spent

**exhausting** ADJECTIVE

*an exhausting journey*
► tiring, wearying, fatiguing, wearing, arduous, strenuous, taxing, gruelling, demanding, laborious, punishing, sapping, difficult, hard, severe
AN OPPOSITE IS refreshing

**exhaustion** NOUN

*He had to stop from sheer exhaustion.*
► fatigue, weariness, tiredness, debility, weakness
AN OPPOSITE IS vigour

**exhaustive** ADJECTIVE

*An exhaustive search failed to produce the missing ring.*
► comprehensive, thorough, intensive, meticulous, extensive, far-reaching, full-scale, all-out, careful

**exhibit** VERB

1 *The gallery will exhibit a collection of new paintings.*
► show, display, put on display, present, set up

2 *He exhibited great pride in his family.*
► show, reveal, display, demonstrate, manifest, disclose, express
OPPOSITES ARE hide, conceal

**exhibition** NOUN

*an exhibition of Greek sculpture*
► display, presentation, show, showing, demonstration

# exhilarated ADJECTIVE

*The day's events left them feeling exhilarated.*
► excited, elated, thrilled, animated, stimulated, worked up
AN OPPOSITE IS dejected

# exhilarating ADJECTIVE

*The ride was an exhilarating experience.*
► exciting, thrilling, stirring, rousing, stimulating, invigorating, enthralling, gripping, dramatic, sensational
OPPOSITES ARE dull, unexciting

# exhilaration NOUN

*a feeling of exhilaration*
► excitement, enthusiasm, elation, eagerness, stimulation

# exile NOUN

1 *The poet was punished with exile.*
► banishment, expulsion, deportation, expatriation, extradition

2 *a group of political exiles*
► émigré, exiled person, displaced person, deportee, expatriate, outcast, refugee

# exile VERB

*The new regime immediately exiled the dictators.*
► expel, banish, deport, drive out, eject, expatriate, send away

# exist VERB

1 *animals that no longer exist*
► live, occur, be alive, be in existence

2 *They had to exist for years on a meagre income.*
► survive, subsist, live, hold out, keep going, continue, endure, last

# existence NOUN

1 *The new law threatens the very existence of these old institutions.*
► survival, continuance, continuation, being, actuality, life, living, reality
AN OPPOSITE IS non-existence

2 *a dreary existence in a remote part of the country*
► way of life, livelihood, lifestyle

# existing ADJECTIVE

*The existing arrangements were proving inadequate.*
► current, present, available, prevailing, actual, existent, extant

**USAGE** You can also say the arrangements already in place or the arrangements already in force.

# exit NOUN

1 *A passage on the right leads to the exit.*
► way out, door, doorway, egress, gate, gateway
AN OPPOSITE IS entrance

2 *They made a quick exit.*
► departure, withdrawal, retreat, leaving, exodus
OPPOSITES ARE entrance, arrival

3 *Take the exit marked Leeds.*
► turning, turn-off, turn, road

# exit VERB

*A regal-looking woman then exited.*
► leave, depart, go out
OPPOSITES ARE enter, arrive

# exonerate VERB

*The letter exonerated him.*
► clear, absolve, vindicate, acquit

# exorbitant ADJECTIVE

*The cost of rail travel can be exorbitant.*
► extortionate, excessive, unreasonable, prohibitive, inordinate, unrealistic, outrageous, expensive, extravagant, high, overpriced
OPPOSITES ARE reasonable, competitive

# exotic ADJECTIVE

1 *exotic places in the Far East*
► faraway, distant, remote, foreign, romantic, unfamiliar, alien
AN OPPOSITE IS familiar

2 *an exhibition of exotic birds*
► foreign, non-native, tropical, alien, unnaturalized, imported
AN OPPOSITE IS native

3 *exotic dress*
► colourful, striking, unusual, unfamiliar, unconventional, outlandish
AN OPPOSITE IS conventional

# expand VERB

1 *a good opportunity to expand the business*
► develop, enlarge, extend, broaden, build up, diversify, increase, amplify, augment, elaborate, fill out, make bigger
OPPOSITES ARE contract, reduce

2 *Metal expands when heated.*
► increase in size, become larger, swell, dilate, grow, stretch, thicken, widen
AN OPPOSITE IS contract

# expanse NOUN

*a vast expanse of water*
► extent, area, stretch, surface, sweep, range, breadth, sheet, tract

# expansive ADJECTIVE

*After a few drinks be became quite expansive.*
► talkative, communicative, forthcoming, outgoing, sociable, unreserved, uninhibited, voluble, conversational, open
OPPOSITES ARE curt, unfriendly

# expect VERB

1 *We expect a large number of visitors this year.*
► hope for, look for, look forward to, envisage, predict, anticipate, await, bank on

2 *We expect complete discretion.*
► demand, insist on, require, call for, count on, rely on, want

3 *I expect they missed the train.*
► suppose, assume, presume, imagine, believe, guess, judge, think, (*more informal*) reckon

## expectant ADJECTIVE

**1** *Hundreds of expectant fans waited outside the theatre.*
▶ eager, excited, hopeful, watchful, anxious

**2** *an expectant mother*
▶ pregnant, expecting

## expedient ADJECTIVE

*It seemed expedient to leave.*
▶ advantageous, convenient, suitable, useful, beneficial, prudent, in your own interests

## expedition NOUN

*a major scientific expedition*
▶ journey , voyage , mission, quest, exploration, mission, safari

## expel VERB

**1** *He was expelled from the country.*
▶ banish, exile, deport, drive out, throw out, cast out, evict, expatriate

**2** *The machinery was expelling thick smoke.*
▶ discharge, emit, let out, release, disgorge, spew out

## expend VERB

*It may not be worth expending a lot of effort on this task.*
▶ use up, consume, spend, drain, devote (to)

## expendable ADJECTIVE

*the theory that males are expendable*
▶ dispensable, replaceable, superfluous, non-essential, unnecessary, unimportant
OPPOSITES ARE indispensable, essential

## expenditure NOUN

*the need to cut back on local expenditure*
▶ spending, outlay, expense, outgoings, payment

## expense NOUN

**1** *the increasing expense of running a car*
▶ cost, price, spending

**2** *unexpected expenses*
▶ expenditure, outlay, charges, outgoings, overheads, payment

## expensive ADJECTIVE

*an expensive holiday*
▶ costly, dear, high-priced, extravagant, lavish, exorbitant, (more informal) pricey
OPPOSITES ARE cheap, inexpensive

## experience NOUN

**1** (informal) *You learn by experience.*
▶ practice, involvement, participation, familiarity, observation, taking part

**2** (informal) *Salary will depend partly on experience.*
▶ skill, knowledge, background, understanding, (more formal) know-how

**3** *a terrifying experience*
▶ incident, event, episode, affair, happening, occurrence, ordeal, adventure

## experience VERB

*She experienced some harassment at work.*
▶ meet, encounter, undergo, face, run into, suffer

## experienced ADJECTIVE

**1** *an experienced actor*
▶ expert, skilled, skilful, qualified, trained, practised, knowledgeable, professional, specialized, well-versed
AN OPPOSITE IS inexperienced

**2** *an experienced man of the world*
▶ mature, seasoned, sophisticated, worldly-wise, knowing, wise
OPPOSITES ARE innocent, naive

## experiment NOUN

**1** *She conducted experiments using laser technology.*
▶ test, investigation, trial, enquiry, demonstration, observation, analysis, piece of research

**2** *The new library hours are an experiment.*
▶ trial, trial run, try-out

## experiment VERB

**experiment with** *You need to experiment with the camera's different settings.*
▶ test, try out, investigate, explore, do tests on, conduct an experiment on, do research on

## experimental ADJECTIVE

**1** *The new designs are still at an experimental stage.*
▶ exploratory, investigatory, provisional, tentative, preliminary, speculative, trial, test

**2** *experimental forms of music*
▶ innovative, innovatory, radical, avant-garde, original

## expert ADJECTIVE

**1** *You can get independent expert advice quite cheaply.*
▶ skilled, professional, qualified, specialist

**2** *I am an expert swimmer.*
▶ skilful, skilled, accomplished, proficient, competent, talented, outstanding, exceptional, formidable

## expert NOUN

**1** *You need to get advice from an expert.*
▶ specialist, professional, authority, (more informal) pro

**2** (informal) *He is an expert at board games.*
▶ authority, master, past master, connoisseur, genius, virtuoso, (more informal) ace, (more informal) whizz, (more informal) wizard, (more informal) dab hand, (disapproving) know-all
AN OPPOSITE IS novice

## expertise NOUN

*A high level of expertise is required.*
▶ skill, competence, proficiency, ability, knowledge, capability, professionalism

## expire VERB

**1** *Animals were expiring in the heat.*
▶ die, perish, pass away

**2** *Our television licence has expired.*
▶ run out, become invalid, lapse, finish

## explain VERB

**1** *I will try to explain the problem.*
▶ describe, clarify, make clear, spell out, elucidate, interpret, demonstrate, express, put into words
**2** *It is hard to explain such stupidity.*
▶ account for, justify, excuse, defend, vindicate, give reasons for, make excuses for, rationalize

## explanation NOUN

**1** *I owe you an explanation for what happened.*
▶ justification, reason, account, excuse, defence, rationale
**2** *What on earth can the explanation be?*
▶ cause, motive, reason
**3** *The summary at the end gives a brief explanation of the ideas discussed.*
▶ account, clarification, elucidation, interpretation, demonstration

## explanatory ADJECTIVE

*a few explanatory comments*
▶ descriptive, explaining, illustrative, interpretive, revelatory, helpful, illuminating, (*more formal*) expository

## explicit ADJECTIVE

**1** *The advance party had received explicit instructions to turn back.*
▶ clear, plain, direct, definite, express, precise, distinct, exact, emphatic, specific, positive, categorical, unambiguous, unmistakable, unequivocal
AN OPPOSITE IS vague
**2** *The film contains a number of sexually explicit scenes.*
▶ candid, open, direct, frank, unreserved, undisguised, plain
OPPOSITES ARE implicit, suggestive

## explode VERB

**1** *A bomb exploded in the centre of the city.*
▶ go off, blow up, detonate
**2** *The findings explode a number of myths about cancer treatment.*
▶ disprove, rebut, refute, expose, debunk, discredit, destroy, put an end to

## exploit NOUN (with the stress on *ex-*)

*Their exploits gave them a fearsome reputation.*
▶ feat, deed, adventure, accomplishment, achievement

## exploit VERB (with the stress on -*ploit*)

**1** *The newcomers exploited the land's mineral resources.*
▶ make use of, utilize, use, take advantage of, draw on, benefit from, capitalize on
**2** (*informal*) *They are accused of exploiting an impoverished workforce.*
▶ take advantage of, mistreat, ill-treat, abuse, oppress, manipulate, cheat, swindle, (*more informal*) fleece

## explore VERB

**1** *an outing to explore the neighbourhood*
▶ tour, travel through, reconnoitre, survey, inspect, take a look at
**2** *We'd like to explore the possibility of working together.*
▶ investigate, examine, look into, consider, study, review, probe, analyse

## explorer NOUN

*Roberts was a keen explorer as well as an artist.*
▶ traveller, discoverer, voyager, rover, globetrotter

## explosion NOUN

*A loud explosion shook the building.*
▶ blast, bang, boom, burst, crash, report, detonation, discharge

## explosive ADJECTIVE

**1** *explosive substances*
▶ volatile, inflammable, combustible, unstable
**2** *an explosive situation*
▶ tense, highly charged, critical, fraught, hazardous, dangerous, perilous, sensitive
AN OPPOSITE IS stable

## explosive NOUN

*a large supply of explosives*
▶ bomb, device, incendiary device

## export VERB

*Most of the country's produce is exported.*
▶ sell abroad, trade abroad, send abroad
**USAGE** You can use *overseas* instead of *abroad* in all these synonyms.

## expose VERB

**1** *The investigation exposed many faults.*
▶ reveal, uncover, bring to light, disclose, unveil, unmask
**2 expose someone to** *They were exposed to serious danger.*
▶ put at risk of, subject to, lay open to

## exposure NOUN

**1** *He feared exposure of the scandal in the tabloid press.*
▶ revelation, disclosure, uncovering, unmasking, divulgence
**2 exposure to** *exposure to criticism*
▶ experience of, contact with, introduction to, acquaintance with

## express VERB

*They expressed their wishes clearly.*
▶ communicate, articulate, utter, convey, voice, vent, give vent to, release, air, phrase, put into words, ventilate

## express ADJECTIVE

**1** *It was his express wish.*
▶ explicit, clear, plain, direct, definite, precise, distinct, exact, emphatic, specific, positive, categorical, unambiguous, unmistakable, unequivocal
**2** *an express train*
▶ fast, rapid, high-speed, non-stop

**expression** NOUN

1 *He liked to use old-fashioned expressions.*
▶ phrase, idiom, statement, saying, turn of phrase, phraseology, wording, cliché, formula, remark, term

2 *She bore a puzzled expression.*
▶ look, countenance, aspect, air, face, appearance, mien

3 *She read out the letter with expression.*
▶ emotion, feeling, passion, intensity, poignancy, sensibility, sensitivity, sympathy, understanding

4 *The regime forbids the expression of opposing ideas.*
▶ utterance, uttering, voicing, assertion

**expressive** ADJECTIVE

1 *He raised his hand in an expressive gesture.*
▶ meaningful, telling, revealing, informative, emphatic, communicative, demonstrative, significant

2 *an expressive voice*
▶ eloquent, articulate, lively, modulated, varied
AN OPPOSITE IS expressionless

3 *an expressive piece of music*
▶ emotional, passionate, intense, poignant, evocative, powerful
AN OPPOSITE IS unemotional

**expulsion** NOUN

*The culprits faced expulsion.*
▶ dismissal, removal, exclusion, banishment, eviction

**exquisite** ADJECTIVE

1 *a ring with exquisite little jewels*
▶ beautiful, lovely, delicate, dainty

2 *She always showed exquisite taste.*
▶ refined, discriminating, discerning, sensitive, impeccable

**extend** VERB

1 *The emperor sought to extend his power.*
▶ expand, enlarge, develop, build up, broaden, spread
AN OPPOSITE IS reduce

2 *The meeting was extended to allow for questions.*
▶ prolong, lengthen, continue, protract, draw out, make longer

3 *We extend our thanks to all contributors.*
▶ offer, proffer, advance, bestow, confer, hold out, present, accord

4 *The fields extend as far as the river.*
▶ reach, go, continue, carry on, spread

**extension** NOUN

1 *The new owners built a huge extension to the house.*
▶ addition, annexe, wing

2 *We needed an extension of the deadline.*
▶ postponement, deferral, delay

3 *the extension of the royal territories the extension of knowledge*
▶ enlargement, increase, expansion, broadening, development, growth

**extensive** ADJECTIVE

1 *a country house with extensive gardens*
▶ large, large-scale, substantial, considerable, spacious, expansive

2 *an extensive knowledge of Indian languages*
▶ comprehensive, thorough, complete, exhaustive, wide-ranging, broad, vast, wide

**extent** NOUN

1 *The estate is about three acres in extent.*
▶ area, size, expanse, scope, dimensions, spread, distance

2 *It was only later that we saw the extent of the damage.*
▶ degree, scale, scope, size, magnitude, amount, measure, quantity, range

**exterior** NOUN

*the exterior of the building*
▶ outside, outside surface, outward aspect, facade, shell
AN OPPOSITE IS interior

**exterior** ADJECTIVE

*the exterior walls*
▶ outer, outside, external, outermost
AN OPPOSITE IS interior

**exterminate** VERB

*They came with orders to exterminate all alien life.*
▶ eradicate, annihilate, eliminate, wipe out, do away with, massacre, kill

**external** ADJECTIVE

*an external surface*
▶ outer, outside, exterior, outermost

**extinct** ADJECTIVE

1 *an extinct volcano*
▶ inactive, extinguished
OPPOSITES ARE active, dormant

2 *an extinct species*
▶ lost, vanished, defunct, died out, dead, destroyed, obsolete, exterminated
OPPOSITES ARE extant, living, surviving

**extinction** NOUN

*Some breeds face extinction.*
▶ disappearance, extermination, eradication, annihilation, death, obliteration

**extinguish** VERB

*Extinguish all fires before leaving the site.*
▶ put out, douse, quench, smother, damp down, snuff out
AN OPPOSITE IS light

**extort** VERB

*He went around extorting money from local residents.*
▶ force, exact, extract, wrest, coerce, bully, (more informal) screw

**extortionate** ADJECTIVE

*Rents have become extortionate in this area.*
▶ exorbitant, excessive, unreasonable, prohibitive, inordinate, unrealistic, outrageous, expensive, extravagant, high, overpriced
OPPOSITES ARE reasonable, competitive

**extra** ADJECTIVE

**1** *She had a second job to bring in extra money.*
▶ additional, more, further, added, increased, supplementary, fresh

**2** *There was a lot of extra food in the house.*
▶ spare, excess, surplus, superfluous, unused, leftover

**3** *The large stores take on extra staff before Christmas.*
▶ temporary, ancillary, auxiliary, supernumerary

**extra** ADVERB

*He worked extra hard just before the exams.*
▶ especially, exceptionally, particularly, extremely, unusually

**extra** NOUN

*The Monday holiday was a welcome extra.*
▶ addition, supplement, bonus, extension

**extract** VERB

**1** *The dentist extracted her tooth.*
▶ pull out, take out, draw out, remove, withdraw
AN OPPOSITE IS insert

**2** *It was difficult to extract any information from them.*
▶ obtain, wrest, draw, glean, elicit, derive, gather, get

**extract** NOUN

**1** *a drink of beef extract*
▶ essence, concentrate, distillation, decoction

**2** *He was copying out extracts from a newspaper.*
▶ excerpt, passage, selection, clipping, cutting, piece, citation, quotation, clip

**extraordinary** ADJECTIVE

*What an extraordinary story! Their behaviour was quite extraordinary.*
▶ remarkable, exceptional, amazing, astonishing, astounding, wonderful, startling, staggering, stunning, breathtaking, fantastic, phenomenal, incredible
AN OPPOSITE IS ordinary

**extravagance** NOUN

*The new outfit was bought in a fit of extravagance.*
▶ indulgence, lavishness, prodigality, profligacy, excess, squandering, improvidence, wastefulness
AN OPPOSITE IS thrift

**extravagant** ADJECTIVE

*an extravagant lifestyle*
▶ indulgent, lavish, spendthrift, improvident, squandering, wasteful
AN OPPOSITE IS thrifty

**extreme** ADJECTIVE

**1** *a sure sign of extreme tiredness*
▶ great, intense, exceptional, extraordinary, utter, acute, downright
AN OPPOSITE IS slight

**2** *The situation called for extreme measures.*
▶ drastic, serious, radical, dire, desperate, severe, tough, harsh, strict
AN OPPOSITE IS mild

**3** *in the extreme north of the country*
▶ farthest, furthest, far-off, distant, remotest, faraway

**4** *a person of extreme political opinions*
▶ radical, fanatic, fanatical, diehard, zealous
AN OPPOSITE IS moderate

**extreme** NOUN

*These theories go from one extreme to the other.  an attitude pushed to its extreme*
▶ limit, extremity, height, end

**extremity** NOUN

*at the southern extremity of the island*
▶ limit, edge, end, tip, boundary, margin

**extrovert** NOUN

*Most of the volunteers are extroverts by nature.*
▶ socializer, outgoing person, mixer
AN OPPOSITE IS introvert

**extrovert** ADJECTIVE

*an extrovert personality*
▶ outgoing, extroverted, sociable, gregarious, positive, active, confident
AN OPPOSITE IS introvert

**exuberant** ADJECTIVE

*a witty and exuberant style of humour*
▶ lively, ebullient, high-spirited, sparkling, effusive, enthusiastic, exhilarated, cheerful, outgoing

**exult** VERB

*The staff exulted at the good news about the business.*
▶ rejoice, delight, celebrate, be joyful, be glad, be delighted

**exultant** ADJECTIVE

*The exultant winners waved to the crowd.*
▶ jubilant, joyful, triumphant, exhilarated, joyous, ecstatic

**eye** NOUN

**1** *He has a sharp eye.*
▶ eyesight, vision, power of sight, visual perception
RELATED ADJECTIVES ocular, ophthalmic

**2** *Not much escaped her attentive eye.*
▶ watch, observation, vigilance, notice

**3** **eyes** *It was a dreadful mistake in our eyes.*
▶ opinion, view, judgement, way of thinking, viewpoint, (to our) mind

**an eye for** *an eye for detail*
▶ an appreciation of, an awareness of, an understanding of, a perception of, a sensitivity for, an instinct for

**eye** VERB

*He eyed the visitors carefully.*
▶ look at, watch, observe, view, gaze at, glance at, scrutinize, examine

**eye-witness** NOUN

*The police case depends on the evidence of an eye-witness.*
▶ bystander, looker-on, onlooker, witness, observer, spectator, watcher

a b c d e f g h i j k l m n o p q r s t u v w x y z

# Ff

**fable** NOUN
*the fable of the fox and the crow*
▶ story, tale, parable, moral tale

**fabric** NOUN
**1** *Special fabrics are often used for the seats.*
▶ cloth, material, stuff, textile
**2** *The bomb did some damage to the fabric of the building.*
▶ structure, framework, frame, construction, make-up

**fabricate** VERB
*The witness had fabricated his evidence.*
▶ invent, falsify, make up, concoct, trump up

**fabulous** ADJECTIVE
**1** *They had a fabulous time in Morocco.*
▶ wonderful, marvellous, fantastic, splendid, magnificent
**2** *fabulous places you read about in stories*
▶ legendary, mythical, imaginary, fictitious, fantastic

**façade** NOUN
**1** *the façade of the house*
▶ front, frontage, exterior, aspect
**2** *their constant joking was just a façade*
▶ show, front, display, pretence, affectation, posture, act, pose, sham

**face** NOUN
**1** *She has a lovely face.*
▶ features, countenance, visage, profile, physiognomy
**2** *His face became angry.*
▶ expression, look, appearance, manner, bearing, countenance
**3** *A cube has six faces.*
▶ side, surface, plane, aspect
**4** *the north face of the house*
▶ aspect, façade
**5** *He put on a brave face for the sake of his visitors.*
▶ front, show, display, act

**face** VERB
**1** *The hotel faces the lake.*
▶ overlook, be opposite (to), front, give on to
**2** *You will face a lot of criticism.*
▶ meet, encounter, experience, confront
**face up to** *She faced up to all her obligations.*
▶ accept, come to terms with, recognize, acknowledge, deal with, cope with

**facet** NOUN
*every facet of the situation*
▶ aspect, feature, characteristic, detail, particular

**facetious** ADJECTIVE
*That's enough of the facetious remarks, thank you.*
▶ flippant, frivolous, jocular, humorous, funny, witty, amusing, comical, glib
AN OPPOSITE IS serious

**facile** ADJECTIVE
*a facile explanation*
▶ simplistic, superficial, over-simple, shallow, glib, pat
AN OPPOSITE IS profound

**facilitate** VERB
*Use of video and other classroom aids will facilitate rapid learning.*
▶ assist, support, enable, allow, promote, encourage, further, make way for

**facility** NOUN
**1** *She has a great facility for singing.*
▶ aptitude, talent, flair, faculty, adeptness, skill (in), expertise (in)
**2** *This facility is used for copying music to a CD.*
▶ function, device, provision
**3** **facilities** *the use of a sauna and sports facilities*
▶ amenities, resources, services, equipment, provisions

**fact** NOUN
*It is a fact that car use has risen steeply in the last decade.*
▶ reality, truth, actuality, certainty, fait accompli
AN OPPOSITE IS fiction
**the facts** *The jury has to take all the facts into account.*
▶ evidence, information, details, data, circumstances, particulars, aspects

**faction** NOUN
*Fighting between the two rival factions began almost immediately.*
▶ group, side, party, section, contingent, camp, clique, cabal

**factor** NOUN
*Cost was a key factor in the decision.*
▶ circumstance, element, feature, component, ingredient, influence, aspect, determinant

**factory** NOUN
*I worked in a factory that made parts for tractors.*
▶ manufacturing plant, workshop, works, assembly line

**factual** ADJECTIVE
*a factual description of the events*
▶ truthful, accurate, historical, authentic, genuine, realistic, faithful, objective

**faculty** NOUN
**1** *the faculty of speech*
▶ power, capability, capacity, facility
**2** *a faculty for settling disputes*
▶ aptitude, talent, facility, flair, adeptness, skill (in), expertise (in)
**3** **faculties**
▶ senses, wits, intelligence, reason, powers

**fad** NOUN

*Rap music was not just a passing fad.*
► craze, fashion, trend, vogue, whim, passion, enthusiasm, obsession, compulsion, (*more informal*) rage, (*more informal*) thing

**faddy** ADJECTIVE

(*informal*) *Luke was such a faddy eater.*
► fussy, finicky, (*informal*) picky, (*informal*) choosy

**fade** VERB

**1** *The light has faded the colours.*
► blanch, bleach, discolour, whiten
AN OPPOSITE IS brighten

**2** *The music began to fade.*
► weaken, decline, decrease, diminish, dwindle, dim, wane, disappear, evanesce, fail, melt away, pale, vanish
AN OPPOSITE IS intensify

**3** *The flowers had faded by now.*
► wither, wilt, droop, flag, perish, shrivel
AN OPPOSITE IS bloom

**4** *Their enthusiasm was fading.*
► decline, diminish, dwindle, fail, flag, sink, disappear

**fail** VERB

**1** *In the end all attempts failed.*
► be unsuccessful, go wrong, miscarry, fall through, come to grief, collapse
AN OPPOSITE IS succeed

**2** *The business had failed and the family faced ruin.*
► collapse, founder, go under, go bankrupt, (*more informal*) fold
AN OPPOSITE IS prosper

**3** *She was angry with her daughter who had failed to contact her.*
► neglect, forget, omit

**4** *Her health was failing.*
► deteriorate, decline, weaken, sink, collapse
AN OPPOSITE IS improve

**5** *They believe we have failed them.*
► let down, disappoint, betray, desert
AN OPPOSITE IS support

**6** *He failed one of his exams.*
► be unsuccessful in, not pass
AN OPPOSITE IS pass

**failing** NOUN

*She loved him despite his failings.*
► fault, weakness, shortcoming, flaw, defect
OPPOSITES ARE strength, strong point

**failure** NOUN

**1** *The negotiations ended in failure.*
► disappointment, lack of success, defeat, disaster

**2** *The plan proved to be a failure.*
► disaster, catastrophe, fiasco, debacle, blunder, mistake, (*more informal*) flop, (*more informal*) damp squib

**3** *a failure in the power supply*
► breakdown, fault, malfunction

**4** *To do nothing might be regarded as a failure of duty.*
► dereliction, neglect, omission, deficiency

**faint** ADJECTIVE

**1** *There was a faint smell of gas.*
► slight, indistinct, vague, weak
AN OPPOSITE IS strong

**2** *The sky had a faint pink colour.*
► pale, light, hazy, weak
AN OPPOSITE IS bright

**3** *We heard a faint cry from the next room.*
► quiet, muted, muffled, feeble, weak
AN OPPOSITE IS loud

**4** *There is a faint possibility of an improvement in the weather.*
► slight, slim, slender, remote, small, vague, doubtful
AN OPPOSITE IS strong

**5** *She was feeling faint and had to lie down.*
► dizzy, giddy, light-headed, weak, (*more informal*) woozy

**faint** VERB

*He grew pale and seemed about to faint.*
► pass out, lose consciousness, black out, collapse, (*more informal*) flake out, (*literary*) swoon

**fair** ADJECTIVE

**1** *It doesn't seem fair to blame the children.*
► just, equitable, reasonable, honourable
AN OPPOSITE IS unfair

**2** *They gave a fair assessment of the situation.*
► honest, impartial, reasonable, objective, dispassionate, neutral, even-handed
OPPOSITES ARE unreasonable, biassed

**3** *She believes she has a fair chance of success. He had achieved a fair result in his exams.*
► moderate, reasonable, average, satisfactory, adequate, acceptable, tolerable, respectable, decent
OPPOSITES ARE excellent, outstanding

**4** *There was a fair amount of traffic going past.*
► considerable, moderate, average

**5** *She had blue eyes and fair hair.*
► blond(e), light, pale, yellow

**6** *It was a good match played in fair weather.*
► fine, dry, bright, clear, sunny, warm
OPPOSITES ARE bad, wet, inclement

**fair** NOUN

**1** *a country fair*
► fete, gala, carnival, funfair, festival

**2** *an antiques fair*
► market, sale, mart, bazaar

**3** *a book fair*
► exhibition, display, show, presentation

**fairly** ADVERB

*The news is fairly good.*
► reasonably, moderately, tolerably, quite, rather, somewhat, (*more informal*) pretty
AN OPPOSITE IS extremely

**fairy tale, fairy story** NOUN

*fairy tales about witches and dragons*
► folk tale, legend, myth, story

a
b
c
d
e
f
g
h
i
j
k
l
m
n
o
p
q
r
s
t
u
v
w
x
y
z

**faith** NOUN
  **1** *His employers had complete faith in him.*
  ▶ trust, confidence, hope, belief, reliance
  **2** *Her faith is very precious to her.*
  ▶ religion, belief, religious conviction

**faithful** ADJECTIVE
  **1** *He wondered if Clara had a faithful partner waiting for her at home.*
  ▶ loyal, devoted, constant, dependable, dutiful, reliable, staunch, steadfast, trusty, trustworthy, close, consistent, unswerving
  OPPOSITES ARE unfaithful, disloyal
  **2** *He kept a faithful record of the events of that day.*
  ▶ accurate, true, truthful, precise, exact, authentic
  AN OPPOSITE IS inaccurate

**fake** ADJECTIVE
  **1** *You could tell the diamonds were fake.*
  ▶ imitation, artificial, simulated, synthetic, unreal, false, bogus, sham, (*more informal*) phoney
  **2** *He brought out a wad of fake banknotes.*
  ▶ counterfeit, forged, false, sham, bogus, fraudulent, (*more informal*) phoney
  AN OPPOSITE IS genuine

**fake** NOUN
  **1** *One of the paintings was a fake.*
  ▶ forgery, copy, imitation, reproduction, replica, duplicate, hoax, sham, simulation, (*more informal*) phoney
  **2** *The man who claimed to be a surgeon is a fake.*
  ▶ fraud, charlatan, impostor, cheat, (*more informal*) quack, (*more informal*) phoney

**fake** VERB
  *They would have to fake a death certificate.*
  ▶ forge, fabricate, counterfeit, falsify, (*more informal*) fiddle

**fall** VERB
  **1** *He stumbled and fell.*
  ▶ tumble, fall over, topple, trip over, keel over, collapse
  AN OPPOSITE IS get up
  **2** *Flood levels began to fall at last.*
  ▶ drop, go down, subside, recede
  AN OPPOSITE IS rise
  **3** *Bombs continued to fall all night.*
  ▶ drop, descend, plummet, rain down
  **4** *Prices are expected to fall soon.*
  ▶ go down, decrease, decline, diminish
  OPPOSITES ARE rise, increase
  **5** *The Empire in the East did not fall for several more centuries.*
  ▶ decline, collapse, disintegrate, deteriorate
  AN OPPOSITE IS flourish
  **6** *Thousands fell in the war.*
  ▶ die, be killed, be lost, lose your life, perish, (*literary*) be slain
  **7** *Her birthday falls on a Saturday this year.*
  ▶ occur, come, happen, take place
  **fall apart** *The sheds fell apart in the high winds.*
  ▶ collapse, disintegrate, break up, fragment, crumble, fall to pieces, shatter

**fall asleep** *She couldn't help falling asleep.*
  ▶ doze off, drop off, go to sleep, (*more informal*) nod off

**fall in** *The roof has fallen in.*
  ▶ collapse, come down, cave in

**fall off** *Demand for these products has fallen off lately.*
  ▶ decline, slacken, decrease, lessen, drop off

**fall out** *They fell out over money.*
  ▶ quarrel, argue, disagree, fight, squabble, bicker, clash

**fall through** *In the end the plan fell through.*
  ▶ come to nothing, fail, miscarry, founder, collapse
  OPPOSITES ARE go ahead, succeed

**fall** NOUN
  **1** *He was hurt in a fall.*
  ▶ tumble, spill, topple, stumble
  **2** *Economists expect a fall in house prices.*
  ▶ drop, decline, fall-off, decrease, dip, lessening, reduction, slump
  OPPOSITES ARE rise, increase
  **3** *an epic poem on the fall of Troy*
  ▶ surrender, capitulation, submission, defeat
  **4** *the fall of the Roman Empire*
  ▶ downfall, collapse, ruin, failure, demise, destruction

**fallacy** NOUN
  *It is a fallacy to think we can change our character.*
  ▶ misconception, delusion, mistake, falsehood, error, myth

**fallible** ADJECTIVE
  *Humans are fallible beings.*
  ▶ imperfect, erring, error-prone, weak
  AN OPPOSITE IS infallible

**false** ADJECTIVE
  **1** *a false alibi*
  ▶ untrue, fictitious, invented, concocted, fabricated, invalid, spurious
  AN OPPOSITE IS genuine
  **2** *a false friend*
  ▶ unfaithful, disloyal, unreliable, dishonourable, untrustworthy
  AN OPPOSITE IS faithful
  **3** *false hair*
  ▶ artificial, unreal, imitation, synthetic, simulated, fake, sham
  AN OPPOSITE IS real
  **4** *a false belief*
  ▶ incorrect, erroneous, mistaken, fallacious, wrong
  AN OPPOSITE IS correct

**falsify** VERB
  *The date of the entry had been falsified.*
  ▶ tamper with, fake, fabricate, alter, pervert

**falter** VERB
  **1** *The country must not falter in the face of such danger.*
  ▶ hesitate, waver, delay, vacillate, flinch, hold back, lose confidence, be indecisive, get cold feet
  AN OPPOSITE IS persevere
  **2** *He faltered for a moment over an awkward name.*
  ▶ stammer, stumble, stutter

## fame NOUN

*Their fame spread all over the world.*
▶ renown, celebrity, stardom, popularity, notability, prestige, reputation, glory, name, stature, standing, prominence

## familiar ADJECTIVE

1 *The room was full of familiar faces.*
▶ well-known, recognizable, accustomed, everyday, commonplace
2 *a familiar friend*
▶ close, intimate, dear
3 *The atmosphere in the house was friendly and familiar.*
▶ informal, casual, relaxed, natural, open, unreserved, free and easy, unceremonious

## familiarity NOUN

1 *A familiarity with at least one European language is needed.*
▶ acquaintance, knowledge (of), understanding (of)
2 *They spoke to one another with a great deal of familiarity.*
▶ informality, intimacy, closeness, friendliness, naturalness, casualness

## familiarize VERB

**familiarize with** *Our aim is to familiarize the public with basic word-processing programs.*
▶ introduce (to), accustom (to), acclimatize (to), make familiar (with), teach

> ## family NOUN
>
> 1 *a large house divided to accommodate two families*
> ▶ household
> 2 *She sends a yearly newsletter to family and friends.*
> ▶ relatives, relations, kin, kinsmen, clan
> **USAGE** Kin and kinsmen are words you normally find only in stories and literature.
> 3 *parents clearly devoted to their family*
> ▶ children, offspring, daughters and sons
> RELATED ADJECTIVE domestic
>
> **same generation:** sister, brother, sibling (= brother or sister), twin, triplet; half-sister, half-brother (= a sister or brother having one parent the same); stepbrother, stepsister (= a child of a step-parent from a previous marriage); cousin; fiancé (= the man a woman is going to marry), fiancée (= the woman a man is going to marry), husband, wife, spouse (= a husband or wife), partner; widow (= a woman whose husband has died), widower (= a man whose wife has died).
>
> **older generation:** ancestor, forebear, forefather; grandparent, grandmother, grandfather; parent, mother, father; step-parent, stepmother, stepfather; guardian, godparent, godmother, godfather; aunt, uncle. ▶▶

> **younger generations:** descendant, offspring, heir; child, daughter, son; stepchild, stepdaughter, stepson; ward (= a child looked after by a guardian); godchild, goddaughter, godson; niece, nephew; grandchild, granddaughter, grandson.

## famine NOUN

*a country constantly threatened by famine*
▶ hunger, malnutrition, scarcity, shortage, starvation, dearth, want
AN OPPOSITE IS plenty

## famous ADJECTIVE

*a famous singer*
▶ well-known, celebrated, renowned, acclaimed, admired, prominent, revered, distinguished, honoured, eminent, exalted, illustrious, great, notable, noted
OPPOSITES ARE unknown, obscure

## fan NOUN

1 *a fan of rock music*
▶ devotee, enthusiast, admirer, lover, fanatic, addict, aficionado, (more informal) freak
2 *A ceiling fan cooled the room.*
▶ ventilator, blower, extractor, air-conditioner

## fanatic NOUN

1 *a religious fanatic*
▶ extremist, zealot, militant, activist, diehard
2 *a fitness fanatic*
▶ enthusiast, devotee, admirer, fan, addict, aficionado, (more informal) freak

## fanatical ADJECTIVE

*His ancestors had been fanatical royalists.*
▶ extreme, fervent, passionate, zealous, militant, single-minded, rabid, frenzied, immoderate, irrational, obsessive, bigoted
AN OPPOSITE IS moderate

## fanciful ADJECTIVE

*full of fanciful ideas*
▶ unrealistic, far-fetched, fantastic, imaginary, whimsical, illusory, visionary, romantic

## fancy ADJECTIVE

1 *The belts are decorated with fancy patterns.*
▶ elaborate, decorative, ornamental, ornate
2 *They don't like wearing fancy clothes.*
▶ showy, ostentatious, gaudy

## fancy NOUN

1 *The little cottage caught our fancy.*
▶ imagination, ingenuity, whim
2 *I had a fancy they might be there.*
▶ notion, idea, belief, impression, suspicion, hunch

## fancy VERB

1 *I fancied I could see a light in the sky.*
▶ imagine, think, suppose, believe, suspect
2 *I fancy a doughnut.*
▶ feel like, wish for, want, desire

a b c d e f g h i j k l m n o p q r s t u v w x y z

**3** *This was the boy she had fancied for so long.*
► be attracted to, find attractive, have a crush on, desire, want

**fantastic** ADJECTIVE
**1** *We had a fantastic time.*
► wonderful, marvellous, fabulous, splendid, magnificent
**2** *It's a fantastic idea.*
► fanciful, extraordinary, incredible, unbelievable

**fantasy** NOUN
*a fantasy about living on a desert island*
► dream, daydream, pipe dream, delusion, fancy

**far** ADJECTIVE
*He'd been to many far places.*
► distant, faraway, far off, remote, out of the way, outlying

**farce** NOUN
**1** *They went to see a farce at the local theatre.*
► comedy, slapstick
**2** *The trial had been a farce.*
► travesty, absurdity, sham, mockery, charade

**fare** NOUN
*a standard-class rail fare*
► price, charge, cost, payment, fee

**far-fetched** ADJECTIVE
*The storyline was too far-fetched and the acting was poor.*
► improbable, unlikely, implausible, incredible, dubious, doubtful, unconvincing

**farm** NOUN
*a farm of 200 acres*
► smallholding, farmstead, estate, grange

**farm** VERB
*The same family had farmed the land for centuries.*
► cultivate, work, till, plough

**farming** NOUN
*Farming makes an important contribution to the country's economy.*
► agriculture, cultivation, husbandry, land management, tillage, crofting, agronomy
RELATED ADJECTIVES agricultural, pastoral

**fascinate** VERB
*Most people are fascinated by the way words change their meaning.*
► interest (in), engross, captivate, enthrall, absorb, beguile, entrance, attract, charm

**fascinating** ADJECTIVE
*a fascinating book about the invention of the camera*
► interesting, engrossing, intriguing, captivating, enthralling, absorbing, beguiling, entrancing, attractive, charming

**fashion** NOUN
**1** *the fashion for long dresses*
► trend, vogue, craze
**2** *She was behaving in a very odd fashion.*
► way, manner, mode, method

**fashionable** ADJECTIVE
*a fashionable hotel in central London*
► stylish, popular, chic, elegant, modish, (more informal) trendy
AN OPPOSITE IS unfashionable

**fast** ADJECTIVE
**1** *She drives a fast car* *The race was run at a fast pace* *Delivery is always fast.*
► quick, rapid, speedy, swift, brisk, lively, sprightly, flying, high-speed, (more informal) nippy
AN OPPOSITE IS slow

**fast** ADVERB
**1** *The train was travelling fast towards the tunnel.*
► quickly, rapidly, swiftly, speedily, at full speed, at full tilt, briskly
AN OPPOSITE IS slowly
**2** *The wheels were stuck fast in the mud.*
► tightly, securely, immovably
**3** *By now she was fast asleep.*
► deeply, sound, completely

**fast** VERB
*a month in which many people are fasting*
► go without food, abstain, deny yourself
AN OPPOSITE IS overeat

**fasten** VERB
**1** *a sleeveless jacket that you fasten at the back*
► do up, tie, close, button up
OPPOSITES ARE unfasten, undo
**2** *We were told to fasten all windows.*
► close, secure, lock, bolt
AN OPPOSITE IS unfasten
**3** *Brackets are fastened to the wall.*
► fix, attach, secure, bolt
AN OPPOSITE IS remove

**fastidious** ADJECTIVE
*Louise had always been fastidious about her appearance.*
► particular, punctilious, discriminating, scrupulous, fussy, choosy, finicky, (more informal) pernickety

> **fat** ADJECTIVE This word is often overused. Here are some alternatives:
> **1** *A fat woman came into the room.*
> ► plump, stout, large, overweight, corpulent, rotund, podgy, obese, tubby, portly
> OPPOSITES ARE thin, slim
> **2** *He was reading a fat book.*
> ► thick, bulky, chunky, substantial
> **3** (informal) *A fat cheque arrived just before Christmas.*
> ► large, substantial, sizeable, generous

**fat** NOUN
*He has a lot of fat to get rid of.*
► fatness, obesity, blubber, (technical) adipose tissue, (more informal) flab

**fatal** ADJECTIVE
**1** *He delivered a fatal blow with the axe.*
► deadly, mortal, lethal

**2** *She contracted a fatal illness in the Far East.*
► deadly, terminal, mortal, incurable, malignant
**3** *That decision proved to be a fatal mistake.*
► disastrous, catastrophic, calamitous, destructive

**fatality** NOUN
*There were several fatalities from the blast.*
► casualty, death, loss

**fate** NOUN
**1** *I am ready for whatever fate has to offer.*
► destiny, chance, providence, fortune, the future, luck, the stars, karma, kismet
**2** *He was to meet a terrible fate.*
► death, demise, end, ruin, doom

**fated** ADJECTIVE
*They were fated not to meet again.*
► destined, doomed, predestined, preordained, predetermined, meant, bound, certain, intended

**fateful** ADJECTIVE
*The fateful meeting took place that week.*
► momentous, decisive, crucial, critical, historic
OPPOSITES ARE trivial, unimportant

**father** NOUN
*His father was now living in Bristol.*
► male parent, (*more informal*) dad, (*more informal*) daddy, (*more informal*) pop, (*old-fashioned*) pater
RELATED ADJECTIVE paternal

**fathom** VERB
*There was a look on his face that she couldn't quite fathom.*
► understand, comprehend, work out, make out, get to the bottom of

**fatigue** NOUN
*Fatigue got the better of them.*
► tiredness, weariness, exhaustion, lethargy, debility, feebleness, weakness
OPPOSITES ARE vitality, energy

**fatten** VERB
*Farmers fatten their livestock.*
► feed up, build up, make fat

**fatty** ADJECTIVE
*fatty food*
► greasy, oily, fat, (*technical*) oleaginous

**fault** NOUN
**1** *a fault in the manufacturing process*
► defect, deficiency, failure, failing, flaw, weakness, imperfection, shortcoming, blemish, malfunction, snag
**2** *There is a fault in their argument.*
► flaw, error, fallacy, inaccuracy, miscalculation, mistake
**3** *He had his faults, but carelessness was not one of them.*
► failing, weakness, shortcoming, flaw, defect
OPPOSITES ARE strength, strong point
**4** *The problem was my fault.*
► responsibility, liability, mistake, error

**fault** VERB
*I cannot fault your reasoning.*
► criticize, find fault with, censure, impugn, (*more informal*) pick holes in

**faultless** ADJECTIVE
*Her French is faultless.*
► perfect, flawless, impeccable, exemplary, fluent

**faulty** ADJECTIVE
*The light bulb was faulty.*
► broken, defective, not working, malfunctioning, inoperative, out of order, deficient

**favour** NOUN
**1** *She regards us with great favour.*
► approval, approbation, commendation, goodwill, kindness, friendliness, benevolence, esteem
OPPOSITES ARE disfavour, disapproval
**2** *Could you do me a favour?*
► good turn, benefit, kindness, kind act, courtesy, indulgence, good deed

**favour** VERB
**1** *I favour casual clothes.*
► prefer, choose, opt for, approve of, like
**2** *The government favours a policy of peace.*
► recommend, support, back, subscribe to, promote, advocate, espouse, endorse, champion

**favourable** ADJECTIVE
**1** *CDs at favourable prices*
► advantageous, beneficial, competitive, convenient
**2** *a favourable assessment of their ability*
► positive, encouraging, enthusiastic, complimentary, sympathetic, approving, agreeable

**favourite** ADJECTIVE
*John was her favourite nephew.*
► best-loved, most-liked, preferred, favoured, treasured, dearest, special, chosen, pet

**favourite** NOUN
(*informal*) *Sarah had always been one of his favourites.*
► first choice, preference, darling, pet, idol, apple of your eye

**favouritism** NOUN
*We want to be fair and avoid favouritism.*
► preferential treatment, partiality, one-sidedness, partisanship, bias, prejudice

**fear** NOUN
**1** *I remember the shock of fear when I heard her scream.*
► terror, fright, horror, alarm, panic, dread, trepidation
**2** *He found it hard to overcome his fears.*
► anxiety, concern, foreboding, unease, misgiving

**fear** VERB
**1** *They all feared Ted and kept away from him.*
► be afraid of, be scared of, dread, be terrified of, tremble at, worry about
**2** *We fear a bad outcome. I fear you may be right.*
► suspect, expect, foresee, anticipate

**fearful** ADJECTIVE

**1** *The generals were fearful of enemy reprisals.*
▶ afraid, frightened, scared, nervous, apprehensive (about), anxious (about), uneasy (about), (*more informal*) jittery (about)

**2** *She felt a fearful pain in her leg.*
▶ terrible, dreadful, frightful, horrible, awful

**3** (*informal*) *There would be a fearful row if anyone found out.*
▶ major, very great, dreadful, terrible, awful

**feasible** ADJECTIVE

*With luck the plan might be feasible.*
▶ practicable, practical, workable, achievable, realizable, attainable, possible, viable
OPPOSITES ARE impractical, impossible

**feast** NOUN

*a feast fit for a king*
▶ banquet, meal, dinner, (*more formal*) repast, (*more informal*) spread, (*more formal*) binge

**feast** VERB

*They feasted for three whole days.*
▶ eat your fill, wine and dine, gorge yourself

**feat** NOUN

*a feat of great daring*
▶ deed, exploit, act, accomplishment, achievement, undertaking, action, attainment, performance

**feature** NOUN

**1** *This latest incident has some notable features.*
▶ characteristic, circumstance, aspect, point, facet, detail, peculiarity, quality, trait

**2** *a magazine feature*
▶ article, report, story, item, piece, column

**3** **features** *Her coiled hair accentuated her fine features.*
▶ face, countenance, expression, lineaments, look, (*more formal*) physiognomy

**feature** VERB

**1** *This year's concerts will feature new young performers.*
▶ present, promote, highlight, focus on, give prominence to, spotlight

**2** *The players will feature in a charity promotion.*
▶ appear, participate, take part, play a role, star

**fed up** ADJECTIVE

**1** *You look tired and fed up.*
▶ depressed, dejected, dispirited, despondent, disheartened, miserable, cast down, sad, down, glum

**2** **be fed up with** *I was totally fed up with all their whinging.*
▶ be sick of, be tired of, be weary of, have had enough of

**fee** NOUN

**1** *You can have your order delivered for a small fee.*
▶ charge, payment, cost, sum, price

**2** *The membership fee is due in April.*
▶ subscription, charge, dues

**feeble** ADJECTIVE

**1** *My feeble attempts to protest were ignored.*
▶ weak, ineffective, inadequate, tame, poor, flimsy, shallow

**2** *The illness left him too feeble to stand.*
▶ weak, weakened, frail, delicate, sickly, poorly, infirm, incapacitated, helpless

**3** *Her brother was a feeble character.*
▶ spineless, timid, weak, ineffective, ineffectual

**feed** VERB

**1** *She has a large family to feed.*
▶ nourish, sustain, provide for, cater for

**2** *He was feeding information to the enemy.*
▶ supply, provide, deliver, present

**3** *They spend all their time feeding and sleeping.*
▶ eat, take food, have a meal, dine

**4** **feed on** *The local wildlife feeds on these plants.*
▶ eat, live on, exist on, consume, devour

**feel** VERB

**1** *He felt the back of his head with his hand.*
▶ touch, stroke, finger, handle, caress, fondle

**2** *She felt the muzzle of a gun in her side.*
▶ sense, perceive, detect, be aware of, be conscious of, discern

**3** *Did you feel any pain?*
▶ experience, suffer, undergo, endure, go through

**4** *We feel you should apologize to her.*
▶ believe, think, consider, consider it right, reckon, judge

**5** *The fabric feels soft.*
▶ seem, appear, strike you as

**feel for** *She had had a bad time and I felt for her.*
▶ feel sorry for, sympathize with, pity, commiserate with

**feel like** *Do you feel like a drink?*
▶ fancy, wish for, want, desire

**feel** NOUN

**1** *The wood had a warm feel.*
▶ texture, quality, surface, touch, impression

**2** *She has a good feel for the music.*
▶ aptitude, flair, talent, gift, knack

**feeling** NOUN

**1** *They enjoyed the feeling of power and superiority.*
▶ sensation, sense, awareness, consciousness, perception

**2** *I had a feeling she wouldn't be coming.*
▶ suspicion, inkling, notion, idea, hunch, fancy, premonition

**3** *There was a friendly feeling about the place.*
▶ atmosphere, aura, air, ambience, climate, quality, mood

**4** *She spoke with great feeling.*
▶ emotion, passion, intensity, concern, tenderness, warmth, ardour

**5** *He had lost all feeling in his arm.*
▶ sensation, perception, sense of touch

**fell** VERB

**1** *A guard felled him with a single blow.*
▶ knock down, knock over, bring down, flatten, prostrate, (*more informal*) floor

**fellow**

2 *Dead trees have to be felled fairly quickly.*
► chop down, cut down

**fellow** NOUN
*He's a decent fellow, always ready to help out.*
► chap, man, boy, individual, (*more informal*) bloke, (*more informal*) guy

**female** ADJECTIVE
*female characteristics*
► feminine, womanly

**feminine** ADJECTIVE
*a feminine young woman who revels in her freedom*
► womanly, ladylike, girlish, female

**fence** NOUN
*The area was surrounded by a tall fence.*
► railing, enclosure, barrier, wall, paling, hedge

**fence** VERB
**fence in** *You will need to fence in the hens.*
► confine, pen in, coop up, shut in, close in, hedge in
**fence off** *More land would be fenced off.*
► enclose, surround, encircle, separate off, section off, partition off, cut off

**fend** VERB
**fend for yourself** *They can fend for themselves for a few days.*
► look after yourself, care for yourself, take care of yourself, manage, cope, (*more informal*) get by
**fend off** *A small force might not be enough to fend off an attack.*
► repel, repulse, resist, ward off, beat off, fight off, hold back, thwart

**ferment** NOUN (with the stress on *fer-*)
*Constant change leaves the organization in a state of ferment.*
► turmoil, upheaval, agitation, unrest, commotion, excitement, disruption, confusion, disorder

**ferment** VERB (with the stress on -*ment*)
*Low pay ferments resentment.*
► cause, bring about, rouse, stir up, foment, engender, provoke, incite, stimulate

**ferocious** ADJECTIVE
*He was the victim of a ferocious attack.*
► fierce, brutal, violent, savage, cruel, vicious, barbaric, callous, heartless, cold-blooded, pitiless, ruthless, merciless, vile, sadistic, brutish
OPPOSITES ARE gentle, humane

**ferocity** NOUN
*The police were surprised by the ferocity of the attack.*
► savagery, brutality, cruelty, viciousness, fierceness, barbarity, callousness, heartlessness, cold-bloodedness, ruthlessness
AN OPPOSITE IS gentleness

**fertile** ADJECTIVE
1 *fertile soil*
► fruitful, productive, prolific, rich, fecund
AN OPPOSITE IS infertile
2 *a fertile mind*
► imaginative, inventive, creative, resourceful, ingenious

**fertilize** VERB
1 *The sperm has a tail that allows it to swim before fertilizing the egg.*
► impregnate, inseminate
2 *Insects fertilize the plants.*
► pollinate
3 *After ploughing the land is fertilized.*
► enrich, feed, dress, compost, manure

**fertilizer** NOUN
*Farmers depend on good fertilizer.*
► manure, dung, compost, dressing

**fervent** ADJECTIVE
1 *a fervent hope that we can be friends*
► heartfelt, earnest, eager, intense, keen, strong
2 *a fervent cricket supporter*
► eager, ardent, passionate, impassioned, avid, zealous, keen, enthusiastic

**fester** VERB
1 *The wound in his side had festered.*
► become infected, turn septic, suppurate, ulcerate, putrefy, discharge, gather, go bad, decay
2 *He did not want to spend years festering in jail.*
► languish, waste away, wither, rot, moulder

**festival** NOUN
*The city has a music festival in the spring.*
► jubilee, pageant, carnival, gala, fête, jamboree, celebration, festivities, anniversary

**NAMES FOR RELIGIOUS FESTIVALS**
**Buddhist festivals**: Buddha Day, Nirvana Day.
**Christian festivals**: Lent, Easter, Christmas Day.
**Hindu festivals**: Holi, Diwali.
**Muslim festivals**: Ramadan, Eid.
**Jewish festivals**: Passover, Rosh Hashanah, Yom Kippur, Hanukkah.
**Sikh festivals**: Baisakhi, Birth of Guru Nanak.

**festive** ADJECTIVE
*A festive atmosphere encourages the children to have a good time.*
► jolly, joyous, joyful, happy, merry, cheerful, cheery, jubilant, convivial, celebratory, gay, gleeful, jovial, light-hearted
OPPOSITES ARE gloomy, sombre

**festivities** PLURAL NOUN
*The family returned home in time for the New Year festivities.*
► celebrations, revels, revelry, festival, party, entertainments, amusements, fun, jollification

**fetch** VERB
1 *She went to fetch a bucket from the cupboard.*
► get, bring, collect, pick up, retrieve, obtain, bear, call for, carry, convey, import, transfer, transport
2 *Will you fetch your brother from the station?*
► collect, pick up, transport, bring, get, convey, conduct
3 *We had better fetch the doctor.*
► send for, call for, summon, go for, get, bring

a b c d e **f** g h i j k l m n o p q r s t u v w x y z

**4** *By this time he reckoned the house might fetch a cool million.*
► sell for, be sold for, be bought for, raise, realize, bring in, earn, go for, make, produce

**fetching** ADJECTIVE
*The children wore fetching little outfits.*
► pretty, attractive, appealing, delightful, charming
AN OPPOSITE IS unattractive

**fete** NOUN
*a village fete*
► gala, fair, festival, pageant, bazaar, garden party, jubilee, carnival

**feud** NOUN
*The family feud came to a head this week.*
► vendetta, dispute, conflict, rivalry, strife, quarrel, antagonism, hostility, enmity, animosity

**fever** NOUN
**1** *He caught some sort of fever and never got over it.*
► feverishness, high temperature, delirium
**2** *We were in a fever of impatience waiting for them to return.*
► frenzy, ferment
**3** *World Cup football fever*
► excitement, agitation, passion, frenzy

**feverish** ADJECTIVE
**1** *She looked flushed and feverish.*
► fevered, burning, hot, febrile, inflamed, delirious
**2** *The house was a scene of feverish activity.*
► frenzied, frantic, frenetic, excited, hectic, agitated, hurried, hasty, impatient, restless
OPPOSITES ARE calm, gentle

**few** ADJECTIVE
**1** *Few details are available about the crash* (*informal*) *A few people had gathered at the gates.*
► not many, hardly any, a small number of, a handful of
AN OPPOSITE IS many
**2** *Buses are few at this time of night.*
► scarce, scant, meagre, in short supply, thin on the ground, few and far between

**few** PRONOUN
*I only have a few left.*
► small number, handful, sprinkling, couple, one or two
AN OPPOSITE IS lot

**fiasco** NOUN
*The invasion attempt ended up as a fiasco.*
► failure, debacle, catastrophe, disaster, shambles, farce, (*more informal*) washout, (*more informal*) cock-up

**fib** NOUN
*It was obvious that he was telling fibs.*
► lie, untruth, story, falsehood

**fibre** NOUN
**1** *The fibres are then spun, either by hand or by machine.*
► thread, strand, hair, filament

**2** *clothes in natural fibres*
► cloth, fabric, stuff, material, substance
**3** *a diet low in fat and high in fibre*
► roughage, bulk, fibrous material
**4** *a person of great moral fibre*
► character, backbone, toughness, courage, determination, spirit, tenacity

**fickle** ADJECTIVE
*His fickle supporters soon deserted him.*
► changeable, disloyal, unfaithful, inconstant, changing, erratic, faithless, variable, unreliable, unstable, vacillating, volatile, unpredictable
OPPOSITES ARE loyal, faithful, constant

**fiction** NOUN
**1** *a course in twentieth-century fiction*
► novels, stories, creative writing
AN OPPOSITE IS non-fiction
**2** *The allegations were a total fiction.*
► invention, fabrication, concoction, deception, fantasy, figment, flight of fancy, pack of lies, (*more informal*) tall story
OPPOSITES ARE fact, truth

**NAMES FOR TYPES OF FICTION**

novel, short story; drama, play, poetry; gothic novel (19th-century horror and mystery), ghost story, adventure story, picaresque (adventures of a hero), romantic novel, epistolary novel (story told through exchanges of letters), historical novel (set in a historical period), detective story, science fiction (or sci fi), spy fiction, fantasy, myth, fairy story.

**fictional** ADJECTIVE
*a fictional character*
► imaginary, invented, fabulous, fanciful, legendary, made-up, make-believe, mythical
AN OPPOSITE IS factual

**fictitious** ADJECTIVE
*He used a fictitious name.*
► invented, false, fake, assumed, spurious, fabricated, fraudulent, unreal, untrue, apocryphal
OPPOSITES ARE genuine, true

**fiddle** NOUN
**1** *a group of fiddle players*
► violin
**2** (*informal*) *He was involved in a huge tax fiddle.*
► fraud, swindle, cheat, trick

**fiddle** VERB
**1** **fiddle with** *Stephen was fiddling with the CD player.*
► tinker with, play about with, tamper with, meddle with, twiddle, finger
**2** (*informal*) *The auditors will find out if anyone has fiddled the accounts.*
► falsify, misrepresent, rig, alter, interfere with, tamper with, (*more informal*) doctor, (*more informal*) cook

**fiddling** ADJECTIVE
*I get fed up with the fiddling little details*
► trivial, petty, trifling, paltry, unimportant

**fiddly** ADJECTIVE

*(informal) a row of fiddly buttons and switches*
▶ intricate, complicated, inaccessible

**fidelity** NOUN

*The nobles were expected to show fidelity to the king.*
▶ loyalty, allegiance, obedience, fealty

**fidget** VERB

*The heat in the room made me fidget.*
▶ wriggle, twitch, jiggle, shuffle about, be jittery

**fidgety** ADJECTIVE

*The audience became bored and fidgety.*
▶ restless, twitchy, jittery, impatient, restive,
uneasy, agitated, nervous, on edge
OPPOSITES ARE controlled, still

**field** NOUN

1 *There was a bull in the next field.*
▶ enclosure, paddock, pasture
2 *The field was too wet to play on.*
▶ pitch, ground, sports field, playing field, *(more informal)* park
3 *great names in the field of medicine*
▶ sphere, domain, area, speciality, subject,
discipline
4 *The house lay outside our field of vision.*
▶ range, scope, extent

**fiend** NOUN

1 *It was as if he had been possessed by some fiend.*
▶ demon, devil, evil spirit, imp, bogie
2 *the fiend who had attacked her*
▶ brute, beast, monster, villain
3 *She was a bit of a fitness fiend.*
▶ fanatic, enthusiast, addict, devotee, *(more informal)* freak, *(more informal)* nut

**fiendish** ADJECTIVE

1 *All sorts of fiendish tortures might be awaiting them.*
▶ wicked, cruel, diabolical, brutal, barbaric, vicious,
unspeakable
2 *a fiendish plot to kill the king*
▶ cunning, clever, ingenious, canny, devious, wily

**fierce** ADJECTIVE

1 *a fierce dog*
▶ ferocious, vicious, savage, wild, brutal
OPPOSITES ARE gentle, tame
2 *fierce competition*
▶ strong, intense, powerful, keen, aggressive,
cutthroat
AN OPPOSITE IS mild
3 *fierce resentment*
▶ passionate, ardent, intense, strong, powerful
4 *a fierce pain*
▶ acute, severe, strong, powerful, intense

**fiery** ADJECTIVE

1 *a fiery furnace*
▶ burning, blazing, flaming, raging, glowing,
scorching, red-hot
2 *She remained calm, despite her fiery temperament.*
▶ passionate, ardent, fervent, excitable, spirited,
lively, volatile, explosive, violent, hot-headed

3 *The sky was a fiery red.*
▶ bright, vivid, brilliant, intense, vibrant, rich, strong

**fight** NOUN

1 *He had got into a fight on the way home.*
▶ brawl, fracas, tussle, struggle
2 *She hated having fights with her boyfriend.*
▶ quarrel, argument, row, squabble, wrangle,
contretemps, altercation, difference of opinion,
*(more informal)* bust-up, *(more informal)* slanging
match
3 *the fight for women's rights*
▶ struggle, battle, campaign, effort
4 *a championship fight*
▶ contest, match, bout, meeting, fixture

**fight** VERB

1 *Some men were fighting in the street.*
▶ brawl, tussle, struggle, grapple, wrestle, have a
fight, exchange blows
2 *Her sons all fought in the war.*
▶ serve, be a soldier, join up, take up arms
3 *She and her boyfriend are always fighting.*
▶ quarrel, argue, row, squabble, wrangle
4 *The unions will fight any proposals to cut jobs.*
▶ oppose, resist, contest, challenge, defy, object to,
combat, withstand
5 *women who fought for their basic freedoms*
▶ campaign, battle, strive, crusade

**fighter** NOUN

*an enemy fighter*
▶ soldier, combatant, fighting man, fighting
woman, warrior

**figurative** ADJECTIVE

*a figurative expression*
▶ metaphorical, symbolic, allegorical, fanciful,
non-literal
AN OPPOSITE IS literal

**figure** NOUN

1 *The final figure was higher than last year.*
▶ total, sum, amount, number
2 *The third figure is an eight.*
▶ digit, numeral, character, number
3 *It's hard to put an exact figure on it.*
▶ amount, price, cost, sum
4 *Jane has a lovely figure.*
▶ shape, physique, build, proportions, body, frame
5 *By now she had become a public figure.*
▶ personality, character, celebrity, dignitary,
person, individual, personage
6 *He did not want to be seen as a figure of fun.*
▶ symbol, personification, embodiment, epitome

**figure** VERB

*an animal that figures in many ancient myths*
▶ feature, appear, play a role, has a place

**file** NOUN

1 *He keeps his business letters in A4 files.*
▶ folder, binder, portfolio, wallet, sleeve
2 *There is a file on these people at headquarters.*
▶ dossier, record, set of notes

**3** *A file of soldiers was walking up the road.*
▶ line, column, string, train, procession, convoy, stream

**file** VERB
**1** *Completed forms are filed by year in the top drawer.*
▶ classify, arrange, organize, put in order, enter, store, keep, archive
**2** *She was sitting filing her nails.*
▶ smooth, shape, rub, polish
**3** *The children filed through the door into the sunshine.*
▶ stream, troop, march, parade, walk in a line, proceed in a line

**fill** VERB
**1** *She soon filled a suitcase with the things she needed.*
▶ pack, load
**2** *Fill the holes and gaps before you start papering.*
▶ plug, stop, stop up, bung up, block up, seal
**3** *With thirty guests we will fill the house.*
▶ crowd, throng, pack, pack into, congest
**4** *A smell of coffee filled the room.*
▶ spread through, pervade, permeate, penetrate
**5** *Recruits will fill the new posts by the end of the year.*
▶ occupy, take up, be appointed to, move into
**6** *A bank loan will fill their needs for now.*
▶ fulfil, satisfy, meet, supply, furnish

**fill in**
**1** *You have to fill in this form.*
▶ complete, fill out, answer
**2** *I am filling in for Shirley while she is away.*
▶ deputize, cover, stand in, substitute
**3** *Ken will fill us in on the details.*
▶ brief, inform (of), advise (of), apprise (of)

**filling** NOUN
*The cushion was losing its filling.*
▶ stuffing, padding, wadding, insides, contents

**filling** ADJECTIVE
*a filling meal*
▶ satisfying, nourishing, nutritious, ample, square, solid, substantial

**film** NOUN
**1** *There was a film of dust on the table.*
▶ layer, covering, coat, coating, dusting, patina, sheet, veil, skin, screen
**2** *The boys are going to see a film this evening.*
▶ movie, picture, feature, (*old-fashioned*) motion picture

**NAMES FOR TYPES OF CINEMA FILM**

feature film, documentary, cartoon, war film, western, romance, (*informal*) weepie, love story, (*informal*) biopic, science fiction film, horror film, comedy film.

**filter** NOUN
*Pass the liquid through a filter.*
▶ sieve, strainer, gauze, membrane, mesh, screen

**filter** VERB
*You have to filter the rainwater.*
▶ sieve, strain, sift, filtrate, purify, clarify, percolate

**filth** NOUN
**1** *I needed a hose to get the filth off my boots.*
▶ dirt, muck, grime, mud, slime, sludge, garbage, excrement
**2** *The newspaper had several pages of filth.*
▶ pornography, smut, indecency, obscenity, (*more informal*) porn

**filthy** ADJECTIVE
**1** *The house was filthy.*
▶ dirty, grubby, mucky, squalid, uncleaned, unwashed
AN OPPOSITE IS clean
**2** *Everyone agreed it was a filthy trick.*
▶ nasty, mean, vile, despicable, contemptible, disgusting, shabby
**3** *They were accused of using filthy language.*
▶ rude, indecent, coarse, vulgar, lewd, improper, obscene
OPPOSITES ARE clean, polite
**4** *He was in a filthy mood.*
▶ bad, foul, bad-tempered, irritable

**final** ADJECTIVE
**1** *the final month of their course*
▶ last, closing, concluding, finishing, end
OPPOSITES ARE first, initial
**2** *the final minutes of the match*
▶ last, closing, dying
**3** *The judges' decision is final.*
▶ irrevocable, definitive, absolute, indisputable, unalterable, decisive, incontrovertible

**finalize** VERB
*We can now finalize the arrangements for the trip.*
▶ complete, conclude, settle, clinch, resolve, decide, confirm, (*more informal*) wrap up

**finally** ADVERB
*The bank finally agreed to loan the money.*
▶ eventually, ultimately, in the end, at length, at last

**finance** NOUN
**1** *He needs to learn more about finance.*
▶ economics, money management, accounting, banking, fiscal matters
**2** *The company is seeking longer-term finance.*
▶ funding, funds, capital, assets, revenue, income, financial backing
**3** *His finances are in a fairly good state.*
▶ resources, assets, financial affairs, money affairs

**finance** VERB
*Private sponsors will finance the venture.*
▶ fund, back, subsidize, support, provide money for, invest in, underwrite, pay for, sponsor

**financial** ADJECTIVE
*financial affairs*
▶ monetary, fiscal, pecuniary, economic

**find** VERB
**1** *I found some old coins in the cupboard.*
▶ discover, locate, retrieve, track down, come across, chance on, unearth, uncover

**2** *We found it odd that there were so many complaints.*
► consider, think, believe, reckon, see as, regard as, look on as, view as
**3** *You will find that it's helpful to number each paragraph.*
► realize, discover, learn, perceive, notice, become aware
**4** *I hope you find the success you deserve.*
► achieve, attain, win, obtain, acquire, reach, secure, get

**find out**
**1** *At last we will find out what happened.*
► learn, ascertain, discover, perceive
**2** *The culprits were soon found out.*
► reveal, expose, unmask, uncover, (*more informal*) rumble

**find** NOUN
*An ancient ship burial was among the exciting finds.*
► discovery, acquisition

**findings** NOUN
*The inquiry will announce its findings tomorrow.*
► judgement, conclusion, recommendation, verdict, decision

**fine** ADJECTIVE
**1** *It was a fine achievement.*
► excellent, outstanding, admirable, remarkable, exceptional, commendable, first-class, good
**2** *The next day was fine.*
► bright, fair, dry, clear, sunny, warm, cloudless
OPPOSITES ARE bad, wet, inclement
**3** *He brought out the fine china.*
► delicate, fragile
**4** *A pen with a fine tip.*
► thin, narrow, slender, slim
**5** *a beach of fine warm sand*
► powdery, minute
**6** *He likes fine clothes*
► elegant, stylish, smart, chic, fashionable
**7** *The mechanism needs a fine adjustment.*
► small, minor, subtle
**8** *It's fine to write to me here.*
► all right, acceptable, suitable, agreeable

**fine** NOUN
*He got a parking fine.*
► penalty, charge

**finger** VERB
*He fingered the ring on his finger.*
► touch, feel, handle, stroke, rub, fondle, caress, twiddle

**finicky** ADJECTIVE
*a finicky eater*
► fussy, fastidious, particular, choosy, (*more informal*) picky

**finish** NOUN
**1** *The race had an exciting finish.*
► ending, end, close, last stage, conclusion, result
**2** *They went out to celebrate the finish of the work.*
► completion, conclusion, end, cessation, termination

**3** *Mix the paint well for an even finish.*
► appearance, surface, texture, lustre, polish, shine, gloss, smoothness

**finish** VERB
**1** *We have to finish the work today.*
► complete, conclude, end, finalize
**2** *They never seem to finish complaining.*
► stop, cease, end
**3** *We've finished the biscuits.*
► use up, eat, consume, devour, exhaust, (*more informal*) polish off
**4** *The film finishes at ten.*
► end, conclude, terminate
**5** *Another year of losses will finish the company.*
► destroy, ruin, overwhelm, overpower

**finite** ADJECTIVE
*We have a finite amount of land to build on.*
► limited, restricted, fixed, definable, defined, known, measurable, numbered, calculable
OPPOSITES ARE infinite, limitless

**fire** NOUN
**1** *The building was destroyed in a fire.*
► blaze, conflagration, inferno, flames, burning, combustion, holocaust, pyre
**2** *She spoke with fire in her eyes.*
► passion, feeling, enthusiasm, intensity, vigour, fervour, ardour, dynamism, exuberance

**fire** VERB
**1** *The engine began to fire.*
► ignite, start, catch, (*more informal*) get going
**2** *The guerrillas fired a rocket.*
► launch, discharge, shoot, detonate, set off, let off, let fly with
**3** *The idea fired their imagination.*
► excite, stimulate, arouse, inspire, enliven, stir up
**4** *(informal) They fired him for misconduct.*
► dismiss, discharge, sack, give someone notice, lay off

**firm** ADJECTIVE
**1** *The ground is fairly firm at this point.*
► hard, solid, unyielding, hardened, compact, compressed, resistant, stable
AN OPPOSITE IS soft
**2** *The house lacked firm foundations.*
► secure, steady, strong, sturdy, fast, fixed, stable, tight, anchored
**3** *Firm action is essential.*
► resolute, determined, decided, steadfast, adamant, dogged, obstinate, persistent, unshakeable, unwavering, unflinching
**4** *We need a firm commitment*
► definite, agreed, settled, unchangeable
**5** *Sally was a firm friend of hers.*
► devoted, constant, faithful, loyal, reliable, dependable

**firm** NOUN
*Dave joined an accountancy firm.*
► company, establishment, organization, business, concern, corporation

# first ADJECTIVE

**1** *Our first attempts didn't work.*
► initial, opening, preliminary
**2** *The first inhabitants were hunters.*
► original, earliest, oldest, primeval, primitive
**3** *The first consideration is the welfare of the children.*
► principal, prime, paramount, primary, main, chief, key, foremost, supreme, overriding

# first-class ADJECTIVE

*a first-class meal*
► excellent, first-rate, top-quality, outstanding, superb, superlative, top-flight

# first-hand ADJECTIVE

*She has first-hand knowledge of the city.*
► direct, personal

# firstly ADVERB

*Firstly, we must learn each other's names.*
► first, to begin with, to start with, at the outset, as a start

# first-rate ADJECTIVE

*a first-rate piece of work*
► excellent, outstanding, first-class, top-quality, superb, superlative, top-flight

---

**fish** NOUN

**SOME COMMON TYPES OF FISH**

**flatfish**: brill, dab, Dover sole, flounder, fluke, halibut, lemon sole, megrim, plaice, scaldfish, sole, turbot.

**freshwater fish**: barb, barbel, barramundi, bass, bream, carp, catfish, chub, dace, grayling, gudgeon, guppy, loach, lungfish, minnow, perch, pike, piranha, roach, rudd, salmon (partly freshwater), stickleback, sucker, tench, trout.

**sea fish**: angler fish, barracuda, brisling, catfish, cod, coelacanth, conger (eel), dory, eel, garfish, goby, goldfish (kind of carp), gunnel, haddock, hake, herring, jellyfish, ling (type of cod), mackerel, monkfish, moonfish, mullet, pilchard, rockfish, salmon (partly sea fish), sardine, shad, shark, skate, snapper, sprat, starfish, surgeon, swordfish, tuna, whitebait, whiting, wrasse.

**crustaceans and molluscs**: barnacle, crab, crayfish, cuttlefish, lobster, prawn, shellfish, shrimp; clam, cockle, conch, cowrie, cuttlefish, limpet, mussel, nautilus, octopus, oyster, scallop, sea slug, sea snail, shellfish, squid, triton, whelk, winkle.

**RELATED ADJECTIVE** piscine

---

# fish VERB

**fish for** *He seemed to be fishing for compliments.*
► invite, seek, solicit

# fishy ADJECTIVE

*(informal) The price was so low it all seemed a bit fishy.*
► suspicious, dubious, doubtful, suspect, peculiar, strange, odd, queer, funny

# fit ADJECTIVE

**1** *She looked remarkably fit for a fifty-two-year-old.*
► healthy, well, able-bodied, robust, hale and hearty, in good form
OPPOSITES ARE unfit, unhealthy
**2** *The vehicles are all fit for commercial use.*
► suitable, appropriate, prepared, equipped, ready, proper, right, correct
OPPOSITES ARE unfit, unsuitable
**3** *Do you think he is fit to be a parent?*
► competent, able, capable (of being), qualified, worthy
OPPOSITES ARE unfit, incapable

# fit NOUN

**1** *He might have an epileptic fit at any time.*
► seizure, convulsion, paroxysm, spasm, attack
**2** *She was having a fit of hysterics.*
► outbreak, outburst, spell, bout, attack, explosion

# fit VERB

**1** *It takes a long time to fit all the pieces together.*
► arrange, assemble, build, construct, dovetail, install, interlock, join, match, position, put in place, put together
**2** *Make the punishment fit the crime.*
► suit, match, accord with, be appropriate to, correspond with or to, be fitting for, conform with

# fitful ADJECTIVE

*There was time for a few hours' fitful sleep.*
► spasmodic, intermittent, disturbed, uneven, broken, patchy, irregular
OPPOSITES ARE constant, regular

# fitted ADJECTIVE

**1** *He clearly isn't fitted for the job.*
► suited, suitable, right, equipped, appropriate
**2** *It was a modern house with fitted cupboards everywhere you looked.*
► built-in, integral, incorporated, customized

# fitting ADJECTIVE

*The concert was a fitting tribute to a fine singer.*
► suitable, apt, appropriate, apposite, proper, timely, felicitous
OPPOSITES ARE inappropriate, unsuitable

# fittings PLURAL NOUN

*The bathroom fittings were cheap and flimsy.*
► fixtures, fitments, equipment, accessories, furnishings

# fix VERB

**1** *You can fix the notice to a lamppost.*
► fasten, tie, pin, attach, affix, secure
**2** *The farmer had fixed posts into the ground.*
► set, embed, cement, place, position
**3** *I can fix it for you to get an invitation.*
► arrange, organize, manage
**4** *Let's fix a date to meet.*
► set, decide on, agree on, arrange, settle, determine
**5** *The television needs to be fixed.*
► mend, repair, put right

**fix** NOUN
(*informal*) I'm in a bit of a fix.
► difficulty, predicament, mess, plight, dilemma, (*informal*) hole, (*informal*) jam, quandary, corner

**fixed** NOUN
The licence is for a fixed period.
► set, definite, decided, established, settled, predetermined, firm

**fizz** VERB
She dropped in a tablet and the water fizzed.
► bubble, effervesce, foam, froth, fizzle, sizzle, hiss

**fizzy** ADJECTIVE
There are fizzy drinks in the garden.
► sparkling, effervescent, bubbly, carbonated, foaming
AN OPPOSITE IS still

**flabbergasted** ADJECTIVE
He just stood there, flabbergasted.
► astonished, amazed, astounded, surprised, staggered, startled, disconcerted, dumbfounded, speechless, shocked, perplexed, stunned, stupefied, bewildered, (*more informal*) thunderstruck

**flabby** ADJECTIVE
(*informal*) When he took her hand in his, it was soft and flabby.
► slack, limp, loose, floppy, flaccid, weak, feeble
OPPOSITES ARE firm, stiff

**flag** NOUN
The route was decorated with flags.
► banner, standard, ensign, pennant, pennon, streamer, bunting, colours

**flag** VERB
Our energy was beginning to flag.
► fade, fail, decline, diminish, dwindle, sink, disappear

**flair** NOUN
1 He has a flair for games.
► talent, aptitude, gift, ability, genius, faculty, capacity, adeptness
2 She dresses with great flair.
► style, elegance, taste, discernment, panache, finesse

**flake** NOUN
First remove any loose flakes of old paint.
► scale, sliver, chip, splinter, shaving, bit, leaf, slice, wafer

**flamboyant** ADJECTIVE
He was well known for his flamboyant appearance.
► ostentatious, showy, colourful, gaudy, brilliant, resplendent, extravagant

**flaming** ADJECTIVE
a flaming torch
► burning, blazing, fiery, glowing, brilliant

**flap** VERB
1 The washing was flapping in the wind
► flutter, sway, swing, quiver, wave about

2 The swan flapped its wings angrily.
► beat, flutter, shake, agitate, quiver, thrash
3 He tried hard to avoid flapping.
► panic, fuss, become agitated, become flustered

**flare** VERB
The match flared in his cupped hands.
► blaze, flame, flash, burn, erupt, sparkle

**flare up**
1 This border war could flare up at any time.
► break out, burst out, erupt, blow up, recur
2 They annoyed her and she flared up at them.
► lose your temper, lose control, fly into a rage, become angry

**flash** VERB
Lights flashed in the distance.
► shine, blaze, flare, gleam, beam, glint, sparkle, spark

**flash** NOUN
1 a flash of light
► blaze, burst, flare, glare, gleam, glint, sparkle, flicker, twinkle, ray
2 a flash of inspiration
► burst, wave, surge, rush

**flashy** ADJECTIVE
Lily held out her hand with a flashy ring on her finger.
► showy, gaudy, ostentatious, vulgar, (*more informal*) tacky

**flat** ADJECTIVE
1 a flat surface
► level, smooth, even, horizontal, plane
OPPOSITES ARE bumpy, uneven
2 She lay flat on the bed.
► outstretched, prostrate, spread out, recumbent
3 a flat sea
► calm, still, smooth, waveless, tranquil
OPPOSITES ARE rough, choppy
4 His voice was flat and lifeless.
► dull, monotonous, uninteresting, unexciting, tedious, boring, bland, dreary, insipid, colourless, featureless, unexpressive, weak
AN OPPOSITE IS emotional
5 The request met with a flat refusal.
► outright, direct, straight, plain, absolute, positive

**flat** NOUN
They lived in a small flat for several years.
► apartment, maisonette, set of rooms, flatlet, penthouse

**flatten** VERB
1 Tom flattened the crumpled paper against his knee.
► smooth, press, even out, iron out, level out, roll
OPPOSITES ARE roughen, crumple
2 People had walked over the beds and flattened the plants.
► squash, trample, crush, compress, run over
3 The hurricane had flattened hundreds of buildings.
► demolish, destroy, devastate, knock down, level, raze

**4** (*informal*) *He's quite capable of flattening you with a single blow.*
▶ knock down, knock over, fell, prostrate, (*informal*) floor, (*informal*) lay out

**flatter** VERB
**1** *He enjoyed teasing and flattering her.*
▶ praise, compliment, humour, fawn on, play up to, (*more informal*) sweet-talk, (*more informal*) butter up
**USAGE** Note that *to flatter* is to compliment someone in an insincere way, whereas to *praise* is to pay genuine compliments.
**2** *She wore a dress that flattered her small figure.*
▶ suit, enhance, set off, look good on, show to advantage

**flattering** ADJECTIVE
**1** *flattering remarks*
▶ complimentary, favourable, appreciative, adulatory, effusive, obsequious, fawning, fulsome, ingratiating
OPPOSITES ARE insulting, sincere
**2** *a flattering outfit*
▶ becoming, fetching, enhancing

**flattery** NOUN
*We succumb to flattery because it makes us feel good.*
▶ praise, compliments, adulation, blandishments, admiration, fawning, obsequiousness, servility
**USAGE** Note that *flattery* is always insincere, whereas *praise* is usually genuine.

**flaunt** VERB
*He loved flaunting his knowledge about cars.*
▶ show off, display, parade, exhibit, flourish, vaunt, make a show of

**flavour** NOUN
**1** *The food had a spicy flavour.*
▶ taste, tang, savour
**2** *a story with an oriental flavour*
▶ character, quality, atmosphere, aura, ambience, mood, feel, style, feeling, aspect

**flavour** VERB
*You can flavour the stew with mixed herbs.*
▶ season, spice, enliven, liven up, enrich

**flavouring** NOUN
*Add some gentle flavouring.*
▶ seasoning, additive, spice, essence, extract

**flaw** NOUN
*There is a flaw in this reasoning.  a glass with a tiny flaw you can hardly see*
▶ defect, blemish, fault, imperfection, deficiency, weakness, failing, shortcoming

**flawed** ADJECTIVE
*The argument was obviously flawed.*
▶ defective, unsound, faulty, imperfect, weak, deficient

**flawless** ADJECTIVE
*Her skin was flawless.*
▶ perfect, faultless, immaculate, unblemished, unmarked, spotless

**fleck** NOUN
*white with flecks of blue*
▶ speck, patch, dot, point, streak, dab, splash

**flee** VERB
*She left the others and fled to her room.*
▶ run off, bolt, fly, take off, clear off, hurry off, escape, disappear

**fleet** NOUN
*A large fleet of ships sailed out.*
▶ flotilla, armada, naval force, convoy, navy, squadron, task force

**fleeting** ADJECTIVE
*We had a fleeting glimpse of the queen.*
▶ brief, momentary, transient, cursory, passing, short
AN OPPOSITE IS lasting

**flesh** NOUN
*an animal's flesh*
▶ meat, muscle, tissue, carrion, fat
**USAGE** Note that *carrion* is the decaying flesh of a dead animal.

**flex** NOUN
*a flex for an electric iron*
▶ cable, lead, wire

**flex** VERB
*She flexed her arms and swept back her hair.*
▶ bend, bow, curve, double up, hook, cock, angle

**flexible** ADJECTIVE
**1** *flexible working practices*
▶ adaptable, adjustable, variable, fluid, open
OPPOSITES ARE inflexible, rigid
**2** *a flexible rod used as an aerial*
▶ bendable, pliable, pliant, malleable, stretchable
OPPOSITES ARE rigid, fixed

**flick** VERB
*He flicked a finger lightly against her cheek.*
▶ stroke, wag, brush, wave, sweep, flip, jerk

**flick** NOUN
**1** *The king dismissed his page with a flick of his head.*
▶ jerk, toss, flip, sweep
**2** *He gave the table a few flicks with a duster.*
▶ dab, touch, brush, swipe, stroke

**flicker** VERB
**1** *The candle flickered in the breeze.*
▶ glimmer, twinkle, sparkle, shimmer, blink
**2** *The eyelids can flicker when you dream.*
▶ tremble, quiver, waver, flutter

**flight** NOUN
**1** *a short history of flight*
▶ flying, aviation, aeronautics, air travel
**2** *the flight of a missile*
▶ path, trajectory, track
**3** *the king's flight to safety*
▶ escape , getaway, retreat, fleeing

## flimsy ADJECTIVE

**1** *He moved the flimsy barrier and walked past.*
► fragile, rickety, shaky, makeshift, insubstantial, frail, weak
AN OPPOSITE IS substantial

**2** *She wore a flimsy nightdress.*
► light, lightweight, thin, fine, diaphanous, silky, filmy

**3** *We heard the usual flimsy excuses.*
► feeble, weak, poor, thin, unconvincing, implausible

## flinch VERB

*She flinched as he put out his hand.*
► wince, recoil, start, shrink, pull back, draw back, shy away, shrink back
**flinch from** *He never flinches from his duty.*
► shrink from, shirk, avoid, evade, balk at

## fling VERB

*He flung the gun over the bridge.*
► throw, hurl, toss, sling, cast, pitch, heave

## flip VERB

**1** *He flipped a coin in the air.*
► toss, flick, spin, threw

**2** *The beetle flipped on to its back.*
► turn, spin, tip, topple
**flip through** *She was flipping through the pages of a magazine.*
► flick through, thumb through, skim through, scan, peruse

## flippant ADJECTIVE

*a flippant remark*
► facetious, frivolous, jocular, humorous, funny, witty, amusing, comical, glib
AN OPPOSITE IS serious

## flirt VERB

**flirt with**
**1** *He loves flirting with the girls.*
► tease, trifle with, lead on, make up to, (*more informal*) chat up

**2** *an idea I had been flirting with for some time*
► consider, entertain, toy with, trifle with, dabble in

## flit VERB

*insects flitting from plant to plant*
► dart, flip, fly, flutter, whisk, skim, dance

## float VERB

**1** *little boats floating on the water*
► sail, bob, drift

**2** *A cloud floated across the sun.*
► drift, glide, hover, slip, slide, waft

**3** *We want to float a few ideas.*
► suggest, propose, put forward, submit, raise, present, come up with, moot

**4** *The company was floated on the Stock Market.*
► launch, set up, promote, initiate, offer

## flock NOUN

**1** *a flock of sheep*
► herd, drove, group

**2** *a flock of birds*
► flight, group

**3** *a flock of anxious relatives*
► crowd, throng, horde, gathering, bunch, huddle, mob, mass

## flock VERB

*People flocked from all quarters.*
► gather, collect, assemble, come together, congregate, crowd, convene, converge, muster

## flog VERB

*The executioner flogged the woman on her back.*
► whip, beat, flay, lash, scourge, thrash, flagellate, birch, cane

## flood NOUN

**1** *The flood cut off several villages.*
► inundation, deluge, torrent, downpour

**2** *a flood of protests*
► succession, torrent, barrage, spate, storm, volley, excess, abundance, profusion, plethora
AN OPPOSITE IS trickle

## flood VERB

**1** *The dam burst, flooding the town.*
► inundate, swamp, submerge, engulf, overwhelm, drown, deluge, immerse

**2** *Light flooded the room.*
► fill, swamp, saturate

**3** *The loo flooded yesterday.*
► overflow, run over, brim over

**4** *The press flooded back into the courtroom.*
► pour, stream, surge, swarm, flock, crowd, throng

## floor NOUN

**1** *The floor was sopping wet.*
► ground, flooring, base

**2** *Take the lift to the third floor.*
► level, storey, stage, landing

## flop VERB

**1** *His white hair flopped over his eyes.*
► dangle, droop, hang down, slump, flag, sag, wilt

**2** *All she wanted was to flop into a chair.*
► drop, fall, sink, slump, collapse, tumble

**3** *The idea flopped spectacularly.*
► fail, founder, misfire, be unsuccessful, fold

## flop NOUN

*The show was a flop.*
► failure, disaster, debacle, fiasco, (*more informal*) washout

## floppy ADJECTIVE

*a girl in pigtails, wearing a large floppy woollen hat*
► limp, droopy, drooping, dangling, loose, saggy, sagging, hanging
AN OPPOSITE IS stiff

## flounder VERB

*The infantry floundered in the swampy ground. He was floundering in a situation of his own making.*
► struggle, falter, grope, wallow, stumble, fumble, stagger

**flourish** VERB

1 *Plants flourish in this good soil.*  *The farmers flourished, aided by good weather.*
▶ thrive, prosper, bloom, blossom, succeed, boom, be strong, be vigorous, progress
2 *She went out, flourishing an umbrella.*
▶ brandish, wave, wield, swirl, swing, flaunt

**flourish** NOUN

*With a flourish he produced a small bag of sweets.*
▶ gesture, wave, sweep, show, fanfare

**flourishing** ADJECTIVE

*a flourishing chain of supermarkets*
▶ thriving, successful, prosperous, booming, vigorous, buoyant, productive, lucrative

**flout** VERB

*He had no intention of flouting a court order.*
▶ disobey, defy, violate, contravene, infringe, break, spurn, scorn
OPPOSITES ARE respect, observe

**flow** VERB

1 *Water was flowing through the pipes.*
▶ run, stream, spurt, trickle, ooze, squirt, gush, flood, cascade
2 *Several issues flow from these proposals.*
▶ result, proceed, follow, arise, spring, proceed, emerge, emanate

**flow** NOUN

1 *Alcohol increases the flow of blood to the brain.*
▶ movement, circulation, stream, motion, course, current, passage, surge
2 *a steady flow of correspondence*
▶ stream, current, deluge, cascade, flood, gush, spate

**flower** NOUN

1 *Mandy picked flowers from the garden*
▶ bloom, blossom, floret, bud
2 *the flower of a nation's youth*
▶ finest, best, pick, cream, choice, elite

**flowery** ADJECTIVE

*flowery language*
▶ fancy, elaborate, florid, ornate, flamboyant, overblown

**fluctuate** VERB

*Their income fluctuates from year to year.*
▶ vary, change, alter, shift, differ, rise and fall

**fluent** ADJECTIVE

1 *She is fluent in five European languages.*
▶ articulate, able to speak
2 *It is important to speak in a fluent and interesting manner.*
▶ articulate, natural, expressive, eloquent, effortless, flowing, polished, ready, smooth, unhesitating, (*disapproving*) glib, (*disapproving*) facile
AN OPPOSITE IS inarticulate

**fluff** NOUN

*The sofa is covered in fluff.*
▶ fuzz, dust, nap, down, floss, thistledown

**fluffy** ADJECTIVE

*She padded into the bedroom wrapped in a big fluffy towel.*
▶ furry, woolly, fleecy, fuzzy, downy, velvety, soft

**fluid** ADJECTIVE

1 *fluid substances*
▶ liquid, aqueous, flowing, watery, running, gaseous, liquefied, melted, molten, (*more informal*) runny
AN OPPOSITE IS solid
2 *fluid movements*
▶ graceful, flowing, smooth
3 *My plans are still fairly fluid.*
▶ flexible, adaptable, adjustable, variable, open, changeable, unstable, indefinite, unsettled
OPPOSITES ARE firm, fixed, definite
**USAGE** Be careful when you use *changeable* or *indefinite*, because they have other meanings.

**fluid** NOUN

*Drink lots of fluids and eat fibre-rich foods.*
▶ liquid, juice

**fluke** NOUN

*By a lucky fluke she came along at that moment.*
▶ chance, accident, piece of luck, stroke of luck

**flurry** NOUN

1 *a snow flurry*
▶ swirl, whirl, gust
2 *a flurry of activity*
▶ spate, wave, burst, spell, stir, spurt, outbreak, commotion

**flush** ADJECTIVE

1 *He had just been paid and was feeling flush.*
▶ rich, wealthy, well off, prosperous
2 *The opening needs to be flush with the wall.*
▶ level, flat, even, square, true

**flush** VERB

1 *Nancy flushed with embarrassment.*
▶ blush, go red, redden, colour, glow
2 *Fruit helps flush toxins from the body.*
▶ cleanse, rinse out, wash out, swill
3 *The police tried to flush the suspects out.*
▶ chase out, drive out, expel, send up

**flustered** ADJECTIVE

*She looked shocked and flustered.*
▶ confused, bewildered, bemused, perplexed, baffled, puzzled, mystified, disconcerted, confounded

**flutter** VERB

1 *Butterflies fluttered around the garden.*
▶ flit, flitter, dance
2 *The bird fluttered its wings.*
▶ flap, beat, shake, agitate, quiver, thrash

**fly** VERB

1 *A flock of birds flew past.*
▶ glide, flit, flutter, hover, soar, wing
2 *A gull flew into the air.*
▶ rise, soar, ascend, mount

**3** *He refused to fly the aircraft until it had been checked.*
▶ pilot, operate, take off in, travel in

**4** *A flag was flying at half mast.*
▶ flutter, flap, wave

**5** *The ship was flying a neutral flag.*
▶ display, show, exhibit

**6 fly at** *Charley flew at him, shaking his fist.*
▶ attack, assault, go for, set upon, weigh into, let fly at, hit out at, lash out at

**foam** NOUN
**1** *The sea looked like white crests of foam.*
▶ froth, spume, surf, spray, lather, scum, suds

**2** *There was at least an inch of foam on his beer.*
▶ head, bubbles, effervescence

**foam** VERB
*The water heaved and foamed.*
▶ froth, fizz, seethe, ferment, bubble, effervesce, lather, boil

**fob** VERB
**fob off**
**1** *It's no good fobbing us off with promises.*
▶ stall, put off, palm off, deceive, saddle

**2** *He fobbed off the most difficult job on Trevor.*
▶ inflict, impose, dump, unload

**focus** NOUN
**1** *Get the camera into focus*
▶ clarity, correct adjustment, sharpness

**2** *The television has become a main focus of the living room.*
▶ centre, focal point, heart, hub, core, pivot

**focus** VERB
**focus on** *We need to focus on the events of this coming week.*
▶ concentrate on, direct attention to, fix attention on, home in on, zero in on, spotlight, think about, aim at, centre on, look mainly at

**fog** NOUN
*Don't go out if there's fog.*
▶ mist, smog, bad visibility, haze

**foggy** ADJECTIVE
*Outside it was dull and foggy.*
▶ misty, smoggy, hazy, murky, gloomy, dingy, dim
AN OPPOSITE IS clear

**foil** VERB
*She foiled their efforts by walking in at the wrong moment.*
▶ thwart, frustrate, obstruct, impede, hamper, hinder, baffle, scotch, check, prevent, stop

**foist** VERB
*She doesn't want to foist her opinions on her kids.*
▶ impose, force, thrust, offload, palm off, saddle someone with

**fold** VERB
**1** *Fold the sheets and put them in a drawer.*
▶ double, double over, turn over, bend, tuck, overlap, crease, pleat

**2** *She stood there, folding her arms.*
▶ clasp, wrap, cradle, enfold, enclose, embrace, entwine, envelop, hug

**3** *I'll fold the chair and put it away.*
▶ close, collapse, let down, put down

**4** *The business folded during the recession.*
▶ fail, collapse, crash, founder, close down

**fold** NOUN
**1** *Neatly arrange the folds in the curtains.*
▶ pleat, crease, tuck, furrow, bend

**2** *a fold for sheep*
▶ enclosure, pen, paddock, compound

**folder** NOUN
*I need a folder for these papers.*
▶ file, binder, portfolio, wallet, sleeve

**folk, folks** PLURAL NOUN
**1** *It was good news for the folk back home.*
▶ people, individuals, citizens, inhabitants

**2** *She would visit her folks at the weekend.*
▶ family, parents, relatives, people, kinsfolk

**follow** VERB
**1** *He followed them as far as the corner.*
▶ go after, come after, walk behind, tread on the heels of, trace the footsteps of

**2** *She hoped to follow her father as chief executive of the company.*
▶ succeed, replace, take the place of, take over from, supplant, supersede, step into someone's shoes

**3** *An undercover police officer followed him everywhere.*
▶ pursue, stalk, track, shadow, trail, go after, (more informal) tail

**4** *Make sure you follow the instructions on the packet.*
▶ observe, comply with, adhere to, carry out, obey, note, heed, conform to, keep to

**5** *Many benefits followed from their membership of the community.*
▶ result, ensue, emanate, arise, develop

**6** *I found it hard to follow his meaning.*
▶ understand, comprehend, grasp, fathom, take in, catch

**7** *Which team do you follow?*
▶ support, be a fan of

**follower** NOUN
*the leader's closest followers*
▶ supporter, adherent, devotee, backer, disciple, companion

**following** ADJECTIVE
*She went home on the following day*
▶ next, ensuing, subsequent, succeeding
OPPOSITES ARE preceding, previous

**following** NOUN
*These successes brought him a strong following.*
▶ support, backing, retinue, patronage, body of adherents

**folly** NOUN

*It would be an act of folly to start a war.*
▶ foolishness, stupidity, senselessness, recklessness, silliness, madness, lunacy, idiocy

**fond** ADJECTIVE

**1** *her fond father*
▶ loving, adoring, devoted, doting, caring, attentive, kind

**2** *a fond hope*
▶ foolish, unrealistic, naive, vain, empty

**3 be fond of** *She's fond of dancing I'm very fond of Jo.*
▶ be keen on, be partial to, be attached to, like, love, (*more informal*) be hooked on, (*more informal*) be wild about, (*more informal*) be crazy about

**fondle** VERB

*He stooped down to fondle the cat.*
▶ stroke, caress, pat, pet, cuddle, play with

---

**food** NOUN

**1** *He had gone a week without food.*
▶ nourishment, sustenance, nutriment, subsistence
RELATED ADJECTIVE alimentary

**2** *Have you brought any food?*
▶ provisions, refreshments, eatables, something to eat, (*old use*) victuals, (*more informal*) grub

**WORDS FOR BASIC TYPES OF FOOD**

**cereals and cereal products:** barley, maize, oats, rice, rye, sweetcorn, wheat; bread, chapatti, chollah, ciabatta, naan, roll, pitta, matzo, croissant, baguette, bagel, pumpernickel, tortilla, flour; branflakes, cornflakes; semolina; pasta, lasagne, macaroni, noodles, spaghetti; dumplings; porridge.

**dairy products:** butter, cheese, cream, curds, eggs, milk, yoghurt.

**fish:** carp, cod, brill, flounder, haddock, halibut, kipper, mackerel, plaice, salmon, sardine, sole, trout, turbot, whitebait.

**fruit:** ackee, apple, apricot, banana, berry, cherry, citrus fruits, coconut, currant, date, fig, grape, grapefruit, kiwi, lemon, lime, lychee, mango, melon, olive, orange, papaya, paw-paw, peach, pear, pineapple, plantain, plum, prune, raisin, raspberry, rhubarb, strawberry, sultana, tangerine, tomato.

**meat:** bacon, beef, chicken, corned beef, game, gammon, ham, lamb, mutton, pork, poultry, tripe, turkey, veal, venison.

**puddings and other sweet foods:** biscuit, cake, chocolate, cookie, custard, fruit salad, ice-cream, jelly, mousse, pie, tart.

**savoury foods:** broth, chop suey, crisps, curry, fritter, goulash, lasagne, moussaka, nuts, pastry, pie, pizza, quiche, pudding, risotto, seafood, soup.

**vegetables:** asparagus, aubergine, brinjal, sweet potato, courgette, yam, zuchinni, beans, beetroot, Brussels sprouts, cabbage, carrot, cauliflower, celery, greens, kale, leek, marrow, onion, parsnip, pea, potato, pumpkin, runner bean, spinach, swede, tomato, turnip.

---

**fool** NOUN

**1** *He was acting like a fool.*
▶ idiot, ass, halfwit, dimwit, blockhead, dunderhead, nincompoop, imbecile, moron, clown, buffoon, clot, chump, (*more informal*) dope, (*more informal*) prat, (*more informal*) ninny, (*more informal*) twit, (*more informal*) twerp

**2** (*old-fashioned*) *a fool at the court of the king*
▶ jester, clown, buffoon, comic, stooge

**fool** VERB

**1** *We easily fooled him.*
▶ deceive, trick, hoodwink, hoax, dupe

**2** *I thought you were just fooling.*
▶ pretend, joke, jest, tease, make believe, put on an act

**fool about** *Some children were fooling about.*
▶ play about, lark about, misbehave

**USAGE** You can use *around* instead of *about* in all these synonyms.

**foolhardy** ADJECTIVE

*a foolhardy venture*
▶ reckless, rash, impetuous, imprudent, ill-advised, unwise, irresponsible

**foolish** ADJECTIVE

*a foolish remark She had been extremely foolish.*
▶ stupid, silly, ill-advised, unwise, crazy, mad, insane, (*more informal*) daft
OPPOSITES ARE wise, sensible

**foolishness** NOUN

*They shook their heads at her foolishness in going back to France.*
▶ stupidity, folly, senselessness, recklessness, silliness, madness, lunacy, idiocy

**foolproof** ADJECTIVE

*The system is foolproof if you follow the instructions carefully.*
▶ infallible, unfailing, dependable, straightforward, simple, (*more informal*) idiot-proof

**foot** NOUN

**1** *The animal had hurt its foot.*
▶ paw, hoof, trotter, claw

**2** *The house was at the foot of the hill.*
▶ bottom, base

**footing** NOUN

**1** *He tried not to lose his footing on the narrow stairs.*
▶ foothold, hold, grip, balance

**2** *They would put the club on a sound financial footing.*
▶ basis, base, foundation, standing, support, terms

▶▶

## footprint NOUN
*There were huge footprints in the snow.*
▶ footmark, footstep, track, print, trace, spoor
**USAGE** You use *spoor* only when referring to an animal.

## footstep NOUN
*She heard footsteps in the hall.*
▶ step, footfall, tread

## forbid VERB
*She forbids the use of calculators in this exercise.*
▶ ban, prohibit, bar, disallow, rule out, exclude, proscribe, veto, outlaw, refuse, preclude
OPPOSITES ARE permit, allow

## forbidden ADJECTIVE
**1** *Ball games are forbidden on the grass outside the building.*
▶ banned, prohibited, barred, disallowed, proscribed, illegal, against the law, outlawed, unauthorized, unlawful
AN OPPOSITE IS permissible
**2** *This part of the house is forbidden to them.*
▶ out of bounds, restricted, closed

## forbidding ADJECTIVE
*The house has a dark, forbidding appearance.*
▶ grim, ominous, menacing, threatening, gloomy, stern, unfriendly, uninviting, unwelcoming
AN OPPOSITE IS friendly

## force NOUN
**1** *It needed some force to get the door open.*
▶ strength, might, vigour, effort, energy, muscle, power, drive, pressure, weight
**2** *The force of the explosion was felt for miles.*
▶ intensity, impact, effect, shock, momentum
**3** *They used force to get their way.*
▶ violence, coercion, compulsion, aggression, constraint, duress
**4** *I could see the force of the argument.*
▶ strength, cogency, effectiveness, validity, persuasiveness, weight, rightness
**5** *a peace-keeping force*
▶ body, group, corps, unit, team, detachment, troops, army

## force VERB
**1** *If necessary we will force them to do it.*
▶ compel, make, oblige, coerce, constrain, pressure, pressurize, order, impel, bulldoze, drive, press-gang
**2** *The intruders had to force a door.*
▶ break open, burst open, prise open, smash, use force on, wrench
**3** *They tried to force their opinions on us*
▶ impose, inflict, thrust

## forceful ADJECTIVE
**1** *a forceful personality*
▶ strong, dynamic, powerful, assertive, commanding, self-assured, energetic
**2** *forceful arguments*
▶ strong, cogent, compelling, convincing, potent, plausible, effective

## foreboding NOUN
**1** *Lucy was full of foreboding about the day ahead.*
▶ anxiety, fear, apprehension, misgiving, trepidation, dread, worry
**2** *Their forebodings proved right.*
▶ premonition, presentiment, suspicion, intuition, inkling, hunch, portent, bad omen

## forecast NOUN
*The figures were based on an inaccurate forecast and had to be revised.*
▶ prediction, prophecy, projection, prognosis, calculation, outlook, expectation, prognostication

## forecast VERB
*We forecast increased rain levels over the coming months.*
▶ predict, foretell, foresee, prophesy, expect, anticipate, reckon on

## foreign ADJECTIVE
**1** *I like travelling to foreign countries.*
▶ overseas, distant, remote, exotic, faraway, far-flung
**2** *the Company's foreign branches*
▶ overseas, international, external
AN OPPOSITE IS domestic
**3** *Jealousy is foreign to her nature.*
▶ unknown, familiar, alien, strange
AN OPPOSITE IS natural

## foreigner NOUN
*Many foreigners come to live in this city.*
▶ overseas visitor, visitor, immigrant, alien, outsider, newcomer, stranger
AN OPPOSITE IS native

## foreman NOUN
*He asked the foreman what to do next.*
▶ supervisor, manager, overseer, superintendent, team leader

## foremost ADJECTIVE
*the foremost musicians of the day*
▶ leading, principal, chief, main, greatest, supreme, primary

## foresee VERB
*We could never have foreseen what would happen.*
▶ forecast, anticipate, predict, foretell, expect, envisage, prophesy

## foresight NOUN
*She had the foresight to write a will.*
▶ forethought, prudence, perspicacity, farsightedness, prescience, vision, circumspection, preparedness
AN OPPOSITE IS improvidence

## forestall VERB
*The Government will try to forestall criticism by conceding some of the objections.*
▶ prevent, pre-empt, anticipate, stave off, fend off, thwart, frustrate

## foretell VERB
*We could not foretell what might happen.*
► predict, forecast, foresee, anticipate, prophesy, forewarn

## forever ADVERB
*They are forever complaining.*
► constantly, continually, always, perpetually, incessantly, endlessly, ceaselessly

## forfeit NOUN
*You are liable to a forfeit if you disobey.*
► penalty, fine, charge, damages

## forfeit VERB
*The original owner can forfeit his right to claim back his property.*
► lose, relinquish, surrender, sacrifice, forgo, renounce, give up

## forge NOUN
*a blacksmith's forge*
► smithy, workshop, furnace

## forge VERB
1 *The smithy forged swords and knives for the army.*
► work, cast, make, mould, shape, hammer out, beat into shape
2 *He would have a go at forging the signature.*
► fake, falsify, counterfeit, imitate, copy, reproduce
3 *He had been highly successful in forging a strong team.*
► build, create, develop, establish, set up
**forge ahead** *The Persians forged ahead through Thrace.*
► advance, make progress

## forgery NOUN
*He thinks they sold him a forgery.*
► fake, copy, imitation, reproduction, replica, duplicate, hoax, sham, simulation, (*more informal*) phoney

## forget VERB
1 *I forgot my passport.*
► leave behind, overlook, mislay
AN OPPOSITE IS **remember**
2 *She forgot to lock the door.*
► omit, neglect, fail
AN OPPOSITE IS **remember**
3 *This is not something we can easily forget.*
► ignore, disregard, overlook, dismiss, think no more of, stop thinking about

## forgetful ADJECTIVE
*As he grew older he became more forgetful.*
► absent-minded, inattentive, neglectful, abstracted, oblivious, vague, dreamy, lax, heedless

## forgive VERB
1 *He found it hard to forgive them.*
► excuse, pardon, exonerate, absolve, let off, spare, (*more formal*) exculpate
2 *We cannot forgive such rudeness.*
► excuse, condone, overlook, ignore, disregard

## forgiveness NOUN
*He begged their forgiveness.*
► pardon, absolution, exoneration, understanding, tolerance, mercy

## forgiving ADJECTIVE
*He seemed kind and forgiving.*
► merciful, lenient, tolerant, compassionate, understanding, clement, humane
AN OPPOSITE IS **vindictive**

## forgo VERB
*They would have to forgo their morning swim.*
► do without, go without, miss, give up, sacrifice, eschew, abandon, renounce

## fork VERB
1 *The road forks at the bottom of the hill.*
► branch, split, separate
**fork out** (*informal*) *If necessary they would just have to fork out the money.*
► pay, produce, (*informal*) cough up

## forked ADJECTIVE
*a bird with a forked tail*
► split, branched, divided, pronged, V-shaped, (*technical*) bifurcate

## forlorn ADJECTIVE
*She looked so forlorn.*
► sad, unhappy, miserable, sorrowful, dejected, wretched, disconsolate, downcast, crestfallen, pitiful

## form NOUN
1 *a form of blackmail*
► kind, type, sort, class, order, variety
2 *the human form*
► body, frame, shape, figure, build
3 *They wanted to know the correct form for these occasions.*
► etiquette, custom, protocol, usage, procedure, convention
4 *There is a form to fill in.*
► document, questionnaire, sheet
5 *Her son moved into a new form at school.*
► class, year, grade, set, group, stream
6 *The form of the landscape has hardly changed for centuries.*
► appearance, shape, formation, configuration, structure, outline, silhouette
7 *He exercised hard to get into good form.*
► condition, shape, health, fettle, fitness

## form VERB
1 *We must form a plan.*
► devise, formulate, develop, prepare, draw up, put together, work out, conceive
2 *The pots were formed from clay.*
► make, fashion, shape, model
3 *They decided to form a club.*
► set up, establish, found, launch, institute, begin
4 *Ice was forming on the windows.*
► materialize, appear, take shape, develop, emerge, grow

**formal**

5 Six players form a team.
► make up, constitute, compose, comprise

**formal** ADJECTIVE

1 a formal manner
► aloof, prim, staid, stiff, starchy, punctilious

2 a formal occasion
► solemn, official, ceremonious, conventional, dignified

3 a formal education
► prescribed, conventional, institutional

**formality** NOUN

1 He behaved towards her with greater formality.
► aloofness, remoteness, staidness, correctness, decorum, ceremony

2 formalities Certain formalities have to be observed.
► procedures, conventions, rules, customs, protocol

**formation** NOUN

the formation of a joint company
► establishment, setting up, institution, inauguration, creation, inception

**former** ADJECTIVE

1 She met her former husband in town.
► ex-, past, one-time, previous, late

2 The fields were a lake in former times.
► earlier, past, bygone, ancient

**formerly** ADVERB

The work had formerly been done by volunteers.
► previously, in the past, at one time, once, earlier, hitherto

**formidable** ADJECTIVE

We face a formidable task.
► difficult, daunting, demanding, challenging, onerous, strenuous, awesome, overwhelming

**formula** NOUN

1 a legal formula
► form of words, phrase, rubric

2 a formula for success
► recipe, prescription, blueprint, procedure, method, rule, way

**formulate** VERB

The party formulated a ten-point programme.
► form, devise, develop, prepare, draw up, put together, work out, conceive

**forsake** VERB

1 He found it hard to forsake his old ways.
► give up, renounce, abandon, relinquish, discard, set aside

2 He would not forsake his wife and family.
► abandon, desert, disown, leave behind, turn your back on

**fort** NOUN

A small garrison was left to defend the fort.
► fortress, fortification, stronghold, castle, citadel, tower

**forthcoming** ADJECTIVE

1 He would be a candidate in the forthcoming election.
► imminent, impending, approaching, coming, future, next

2 She is not always particularly forthcoming.
► communicative, talkative, expansive, informative, voluble, chatty, sociable
AN OPPOSITE IS uncommunicative

3 No reply was forthcoming.
► available, ready, on offer, at hand
AN OPPOSITE IS unavailable

**forthright** ADJECTIVE

She was forthright in her reply.
► frank, candid, direct, blunt, outspoken, plain-speaking, straightforward, unequivocal
AN OPPOSITE IS cautious

**fortify** VERB

1 The knights fortified the citadel.
► strengthen, reinforce, secure, defend, protect, garrison

2 She fortified herself with a strong drink.
► strengthen, support, sustain, invigorate, hearten, reassure, encourage, boost, cheer
OPPOSITES ARE weaken, subdue

**fortitude** NOUN

He accepted his fate with great fortitude.
► courage, bravery, resolution, determination, valour, firmness, hardihood, willpower, strong-mindedness

**fortuitous** ADJECTIVE

It was fortuitous that they arrived on the same day.
► accidental, coincidental, unintentional, chance

**fortunate** ADJECTIVE

1 He was fortunate not to be shown a red card.
► lucky, favoured

2 These events provided them with a fortunate opportunity.
► favourable, advantageous, auspicious, providential, welcome, happy, lucky

**fortune** NOUN

1 a major change of fortune
► fate, destiny, luck

2 By good fortune he was able to take up the offer.
► chance, luck, accident, providence

3 She decided she would leave her fortune to charity.
► wealth, riches, property, possessions, (more informal) pile

**fortune-teller** NOUN

He had the solemn voice of a fortune-teller.
► clairvoyant, crystal-gazer, soothsayer, palmist, prophet

**forward** ADJECTIVE

1 The animal's long rear legs enable a fast forward movement.
► onward, advancing, frontal, front, leading, progressive
AN OPPOSITE IS backward

**2** *forward planning*
► advance, future, early, prospective, forward-looking
AN OPPOSITE IS retrospective.

**3** *His manner on the phone had been a little too forward.*
► bold, brazen, barefaced, brash, audacious, daring, presumptuous, familiar, uninhibited, precocious, assertive, over-confident, cheeky, (*more informal*) fresh, (*more informal*) pushy
OPPOSITES ARE shy, diffident

**forward** VERB
**1** *Will you forward my letter?*
► send on, redirect

**2** *The goods are forwarded by air.*
► dispatch, send, transport, transmit, convey, carry

**3** *I will try to forward my plans during my visit.*
► advance, progress, develop, expedite, promote

**forwards, forward** ADVERB
*The car shot forwards.*
► ahead, in front, onwards

**foster** VERB
**1** *activities that foster good health*
► encourage, promote, cultivate, stimulate, nurture, advance, further

**2** *The couple had fostered several children.*
► bring up, rear, raise, care for, take care of, look after, nurture, parent, mother
**USAGE** You can also use *adopt*, but it has a special legal meaning.

**foul** ADJECTIVE
**1** *You can recognize the animal from its foul smell.*
► nasty, horrible, unpleasant, disgusting, revolting, repulsive, repellent, dreadful, terrible, vile
AN OPPOSITE IS pleasant

**2** *There was a foul mess on the floor.*
► dirty, filthy, unclean, nasty, mucky
AN OPPOSITE IS clean

**3** *He had committed a foul crime*
► wicked, evil, vile, contemptible, despicable, obnoxious, shameful, abhorrent, repellent, loathsome
AN OPPOSITE IS pleasant

**4** *She had been subjected to taunts and foul language.*
► obscene, indecent, coarse, vulgar, offensive, crude, lewd
AN OPPOSITE IS mild

**5** *The game was spoilt by a series of foul tackles.*
► illegal, unfair, prohibited
OPPOSITES ARE legal, fair

**6** *The weather was foul all day.*
► unpleasant, bad, vile, disagreeable, inclement
AN OPPOSITE IS fine

**7** *He apologized for having been so foul to her.*
► unkind, unfriendly, unpleasant, disagreeable, bad-tempered
OPPOSITES ARE kind, friendly

**foul** VERB
**1** *Chemical waste was fouling the water.*
► pollute, contaminate, dirty, soil, sully, stain

**2** *Silt was fouling the river mouth.*
► clog, choke, block, obstruct, stop up

**3** *The ship had fouled its own nets.*
► entangle, snarl, catch, ensnare, twist

**found** VERB
**1** *He founded the business in the 1880s.*
► establish, set up, start, create, begin, institute, inaugurate, initiate, organize, endow, fund

**2** *Democracy is founded on the principle of free speech.*
► base, build, ground, construct, erect

**foundation** NOUN
**1** *the foundation of the company in the eighteenth century*
► founding, establishment, institution, inauguration, initiation, setting up, starting, beginning

**2** *There was no foundation for the claim.*
► basis, ground, reason, justification, rationale

**3** **foundations** *The building had weak foundations*
► base, substructure, footing, underpinning, basis, bottom, cornerstone, bedrock

**4** **foundations** *the foundations of the subject*
► fundamentals, rudiments, basic principles, elements, essentials, origins

**founder** NOUN
*His grandfather had been the founder of the college.*
► originator, creator, initiator, benefactor

**founder** VERB
*The scheme foundered for lack of money.*
► fail, collapse, miscarry, come to grief, come to nothing, (*more informal*) fold

**fountain** NOUN
*The fountains are switched off in the cold months.*
► jet, spout, spray, spring, fount

**fox** VERB
*The question completely foxed them.*
► baffle, confuse, perplex, bemuse, disconcert, confound, (*more informal*) flummox, (*more informal*) floor

**fraction** NOUN
*They could only raise a fraction of the amount needed.*
► part, division, portion, percentage, section, subdivision
**USAGE** You can use *small* or *tiny* with any of these words to help with the meaning.

**fractious** ADJECTIVE
*He was feeling tired and fractious.*
► irritable, bad-tempered, peevish, disagreeable, tetchy

**fracture** NOUN
*She suffered a fracture in her leg.*
► break, crack, breakage, fissure, split, chip, cleft, gap, opening, rent, rift

**fracture** VERB
*He had fallen and fractured his skull.*
► break, crack, split, cause a fracture in, suffer a fracture in

**fragile** ADJECTIVE

**1** *She put away her fragile china.*
▶ breakable, brittle, delicate, weak, easily damaged
AN OPPOSITE IS strong

**2** *The fragile ceasefire was barely holding.*
▶ precarious, tenuous, insecure, flimsy, vulnerable, (*more informal*) dodgy

**fragment** NOUN (with the stress on *frag-*)
*Fragments of broken pottery lay around.*
▶ piece, bit, particle, chip, sliver, scrap, shiver, shred, remnant, snippet, speck, atom, crumb, part

**fragment** VERB (with the stress on *-ment*)
*The impact made the glass fragment.*
▶ break, shatter, splinter, split, disintegrate, shiver, crumble, come to pieces

**fragmentary** ADJECTIVE
*They couldn't tell much from the fragmentary information available.*
▶ scrappy, incomplete, piecemeal, partial, disconnected, disjointed, bitty
**USAGE** Be careful when you use *partial*, because it has other meanings.

**fragrance** NOUN
*The herbs gave off a gentle aromatic fragrance.*
▶ scent, smell, perfume, bouquet, aroma, balm

**fragrant** ADJECTIVE
*She went back to her own pretty and fragrant bedroom.*
▶ sweet-scented, sweet-smelling, scented, perfumed, aromatic

**frail** ADJECTIVE

**1** *The old lady was very frail since breaking her hip.*
▶ weak, infirm, feeble, puny
OPPOSITES ARE strong, robust

**2** *houses made of frail materials*
▶ flimsy, fragile, insubstantial, delicate, brittle, breakable

**3** *She clung to her frail memories.*
▶ weak, faint, dim

**frailty** NOUN

**1** *the frailty of the very old*
▶ weakness, infirmity, debility, incapacity

**2** *human frailties*
▶ weakness, failing, foible, deficiency, imperfection, susceptibility

**frame** NOUN

**1** *The vehicle has a strong lightweight frame.*
▶ framework, shell, skeleton, chassis, structure, construction, bodywork

**2** *a portrait in a gilt frame*
▶ surround, mount, mounting, border, setting, edging

**frame** VERB

**1** *The artists frame their own pictures.*
▶ mount, surround, encase, set

**2** *The lawyers will frame the proposals.*
▶ compose, formulate, draw up, plan

**framework** NOUN

**1** *The models are built round a wooden framework.*
▶ frame, shell, skeleton, structure, construction, armature

**2** *the changing framework of human life*
▶ structure, fabric, scheme, organization

**frank** ADJECTIVE
*At least he is frank about his opinions.*
▶ honest, candid, sincere, genuine, direct, open, forthright, ingenuous, straightforward, straight, truthful, unequivocal
OPPOSITES ARE insincere, disingenuous

**frantic** ADJECTIVE

**1** *Her parents were frantic about her safety.*
▶ anxious, agitated, worried, distraught, fraught, overwrought, (*more informal*) beside yourself
OPPOSITES ARE calm, composed

**2** *There are frantic attempts to locate the luggage.*
▶ hectic, feverish, frenzied, wild
AN OPPOSITE IS calm

**fraud** NOUN

**1** *He was accused of fraud.*
▶ fraudulence, swindling, cheating, sharp practice, deceit, deception

**2** *The offer turned out to be a fraud.*
▶ swindle, deception, trick, hoax, sham

**3** *They exposed him as a fraud.*
▶ impostor, charlatan, cheat, trickster, (*more informal*) phoney

**fraudulent** ADJECTIVE
*fraudulent dealings on the stock exchange*
▶ dishonest, illegal, unlawful, illicit, corrupt, criminal, bogus, (*more informal*) crooked
AN OPPOSITE IS honest

**fraught** ADJECTIVE
*By the end of the day she looked tired and fraught.*
▶ anxious, apprehensive, agitated, tense, worried, concerned, nervous, fearful, uneasy, troubled, distressed
AN OPPOSITE IS calm

**frayed** ADJECTIVE
*He wore a shirt with a frayed collar*
▶ worn, tattered, ragged, threadbare, shabby, untidy

**freak** ADJECTIVE
*The south of the country was battered by freak storms.*
▶ unusual, exceptional, abnormal, untypical, anomalous, unpredictable, extraordinary
AN OPPOSITE IS normal

**freak** NOUN

**1** *The animal is a genetically engineered freak.*
▶ oddity, aberration, abnormality, irregularity, anomaly, quirk, monster, monstrosity, mutant, malformation

**2** (*Informal*) *a weight-training freak*
▶ fanatic, devotee, enthusiast, admirer, lover, fan, addict, aficionado

**free** ADJECTIVE

**1** *Tickets to the concert are free.*
► without charge, free of charge, gratis, complimentary, gratuitous, on the house
AN OPPOSITE IS to be paid for

**2** *The people longed to be free.*
► independent, self-governing, autonomous, emancipated
OPPOSITES ARE subjugated, dependent

**3** *The wanted man is still free.*
► at liberty, on the loose, at large, unrestrained
AN OPPOSITE IS captive

**4** *We don't have much free time.*
► spare, available, idle, unused

**5** *The bathroom is free now.*
► vacant, unoccupied, empty, available, not in use
OPPOSITES ARE occupied, engaged

**6** *She is very free with her money.*
► generous, lavish, liberal, unstinting, bounteous
OPPOSITES ARE mean, tight

**7** *Are you free on Friday?*
► available, unoccupied, able to come
AN OPPOSITE IS occupied

**8** *They are free to choose.*
► able, allowed, permitted, in a position, at leisure
AN OPPOSITE IS unable

**9** *free of We are free of any commitments now.*
► relieved of, unaffected by, unencumbered by, unhindered by, lacking, without
AN OPPOSITE IS encumbered by

**10** *the free movement of people and goods*
► unrestricted, unimpeded, unobstructed, unhindered, unlimited, clear, open
AN OPPOSITE IS obstructed

**free** VERB

**1** *The new government freed all political prisoners.*
► release, liberate, set free, set at liberty, let loose, set loose, turn loose, deliver
OPPOSITES ARE confine, lock up

**2** *The jury freed all three accused.*
► acquit, clear, exonerate, absolve, discharge, pardon
AN OPPOSITE IS condemn

**3** *Firefighters managed to free the trapped victims.*
► rescue, release, extricate, remove, pull out, pull free

**4** *She struggled hard to free her hand.*
► clear, loose, extricate, disentangle, disengage, untie, untangle
AN OPPOSITE IS tangle

**freedom** NOUN

**1** *The prisoners longed for their freedom.*
► liberty, liberation, release, deliverance
OPPOSITES ARE captivity, confinement

**2** *Only a revolution would give the country its freedom.*
► independence, self-government, self-determination
AN OPPOSITE IS dependence

**3** *Parents should have the freedom to choose the education for their children.*
► ability, opportunity, chance, facility, power, licence, scope, leeway
AN OPPOSITE IS restriction

**freely** ADVERB

*He found it hard to talk freely.*
► openly, candidly, frankly, plainly, honestly

**freeze** VERB

**1** *In winter the river freezes.*
► ice over, become ice, become solid, solidify, harden

**2** *We had no fire and were beginning to freeze.*
► feel cold, go numb with cold

**3** *If you have too much fruit you can freeze it.*
► deep-freeze, dry-freeze, refrigerate, chill, preserve

**4** *a government plan to freeze prices*
► fix, peg, hold, curb, limit, keep as they are

**freezing** ADJECTIVE

*It was a freezing morning.*
► bitterly cold, frosty, raw, biting, piercing

**freight** NOUN

**1** *a mixture of passenger and freight services*
► cargo, goods, merchandise

**2** *Air freight charges are extremely high.*
► transportation, shipment, carriage, conveyance

**frenzy** NOUN

**1** *The audience was in a state of frenzy.*
► hysteria, fever, delirium, turmoil, agitation, mania, derangement

**2** *a frenzy of anger*
► fit, spasm, outburst, paroxysm, ferment

**frequent** ADJECTIVE (with the stress on *fre-*, pronounced like *free*)

**1** *An airport bus leaves at frequent intervals.*
► regular, numerous, repeated, constant, recurring, continual

**2** *Claire is a frequent visitor here.*
► habitual, constant, regular, common

**frequent** VERB (with the stress on *-quent*)

*He frequents wine bars in the town.*
► visit, patronize, haunt, attend

**fresh** ADJECTIVE

**1** *Good eating habits include fresh fruit and vegetables*
► natural, raw

**2** *The party needs new members and fresh ideas*
► new, original, innovative, novel, recent, up-to-date

**3** *The army has a batch of fresh recruits*
► young, youthful, inexperienced, callow

**4** *Next day was fresh and bright.*
► cool, crisp, refreshing, clear

**5** *She was feeling fresh after her shower.*
► refreshed, rested, restored, revived, invigorated

**6** *They walked out to a fresh wind.*
► cold, brisk, bracing, invigorating

**7** *She told him not to get fresh.*
▶ impudent, impertinent, insolent, cheeky, saucy, familiar, disrespectful, forward

**freshen** VERB
*The cool water freshened him.*
▶ refresh, invigorate, restore, revive, stimulate, fortify

**fret** VERB
*He stopped fretting about his life and the future.*
▶ worry, be anxious, agonize, concern yourself, brood, mope, be upset

**friction** NOUN
**1** *The rope is restrained by friction.*
▶ rubbing, abrasion, grip, chafing, resistance, scraping
**2** *There was some friction between the different ethnic groups.*
▶ conflict, disagreement, antagonism, discord, strife, dissension, contention, clashing, quarrelling, fighting, rivalry

**friend** NOUN
*He can stay with a friend while his parents are away.*
▶ acquaintance, companion, associate, (more informal) mate, (more informal) pal, (more informal) buddy, (more informal) chum

**friendliness** NOUN
*They liked him for his friendliness and humour.*
▶ kindness, sociability, goodwill, hospitality, warmth

**friendly** ADJECTIVE
**1** *The staff are very friendly and helpful.*
▶ pleasant, agreeable, kind, amiable, kindly, kind-hearted, well-disposed, likeable, genial, congenial, sympathetic, approachable, receptive, sociable, outgoing
**2** *Volunteers are on hand to give friendly advice. The hotel is small with a friendly atmosphere.*
▶ cordial, good-natured, sympathetic, amicable, warm, welcoming
**3** *The girls had been friendly since their childhood.*
▶ close, affectionate, intimate, familiar, (more informal) chummy, (more informal) pally, (more informal) matey

**friendship** NOUN
**1** *He thanked his colleagues for their friendship and support.*
▶ friendliness, affection, goodwill, comradeship, cordiality
OPPOSITES ARE hostility, enmity
**2** *Their friendship grew over the coming months.*
▶ relationship, affection, intimacy, closeness, love, attachment

**fright** NOUN
**1** *The blast gave everyone a fright.*
▶ scare, shock, surprise, start, turn, jolt
**2** *Amy was overcome by fright.*
▶ fear, alarm, terror, trepidation, consternation, horror, dismay, dread, panic

**frighten** VERB
*The noises outside began to frighten them.*
▶ scare, startle, alarm, terrify, shock, agitate, disturb, fluster, panic, intimidate, disconcert
AN OPPOSITE IS reassure

**frightened** ADJECTIVE
*The children were tired and frightened.*
▶ scared, afraid, alarmed, terrified, petrified, fearful, shaken, shocked, panicky

**frightening** ADJECTIVE
*a frightening experience*
▶ terrifying, alarming, fearsome, daunting, (more informal) scary

**frightful** ADJECTIVE
**1** *We had to eat frightful food.*
▶ awful, terrible, dreadful, ghastly, appalling, horrible
**2** *a scene of frightful devastation*
▶ shocking, horrible, terrible, gruesome, harrowing, hideous, grisly, horrid, macabre

**frigid** ADJECTIVE
**1** *the frigid northern climate*
▶ bitter, bitterly cold, freezing, frozen, icy, arctic
**2** *Leo glared back in frigid indignation.*
▶ stiff, stony, formal, unfeeling, austere, distant, aloof

**frill** NOUN
**1** *a skirt with deep frills*
▶ fringe, ruff, ruffle, flounce
**2** *a small hotel with no frills*
▶ extra, luxury, embellishment, extravagance

**fringe** NOUN
**1** *a fringe round the edge of a curtain*
▶ border, edging, flounce, frill, gathering, trimming, valance
**2** *on the fringe of the town*
▶ edge, outskirts, limits, periphery, perimeter, borders, margin
AN OPPOSITE IS centre

**frisk** VERB
**1** *The dogs frisked about on the grass.*
▶ leap, cavort, frolic, caper, bound, jump, play, sport, spring, bounce, gambol, skip
**2** *She was frisked by a police officer.*
▶ search, body-search, examine, inspect

**frisky** ADJECTIVE
*a frisky young calf*
▶ lively, playful, skittish, high-spirited, spirited, frolicsome, jaunty, sprightly

**fritter** VERB
*He frittered away all the money he had been given.*
▶ squander, waste, misspend, dissipate, get through

**frivolous** ADJECTIVE
*They often made frivolous comments.*
▶ flippant, facetious, trivial, trifling, silly, shallow, stupid, foolish, jocular, flighty, ridiculous, superficial, unimportant, vacuous
AN OPPOSITE IS serious

**frock** NOUN
*a red cotton frock*
▶ dress, gown, shift, robe

**frolic** VERB
*Lambs frolicked in the fields.*
▶ play, cavort, frisk, caper, leap, jump, sport, spring, bounce, gambol, skip, bound

**front** NOUN
1 *the front of the house*
▶ facade, facing, exterior
AN OPPOSITE IS back
2 *the front of a boat*
▶ prow, bow, forepart
OPPOSITES ARE back, stern
3 *the front of a car*
▶ nose, forepart
AN OPPOSITE IS rear
4 *the front of the queue*
▶ head, start, beginning, lead
OPPOSITES ARE back, end
5 *Young recruits were sent to the front.*
▶ front line, battle line, combat zone
6 *He managed to keep up a brave front.*
▶ appearance, manner, show, pose, bearing

**front** ADJECTIVE
*The front runners came into view.*
▶ first, leading, foremost, most advanced
AN OPPOSITE IS back

**frontier** NOUN
*the French-German frontier*
▶ border, boundary, borderline, dividing line, limit

**frosty** ADJECTIVE
1 *a frosty autumn morning*
▶ freezing, bitter, ice-cold, crisp
2 *I'm afraid we'll get a frosty reception.*
▶ unfriendly, unwelcoming, unsympathetic, cool, stony

**froth** NOUN
1 *Claude wiped the champagne froth from his moustache.*
▶ foam, bubbles, effervescence, head
2 *He shook his hand in the water to make a froth.*
▶ lather, suds, foam

**frown** VERB
*The woman frowned at them.*
▶ scowl, glower, glare, lour, grimace, knit your brow, look sullen, (*more informal*) give a dirty look
**frown on** *They frown on bad language.*
▶ disapprove of, view with disfavour, look askance at, object to, disfavour, dislike, discourage

**frown** NOUN
*He had a frown on his face.*
▶ scowl, glare, grimace, black look, (*more informal*) dirty look

**frozen** ADJECTIVE
1 *The lake is frozen.*
▶ iced over, ice-covered, icebound, solidified
2 *She felt frozen in the keen wind.*
▶ freezing, very cold, numbed

**frugal** ADJECTIVE
1 *a frugal meal*
▶ meagre, paltry, plain, simple
2 *They lead a frugal life.*
▶ economical, thrifty, sparing, parsimonious, abstemious

---

**fruit** NOUN
**SOME COMMON TYPES OF FRUIT**
**apples:** Blenheim orange, Bramley, Cox (Cox's orange pippin), crab apple (small and sour), Golden Delicious, Granny Smith, Gravenstein, Pearmain, pippin, Red Delicious, russet ; eating apple, cooking apple; crab apple.
**pears:** Bartlett, Comice, Conference, Jargonelle, Williams.
**citrus fruits:** clementine (tangerine), grapefruit, Jaffa (orange), kumquat, lemon, lime, mandarin (orange), navel orange (seedless), orange, ortanique (cross between orange and tangerine), pomelo, satsuma (tangerine), Seville orange (bitter, used for marmalade), tangerine, Ugli fruit.
**stone fruits:** apricot, avocado, cherry, damson, date, greengage, lychee, nectarine, olive, peach, plum.
**fleshy fruits:** banana, cantaloupe (small melon), cucumber, fig, guava, honeydew (melon), kiwi fruit, mango, mangosteen, melon, persimmon, pineapple, pomegranate, pumpkin, tomato.
**berries:** bilberry, blackcurrant, blueberry, cranberry, elderberry, gooseberry, grape, jujube, loganberry, raspberry, redcurrant, strawberry.

---

**fruitful** ADJECTIVE
1 *a fruitful crop*
▶ abundant, copious, productive, rich, prolific, fertile, plenteous, profuse
AN OPPOSITE IS unproductive
2 *Talks have proved fruitful.*
▶ successful, productive, beneficial, profitable, useful, effective, worthwhile, gainful, rewarding
AN OPPOSITE IS fruitless

## fruitless ADJECTIVE
*three days of fruitless negotiations*
▶ futile, vain, abortive, unsuccessful, unfruitful, unproductive, profitless, unavailing, pointless, useless, disappointing, unprofitable, unrewarding
AN OPPOSITE IS fruitful

## frustrate VERB
**1** *The lack of progress was clearly frustrating them.*
▶ exasperate, discourage, dispirit, irritate
OPPOSITES ARE satisfy, please
**2** *Bad weather frustrated all attempts at a rescue.*
▶ thwart, foil, defeat, forestall, inhibit, prevent

## frustrated ADJECTIVE
*He felt let down and frustrated.*
▶ disappointed, thwarted, inhibited

## frustration NOUN
*He shook his head in frustration.*
▶ exasperation, annoyance, anger, irritation, disappointment, dissatisfaction

## fudge VERB
**1** *The Government were accused of trying to fudge the issue.*
▶ evade, dodge, skirt, gloss over
**2** *The accountants won't let you fudge the figures.*
▶ falsify, fake, distort, misrepresent

## fudge NOUN
*The proposals are regarded as a bit of a fudge.*
▶ compromise, evasion, equivocation, (more informal) cop-out

## fuel NOUN
**1** *Vehicles were running out of fuel on the motorway jams.*
▶ petrol, propellant, diesel oil
**2** *The inspectors' report added fuel to the war cause.*
▶ encouragement, provocation, incentive

## fuel VERB
*The pictures fuelled rumours of an affair.*
▶ encourage, stimulate, intensify, sustain, stoke up, feed, nurture

## fugitive NOUN
*He spent three months as a fugitive and was finally captured.*
▶ escapee, runaway, escaper, deserter, renegade, refugee

## fulfil VERB
**1** *She was fulfilling her life's ambition of seeing the world.*
▶ achieve, realize, carry out, accomplish, succeed in, attain, effect, perform
**2** *They have to work twelve hours a day to fulfil their obligations.*
▶ meet, complete, implement, execute, comply with, satisfy, respond to, answer, conform to
OPPOSITES ARE fail in, neglect

## fulfilment NOUN
*The fulfilment of these plans would take time.*
▶ achievement, completion, accomplishment, execution, performance, discharge

## full ADJECTIVE
**1** *His glass was still full.*
▶ filled, loaded, topped up
AN OPPOSITE IS empty
**2** *The trains would be full on a Friday afternoon.*
▶ crowded, packed, crammed, congested, thronged, teeming, swarming, stuffed, mobbed, (more informal) jam-packed
AN OPPOSITE IS empty
**3** *By the end of the meal they were too full to talk.*
▶ well fed, satisfied, satiated, replete, sated, (more informal) bursting
**4** *The bureau can give you a full list of local hotels and guest houses.*
▶ complete, comprehensive, exhaustive, thorough, copious
**5** *The article did not tell the full story.*
▶ entire, complete, total, unabridged, unexpurgated
**6** *She had led a full life and was looking forward to a period of quiet.*
▶ exciting, eventful, interesting, busy, lively, hectic
**7** *The new piano had a full sound.*
▶ rich, resonant, sonorous, full-bodied, deep

## fully ADVERB
*We fully accept that there must be changes. I don't think you fully understand.*
▶ completely, entirely, wholly, totally, thoroughly, quite, altogether, positively, without reserve
AN OPPOSITE IS partially

## fumble VERB
**1** *He fumbled for his wallet.*
▶ grope, feel about, fish, delve
**2** *Without any light he could only fumble about.*
▶ stumble, blunder, flounder, lurch, stagger, totter
**3** *Then, unfortunately, the keeper fumbled the ball.*
▶ mishandle, miss, drop, fail to catch, fail to keep

## fumes PLURAL NOUN
*fumes from an old tractor*
▶ exhaust, smoke, gases, vapour, fog, pollution, smog

## fuming ADJECTIVE
*Dad was pacing back and forth, fuming.*
▶ angry, furious, enraged, seething, raging, incensed

## fun NOUN
*After their exams they just wanted some fun.*
▶ enjoyment, entertainment, amusement, recreation, diversion, distraction, relaxation, jollity, play

## function NOUN
**1** *The organization has several functions.*
▶ role, responsibility, obligation, purpose, concern, use, job, task
**2** *I had seen him at an official function*
▶ event, occasion, party, gathering, reception, dinner, (more informal) do

a
b
c
d
e
f
g
h
i
j
k
l
m
n
o
p
q
r
s
t
u
v
w
x
y
z

## function VERB

**1** *To stop the machine functioning, switch it off.*
▶ work, operate, run, perform

**2 function as** *The office also functions as an advice centre.*
▶ act as, serve as, operate as, constitute, form, have the role of

## functional ADJECTIVE

**1** *an ugly functional building*
▶ practical, utilitarian, serviceable, useful
OPPOSITES ARE impractical, decorative

**2** *The drinks machine is not yet functional.*
▶ working, operational, operative, in working order
OPPOSITES ARE inoperative, out of order

## fund NOUN

**1** *an emergency fund for refugees*
▶ pool, kitty, store, reserve, cache, source, supply

**2** *Funds are running low.*
▶ money, cash, capital, finances, assets, reserves, savings

## fund VERB

*Private capital will help fund the railways.*
▶ pay for, finance, capitalize, sponsor, subsidize, back, endow, maintain

## fundamental ADJECTIVE

*fundamental political principles*
▶ basic, elementary, essential, primary, underlying, axiomatic, key, prime, principal, important, main, necessary
OPPOSITES ARE secondary, inessential

## funeral NOUN

*I attended his funeral last week.*
▶ burial, interment, cremation, committal, laying to rest, obsequies, wake

## funnel NOUN

*Smoke poured from the funnel.*
▶ chimney, flue, vent, shaft

## funny ADJECTIVE

**1** *a funny story*
▶ amusing, humorous, comic, comical, witty, hilarious, facetious, droll, entertaining, silly, absurd, ridiculous
AN OPPOSITE IS serious

**2** *a funny coincidence*
▶ peculiar, strange, odd, curious, puzzling, queer, weird, bizarre

## furious ADJECTIVE

*She was furious when she found out.*
▶ angry, enraged, infuriated, incensed, fuming, annoyed, cross, displeased, irritated, irate, indignant, outraged
OPPOSITES ARE pleased, calm

## furnish VERB

*They have furnished the rooms tastefully.*
▶ decorate, appoint, fit out, fit up, equip

## furniture NOUN

*After the fire they had to buy new furniture.*
▶ furnishings, fitments, fittings, effects, household goods, equipment, movables, possessions

## furrow NOUN

*a potato field with deep furrows*
▶ channel, trench, groove, rut, ditch

## furrow VERB

*He furrowed his brow.*
▶ crease, wrinkle, crinkle, pucker, knit, screw up

## furry ADJECTIVE

*All her furry little pets had died.*
▶ fleecy, woolly, fuzzy, hairy, downy, feathery

## further ADJECTIVE

*We need further information*
▶ more, additional, extra, fresh, new, supplementary

## further VERB

*She wants to further her career in business.*
▶ advance, promote, foster, forward, develop, boost, assist, expedite, accelerate

## furtive ADJECTIVE

*They cast furtive glances round the room.*
▶ secret, secretive, surreptitious, covert, stealthy, shifty, sly, concealed, disguised, hidden, conspiratorial, underhand, (*more informal*) sneaky
AN OPPOSITE IS open

## fury NOUN

**1** *She could not hide her fury.*
▶ anger, rage, wrath, passion

**2** *The storm hit the town with immense fury.*
▶ force, ferocity, fierceness, violence, turbulence, severity, savagery

## fuse VERB

*The programme fuses news information with comment.*
▶ blend, combine, merge, join, amalgamate, compound, unite, meld, weld

## fuss NOUN

**1** *There was a lot of fuss about the missing money.*
▶ commotion, agitation, excitement, confusion, upset, worry

**2** *He wanted to get the job done with as little fuss as possible.*
▶ bother, trouble, difficulty, inconvenience, effort, (*more informal*) hassle

## fuss VERB

*He begged her not to fuss.*
▶ fret, worry, get worked up, agitate, bother, complain, (*more informal*) flap, (*more informal*) create

## fussy ADJECTIVE

**1** *They are both fussy about their food.*
▶ finicky, fastidious, particular, choosy, (*more informal*) picky

**2** *The menu is a little fussy and over-rich.*
▶ fancy, elaborate, ornate, florid, detailed

**futile** ADJECTIVE

*In the end the rebels abandoned the futile struggle.*
► fruitless, pointless, vain, ineffectual, unsuccessful, useless, abortive, unavailing, unproductive, barren
AN OPPOSITE IS fruitful

**futility** NOUN

*She shook her head, aware of the futility of trying to explain herself.*
► pointlessness, uselessness, ineffectiveness, unproductiveness, absurdity, aimlessness, emptiness, hollowness, vanity, wasted effort
OPPOSITES ARE usefulness, effectiveness

**future** NOUN

**1** *There is a bright future for them.*
► outlook, prospects, expectations, destiny
**2** *our plans for the future*
► time to come, time ahead
AN OPPOSITE IS past

**future** ADJECTIVE

*Future generations may find themselves living on a warmer planet.*
► later, following, coming, succeeding, subsequent, prospective, approaching, forthcoming, impending
AN OPPOSITE IS past

**fuzzy** ADJECTIVE

**1** *The baby had a large fuzzy head.*
► downy, frizzy, fluffy, woolly, fleecy, velvety, feathery
**2** *good sound but a fuzzy picture*
► blurred, bleary, unfocused, ill-defined, indistinct, vague, hazy, shadowy, unclear, cloudy, dim, faint, misty
OPPOSITES ARE clear, sharp

# Gg

**gadget** NOUN

*a kitchen full of gadgets*
► tool, utensil, appliance, contraption, contrivance, device, implement, machine, invention, instrument

**gaffe** NOUN

*Anne was taking a day off trying to forget her gaffe.*
► mistake, blunder, error, slip, indiscretion

**gag** NOUN

*His latest gag was quite funny for a change.*
► joke, jest, quip, funny remark, witticism, wisecrack

**gag** VERB

**1** *The food had a strange taste that made her gag.*
► retch, choke, heave
**2** *The regime found effective ways of gagging the press.*
► silence, muzzle, stifle, keep quiet, suppress, smother, restrain, prevent from speaking

**gaiety** NOUN

**1** *There was gaiety in her voice.*
► cheerfulness, cheer, joy, happiness, merriment, jollity, delight
**2** *They headed for the gaiety of a London bar.*
► festivity, fun, celebration, revelry, jollification

**gaily** ADVERB

**1** *She waved gaily back.*
► merrily, cheerfully, cheerily, happily, joyfully, blithely
OPPOSITES ARE sadly, drearily
**2** *She wore a gaily coloured sari.*
► brightly, brilliantly, flamboyantly
AN OPPOSITE IS drably
**3** *There was Ben, gaily waving the traffic past.*
► casually, nonchalantly, heedlessly, airily, breezily, lightly, unthinkingly, uncaringly
AN OPPOSITE IS anxiously

**gain** NOUN

**1** *We are all motivated by the prospect of financial gain. There was no personal gain in it for me.*
► profit, earnings, income, advantage, benefit, return, reward, proceeds, yield, acquisition, asset, attainment, dividend, increase, winnings
AN OPPOSITE IS loss
**2** gain or gains *Labour made modest gains in the local elections in the spring.*
► advances, progress, advancement, headway

**gain** VERB

**1** *She gained a huge income from her investments.*
► earn, gross, clear, bring in, obtain, acquire, procure
**2** *They gained a wide reputation from the publicity.*
► earn, achieve, acquire, win, secure
**3** *Trevor raised his head to gain a better view.*
► get, achieve, attain
**4** *The car began to gain speed.*
► increase, gather, pick up
**USAGE** You can also say *the car began to accelerate.*
**5** gain on *We were gaining on the vehicle in front.*
► catch up with, draw nearer to, narrow the gap between, creep up on, approach

**gala** NOUN

*the annual summer gala*
► festival, carnival, jamboree, fete, fair, fiesta, celebration, revelry, party

**gale** NOUN

**1** *Rain and gales are frequent.*
► storm, squall, high wind, hurricane
**2** *She collapsed in gales of laughter.*
► outburst, burst, eruption, paroxysm, fit, peal, howl, hoot, roar

**gallant** ADJECTIVE

**1** *a gallant band of soldiers*
► brave, courageous, valiant, daring, fearless, intrepid, heroic, doughty, noble, manly
AN OPPOSITE IS cowardly

a b c d e **f** **g** h i j k l m n o p q r s t u v w x y z

## gallery

2 *A gallant gentleman at the next table came over to help her.*
▶ courteous, chivalrous, respectful, considerate, obliging, gracious
OPPOSITES ARE discourteous, rude

## gallery NOUN

1 *She walked to the end of the gallery and through a door at the end.*
▶ passage, passageway, corridor
2 *They had seats up in the gallery.*
▶ balcony, circle, upper circle, (*more informal*) gods

## gallop VERB

*A horse galloped past.*
▶ race, run, canter, rush, dash, speed, sprint

## galvanize VERB

*Seeing her in this state galvanized him into action.*
▶ jolt, shock, spur, prod, urge, stimulate

## gambit NOUN

*It was a daring gambit and might just work.*
▶ plan, stratagem, tactic, ruse, move, manoeuvre, trick

## gamble VERB

1 *He drinks and gambles and chases women.*
▶ bet, game, risk money, wager, (*more informal*) have a flutter
2 *We gambled and were lucky.*
▶ take a risk, take a chance, try your luck, speculate, venture

---

## game NOUN

1 *The children were playing a new game.*
▶ pastime, diversion, amusement, entertainment, sport, activity
2 *I know how to deal with his little game.*
▶ scheme, trick, plot, plan, dodge
3 *It was the big game on Saturday.*
▶ match, contest, tournament, competition, event, meeting
4 *They were just playing a game on us.*
▶ joke, trick, prank, hoax

**NAMES FOR TYPES OF GAME**

**board games:** chess, draughts, ludo, Monopoly, Scrabble; backgammon.

**card games:** beggar-my-neighbour, blackjack or pontoon or vingt-et-un, bridge, bezique, canasta, cribbage, faro, old maid, patience (for one player), piquet, poker, rummy, snap, whist.

**other indoor games:** billiards, snooker, pool; cards, solitaire; darts; dominoes; dice; lotto, bingo; marbles, tiddlywinks; table tennis, (*informal*)ping-pong); bagatelle; charades, eye spy, consequences, hide-and-seek, pass the parcel; computer games.

**outdoor games:** roller skating, rollerblading, skateboarding; skating, sledging; hopscotch, leapfrog; conkers.

---

## game ADJECTIVE

1 *She was always game for anything.*
▶ willing, ready, eager, keen, prepared, in the mood
2 *You will need to be game to take on this job.*
▶ brave, daring, bold, courageous, plucky, intrepid

## gang NOUN

1 *a gang of teenagers*
▶ band, group, crowd, pack, mob
2 *a gang working on the road*
▶ team, squad, troop, shift, detachment, working party
3 *I was never a part of his gang.*
▶ circle, set, group, ring, clan, clique

## gang VERB

**gang together** or **up** *They always gang up to get their way.*
▶ combine, conspire, cooperate, work together, team up

## gangster NOUN

*a mob of armed gangsters*
▶ hoodlum, bandit, robber, mobster, brigand, criminal, crook, desperado, gunman, thug

## gaol NOUN, VERB, SEE **jail**

## gap NOUN

1 *a gap in a wall*
▶ opening, breach, break, chink, space, hole, cleft, crack, cranny, crevice, rift, void
2 *a gap in the fighting*
▶ pause, break, interruption, lull, intermission, interval
3 *the gap between rich and poor*
▶ divide, gulf, rift, chasm, disparity, imbalance

## gape VERB

*He gaped at her in surprise.*
▶ stare, gaze, goggle, (*more informal*) gawk, (*more informal*) gawp

## garage NOUN

1 *The house had a large garage, which the new owner turned into a study.*
▶ car-port
2 *She had stopped to fill up the tank at a local garage.*
▶ filling-station, petrol station, service station

## garbled ADJECTIVE

*The story seems garbled and may be nonsense.*
▶ confused, muddled, mixed up, twisted, jumbled, scrambled
AN OPPOSITE IS clear

## garden NOUN

1 *a house with a garden*
▶ plot, allotment, patch, yard
2 **gardens** *a walk through the gardens*
▶ grounds, park
RELATED ADJECTIVE horticultural
RELATED NOUN horticulture

## garland NOUN

*a garland of flowers*
► wreath, chain, festoon, circle, loop, ring

## garment NOUN

*These fabrics are ideal for children's garments.*
► piece of clothing, item of clothing, costume, outfit, habit, robe

## garnish VERB

*Garnish the fish with cucumber.*
► decorate, adorn, trim, embellish, enhance

## garrison NOUN

**1** *A small garrison defended the town.*
► force, unit, platoon, contingent, detachment
**2** *An enemy force surrounded the garrison.*
► stronghold, fortress, fort, fortification, barracks, post, camp, citadel

## gash NOUN

*Blood was pouring from a gash on his head.*
► cut, slash, wound, injury, slit, laceration, abrasion

## gash VERB

*Frank gashed his hand on a broken glass.*
► cut, slash, lacerate, wound, injure, gouge

## gasp VERB

*She gasped and sat back, her face pale.*
► catch your breath, pant, choke, gulp, blow

## gasp NOUN

*The boy fell back with a gasp.*
► pant, heave, wheeze, puff, blow

## gasping ADJECTIVE

*The effort left them gasping.*
► breathless, exhausted, tired out, puffed

## gate NOUN

*Some children came through the gate.*
► gateway, doorway, door, entrance, entry, exit, (*poetic*) portal

## gather VERB

**1** *A crowd gathered near the entrance.*
► assemble, collect, come together, congregate, crowd round, convene, converge, flock, group, muster
AN OPPOSITE IS disperse
**2** *She spent some time gathering her books.*
► collect, assemble, accumulate, bring together, heap up
**3** *They went into the garden to gather flowers and berries.*
► pick, pluck, garner, harvest
**4** *I gather you have been unwell.*
► understand, believe, be told, be given to understand, learn, hear, be informed, deduce, infer, surmise
**5** *You can gather the dress at the waist.*
► pleat, fold, crimp, ruffle, pucker

## gathering NOUN

*a gathering of families*
► assembly, meeting, company, group , mass, party, function, social, (*informal*) get-together

## gauche ADJECTIVE

*a gauche young man with a slight stammer*
► awkward, ungainly, gawky, inelegant, graceless
OPPOSITES ARE elegant, sophisticated

## gaudy ADJECTIVE

*She wore dull clothes, nothing gaudy.*
► garish, lurid, flashy, loud, glaring, vulgar
OPPOSITES ARE sober, dull

## gauge NOUN

**1** *He checked the pressure gauge.*
► meter, instrument, dial, reading
**2** *The track was the wrong gauge for the new rolling stock.*
► size, width, measure, standard
**3** *The local elections will be seen as a gauge of public opinion.*
► measure, indicator, test, guide (to), touchstone, benchmark

## gauge VERB

**1** *A special scoring table will gauge which competitor does best.*
► assess, evaluate, appraise, calculate, reckon
**2** *Instruments can gauge the distance precisely.*
► measure, calculate, compute, quantify, determine

## gaunt ADJECTIVE

*His arms were wrapped round his gaunt body.*
► haggard, drawn, lank, emaciated, wasted, skinny, scrawny, shrivelled, skeletal, cadaverous

## gawky ADJECTIVE

*She had been a thin, gawky adolescent*
► awkward, ungainly, inelegant, ungraceful, graceless, gangling, gauche, inept, lumbering, bumbling, maladroit, uncoordinated
AN OPPOSITE IS graceful

## gay ADJECTIVE

**1** *a club for gay people*
► homosexual, (*female*) lesbian, (*more informal*) queer
**2** *He was so gay and lively.*
► cheerful, happy, carefree, lively, merry, jolly, jovial, glad

## gaze VERB

*He continued to gaze out of the window.*
► stare, look, gape

## gear NOUN

(*informal*) *You can put your gear in here.*
► equipment, paraphernalia, belongings, possessions, stuff, things, tackle

**gem** NOUN

1 *a tiara made of gems and pearls*
▶ jewel, precious stone, gemstone
2 *The anthology contains some real gems.*
▶ pearl, wonder, treasure, masterpiece, outstanding example

SOME COMMON TYPES OF GEM AND GEMSTONES

agate, alexandrine, almandine, amber, amethyst, aquamarine, beryl, bloodstone, cairngorm, carbuncle, carnelian, cat's-eye, chalcedony, chrysolite, chrysoprase, corundum, diamond, emerald, garnet, girasol, greenstone, jacinth, jade, jasper, lapis lazuli, marcasite, moonstone, morganite, moss agate, onyx, opal, rhodolite, rose quartz, ruby, sapphire, sardonyx, sunstone, tanzanite, topaz, tourmaline, turquoise, zircon.

**general** ADJECTIVE

1 *The idea is sound in general terms*
▶ broad, rough, sweeping, vague, loose, indefinite
AN OPPOSITE IS specific
2 *This model is more suitable for general use.*
▶ widespread, universal, popular, regular, typical, normal, ordinary, everyday, conventional
OPPOSITES ARE specialist, restricted
3 *a general pay increase*
▶ comprehensive, inclusive, overall, universal

**generally** ADVERB

*It is generally a mistake to ignore these factors.*
▶ normally, as a rule, by and large, on the whole, broadly, mainly, mostly, in the main, predominantly, usually

**generate** VERB

*a move to generate more business*
▶ create, produce, bring about, make, cause, give rise to, propagate, engender, beget, breed, (*more informal*) whip up

**generation** NOUN

1 *people of an earlier generation*
▶ age, age group
2 *the generation of new jobs*
▶ creation, production, origination, initiation, genesis

**generosity** NOUN

*Thanks to the generosity of sponsors the games can continue.*
▶ kindness, munificence, liberality, philanthropy, benevolence, bounty, charity, largess

**generous** ADJECTIVE

1 *a person of a good and generous nature*
▶ kind, kind-hearted, magnanimous, benevolent, unselfish, charitable, big-hearted, beneficent, philanthropic

2 *She was always generous on the children's birthdays.*
▶ bountiful, liberal, lavish, munificent, indulgent, bounteous
3 *a generous helping of pudding*
▶ large, lavish, ample, copious, plentiful, abundant

**genial** ADJECTIVE

*The guests were welcomed by their genial host.*
▶ friendly, affable, cordial, congenial, kindly, pleasant, cheerful, good-natured, companionable, hospitable, jolly, warm-hearted, easygoing
AN OPPOSITE IS unfriendly

**genius** NOUN

1 *They have a genius for getting attention.*
▶ talent, gift, flair, aptitude, bent, intellect, knack
2 *It doesn't take a genius to work out his little game.*
▶ mastermind, great thinker, great brain, prodigy, past master, expert, intellectual

**gentle** ADJECTIVE

1 *The mild, gentle face looked back at him.*
▶ kind, kindly, tender, sympathetic, compassionate, warm-hearted, soft-hearted, placid, calm
OPPOSITES ARE unkind, harsh
2 *A gentle breeze was blowing.*
▶ light, faint, soft
OPPOSITES ARE strong, fierce
3 *There was a gentle slope up to the house.*
▶ gradual, slight, easy
AN OPPOSITE IS steep

**genuine** ADJECTIVE

1 *A genuine Picasso hung on the wall.*
▶ authentic, original, bona fide, actual, real, true, authenticated
AN OPPOSITE IS fake
2 *She's a very genuine person.*
▶ sincere, honest, unaffected, frank, truthful, devout, candid, earnest, true
AN OPPOSITE IS insincere

**germ** NOUN

1 *the germ of a great idea*
▶ beginning, nucleus, seed, start, genesis, embryo, cause, origin
2 *a cleaner that also kills germs*
▶ microbe, micro-organism, bacterium, (*more informal*) bug, virus

**gesture** NOUN

1 *She sent them away with an irritable gesture of her hand.*
▶ signal, sign, motion, movement, flourish, gesticulation
2 *a gesture of goodwill*
▶ act, action, indication, deed

**gesture** VERB

*He gestured for them to leave.*
▶ signal, motion, gesticulate, make a gesture, sign

**get** VERB This word is often overused. Here are some alternatives:

**1** *She got her degree at St Andrews.*
► obtain, receive, acquire, come by, achieve, procure

**2** *It's getting cold.*
► become, turn, grow

**3** *We'll get there soon.*
► arrive, reach, come to

**4** *Will you get my book?*
► fetch, bring, collect, pick up

**5** *I got a cold.*
► catch, come down with, develop

**6** *I'll get her to come tomorrow.*
► persuade, urge, induce, make

**get across** *It's hard to get the idea across.*
► communicate, convey, impart, transmit

**get ahead** *people who want to get ahead*
► succeed, prosper, flourish, get on well

**get along**
**1** *They do seem to get along with each other.*
► agree, see eye to eye, be friendly, be compatible
**2** *We are getting along quite well now.*
► manage, cope, get on, make out, progress, advance

**get at** *What are you getting at?*
► suggest, imply, intend, insinuate, mean

**get away** *Tom and Fiona wanted to get away for the weekend*
► escape, leave, (*more informal*) make off

**get back** *We won't get our money back.*
► recover, recoup, regain, retrieve

**get by** *We have enough money to get by.*
► survive, manage, cope, make do, muddle along, muddle through

**get down** *All the talk of war got them down.*
► depress, deject, dishearten, dispirit, sadden

**get in** *The train gets in at 7 o'clock.*
► arrive, come

**get on**
**1** *We'd better get on the bus.*
► board, embark, mount, ascend
**2** *How did they get on during their holiday?*
► cope, manage, fare, get along, make out

**get out** *Some of the prisoners had got out.*
► escape, break out, break free, get away, flee

**get over**
**1** *She's just got over flu.*
► recover from, shake off, survive
**2** *difficulties that we can never get over*
► overcome, surmount, deal with

**get round**
**1** *a problem they tried to get round*
► avoid, evade, overcome, get the better of
**2** *He always got round his mother when he needed something.*
► persuade, cajole, prevail on, win over, beguile

**get together** *Let's get together next week.*
► meet, meet up, see one another ►►

**get up**
**1** *She got up from her chair.*
► rise, stand, stand up
**2** *They would have to get up early to leave for the airport.*
► rise, get out of bed

**getaway** NOUN
*a quick getaway*
► escape, breakout, breakaway

**ghastly** ADJECTIVE
**1** *a ghastly murder*
► terrible, frightful, horrible, horrific, horrifying, gruesome
**2** *a ghastly time*
► unpleasant, disagreeable, nasty, horrid, revolting
AN OPPOSITE IS lovely

**ghost** NOUN
**1** *They say there's a ghost in the house.*
► phantom, spectre, spirit, wraith, vision
**2** *a ghost of a smile*
► trace, hint, suggestion, glimmer, semblance, shadow

**ghostly** ADJECTIVE
*The ghostly figure seemed to belong to a dream.*
► unearthly, spectral, eerie, phantom, uncanny, weird, supernatural, (*informal*) spooky, (*informal*) creepy, (*informal*) scary

**giant** NOUN
*A giant of a man stood in the doorway.*
► monster, colossus, titan, Goliath, ogre
AN OPPOSITE IS dwarf

**giant** ADJECTIVE
*The thrust from the four giant engines pushed him back in his seat.*
► huge, enormous, gigantic, colossal, immense, massive, mighty, vast, large, elephantine, gargantuan, mammoth, monstrous, prodigious, titanic, (*more informal*) whopping, (*more informal*) jumbo, (*more informal*) king-size
OPPOSITES ARE tiny, miniature

**gibberish** NOUN
*He kept up a stream of gibberish.*
► nonsense, rubbish, balderdash, (*more informal*) drivel, (*more informal*) gobbledegook, (*more informal*) hogwash

**gibe** VERB, SEE **jibe**

**giddy** ADJECTIVE
*The heat of the sun made her giddy.*
► dizzy, faint, weak, light-headed, unsteady, wobbly, (*more informal*) woozy

**gift** NOUN
**1** *He made the library a generous gift.*
► present, donation, benefaction, contribution, largesse, handout, offering, grant, gratuity, bequest, endowment

**gifted**

2 *a gift for languages*
▶ talent, flair, aptitude, capacity, genius, knack, ability, bent, capability

**gifted** ADJECTIVE

*a gifted young musician*
▶ talented, able, accomplished, capable, skilful, skilled

**gigantic** ADJECTIVE

*a gigantic old building*
▶ huge, enormous, colossal, immense, massive, mighty, vast, large, giant, (*more informal*) whopping, (*more informal*) jumbo, (*more informal*) king-size

**giggle** VERB

*The silly hat made them giggle.*
▶ snigger, titter, chuckle, laugh

**gimmick** NOUN

*the latest publicity gimmicks*
▶ stunt, trick, device, ploy, stratagem

**gingerly** ADVERB

*They stepped gingerly into the road.*
▶ cautiously, carefully, warily, charily, hesitantly, nervously, timidly, tentatively, guardedly

**girdle** NOUN

*They wore girdles round their waists.*
▶ belt, sash, band, waistband, corset

**girl** NOUN

*a pretty little girl*
▶ lass, daughter, female child

**gist** NOUN

*The gist of the story is clear.*
▶ main idea, drift, point, meaning, essence, substance, significance, general sense, quintessence, nub, direction

**give** VERB

1 *He would give them another hundred pounds.*
▶ provide with, present with, supply with, allow, award, bestow on, donate, make over

2 *Will you give her a message?*
▶ pass on, convey, communicate, transmit, send, deliver

3 *three brothers who had given their lives in the Great War*
▶ sacrifice, lose, relinquish, devote

4 *a note giving details of Christmas opening times*
▶ show, list, provide, display

5 *The boys gave no trouble.*
▶ cause, make, create, start

6 *The right herbs will give your food a better flavour.*
▶ afford, produce, yield, lend

7 *We are going to give a party*
▶ hold, lay on, organize, arrange

8 *He saw her and gave a shout.*
▶ utter, emit, let out

9 *The roof was giving under the weight.*
▶ collapse, yield, break, fall in

10 *She would give them a warning.*
▶ issue, deliver, administer, impose on

**give away** *She tried not to give away their secret.*
▶ reveal, disclose, divulge, betray

**give in** *They had to give in after a while.*
▶ submit, surrender, capitulate, yield, succumb, comply

**give off** *The fire gave off grey fumes.*
▶ produce, emit, send out, discharge, exude, release

**give out**

1 *Please give out the books.*
▶ hand out, hand round, distribute, dole out, deal out

2 *The money gave out after four days.*
▶ run out, be used up, be exhausted, dry up

**give up** *Don't give up now.*
▶ quit, stop, concede defeat, admit defeat, resign, despair

**glad** ADJECTIVE

1 *I am glad you came.*
▶ pleased, happy, delighted, thrilled, overjoyed

2 *They were glad to help*
▶ pleased, willing, eager, keen

**glamorous** ADJECTIVE

1 *a glamorous woman*
▶ beautiful, elegant, captivating, alluring, gorgeous, smart, lovely, entrancing, stylish, fashionable

**USAGE** Be careful when you use *smart*, because it has another important meaning.

2 *a glamorous lifestyle*
▶ exciting, colourful, dazzling, glittering, alluring, smart

**glamour** NOUN

1 *She offered that extra bit of glamour.*
▶ beauty, attractiveness, elegance, style, charm, seductiveness

2 *the glamour of living in a big city*
▶ appeal, excitement, attraction, allure, glitter, lustre, magic

**glance** VERB

1 *She glanced at her watch.*
▶ look, peek, peep, take a look at

2 *glance at* or *through I only had time to glance at the article.*
▶ scan, skim, read quickly, run your eye over

**glance** NOUN

*He gave us a quick glance.*
▶ look, peek, peep, glimpse

**glare** VERB

1 *She glared at him.*
▶ stare angrily, glower, scowl, frown

2 *The lights of oncoming cars glared in the darkness.*
▶ dazzle, blaze, be blinding, flare, beam

**glare** NOUN

1 *an angry glare*
▶ stare, scowl, glower, frown, black look

## glaring

**2** *the glare of the lights*
▶ dazzle, shine, blaze, brilliance, beam, flare

**glaring** ADJECTIVE
*a glaring error*
▶ obvious, conspicuous, blatant, flagrant, patent, plain, overt, inescapable

**glaze** NOUN
*pots with a bright glaze*
▶ varnish, coating, lustre, gloss, shine

**gleam** VERB
*The brass door knob gleamed in the moonlight.*
▶ glimmer, glint, glow, shine, flash, glisten, glitter, sparkle, shimmer

**gleam** NOUN
*the gleam of lights in the distance*
▶ glimmer, glint, glow, glitter, sparkle, shimmer

**glib** ADJECTIVE
*a glib talker   an answer that was merely glib*
▶ slick, pat, smooth, facile, superficial, insincere, articulate, fluent, plausible, quick, ready
OPPOSITES ARE sincere, thoughtful

**glide** VERB
**1** *A boat glided past.*
▶ slide, move smoothly, slip, sail, coast, skim
**2** *The gulls were gliding overhead.*
▶ drift, soar, wheel, hover, sail, float, fly

**glimmer** VERB
*The moonlight glimmered on the great sweep of lawn.*
▶ gleam, glint, glow, shine, flash, glisten, glitter, sparkle, shimmer, twinkle

**glimmer** NOUN
*There was a faint glimmer in his eyes.*
▶ gleam, glint, glow, glitter, sparkle, shimmer, twinkle

**glimpse** VERB
*I glimpsed Auntie sitting on the bottom stair.*
▶ spot, spy, catch sight of, make out

**glimpse** NOUN
*I caught a quick glimpse of the house.*
▶ glance, peep, look, sight, sighting, view, (more *Informal*) squint

**glint** VERB
*Her blue eyes glinted like ice.*
▶ gleam, glow, shine, flash, glisten, glitter, sparkle, shimmer

**glint** NOUN
*a glint in the mirror*
▶ gleam, glimmer, glow, glitter, sparkle, shimmer

**gloat** VERB
*A group of lads was gloating over a rugby victory.*
▶ boast, brag, crow, triumph, exult, rejoice, show off

**global** ADJECTIVE
**1** *global communications*
▶ worldwide, international, world, intercontinental, universal

**2** *a global solution to the problem*
▶ total, comprehensive, general, all-inclusive, wide-ranging

**globe** NOUN
**1** *people from all over the globe*
▶ world, earth, planet
**2** *the shape of a globe*
▶ ball, orb, sphere, round

**gloom** NOUN
**1** *They peered out into the gloom*
▶ darkness, dimness, semi-darkness, murk, murkiness, shade, shadow, twilight, cloudiness, dullness, dusk, obscurity
**2** *Her feeling of gloom lifted.*
▶ depression, dejection, despondency, low spirits, melancholy

**gloomy** ADJECTIVE
**1** *They walked through the front door into a gloomy hall.*
▶ dark, dingy, dim, dismal, dreary, dull, shadowy, sombre, cheerless
AN OPPOSITE IS bright
**2** *a gloomy expression*
▶ miserable, downcast, downhearted, dejected, dispirited, glum, unhappy
OPPOSITES ARE cheerful, happy
**3** *a gloomy outlook for the economy*
▶ pessimistic, unfavourable, unpromising, depressing, bleak, downbeat
OPPOSITES ARE optimistic, upbeat

**glorious** ADJECTIVE
**1** *a glorious victory*
▶ magnificent, splendid, illustrious, celebrated, acclaimed, distinguished, renowned, great
**2** *a glorious view across the hills*
▶ wonderful, spectacular, magnificent, superb, beautiful, stunning

**glory** NOUN
**1** *the glory of competing for your country   successes that bring much glory*
▶ distinction, honour, renown, prestige, kudos, fame, credit, triumph, success
**2** *glory to God*
▶ adoration, homage, praise, thanksgiving, veneration, worship
**3** *the glories of New England in the autumn*
▶ beauty, magnificence, grandeur, majesty, radiance, splendour

**gloss** NOUN
*The new paint has a fine gloss.*
▶ shine, sheen, brightness, brilliance, lustre, burnish, polish

**gloss** VERB
**gloss over** *He tended to gloss over arguments that didn't fit his theories.*
▶ conceal, cover up, disguise, evade, explain away
OPPOSITES ARE highlight, emphasize

**gloss**

a b c d e f **g** h i j k l m n o p q r s t u v w x y z

**glossy** ADJECTIVE

*a glossy tile floor*
▶ bright, burnished, glassy, glazed, gleaming, lustrous, polished, reflective, shiny, silky, sleek, smooth
AN OPPOSITE IS dull

**glow** VERB

1 *Lights glowed from the windows.*
▶ shine, gleam, glimmer, flicker, flare
2 *She glowed with pleasure at having said the right thing.*
▶ shine, flush, blush, colour, redden

**glow** NOUN

1 *the glow of the street lights*
▶ shine, gleam, glimmer, radiance, luminosity, brilliance
2 *There was a distinct glow in her cheeks.*
▶ flush, blush, rosiness, pinkness, warmth
3 *We felt a glow of excitement.*
▶ ardour, fervour, enthusiasm, feeling, intensity, passion

**glower** VERB

*Harry glowered at him from the table.*
▶ scowl, glare, stare angrily, frown, lour

**glowing** ADJECTIVE

1 *glowing street lights*
▶ bright, shining, luminous, radiant
2 *glowing cheeks*
▶ bright, rosy, red, pink, blushing, flushed
3 *a glowing report*
▶ complimentary, enthusiastic, highly favourable, fervent, admiring, eulogistic, ecstatic

**glue** NOUN

*a tube of glue*
▶ adhesive, paste, gum, fixative, sealant, cement

**glue** VERB

*Glue the pieces together.*
▶ fix, stick, fasten, affix, paste, cement, bond, gum, seal

**glum** ADJECTIVE

*Tony looked glum.*
▶ miserable, downcast, downhearted, dejected, dispirited, gloomy, unhappy
OPPOSITES ARE cheerful, happy

**glut** NOUN

*a glut of fresh fruit*
▶ surplus, surfeit, excess, superfluity, plenty, abundance
AN OPPOSITE IS a scarcity

**gnaw** VERB

1 *The dog was gnawing a bone.*
▶ chew, bite, nibble, munch, eat
2 **gnaw at** *Doubts continued to gnaw at her.*
▶ worry, torment, plague, niggle, distress

**go** VERB This word is often overused. Here are some alternatives:

1 *She started to go towards the entrance.*
▶ move, advance, proceed, walk, make your way, progress
2 *We are going to London on Friday.*
▶ travel, journey, make a trip
3 *Several of the guests had already gone.*
▶ leave, depart, go away, withdraw, make off, (more informal) clear off
4 *My purse had gone.*
▶ disappear, vanish, be taken, be stolen
5 *The path goes to the village.*
▶ lead, take you, continue, extend, stretch
6 *All the money goes to charity.*
▶ be given, be donated, be granted, be presented
7 *All our money has gone.*
▶ be used up, be spent, be exhausted
8 *His hair had gone grey.*
▶ turn, become, grow
9 *I hope things go well for them.*
▶ work out, turn out, develop
10 *The coat and hat don't go.*
▶ match, harmonize, blend, suit one another
11 *The car won't go.*
▶ start, work, function, operate, run
12 *Where do these books go?*
▶ belong, be placed, be kept, have a place
13 *Has the bell gone?*
▶ sound, ring, chime, peal
14 *The time will go quickly.*
▶ pass, go by, elapse, lapse

**go ahead** *The plan will go ahead*
▶ begin, proceed, continue, take place
**go away** *She wanted them all to go away.*
▶ leave, depart, (more informal) clear off
**go back** *I'll have to go back and look for it.*
▶ return, turn round
**go down** *Prices are expected to go down.*
▶ fall, drop, decrease, get lower
**go for**
1 *Which one will you go for?*
▶ choose, take, favour, prefer
2 *He went for her with a hammer.*
▶ attack, assault, set at, lunge at
**go in for** *We are going in for a competition.*
▶ enter, take part in, participate in
**go into** *The lawyers will go into it in detail.*
▶ discuss, consider, think about, investigate, probe, delve into, review
**go off**
1 *A bomb went off.*
▶ explode, detonate, blow up
2 *The milk's gone off.*
▶ go bad, go sour, turn

▶▶

### go on
**1** *The programme went on for over two hours.*
► continue, extend, carry on, run
**2** *She went on about how lucky we were.*
► chatter, witter, ramble, (*more informal*) rabbit

### go over
*Shall we go over the figures?*
► study, check, review, examine, analyse, scrutinize, investigate

### go through
*It's hard to comprehend what they must have gone through.*
► suffer, experience, undergo, endure, withstand

### go with
**1** *Will you go with them?*
► accompany, escort
**2** *I'm not sure this tie goes with my shirt.*
► match, suit, harmonize with, blend with

---

### goad VERB
*The latest unemployment figures might goad the minister to take action.*
► provoke, stimulate, spur, move, rouse, urge, motivate, encourage

### go-ahead NOUN
*The plan will be given the go-ahead next week.*
► approval, permission, authorization, clearance, consent, assent, agreement

### goal NOUN
*The overall goal is to promote the use of good English.*
► aim, objective, object, ambition, intention, purpose, target, aspiration, design, end

### gobble VERB
*He stopped talking to gobble his food.*
► guzzle, devour, bolt, gulp, eat

### god, goddess NOUN
*the gods and goddesses of ancient Olympus*
► deity, divinity, divine being, immortal
RELATED ADJECTIVE divine

### godsend NOUN
*A cut in interest rates would be a godsend to homeowners.*
► blessing, boon, miracle, stroke of good luck, windfall

### golden ADJECTIVE
**1** *a golden carriage*
► gilt, gilded
**2** *golden hair*
► blond, blonde, yellow
**3** *a golden opportunity*
► excellent, unique, special, promising, auspicious, propitious

---

### good ADJECTIVE
This word is often overused. Here are some alternatives:

**1** *She is basically a good person.*
► virtuous, exemplary, righteous, moral, honest, upright, worthy, trustworthy
OPPOSITES ARE bad, wicked, immoral

**2** *Can you recommend a good hotel?*
► fine, high-quality, satisfactory, acceptable, excellent, superb, outstanding
AN OPPOSITE IS poor

**3** *The children were exceptionally good all evening.*
► well-behaved, obedient, well-mannered
AN OPPOSITE IS naughty

**4** *That would be a good thing to do.*
► proper, right, correct, appropriate, auspicious
AN OPPOSITE IS inappropriate

**5** *He is not a good swimmer. She has always been good at music.*
► capable, able, proficient, accomplished, talented, skilled
OPPOSITES ARE poor, inept

**6** *She was a good friend.*
► true, loyal, close, dear, trusty, reliable, trustworthy, dependable
AN OPPOSITE IS distant

**7** *It was a good party.*
► enjoyable, pleasant, agreeable, pleasing

**8** *Tom gave the car a good clean*
► thorough, complete

**9** *a good number of people*
► considerable, substantial, appreciable, sizeable, fair, ample

**10** *It is good of you to come.*
► kind, generous, considerate, obliging
AN OPPOSITE IS unkind

**11** *When is a good time to call?*
► convenient, suitable, appropriate, opportune, fitting
OPPOSITES ARE bad, unsuitable

**12** *food that is good for you*
► healthy, wholesome, nutritious, nourishing
OPPOSITES ARE bad, unhealthy

**13** *a pub that serves good food*
► delicious, appetizing, tasty

**14** *There are several good reasons for going.*
► valid, genuine, cogent, real, convincing
AN OPPOSITE IS poor

### goodbye NOUN
*Roddy said goodbye and left us*
► farewell, (*more informal*) cheerio, (*French*) adieu, (*French*) au revoir

### good-for-nothing ADJECTIVE
*a good-for-nothing layabout*
► worthless, useless, inept, lazy, idle, (*more informal*) no-good

**good-humoured** ADJECTIVE

He was patient and good-humoured.
► genial, affable, cordial, congenial, amiable, easygoing
AN OPPOSITE IS ill- humoured

**good-looking** ADJECTIVE

a good-looking woman
► attractive, handsome, nice-looking, presentable, beautiful, pretty, lovely
AN OPPOSITE IS ugly

**good-natured** ADJECTIVE

He had a blunt good-natured face.
► kind, kindly, gentle, warm-hearted, amiable, friendly, neighbourly, benevolent
AN OPPOSITE IS ill- natured

**goodness** NOUN

There is a lot of goodness in these people, criminals though they are.
► virtue, good, uprightness, generosity, goodwill, honesty
AN OPPOSITE IS wickedness

**goods** PLURAL NOUN

1 the supply of goods and services
► merchandise, produce, products, articles, stock
2 The dead man's goods did not amount to much.
► property, possessions, effects, chattels

**good-tempered** ADJECTIVE

He remained patient and good-tempered despite the difficulties.
► calm, placid, equable, unflustered, composed, self-possessed, tranquil
AN OPPOSITE IS bad- tempered

**goodwill** NOUN

People come here full of goodwill and good intentions.
► kindness, benevolence, generosity, friendliness, consideration
OPPOSITES ARE hostility, ill- will

**gorge** NOUN

The drive is spectacular: gorges and tropical rain forests.
► ravine, gully, canyon, defile, chasm, pass, fissure

**gorge** VERB

gorge on We gorged on fresh sardines and salads from the local market.
► gobble, guzzle, wolf, devour, cram down, (more informal) tuck into, (more informal) stuff yourself with

**gorgeous** ADJECTIVE

1 a gorgeous young woman
► beautiful, lovely, glamorous, dazzling, pretty, stunning, striking
2 a gorgeous view
► magnificent, spectacular, splendid, superb, glorious

**gory** ADJECTIVE

an account of the battle with all the gory details
► grisly, gruesome, ghastly, violent, bloody, brutal, horrific, repulsive

**gossip** NOUN

1 He liked gossip and knew something about everybody.
► idle talk, tittle-tattle, tattle, prattle, rumour, hearsay, chatter, scandal

2 The sisters were both dreadful gossips.
► scandalmonger, gossipmonger, talebearer, busybody, tattler

**gossip** VERB

The landlord was busy gossiping to the other customers.
► chat, chatter, prattle, spread stories, (informal) natter, (informal) tattle

**gouge** VERB

Engineers had gouged a tunnel out of the rock.
► dig, hollow, scoop, chisel, excavate, cut

**govern** VERB

1 A coalition was formed to govern the country.
► run, rule, administer, be in charge of, conduct the affairs of, direct, manage, preside over

2 the rules that govern the way we treat each other
► regulate, determine, control, direct, affect, influence, shape

3 She tried to govern her feelings.
► control, master, restrain, curb, check, bridle, discipline, regulate, tame, keep in check, keep under control

---

**government** NOUN

1 The new government takes office next week.
► administration, executive, regime, ministry
2 a country that badly needs a period of stable government
► rule, direction, leadership, management, guidance, regulation

NAMES FOR TYPES OF GOVERNMENT

**terms ending in -cracy (from a Greek word kratia meaning 'power or rule'):** autocracy (by one ruler), bureaucracy (by state officials), democracy (by representatives elected by the people), meritocracy (by able or qualified people), plutocracy (by the rich), theocracy (by a god through priests).

**terms ending in -archy (from a Greek word arkhein meaning 'to rule'):** monarchy (by a king or queen), oligarchy (by a few powerful people).

**terms ending in -ism:** communism (with public ownership of wealth and resources), constitutionalism (according to a constitution), despotism (by a despot), fascism (by an extreme right-wing group), federalism (by a union of states running their own internal affairs), imperialism (by an empire or emperor), totalitarianism (by an oppressive ruler or rulers).

**other terms:** dictatorship (by a dictator), tyranny (by a tyrant).

---

**governor** NOUN

1 a prison governor
► administrator, director, principal, superintendent

**gown**

2 *the governor of a province*
► ruler, overseer, viceroy, commissioner, administrator

**gown** NOUN
*a beautiful silk gown*
► dress, robe, costume, frock

**grab** VERB
1 *She grabbed him by his arm.*
► seize, grasp, catch, grip, take hold of, clutch at
2 *Someone grabbed her credit card while she wasn't looking.*
► snatch, steal, take, (*more informal*) nab, (*more informal*) pinch

**grace** NOUN
1 *The dancers moved with considerable grace.*
► elegance, poise, gracefulness, refinement
2 *He conceded the point with good grace.*
► courtesy, civility, decorum, decency, charm, generosity
3 *They did not want to see another president fall from grace.*
► favour, approval, esteem, regard, support
4 *by the grace of the monarch*
► generosity, favour, benevolence, indulgence, goodwill

**graceful** ADJECTIVE
*Mary's clothes were light and graceful.*
► elegant, flowing, stylish, tasteful, smooth, beautiful

**gracious** ADJECTIVE
1 *a kind and gracious man*
► courteous, polite, civil, refined, considerate, compassionate, benevolent, generous, magnanimous, decorous
2 *a gracious building*
► elegant, handsome, graceful, opulent, grand

**grade** NOUN
1 *She is trying for a higher grade in the exam.*
► mark, score, level, grading, assessment, standard
2 *a hotel in the top grade*
► class, category, classification
3 *officers in the lower grades*
► rank, level, status, echelon, step

**grade** VERB
1 *Eggs are graded according to size.*
► sort, classify, categorize, differentiate, group, range, arrange, rank
2 *An external examiner will grade the coursework.*
► mark, assess, evaluate, rank, rate

**gradient** NOUN
*The road is on a steep gradient*
► slope, incline, rise, ascent, bank, declivity, hill

**gradual** ADJECTIVE
1 *a gradual change in the weather*
► steady, slow, moderate, progressive, continuous, regular, step-by-step
AN OPPOSITE IS sudden
2 *a gradual slope*
► gentle, moderate, slight, easy
AN OPPOSITE IS steep

**gradually** ADVERB
*The colours fade gradually in the sunlight.* *Gradually she eased the drawer back in its place.*
► slowly, little by little, steadily, gently, cautiously, progressively, imperceptibly

**grain** NOUN
1 *a good grain harvest*
► corn, cereal, seed
2 *grains of sand*
► granule, particle, speck, crumb, fragment
3 *not a grain of truth in the story*
► trace, hint, ounce, scrap
4 *wood with a strong grain*
► texture, marking, surface, pattern

**grand** ADJECTIVE
1 *a grand palace*
► magnificent, splendid, majestic, glorious, stately, imposing
2 *a grand old lady*
► distinguished, illustrious, august, eminent, prominent, celebrated
3 (*informal*) *They are doing a grand job.*
► excellent, very good, fine, splendid, first-class, first-rate

**grandeur** NOUN
*the grandeur of the royal ceremonies*
► splendour, magnificence, glory, resplendence, stateliness

**grandiose** ADJECTIVE
*a grandiose scheme*
► ambitious, bold, daring, grand, ostentatious, pretentious, showy, extravagant, flamboyant, (*more informal*) over the top
AN OPPOSITE IS modest

**grant** VERB
1 *The award body can grant you a scholarship.*
► give, award, allow, confer on you, pay, provide you with
2 *The court granted her request.*
► allow, consent to, accede to, permit
3 *We grant that the difference is small.*
► admit, concede, acknowledge, agree, accept, confess

**grant** NOUN
1 *They were given a local authority grant to repair their roof.*
► award, allowance, subsidy, subvention, endowment, contribution, donation, allocation
2 *a student grant*
► bursary, scholarship, sponsorship, loan

**graph** NOUN
*a graph showing the rise in house prices*
► table, chart, diagram, grid, pie chart, column-graph

**graphic** ADJECTIVE
*a graphic description of the accident*
► vivid, explicit, striking, forceful, dramatic, lurid, detailed, colourful
AN OPPOSITE IS vague

## grapple VERB

**1** *They grappled for the gun on the wet grass.*
► struggle, wrestle , tussle, scuffle, brawl, fight
**2** *grapple with The Prime Minister has a major problem to grapple with.*
► contend with, tackle, attend to, cope with, deal with, manage, handle, come to grips with, engage with, get involved with, try to solve, (*more informal*) have a go at
AN OPPOSITE IS avoid

## grasp VERB

**1** *He got up and grasped her hand.*
► grip, clasp, clutch, grab, seize, catch, snatch, hold, get hold of, hang on to
**2** *He got impatient if they failed to grasp a point.*
► understand, comprehend, follow, take in, apprehend, perceive, master, learn, realize, (*more informal*) cotton on to

## grasp NOUN

**1** *She managed to escape his grasp.*
► grip, hold, clutch, embrace, control
**2** *His ultimate goal was within his grasp.*
► reach, power, command
**3** *They now have a good grasp of the subject.*
► understanding, comprehension, perception, mastery, familiarity (with)

## grass NOUN

*A notice told them to keep off the grass.*
► lawn, turf, green

## grate VERB

**1** *She started to grate some cheese.*
► shred, grind, cut up, mince
**2** *His whining voice began to grate.*
► irritate, jar, rankle, be irksome

## grateful ADJECTIVE

*The families are grateful for all the support they have received.*
► thankful, appreciative (of), indebted, obliged
AN OPPOSITE IS ungrateful

## gratitude NOUN

*His letter expressed gratitude for the help he had been given.*
► thanks, appreciation (of), acknowledgement (of), indebtedness

## gratuitous ADJECTIVE

*This is no time for gratuitous insults.*
► unjustified, unwarranted, uncalled for, undeserved, needless, unmerited, superfluous, inappropriate
OPPOSITES ARE justifiable, unnecessary

## grave ADJECTIVE

**1** *a grave error  grave matters*
► serious, important, significant, crucial, critical, momentous, vital, acute, weighty
AN OPPOSITE IS unimportant
**2** *a grave offence*
► criminal, indictable, punishable
AN OPPOSITE IS minor

**3** *a grave expression*
► serious, solemn, sombre, earnest, severe, subdued, dignified, gloomy, thoughtful, unsmiling, grim, long-faced
AN OPPOSITE IS happy

## grave NOUN

*He visited the graves of his ancestors.*
► burial place, tomb, vault, mausoleum, sepulchre

## gravity NOUN

**1** *the gravity of the situation*
► seriousness, severity, acuteness, magnitude, momentousness, danger, importance
**2** *the gravity of his manner*
► solemnity, dignity, sobriety, earnestness, ceremony, pomp, sedateness
**3** *the force of gravity*
► gravitation, pull, weight, heaviness, downward force

## graze VERB

**1** *She fell and grazed her knee.*
► scrape, cut, scratch, scuff, abrade
**2** *Cattle grazed in the fields.*
► feed, browse, crop, ruminate, pasture

## graze NOUN

*a graze on his elbow*
► cut, abrasion, laceration, raw spot

## greasy ADJECTIVE

**1** *She had greasy hair and worried about her weight.*
► oily, shiny, waxy
AN OPPOSITE IS dry
**2** *His hand left greasy fingerprints on the glass.*
► fatty, oily, smeary, slimy, buttery
**3** *He sidled up in his usual greasy manner.*
► obsequious, ingratiating, unctuous, sycophantic, fawning, grovelling, flattering, fulsome, (*more informal*) smarmy

---

**great** ADJECTIVE This word is often overused. Here are some alternatives:
**1** *A great hill rose before them.*
► large, huge, big, enormous, gigantic, massive, colossal
AN OPPOSITE IS small
**2** *Speaking a foreign language is a great advantage. She is a person of great courage.*
► considerable, special, much, extreme
OPPOSITES ARE small, little
**3** *He read through the list of great statesmen.*
► famous, eminent, celebrated, distinguished, honoured, renowned, acclaimed, prominent, revered, exalted, illustrious
OPPOSITES ARE unknown, obscure
**4** *The invasion proved a great mistake.  a talk on the great advances in medicine*
► important, significant, crucial, critical, big, vital
OPPOSITES ARE insignificant, unimportant
**5** *We went to a great party.*
► excellent, enjoyable, marvellous, wonderful, fantastic, first-rate
AN OPPOSITE IS poor

## greed NOUN

**1** *I ate my supper with undisguised greed.*
▶ hunger, gluttony, ravenousness, overeating, over-indulgence

**2** *Material greed is not one of their faults.*
▶ avarice, acquisitiveness, covetousness, rapacity, cupidity, craving, desire, selfishness

**3** *He was clearly motivated by a greed for power.*
▶ appetite, desire, urge, need, lust, longing, craving

## greedy ADJECTIVE

**1** *a greedy eater*
▶ gluttonous, ravenous, voracious, insatiable

**2** *greedy for money*
▶ avaricious, covetous, acquisitive, mercenary, grasping

**3** *greedy for power*
▶ eager, avid, longing, craving, (more informal) itching

## green ADJECTIVE

**1** *a green garden*
▶ leafy, grassy, verdant
OPPOSITES ARE barren, bare

**2** *green with envy*
▶ envious, covetous, jealous, resentful

**3** *a green recruit*
▶ inexperienced, raw, naive, innocent, immature, untried, credulous, gullible
OPPOSITES ARE experienced, worldly wise

**4** *green issues*
▶ environmental, ecological, conservationist

## greenery NOUN

*vases stuffed with flowers and greenery*
▶ foliage, leaves, leafage, plants, vegetation

## greet VERB

*She greeted her visitors one by one.*
▶ welcome, say hello to, acknowledge, receive, give a greeting to, hail, salute

## greeting NOUN

**1** *She called out a greeting.*
▶ hello, salutation, welcome

**2** *greetings birthday greetings*
▶ good wishes, best wishes, congratulations, compliments

## gregarious ADJECTIVE

*He is cheerful, hard-working, and gregarious.*
▶ sociable, outgoing, extrovert, friendly, convivial, companionable, affable

## grey ADJECTIVE

**1** *His grey beard had grown very long.*
▶ silver, silvery, slate-grey, whitish, greying, grizzled, grizzly, hoary

**2** *Her face was grey with worry.*
▶ pale, ashen, leaden, wan, sallow, pasty, drawn

**3** *The day began grey and dull.*
▶ cloudy, overcast, gloomy, dismal, dreary, bleak

## grid NOUN

**1** *He had broken the stone to which the iron grid was fixed.*
▶ grating, grille, lattice, mesh, framework

**2** *The information is shown in the form of a grid.*
▶ graph, matrix, network

## grief NOUN

*His letters made her grief for her mother more bearable.*
▶ sadness, sorrow, mourning, bereavement, unhappiness, distress, misery, affliction, desolation
AN OPPOSITE IS joy

**come to grief** *The scheme came to grief from lack of financial support.*
▶ fail, go wrong, miscarry, be unsuccessful, fall through, collapse

## grievance NOUN

*The public can call in with any grievances about local services.*
▶ complaint, protest, criticism, objection, grudge, (more informal) moan, (more informal) grouse

## grieve VERB

**1** *She grieved for her mother constantly.*
▶ mourn, sorrow, lament, weep, cry

**2** *They were deeply grieved by the unkind newspaper reports.*
▶ hurt, wound, upset, sadden, distress

## grim ADJECTIVE

**1** *His face bore a grim expression.*
▶ stern, severe, harsh, dour, forbidding, sullen, morose, gloomy
OPPOSITES ARE cheerful, pleasant

**2** *the grim knowledge that she might die*
▶ unpleasant, dreadful, terrible, grisly, gruesome, macabre, distressing, fearsome, horrid, shocking
AN OPPOSITE IS pleasant

**3** *a grim little mining town*
▶ dreary, bleak, dismal, gloomy, dingy

## grime NOUN

*The shelves were covered in grime.*
▶ dirt, filth, muck, dust, soot

## grimy ADJECTIVE

*The other office was dark and grimy.*
▶ dirty, grubby, filthy, messy, smutty, soiled

## grin VERB

*She grinned at us and left the room.*
▶ smile, beam, smirk

## grin NOUN

*He had a silly grin on his face.*
▶ smile, smirk

## grind VERB

**1** *He ground the coffee into a fine powder.*
▶ crush, pound, grate

**2** *The kitchen had a wheel for grinding knives.*
▶ sharpen, whet, hone, file

**3** *The old car grinds slowly up the hill.*
▶ struggle, crawl, strain, chug

A B C D E F **G** H I J K L M N O P Q R S T U V W X Y Z

**grip** VERB
1 *He gripped Helen's hand.*
▶ grasp, clasp, clutch, grab, seize, catch, snatch, hold, get hold of, hang on to
2 *The story gripped everyone.*
▶ engross, enthral, absorb, captivate, fascinate, rivet, mesmerize

**grip** NOUN
*She kept a firm grip on the back of the chair.*
▶ hold, grasp, clasp, clutch
**get to grips with** *a book that gets to grips with the main issues*
▶ deal with, cope with, grasp, tackle
AN OPPOSITE IS avoid

**gripe** VERB
*(informal) I was griping to her about the people at work.*
▶ complain, grumble, protest, whine, grouch, *(informal)* moan, *(informal)* whinge, *(more informal)* bellyache

**grisly** ADJECTIVE
*a grisly little story about a serial murderer*
▶ gruesome, gory, ghastly, violent, bloody, brutal, horrific, repulsive, frightful, hideous, macabre, revolting, repellent

**grit** NOUN
1 *The problem was caused by pieces of grit in the carburettor.*
▶ gravel, dust, sand
2 *(informal) Ambition and sheer grit got them where they are today.*
▶ determination, toughness, stamina, tenacity, perseverance, courage, bravery, pluck, spirit, *(informal)* guts

**grit** VERB
1 *Sara gritted her teeth and said nothing.*
▶ clench, gnash, grind, grate
2 *Lorries have gone out to grit the roads.*
▶ treat, salt, sand

**grizzle** VERB
*(informal) a grumpy child who was always grizzling*
▶ cry, whimper, snivel, whine, *(informal)* whinge

**groan** VERB
*She heard him groaning in his sleep.*
▶ moan, cry out, sigh, wail

**groan** NOUN
*He let out a weary groan.*
▶ moan, sigh, cry, wail

**groom** VERB
*Martha was grooming her hair.*
▶ brush, comb, smooth, dress, arrange, tidy

**groove** NOUN
*The water had worn a groove in the rock.*
▶ channel, furrow, hollow, rut, indentation, slot, track

**grope** VERB
*She groped around for her clothes.*
▶ fumble, cast about, feel about, flounder, search blindly

**gross** ADJECTIVE
1 *a gross exaggeration*
▶ extreme, blatant, flagrant, glaring, obvious, conspicuous, sheer, outright
2 *gross indecency*
▶ coarse, vulgar, crude, obscene, lewd, improper
3 *He looked gross and he knew it.*
▶ obese, fat, corpulent, overweight, big
4 *gross income*
▶ total, inclusive, overall, aggregate, whole, full
5 *gross misshapen versions of the human form*
▶ disgusting, repellent, abhorrent, loathsome, sickening

**grotesque** ADJECTIVE
*a grotesque creature with a flattened body and a squashed-looking head*
▶ deformed, malformed, misshapen, distorted, weird, freakish, bizarre, hideous, mangled

**ground** NOUN
1 *The ground was wet and spongy.*
▶ earth, terrain, soil, turf, loam
2 *The little plane slowly rose from the ground.*
▶ land, surface
3 **grounds** *a large house in its own grounds*
▶ land, estate, gardens, surroundings

**groundless** ADJECTIVE
*Their fears proved to be groundless.*
▶ baseless, needless, unfounded, unjustified, unwarranted, unsubstantiated, uncalled for, false, gratuitous, imaginary, irrational
AN OPPOSITE IS justifiable

**group** NOUN
1 *Divide the children into groups for a game.*
▶ set, circle, section
2 *The reading group meets once a month.*
▶ club, circle, society, association
3 *a small group of islands off the north-east coast*
▶ cluster, collection, formation, bunch, mass, clump
4 *A group of fans waited at the stage door.*
▶ crowd, band, body, gathering, flock, assembly, gang, pack
5 *They sorted the books into different groups.*
▶ category, class, type, sort, kind, set

**group** VERB
**group together**
1 *Farmers began to group together to form cooperatives.*
▶ unite, join together, join forces, team up, come together
2 *Comfortable chairs are grouped around coffee tables.*
▶ arrange, organize, dispose, assemble, collect, cluster
3 *We group the books according to their size.*
▶ classify, categorize, sort, range, band

# grovel VERB

**1** *grovelling on the floor*
► crawl, creep, crouch
**2** *I don't like to see them grovelling to him.*
► kowtow, crawl, behave obsequiously, demean yourself, (*more informal*) suck up

# grow VERB

**1** *The baby grew fast.*
► get bigger, get larger, increase in size, fill out, put on growth
**2** *Their debts are growing.*
► increase, mount up, multiply
AN OPPOSITE IS decrease
**3** *She grows roses in her garden.*
► cultivate, produce, propagate, farm
**4** *At about 4 o'clock it grows dark.*
► become, turn, come to be
**5** *The business was growing.*
► expand, develop, flourish, thrive, prosper, succeed, boom
OPPOSITES ARE decline, fail

# growl VERB

*The dog growled at him.*
► snarl, snap, yap

# grown-up ADJECTIVE

*Chris has a grown-up sister.*
► adult, fully grown, mature

# growth NOUN

**1** *a steady growth in population*
► increase, expansion, development
OPPOSITES ARE decline, decrease
**2** *hormones that aid growth*
► growing, development, maturing
**3** *measures to increase economic growth*
► expansion, development, progress, advance
AN OPPOSITE IS decline
**4** *She has to have a growth removed.*
► tumour, lump, swelling, cyst

# grub NOUN

*The fruit was riddled with grubs.*
► larva, maggot, caterpillar

# grub VERB

**grub about** or **around** *He began grubbing around under the table.*
► rummage, delve, scrabble, ferret, poke

# grubby ADJECTIVE

*He had not yet changed out of his grubby overalls.*
► dirty, filthy, grimy, soiled, messy

# grudge NOUN

*The letter was written by someone with a grudge.*
► grievance, resentment, umbrage, pique, bitterness, rancour, bad feelings

# grudge VERB

*He grudged the money he would have to pay out.*
► resent, begrudge, object to, be angry about

# grudging ADJECTIVE

*She was pleased by this approval, grudging though it was.*
► reluctant, unwilling, unenthusiastic, half-hearted, resentful, hesitant, guarded, cautious, ungracious
AN OPPOSITE IS enthusiastic

# gruelling ADJECTIVE

*a gruelling journey back from the Himalayas*
► exhausting, arduous, tiring, wearying, exacting, demanding, punishing, hard, taxing, strenuous, laborious, (*more informal*) killing
AN OPPOSITE IS easy

# gruesome ADJECTIVE

*The gruesome remains had to be analysed.*
► grisly, gory, ghastly, bloody, horrific, repulsive, frightful, hideous, macabre, revolting, repellent

# gruff ADJECTIVE

**1** *His voice was gruff in the darkness.*
► harsh, rough, hoarse, husky, throaty
**2** *his unique gruff manner*
► abrupt, brusque, curt, blunt, bad-tempered, churlish

# grumble VERB

*Everyone was grumbling about the heat.*
► complain, carp, protest, whine, grouch, (*informal*) moan, (*informal*) whinge, (*more informal*) bellyache, (*more informal*) gripe

# grumble NOUN

*constant grumbles about the weather*
► complaint, moan, groan, protest, objection

# grumpy ADJECTIVE

*I'm always grumpy early in the morning.*
► bad-tempered, irritable, irascible, testy, grouchy, touchy, crotchety, cantankerous, peevish, fractious, cross, (*more informal*) stroppy, (*more informal*) shirty
OPPOSITES ARE good-humoured, good-tempered

# guarantee NOUN

**1** *Used cars come with a six-month guarantee.*
► warranty, warrant, covenant
**2** *We cannot give a guarantee that these measures will succeed.*
► assurance, pledge, promise, commitment, surety, oath

# guarantee VERB

**1** *He could not guarantee that they would keep their jobs.*
► promise, swear, pledge, assure, certify, give a guarantee, give your word, vouch, vow
**2** *You need a reservation to guarantee a seat.*
► secure, ensure, make sure of

# guard VERB

**1** *Troops guarded the house.*
► protect, stand guard over, watch over, shield, safeguard, defend, cover
**2** *An escort guarded the prisoners.*
► supervise, watch over, control

**3 guard against** *Take care to guard against over-tiredness in the first few weeks.*
▶ beware of, be alert to, try to prevent

**guard** NOUN

**1** *We were turned back by the guards at the border.*
▶ sentry, sentinel, custodian, lookout, patrol, watchman

**2** *He felt the guard's hand on his shoulder.*
▶ jailer, prison officer, warder, warden

**off your guard** or **off guard** *He was caught off guard for a moment and the water surged over him.*
▶ unprepared, unready, unsuspecting

**on your guard** *Thieves are operating in this area, so be on your guard.*
▶ alert, watchful, vigilant, heedful, circumspect, chary

**guarded** ADJECTIVE

*Their reaction was guarded and unfriendly.*
▶ cautious, wary, chary, unenthusiastic, non-committal, discreet

**guardian** NOUN

**1** *the child's guardian*
▶ adoptive parent, foster parent

**2** *the guardian of international peace*
▶ protector, defender, preserver, custodian, keeper, minder, steward

**guess** VERB

**1** *You have to guess the weight of a large cake.*
▶ estimate, reckon, judge, predict, gauge, determine

**2** *I guess I should say sorry.*
▶ suppose, believe, think, imagine, expect, assume, consider, reckon

**guess** NOUN

*My guess was he would head for the motorway.*
▶ theory, hypothesis, prediction, feeling, belief, opinion, conjecture, supposition, notion, idea, intuition

**guest** NOUN

**1** *They joined their guests for dinner.*
▶ visitor, company, caller

**2** *The hotel could take up to thirty guests.*
▶ resident, patron, client, lodger, boarder, customer, tenant

**guidance** NOUN

*His supervisor offered him guidance.*
▶ advice, direction, instruction, help, counsel, teaching, support, pointers, guidelines

**guide** VERB

**1** *I asked her to guide me back to the town.*
▶ lead, direct, show, show the way, take, accompany, escort, conduct

**2** *The students have to be guided carefully through this stage of their work.*
▶ advise, counsel, direct, supervise, instruct, teach

**guide** NOUN

**1** *Your guide will show you the way.*
▶ escort, leader, courier, navigator, pilot, attendant

**2** *The sample is only meant to be a guide.*
▶ model, indication, example, gauge, guideline, pointer

**3** *We explored the city with the help of a pocket guide.*
▶ guidebook, tourist guide, handbook, manual

**guilt** NOUN

**1** *The jury was quite sure of his guilt.*
▶ guiltiness, culpability, liability, responsibility, blame, blameworthiness, wrongfulness, criminality
AN OPPOSITE IS innocence

**2** *There is no need to feel guilt about it.*
▶ shame, remorse, self-reproach, self-accusation, bad conscience, penitence, contrition, dishonour, guilty feelings, regret
AN OPPOSITE IS virtue

**guilty** ADJECTIVE

**1** *Brown was found guilty of assault.*
▶ culpable, blameworthy, at fault, liable, responsible, blameable, in the wrong, reprehensible
AN OPPOSITE IS innocent

**2** *She felt guilty about deceiving her friends.*
▶ ashamed, remorseful, sorry, repentant, regretful, contrite, penitent, conscience-stricken, shamefaced, sheepish
AN OPPOSITE IS unrepentant

**gulf** NOUN

**1** *Here ships turn into the gulf.*
▶ bay, inlet, creek, estuary, sound

**2** *the gulf between rich and poor*
▶ gap, contrast, chasm, divergence, divide, rift, split, division

**gullible** ADJECTIVE

*Wayne is very gullible when he's had too much to drink.*
▶ credulous, over-trusting, trustful, suggestible, easily taken in
OPPOSITES ARE suspicious, astute

**gulp** VERB

*Brian gulped his beer and stood to leave.*
▶ swallow, swill down, (more informal) swig, (more informal) knock back
AN OPPOSITE IS sip

**gulp** NOUN

*She finished her juice in one gulp.*
▶ swallow, mouthful, (more informal) swig

**gum** NOUN

*You can stick the pictures in with gum.*
▶ glue, adhesive, paste

**gum** VERB

*The photos were gummed to the page.*
▶ stick, glue, paste, fix

# gun NOUN
*He threatened her with a gun.*
► firearm, weapon, pistol, revolver, rifle, shotgun, (*more informal*) shooter

# gurgle VERB
**1** *The baby gurgled in a corner.*
► burble, babble, chuckle
**2** *The stream gurgled beside the path.*
► babble, burble, trickle, murmur

# gurgle NOUN
*The water rushed out with a loud gurgle.*
► burble, babble, trickle, ripple

# gush VERB
**1** *Blood gushed from the wound in his head.*
► pour, spurt, squirt, stream, flow, rush, cascade, spout, surge
OPPOSITES ARE trickle, ooze
**2** *They gushed all afternoon about their holiday plans.*
► enthuse, rave, effuse, chatter, jabber, (*more informal*) go on

# gush NOUN
*Turning the tap slightly produced a gush of scalding water.*
► rush, spurt, surge, stream, torrent, cascade, flood, flow, jet, spout, squirt, burst

# gust NOUN
*They felt a sudden gust of wind.*
► blast, flurry, rush, puff, squall

# gusto NOUN
*He ate his dinner with gusto.*
► enthusiasm, vigour, relish, enjoyment, satisfaction, liveliness, spirit, verve, zest

# gut NOUN
**1** *gut* or *guts* (*informal*) *He felt a sharp pain in his gut.*
► stomach, belly, bowels, intestines, innards, insides
RELATED ADJECTIVE visceral
**2** *guts* (*informal*) *It takes guts to say what you think.*
► courage, nerve, bravery, audacity, boldness, daring, (*informal*) bottle

# gut ADJECTIVE
*I had a gut feeling Eric was the right man for us.*
► instinctive, intuitive, deep-seated, spontaneous, innate, reflex

# gutter NOUN
*The recent rains had filled the gutters.*
► guttering, channel, conduit, drain, duct, sluice

# guy NOUN
*He's a clever guy.*
► bloke, chap, fellow, man, boy, individual

# guzzle VERB
*They came in and guzzled all the food.*
► gobble, gobble up, wolf, wolf down, devour, (*more informal*) scoff, (*more informal*) tuck into, (*more informal*) polish off

# gyrate VERB
*Couples were gyrating to loud music.*
► turn, twirl, rotate, wheel, revolve, spin, swirl, circle, spiral, pirouette

# Hh

# habit NOUN
**1** *healthy eating habits*
► practice, custom, pattern, routine, tendency, way, rule
**2** *her habit of twirling her hair as she spoke*
► mannerism, quirk, trick, gesture, custom, practice
**3** *They stole money to fund their drug habit*
► addiction, dependence, craving, fixation, compulsion, obsession, weakness
**4** *a nun's habit*
► costume, robe, garment, outfit, attire, garb
**in the habit of** *He was in the habit of practising on his flute when he went to bed.*
► used to, accustomed to, given to, inclined to

---

# habitat NOUN
*the panda's natural habitat*
► environment, surroundings, element, territory, terrain, haunt, domain, ecosystem
**WORDS FOR ANIMAL HABITATS**
**terrestrial habitats (land):** burrow, copse, desert, ditch, field, forest, garden, grassland, heathland, meadow, moorland, mountain, pasture, rainforest, scrub, soil, tree, towns and cities, tundra, walls, woodland
**aquatic and semi-aquatic habitats (water):** bog, coral reef, ditch, fen, lake, mangrove swamp, marsh, ocean, pond, river, rock pool, sea, seashore, stream, swamp.

---

# habitual ADJECTIVE
**1** *She expected his habitual response to such suggestions.*
► usual, customary, normal, regular, characteristic, typical, fixed, routine, accustomed, established
AN OPPOSITE IS unaccustomed
**2** *their habitual criticism of everything we did*
► constant, persistent, continual, recurrent, incessant, interminable, unremitting, endless, relentless
AN OPPOSITE IS infrequent
**3** *habitual smokers*
► confirmed, regular, addicted, persistent, inveterate, hardened, compulsive, chronic
AN OPPOSITE IS occasional

# hack VERB
*The victim's head had been hacked off.*
► cut, chop, lop, slash, saw

# hackneyed ADJECTIVE
*hackneyed expressions*
► overused, clichéd, banal, commonplace, stale, tired, worn, trite, (*more informal*) corny
OPPOSITES ARE original, fresh

# hag NOUN
*an old hag*
► crone, witch, gorgon, termagant, woman

## haggard ADJECTIVE

*He saw tears on her white, haggard cheeks.*
▶ drawn, careworn, shrunken, pinched, gaunt, wan, withered, wasted
OPPOSITES ARE fresh, healthy

## haggle VERB

*He could spend all afternoon haggling over a few dollars.*
▶ barter, bargain, negotiate, argue, quibble, discuss terms, wrangle

## hail VERB

*A friend hailed him from a top window.*
▶ greet, call out to, shout to, wave to, salute

## hail NOUN

*a hail of bullets*
▶ barrage, volley, shower, deluge, torrent, stream, flood, burst

## hair NOUN

1 *She ran her hand through her hair.*
▶ locks, tresses, curls, (*more informal*) mop
2 *a dog with short hair*
▶ coat, fur, hide

## hairdresser NOUN

*an appointment with the hairdresser*
▶ hair stylist, stylist, coiffeur, (*for men*) barber

## hair-raising ADJECTIVE

*the hair-raising events of the days leading up to war*
▶ terrifying, frightening, horrifying, shocking, alarming, chilling, petrifying

## hairstyle NOUN

*A new hairstyle will give you a new lease of life.*
▶ haircut, cut, coiffure, style, (*more informal*) hairdo

## hairy ADJECTIVE

*His shirt was open, revealing a hairy chest.*
▶ shaggy, fuzzy, bristly, downy, hirsute, fleecy, furry, long-haired, stubbly, woolly
OPPOSITES ARE hairless, smooth-skinned

## half-hearted ADJECTIVE

*She made a half-hearted attempt to brush away his hand.*
▶ unenthusiastic, weak, feeble, apathetic, indifferent
AN OPPOSITE IS committed

## halfway ADJECTIVE

*the halfway point in the journey*
▶ midway, central, part-way

## halfway ADVERB

*He stopped halfway along the path.*
▶ midway, part-way, in the middle

## hall NOUN

1 *The meeting will be in the village hall.*
▶ assembly hall, meeting room, auditorium, concert hall, theatre
2 *You can leave your coat in the hall.*
▶ hallway, entrance hall, lobby, foyer, corridor, passage, vestibule

## hallucination NOUN

*He suffered from hallucinations for weeks after the accident.*
▶ delusion, illusion, apparition, fantasy, figment of the imagination, mirage, vision, daydream, dream

## halo NOUN

*Her hair sparkled like a halo round her head.*
▶ ring of light, aureole, aureola, corona, nimbus

## halt VERB

1 *A series of strikes halted production for several weeks.*
▶ stop, terminate, obstruct, arrest, impede, block, check, curb
OPPOSITES ARE start, continue
2 *Traffic halted on the bridge.*
▶ stop, wait, come to a halt, come to rest, draw up, pull up
OPPOSITES ARE start, continue
3 *Work on the building halted during the holiday period.*
▶ cease, stop, break off, end, terminate
OPPOSITES ARE start, resume

## halt NOUN

1 *The train came to a halt.*
▶ stop, standstill, break, interruption, pause, stoppage
2 *a halt in the output of spare parts*
▶ stoppage, cessation, break, interruption, pause

## halting ADJECTIVE

*She spoke at best a halting English.*
▶ hesitant, faltering, stumbling, uncertain, underconfident, unsure, erratic, irregular, stammering, stuttering
AN OPPOSITE IS fluent

## halve VERB

1 *Halve the pears and remove the cores.*
▶ cut in half, split in two, divide in two, bisect
2 *Their income halved over the next year.*
▶ lessen by half or by fifty percent, decrease by half or by fifty percent

## hammer NOUN

*He hit the nail with a hammer.*
▶ mallet, gavel

## hammer VERB

*The soldiers hammered on the door.*
▶ beat, batter, bash, pummel, pound, strike, knock

## hamper VERB

1 *Bad weather hampered the rescue operation.*
▶ obstruct, hinder, hold up, interfere with, restrict, thwart, prevent, curb, curtail, foil
AN OPPOSITE IS facilitate
2 *Her bandaged hand hampered her.*
▶ hinder, encumber, impede, restrain, entangle, handicap, hold back
AN OPPOSITE IS aid

## hand NOUN

1 *a person's hand*
▶ fist, palm
RELATED ADJECTIVE manual

**2** *the hand of a gauge*
▶ pointer, indicator

**3** *The factory took on more hands.*
▶ worker, employee, labourer

**4 hands** *The property came into his sister's hands.*
▶ possession, control, charge, custody, power, responsibility

**at** or **on** or **to hand**
▶ close by, handy, accessible, available, present, waiting, within reach

**give somebody a hand** *Let me give you a hand with the dinner.*
▶ help, assist

## hand VERB

*He handed her a letter.*
▶ give, offer, pass, present (her with a letter), submit (a letter to her), convey, deliver

**hand down** *The family property is handed down from one generation to the next.*
▶ pass down, pass on, bequeath, leave as a legacy, will

**hand out** or **round** *A flight attendant handed out forms.*
▶ distribute, circulate, give out, deal out, share out

**hand over**
**1** *She handed over a large sum.*
▶ pay, donate, tender, surrender
**2** *The prisoners were handed over to the local police.*
▶ deliver up, entrust, turn over

## handbook NOUN

*a UCAS handbook and application form*
▶ guide, instruction book, manual, reference manual

## handful NOUN

*a handful of complaining letters*
▶ small number, smattering, sprinkling, trickle

## handicap NOUN

**1** *Their poor French was a handicap when travelling.*
▶ disadvantage, difficulty, drawback, shortcoming, hindrance, inconvenience, limitation, encumbrance, stumbling block, restriction, obstacle, problem, nuisance
OPPOSITES ARE advantage, benefit
**2** *He was born with a severe physical handicap.*
▶ disability, defect, abnormality, impairment, impediment
**USAGE** Note that *handicap* is often regarded as offensive in this meaning.

## handicap VERB

*They were handicapped by the fact that they had not been taught science.*
▶ hamper, impede, limit, disadvantage, restrict, hinder, hold back
AN OPPOSITE IS help

## handicapped ADJECTIVE

*learning methods for handicapped pupils*
▶ disabled, disadvantaged, incapacitated
**USAGE** Note that *handicapped* is often regarded as offensive in this meaning.

## handiwork NOUN

*I stood back to admire my handiwork.*
▶ creation, work, product, handicraft, craftwork, achievement, invention

## handle NOUN

*The head flew off the handle and cracked our only mirror.*
▶ haft, shank, stock, shaft, grip

## handle VERB

**1** *A notice asked visitors not to handle the exhibits.*
▶ touch, feel, hold, finger, fondle, pick up, grip, grasp
**2** *It would not be easy to handle such a tense meeting. He was used to handling temperamental singers.*
▶ manage, deal with, cope with, control, tackle, contend with
**3** *The firm handles a lot of overseas business.*
▶ deal in, trade in, market
**4** *He needed a smaller car that he could handle more easily.*
▶ control, drive, manoeuvre, operate, steer

## handout NOUN

**1 handouts** *They lived on benefits and handouts for several months.*
▶ donations, charity, aid
**2** *There are handouts for each talk at the back of the room.*
▶ leaflet, circular, pamphlet, notice, brochure

## handsome ADJECTIVE

**1** *a handsome man*
▶ good-looking, nice-looking, attractive, comely, personable, (more informal) dishy
OPPOSITES ARE ugly, unattractive
**2** *a handsome building*
▶ elegant, striking, imposing, stately, well-proportioned, attractive
OPPOSITES ARE ugly, hideous
**3** *a handsome profit*
▶ large, big, sizeable, substantial, considerable, ample
AN OPPOSITE IS meagre
**4** *a handsome offer*
▶ generous, gracious, liberal, magnanimous, munificent
AN OPPOSITE IS mean

## handwriting NOUN

*large clear handwriting*
▶ writing, script, hand, calligraphy, penmanship

## handy ADJECTIVE

**1** *The brush is handy for cleaning up stubborn dust.*
▶ useful, convenient, practical, helpful, effective
**2** *He's handy with a screwdriver.*
▶ skilful, adept, dexterous, proficient, practical, able, deft
**3** *Keep your timer handy.*
▶ accessible, available, ready, at or to hand, close by, nearby

# hang VERB

**1** *Baskets of flowers hung from the lampposts.*
► be suspended, dangle, swing, sway

**2** *Rich exotic curtains hang from every window.*
► drape, drop, droop, cascade, trail

**3** *Make sure you hang the pictures at eye level.*
► fix, attach, fasten, display, suspend, stick

**4** *A damp mist hung in the air.*
► float, hover, drift, linger, cling, remain

**hang about** *(informal) Don't hang about if you want to take advantage of this offer.*
► delay, wait, procrastinate

**hang around** *(informal) small groups hanging around coffee bars*
► linger in, loiter in, frequent, haunt

**hang back** *He hung back, afraid to go in.*
► hesitate, demur, hold back, recoil, shy away

**hang on** *If they can hang on a few more days it will help us.*
► stay, persevere, remain, continue, carry on, persist

**hang on to** *If you have cash, hang on to it.*
► keep, hold on to, retain, preserve

**hang out** *(informal) She enjoyed hanging out with members of the band.*
► associate, mix, spend time, keep company, fraternize, socialize

# hang-up NOUN

*(informal) Wally has a hang-up about his appearance.*
► fixation, obsession, neurosis, inhibition, anxiety, *(more informal)* thing

# hanker VERB

**1** *He could see that she hankered to go back.*
► long, yearn, be aching, crave, want, wish

**2 hanker after** or **for** *They hankered after the bright city lights.*
► long for, crave, miss, be pining for

# haphazard ADJECTIVE

*the haphazard spray of machine-gun fire   things strewn about in a haphazard fashion*
► random, indiscriminate, arbitrary, chaotic, disorderly, disorganized, casual, irregular, unmethodical
AN OPPOSITE IS orderly

# happen VERB

**1** *The collision happened as the pursuing boat tried to turn.   Something strange was happening that day.*
► occur, take place, come about, arise, result, ensue, transpire

**2 happen to** *We never knew what happened to her.*
► become of, befall

# happening NOUN

*There is a record of all the happenings of that week.*
► event, incident, occurrence, circumstance, episode, affair

# happiness NOUN

*A feeling of great happiness filled her.*
► contentment, joy, joyfulness, gladness, pleasure, bliss, elation, ecstasy
OPPOSITES ARE unhappiness, sorrow

**happy** ADJECTIVE This word is often overused. Here are some alternatives:
**1** *a room full of happy faces*
► contented, cheerful, joyful, jolly, delighted, merry, smiling
**2** *I will be happy to help.*
► pleased, glad, willing, disposed, delighted
**3** *By a happy chance a film crew was there to record the scene.*
► fortunate, lucky, felicitous, favourable, fitting

# harass VERB

*The men continued to harass her.*
► pester, torment, badger, hound, persecute, trouble, harry, hassle, annoy, vex

# harassed ADJECTIVE

*good news for harassed mums and dads*
► stressed, harried, worn, troubled, *(informal)* exhausted
AN OPPOSITE IS carefree

# harbour NOUN

*Boats bobbed up and down in the harbour.*
► port, dock, marina, mooring, quay, waterfront

# harbour VERB

**1** *He was arrested for harbouring a criminal.*
► hide, protect, shelter, conceal, shield, give refuge to, give asylum to, give sanctuary to

**2** *Better not to harbour a grudge.*
► bear, hold, nurse, nurture, entertain, foster, cling to

**hard** ADJECTIVE This word is often overused. Here are some alternatives:
**1** *The ground is too hard to play on.*
► solid, firm, unyielding, hardened, tough, compact
AN OPPOSITE IS soft
**2** *three weeks of hard work*
► strenuous, arduous, exhausting, fatiguing, demanding
AN OPPOSITE IS easy
**3** *a hard problem to solve*
► difficult, complicated, complex, involved, knotty, baffling, puzzling
AN OPPOSITE IS simple
**4** *a hard taskmaster*
► strict, harsh, firm, stern, demanding, severe
OPPOSITES ARE mild, easy-going
**5** *a hard blow*
► heavy, forceful, strong, powerful, violent
AN OPPOSITE IS light
**hard up** *We were too hard up to buy fancy clothes.*
► poor, impoverished, poverty stricken, badly off, impecunious

## hard ADVERB

**1** *She works hard at school.*
▶ diligently, industriously, steadily, earnestly, energetically

**2** *It has been raining hard.*
▶ heavily, steadily, (*more informal*) cats and dogs

**3** *She looked hard at them.*
▶ intently, intensely, closely, attentively, keenly

## harden VERB

**1** *The cement hardens after two hours.*
▶ set, solidify, become hard, stiffen

**2** *These experiences hardened their determination to continue.*
▶ strengthen, reinforce, increase, intensify, fortify, toughen

## hard-hearted ADJECTIVE

*No one could be so hard-hearted as to ignore such desperate appeals for help.*
▶ unfeeling, heartless, unsympathetic, callous, uncaring, unconcerned

## hardly ADVERB

**1** *It is hardly surprising that so many people have considered leaving.*
▶ not at all, by no means, barely, scarcely

**2** *John said he hardly knew her.*
▶ scarcely, barely, only just, only slightly, only faintly

## hardship NOUN

*Drought caused the population much hardship.*
▶ suffering, privation, misery, misfortune, adversity, affliction, austerity, destitution, difficulty, need, trouble, unhappiness, want

## hardware NOUN

*tanks and other military hardware   computer hardware*
▶ equipment, machinery, implements, tools, instruments

## hard-wearing ADJECTIVE

*outdoor clothes that are hard-wearing*
▶ durable, strong, tough, resilient, lasting, sturdy, well-made, stout
OPPOSITES ARE flimsy, delicate

## hardy ADJECTIVE

*a good expedition for hardy walkers*
▶ fit, robust, sturdy, hearty, healthy, tough, vigorous, strong, resilient, rugged
OPPOSITES ARE tender, delicate

## harm NOUN

**1** *a way of dealing with waste without causing any harm to the public*
▶ injury, damage, suffering, hurt, detriment, inconvenience
AN OPPOSITE IS benefit

**2** *We can't see any harm in their idea.*
▶ wrong, disadvantage, snag

## harm VERB

**1** *If they harmed any of the hostages the police would have to go in.*
▶ hurt, injure, maltreat, mistreat, ill-treat, wound, molest, abuse, (*more informal*) lay a finger on

**2** *effluent that harms the environment*
▶ damage, spoil, ruin, hurt, do damage to, do harm to

## harmful ADJECTIVE

*the harmful effects of smoking*
▶ damaging, detrimental, injurious, dangerous, noxious, destructive, unhealthy
OPPOSITES ARE harmless, beneficial

## harmless ADJECTIVE

**1** *a harmless substance*
▶ safe, innocuous, non-toxic, non-poisonous, benign
AN OPPOSITE IS harmful

**2** *It was just a bit of harmless fun.   He looked as harmless as a tired sparrow.*
▶ safe, inoffensive, innocuous, unobjectionable, gentle
AN OPPOSITE IS objectionable

## harmonious ADJECTIVE

**1** *harmonious sounds*
▶ tuneful, melodious, melodic, euphonious, sweet-sounding, mellifluous
AN OPPOSITE IS discordant

**2** *a harmonious relationship*
▶ friendly, cordial, amicable, congenial
OPPOSITES ARE unfriendly, hostile

**3** *a harmonious balance of colour and tone*
▶ matching, coordinated, proportional, balanced, pleasing, congruous
OPPOSITES ARE unbalanced, incongruous

## harmonize VERB

**1** *The colours harmonize well.*
▶ match, blend, tone in, go together, coordinate, balance, fit together

**2** *There is an argument for harmonizing taxes across Europe.*
▶ coordinate, correlate, reconcile, bring together, make uniform, make consistent

## harmony NOUN

**1** *different ethnic groups living in harmony*
▶ friendship, agreement, concord, peace, amity, fellowship, goodwill, unity
OPPOSITES ARE disagreement, enmity

**2** *musical harmony*
▶ tunefulness, euphony, concord, melody
AN OPPOSITE IS discord

## harness VERB

*attempts to harness the forces of nature*
▶ use, control, utilize, make use of, exploit, tame, keep under control, mobilize

## harrowing ADJECTIVE

*a harrowing tale of betrayal and murder*
▶ distressing, traumatic, disturbing, upsetting, shocking, frightening

## harry VERB

**1** *They were harried all morning by news reporters.*
▶ harass, pester, torment, persecute, badger, trouble, annoy, vex

**2** *The fleet was given a free hand to harry the enemy's supply lines.*
▶ attack, ravage, ransack, plunder, devastate

## harsh ADJECTIVE

**1** *He spoke in a high, harsh voice.*
▶ shrill, grating, strident, rasping

**2** *harsh measures to combat street crime*
▶ severe, punitive, strict, draconian

**3** *They exchanged harsh words.*
▶ sharp, bitter, unfriendly, unkind

**4** *the harsh rule of a tyrant*
▶ cruel, savage, brutal, despotic, hard, strict, intolerant

## harvest NOUN

*a bumper harvest*
▶ crop, yield, produce, return

## harvest VERB

*crops that have to be harvested by hand*
▶ gather, reap, take in, bring in, collect, garner, mow, pick

## hash NOUN

**make a hash of**
▶ bungle, botch, mismanage, mishandle, muff, make a mess of

## hassle NOUN

**1** *It's always such a hassle trying to park.*
▶ bother, nuisance, inconvenience, struggle, difficulty

**2** *She started getting hassle from the kids coming to her.*
▶ harassment, trouble, annoyance, argument, (*more informal*) aggravation

## hassle VERB

*Some of the passengers were hassling the driver.*
▶ harass, pester, badger, trouble, harry, annoy

## haste NOUN

*He was working with great haste.*
▶ speed, hurry, urgency, swiftness, rapidity, promptness, impetuosity

## hasten VERB

**1** *The king hastened back from Berwick.*
▶ hurry, rush, speed, make haste

**2** *A rise in interest rates will hasten the ruin of many small businesses.*
▶ quicken, accelerate, speed up, bring nearer, precipitate

## hasty ADJECTIVE

**1** *They made a hasty retreat back to the house.*
▶ hurried, swift, rapid, brisk, quick, headlong

**2** *The decision seemed hasty.*
▶ rash, precipitate, impulsive, imprudent, impetuous, reckless

## hat NOUN

**SOME COMMON TYPES OF HAT**

**men's hats:** bowler, trilby, top hat, Homburg, porkpie, deerstalker, stetson, boater, sun-hat, sombrero, panama, straw hat.

**women's hats:** bonnet, Juliet cap, cloche, toque.

**soft informal hats:** cap, beret, baseball cap, balaclava, skull cap, beanie.

**ceremonial and official hats:** busby, helmet, mortar board, biretta, mitre.

**some other hats:** bobble hat, glengarry, yarmulke, taj, tam-o'-shanter, turban.

## hatch VERB

*A plan was hatching in her mind.*
▶ develop, form, grow

**hatch up** *The little scheme they hatched up.*
▶ devise, concoct, conceive, contrive, formulate, think up, brew up, dream up, cook up

## hate VERB

**1** *The brothers hated each other.*
▶ loathe, detest, abhor, dislike, abominate, (*more informal*) can't bear, (*more informal*) can't stand

**2** *I hate to bother them.*
▶ be sorry, hesitate, regret, be reluctant

## hate NOUN

**1** *feelings of hate*
▶ hatred, loathing, detestation, dislike, distaste, revulsion, abhorrence

**2** *They made a list of their pet hates.*
▶ dislike, bugbear, bane, bête noire

## hateful ADJECTIVE

*I'll never come back to this hateful country.*
▶ detestable, loathsome, horrible, horrid, awful, nasty
AN OPPOSITE IS lovable

## hatred NOUN

*The war left a legacy of fear and hatred.*
▶ hate, loathing, detestation, revulsion, repugnance, hostility, enmity, bad feeling
OPPOSITES ARE love, liking

## haughty ADJECTIVE

*He walked out with a haughty toss of his head.*
▶ proud, arrogant, self-important, supercilious, disdainful, contemptuous, scornful, superior, lofty, overbearing
AN OPPOSITE IS modest

## haul VERB

*A special locomotive is needed to haul these trains. She hauled him up from the floor.*
▶ pull, drag, heave, tug, tow
AN OPPOSITE IS push

## haunt VERB

**1** *He likes to haunt old junk shops.*
▶ frequent, spend time in, keep returning to, visit frequently, (*more informal*) hang around in

2 *Her words came back to haunt her.*
▶ obsess, torment, trouble, worry, prey on

**haunt** NOUN
*one of their favourite haunts in town*
▶ meeting place, retreat, rendezvous, spot

**haunting** ADJECTIVE
*haunting and lyrical poetry*
▶ evocative, touching, emotive, memorable, poignant, nostalgic, wistful, plaintive
AN OPPOSITE IS unmemorable

**have** VERB
1 *They have a house in France.*
▶ own, possess, be the owner of, boast, keep, enjoy
AN OPPOSITE IS lack
2 *We have coffee at eleven.*
▶ drink, take
3 *What did you have for lunch?*
▶ eat, consume
4 *She had a letter from her boyfriend.*
▶ receive, get, be sent, obtain, acquire
OPPOSITES ARE send, reject
5 *They are having a party next door.*
▶ hold, give, organize, arrange, throw, provide, lay on
6 *The apartment has five rooms.*
▶ contain, comprise, consist of, include, incorporate, be made up of
7 *We had trouble parking.*
▶ experience, encounter, undergo, meet with, run into, suffer, face
8 *I have a cold.*
▶ be suffering from, be afflicted by, be affected by, be troubled by
9 *The boys had a lot of fun.*
▶ enjoy, experience, go through
10 *Mike had guests at the weekend.*
▶ entertain, receive, be host to, cater for, invite
11 *Julia has had her baby.*
▶ give birth to, bear, produce, be delivered of, bring into the world

**haven** NOUN
1 *a haven for ships on the north coast*
▶ harbour, port, anchorage, mooring
2 *a safe haven in time of trouble*
▶ refuge, retreat, shelter, sanctuary, asylum

**havoc** NOUN
*Frost and snow caused havoc in the area.*
▶ chaos, confusion, disruption, mayhem, disorder, devastation, destruction

**haywire** ADJECTIVE
*A virus can make your PC go haywire.*
▶ out of control, erratic, faulty, chaotic, disorganized, topsy-turvy

**hazard** NOUN
*a serious health hazard*
▶ risk, threat, danger, menace

**hazard** VERB
1 *a business that is too risky to hazard money on*
▶ risk, chance, jeopardize
2 *I wouldn't want to hazard a guess about that.*
▶ offer, put forward, venture, advance

**hazardous** ADJECTIVE
*He knew how hazardous the road could be in the dark.*
▶ dangerous, risky, perilous, precarious, uncertain, unpredictable, unsafe, chancy, (*more informal*) dicey
OPPOSITES ARE safe, secure

**haze** NOUN
*The clear sky suddenly filled with haze.*
▶ mist, fog, cloud, vapour, film, obscurity

**hazy** ADJECTIVE
1 *The weather was good, if a little hazy.*
▶ misty, cloudy, foggy, smoky
2 *hazy memories of childhood*
▶ vague, indistinct, blurred, fuzzy, unclear, faint, dim

**head** NOUN
1 *He hit his head on a beam.*
▶ skull, crown, cranium, (*more informal*) nut, (*more informal*) bonce
RELATED ADJECTIVE cephalic
2 *the head of a publishing firm*
▶ chief, chairman, chief executive, president, principal
3 *You need a good head for this work.*
▶ brain, intellect, intelligence, wit
4 *She has quite a head for figures.*
▶ aptitude, gift, talent, bent, knack
**lose your head** *Connie lost her head and ran off.*
▶ panic, lose control, go to pieces, (*more informal*) lose your cool
**off your head** *He was quite off his head, spouting complete nonsense.*
▶ mad, crazy, insane, out of your mind, unbalanced, demented, deranged

**head** ADJECTIVE
*the head chef*
▶ chief, senior, principal, leading

**head** VERB
1 *She headed a team of researchers.*
▶ lead, be in charge of, be at the head of, manage, direct, oversee, supervise
2 *head for They were heading for the station.*
▶ go or move towards, make for, aim for, point to

**heading** NOUN
1 *He turned the page and read the chapter heading.*
▶ title, headline, caption, rubric
2 *The subject is discussed under several headings.*
▶ category, division, section, class, group

**headland** NOUN
*You can gaze out over the headland to the sea.*
▶ promontory, cape, head, point, foreland

### headline NOUN
*a newspaper headline*
▶ heading, title, caption

### headlong ADJECTIVE
*a headlong dash to the river*
▶ hasty, breakneck, precipitate, impetuous, reckless

### headstrong ADJECTIVE
*Imaginative and headstrong, he became an art student.*
▶ stubborn, wilful, obstinate, intractable, perverse, contrary

### headway NOUN
**make headway** *The sales team has begun to make good headway.*
▶ make progress, progress, advance, gain ground, move forward

### heady ADJECTIVE
*a mood of heady excitement*
▶ exhilarating, intoxicating, thrilling, euphoric, ecstatic, elated

### heal VERB
1 *Madra's wounds began to heal.*
▶ get better, recover, knit, mend, unite
2 *an ointment to heal her injured finger*
▶ make better, cure, treat, remedy, restore
3 *The rift between father and son was never completely healed.*
▶ mend, repair, put right, settle, remedy, reconcile, patch up

### health NOUN
1 *He is now in excellent health and back at work.*
▶ condition, shape, form, fettle, constitution
2 *Hormone levels are important to health.*
▶ fitness, wellbeing, healthiness, good health
RELATED ADJECTIVE sanitary

### healthy ADJECTIVE
1 *We try to promote a healthy lifestyle.*
▶ health-giving, wholesome, beneficial, bracing, invigorating
2 *I think I am fit, healthy, and looking good again.*
▶ well, in good health, in good condition, in good shape, in good trim
3 *a healthy respect for the opposite sex*
▶ sound, strong, rigorous

### heap NOUN
1 *a heap of old newspapers*
▶ pile, stack, mass, mound, mountain, collection, hoard
2 **heaps** *We've got heaps of time.*
▶ plenty, a lot, a great deal, (*more informal*) lots, (*more informal*) masses, (*more informal*) piles

### heap VERB
1 *She heaped more cakes on their plates.*
▶ pile, stack, mass, bank, collect
2 *The praise heaped on them was well deserved.*
▶ lavish, shower, bestow, confer

### hear VERB
1 *You can hear the traffic in the distance.*
▶ make out, catch, listen to, perceive, discern, detect.
RELATED ADJECTIVE audible
**USAGE** Note that all these words, except for listen to, can also be used about seeing, and so you might need to make the meaning clear by saying, for example, *You can make out the sound of traffic in the distance.* Note also that listen to implies something you try to do, whereas hear can refer to sounds that you might be aware of by chance.
2 *I heard that you were leaving.*
▶ be told, be informed, learn, gather, find out, discover
3 *A female judge heard the case.*
▶ try, judge, sit in judgement on

### hearing NOUN
1 *He made the comment out of our hearing.*
▶ earshot, range, reach.
RELATED ADJECTIVE acoustic
2 *a judicial hearing*
▶ trial, court case, inquiry, investigation, tribunal, review, proceedings

### hearsay NOUN
*evidence based on hearsay*
▶ rumour, gossip, talk, word of mouth, tittle-tattle

### heart NOUN
1 *His heart had stopped beating.*
▶ organ of circulation, (*more informal*) ticker
RELATED ADJECTIVE cardiac
2 *an air link into the heart of the city*
▶ centre, middle, nucleus, core, hub, inside, kernel
3 *the heart of the problem*
▶ essence, nub, crux, root, focus
4 *He won't allow his heart to rule his head.*
▶ feelings, emotion, sentiment
5 *The lack of support made them lose heart.*
▶ enthusiasm, eagerness, courage, bravery, resolution, determination
6 *She may be stern but she has a lot of heart.*
▶ compassion, feeling, sympathy, tenderness, understanding, affection, humanity, kindness, love

### heartbreaking ADJECTIVE
*heartbreaking sobs from the bedroom*
▶ distressing, harrowing, pitiful, saddening, tragic, grievous, heart-rending

### heartbroken ADJECTIVE
*He was heartbroken at having to sell his home.*
▶ broken-hearted, inconsolable, devastated, grief-stricken, desolate, despairing
AN OPPOSITE IS happy

### hearten VERB
*It had heartened her that she could still win against Ivor.*
▶ encourage, comfort, reassure, console, cheer, cheer up, (*more informal*) buck up
AN OPPOSITE IS dishearten

**heartfelt** ADJECTIVE

*a heartfelt message of good luck*
► sincere, genuine, deeply felt, profound, wholehearted, enthusiastic, earnest, ardent, fervent

**heartless** ADJECTIVE

*heartless thieves who stole a boy's bicycle*
► callous, hard-hearted, mean-spirited, insensitive, cruel

**hearty** ADJECTIVE

1 *The remark brought a loud hearty laugh.*
► enthusiastic, sincere, warm, jovial, cordial, exuberant, cheerful, uninhibited
2 *Beth always had a hearty appetite.*
► big, healthy, strong, robust, vigorous
3 *They looked forward to a hearty meal and a good night's sleep.*
► substantial, generous, sizeable, solid, large, ample, wholesome

**heat** NOUN

1 *The fire gave out a lot of heat.*
► warmth, hotness, glow
RELATED ADJECTIVES thermal, calorific
2 *The summer heat was exhausting.*
► hot weather, warmth, humidity, sultriness, swelter
3 *There is too much heat in these arguments.*
► passion, intensity, ardour, warmth, vehemence, anger, fury

**heat** VERB

1 *You can heat the food under the grill, if you prefer.*
► cook, heat up, reheat
2 *The room has two external walls and is difficult to heat.*
► keep warm, warm up

**heated** ADJECTIVE

1 *The discussion soon became heated.*
► passionate, vehement, animated, impassioned, bitter, tempestuous
OPPOSITES ARE dispassionate, calm
2 *Rachael grew heated as she talked about her ordeal.*
► excited, roused, worked up, keyed up, animated, impassioned
AN OPPOSITE IS calm

**heave** VERB

*Two men heaved back the great iron gates.*
► haul, drag, pull, throw, draw, tow, tug, hoist, lift, lug, raise

**heaven** NOUN

1 *You might get your reward in heaven, if you are lucky.*
► paradise, the next world, the hereafter, the afterlife
2 *In that heat a cool drink was absolute heaven.*
► ecstasy, bliss, joy, rapture, delight
AN OPPOSITE IS hell
3 **the heavens** *The moon caused a glow in the heavens.*
► the sky, the skies, the firmament, the blue
RELATED ADJECTIVE celestial

**heavenly** ADJECTIVE

1 *the sound of joyful, heavenly music*
► beautiful, celestial, divine, angelic, blissful, exquisite
OPPOSITES ARE devilish, infernal
2 *They had a heavenly time.*
► delightful, marvellous, wonderful, lovely, pleasant

**heavy** ADJECTIVE

1 *too heavy to lift*
► weighty, massive, bulky, hefty
2 *a heavy man*
► large, fat, corpulent, overweight
3 *heavy smoking*
► excessive, immoderate, intensive, uncontrolled
4 *a heavy meal*
► substantial, hearty, filling, sizeable, solid, stodgy
5 *a heavy blow*
► hard, forceful, violent, powerful, hefty
6 *heavy losses  a heavy fine*
► large, substantial, considerable
7 *a heavy burden of responsibility*
► onerous, demanding, formidable, challenging, severe
8 *heavy work*
► arduous, strenuous, taxing
9 *heavy reading*
► serious, tedious, dull
10 *heavy rain*
► strong, intense, teeming, torrential

**heckle** VERB

*Some of the speakers came close to being heckled.*
► barrack, jeer, shout down, interrupt, harass, disrupt

**hectic** ADJECTIVE

*We spent three hectic days getting the house in order.*
► busy, frantic, feverish, frenzied, manic, chaotic
OPPOSITES ARE leisurely, quiet

**hector** VERB

*An official hectored them into leaving.*
► bully, browbeat, intimidate, chivvy, harass

**hedge** NOUN

1 *The garden was enclosed by a hedge.*
► fence, hedgerow, barrier, screen
2 *Savings form a hedge against loss of income.*
► safeguard, protection, shield, buffer, cushion

**hedge** VERB

*The next question made him hedge.*
► prevaricate, equivocate, vacillate, stall, be evasive, quibble, hesitate, temporize, (more informal) beat about the bush
**hedge in** *They were hedged in by their lack of information.*
► confine, hinder, obstruct, impede, restrict, limit

**heed** VERB

*She refused to heed him.*
► listen to, pay attention to, take notice of, regard, obey, follow
AN OPPOSITE IS disregard

## heedless ADJECTIVE

**heedless of** *They were heedless of the suffering around them.*
▶ inattentive to, unconcerned about, unmindful of, neglectful of, uncaring of, careless about, unsympathetic towards
AN OPPOSITE IS heedful

## hefty ADJECTIVE

*A hefty young man stood in their way.*
▶ burly, beefy, sturdy, well-built, strapping, brawny, hulking, muscular, powerful, stocky, stout, athletic, big, heavy
OPPOSITES ARE slight, thin

## height NOUN

**1** *We wanted to know the height of the tower.*
▶ tallness, highness, vertical measurement, elevation, altitude
**2** **heights** *reaching the mountain heights*
▶ summit, top, peak, crest, crown, tip
**3** *They were at the height of their fame.*
▶ peak, high point, acme, climax, zenith
OPPOSITES ARE nadir, low point

## heighten VERB

**1** *The architects proposed heightening the roof levels.*
▶ raise, make higher, lift up, elevate, build up
AN OPPOSITE IS lower
**2** *The presence of police heightened their sense of alarm.*
▶ increase, magnify, intensify, add to, sharpen, strengthen, augment, boost, enhance
AN OPPOSITE IS lessen

## hell NOUN

**1** *religions that believe in a hell*
▶ netherworld, eternal punishment, infernal regions, lower regions
AN OPPOSITE IS heaven
RELATED ADJECTIVE infernal
**2** *Living with Patrick must be hell.*
▶ agony, torture, a misery, a nightmare, an ordeal, a torment

## hellish ADJECTIVE

*It was a hellish experience they wanted never to repeat.*
▶ dreadful, ghastly, horrible, terrible, frightful

## help VERB

**1** *Will you help me move this bed?*
▶ assist, aid, lend a hand
**2** *I couldn't help laughing.*
▶ prevent yourself, restrain yourself from, refrain from, resist
**3** *A small donation will help those in need.*
▶ support, contribute to, encourage, promote
**4** *Foreign visits will help your languages.*
▶ improve, enhance, bolster
**5** *She took aspirin to help her headache.*
▶ relieve, reduce, ease, soothe, alleviate, remedy, lessen

## help NOUN

**1** *We could do with some help.*
▶ assistance, support, aid, guidance, cooperation, advice
AN OPPOSITE IS hindrance
**2** *Would a screwdriver be of help?*
▶ use, service, benefit, utility

## helper NOUN

**1** *A chain of helpers passed buckets of water along.*
▶ supporter, volunteer, worker
**2** *All her helpers were away that day.*
▶ assistant, colleague, collaborator, subordinate, associate, co-worker

## helpful ADJECTIVE

**1** *The shop assistant was friendly and helpful.*
▶ obliging, willing, cooperative, thoughtful, considerate, sympathetic, eager to please, friendly
**2** *A hammer might be helpful. A sceptical attitude won't be helpful.*
▶ useful, of use, beneficial, worthwhile, productive, constructive, valuable

## helping NOUN

*a good helping of pudding*
▶ portion, serving, plateful, bowlful, share, amount, ration, (more informal) dollop

## helpless ADJECTIVE

*She felt helpless and frustrated.*
▶ powerless, impotent, incapable, dependent, weak, forlorn, vulnerable, defenceless, destitute

## hem NOUN

*She lowered the hem of her skirt.*
▶ hemline, edge, border, fringe

## hem VERB

**hem in** *We were hemmed in by a group of tourist buses.*
▶ shut in, close in, box in, enclose, surround, confine, restrict

## herald NOUN

**1** *A herald announced the end of hostilities.*
▶ courier, messenger, town crier, crier
**2** *The buds in the park are a herald of spring.*
▶ harbinger, sign, indicator, indication, prelude, forerunner, precursor

---

## herb NOUN

**SOME COMMON HERBS**

angelica, anise, balm, balsam, basil, bay leaf, bergamot, borage, camomile, caraway, chervil, chicory, chive, coriander, cumin, dill, fennel, fenugreek, hyssop, lavender, lemon balm, lovage, marjoram, mint, oregano, parsley, peppermint, rosemary, rue, saffron, sage, savory, sorrel, spearmint, tansy, tarragon, thyme, wintergreen.

**herd** NOUN

**1** *herds of farm animals*
► drove, pack, flock, fold
**2** *She cut her way through the herd of lunchtime drinkers.*
► crowd, mass, throng, horde, crush

**herd** VERB

**1** *They herded the sheep into the pens.*
► drive, lead, guide, round, collect
**2** *We all herded into a meeting room.*
► crowd, pack, throng, flock, huddle, squash

**hereditary** ADJECTIVE

**1** *the hereditary right to place the crown on the king's head*
► ancestral, inherited, bequeathed, handed down, transmitted, family
**2** *a hereditary disease hereditary characteristics*
► genetic, congenital, inherent, transmissible, transmittable, inborn, inbred, innate
AN OPPOSITE IS acquired

**heritage** NOUN

*part of our national heritage*
► tradition, culture, history, inheritance, legacy

**hermit** NOUN

*caves occupied by hermits*
► recluse, solitary, ascetic, anchorite

**hero** NOUN

**1** *His father had been decorated as a war hero.*
► champion, brave man
**2** *James had always been her hero.*
► idol, star, ideal, paragon, favourite, darling
**3** *The story had no real hero.*
► principal character, lead character, protagonist

**heroic** ADJECTIVE

*All his heroic efforts might come to nothing.*
► brave, courageous, noble, valiant, bold, daring, gallant, intrepid
AN OPPOSITE IS cowardly

**heroine** NOUN

*the heroine of the film*
► leading or principal female character, female lead, female star, leading lady

**hesitant** ADJECTIVE

*They were hesitant about what to do next. He took a hesitant step back.*
► uncertain, tentative, cautious, faltering, doubtful, half-hearted, irresolute, indecisive, undecided, dithering
OPPOSITES ARE decisive, resolute

**hesitate** VERB

*She hesitated before searching in her bag for her keys.*
► pause, delay, falter, dither, hold back, vacillate, waver, wait, have second thoughts

**hesitation** NOUN

*He answered without any hesitation.*
► pause, delay, equivocation, reluctance, vacillation, misgivings, second thoughts, qualms, reservation, doubt, uncertainty

**hidden** ADJECTIVE

**1** *a hidden entrance a hidden camera*
► concealed, secret, unseen, invisible, disguised, camouflaged, covered
**2** *The message may have a hidden meaning.*
► unknown, obscure, cryptic, secret, abstruse, mysterious, ulterior

**hide** VERB

**1** *Sam hid in a cupboard.*
► conceal yourself, take cover, keep hidden, lie low, keep out of sight
**2** *Where did they hide the jewels?*
► conceal, secrete, store away, bury, (more informal) stash
AN OPPOSITE IS expose
**3** *Richard tried to hide his disapproval.*
► disguise, conceal, keep hidden, suppress, repress, mask
OPPOSITES ARE disclose, flaunt
**4** *Passing clouds hid the moon.*
► obscure, shadow, block out, conceal, obstruct
AN OPPOSITE IS reveal

**hide** NOUN

*an animal's hide*
► skin, pelt, coat, fur, leather

**hideous** ADJECTIVE

**1** *His mouth was twisted in a hideous grin.*
► ugly, unsightly, repulsive, repellent, revolting, gruesome, disgusting, macabre
AN OPPOSITE IS beautiful
**2** *It is one of the most hideous experiences we have had in our lives.*
► horrible, ghastly, horrific, terrible, appalling, shocking, sickening, dreadful, frightful, grim, grisly, odious

**hide-out** NOUN

*Police stormed his hideout in the suburbs.*
► hiding place, hideaway, retreat, refuge, lair, den, shelter, sanctuary, bolt-hole

**hiding** NOUN

*I was given a good hiding.*
► beating, thrashing, caning, spanking, belting, whacking

**high** ADJECTIVE

**1** *a high mountain a high building*
► tall, lofty, elevated, towering
OPPOSITES ARE low, short
**2** *a high position in the government*
► senior, prominent, high-ranking, top-ranking, leading, distinguished, important, influential, powerful
OPPOSITES ARE junior, low-ranking
**3** *high moral principles*
► noble, lofty, honourable, high-minded
AN OPPOSITE IS base
**4** *high prices*
► inflated, excessive, exorbitant, top, costly
AN OPPOSITE IS low

a b c d e f g **h** i j k l m n o p q r s t u v w x y z

**5** *the high notes*
► high-pitched, soprano, treble, shrill, sharp, piercing
OPPOSITES ARE low, bass
**6** *the highest standards*
► excellent, outstanding, exceptional, exemplary
OPPOSITES ARE low, poor
**7** *high winds*
► strong, powerful, violent, stiff, blustery
AN OPPOSITE IS gentle
**8** *I have a high opinion of them.*
► favourable, positive, good, approving
OPPOSITES ARE low, unfavourable

**highbrow** ADJECTIVE
*highbrow tastes in music*
► intellectual, sophisticated, cultivated, cultured, serious

**high-class** ADJECTIVE
*The restaurant is high-class and in a good location.*
► superior, high-quality, high-grade, exclusive, excellent

**highlight** NOUN
*one of the highlights of a long career*
► high point, high spot, climax, peak, best moment

**highlight** VERB
*The news reports tend to highlight party disagreements.*
► emphasize, accentuate, spotlight, focus on, play up, show up

**highly** ADVERB
*a form of waste that is highly toxic*
► very, extremely, considerably, exceedingly, distinctly, decidedly, immensely

**highly-strung** ADJECTIVE
*a young highly-strung performer*
► nervous, nervy, sensitive, excitable, jumpy, temperamental, tense

**hijack** VERB
*A man was charged with hijacking a Russian plane to Stockholm.*
► seize, commandeer, take over, skyjack, expropriate

**hike** VERB
*They hiked across the moors for several miles.*
► trek, go on foot, walk , ramble, tramp, trudge, traipse, slog

**hike** NOUN
*a twenty-mile hike*
► trek, walk , ramble, tramp, trudge, slog

**hilarious** ADJECTIVE
*A group clustered round a hilarious puppet show.*
► comical, funny, amusing, entertaining, uproarious, riotous, (*more informal*) hysterical, (*more informal*) side-splitting

**hill** NOUN
**1** *the house at the top of the hill*
► high ground, elevation, hillock, ridge, peak, mount

**2** *The car stalled on a steep hill.*
► slope, rise, gradient, incline, ascent

**hinder** VERB
*Power failures have hindered production.*
► hamper, hold up, interfere with, obstruct, restrict, thwart, prevent, curb, curtail, foil
AN OPPOSITE IS facilitate

**hindrance** NOUN
*Our presence might be as much a hindrance to you as a help.*
► impediment, obstacle, obstruction, encumbrance, handicap, restriction, limitation, restraint, inconvenience, complication, disadvantage, drawback
AN OPPOSITE IS help

**hinge** VERB
*Everything hinges on next month's elections.*
► depend, rest, hang, revolve, turn

**hint** NOUN
**1** *She would drop a few casual hints about leaving. I can take a hint that I'm not wanted.*
► clue, sign, signal, indication, reminder, inkling, intimation
**2** *His father kept turning up to offer handy hints.*
► tip, piece of advice, pointer
**3** *There was a hint of sadness in her voice.*
► trace, tinge, touch, suggestion

**hint** VERB
**1** *He hinted that a new project was being considered.*
► suggest, imply, indicate, intimate
**2** hint at *I'm not sure what she was hinting at.*
► allude to, refer to, imply, suggest

**hire** VERB
**1** *We could hire a car and drive to London.*
► rent, lease, book, charter
**2** *The new bosses want to hire more freelance workers.*
► employ, engage, recruit, appoint

**hiss** VERB
**1** *She turned the tap until she heard the gas hiss.*
► fizz, fizzle, whistle
**2** *The audience hissed him and threw things on the stage.*
► jeer, boo, catcall

**historic** ADJECTIVE
*a historic meeting of the heads of state*
► famous, notable, epoch-making, celebrated, momentous, significant, important
AN OPPOSITE IS unimportant

**historical** ADJECTIVE
*a story based on historical events*
► real, real-life, true, actual, authentic, documented, attested, verifiable
OPPOSITES ARE fictitious, fictional

**history** NOUN
**1** *their interest in history*
► the past, former times, days of old, antiquity
**2** *a history of the civil wars*
► chronicle, record, narrative

**hit** VERB This word is often overused. Here are some alternatives:
1 *He hit the tree with his fist.*
▶ strike, smack, slap, thump, whack, (*more informal*) slug
2 *Several lorries hit the central barrier.*
▶ crash into, run into, collide with, smash into
3 *The industry has been hit by lightning strikes.*
▶ affect, hurt, harm, damage
4 *It suddenly hit me that I should have confirmed the booking.*
▶ strike, occur to, dawn on, come to, cross your mind
5 *Contributions should hit the million mark.*
▶ reach, achieve

**hit** NOUN
1 *He got a hit on the head.*
▶ blow, punch, thump, knock, smack, slap, whack
2 *The party had been a huge hit.*
▶ success, triumph, winner, best-seller, (*more informal*) knockout

**hitch** NOUN
*The moves all went without any hitch.*
▶ problem, difficulty, snag, setback, hindrance

**hitch** VERB
1 *The farmer hitched a tractor to the cart.*
▶ fasten, attach, hook, couple, connect
2 *Diana hitched up her skirts and entered the water.*
▶ pull, lift, raise, hoist, jerk, (*more informal*) hike

**hoard** NOUN
*The tomb contained a huge hoard of jewellery.*
▶ cache, store, stock, pile, stockpile, heap, supply, treasure-trove

**hoard** VERB
*The refugees had hoarded their supplies.*
▶ store, amass, accumulate, mass, put by, save, stockpile, pile up, collect, gather, keep, lay up, treasure, (*more informal*) stash away
AN OPPOSITE IS squander

**hoarse** ADJECTIVE
*a voice that was hoarse from shouting*
▶ rough, harsh, gruff, husky, throaty, rasping, croaking, grating, gravelly, growling, raucous

**hoax** NOUN
*The virus warning was a hoax*
▶ joke, practical joke, prank, trick, spoof, deception, fake, fraud, imposture, cheat, swindle, (*more informal*) leg-pull, (*more informal*) con

**hoax** VERB
*It's not a good time to hoax people.*
▶ trick, fool, dupe, deceive, take in, hoodwink, cheat, (*more informal*) con, (*more informal*) pull someone's leg

**hobble** VERB
*The old man hobbled down the road.*
▶ limp, shuffle, shamble, totter, falter, stagger

**hobby** NOUN
*Kevin took up fishing as a hobby.*
▶ pastime, leisure activity, leisure pursuit, recreation, diversion, interest, relaxation

**hoist** VERB
*The crew hoisted more cargo on deck.*
▶ raise, lift, pull up, heave, winch up

**hoist** NOUN
*a hand-operated pneumatic hoist*
▶ crane, jack, pulley, winch, lift, lifting gear, block and tackle, davit, windlass, derrick

**hold** VERB
1 *He was holding a black briefcase.*
▶ clasp, clutch, grip, cling to, cling on to
2 *I wanted to hold her in my arms.*
▶ hug, embrace, clasp, fold, cradle
3 *Visitors must hold a valid passport.*
▶ possess, bear, have, own
4 *The society holds a general meeting in March.*
▶ call, convene, summon, conduct, assemble
5 *Police are holding him pending further investigation.*
▶ detain, keep in custody, imprison, lock up, arrest
6 *She held a senior position in a bank.*
▶ occupy, fill, (*more informal*) hold down
7 *The house holds six to eight people.*
▶ take, accommodate, have room for, have space for, contain
8 *The sect holds that killing animals is a sin.*
▶ believe, consider, maintain, contend, think, take the view
9 *I hope the good weather will hold.*
▶ continue, last, carry on, persist, endure
**hold back**
1 *Joe held back his anger.*
▶ suppress, control, restrain, curb, check, keep back, hold in
AN OPPOSITE IS release
2 *The lack of information held us back.*
▶ hinder, hamper, inhibit, impede, thwart, restrain
AN OPPOSITE IS help
3 *There is no need to hold back if you have things to say.*
▶ hesitate, pause, desist, shrink
AN OPPOSITE IS proceed
**hold forth** *Ivor was holding forth about his adventures.*
▶ discourse, declaim, speak at length, spout, rant
**hold off**
1 *The rain held off until lunch time.*
▶ stay away, desist
2 *He held the attackers off as long as he could.*
▶ resist, fend off, ward off, stave off, repel, rebuff
**hold out**
1 *Supplies will not hold out much longer.*
▶ last, remain, continue
AN OPPOSITE IS run out
2 *The garrison held out for a whole month.*
▶ resist, persevere, stand fast, hang on
OPPOSITES ARE give in, yield
**hold up**
1 *The bridge is held up by concrete columns.*
▶ support, bear, shore up, carry, raise

a b c d e f **g** **h** i j k l m n o p q r s t u v w x y z

**hold** (continued)

2 *Work on the roof was held up by bad weather.*
▶ delay, detain, hinder, impede
AN OPPOSITE IS facilitate

**hold with** *We do not hold with violence.*
▶ approve of, agree with, support, condone, countenance, subscribe to
AN OPPOSITE IS disapprove of

**hold** NOUN
1 *She released her hold on the handle.*
▶ grip, grasp, clutch
2 *Tim had some kind of hold over them.*
▶ influence, power, control, sway, (*more informal*) clout

**holder** NOUN
1 *She put the knife back in its holder.*
▶ case, container, receptacle, casing, cover, sheath, stand, rest
2 *holders of EU passports*
▶ bearer, possessor, owner

**hold-up** NOUN
1 *There was a hold-up at the bank.*
▶ robbery, raid, burglary
2 *We faced several hold-ups on the motorway.*
▶ delay, wait, hitch, setback, stoppage

**hole** NOUN
1 *The work gang dug a large hole in the road.*
▶ opening, orifice, trench, ditch
2 *There were holes in the plaster caused by damp.*
▶ gap, split, cavity, crack, fissure, pit, puncture, hollow, depression, tear
3 *The animal crawled out of its hole.*
▶ burrow, lair, retreat
4 *We were out of money and in a bit of a hole.*
▶ predicament, mess, difficulty, tight corner, quandary, plight, crisis, emergency

**holiday** NOUN
1 *Her doctor told her she needed a holiday.*
▶ vacation, break, rest, time off, leave
2 *Monday is a public holiday.*
▶ bank holiday, festival, feast day

**holiness** NOUN
*Her holiness affected everyone who saw her.*
▶ sanctity, devoutness, spirituality, piety, saintliness, godliness, righteousness

**hollow** ADJECTIVE
1 *a hollow space*
▶ empty, concave, sunken, deep, depressed
AN OPPOSITE IS solid
2 *a hollow laugh*
▶ dull, low, flat, muffled, muted
3 *a hollow promise*
▶ insincere, artificial, false, empty, deceptive
AN OPPOSITE IS sincere
4 *a hollow victory*
▶ worthless, futile, vain, meaningless, pointless, pyrrhic
AN OPPOSITE IS worthwhile

**hollow** NOUN
*an ancient theatre built in the hollow of a hillside*
▶ depression, cavity, dimple, dip, crater, hole, indentation, bowl, concavity, dent, dint, dish

**hollow** VERB
**hollow out** *Engineers hollowed out a tunnel.*
▶ dig out, excavate, gouge out, burrow, scoop

**holy** ADJECTIVE
1 *holy men and women*
▶ saintly, godly, pious, devout, religious, spiritual, virtuous, pure
2 *a holy place*
▶ sacred, hallowed, consecrated, sanctified, revered, venerated

**homage** NOUN
*an act of homage to the king*
▶ respect, recognition, acknowledgement, devotion, tribute, honour, admiration, esteem, deference, veneration
**pay homage to** *He paid homage to all who had sacrificed their lives in the war.*
▶ honour, praise, salute, acclaim, applaud

**home** NOUN
1 *People were forced to leave their homes.*
▶ house, dwelling, place of residence, address, accommodation
RELATED ADJECTIVE domestic
2 *They had travelled thousands of miles from home.*
▶ native land, homeland, birthplace, motherland, fatherland
3 *He refused to go into a home.*
▶ institution, nursing home, residential home, hospice, shelter

**homeless** ADJECTIVE
*increasing numbers of homeless people*
▶ destitute, vagrant, down-and-out, outcast, unhoused, wandering, evicted, forsaken, abandoned, itinerant, nomadic

**homely** ADJECTIVE
*The hotel offers a warm welcome and a homely atmosphere.*
▶ friendly, informal, relaxed, easygoing, familiar, intimate, congenial, comfortable, cosy, natural, simple, unaffected, unpretentious
AN OPPOSITE IS formal

**homosexual** ADJECTIVE
*homosexual couples*
▶ gay, queer, (*female*) lesbian
AN OPPOSITE IS heterosexual

**honest** ADJECTIVE
1 *He's a fair and honest man.*
▶ upright, honourable, virtuous, law-abiding, high-minded, scrupulous, moral, decent, principled, upstanding
AN OPPOSITE IS dishonest
2 *business practices that are barely honest*
▶ legal, lawful, ethical, legitimate, above-board, (*more informal*) on the level
AN OPPOSITE IS dishonest

**3** *It was an honest mistake.*
▶ genuine, real, authentic, legitimate
AN OPPOSITE IS deliberate

**4** *Let us have your honest opinion.* *I've tried to be perfectly honest with you.*
▶ sincere, objective, candid, direct, open, frank, truthful, impartial, unbiased, unprejudiced, balanced
OPPOSITES ARE insincere, untruthful, biased

## honestly ADVERB

**1** *He said he had come by the money honestly.*
▶ fairly, legally, lawfully, legitimately, honourably
**2** *She could honestly say she had had nothing to do with the incident.*
▶ frankly, sincerely, truthfully, genuinely

## honesty NOUN

**1** *She demanded complete honesty from her staff.*
▶ truthfulness, trustworthiness, integrity, goodness, morality, honour, uprightness, veracity, fairness, probity, rectitude, reliability, scrupulousness
AN OPPOSITE IS dishonesty

**2** *They were encouraged to speak with complete honesty.*
▶ sincerity, candour, directness, frankness, straightforwardness, bluntness, outspokenness, plainness
AN OPPOSITE IS insincerity

## honour NOUN

**1** *He defended the President, calling him a man of honour.*
▶ honesty, integrity, morality, principle, distinction, decency, probity

**2** *She received many honours from the film industry.*
▶ award, accolade, tribute, distinction, commendation, acknowledgement, recognition

**3** *I appreciate the honour of speaking at this assembly.*
▶ privilege, distinction, cachet, kudos

**4** *They were received with honour by the king.*
▶ praise, acclaim, homage, admiration, adulation

## honour VERB

**1** *a grand parade to honour the distinguished visitors*
▶ praise, applaud, acclaim, salute, celebrate, commend, pay homage to

**2** *They intend to honour their commitment to the peace process.*
▶ fulfil, respect, observe, carry out, keep, discharge

## honourable ADJECTIVE

**1** *No one doubted that her motives were entirely honourable. honourable people who were fighting for the common good*
▶ honest, sincere, reputable, noble, worthy, just, straight, trustworthy, principled, virtuous, upright, proper

**2** *a respected politician who has done honourable service in the Treasury*
▶ distinguished, illustrious, eminent, great

## hoodwink VERB

*The man had hoodwinked him into parting with a large sum of money.*
▶ deceive, trick, dupe, cheat, swindle, fool, mislead, delude, (more informal) take in

## hook NOUN

**1** *He hung his coat on one of the hooks.*
▶ peg, nail
**2** *a dress fastened at the back with a hook and eye*
▶ fastener, fastening, clasp, clip, hasp
**3** *a fishing hook*
▶ barb, snare

## hook VERB

**1** *David hooked a 64 pound carp.*
▶ catch, take, land, net, bag
**2** *He hooked a trailer to the car.*
▶ hitch, fasten, attach, couple, connect

## hooligan NOUN

*hooligans messing around in the dodgems*
▶ troublemaker, hoodlum, lout, ruffian, vandal, thug, bully, delinquent, tough, rough, tearaway, (more informal) yob

## hoop NOUN

*a hoop of metal*
▶ band, loop, ring, round, circle, circlet, girdle

## hoot VERB

**1** *An owl hooted.*
▶ screech, call, tu-whit tu-whoo
**2** *The driver became impatient and hooted.*
▶ beep, toot, honk, sound the horn
**3** *The audience hooted in derision.*
▶ shout, shriek, yell, jeer, call out

## hoot NOUN

**1** *the hoot of an owl*
▶ screech, call, tu whit tu-whoo
**2** *hoots of laughter*
▶ shriek, shout, scream, yell, jeer

## hop VERB

*He hopped along beside her.* *She hopped on a bus and went home.*
▶ jump, leap, skip, spring, trip, bound, dance, flit, limp, prance, caper

## hop NOUN

**1** *With one hop he was free.*
▶ jump, leap, skip, spring, bound
**2** *a short hop across the Channel*
▶ trip, journey, jaunt, ride, distance

## hope VERB

**1** *I hope to answer all your questions.*
▶ aim, intend, plan, have it in mind, aspire
**2** **hope for** *We are hoping for a quick response.*
▶ expect, look for, wish for, want
USAGE It is better to avoid *anticipate* in this sense, because it has other meanings.

## hope NOUN

**1** *She has the hope of being in the national team.*
▶ ambition, aspiration, expectation, dream, desire, wish

# hopeful

**2** *There's some hope of a better future.*
▶ prospect, expectation, likelihood, optimism, assumption

## hopeful ADJECTIVE

**1** *We are still hopeful about avoiding a conflict.*
▶ optimistic, confident, positive, expectant, sanguine
AN OPPOSITE IS pessimistic

**2** *hopeful signs of an economic recovery*
▶ promising, encouraging, favourable, heartening, reassuring, propitious, auspicious, cheering
AN OPPOSITE IS discouraging

## hopefully ADVERB

**1** *'Are we going back?' she asked hopefully.*
▶ expectantly, optimistically, confidently, with hope
AN OPPOSITE IS pessimistically

**2** *Hopefully the work will be completed next week.*
▶ all being well, most likely, with luck, conceivably, probably

## hopeless ADJECTIVE

**1** *He looked at her in hopeless bewilderment.*
▶ despairing, desperate, dejected, downhearted, downcast, wretched, pessimistic

**2** *The doctors regarded his case as hopeless.*
▶ impossible, incurable, irremediable, beyond hope, beyond recovery, lost, unattainable

**3** *The situation seemed hopeless, now that the food had run out.*
▶ desperate, critical, serious, dire, impossible, beyond hope, useless, futile

**4** *He is hopeless at board games.*
▶ incompetent, ineffective, ineffectual, poor, inept, (more informal) pathetic, (more informal) useless, (more informal) rubbish

## horde NOUN

*A horde of journalists waited outside the house.*
▶ crowd, throng, pack, mob, swarm, band, gang, group

## horizon NOUN

*A ship was visible on the horizon*
▶ skyline, vista, range of view

## horrible, horrid ADJECTIVE

**1** *a horrible accident on the bypass*
▶ dreadful, horrific, horrifying, horrendous, frightful, fearful, terrible, ghastly, hideous, sickening

**2** *Saturday was a wet, horrible day. The smell was horrid.*
▶ unpleasant, nasty, disagreeable, awful, beastly, dreadful, ghastly, revolting, terrible
OPPOSITES ARE pleasant, agreeable

**3** *Nora was a horrible person. The teachers were horrid to him.*
▶ nasty, disagreeable, odious, objectionable, loathsome, hateful, offensive
OPPOSITES ARE nice, kind

## horrific ADJECTIVE

*He died from horrific head injuries.*
▶ dreadful, appalling, horrific, horrifying, horrendous, frightful, fearful, terrible, hideous, ghastly, sickening

## horrified ADJECTIVE

*Horrified residents escaped the flames over garden fences.*
▶ frightened, horror-stricken, horror-struck, shocked, appalled, disgusted, sickened, stunned

## horrify VERB

**1** *He wrote stories that horrified his readers.*
▶ terrify, frighten, scare, alarm, petrify, terrorize

**2** *The news would have horrified her.*
▶ shock, appal, outrage, scandalize, offend, sicken, disgust, revolt, nauseate, unnerve, alarm
OPPOSITES ARE please, delight

## horror NOUN

**1** *People screamed in horror.*
▶ terror, fear, fright, alarm

**2** *Public opinion reacted with horror.*
▶ shock, outrage, disgust, revulsion, repugnance, consternation
AN OPPOSITE IS delight

**3** *Newspaper reports described the full horror of the attack.*
▶ ghastliness, awfulness, frightfulness, hideousness, savagery, barbarity

## horse NOUN

*a woman on a horse*
▶ (for riding) mount, (small breed) pony, (adult male) stallion, (young male) colt, (large and strong) cob, (adult female) mare, (young female) filly, (new-born horse) foal
RELATED ADJECTIVES equestrian, equine

## hospitable ADJECTIVE

*a kind, hospitable family*
▶ friendly, sociable, welcoming, congenial, cordial, convivial, amicable, generous, gracious, receptive
OPPOSITES ARE inhospitable, unfriendly

## hospital NOUN

*Joe was lying in a bed in the hospital.*
▶ infirmary, clinic, nursing home, sanatorium, medical institution, convalescent home, hospice

## hospitality NOUN

**1** *We needed hospitality for the night.*
▶ accommodation, catering, entertainment

**2** *Thank you for your hospitality.*
▶ kindness, friendliness, sociability, welcome, conviviality, warm reception

## host NOUN

**1** *A host of people headed for the town.*
▶ crowd, throng, band, horde, swarm, group

**2** *The host of the restaurant welcomed his guests.*
▶ proprietor, landlord

**3** *the host of a television programme*
▶ presenter, compère, anchorman, anchorwoman, announcer, link person

# hostage

**hostage** NOUN
*The hijackers released some of the hostages.*
▶ captive, prisoner, detainee

**hostel** NOUN
*We could stay at a hostel near the city.*
▶ boarding house, guest house

**hostile** ADJECTIVE
**1** *a hostile crowd  a hostile attack*
▶ aggressive, antagonistic, belligerent, confrontational, bellicose, pugnacious, angry, militant, unfriendly, malevolent, ill-disposed, warlike
AN OPPOSITE IS friendly
**2** *a hostile climate*
▶ harsh, unfavourable, adverse, inhospitable, bad, contrary, unpropitious
AN OPPOSITE IS favourable
**3** *hostile to They are hostile to the idea.*
▶ opposed to, averse to, unsympathetic to, antagonistic to, against

**hostility** NOUN
**1** *They reacted with hostility.*
▶ antagonism, enmity, animosity, opposition, malice, hatred, ill-will
AN OPPOSITE IS friendship
**2** *their hostility to our suggestion*
▶ opposition, antipathy, disapproval (of), aversion, antagonism

**hot** ADJECTIVE
**1** *hot weather*
▶ warm, balmy, summery, boiling, blazing, roasting, scorching, sweltering, sultry
OPPOSITES ARE cold, chilly
**2** *What we need is a hot meal.*
▶ cooked, heated, piping, sizzling
**3** *a hot dish with peppers*
▶ spicy, peppery, piquant, sharp, pungent
AN OPPOSITE IS mild
**4** *a hot temper*
▶ fierce, angry, raging, intense, violent, passionate

**hotchpotch** NOUN
*a hotchpotch of different plants and shrubs.*
▶ mixture, assortment, jumble, miscellany, ragbag, mishmash, confusion, mess

**hotel** NOUN
*We stayed in a hotel by the river.*
▶ guest house, boarding house, inn, pension, motel

**hound** VERB
*The reporters went on hounding her.*
▶ harass, pursue, harry, hassle, pester, persecute, trouble

**house** NOUN
**1** *a row of terraced houses*
▶ home, dwelling, abode, residence
**2** *the house of Stuart*
▶ dynasty, clan, family, tribe

# huff

**house** VERB
*The cabins housed twenty people.*
▶ accommodate, provide room for, lodge, quarter, shelter, take in, billet, board, (more informal) put up

**household** NOUN
*a large household with lots of children*
▶ family, home, ménage, establishment, (more informal) set-up

**housing** NOUN
*an acute need for better housing*
▶ accommodation, houses, homes, habitation, shelter

**hovel** NOUN
*The little cottage was not much better than a hovel.*
▶ shack, shanty, shed, slum, hut

**hover** VERB
**1** *A police helicopter hovered above the crowd.*
▶ float, hang, flutter, drift, fly
**2** *He hovered outside the room waiting to be called in.*
▶ linger, dally, pause, wait about, waver, loiter, hesitate, (informal) hang about

**howl** VERB
*A dog howled in the distance.*
▶ yowl, bay, cry

**howl** NOUN
*howls of laughter*
▶ shriek, hoot, roar, gale, scream, yell

**hub** NOUN
**1** *He gripped the hub of the rear wheel.*
▶ centre, middle, pivot, axis
**2** *The foyer will be the hub of activity in this part of the building.*
▶ focus, focal point, heart, pivot, nucleus

**hubbub** NOUN
*Seb listened to the growing hubbub.*
▶ commotion, noise, din, disturbance, uproar, racket, tumult, hullabaloo, rumpus

**huddle** VERB
**1** *They huddled together in twos and threes.*
▶ crowd, gather, cluster, squeeze, pack, throng, flock, herd, pile, press
AN OPPOSITE IS scatter
**2** *He huddled under the duvet.*
▶ cuddle, curl up, nestle, snuggle

**huddle** NOUN
*There was a huddle of people round the enquiry desk.*
▶ crowd, throng, crush, knot, flock, cluster

**hue** NOUN
**1** *gloss paint in a range of hues*
▶ colour, shade, tone, tint, tinge
**2** *people of all political hues*
▶ complexion, kind, type, nature, character

**huff** NOUN
*He went off in a huff.*
▶ sulk, fit of pique, rage, bad mood

A
B
C
D
E
F
G
**H**
I
J
K
L
M
N
O
P
Q
R
S
T
U
V
W
X
Y
Z

**huffy** ADJECTIVE

*They didn't have an answer and became huffy when we asked.*
▶ irritable, irritated, annoyed, unfriendly, grumpy, prickly, piqued, testy, petulant
AN OPPOSITE IS friendly

**hug** VERB

*Mary was kissed and hugged by her workmates.*
▶ embrace, clasp, cuddle, squeeze, cling to, enfold, fold in your arms, hold close, nurse, snuggle against

**hug** NOUN

*They met with tears and hugs.*
▶ embrace, clasp, cuddle, squeeze

**huge** ADJECTIVE

*a huge building  a huge tax increase*
▶ enormous, gigantic, immense, massive, colossal, vast, large, big, great, giant, *(more informal)* whopping, *(more informal)* ginormous
AN OPPOSITE IS tiny

**hulk** NOUN

*the hulk of an old ship*
▶ wreck, shell, ruin, body, carcass, frame, hull

**hulking** ADJECTIVE

*A hulking figure came through the door.*
▶ huge, large, bulky, clumsy, cumbersome, awkward, heavy, ungainly, unwieldy
OPPOSITES ARE small, delicate

**hum** VERB

*The engine was still humming.*
▶ purr, whirr, drone, murmur, throb, vibrate

**human** ADJECTIVE

1 *the human race*
▶ anthropoid

2 *They are only human and make mistakes.*
▶ mortal, fallible, imperfect, weak

3 *a very human reaction to the problem*
▶ compassionate, humane, kind, considerate, understanding, sympathetic, merciful, philanthropic
AN OPPOSITE IS inhuman

**human beings**
▶ men and women, humankind, humanity, mortals, people, folk

**humane** ADJECTIVE

*a humane way to control the fox population*
▶ kind, compassionate, considerate, understanding, sympathetic, merciful

**humanity** NOUN

1 *If they have a shred of humanity in them they will hand over the suspects.*
▶ compassion, understanding, sensitivity, fellow feeling, sympathy, tolerance

2 *A decision that could affect the whole of humanity*
▶ humankind, the human race, mankind, mortals, people

**humble** ADJECTIVE

1 *He acted in a humble and contrite manner.*
▶ meek, self-effacing, unassuming, deferential, respectful, submissive
AN OPPOSITE IS proud

2 *I live in a humble house in the suburbs.*
▶ modest, simple, plain, ordinary, unpretentious, unostentatious
OPPOSITES ARE grand, pretentious

3 *She comes from a humble background.*
▶ lowly, undistinguished, poor, common, ordinary
OPPOSITES ARE distinguished, noble

**humdrum** ADJECTIVE

*Most of the work is repetitive and humdrum.*
▶ tedious, dull, mundane, dreary, boring, routine, monotonous, ordinary, banal

**humid** ADJECTIVE

*a hot and humid day*
▶ muggy, clammy, sultry, sticky, damp, dank, moist, steamy, sweaty
AN OPPOSITE IS fresh

**humiliate** VERB

*He liked to humiliate them with constant reminders of their mistakes.*
▶ embarrass, humble, mortify, demean, shame, put to shame

**humiliating** ADJECTIVE

*Rome inflicted a humiliating defeat on its neighbour.*
▶ embarrassing, mortifying, ignominious, degrading, demeaning, humbling, chastening, crushing, inglorious, discreditable, dishonourable, shaming, undignified
AN OPPOSITE IS glorious

**humiliation** NOUN

*At immigration he suffered the humiliation of a body search.*
▶ embarrassment, indignity, ignominy, mortification, shame, disgrace, degradation, dishonour

**humility** NOUN

*I'm not sure I have the humility to admit my mistakes.*
▶ modesty, deference, humbleness, meekness, self-effacement, unpretentiousness, lowliness
AN OPPOSITE IS pride

**humorous** ADJECTIVE

*a love story with humorous episodes*
▶ amusing, funny, comic, comical, jocular, hilarious, entertaining

**humour** NOUN

1 *a conversation spiced with humour*
▶ wit, jocularity, badinage, repartee, jokes, jesting, hilarity, comedy, drollery

2 *in a bad humour*
▶ mood, temper, frame of mind, state of mind, disposition, spirits

## humour VERB

*She humoured him to keep him happy.*
► indulge, pander to, gratify, pamper, mollify, cater to, give way to, go along with

## hump NOUN

*a hump in the road*
► bump, protuberance, bulge, mound, rise, curve, knob, lump, swelling

## hunch NOUN

*The theory was no more than a hunch.*
► feeling, intuition, inkling, guess, impression, suspicion, idea

## hunch VERB

*He sat in a corner and hunched his shoulders.*
► arch, curve, bend, hump, shrug, huddle, curl up

## hunger NOUN

1 *She had no hunger that day.*
► appetite, desire for food
2 *He grew faint with hunger.*
► lack of food, malnutrition, starvation, deprivation, famine
3 *a hunger for knowledge*
► desire, yearning, longing, craving, appetite, thirst

## hungry ADJECTIVE

*I was hungry again by 3 o'clock.*
► in need of food, ravenous, famished, starving, (more informal) peckish

## hunk NOUN

*a hunk of bread*
► lump, chunk, block, wedge, piece, portion, slab

## hunt NOUN

*the hunt for clues*
► search, quest, pursuit (of), chase

## hunt VERB

1 *They hunt foxes and deer.*
► chase, give chase to, stalk, track, trail, course, pursue
2 *She spent ages hunting for her keys.*
► search, look, rummage, scour, root around

## hurdle NOUN

1 *He hit the last hurdle and fell.*
► fence, jump, barrier, obstacle
2 *There was one more hurdle to overcome before they could claim success.*
► obstacle, difficulty, handicap, problem, snag, stumbling block

## hurl VERB

*She hurled a book at Roger.*
► throw, fling, toss, cast, pitch, heave

## hurly-burly NOUN

*the hurly-burly of city life*
► bustle, hustle, commotion, hubbuh, turmoil

## hurricane NOUN

*a region hit by floods and hurricanes*
► gale, tornado, storm, typhoon, whirlwind, cyclone

## hurried ADJECTIVE

1 *hurried attempts to change the venue.*
► hasty, hectic, rushed, speedy, precipitate, swift, rapid
2 *He gave the paper a hurried read.*
► brief, cursory, superficial, swift, rapid

## hurry VERB

1 *If I don't hurry I'll be late.*
► be quick, hurry up, hasten, make speed, move faster, (more informal) buck up, (more informal) shift, (more informal) step on it
AN OPPOSITE IS dawdle
2 *Sarah hurried to the library.*
► rush, hasten, dash, speed, chase, hurtle, hustle, move quickly, (more informal) belt
OPPOSITES ARE go slowly, amble
3 *She hurried the children into the bathroom.*
► hustle, hasten, push on, urge on, drive
AN OPPOSITE IS delay

## hurry NOUN

*In our hurry we forgot the food.*
► haste, bustle, confusion, urgency, agitation

## hurt VERB

1 *My arm hurts.*
► be sore, be painful, ache, throb, sting
2 *Derek hurt his leg.*
► injure, wound, maim, bruise, damage, disable
3 *The criticism hurt her deeply.*
► upset, distress, offend, grieve

## hurt NOUN

1 *She rubbed the hurt on her leg.*
► injury, wound, soreness, pain, aching
2 *She loved him in spite of the hurt he had caused her.*
► distress, suffering, pain, wrong, sadness, anguish, torment

## hurt ADJECTIVE

1 *A hurt animal lay in the road.*
► injured, wounded, maimed, bruised, scarred
2 *He felt hurt by the words she had used.*
► upset, pained, distressed, wounded

## hurtful ADJECTIVE

*She forgot all the hurtful remarks and remembered the good times.*
► upsetting, distressing, unkind, spiteful, mean, cruel, malicious, wounding, painful
OPPOSITES ARE kind, comforting

## hurtle VERB

1 *A train was hurtling towards them.*
► speed, rush, race, career, charge, dash, fly, tear, chase, shoot
2 *The plane hurtled to the ground.*
► plunge, plummet, nosedive, drop

## husband NOUN

*Their husbands had taken their cars to the rally.*
► spouse, partner, (more formal) consort, (more informal) man, (more informal) mate, (more informal) better half

## hush

**hush** NOUN
*A hush fell on the room.*
▶ silence, quiet, quietness, calm, stillness, tranquillity
OPPOSITES ARE noise, clamour

**hush** VERB
*She wanted to hush their fears.*
▶ calm, soothe, allay, ease, assuage, quieten
**hush up** *The government is accused of hushing up the dangers.*
▶ conceal, cover up, keep secret, keep quiet, hide, stifle, suppress

**hush-hush** ADJECTIVE
*The news is still rather hush-hush.*
▶ secret, confidential, restricted, classified, (more informal) under wraps

**husk** NOUN
*There were seed husks scattered over the floor.*
▶ shell, case, pod, covering

**husky** ADJECTIVE
**1** *He gave a low husky laugh.*
▶ gruff, throaty, hoarse, croaky
**2** *Eyes turned to the big husky guy who came.*
▶ hefty, beefy, burly, brawny, strong, muscular

**hustle** VERB
*The MPs were hustled out of the building.*
▶ rush, hasten, bustle, jostle, bundle, force, shove

**hut** NOUN
*a hut in the woods*
▶ cabin, shack, shed, shelter, shanty, den, hovel

**hybrid** NOUN
*a hybrid of two species*
▶ cross, cross-breed, mixed breed, blend, amalgam, combination, composite, compound, mixture, fusion

**hybrid** ADJECTIVE
*hybrid roses*
▶ cross-bred, composite, mixed, compound, mongrel
AN OPPOSITE IS pure-bred

**hygiene** NOUN
*acceptable standards of hygiene*
▶ cleanliness, sanitariness, sanitation, health, wholesomeness
RELATED ADJECTIVE sanitary

**hygienic** ADJECTIVE
*Hygienic conditions are essential.*
▶ sanitary, clean, germ-free, sterilized, sterile, aseptic, disinfected, healthy, pure, salubrious, unpolluted, wholesome
OPPOSITES ARE unhygienic, insanitary, dirty

**hypnotic** ADJECTIVE
*The music has a hypnotic beat.*
▶ mesmeric, mesmerizing, soporific, sleep-inducing, spellbinding, compelling, fascinating, irresistible, magnetic, soothing

**hypnotism** NOUN
*She returned under hypnotism to an earlier part of her life.*
▶ hypnosis, (old use) mesmerism

**hypnotize** VERB
*She was hypnotized by the sight of the body on the floor.*
▶ mesmerize, bewitch, entrance, captivate, enthral, transfix, fascinate, dominate, magnetize, stupefy

**hypocrisy** NOUN
*He wanted to be completely honest and avoid accusations of hypocrisy.*
▶ insincerity, double-talk, duplicity, sanctimoniousness, sanctimony, pretence, deceit, deception, cant, falsity, inconsistency, (more informal) humbug

**hypocritical** ADJECTIVE
*It would be hypocritical to condemn them for something I'd like to do myself.*
▶ insincere, false, inconsistent, sanctimonious, deceptive, (more informal) phoney, (more informal) two-faced

**hypothesis** NOUN
*a hypothesis about the origin of the universe*
▶ theory, thesis, premise, conjecture, proposition, supposition, guess

**hypothetical** ADJECTIVE
*There is a hypothetical risk of damage.*
▶ theoretical, speculative, conjectural, notional, putative, imaginary, assumed, supposed, suppositional, unreal

**hysteria** NOUN
*He was overexcited, on the verge of hysteria.*
▶ frenzy, hysterics, panic, mania, madness
OPPOSITES ARE composure, calmness

**hysterical** ADJECTIVE
**1** *The fans were screaming and hysterical.*
▶ overwrought, frenzied, uncontrollable, uncontrolled, crazed, berserk, delirious, demented, frantic, wild, raving, distraught
**2** (informal) *A dog set off the security alarm with hysterical results.*
▶ hilarious, crazy, comical, funny, amusing, uproarious, (informal) killing, (informal) side-splitting

# Ii

**icy** ADJECTIVE
**1** *An icy blast of air hit Dad full in the face.*
▶ freezing, biting, bitter, frosty, arctic, cold
**2** *Few people had braved the icy streets.*
▶ frozen, frozen over, ice-covered, glacial, glassy, slippery, (more informal) slippy
**3** *She looked at him with an icy stare.*
▶ unfriendly, hostile, cold, frosty, stony

**idea** NOUN

**1** *The idea of an afterlife appeals to him.*
▶ concept, notion, conception, image, perception, hypothesis
**2** *Our idea is to go abroad this year.*
▶ plan, intention, scheme, object, objective, aim, goal, proposal, project
**3** *I have other ideas on that subject.*
▶ view, thought, opinion, viewpoint, theory, feeling
**4** *Did you have an idea this might happen?*
▶ suspicion, feeling, fancy, inkling, impression, notion
**5** *We need some idea of the cost.*
▶ estimate, estimation, approximation, guess, (*more informal*) guesstimate

**ideal** ADJECTIVE

**1** *The conditions for skiing were ideal.*
▶ perfect, excellent, optimum, exemplary, suitable, best, classic, faultless, model
**2** *Such things are only possible in an ideal world.*
▶ Utopian, visionary, unattainable, hypothetical, imaginary, unreal, impractical

**ideal** NOUN

**1** *an ideal to aim at*
▶ model, example, pattern, standard, yardstick, epitome, paradigm, archetype
**2** *a person of high ideals*
▶ principle, standard, value, belief, conviction

**idealistic** ADJECTIVE

*an idealistic picture of family life*
▶ unrealistic, perfectionist, utopian, visionary, over-optimistic, romantic, quixotic, starry-eyed
AN OPPOSITE IS realistic

**identical** ADJECTIVE

**1** *The two houses looked identical.*
▶ alike, similar, the same, indistinguishable
**2** *Successive tests produced identical results.*
▶ the same, corresponding, matching, equal, equivalent

**identification** NOUN

**1** *The Bank will need to see your identification.*
▶ ID, proof of identity, identity card, papers, credentials, documents
**2** *An early identification of problems is important.*
▶ recognition, detection, diagnosis, discovery, classification, establishment
**3** *their identification with independence struggles in Africa*
▶ association, sympathy, empathy, involvement, rapport, fellow feeling

**identify** VERB

**1** *The suspect was identified by three witnesses.*
▶ recognize, pick out, single out, name
**2** *The report identifies three areas for action.*
▶ establish, determine, recognize, diagnose, detect, discover, distinguish, pinpoint, spot
**3** *identify with* *Readers can easily identify with the chief character in the story.*
▶ empathize with, relate to, feel for, sympathize with, (*informal*) put yourself in the shoes of

**identity** NOUN

**1** (*informal*) *There was nothing to show the owner's identity.*
▶ name, ID
**2** *a case of mistaken identity*
▶ identification, recognition, picking out
**3** *She might lose her identity if she married him.*
▶ individuality, character, personality, selfhood, uniqueness, distinctiveness, singularity

**idiom** NOUN

**1** *He uses 'spiffing' and other outdated idioms.*
▶ expression, phrase, turn of phrase, choice of words, manner of speaking, colloquialism, usage
**2** *the poet's idiom*
▶ language, mode of expression, style, usage, phraseology

**idiomatic** ADJECTIVE

*idiomatic expressions*
▶ colloquial, natural, well-phrased

**idiosyncrasy** NOUN

*One of his idiosyncrasies is sleeping in his clothes.*
▶ oddity, peculiarity, eccentricity, quirk, whim, trait, habit, mannerism

**idiosyncratic** ADJECTIVE

*The grammar was faulty and the spelling idiosyncratic.*
▶ odd, peculiar, eccentric, distinctive, unconventional, quirky, individual, personal, singular
AN OPPOSITE IS common

**idiot** NOUN

*The mistake made him feel an idiot.*
▶ fool, ass, dolt, imbecile, simpleton, blockhead, ignoramus, dunderhead, dunce, halfwit, moron, cretin, (*more informal*) dope, (*more informal*) dimwit, (*more informal*) nitwit, (*more informal*) chump, (*more informal*) ninny

**idiotic** ADJECTIVE

*How idiotic it seemed for a man of his age to fall in love.*
▶ stupid, silly, foolish, absurd, senseless, nonsensical, (*more informal*) daft
AN OPPOSITE IS sensible

**idle** ADJECTIVE

**1** *The chief problem with Jack was that he was idle.*
▶ lazy, indolent, slothful, work-shy
**2** *The computers had been idle all day.*
▶ out of use, unused, dormant, out of service, inoperative
**3** *She refused to indulge in idle speculation*
▶ futile, pointless, aimless, vain, meaningless, trivial, frivolous, fatuous

**idle** VERB

**1** *Jane idled across the park.*
▶ saunter, amble, dawdle, wander
**2** *Richard had finished his work and idled until it was time to go home.*
▶ do nothing, laze, take it easy, kill time, loaf, slack

**idol**

3 *A car was idling in the driveway.*
► tick over

**idle away** *We idled away an hour or two.*
► fritter away, while away, pass, spend

**idol** NOUN
1 *a temple in which idols were worshipped*
► image, icon, statue, deity, god
2 *the newest pop idols*
► star, superstar, icon, hero, heroine, favourite

**idolize** VERB
*The man she had once idolized was now a racist.*
► hero-worship, worship, revere, admire, look up to, adulate, adore, venerate
AN OPPOSITE IS vilify

**idyllic** ADJECTIVE
*They spent an idyllic week in Paris.*
► blissful, delightful, heavenly, perfect, lovely, peaceful, happy, unspoiled
AN OPPOSITE IS desolate

**ignite** VERB
1 *The fuel will not ignite.*
► fire, burn, catch fire, light
2 *Resentment can ignite disobedience or even rioting.*
► cause, kindle, trigger, spark, set off, whip up

**ignoble** ADJECTIVE
*They were accused of starting a war for ignoble motives.*
► dishonourable, unworthy, base, shameful, despicable, disgraceful, vile
AN OPPOSITE IS noble

**ignominious** ADJECTIVE
*an ignominious defeat*
► humiliating, undignified, mortifying, degrading, inglorious, shameful, disgraceful

**ignorance** NOUN
1 *She seemed amused by Rashid's obvious ignorance of the subject.*
► unawareness, unfamiliarity (with), incomprehension, lack of knowledge, inexperience
OPPOSITES ARE knowledge, familiarity (with)
2 *They could not hide their ignorance.*
► foolishness, unintelligence, naivety, stupidity

**ignorant** ADJECTIVE
1 *He called his wife an ignorant peasant.*
► uneducated, illiterate, unread, unschooled, untaught, untutored, simple, stupid
2 *We are hopelessly ignorant of events in this part of the world.*
► unaware, uninformed (about), unenlightened (about), ill-informed, oblivious, (more informal) clueless (about)

**ignore** VERB
1 *The complaints are too serious to ignore.*
► disregard, overlook, take no notice of, neglect, pass over, set aside
2 *Helen had ignored him, out of spite.*
► snub, spurn, shun, give the cold shoulder to

**ill** ADJECTIVE
1 *Jenny began to feel ill in the taxi home.*
► sick, unwell, poorly, out of sorts, off colour, indisposed, ailing, peaky, queasy, nauseous
2 *She suffered no ill effects from her night out.*
► harmful, damaging, adverse

**illegal** ADJECTIVE
*Under-age drinking is illegal.*
► unlawful, prohibited, criminal, wrong, forbidden, barred
OPPOSITES ARE legal, lawful, permitted

**illegible** ADJECTIVE
*The signature was illegible.*
► unreadable, indecipherable, unintelligible, indistinct, obscure, unclear
OPPOSITES ARE legible, readable

**illegitimate** ADJECTIVE
1 *There were three illegitimate children from an earlier affair.*
► natural, (old use) bastard
2 *Support from the Church was propping up an illegitimate regime.*
► illegal, unlawful, illicit, spurious

**illicit** ADJECTIVE
*trade in illicit drugs*
► illegal, unlawful, prohibited, proscribed, unauthorized

**illiterate** ADJECTIVE
*Though not as good a singer as her sister, she was by no means musically illiterate.*
► uneducated, ignorant, backward, untaught, untrained, unlearned, unschooled
AN OPPOSITE IS literate

**illness** NOUN
*The doctors were unsure of the exact nature of the illness.*
► disease, disorder, sickness, infirmity, complaint, indisposition, ailment, malady, affliction

**illogical** ADJECTIVE
*The conclusion, however illogical it seems, was correct.*
► irrational, unreasonable, fallacious, invalid, unsound, absurd, inconsequential, inconsistent, senseless
AN OPPOSITE IS logical

**ill-treat** VERB
*Their father had ill-treated them.*
► maltreat, mistreat, abuse, misuse, harm, injure, (more informal) knock about

**illuminate** VERB
1 *Blazing torches illuminated the path.*
► light, light up, brighten, floodlight, make brighter, shine on
2 *a series of articles illuminating current events*
► clarify, elucidate, throw or shed light on, illustrate, clear up, enlighten, explain

**illumination** NOUN
*The full moon provided some illumination.*
► light, lighting, radiance, brightness

**illusion** NOUN

**1** *an illusion created by mirrors*
▶ hallucination, apparition, mirage, deception, delusion, fantasy, figment of the imagination, trick
**2** *We have no illusions about the difficulty of the task.*
▶ delusion, misapprehension, misconception, fantasy

**illusory** ADJECTIVE

*These signs of progress may be illusory.*
▶ deceptive, misleading, delusive, deluding, false, illusive, imaginary, unreal, sham
OPPOSITES ARE real, genuine

**illustrate** VERB

**1** *The book is illustrated with photographs and drawings.*
▶ decorate, adorn, embellish
**2** *A few examples will illustrate the argument.*
▶ clarify, elucidate, throw or shed light on, illuminate, clear up, enlighten, explain

**illustration** NOUN

**1** *a children's book with beautiful illustrations*
▶ picture, drawing, plate, sketch, photograph, figure, depiction
**2** *a good illustration of the difficulties involved*
▶ example, instance, specimen, demonstration, case

**illustrious** ADJECTIVE

*an illustrious naval commander*
▶ distinguished, eminent, famous, prominent, well known, celebrated, acclaimed, renowned, famed, notable, noteworthy, esteemed, respected, honoured, outstanding

**image** NOUN

**1** *There were images of the saints along the church walls.*
▶ picture, portrait, representation, likeness, icon, effigy, figure
**2** *The image on the screen was a little fuzzy.*
▶ picture, reproduction
**3** *The image the company gives is one of ruthless profiteering.*
▶ impression, perception, conception, idea, notion

**imaginable** ADJECTIVE

*It was the worst outcome imaginable.*
▶ conceivable, thinkable, possible
OPPOSITES ARE unimaginable, inconceivable

**imaginary** ADJECTIVE

*a story set in an imaginary country*
▶ imagined, fictitious, fictional, invented, made-up, make-believe, fanciful, unreal, non-existent, hypothetical, mythical, fabulous
OPPOSITES ARE real, actual

**imagination** NOUN

*The writing shows a great deal of imagination.*
▶ creativity, inventiveness, originality, inspiration, vision, ingenuity, insight, sensitivity, resourcefulness, artistry, cleverness, fancy, thought

**imaginative** ADJECTIVE

*an imaginative dramatization for television*
▶ creative, inventive, original, inspired, ingenious, resourceful, enterprising, fanciful, clever
AN OPPOSITE IS unimaginative

**imagine** VERB

**1** *Can you imagine life on a desert island?*
▶ visualize, envisage, picture, conceive, conceptualize
**2** *I imagine you'd like us to pay you now.*
▶ suppose, assume, presume, expect, take it

**imbecile** NOUN

*I'd have to be an imbecile to do such a thing.*
▶ fool, idiot, ass, simpleton, blockhead, dunderhead, halfwit, moron, cretin

**imitate** VERB

**1** *June liked to imitate her mother's social life.*
▶ copy, emulate, follow, model yourself on, echo
**2** *He was good at imitating politicians.*
▶ mimic, impersonate, do an impression of, parody, caricature, send up, spoof

**imitation** NOUN

**1** *a good imitation of the human voice*
▶ impersonation, impression, parody, travesty
**2** *The stolen jewels turned out to be imitations.*
▶ copy, reproduction, replica, duplicate, fake, counterfeit

**imitation** ADJECTIVE

*The weapon was an imitation firearm.*
▶ fake, artificial, simulated, sham, counterfeit, dummy, mock, model
OPPOSITES ARE real, genuine

**imitative** ADJECTIVE

*a painting done in an imitative style*
▶ derivative, unoriginal, conventional, copied, plagiarized, unimaginative
AN OPPOSITE IS original

**immaculate** ADJECTIVE

*She wore an immaculate blue suit.*
▶ perfect, spotless, pristine, impeccable

**immature** ADJECTIVE

*an immature young man behaving in a silly way*
▶ childish, babyish, inexperienced, callow

**immediate** ADJECTIVE

**1** *We need to take immediate action*
▶ instant, instantaneous, prompt, urgent, speedy, swift, quick, rapid, direct, pressing, top-priority
OPPOSITES ARE delayed, low- priority
**2** *our immediate neighbours*
▶ nearest, closest, close, near, adjacent, next
AN OPPOSITE IS remote

**immediately** ADVERB

**1** *I went back to London immediately.*
▶ straight away, at once, directly, forthwith, instantly, promptly, right away, unhesitatingly
**2** *The wall has a damp patch immediately below the window.*
▶ directly, exactly, precisely, squarely, dead, close

**immense** ADJECTIVE
*a cathedral with two immense towers*
▶ huge, great, enormous, gigantic, massive, colossal, vast, giant, (*more informal*) whopping, (*more informal*) ginormous
AN OPPOSITE IS tiny

**immerse** VERB
*You need to immerse your hair in warm water.*
▶ plunge, submerge, submerse, bathe, dip, dunk, drench, douse, duck, lower

**immersed** ADJECTIVE
*I was immersed in my work.*
▶ absorbed, engrossed, preoccupied (by), occupied (by), busy (with), involved, wrapped up, interested, engaged

**immigrant** NOUN
*a large number of Spanish-speaking immigrants*
▶ incomer, settler, newcomer
AN OPPOSITE IS emigrant

**imminent** ADJECTIVE
*An invasion of Crete seemed imminent.*
▶ close, near, at hand, in the offing, in the air, impending, threatening, about to happen, approaching, looming, coming, foreseeable

**immobilize** VERB
*The authorities will immobilize illegally parked vehicles.*
▶ put out of action, make immobile, make inoperative, deactivate, disable, clamp

**immoral** ADJECTIVE
*immoral behaviour*
▶ wrong, unethical, morally wrong, wrongful, disreputable, degenerate, sinful, wicked, unscrupulous, unprincipled, evil, bad
AN OPPOSITE IS moral

**immortal** ADJECTIVE
*She might place her immortal soul in deadly peril.*
▶ eternal, undying, everlasting, ageless, timeless, deathless, endless, perpetual, unchanging
AN OPPOSITE IS mortal

**immortality** NOUN
*the gods' immortality*
▶ eternal life, endless life, agelessness, permanence, timelessness

**immune** ADJECTIVE
*immune to the disease  immune from prosecution*
▶ safe (from), free (from), resistant, invulnerable, exempt (from), protected (from), unaffected (by)

**immunity** NOUN
**1** *immunity to malaria*
▶ resistance, resilience, protection (from)
**2** *immunity from prosecution*
▶ exemption, freedom, impunity, dispensation, protection

**impact** NOUN
**1** *She suffered a broken ankle in the impact.*
▶ crash, collision, smash, clash, blow, jolt, bump, bang, knock

**2** *High street technology is having a huge impact on modern life.*
▶ effect, influence, impression, repercussions, consequences (for)

**impair** VERB
*An illness has impaired his hearing.*
▶ damage, injure, weaken, harm, diminish

**impartial** ADJECTIVE
*Counsellors are on hand to give you free and impartial advice.*
▶ objective, unbiased, disinterested, dispassionate, balanced, detached, neutral, non-partisan, open-minded, equitable, even-handed, fair, fair-minded, just, unprejudiced
AN OPPOSITE IS biased

**impatience** NOUN
**1** *There was a tremor of impatience in her voice.*
▶ irritability, agitation, shortness, intolerance, brusqueness, frustration, nervousness
**2** *his impatience to start work*
▶ eagerness, keenness, haste

**impatient** ADJECTIVE
**1** *As time passed Michael grew impatient.*
▶ restless, agitated, fretful, irritated, tetchy, testy, anxious, ill at ease, keyed up, jumpy
**2** *The army was impatient to engage the enemy.*
▶ anxious, eager, keen, avid

**impeccable** ADJECTIVE
*a young person of impeccable character*
▶ perfect, exemplary, flawless, spotless, blameless, model, untarnished, irreproachable

**impede** VERB
*Various problems have impeded progress on the project.*
▶ obstruct, hinder, hold up, hamper, interfere with, restrict, inhibit, thwart, check, curb, handicap
AN OPPOSITE IS facilitate

**impediment** NOUN
**1** *Her humble origins were not seen as an impediment to the marriage.*
▶ obstacle, obstruction, barrier, bar, hindrance, handicap, block, check, curb
AN OPPOSITE IS aid
**2** *a speech impediment*
▶ handicap, defect, stammer, stutter

**impel** VERB
*Her love for Gerry impelled her to stand by him.*
▶ force, compel, oblige, constrain, motivate, inspire, urge, instigate, propel

**impending** ADJECTIVE
*There were looks of dismay at her impending departure.*
▶ imminent, approaching, coming, forthcoming, looming

**imperative** ADJECTIVE
*It is imperative that we find them.*
▶ essential, vital, crucial, necessary, obligatory, compulsory, urgent
OPPOSITES ARE unimportant, optional

**imperceptible** ADJECTIVE

*The movement was slow and imperceptible.*
▶ indiscernible, undetectable, indistinguishable, unnoticeable, infinitesimal, insignificant, negligible, slight, small, subtle
AN OPPOSITE IS noticeable

**USAGE** You can also use *inaudible* when you are referring to sounds, and *invisible* when you are referring to sight.

**imperfect** ADJECTIVE

*The goods were imperfect and had to be sent back.*
▶ faulty, defective, deficient, flawed, damaged, broken, incomplete, shop-soiled
AN OPPOSITE IS perfect

**imperfection** NOUN

*She handed over her work, hoping they would not notice its many imperfections.*
▶ defect, fault, deficiency, shortcoming, weakness, flaw, failing, blemish, inadequacy
AN OPPOSITE IS perfection

**imperial** ADJECTIVE

**1** *The imperial armies moved east.*
▶ royal, regal, sovereign
**2** *her imperial manner*
▶ majestic, grand, dignified, imposing, magnificent

**imperil** VERB

*He did not wish to imperil their chances of success.*
▶ endanger, harm, risk, jeopardize, threaten, compromise

**impersonal** ADJECTIVE

*His manner was brusque and impersonal.*
▶ detached, aloof, distant, formal, unemotional, unfriendly, unsympathetic, businesslike, remote, cold, cool
AN OPPOSITE IS friendly

**impersonate** VERB

*She tried to impersonate the queen.*
▶ imitate, mimic, parody, caricature, mock, pose as

**impertinence** NOUN

*They were unclear whether the remark was a joke or a piece of impertinence.*
▶ rudeness, cheek, insolence, impudence, effrontery, audacity, impoliteness, discourtesy, disrespect
AN OPPOSITE IS politeness

**impertinent** ADJECTIVE

*A question like that would seem impertinent from anyone else.*
▶ rude, impolite, insolent, impudent, disrespectful, audacious, brazen
OPPOSITES ARE respectful, polite

**impetuous** ADJECTIVE

*With hindsight the decision looked impetuous rather than decisive.*
▶ impulsive, rash, hasty, reckless, foolhardy
AN OPPOSITE IS cautious

**impetus** NOUN

**1** *Their enthusiasm began to lose impetus.*
▶ momentum, force, power, drive, motivation, stimulus, energy, impulse, incentive, push, spur
**2** *A new product would give the sales campaign an added impetus.*
▶ boost, stimulus, inducement, incentive, push, spur

**impinge** VERB

**impinge on** *The noise in the next room was impinging on her concentration.*
▶ encroach on, intrude on, affect, interfere with, influence, invade

**implacable** ADJECTIVE

*They voiced their implacable opposition.*
▶ relentless, inexorable, remorseless, adamant, unswerving, unrelenting, inflexible, outright, utter

**implausible** ADJECTIVE

*The suggestion seemed implausible.*
▶ unconvincing, improbable, unlikely, questionable, unreasonable, doubtful, dubious, far-fetched, incredible, fanciful, suspect, flimsy, weak, feeble
AN OPPOSITE IS plausible

**implement** NOUN

*garden implements*
▶ tool, utensil, appliance, device, gadget, instrument, contraption

**implement** VERB

*The measures would be costly to implement.*
▶ put into practice, carry out, execute, bring about, accomplish, effect, realize, enforce, fulfil, perform, try out

**implicate** VERB

*The evidence implicated them in several crimes.*
▶ involve, embroil, entangle, incriminate, inculpate, associate (with), connect (with)

**implication** NOUN

**1** *He did not like the implication that he had been dishonest.*
▶ suggestion, insinuation, intimation, imputation, innuendo, inference

**USAGE** Strictly, *inference* means 'a conclusion you draw' rather than 'a conclusion you suggest', so it is better to use one of the other words given here.

**2** *They are suspected of implication in the crime.*
▶ involvement, association, connection, entanglement, incrimination

**implicit** ADJECTIVE

**1** *The article makes a number of implicit assumptions.*
▶ implied, indirect, tacit, hinted at, insinuated, unspoken, unstated
AN OPPOSITE IS explicit

**2** *an implicit belief in their ability*
▶ absolute, utter, total, wholehearted, complete, unqualified, unreserved, unquestioning

**implore** VERB
*His family implored him to come home.*
▶ beg, entreat, urge, appeal to, call on, exhort, (*literary*) beseech

**imply** VERB
**1** *He seemed to imply that we were wrong.*
▶ suggest, hint, insinuate, intimate, indicate
**USAGE** You will sometimes see *infer* used as a synonym of *imply*, but *infer* properly means 'to draw a conclusion' rather than 'to suggest a conclusion', so it is better to use one of the other words given here.
**2** *The traffic measures imply a need for better public transport.*
▶ entail, involve, point to, indicate, suggest, signify, necessitate

**impolite** ADJECTIVE
*It would have been impolite to leave the party so early.*
▶ rude, bad-mannered, discourteous, disrespectful, inconsiderate, ungracious

**importance** NOUN
**1** *an event of the greatest importance*
▶ significance, consequence, seriousness, import, substance, gravity, urgency
**2** *a person of importance*
▶ power, influence, authority, prominence, status, distinction, eminence

**important** ADJECTIVE
**1** *an important decision*
▶ significant, momentous, crucial, critical, vital, far-reaching, consequential, historic
**2** *It is important to get there early.*
▶ crucial, vital, essential
**3** *an important person*
▶ powerful, influential, prominent, distinguished, eminent

**impose** VERB
**1** *The library will impose a fine on the late return of books.*
▶ exact, enforce, introduce, fix, inflict, levy, prescribe, set, place
**2** *impose on They were afraid they might be imposing on us.*
▶ intrude on, presume on, inconvenience, encroach on, obtrude on, force yourself on, take advantage of

**imposing** ADJECTIVE
*an imposing mock-baronial building*
▶ grand, stately, impressive, magnificent, majestic, splendid, distinguished, striking, dignified, grandiose
OPPOSITES ARE unimposing, modest

**imposition** NOUN
**1** *the imposition of a windfall tax*
▶ introduction, levying, charging, exacting, enforcing, fixing, setting
**2** *Asking for help might seem an imposition.*
▶ intrusion, encroachment, presumption, liberty, burden, encumbrance

**impossibility** NOUN
*They had to admit to the impossibility of the task.*
▶ impracticality, unlikelihood, hopelessness
OPPOSITES ARE possibility, feasibility

**impossible** ADJECTIVE
**1** *The tears made speaking impossible.*
▶ impractical, hopeless, inconceivable, unthinkable, out of the question, unachievable
**2** *They had succeeded against impossible odds.*
▶ unrealistic, hopeless, overwhelming, insurmountable, implausible, unbelievable, preposterous, ludicrous, unattainable
AN OPPOSITE IS possible

**impostor** NOUN
*The official turned out to be an impostor.*
▶ impersonator, masquerader, charlatan, fraud, cheat, hoaxer, trickster, (*more informal*) phoney

**impotent** ADJECTIVE
*They felt impotent against the power pitted against them.*
▶ powerless, helpless, ineffectual, weak, useless, feeble, inadequate, incapable, incompetent, ineffective, unable
OPPOSITES ARE powerful, effective

**impoverished** ADJECTIVE
*an impoverished family*
▶ poor, poverty-stricken, penniless, destitute, impecunious, insolvent, ruined

**impractical** ADJECTIVE
*an impractical suggestion*
▶ unrealistic, unworkable, impossible, unreasonable
AN OPPOSITE IS practical

**imprecise** ADJECTIVE
*an imprecise description*
▶ vague, loose, inexact, inaccurate, hazy, woolly, equivocal
OPPOSITES ARE precise, exact

**impregnable** ADJECTIVE
*The enemy were in an impregnable position.*
▶ invulnerable, invincible, unassailable, unconquerable, safe, secure, strong, impenetrable
AN OPPOSITE IS vulnerable

**impress** VERB
**1** *This evidence did not impress the jury.*
▶ move, stir, influence, affect, excite, make an impression on, have an impact on, (*more informal*) grab
**2** *impress on We must impress on Chris what good work he has done.*
▶ emphasize to, bring home to, instil in, inculcate in

**impression** NOUN
**1** *We got the impression they were hiding something.*
▶ feeling, sense, suspicion, conviction, awareness, notion, idea, hunch, inkling
**2** *The experience left a good impression on him.*
▶ effect, impact, influence

3 *He had formed a favourable impression of them.*
▶ opinion, view, perception, assessment, estimation, judgement, verdict

4 *She did a good impression of the Queen Mother.*
▶ imitation, impersonation, parody, caricature, (*more informal*) send-up

5 *The mug had left a circular impression in the cloth.*
▶ indentation, dent, hollow, stamp, mark, print, outline

## impressive ADJECTIVE

1 *She has made an impressive concert debut.*
▶ striking, accomplished, masterly, first-class, exciting, stirring
AN OPPOSITE IS insignificant

2 *The conference is held in an impressive building near the university.*
▶ magnificent, imposing, splendid, grand, stately, monumental

## imprison VERB

*The judge imprisoned him for five years.*
▶ jail, incarcerate, send to prison, put in prison, detain, lock up, confine, (*more informal*) put away, (*more informal*) send down

## imprisonment NOUN

*The penalty is life imprisonment.*
▶ incarceration, internment, detention, confinement, custody

## improbable ADJECTIVE

*The excuse was most improbable.*
▶ unlikely, implausible, incredible, doubtful, questionable, far-fetched, unbelievable, unconvincing, preposterous
AN OPPOSITE IS probable

## impromptu ADJECTIVE

*an impromptu talk on famous battles*
▶ unrehearsed, improvised, extempore, unscripted, spontaneous, ad-lib
AN OPPOSITE IS rehearsed

## improper ADJECTIVE

1 *It would be improper to accept payment.*
▶ wrong, inappropriate, unsuitable, irregular, out of place, unacceptable, unprofessional, incorrect, inopportune, uncalled for, unwarranted

2 *In those days such behaviour would have been thought improper.*
▶ indecent, unseemly, indecorous, unbecoming, unfitting, shocking, vulgar
AN OPPOSITE IS proper

## improve VERB

1 *We are always looking for ways to improve the service.*
▶ make better, better, enhance, reform, upgrade, develop

2 *Relations between the employers and unions have improved markedly.*
▶ get better, progress, advance, develop, make headway, rally, (*more informal*) look up

3 *Reduce the dose as soon as the patient begins to improve.*
▶ recover, get better, recuperate, regain strength

4 *They are hoping to improve their offer shortly.*
▶ increase, raise, supplement, enlarge, augment, top up

5 **improve on** *It will be hard to improve on work of that quality.*
▶ surpass, outdo, do better than, exceed

## improvement NOUN

1 *The weather showed a little improvement. an improvement in East-West relations*
▶ recovery, advance, upturn, progress, enhancement, amelioration, development, rectification, betterment, gain, rally, reformation

2 *We have carried out a lot of improvements to the house.*
▶ renovation, alteration, extension, modernization, modification, (*informal*) face-lift

## improvise VERB

1 *The boys improvised a raft.*
▶ devise, contrive, rig, put together, concoct

2 *an entertainer who is good at improvising.*
▶ extemporize, ad-lib

## impudence NOUN

*They soon forgave him his impudence.*
▶ cheek, insolence, impertinence, effrontery, audacity, rudeness, impoliteness, discourtesy, disrespect
AN OPPOSITE IS politeness

## impudent ADJECTIVE

*She thought him an impudent bully.*
▶ rude, insolent, impertinent, impolite, disrespectful, audacious, brazen
OPPOSITES ARE respectful, polite

## impulse NOUN

1 *His first impulse was to call the police.*
▶ instinct, urge, inclination, compulsion, whim, caprice, desire

2 *His actions were so often governed by impulse.*
▶ impetuosity, spontaneity, rashness, recklessness

3 *Emotion is one of the main impulses of poetry.*
▶ stimulus, inspiration, motivation

## impulsive ADJECTIVE

*With an impulsive gesture she flounced out of the room.*
▶ impetuous, spontaneous, rash, reckless, hasty, uninhibited, instinctive, passionate
AN OPPOSITE IS deliberate

## impure ADJECTIVE

1 *The water was found to be impure.*
▶ contaminated, polluted, tainted, unclean, foul, defiled, dirty, filthy, infected, unhygienic, unwholesome, adulterated

2 *impure thoughts*
▶ immoral, indecent, unclean, corrupt, wicked, degenerate

## impurity NOUN

1 *An instrument measured the impurity of the air.*
▶ contamination, pollution, dirtiness, uncleanliness, foulness, filthiness

a
b
c
d
e
f
g
h
i
j
k
l
m
n
o
p
q
r
s
t
u
v
w
x
y
z

**2** *water full of impurities*
► contaminant, pollutant, adulterant, foreign matter

**inability** NOUN
*their inability to agree on a single point*
► incapacity, incapability, impotence, powerlessness, lack of ability

**inaccessible** ADJECTIVE
*More of the countryside is becoming inaccessible.*
► unreachable, cut off, out of reach, isolated, remote, godforsaken, hard to find, out-of-the-way, in the middle of nowhere, in the back of beyond, secluded, unfrequented, (*informal*) unget-at-able
AN OPPOSITE IS accessible

**inaccuracy** NOUN
*The information is marred by inaccuracies*
► mistake, error, miscalculation, blunder, imprecision, fault, defect, flaw, slip, oversight
OPPOSITES ARE accuracy, precision

**inaccurate** ADJECTIVE
*The road map is very inaccurate.*
► inexact, imprecise, incorrect, erroneous, faulty, imperfect, defective, unsound

**inactive** ADJECTIVE
**1** *Illness left me inactive for several weeks.*
► idle, immobile, inert, lethargic, listless, sluggish
**2** *The alarm was inactive at the time of the break-in.*
► inoperative, idle, non-functioning, turned off, out of action, out of use

**inadequate** ADJECTIVE
**1** *The army suffered from bad pay and inadequate training.*
► insufficient, unsatisfactory, not enough, deficient, scanty, sparse
**2** *It's a difficult job and they may prove inadequate.*
► incapable, ineffectual, incompetent, not up to scratch

**inadvisable** ADJECTIVE
*It was inadvisable for him to drive or operate machinery.*
► unwise, ill-advised, imprudent, foolish, misguided, silly
AN OPPOSITE IS advisable

**inane** ADJECTIVE
*a series of inane remarks*
► silly, foolish, stupid, fatuous, idiotic, absurd, mindless, vacuous, futile, pointless

**inanimate** ADJECTIVE
*an inanimate object*
► lifeless, insentient, inert, dead, dormant, inactive, unconscious
OPPOSITES ARE animate , living

**inappropriate** ADJECTIVE
*The police decided a prosecution would be inappropriate.*
► unsuitable, out of place, inapt, ill-suited, unfitting, untimely, ill-timed, improper, incongruous
OPPOSITES ARE appropriate, suitable

**inattentive** ADJECTIVE
*The performance suffered from an inattentive audience.*
► distracted, preoccupied, heedless, unobservant, dreamy, daydreaming, dreaming, absent-minded, lacking concentration
OPPOSITES ARE attentive, alert

**inaudible** ADJECTIVE
*From that distance the voices were inaudible.*
► indistinct, hard to hear, unclear, quiet, silent, weak, undetectable, unidentifiable, muted, faint, low, muffled, mumbled
AN OPPOSITE IS audible

**incapable** ADJECTIVE
*Those who feel incapable in their work can get advice.*
► incompetent, ineffective, ineffectual, inadequate, impotent, inept, unable, useless, weak
AN OPPOSITE IS capable

**incentive** NOUN
*the introduction of more financial incentives*
► inducement, stimulus, motivation, spur, encouragement, reward, (*more informal*) sweetener, (*more informal*) carrot

**incessant** ADJECTIVE
*incessant noise from the road works outside*
► continuous, continual, constant, ceaseless, endless, unceasing, interminable, non-stop
OPPOSITES ARE temporary, intermittent

**incident** NOUN
**1** *He recalled an amusing incident from his childhood.*
► event, episode, occurrence, happening, occasion, affair, experience, activity, business, circumstance
**2** *Police were called to an incident in the centre of town.*
► disturbance, commotion, fracas, scene, brawl, rumpus, fight

**incidental** ADJECTIVE
*We can ignore the incidental details.*
► secondary, subsidiary, ancillary, subordinate, inessential, unimportant, minor, trivial, petty, peripheral
AN OPPOSITE IS essential

**incite** VERB
**1** *She had incited him to commit the crime.*
► urge, encourage, provoke, goad, push, impel, egg on
**2** *They were accused of inciting racial hatred.*
► stir up, instigate, rouse, whip up, foment

**inclination** NOUN
**1** *He showed no inclination to leave.*
► readiness, desire, impulse, wish, disposition, predisposition, predilection
AN OPPOSITE IS disinclination
**2** *She had no inclination for work that day.*
► liking, partiality, appetite, taste, fondness, penchant
AN OPPOSITE IS dislike
**3** *an inclination of 45°*
► gradient, incline, slope, angle, slant

## incline VERB

*The uprights incline slightly to the right.*
▶ lean, slant, tilt, tip, slope, veer

**be inclined** *We are inclined to believe him.*
▶ be disposed, be minded, be willing, be ready

## include VERB

1 *Sports activities include swimming and aerobics.*
▶ incorporate, involve, comprise, contain, embrace, encompass, consist of, take in, make room for, subsume
2 *The package includes flights, hotels costs, and all outings.*
▶ cover, allow for, take into account, add in
AN OPPOSITE IS exclude

## incoherent ADJECTIVE

*The letter was long and incoherent.*
▶ unclear, confused, muddled, unintelligible, disorganized, incomprehensible, inarticulate, garbled, rambling, hard to follow, disjointed, disordered, illogical
OPPOSITES ARE coherent, intelligible

## income NOUN

1 *Her income has gone up significantly in the last year.*
▶ earnings, salary, pay, remuneration, wages, money
2 *taxes on business income*
▶ revenue, receipts, takings, profits, gains, proceeds, takeover
OPPOSITES ARE expenditure, outgoings

## incomparable ADJECTIVE

*the city's incomparable beauty*
▶ unparalleled, unequalled, unrivalled, matchless, peerless, inimitable

## incompatible ADJECTIVE

1 *The two versions of the incident are incompatible.*
▶ inconsistent, irreconcilable, conflicting, contradictory, discrepant, incongruous, at variance, clashing, contrasting, different
2 *She and her partner seem totally incompatible*
▶ unsuited, mismatched, (more informal) poles apart
AN OPPOSITE IS compatible

## incompetent ADJECTIVE

*They were all either too lazy or too incompetent to do an honest day's work.*
▶ inept, incapable, unqualified, inefficient, unskilful, unfit, inadequate, unproficient, bungling, blundering, clumsy, ineffectual
AN OPPOSITE IS competent

## incomplete ADJECTIVE

*They have to move into the house even though it's still incomplete.*
▶ unfinished, uncompleted, half-finished, not finished, unready

## incomprehensible ADJECTIVE

1 *She made some incomprehensible remark.*
▶ unintelligible, incoherent, unfathomable, baffling, confusing, perplexing, obscure, cryptic, opaque, mysterious, inscrutable, enigmatic
AN OPPOSITE IS comprehensible

2 *The writing was incomprehensible.*
▶ illegible, indecipherable, unintelligible
OPPOSITES ARE intelligible, legible

## inconceivable ADJECTIVE

*It was inconceivable that the king would agree to these demands.*
▶ unimaginable, unthinkable, implausible, incredible, unbelievable, undreamed of, (more informal) mind-boggling
OPPOSITES ARE conceivable, credible

## inconclusive ADJECTIVE

*The opinion polls are inconclusive.*
▶ unconvincing, indefinite, undecided, ambiguous, equivocal, indecisive, indeterminate, uncertain, unsettled, open
AN OPPOSITE IS conclusive

## incongruous ADJECTIVE

*the incongruous sound of an electric doorbell*
▶ inappropriate, out of place, discordant, unsuitable, ill-suited, incompatible, inconsistent, conflicting, odd, clashing, contrasting, ill-matched, uncoordinated, irreconcilable
AN OPPOSITE IS appropriate

## inconsiderate ADJECTIVE

*inconsiderate behaviour It was very inconsiderate of them.*
▶ thoughtless, insensitive, unthinking, uncaring, unkind, discourteous, impolite, unconcerned, tactless

## inconsistent ADJECTIVE

1 *Their attitudes are inconsistent and hard to understand.*
▶ changeable, unreliable, erratic, capricious, unstable, variable, fickle, inconstant, unpredictable, (more informal) up-and-down
2 *There are several inconsistent versions of the legend.*
▶ conflicting, contradictory, incompatible, irreconcilable, discrepant, incongruous, at variance, clashing, contrasting, different
AN OPPOSITE IS consistent

## inconsolable ADJECTIVE

*Lisa was inconsolable when she arrived back from the accident.*
▶ heartbroken, broken-hearted, devastated, grief-stricken, desolate, despairing

## inconspicuous ADJECTIVE

1 *The building is small and inconspicuous.*
▶ unobtrusive, undistinguished, unremarkable, unostentatious, camouflaged, hidden, out of sight, insignificant, ordinary, invisible
2 *Jane did her best to remain inconspicuous.*
▶ retiring, self-effacing, unassuming, modest, restrained
OPPOSITES ARE conspicuous, noticeable

## incontrovertible ADJECTIVE

*These are all incontrovertible facts.*
▶ indisputable, incontestable, irrefutable, undeniable, unquestionable, unarguable, self-evident

## inconvenience NOUN

*The road works have caused a great deal of inconvenience.*
▶ trouble, bother, difficulty, disruption, awkwardness, nuisance, hindrance, irritation, fuss, upset, annoyance, disadvantage, drawback, encumbrance
AN OPPOSITE IS convenience

## inconvenience VERB

*We hope the delay will not inconvenience you too much.*
▶ trouble, bother, disturb, put out, incommode, annoy, irritate, disadvantage, embarrass, (*informal*) put you out

## inconvenient ADJECTIVE

*Shirley arrived at an extremely inconvenient moment.*
▶ awkward, difficult, unsuitable, inappropriate, inopportune, untimely, ill-timed, embarrassing, annoying, bothersome, irritating, troublesome
AN OPPOSITE IS convenient

## incorporate VERB

**1** *The peace treaty incorporated the region into Italy.*
▶ absorb, merge, assimilate, subsume, embody, include (in), contain (in)
**2** *The leaflet incorporates a sponsorship form.*
▶ include, contain, embrace

## incorrect ADJECTIVE

*The next three answers were incorrect.*
▶ wrong, erroneous, mistaken, inaccurate, imprecise, inexact, false, untrue

## incorrigible ADJECTIVE

*an incorrigible flirt*
▶ incurable, inveterate, irredeemable, hardened, hopeless

## increase NOUN

*an increase in size   an increase in demand*
▶ growth, rise, development, enlargement, expansion, swelling, intensification, upsurge, upturn
AN OPPOSITE IS decrease

## increase VERB

**1** *Applications for jobs have increased.*
▶ rise, grow, swell, multiply, expand, spread, proliferate
OPPOSITES ARE decrease, decline
**2** *Prosperity increases consumer demand.*
▶ raise, heighten, boost, enhance, add to, strengthen, intensify, develop, expand, escalate, augment
OPPOSITES ARE reduce, lower

## incredible ADJECTIVE

**1** *an incredible feat of engineering*
▶ magnificent, marvellous, spectacular, remarkable, wonderful, extraordinary, amazing, astounding
**2** *Their story is incredible.*
▶ unbelievable, implausible, far-fetched, improbable, unlikely, questionable, unreasonable, doubtful, dubious
AN OPPOSITE IS credible

## incredulous ADJECTIVE

*She was incredulous when they told her the cost.*
▶ disbelieving, unbelieving, doubtful, dubious, sceptical, unconvinced, distrustful, questioning, suspicious, uncertain
AN OPPOSITE IS credulous

## incriminate VERB

*The evidence incriminated the whole family.*
▶ implicate, involve, accuse, blame, embroil, (*more formal*) inculpate, (*more informal*) point the finger at
OPPOSITES ARE exonerate, clear

## incur VERB

*actions that might incur a penalty*
▶ earn, sustain, attract, provoke, run up, suffer, get, expose you to, bring upon yourself

## incurable ADJECTIVE

**1** *an incurable illness*
▶ untreatable, inoperable, irremediable, irreparable, terminal, fatal, chronic, hopeless
AN OPPOSITE IS curable
**2** *Jenny is an incurable romantic.*
▶ inveterate, incorrigible, hardened, dyed-in-the-wool

## indecent ADJECTIVE

*Customs officers discovered indecent photographs in his luggage.*
▶ obscene, pornographic, dirty, filthy, bawdy, lewd, licentious

## indecision NOUN

*She wanted to act, but indecision prevented her.*
▶ hesitation, irresolution, indecisiveness, uncertainty, doubt, ambivalence, vacillation, equivocation
OPPOSITES ARE decisiveness, resolution

## indecisive ADJECTIVE

**1** *He came across as an indecisive leader.*
▶ hesitant, irresolute, tentative, equivocating, uncertain, weak, dithering
**2** *The result of the tests was indecisive.*
▶ uncertain, doubtful, unsure

## indefensible ADJECTIVE

*That sort of abusive talk is quite indefensible.*
▶ inexcusable, unjustifiable, unpardonable, unacceptable, unsupportable, untenable, wrong, misguided

## indefinite ADJECTIVE

**1** *The inspectors are here for an indefinite period.*
▶ unspecified, unknown, uncertain, unlimited
AN OPPOSITE IS definite
**2** *a word like 'get', with an indefinite meaning*
▶ vague, unclear, unspecific, imprecise, hazy

## indefinitely ADVERB

*A problem could be with us indefinitely.*
▶ for ever, continuously, continually, endlessly, for all time

**indelible** ADJECTIVE

**1** *indelible ink*
▶ permanent, ineradicable, fixed, lasting, fast, ingrained

**2** *The experience left an indelible impression on her.*
▶ unforgettable, ineradicable, lasting, enduring
AN OPPOSITE IS erasable.

**indelicate** ADJECTIVE

**1** *It seemed a little indelicate to ask.*
▶ insensitive, tactless, indiscreet, undiplomatic, indecent

**2** *His sense of humour could be indelicate at times.*
▶ indecent, coarse, vulgar, gross, crude, lewd, bawdy, obscene

**independence** NOUN

**1** *The country gained its independence in the 1950s.*
▶ self-government, autonomy, freedom, individualism, liberty, nonconformity
AN OPPOSITE IS dependence

**2** *The judges must be able to act with complete independence.*
▶ impartiality, neutrality, disinterest, detachment, objectivity, freedom

**independent** ADJECTIVE

**1** *an independent country*
▶ autonomous, sovereign, self-governing

**2** *an independent person*
▶ free, unconstrained, self-reliant, self-sufficient, free-thinking, liberated
AN OPPOSITE IS dependent

**3** *an independent opinion*
▶ impartial, unbiased, disinterested, objective

**indicate** VERB

**1** *A linesman raised his flag to indicate a goal.*
▶ signify, denote, register, record, designate

**2** *Good sales indicate the book's popularity.*
▶ show, demonstrate, be a sign of, testify to, suggest, imply, attest

**3** *Indicate your choice of prize on the form.*
▶ specify, point out

**indication** NOUN

**1** *His secretary could give no clear indication of when he was expected back.*
▶ clue, hint, inkling, intimation, suggestion, explanation

**2** *Pain may be an indication of injury.*
▶ sign, indicator, symptom, mark, evidence, manifestation

**indifference** NOUN

*He reacted with complete indifference to their predicament.*
▶ unconcern, apathy, coolness, disregard, nonchalance, inattention

**indifferent** ADJECTIVE

**1** *His voice showed how indifferent he was.*
▶ unconcerned, apathetic, uncaring, nonchalant

**2** *After an indifferent meal he went off to bed.*
▶ mediocre, ordinary, inferior, unexceptional, average

**indigenous** ADJECTIVE

*indigenous people from rainforests across the world*
▶ native, aboriginal, original, local

**indignant** ADJECTIVE

*The newspaper received indignant letters from outraged readers.*
▶ irate, angry, affronted, aggrieved, incensed, outraged, resentful, offended, vexed, piqued, heated, furious, fuming

**indignation** NOUN

*The false accusations filled him with indignation.*
▶ anger, fury, resentment, outrage, affront, umbrage, vexation

**indignity** NOUN

*He suffered the indignity of having his application rejected.*
▶ humiliation, shame, embarrassment, mortification, disgrace, dishonour, stigma

**indirect** ADJECTIVE

**1** *The convoy took a quieter indirect route.*
▶ roundabout, circuitous, meandering, out-of-the-way

**2** *It was an insult, if only an indirect one.*
▶ disguised, ambiguous, equivocal, oblique, implicit, implied, inexplicit
AN OPPOSITE IS direct

**indiscreet** ADJECTIVE

*Her mum would never have done anything so indiscreet.*
▶ imprudent, unwise, injudicious, tactless, ill-advised, ill-considered, ill-judged, unthinking, impolite, impolitic, undiplomatic, careless, incautious, unguarded
OPPOSITES ARE discreet, careful

**indiscretion** NOUN

*It is important to be careful and avoid any indiscretion.*
▶ imprudence, rashness, recklessness, tactlessness, foolhardiness

**indiscriminate** ADJECTIVE

*Congestion soon occurs if indiscriminate parking is allowed.*
▶ haphazard, random, unsystematic, general, wholesale, undiscriminating, aimless, desultory, general
OPPOSITES ARE selective, systematic

**indispensable** ADJECTIVE

*Charles regarded him as an indispensable source of wisdom and experience.*
▶ essential, vital, crucial, required, requisite, basic, central, imperative, key, necessary, much-needed
AN OPPOSITE IS unnecessary

**indisposed** ADJECTIVE

*Mark had to stand in for the soloist, who was indisposed.*
▶ ill, unwell, sick, infirm, poorly

**indisputable** ADJECTIVE

*Charles returned in triumph, indisputable King of Aquitaine.*
▶ incontrovertible, incontestable, acknowledged, undeniable, indubitable, unassailable, unequivocal
OPPOSITES ARE questionable, debatable

**indistinct** ADJECTIVE

1 *In the photocopies, some of the letters were indistinct.*
▶ blurred, fuzzy, unclear, out of focus, ill-defined, dim, faint, hazy, misty, obscure, vague, shadowy, bleary
2 *She murmured, but her voice was indistinct.*
▶ muffled, muted, faint, weak, inaudible, slurred
AN OPPOSITE IS distinct

**indistinguishable** ADJECTIVE

*The boys are indistinguishable.*
▶ identical, interchangeable, alike, the same
AN OPPOSITE IS different

**individual** ADJECTIVE

1 *music with an individual style*
▶ characteristic, distinctive, distinct, particular, special, specific, unique, peculiar, exclusive, idiosyncratic, private, personal
2 *Individual countries can make their own decisions.*
▶ separate, single, discrete
AN OPPOSITE IS collective

**individual** NOUN

*In the corner sat a strange individual.*
▶ person, being, human being, soul, mortal

**indoctrinate** VERB

*With their psychological techniques they were able to indoctrinate large numbers of people.*
▶ brainwash, propagandize, re-educate, instruct, train, teach

**induce** VERB

1 *Their leaders induced them to continue fighting.*
▶ persuade, convince, prevail upon, press, urge, encourage
2 *Conversations like these induce close friendship.*
▶ bring about, cause, create, effect, instigate, engender, develop, produce, lead to, give rise to, arouse, kindle

**inducement** NOUN

*Paying off student loans is an inducement to join the profession.*
▶ incentive, encouragement, enticement, stimulus, motivation, spur, lure, bait

**indulge** VERB

1 *She decided to indulge her passion for music.*
▶ satisfy, gratify, fulfil, pander to, go along with, humour
2 *She could not be accused of indulging her children.*
▶ spoil, pamper, cosset, mollycoddle
3 **indulge in** *Here we stopped and indulged in a cream tea.*
▶ enjoy, revel in

**indulgent** ADJECTIVE

*He could see the looks of indulgent amusement on their faces.*
▶ tolerant, compliant, patient, permissive, easygoing, lenient, liberal, overgenerous, fond, genial, kind
AN OPPOSITE IS strict

**industrial** ADJECTIVE

*an industrial area north of the city*
▶ industrialized, manufacturing, business

**industrious** ADJECTIVE

*an industrious and studious youth*
▶ diligent, hard-working, conscientious, assiduous, enterprising, painstaking, energetic, active, keen, productive, zealous, sedulous, tireless
OPPOSITES ARE lazy, indolent

**industry** NOUN

1 *the American oil industry*
▶ business, trade, commerce, manufacturing
2 *The garden looked a hive of industry.*
▶ activity, hard work, industriousness, diligence, effort, toil, energy, vigour, application, commitment, determination, keenness, labour, perseverance, persistence, tirelessness, zeal
OPPOSITES ARE laziness, indolence

**inedible** ADJECTIVE

*a joke recipe for baking an inedible cake*
▶ uneatable, unpalatable, unwholesome, poisonous, noxious
AN OPPOSITE IS edible

**ineffective** ADJECTIVE

1 *The protests were quite ineffective.*
▶ unsuccessful, unproductive, useless, futile, vain, fruitless, unavailing, worthless
OPPOSITES ARE effective, fruitful
2 *an ineffective leader*
▶ inadequate, ineffectual, weak, feeble, inept, incompetent
AN OPPOSITE IS effective

**inefficient** ADJECTIVE

1 *He must be the world's most inefficient gardener.*
▶ ineffective, ineffectual, unproductive, disorganized, incompetent, inept, inexpert
2 *The wood stoves are extremely inefficient for cooking food.*
▶ uneconomical, unproductive, extravagant, wasteful, awkward, clumsy
AN OPPOSITE IS efficient

**inelegant** ADJECTIVE

*'Sunken building' is an inelegant term for these small structures.*
▶ unattractive, graceless, awkward, cumbersome, unrefined, ugly, crude

**ineligible** ADJECTIVE

*The club was fined for fielding ineligible players.*
▶ disqualified, inappropriate, unacceptable, unfit, unsuitable
AN OPPOSITE IS eligible

**inept** ADJECTIVE
*The Banks have proved inept at merging.*
► unskilful, incompetent, bungling, clumsy, maladroit

**inequality** NOUN
*a growth in crime, caused by unemployment and social inequality*
► imbalance, disparity, unfairness, divergence, difference, dissimilarity
AN OPPOSITE IS equality

**inert** ADJECTIVE
*He prodded the inert body on the floor.*
► motionless, lifeless, immobile, inanimate, dormant, inactive

**inertia** NOUN
*There was a danger of lapsing into inertia.*
► inactivity, inaction, passivity, lethargy, listlessness, apathy, torpor, immobility, lassitude, indolence, idleness, laziness, numbness, sluggishness
AN OPPOSITE IS liveliness

**inescapable** ADJECTIVE
*For the king, Parliament was an inescapable reality when taxes had to be raised.*
► unavoidable, inevitable, necessary, obligatory, mandatory
AN OPPOSITE IS avoidable

**inevitable** ADJECTIVE
*There have been the inevitable delays.*
► unavoidable, inescapable, obligatory, mandatory, ineluctable

**inexcusable** ADJECTIVE
*The insult was inexcusable.*
► indefensible, unforgivable, intolerable, unpardonable, reprehensible

**inexpensive** ADJECTIVE
*a simple and inexpensive method*
► cheap, low-priced, low-cost, economical, affordable, modest
AN OPPOSITE IS expensive

**inexperienced** ADJECTIVE
*School-leavers and inexperienced people often get jobs in riding schools.*
► inexpert, untrained, unskilled, unpractised, unaccustomed, immature, callow, amateur, fresh, green, raw
AN OPPOSITE IS experienced.

**inexplicable** ADJECTIVE
*For some inexplicable reason she felt suddenly afraid.*
► unexplainable, mysterious, puzzling, strange, unaccountable, incomprehensible, unfathomable, baffling, mystifying, enigmatic
AN OPPOSITE IS understandable

**infallible** ADJECTIVE
**1** *The idea works well, but it is not infallible.*
► foolproof, unfailing, guaranteed, perfect, certain
AN OPPOSITE IS fallible

**2** *Kate always adopted her infallible routine.*
► dependable, reliable, unerring, accurate

**infamous** ADJECTIVE
*a series of infamous murders*
► notorious, scandalous, shameful, ill-famed, disreputable
AN OPPOSITE IS reputable

**infant** NOUN
*an age at which infants are learning to walk*
► baby, child, tot, (*informal*) toddler

**infatuated** ADJECTIVE
*He seemed to be infatuated with every girl her met.*
► besotted, obsessed, taken, (*more informal*) smitten, (*more informal*) head over heels

**infatuation** NOUN
(*informal*) *Her mother regarded Sarah's feelings for him as a girlish infatuation.*
► obsession, fixation, passion, (*more informal*) crush

**infect** VERB
**1** *The organism may infect the eye of the infant with a 'sticky eye'.*
► cause an infection in, spread disease to
**2** *The water supply had become infected.*
► contaminate, pollute, poison, taint, blight
**3** *Her cheerful humour infects everyone she meets.*
► affect, influence, inspire, animate, touch

**infection** NOUN
**1** *a bladder infection*
► disease, virus, disorder, complaint
**2** *The dressing will keep the wound free of infection.*
► contamination, contagion, bacteria, poisoning

**infectious** ADJECTIVE
**1** *the conquest of infectious diseases*
► contagious, communicable, catching, transmissible, transmittable, spreading
**2** *infectious laughter*
► contagious, irresistible, spreading

**infer** VERB
*What can we infer from the table of results?*
► conclude, deduce, extrapolate, reason, gather, assume, work out, guess, understand
**USAGE** See the note at *imply*.

**inferior** ADJECTIVE
**1** *inferior rank*
► lesser, lower, subsidiary, subordinate, junior, secondary, second-class, ancillary, low, humble
**2** *inferior quality*
► poor, mediocre, substandard, shoddy, tawdry, bad, cheap, indifferent

**infernal** ADJECTIVE
**1** *the infernal regions of the underworld*
► hellish, nether, lower, diabolical, devilish
**2** *Having to leave so early was an infernal nuisance.*
► wretched, damned, diabolical, accursed

**infinite** ADJECTIVE

1 *You will need infinite patience in detailed work like this.*
▶ endless, limitless, boundless, immeasurable, unlimited, incalculable, immense, prodigious
OPPOSITES ARE limited, finite

2 *Along the rooflines were infinite numbers of chimneys.*
▶ countless, innumerable, numberless, incalculable
OPPOSITES ARE limited, finite

**inflamed** ADJECTIVE

*Her skin had become inflamed.*
▶ swollen, reddened, raw, smarting, infected, poisoned, septic, festering

**inflammable** ADJECTIVE

*inflammable chemicals*
▶ flammable, combustible, volatile, burnable
OPPOSITES ARE non-flammable, incombustible

**inflammation** NOUN

*inflammation of the skin*
▶ swelling, redness, soreness, burning, tenderness, infection

**inflate** VERB

1 *We have ten minutes to inflate fifty balloons.*
▶ pump up, blow up, puff up, dilate, distend, swell

2 *News reports have greatly inflated the number of casualties.*
▶ exaggerate, magnify, overstate, overplay, overdramatize

**inflexible** ADJECTIVE

1 *The boots felt rather narrow and inflexible.*
▶ rigid, stiff, firm, hard, unbending, unyielding, hardened, immovable, fixed, solid

2 *An inflexible approach to the problem won't work.*
▶ strict, stubborn, obstinate, entrenched, immutable, intractable, intransigent, unaccommodating, unalterable, uncompromising, unhelpful
AN OPPOSITE IS flexible

**inflict** VERB

1 *He was determined to inflict some sort of penalty on them.*
▶ impose, administer (to), mete out (to), deal out (to), apply (to), perpetrate, wreak, enforce, force

2 *No one really wants an elderly relative inflicted on them for months.*
▶ impose, foist, thrust, saddle someone (with), burden someone (with)

**influence** NOUN

*The local organizations can have a large influence on the party at national level.*
▶ effect, impact, control, sway, hold, pressure, pull, power (over), direction (over), authority (over), dominance (over)

**influence** VERB

1 *Parents influence their children enormously in the first few years.*
▶ affect, have an effect on, guide, exert an influence on, direct, control

2 *There had been several attempts to influence the jury.*
▶ sway, bias, coerce, pressurize, prejudice, suborn, lead astray, bribe, corrupt

**influential** ADJECTIVE

1 *a respected and influential politician*
▶ important, authoritative, leading, powerful, dominant
OPPOSITES ARE uninfluential, insignificant

2 *a piece of writing that has been highly influential*
▶ significant, persuasive, pivotal, seminal, crucial, effective, far-reaching, telling
OPPOSITES ARE uninfluential, unimportant

**influx** NOUN

*a huge influx of tourists*
▶ rush, stream, flood, flow, inflow, inundation, invasion

**inform** VERB

1 *I'll inform them that we are ready to leave.*
▶ tell, notify, advise, let someone know, send word to, apprise

2 **inform on** *No one wants to inform on a friend.*
▶ denounce, betray, report, incriminate, tell on, (*more informal*) shop

**informal** ADJECTIVE

1 *We were having an informal conversation.*
▶ casual, relaxed, natural, easy-going

2 *The style of the article was very informal.*
▶ colloquial, idiomatic, vernacular, demotic, popular

3 *You can wear informal clothes.*
▶ casual, everyday, comfortable, leisure

**information** NOUN

*You can get more information from the website.*
▶ details, particulars, facts, data, guidance, material, documentation, advice, knowledge, (*more informal*) info

**informative** ADJECTIVE

*The two-day course is too short to be informative.*
▶ instructive, useful, helpful, communicative, enlightening, revealing, illuminating, factual
OPPOSITES ARE uninformative, uncommunicative

**informed** ADJECTIVE

*She seems highly informed on the subject.*
▶ knowledgeable, enlightened, conversant (with), familiar (with), abreast (of), au fait (with)
OPPOSITES ARE ill-informed, ignorant

**infringe** VERB

1 *behaviour that infringes all the rules*
▶ break, violate, contravene, disobey, breach, flout, transgress

2 *measures that infringe civil liberties*
▶ undermine, encroach on, impair, compromise, damage

**infuriate** VERB

*His stubborn refusal began to infuriate her.*
▶ anger, enrage, exasperate, incense, annoy, irritate, vex, madden, aggravate, antagonize,

displease, make angry, (*more informal*) needle, (*more informal*) rile
OPPOSITES ARE placate, appease, please

**ingenious** ADJECTIVE
*an ingenious solution to the difficulty*
► inventive, imaginative, creative, clever, original, cunning, resourceful, astute, shrewd, inspired, skilful, subtle
AN OPPOSITE IS unimaginative

**ingenuity** NOUN
*You need ingenuity to write computer programs like these.*
► inventiveness, imagination, creativity, originality

**ingenuous** ADJECTIVE
*The look on his face was ingenuous and sincere.*
► innocent, naive, frank, guileless, honest, open, artless
OPPOSITES ARE disingenuous, artful

**ingredient** NOUN
*Fruit is the missing ingredient in their diet.*
► component, constituent, element, part, piece, portion

**inhabit** VERB
(*old-fashioned*) *a cave complex that hermits used to inhabit*
► live in, occupy, dwell in, people, populate, settle in

**inhabitant** NOUN
*the inhabitants of the town*
► resident, citizen, native, local, occupant, dweller, (*plural*) population, (*plural*) townsfolk

**inhabited** ADJECTIVE
*an inhabited island*
► populated, settled, occupied, peopled, colonized
AN OPPOSITE IS uninhabited

**inherent** ADJECTIVE
*the inherent goodness of humankind*
► intrinsic, innate, inborn, inbred, ingrained, congenital, fundamental, essential, hereditary, immanent, native, natural
AN OPPOSITE IS acquired

**inherit** VERB
*His son will inherit the business on his death.*
► receive, be left, be bequeathed, succeed to

**inheritance** NOUN
*She bought a house with her inheritance.*
► legacy, bequest, estate, fortune, heritage

**inhibit** VERB
*the problems that inhibit progress*
► obstruct, hinder, hold up, hamper, impede, interfere with, restrict, thwart, check, curb, handicap

**inhibited** ADJECTIVE
*He felt inhibited about discussing money.*
► shy, reticent, embarrassed, awkward, self-conscious, reserved, diffident, bashful, (*more informal*) hung up

**inhibition** NOUN
**1** *The state places no inhibition on press freedom.*
► restraint, bar, check, barrier, interference, impediment
**2** *inhibitions Not everyone can overcome their inhibitions so easily.*
► shyness, reticence, diffidence, reserve, self-consciousness, insecurity, repression, (*informal*) hang-ups

**inhuman** ADJECTIVE
*the inhuman treatment of political prisoners*
► inhumane, brutal, cruel, barbaric, barbarous, harsh, callous, bestial, savage, merciless, pitiless, ruthless, unnatural, bloodthirsty, diabolical, fiendish, heartless
OPPOSITES ARE humane, compassionate

**inhumane** ADJECTIVE
*It would be inhumane to take away their freedom.*
► cruel, inhuman, harsh, callous, sadistic, barbaric, barbarous, uncivilized
AN OPPOSITE IS humane

**initial** ADJECTIVE
**1** *Their initial reaction was one of anger.*
► first, original, provisional, earliest
OPPOSITES ARE final, eventual
**2** *an initial payment of £100*
► opening, preliminary, starting, commencing, inaugural, introductory
OPPOSITES ARE final, closing

**initially** ADVERB
*I had initially intended to send an email.*
► at first, originally, to begin with, to start with, at the start

**initiate** VERB
*The local authority has initiated a youth enterprise scheme.*
► institute, inaugurate, instigate, launch, begin

**initiative** NOUN
**1** *Employers are looking for initiative in candidates for jobs.*
► enterprise, resourcefulness, drive, inventiveness, innovativeness, energy, dynamism, leadership, originality, ambition
**2** *We are in danger of losing the initiative.*
► advantage, upper hand, edge, lead
**3** *a new initiative for peace*
► proposal, plan, scheme, strategy, measure

**injure** VERB
**1** *He was injured in a street fight.*
► hurt, harm, wound, maim, cripple, disfigure
**2** *She injured her arm.*
► hurt, damage, break, crush

**injury** NOUN
**1** *His hand injury had fully recovered.*
► wound, cut, damage, fracture, lesion
**2** *The suit will protect you from personal injury*
► harm, hurt, suffering

a
b
c
d
e
f
g
h
**i**
j
k
l
m
n
o
p
q
r
s
t
u
v
w
x
y
z

## injustice NOUN

1 *He shook his head at the cruel injustice of the world.*
► unfairness, unjustness, inequality, inequity, oppression, discrimination, dishonesty, partiality, wrongness
AN OPPOSITE IS justice

2 *She felt her treatment to be a grave injustice.*
► wrong, injury, affront, grievance, offence, crime, iniquity, outrage

## inkling NOUN

*I got some inkling that this one would be different.*
► idea, notion, impression, suspicion

## innate ADJECTIVE

*a decor that shows innate good taste.*
► inherent, inborn, inbred, intrinsic, natural, ingrained, congenital, fundamental, essential
AN OPPOSITE IS acquired

## inner ADJECTIVE

1 *The inner part of the building*
► interior, central, innermost, internal, inside
AN OPPOSITE IS outer

2 *She kept her inner feelings to herself.*
► private, secret, personal, intimate

## innocent ADJECTIVE

1 *He always swore that he was innocent.*
► guiltless, blameless, free from blame
AN OPPOSITE IS guilty

2 *At her age she looked so innocent.*
► pure, virtuous, chaste, fresh, childlike, trusting, guileless, artless

3 *They claimed it had just been innocent fun.*
► harmless, innocuous, inoffensive

## innovation NOUN

*There will be some innovations when the new management takes over.*
► change, alteration, reform, departure, new feature, novelty, revolution

## innovative ADJECTIVE

*innovative ideas*
► new, fresh, original, inventive, resourceful

## innuendo NOUN

*language full of double meanings and innuendo*
► insinuation, intimation, aspersion, slur

## innumerable ADJECTIVE

*the light from innumerable fires*
► countless, numerous, very many, untold, numberless, unnumbered, incalculable, infinite

## inoffensive ADJECTIVE

*a few inoffensive remarks about their local MP*
► harmless, innocuous, unobjectionable, unexceptionable

## input NOUN

*They went to the meeting armed with input from their survey.*
► information, data, facts and figures, statistics

## inquire VERB

**inquire into** *The committee will inquire into all these matters.*
► investigate, look into, examine, probe, scrutinize, explore

**USAGE** Note that *enquire* is normally used in the more general meaning 'to ask about something', as in *'She enquired about his health'*.

## inquiry NOUNS

*The government has set up a formal inquiry into the incident.*
► investigation, inquest, scrutiny, inquisition, inspection

## inquisitive ADJECTIVE

*Gareth possessed a sharp and inquisitive mind.*
► curious, questioning, inquiring, interested, probing, prying

## insane ADJECTIVE

1 *She was declared insane on the recommendation of two doctors.*
► mad, deranged, crazy, demented, mentally ill

2 *It would be insane to think they could do the journey in a day.*
► crazy, foolish, stupid, senseless, ludicrous, absurd, mad

## insanity NOUN

1 *Insanity ran in the family.*
► madness, mental disorder, mental illness, derangement, lunacy, dementia

2 *A loan at such a high rate of interest would be insanity.*
► folly, foolishness, stupidity, madness, lunacy

## insatiable ADJECTIVE

*an insatiable appetite for debate*
► unquenchable, unsatisfiable, voracious, ravenous, immoderate, prodigious

---

**insect** NOUN
*Some insects are disguised as a leaf or a twig.*
► bug, pest, *(more informal)* creepy-crawly

**SOME COMMON INSECTS**

**flies:** fly, blackfly, bluebottle, gadfly, gnat, horsefly, housefly, hoverfly, midge, mosquito, sandfly, tsetse fly.

**bees:** bee, worker, drone, queen bee; bumblebee, carpenter bee, drone, honeybee, mason bee.

**wasps:** wasp, hornet, ichneumon (= 'tracker'), sawfly, *(informal)* yellow jacket.

**beetles:** beetle, black beetle (= cockroach), chafer, click beetle, cockchafer, Colorado beetle, death-watch beetle, dung beetle, firefly (having soft body), glow-worm (having soft body), ladybird, soldier beetle, stag beetle, weevil.
►►

**other flying insects**: ant; aphid (blackfly, greenfly); crane fly (daddy-long-legs), damselfly, dragonfly, lacewing; locust; mayfly; butterfly, moth.

**jumping insects**: flea, grasshopper, cricket, cicada.

**non-flying insects**: ant, cockroach, earwig, louse, mantis, sawyer, stick insect, termite, thrip, water boatman.

**other creatures loosely called insects**: centipede, worm, earthworm, mite, slug, woodlouse.

**other words**: larva (e.g. caterpillar or tadpole), grub (larva), maggot (larva), leatherjacket (larva of crane fly), woodworm (larva of a beetle), nit (egg), pupa (stage between larva and adult), chrysalis (butterfly or moth pupa), imago (adult stage).

**insecure** ADJECTIVE
1 *Police warned that the house was insecure.*
▶ unsafe, unprotected, ill-protected, vulnerable, exposed, ill-defended, defenceless
2 *All this bold talk made him feel insecure.*
▶ anxious, worried, concerned, unconfident, diffident

**insensible** ADJECTIVE
1 *She lay insensible on a couch.*
▶ unconscious, inert, senseless
2 **insensible to** *We are not insensible to the risks involved.*
▶ unaware of, ignorant of, unconscious of, unresponsive to
**USAGE** Note that *insensible* is not the opposite of *sensible* in its normal meaning 'having good sense'.

**insensitive** ADJECTIVE
1 *It was insensitive to criticize them at a time like this.*
▶ unfeeling, uncaring, tactless, thoughtless, callous
2 *a part of the body insensitive to pain*
▶ hardened, resistant, impervious, immune, unaffected (by)

**insert** VERB
*He inserted a new film in the camera.*
▶ put, place, push, slip, install, locate

**inside** ADJECTIVE
*The inside walls of the house were damp.*
▶ inner, interior, internal, innermost, indoor
OPPOSITES ARE outside , outer, exterior

**inside** NOUN
*The inside of the box should be lined with silver paper.*
▶ interior, inner surface, inner part, core

**insides** PLURAL NOUN
*He felt total panic in his insides.*
▶ guts, stomach, intestines, organs, (more informal) tummy

**insidious** ADJECTIVE
*Mocking little phrases found their insidious way into her mind.*
▶ stealthy, surreptitious, sneaking, cunning, furtive

**insight** NOUN
*Her experience and insight proved invaluable.*
▶ understanding, appreciation, awareness, grasp, perception, intuition, acumen, discernment

**insignificant** ADJECTIVE
*The differences are mostly insignificant.*
▶ unimportant, negligible, trivial, trifling, small, footling, inconsequential, inconsiderable, irrelevant, meaningless
AN OPPOSITE IS significant

**insincere** ADJECTIVE
*He flashed a gleaming, insincere smile.*
▶ false, deceitful, dishonest, disingenuous, pretended, feigned, hypocritical, devious
AN OPPOSITE IS sincere

**insinuate** VERB
*He insinuated that they had lied.*
▶ imply, suggest, hint, intimate, give to understand

**insipid** ADJECTIVE
*They sipped bowls of pale insipid soup.*
▶ bland, tasteless, weak, watery

**insist** VERB
1 *He insisted he had done everything they had asked.*
▶ maintain, contend, assert, hold, aver, claim, declare, state, stress
2 **insist on** *parents who insist on an early bedtime*
▶ demand, enforce, require, stipulate

**insistence** NOUN
1 *her insistence that they should go with her*
▶ demand, requirement, entreaty, urging
2 *Jane's insistence that she loved him*
▶ assertion, declaration, contention, claim, avowal

**insistent** ADJECTIVE
*There were insistent requests for financial support.*
▶ persistent, demanding, unrelenting, unremitting, urgent, emphatic, relentless, repeated, forceful, assertive

**insolence** NOUN
*She accused him of insolence.*
▶ cheek, impertinence, impudence, effrontery, audacity, rudeness, impoliteness, discourtesy, disrespect

**insolent** ADJECTIVE
*The boy was constantly insolent.*
▶ rude, impolite, impertinent, impudent, disrespectful, audacious, brazen
OPPOSITES ARE respectful, polite

**insoluble** ADJECTIVE
*one of the world's insoluble problems*
▶ unsolvable, unresolvable, inexplicable, unanswerable, unfathomable, incomprehensible, mysterious, mystifying, baffling, enigmatic, puzzling
AN OPPOSITE IS soluble

a b c d e f g h **i** j k l m n o p q r s t u v w x y z

**inspect** VERB

*The houses had been inspected by a surveyor.*
► check, examine, investigate, scrutinize, supervise, oversee

**inspection** NOUN

*The machinery needs a regular inspection.*
► examination, check, check-up, investigation, review, scrutiny, survey

**inspector** NOUN

*Inspectors are sent out each week to assess the work done.*
► examiner, investigator, supervisor, tester, controller, official, superintendent

**inspiration** NOUN

1 *writing that relies on inspiration*
► creativity, imagination, inventiveness, ingenuity, enthusiasm, genius, influence
2 *The success proved an inspiration to everyone involved in the project.*
► stimulus, spur, motivation, filip, boost
3 *Emma had a sudden inspiration*
► idea, thought, brainwave, revelation

**inspire** VERB

*a simple tune that inspired him to write a musical*
► stimulate, influence, motivate, prompt, encourage, enthuse, galvanize, reassure, spur, stir, animate, arouse, (*more informal*) egg on

**instability** NOUN

*The world economy is in a state of instability.*
► unsteadiness, variability, unreliability, changeability, precariousness, fluctuation, unpredictability

**install** VERB

1 *We want to install central heating on all floors.*
► put in, establish, fix, introduce, set up
2 **install yourself** *She installed herself in a sofa by the fire.*
► ensconce yourself, settle, place yourself, plant yourself, (*more informal*) park yourself

**instalment** NOUN

1 *You can pay for your licence in monthly instalments.*
► payment, part
2 *a serial in four instalments*
► episode, part, section

**instance** NOUN

*We could not find a single instance of discrimination.*
► example, occurrence, case, illustration, sample

**instant** ADJECTIVE

*The website gives you instant access to the information you need.*
► immediate, instantaneous, on-the-spot, prompt, fast, quick, rapid, speedy, direct, swift

**instant** NOUN

*The incident was over in an instant.*
► moment, second, minute, flash, split second, (*more informal*) tick, (*more informal*) twinkling

**instantly** ADVERB

*He fell asleep instantly.*
► immediately, at once, straight away, right away, there and then, in a trice, directly

**instigate** VERB

1 *The police will instigate formal inquiries.*
► initiate, set in motion, establish, institute
2 *A few troublemakers managed to instigate a disturbance.*
► start, spark, incite, generate, encourage, prompt, whip up, kindle

**instinct** NOUN

*Her instinct was to find out more about them.*
► impulse, inclination, intuition, hunch, feeling, presentiment, sixth-sense, tendency, urge

**instinctive** ADJECTIVE

*Their instinctive reaction is to find someone to blame.*
► intuitive, natural, innate, automatic, reflex
OPPOSITES ARE deliberate, conscious

**institute** VERB

*The Academy has instituted a new research programme.*
► establish, inaugurate, initiate, launch, introduce, found, create, originate, set up, begin, start

**institution** NOUN

1 *the institution of a new language course*
► introduction, establishment, setting up, formation, creation, launching, inauguration, inception, initiation, founding, opening
2 *He did not want to spend the rest of his life in an institution.*
► home, hospital, asylum
3 *an academic institution*
► establishment, school, academy, college
4 *A spring holiday has become a family institution.*
► custom, convention, tradition, routine, practice, ritual, habit

**instruct** VERB

1 *A private tutor instructed the children in French.*
► coach, educate, train, drill, ground, teach
2 *The officials instructed us to wait.*
► order, direct, command, require, call on, advise

**instruction** NOUN

1 *It is important to listen out for instructions.*
► direction, directive, order, command, guidance
2 *basic instruction in mathematics*
► education, tuition, teaching, schooling, coaching, tutoring, grounding

**instructive** ADJECTIVE

*an instructive experience*
► educational, enlightening, informative, illuminating, revealing, edifying, helpful, improving

**instrument** NOUN

*a sharp instrument*
► implement, tool, device, utensil, contrivance, contraption, apparatus, appliance, equipment, gadget, machine, mechanism

## instrumental ADJECTIVE

*He was instrumental in getting the information we needed.*
▶ active, influential, involved, contributory (to), helpful, useful

## insubordinate ADJECTIVE

*His older son had been difficult and insubordinate.*
▶ disobedient, unruly, rebellious, badly behaved, wayward, undisciplined, defiant, mutinous
AN OPPOSITE IS obedient

## insult NOUN (with the stress on *in-*)

*The two men threw insults at each other.*
▶ affront, abuse, indignity, slight, snub
AN OPPOSITE IS compliment

## insult VERB (with the stress on -*sult*)

*She put her head out of the window to insult passers-by.*
▶ abuse, affront, malign, revile, offend, mock, snub, vilify, sneer at
AN OPPOSITE IS compliment

## insulting ADJECTIVE

*They directed their insulting remarks at anyone they happened to see.*
▶ abusive, rude, offensive, disparaging, contemptuous, deprecatory, scornful, scurrilous, slanderous, insolent, condescending, mocking, patronizing, (*more informal*) snide
OPPOSITES ARE polite, complimentary

## intact ADJECTIVE

*Several buildings remained intact despite heavy bombing.*
▶ whole, undamaged, untouched, unharmed, complete, entire

## intangible ADJECTIVE

*Dusk gave the scene an intangible quality.*
▶ impalpable, untouchable, imperceptible, unreal, ethereal, incorporeal, shadowy, disembodied, elusive, abstract, airy
AN OPPOSITE IS tangible

## integral ADJECTIVE

**1** *Speech is an integral part of human interaction.*
▶ essential, constituent, indispensable, intrinsic, irreplaceable, necessary, requisite
AN OPPOSITE IS incidental
**2** *The equipment is sold as an integral system.*
▶ complete, integrated, combined, indivisible, whole

## integrate VERB

*The army command integrated several units into a single force.*
▶ merge, amalgamate, combine, consolidate, unify, unite, fuse, join, blend, bring together
AN OPPOSITE IS separate

## integrity NOUN

*No one doubts their integrity.*
▶ honesty, honour, morality, sincerity, reliability, virtue, fidelity, uprightness, honourableness, righteousness, goodness, incorruptibility, loyalty, principle
AN OPPOSITE IS dishonesty

## intellect NOUN

*a story that appeals to the intellect rather than the emotions*
▶ mind, reason, intelligence, judgement, wits

## intellectual ADJECTIVE

**1** *intellectual powers.*
▶ mental, cerebral, rational, cognitive, conceptual
**2** *an intellectual person*
▶ intelligent, academic, cultured, scholarly, studious, thoughtful, highbrow

## intellectual NOUN

*Opposition to the regime is strongest among intellectuals.*
▶ academic, scholar, highbrow, thinker, member of the intelligentsia, intelligent person

## intelligence NOUN

**1** *a person of great intelligence*
▶ intellect, brainpower, powers of reasoning, perceptiveness, acumen, wisdom, wits, understanding, comprehension, (*more informal*) nous
AN OPPOSITE IS stupidity
**2** *constant intelligence regarding terrorist attacks*
▶ information, report, warning, news, notification, data, facts, knowledge, (*more informal*) tip-off

## intelligent ADJECTIVE

*She is a highly intelligent writer.*
▶ clever, bright, acute, sharp, perceptive, profound, shrewd

## intelligible ADJECTIVE

*The message was barely intelligible.*
▶ understandable, comprehensible, coherent, decipherable, legible, clear, lucid, meaningful
OPPOSITES ARE unintelligible, incomprehensible

## intend VERB

**1** *I intend to apply for a grant.*
▶ propose, mean, plan, have it in mind, have a mind, aim, contemplate (applying), determine, purpose
**2** *The book is intended for learners of English.*
▶ design, destine, mean

## intense ADJECTIVE

*She was suffering from intense pain. The experience rouses intense emotions.*
▶ extreme, acute, severe, fierce, sharp, strong, powerful, profound, potent
OPPOSITES ARE moderate, mild

## intensify VERB

**1** *The dizzy feeling in his head intensified.*
▶ increase, strengthen, grow, escalate
AN OPPOSITE IS weaken
**2** *We must intensify our efforts.*
▶ increase, escalate, step up, reinforce, sharpen, concentrate
AN OPPOSITE IS reduce

a
b
c
d
e
f
g
h
i
j
k
l
m
n
o
p
q
r
s
t
u
v
w
x
y
z

## intensive ADJECTIVE
*Police have made an intensive search of the area.*
▶ thorough, exhaustive, comprehensive, rigorous, detailed, complete, full, all-out, concentrated

## intent ADJECTIVE
1 *She was intent on visiting her friends in Spain.*
▶ keen (to), resolved (to), determined (to), bent, fixed
AN OPPOSITE IS reluctant

2 *He had an intent look on his face.*
▶ attentive, engrossed, absorbed, preoccupied, steadfast
OPPOSITES ARE vacant, blank

## intention NOUN
*Our intention is to accept the offer.*
▶ aim, purpose, objective, object, plan, ambition, design, end, goal

## intentional ADJECTIVE
*The remarks were intentional.*
▶ deliberate, premeditated, intended, planned, calculated, conscious, considered, meant, designed, prearranged, wilful
AN OPPOSITE IS unintentional

## interaction NOUN
*the interaction of two influences*
▶ effect on each other, exchange, (*informal*) give and take, interplay, reciprocal effect, (*informal*) to and fro

## intercept VERB
*He intercepted her at the kitchen door.*
▶ stop, catch, check, interrupt, obstruct, cut off, block, deflect, head off, thwart, trap

## interest NOUN
1 *a matter of great interest to both of them*
▶ importance, significance, consequence, moment, note, value

2 *Her interests include rock-climbing.*
▶ activity, pursuit, hobby, pastime, diversion, preoccupation

**show interest in** *John was showing interest in the idea.*
▶ take notice of, pay attention to, be concerned about, be curious about, have regard for, show involvement in, show commitment to

## interest VERB
*an idea that interests me*
▶ appeal to, attract, excite, fascinate, intrigue, engage, engross, concern, stimulate, arouse the curiosity of, capture the imagination of, divert, entertain, involve, (*more informal*) turn on
AN OPPOSITE IS bore

## interested ADJECTIVE
1 *None of them appeared to be interested.*
▶ curious, enthusiastic, excited, keen, responsive, fascinated, absorbed, attentive, engrossed, intent
AN OPPOSITE IS uninterested.

2 *At the meeting various problems were explained to the interested parties.*
▶ affected, involved, concerned, connected
AN OPPOSITE IS disinterested

**be interested in** *The owners were interested in the idea of selling off part of the land.*
▶ like, be attracted by, fancy

## interesting ADJECTIVE
*an interesting idea*
▶ attractive, appealing, engrossing, stimulating, exciting, intriguing, fascinating, thought-provoking

## interfere VERB
1 *interfere in She did not wish to interfere in her friends' lives.*
▶ intervene, intrude in, meddle in, butt into, pry into, snoop into, encroach on
2 *interfere with A headache interfered with his thoughts.*
▶ inhibit, hinder, hamper, impede, get in the way of

## interference NOUN
*He would not tolerate any interference.*
▶ intrusion, intervention, meddling, snooping, involvement

## interfering ADJECTIVE
*She blamed his interfering brother.*
▶ meddlesome, meddling, nosy, prying, snooping, intrusive

## interim ADJECTIVE
*An interim report is being prepared.*
▶ provisional, temporary, stopgap, short-term, acting, halfway

## interior NOUN
*the interior of the building*
▶ inside, inside surface, inward aspect, heart, core
AN OPPOSITE IS exterior

## interior ADJECTIVE
*the interior walls*
▶ inner, inside, internal, innermost
AN OPPOSITE IS exterior

## interlude NOUN
*a quiet interlude in a hectic day*
▶ interval, pause, respite, spell, break, breathing space

## intermediary NOUN
*They used an intermediary to conclude the agreement.*
▶ mediator, go-between, negotiator, conciliator, middleman

## intermediate ADJECTIVE
*French classes at intermediate level*
▶ midway, halfway, transitional

## interminable ADJECTIVE
*It was a week of interminable meetings and interviews.*
▶ endless, never-ending, ceaseless, incessant, constant, continuous, continual, perpetual, everlasting

**intermittent** ADJECTIVE
*A day of intermittent rainstorms followed.*
▶ sporadic, periodic, occasional, irregular, recurrent, spasmodic, fitful, (*informal*) on and off
AN OPPOSITE IS continuous

**internal** ADJECTIVE
**1** *The house was built round an internal courtyard.*
▶ inner, interior, inside, central
AN OPPOSITE IS external
**2** *the country's internal affairs*
▶ domestic, home, interior, local, civil

**international** ADJECTIVE
*the growth of fast international travel*
▶ global, worldwide, intercontinental, universal

**interpret** VERB
*wise men who interpret the sacred laws*
▶ explain, expound, clarify, elucidate, translate

**interpretation** NOUN
*We have a different interpretation of the story.*
▶ explanation, understanding, clarification, reading, analysis, definition, gloss, version

**interrogate** VERB
*The secret police wanted to interrogate them.*
▶ question, cross-examine, examine, investigate, (*more informal*) grill, (*more informal*) quiz

**interrogation** NOUN
*The police interrogation continued all morning.*
▶ questioning, cross-examination, investigation, examination, (*more informal*) grilling

**interrupt** VERB
**1** *He opened his mouth to interrupt.*
▶ butt in, break in, cut in, intervene
**2** *People at the back of the hall began to interrupt her.*
▶ heckle, disrupt, butt in on, cut in on
**3** *The news from home led them to interrupt their holiday.*
▶ suspend, break off, discontinue, delay, postpone, put off, defer
**4** *The new building will interrupt the view.*
▶ break, break up, divide, disturb

**interruption** NOUN
**1** *There were several interruptions during the speech.*
▶ intervention, intrusion, disruption, cutting in, disturbance
**2** *A note through the letterbox warned of interruptions in the water supply.*
▶ break, disruption, suspension, pause, check, hiatus, stop

**interval** NOUN
**1** *There will be an interval of 20 minutes halfway through the show.*
▶ intermission, interlude, break, pause
**2** *The next class will be in a week's time and you can revise in the interval.*
▶ interim, meantime, meanwhile, pause, delay

**intervene** VERB
**1** *A week intervened before I saw her again*
▶ come between, happen, intrude, occur

**2** *Someone has to intervene to sort out the disagreement.*
▶ step in, intercede, interrupt, interfere, intrude, mediate, arbitrate, butt in

**intervention** NOUN
*Their intervention was resented by both sides in the dispute.*
▶ intrusion, involvement, intercession, mediation

**interview** NOUN
*Interviews for the job will be held next week.*
▶ meeting, discussion, conference, audience, questioning

**interview** VERB
*A journalist wants to interview her about her new book.*
▶ talk to, question, ask questions, have a discussion with, interrogate, examine

**intimate** ADJECTIVE
**1** *an intimate friendship*
▶ close, loving, affectionate, personal, familiar, friendly, informal, sexual
**2** *an intimate atmosphere*
▶ friendly, welcoming, warm, informal, relaxed, cosy
**3** *intimate thoughts*
▶ personal, private, secret, confidential
**4** *an intimate knowledge of the area*
▶ detailed, exhaustive, profound, deep, in-depth

**intimidate** VERB
*He wanted to get his way without appearing to intimidate them.*
▶ threaten, bully, frighten, coerce, browbeat, menace, persecute, scare, terrify, terrorize, cow, daunt, hector, make afraid

**intolerable** ADJECTIVE
*The noise had become intolerable.*
▶ unbearable, unendurable, unacceptable, insufferable, insupportable, excruciating, impossible
OPPOSITES ARE tolerable, bearable

**intolerant** ADJECTIVE
*He was extremely intolerant about religion.*
▶ bigoted, dogmatic, narrow-minded, opinionated, prejudiced, chauvinistic, illiberal
AN OPPOSITE IS tolerant

**intrepid** ADJECTIVE
*The four intrepid climbers had to turn back because of fierce winds.*
▶ bold, courageous, daring, brave, gallant, fearless, plucky, valiant

**intricate** ADJECTIVE
*intricate designs  intricate relationships*
▶ complex, elaborate, ornate, detailed, complicated, convoluted, tangled, delicate, involved, sophisticated, tortuous
AN OPPOSITE IS simple

a b c d e f g h **i** j k l m n o p q r s t u v w x y z

**intrigue** NOUN

**1** *a leader vulnerable to jealousy and intrigue*
► conspiracy, plotting, scheming, machination, trickery, subterfuge

**2** *a family abuzz with romantic intrigues*
► affair, liaison, amour, flirtation, dalliance, intimacy

**intrigue** VERB

**1** *These stories have always intrigued young children.*
► interest, fascinate, engross, captivate, enthrall, absorb, beguile

**2** *The men were suspected of intriguing against the king*
► plot, conspire, scheme, connive, manoeuvre

**intriguing** ADJECTIVE

*an intriguing account of a trip round the world*
► interesting, fascinating, engrossing, captivating, enthralling, absorbing, beguiling

**intrinsic** ADJECTIVE

*The jewellery has little intrinsic value.*
► inherent, innate, fundamental, essential, basic, real

**introduce** VERB

**1** *Jane introduced us to her husband.*
► present, make known, acquaint

**2** *The new owners have introduced some new features.*
► bring in, institute, initiate, establish, set up, start, begin, create, offer, propose, suggest, pioneer

**3** *a new star to introduce the show*
► present, host, compère, announce

**introduction** NOUN

**1** *the introduction of a democratic government*
► institution, establishment, foundation, inauguration, beginning, development

**2** *The author thanks his friends in the book's introduction.*
► foreword, preface, preamble, front matter, opening

**introductory** ADJECTIVE

**1** *The speaker began with some introductory remarks.*
► opening, preliminary, preparatory, initial, prefatory
AN OPPOSITE IS concluding

**2** *a short introductory course*
► basic, elementary, preliminary, preparatory, primary

**introvert** NOUN

*He enjoyed a social life despite being an introvert.*
► shy person, reserved person
AN OPPOSITE IS extrovert

**USAGE** For other synonyms see the words in the next entry.

**introverted** ADJECTIVE

*a quiet and introverted character*
► shy, reserved, retiring, introvert, introspective, inward-looking, thoughtful, meditative, withdrawn, contemplative, pensive, self-contained, unsociable
AN OPPOSITE IS extrovert

**intrude** VERB

**intrude on** *No one has the right to intrude on a person's privacy in this way.*
► encroach on, break in on, interrupt, interfere with, butt in on, eavesdrop on, intervene in, gatecrash

**intruder** NOUN

*Intruders had left the house in a mess.*
► trespasser, interloper, invader, burglar, housebreaker, prowler, robber, thief, raider

**intrusion** NOUN

*Please forgive this intrusion.*
► interruption, interference, encroachment, intervention, disruption
AN OPPOSITE IS withdrawal

**intuition** NOUN

**1** *He relied on his intuition to get him out of the difficulty.*
► instinct, intuitiveness, sixth sense, insight

**2** *What you say confirms all my intuitions.*
► feeling, gut feeling, hunch, suspicion, premonition

**intuitive** ADJECTIVE

*She has an intuitive understanding of languages.*
► instinctive, innate, inborn, inherent, natural, unconscious, involuntary

**inundate** VERB

*The waters inundated the city. We were inundated with letters.*
► flood, deluge, engulf, submerge, overrun, overwhelm

**invade** VERB

*The allies invaded the country from the south.*
► march into, occupy, enter, penetrate, overrun, raid, subdue, violate, attack, descend on, encroach on

**invalid** ADJECTIVE (with the stress on -*val*-)

**1** *His licence would be invalid in America.*
► void, unacceptable, unusable, worthless, null and void
AN OPPOSITE IS valid

**2** *It was not difficult to prove the idea invalid.*
► false, fallacious, unfounded, unreasonable, unsound, incorrect, untrue, illogical, irrational, unconvincing, unscientific
AN OPPOSITE IS valid

**invalid** ADJECTIVE (with the stress on *in*-)

*Kate has an invalid husband.*
► sick, ailing, infirm, disabled, incapacitated, bedridden

**invaluable** ADJECTIVE

*James is an invaluable member of the team.*
► crucial, indispensable, irreplaceable, precious, priceless, useful, valuable, incalculable, inestimable
AN OPPOSITE IS worthless

**USAGE** Note that *invaluable* is not the opposite of *valuable*: for this you should use *valueless*.

**invasion** NOUN

**1** *an air invasion of the island*
▶ attack (on), occupation, incursion, seizure, annexation, overrunning, onslaught, raid
**2** *the annual invasion of tourists*
▶ influx, incursion, inundation, flood, horde, spate, stream, swarm, throng, infestation

**invent** VERB

**1** *He invented a new board game.*
▶ create, devise, conceive, formulate, improvise, originate
**2** *They invented any excuse to avoid going near the swimming pool.*
▶ make up, concoct, fabricate, manufacture, (*more informal*) cook up

**invention** NOUN

**1** *the invention of printing*
▶ development, origination, creation, devising, innovation, pioneering
**2** *writing that shows a lot of invention*
▶ originality, creativity, imagination, ingenuity, inventiveness, resourcefulness, inspiration
**3** *The excuse was pure invention.*
▶ fabrication, fantasy, fiction, deceit, concoction

**inventive** ADJECTIVE

*an inventive artist*
▶ creative, original, imaginative, innovative, ingenious, resourceful, enterprising, fertile, inspired
AN OPPOSITE IS imitative

**inventor** NOUN

*the inventor of the telephone*
▶ creator, originator, designer, discoverer, architect, author, maker

**invert** VERB

*A storm inverted the little boat.*
▶ overturn, reverse, turn upside down, upset, capsize

**invest** VERB

*invest in She invested in her son's business.*
▶ put money into, buy shares in, fund, back

**investigate** VERB

*Police are investigating the discovery of a body.*
▶ inquire into, look into, follow up, probe, examine, explore, consider, study, gather evidence about, scrutinize, (*more informal*) go into

**investigation** NOUN

*The problem needs further investigation. There will have to be an official investigation.*
▶ examination, inquiry, research, scrutiny, study, survey, inspection, inquisition, (*informal*) probing

**investment** NOUN

*You need good advice before you make any investments.*
▶ venture, expenditure, outlay

**invigorating** ADJECTIVE

*an invigorating early morning walk*
▶ stimulating, exhilarating, refreshing, bracing, enlivening, fresh, health-giving, healthy, rejuvenating
AN OPPOSITE IS tiring

**invincible** ADJECTIVE

*the invincible power of the invading armies*
▶ unbeatable, unassailable, indestructible, indomitable, unconquerable, invulnerable, mighty

**invisible** ADJECTIVE

*The house was invisible in the dark.*
▶ hidden, obscured, concealed, undetectable, unnoticeable, imperceptible, unnoticed, unseen, out of sight, covered, disguised, inconspicuous
AN OPPOSITE IS visible

**invitation** NOUN

**1** *an invitation to attend the conference*
▶ call, summons, request
**2** *An open door is an invitation to any passing thief.*
▶ temptation, encouragement, enticement, lure, provocation, inducement

**invite** VERB

**1** *They've invited us to dinner on Saturday.*
▶ ask, request the company of, welcome, summon
**2** *Using emotive language might invite trouble.*
▶ provoke, cause, generate, engender, foster, elicit

**inviting** ADJECTIVE

*the inviting sight of a buffet lunch*
▶ attractive, appealing, welcome, pleasant, enticing, agreeable, appetizing, seductive

**invoke** VERB

**1** *The prosecutor invoked an old law of the previous century.*
▶ refer to, appeal to, cite
**2** *She clasped her hands and invoked her patron saint.*
▶ pray to, appeal to, entreat, supplicate, beseech, implore

**involuntary** ADJECTIVE

*She gave an involuntary shudder.*
▶ reflex, automatic, unconscious, spontaneous, unthinking, unintentional, conditioned, impulsive, instinctive
AN OPPOSITE IS deliberate

**involve** VERB

**1** *Her job involves a lot of travel.*
▶ necessitate, entail, require, demand, mean
**2** *These are decisions that involve everybody.*
▶ affect, concern, interest, include, embrace, take in, touch
**3** *The project involved them in community work.*
▶ occupy, engage, absorb, engross
**4** *A drug habit can rapidly involve them in crime.*
▶ implicate, associate, embroil, entangle

**involved** ADJECTIVE

**1** *a long and involved story*
▶ complex, complicated, convoluted, elaborate, intricate, tangled, confusing, difficult, (*more informal*) knotty
AN OPPOSITE IS straightforward

**2** *She is totally involved in her work.*
▶ occupied, engrossed, absorbed, engaged, preoccupied, caught up, committed (to), dedicated (to)
AN OPPOSITE IS uninvolved

**involvement** NOUN

**1** *her involvement in charity work.*
▶ interest, participation, activity

**2** *There was no doubting their involvement in the plot.*
▶ complicity, connivance, participation, entanglement, association

**invulnerable** ADJECTIVE

*No one is invulnerable to these dangers.*
▶ safe (from), secure (from), impervious, immune, insusceptible
AN OPPOSITE IS vulnerable

**irate** ADJECTIVE

*The helpline has to deal with hundreds of irate callers.*
▶ angry, enraged, furious, incensed, infuriated, indignant, displeased, outraged

**ironic** ADJECTIVE

**1** *The tone of Sarah's voice was sharply ironic.*
▶ sarcastic, ironical, satirical, wry, derisive, double-edged, mocking

**2** *It is ironic that after criticizing London so much he should end up living there.*
▶ paradoxical, strange, peculiar, odd, weird, incongruous

**irrational** ADJECTIVE

*an irrational fear of flying*
▶ illogical, baseless, unreasonable, senseless, arbitrary, unsound, absurd
AN OPPOSITE IS rational

**irregular** ADJECTIVE

**1** *an irregular surface*
▶ uneven, rough, coarse, bumpy, pitted

**2** *an irregular heartbeat   an irregular pattern*
▶ variable, fluctuating, erratic, fitful, haphazard, unsystematic, intermittent

**3** *Her appointment was most irregular.*
▶ improper, abnormal, unorthodox, anomalous, unconventional, against the rules

**irrelevant** ADJECTIVE

*Don't waste time on irrelevant details.*
▶ inappropriate, unnecessary, inessential, extraneous, peripheral, immaterial, inapplicable, pointless, unconnected, unrelated
AN OPPOSITE IS relevant

**irreparable** ADJECTIVE

*A power failure can cause irreparable damage.*
▶ permanent, irretrievable, irreversible, irremediable, unrectifiable, lasting, irrecoverable, unalterable, incurable
AN OPPOSITE IS reparable

**irreplaceable** ADJECTIVE

*a work of art that is irreplaceable*
▶ unique, inimitable, indispensable, matchless, priceless, rare
OPPOSITES ARE replaceable, common

**irrepressible** ADJECTIVE

*He loved her irrepressible high spirits*
▶ ebullient, lively, boisterous, uninhibited, unstoppable, sparkling, bubbling, vivacious, vigorous, bouncy, resilient, uncontrollable, ungovernable
AN OPPOSITE IS sluggish

**irresistible** ADJECTIVE

**1** *The temptation to laugh was irresistible.*
▶ overpowering, overwhelming, inescapable, inexorable, powerful, seductive, unavoidable, compelling, persuasive

**2** *She has an irresistible laugh.*
▶ attractive, appealing, enticing, alluring, seductive, fetching, captivating, beguiling

**irresponsible** ADJECTIVE

**1** *an irresponsible attitude*
▶ reckless, rash, inconsiderate, thoughtless, careless, immoral, selfish, shiftless
AN OPPOSITE IS responsible

**2** *They sometimes behave like irresponsible teenagers.*
▶ immature, unreliable, feckless, unthinking, untrustworthy

**irreverent** ADJECTIVE

*an irreverent approach to authority*
▶ disrespectful, discourteous, disdainful, insolent, impertinent, impudent, scornful, flippant, casual, rude
OPPOSITES ARE reverent, respectful

**irrevocable** ADJECTIVE

*an irrevocable decision*
▶ unalterable, unchangeable, irreversible, immutable, binding, final, firm, fixed, settled, hard and fast
AN OPPOSITE IS reversible

**irritable** ADJECTIVE

*Harry sat back with an irritable look on his face.*
▶ bad-tempered, irascible, grumpy, testy, grouchy, touchy, tetchy, crotchety, cantankerous, peevish, fractious, cross, (*more informal*) stroppy, (*more informal*) shirty
OPPOSITES ARE good-tempered, good-humoured, affable

**irritate** VERB

*I was letting silly things irritate me.*
▶ annoy, displease, anger, infuriate, enrage, exasperate, incense, peeve, vex, madden, aggravate, antagonize, inflame, make angry, (*more*

**irritation**

*informal*) needle, (*more informal*) rile, (*more informal*)
bug, (*more informal*) rub up the wrong way
OPPOSITES ARE please, gratify

**irritation** NOUN
*It was hard to hide our irritation at his rudeness.*
▶ annoyance, indignation, displeasure,
exasperation, pique, chagrin, vexation

**isolate** VERB
**1** *Their extreme political views tended to isolate them
from their contemporaries.*
▶ separate, set apart, keep apart, cut off, segregate,
detach, insulate, seclude, alienate, exclude, single
out
**2** *Sophisticated cameras can easily isolate offending
vehicles.*
▶ identify, recognize, pick out, single out, pinpoint,
distinguish

**isolated** ADJECTIVE
**1** *an isolated town in eastern Malaysia*
▶ remote, outlying, secluded, solitary, inaccessible,
out of the way, deserted
AN OPPOSITE IS accessible
**2** *an isolated occurrence*
▶ unique, special, exceptional, untypical, abnormal

**issue** NOUN
**1** *The society debates political issues.*
▶ matter, concern, subject, topic, affair, point,
question, argument, controversy, dispute, problem
**2** *a special issue of the magazine*
▶ edition, number, instalment, publication, printing

**issue** VERB
**1** *Smoke issued from the top of the building.*
▶ emerge, emanate, erupt, flow out, rise, appear,
come out, gush, leak, spring
**2** *The ambassador issued a formal statement.*
▶ publish, publicize, release, circulate, distribute,
give out, print, produce, send out

**itch** NOUN
**1** *I have an itch in my back.*
▶ itchiness, tickle, tingling, irritation, need to
scratch
**2** *She felt an itch to start painting.*
▶ desire, hankering, longing, yearning, urge, wish,
impulse, lust, need, ache, impatience, restlessness,
(*more informal*) yen

**itch** VERB
**1** *The warmth made my skin itch.*
▶ tickle, tingle, be irritated
**2** *They were itching to leave.*
▶ long, hanker, yearn, be eager, be keen

**item** NOUN
**1** *an item of equipment*
▶ article, bit, object, component, ingredient
**2** *a news item*
▶ report, article, account, feature, notice, piece
**3** *several items on the agenda*
▶ topic, subject

# Jj

**jab** VERB
*He laughed and jabbed his friend in the ribs.*
▶ poke, prod, dig, nudge, elbow, shove

**jack** VERB
**jack up** *He got a passer-by to help him jack up the car
and change the tyre.*
▶ lift, raise, hoist, lever up

**jacket** NOUN
**1** *He wore a blue jacket and cream shirt.*
▶ coat
**2** *books with lurid jackets*
▶ cover, wrapper, coat, covering, folder
**3** *The boiler needs an insulating jacket.*
▶ casing, sheath, sleeve, envelope, skin, wrapping

**jackpot** NOUN
*Three winners will share the jackpot this week.*
▶ top prize, first prize, big prize
**hit the jackpot** (*informal*)
▶ be successful, win a fortune, strike it lucky, make a
packet

**jaded** ADJECTIVE
*The long day left me feeling jaded.*
▶ weary, tired, drained, exhausted, fatigued, listless,
spent, (*more informal*) done in
AN OPPOSITE IS fresh

**jagged** ADJECTIVE
*He gashed his head against a jagged branch.*
▶ spiky, uneven, broken, irregular, ragged, rough,
toothed, serrated, zigzag
OPPOSITES ARE even, smooth

**jail** NOUN
*a building that used to be the town jail*
▶ prison, jailhouse, guardhouse, (*more informal*) nick,
(*more informal*) clink

**jail** VERB
*If he's found guilty he'll be jailed.*
▶ send to prison, put in prison, imprison, give a
custodial sentence to

**jailer** NOUN
*The jailer's wife brought the prisoner some food.*
▶ prison guard, prison officer, guard, warder,
warden

**jam** NOUN
**1** *a long jam on the motorway*
▶ tailback, hold-up, obstruction, blockage,
bottleneck
**2** *We're in a bit of a jam.*
▶ predicament, quandary, embarrassment,
difficulty, dilemma, tight corner, trouble, plight,
(*more informal*) fix, (*more informal*) hole
**3** *Have some home-made jam.*
▶ preserve, conserve, jelly, marmalade

## jam VERB

1 *They try to jam too many people in the lifts.*
► cram, pack, squeeze, stuff, crowd, crush, ram, squash

2 *Protesters jammed one side of the motorway.*
► block, clog, obstruct, congest

3 *I'll jam the door open with a newspaper.*
► prop, stick, wedge

4 *The window has jammed.*
► stick, become stuck, become wedged, become lodged, seize

## jangle VERB

*He jangled his keys as he walked to the door. Bracelets jangled on her wrists.*
► jingle, clink, tinkle, clang

## janitor NOUN

*a school janitor*
► caretaker, custodian, watchman, maintenance man

## jar NOUN

*a jar of honey*
► pot, drum, glass, crock, container

## jar VERB

1 *jar on His whining voice jarred on me.*
► grate on, annoy, irritate, irk, exasperate, set your teeth on edge

2 *The fall jarred her whole body.*
► jolt, jerk, shake, shock, vibrate

## jargon NOUN

*The instructions are full of difficult jargon.*
► technical language, parlance, idiom, (more informal) gobbledegook

## jarring ADJECTIVE

*a sequence of jarring chords*
► clashing, discordant, conflicting, harsh, grating, grinding, raucous, jangling, unpleasant, disagreeable

## jaundiced ADJECTIVE

*a jaundiced view of life*
► bitter, pessimistic, resentful, disillusioned, cynical, sceptical

## jaunt NOUN

*a jaunt round the old city*
► trip, outing, excursion, tour, expedition, journey

## jaunty ADJECTIVE

*His cap was pushed to one side, giving him a jaunty air.*
► cheerful, bright, lively, jolly, carefree, spirited, perky, airy, breezy, frisky, sprightly
OPPOSITES ARE dejected, dismal

## jazzy ADJECTIVE

1 *jazzy music*
► animated, lively, rhythmic, spirited, syncopated

2 *a jazzy colour scheme*
► bright, bold, colourful, gaudy, showy, loud, flashy
OPPOSITES ARE sober, dull

## jealous ADJECTIVE

1 *Jason was jealous of her ability to come up with good ideas.*
► envious, resentful, grudging, covetous, desirous
OPPOSITES ARE proud, admiring

2 *the story of a beautiful woman who is locked away by her jealous lover*
► suspicious, distrustful, possessive, protective, dominating
AN OPPOSITE IS trusting

3 *They are very jealous of their privileges.*
► protective, defensive, watchful, mindful
AN OPPOSITE IS unconcerned (about)

## jealousy NOUN

1 *He was overcome by jealousy at their good fortune.*
► envy, resentment, bitterness, discontent, covetousness

2 *She could no longer stand her lover's jealousy.*
► suspicion, distrust, mistrust, possessiveness

## jeer VERB

*The demonstrators were jeering the police.*
► mock, taunt, scoff, deride, sneer at, abuse, insult, barrack, heckle
AN OPPOSITE IS cheer

## jeer NOUN

*comments that brought jeers from his schoolmates*
► taunt, sneer, jibe, insult, boo, hiss, ridicule, disapproval
AN OPPOSITE IS cheer

## jeopardize VERB

*He wouldn't jeopardize his career by taking risks now.*
► threaten, endanger, put at risk, compromise, harm, imperil, expose

## jeopardy NOUN

*in jeopardy With the country at war the empire was in jeopardy*
► in danger, in peril, at risk, vulnerable, under threat
AN OPPOSITE IS secure

## jerk VERB

1 *She jerked her hand from his and turned away.*
► pull, tug, pluck, wrench, yank, tweak

2 *The car jerked forward.*
► jolt, lurch, bump, bounce

## jerk NOUN

1 *He pulled away his hand with a jerk.*
► tug, pull, wrench, yank, twitch

2 *The bus stopped with a jerk.*
► jolt, lurch, start, bump, shock

## jerky ADJECTIVE

*Her voice had grown jerky and breathless.*
► fitful, spasmodic, convulsive, shaky, twitchy, jumpy, uncoordinated, incoherent
OPPOSITES ARE steady, smooth

## jest NOUN

*The men talked and exchanged jests.*
► joke, witticism, quip, banter

## jest

**jest** VERB

*He admitted that he had been jesting.*
▶ joke, fool, hoax, tease, (*more informal*) kid

**jet** NOUN

**1** *a jet of water*
▶ stream, spurt, squirt, gush, spout, spray, flow, fountain, rush

**2** *He pointed the jet at the flames.*
▶ nozzle, sprinkler

**jetty** NOUN

*We landed at a rickety jetty.*
▶ pier, quay, wharf, landing stage, breakwater, groyne, mole

**jewel** NOUN

**1** *a tiara encrusted with jewels*
▶ gem, gemstone, precious stone

**2** *His girlfriend was a jewel.*
▶ treasure, angel, paragon, pearl, wonder

---

**jewellery** NOUN

*A street fair was selling ethnic jewellery.*
▶ gems, jewels, ornaments, (*more informal*) sparklers

**ITEMS OF JEWELLERY**

**worn on the head and neck:** diadem, tiara; earring, ear stud; nose ring, nose stud; necklace, beads, chain, pendant; choker.

**worn on the arms and hands:** armlet, bangle, bracelet, charm bracelet, circlet, wristlet; cuff links; ring, eternity ring, signet ring.

**worn on the body:** anklet, brooch, clasp, locket, pin, tiepin, stud.

**JEWELS AND JEWELLERY STONES**

amber, cairngorm, carnelian or cornelian, coral, diamond, emerald, garnet, ivory, jade, jasper, jet, lapis lazuli, moonstone, onyx, opal, pearl, rhinestone, ruby, sapphire, topaz, turquoise.

**METALS USED TO MAKE JEWELLERY**

gold, platinum, silver.

---

**jibe** NOUN

*He'll have to put up with the jibes of his friends.*
▶ taunt, jeer, sneer, snide remark

**jiggle** VERB

*The boy was jiggling in his chair.*
▶ fidget, wriggle, squirm

**jilt** VERB

*Perhaps Hugh had done her a favour by jilting her.*
▶ reject, desert, discard, abandon, (*more informal*) ditch

**jingle** NOUN

**1** *He could hear the jingle of her bracelet.*
▶ jangle, clink, tinkle

**2** *An advertising jingle kept coming into his head.*
▶ slogan, song, catchline, ditty, refrain

**jingle** VERB

*The coins jingled in their pockets.*
▶ jangle, clink, tinkle, clang

**jingoism** NOUN

*the jingoism of some war films*
▶ chauvinism, nationalism, extreme patriotism, xenophobia

**jinx** NOUN

*They wondered whether the jinx would strike again.*
▶ curse, spell, evil eye, bad luck

**jinxed** ADJECTIVE

*It was almost as if the house was jinxed.*
▶ cursed, bewitched, bedevilled, under a spell

**jitters** PLURAL NOUN

*a fit of jitters*
▶ nervousness, nerves, anxiety, agitation, tension, edginess, restlessness

**jittery** ADJECTIVE

*He felt jittery about meeting her again.*
▶ nervous, anxious, agitated, tense, edgy, fretful, restless, ill at ease

**job** NOUN

**1** *The job involves some weekend work.*
▶ occupation, employment, position, situation, post, work, career

**2** *Painting the house will be a long job.*
▶ task, piece of work, undertaking, operation, assignment, project, chore

**3** *It's my job to lock up in the evenings.*
▶ responsibility, duty, task, concern, role, function

**4** (*informal*) *We had a job finding the house.*
▶ problem, difficulty, difficult task, hard time, struggle

**jobless** ADJECTIVE

*Two percent of the population is jobless.*
▶ unemployed, out of work, laid off, redundant
OPPOSITES ARE employed, in work

**jocular** ADJECTIVE

*a few jocular remarks*
▶ humorous, funny, witty, comical, amusing, droll, joking
AN OPPOSITE IS serious

**USAGE** Remember that *funny* can mean 'peculiar' as well as 'jocular', and it is sometimes better to use another word.

**jog** VERB

**1** *He jogged her elbow as he walked past.*
▶ nudge, prod, jolt, jar, bump, jostle

**2** *I need a clue to jog my memory.*
▶ prompt, stir, arouse, stimulate, remind

**3** *They were jogging through the park.*
▶ trot, run, jogtrot

**join** VERB

**1** *Join the two pieces together.*
▶ connect, fasten, attach, couple, merge, stick, tie, glue

**2** *Her son wanted to join the army.*
► enlist in, enrol in, sign up in, enter, volunteer for, become a member of
**3** *We joined the peace march along the route.*
► follow, go along with, tag along with, accompany
**4** *The two roads join here.*
► meet, come together, converge

**join** NOUN
*You have to look hard to see the join.*
► joint, connection, seam, knot, link, mend

**joint** NOUN
*the joint between the wall and the flat roof*
► join, connection, junction, seam

**joint** ADJECTIVE
*The two artists are holding a joint exhibition.*
► combined, shared, common, collaborative, coordinated, cooperative, collective, communal, concerted, united, mutual
OPPOSITES ARE separate, discrete, individual

**joke** NOUN
*(informal) They sat all evening telling each other jokes.*
► funny story, jest, witticism, wisecrack, pleasantry, quip, crack, (more informal) gag

**joke** VERB
**1** *He laughed and joked with his friends.*
► tell jokes, crack jokes, jest, clown, have a laugh, be facetious
**2** *From the look on her face I'd say she was only joking.*
► fool, tease, hoax, (more informal) kid

**joker** NOUN
*She seems quite a joker, but she has her serious side.*
► jester, comedian, comic, humorist, wag, wit, clown

**jolly** ADJECTIVE
*We had a jolly time. He was in a jolly mood when he came back.*
► cheerful, merry, cheery, happy, jovial, exuberant, hearty

**jolt** VERB
**1** *The car jolted along the rough roads.*
► bump, bounce, jerk, jog, shake, shudder
**2** *The fierceness of his remarks jolted her.*
► startle, surprise, shock, disturb, disconcert, upset, discompose, astonish, nonplus

**jostle** VERB
**1** *She was afraid of being jostled by the crowds.*
► push, shove, hustle, press, crowd in on
**2** *People jostled for a good view.*
► struggle, scramble, jockey

**jot** VERB
**jot down** *The man jotted down my details.*
► write down, note down, take down, scribble, make a note of

**journal** NOUN
**1** *an academic journal*
► periodical, publication, magazine, gazette, digest
**2** *She kept a journal of the voyage.*
► diary, log, record, chronicle, account

**journalist** NOUN
*A journalist wanted to hear his story.*
► reporter, correspondent, columnist, feature-writer, contributor, writer

**journey** NOUN
*The journey takes you through three countries.*
► trip, route, itinerary, travels, voyage, peregrination
**USAGE** You normally use *voyage* to mean a long journey by sea.

**journey** VERB
*They journeyed north.*
► travel, go, voyage, go on a journey, sail, cruise, trek

**jovial** ADJECTIVE
*A jovial old man greeted them.*
► jolly, cheerful, cheery, affable, genial, merry

**joy** NOUN
*There was a look of joy on her face.*
► delight, bliss, pleasure, happiness, gladness, ecstasy, elation, joyfulness, exultation, rapture, euphoria, exuberance
OPPOSITES ARE sorrow, misery

**joyful** ADJECTIVE
*Kate set off with joyful enthusiasm.*
► cheerful, happy, joyous, jubilant, bright, sunny, lively, elated, animated, contented, buoyant, good-humoured, light-hearted, chirpy
AN OPPOSITE IS sad

**jubilant** ADJECTIVE
*Jubilant fans surged on to the pitch.*
► delighted, joyful, overjoyed, exultant, joyous, elated, ecstatic, thrilled

**jubilee** NOUN
*a royal jubilee*
► anniversary, celebration, festival, gala, carnival, commemoration

**judge** NOUN
**1** *The judges could not agree on a winner.*
► adjudicator, arbiter, arbitrator, assessor, moderator, referee, umpire
**2** *a good judge of art*
► connoisseur, authority (on), expert (on), critic

**judge** VERB
**1** *A magistrate will judge the case.*
► try, hear, sit in judgement on, adjudicate on, decide
**2** *A panel of experts will judge the ten best entries.*
► assess, appraise, decide, evaluate, review, examine
**3** *We judged that she had been misled.*
► conclude, decide, consider, believe, think, reckon, determine, come to the view, form the opinion

**judgement** NOUN
**1** *the judgement of the court*
► verdict, decision, adjudication, ruling, finding, pronouncement, sentence

281

**2** *He showed a lack of judgement.*
▶ understanding, discernment, perception, wisdom, sense, common sense, acumen, prudence
**3** *my judgement of the situation*
▶ assessment, appraisal, evaluation, estimate, analysis, view, opinion, belief

**judicial** ADJECTIVE
*a judicial review*
▶ legal, judiciary, official, impartial

**judicious** ADJECTIVE
*a judicious approach to the teaching of English*
▶ sensible, prudent, appropriate, shrewd, thoughtful, well judged, wise, astute, expedient

**jug** NOUN
*a jug of water*
▶ pitcher, carafe, flagon, ewer, crock, vessel

**juggle** VERB
*She learned to juggle her hours so she could spend more time at home.*
▶ manipulate, rearrange, alter, change, move about

**juice** NOUN
*Add the juice of a lemon.*
▶ liquid, fluid, extract, essence

**juicy** ADJECTIVE
**1** *a juicy pear*
▶ succulent, tender, moist, soft, ripe
AN OPPOSITE IS dry
**2** *a juicy piece of gossip*
▶ interesting, lurid, spicy, colourful, racy

**jumble** NOUN
*Clothes lay on the floor in a jumble.*
▶ muddle, hotchpotch, mess, clutter, chaos, confusion, disorder

**jumble** VERB
*I'll try not to jumble the photographs.*
▶ muddle, disorganize, mix up, shuffle, confuse, disarrange, (more informal) mess up
AN OPPOSITE IS organize

**jump** VERB
**1** *A dog jumped off the chair.*
▶ leap, spring, bound, bounce, hop
**2** *All the horses jumped the first fence.*
▶ vault, clear
**3** *The children were jumping about in the garden.*
▶ skip, dance, frolic, prance, cavort
**4** *A noise made him jump.*
▶ start, jerk, jolt, flinch, recoil
**5** *Attendance had jumped by more than 20 percent.*
▶ rise, increase, leap, go up, escalate

**jump** NOUN
**1** *With a jump he reached the other side.*
▶ leap, bound, spring, vault, hop
**2** *The horse cleared the last jump comfortably.*
▶ fence, hurdle, ditch, barrier, obstacle, gap, gate
**3** *a huge jump in house prices*
▶ rise, increase, escalation, upturn
**4** *She woke up with a jump.*
▶ start, jerk, jolt, shock, shudder, lurch

**jumpy** ADJECTIVE
*He was tired and jumpy.*
▶ nervous, edgy, jittery, tense, anxious, agitated, apprehensive

**junction** NOUN
**1** *a road junction*
▶ intersection, crossing, interchange, turn-off
**2** *the junction of two rivers*
▶ confluence, convergence, meeting

**junior** ADJECTIVE
*a junior official*
▶ low-ranking, lower-ranking, subordinate, subsidiary, younger, lesser, minor, secondary
AN OPPOSITE IS senior

**junk** NOUN
*a cupboard full of old junk*
▶ rubbish, clutter, oddments, odds and ends, garbage, refuse, scrap, trash, waste

**just** ADJECTIVE
**1** *a just ruler   a just settlement*
▶ fair, equitable, fair-minded, honourable, even-handed, unprejudiced, unbiased, neutral, non-partisan
AN OPPOSITE IS unjust
**2** *a just punishment*
▶ fair, fitting, deserved, merited, appropriate, suitable, reasonable, legitimate
OPPOSITES ARE undeserved, unfair

**justice** NOUN
**1** *He appealed to their sense of justice.*
▶ fairness, justness, fair play, integrity, equity, honesty, impartiality, legality, right
AN OPPOSITE IS injustice
**2** *the administration of justice*
▶ the law, legal proceedings

**justifiable** ADJECTIVE
*a justifiable reaction*
▶ reasonable, justified, valid, legitimate, defensible, excusable, well-founded, understandable, warranted, acceptable
AN OPPOSITE IS unjustifiable

**justification** NOUN
**1** *There is no justification for such callousness.*
▶ excuse, reason, grounds, basis, warrant, foundation
**2** *Such extreme measures call for some justification*
▶ explanation, defence, vindication, argument, rationalization

**justify** VERB
*Tiredness cannot justify this kind of reckless behaviour.*
▶ excuse, defend, absolve, mitigate, account for, vindicate, exonerate, warrant, validate, uphold, support

**jut** VERB
*jut out A set of shelves jutted out on one wall.*
▶ project, protrude, stick out, extend, overhang, poke out

## juvenile ADJECTIVE

**1** *juvenile behaviour*
▶ immature, childish, babyish, infantile, puerile
AN OPPOSITE IS mature
**2** *juvenile novels*
▶ adolescent, young, youthful

## juvenile NOUN

*The people involved were all juveniles.*
▶ youth, young person, minor, under-age person

# Kk

## keen ADJECTIVE

**1** *Competition is keen and a good honours degree is essential.*
▶ intense, acute, fierce, extreme, strong
**2** *France was keen to attract more foreign investment.*
▶ eager, anxious, determined, impatient, ambitious, intent (on attracting)
**3** *William is a keen devotee of science fiction.*
▶ enthusiastic, eager, avid, fervent, impassioned, committed, conscientious
**4** *a knife with a keen cutting edge*
▶ sharp, sharp-edged, razor-sharp, honed
**5** *Patience, nimble fingers, and keen eyesight are needed to operate the tool.*
▶ sharp, acute, clear, sensitive, strong, powerful
**6** *She still displays a keen sense of humour.*
▶ sharp, piercing, incisive, penetrating, pungent, trenchant

## keep VERB

**1** *an in-flight magazine for you to read and keep*
▶ retain, hold on to, hang on to, possess
**2** *They did their best to keep quiet.*
▶ remain, stay, continue to be, carry on being
**3** *He keeps twitching his ears.*
▶ persist in, go on, continue, carry on
**4** *We'll try not to keep you too long.*
▶ detain, delay, hold up, keep waiting
**5** *These problems shouldn't keep you from continuing.*
▶ deter, constrain, hinder, impede, obstruct
**6** *You must keep your promise.*
▶ observe, fulfil, comply with, obey, respect, keep faith with
**7** *Where do you keep the coats?*
▶ store, put, stow, house
**8** *Keeping a family can be expensive.*
▶ support, maintain, provide for, look after, care for, be responsible for

## keeper NOUN

**1** *the keeper of the museum*
▶ curator, custodian, administrator, superintendent
**2** *the prisoners and their keeper*
▶ jailer, warden, guard, custodian
**3** *He said he was not his brother's keeper.*
▶ guardian, protector, minder

## keepsake NOUN

*She gave him a ring as a keepsake.*
▶ memento, souvenir, reminder, token

## kernel NOUN

*the juicy kernel of the nut*
▶ core, heart, seed, middle

## key NOUN

**1** *the key to a problem*
▶ clue, indicator, pointer, lead, secret, solution, answer, interpretation
**2** *a key to a map*
▶ guide, legend, index, table, explanation, glossary

## key ADJECTIVE

*the key question*
▶ fundamental, crucial, vital, critical, essential, important

---

## keyboard NOUN

**THE MAIN KEYBOARD MUSICAL INSTRUMENTS**

**large standing instruments**: piano, pianoforte, grand piano, fortepiano, clavier; harpsichord, clavichord, spinet, virginals, celesta; organ, harmonium.
**electronic instruments**: electric organ, synthesizer.
**other instruments**: accordion.

---

## kick NOUN

**1** *He gave the television a kick.*
▶ hit, boot, blow
**2** (informal) *Some people might get a kick out of crossing the Atlantic in an old bath.*
▶ thrill, excitement, (informal) buzz

## kick VERB

**1** *Merv kicked the ball out.*
▶ boot, hit , drive, send, punt, heel
**2** (informal) *a habit I have to kick*
▶ give up, quit, break, abandon, cease, desist from

## kid VERB

(informal)
**1** *I think they were only kidding.*
▶ tease, fool, bluff, lie
**2** *Are you kidding me?*
▶ hoodwink, pull your leg, have you on, deceive

## kidnap VERB

*The group was allegedly preparing to kidnap a businessman.*
▶ abduct, capture, seize, carry off, run away with, snatch

## kill VERB

**1** *The gang would not hesitate to kill the prisoners.*
▶ murder, put to death, slay, slaughter, dispatch, eliminate, exterminate, assassinate, (more informal) bump off
**USAGE** You use *assassinate* to refer to an important person, especially a statesman or stateswoman. *Slay* and *dispatch* are literary words.

2 *The war killed all hopes of continuing archaeological investigation at the site.*
▶ end, destroy, put an end to, dash, extinguish, finish

3 *Take aspirin to kill the pain.*
▶ soothe, alleviate, assuage, deaden, suppress, dull, blunt, reduce, stifle, extinguish

4 (*informal*) *She complained that her back was killing her.*
▶ hurt, pain, torment, torture, give discomfort to, give pain to

5 *We arrived early and had an hour to kill.*
▶ occupy, fill up, while away, pass, spend

6 (*informal*) *She nearly killed herself getting the work finished in time.*
▶ exhaust, wear out, tire out, sap, debilitate

**killer** NOUN
*A witness was able to identify the killers.*
▶ murderer, assassin, gunman, (*more informal*) hitman

**killing** NOUN
*a brutal killing that shocked the community*
▶ murder, assassination, slaughter, massacre, execution
**USAGE** Note that *slaughter* and *massacre* refer to the killing of a large number of people.

**kind** ADJECTIVE
*A kind friend helped him home.  It was kind of her to ring.*
▶ caring, good, kind-hearted, kindly, considerate, sympathetic, thoughtful, obliging, tender-hearted, benevolent
OPPOSITES ARE unkind, unfriendly

**kind** NOUN
*a new kind of rock music*
▶ sort, type, style, form, variety, category, genre

**kindle** VERB
1 *Bonfires are kindled on Midwinter's Day.*
▶ light, burn, ignite, fire, set fire to
2 *These events kindled strong feelings.*
▶ stir up, stimulate, arouse, give rise to, evoke, induce, inflame, call forth

**kindly** ADJECTIVE
*a kindly old man*
▶ kind, kind-hearted, benevolent, caring, good, considerate, sympathetic, thoughtful, obliging, tender-hearted

**kindness** NOUN
*She had shown them much kindness over many years.*
▶ consideration, thoughtfulness, generosity, goodwill, benevolence, favour, understanding

**king** NOUN
*After the war the country expelled its king.*
▶ ruler, monarch, sovereign, crowned head
RELATED ADJECTIVES regal, royal

**kingdom** NOUN
*a small kingdom in Asia Minor*
▶ monarchy, realm, dominion

**kink** NOUN
1 *a kink in the road.*
▶ bend, corner, angle
2 *kinks in the line*
▶ twist, curl, loop, knot, tangle

**kiss** VERB
*She stooped to kiss the little boy.*
▶ caress, embrace, (*more informal*) peck

**kiss** NOUN
*He gave her a long kiss.*
▶ caress, embrace, (*more informal*) peck, (*more informal*) snog

**kit** NOUN
1 *a tool kit*
▶ equipment, gear, implements, appliances, tackle
2 *They made the furniture from kits.*
▶ outfit, set of parts, self-assembly set, flatpack
3 *a football kit*
▶ outfit, strip, colours, clothes

**knack** NOUN
*He has a knack of hitting the nail on the head.*
▶ gift, flair (for), talent (for), instinct (for), ability (to hit), skill (for)

**knead** VERB
*Knead the dough until it is smooth.*
▶ work, squeeze, press, pummel, manipulate, pound

**kneel** VERB
*She knelt by the bed to pray.*
▶ bend, bow, crouch, stoop, squat, fall to your knees, genuflect

**knickers** NOUN
*She wore bright blue knickers.*
▶ panties, pants, underpants, briefs, drawers

**knife** VERB
*The victim had been knifed repeatedly.*
▶ stab, gash, slash, pierce, cut, wound

**knit** VERB
**knit together** *The new arrangements took a few months to knit together.*
▶ unite, become unified, come together, combine, connect

**knob** NOUN
1 *He held the door knob as he looked into the room.*
▶ handle
2 *She wore her hair in a knob on top.*
▶ bump, lump, bulge, swelling, boss, projection, protuberance

**knock** VERB
1 *He swore as he knocked his knee on the edge of the desk.*
▶ bump, hit, strike, bang, crack, rap
2 *The man knocked on the door and waited.*
▶ bang, rap, tap, thump, pound
**knock about** *He knocks about with some lads from Walsall.*

a b c d e f g h i j **k** l m n o p q r s t u v w x y z

► mix, associate, go around

**knock down**

**1** *They are going to knock down the entire row of houses.*
► demolish, level, raze, destroy

**2** *He knocked her down with one blow.*
► fell, topple, flatten, floor

**knock off** *(informal)*

**1** *We knock off early tonight.*
► finish work, go home

**2** *Someone had knocked off the vicar's car.*
► steal, take, *(informal)* pinch, *(informal)* nick

**knock out**

**1** *I hit him and knocked him out.*
► stun, strike unconscious

**2** *(informal) The long walk knocked us out.*
► exhaust, tire out, wear out

**3** *(informal) music that knocked me out*
► overwhelm, amaze, astound

**knock** NOUN

*The car has taken a few knocks.*
► blow, bump, bang, shock, collision, smash

**knockout** NOUN

*The event was a knockout.*
► success, sensation, triumph, winner, hit

**knot** NOUN

**1** *a knot in a rope*
► tie, twist, splice, hitch

**2** *a knot of people*
► cluster, bunch, clump, group

**knot** VERB

*She knotted a scarf round her neck.*
► tie, secure, bind, fasten, do up, entwine
OPPOSITES ARE unknot, untie

**know** VERB

**1** *Does she know we are here?*
► realize, be aware, understand, appreciate

**2** *I speak French but don't know any German.*
► understand, speak, have knowledge of, be familiar with, be conversant with, have a grasp of

**3** *Gerry knows me from our student days.*
► be acquainted with, have met, be friendly with, have had dealings with

**4** *He had known much better times.*
► experience, live through, go through, undergo

**know-all** NOUN

*(informal) He's such a know-all he's bound to be able to tell us.*
► smart alec, wise guy, show-off, wiseacre, expert, pundit

**know-how** NOUN

*(informal) technical know-how*
► expertise, knowledge, skill, proficiency, understanding

**knowing** ADJECTIVE

**1** *She gave a knowing look.*
► meaningful, expressive, significant, suggestive, eloquent, shrewd, artful
AN OPPOSITE IS innocent

**2** *a knowing young woman*
► clever, astute, crafty, cunning

**knowledge** NOUN

**1** *an extensive knowledge of the local history*
► understanding, comprehension, mastery, command, grasp

**2** *technical knowledge*
► expertise, skill, proficiency, understanding, *(more informal)* know-how

**3** *I have no knowledge of these people.*
► acquaintance (with), familiarity (with)

**4** *people with a wide range of knowledge*
► learning, education, erudition, scholarship

**knowledgeable** ADJECTIVE

**1** *a knowledgeable man*
► educated, erudite, learned, well informed

**2** *knowledgeable about modern art*
► well informed, versed (in), acquainted (with), conversant (with), familiar (with), au fait (with)
AN OPPOSITE IS ignorant

**kowtow** VERB

*kowtow to It's good not to have to kowtow to the bosses any more.*
► grovel to, defer to, pander to, fawn on, toady, flatter, curry favour with, make up to, *(more informal)* suck up to

# Ll

**label** NOUN

**1** *Always read the label on the packet.*
► tag, tab, sticker, ticket, docket, marker

**2** *a new independent record label*
► brand, company, organization

**label** VERB

*The authorities were too ready to label people as troublemakers.*
► identify, mark, categorize, class, classify, define, describe, regard, name, stamp, brand, call

**laborious** ADJECTIVE

*Restoring your data is a long and laborious process.*
► arduous, hard, heavy, difficult, stiff, tough, exhausting, fatiguing, gruelling, wearisome, onerous, strenuous, burdensome, back-breaking, tiresome, uphill
OPPOSITES ARE easy, straightforward

**labour** NOUN

**1** *(informal) Keeping the place clean involved a lot of labour.*
► work, toil, effort, exertion, industry, drudgery, donkey work, *(more informal)* grind, *(more informal)* sweat

**2** *The company took on extra labour to cope with the seasonal rush.*
▶ staff, workers, employees, workforce, (more informal) hands

**3** *Agnes went into labour about lunchtime.*
▶ childbirth, labour pains, contractions, delivery, (technical) parturition

**labour** VERB

**1** *Levin laboured day and night on the project.*
▶ work , work hard, toil, drudge, grind, exert yourself, (more informal) beaver, (more informal) slave, (more informal) sweat

**2** *As he laboured to get back on course another blast threw the boat lopsided.*
▶ struggle, strive, endeavour, work, do your utmost, go all out

**3** *We have made our point and there is no need to labour it.*
▶ overdo, overemphasize, dwell on, elaborate, exaggerate, make heavy weather of

**labourer** NOUN

*labourers working in the fields*
▶ worker, workman, workperson, hired hand

**labyrinth** NOUN

*a labyrinth of streets and lanes*
▶ maze, warren, network, complex, jungle, tangle

**lace** NOUN

**1** *a cloth trimmed with lace*
▶ lacework, openwork, filigree, net, tatting

**2** *One shoe had a lace missing.*
▶ shoelace, bootlace, shoestring, cord, string, thong

**lace** VERB

**1** *He laced his shoes.*
▶ fasten, do up, tie up, secure

**2** *She laced her fingers into his.*
▶ twine, entwine, intertwine, interweave

**lack** NOUN

*suffering from a lack of vitamins*
▶ deficiency, shortage, want, scarcity, absence, dearth, paucity, deprivation, need, privation, famine
OPPOSITES ARE sufficiency, abundance

**lack** VERB

*The film lacks drama.*
▶ be without, be short of, be deficient in, miss, want, need, require

**lacking** ADJECTIVE

**1** *lacking* or *lacking in* *a relationship lacking in affection*
▶ wanting, needing, without, missing, short of, weak in, deficient in, inadequate in, defective in

**2** *Convincing arguments are lacking.*
▶ absent, missing, unavailable, non-existent

**lad** NOUN

*a young lad of ten*
▶ boy, youth, youngster, schoolboy, fellow, (more informal) kid, (more informal) guy

**laden** ADJECTIVE

*an old man laden with shopping*
▶ loaded, burdened, encumbered, weighed down, hampered, oppressed

**lady** NOUN

*He met the lady again on his way out.*
▶ woman, female, (more informal) dame

**ladylike** ADJECTIVE

*behaviour that was not especially ladylike*
▶ proper, genteel, refined, respectable, polite, dainty, modest, prim and proper, well-bred

**lag** VERB

**1** (informal) *Some of the runners were lagging behind.*
▶ straggle, trail, fall behind, drop behind, hang back, linger, dally, dawdle, bring up the rear, come last, idle
OPPOSITES ARE keep up, take the lead

**2** *material for lagging water pipes*
▶ insulate, wrap up

**laid-back** ADJECTIVE

*He took a laid-back attitude despite the difficulties.*
▶ relaxed, unruffled, nonchalant, philosophical, casual, easygoing, at ease, informal
OPPOSITES ARE tense, uptight

**lair** NOUN

**1** *an animal's lair*
▶ den, burrow, haunt, hole, earth

**2** *a criminal's lair*
▶ hideaway, hideout, hiding place, refuge, retreat, shelter, sanctuary

**lake** NOUN

*a house by the lake*
▶ lagoon, sea, tarn, lido, pond, pool, reservoir, water, (Scottish) loch, (literary) mere

**lame** ADJECTIVE

**1** *a young child who was sick and lame*
▶ disabled, handicapped, incapacitated, crippled

**2** *As excuses went, this one was pretty lame.*
▶ feeble, weak, flimsy, thin, unconvincing, implausible, hard to believe
OPPOSITES ARE convincing, persuasive

**lament** NOUN

*The villagers sang a lament for their dead.*
▶ dirge, elegy, lamentation, requiem, threnody

**lament** VERB

*We sat on the beach, lamenting the loss of our dry clothes.*
▶ bemoan, bewail, regret, mourn, grieve over, deplore, complain about, express sorrow about, weep over

**lamentable** ADJECTIVE

*a lamentable failure*
► regrettable, deplorable, woeful, unfortunate, distressing, pitiful, ignominious

**land** NOUN

1 *a large house with several acres of land*
► grounds, ground, estate, property, farmland, open space
2 *Egypt is a land steeped in history.*
► country, nation, state, region
3 *The ship reached land at last.*
► dry land, terra firma, shore

**land** VERB

1 *Allied troops landed in Kuwait.*
► disembark, debark, go ashore, alight, arrive, berth, come ashore, dock, end a journey, reach landfall
AN OPPOSITE IS embark
2 *The ship will land at Calais.*
► dock, berth, moor, anchor, reach shore
OPPOSITES ARE set sail, put to sea
3 *The plane landed ten minutes ahead of schedule.*
► touch down, come in to land
AN OPPOSITE IS take off

**landmark** NOUN

1 *The church steeple was a landmark visible for miles around.*
► feature, sight, spectacle, marker, high point
2 *a landmark in history*
► turning point, milestone, watershed, new era

**landscape** NOUN

1 *the landscape of the Scottish Highlands.*
► scenery, countryside, topography, terrain, environment, rural scene, scene
2 *a landscape painting*
► panorama, vista, view, outlook, prospect

**landslide** NOUN

*After the flooding came the landslides.*
► landslip, earthfall, rockfall, avalanche

**landslide** ADJECTIVE

*a landslide election victory*
► decisive, overwhelming, runaway, emphatic

**lane** NOUN

*a country lane*
► road, byroad, byway, track, trail, path

**language** NOUN
1 *the language of the media*
► vocabulary, usage, style, speech
2 *The forms are written in plain language.*
► wording, phraseology, phrasing
3 *the grammar of language*
► speech, writing, communication, utterance, discourse
4 *How many languages do you know?*
► tongue
RELATED ADJECTIVE linguistic ►►

**Indo-European languages:** Abanian, Armenian, Belorussian, Bengali, Breton, Bulgarian, Catalan, Croatian, Czech, Danish, Dutch, English, Flemish, French, Frisian, Gaelic, German, Greek, Gujarati, Hindi, Hindustani, Icelandic, Iranian, Irish, Italian, Kashmiri, Kurdish, Latvian, Lithuanian, Macedonian, Manx, Moldavian, Nepali, Norwegian, Pashto, Polish, Portuguese, Provençal, Punjabi, Romanian, Romany, Russian, Serbian, Sinhalese, Slovak, Slovenian, Spanish, Swedish, Tajik, Ukrainian, Urdu, Welsh, Yiddish.

**Finno-Ugric languages:** Estonian, Finnish, Hungarian (Magyar), Lappish (Sami).

**Turkic languages** Azerbaijani, Turkish, Uzbek.

**Languages of the Caucasus:** Armenian, Azerbaijani, Chechen, Georgian, Ossetian.

**Dravidian languages:** Malayalam, Tamil.

**Sino-Tibetan languages:** Burmese, Chinese, Laotian, Thai, Tibetan.

**Semitic languages:** Arabic, Aramaic, Assyrian, Chaldean, Hebrew, Maltese.

**African languages:** Congolese, Coptic, Sesotho, Setswana, Kiswahili.

**Asian and Polynesian languages:** Balinese, Fijian, Hawaiian, Javanese, Khmer, Malagasy, Malay, Maori, Samoan, Sundanese, Tagalog, Tahitian, Tongan, Vietnamese.

**Languages of unknown origin:** Basque, Korean, Japanese.

**Extinct languages:** Akkadian, Anglo-Saxon, Avestan, Babylonian, Gaulish, Gothic, Hittite, Latin, Norn, Old Norse, Old Prussian, Phoenician, Phrygian, Pictish, Prakrit, Sanskrit, Sogdian, Sumerian, Syriac, Tocharian, Ugaritic.

**Artificial languages:** Esperanto, Ido, Volapük.

**languish** VERB

1 *All the plants languished and died.*
► wilt, droop, wither, weaken, waste away
2 *Political prisoners languished for years in the country's jails*
► rot, moulder, decline, waste away, be abandoned, be neglected, be forgotten

**lanky** ADJECTIVE

*a lanky young man*
► tall, gangling, gaunt, gawky, lean, spindly, scraggy

**lap** NOUN

1 *A cat was sitting on her lap.*
► knee or knees, thighs
2 *They managed three laps of the track.*
► circuit, round, orbit, circle, loop, stretch, course

**lap** VERB

1 *Waves lapped against the rocks.*
► wash, splash, dash, beat, strike, surge, rush
2 *The dog lapped a bowl of water.*
► drink, sip, lick, slurp, gulp

**lapse** NOUN

**1** *a temporary lapse of attention*
▶ failure, error, weakness, relapse, failing, fault, slip, mistake, omission, flaw, shortcoming

**2** *a lapse into crime*
▶ decline, descent, fall, falling, deterioration

**3** *The family returned after a lapse of ten years.*
▶ interval, gap, pause, break, interruption

**lapse** VERB

**1** *They soon lapsed into their bad old habits.*
▶ slide, slip, drop, fall, decline, deteriorate, degenerate

**2** *Membership will lapse at the end of the month.*
▶ expire, run out, finish, stop, terminate, become invalid

**large** ADJECTIVE

**1** *a large house  elected with a large majority*
▶ big, great, huge, sizeable, substantial, enormous, gigantic, immense, massive, colossal, vast, giant, (*more informal*) whopping, (*more informal*) ginormous

**2** *a large man*
▶ big, burly, hefty, bulky, stocky, hulking, strapping

**3** *a large supply of food*
▶ plentiful, abundant, copious, generous, lavish, profuse, ample, liberal

**4** *large areas of conifers*
▶ widespread, extensive, wide-ranging, large-scale

**largely** ADVERB

*She was largely responsible for getting us into this mess.*
▶ mainly, chiefly, principally, primarily, mostly, to a large extent

**lark** NOUN

(*informal*) *It all seemed just a lark to them.*
▶ prank, bit of fun, joke, laugh, game, escapade, amusement

**lash** VERB

**1** *Driving rain lashed the windows.*
▶ beat against, dash against, batter, pound

**2** *She lashed him with a belt.*
▶ whip, beat, thrash

**lash out at** *The speaker lashed out at his critics.*
▶ attack, condemn, denounce, lambaste, castigate, censure

**last** ADJECTIVE

**1** *There was none of the violence associated with the last protest.*
▶ previous, preceding, recent, former

**2** *She realized she was still the last person in the queue.*
▶ final, rearmost, endmost
OPPOSITES ARE first, leading

**3** *She decided to have one last look.*
▶ final, concluding, ultimate
OPPOSITES ARE initial, opening

**4** *I am the last person to complain.*
▶ least likely, most unlikely
OPPOSITES ARE first, most likely

**last** VERB

*The storm lasted all night.*
▶ continue, carry on, keep on, persist, endure, linger, remain, stay, hold, hold out, live, survive
OPPOSITES ARE stop, cease, fade

**lasting** ADJECTIVE

*The reforms will produce lasting change.*
▶ permanent, enduring, continuing, long-lasting, long-standing, unceasing, undying, unending, long-term, long-lived, durable, indestructible, indissoluble, lifelong, stable, abiding
AN OPPOSITE IS temporary

**latch** NOUN

*He lifted the latch and opened the door.*
▶ catch, fastening, bolt, clasp, lock

**late** ADJECTIVE

**1** *The train was over an hour late.*
▶ overdue, delayed, slow, behind-hand, belated, dilatory, tardy, unpunctual
AN OPPOSITE IS early

**2** *her father, the late king*
▶ deceased, dead, departed, former

**3** *He had taken part in the late conflict.*
▶ recent, previous, preceding, former

**lately** ADVERB

*He had been out a lot lately.*
▶ recently, latterly, of late

**latent** ADJECTIVE

*the latent power of the media*
▶ dormant, potential, hidden, undeveloped, undiscovered, invisible

**later** ADJECTIVE

*The issue would be dealt with at a later meeting.*
▶ subsequent, future, following, succeeding

**later** ADVERB

*We will meet you later.*
▶ afterwards, in a while, subsequently, eventually, next

**lateral** ADJECTIVE

**1** *lateral movements*
▶ side, sideways, sideward, sidelong, edgeways

**2** *lateral thinking*
▶ unorthodox, creative, inventive, original, ingenious

**lather** NOUN

**1** *soapy lather*
▶ foam, froth, suds, bubbles

**2** *in a lather*
▶ state of excitement, dither, frenzy, fluster, flutter, flap, fever

**latitude** NOUN

(*informal*) *The brief gives some latitude for on-the-spot decisions.*
▶ freedom, leeway, liberty, scope, room, elbow room, space

**latter** ADJECTIVE

*There are more games in the latter part of the month.*
► later, closing, concluding, last, recent, second
AN OPPOSITE IS former

**laudable** ADJECTIVE

*the laudable objective of controlling pollution*
► admirable, praiseworthy, commendable,
creditable, worthy
AN OPPOSITE IS shameful

**USAGE** Do not confuse *laudable* with *laudatory*
(see next entry), which has a different
meaning.

**laudatory** ADJECTIVE

*a highly laudatory character reference*
► complimentary, congratulatory, approving,
approbatory, flattering

**USAGE** Do not confuse *laudatory* with *laudable*
(see previous entry), which has a different
meaning. Note that *flattering* suggests praise
beyond what is really deserved, and you
should only use it when you mean this.

> **laugh** VERB This word is often overused. Here are
> some alternatives:
> **1** *Joe's antics began to make them laugh.*
> ► giggle, chuckle, chortle, snigger, titter, guffaw,
> (*more informal*) scream
> **2** *laugh at* I *didn't say anything in case the others
> laughed at me.*
> ► mock, ridicule, make fun of, scoff at, deride, jeer

**laugh** NOUN

**1** *She gave a loud laugh.*
► chuckle, chortle, snigger, titter, guffaw
**2** *Being with Henry was always a laugh.*
► joke, piece of fun, adventure, (*more informal*)
scream

**laughable** ADJECTIVE

**1** *The money they were offering was laughable.*
► absurd, ridiculous, ludicrous, preposterous,
risible, derisory
**2** *laughable attempts to steer the boat*
► funny, comic, comical, amusing, hilarious, farcical

**laughter** NOUN

*sounds of conversation and laughter from the next room*
► laughing, mirth, laughs, chuckling, sniggering,
hilarity, tittering, giggling, guffaws, merriment,
(*more informal*) hysterics

**launch** VERB

**1** *In its heyday the dockyard launched a ship every year.*
► float, set afloat, put in the water
**2** *It was decided to launch the shuttle from a different
site.*
► fire, propel, send off, blast off, set off
**3** *The enemy launched a counter-offensive. A new
business will be launched next year.*
► begin, start, initiate, open, set up, embark on,
establish, found, inaugurate

**lavatory** NOUN

*There's another lavatory downstairs.*
► toilet, cloakroom, convenience, (*more informal*)
loo, (*old-fashioned*) WC

**lavish** ADJECTIVE

*After the show there will be a lavish supper.*
► sumptuous, elaborate, copious, extravagant,
luxurious, generous, liberal, abundant, plentiful,
bountiful, exuberant, munificent, opulent,
unstinting
AN OPPOSITE IS meagre

**law** NOUN

**1** *a new law closing tax loopholes*
► regulation, statute, act, bill, ruling, rule,
enactment, edict
**USAGE** Note that a *bill* is a government's
proposal for a law, and an *act* is the bill after
it has been passed and received the royal
assent.
RELATED ADJECTIVE legal, judicial
**2** *the laws of logic*
► rule, principle, precept, prescription, guideline,
tenet, maxim, doctrine
**3** (*informal*) *on the run from the law*
► police, authorities

**law-abiding** ADJECTIVE

*law-abiding citizens*
► well-behaved, respectable, honest, decent,
orderly, peaceable, peaceful, compliant, disciplined,
good, obedient
OPPOSITES ARE lawless, criminal

**lawful** ADJECTIVE

**1** *The police were making a lawful arrest.*
► legal, legitimate, permissible, permitted,
allowable, allowed, just, right
**2** *people going about their lawful business*
► legitimate, rightful, proper, valid, recognized,
authorized, regular, legal, documented, prescribed
AN OPPOSITE IS illegal

**lawless** ADJECTIVE

*a lawless rabble*
► disorderly, unruly, riotous, mutinous, wild, rowdy,
rebellious, disruptive, undisciplined, seditious,
reckless, anarchic, anarchical, chaotic
AN OPPOSITE IS law-abiding

**lawlessness** NOUN

*The toppling of the regime was followed by weeks of
lawlessness.*
► anarchy, disorder, chaos, unruliness, insurrection,
mob rule, rebellion, rioting
AN OPPOSITE IS order

**lawsuit** NOUN

*The newspaper did not want to provoke a lawsuit.*
► legal action, suit, litigation, proceedings

**lawyer** NOUN

*This is a matter for the lawyers.*
► solicitor, legal practitioner, legal adviser, barrister,
QC, advocate, attorney

**USAGE** A *barrister* is a lawyer who presents a case in a lawcourt, and an *advocate* is a name for a barrister in Scotland. A *QC* (= Queen's Counsel) is a specially appointed senior barrister. *Attorney* has special meanings in the USA.

**lax** ADJECTIVE

*lax discipline in schools*
▶ slack, slipshod, casual, easygoing, lenient, permissive, careless, loose, neglectful, negligent, remiss, vague
AN OPPOSITE IS strict

**lay** VERB

**1** *He laid the map on the seat beside him.*
▶ put, place, set, set down, spread, deposit, leave

**2** *We began to lay plans for a spring holiday.*
▶ form, make, devise, prepare, work out, hatch, concoct

**3** *Be careful where you lay the blame for this.*
▶ assign, attach, attribute, ascribe, allot, apportion, fix, impute

**4** *The landlady laid a table for breakfast.*
▶ arrange, set out, organize

**lay in** *The men laid in a supply of beer.*
▶ stock up with, put aside, put by, collect, store

**lay into** (*informal*) *His father laid into him when he got home.*
▶ scold, rebuke, berate, castigate, criticize, censure

**lay off**
**1** (*informal*) *You really should lay off smoking.*
▶ give up, stop, cut out

**2** *Over a hundred staff were laid off just before Christmas.*
▶ make redundant, dismiss, discharge, release, (*more informal*) sack

**lay on** *His mother laid on a marvellous tea.*
▶ provide, supply, furnish, give

**lay out**
**1** *Richard laid out the plans on the table.*
▶ arrange, set out, spread, display

**2** (*informal*) *The blow laid him out for an hour.*
▶ knock out, make unconscious, flatten

**layabout** NOUN

*It's odd for such a lively lad to have a layabout for a brother.*
▶ idler, loafer, good-for-nothing, sluggard, (*more informal*) slob, (*more informal*) couch potato
OPPOSITES ARE hard-worker, beaver

**layer** NOUN

**1** *an extra layer of paint*
▶ coating, coat, covering, surface, film, sheet, skin, thickness

**2** *a layer of rock*
▶ seam, stratum, substratum

**layout** NOUN

*The layout of the house takes some getting used to.*
▶ arrangement, organization, design, plan, disposition, (*more informal*) set-up

**laze** VERB

*Young girls lazed in the sun.*
▶ relax, idle, lounge, loll
AN OPPOSITE IS work

**laziness** NOUN

*His report mentioned lateness and laziness.*
▶ idleness, indolence, slothfulness, sloth, lethargy, loafing, lounging about, dilatoriness, inactivity, slowness, sluggishness
AN OPPOSITE IS industry

**lazy** ADJECTIVE

**1** *No one can accuse them of being lazy after all they've achieved.*
▶ idle, indolent, slothful, work-shy, inactive, lethargic, slack
AN OPPOSITE IS industrious

**2** *They headed for a lazy weekend in the country.*
▶ quiet, relaxing, peaceful

**lead** NOUN

**1** *The older students provide a lead for the younger ones.*
▶ example, guidance, leadership, direction

**2** (*informal*) *Detectives are following an important new lead.*
▶ clue, hint, tip, tip-off, line of inquiry

**3** *One of the Ferrari team took the lead.*
▶ first place, front position, spearhead, vanguard

**4** *She will play the lead in his new film.*
▶ principal role, chief part, starring role, title role

**5** *The toaster needs a new lead.*
▶ cable, flex, wire

**6** *He let the dog off the lead.*
▶ leash, tether, rein, chain, strap, cord

**lead** VERB

**1** *She led her guests out on the terrace.*
▶ conduct, guide, show, escort, usher, marshal, shepherd, steer, pilot
AN OPPOSITE IS follow

**2** *Smith was appointed to lead the delegation.*
▶ head, be in charge of, be the leader of, preside over, direct, manage, command, govern, supervise, rule

**3** *The Oxford boat was leading for most of the distance.*
▶ be in front, be in the lead, head the field
AN OPPOSITE IS trail

**4** *They have led a very happy life.*
▶ pass, spend, have, experience, undergo

**lead to** *Asking awkward questions might lead to trouble.*
▶ cause, bring about, result in, give rise to, produce, generate, create, precipitate, induce, stimulate

**lead on** *She was accused of leading them on.*
▶ mislead, deceive, entice, beguile, hoodwink, string along

**leader** NOUN

**1** *the leader of the marketing team*
▶ head, chief, director, manager, principal, superior, (*more informal*) boss

**2** *one of the country's former leaders*
▶ ruler, chief, governor

## leading ADJECTIVE

*The book is acknowledged as the leading authority on the subject.*
▶ principal, foremost, chief, major, key, main, primary, pre-eminent, outstanding, dominant, important, inspiring, prominent, well-known

## leaflet NOUN

*Adam grabbed a leaflet from the counter.*
▶ handout, flyer, brochure, circular, pamphlet, booklet

## league NOUN

1 *The countries came together to form a league.*
▶ association, alliance, federation, confederation, confederacy, syndicate
2 *On Saturday they face the league leaders.*
▶ group, class, championship

## leak VERB

1 *Oil was leaking from the tank.*
▶ seep, escape, ooze, spill, trickle, drip, exude
2 *We still haven't discovered who leaked the information.*
▶ reveal, disclose, divulge, pass on, give away, let out, make known

## leak NOUN

1 *several leaks in the roof*
▶ hole, opening, crack, drip, perforation, puncture
2 *a gas leak*
▶ escape, seepage, discharge
3 *a leak of information*
▶ disclosure, divulgence, revelation

## leaky ADJECTIVE

*a leaky roof*
▶ leaking, dripping, cracked, holed, perforated, punctured
AN OPPOSITE IS watertight

## lean ADJECTIVE

1 *a tall lean figure*
▶ thin, spare, skinny, slender, slim, gaunt, lanky, wiry, bony, emaciated
AN OPPOSITE IS fat
2 *a lean harvest*
▶ meagre, scanty, sparse, poor, mean, barren, inadequate

## lean VERB

1 *The trees were leaning in the wind.*
▶ slant, incline, bend, tilt, tip, bank, heel over, list, loll, slope
2 *Mary leaned against the fence.*
▶ rest, support yourself, prop yourself up, recline
3 **lean towards** *We lean towards a peaceful solution.*
▶ favour, prefer, tend towards, incline towards

## leaning NOUN

*He had a leaning towards socialism.*
▶ inclination, tendency, bent, bias, partiality (for), penchant (for), predilection (for), propensity (for), instinct (for), liking (for), preference (for), taste (for)

## leap VERB

1 *The dog leapt over the gate.*
▶ jump, spring, vault, bound
2 *Claire leapt to her feet*
▶ spring, jump
3 *Prices have leapt in the last few months.*
▶ soar, rise, rocket, surge, increase
OPPOSITES ARE tumble, plummet, fall
4 **leap at** *He leapt at the opportunity.*
▶ seize, grasp, accept eagerly, (*more informal*) go for
OPPOSITES ARE turn down, reject

## learn VERB

1 *It is important to learn the language when living in a foreign country.*
▶ master, acquire a knowledge of, acquire, understand, assimilate, pick up
2 *If I want to learn a poem I stick it on the fridge.*
▶ memorize, learn by heart, know

## learned ADJECTIVE

*a learned piece of writing*
▶ scholarly, erudite, intellectual, academic, cultured, educated, highbrow

## learner NOUN

*At this stage he is just a learner.*
▶ beginner, novice, apprentice, pupil, starter, newcomer, cadet, trainee, tiro

## learning NOUN

*a person of great learning*
▶ scholarship, erudition, knowledge, culture, education, schooling, wisdom, information

## least ADJECTIVE

1 *I haven't the least idea what he means.*
▶ slightest, smallest, tiniest
2 *Choose a place that involves the least travel.*
▶ minimum, minimal, smallest amount of
OPPOSITES ARE maximum, most

## leave VERB

1 *It is time to leave now.*
▶ depart, set off, go, go away, go out, take your leave, withdraw, retire, say goodbye, (*more informal*) disappear
AN OPPOSITE IS arrive
2 *She left the house that afternoon.*
▶ depart from, quit, vacate
3 *His wife has left him.*
▶ desert, abandon, forsake
4 *He's going to leave his job at the end of the month.*
▶ quit, give up, resign from, relinquish
5 *I've left my case on the train.*
▶ lose, mislay, leave behind
6 *Leave it to me to sort out.*
▶ entrust, refer, hand over, consign
7 *When he died he left them the house.*
▶ bequeath, will, endow

# leave

**leave** NOUN

**1** *The judge granted him leave to appeal against the verdict.*
▶ permission, consent, authorization, approval, liberty

**2** *Greg was having some leave from the army.*
▶ free time, time off, holiday, absence, sabbatical, vacation

**lecture** NOUN

**1** *a lecture on modern poetry*
▶ talk, discourse, speech, address, lesson

**2** *He got a stern lecture about being late.*
▶ reprimand, scolding, rebuke, harangue

**lecture** VERB

**1** *Anna lectures at the university.*
▶ teach, give lectures, give lessons, take students

**2** *Professor Jones will lecture on advances in genetics.*
▶ give a lecture, speak, talk, discourse, (more informal) hold forth

**3** *She lectured us on our bad manners*
▶ reprimand, scold, rebuke, admonish, chide

**leg** NOUN

**1** *the first leg of the journey*
▶ stage, part, phase, stretch, lap, step

**2** *a table leg*
▶ support, upright, prop

**legal** ADJECTIVE

**1** *legal advice*
▶ judicial, judiciary

**2** *activity that is not legal*
▶ lawful, legitimate, licit, permissible, authorized, permitted, aboveboard, allowable, allowed, rightful, proper, constitutional, valid
AN OPPOSITE IS illegal

**legend** NOUN

*legends from the past*
▶ myth, story, folk tale, fable, tradition

**legendary** ADJECTIVE

*legendary beasts and heroes*
▶ mythical, fabled, fabulous, fictional, fictitious, story-book, invented, made-up, non-existent
AN OPPOSITE IS real

**legible** ADJECTIVE

*The writing was barely legible.*
▶ readable, clear, decipherable, intelligible, distinct, neat, plain
AN OPPOSITE IS illegible

**legitimate** ADJECTIVE

**1** *They have legitimate reasons for the action they took.*
▶ valid, sound, cogent, admissible, well-founded, acceptable, justifiable

**2** *The Duke lacked a legitimate heir.*
▶ lawful, legal, rightful, acknowledged, true, proper

**leisure** NOUN

**1** *They lead a life of leisure.*
▶ ease, relaxation, enjoyment, inactivity, pleasure, amusement, recreation, retirement

**2** *She never had enough leisure to do the things she wanted.*
▶ free time, spare time, time off, freedom, liberty, rest

**leisurely** ADJECTIVE

*a leisurely stroll through the park*
▶ slow, gentle, unhurried, relaxed, relaxing, restful, sedate, comfortable, easy, lingering, peaceful
OPPOSITES ARE brisk, hurried

**lend** VERB

**1** *He asked me to lend him the money.*
▶ loan, advance, let someone have
AN OPPOSITE IS borrow

**2** *Her presence lent dignity to the occasion.*
▶ add, give, bring, impart, afford, bestow (on), confer (on)
AN OPPOSITE IS detract (from)

**length** NOUN

**1** *The snakes grew to a length of twenty feet or more.*
▶ extent, measurement, stretch, distance

**2** *People began to grumble about the length of the wait.*
▶ duration, extent, protractedness, period, time

**lengthen** VERB

**1** *The days begin to lengthen in March.*
▶ grow longer, get longer, draw out, stretch, enlarge, elongate, expand, extend, get longer, increase, prolong, pull out
AN OPPOSITE IS shorten

**2** *You will need to lengthen the cooking time.*
▶ extend, increase, prolong, continue
AN OPPOSITE IS shorten

**lengthy** ADJECTIVE

*The family faced a lengthy journey.*
▶ long, protracted, drawn out, tedious, extended
OPPOSITES ARE short, brief

**lenient** ADJECTIVE

*He always said his mother had been too lenient with him.*
▶ soft, easygoing, tolerant, soft-hearted, indulgent, merciful, forgiving, mild, kind
OPPOSITES ARE strict, severe

**lessen** VERB

**1** *He took an aspirin to lessen the pain.*
▶ reduce, lower, decrease, deaden, alleviate, assuage, mitigate, make less, minimize, tone down

**2** *Her love for him would never lessen.*
▶ diminish, decrease, abate, fade, dwindle, weaken, grow less, recede, shrink
AN OPPOSITE IS increase

# lesson

**lesson** NOUN

**1** *a French lesson*
▶ class, period, lecture, seminar, tutorial, instruction

**2** *The experience might be a lesson to all of them.*
▶ example, warning, deterrent, moral

## let VERB

**1** *His parents wouldn't let him go on the trip.*
▶ allow, permit, give permission, authorize, consent to, agree to
OPPOSITES ARE prevent, forbid
**USAGE** If you use *allow*, *permit*, or *authorize* you have to add *to*, e.g. *His parents wouldn't allow him to go.* If you use *give permission*, you have to say *His parents wouldn't give him permission to go* or *His parents wouldn't give him permission for him to go.* If you use *consent* or *agree* you have to say *His parents wouldn't agree or consent to his or him going.*
**2** *The landlord will let rooms for six months.*
▶ rent out, lease out, hire out
**let down** *They felt the manager had let them down.*
▶ fail, disappoint, betray, abandon, desert
**let off** *They decided to let him off with a warning.*
▶ pardon, forgive, excuse, spare, release
**let up** *The rain let up for a while.*
▶ ease, subside, abate, slacken, diminish
AN OPPOSITE IS intensify

## let-down NOUN

*After all the excitement, the holiday was a complete let-down.*
▶ disappointment, anticlimax, comedown, (*more informal*) washout, (*more informal*) damp squib

## lethal ADJECTIVE

*execution by lethal injection*
▶ deadly, fatal, mortal, poisonous

## lethargic ADJECTIVE

*I felt tired and lethargic all weekend.*
▶ sluggish, inactive, inert, listless, languid, lazy, sleepy, slow, torpid, apathetic
OPPOSITES ARE vigorous, energetic

## lethargy NOUN

*The best way to shake off winter lethargy is with a good long stretch.*
▶ sluggishness, listlessness, inactivity, inertia, apathy, laziness, slowness, torpor

## letter NOUN

**1** *She wrote a letter to her MP.*
▶ message, note, communication, dispatch, missive, (*more formal*) epistle
RELATED ADJECTIVE epistolary
**2** *The wall was daubed with large letters.*
▶ character, figure, sign, symbol, device

## level ADJECTIVE

**1** *Make sure the surface is level before spreading the paper on it.*
▶ flat, even, smooth, uniform, flush, regular, horizontal, plane
AN OPPOSITE IS uneven
**2** *The scores were level at half time.*
▶ equal, even, matching, balanced, the same, (*more informal*) neck-and-neck

## level NOUN

**1** *Soon she was promoted to a senior level.*
▶ rank, status, position, class, echelon

**2** *There is a high level of absenteeism.*
▶ amount, quantity, extent, degree, proportion
**3** *The water rose to a dangerous level.*
▶ height, elevation, altitude
**4** *There are offices on this level of the building.*
▶ floor, storey, tier

## level VERB

**1** *He piled on the earth, levelling it with his hands.*
▶ smooth, even out, flatten, rake
**2** *A series of violent tremors levelled the area.*
▶ raze, demolish, destroy, devastate, knock down, lay low
**3** *His hand was shaking, making it difficult to level the gun.*
▶ aim, point, direct, train

## level-headed ADJECTIVE

*Belinda was too level-headed to fool herself in this way.*
▶ sensible, balanced, practical, prudent, realistic, self-possessed, commonsensical, judicious

## lever NOUN

*You push the lever down and leave it there.*
▶ switch, handle, knob, bar

## lever VERB

*He picked up a crowbar and levered open the window.*
▶ prise, force, wrench, heave

## liability NOUN

**1** *The driver of the other car admitted liability for the accident.*
▶ responsibility, blame, culpability, accountability
**2** *Taking the dog with us could prove a liability.*
▶ nuisance, inconvenience, encumbrance, hindrance, burden, handicap, drawback, (*more informal*) drag

## liable ADJECTIVE

**1** *The company is not liable for any damage that might be caused.*
▶ responsible, accountable, answerable, to blame
AN OPPOSITE IS exempt (from)
**2** *The shaft is liable to break under pressure.*
▶ likely, apt, prone, inclined, given (to falling), disposed, predisposed, ready
AN OPPOSITE IS unlikely

## liar NOUN

*Parkin was either a coward or a liar, or both.*
▶ deceiver, fabricator, falsifier, (*more informal*) storyteller, (*more informal*) fibber

## libel NOUN

*He said the newspaper article amounted to libel.*
▶ defamation of character, misrepresentation, an insult, a slur, a smear
**USAGE** You can also use *slander* when the insult is spoken rather than printed.

## libellous ADJECTIVE

*Lawyers check whether there is anything libellous in the writing.*
▶ defamatory, derogatory, false, insulting
**USAGE** You can also use *slanderous* when the insult is spoken rather than printed.

# liberal ADJECTIVE

1 *a liberal supply of liquid refreshment*
▶ copious, generous, plentiful, lavish, abundant, ample, bounteous, bountiful, munificent, unstinting
AN OPPOSITE IS mean

2 *liberal social attitudes*
▶ broad-minded, tolerant, enlightened, moderate, easygoing, magnanimous, lenient, unbiased, unprejudiced, permissive, free
AN OPPOSITE IS narrow-minded

3 *liberal political views*
▶ progressive, radical, forward-looking
AN OPPOSITE IS conservative

# liberate VERB

*the intention to liberate all people from every kind of slavery*
▶ free, set free, release, discharge, deliver, rescue, save, emancipate, unfetter, loose, ransom, untie
OPPOSITES ARE enslave, subjugate

# liberty NOUN

*You can enjoy the liberty to follow your own interests.*
▶ freedom, independence, emancipation, liberation, release

## at liberty

1 *The escaped prisoners were at liberty for three months.*
▶ free, on the run, on the loose

2 *She is at liberty to use her money as she wishes.*
▶ free, entitled, permitted, allowed, authorized
AN OPPOSITE IS forbidden

# licence NOUN

1 *I needed a licence to play music in my shop.*
▶ permit, certificate, document, authorization, warrant

2 *the licence to act as you see fit*
▶ authority, authorization, permission, entitlement, prerogative, privilege

# license VERB

*The local authority will license the restaurant to serve alcoholic drinks.*
▶ authorize, permit, give a licence to, entitle, allow, empower
OPPOSITES ARE prohibit (from serving), ban (from serving)

# lick VERB

1 *Tessa was licking a lollipop.*
▶ suck, taste

2 *(more informal) They licked the visiting side 4-0.*
▶ beat, defeat, overcome, trounce, rout, thrash

3 *By now the flames were licking the ceiling.*
▶ touch, reach, brush, flicker round, dance round

# lid NOUN

*The lid was stuck to the jar.*
▶ top, cap, stopper, cover, covering

# lie NOUN

*He can't help telling lies.*
▶ untruth, falsehood, falsification, fabrication, deception, invention, falsity, deceit, fiction, (more informal) fib
OPPOSITES ARE truth, fact

# lie VERB

1 *He lied about where he'd been.*
▶ tell an untruth, invent a story, dissemble, (more informal) fib

2 *She was lying on the bed.*
▶ recline, stretch out, rest, lounge, sprawl

3 *The town lies twenty miles from the coast.*
▶ be situated, be located, be placed, be found, be sited

# life NOUN

1 *the joy of giving life*
▶ existence, breath, being

2 *Their dog still looked full of life*
▶ vitality, energy, liveliness, vigour, verve, spirit, vivacity, zest, activity, (more informal) go

3 *He's reading a life of John Lennon*
▶ biography, autobiography, life story

4 *The contract covers the life of the project.*
▶ duration, course, span, extent

# lifeless ADJECTIVE

1 *The lifeless body fell into the grave.*
▶ dead, deceased, inanimate, defunct, comatose, inert
AN OPPOSITE IS living

2 *a lifeless desert*
▶ barren, arid, bare, sterile
AN OPPOSITE IS fertile

3 *The voice was dull and lifeless.*
▶ lacklustre, lethargic, unexciting, apathetic, tedious, boring, flat, slow
AN OPPOSITE IS animated

# lifelike ADJECTIVE

*The new portrait was unusually lifelike.*
▶ realistic, true to life, authentic, natural, graphic, convincing, photographic
AN OPPOSITE IS unrealistic

# lifelong ADJECTIVE

*Ramesh had been his lifelong friend.*
▶ lasting, constant, long-term

# lift VERB

1 *She lifted the twins into their special chairs.*
▶ raise, pick up, hoist, heave
OPPOSITES ARE lower, drop

2 *The plane lifted off the ground*
▶ rise, ascend, go up, soar
OPPOSITES ARE land, touch down

3 *The sight of the sea lifted their spirits.*
▶ raise, boost, buoy up, revive, enliven, perk up
OPPOSITES ARE lower, subdue

4 *The six-month ban has now been lifted.*
▶ cancel, revoke, rescind, remove, withdraw
AN OPPOSITE IS impose

**5** *By now the mist had lifted.*
▶ clear, disperse, disappear, vanish, dissolve, rise
OPPOSITES ARE come down, appear

**lift** NOUN
*She took the lift to the top floor.*
▶ elevator, escalator, hoist

**light** ADJECTIVE
**1** *a light load*
▶ slight, lightweight, portable, insubstantial, weightless, flimsy, feathery
AN OPPOSITE IS heavy
**2** *a light blue*
▶ pale, faint, pastel, fair
AN OPPOSITE IS dark
**3** *a light meal*
▶ modest, frugal, simple, skimpy, insubstantial
OPPOSITES ARE heavy, rich
**4** *light music   a little light reading*
▶ entertaining, lightweight, diverting, undemanding, easy
**5** *She looked light on her feet.*
▶ nimble, deft, agile, graceful

**light** NOUN
**1** *The gas lamp did not give out much light.*
▶ brightness, illumination, radiance, luminescence, glow, lustre
**2** *There was a light on in the bedroom.*
▶ lamp, lantern, torch, bulb
**3** *She saw the problem in a new light.*
▶ aspect, complexion, angle, standpoint, point of view, slant, approach
USAGE With the last five synonyms you use *from* instead of *in*, e.g. *She saw the problem from a new standpoint.*
**4** *In an hour they would be working in the light.*
▶ daylight, light of day, daytime, sunlight

**light** VERB
**1** *The boys wanted to light a fire.*
▶ kindle, ignite, set alight, set burning, put a match to, set fire to, switch on
OPPOSITES ARE put out, extinguish
**2** *Hundreds of searchlights lit the sky.*
▶ illuminate, light up, lighten, brighten, irradiate, floodlight, cast light on, shed light on, shine on
AN OPPOSITE IS darken

**lighten** VERB
**1** *Pale streaks lightened the sky.*
▶ light, light up, illuminate, brighten, irradiate
AN OPPOSITE IS darken
**2** *The sky lightened in the east.*
▶ brighten, grow lighter
AN OPPOSITE IS darken
**3** *The gift lightened their financial burden.*
▶ ease, reduce, relieve, alleviate, mitigate, moderate
OPPOSITES ARE increase, intensify

**light-headed** ADJECTIVE
*She felt nauseous and light-headed from the shock.*
▶ dizzy, giddy, faint, shaky, (*more informal*) woozy

**light-hearted** ADJECTIVE
*His light-hearted banter had a serious side.*
▶ cheerful, carefree, jolly, playful, jovial, bright

**like** ADJECTIVE
*The cousins are very like each other.*
▶ similar to, the same as, identical
AN OPPOSITE IS unlike

**like** VERB This word is often overused. Here are some alternatives:
**1** *I have always liked Rosamund.*
▶ be fond of, be attached to, care for, adore, admire, respect, esteem, (*old-fashioned*) hold dear, (*more informal*) have a soft spot for, (*more informal*) take a shine to, (*more informal*) fancy
**2** *Do you like dancing?*
▶ enjoy, care for, appreciate, be keen on, be partial to, (*more informal*) love, (*more informal*) fancy

**likeable** ADJECTIVE
*The person appointed needs to be likeable and a good mixer.*
▶ pleasant, personable, nice, friendly, attractive, charming, congenial, pleasing, endearing
AN OPPOSITE IS hateful

**likelihood** NOUN
*Neither side has shown any likelihood of winning.*
▶ possibility, probability, prospect, chance, hope

**likely** ADJECTIVE
**1** *It was likely that there would be an inquiry.*
▶ probable, possible, expected, foreseeable, envisaged, (*more informal*) odds-on
**2** *Try to think of a more likely explanation.*
▶ credible, believable, plausible, convincing, reasonable
**3** *It was a likely place for them to meet.*
▶ suitable, appropriate, proper, apposite, promising, hopeful

**liken** VERB
*He likened a computer to the human brain.*
▶ compare, equate, match, parallel, relate, correlate, associate (with)

**likeness** NOUN
**1** *The photograph was a good likeness of their mother.*
▶ representation, image, depiction, portrayal, picture, portrait, copy, replica
**2** *His likeness to Alan is remarkable.*
▶ resemblance, similarity, affinity, correspondence
AN OPPOSITE IS dissimilarity

**liking** NOUN
*a liking for rock music*
▶ fondness, partiality, taste, desire, attraction, weakness, penchant, predilection, fancy
OPPOSITES ARE dislike (of), aversion (to)

**limb** NOUN
**1** *His limbs ached.*
▶ arm, leg, extremity, appendage
**2** *the limbs of a tree*
▶ branch, bough

**limber** VERB

**limber up** *She was limbering up for the next race.*
▶ warm up, loosen up, work out, prepare, get ready, exercise

**limelight** NOUN

*Peter was excited about being back in the limelight again.*
▶ spotlight, stardom, focus of attention, prominence

**limit** NOUN

1 *There was a limit to what they could do to help.  There is a limit of ten thousand tickets for away supporters.*
▶ restriction, maximum, ceiling, cut-off point, curb, restraint, limitation

2 *They drove out as far as the city limits.*
▶ boundary, border, edge, perimeter, confine

**limit** VERB

*The organizers have to limit numbers in the interests of safety.*
▶ restrict, curb, put a limit on, restrain, check, control, circumscribe, demarcate, confine, fix

**limitation** NOUN

1 *a limitation on numbers*
▶ limit, restriction, ceiling, cut-off point, curb, restraint

2 *I am aware of my limitations.*
▶ weakness, shortcoming, deficiency, imperfection, inadequacy, defect

**limited** ADJECTIVE

*Resources are limited.*
▶ restricted, circumscribed, finite, short, controlled, rationed, defined, determinate, fixed, inadequate, insufficient, narrow, reduced, small
OPPOSITES ARE unlimited, limitless

**limitless** ADJECTIVE

*The opportunities are limitless.*
▶ endless, unending, never-ending, boundless, unbounded, unlimited, without limit, countless, incalculable, inexhaustible, infinite, vast, unimaginable
AN OPPOSITE IS limited

**limp** ADJECTIVE

(*informal*) *The man held out a limp hand.*
▶ soft, loose, flabby, drooping, slack, weak, sagging, wilting, bendy, flexible, pliable, yielding, (*more informal*) floppy
OPPOSITES ARE firm, rigid

**limp** VERB

*She limped back into the house.*
▶ hobble, hop, falter, shuffle, stumble, totter

**line** NOUN

1 *A line of cars was waiting at the lights.*
▶ queue, row, file, column, procession, chain, string

2 *He drew a line under his signature.  From their window they could see lines in the sand.*
▶ stroke, rule, underline, strip, band, bar, streak

3 *As she grew older the lines on her face increased.*
▶ crease, wrinkle, furrow, groove

4 *They walked in a straight line across the field*
▶ direction, path, route, course, track

5 *The courts are taking a tough line with repeat offenders.  Cabinet members are obliged to support the government line.*
▶ approach, course, course of action, procedure, policy, position, stance, tactic

6 *There aren't many opportunities in my line.*
▶ field, line of work, occupation, business, calling, speciality, trade, work, province, domain

7 *Mark attached a line to the post.*
▶ cord, rope, string, cable, wire, thread, flex

8 *the handsome lines of a classical building*
▶ shape, contour, profile, figure, features, silhouette

9 *The ball had not crossed the line.*
▶ limit, boundary, border, edge, demarcation

10 *She comes from a noble line related to the royal family.*
▶ ancestry, family, descent, lineage, extraction, pedigree, genealogy, stock, background

**line** VERB

1 *She lined the cat's box with blankets.*
▶ cover, face, pad, stuff, reinforce

2 *The drive was lined with trees.*
▶ border, edge, fringe, bound, skirt

**line up** *The children lined up by the door.*
▶ form a line, form a queue, queue, queue up, fall in, form a crocodile

**lineage** NOUN

*a noble lineage*
▶ ancestry, line, family, descent, extraction, pedigree, genealogy, stock, background

**line-up** NOUN

*a dazzling line-up of performers*
▶ cast, list, bill, programme, array

**linger** VERB

1 *Most of the crowd leave promptly but some tend to linger.*
▶ wait around, lag behind, loiter, dally, tarry, hang on, stay put, delay

2 *An aroma of coffee lingered all morning.*
▶ persist, last, continue, remain, endure, stay

**lining** NOUN

*a coat with a thick lining*
▶ padding, inner layer, interfacing, inlay, liner, interlining

**link** NOUN

1 *She fostered links between the two families*
▶ bond, tie, relationship, attachment

2 *a rail link between the city centre and the airport*
▶ connection, communication, line

3 *an important link in the organization*
▶ element, component, constituent, piece

4 *a chain of hardened steel links*
▶ loop, ring, connector, connection

**link** VERB

**1** *Police are linking this crime with a series of other robberies.*
▶ connect, associate, relate (to), draw a connection between

**2** *The two trains were linked together.*
▶ couple, join, connect, attach, fasten

**lip** NOUN

*Coffee poured over the lip of the jug.*
▶ rim, brim, brink, mouth, edge

**liquefy** VERB

*The gas will only liquefy at a low temperature.*
▶ become liquid, condense, dissolve, liquidize, melt
AN OPPOSITE IS solidify

**liquid** NOUN

*The doctor says he can only take liquids for a few days.*
▶ fluid, liquid substance, juice, drink, solution

**liquid** ADJECTIVE

*The pudding had become liquid in the heat.*
▶ runny, fluid, thin, watery, sloppy, sloshy, wet, aqueous, molten, running, flowing
AN OPPOSITE IS solid

**liquidate** VERB

USAGE Do not confuse this word with *liquidize*, which has a different meaning.

**1** *The ruling clan liquidated all its rivals.*
▶ kill, slaughter, annihilate, massacre, eliminate, destroy, purge, (more informal) do away with, (more informal) get rid of

**2** *The company was liquidated at the cost of a hundred jobs.*
▶ close down, wind up, dissolve, put into liquidation

**liquidize** VERB

USAGE Do not confuse this word with *liquidate*, which has a different meaning.

*Liquidize the vegetables to make a smooth paste*
▶ blend, crush, purée, pulp, make into liquid

**liquor** NOUN

*Persons under 18 may not buy liquor.*
▶ alcohol, alcoholic drink, spirits, strong drink, intoxicant, (more informal) hard stuff

**list** NOUN

*I had a list of over 7,000 names.*
▶ register, inventory, catalogue, index, file, roll, roster, schedule

**list** VERB

**1** *We have listed names of contributors in alphabetical order.*
▶ record, register, itemize, enter, index, file, enumerate, catalogue

**2** *The ship was listing in the heavy seas.*
▶ tilt, lean, lean over, tip, heel, pitch, keel over

**listen** VERB

**1** *I don't think they were listening.*
▶ pay attention, take notice

**2** *listen to a doctor who listens to what his patients tell him*
▶ pay attention to, take notice of, hear, heed, attend to, concentrate on, (old-fashioned) hark
AN OPPOSITE IS ignore

**listless** ADJECTIVE

*a young woman clutching a pale, listless child*
▶ lethargic, sluggish, enervated, lackadaisical, torpid, inert, apathetic, unenthusiastic
AN OPPOSITE IS lively

**literal** ADJECTIVE

**1** *a literal translation*
▶ word-for-word, verbatim, faithful, strict, exact, close, plain, prosaic, unimaginative

**2** *the literal truth of the Bible*
▶ strict, plain, bare, exact, precise, straightforward, unvarnished, narrow

**literary** ADJECTIVE

**1** *a collection of literary works*
▶ written, printed, published, dramatic, poetic, imaginative

**2** *a literary style of writing*
▶ formal, stylish, ornate, polished, sophisticated, imaginative, recognized as literature

**3** *a group of literary friends*
▶ cultured, educated, literate, scholarly, refined, well-read, widely read, erudite, learned

**literate** ADJECTIVE

**1** *At 15 he was barely literate.*
▶ able to read and write, educated

**2** *a literate piece of writing*
▶ well-written, readable, lucid, eloquent, stylish

**3** *a literate society*
▶ cultured, educated, literary, scholarly, refined, well-read, widely read, erudite, learned

**literature** NOUN

**1** *We can pick up some literature about the place from the tourist office.*
▶ brochures, leaflets, pamphlets, handouts, circulars

**2** *a class in English literature*
▶ writings, books

**lithe** ADJECTIVE

*a lithe young gymnast*
▶ agile, graceful, pliant, supple, flexible, limber, lissom, loose-jointed

**litter** NOUN

**1** *It took days to clear up all the litter.*
▶ rubbish, refuse, junk, waste, debris, clutter, garbage, mess, scraps, bits and pieces, odds and ends, trash, jumble

**2** *a litter of puppies*
▶ brood, family, (more formal) progeny

**litter** VERB

*They had littered the room with a half-eaten takeaway.*
▶ clutter, mess up, make untidy, scatter, strew

**little** ADJECTIVE This word is often overused. Here are some alternatives:
**1** *a little book*
► small, tiny, minute, miniature, mini, petite, (*Scottish*) wee, (*more informal*) teeny
**2** *a little person*
► small, slight, short, diminutive, (*Scottish*) wee
**3** *in a little while*
► short, brief, fleeting, (*Scottish*) wee
**4** *We have a little problem*
► minor, trivial, unimportant, insignificant, inconsequential, negligible
**5** *a little* Add a little water.
► some, a small amount of, a bit of, a touch of, a spot of, a taste of

**little** NOUN
*You only need a little.*
► bit, dash, pinch, small amount, touch, modicum

**little** ADVERB
*The singers are little known in this country.*
► scarcely, barely, hardly, slightly, not much

**live** VERB
**1** *We live in Glasgow.*
► reside, have a home, dwell, lodge
**2** *He hardly earns enough to live on.*
► exist, subsist, survive, endure, stay alive
**3** *I'm not sure these plants will live much longer.*
► last, survive, stay alive
**4** *She has led a happy life.*
► pass, spend, experience, undergo

**live** ADJECTIVE
**1** *live animals*
► living, alive, breathing, animate
**2** *a live show*
► real-time, actual, unrecorded
**3** *a live rail*
► electrified, charged, powered, connected
**4** *a live issue*
► topical, current, relevant, pertinent, contemporary, vital, controversial

**livelihood** NOUN
*The printing business was his main livelihood.*
► income, source of income, means of support, living, subsistence, occupation, employment

**liveliness** NOUN
*She has a liveliness which is quite extraordinary for her age.*
► enthusiasm, exuberance, vitality, vigour, sprightliness, verve, vivacity, energy, dynamism, activity, boisterousness, (*more informal*) go
OPPOSITES ARE tiredness, inactivity

**lively** ADJECTIVE
**1** *The bars are lively late in the evening.*
► busy, hectic, bustling, crowded, swarming
OPPOSITES ARE quiet, dead

**2** *an attractive and lively young woman*
► vivacious, high-spirited, exuberant, animated, alert, active, spirited, exciting, cheerful
OPPOSITES ARE lifeless, dull
**3** *a lively colour scheme*
► bright, vivid, colourful, striking, bold
OPPOSITES ARE dull, bland

**liven** VERB
**liven up** *The room needed a few pictures to liven it up.*
► brighten up, animate, cheer up, vitalize, put life into, (*more informal*) perk up, (*more informal*) pep up

**livery** NOUN
**1** *the pageboys in their blue livery*
► uniform, costume, outfit, suit, regalia, garb, (*more informal*) get-up
**2** *railway coaches repainted in their old maroon livery*
► colours, colour scheme, paintwork

**livestock** NOUN
*If you plan to keep livestock, the security of fences and gates is vital.*
► cattle, farm animals

**livid** ADJECTIVE
**1** *A row of livid bruises began to form on his skin.*
► bluish-grey, purplish, dark, discoloured
**2** *He was livid with me.*
► furious, angry, fuming, seething, raging, enraged, infuriated

**living** ADJECTIVE
*all living creatures*
► live, alive, breathing, animate, existing, vital, active, sentient, surviving, vigorous
OPPOSITES ARE dead, extinct

**living** NOUN
*He was washing cars for a living.*
► livelihood, income, source of income, means of support, subsistence, occupation, employment

**living room** NOUN
*Music was playing in the living room.*
► sitting room, drawing room, lounge, reception room

**load** NOUN
**1** *a load of goods*
► cargo, consignment, freight, vanload, lorryload, truckload, shipment, boatload, (*more formal*) lading
**2** *a heavy load of work*
► burden, commitment, obligation, weight
**3** **a load of** (*informal*) *a load of rubbish*
► a lot of, a great deal of, a wealth of

**load** VERB
**1** *We loaded the luggage into the car.*
► pack, stow, store, stack, cram, heap, pile
AN OPPOSITE IS unload (from)
**2** *They've loaded me with more responsibilities.*
► burden, encumber, weigh down, saddle
AN OPPOSITE IS relieve (of)

**loaded** ADJECTIVE
**1** *He had a loaded gun in his hand.*
► primed, charged, filled, ready

## loaf

**2** *A loaded trolley trundled up the platform.*
▶ full, filled, laden, burdened, inundated, piled high, weighed down, crammed

**3** *a loaded argument*
▶ one-sided, biased, tendentious, prejudiced, unfair, distorted, emotive, partial

**4** (*informal*) *Their parents are loaded and can easily afford the fees.*
▶ wealthy, well-off, rich, affluent, prosperous, moneyed

## loaf VERB

*He can't go on loafing around any longer.*
▶ laze, idle, lounge, waste time, kill time
OPPOSITES ARE work, toil

## loafer NOUN

(*informal*) *education that produces a generation of loafers*
▶ layabout, idler, lounger, shirker, wastrel, (*informal*) skiver, (*informal*) lazybones, (*informal*) good-for-nothing

## loan NOUN

*A bank loan would help develop the business.*
▶ advance, credit, mortgage

## loan VERB

**1** *We will loan you the money for a period of 5 years.*
▶ lend, advance, credit

**2** *The gallery loans pictures all over the world.*
▶ lend, give on loan, provide on loan

## loath ADJECTIVE

*They were loath to admit their mistake.*
▶ reluctant, unwilling, disinclined, averse (to admitting)

## loathe VERB

*She loathed living in the suburbs.*
▶ hate, detest, abhor, abominate, dislike, despise
OPPOSITES ARE love, like, adore

## loathing NOUN

*Loathing for the other woman rose in her chest.*
▶ hatred, detestation, abhorrence, repugnance (for), revulsion (for)
AN OPPOSITE IS love

## loathsome ADJECTIVE

*a loathsome crime*
▶ detestable, horrible, horrid, awful, nasty
OPPOSITES ARE pleasant, likeable

## lob VERB

*He lobbed the ball in the air.*
▶ throw, toss, hurl, pitch, fling, loft, shy, bowl, cast, chuck, sling

## lobby NOUN

**1** *We can wait for her in the hotel lobby.*
▶ entrance hall, foyer, vestibule, hallway

**2** *the anti-abortion lobby*
▶ pressure group, campaign, ginger group, campaigners, supporters

## lobby VERB

**1** *The paper urged readers to lobby their MPs.*
▶ petition, pressurize, solicit, persuade, seek to influence, urge

**2** **lobby for** *a group lobbying for lower rail fares*
▶ campaign for, crusade for, press for, advocate, champion, demand, promote

## local ADJECTIVE

**1** *the local library*
▶ nearby, neighbourhood, neighbouring

**2** *Try the local cuisine.*
▶ regional, district, provincial, community
OPPOSITES ARE national, global

**3** *a local infection*
▶ confined, restricted, limited, localized, circumscribed
AN OPPOSITE IS general

## local NOUN

*The restaurant is filled with locals.*
▶ inhabitant, resident, parishioner, native

## locality NOUN

**1** *There are several good schools in the locality.*
▶ region, area, neighbourhood, vicinity, location, district, community, parish

**2** *new housing in an attractive locality*
▶ position, location, setting, situation, place

## locate VERB

**1** *He located the skylight window he had noticed from the outside.*
▶ find, discover, identify, pinpoint, track down, detect, light on

**2** *The boiler room is located in the basement.*
▶ situate, site, position, place

## location NOUN

*The firm is moving to a new location.*
▶ position, site, locality, locale, place, point, situation, spot, venue, whereabouts

## lock NOUN

**1** *a lock on a door*
▶ fastening, latch, clasp

**2** *a lock of hair*
▶ curl, tress, tuft

## lock VERB

*We lock the door at night.*
▶ fasten, secure, shut, bolt, close, seal
**lock up** *He was locked up for causing criminal damage.*
▶ jail, imprison, put behind bars

## lodge NOUN

*a hunting lodge*
▶ cabin, cottage, hut, chalet

## lodge VERB

**1** *The family lodged at a guest house for a few weeks.*
▶ board, stay, live, reside

**2** *I will lodge a formal complaint.*
▶ submit, register, enter, place, present

**lodger** NOUN
*Her husband had once been a lodger of hers.*
► boarder, paying guest, tenant, resident, inmate, guest

**lodgings** NOUN
*She had lodgings in Camden Town.*
► accommodation, rooms, quarters, apartments, residence, (*more informal*) digs, (*more informal*) pad

**log** NOUN
*a log of telephone calls*
► record, register, tally, list, account, journal

**log** VERB
*All calls are logged and monitored.*
► record, register, book, file, note, write down

**logic** NOUN
*We accept the logic of your case.*
► reasoning, rationale, sense, validity, argumentation, rationality, cogency

**logical** ADJECTIVE
*The conclusions are logical.*
► rational, reasonable, cogent, coherent, clear, sound, valid, consistent, intelligent, methodical, sensible, systematic
AN OPPOSITE IS illogical

**loiter** VERB
*With so much to do there was no time to loiter in the shopping malls.*
► linger, dally, potter, dawdle, tarry, (*more informal*) loaf about, (*more informal*) mooch about

**lone** ADJECTIVE
*a lone cyclist   a lone tree*
► solitary, single, solo, isolated, individual, unaccompanied, separate

**loneliness** NOUN
*The feeling of loneliness drove him to move on.*
► isolation, solitude, solitariness, friendlessness, seclusion, rejection, unpopularity

**lonely** ADJECTIVE
1 *I walked through the garden feeling very lonely.*
► alone, solitary, friendless, abandoned, lonesome, neglected, forlorn
AN OPPOSITE IS popular
2 *The cart drove along the lonely road*
► deserted, unfrequented, remote, secluded, isolated, abandoned, desolate, forsaken, out of the way, uninhabited, (*informal*) off the beaten track
AN OPPOSITE IS crowded

**loner** NOUN
*Although most of the group are sociable, Tony is a loner.*
► recluse, introvert, lone wolf, hermit, outsider

**long** ADJECTIVE
1 *long blonde hair*
► lengthy
AN OPPOSITE IS short
2 *a long wait*
► lengthy, prolonged, extended, extensive, long-lasting
OPPOSITES ARE short, brief

**long** VERB
**long for** *We longed for the holidays.*
► yearn for, crave, dream of, hanker after, hunger for, pine for

**longing** NOUN
*He felt a longing for his home*
► yearning, hankering (after), craving, desire, hunger, need, thirst, urge, wish, (*informal*) yen

**long-lasting** ADJECTIVE
*We need long-lasting solutions to these problems.*
► enduring, abiding, long-running, durable, permanent, prolonged

**long-standing** ADJECTIVE
*a long-standing arrangement*
► well-established, long-established, time-honoured, firm

**long-suffering** ADJECTIVE
*He went home to his long-suffering mother.*
► patient, forbearing, tolerant, uncomplaining

**long-winded** ADJECTIVE
*a long-winded speech*
► lengthy, long, rambling, diffuse, verbose, wordy, tedious, boring

---

**look** VERB This word is often overused. Here are some alternatives:
1 *Everywhere you look there are trees.*
► see, observe, regard, survey, glance, scrutinize, scan
2 *Things looked difficult that day.*
► seem, appear
**look after** *Jane had to look after her father during his last illness.*
► take care of, care for, tend, attend to, provide for, mind, nurse, supervise, watch over, (*more informal*) keep an eye on
**look at** *I knew if I looked at her we'd both start laughing.*
► glance at, watch, observe
**look down on** *The family looked down on all their neighbours.*
► despise, disdain, scorn, hold in contempt, sneer at, (*more informal*) look down one's nose at
**look for**
1 *I was still looking for my wallet.*
► search for, hunt for, seek, try to find
2 *Behaviour like that is looking for trouble.*
► ask for, provoke, invite, attract, court, incite, tempt, cause, encourage, generate, (*more informal*) stir up
**look into** *The official said he would look into the complaint.*
► investigate, find out about, inquire into, study, explore, examine
**look out** *A ball can easily hit you if you don't look out.*
► beware, watch out, be careful, be vigilant, pay attention, keep your eyes open ►►

> **look up**
> 1 *You can look up the answer in an encyclopedia.*
> ▶ find, search for, research, track down
> 2 (informal) *We can look up some friends on our way home.*
> ▶ visit, call on, stop by, (informal) drop in on, (informal) look in on
> 3 *Things were beginning to look up.*
> ▶ improve, progress, show an improvement, revive
> **look up to** *Susan looked up to her father.*
> ▶ admire, respect, esteem, revere, have a high regard for, have a high opinion of, think highly of

**look** NOUN
1 *We had a look at the house.*
▶ glance, glimpse, peek, peep, sight (of), observation (of), view (of), (informal) squint
2 *You could see he was angry from the look on his face.*
▶ expression, mien
3 *a house with a Tudor look*
▶ appearance, aspect, facade, guise, quality, atmosphere, semblance
4 *this year's new look*
▶ fashion, vogue, style, trend, craze, rage
5 **looks** *All the sisters enjoyed stunning good looks.*
▶ appearance, features

**lookalike** NOUN
*a Madonna lookalike*
▶ double, twin, exact likeness, spitting image, replica, clone, (more informal) spit

**lookout** NOUN
1 *a lookout on the bridge*
▶ sentry, guard, sentinel, scout, watchman
2 *It might not work but that's their lookout.*
▶ concern, responsibility, business, affair, problem

**loom** VERB
1 *The cathedral loomed above them.*
▶ soar, tower, rise, appear, rear up
2 *Blurred shapes loomed out of the mist.*
▶ appear, emerge, come into view, reveal itself
3 *Without action, big problems loom.*
▶ threaten, impend, be imminent, menace, overshadow

**loop** NOUN
*He slipped a loop of wire over the handle and pulled it tight.*
▶ coil, noose, ring, twist, curl, hoop, turn, bend, circle, kink

**loop** VERB
*Loop a rope round the animal's neck.*
▶ coil, wind, twist, bend, curl, entwine, turn

**loophole** NOUN
*a loophole in the regulations*
▶ means of escape, ambiguity, flaw, (more informal) get-out, (more informal) let-out

**loose** ADJECTIVE
1 *a loose screw*
▶ insecure, unfastened, untied, unfixed, wobbly
OPPOSITES ARE tight, secure
2 *a wild animal loose in the grounds*
▶ free, at large, unconfined, on the loose, at liberty
AN OPPOSITE IS confined
3 *loose trousers*
▶ baggy, slack, loose-fitting, roomy
OPPOSITES ARE tight, close-fitting
4 *a loose translation*
▶ free, imprecise, vague, inexact
OPPOSITES ARE literal, exact

**loosen** VERB
1 *He tried to loosen the knots.*
▶ ease, free, slacken, undo, untie, unfasten, release
2 *She loosened her grip.*
▶ weaken, relax, lessen
AN OPPOSITE IS tighten

**loot** NOUN
*a bag full of the thieves' loot*
▶ booty, spoils, plunder, haul, (more informal) swag

**loot** VERB
*Soldiers looted the deserted buildings.*
▶ raid, plunder, pillage, ransack, rifle, rob, steal from

**lop** VERB
*With a single blow he lopped off the mighty branch.*
▶ cut, chop, hack, slice, pare

**lopsided** ADJECTIVE
*a tractor pulling a lopsided load*
▶ uneven, unbalanced, tilting, askew, asymmetrical, crooked, (more informal) cock-eyed

**lord** NOUN
1 *the lord of the manor*
▶ master, overlord, leader, chief, prince
2 *He has been made a lord.*
▶ peer, noble, baron, earl, duke

**lordly** ADJECTIVE
1 *lordly titles*
▶ noble, aristocratic, princely, courtly
2 *He spoke in a lordly manner.*
▶ haughty, imperious, disdainful, condescending, domineering, overbearing, high-handed

**lose** VERB
1 *I've lost my passport.*
▶ mislay, misplace, lose track of, forget
AN OPPOSITE IS find
2 *We've already lost a lot of time. They lost money on the deal.*
▶ waste, use up, squander, dissipate, forfeit, exhaust
OPPOSITES ARE gain, make
3 *The home side lost 3-0.*
▶ be beaten, be defeated, fail, suffer defeat
AN OPPOSITE IS win

## loser NOUN

1 *There are many losers and few winners in this game.*
▶ runner-up
AN OPPOSITE IS winner

2 (*informal*) *He's a complete loser.*
▶ failure, non-achiever, nobody, (*informal*) no-hoper

## loss NOUN

1 *The loss of all his money ruined the holiday.*
▶ losing, theft, deprivation, disappearance

2 *The loss of her husband devastated her.*
▶ death, demise, passing, decease

3 *The company faced a huge loss.*
▶ deficit, debit, debt, lack of profit

4 *Loss of the game was a major blow.*
▶ defeat (in), failure (in), forfeiture

5 *The army suffered heavy losses.*
▶ casualty, fatality, mortality, victim

## lost ADJECTIVE

1 *The lost keys never turned up.*
▶ missing, mislaid, misplaced, vanished

2 *I became lost in the complications of the plot.*
▶ confused, baffled, bewildered, perplexed

3 *many lost opportunities*
▶ missed, neglected, wasted, squandered

4 *She appeared to be lost in thought.*
▶ absorbed, engrossed, preoccupied

## lot NOUN

1 *a lot of* or *lots of She has a lot of friends. We need lots of money.*
▶ many, plenty of, a large amount or number of, a great deal of

2 *On Monday a new lot of tourists arrives.*
▶ set, collection, group, batch, crowd

3 *He was not at all happy with his lot.*
▶ fate, destiny, fortune, future

4 *The money was divided into three lots.*
▶ share, portion, allocation, quota

## lottery NOUN

*She won a thousand pounds in a lottery.*
▶ draw, raffle, sweepstake, sweep, gamble

## loud ADJECTIVE

1 *loud music*
▶ noisy, blaring, deafening, booming, thunderous
AN OPPOSITE IS quiet

2 *loud colours*
▶ gaudy, garish, bold, lurid, flashy, showy
AN OPPOSITE IS subdued

## lounge VERB

*Miranda lounged on the sofa all morning.*
▶ laze, loll, recline, relax, sprawl, slump, slouch, luxuriate, idle, waste time

## lounge NOUN

*We will have our drinks in the lounge.*
▶ living room, sitting room, drawing room, day room

## lousy ADJECTIVE

(*informal*) *He had been a lousy father.*
▶ awful, terrible, dreadful, atrocious, appalling, frightful, poor, bad
OPPOSITES ARE wonderful, lovely

## lout NOUN

*a group of drunken louts*
▶ hooligan, hoodlum, ruffian, (*more informal*) yob

## loutish ADJECTIVE

*loutish behaviour*
▶ uncouth, rude, ill-mannered, coarse, crude, vulgar, (*more informal*) yobbish

## lovable ADJECTIVE

*a lovable little kitten*
▶ adorable, dear, sweet, charming, appealing, likeable, attractive, cuddly, enchanting, endearing, engaging, lovely, pleasing, taking, winning
AN OPPOSITE IS hateful

## love VERB

1 *She told him she loved him.*
▶ care for, feel deeply for, adore, cherish, hold dear, treasure
OPPOSITES ARE hate, loathe, detest

2 *We all love the holidays.*
▶ like, like very much, enjoy, take pleasure in, appreciate, desire, look forward to, (*more informal*) fancy
AN OPPOSITE IS dislike

## love NOUN

1 *He gave her flowers to show his love.*
▶ fondness, affection, adoration, devotion, admiration, ardour, desire, friendship, infatuation, liking, passion

2 *Emma was his true love.*
▶ beloved, loved one, darling, dear, dearest, lover
**in love with** *He had been in love with her all his life.*
▶ devoted to, enamoured with, fond of, infatuated with
RELATED ADJECTIVES amatory, erotic

## love affair NOUN

*a passionate love affair*
▶ relationship, romance, affair, liaison, intrigue, courtship

## loveless ADJECTIVE

*a loveless marriage*
▶ passionless, unloving, unfeeling, heartless, unresponsive, cold, frigid, undemonstrative
AN OPPOSITE IS loving

---

**lovely** ADJECTIVE This word is often overused. Here are some alternatives:
1 *a lovely young woman You look lovely.*
▶ beautiful, attractive, good-looking, exquisite, pretty, enchanting, charming, delightful, appealing
OPPOSITES ARE unattractive, hideous, ugly
2 *a lovely spring morning*
▶ pleasant, delightful, glorious, wonderful, fine
OPPOSITES ARE horrible, unpleasant

---

## lover NOUN
*There is a rumour that she has a secret lover.*
► admirer, sweetheart, boyfriend, girlfriend, man friend, lady friend

## loving ADJECTIVE
*He adored her loving nature*
► affectionate, tender, fond, friendly, kind, warm, amorous, ardent, demonstrative, devoted, doting, passionate
AN OPPOSITE IS loveless

## low ADJECTIVE
1 *a low wall*
► short, small, squat, shallow
AN OPPOSITE IS high
2 *Prices are now low.*
► reasonable, cheap, inexpensive
OPPOSITES ARE high, exorbitant
3 *Supplies were getting low.*
► sparse, scarce, meagre, inadequate, depleted, paltry
OPPOSITES ARE plentiful, abundant
4 *He was feeling low that day.*
► depressed, dispirited, downcast, unhappy
AN OPPOSITE IS happy
5 *a low trick*
► mean, base, despicable, shameful, contemptible
AN OPPOSITE IS admirable
6 *a low rumbling sound*
► muted, soft, deep
AN OPPOSITE IS loud

## lower VERB
1 *The soldier lowered the flag.*
► bring down, drop, let down, take down
OPPOSITES ARE raise, hoist
2 *a need to lower interest rates*
► reduce, decrease, bring down, lessen
OPPOSITES ARE raise, increase
3 *Did he have to lower himself in this way?*
► demean, degrade, humiliate, shame, discredit

## lowly ADJECTIVE
*He is just a lowly administrator.*
► modest, simple, humble, obscure, insignificant, meek, low

## loyal ADJECTIVE
*a loyal friend*
► faithful, true, devoted, steadfast, staunch, constant, dependable, reliable, sincere
AN OPPOSITE IS disloyal

## loyalty NOUN
*His first loyalty was to his family.*
► allegiance, faithfulness, fidelity, devotion, constancy, dependability, fealty, honesty, patriotism, reliability, staunchness, steadfastness, trustworthiness
AN OPPOSITE IS disloyalty

## lubricate VERB
*She went out to lubricate her cycle.*
► grease, oil

## lucid ADJECTIVE
*a lucid explanation of the problem*
► clear, intelligible, coherent, cogent, plain, simple

## luck NOUN
1 *They could not believe their luck.*
► good fortune, good luck, success
2 *She hopes her luck will change.*
► fate, fortune, lot, destiny
3 *It was luck that brought them here.*
► chance, accident, serendipity

## lucky ADJECTIVE
1 *a lucky chance   a lucky guess*
► fortunate, auspicious, providential, opportune, expedient, timely
2 *He is lucky to have such a good friend as you.*
► fortunate, blessed, favoured, advantaged

## lucrative ADJECTIVE
*a lucrative business*
► profitable, profit-making, productive, rewarding, gainful

## ludicrous ADJECTIVE
*a ludicrous suggestion*
► absurd, ridiculous, laughable, incredible, farcical, preposterous, risible, foolish, idiotic, (more informal) crazy, (more informal) daft, (more informal) barmy, (more informal) zany
OPPOSITES ARE reasonable, sensible

## lug VERB
*He lugged his old suitcase up the hill.*
► drag, pull, haul, carry, heave, hump

## luggage NOUN
*Trevor put his luggage on the rack.*
► bags, cases, baggage, things, paraphernalia, belongings

## lukewarm ADJECTIVE
1 *She pulled a face over her lukewarm tea.*
► tepid, warm
2 *a lukewarm response*
► unenthusiastic, indifferent, half-hearted, offhand, cool, apathetic

## lull NOUN
*a lull in the fighting*
► pause, respite, break, calm, gap, interval, rest, (more informal) let-up

## lull VERB
*The singing lulled her to sleep.*
► soothe, calm, subdue, hush, pacify, quell, quieten, tranquillize
AN OPPOSITE IS agitate

## lumber VERB
1 (informal) *We were lumbered with paying the bill.*
► saddle, burden, encumber, load
2 *Henry lumbered down the stairs.*
► shamble, trudge, tramp, plod, shuffle, blunder, move clumsily

## lumber NOUN
1 *cutting lumber in the forest*
► timber, wood

**luminous**

**2** *a loft full of lumber*
▶ jumble, clutter, junk, odds and ends, bits and pieces, rummage, rubbish, trash

**luminous** ADJECTIVE
*a luminous dial*
▶ glowing, luminescent, lustrous, radiant, bright, phosphorescent, shining

**lump** NOUN
**1** *a lump of bread*
▶ chunk, hunk, block, wedge, piece, portion, slab, wad
**2** *The blow left a lump on his head*
▶ swelling, bump, growth, protuberance

**lump** VERB
**lump together** *The newspaper reports lumped together several stories.*
▶ combine, amalgamate, merge, bunch
**lump it** (*informal*) *We're not going and we'll just have to lump it.*
▶ accept it, put up with it, tolerate it, endure it

**lunacy** NOUN
**1** *a scene of despair and lunacy*
▶ insanity, madness, mental disorder, mental illness, derangement, dementia
**2** *It would be lunacy to try a rescue in this weather.*
▶ folly, foolishness, stupidity, madness, insanity

**lunatic** NOUN
*a dangerous lunatic*
▶ maniac, madman, madwoman, (*more informal*) loony

**lunatic** ADJECTIVE
*a lunatic scheme*
▶ crazy, foolish, stupid, senseless, ludicrous, absurd, mad

**lunge** VERB
*The man lunged at him.*
▶ thrust, charge, pounce, rush, throw yourself, dash, dive, lurch

**lurch** VERB
*James lurched into the bathroom.*
▶ stagger, stumble, totter, reel, roll, list, lunge, sway, pitch, heave, lean, plunge, wallow

**lurch** NOUN
**leave in the lurch** *They felt they had been left completely in the lurch.*
▶ let down, desert, abandon, forsake

**lure** VERB
*Advertising can lure people into debt.*
▶ tempt, entice, allure, attract, induce, coax, seduce, draw, inveigle, invite, lead on, persuade

**lurid** ADJECTIVE
**1** *window blinds of lurid colours*
▶ garish, gaudy, flashy, loud, glaring, vulgar
OPPOSITES ARE sober, dull
**2** *The report included all the lurid details.*
▶ sensational, melodramatic, graphic, salacious, gruesome, macabre

**lurk** VERB
*men lurking in doorways*
▶ skulk, loiter, lie in wait, lie low, crouch, hide

**luscious** ADJECTIVE
*luscious fruit hanging from the trees*
▶ delicious, juicy, succulent, mouth-watering, appetizing

**lush** ADJECTIVE
**1** *lush vegetation*
▶ rich, luxuriant, abundant, profuse, exuberant, prolific, flourishing
**2** *a lush penthouse*
▶ luxurious, sumptuous, grand, opulent, lavish

**lust** NOUN
**1** *He watched her with obvious lust.*
▶ sexual desire, sexual longing, ardour, passion, lechery, licentiousness
**2** *a lust for power*
▶ greed, desire, craving, longing, hunger, appetite, itch

**luxurious** ADJECTIVE
*luxurious surroundings*
▶ sumptuous, grand, opulent, lavish, comfortable, lush, magnificent, plush, splendid
OPPOSITES ARE austere, simple, spartan

**luxury** NOUN
*They led a life of luxury.*
▶ opulence, sumptuousness, splendour, affluence, extravagance, comfort, ease, enjoyment, indulgence, pleasure, relaxation, self-indulgence, voluptuousness

**lying** ADJECTIVE
*He was just a lying schemer.*
▶ deceitful, dishonest, double-dealing, two-faced, false, untrustworthy, untruthful
AN OPPOSITE IS truthful

**lying** NOUN
*She was no good at lying, even to save her own skin.*
▶ falsehood, untruthfulness, deceit, dishonesty, mendacity, (*more formal*) perjury

**lyrical** ADJECTIVE
*a lyrical poem   a lyrical description*
▶ expressive, poetic, emotional, inspired, songlike, rhapsodic

# Mm

**macabre** ADJECTIVE
*the macabre business of the switched bodies*
▶ gruesome, grisly, grim, gory, morbid, eerie, weird, lurid, dreadful, horrible, ghoulish

**machine** NOUN
*The machine started to make a noise.*
▶ apparatus, contrivance, device, contraption, instrument, tool, gadget, mechanism
RELATED ADJECTIVE mechanical

**machinery** NOUN
1 *a factory equipped with modern machinery*
▶ equipment, machines, plant, instruments, hardware, gear
2 *the agreed machinery for resolving disputes*
▶ procedure, organization, structure, system, constitution, method

**macho** NOUN
*macho jobs like bricklaying*
▶ manly, male, masculine, virile, (*more informal*) butch, (*more informal*) laddish

**mad** ADJECTIVE
1 *He thought he was going mad.*
▶ insane, mentally ill, deranged, demented, crazy, (*more informal*) out of your mind, (*more informal*) off your head, (*more informal*) potty, (*more informal*) nutty, (*more informal*) nuts
2 *It was a mad idea but they liked it.*
▶ foolish, crazy, insane, absurd, senseless, wild, preposterous
3 (*informal*) *Is she still mad with you for ditching her?*
▶ angry, cross, furious, enraged, infuriated, irate
4 *mad about* (*informal*) *Jenny is mad about jazz.*
▶ keen on, crazy about, enthusiastic about, eager for, devoted to, addicted to

**madden** VERB
*It's their pretence that maddens me most.*
▶ infuriate, exasperate, anger, enrage, incense, annoying, craze, irritate, vex, provoke

**maddening** ADJECTIVE
*The traffic moved with maddening slowness.*
▶ infuriating, exasperating, irritating, annoying, vexing, irksome

**madness** NOUN
1 *There was a gleam of madness in his eyes.*
▶ insanity, dementia, lunacy, delirium, frenzy, hysteria, derangement, eccentricity, mania, mental illness, psychosis
2 *It is madness to let children roam about after dark.*
▶ foolishness, folly, stupidity, insanity, lunacy

**magazine** NOUN
1 *a pile of magazines on the dining-room table*
▶ journal, periodical, colour supplement, weekly, monthly, comic
2 *a magazine of weapons*
▶ arsenal, ammunition dump, storehouse, depot

**magic** NOUN
1 *It was so real it had to be magic.*
▶ sorcery, wizardry, witchcraft, devilry, the black arts, the supernatural
2 *No children's party is complete without the magic.*
▶ conjuring, conjuring tricks, illusion, sleight of hand, (*technical*) prestidigitation

3 *The place had lost none of its magic.*
▶ charm, fascination, appeal, allure, glamour

**magic** ADJECTIVE
*a magic spell*
▶ supernatural, magical, miraculous

**magical** ADJECTIVE
*They would remember this magical day for the rest of their lives.*
▶ wonderful, marvellous, extraordinary, delightful, enchanting

**magician** NOUN
*A magician would finish off the day's entertainment.*
▶ conjuror, entertainer, illusionist, wizard, sorcerer

**magnanimous** ADJECTIVE
*With luck on her side Dora could afford to be magnanimous.*
▶ generous, bountiful, beneficent, liberal, unstinting

**magnate** NOUN
*an oil magnate*
▶ industrialist, tycoon, mogul, baron, businessman, captain of industry

**magnetic** ADJECTIVE
*her magnetic personality*
▶ attractive, fascinating, captivating, alluring, charming, appealing, charismatic, seductive, compelling, hypnotic, irresistible
AN OPPOSITE IS repulsive

**magnetism** NOUN
*the sheer magnetism of her personality*
▶ attraction, charm, appeal, fascination, allure, charisma, seductiveness, lure, power

**magnificent** ADJECTIVE
1 *a magnificent view*
▶ spectacular, splendid, impressive, imposing, noble, glorious, gorgeous, sumptuous
2 *a magnificent achievement*
▶ brilliant, masterly, superb, marvellous, wonderful, very fine

**magnify** VERB
1 *The device magnifies the image.*
▶ enlarge, maximize, amplify, make larger, augment, expand, increase, intensify, (*more informal*) blow up
AN OPPOSITE IS reduce
2 (*informal*) *It is easy to magnify the difficulties involved.*
▶ exaggerate, inflate, maximize, overdo, overestimate, overstate, make too much of, blow up out of all proportion, dramatize
AN OPPOSITE IS minimize

**magnitude** NOUN
1 *They realized the magnitude of the task.*
▶ size, immensity, vastness, hugeness, extent, enormousness
2 *events of tragic magnitude*
▶ importance, significance, consequence, import, moment

**maid** NOUN
*A maid cleared the room.*
▶ servant, serving girl, maidservant, domestic

**maiden** NOUN
*a young maiden*
▶ girl, lass, (*literary*) damsel

**mail** NOUN
*The letter came with the morning mail.*
▶ post, letters, delivery, packages, packets, parcels, correspondence

**mail** VERB
*I'll mail you the package tomorrow.*
▶ post, send, dispatch, forward

**maim** VERB
*Many people were killed or maimed in the attack.*
▶ injure, disable, mutilate, wound , disfigure, cripple, handicap

**main** ADJECTIVE
*These are the main issues.*
▶ chief, principal, primary, prime, most important, overriding, foremost, fundamental, key, crucial, central, paramount, predominant, basic, essential

**mainly** ADVERB
*The staff are mainly trainees.*
▶ chiefly, primarily, principally, mostly, predominantly, especially, essentially

**maintain** VERB
1 *The villagers pay to maintain the private road.*
▶ keep up, preserve, service, look after, take care of
2 *We need to maintain our links with industry.*
▶ sustain, continue, keep up, conserve, retain, preserve, prolong
3 *They maintain that they were never there.*
▶ assert, claim, affirm, insist, make out, declare, contend, argue

**maintenance** NOUN
1 *The buildings need a good deal of regular maintenance.*
▶ upkeep, repairs, preservation, care, servicing, conservation, looking after
2 *Absent fathers have to pay maintenance.*
▶ financial support, subsistence, alimony, allowance

**majestic** ADJECTIVE
*a majestic range of mountains*
▶ magnificent, grand, spectacular, splendid, impressive, imposing, noble, glorious, gorgeous, sumptuous

**majesty** NOUN
1 *The procession continued with great majesty.*
▶ dignity, stateliness, solemnity, glory, splendour, grandeur, nobility
2 *the Queen's majesty*
▶ sovereignty, royalty, dominion, authority

**major** ADJECTIVE
*a major achievement*
▶ important, considerable, significant, noteworthy, substantial, sizeable, appreciable

**majority** NOUN
1 *The majority of older people are poor.*
▶ greater number, preponderance, bulk
2 *the age of majority*
▶ adulthood, coming of age, manhood, maturity, womanhood
AN OPPOSITE IS minority

**be in the majority**
▶ predominate, preponderate, be greater, dominate, outnumber, prevail

**make** VERB
1 *He makes reproduction furniture.*
▶ build, construct, assemble, put together, manufacture, produce
2 *She made me tell her the whole story.*
▶ force, coerce, oblige, compel, prevail on, pressure, urge

**USAGE** You need to use the word *to* after all these synonyms, e.g. *She forced me to tell her the whole story.* If you use *prevail* you have to say *She prevailed on me to tell her the whole story.*

3 *The animals make such a noise.*
▶ cause, create, generate, engender, give rise to
4 *She made a little bow.*
▶ perform, execute, give, do, effect, carry out
5 *The town made him their mayor.*
▶ appoint, name, designate, nominate, elect, vote
6 *We seem to have made some mistakes.*
▶ commit, perpetrate, be responsible for, be guilty of
7 *The scheme is bound to make money.*
▶ earn, bring in, gain, acquire
AN OPPOSITE IS lose
8 *James's mother went out to make the lunch.*
▶ prepare, get ready, cook, put together, concoct
9 *I make the total over £500.*
▶ estimate, calculate, work out

**USAGE** You need to use the word *at* after all these synonyms, e.g. *I estimate the total at over £500.*

10 *We must make a decision.*
▶ reach, come to, arrive at, settle on
11 *I think she'll make a good leader.*
▶ be, constitute, act as, serve as

**make off** *The thieves made off with the money.*
▶ escape, run off, get away, leave, bolt, (*more informal*) clear off

**make out**
1 *We could make out a tower in the distance.*
▶ see, discern, distinguish, perceive, detect, recognize, catch sight of, glimpse
2 *They made out we owed them money.*
▶ maintain, assert, claim, affirm, insist, declare, contend, argue
3 *How did you make out at the interview?*
▶ manage, get on, get along, do, cope, (*more formal*) fare

**4** *The old man had made out a will.*
► draw up, write, complete

**make up**

**1** *Such a story is not something anyone could make up.*
► invent, fabricate, contrive, concoct, think up, devise, create, (*more informal*) cook up

**2** *They decided to kiss and make up.*
► be friends again, make peace, settle your differences, bury the hatchet, mend fences
AN OPPOSITE IS quarrel

**make up for** *The fine acting made up for all the problems with the production.*
► compensate for, offset, counterbalance, counteract, make amends for, redress

**make** NOUN
*a new make of car*
► brand, marque, model, sort, kind, type, variety

**make-believe** NOUN
*The secret garden was only make-believe.*
► fantasy, pretence, fiction, fancy, illusion, invention, imagination
AN OPPOSITE IS reality

**make-believe** ADJECTIVE
*a make-believe world of elves and fairies*
► imaginary, fanciful, pretended, sham, simulated, unreal, feigned, made-up, mock, (*more informal*) pretend
AN OPPOSITE IS real

**maker** NOUN
*a maker of toy cars*
► manufacturer, producer, creator, designer, originator, constructor, builder

**makeshift** ADJECTIVE
*He arranged a row of chairs to form a makeshift bed.*
► temporary, standby, rough-and-ready, improvised, stopgap, pernicious, hurtful

**make-up** NOUN
**1** *Ambition is an important part of his make-up.*
► character, nature, temperament, constitution, disposition

**1** *Her make-up started to run.*
► cosmetics, powder, paint

**male** ADJECTIVE
*male characteristics*
► masculine, manly, virile

**malevolent** ADJECTIVE
*the malevolent gaze of his eyes*
► malicious, hostile, spiteful, baleful, malign, vindictive, malignant, pernicious, hurtful, offensive, venomous

**malice** NOUN
*actions prompted by malice*
► malevolence, ill will, spite, spitefulness, animosity

**malicious** ADJECTIVE
*malicious remarks*
► malevolent, hostile, spiteful, baleful, malign, vindictive, malignant, mischievous, pernicious, offensive, hurtful, venomous
OPPOSITES ARE benevolent, kind

**malign** ADJECTIVE
*a malign influence*
► harmful, malevolent, hostile, spiteful, baleful, vindictive, malignant, pernicious, offensive, hurtful, venomous
OPPOSITES ARE benevolent, kind

**malign** VERB
*She accused them of maligning her.*
► defame, vilify, disparage, smear, slander, libel

**malignant** ADJECTIVE
**1** *a malignant disease*
► fatal, incurable, terminal, virulent, destructive
**2** *a malignant growth*
► cancerous, poisonous, non-benign, spreading
AN OPPOSITE IS benign
**3** *a malignant stare*
► malevolent, hostile, spiteful, baleful, malign, pernicious, offensive, hurtful, venomous
OPPOSITES ARE benevolent, kind

**malinger** VERB
*We do all the work while Charlie goes on malingering.*
► shirk, sham, (*more informal*) skive, (*more informal*) swing the lead

**malleable** ADJECTIVE
*a malleable substance*
► soft, pliable, tractable, workable, ductile, plastic
AN OPPOSITE IS brittle

**malnutrition** NOUN
*a country blighted by poverty and malnutrition*
► hunger, starvation, under-nourishment, famine

**malpractice** NOUN
*a lawyer accused of malpractice*
► misconduct, wrongdoing, impropriety, dereliction of duty, negligence

**maltreat** VERB
*He was a bully and often maltreated his wife.*
► ill-treat, mistreat, abuse, misuse, harm, injure, molest, (*more informal*) knock about

**mammoth** ADJECTIVE
*It would be a mammoth task getting the house to rights again.*
► huge, enormous, gigantic, immense, massive, colossal, vast, large, big, giant, (*more informal*) whopping, (*more informal*) ginormous
AN OPPOSITE IS tiny

**man** NOUN
**1** *a man in a smart suit*
► male, gentleman, fellow, (*more informal*) chap, (*more informal*) bloke
**2** *All men are fallible.*
► person, individual, human being

**3** *the evolution of modern man*
▶ humanity, humankind, mankind, the human race, humans, Homo sapiens
**4** *The men have gone on strike.*
▶ worker, employee
RELATED ADJECTIVES male, masculine

## man VERB
*We need to man the reception desk from 8 till 5.*
▶ staff, provide personnel for, provide staff for, occupy

## manage VERB
**1** *She manages a team of 20.*
▶ be in charge of, run, head, lead, supervise, oversee, control
**2** *a course in managing money*
▶ organize, administer, deal with, regulate
**3** *I could only just manage the extra work I had to do.*
▶ undertake, accomplish, achieve, finish, complete, carry out
**4** *I don't know how we'll manage without her.*
▶ cope, get along, survive, fare, make do
**5** *a horse that's difficult to manage*
▶ control, handle, master, cope with, deal with

## manageable ADJECTIVE
**1** *a manageable task*
▶ achievable, doable, practicable, feasible, reasonable, attainable, viable
AN OPPOSITE IS awkward
**2** *a manageable horse*
▶ controllable, obedient, tractable, compliant, amenable, disciplined, docile
OPPOSITES ARE unmanageable, disobedient

## management NOUN
**1** *The local cinema is under new management.*
▶ administration, control, direction, supervision, charge, care
**2** *The union is in dispute with the management.*
▶ managers, employers, directors, proprietors, executives

## manager NOUN
*a meeting of departmental managers*
▶ director, administrator, head, executive, supervisor, principal, controller, boss, chief

## mandate NOUN
*The government claims it has an election mandate for these measures.*
▶ authority, authorization, approval, endorsement, sanction

## mandatory ADJECTIVE
*a mandatory UN resolution*
▶ compulsory, obligatory, binding, required

## mangle VERB
*Henry was staring at the man's mangled hand.*
▶ maul, mutilate, maim, crush, damage, disfigure, injure, wound, lacerate, squash, tear

## mangy ADJECTIVE
**1** *a mangy dog*
▶ dirty, unkempt, scabby

**2** *a mangy old sofa*
▶ scruffy, shabby, worn, moth-eaten, shoddy, (*more informal*) tatty

## manhandle VERB
**1** *The gun crews manhandled the weapons into position.*
▶ heave, haul, shove, push, manoeuvre
**2** *We were spat on, sworn at, and manhandled.*
▶ maltreat, mistreat, maul, abuse, (*more informal*) knock about

## mania NOUN
*a mania for old cars*
▶ obsession, passion, enthusiasm, fad, craze, infatuation (with), preoccupation (with)

## maniac NOUN
*a homicidal maniac*
▶ lunatic, madman or madwoman, psychopath, (*more informal*) loony

## manifest ADJECTIVE
*a manifest error*
▶ clear, obvious, plain, apparent, patent, unmistakable

## manifesto NOUN
*a political manifesto*
▶ statement, programme, declaration, policy

## manipulate VERB
**1** *You need to know how to manipulate all the machine's knobs and levers.*
▶ operate, work, wield, control, negotiate, twiddle
**2** *Governments try to manipulate the economy before elections.*
▶ influence, control, exploit
**3** *It is not difficult to manipulate the data to get the result you want.*
▶ alter, distort, falsify, doctor, massage, tinker with, fiddle with, fudge, rig, (*more informal*) cook

## mankind NOUN
*They want to save nature from mankind.*
▶ humanity, humankind, the human race, humans, man, Homo sapiens

## manly ADJECTIVE
**1** *a manly physique*
▶ virile, masculine, muscular, sturdy, robust, well-built
**2** *manly deeds*
▶ brave, courageous, bold, heroic, valiant, gallant, chivalrous

## man-made ADJECTIVE
*a man-made fibre*
▶ synthetic, artificial, manufactured, simulated, imitation
AN OPPOSITE IS natural

## manner NOUN
**1** *They dealt with the problem in a very efficient manner.*
▶ way, fashion, style, method, means, procedure, process, mode

**2** *I don't much like his unfriendly manner.*
► attitude, demeanour, disposition, air, look, bearing, behaviour, character, conduct, mien
**3** *We've seen all manner of things there.*
► kind, sort, type, variety, category, class
**4 manners** *He needs to learn some manners.*
► politeness, refinement, civility, courtesy, etiquette, good behaviour, good conduct, breeding, gentility

**mannerism** NOUN
*He has the annoying mannerism of impatiently snapping his fingers.*
► peculiarity, idiosyncrasy, quirk, trait, oddity, habit, characteristic

**manoeuvre** NOUN
**1** *She parked the car with a deft manoeuvre.*
► movement, move, action, operation
**2** *a diplomatic manoeuvre*
► stratagem, strategy, tactic, move, plan, plot, ploy, ruse, dodge, gambit, trick
**3** *military manoeuvres*
► exercise, movement, operation, training

**manoeuvre** VERB
*He manoeuvred the trunk down the stairs.*
► manipulate, negotiate, move, engineer, guide, navigate, pilot, steer

**manual** ADJECTIVE
*manual work*
► labouring, physical, by hand

**manual** NOUN
*a training manual*
► handbook, guide, guidebook, reference book

**manufacture** VERB
*The country could manufacture a nuclear weapon within five years.*
► make, construct, create, build, prefabricate, assemble, fabricate, mass-produce, process, (*informal*) turn out

**manufacturer** NOUN
*a manufacturer of cosmetics*
► maker, producer, creator

**many** ADJECTIVE
*There are many reasons.*
► a lot of, plenty of, numerous, countless, various, copious, profuse, innumerable, umpteen, (*more informal*) lots of
AN OPPOSITE IS few

**map** NOUN
*a map of Europe*
► chart, diagram, plan
RELATED ADJECTIVE cartographic
RELATED NOUN cartography

**map** VERB
*Aircraft were used to map the region.*
► chart, survey
**map out** *We mapped out a plan.*
► outline, set out, formulate, detail

**mar** VERB
*His good looks were marred by stubble and red eyes.*
► spoil, impair, disfigure, ruin, deface, detract from, tarnish

**marauder** NOUN
*An array of jagged glass kept out marauders.*
► bandit, brigand, raider, robber, buccaneer, pirate, plunderer, invader

**march** VERB
*A company of soldiers marched past.*
► file, troop, parade, stride, pace, walk

**march** NOUN
**1** *a three-day march*
► trek, hike, tramp, slog
**2** *a protest march*
► procession, rally, demonstration, parade, (*more informal*) demo
**3** *the march of time*
► advance, progress, progression, passage, evolution

**margin** NOUN
**1** *the margin of the lake*
► edge, border, boundary, verge, perimeter, side
**2** *They won by a narrow margin.*
► difference, gap, surplus

**marginal** ADJECTIVE
*The extra cost is marginal.*
► negligible, minimal, insignificant, unimportant, minimal, borderline
OPPOSITES ARE significant, important

**mark** NOUN
**1** *a dirty mark*
► spot, stain, blot, blotch, smudge, blemish
**2** *a mark of respect*
► sign, token, symbol, indication, proof, evidence, gesture
**3** *Donations have passed the million mark.*
► stage, point, level
**4** *a comment that hit the mark*
► target, objective, purpose, aim
**5** *He got a better mark for French than for German.*
► grade, grading, score, assessment, evaluation

**mark** VERB
**1** *She took great care not to mark her white dress.*
► stain, blemish, smudge, dirty, discolour, blot
**2** *All possessions should be clearly marked.*
► label, tag
**3** *The capture of the rebel stronghold marked a new stage in the war.*
► represent, signify, herald, denote, identify, characterize
**4** *a festival to mark the Golden Jubilee*
► celebrate, recognize, observe, commemorate, remember
**5** *Mark my words carefully.*
► heed, note, mind, take notice of, listen to, regard
**6** *She had exam papers to mark that evening.*
► assess, grade, correct, evaluate, appraise

## marked ADJECTIVE

*a marked improvement in health*
▶ distinct, noticeable, decided, pronounced, plain, clear, emphatic, palpable
AN OPPOSITE IS slight

## market NOUN

**1** *The local market is every Saturday.*
▶ bazaar, fair, sale, marketplace

**2** *The market for second-hand cars is thriving.*
▶ demand, call, need, requirement

## market VERB

*The firm markets reproduction furniture*
▶ sell, trade in, merchandise, retail

## maroon VERB

*a story about a group of boys marooned on a desert island*
▶ strand, cast away, abandon, isolate, leave, desert, forsake

## marriage NOUN

**1** *The couple will celebrate their 50 years of marriage.*
▶ matrimony, wedlock, partnership, union

**2** *The marriage took place in the local register office.*
▶ wedding, wedding ceremony, match, nuptials
RELATED ADJECTIVES conjugal, marital, matrimonial, nuptial

## marry VERB

**1** *They never married.*
▶ get married, wed, (*more informal*) tie the knot
OPPOSITES ARE separate, divorce

**2** *He married Jessica in Italy.*
▶ wed, (*more informal*) get hitched to
OPPOSITES ARE separate from, divorce

**3** *The exhibition marries information with entertainment.*
▶ combine, unite, link, merge, connect, join, ally

## marsh NOUN

*The car had plunged into a marsh.*
▶ swamp, bog, marshland, wetland, mire, morass, quagmire, quicksands, fen, slough, mudflats, saltmarsh, saltings

## marshal VERB

*The king marshalled a huge army. The police marshalled their evidence with great care.*
▶ gather, assemble, collect, organize, muster, set out, deploy, draw up, group, line up, arrange
OPPOSITES ARE disperse, scatter

## martial ADJECTIVE

**1** *martial law*
▶ military
AN OPPOSITE IS civil

**2** *a martial nation*
▶ warlike, bellicose, militant, aggressive, belligerent, pugnacious
AN OPPOSITE IS peaceable

**3** *martial exploits*
▶ military, soldierly, valiant, brave, courageous

## marvel VERB

**marvel at** *Everyone marvelled at their courage.*
▶ admire, be amazed by, wonder at, applaud, praise, appreciate, respect, be astonished by, be surprised by

## marvel NOUN

*a marvel of precision engineering*
▶ miracle, wonder, sensation, phenomenon

## marvellous ADJECTIVE

**1** *a marvellous achievement*
▶ remarkable, amazing, extraordinary, wonderful, magnificent, astonishing, astounding
AN OPPOSITE IS ordinary

**2** *We had a marvellous time*
▶ excellent, wonderful, fantastic, splendid, lovely, delightful, smashing, (*more informal*) terrific
OPPOSITES ARE awful, dreadful

## masculine ADJECTIVE

**1** *She wore a masculine shirt with rolled-up sleeves.*
▶ male, man's or men's, manlike
AN OPPOSITE IS feminine

**2** *a powerfully masculine man*
▶ manly, virile, muscular, well-built, strapping, vigorous
OPPOSITES ARE weak, timid

## mash VERB

*Mash the potatoes and put them on top.*
▶ crush, pulp, cream, purée, pulverize, pound, smash, squash, grind, mangle, beat

## mask NOUN

*They wore masks to hide their faces.*
▶ disguise, veil, camouflage, cover, screen, shield, façade

## mask VERB

*A row of trees masked the view.*
▶ conceal, cover, obscure, screen, shield, hide, shroud, veil, blot out, camouflage, cloak, disguise

## mass NOUN

**1** *a mass of wet leaves*
▶ pile, heap, load, accumulation, collection, conglomeration

**2** *a mass of cars heading for the coast*
▶ multitude, throng, crowd, troop, mob, quantity, large number

**3** *The mass of people declined to vote at all.*
▶ majority, greater part, bulk, body

**4** *an object having a large mass*
▶ weight, size, magnitude, bulk

## mass ADJECTIVE

*a mass protest*
▶ wholesale, universal, large-scale, widespread, comprehensive, general, popular
AN OPPOSITE IS small-scale

## mass VERB

*Spectators massed under the trees during the downpour.*
▶ gather, assemble, collect, flock

**massacre** NOUN
*the massacre of innocent civilians*
▶ slaughter, killing, mass murder, extermination, butchery, carnage, annihilation

**massacre** VERB
*The army massacred most of the population.*
▶ slaughter, butcher, exterminate, annihilate, murder, liquidate, eliminate

**massive** ADJECTIVE
*a massive building  massive debts*
▶ huge, enormous, gigantic, immense, colossal, vast, large, big, giant, (*more informal*) whopping, (*more informal*) ginormous
AN OPPOSITE IS tiny

**mast** NOUN
1 *a tall mast*
▶ flagpole, maypole, aerial, pylon, transmitter
2 *a ship's mast*
▶ spar, boom, yard

**master** NOUN
1 *He became master of the country after a bloody coup.*
▶ ruler, chief, head, lord, overlord, governor
2 *a dog's master*
▶ owner, keeper
3 *a master of disguises*
▶ expert (at), genius, past master, maestro, virtuoso

**master** VERB
1 *He managed to master his feelings.*
▶ control, restrain, check, contain, curb, confine, keep in check, repress, subdue, suppress
2 *She mastered the language after a few months.*
▶ learn, grasp, acquire, be expert in, (*more informal*) get the hang of

**masterful** ADJECTIVE
USAGE Do not confuse this word with *masterly*, which has a different meaning.
*the most masterful sovereign in English history*
▶ authoritative, commanding, powerful, domineering, overbearing, arrogant, dictatorial, tyrannical, bossy

**masterly** ADJECTIVE
USAGE Do not confuse this word with *masterful*, which has a different meaning.
*a masterly survey of the subject*
▶ expert, skilful, adept, adroit, accomplished, consummate, intelligent, fine

**mastermind** NOUN
*the mastermind behind the robbery*
▶ originator, planner, creator, engineer, prime mover, architect, inventor, manager, (*more informal*) brain, (*more informal*) brains

**mastermind** VERB
*They brought him back to mastermind the new operation.*
▶ control, direct, plan, organize, coordinate, conduct, supervise, carry through

**masterpiece** NOUN
*The portrait is the artist's masterpiece.*
▶ masterwork, finest work, (*Latin*) magnum opus, (*French*) chef-d'oeuvre

**mastery** NOUN
1 *a mastery of languages*
▶ command, knowledge, grasp, comprehension, understanding, proficiency (in)
2 *work done with great mastery*
▶ proficiency, capability, expertness, skill, adroitness, dexterity

**match** NOUN
1 *a cricket match*
▶ game, contest, competition, fixture, test match, tie, tournament
2 *The dress and shoes are a good match.*
▶ combination, pair
3 *She found a match for the tall vase.*
▶ copy, replica, complement, counterpart, duplicate, twin
4 *The enemy tanks were no match for ours in speed and range.*
▶ equal, rival, equivalent, counterpart
5 *a love match*
▶ marriage, union, friendship, partnership, relationship, alliance

**match** VERB
1 *The hat matches her dress.*
▶ go with, suit, harmonize with, tone with, blend with, complement
AN OPPOSITE IS
2 *The two versions of the story don't match.*
▶ agree, correspond, tally
3 *No one can match him at Scrabble.*
▶ equal, rival, compete with

**matching** ADJECTIVE
*The curtains have a matching duvet cover.*
▶ corresponding, coordinating, equivalent, harmonizing, toning, complementing
AN OPPOSITE IS incongruous

**matchless** ADJECTIVE
*her matchless beauty*
▶ incomparable, unequalled, inimitable, unmatched, unrivalled, peerless, unique

**mate** NOUN
1 *a plumber's mate*
▶ assistant, helper, apprentice, colleague
2 *He went to see a film with his mates.*
▶ friend, pal, chum, companion
3 *He's still looking for his ideal mate.*
▶ partner, wife or husband, spouse, lover, consort

**mate** VERB
*The zoo is trying to get the pandas to mate.*
▶ breed, copulate, couple

**material** NOUN
1 *material for making curtains*
▶ fabric, cloth, textile, stuff

**2** *organic material*
▶ matter, substance, stuff

**3** *We are collecting material for an article on surfing.*
▶ data, information, facts, statistics, evidence, particulars

**material** ADJECTIVE

**1** *The material world as distinct from the spiritual world*
▶ physical, corporeal, tangible, earthly, concrete
OPPOSITES ARE spiritual, abstract

**2** *information that is material to our enquiries*
▶ relevant, pertinent, applicable, germane
OPPOSITES ARE irrelevant, immaterial

**materialize** VERB

**1** *A vague form materialized at the end of the path.*
▶ appear, take shape, form, loom, arise
AN OPPOSITE IS disappear

**2** *The expected deliveries had not in fact materialized.*
▶ happen, occur, come about, take place

**matter** NOUN

**1** *Excess vegetable matter can be kept in a separate waste bin.*
▶ material, substance, stuff

**2** *The last sentence of his statement goes to the heart of the matter.*
▶ affair, business, subject, topic, issue, concern

**3** *It's of little matter now.*
▶ importance, consequence, significance, moment

**matter** VERB

*Does it matter what I wear?*
▶ make a difference, be important, count, signify

**matter-of-fact** ADJECTIVE

*(informal) He described the place in a very matter-of-fact way.*
▶ deadpan, down-to-earth, factual, mechanical, prosaic, unemotional, unimaginative, to the point, unadorned
OPPOSITES ARE emotional, imaginative

**mature** ADJECTIVE

**1** *a mature woman*
▶ adult, grown-up, grown, full-grown, advanced, well-developed
OPPOSITES ARE immature, adolescent

**2** *He seems very mature for his age.*
▶ responsible, sensible, dependable, reliable
OPPOSITES ARE immature, childish

**3** *mature cheese  mature fruit*
▶ mellow, ready, ripened, seasoned
AN OPPOSITE IS unripe

**mature** VERB

**1** *Bella had matured into a beautiful young woman.*
▶ grow, grow up, develop, blossom

**2** *Their friendship matured rapidly.*
▶ develop, grow, blossom, bloom, flourish, thrive

**maul** VERB

**1** *He pulled me to the ground and started mauling me on my back and neck.*
▶ savage, attack, claw, manhandle, molest, maltreat, ill-treat, mutilate, lacerate

**2** *The new production was mauled by the critics.*
▶ criticize, attack, savage, pillory, lambaste, (*more informal*) hammer, (*more informal*) slam

**maximum** ADJECTIVE

*a maximum speed of 80 kph*
▶ greatest, highest, top, full, utmost, extreme, fullest, largest, most, biggest, supreme
AN OPPOSITE IS minimum

**maximum** NOUN

*Production has reached its maximum.*
▶ upper limit, limit, peak, ceiling, highest point, pinnacle, top level
AN OPPOSITE IS minimum

**mayhem** NOUN

*I decided I'd caused enough mayhem for one day.*
▶ confusion, chaos, disorder, muddle, bedlam, pandemonium, anarchy, disorganization, lawlessness, shambles, tumult
AN OPPOSITE IS order

**maze** NOUN

*a maze of rooms and corridors*
▶ labyrinth, warren, network, web, tangle, confusion

**meadow** NOUN

*sheep grazing in a meadow*
▶ field, paddock, pasture, (*poetic*) mead, (*poetic*) lea

**meagre** ADJECTIVE

**1** *He had a few coins in his pocket, his meagre earnings for the day.*
▶ paltry, scanty, scant, sparse, negligible, pitiful, miserable, modest, (*more informal*) mingy, (*more informal*) measly
OPPOSITES ARE plentiful, abundant

**2** *a tall, meagre youth*
▶ thin, lean, skinny, scrawny, scraggy, lanky

---

**meal** NOUN

*A meal would be waiting for them when they got home.*
▶ bite to eat, (*literary*) repast, (*more informal*) spread, (*more informal*) feed
RELATED ADJECTIVE prandial

SOME WORDS FOR MEALS

**main meals:** breakfast, continental breakfast, lunch ((*more formal*) luncheon), tea, high tea, dinner.

**large or grand meals:** banquet, dinner party, feast; (*more informal*) blowout, beanfeast.

**outdoor meals:** picnic, barbecue.

**light or informal meals:** snack, elevenses, brunch (combined breakfast and lunch), buffet, supper, fork supper, takeaway, TV dinner.

---

**mean** ADJECTIVE

**1** *He was too mean to leave a tip.*
▶ miserly, niggardly, stingy, parsimonious, (*more informal*) mingy, (*more informal*) tight-fisted, (*more informal*) penny-pinching

**2** *It was mean of them to leave her like that.*
► unkind, nasty, shameful, unpleasant, callous, cruel, spiteful

**3** *His room was a cold mean affair.*
► squalid, shabby, wretched, dismal, humble, lowly

### mean VERB

**1** *The sign means you have to stop.*
► indicate, signify, denote, convey, show

**2** *What do you think they mean by these remarks?*
► intend, suggest, imply

**3** *I mean to find him come what may.*
► intend, plan, aim, want, wish, propose, purpose, aspire

**4** *Her promotion meant a lot more travel.*
► involve, entail, necessitate, lead to, result in

**5** *Your help means a lot to me.*
► matter, be important, have importance

### meander VERB

*A group of tourists meandered across the square.*
► wander, stroll, ramble, amble, roam, saunter

### meaning NOUN

**1** *I didn't understand the meaning of her remarks.*
► significance, sense, import, implication, force, thrust, connotation

**2** *Some words have several meanings.*
► sense, definition, denotation, explanation

**3** *Life has little meaning for them now.*
► value, worth, point, purpose, significance

### meaningful ADJECTIVE

*meaningful remarks*
► expressive, significant, relevant, consequential, pointed, suggestive, meaning
AN OPPOSITE IS meaningless

### meaningless ADJECTIVE

**1** *a meaningless compliment*
► empty, worthless, insincere, hollow, fatuous, nonsensical
AN OPPOSITE IS meaningful

**2** *Life seemed meaningless.*
► pointless, senseless, worthless, inconsequential, insignificant

### means NOUN

**1** *modern means of communication*
► method, mode, way, medium, channel, vehicle, instrument, course

**2** *I don't have the means for such a lifestyle.*
► resources, funds, money, wherewithal, income, finance

**3** *a person of means*
► wealth, riches, substance, property

### measly ADJECTIVE

*(informal) All he could find was a measly ten-pence piece.*
► meagre, paltry, scanty, scant, sparse, negligible, pitiful, miserable, modest, (more informal) mingy
AN OPPOSITE IS generous

### measure NOUN

**1** *These successes earned them a measure of glory.* Add three measures of liquid.
► share, portion, amount, allocation, quota, ration

**2** *personal income as a measure of success*
► gauge, criterion, yardstick, standard, touchstone, meter, test

**3** *special measures to monitor noise levels*
► step, action, procedure, process, means, control, operation

### measure VERB

**1** *It's not easy to measure the effects of such a disaster.*
► evaluate, assess, gauge, appraise, determine, fathom

**2 measure up to** *attempts to measure up to the expected standards.*
► achieve, meet, satisfy, match, comply with

### measured ADJECTIVE

*He was walking at a measured pace.*
► steady, regular, even, rhythmic, constant, sustained, sedate, slow, firm, resolute

---

### measurement NOUN

**1** *Measurements are given in metric units.*
► dimension, size, extent, proportions

**2** *an instrument used in the measurement of air speed*
► calculation, computation, mensuration, evaluation, assessment

**SOME METRIC MEASUREMENTS WITH UNITS (* = SI UNITS)**

**length:** kilometre (km, = 1,000 metres), metre (m) centimetre (cm), milimetre (mm).

**mass:** *kilogram (kg, = 1,000 grams), gram (g).

**time:** millennium (1,000 years), century (100 years), year, month, week, minute, second.

**temperature:** *kelvin (K), degree Celsius, Centigrade.

**strength of light:** *candela (cd).

**amount of substance:** *mole (mol).

**force:** *newton (N).

**work, nergy, heat:** *joule (j).

**power:** watt (W).

**electric current:** *ampere (A).

**electric charge:** coulomb (C).

**electrical resistance:** *ohm (Ω).

**electric voltage:** *volt.

**frequency:** *hertz.

**pressure:** *pascal (Pa).

**radioactivity:** *becquerel (Bq).

---

### mechanic NOUN

*a motor mechanic*
► engineer, technician

### mechanical ADJECTIVE

**1** *a mechanical doll*
► mechanized, automated, machine-driven, motor-driven, automatic
AN OPPOSITE IS manual

2 *The voice sounded detached and mechanical.*
▶ unemotional, unfeeling, matter-of-fact, perfunctory, unthinking, cold, inhuman, lifeless, routine, soulless
AN OPPOSITE IS thoughtful

**mechanism** NOUN
1 *A trigger mechanism activates the bolt.*
▶ apparatus, machine, device, appliance, system, tool
2 *Mechanisms are in place for correcting mistakes.*
▶ procedure, process, system, means, channel, structure

**medal** NOUN
*Their son had won a medal for bravery.*
▶ medallion, honour, decoration, award, reward, trophy, prize

**meddle** VERB
*We don't want them meddling in our affairs.*
▶ interfere, pry, intrude, poke, nose, snoop, (more informal) stick your nose in

**meddlesome** ADJECTIVE
*We can do without meddlesome relatives.*
▶ interfering, meddling, prying, intrusive, officious, intruding

**mediate** VERB
*He tried to mediate between Franklin and the British government.*
▶ negotiate, arbitrate, intercede, act as mediator, liaise

**mediator** NOUN
*last-minute pressure from diplomat and UN mediators*
▶ arbitrator, negotiator, intermediary, broker, go-between, peacemaker

**medicinal** ADJECTIVE
*They collected berries, nuts, and medicinal plants.*
▶ healing, curative, remedial, restorative, therapeutic, medical

**medicine** NOUN
1 *examples of how modern medicine has helped to prolong life*
▶ medical science, healing, surgery, therapeutics, treatment of diseases
2 *He poured a dose of the medicine into the glass.*
▶ medication, medicament, remedy, cure, drug, prescription, treatment
RELATED ADJECTIVES clinical, pharmaceutical

**mediocre** ADJECTIVE
*Fred turned a mediocre business into one that was thriving.*
▶ ordinary, commonplace, indifferent, average, undistinguished, middle-of-the-road, run-of-the-mill, unexceptional, middling, passable, tolerable, second-rate
OPPOSITES ARE exceptional, outstanding

**meditation** NOUN
*He fell silent for a while, as if in meditation.*
▶ contemplation, prayer, reflection, yoga

**meditate** VERB
**meditate on** *They were meditating on the meaning of life.*
▶ consider, contemplate, ponder, cogitate, reflect on, brood on, mull over, speculate on

**medium** ADJECTIVE
*She is of medium height.*
▶ average, middling, middle, normal, ordinary, standard, usual, intermediate, midway, moderate

**medium** NOUN
1 *Television is a powerful medium of communication.*
▶ method, means, channel, mode, way, vehicle, instrument, course
2 *a happy medium between quality and quantity*
▶ average, midpoint, middle way, middle ground, compromise
3 *I went to see a medium and she told me I would be rich one day.*
▶ clairvoyant, spiritualist, psychic

**medley** NOUN
*a medley of popular tunes*
▶ mixture, assortment, miscellany, variety, selection, collection, hotchpotch, assembly

**meek** ADJECTIVE
*She seemed meek but could be fiercely passionate.*
▶ gentle, mild, demure, submissive, compliant, modest, docile, unassuming, self-effacing, unassertive, forbearing
AN OPPOSITE IS assertive

**meet** VERB
1 *She met an old friend in town.*
▶ encounter, come across, run across, run into, chance on, stumble on
2 *I'll meet you at the airport.*
▶ collect
3 *They met the challenge bravely.*
▶ face, undergo, encounter, experience, endure, suffer
4 *The equipment does not meet our requirements.*
▶ satisfy, fulfil, answer, measure up to, match up to, conform to
5 *The board meets every month.*
▶ gather, assemble, come together, convene, hold a meeting
6 *The two roads meet north of the city.*
▶ join, converge, merge, come together, connect, intersect

**meeting** NOUN
1 *He rushed back to be in time for the meeting.*
▶ gathering, assembly, conference, forum, convention
2 *He adored her from their very first meeting.*
▶ encounter, rendezvous, contact, assignation, get-together, date
3 *The town stands at the meeting of three mighty rivers.*
▶ convergence, coming together, junction, confluence, union, concourse

**melancholy** ADJECTIVE

1 *melancholy music*
▶ sad, sorrowful, mournful, reflective

2 *a melancholy mood*
▶ unhappy, downhearted, despondent, gloomy, dispirited, depressed, dejected, downcast
OPPOSITES ARE joyful, happy, elated

**melancholy** NOUN

*a feeling of melancholy*
▶ sadness, sorrow, dejection, unhappiness, depression, dejection, despondency, gloom
OPPOSITES ARE joy, happiness, elation

**mellow** ADJECTIVE

1 *a mellow voice*
▶ smooth, melodious, dulcet, tuneful, sweet

2 *a mellow temperament*
▶ easy-going, tolerant, amiable, good-natured, affable, kind-hearted

3 *mellow fruit*
▶ ripe, mature, juicy, tender, sweet

**melodious** ADJECTIVE

*melodious sounds*
▶ tuneful, musical, melodic, harmonious, euphonious, lyrical, sweet-toned

**melody** NOUN

*a beautiful melody*
▶ tune, air, strain, theme, song

**melt** VERB

*The sun soon melted the snow, The ice was beginning to melt.*
▶ thaw, unfreeze, defrost, liquefy, soften, dissolve

**melt away** *The crowds rapidly melted away.*
▶ disperse, dissolve, dwindle, vanish, evaporate, disappear, fade

**member** NOUN

*new members of the sports club*
▶ associate, subscriber, fellow, adherent

**memento** NOUN

*a memento of the occasion*
▶ souvenir, keepsake, token, reminder, memorial

**memoirs** PLURAL NOUN

*He published his memoirs in 1990.*
▶ reminiscences, recollections, autobiography, life story

**memorable** ADJECTIVE

1 *a memorable event*
▶ unforgettable, notable, remarkable, outstanding, extraordinary
OPPOSITES ARE commonplace, forgettable

2 (*informal*) *a memorable tune*
▶ catchy, haunting

**memorial** NOUN

*a memorial to victims of the war*
▶ monument, remembrance, shrine, cenotaph, plaque, tablet

**memorize** NOUN

*Long numbers are hard to memorize.*
▶ remember, commit to memory, learn by heart, retain
AN OPPOSITE IS forget

**memory** NOUN

1 *My mother always had a good memory.*
▶ recall, retention, ability to remember, recollection

2 *happy memories of a lovely occasion*
▶ reminiscence, recollection, remembrance, reminder, souvenir, impression

3 *a plaque in memory of local writers*
▶ commemoration, remembrance, tribute, honour, recognition

**menace** NOUN

1 *a menace to society*
▶ danger, threat, hazard, risk

2 *That child is a menace.*
▶ nuisance, pest, annoyance

3 *a situation full of menace*
▶ threat, ominousness, intimidation

**menace** VERB

*The state should not menace its own citizens.*
▶ threaten, intimidate, frighten, bully

**mend** VERB

1 *An electrician was mending faulty wiring.*
▶ repair, fix, restore, renovate
AN OPPOSITE IS break

2 *a pile of socks to mend*
▶ patch, repair, darn

3 *a quarrel that a few kind words can mend*
▶ put right, resolve, sort out, straighten out, remedy, rectify, redress
AN OPPOSITE IS make worse

**menial** ADJECTIVE

*Someone has to do the menial tasks.*
▶ humble, lowly, routine, unskilled, low-grade, humdrum, inferior, degrading, demeaning
OPPOSITES ARE skilled, important

**menial** NOUN

*They are treated like menials.*
▶ servant, drudge, minion, domestic, (*more informal*) skivvy

**mental** ADJECTIVE

1 *The work calls for considerable mental concentration.*
▶ intellectual, cerebral, abstract, rational, cognitive, theoretical

2 *Your mental attitude affects your behaviour.*
▶ psychological, temperamental, emotional, subjective

**mentality** NOUN

*They seem to have an ostrich-like mentality.*
▶ attitude, way of thinking, outlook, predisposition, disposition, frame of mind, character, temperament, personality, (*more informal*) make-up

## mention VERB

**1** *Nick mentioned that he would be here next week.*
▶ state, say, remark, observe, reveal, indicate, disclose, divulge

**2** *Better not to mention the score.*
▶ refer to, allude to, touch on, speak about, comment on, disclose, hint at, let out, reveal, (*more informal*) let drop

## merciful ADJECTIVE

*They believe in a merciful God.*
▶ compassionate, forgiving, humane, gracious, understanding, sympathetic, generous, beneficent
OPPOSITES ARE merciless, cruel

## merciless ADJECTIVE

*a leader who was merciless to his enemies*
▶ cruel, pitiless, ruthless, heartless, unsparing, unforgiving, unrelenting, harsh, severe
AN OPPOSITE IS merciful

## mercy NOUN

**1** *The prisoners begged for mercy.*
▶ clemency, compassion, leniency, pity, sympathy, forbearance, forgiveness, understanding
AN OPPOSITE IS cruelty

**2** *It is a mercy that more people weren't killed.*
▶ blessing, godsend, boon, favour, piece of good fortune

## merge VERB

**1** *It seems a good idea to merge the two organizations.*
▶ combine, amalgamate, integrate, unite, join together, consolidate, coalesce, blend, fuse, link up, put together

**2** *The two parties have agreed to merge.*
▶ unite, join together, come together, amalgamate, unify, combine

**3** *The motorways merge ahead.*
▶ join, meet, converge
OPPOSITES ARE split, separate

## merit NOUN

*writers of merit*
▶ excellence, goodness, value, virtue, worth, importance, quality, credit, eminence

## merit VERB

*The idea certainly merits consideration.*
▶ deserve, warrant, be worth, be worthy of, be entitled to, justify, rate, earn, incur

## merriment NOUN

*They could hear bursts of laughter and ripples of merriment.*
▶ jollity, enjoyment, cheerfulness, mirth, festivity, conviviality, amusement, revelry, high spirits
OPPOSITES ARE misery, gloom

## merry ADJECTIVE

*merry crowds of holiday-makers   a merry ringing of bells*
▶ jolly, cheerful, light-hearted, carefree, joyful, joyous, festive, happy, gleeful

## mesh NOUN

**1** *A wire mesh covered the hutch.*
▶ netting, lattice, net, network, web

**2** *a mesh of political intrigue*
▶ tangle, entanglement, snare, trap

## mesmerize VERB

*His hand gripped hers across the table and his voice mesmerized her.*
▶ hypnotize, bewitch, entrance, captivate, enthral, transfix, fascinate, dominate, magnetize

## mess NOUN

**1** *There's quite a mess in the kitchen.*
▶ muddle, untidiness, disarray, jumble, confusion, clutter, shambles

**2** *It was a mess of his own making and he would have to find a way out.*
▶ predicament, quandary, difficulty, trouble, (*more informal*) fix

**make a mess of** *I'm afraid I've made a mess of the assignment.*
▶ ruin, spoil, botch, bungle, mishandle, mismanage, fluff, muff, mess up, (*more informal*) make a hash of, (*much more informal*) cock up, (*much more informal*) screw up
OPPOSITES ARE succeed in, bring off

## mess VERB

**mess about** or **around** *They need to stop messing around and get on with something.*
▶ fool about or around, play about or around, (*more informal*) muck about or around

**mess up**

**1** *They had messed up the garden in less than ten minutes.*
▶ jumble, muddle, make a mess of, dirty, dishevel, disrupt, disarrange

**2** *A new assignment: try not to mess this one up.*
▶ ruin, spoil, botch, bungle, mishandle, mismanage, fluff, muff, make a mess of, (*more informal*) make a hash of, (*much more informal*) cock up, (*much more informal*) screw up

## message NOUN

*Sarah sent a message with her brother.*
▶ communication, note, letter, word, memo, dispatch, missive

## messenger NOUN

*A messenger brought the news.*
▶ courier, emissary, go-between, envoy, runner, dispatch-rider

## messy ADJECTIVE

**1** *All these jobs can be messy and produce a lot of debris.*
▶ dirty, filthy, mucky, grubby, grimy

**2** *The bathroom had become very messy.  Her hair was tangled and messy.*
▶ untidy, dishevelled, unkempt, disorganized, chaotic, sloppy
OPPOSITES ARE tidy, neat, organized

**metal** NOUN

**a lump of metal**
▶ ingot, nugget

**WORDS FOR TYPES OF METAL**

**metals**: lithium, beryllium, sodium, magnesium, aluminium, potassium, calcium, scandium, titanium, vanadium, chromium, manganese, iron, cobalt, nickel, copper, zinc, gallium, strontium, zirconium, molybdenum, silver, cadmium, tin, barium, tungsten, platinum, gold, mercury, lead, bismuth, uranium.

**metal alloys**: brass (copper and zinc), bronze (copper and tin), cast iron (iron and carbon), electrum (gold and silver), pewter (tin and lead, or tin, copper and antimony), solder (lead and tin), steel (iron, carbon and other elements).

**method** NOUN

*a new method of gathering vital data*
▶ way, approach (to), procedure (for), manner, mode, technique (for), style, plan (for)

**methodical** ADJECTIVE

*a methodical approach to working*
▶ organized, orderly, systematic, meticulous, painstaking, efficient, businesslike, meticulous, logical, tidy, precise, neat
OPPOSITES ARE disorganized, inefficient

**meticulous** ADJECTIVE

*He continued his meticulous inspection of the machine.*
▶ careful, methodical, scrupulous, diligent, painstaking, systematic, thorough, rigorous

**middle** ADJECTIVE

*Remove the middle pin.*
▶ central, midway, mean, medial, median, half-way, inner, inside

**middle** NOUN

**1** *There was a large table in the middle of the room.*
▶ centre, midpoint
OPPOSITES ARE edge, border

**2** *a journey to the middle of the earth*
▶ centre, core, heart, kernel
OPPOSITES ARE surface, circumference

**middling** ADJECTIVE

*She speaks middling to good Japanese.*
▶ average, medium, fair, ordinary, moderate, everyday, modest, passable

**midget** NOUN

*houses so small they must have been occupied by midgets*
▶ person of restricted growth, small person, dwarf, pygmy

**USAGE** *Person of restricted growth* is the term you should use to avoid causing offence, as all the other words have derogatory overtones.

**midget** ADJECTIVE

*a midget car*
▶ miniature, baby, dwarf, small

**miffed** ADJECTIVE

*(informal) She felt miffed at being ignored.*
▶ annoyed, irritated, angry, cross, displeased, vexed, infuriated, incensed, enraged, (more informal) put out

**might** NOUN

*I hit it with all my might.*
▶ strength, force, power, energy, vigour

**mighty** ADJECTIVE

*a mighty blow to the head*
▶ powerful, forceful, violent, vigorous, ferocious, hefty, savage
AN OPPOSITE IS weak

**mild** ADJECTIVE

**1** *She spoke in a mild voice.*
▶ gentle, soft, tender, calm, tender-hearted, easygoing, sympathetic
AN OPPOSITE IS harsh

**2** *The weather turned mild.*
▶ warm, calm, fair, temperate
OPPOSITES ARE severe, cold

**militant** ADJECTIVE

*militant opponents of the regime*
▶ belligerent, active, aggressive, combatant, assertive, positive
OPPOSITES ARE restrained, peaceful

**military** ADJECTIVE

*a military command   military units*
▶ fighting, service, armed, martial, belligerent, enlisted, uniformed
AN OPPOSITE IS civilian

**military** NOUN

*The town came under the control of the military.*
▶ army, armed forces, services, militia, soldiers, soldiery
AN OPPOSITE IS civilian

**milk** VERB

*Unscrupulous moneylenders can milk unwary clients.*
▶ exploit, take advantage of, cash in on, squeeze, bleed

**milky** ADJECTIVE

**1** *her beautiful milky skin*
▶ pale, white, cream, creamy

**2** *a milky liquid*
▶ cloudy, chalky, misty, opaque, whitish
AN OPPOSITE IS clear
RELATED ADJECTIVE lactic

**mill** NOUN

**1** *a paper mill*
▶ factory, plant, processing plant, works, workshop

**2** *a pepper mill*
▶ grinder, crusher, roller

## mill VERB

*The wheat is milled into flour.*
▶ grind, crush, roll, pulverize, powder

**mill about** or **around** *Outside, people were still milling about.*
▶ throng, swarm, stream, surge, wander about, move aimlessly

## mime VERB

*She mimed a telephone conversation.*
▶ act out, mimic, simulate, gesture, impersonate

## mimic NOUN

*He was entertaining and a good mimic.*
▶ impersonator, impressionist, imitator

## mimic VERB

*She could mimic anyone after a few minutes listening to them.*
▶ imitate, impersonate, copy, ape, caricature, do an impression of, parody, parrot, pretend to be, simulate, (more informal) take off

## mince VERB

**1** *He took the meat and minced it.*
▶ grind, chop, dice, crumble, cube

**2 not mince words** *She doesn't mince her words when she's angry.*
▶ speak plainly, speak straight, get to the point, not pull your punches

## mind NOUN

**1** *people with brilliant minds*
▶ brain, intellect, intelligence, sense, wits, understanding, mentality, power of reasoning, (more informal) grey matter
RELATED ADJECTIVE mental

**2** *It's hard to keep my mind on my work.*
▶ attention, concentration, thinking

**3** *I couldn't get her words out of my mind.*
▶ memory, recollection, remembrance

**4** *I've a mind to go and complain.*
▶ inclination, wish, desire, fancy, intention, disposition, tendency

## mind VERB

**1** *I'll mind your bags while you're gone.*
▶ look after, watch, guard, take care of, attend to, (more informal) keep an eye on

**2** *You'd better mind what they say.*
▶ be careful of, beware of, heed, pay attention to, look out for, watch out for, take notice of, note, remember

**3** *Will you mind if I eat my lunch?*
▶ care, object, bother, disapprove, grumble, take offence, worry, be resentful, complain

## mindful ADJECTIVE

**mindful of** *Rob flew with care, mindful of the lives of his crew.*
▶ aware of, conscious of, heedful of, alive to, attentive to, careful of
OPPOSITES ARE heedless of, oblivious to

## mindless ADJECTIVE

**1** *The occasion was spoilt by incidents of mindless violence.*
▶ senseless, wanton, gratuitous, thoughtless

**2** *People are reduced to mindless automatons, unable to think for themselves.*
▶ stupid, idiotic, brainless, witless, foolish

## mine NOUN

**1** *a coal mine*
▶ pit, colliery, coalfield, deposit, mineshaft

**2** *He was killed by a mine.*
▶ landmine, explosive

**3** *The book is a mine of information.*
▶ store, wealth, fund, treasury, repository, hoard, rich supply

## mine VERB

*Gold is mined in these hills.*
▶ excavate, extract, quarry, dig for, remove

---

## mineral NOUN

**SOME COMMON MINERALS**

alabaster, albite, anhydrite, asbestos, aventurine, azurite, bentonite, bloodstone, Blue John, borax, cairngorm, calamine, calcite, cassiterite, chalcedony, chlorite, chrysoberyl, cinnabar, corundum, dolomite, emery, feldspar, fluorite or fluorspar, fool's gold, galena, graphite, gypsum, haematite, halite, hornblende, idocrase, jacinth, jargoon, kaolinite, lapis lazuli, lazurite, magnetite, malachite, mica, microcline, montmorillonite, orthoclase, pitchblende, pyrites, quartz, realgar, rock salt, rutile, sanidine, siderite, smithsonite, sodalite, spar, sphalerite, spinel, talc, uraninite, vesuvianite, wurzite, zircon.

---

## mingle VERB

**1** *Guests mingled in the gardens.*
▶ socialize, circulate, get together, merge, mix, fraternize, associate, move about, rub shoulders, intermingle

**2** *Open air smells mingled with the aroma of food cooking.*
▶ combine, merge, fuse, unite, join, coalesce

## mingy ADJECTIVE

*(informal) All I got was a mingy five pounds.*
▶ meagre, measly, paltry, miserable, scanty, scant, sparse, negligible, pitiful, modest, (informal) mouldy
AN OPPOSITE IS generous

## miniature ADJECTIVE

*a miniature village*
▶ tiny, small-scale, scaled-down, diminutive, minute, baby, model

## minimal ADJECTIVE

*Increases in rent this year have been minimal.*
▶ very little, negligible, slight, least, smallest, minimum, token, nominal

**minimize** VERB

1 *They banned smoking to minimize the danger of fire*
▶ reduce, keep down, cut down, lessen, curtail, diminish
OPPOSITES ARE maximize, increase

2 *He should not minimizes the value of their contribution.*
▶ underestimate, gloss over, make light of, play down
OPPOSITES ARE maximize, exaggerate

**minimum** ADJECTIVE
*The pay is well above the minimum wage.*
▶ lowest, least, smallest, minimal, bottom

**minimum** NOUN
*Costs are kept to a minimum*
▶ lower limit, limit, base, lowest point, bottom level
AN OPPOSITE IS maximum

**minion** NOUN
*He gives the worst jobs to his minions.*
▶ assistant, underling, lackey, hireling, stooge, hanger-on, attendant

**minister** NOUN

1 *a minister of the church*
▶ clergyman, clergywoman, cleric, parson, priest, vicar, preacher

2 *a government minister*
▶ official, office-holder, executive, secretary of state
**USAGE** A *secretary of state* is a head of a government department (such as transport) and a member of the cabinet; not all ministers are secretaries of state.

**minister** VERB
**minister to** *Paramedics were ministering to the injured.*
▶ tend, attend to, care for, look after, nurse, treat, assist, help

**minor** ADJECTIVE
*minor alterations to the treaty*
▶ small, trivial, unimportant, insignificant, inconsequential, negligible, secondary, lesser, trifling, petty
AN OPPOSITE IS major

**minority** NOUN
*A minority voted for a return to work.*
▶ small number, lesser number, smaller number
**be in a minority**
▶ be outnumbered, be less, be the smaller number

**mint** ADJECTIVE
*in mint condition*
▶ brand new, pristine, immaculate, perfect, new, unblemished, unmarked, unused, fresh

**mint** NOUN
*(informal) They made a mint from the deal.*
▶ fortune, heap, (informal) packet, (informal) pile, (informal) stack

**mint** VERB
*Special coins were minted to celebrate the jubilee.*
▶ strike, cast, manufacture, stamp out, coin, forge, make

**minuscule** ADJECTIVE
*a minuscule room*
▶ tiny, minute, infinitesimal, microscopic

**minute** ADJECTIVE
*a minute insect*
▶ tiny, minuscule, infinitesimal, diminutive, miniature

**minute** NOUN
*I'll only be a minute.*
▶ moment, short while, second, (more informal) tick

**miracle** NOUN
*a miracle of modern technology*
▶ marvel, wonder, sensation, phenomenon, feat

**miraculous** ADJECTIVE
*a miraculous escape*
▶ amazing, astounding, astonishing, extraordinary, unbelievable, incredible, inexplicable, marvellous, wonderful, mysterious

**mirage** NOUN
*The lake turned out to be a mirage.*
▶ illusion, optical illusion, hallucination, vision, delusion

**mirror** NOUN

1 *She took a quick look in the mirror on her way out.*
▶ looking glass, glass, reflector

2 *art as a mirror of life*
▶ reflection, image, likeness, copy, double

**mirror** VERB
*Jody's views mirrored her own.*
▶ reflect, correspond to, match, imitate, copy, echo

**mirth** NOUN
*sounds of mirth from the terrace*
▶ merriment, amusement, revelry, jollity, enjoyment, cheerfulness, festivity, conviviality, high spirits
OPPOSITES ARE misery, gloom

**misbehave** VERB
*Little Mary was misbehaving again.*
▶ behave badly, be naughty, be disobedient, (more informal) play up, (more informal) fool about

**misbehaviour** NOUN
*In those days any form of misbehaviour was punished.*
▶ bad behaviour, misconduct, naughtiness, disobedience, indiscipline, insubordination, mischief, mischief-making, wrongdoing

**miscalculate** VERB
*We miscalculated the amount of fuel we would need.*
▶ misjudge, make a mistake over, get wrong, underestimate or overestimate, blunder over

**miscalculation** NOUN
*The problem arises from miscalculations by officials.*
▶ mistake, error, error of judgement, blunder

## miscellaneous ADJECTIVE

*He made money from gardening and miscellaneous jobs.*
▶ various, varied, different, assorted, mixed, sundry, multifarious

## mischief NOUN

**1** *He was always plotting some mischief with his brother.*
▶ misbehaviour, naughtiness, bad behaviour, mischievousness, misconduct, disobedience, pranks

**2** *A faulty fuel pipe can cause much mischief.*
▶ trouble, difficulty, harm, damage, injury, bother, nuisance

## mischievous ADJECTIVE

**1** *mischievous children*
▶ naughty, badly behaved, misbehaving, disobedient, insubordinate, troublesome, vexatious

**2** *There was a mischievous grin on his face.*
▶ playful, impish, roguish, teasing

**3** *The house was full of mischievous rumours.*
▶ malicious, malevolent, hostile, unfriendly, spiteful, vicious, pernicious

## misconception NOUN

*a popular misconception about volcanoes*
▶ misunderstanding, misapprehension, misbelief, delusion, fallacy

## misconduct NOUN

**1** *They were accused of professional misconduct.*
▶ wrongdoing, malpractice, impropriety, misbehaviour, negligence

**2** *Any misconduct will be reported.*
▶ misbehaviour, bad behaviour, naughtiness, misdemeanour

## miser NOUN

*an old miser who kept his money hidden under the floorboards*
▶ scrooge, penny-pincher, hoarder, niggard, (*informal*) skinflint
AN OPPOSITE IS spendthrift

## miserable ADJECTIVE

**1** *She was too miserable to eat.*
▶ unhappy, sad, dejected, despondent, downcast, downhearted, down, disheartened, disconsolate, glum, melancholy, cast down

**2** *The house was cramped and miserable.*
▶ dreary, dismal, gloomy, cheerless, joyless, squalid

**3** *It was a miserable way to treat people.*
▶ contemptible, despicable, disgraceful, deplorable, shameful

**4** *They kept us waiting for hours and all we got was a miserable cup of tea.*
▶ measly, paltry, meagre, wretched, niggardly, pitiful, (*more informal*) mingy, (*more informal*) mouldy

## miserly ADJECTIVE

*He was miserly for all his life and died rich as a result.*
▶ mean, niggardly, penny-pinching, parsimonious, tight, stingy
AN OPPOSITE IS generous

## misery NOUN

**1** *the misery of unemployment*
▶ hardship, suffering, privation, affliction, distress, misfortune, tribulation, anguish

**2** *She put her hands to her face in silent misery.*
▶ unhappiness, distress, wretchedness, despair, grief, suffering

**3** (*more informal*) *He can be fun but a lot of the time he's a real misery.*
▶ spoilsport, killjoy, pessimist, (*more informal*) wet blanket

## misfire VERB

*The plan had misfired.*
▶ fail, fall through, founder, miscarry, go wrong, (*more informal*) flop
AN OPPOSITE IS succeed

## misfit NOUN

*a bunch of misfits and weirdos*
▶ eccentric, nonconformist, maverick, dropout, individualist, (*more informal*) oddball

## misfortune NOUN

*Bruce had the misfortune to break a bone in his wrist. The family had suffered several generations of misfortune*
▶ bad luck, mischance, mishap, trouble, setback, tribulation, hardship
AN OPPOSITE IS good luck

## misgiving NOUN

*We agreed to the proposal with several misgivings.*
▶ doubt, reservation, qualm, scruple, diffidence
AN OPPOSITE IS confidence

## misguided ADJECTIVE

*a misguided policy on immigration*
▶ mistaken, misconceived, erroneous, fallacious, unsound, unfounded, ill-judged, ill-considered

## mishap NOUN

*an unfortunate mishap in the kitchen*
▶ accident, misfortune, misadventure, setback, problem, difficulty

## misjudge VERB

*He misjudged the distance and hit a parked car.*
▶ miscalculate, overestimate, underestimate, get wrong, guess wrongly, make a mistake about, misinterpret, misunderstand

## mislay VERB

*I seem to have mislaid my passport.*
▶ lose, misplace, lose track of, forget

## mislead VERB

*Colin had evidently tried to mislead her.*
▶ deceive, delude, fool, hoodwink, take in, misguide, misinform, lead astray

## misleading ADJECTIVE

*a misleading answer*
▶ confusing, deceptive, equivocal, ambiguous, evasive, dishonest, unreliable

## mismanage VERB
*The redundancies had been badly mismanaged..*
▶ mishandle, bungle, botch, ruin, spoil, fluff, muff, mess up, make a mess of, *(more informal)* make a hash of, *(much more informal)* cock up, *(much more informal)* screw up

## misrepresent VERB
*The statement misrepresented the views of the government.*
▶ misreport, misstate, falsify, distort, pervert, misconstrue

## miss VERB
**1** *The bullet missed him by inches.*
▶ fail to hit, fall short of
**2** *It was an easy catch but he still missed it.*
▶ drop, fumble, fail to catch, let slip, mishandle
**3** *If we're not careful we'll miss the last train.*
▶ be too late for, fail to catch
**4** *He was ill and had to miss the party.*
▶ be absent from, skip
**5** *I will miss Debbie terribly.*
▶ pine for, long for, yearn for, feel the loss of
**6** *He swerved and managed to miss an oncoming car.*
▶ avoid, dodge, evade, escape, circumvent
**7** *Don't miss your chance.*
▶ let slip, let go, forfeit, pass by, pass up, disregard

## missing ADJECTIVE
*A few books are still missing.*
▶ lost, mislaid, misplaced, gone astray, straying, unaccounted for, absent, disappeared

## mission NOUN
**1** *a mission to Africa*
▶ expedition, assignment, operation, exploration, journey, sortie, voyage
**2** *his mission in life*
▶ calling, vocation, goal, aim, purpose, function

## mist NOUN
**1** *The sun was breaking through the early morning mist.*
▶ haze, fog, vapour, cloud, mistiness
**2** *She wiped a hole to peep through the mist on the windows*
▶ condensation, film, steam

## mistake NOUN
*It's easy to make mistakes when you are tired.*
▶ error, slip, blunder, lapse, misjudgement, miscalculation, oversight, *(more informal)* gaffe

## mistake VERB
*I mistook the meaning of the instruction.*
▶ misunderstand, misinterpret, confuse, get wrong, misjudge, misread, misconstrue, *(informal)* get the wrong end of the stick about, mix up

## mistaken ADJECTIVE
*These conclusions are mistaken, in our view.*
▶ wrong, incorrect, erroneous, misguided, unfounded, unsound, ill-judged, inappropriate

## mistreat VERB
*Some of the prisoners had been mistreated.*
▶ ill-treat, maltreat, abuse, misuse, harm, injure, molest, *(more informal)* knock about

## mistress NOUN
*His wife never knew he had a mistress.*
▶ lover, girlfriend, *(more informal)* bit on the side, *(more informal)* fancy woman

## mistrust VERB
*I mistrust their intentions.*
▶ distrust, suspect, be suspicious of, be sceptical about, have misgivings about, have qualms about, be wary of, disbelieve, doubt, question
AN OPPOSITE IS trust

## misty ADJECTIVE
**1** *misty weather*
▶ hazy, foggy, murky, cloudy
AN OPPOSITE IS clear
**2** *a misty window*
▶ misted, clouded
**3** *misty memories*
▶ indistinct, vague, hazy, unclear, obscure, nebulous
OPPOSITES ARE sharp, distinct

## misunderstand VERB
*I must have misunderstood - I thought you were coming with us.*
▶ make a mistake, misapprehend, misinterpret, mishear, get it wrong, *(more informal)* get hold of the wrong end of the stick

## misunderstanding NOUN
**1** *The suggestion was based on a misunderstanding of the issues.*
▶ misapprehension, misconception, misinterpretation, misjudgement, false impression, delusion (about), mix-up
**2** *It wasn't a row, just a slight misunderstanding.*
▶ difference of opinion, disagreement, dispute, quarrel , squabble, argument, contretemps

## misuse NOUN
**1** *the misuse of confidential information*
▶ wrong use, misappropriation, misapplication, exploitation
**2** *the misuse of innocent people*
▶ ill-treatment, maltreatment, mistreatment
**3** *the misuse of drugs*
▶ abuse, careless use, ill-use, mishandling

## misuse VERB
**1** *He was accused of misusing public money.*
▶ misapply, misemploy, embezzle, put to wrong use
**2** *She had been misused by successive partners.*
▶ ill-treat, maltreat, mistreat, abuse, harm, injure, molest, *(more informal)* knock about

## mitigate VERB
*The treatment mitigated the worst effects of the injury.*
▶ alleviate, lessen, reduce, diminish, allay, deaden, temper, soften

**mitigating** ADJECTIVE
*The defence lawyers pointed to mitigating circumstances.*
▶ extenuating, moderating, vindicating, justifying, qualifying

**mix** VERB
1 *Mix the ingredients together. Oil and water don't mix.*
▶ blend, mingle, combine, merge, fuse, unite, coalesce, amalgamate
2 *He mixes with all sorts of people.*
▶ associate, consort, fraternize, socialize, mingle, (*more informal*) hang about with
**mix up** *I've mixed up the two dates.*
▶ confuse, muddle, muddle up, jumble up, mistake

**mix** NOUN
*The work calls for a good mix of basic skills.*
▶ mixture, combination, blend, assortment, fusion, set

**mixed** ADJECTIVE
1 *a mixed collection*
▶ assorted, varied, diverse, miscellaneous, heterogeneous, different
2 *mixed ingredients*
▶ combined, integrated, amalgamated, united, composite, hybrid, joint
3 *Their reactions were mixed.*
▶ ambivalent, equivocal, uncertain, unsure, confused, muddled, ambiguous

**mixture** NOUN
*a strange mixture of people*
▶ assortment, variety, medley, combination, blend, miscellany, jumble, hotchpotch, assemblage, gathering

**moan** VERB
1 *The injured man was moaning with pain.*
▶ groan, cry, howl, whimper
2 *Everyone moaned about the food.*
▶ complain, grumble, grouse, grouch, carp, whine, (*more informal*) whinge

**moan** NOUN
1 *moans of pain*
▶ groan, cry, howl, whimper
2 *moans about the awful food*
▶ complaint, grumble, grouse, grouch, carping, whining, (*more informal*) whinging

**mob** NOUN
(*informal*) *An angry mob gathered at the gate.*
▶ crowd, throng, mass, horde, rabble, swarm, bunch, gang, group, herd, pack, riot

**mob** VERB
*Her fans mobbed her all the way to her car.*
▶ crowd round, swarm round, throng round, jostle, surround, besiege, hem in, harass, hassle

**mobile** ADJECTIVE
1 *She was soon mobile again after her operation.*
▶ moving, walking, able to move

2 *The village is visited by a mobile library once a week.*
▶ travelling, itinerant, peripatetic, roving, wandering
3 *It helps to be mobile in furthering a career.*
▶ adaptable, flexible, versatile, adjustable
4 *Her mobile features showed anger and regret.*
▶ expressive, suggestive, changing, changeable

**mobilize** VERB
1 *The army was mobilized to fight the rebels.*
▶ summon, assemble, call up, enlist, levy, marshal, muster
2 *The spin doctors mobilize support for government policy.*
▶ rally, generate, activate, stir up, stimulate, promote, galvanize, organize

**mock** VERB
*Her brother had grinned and mocked her behind her back.*
▶ ridicule, jeer, make fun of, laugh at, taunt, scorn, sneer at, deride, disparage, tease

**mock** ADJECTIVE
*He shook his head in mock disbelief.*
▶ pretend, imitation, simulated, false, fake, sham, feigned

**mockery** NOUN
1 *There was a note of mockery in her voice.*
▶ ridicule, derision, contempt, scorn, sarcasm, disdain
2 *The trial was a mockery of justice.*
▶ travesty, parody, caricature, sham

**mocking** ADJECTIVE
*His smile was coldly mocking.*
▶ derisive, contemptuous, scornful, sarcastic, disdainful
AN OPPOSITE IS friendly

**mode** NOUN
*The normal mode of transport is by road.*
▶ method, means, manner, system

**model** ADJECTIVE
1 *a model railway*
▶ miniature, toy, replica
2 *a model pupil*
▶ ideal, perfect, exemplary, impeccable, faultless

**model** NOUN
1 *a working model of a high-speed train*
▶ replica, copy, representation, facsimile, imitation
2 *a model of good behaviour*
▶ ideal, paragon, epitome, personification
3 *laws based on the American model*
▶ pattern, example, type, standard, paradigm, prototype, version, mould

**model** VERB
1 *The artist modelled the figure in bronze.*
▶ form, make, fashion, mould, sculpt, design
2 *Characters who are modelled on real life.*
▶ base, draw (from), derive (from)

a b c d e f g h i j k l **m** n o p q r s t u v w x y z

## moderate ADJECTIVE

**1** *a moderate success*
▶ average, modest, mediocre, tolerable, passable
**2** *a moderate drinker*   *Prices are moderate this year.*
▶ reasonable, sensible, restrained, controlled, modest, fair

## moderate VERB

**1** *The wind has moderated.*
▶ abate, die down, ease off, subside, decrease, become less extreme
**2** *Can we do something to moderate the noise?*
▶ control, curb, check, reduce, lessen, mitigate, alleviate, allay, subdue

## moderately ADVERB

*a moderately successful attempt*
▶ fairly, reasonably, somewhat, passably, quite, rather, slightly, (*more informal*) pretty

## moderation NOUN

*He always showed moderation in exercising authority.*
▶ restraint, caution, fairness, reasonableness, sobriety, temperance

## modern ADJECTIVE

**1** *modern art*
▶ contemporary, present-day, current
**2** *She wears very modern clothes.*
▶ fashionable, stylish, modish, voguish, advanced

## modernize VERB

(*informal*) *The factory needs to modernize its production methods.*
▶ update, renovate, refurbish, renovate, regenerate, improve, rebuild

## modest ADJECTIVE

**1** *a modest increase in income*
▶ moderate, reasonable, limited, slight, small
AN OPPOSITE IS large
**2** *He is always modest about his achievements.*
▶ unassuming, unpretentious, humble, reserved, discreet, retiring, bashful
AN OPPOSITE IS boastful

## modesty NOUN

*She shows admirable modesty about her abilities.*
▶ humility, reserve, reticence, discretion, self-effacement, shyness, lack of pretension

## modify VERB

*These events have led us to modify our views.*
▶ change, alter, amend, adapt, revise, adjust, reform

## moist ADJECTIVE

*He dug into the dark moist earth.*
▶ damp, soggy, clammy, wet, watery

## moisten VERB

*Moisten the compost if it becomes dry.*
▶ dampen, wet, damp, soak, moisturize, make moist, humidify
AN OPPOSITE IS dry

## moisture NOUN

*The windows were covered in moisture.*
▶ dampness, condensation, damp, humidity, liquid, steam, vapour, wetness, wet

## molest VERB

*The woman had been molested by a group of men.*
▶ harass, pester, beset, torment, persecute, harry

## moment NOUN

**1** *She waited for a moment before going in.*
▶ minute, second, little while, short time
**2** *We can leave the moment the rain stops.*
▶ instant, minute, second, point
**3** *These matters are of little moment to most people.*
▶ importance, import, significance, consequence, interest, weight, value

## momentary ADJECTIVE

*He had a momentary glimpse of her face.*
▶ brief, fleeting, passing, quick, temporary, transient, transitory
AN OPPOSITE IS permanent

## momentous ADJECTIVE

*a momentous decision*
▶ important, significant, fateful, epoch-making, historic, critical, crucial, decisive
AN OPPOSITE IS unimportant

## momentum NOUN

*The car began to gain momentum.*   *a momentum for change*
▶ impetus, force, velocity, power, impulse, incentive, thrust

## monarch NOUN

*They swore loyalty to the monarch.*
▶ sovereign, ruler, king, queen
RELATED ADJECTIVES regal, royal

## monarchy NOUN

*the abolition of the monarchy*
▶ royalty, kingship, kingdom, realm

## money NOUN

**1** *I don't have enough money to buy it.*
▶ cash, means, funds, capital, finance, change, (*more informal*) dosh
**2** *How much money shall we take on holiday?*
▶ currency, cash
RELATED ADJECTIVES financial, monetary, pecuniary

## monitor NOUN

**1** *Watch the monitor.*
▶ screen, set, television, VDU = visual display unit
**2** *a heart monitor*
▶ scanner, detector

## monitor VERB

*Special equipment will monitor noise levels.*
▶ check, watch, keep track of, observe, record, scan

## monopolize VERB

*He tends to monopolize the conversation.*
▶ dominate, control, corner, take over, shut others out of, (*more informal*) hog
AN OPPOSITE IS share

**monotonous** ADJECTIVE

*a monotonous piece of work*
▶ boring, tedious, dull, dreary, uninteresting, tiresome, wearisome, repetitive, repetitious
OPPOSITES ARE interesting, varied

**monotony** NOUN

*the monotony of their working lives*
▶ dullness, boredom, tedium, sameness, repetitiveness, repetitiousness, weariness, dreariness, routine, uniformity

**monster** NOUN

1 *a huge monster of a man*
▶ giant, colossus, mammoth, leviathan
2 *He was behaving like a monster.*
▶ beast, brute, fiend, savage, ogre

**monster** ADJECTIVE

*She came in eating a monster ice cream. The film was a monster hit.*
▶ huge, enormous, massive, colossal, gigantic, immense, (*informal*) ginormous

**monstrous** ADJECTIVE

1 *A monstrous wave loomed over the ship.*
▶ huge, enormous, massive, colossal, gigantic, immense, (*informal*) ginormous
2 *a monstrous winged creature*
▶ grotesque, hideous, gruesome, horrible, grisly, repulsive
3 *a monstrous injustice*
▶ appalling, dreadful, shocking, outrageous, abominable, disgraceful, scandalous, hideous, wicked, vile, foul, evil

**monument** NOUN

1 *a monument to local heroes*
▶ memorial, obelisk, statue, shrine, mausoleum
2 *a monument over his grave*
▶ gravestone, headstone, tombstone
3 *The book is a monument to years of research.*
▶ testament, record, token, evidence

**monumental** ADJECTIVE

1 *a monumental plaque*
▶ commemorative, memorial
2 *a monumental task*
▶ huge, great, enormous, immense, awesome, grand, impressive

**mood** NOUN

1 *He was in a bad mood for most of the day.*
▶ temper, humour, disposition, spirit, frame of mind, state of mind, vein
2 *The music sets the right mood for the story.*
▶ atmosphere, feeling, tone, spirit, ambience

**moody** ADJECTIVE

*Charles was quiet and moody, and this worried her.*
▶ changeable, temperamental, volatile, unpredictable, sulky, sullen, gloomy, morose

**moon** NOUN

*by the light of a full moon*
RELATED ADJECTIVE lunar

**moon** VERB

*There was not much to do and the young ones were mooning about.*
▶ mope, loaf, idle, waste time, (*more informal*) mooch

**moor** NOUN

*a windswept moor*
▶ heath, moorland, upland, fell

**moor** VERB

*The boat was moored by a jetty.*
▶ tie up, secure, fasten, anchor, berth, dock

**mop** VERB

*A man was mopping the floor.*
▶ wash, clean, sponge, wipe

**mope** VERB

*She realized it was no use moping.*
▶ brood, fret, sulk, pine, be miserable, grieve

**moral** ADJECTIVE

1 *moral issues*
▶ ethical, social, behavioural
2 *a very moral person*
▶ good, honest, virtuous, upright, principled, honourable, decent, proper, pure, blameless, upstanding, responsible, trustworthy
AN OPPOSITE IS immoral
3 *moral support*
▶ emotional, psychological

**moral** NOUN

*There's a clear moral to this story.*
▶ lesson, message, meaning, point, significance, import, principle

**morale** NOUN

*A series of wins boosted the team's morale.*
▶ confidence, self-confidence, self-esteem, state of mind, spirit, mood, (*informal*) heart

**morality** NOUN

*standards of morality*
▶ ethics, morals, ideals, principles, integrity, honesty, goodness, propriety, conduct, behaviour, manners
AN OPPOSITE IS immorality

**morbid** ADJECTIVE

1 *a morbid obsession with death*
▶ macabre, ghoulish, unhealthy, gruesome, grisly, unwholesome
2 *The thought of old age made her morbid.*
▶ gloomy, depressed, dejected, melancholy, downhearted, pessimistic
AN OPPOSITE IS cheerful

**more** ADJECTIVE

*They want more money.*
▶ additional, extra, further, added, increased, fresh, supplementary, other
AN OPPOSITE IS less

**morning** NOUN

*It was nearly morning when they finally reached home.*
▶ daybreak, dawn, daylight, sunrise, first light

a
b
c
d
e
f
g
h
i
j
k
l
**m**
n
o
p
q
r
s
t
u
v
w
x
y
z

A B C D E F G H I J K L M N O P Q R S T U V W X Y Z

**morose** ADJECTIVE
*Back home dad was looking very morose.*
► sullen, gloomy, bad-tempered, ill-tempered, glum, sour, surly, moody, tetchy, crabby
AN OPPOSITE IS cheerful

**morsel** NOUN
*a few morsels of food*
► bite, mouthful, nibble, taste, fragment, piece, scrap, crumb, titbit

**mortal** ADJECTIVE
1 *The coffins contained the mortal remains of the victims.*
► physical, bodily, corporeal, earthly, worldly, perishable
2 *She struck him a mortal blow.*
► deadly, fatal, lethal
3 *mortal enemies*
► deadly, bitter, irreconcilable
4 *living in mortal fear*
► extreme, intense, grave, dire

**mortal** NOUN
*a tale of mortals battling with divine forces.*
► human being, human, mortal creature, individual, person, man or woman, earthling

**mortified** ADJECTIVE
*He would be mortified if his friends knew.*
► humiliated, embarrassed, shamed, ashamed, crushed

**mostly** ADVERB
*She reads books all day, mostly novels.*
► mainly, chiefly, predominantly, primarily, principally, normally, typically, usually, generally, largely
OPPOSITES ARE rarely, hardly

**mother** NOUN
*Her mother picked her up every day from school.*
► female parent, (*more informal*) mum, (*more informal*) mummy, (*more informal*) ma, (*old-fashioned*) mater
RELATED ADJECTIVE maternal

**mother** VERB
*She was fond of mothering the residents when they were sick.*
► look after, care for, nurse, comfort, pamper, protect, cherish, fuss over

**motherly** ADJECTIVE
*a motherly woman*
► maternal, protective, caring, kind, loving

**motif** NOUN
*wallpaper with a repeated floral motif*
► design, device, pattern, symbol, ornament, figure, emblem

**motion** NOUN
*The motion of the bus made her queasy.*
► movement, moving, action, shifting, progress
RELATED ADJECTIVES dynamic, kinetic

**motion** VERB
*He motioned to them to go in.*
► gesture, signal, beckon, direct

**motionless** ADJECTIVE
1 *The traffic ahead was motionless.*
► static, stationary, immobile, still, at a standstill, at rest
AN OPPOSITE IS moving
2 *They stood motionless for several minutes, neither wanting to speak first.*
► still, stock-still, immobile, unmoving, paralysed, rooted to the spot, frozen, inert
OPPOSITES ARE moving, active

**motivate** VERB
*Money is what motivated them most.*
► prompt, drive, urge, stimulate, provoke, influence, activate, incite, persuade, impel

**motivation** NOUN
*the motivation to learn*
► incentive, stimulus, impulse, drive, inspiration, inducement, encouragement, spur

**motive** NOUN
*The police could not establish any motive for the attacks.*
► reason, grounds, rationale, motivation, object, intention, purpose, thinking, aim, cause

**motto** NOUN
*Their guiding motto was 'You scratch my back, and I'll scratch yours'.*
► saying, maxim, watchword, dictum, proverb, adage, precept, slogan, axiom

**mould** NOUN
1 *The cheese had mould on it.*
► mildew, fungus, must, growth
2 *The molten metal is poured into a mould.*
► cast, die, form, matrix, template

**mould** VERB
1 *The figures are moulded in bronze.*
► shape, form, fashion, forge, model, create, sculpt
2 *Education helps to mould your character.*
► form, shape, influence, determine, direct

**mouldy** ADJECTIVE
1 *a hunk of mouldy bread*
► mildewed, mildewy, mouldering, decaying, musty, rotten, stale
2 (*informal*) *The prize was just a mouldy book token.*
► measly, paltry, miserable, meagre, wretched, niggardly, pitiful, (*informal*) mingy

**mound** NOUN
1 *a mound of dirty socks*
► pile, heap, stack
2 *The common had several mounds to climb.*
► hill, hillock, hummock, rise, ridge, embankment

**mount** VERB

**1** *The gallery mounts a special exhibition every year.*
▶ put on, organize, present, display, show, exhibit
**2** *June mounted her pony.   The guest of honour mounted the platform.*
▶ climb on to, jump on to, get on, get up on, get astride
OPPOSITES ARE get off, climb down from
**3** *Our savings were mounting at last.*
▶ grow, increase, accumulate, pile up
OPPOSITES ARE dwindle, decrease

**mountain** NOUN

**1** *several mountains to climb in the area*
▶ peak, summit, height
RELATED ADJECTIVE alpine
**2** *a mountain of work to get through*
▶ heap, pile, load, mound, stack, mass, great deal, backlog

**mountainous** ADJECTIVE

**1** *mountainous country*
▶ hilly, craggy, rocky, alpine, highland, precipitous
**2** *mountainous waves*
▶ huge, enormous, gigantic, colossal, immense, towering, (*more informal*) ginormous

**mourn** VERB

**1** *He hid himself away, mourning his dead wife.*
▶ grieve for, sorrow over, lament for, weep for, pine for
**2** *We all mourn the loss of so many precious artefacts.*
▶ regret, deplore, bewail
AN OPPOSITE IS rejoice over

**mournful** ADJECTIVE

*mournful music   a mournful cry*
▶ sad, sorrowful, melancholy, unhappy, doleful, desolate, heartbroken, tragic, sombre

**mouth** NOUN

**1** *He opened his mouth.*
▶ jaws, lips, (*more informal*) gob
RELATED ADJECTIVE oral
**2** *the mouth of the cave*
▶ entrance, opening, entry, aperture
**3** *the mouth of a river*
▶ outfall, outlet, estuary, firth

**mouth** VERB

*Thank you, I answered, mouthing the words carefully.*
▶ utter, enunciate, pronounce, articulate, form, say

**mouthful** NOUN

**1** *a mouthful of food*
▶ bite, taste, morsel, nibble, gobbet, spoonful, swallow
**2** *a mouthful of water*
▶ gulp, draught, sip, swallow, (*more informal*) swig

**movable** ADJECTIVE

*They took all the movable furniture when they left.*
▶ portable, transportable, transferable, mobile, detachable
AN OPPOSITE IS immobile

**move** VERB This word is often overused. Here are some alternatives:
**1** *He got up and moved to the bench under the tree.*
▶ go, walk, march, proceed, advance, stroll, amble
**2** *The traffic moved slowly forward.*
▶ edge, creep, crawl, slide
**3** *I'll move the chair closer to the table.*
▶ carry, take, shift, transport
**4** *We need to move quickly to secure a place.*
▶ act, take action, take steps, make a move, take the initiative
**5** *At long last things are starting to move.*
▶ progress, make progress, make headway, develop, (*more informal*) get somewhere
**6** *She moved from London to the country last year.*
▶ relocate, move house, move home, migrate, decamp, depart
**7** *The beautiful performance moved them deeply.*
▶ touch, affect, impress, disturb, agitate
**8** *The language course moved her to find out about living abroad.*
▶ prompt, stimulate, motivate, persuade, rouse, impel, induce, inspire

**move** NOUN

**1** *The group got together to talk over their next move.*
▶ step, action, initiative, tactic, ploy, ruse
**2** *It's your move.*
▶ turn, go, opportunity, chance

**movement** NOUN

**1** *the movement of goods and animals*
▶ transportation, carrying, relocation, conveyance, transferral, repositioning
**2** *She joined a left-wing political movement in her student days.*
▶ party, organization, faction, group, grouping, campaign
**3** *A movement in the bushes caught his eye.*
▶ motion, move, activity, action
**4** *There has been little movement on our grant application.*
▶ progress, change, advance
**5** *a movement towards equal pay for men and women*
▶ trend, tendency, swing, current

**movie** NOUN

**1** *a horror movie*
▶ film, picture, feature, motion picture
**2** *Let's go to the movies.*
▶ cinema, films

**moving** ADJECTIVE

**1** *a moving train*
▶ travelling, mobile, active, on the move, under way
OPPOSITES ARE stationary, motionless
**2** *a moving story*
▶ touching, affecting, poignant, emotive, stirring, emotional, heart-warming, inspiring, exciting, stimulating
AN OPPOSITE IS unemotional

**mow** VERB
*Someone should mow the grass.*
▶ cut, trim, clip, crop

**much** NOUN
*We don't have much to do.*
▶ a lot, a great deal, plenty

**much** ADJECTIVE
*Do you need much help?*
▶ a lot of, a great deal of, plenty of, considerable, substantial

**muck** NOUN
1 *He went out to clean the muck off the windows.*
▶ dirt, grime, filth, slime, sludge, mess, mud, (*more informal*) gunge
2 *spreading muck in the fields*
▶ manure, dung

**muck** VERB
**muck about** or **around** (*informal*) *John was mucking about with an old engine.*
▶ fool about or around, play about or around, tinker, (*informal*) mess about or around

**mucky** ADJECTIVE
*She took off her mucky shoes.*
▶ dirty, messy, muddy, filthy, grubby, soiled, foul, grimy
AN OPPOSITE IS clean

**mud** NOUN
*He slipped and fell in the mud.*
▶ sludge, slime, slurry, clay, soil, dirt, mire, muck, ooze, silt

**muddle** NOUN
1 *a muddle over the time of the train*
▶ confusion, misunderstanding, mistake, mix-up
2 *Look at the muddle in the kitchen.*
▶ mess, shambles, jumble, clutter, chaos, untidiness, disorder, tangle

**muddle** VERB
1 *Her explanation merely muddled him.*
▶ confuse, bewilder, mix up, perplex, puzzle, disorientate, mislead
AN OPPOSITE IS enlighten
2 *Don't muddle the papers on the desk.*
▶ disorganize, disarrange, mix up, mess up, jumble up, make a mess of, disorder
OPPOSITES ARE tidy, clear up

**muddled** ADJECTIVE
*He felt muddled and couldn't think what to do.*
▶ confused, disorganized, bewildered, mixed up, perplexed, puzzled, disorientated

**muddy** ADJECTIVE
1 *They came in to change their muddy boots.*
▶ dirty, messy, mucky, filthy, grubby, soiled, foul, grimy
AN OPPOSITE IS clean
2 *The ground was wet and muddy.*
▶ waterlogged, boggy, marshy, sodden, soft, spongy, sloppy

3 *The water looked muddy.*
▶ cloudy, misty, opaque, messy
AN OPPOSITE IS clear

**muffle** VERB
*He muffled the sound of the gun with cushions.*
▶ deaden, dull, dampen, smother, soften, suppress, muzzle
**muffle up** *She went out, muffling herself up against the cold.*
▶ wrap up, cover up, envelop, swathe, enclose

**muffled** ADJECTIVE
*a muffled cry*
▶ faint, indistinct, muted, deadened, dull, unclear
OPPOSITES ARE distinct, loud

**mug** NOUN
1 *We drank tea from mugs.*
▶ beaker, cup
2 *He was rather a mug to drive so fast.*
▶ fool, simpleton, idiot, clot

**mug** VERB
*They were mugged on their way home.*
▶ attack, assault, molest, rob, steal from, set on, jump on
**mug up** *He's mugging up for his driving test.*
▶ study, learn, read up, cram

**muggy** ADJECTIVE
*muggy weather*
▶ humid, close, clammy, sultry, oppressive, sticky, stuffy, airless

**mull** VERB
**mull over** *a few suggestions to mull over*
▶ consider, ponder, think about, contemplate, reflect on, weigh up, turn over in your mind

**multiply** VERB
1 *The problems began to multiply.*
▶ increase, proliferate, grow, mount up, spread, become numerous
OPPOSITES ARE decrease, diminish
2 *The hedgehogs multiplied rapidly.*
▶ breed, propagate, reproduce, procreate

**multitude** NOUN
*a multitude of people a multitude of questions to answer*
▶ mass, host, myriad, swarm, throng, lots, large number, legion

**mumble** VERB
*She walked off, mumbling quietly.*
▶ mutter, murmur, whisper, burble

**mumbo-jumbo** NOUN
*The form was covered in mumbo-jumbo.*
▶ jargon, gobbledegook, gibberish, nonsense

**munch** VERB
*The children waited, munching their rolls.*
▶ chomp, crunch, eat, bite, chew, gnaw

## mundane

**mundane** ADJECTIVE

_She hoped such mundane matters would keep him occupied for a while._
► everyday, routine, commonplace, day-to-day, humdrum, tedious, dull, boring, unexceptional
OPPOSITES ARE extraordinary, exceptional

**murder** NOUN
_Reports are coming in of a brutal murder._
► killing , homicide, slaughter (= killing of many people), assassination (= killing of an important person), fratricide (= killing of a brother), infanticide (= killing of a child), matricide (= killing of a mother), parricide (= killing of a parent or close relative), patricide (= killing of a father), regicide (= killing of a king or queen)

**murder** VERB
_A gang had tried to murder him._
► kill, put to death, assassinate

**murderer** NOUN
_The murderer was never caught._
► killer, assassin

**murderous** ADJECTIVE
_a murderous assault_
► homicidal, deadly, lethal, brutal, bloodthirsty, barbarous, savage, ferocious, vicious

**murky** ADJECTIVE
_The sky was murky and drizzle was falling._
► gloomy, grey, dark, overcast, leaden, misty, dim, dull, cloudy, foggy, sombre
AN OPPOSITE IS clear

**murmur** VERB
_He murmured an apology and left._
► mutter, mumble, whisper, burble

**muscular** ADJECTIVE
_He's tall and muscular._
► brawny, muscly, athletic, strong, well built, beefy, strapping, sinewy

**mushy** ADJECTIVE
1 _The fruit was mushy and overripe._
► soft, pulpy, pappy, slushy, sloppy, squidgy
2 _They read a mushy article about being good neighbours._
► sentimental, mawkish, emotional, slushy

**music** NOUN
NAMES FOR TYPES OF MUSIC
**traditional music**: classical music, chamber music, instrumental music, orchestral music, choral music, opera; ballet music; folk music.
**rock and popular music**: pop music, rock, rock and roll, reggae, soul, jive, swing; acid house, funk, rap, hip-hop, garage, goth, grunge, heavy metal, punk, new wave, techno.
**jazz music**: jazz, traditional jazz (or trad), blues, ragtime, salsa, bebop, skiffle; .
**religious music**: church music, gospel music; hymn, anthem, cantata, spiritual, qawwali, bhjan.

NAMES FOR MUSICAL INSTRUMENTS
**keyboard instruments**: piano, pianoforte, grand piano, fortepiano, clavier; harpsichord, clavichord, spinet, virginals, celesta; organ, harmonium; electric organ, synthesizer; accordion.
**wind instruments**: bassoon, clarinet; oboe, cor anglais; flute, piccolo; recorder; saxophone; harmonica, mouth organ; bagpipes; ocarina (bird-shaped).
**brass instruments**: trumpet, bugle, cornet; trombone; horn, tuba, sousaphone, euphonium.
**stringed instruments**: violin, viola, cello, double bass; guitar, banjo, mandolin, lute, lyre, ukulele; balalaika (Russian guitar with triangular body), bouzouki (Greek mandolin), harp; sitar (Indian lute with a long neck), sarod (classical Indian lute), tamboura (large four-stringed Indian lute).
**percussion instruments**: drum, timpani (plural), kettledrum, snare drum, side drum, bongo, tom-tom, tam-tam, cymbal, triangle; tambourine, xylophone, glockenspiel, gongs, chimes; castanets, maracas, marimba; gamelan (band in Java and Bali), tabla (small hand drums used in Indian music), goombay (West Indian goatskin drum).

**musical** ADJECTIVE
_musical sounds_
► tuneful, melodic, melodious, euphonious, harmonious, lyrical, pleasant, sweet-sounding
AN OPPOSITE IS discordant

**musician** NOUN
_A small group of musicians were playing on the terrace._
► performer, player, instrumentalist

**muster** VERB
_The king mustered a large army._
► assemble, marshal, mobilize, gather, call together, summon, rally, convene, collect, get together

**musty** ADJECTIVE
_There is a musty smell in the room._
► mouldy, stale, stuffy, airless, damp, dank, fusty, mildewy

**mute** ADJECTIVE
_Yvonne remained mute._
► silent, speechless, unspeaking, dumb, tongue-tied, voiceless

**mutilate** VERB
_Some of the bodies had been mutilated._
► mangle, disfigure, cripple, dismember, cut up, lacerate, maim, disable, injure, lame, wound

**mutinous** ADJECTIVE
_mutinous soldiers_
► rebellious, insubordinate, seditious, insurgent, rebel

## mutiny NOUN

*a mutiny on board ship  a mutiny by government MPs*
▶ rebellion, revolt, protest, uprising, insurrection

## mutiny VERB

*The troops mutinied over pay.*
▶ rebel, revolt, rise up, protest, go on strike

## mutter VERB

*Her husband mutters in his sleep.*
▶ mumble, murmur, whisper, burble

## mutual ADJECTIVE

*an agreement based on mutual trust*
▶ joint, shared, reciprocal, reciprocated, common, complementary

## muzzle NOUN

*the dog's muzzle*
▶ snout, nose, mouth, jaws

## muzzle VERB

*crude attempts to muzzle the press*
▶ silence, restrain, stifle, suppress, censor, gag

## muzzy ADJECTIVE

*a muzzy feeling in the head*
▶ dazed, hazy, blurred, confused, muddled

## mysterious ADJECTIVE

*His friends had disappeared in mysterious circumstances.*
▶ strange, puzzling, odd, peculiar, curious, weird, obscure, baffling, unexplained, unknown
AN OPPOSITE IS straightforward

## mystery NOUN

1 *Their disappearance remains a mystery.*
▶ puzzle, enigma, riddle, conundrum
2 *events surrounded in mystery*
▶ secrecy, obscurity, uncertainty, ambiguity

## mystical ADJECTIVE

*a mystical experience*
▶ spiritual, religious, supernatural, metaphysical, transcendental, mysterious, abnormal, occult

## mystify VERB

*The work he did mystified his contemporaries.*
▶ puzzle, perplex, baffle, bewilder, bamboozle, confuse

## mythical ADJECTIVE

*a story based on mythical events*
▶ legendary, mythological, imaginary, fabled, fabulous, fictional, invented, fanciful, make-believe
AN OPPOSITE IS real

## mythological ADJECTIVE

*mythological gods and heroes*
▶ mythical, fabled, legendary, traditional

## mythology NOUN

*creatures in mythology*
▶ legend, myth, tradition, folklore

# Nn

## nab VERB

*(informal) A police car nabbed him on his way home.*
▶ catch, arrest, apprehend, take into custody

## nag VERB

*He's been nagging me about it for weeks.*
▶ harass, badger, pester, chivvy, hound, (*more informal*) keep on at, (*more informal*) go on at, (*more informal*) moan at

## nail NOUN

1 *The nail's fallen out so I'll have to use a screw.*
▶ tack, pin, stud
2 *He broke his nail opening a carton.*
RELATED ADJECTIVE ungual

## nail VERB

*Nail it to the wall.*
▶ hammer, pin, tack, fasten, attach, secure, fix

## naive ADJECTIVE

*I was very naive in those days but I've learned a lot since then.*
▶ innocent, ingenuous, unsophisticated, inexperienced, credulous, artless, raw, green
OPPOSITES ARE sophisticated, experienced, knowing

## naked ADJECTIVE

1 *a naked statue*
▶ nude, bare, unclothed, uncovered, undressed, unclad
AN OPPOSITE IS clothed
2 *the naked truth*
▶ plain, undisguised, unadorned, unvarnished, simple, bald, unmitigated

## name NOUN

*His name is Carl.*
▶ first name, forename, (*more formal*) denomination, (*more formal*) appellation
RELATED ADJECTIVES nominal, onomastic

## name VERB

1 *Her father had wanted to name her Clio.*
▶ call, dub, style, christen, baptize
2 *The victim will not be be named until relatives have been notified.*
▶ identify, specify
3 *The king has to name a successor.*
▶ choose, designate, nominate, decide on, specify, appoint

## nameless ADJECTIVE

*pictures by a nameless artist*
▶ unnamed, unidentified, anonymous, unheard of

## nap NOUN

*He was on the sofa, having a nap.*
▶ snooze, doze, sleep, rest, lie-down, (*more informal*) forty winks

## narrate VERB
*The story is narrated by the governess.*
▶ tell, relate, recount, report, describe, unfold, detail, relay, chronicle

## narrative NOUN
*a chronological narrative of the events of the last five years*
▶ account, summary, narration, commentary, description, sketch

## narrow ADJECTIVE
**1** *a narrow path* She was elected by a narrow majority.
▶ slim, thin, slender, fine
**2** *a narrow space*
▶ tight, close, confined, cramped, enclosed, limited, constricting
AN OPPOSITE IS wide
**3** *a narrow point of view*
▶ narrow-minded, intolerant, conservative, illiberal, insular, parochial, small-minded, bigoted, hidebound
OPPOSITES ARE broad-minded, open-minded, tolerant

## narrow-minded ADJECTIVE
*a narrow-minded outlook*
▶ small-minded, intolerant, narrow, bigoted, conservative, illiberal, insular, parochial, short-sighted, hidebound
OPPOSITES ARE broad-minded, open-minded, tolerant

## nasty ADJECTIVE
**1** *The pudding had a nasty taste*
▶ unpleasant, disagreeable, disgusting, horrible, disgusting, repellent
OPPOSITES ARE pleasant, nice, lovely
**2** *He can be very nasty at times.*
▶ unkind, unfriendly, unpleasant, disagreeable, malicious, mean, spiteful, vindictive
**3** *The weather turned nasty.*
▶ unpleasant, rough, squally
OPPOSITES ARE fine, pleasant

## nation NOUN
**1** *The president will broadcast to the nation.*
▶ people, population, country, community, society
**2** *the nations of the world*
▶ country, people, civilization, land, power, race, state
RELATED ADJECTIVE ethnic

## national ADJECTIVE
**1** *a national strike*
▶ nationwide, countrywide, general, widespread
**2** *national costume*
▶ ethnic, popular, domestic

## national NOUN
*an Italian national*
▶ citizen, subject, native, resident, inhabitant

## nationalism NOUN
*the surge of nationalism in Europe*
▶ patriotism, (*disapproving*) chauvinism, (*disapproving*) jingoism, (*disapproving*) xenophobia

## native ADJECTIVE
**1** *native inhabitants*
▶ original, aboriginal, indigenous
**2** *a native instinct for politics*
▶ innate, inherent, inborn, inbred, natural, congenital, hereditary, inherited

## native NOUN
*a native of New York*
▶ inhabitant, resident, citizen, national

## natter VERB
*It was natural for them to make complaints.*
▶ chatter, chat, prattle, blather, burble, talk

## natural ADJECTIVE
**1** *a natural tendency to self-preservation*
▶ innate, inborn, instinctive, intuitive, inherent
**2** *Her manner is fresh and natural.*
▶ genuine, sincere, unaffected, uninhibited, ingenuous, open
**3** *It was natural for them to want more information.*
▶ understandable, reasonable, logical, unsurprising, predictable
**4** *Kim proved to be a natural leader.*
▶ born, spontaneous, untaught
**5** *The bay forms a natural port on this side of the island.*
▶ ready-made

## nature NOUN
**1** *the beauties of nature*
▶ the natural world, the living world, the environment, the countryside, the landscape
**2** *It's not in his nature to make complaints.*
▶ character, personality, temperament, disposition, constitution, make-up
**3** *decisions that by their nature cause resentment*
▶ essence, characteristics
**4** *coins, medals, and things of that nature*
▶ kind, type, sort, category, description

## naughty ADJECTIVE
**1** *a naughty child*
▶ badly behaved, mischievous, misbehaving, disobedient, insubordinate, troublesome, vexatious
**2** *a naughty film*
▶ indecent, suggestive, obscene, pornographic

## nausea NOUN
*He had a bad headache and a feeling of nausea.*
▶ sickness, queasiness, biliousness, retching, vomiting

## nauseating ADJECTIVES
*She disliked his nauseating self-importance.*
▶ sickening, disgusting, revolting, repulsive, repellent, loathsome, offensive

## nauseous ADJECTIVE
*The stench made him feel nauseous.*
▶ sick, disgusted, queasy, bilious

## nautical ADJECTIVE
*eating seafood in a nautical atmosphere*
▶ maritime, naval, marine, seafaring, seagoing

a b c d e f g h i j k l m **n** o p q r s t u v w x y z

**naval** ADJECTIVE
*Mediterranean naval bases*
▶ nautical, maritime, marine

**navel** NOUN
*She wore a bright stud in her navel.*
▶ (*more informal*) belly button, (*more informal*) tummy button, (*technical*) umbilicus
RELATED ADJECTIVE umbilical

**navigate** VERB
**1** *She navigated the yacht round the world.*
▶ steer, pilot, direct, handle, manoeuvre, (*more informal*) skipper
**2** *Parts of the river are hard to navigate.*
▶ negotiate, cross, traverse, sail over

**navy** NOUN
*an officer in the navy*
▶ fleet, armada, convoy, flotilla, naval force

**near** ADJECTIVE
**1** *She is a near neighbour of ours.*
▶ nearby, close, adjacent, adjoining, next-door, bordering, connected, neighbouring
OPPOSITES ARE distant, faraway
**2** *A decision is near.*
▶ close, approaching, imminent, coming, forthcoming, impending, (*more informal*) round the corner
**3** *near relatives*
▶ close, dear, familiar, intimate
AN OPPOSITE IS distant

**nearby** ADVERB
*Her children all live nearby.*
▶ close by, not far away, at hand, within reach, in the vicinity

**nearly** ADVERB
*The work is nearly finished.*
▶ almost, practically, virtually, about, more or less, as good as, just about, around

**neat** ADJECTIVE
**1** *The room was neat and newly decorated.*
▶ tidy, orderly, trim, spick-and-span, spruce, immaculate
OPPOSITES ARE untidy, messy
**2** *hair tied in a neat bun at the back*
▶ compact, elegant, trim, well formed, simple
OPPOSITES ARE clumsy, awkward
**3** *neat writing*
▶ regular, precise, well formed, elegant
**4** *a neat solution to the problem*
▶ clever, ingenious, adroit, deft, inventive, resourceful, slick
AN OPPOSITE IS inept
**5** *a glass of neat whisky*
▶ undiluted, straight, pure, unmixed, unadulterated
AN OPPOSITE IS diluted

**nebulous** ADJECTIVE
*We need more than a few nebulous ideas.*
▶ vague, hazy, uncertain, muddled, confused, half-formed, (*more informal*) half-baked

**necessary** ADJECTIVE
*necessary repairs to the bridge*
▶ essential, indispensable, vital, unavoidable, requisite, needed, needful, obligatory, imperative, compulsory, mandatory
AN OPPOSITE IS unnecessary

**necessitate** VERB
*Measures as drastic as these would necessitate legislation.*
▶ require, involve, entail, demand, call for, mean, compel

**necessity** NOUN
**1** *A mobile phone is now regarded as a necessity by most people.*
▶ essential, requirement, prerequisite
**2** *Necessity compelled thousands to emigrate.*
▶ need, poverty, hardship, destitution, penury, deprivation
**3** *the necessity for caution*
▶ need, demand, indispensability (of)

**need** VERB
**1** *The room needs redecorating.*
▶ require, want, be in need of, demand, call for
**2** *We need more milk.*
▶ require, want, be short of, lack
**3** *He needed her so much now.*
▶ yearn for, long for, pine for, crave, depend on, rely on
**4** **need to** *Do we need to come?*
▶ have to, be obliged to, be required to, be compelled to, be under an obligation to

**need** NOUN
**1** *There is no need to say anything.*
▶ necessity, obligation, call, requirement
**2** *basic human needs like food and water*
▶ requirement, essential, necessity, want, prerequisite

**needle** VERB
*You shouldn't let them needle you like that.*
▶ annoy, irritate, goad, hassle, rile, niggle

**needless** ADJECTIVE
*a lot of needless expense*
▶ unnecessary, unwanted, inessential, unneeded, gratuitous, superfluous, pointless

**needy** ADJECTIVE
*day centres for the frail and needy*
▶ poor, deprived, destitute, impoverished, underprivileged, penniless

**negate** VERB
*The decision negates years of hard work.*
▶ nullify, invalidate, undo, reverse, cancel, neutralize, abrogate, countermand

**negative** ADJECTIVE
**1** *a negative response*
▶ dissenting, saying 'no', rejecting, refusing
OPPOSITES ARE affirmative, positive

**2** *They have been criticized for their negative attitudes.*
▶ pessimistic, unenthusiastic, uncooperative, defeatist, dismissive, antipathetic
AN OPPOSITE IS positive

**neglect** VERB
**1** *He'd been neglecting his work for the past week.*
▶ pay no attention to, ignore, let slide, shirk, skip, disregard, overlook, forget, leave alone
AN OPPOSITE IS concentrate on
**2** *She neglected her son and had a succession of boyfriends.*
▶ fail to take care of, fail to look after, abandon, spurn, forsake
AN OPPOSITE IS look after
**3** *He was being neglected by all his friends.*
▶ ignore, disregard, abandon, rebuff, disdain, slight
AN OPPOSITE IS appreciate

**neglect** NOUN
*The building had suffered from years of neglect.*
▶ negligence, carelessness, dereliction of duty, inattention, indifference, slackness
OPPOSITES ARE attention, care

**neglected** ADJECTIVE
*The back of the house overlooked a neglected garden.*
▶ untended, uncared for, derelict, dilapidated, run-down, ramshackle, overgrown

**negligence** NOUN
*The company was accused of negligence.*
▶ dereliction of duty, remissness, irresponsibility, carelessness, failure to take proper care
AN OPPOSITE IS conscientiousness

**negligent** ADJECTIVE
*He claimed that the doctors had been negligent.*
▶ neglectful, careless, irresponsible, inattentive
OPPOSITES ARE conscientious, careful

**negligible** ADJECTIVE
*The difference in price is negligible.*
▶ tiny, trifling, trivial, insignificant, unimportant, inconsequential, imperceptible, inconsiderable, minor, slight, small
OPPOSITES ARE considerable, significant

**negotiate** VERB
**1** *We would like to negotiate a better deal.*
▶ work out, hammer out, agree on, reach agreement on, settle, transact
**2** *The other side refused to negotiate.*
▶ consult, confer, discuss terms, deal, talk, parley
**3** *The road has several sharp bends to negotiate.*
▶ get round, clear, pass round, deal with, overcome

**negotiation** NOUN
*The negotiations will begin in Rome next week.*
▶ discussion, consultation, bargaining, arbitration, mediation, conciliation, transaction, debate, diplomacy

**neighbourhood** NOUN
*a quiet neighbourhood*
▶ district, area, locality, vicinity, region, place, community, environs, surroundings, zone

**neighbouring** ADJECTIVE
*The neighbouring buildings have parking facilities.*
▶ nearby, adjacent, adjoining, nearest, closest, next-door, bordering, close
OPPOSITES ARE distant, remote

**neighbourly** ADJECTIVE
*a neighbourly offer of help*
▶ friendly, amiable, obliging, considerate, kind, helpful, genial, sociable, companionable

**nerve** NOUN
**1** *The manoeuvre takes some nerve and a good sense of timing. He lost his nerve at the last moment and couldn't go through with it.*
▶ courage, bravery, boldness, daring, gallantry, determination, fearlessness, fortitude, heroism, (more informal) bottle, (more informal) grit, (more informal) guts, (more informal) pluck, (much more informal) spunk
**2** *They had the nerve to ask for more money.*
▶ cheek, audacity, effrontery, temerity, impertinence, impudence, insolence, presumptuousness, shamelessness, (more informal) sauce
**3** *the nerves in your body*
RELATED ADJECTIVE neural

**nervous** ADJECTIVE
**1** *a nervous girl who always wore black*
▶ highly-strung, nervy, anxious, excitable
**2** *He was getting a little nervous out there, all by himself.*
▶ anxious, worried, apprehensive, agitated, concerned, (more informal) jumpy, (more informal) jittery

**nestle** VERB
*The children nestled together in the back of the car.*
▶ huddle, cuddle, nuzzle, snuggle, curl up, lie comfortably

**net** NOUN
*The gardener put nets on the trees to catch falling fruit.*
▶ mesh, netting, webbing, lattice

**net** VERB
**1** *He managed to net the fish at last.*
▶ catch, land
**2** *Top executives can net enormous bonuses as well as their massive salaries.*
▶ earn, get, make, receive, bring in, clear, accumulate

**nettle** VERB
*remarks that began to nettle him*
▶ annoy, irritate, displease, anger, infuriate, enrage, exasperate, incense, vex, madden, aggravate, antagonize, inflame, make angry, (more informal) needle, (more informal) rile, (more informal) bug, (more informal) rub up the wrong way

**network** NOUN

**1** *a network of tiny tubes*
▸ web, grid, mesh, net, netting, crisscross pattern, labyrinth, lattice, maze, tracery

**2** *a computer network   the rail network*
▸ system, complex, organization

**neurotic** ADJECTIVE

*He always tries to depict me as incompetent and neurotic.*
▸ unstable, mentally unbalanced, disturbed, maladjusted, nervous, obsessive, overwrought

**neutral** ADJECTIVE

**1** *He would be the perfect neutral umpire.*
▸ impartial, unbiased, objective, disinterested, unprejudiced, even-handed
OPPOSITES ARE biased, prejudiced

**2** *neutral colours*
▸ dull, indefinite, indeterminate, intermediate, characterless, colourless, middle
AN OPPOSITE IS distinctive

**neutralize** VERB

*Alkalis neutralize acids.*
▸ counteract, counterbalance, cancel out, invalidate, make ineffective, negate, nullify, offset

**never-ending** ADJECTIVE

*They were having never-ending rows.*
▸ constant, continual, endless, incessant, persistent, interminable

---

**new** ADJECTIVE This word is often overused. Here are some alternatives:
**1** *new ways of beating crime*
▸ modern, recent, up-to-date, advanced
**2** *We need some new ideas.*
▸ fresh, original, innovative, novel, creative, different
**3** *The school has had some new labs built.*
▸ additional, extra, more, further, supplementary, fresh
**4** *After the operation I felt a new person.*
▸ changed, improved, restored, revived, invigorated

---

**newcomer** NOUN

*She watched the newcomers suspiciously from her open door.*
▸ new arrival, outsider, settler, stranger, immigrant, novice, beginner

**news** NOUN

*The news of his death stunned his colleagues.*
▸ report, announcement, story, account, tidings, information (about), disclosure (about), statement, revelation

**next** ADJECTIVE

**1** *Her friend lived in the next street*
▸ adjacent, neighbouring, adjoining, connecting, closest, nearest
AN OPPOSITE IS distant

**2** *The next train is not for another hour.*
▸ following, soonest, succeeding, subsequent
AN OPPOSITE IS previous

**nibble** VERB

*She nibbled her sandwich while she waited.*
▸ munch, pick at, gnaw, eat

---

**nice** ADJECTIVE This word is often overused. Here are some alternatives:
**1** *We had a nice time in Greece.*
▸ pleasant, agreeable, enjoyable, marvellous, wonderful, delightful, splendid
**2** *They are such nice people.*
▸ pleasant, likeable, agreeable, personable, friendly, congenial, genial
**3** *That's rather a nice distinction.*
▸ fine, subtle, delicate, fastidious

---

**niche** NOUN

**1** *A little statue stood in a niche in the wall.*
▸ recess, alcove, nook, cavity
**2** *She felt she had found her niche in life.*
▸ place, slot, position, calling, vocation

**nick** VERB

**1** *He had nicked his skin while shaving.*
▸ cut
**2** (informal) *Someone nicked my pen.*
▸ steal, take, (informal) pinch

**nick** NOUN

**1** *a nick in the wood*
▸ cut, notch, chip, groove, scar
**2** (informal) *The car is in good nick.*
▸ condition, shape, repair, order, trim, fettle

**nickname** NOUN

*Her nickname is 'Posh'.*
▸ pet name, sobriquet, tag, alias

**night** NOUN

*It had rained in the night.*
▸ night-time, dark
RELATED ADJECTIVE nocturnal

**nightmare** NOUN

**1** *After the accident he had a series of nightmares.*
▸ bad dream
**2** *Getting the tyre fixed had been a nightmare.*
▸ ordeal, trial, torment

**nimble** ADJECTIVE

*He was surprisingly light and nimble on his feet.*
▸ agile, lithe, lively, sprightly, deft, quick, graceful, (informal) nippy

**nip** VERB

**1** *The dog nipped her leg.*
▸ bite, peck, snap at, pinch, tweak
**2** (informal) *I'll nip round and see how he's getting on.*
▸ go, dash, drop, (informal) pop

**nippy** ADJECTIVE

**1** (informal) *She drives a nippy two-seater.*
▸ speedy, fast, nimble, quick, rapid
**2** (informal) *The weather's quite nippy for June.*
▸ chilly, cold, raw

**nitty-gritty** NOUN
(*informal*) *Her job involves getting stuck into the nitty-gritty.*
▶ basics, essentials, hard work, (*informal*) slog

**nobility** NOUN
**1** *actions that showed true nobility*
▶ honour, dignity, nobleness, uprightness, virtue, worthiness, greatness, integrity, magnanimity, morality
**2** *The king had the support of the nobility.*
▶ aristocracy, gentry, nobles, lords, peerage

**noble** ADJECTIVE
**1** *He came from a noble family.*
▶ aristocratic, high-born, patrician, princely, (*informal*) blue-blooded
AN OPPOSITE IS humble
**2** *a noble deed*
▶ honourable, virtuous, worthy, brave, chivalrous, courageous, gallant, glorious, heroic, magnanimous
AN OPPOSITE IS ignoble
**3** *a noble building*
▶ imposing, impressive, magnificent, elegant, grand, majestic, splendid, stately, dignified, distinguished, great
AN OPPOSITE IS unimpressive

**noble** NOUN
*War was the principal activity of many of the nobles in Edward's reign.*
▶ aristocrat, nobleman, noblewoman, lord, peer, grandee, lady, peers

**nod** VERB
**1** *She nodded to him to go in.*
▶ signal, gesture, indicate, sign
**2** *He nodded his head in agreement.*
▶ incline, bob, dip, lower
**nod off** *She nodded off and started to snore.*
▶ fall asleep, go to sleep, doze off, drop off

**nod** NOUN
*He gave us a discreet nod.*
▶ signal, gesture, cue

**noise** NOUN
*The noise from below battered her eardrums.*
▶ sound, din, clamour, racket, uproar, tumult, commotion, crash, clatter, clash, (*more informal*) hullabaloo
AN OPPOSITE IS silence

**noisy** ADJECTIVE
**1** *He loved this noisy, busy city.*
▶ loud, clamorous, rackety, tumultuous, turbulent, deafening
**2** *The plane completed its noisy take-off.*
▶ loud, deafening, ear-splitting, thunderous
**3** *They were disturbed by the noisy argument going on in the next room.*
▶ loud, vociferous, raucous, rowdy, strident, shouting, shrieking

**nomad** NOUN
*a group of nomads driving cattle*
▶ traveller, wanderer, itinerant, migrant, rover

**nomadic** ADJECTIVE
*nomadic peoples*
▶ travelling, wandering, itinerant, roving

**nominal** ADJECTIVE
**1** *The president is nominal head of the organization but has few real powers.*
▶ formal, official, ostensible, supposed, theoretical, in name only
**2** *The family continued to live in the house for a nominal rent.*
▶ token, symbolic, minimal, small, peppercorn

**nominate** VERB
*It is a good idea to nominate an adult to supervise the children's activities.*
▶ choose, appoint, designate, name, select, elect

**nonchalant** ADJECTIVE
*Kate leant back, trying to look nonchalant.*
▶ unconcerned, detached, relaxed, indifferent, dispassionate, unemotional, unruffled, blasé, calm, casual, cool, (*more informal*) laid-back
AN OPPOSITE IS anxious

**non-committal** ADJECTIVE
*He held up a hand in a non-committal gesture.*
▶ guarded, cautious, wary, discreet, (*more informal*) cagey

**nondescript** ADJECTIVE
*The town was a nondescript, cheerless place.*
▶ ordinary, undistinguished, commonplace, average, dull, uninspiring
OPPOSITES ARE distinctive, remarkable

**nonentity** NOUN
*a nonentity incapable of making decisions*
▶ nobody, nothing, cipher, person of straw, person of no importance

**non-existent** ADJECTIVE
*The cupboard had a row of hangars for my non-existent dozen suits.*
▶ imaginary, fictitious, mythical, supposed, unreal, hypothetical, imagined, legendary, made-up
AN OPPOSITE IS existing

---

**non-fiction** NOUN

**TYPES OF NON-FICTION WRITING**

anthology (collection of short items), article (short essay in a magazine or newspaper), journalism; autobiography, biography, memoir, essay; travel writing, monograph (short book on a specific subject), reference, encyclopedias, dictionaries, thesauruses, gazetteers, atlases; sacred writing, holy books.

**OTHER TYPES OF NON-FICTION**

report, recount, advice text, persuasive text, revue, instruction, explanation text.

---

**nonplussed** ADJECTIVE
*The confusion left us feeling nonplussed.*
▶ surprised, disconcerted, astonished, astounded, bewildered, stunned, flummoxed, stupefied, perplexed, (*more informal*) thunderstruck

a b c d e f g h i j k l m n o p q r s t u v w x y z

**nonsense** NOUN

**1** *They're talking nonsense.*
▶ rubbish, balderdash, gibberish, claptrap, drivel, gobbledegook, (*more informal*) rot, (*more informal*) twaddle

**2** *The idea was a complete nonsense.*
▶ absurdity, folly, mistake, inanity

**nonsensical** ADJECTIVE

*The suggestion was nonsensical and shouldn't be taken seriously.*
▶ absurd, ludicrous, meaningless, ridiculous, senseless, unreasonable, incomprehensible, foolish, crazy, laughable, silly, stupid, fatuous, inane, illogical, irrational
AN OPPOSITE IS sensible

**non-stop** ADJECTIVE

*non-stop fun and laughter*
▶ continuous, constant, endless, uninterrupted, unending, never-ending, ceaseless

**non-stop** ADVERB

*We worked non-stop to get the job finished.*
▶ continuously, all the time, unceasingly, incessantly, steadily, round the clock

**nook** NOUN

*a nook in the corner with magazines to read*
▶ recess, alcove, niche, hollow, cubbyhole

**norm** NOUN

*Society imposes its own norms of behaviour.*
▶ standard, principle, yardstick, benchmark, pattern, basis, guide (to)

**normal** ADJECTIVE

**1** *They seem like a perfectly normal couple.*
▶ ordinary, average, typical, run-of-the-mill, standard, conventional, everyday

**2** *During the holidays you can borrow books in the normal way.*
▶ usual, customary, standard, regular, routine, habitual, established

**normality** NOUN

*The household returned to something like normality.*
▶ routine, regularity, typicality, usualness

**normally** ADVERB

**1** *Reminders are normally sent out at the beginning of the month.*
▶ usually, ordinarily, customarily, typically
AN OPPOSITE IS exceptionally

**2** *They just wanted to be able to live normally again.*
▶ as normal, in the normal way

**nose** NOUN

**1** *He stood scratching the side of his nose.*
▶ nostrils, (*technical*) proboscis, snout
RELATED ADJECTIVE nasal

**2** *The nose of a boat appeared at the harbour entrance.*
▶ prow, bow, front

**nose** VERB

*He nosed the car into a gap in the traffic.*
▶ ease, inch, edge, move, manoeuvre
**nose about** *Her friend was nosing about downstairs.*
▶ explore, ferret, search, snoop, prowl
**nose into** *I wish they would stop nosing into our business.*
▶ interfere in, meddle in, pry into, snoop in

**nostalgic** ADJECTIVE

*The smell of the place aroused nostalgic feelings.*
▶ evocative, wistful, emotional, yearning, regretful, sentimental, romantic, maudlin

**nosy** ADJECTIVE

*He always wanted to help, but sometimes he seemed too nosy for his own good.*
▶ inquisitive, prying, intrusive, curious, (*more informal*) snoopy

**notable** ADJECTIVE

**1** *Musicians (with some notable exceptions) are highly practical people.*
▶ significant, noteworthy, remarkable, important, memorable
AN OPPOSITE IS insignificant

**2** *a notable American statesman*
▶ prominent, famous, distinguished, noted, eminent, illustrious
OPPOSITES ARE obscure, unknown

**notch** NOUN

**1** *The bow string fits into a notch in the arrow.*
▶ nick, groove, incision, cut
**2** *His spirits lifted a notch.*
▶ degree, step, point, level

**notch** VERB

**notch up** *He hoped to notch up another good mark with Harriet.*
▶ earn, score, gain, achieve, acquire

**note** NOUN

**1** *Leave me a note before you go.*
▶ message, communication, letter, memo, line
**2** *I'll make a note of her new address.*
▶ record, entry, reminder
**3** *Someone had written notes in the margin.*
▶ comment, annotation, gloss, remark
**4** *a writer of some note*
▶ importance, distinction, renown, eminence, acclaim

**note** VERB

**1** *Note the new cafeteria built since our last visit.*
▶ observe, notice, see, remark
**2** *I'll be happy to note your suggestion.*
▶ consider, heed, bear in mind, make a note of, take into account
**3** *Note the dates in your diary.*
▶ write down, jot down, enter, record, scribble

**notebook** NOUN

*She wrote the details in a notebook.*
▶ exercise book, jotter, writing book, diary

**noted** ADJECTIVE
*a noted local celebrity*
► famous, well-known, renowned, notable
OPPOSITES ARE obscure, unknown

**noteworthy** ADJECTIVE
*a noteworthy addition to his collection*
► important, significant, notable, remarkable,
striking
OPPOSITES ARE insignificant, unimportant

**notice** NOUN
**1** *There was a notice pinned on the classroom door.*
► announcement, message, note, information
sheet, poster, sticker, sign, placard, warning
**2** *Nothing escaped her notice that day.*
► attention, observation, awareness, perception,
heed
**take no notice of** *Take no notice of the shouting.*
► ignore, disregard, pay no attention to, pass over

**notice** VERB
**1** *Did you notice the window was open?*
► observe, perceive, see, spot
**2** *I noticed a smell of gas in the kitchen.*
► detect, perceive, note

**noticeable** ADJECTIVE
*a noticeable reduction in the cost*
► perceptible, appreciable, observable,
conspicuous, recognizable, distinct, marked,
significant, unmistakable
AN OPPOSITE IS imperceptible

**notify** VERB
*Parents will be notified of any changes.*
► inform, advise, tell, apprise, let somebody know

**notion** NOUN
**1** *Paul was a dreamer, his head full of wild notions.*
► idea, belief, concept, thought, image, perception,
opinion
**2** *He had no notion of what her words meant.*
► understanding, idea, knowledge, clue

**notional** ADJECTIVE
*the notional line along the horizon*
► theoretical, hypothetical, conjectural, putative,
imaginary

**notoriety** NOUN
*He was fast achieving notoriety as a writer of racy
stories.*
► infamy, ill repute, dishonour, discredit, scandal

**notorious** ADJECTIVE
*one of the most notorious villains in London*
► infamous, disreputable, dishonourable,
ignominious, ill-famed

**nought** NOUN
**1** *Her card number has a lot of noughts in it.*
► zero, nil, O
**2** *One of the contestants scored a resounding nought.*
► nil, zero, nothing, (more informal) zilch

**nourish** VERB
*They had just enough money to nourish their children.*
► feed, provide for, support, sustain, maintain

**nourishing** ADJECTIVE
*a nourishing diet*
► nutritious, wholesome, sustaining, healthy,
nutritive, beneficial, health-giving

**nourishment** NOUN
*the nourishment that elderly people require*
► sustenance, nutriment, nutrition, diet, food,
subsistence, goodness

**novel** ADJECTIVE
*a novel idea for its time*
► new, original, innovative, unconventional,
unfamiliar, unusual, fresh, imaginative, different,
singular, surprising, uncommon
OPPOSITES ARE familiar, common, hackneyed

**novelty** NOUN
**1** *the beauty and novelty of the poetry*
► freshness, originality, unfamiliarity,
unconventionality, imaginativeness, newness
**2** *a little shop selling sweets and novelties*
► knick-knack, trinket, souvenir, bauble, curiosity,
gimmick

**novice** NOUN
*He admitted he was only a novice at sailing.*
► beginner, learner, newcomer, new recruit,
neophyte

**now** ADVERB
**1** *You need to decide now.*
► immediately, straight away, here and now, on the
spot, without delay
**2** *The box office is closed now.*
► at present, at the moment, at the minute,
currently

**noxious** ADJECTIVE
*noxious substances*
► poisonous, harmful, toxic, foul, unwholesome,
destructive, corrosive, noisome
OPPOSITES ARE innocuous, harmless

**nub** NOUN
*Money is the nub of the problem.*
► crux, essence, central point, core, gist

**nucleus** NOUN
*These three chapters form the nucleus of the description.*
► heart, core, centre, kernel

**nude** ADJECTIVE
*Nude bathing is forbidden.*
► naked, unclothed, undressed, uncovered, bare

**nudge** VERB
*Every time he laughed she nudged him in his side.*
► poke, prod, shove, jog, jolt, bump, hit, touch

**nuisance** NOUN
**1** *What a nuisance for you, having to go back into
hospital.*
► inconvenience, annoyance, bother, bore, trial,
irritant, irritation, worry, pest, vexation, trouble,
(more informal) pain
**2** *I'm sorry if I'm being a nuisance.*
► pest, bother, trial, burden

## nullify VERB

*The opposition has promised to nullify the current legislation.*
▶ cancel, repeal, rescind, revoke, abolish, annul, do away with, invalidate, negate, neutralize

## numb ADJECTIVE

*My hands were numb with cold.*
▶ dead, frozen, numbed, benumbed, insensitive, unfeeling
AN OPPOSITE IS sensitive

## numb VERB

*Sheer terror had numbed her senses.*
▶ deaden, paralyse, desensitize, freeze, immobilize, make numb, anaesthetize

## number NOUN

1 *The paper had a line of numbers written on it.*
▶ figure, numeral, integer, digit, unit
RELATED ADJECTIVE numerical
2 *a large number of children*
▶ quantity, amount, collection, sum, total, crowd, multitude, aggregate
3 *The film included a few musical numbers.*
▶ item, piece, song
4 *the spring number of the magazine*
▶ issue, edition, publication, impression, printing

## number VERB

*Visitors to the city this year numbered over ten million.*
▶ total, add up to, amount to, come to

## numeral NOUN

*Items over a hundred are written in numerals.*
▶ figure, digit, integer, number

## numerous ADJECTIVE

*Numerous reasons have been given to justify the invasion.*
▶ many, several, a lot of, plenty of, copious, abundant, profuse, multitudinous, diverse, sundry
AN OPPOSITE IS few

## nurse VERB

1 *She nursed her old father for years.*
▶ look after, care for, take care of, tend, treat
2 *A woman was nursing a baby.*
▶ breastfeed, feed, suckle
3 *hopes that have to be nursed until they become reality*
▶ preserve, sustain, support, cherish, maintain, encourage
4 *They went on nursing their grievance all their lives.*
▶ harbour, foster, bear

## nursery NOUN

*The youngest children were at the nursery.*
▶ nursery school, playgroup, kindergarten, crèche

## nurture VERB

1 *nurturing young children*
▶ bring up, look after, care for, provide for, nourish, educate, rear
2 *She nurtured a deep interest in the classical world.*
▶ foster, cultivate, encourage, promote, stimulate

## nut NOUN

KINDS OF NUT INCLUDE
almond, areca, beechnut, brazil, cashew, chestnut, cob-nut, coconut, filbert, hazel, monkey nut, peanut, pecan, pistachio, walnut.

## nutritious ADJECTIVE

*nutritious food*
▶ nourishing, wholesome, sustaining, healthy, nutritive, beneficial, health-giving

# Oo

## oaf NOUN

*She called him a loud-mouthed oaf.*
▶ lout, fool, dolt, ass, idiot, clod, clot

## oath NOUN

1 *The nobles refused to take the oath of allegiance to the king.*
▶ vow, pledge, promise, affirmation, avowal
2 *He uttered a terrible oath.*
▶ swear word, profanity, expletive, imprecation, curse, obscenity

## obedient ADJECTIVE

*She was described as a good girl, always obedient.*
▶ dutiful, compliant, deferential, respectful, well-behaved, subservient, submissive, acquiescent, amenable, biddable, tractable
AN OPPOSITE IS disobedient

## obese ADJECTIVE

*The proportion of obese men has risen to 8 percent.*
▶ fat, overweight, outsize, corpulent, rotund

## obey VERB

1 *I obeyed him without question.*
▶ do what someone says, take orders from, submit to, defer to
2 *He was not too good at obeying orders.*
▶ follow, carry out, perform, discharge, execute
3 *Her legs wouldn't obey her brain's command to move.*
▶ respond to, respect, abide by

## object NOUN

1 *It's an object I found on the beach.*
▶ article, body, item, thing
2 *Research is published regularly with the object of providing the most up-to-date findings.*
▶ objective, purpose, intention, aim, point, target, end, goal, intent

## object VERB

1 *I'll open a window if you don't object.*
▶ mind, protest, demur
2 *object to I hope they don't object to us coming.*
▶ oppose, protest against, be against, disapprove of, take exception to

## objection NOUN

*The scheme went ahead despite many objections.*
▶ protest, protestation, challenge, complaint, exception, dissent, disapproval, opposition, remonstration

## objectionable ADJECTIVE

*He can be objectionable when he wants to be. There was an objectionable smell in the room.*
▶ unpleasant, offensive, disagreeable, obnoxious, intolerable, unacceptable, nasty, repellent, distasteful

## objective ADJECTIVE

1 *The case lacks objective evidence.*
▶ impartial, unbiased, disinterested, neutral, detached, dispassionate
AN OPPOSITE IS subjective

2 *a research programme based on objective investigation*
▶ factual, scientific, rational

## objective NOUN

*The main objective is to build a strong business.*
▶ object, purpose, intention, aim, point, target, end, goal, intent

## obligation NOUN

*She believed she had an obligation to help.*
▶ responsibility, duty, liability, commitment, requirement, need

## obligatory ADJECTIVE

*Use of seat-belts in the back seats is now obligatory.*
▶ compulsory, mandatory, binding, required, stipulated, unavoidable, de rigueur, imperative, imposed, incumbent, inescapable, official
AN OPPOSITE IS optional

## oblige VERB

*We cannot oblige them to agree, but we can persuade them.*
▶ force, compel, require, constrain, make

## obliged ADJECTIVE

*We'd be obliged if you would let us know when you arrive.*
▶ grateful, indebted, gratified, appreciative, thankful

## obliging ADJECTIVE

*Richard is an obliging sort of chap.*
▶ helpful, accommodating, considerate, cooperative, thoughtful, willing, agreeable, civil, courteous, friendly, kind, neighbourly, polite
OPPOSITES ARE disobliging, unhelpful

## oblique ADJECTIVE

*an oblique line*
▶ slanting, angled, diagonal, inclined, sloping, tilted, aslant

## obliterate VERB

*The explosion might obliterate the entire building.*
▶ destroy, demolish, wipe out, ruin, wreck, devastate, shatter, blow up

## oblivion NOUN

1 *She sank further into oblivion.*
▶ unconsciousness, insensibility, stupor, senselessness, blackness, unawareness
OPPOSITES ARE consciousness, awareness

2 *achievements that history has consigned to oblivion*
▶ obscurity, nothingness, non-existence
AN OPPOSITE IS prominence

## oblivious ADJECTIVE

*oblivious of what is going on*
▶ unaware, unconscious, heedless, unmindful, insensible (to), insensitive (to), disregardful, blind (to), deaf (to), ignorant, unconcerned (with), unresponsive (to)
OPPOSITES ARE conscious, aware

## obnoxious ADJECTIVE

*a thoroughly obnoxious individual*
▶ unpleasant, objectionable, disagreeable, disgusting, loathsome, odious, repulsive, repellent

## obscene ADJECTIVE

*obscene literature*
▶ pornographic, indecent, improper, immodest, immoral, depraved, salacious, shocking, suggestive

## obscenity NOUN

1 *laws against obscenity*
▶ indecency, immodesty, impurity, impropriety, pornography, licentiousness, grossness, indelicacy

2 *The crime was an obscenity.*
▶ atrocity, abomination, outrage, enormity, evil

3 *louts uttering obscenities*
▶ swear word, profanity, curse, expletive

## obscure ADJECTIVE

*He was suffering from an obscure disease that made his hand shaky.*
▶ unknown, little-known, unheard-of, mysterious, dubious

## obscure VERB

1 *Clouds obscured the sun.*
▶ hide, conceal, cover, veil, shroud, mask, envelop

2 *Their evidence has merely obscured the issues.*
▶ confuse, complicate, muddle, obfuscate

## obsequious ADJECTIVE

*the mafia leader and his obsequious followers*
▶ servile, grovelling, unctuous, sycophantic, ingratiating, fawning, toadying, subservient, smarmy

## observant ADJECTIVE

*Her observant eye took in every detail.*
▶ alert, attentive, vigilant, watchful, perceptive, percipient, eagle-eyed, sharp-eyed, heedful, quick
AN OPPOSITE IS inattentive

## observation NOUN

1 *He was sent to hospital for observation.*
▶ monitoring, scrutiny, examination, inspection, surveillance, attention

2 *Put any further observations on a separate sheet of paper.*
▶ remark, comment, statement, opinion

**observe** VERB

**1** *She observed her friends over by the bar.*
► notice, see, perceive, discern, spot, descry, behold
**2** *James observed that Rachel looked unhappy.*
► remark, comment, mention, note, declare, announce, state
**3** *From her window she could observe what was going on in the street.*
► watch, view, survey, regard, monitor, witness, scrutinize

**observer** NOUN

*Brian was merely an observer and took no part in the action.*
► spectator, onlooker, looker-on, bystander, viewer, watcher, commentator, eye-witness, witness

**obsess** VERB

**1** *Thoughts of death obsessed him.*
► preoccupy, dominate, haunt, prey on, engross, possess, take a hold on
**2** **be obsessed with** or **by** *I was totally obsessed with food and controlling my weight.*
► be fixated with or by, be preoccupied with or by, (*more informal*) be hung up on

**obsession** NOUN

*These memories rapidly became an obsession.*
► fixation, preoccupation, mania, passion, infatuation, compulsion, addiction

**obsessive** ADJECTIVE

*His jealousy was becoming obsessive.*
► compulsive, consuming, all-consuming, dominating, controlling, fanatical, addictive

**obsolescent** ADJECTIVE

*obsolescent forms of recording*
► declining, waning, disappearing, ageing, dying out, moribund, (*informal*) on the way out
**USAGE** Note that something is *obsolescent* when it is dying out, i.e. will soon be obsolete, and is *obsolete* when it has died out.

**obsolete** ADJECTIVE

*The machinery installed in the 1990s had become obsolete.*
► out of date, outdated, outmoded, anachronistic, antiquated, extinct, superseded, old-fashioned, passé, disused, dated, primitive
OPPOSITES ARE current, up to date

**obstacle** NOUN

*a major obstacle in the peace process*
► barrier, hurdle, hindrance, stumbling block, obstruction, drawback, difficulty, impediment, problem, snag, bar, interference

**obstinate** ADJECTIVE

*They were too obstinate to see the advantages of the scheme.*
► stubborn, inflexible, intractable, immovable, intransigent, unbending, unyielding, dogged, headstrong
OPPOSITES ARE amenable, open-minded

**obstreperous** ADJECTIVE

*The shop was full of obstreperous customers.*
► unruly, awkward, unmanageable, disorderly, disruptive, rowdy, rough, (*more informal*) stroppy
OPPOSITES ARE well-behaved, restrained

**obstruct** VERB

**1** *The opposite side of the road was obstructed by cars.*
► block, jam, clog up, choke up
**2** *He was charged with obstructing the course of justice.*
► impede, hinder, hamper, frustrate, thwart, hold up, inhibit, retard, interfere with
OPPOSITES ARE assist, further

**obstruction** NOUN

*an obstruction to learning*
► barrier, hurdle, hindrance, stumbling block, drawback, difficulty, impediment, problem, snag, bar, interference

**obstructive** ADJECTIVE

*He accused her of being deliberately obstructive.*
► uncooperative, unhelpful, awkward, difficult, disobliging, stalling
OPPOSITES ARE helpful, cooperative

**obtain** VERB

*You will need to obtain the necessary permission.*
*I obtained the books at half price.*
► get, acquire, secure, procure, come by, achieve

**obtrusive** ADJECTIVE

*A motorway through the valley would be very obtrusive.*
► conspicuous, prominent, noticeable, obvious, out of place, intrusive, protuberant, ugly
OPPOSITES ARE unobtrusive, inconspicuous

**obtuse** ADJECTIVE

*He seemed too obtuse to understand what I was saying.*
► stupid, slow, dense, crass, unintelligent, dull-witted, slow-witted, (*more informal*) thick

**obvious** ADJECTIVE

*It's obvious that she's keen on Bill. He spoke with an obvious French accent.*
► clear, plain, evident, self-evident, patent, apparent, glaring, perceptible
AN OPPOSITE IS imperceptible

**obviously** ADVERB

*She was obviously very upset.*
► clearly, plainly, patently, evidently, discernibly, indubitably, manifestly, unmistakably, without doubt

**occasion** NOUN

**1** *She had spoken to him on several occasions.*
► instance, point, time, moment
**2** *His eighteenth birthday would be a special occasion.*
► event, affair, celebration
**3** *I'll mention it if the occasion arises.*
► opportunity, chance, opening, right moment

**occasional**

4 *I've never had any occasion to complain.*
▶ reason, cause, grounds, excuse, need, justification, pretext

**occasional** ADJECTIVE

*There were still occasional air raids.*
▶ intermittent, periodic, sporadic, infrequent, irregular, isolated, odd, rare, random

**occasionally** ADVERB

*Tess turned her head occasionally to look at him.*
▶ sometimes, from time to time, now and then, every so often, intermittently, periodically, sporadically, infrequently, irregularly

**occult** ADJECTIVE

*the occult power of the priests*
▶ supernatural, mystical, magic, magical, transcendental, paranormal, secret, esoteric, arcane, obscure

**occult** NOUN

*the occult Mary had a strong interest in the occult.*
▶ the supernatural, the paranormal, supernaturalism, black magic, diabolism, witchcraft, sorcery

**occupant** NOUN

*The apartment had two occupants at the time.*
▶ resident, inhabitant, tenant, occupier, lodger, householder

**occupation** NOUN

1 *Passports no longer specify your occupation.*
▶ job, profession, work, line of work, walk of life, employment, business

2 *The occupation of the country continued for much longer than predicted.*
▶ invasion, annexation, seizure, takeover, occupancy, possession

3 *a house built for multiple occupation*
▶ occupancy, residence, habitation, tenancy, possession, use

4 *Board games are one of their favourite leisure occupations.*
▶ pastime, hobby, interest, activity, diversion

**occupy** VERB

1 *Colin occupies the top floor.*
▶ live in, inhabit, be the tenant of, reside in, lodge in, possess, have possession of, own

2 *These problems occupied her mind for several days.*
▶ absorb, engage, hold, preoccupy, engross, divert

3 *The army occupied the country in the spring.*
▶ capture, seize, invade, take over, take possession of, overrun, annex, conquer, garrison

**occur** VERB

1 *We need to know everything that occurred that morning.*
▶ happen, take place, come about

2 *The disease occurs only in tropical climates.*
▶ be found, exist, be prevalent, appear, show itself, manifest itself

3 **occur to** *It occurred to him that she might still be waiting there. It never occurred to us that we'd have to pay extra.*
▶ cross your mind, enter your head

**occurrence** NOUN

*Bicycle theft has become a common occurrence.*
▶ event, happening, incident, experience, circumstance, affair, occasion, phenomenon

**odd** ADJECTIVE

1 *It was an odd thing to do.*
▶ strange, peculiar, weird, unusual, bizarre, curious, eccentric

2 *His friends thought him quite odd.*
▶ eccentric, strange, peculiar, abnormal, weird

3 *the odd numbers*
▶ uneven

4 *Do you have any odd change you could give him?*
▶ spare, leftover, miscellaneous, sundry, available

5 *She noticed he was wearing odd socks.*
▶ unmatched, different, unpaired, clashing

**oddity** NOUN

1 *people remembered chiefly for their oddity*
▶ strangeness, abnormality, peculiarity, idiosyncrasy, quirkiness

2 *He is regarded as a bit of an oddity.*
▶ eccentric, crank, misfit, maverick, curiosity, character

**oddments** PLURAL NOUN

*oddments left over from a jumble sale*
▶ bits and pieces, odds and ends, scraps, fragments, remnants, leftovers, offcuts

**odds** PLURAL NOUN

*The odds are that they have left the country.*
▶ likelihood, probability, chances

**USAGE** If you use *likelihood* or *probability* you should use a singular verb, e.g. *The likelihood is that they have left the country.*

**odious** ADJECTIVE

*odious methods of dealing with their political opponents*
▶ hateful, offensive, repulsive, repellent, obnoxious, unpleasant, abhorrent, detestable, abominable

**odorous** ADJECTIVE

*odorous fumes from parked lorries*
▶ foul-smelling, evil-smelling, smelly, stinking, reeking

**odour** NOUN

1 *an odour of urine*
▶ smell, stink, stench

2 *a delicious odour of hot bread*
▶ aroma, smell, savour

**off** ADJECTIVE

1 *The milk is off.*
▶ bad, rotten, putrid

**2** *The game is now off.*
▶ postponed, cancelled

**3** *I think their remarks were a bit off, to put it mildly.*
▶ unacceptable, objectionable, unsatisfactory, disappointing

**offbeat** ADJECTIVE
*an offbeat humour*
▶ unconventional, unorthodox, idiosyncratic, strange, weird, bizarre, quirky

**off colour** ADJECTIVE
*He was feeling a bit off colour and decided to stay at home.*
▶ unwell, poorly, ill, queasy, peaky, nauseous

**offence** NOUN
**1** *The company might even be guilty of a criminal offence.*
▶ crime, misdemeanour, wrong, wrongdoing, misdeed, fault, transgression
**2** *We don't want to cause any offence.*
▶ annoyance, anger, resentment, hard feelings, indignation, irritation, upset, displeasure, disgust
**take offence** *She made it clear she had taken offence.*
▶ be or feel offended, be upset, be or feel aggrieved, be or feel affronted, take umbrage

**offend** VERB
**1** *I didn't mean to offend you.*
▶ give or cause offence to, upset, hurt, displease, annoy, affront, insult, anger, irritate, disgust, make angry, outrage, provoke, rile, vex
**2** *A large percentage of prisoners released early went on to offend again.*
▶ break the law, commit a crime, do wrong, transgress
**be** or **feel offended**
▶ take offence, be upset, be or feel aggrieved, be or feel affronted, take umbrage

**offender** NOUN
*A higher proportion of offenders were sentenced to three months or less.*
▶ wrongdoer, lawbreaker, criminal, malefactor, miscreant, delinquent, culprit, transgressor

**offensive** ADJECTIVE
*The remarks were clearly offensive.*
▶ insulting, derogatory, depreciatory, disrespectful, abusive, objectionable, provocative, discourteous, insolent, uncivil, rude
OPPOSITES ARE complimentary, courteous

**offer** VERB
**1** *Counsellors are on hand to offer advice and support.*
▶ provide, give, extend, make available, put forward, hold out, suggest
**2** *Many local people offered to help in the search.*
▶ volunteer, come forward, present yourself, show willing
**3** *The job offers good career prospects.*
▶ provide, afford, present, hold out, involve, entail

**offer** NOUN
**1** *a business offer*
▶ bid, proposal, tender, proposition, submission

**2** *kind offers of help*
▶ proposal, proposition, overture

**offering** NOUN
*an offering of a few silver coins*
▶ contribution, donation, gift, benefaction, present

**offhand** ADJECTIVE
*His manner was most offhand.*
▶ casual, indifferent, cool, cavalier, brusque, abrupt, aloof, curt, uncooperative, perfunctory
OPPOSITES ARE polite, courteous

**offhand** ADVERB
*I can't think of a better way offhand.*
▶ on the spur of the moment, at the drop of a hat, right now, without consideration, impromptu

**office** NOUN
**1** *Her office was just a few blocks away.*
▶ workplace, place of work, place of business, bureau
**2** *The new Prime Minister took up his office immediately.*
▶ post, position, appointment, function, task, duty, responsibility, situation

**officer** NOUN
*The trade union had few full-time officers.*
▶ official, functionary, office-holder, representative, executive, administrator

**official** ADJECTIVE
**1** *There were calls for an official inquiry into the matter. a member of an official organization*
▶ authorized, accredited, approved, proper, authentic, authenticated, certified, formal
**2** *They were dressed for an official function.*
▶ formal, ceremonial

**official** NOUN
*An official came down to escort us to the president's office.*
▶ officer, functionary, office-holder, representative, executive, administrator

**officiate** VERB
**officiate at** *The Vice-President officiates at the annual ceremony.*
▶ be in charge of, preside over, conduct, direct, oversee, supervise, manage, be responsible for, have official authority over

**officious** ADJECTIVE
*An officious waiter led us to a table in a poky corner.*
▶ self-important, bumptious, bossy, over-zealous, dictatorial, interfering, meddling, (*more informal*) pushy

**off-putting** ADJECTIVE
*She tried to think of some off-putting remark to make them go away.*
▶ discouraging, unpleasant, intimidating, unnerving, unsettling, disconcerting, unappealing, unattractive, disagreeable, distasteful

## offset VERB

*Charges are offset by interest earned on deposit accounts.*
▶ counterbalance, balance, cancel, neutralize, compensate for, counteract

## offshoot NOUN

*The business has offshoots all over Europe.*
▶ branch, subsidiary, (*more informal*) spin-off

## offspring NOUN

**1** *the core of the family: parents and their offspring*
▶ children, sons and daughters, progeny, family

**2** *Their latest offspring was playing in the garden.*
▶ child, baby, infant, little one, son, daughter, youngster

## often ADVERB

*She often asks about you.*
▶ frequently, regularly, repeatedly, constantly, again and again, many times, time after time

## ogre NOUN

**1** *an ogre who ate children*
▶ giant, monster, bogey

**2** *He was not such an ogre as he seemed.*
▶ fiend, brute, monster, devil

## oil VERB

*She went to the shed to oil her bike.*
▶ lubricate, grease

## oily ADJECTIVE

**1** *oily skin*   *an oily substance*
▶ greasy, oleaginous, slimy

**2** *an oily manner*
▶ smooth, unctuous, fawning, ingratiating, obsequious, (*more informal*) smarmy

## ointment NOUN

*She rubbed ointment on her skin.*
▶ lotion, cream, salve, liniment, embrocation, balm, unguent

## OK, okay ADJECTIVE This word is often overused. Here are some alternatives:

(*informal*) *Is everything OK now?*   *The film is OK.*
▶ all right, satisfactory, fine, in order, acceptable, adequate, reasonable

## OK, okay INTERJECTION

(*informal*) *OK, I'll go with you.*
▶ all right, very well, very good, right you are, right, fine

## OK, okay NOUN

(*informal*) *The manager gave his OK.*
▶ permission, approval, consent, authorization, agreement, assent

## OK, okay VERB

(*informal*) *Get a parent to okay your proposal.*
▶ agree to, approve, authorize, consent to, endorse, ratify

## old ADJECTIVE This word is often overused. Here are some alternatives:

**1** *an old man*
▶ elderly, aged, advanced in years, senile

**2** *old buildings*
▶ antiquated, dilapidated, ramshackle, ruined, historic

**3** *old clothes*
▶ worn, shabby, threadbare, frayed, moth-eaten

**4** *in the old days*
▶ past, former, bygone, early, ancient, olden

**5** *an old practice*
▶ long-standing, time-honoured, traditional, established, familiar

**6** *an old joke*
▶ hackneyed, stale, tired, overworked

## old-fashioned ADJECTIVE

*a big old-fashioned bathroom with noisy pipes*
▶ outdated, out of date, outmoded, antiquated, obsolescent
OPPOSITES ARE up to date, modern, fashionable

## omen NOUN

*an omen of things to come*
▶ sign, portent, signal, token, foreboding, indication, premonition, augury, auspice, presage, warning

## ominous ADJECTIVE

*an ominous dark sky*   *an ominous warning*
▶ threatening, menacing, portentous, sinister, inauspicious, unpropitious, baleful, forbidding, grim
OPPOSITES ARE auspicious, propitious

## omission NOUN

*There are some unfortunate omissions from the list.*
▶ exclusion, gap, oversight, deletion, blank

## omit VERB

**1** *Someone had omitted her name from the list.*
▶ leave out, miss out, exclude, ignore, cut, drop, overlook, edit out, eliminate
OPPOSITES ARE include, add, insert

**2** *I omitted to tell you.*
▶ forget, neglect, fail
AN OPPOSITE IS remember

## once ADVERB

*We were good friends once.*
▶ at one time, in the past, formerly, previously

## onerous ADJECTIVE

*an onerous task*
▶ difficult, burdensome, troublesome, arduous, strenuous

## one-sided ADJECTIVE

**1** *a one-sided account of the conflict*
▶ biased, prejudiced, partisan, partial, preferential, slanted, unfair
OPPOSITES ARE impartial, fair

**2** *a one-sided argument*
▶ unequal, uneven, unbalanced
AN OPPOSITE IS even

**ongoing** ADJECTIVE

**1** *an ongoing problem with noisy neighbours*
▶ continuous, continuing, persistent, constant, ceaseless

**2** *A road improvement programme is ongoing.*
▶ under way, in progress, progressing, evolving, continuing, current, extant, existing

**onlooker** NOUN
*An onlooker had videoed the entire incident.*
▶ observer, bystander, eyewitness, witness, spectator

**only** ADJECTIVE
*She is their only child*
▶ sole, single, solitary, lone, unique

**onset** NOUN
*With the onset of winter came the snow.*
▶ beginning, start, arrival, opening, inception

**onslaught** NOUN
*The onslaught on the city lasted for several days.*
▶ attack, assault, offensive, bombardment

**onus** NOUN
*The onus is on Scott to raise the issue.*
▶ responsibility, obligation, liability, burden, duty

**ooze** VERB
*Blood oozed from a wound on his arm.*
▶ seep, leak, issue, exude, escape, flow, dribble

**opaque** ADJECTIVE
*The glass of the bottle was opaque so the contents could not be seen.*
▶ cloudy, non-transparent, obscure, blurred, misty, dark, hazy, unclear
OPPOSITES ARE clear, transparent

**open** ADJECTIVE

**1** *an open door*
▶ unclosed, ajar, unlocked
AN OPPOSITE IS closed

**2** *an open box*
▶ uncovered, unfastened, unsealed, lidless
OPPOSITES ARE closed, fastened

**3** *open access*
▶ free, unrestricted, clear, unobstructed, wide, available
AN OPPOSITE IS restricted

**4** *open country*
▶ sweeping, rolling, broad, extensive, unenclosed

**5** *an open secret*
▶ plain, evident, overt, obvious, conspicuous, noticeable
AN OPPOSITE IS closed

**6** *an open question*
▶ unresolved, unsettled, undecided, debatable, moot
AN OPPOSITE IS closed

**7** *open about his feelings*
▶ frank, honest, candid, unreserved, natural
OPPOSITES ARE reserved, guarded

**8** *a procedure open to abuse*
▶ vulnerable, subject, susceptible, liable

**open** VERB

**1** *A young woman opened the door.*
▶ unfasten, unlock, unbolt

**2** *He started to open the packet.*
▶ unwrap, undo, untie, unseal

**3** *A new superstore will open next month.*
▶ start trading

**4** *The story opens with a train journey.*
▶ begin, start, (*more formal*) commence

**5** *The chairman then opened the meeting.*
▶ begin, start, inaugurate, set in motion

**open-air** ADJECTIVE
*an open-air swimming pool*
▶ outdoor, out-of-doors, alfresco
AN OPPOSITE IS indoor

**opening** NOUN

**1** *an opening in the wall*
▶ doorway, gateway, entry, aperture, breach, chink, crack, cleft, hole, fissure

**2** *looking for openings in accountancy*
▶ opportunity, chance, (*more informal*) break

**opening** ADJECTIVE
*the opening line of the poem*
▶ first, initial, beginning, introductory, inaugural
AN OPPOSITE IS final

**operate** VERB

**1** *The alarms had been switched off and were not operating.*
▶ work, function, run, act, perform, be operative, go

**2** *a machine that's difficult to operate*
▶ work, use, utilize, handle, manage, deal with, drive

**3** *X-rays will show whether doctors will need to operate on him.*
▶ perform surgery, carry out an operation

**operation** NOUN

**1** *There are few other business operations the size of ours.*
▶ enterprise, undertaking, procedure, proceeding, process, transaction

**2** *Military operations have been delayed by the weather.*
▶ campaign, exercise, action, activity, manuvre, movement, effort

**3** *a committee to ensure the smooth operation of the system*
▶ running, functioning, working, direction, control, management

**4** *a surgical operation*
▶ biopsy, surgery, transplant

**operational** ADJECTIVE
*Two new reactors were operational the following year.*
▶ functioning, operating, working, up and running, going, usable

**operative** ADJECTIVE
*Perhaps you're right: the operative word is 'perhaps'.*
▶ key, significant, important, principal, relevant, crucial, effective

# opinion NOUN

*You can have an opinion but you must back it up with facts or reasons.*
▶ belief, judgement, view, point of view, viewpoint, thought, attitude, standpoint, stance, idea, notion, feeling

# opinionated ADJECTIVE

*He always seemed patronizing and opinionated.*
▶ dogmatic, doctrinaire, inflexible, pompous, cocksure, self-important, arrogant, stubborn, uncompromising

# opponent NOUN

**1** *He threw the ball at an opponent's head.*
▶ adversary, opposer, rival, antagonist, competitor, contestant, enemy, foe, opposition
OPPOSITES ARE ally, partner

**2** *an opponent of reform*
▶ objector (to), opposer, dissident, dissenter

# opportune ADJECTIVE

*It was an opportune moment to speak out.*
▶ appropriate, suitable, timely, auspicious, convenient, favourable, propitious, advantageous, lucky, right
OPPOSITES ARE unsuitable, inconvenient

# opportunity NOUN

*(informal) This was a good opportunity to make some money.*
▶ chance, occasion, possibility, moment, opening, time, (more informal) break

# oppose VERB

**1** *There was a large group of protesters who opposed the plans for a new runway.*
▶ object to, be against, protest against, disapprove of, take exception to
OPPOSITES ARE support, defend

**2** *If you want to go I shan't oppose you*
▶ resist, counter, withstand, take issue with, defy, confront

# opposed ADJECTIVE

**opposed to** *The village was opposed to the scheme for a new hostel.*
▶ against, hostile to, antagonistic to, antipathetic to, unsympathetic to

# opposite ADJECTIVE

**1** *She lived in a house opposite the church.*
▶ facing, across from

**2** *There is a long mirror on the opposite wall.*
▶ opposing, facing

**3** *They were brothers who had fought on opposite sides in the civil war.*
▶ rival, opposing, conflicting, contrary, enemy
AN OPPOSITE IS allied

# opposite NOUN

*He always says one thing and does the opposite.*
▶ contrary, reverse, other extreme, antithesis, converse
AN OPPOSITE IS same

# opposition NOUN

**1** *The suggestion met with fierce opposition.*
▶ resistance, hostility, antagonism, disapproval, scepticism, unfriendliness, competition
AN OPPOSITE IS support

**2** *In the argument she quickly won over the opposition.*
▶ opponents, opposing side, other side

# oppress VERB

**1** *He could not get rid of the gloomy feelings that oppressed him.*
▶ depress, cast down, weigh down, burden, hang over, dispirit

**2** *a people that had been oppressed by successive invaders*
▶ persecute, abuse, maltreat, tyrannize, repress, suppress, subjugate, subdue, keep down

# oppressed ADJECTIVE

*oppressed minorities in the community*
▶ persecuted, downtrodden, repressed, abused, maltreated, tyrannized, suppressed
AN OPPOSITE IS privileged

# oppressive ADJECTIVE

**1** *an oppressive dictatorship*
▶ dictatorial, autocratic, authoritarian, despotic, brutal, cruel, harsh, repressive, tyrannical

**2** *oppressive weather*
▶ humid, muggy, sultry, stuffy, airless, close, hot, stifling, heavy

# oppressor NOUN

*The angry mob thirsted for the blood of its oppressors.*
▶ persecutor, intimidator, tormentor, despot, tyrant, autocrat

# opt VERB

**opt for** *They opted for a hotel near the beach.*
▶ choose, pick, pick out, select, settle on, fix on

# optimism NOUN

*Despite the difficulties he tried to keep up a note of optimism.*
▶ confidence, hopefulness, hope, positiveness, cheerfulness, good cheer
AN OPPOSITE IS pessimism

# optimistic ADJECTIVE

**1** *Women are less optimistic about their health prospects than men.*
▶ cheerful, confident, positive, hopeful, upbeat, sanguine, cheerful, buoyant
AN OPPOSITE IS pessimistic

**2** *The accounts included an optimistic assessment of the financial outlook.*
▶ favourable, encouraging, hopeful, upbeat, bright, rosy
AN OPPOSITE IS pessimistic

# optimum ADJECTIVE

*The announcement is timed to have the optimum effect.*
▶ best, maximum, most favourable, most advantageous, highest, ideal, perfect
AN OPPOSITE IS worst

**option** NOUN
We had little option but to agree.
► choice, alternative, possibility

**optional** ADJECTIVE
The exam consists of two compulsory questions and an optional essay.
► voluntary, discretionary, non-compulsory, elective
OPPOSITES ARE compulsory, obligatory

**opulent** ADJECTIVE
a house with an air of opulent grandeur
► luxurious, sumptuous, lavish, splendid, magnificent, wealthy, rich
OPPOSITES ARE stark, restrained

**oral** ADJECTIVE
Witnesses give oral evidence to the inquiry.
► spoken, unwritten, verbal, by mouth, said
AN OPPOSITE IS written

**orbit** NOUN
1 the earth's orbit round the sun
► course, path, circuit, track, trajectory, rotation, revolution
2 This question is outside the orbit of the ordinary officials.
► domain, sphere, range, scope, ambit

**orbit** VERB
other planets that orbit the sun
► circle, go round, travel round

**ordeal** NOUN
She helped nurse him back to health after his four-year ordeal as a captive.
► trial, tribulation, suffering, difficulty, test, torture, unpleasant experience, nightmare

**order** NOUN
1 He gave the order to charge.
► command, directive, instruction, direction, decree, edict
2 It would not be easy to restore order.
► peace, control, calm, quiet, law and order, discipline, harmony
3 The plants were put in in a set order.
► sequence, arrangement, disposition
4 I've put in an order for a hundred storage boxes.
► request, requisition, booking, demand, application
5 the lowest orders in society
► class, rank, hierarchy
6 an ancient order of craftsmen
► association, society, guild, company, lodge, brotherhood, sisterhood
7 skills of a very high order
► type, kind, sort, nature, variety, category

**out of order**
1 The ticket machine was, as usual, out of order.
► broken, not working, inoperative
2 Remarks like that would be ruled out of order.
► improper, uncalled-for, unacceptable, irregular, unwarranted

**order** VERB
1 She ordered them to leave the room.
► instruct, command, direct, charge, enjoin
2 I ordered the tickets on the Internet.
► book, reserve, apply for, requisition
3 He tried hard to order his thoughts.
► arrange, organize, sort out, set in order, regulate

**orderly** ADJECTIVE
1 The army began an orderly withdrawal.
► methodical, systematic, ordered, regular, well organized, well regulated
AN OPPOSITE IS disorganized
2 The children were told to form an orderly queue.
► neat, tidy, controlled, well behaved
AN OPPOSITE IS disorderly

**ordinary** ADJECTIVE
1 just an ordinary day's work
► usual, normal, typical, habitual, customary
OPPOSITES ARE unusual, abnormal
2 Susan is not like ordinary women.
► average, normal, typical, conventional
OPPOSITES ARE abnormal, unconventional
3 My life seemed so ordinary; I needed a change.
► routine, humdrum, run-of-the-mill, dull, routine, unremarkable, uninteresting, unexceptional, unexciting, commonplace
OPPOSITES ARE exceptional, unique

**organic** ADJECTIVE
1 an organic substance
► natural, animate, live, living, biological
AN OPPOSITE IS inorganic
2 organic foods
► natural, additive-free, pesticide-free, non-chemical
3 society as an organic whole
► integrated, organized, structured, coherent, systematic, harmonious
AN OPPOSITE IS disparate

**organism** NOUN
a living organism
► living thing, being, creature, animal, plant

**organization** NOUN
1 Sara is responsible for the organization of trips and visits.
► planning, administration, coordination, running
2 Organization is an important aspect of essay writing.
► structure, planning, arrangement, composition
3 an international organization with branches throughout the world
► institution, enterprise, operation, company, (more informal) outfit, (more informal) set-up

**organize** VERB
1 The protesters used mobile phones and the Internet to organize a demonstration.
► arrange, coordinate, plan, make arrangements for, assemble, bring together, run
2 Try to organize your ideas on paper.
► order, marshal, structure, assemble, develop, coordinate, establish, systematize, put in order, form, shape

# organized ADJECTIVE
*a well organized sales promotion*
▶ systematic, coordinated, efficient, well ordered, well planned, well run, meticulous, methodical, orderly, scientific, structured
OPPOSITES ARE disorganized, inefficient

# orient, orientate VERB
1 *After her husband's death she had to orientate herself to a new way of life.*
▶ adapt, adjust, accommodate, familiarize, acclimatize, accustom
2 **orient** or **orientate yourself** *They looked out for landmarks to orient themselves.*
▶ get your bearings, get the lie of the land

# oriental ADJECTIVE
*oriental countries*
▶ eastern, Far Eastern, Asian, Asiatic

# origin NOUN
1 *a discussion of the origin of the universe*
▶ beginning, start, birth, genesis, dawning, emergence, inception, source
OPPOSITES ARE end, conclusion
2 *a man of Irish origins*
▶ descent, ancestry, parentage, extraction, family, pedigree, background, stock

# original ADJECTIVE
1 *the original inhabitants of North America*
▶ earliest, first, indigenous, native, aboriginal, initial
AN OPPOSITE IS recent
2 *an original idea for a story*
▶ new, creative, innovative, novel, fresh, unfamiliar, unique, unusual, first-hand, imaginative, inventive, unconventional
OPPOSITES ARE unoriginal, commonplace
3 *an original painting by Picasso*
▶ authentic, genuine, real

# originate VERB
1 *Where did the rumour originate?*
▶ arise, start, begin, emerge, emanate, evolve, be born, crop up
2 *It is not clear who originated the idea.*
▶ conceive, invent, create, initiate, introduce, inaugurate, discover, inspire, pioneer, be the inventor of, give birth to, institute, launch

# ornament NOUN
1 *a plain style of clothing without ornament*
▶ decoration, adornment, embellishment, trimming, accessory, filigree, frill, frippery, finery, garnish, jewel, tracery
2 *a shelf covered with ornaments*
▶ trinket, knick-knack, bauble, gewgaw

# ornamental ADJECTIVE
*an ornamental ceiling*
▶ decorative, fancy, attractive, ornate, ornamented, showy

# ornate ADJECTIVE
1 *an ornate mirror over the fireplace*
▶ ornamented, decorated, elaborate, showy
AN OPPOSITE IS plain

2 *ornate language*
▶ elaborate, florid, fancy, grandiose, affected, pretentious

# orthodox ADJECTIVE
*He has orthodox views on most things.*
▶ conventional, mainstream, established, conservative, standard, traditional, conformist
OPPOSITES ARE unorthodox, unconventional

# ostentatious ADJECTIVE
*Their ostentatious attempts to look busy fools nobody.*
▶ showy, pretentious, conspicuous, flamboyant, obtrusive, vulgar, theatrical, overdone
AN OPPOSITE IS modest

# oust VERB
*The president knew that his opponent would never unite to oust him.*
▶ depose, overthrow, remove, drive out, expel, unseat, defeat

# out-and-out ADJECTIVE
*an out-and-out success*
▶ complete, utter, outright, thoroughgoing, downright, absolute, thorough, unmitigated

# outbreak NOUN
1 *an outbreak of SARS  new outbreaks of violence*
▶ eruption, upsurge, outburst, epidemic, rash, spate
2 *the outbreak of war*
▶ start, beginning, onset

# outburst NOUN
*At this there was a loud outburst of laughter.*
▶ eruption, burst, explosion, outbreak, surge, spasm

# outcast NOUN
*a social outcast*
▶ reject, pariah, leper, outsider, exile, outlaw, castaway

# outclass VERB
*She won every game, outclassing every rival.*
▶ surpass, outdo, outstrip, outshine, beat, exceed, eclipse, excel, be better than

# outcome NOUN
*speculation about the outcome of the next election*
▶ result, consequence, conclusion, upshot, issue, conclusion

# outcry NOUN
*an outcry about the state of the railways*
▶ protest, complaint, furore, clamour, tumult

# outdated ADJECTIVE
*an outdated road network*
▶ out-of-date, obsolete, old-fashioned, dated, decrepit, antiquated, ancient

# outdo VERB
*Everyone tried to outdo each other with stories of how exciting their holidays had been.*
▶ surpass, outstrip, outshine, exceed, eclipse, excel, be better than, outclass, beat

**outdoor** ADJECTIVE

*an outdoor sport such as archery*
▶ open-air, outside, alfresco

**outer** ADJECTIVE

1 *It was so hot they began to shed their outer clothing.*
▶ outermost, exterior, external, outside, outward, surface, superficial

2 *superstores built in the outer areas of cities*
▶ outlying, distant, remote, peripheral, further, suburban
AN OPPOSITE IS inner

**outfit** NOUN

1 *a complete photography outfit*
▶ equipment, kit, apparatus, (*more informal*) gear, (*more informal*) set-up

2 *The weather was still too cold for summer outfits.*
▶ costume, ensemble, suit, dress, clothing, (*informal*) get-up, (*informal*) turn-out, (*more informal*) gear, (*more informal*) togs

**outgoing** ADJECTIVE

1 *She was in a bright, outgoing mood that day.*
▶ sociable, friendly, amiable, genial, congenial, demonstrative, pleasant, agreeable, kind, kindly, kind-hearted, well-disposed, sympathetic, likeable, approachable, receptive

2 *the outgoing president*
▶ departing, leaving, retiring, former, ex-
AN OPPOSITE IS incoming

**outgoings** PLURAL NOUN

*His monthly outgoings had risen alarmingly.*
▶ expenses, expenditure, spending, disbursements, overheads

**outing** NOUN

*family outings to the coast*
▶ trip, excursion, jaunt, expedition, drive, run, ride, joyride

**outlandish** ADJECTIVE

*We could dream up all sorts of outlandish ideas.*
▶ weird, strange, extraordinary, odd, queer, eccentric, bizarre, quirky

**outlast** VERB

*Don't forget that leather outlasts denim.*
▶ outwear, last longer than, survive

**outlaw** NOUN

*those notorious outlaws Jesse and Frank James*
▶ bandit, brigand, fugitive, desperado, renegade, robber, marauder, criminal, outcast

**outlaw** VERB

*The state in effect outlawed political opposition.*
▶ ban, prohibit, bar, forbid, disallow, banish, embargo, condemn, veto

**outlay** NOUN

*The trip involves a small outlay.*
▶ expense, expenditure, cost, price, (*more formal*) disbursement

**outlet** NOUN

1 *The boiler has an outlet for fumes.*
▶ vent, duct, channel, opening, orifice, exit, mouth, way out

2 *We need a better outlet for complaints.*
▶ channel, process, means

3 *High Street outlets for these goods*
▶ shop, store, retailer, market

**outline** NOUN

1 *the outline of a low building*
▶ profile, silhouette, shape, form, contour, shadow, figure

2 (*informal*) *He sat down and wrote an outline of his essay.*
▶ summary, sketch, framework, skeleton, plan, draft, rough idea, bare bones

**outline** VERB

*In this chapter we will outline ways of acting out your chosen scenario.*
▶ sketch out, summarize, indicate, rough out

**outlive** VERB

*She outlived her husband by more than twenty years.*
▶ survive, live longer than, outlast

**outlook** NOUN

1 *The house has a glorious outlook over the downs.*
▶ view, vista, prospect, panorama, aspect, vantage point

2 *The sisters were totally different in character and outlook.*
▶ attitude, way of thinking, standpoint, viewpoint, frame of mind, point of view

3 *Lower interest rates will improve the economic outlook.*
▶ prospects, expectations, forecast, hopes, future, prognosis, prediction, (*more informal*) lookout

**outlying** ADJECTIVE

*Take a boat trip to one of the outlying islands.*
▶ outer, distant, remote, outermost, far-flung, far-off, faraway
AN OPPOSITE IS central

**outmoded** ADJECTIVE

*outmoded ways of storing information*
▶ old-fashioned, outdated, out-of-date, obsolete, dated, obsolescent

**outnumber** VERB

*On these occasions males usually outnumber females.*
▶ exceed, be more than, outstrip

**out-of-date** ADJECTIVE

1 *He handed over an out-of-date passport.*
▶ expired, lapsed, invalid, void

2 *She was using a machine that was totally out of date.*
▶ old-fashioned, outdated, obsolete, dated, obsolescent

**out-of-the-way** ADJECTIVE

*out-of-the-way places*
▶ distant, outlying, faraway, remote, isolated, far-flung, far-off

**output** NOUN
*a marked increase in industrial output*
▶ production, productivity, product, yield,
manufacture

**outrage** NOUN
1 *I can remember the sense of outrage when I first saw
those blancmange-coloured walls.*
▶ anger, indignation, fury, disgust, affront, horror
2 *The country's suffering is an outrage.*
▶ scandal, disgrace, atrocity, enormity, barbarity,
infamy

**outrageous** ADJECTIVE
1 *an outrageous slur on his character*
▶ disgraceful, shocking, scandalous, appalling,
monstrous, shameful, dreadful, intolerable, wicked,
heinous
AN OPPOSITE IS mild
2 *We were invited to tell outrageous stories about
people we knew.*
▶ far-fetched, extravagant, preposterous, unlikely,
questionable, dubious
AN OPPOSITE IS reasonable
3 *If you're not careful about the extras the cost can
become outrageous.*
▶ excessive, exorbitant, extortionate

**outright** ADJECTIVE
*By now it was clear the whole story was an outright
fabrication.*
▶ complete, utter, out-and-out, thoroughgoing,
downright, absolute, thorough, unmitigated
AN OPPOSITE IS indefinite

**outright** ADVERB
*I decided I would have to tell her outright.*
▶ directly, explicitly, candidly, plainly, bluntly,
openly, honestly

**outset** NOUN
*The answer was clear from the outset.*
▶ start, beginning, opening, inception
OPPOSITES ARE conclusion, end

**outside** ADJECTIVE
1 *An outside light will improve security.*
▶ exterior, external, outer, outdoor, outward
AN OPPOSITE IS inside
2 *We must resist all outside interference*
▶ external, extraneous, foreign, alien
AN OPPOSITE IS inside
3 *There is an outside chance of thunder.*
▶ slight, remote, slender, slim, faint, negligible

**outside** NOUN
*The outside of the building is covered in ivy.*
▶ exterior, facade, surface, outer surface, shell, skin
AN OPPOSITE IS inside

**outsider** NOUN
*I still felt an outsider after years of living in the village.*
▶ stranger, visitor, foreigner, alien, newcomer,
incomer, interloper, intruder, immigrant,
non-resident, outcast
AN OPPOSITE IS insider

**outskirts** PLURAL NOUN
*a group of buildings on the outskirts of the city*
▶ outer areas, outlying districts, edge, fringe,
suburbs, margin, periphery, purlieus
OPPOSITES ARE centre, heart

**outspoken** ADJECTIVE
*some outspoken remarks*
▶ frank, forthright, candid, direct, blunt,
plain-speaking, straightforward, unequivocal
OPPOSITES ARE guarded, diplomatic

**outstanding** ADJECTIVE
1 *She is an outstanding musician.*
▶ excellent, exceptional, superb, superlative, fine,
extraordinary, distinguished, celebrated
OPPOSITES ARE mediocre, unexceptional
2 *All outstanding questions will be answered.*
▶ unresolved, unsettled, remaining, pending

**outstrip** VERB
*Demand for fuel was outstripping supply.*
▶ exceed, surpass, outdo, overtake, outdistance,
eclipse

**outward** ADJECTIVE
*His outward manner was bright and cheerful.*
▶ external, outer, outside, surface, apparent,
ostensible, superficial, visible
OPPOSITES ARE inward, inner

**outweigh** VERB
*The benefits of the scheme have to outweigh the costs.*
▶ exceed, be better than, be greater than, prevail
over, override, have the edge on

**outwit** VERB
*The besieged garrison managed to outwit the enemy.*
▶ outsmart, dupe, fool, hoodwink, hoax, cheat,
deceive, trick, (more informal) take in, (more informal)
outfox

**oval** ADJECTIVE
*an oval lawn*
▶ egg-shaped, elliptical, ovoid

**overall** ADJECTIVE
*It was a good overall result.*
▶ general, all-inclusive, all-embracing,
comprehensive, inclusive
AN OPPOSITE IS specific

**overall** ADVERB
*Things have improved overall.*
▶ generally, in general, generally speaking,
altogether, all in all, for the most part, on the whole,
in the main, on balance, on average

**overbearing** ADJECTIVE
*Don't be intimidated by his overbearing attitude.*
▶ arrogant, haughty, conceited, self-important,
high-handed, lordly, superior, condescending,
supercilious, disdainful, cavalier, imperious
AN OPPOSITE IS meek

a
b
c
d
e
f
g
h
i
j
k
l
m
n
**o**
p
q
r
s
t
u
v
w
x
y
z

**overcast** ADJECTIVE

*The sky was dull and overcast.*
▶ cloudy, grey, dull, dark, sombre, sunless, gloomy, stormy
OPPOSITES ARE clear, bright

**overcome** VERB

1 *Neither army was strong enough to overcome the other.*
▶ defeat, beat, conquer, overpower, vanquish, overwhelm, trounce

2 *It would be be easy to overcome his fear of flying.*
▶ control, master, get the better of, repress, subdue

**overcrowded** ADJECTIVE

*an overcrowded beach*
▶ packed, overfull, congested, bursting, jam-packed, chock-full, crammed, overpopulated, swarming, filled to capacity, jammed

**overdo** VERB

*She spoilt her case by overdoing the emotion.*
▶ exaggerate, overstate, overplay, overemphasize, overdramatize
OPPOSITES ARE underplay, play down

**overdue** ADJECTIVE

1 *The train is overdue.*
▶ late, delayed, behind time, tardy, unpunctual, slow
AN OPPOSITE IS early

2 *Our phone bill is overdue.*
▶ unpaid, unsettled, outstanding, owing, in arrears

**overeat** VERB

*The food was so dreadful at least there was no danger of them overeating.*
▶ overindulge, eat too much, be greedy, gorge, guzzle, binge, (more informal) stuff yourself, (more informal) make a pig of yourself
OPPOSITES ARE diet, fast, undereat

**overflow** VERB

*The water tank overflowed, causing damage to the roof.*
▶ spill over, flow over, pour over, run over, brim over, flood

**overgrown** ADJECTIVE

*The garden was overgrown from years of neglect.*
▶ unkempt, untidy, wild, tangled, untrimmed, unweeded, weedy

**overhaul** VERB

*Cars used for hire are overhauled regularly.*
▶ service, maintain, check over, examine, inspect, repair, refurbish

**overhead** ADJECTIVE

*an overhead power line*
▶ aerial, elevated, raised, high, suspended, projecting, overhanging
AN OPPOSITE IS underground

**overhead** ADVERB

*A flock of birds passed overhead.*
▶ above, up above, on high, high up, (more literary) aloft

**overjoyed** ADJECTIVE

*Brian was overjoyed at the birth of his daughter.*
▶ thrilled, delighted, ecstatic, pleased, excited, happy, glad
OPPOSITES ARE dejected, disappointed

**overload** VERB

*At peak times the staff were constantly overloaded with work.*
▶ overburden, weigh down, strain, encumber

**overlook** VERB

1 *a mistake we are willing to overlook*
▶ ignore, disregard, take no notice of, pay no attention to, discount, overlook, pass over, let pass, excuse, forget, make light of, brush aside, (more informal) turn a blind eye to
AN OPPOSITE IS penalize

2 *The house overlooks a car park.*
▶ look out on, have a view of, look on to, look over, face, front

**overpower** VERB

*The prisoners could easily have overpowered their guards.*
▶ overwhelm, subdue, prevail over, get the better of, gain mastery over, get control over, master, overturn

**overpowering** ADJECTIVE

1 *an overpowering feeling of sorrow*
▶ overwhelming, irrepressible, irresistible, uncontrollable, oppressive, intense
OPPOSITES ARE slight, weak

2 *The smell was overpowering.*
▶ stifling, suffocating, nauseating, sickening, pungent
AN OPPOSITE IS mild

3 *overpowering evidence of their guilt*
▶ compelling, irrefutable, undeniable, incontrovertible, conclusive, forceful, powerful, strong
OPPOSITES ARE unconvincing, inconclusive

**overrated** ADJECTIVE

*His achievements are often overrated.*
▶ exaggerated, overvalued, magnified, glorified, rated too highly
AN OPPOSITE IS underrated

**overrule** VERB

*A higher court overruled the decision.*
▶ overturn, override, revoke, reverse, cancel, rescind, quash, set aside, countermand
OPPOSITES ARE confirm, endorse, allow

**overrun** VERB

*The country was overrun by its neighbours.*
▶ invade, occupy, subdue, violate, attack, enter, penetrate, raid

**overshadow** VERB

*Both countries were overshadowed by the superior power of Russia.*
▶ dominate, eclipse, dwarf, overpower, put in the shade, outshine, outclass

## oversight NOUN

*The delay was caused by oversight.*
► omission, lapse, carelessness, neglect, error

## overt ADJECTIVE

*signs of overt racism*
► open, obvious, manifest, plain, blatant, unconcealed, undisguised
OPPOSITES ARE disguised, hidden, covert

## overtake VERB

**1** *Huge lorries were overtaking one another.*
► pass, pull ahead of, go past, overhaul, catch up with

**2** *Fruit had overtaken oil as the country's main export.*
► outstrip, exceed, surpass, outdo

**3** *Another disaster overtook the family.*
► befall, overwhelm, overpower, strike, hit, afflict, engulf

## overthrow VERB

*The emperor was finally overthrown by his own guard.*
► depose, oust, remove, drive out, expel, unseat, defeat

## overthrow NOUN

*the overthrow of the tyrant*
► downfall, defeat, removal, fall, collapse, deposing, ousting, expulsion, unseating

## overtone NOUN

*The word 'compulsory' has threatening overtones*
► connotation, association, implication, undertone, undercurrent, reverberation, suggestion

## overturn VERB

**1** *The boat overturned in a squall.*
► capsize, turn over, tip over, keel over, turn turtle, overbalance

**2** *Someone had overturned a box of tools over the garage floor.*
► upset, spill, knock over, tip over, topple

**3** *The decision was overturned in the House of Lords.*
► overrule, override, revoke, reverse, cancel, rescind, quash, set aside, countermand

## overweight ADJECTIVE

*I had put on two stone and was noticeably overweight.*
► fat, obese, corpulent, gross
OPPOSITES ARE underweight, undernourished

## overwhelm VERB

**1** *The home side overwhelmed the visitors in the league game.*
► defeat, overcome, crush, overpower, rout, trounce, win against, conquer, vanquish, subdue, get the better of, (more informal) thrash

**2** *Monsoons would soon overwhelm the region.*
► overrun, inundate, submerge, engulf, flood, deluge, bury

**3** *She bent her head, overwhelmed by grief.*
► overcome, overpower, strike, crush

## overwhelming ADJECTIVE

**1** *The campaign received overwhelming support.*
► strong, massive, formidable, sweeping, forceful, powerful

**2** *The army suffered another overwhelming defeat.*
► crushing, devastating, great, overpowering

## overwrought ADJECTIVE

*They were overwrought and needed sleep.*
► tense, agitated, keyed up, worked up, nervous, upset, excited
OPPOSITES ARE calm, unexcited

## owing ADJECTIVE

*There is a small amount of money still owing.*
► due, outstanding, unpaid, payable, owed, unsettled, overdue

**owing to** *He would not use the lifts, owing to his claustrophobia.*
► because of, as a result of, on account of, as a consequence of, by reason of, thanks to

## own VERB

*Many more people own their own house.*
► possess, be the owner of, have, hold

**own up to** *He was waiting for a good moment to own up to the mistake.*
► confess, admit, acknowledge, tell the truth about, (more informal) come clean about, (more informal) make a clean breast of

## owner NOUN

**1** *Maintenance of the service road is the responsibility of the properties' owners.*
► possessor, proprietor, freeholder, landlord, landlady

**2** *Dog owners should not let their pets foul the pavements.*
► keeper, master, mistress

# Pp

## pace NOUN

**1** *She moved back a few paces.*
► step, stride

**2** *The traffic was moving at a slow pace.*
► speed, rate, velocity, movement, quickness, gait, (informal) lick

**3** *They quickened their pace to a run.*
► stride, gait, tread, walk, march, speed, progress

## pace VERB

*Richard paced up and down for ages before going in.*
► walk, stride, tread, march

## pacifism NOUN

*a supporter of pacifism and tolerance*
► non-violence, peaceful solutions
AN OPPOSITE IS militarism

## pacifist NOUN

*Her parents had been strong pacifists during the cold war.*
► peace-lover, peacemaker
AN OPPOSITE IS militarist

## pacify VERB

*It was too late to pacify her now, and she stormed off.*
► appease, placate, calm, conciliate, mollify, soothe, assuage, propitiate, quieten
AN OPPOSITE IS anger

## pack NOUN

1 *The bookshelves come in a self-assembly pack. A pack of cigarettes lay on the table.*
► package, packet, container, carton, box, parcel, bundle
2 *a group of walkers with packs on their backs*
► backpack, rucksack, knapsack, kitbag
3 *a pack of wolves*
► group, herd, troop
4 *a pack of youths*
► group, crowd, band, gang, set, throng, horde, mob

## pack VERB

1 *The children helped to pack the hamper.*
► fill, load, stuff, put things in
2 *She decided to pack her belongings and leave.*
► bundle, parcel, wrap, stow, store
3 *On rainy days visitors pack the local museums.*
► throng, crowd into, cram into, squash into, squeeze into, fill, jam

**pack in** (*informal*) *James has decided to pack in his job.*
► give up, leave, resign from, (*informal*) quit, (*informal*) chuck in

**pack up**
1 (*informal*) *The microwave chose that very moment to pack up.*
► break down, stop working, go wrong, fail, develop a fault, (*more formal*) malfunction, (*informal*) play up, (*informal*) act up
2 (*informal*) *If you're not having a good time perhaps it's time to pack up.*
► stop, break off, call it a day

## package NOUN

*A strange package arrived by special delivery.*
► parcel, packet, container, consignment

## packed ADJECTIVE

*a packed room*
► crowded, full, crammed, jam-packed, chock-a-block

## packet NOUN

1 *a packet of sugar*
► pack, carton, bag, box, container
2 **a packet** (*informal*) *new shoes that cost a packet*
► a fortune, a small fortune, a huge amount, a king's ransom, (*informal*) an arm and a leg

## pact NOUN

*The two countries signed a non-aggression pact.*
► treaty, alliance, agreement, settlement, truce, protocol, understanding

## pad NOUN

1 *Take a pad to sit on as the seats are hard.*
► cushion, pillow, padding, squab, bolster, wad
2 *She made notes on a small pad.*
► notebook, notepad, jotter, sketchbook

## pad VERB

1 *You can pad the cushion with plastic foam.*
► stuff, pack, fill, line, upholster
2 *He padded along to the bathroom.*
► walk, creep, tiptoe

**pad out** *Try not to pad out your letter with irrelevant detail.*
► expand, inflate, fill out, elaborate, lengthen, spin out, stretch out

## padding NOUN

1 *The sofa burst open and masses of grey padding fell out.*
► stuffing, wadding, filling, cushioning
2 *The story could be much shorter but for all the tedious padding.*
► verbiage, verbosity, wordiness, (*informal*) waffle

## paddle NOUN

*You'll need to use the paddle to reach the shore.*
► oar, scull

## paddle VERB

1 *We paddled furiously to get to safety.*
► row, scull, pull
2 *You can paddle a long way out at low tide.*
► dabble, wade, splash about

## paddock NOUN

*horses in a paddock*
► field, meadow, pasture, enclosure

## pagan NOUN

*pagans who worshipped nature*
► heathen, infidel, non-believer, unbeliever
**USAGE** You should only use *pagan* with reference to people in the past. It is an unfavourable term used by Christians and other believers in God to refer to non-believers. It is not an ordinary equivalent to words such as *atheist*, which is a more neutral term for someone who believes there is no God.

## pagan ADJECTIVE

*pagan festivals*
► heathen, infidel, ungodly, atheistic, godless, idolatrous, irreligious, unchristian
**USAGE** See the note at the previous entry.

## page NOUN

1 *He had written a whole page by the time she returned.*
► side, sheet, folio, leaf
2 *Clare's little brother had been a page at her friend's wedding.*
► pageboy, attendant, train-bearer

## pageant NOUN

*the annual pageant in the city centre*
► parade, procession, spectacle, extravaganza, display, tableau

## pageantry NOUN

*Visitors love all the pageantry associated with royalty.*
▶ pomp, ceremony, ritual, show, spectacle, splendour, grandeur, glamour, magnificence, display, formality

## pain NOUN

**1** *The pain in his tooth was fading.*
▶ ache, soreness, hurt, tenderness, throb, discomfort

**2** *How could anyone be expected to put up with so much pain?*
▶ suffering, discomfort, agony, affliction

**3** *the pain of losing a child*
▶ grief, sorrow, distress, torment, anguish, misery, trauma

**4** (*informal*) *Younger brothers could be a pain at times like this.*
▶ nuisance, pest, bother, bore, trial, tribulation, inconvenience

## pain VERB

*It pained him to think of all the trouble they had been through.*
▶ hurt, sadden, grieve, distress, mortify

## pained ADJECTIVE

*He wore a pained expression as he told them the news.*
▶ hurt, upset, injured, distressed, aggrieved, offended

## painful ADJECTIVE

**1** *The knight had a painful wound in his side.*
▶ sore, hurting, tender, agonizing, excruciating

**2** *The journey had been a painful experience.*
▶ unpleasant, traumatic, disagreeable, bitter, wretched
OPPOSITES ARE pleasant, agreeable

## painless ADJECTIVE

*There is no completely painless way to travel*
▶ comfortable, easy, effortless, pain-free, simple, trouble-free, undemanding
AN OPPOSITE IS painful

## painstaking ADJECTIVE

*She showed a painstaking attention to detail.*
▶ meticulous, careful, thorough, assiduous, punctilious, scrupulous
OPPOSITES ARE careless, slapdash

## paint NOUN

*They chose a bright paint for the walls.*
▶ colour, pigment, tint, colouring, stain

## paint VERB

**1** *Kim couldn't make up her mind whether to paint the room or paper it.*
▶ colour, tint, use paint on, coat with paint, apply paint to, decorate

**2** *The article paints a vivid picture of life in rural Wales.*
▶ describe, depict, portray, present, sketch, outline, delineate

## painting NOUN

*She was eager to buy one of his larger paintings.*
▶ picture, oil painting, watercolour

**KINDS OF PAINTING INCLUDE**

cave painting, fresco (painted on wet plaster), icon (religious portrait), landscape, miniature, mural (painted on dry wall), nude, oil, panorama, portrait, seascape, still life, wall painting, watercolour.

## pair NOUN

**1** *a pair of earrings*
▶ set, set of two

**2** *The guests drank to the happy pair.*
▶ couple, partners, husband and wife, man and wife

**3** *The pair sang, one standing and the other at the piano.*
▶ couple, duo, two, twosome

## pair VERB

*She couldn't find a jersey to pair with her skirt.*
▶ match, couple, twin, partner, put together

## pal NOUN

(*informal*) *The boys had been pals since primary school.*
▶ friend, companion, (*informal*) mate, (*informal*) buddy, (*informal*) chum

## palace NOUN

*a royal palace open to the public*
▶ official residence, château, mansion, stately home, castle
RELATED ADJECTIVE palatial

## palatable ADJECTIVE

**1** *The little hotel serves meals that are more than palatable.*
▶ tasty, pleasant, appetizing, eatable, edible, nice to eat, enjoyable
AN OPPOSITE IS unpalatable

**2** *Some of the news is not very palatable.*
▶ acceptable, agreeable, easy to take
AN OPPOSITE IS unpalatable

## palatial ADJECTIVE

*a palatial residence in the heart of the old city*
▶ grand, magnificent, splendid, impressive, imposing, noble, luxurious, sumptuous
OPPOSITES ARE modest, humble

## pale ADJECTIVE

**1** *He frowned and turned pale.*
▶ white, pallid, wan, ashen, anaemic, sallow
AN OPPOSITE IS flushed

**2** *a pale shade of pink*
▶ light, soft, muted, pastel, faint, weak
OPPOSITES ARE dark, strong

**3** *a pale light*
▶ dim, weak, watery, feeble
OPPOSITES ARE bright, strong

## pale VERB

*She paled suddenly and clenched her hands.*
▶ turn white or go white, become pale, lose colour, whiten, blanch, lighten

**pall** NOUN
*a thick pall of carbon monoxide*
▶ cloud, cloak, mantle, blanket, covering

**pall** VERB
*The constant business travel soon began to pall*
▶ become tedious, become boring, weary, cloy, irk, lose its attraction, become uninteresting

**pallid** ADJECTIVE
*His face was pallid with fear.*
▶ pale, white, wan, ashen, anaemic, sallow
AN OPPOSITE IS flushed

**pally** ADJECTIVE
*The two men had become quite pally over the years.*
▶ friendly, close, on good terms, intimate, (*informal*) matey, (*informal*) chummy

**palm** VERB
*palm off They palmed off the worst wines on their visitors.*
▶ foist, fob off, get rid of, dispose of, offload, (*more informal*) unload

**palpable** ADJECTIVE
*The tension in the room was palpable.*
▶ perceptible, noticeable, discernible, recognizable, unmistakable, obvious, plain, clear

**paltry** ADJECTIVE
*All he gave was a paltry five pounds.*
▶ meagre, negligible, pitiful, miserable, modest, scanty, scant, sparse, (*more informal*) mingy, (*more informal*) measly
OPPOSITES ARE generous, extravagant

**pamper** VERB
*His mother tended to pamper him.*
▶ spoil, indulge, overindulge, cosset, mollycoddle, coddle, humour, pander to

**pamphlet** NOUN
*a pamphlet on bee-keeping*
▶ leaflet, brochure, booklet, handout, folder, notice

**pan** NOUN
*Fry the mushrooms and onions in a large pan.*
▶ frying-pan, saucepan, container, vessel, pot

**pan** VERB
(*informal*) *The reviews all panned the film mercilessly.*
▶ criticize, attack, lambaste, censure, (*informal*) hammer, (*informal*) take apart, (*informal*) knock
OPPOSITES ARE praise, commend, recommend

**panacea** NOUN
*a panacea for our troubles*
▶ cure, remedy, perfect solution, magic formula

**panache** NOUN
*Julian produced the flowers with all the panache of a successful conjuror.*
▶ confidence, enthusiasm, flourish, spirit, style, verve, zest

**pandemonium** NOUN
*The meeting ended in pandemonium.*
▶ chaos, uproar, bedlam, mayhem, confusion, disorder, muddle

**pander** VERB
*pander to Susan was prepared to pander to some of their foibles, but there were limits.*
▶ gratify, indulge, satisfy, cater to

**pane** NOUN
*She went to the window and pressed her face against the pane.*
▶ glass, sheet of glass, windowpane

**panel** NOUN
1 *He stared at the control panel, looking for the right switch.*
▶ console, fascia, board
2 *The case will be decided by a panel of judges.*
▶ group, team, body, board, council, commission

**pang** NOUN
1 *Pangs of hunger came over them.*
▶ spasm, twinge, stab
2 *She felt a slight pang of regret*
▶ qualm, misgiving, scruple, twinge, prick

**panic** NOUN
*They rushed out in panic.*
▶ alarm, fright, fear, trepidation, consternation, horror, terror, frenzy

**panic** VERB
*There is no need to panic yet.*
▶ be alarmed, take fright, lose your head, lose your nerve, overreact, (*more informal*) flap

**panicky** ADJECTIVE
*Her voice became breathless and panicky.*
▶ panic-stricken, alarmed, frantic, hysterical, frightened, overexcited, terror-stricken, unnerved
AN OPPOSITE IS calm

**panorama** NOUN
*There is a lovely panorama across the city from the top of the tower.*
▶ view, vista, prospect, outlook, landscape, perspective, scene

**panoramic** ADJECTIVE
*a panoramic view of the hills*
▶ wide, sweeping, broad, extensive, comprehensive

**pant** VERB
*He lay there panting from the exertion.*
▶ gasp, puff, heave, wheeze, breathe quickly

**pants** NOUN
*a pair of pants*
▶ underpants, briefs, trunks, shorts, (*for men*) boxer shorts, (*for men*) Y-fronts, (*for women*) panties, (*for women*) knickers

**paper** NOUN
1 *They had to show their papers at the border.*
▶ document, credentials, identification, authorization, certificate
2 *I'll go and buy a paper.*
▶ newspaper, daily, broadsheet (= large newspaper), tabloid (= small newspaper), magazine
3 *Her father was writing a paper for a medical journal.*
▶ article, essay, study, lecture, dissertation, thesis

**parade** NOUN
*a military parade*
► procession, march, cavalcade, spectacle, display, pageant, review, show

**parade** VERB
1 *The teams will parade through the city.*
► process, troop, march past
2 *He paraded up and down in the corridor.*
► stride, strut, walk
3 *She was eager to parade her knowledge.*
► show off, display, demonstrate, exhibit, make a show of

**paradise** NOUN
1 *non-Christian theories about Paradise*
► heaven, Utopia, Eden, Elysium, nirvana
2 *Their holiday had been absolute paradise.*
► bliss, heaven, joy, delight, ecstasy

**paradox** NOUN
*the paradox of high prices at a time of low demand*
► anomaly, contradiction, self-contradiction, incongruity, oddity

**paradoxical** ADJECTIVE
*It seems paradoxical to reduce taxes when more money is needed for public services.*
► absurd, anomalous, conflicting, contradictory, illogical, incongruous, self-contradictory

**parallel** ADJECTIVE
1 *a pair of parallel lines*
► equidistant
2 *parallel methods of achieving the same objective*
► similar, analogous, corresponding, matching

**parallel** NOUN
1 *There is a parallel between her experience and ours.*
► similarity, resemblance, analogy, correspondence, comparison, likeness, match
2 *It would be hard to find an exact parallel to this problem.*
► counterpart, equivalent, analogue, likeness, duplicate

**parallel** VERB
*Their lives parallel each other in many respects.*
► resemble, match, be similar to, compare with, correspond to

**paralyse** VERB
1 *The injury paralysed his right leg for a time.*
► disable, immobilize, cripple, incapacitate, deaden
2 *The country was paralysed by a wave of strikes.*
► bring to a standstill, immobilize, bring to a halt, cripple, halt, freeze

**paralysed** ADJECTIVE
*I had a paralysed right arm.*
► disabled, handicapped, incapacitated, immobilized, crippled, lame, unusable

**paralysis** NOUN
1 *a disease that can cause paralysis*
► immobility, incapacity, paraplegia
2 *paralysis of the country's transport system*
► shutdown, immobilization, stopping, standstill

**parameter** NOUN
*It is important to define the parameters for this research.*
► criterion, guideline, framework, limit, boundary

**paramount** ADJECTIVE
*an issue of paramount importance*
► supreme, prime, primary, central, pre-eminent, highest, cardinal, foremost, utmost

**paraphernalia** NOUN
*all the paraphernalia needed to build our own greenhouse*
► equipment, apparatus, tackle, stuff, things, (more informal) odds and ends

**parcel** NOUN
*a parcel of food*
► package, packet, pack, consignment, bale, bundle, carton

**parcel** VERB
*parcel out Land was parcelled out in small plots.*
► divide up, distribute, share out, apportion, portion out, split up

**parched** ADJECTIVE
1 *The back lawn is so parched it hardly needs cutting.*
► scorched, dry, arid, baked, barren, waterless, dehydrated, lifeless, sterile
2 *We felt parched in the hot afternoon sun.*
► thirsty, dehydrated, dry, (more informal) gasping

**pardon** VERB
1 *The king would pardon them if they admitted their guilt.*
► forgive, excuse, absolve, grant a pardon to, reprieve, amnesty, acquit
AN OPPOSITE IS punish
2 *These are faults we can pardon and even admire.*
► forgive, excuse, condone

**pardon** NOUN
*A pardon was offered to the rebels.*
► amnesty, reprieve, release, discharge

**pare** VERB
*pare down The business has been pared down and several branches closed.*
► reduce, diminish, decrease, cut , prune, slim down, curtail, trim

**parent** NOUN
*She had an elderly parent to look after.*
► mother or father, guardian

**parentage** NOUN
*a young man of Indian parentage*
► origin, ancestry, lineage, pedigree, extraction, descent, heredity, pedigree, roots, stock, derivation, blood, ancestors, forebears

**parish** NOUN
1 *a large London parish*
► district, community
2 *The vicar had a large parish to look after.*
► congregation, flock, fold

**park** NOUN
*The children went off to play in the park.*
▶ recreation ground, public gardens, playground, parkland

**park** VERB
*She parked the car outside her friend's house.*
▶ leave, position, station, stop, place

**parliament** NOUN
*The country's parliament dates back to the Middle Ages.*
▶ legislature, congress, assembly, council, government, senate, conclave, convocation

**parody** NOUN
1 *He swivelled his hips in a parody of the belly dance.*
▶ caricature, lampoon, comic imitation, mimicry, mockery, skit, *(more informal)* take-off, *(more informal)* spoof, *(more informal)* send-up
2 *The article was no more than a parody of the truth.*
▶ travesty, distortion, mockery, caricature

**parody** VERB
*Jane Austen parodied the gothic novel. Alice bit back her tears and parodied a smile.*
▶ caricature, satirize, mimic, lampoon, travesty, ape, imitate, *(more informal)* send up, *(more informal)* take off

**parry** VERB
*Stephen managed to parry the blow.*
▶ fend off, ward off, avert, deflect, block, dodge, stave off, avoid, evade, sidestep, repel, repulse, push away

**parson** NOUN
*The parson shook hands outside the church.*
▶ clergyman, clergywoman, cleric, minister, priest, vicar, preacher

**part** NOUN
1 *This is only one part of the story.*
▶ bit, piece, portion, segment, section, episode, chapter, constituent
OPPOSITES ARE whole, entirety
2 *A part of the house had been closed off.*
▶ section, portion
3 *The washing machine has broken and needs a new part.*
▶ component, element, unit
4 *Deborah would take the lead part in the school play.*
▶ role, character
5 *Her parents lived in another part of town.*
▶ region, district, neighbourhood, quarter, section, sector
6 *Their part in the affair had not been very distinguished.*
▶ involvement, role, function, concern, responsibility, contribution (to)

**part** VERB
1 *They did not want to part on such bad terms.*
▶ separate, leave, say goodbye, say farewell, break up, go away
OPPOSITES ARE meet, reunite
2 *The authorities are anxious not to part the children.*
▶ separate, divide, split

3 **part with** *advertising designed to persuade shoppers to part with their money.*
▶ give up, relinquish, hand over, let go of, give up, forgo, surrender, discard

**partial** ADJECTIVE
1 *The economic collapse was followed by a partial recovery.*
▶ limited, incomplete, qualified, restricted, imperfect, unfinished
AN OPPOSITE IS complete
2 **be partial to** *She had always been partial to a cream tea.*
▶ like, love, enjoy, be fond of, have a fondness for, be keen on, appreciate, *(more informal)* go for

**participant** NOUN
*There were over a hundred participants in the race.*
▶ participator, entrant, competitor

**participate** VERB
*A million people participated in the vote by using their mobiles.*
▶ take part, join in, be involved, cooperate, engage, share, assist, help

**participation** NOUN
*They sought an active participation in the political life of the country*
▶ involvement, cooperation, sharing, contribution (to), partnership, sharing

**particle** NOUN
*There was not a single particle of food left.*
▶ bit, piece, morsel, scrap, shred, crumb, drop, fragment, grain, iota, jot, sliver, speck

**particular** ADJECTIVE
1 *The article criticized a particular group of companies.*
▶ specific, certain, distinct, definite, discrete
2 *This is a matter of particular interest to us.*
▶ special, exceptional, marked, unusual, uncommon, noteworthy, remarkable
3 *He was not too particular about the methods they used.*
▶ fussy, discriminating, finicky, fastidious, *(more informal)* choosy

**particulars** PLURAL NOUN
*A police officer will call to take your particulars.*
▶ details, facts, information, circumstances

**particularly** ADVERB
*The river trip is particularly enjoyable.*
▶ especially, exceptionally, remarkably, unusually, distinctly, notably

**parting** NOUN
1 *It will be an emotional parting.*
▶ farewell, goodbye, departure, leaving
OPPOSITES ARE meeting, reunion
2 *They would tell their son and daughter that evening about their intended parting.*
▶ separation, breakup, split-up, divorce
AN OPPOSITE IS reconciliation

**partisan** NOUN
*The country was swarming with Tito's partisans.*
▶ supporter, follower, adherent, devotee, champion, guerrilla, fighter

**partisan** ADJECTIVE
*the bitterly partisan nature of the debate*
▶ biased, one-sided, prejudiced, coloured, partial, slanted, factional

**partition** NOUN
1 *the partition of the country after the war*
▶ division, dividing, splitting, breaking-up
2 *A partition separated the two parts of the room.*
▶ screen, panel, divider, barrier, dividing wall

**partition** VERB
*A UN resolution partitioned the country into two states.*
▶ divide, split, subdivide, separate

**partly** ADVERB
*The work was now partly finished*
▶ partially, in part, to some extent, up to a point

**partner** NOUN
1 *Jack had been his business partner for many years.*
▶ colleague, associate, collaborator, ally, confederate, comrade, companion
2 *Staff were encouraged to bring their partners to the party.*
▶ girlfriend or boyfriend, husband or wife, spouse, mate

**partnership** NOUN
1 *a business partnership*
▶ company, firm, corporation, organization, syndicate, alliance, combination, cooperative, affiliation
2 *a partnership between nations*
▶ cooperation, association, coalition, collaboration

**party** NOUN
1 *a flat-warming party*
▶ celebration, gathering, festivity, function, merrymaking, (*humorous*) jollification, (*more informal*) get-together, (*more informal*) do
2 *a political party*
▶ group, faction, grouping, league, alliance, association, cabal, coalition
3 *a search party*
▶ team, crew, squad, company, group

**pass** VERB
1 *Lots of heavy traffic passed through the village.*
▶ drive, go, move, stream, progress
2 *She went to pass him the sugar and spilled it.*
▶ hand, give, deliver
3 *Eventually the storm passed.*
▶ blow over, go away, fade, fade away, disappear, come to an end
4 *As time passed he gradually forgot her.*
▶ elapse, go by, advance, progress, tick by
**pass away** *He passed away in his sleep.*
▶ die, pass on, lose your life, meet your end, breathe your last, expire
**pass off** *The meeting passed off without any trouble.*
▶ happen, take place, go off, occur, turn out

**pass out** *She must have passed out.*
▶ faint, lose consciousness, black out, (*more informal*) flake out
**pass over** *Perhaps we can pass over these mistakes.*
▶ disregard, overlook, ignore, forget, take no notice of, pay no attention to, discount
**pass up** *He was not one to pass up a chance of a free holiday.*
▶ turn down, forgo, reject, refuse, miss out on

**pass** NOUN
1 *a pass through the mountains*
▶ route, way, defile, gap, gorge, ravine, canyon
2 *Your pass will get you into all the city's museums.*
▶ permit, ticket, warrant, authority, authorization, licence

**passable** ADJECTIVE
1 *The food was no more than passable.*
▶ adequate, acceptable, satisfactory, tolerable, moderate, ordinary, sufficient, all right, fair, mediocre, middling, (*more informal*) so-so
AN OPPOSITE IS unacceptable
2 *The road is passable again after being closed because of floods.*
▶ open, traversable, navigable, usable, unblocked, clear
AN OPPOSITE IS impassable

**passage** NOUN
1 *the passage of time*
▶ passing, advance, course, march, progress, progression, moving on
2 *a sea passage*
▶ crossing, journey, voyage, trip, cruise, sail
3 *a narrow passage leading to the garden*
▶ corridor, passageway, walkway, thoroughfare, hallway, way through
4 *a passage between the two houses*
▶ alley, alleyway, path, pathway, way, lane, track
5 *a passage from The Amber Spyglass*
▶ excerpt, extract, section, episode, scene, paragraph, piece, quotation

**passenger** NOUN
*Passengers were told to get out at the next station.*
▶ traveller, commuter, voyager, rider

**passer-by** NOUN
*Passers-by stopped and looked.*
▶ bystander, onlooker, observer, spectator, watcher, witness, eyewitness

**passing** ADJECTIVE
*a passing feeling of regret*
▶ brief, temporary, short-lived, transient, momentary, cursory, short

**passion** NOUN
1 *You could talk about your passion for hang-gliding.*
▶ enthusiasm, fondness, eagerness, keenness (on), mania, appetite, interest (in), fanaticism, zeal, craving, commitment (to)
OPPOSITES ARE indifference (to), apathy

**2** *He recalled the passion with which she had kissed him.*
▶ feeling, ardour, intensity, emotion, fervour, love, longing, craving, desire, excitement, fire, heat
AN OPPOSITE IS detachment

**3** *He spoke with a fierce passion.*
▶ emotion, feeling, vehemence, anger, rage, fury, frenzy, paroxysm
OPPOSITES ARE coolness, indifference

### passionate ADJECTIVE

**1** *a passionate appeal for help*
▶ impassioned, emotional, heartfelt, intense, ardent, fervent, impulsive
OPPOSITES ARE half- hearted, cool

**2** *a passionate embrace*
▶ loving, amorous, sensual, lustful, erotic, (*more informal*) steamy
AN OPPOSITE IS cold

**3** *His passionate temperament got the better of him.*
▶ excitable, hot-blooded, intense, fiery, wild, violent
OPPOSITES ARE placid, phlegmatic

### passive ADJECTIVE

**1** *a passive acceptance of hardship*
▶ submissive, resigned, compliant, impassive, docile, long-suffering, non-violent, indifferent, patient, unresisting
OPPOSITES ARE active, lively

**2** *Tim had played a passive role in the affair.*
▶ inactive, uninvolved, non-participating
OPPOSITES ARE active, assertive

### past ADJECTIVE

*memories of past happiness*
▶ former, bygone, previous, earlier, ended, finished, gone, (*more informal*) over and done with
OPPOSITES ARE present, future

### past NOUN

*She was trying hard to forget the past.*
▶ antiquity, days gone by, history, old days, olden days, past times
OPPOSITES ARE present, future

---

### pasta NOUN

*How revolting to want chips with pasta.*
**SOME COMMON KINDS OF PASTA**
cannelloni, fusilli, lasagne, macaroni, noodles, penne, ravioli, rigatoni, spaghetti, tagliatelle, tortellini, vermicelli.

---

### paste NOUN

**1** *He used paste to fix his photos in an album.*
▶ glue, gum, adhesive, fixative
**2** *Mix the ingredients into a smooth paste.*
▶ purée, spread, mixture, pulp

### paste VERB

*She was busy pasting wallpaper.*
▶ fix, fasten, glue, gum, hang

### pastime NOUN

*a time when art was a rich man's pastime*
▶ hobby, activity, recreation, diversion, amusement, entertainment, occupation, game, sport, relaxation

### pastoral ADJECTIVE

**1** *a pastoral scene of trees and cows*
▶ rural, rustic, country, outdoor, agrarian, bucolic, farming, idyllic
AN OPPOSITE IS urban

**2** *the pastoral duties of a vicar's wife*
▶ ecclesiastical, priestly, parochial, ministerial, caring

### pasture NOUN

*a farm with a hundred acres of pasture*
▶ grass, grassland, meadow, field, paddock, pasturage, grazing

### pasty ADJECTIVE

*a row of people with pasty faces*
▶ pale, pallid, white, wan, sickly, anaemic, unhealthy
OPPOSITES ARE healthy, ruddy

### pat VERB

*Les leaned forward to pat her hand.*
▶ tap, touch, dab, stroke, rub, fondle

### pat ADJECTIVE

*His answers sounded pat, as if he'd rehearsed them.*
▶ glib, slick, facile, simplistic, smooth, unconvincing, perfunctory, superficial

### pat ADVERB

**off pat** *They have the right language off pat.*
▶ by heart, by rote, word for word, parrot-fashion

### patch NOUN

**1** *old jeans covered in patches*
▶ mend, repair
**2** *The family was going through a difficult patch.*
▶ period, time, spell, phase, stretch
**3** *Harry had a vegetable patch up the road.*
▶ plot, piece of ground, strip, row, area

### patch VERB

*He had got someone to patch his jacket at the elbow.*
▶ mend, repair, reinforce, put a patch on, cover, darn, fix, sew up, stitch up

### patchy ADJECTIVE

**1** *They drove through stretches of patchy fog.*
▶ irregular, uneven, sporadic, intermittent, variable, erratic, inconsistent, unpredictable, bitty, changeable
AN OPPOSITE IS constant

**2** *a piece of patchy grass*
▶ uneven, speckled, mottled, dappled, multicoloured

**3** *Their story was patchy and confusing.*
▶ fragmentary, deficient, variable, limited, inadequate
OPPOSITES ARE comprehensive, complete

**patent** ADJECTIVE
*The action was a patent violation of the agreement.*
▶ obvious, clear, plain, evident, blatant, manifest, apparent, palpable, undisguised
OPPOSITES ARE hidden, unclear

**path** NOUN
**1** *a path by the railway line*
▶ footpath, pathway, track, alley, lane
**2** *His path was blocked by the barricades.*
▶ way, route, course, passage, progress

**pathetic** ADJECTIVE
**1** *a pathetic wave of the hand*
▶ pitiful, pitiable, poignant, plaintive, sad, touching, moving, affecting, distressing, heartrending, lamentable, wretched
**2** (*informal*) *He added up his pathetic savings.*
▶ inadequate, paltry, meagre, feeble, derisory, miserable, wretched, worthless

**pathos** NOUN
*her speech of pathos and wifely love*
▶ sadness, poignancy, emotion, feeling, pity, tragedy

**patience** NOUN
**1** *Great care and patience is needed to avoid damaging the plants.*
▶ diligence, perseverance, persistence, self-control, stoicism, endurance, fortitude
**2** *Will's behaviour was stretching their patience to the limit.*
▶ toleration, forbearance, composure, calmness, restraint, equanimity, resignation

**patient** ADJECTIVE
**1** *She tried to be patient while her husband hunted for the key.*
▶ calm, self-controlled, composed, restrained, forbearing, indulgent, tolerant, lenient, understanding, philosophical
OPPOSITES ARE impatient, intolerant
**2** *The task called for a great deal of patient work.*
▶ diligent, persistent, persevering, tenacious, determined, dogged, resolved, purposeful

**patient** NOUN
*the relation between doctor and patient*
▶ invalid, sick person, sufferer, case

**patio** NOUN
*In summer they would sit on the patio.*
▶ terrace, courtyard, paved area

**patriotic** ADJECTIVE
*Many of his patriotic songs have a stirring lilt.*
▶ nationalistic, loyal, flag-waving, (*disapproving*) jingoistic, (*disapproving*) chauvinistic

**patrol** NOUN
**1** *Security guards remain on patrol all night.*
▶ surveillance, watch, guard, duty
**2** *A four-man patrol set off through the jungle.*
▶ guard, lookout, party, task force, convoy, detail

**patrol** VERB
*Guards with dogs patrol the estate.*
▶ police, tour, inspect, keep watch on, be on patrol on, go the rounds of

**patron** NOUN
**1** (*informal*) *a patron of the arts*
▶ sponsor, supporter, benefactor, champion, backer, defender
**2** *Parking outside the shops is for patrons only.*
▶ client, customer, (*more informal*) regular

**patronage** NOUN
**1** *State patronage of the arts is a thing of the past.*
▶ sponsorship, backing, support
**2** *The management thanked customers for their patronage over the years.*
▶ custom, business, trade

**patronize** VERB
**1** *The parents of girls like Sally patronized the little shop.*
▶ do business with, be a customer of, frequent, shop at, buy from, deal with
**2** *The nobility patronized music and the arts.*
▶ sponsor, support, finance, back, foster, encourage
**3** *She accused them of patronizing her.*
▶ talk down to, condescend to, look down on, put down

**patronizing** ADJECTIVE
*The British should learn to adopt a less patronizing tone.*
▶ condescending, supercilious, superior, disdainful, haughty, lofty, paternalistic, snobbish
OPPOSITES ARE humble, modest

**patter** VERB
**1** *Rain pattered against the window.*
▶ beat, tap, rattle, clatter, pitter-patter
**2** *The children pattered up to their rooms.*
▶ scurry, scamper, scuttle

**patter** NOUN
**1** *the patter of feet*
▶ pattering, pitter-patter, scurrying, scuttling
**2** *a salesman's patter*
▶ chatter, babble, line, (*more informal*) spiel

**pattern** NOUN
**1** *patterns drawn in the sand*
▶ design, device, figure, motif, shape, figuration, arrangement, decoration, ornamentation
**2** *Their actions might set a pattern*
▶ example, model, standard, guide, norm, original, precedent, archetype, criterion, prototype, sample, specimen
**3** *The insects have a special behaviour pattern.*
▶ system, order, method, scheme

**paunch** NOUN
*He leaned back in his chair and spread his finger over his paunch.*
▶ belly, pot belly, gut, pot

**pauper** NOUN
*The revolution left the family almost paupers.*
▶ beggar, bankrupt, insolvent, down and out

## pause

**pause** VERB

*She paused for a moment before going in.*
► wait, hesitate, stop, delay, halt, waver, hang back, break off, rest, have a pause

**pause** NOUN

*There was a short pause while the band regrouped.*
► break, interruption, interval, delay, rest, wait, interlude, intermission, lull, stoppage, respite, stop, suspension, (*more informal*) breather

**pave** VERB

**1** *She decided to pave part of the garden to put a table on.*
► cover, concrete, flag, tile, asphalt

**2 pave the way for** *Tax cuts paved the way for an economic recovery.*
► prepare for, lay the foundations for, clear the way for, herald, precede

**pavement** NOUN

*A parked car was blocking the pavement.*
► footpath, path, walkway, (*American*) sidewalk

**paw** NOUN

*She stroked the cat's paw.*
► foot, pad

**paw** VERB

*The young animals were pawing one another.*
► touch, poke, maul

**pawn** NOUN

*The nobles used the young prince as a pawn in their power struggle.*
► puppet, dupe, tool, stooge, hostage

**pay** NOUN

*Her pay would go up in April.*
► income, earnings, salary, wages, payment, (*more formal*) remuneration, (*more formal*) emolument

**pay** VERB

**1** *I'd rather pay more and get a better machine.*
► spend, expend, pay out, part with, (*more informal*) shell out, (*more informal*) dish out

**2** *He said he'd pay me for the broken window.*
► reimburse, recompense, refund, repay, pay back

**3** *Stella is trying to pay her debts.*
► settle, discharge, pay off, meet, clear, honour

**4** *I'll make them pay for this.*
► suffer, make amends, atone, answer

**5** *It would pay us to wait until the new model comes out.*
► benefit, profit, be an advantage to

**payment** NOUN

**1** *You can settle in six or twelve monthly payments.*
► instalment, contribution, remittance

**2** *There is a discount for prompt payment.*
► settlement, remittance

**3** *You get extra payment for working late.*
► pay, wages, income, remuneration

**peace** NOUN

**1** *It's not easy to get any peace in this house.*
► calm, quiet, silence, tranquillity, relaxation, hush
OPPOSITES ARE disturbance, noise

**2** *The country longed for peace after years of civil unrest.*
► order, harmony, harmoniousness, non-violence
AN OPPOSITE IS disorder

**3** *A peace will be signed and the war ended.*
► armistice, truce, ceasefire, treaty, agreement, concord

**peaceable** ADJECTIVE

*a peaceable nation*
► peace-loving, unwarlike, non-violent, pacific, peaceful, placid, conciliatory, cooperative, friendly, harmonious
OPPOSITES ARE aggressive, warlike, belligerent

**peaceful** ADJECTIVE

**1** *a peaceful part of the country*
► quiet, restful, serene, tranquil, secluded, undisturbed, unruffled, untroubled, calm, still, pleasant, relaxing, balmy
OPPOSITES ARE noisy, troubled

**2** *The country wants to resolve the dispute in a peaceful manner.*
► non-violent, calm, cordial, amicable, friendly, orderly

**3** *Tanya had a peaceful temperament.*
► calm, placid, serene, amicable, friendly, unruffled, pacific, gentle
OPPOSITES ARE turbulent, agitated

**peak** NOUN

**1** *the peaks of the mountains*
► summit, tip, top, crest, pinnacle, crown, point

**2** *Ruth had reached the peak of her career.*
► height, highest point, zenith, acme, climax, culmination
OPPOSITES ARE nadir, trough

**peaky** ADJECTIVE

*Josh had been looking peaky all morning, and stayed at home.*
► pale, pallid, pasty, unwell, sickly, poorly, queasy, out of sorts

**peal** NOUN

*a peal of bells*
► chime, carillon, ringing, clang

**peal** VERB

*The bells pealed*
► chime, ring, toll, resound, resonate

**peasant** NOUN

**1** *There were rows of peasants picking tomatoes in the fields.*
► countryman, rustic, farmhand, yokel

**2** (*informal*) *He became angry and called them a bunch of peasants.*
► lout, oaf, bumpkin

**peculiar** ADJECTIVE

**1** *Something peculiar was happening to her computer.*
► strange, odd, unusual, weird, curious, funny, extraordinary, bizarre, abnormal
OPPOSITES ARE normal, ordinary

**2** *By that stage of the journey we were all feeling a bit peculiar.*
► unwell, ill, sick, poorly, queasy, out of sorts

**3** *Norman had his own peculiar way of doing things.*
▶ special, characteristic, distinctive, individual, particular, singular, unique, idiosyncratic, (*more informal*) wacky, (*more informal*) screwy

**peculiarity** NOUN
**1** *Find out about the peculiarities of the local weather when you go abroad. He had a strange physical peculiarity.*
▶ oddity, peculiar or special feature, abnormality, foible, idiosyncrasy, quirk, trait, characteristic, eccentricity
**2** *We will have to accept the peculiarity of this arrangement.*
▶ strangeness, abnormality, oddness, oddity, eccentricity, bizarreness

**pedantic** ADJECTIVE
**1** *He has a pedantic style of writing.*
▶ academic, bookish, formal, humourless, learned, old-fashioned, pompous, scholarly, schoolmasterly, stilted
AN OPPOSITE IS informal
**2** *a pedantic application of the rules*
▶ strict, inflexible, precise, over-scrupulous, unimaginative, (*more informal*) nit-picking
AN OPPOSITE IS flexible

**peddle** VERB
*a company peddling cheap software in the third world*
▶ sell, trade in, traffic in, market, vend, tout, (*more informal*) flog

**pedestal** NOUN
*a statue on a tall pedestal*
▶ base, plinth, stand, support, mounting, column, pillar

**pedestrian** ADJECTIVE
**1** *a pedestrian walkway*
▶ pedestrianized, traffic-free
**2** *a pedestrian performance*
▶ dull, tedious, ordinary, mediocre, run-of-the-mill, monotonous, boring

**pedestrian** NOUN
*Pedestrians should use the footbridge.*
▶ walker, person on foot

**pedigree** ADJECTIVE
*a pedigree dog*
▶ pure-bred, thoroughbred

**pedigree** NOUN
*cattle with a pedigree that goes back to Roman Britain*
▶ ancestry, descent, lineage, line, stock, descent, parentage

**pedlar** NOUN
*a pedlar of cheap watches and electronic games*
▶ seller, hawker, travelling salesman, street-trader, vendor

**peek** VERB
*A face peeked round the doorway.*
▶ peep, peer, glance, look

**peek** NOUN
*He took a quick peek at the recipe.*
▶ peep, glance, glimpse, look

**peel** NOUN
*Orange peel lay in a spiral on the table.*
▶ rind, skin, covering, zest

**peel** VERB
*Jeff peeled an apple.*
▶ pare, skin, strip

**peep** VERB
*Jane peeped through the keyhole.*
▶ peek, peer, glance, look

**peep** NOUN
*Have a peep at the baby.*
▶ peek, glance, glimpse, look

**peer** VERB
*A woman peered at us from a corner of the room.*
▶ gaze, look, glance, squint, peep, peek

**peeved** ADJECTIVE
*Paula still felt peeved about it.*
▶ annoyed, irritated, angry, cross, displeased, vexed, infuriated, incensed, enraged, (*more informal*) miffed, (*more informal*) put out
AN OPPOSITE IS pleased

**peevish** ADJECTIVE
*Ellen replied in a slightly peevish tone.*
▶ irritable, petulant, fractious, irascible, fretful, touchy, sullen, snappy, crotchety
OPPOSITES ARE good-humoured, agreeable

**peg** NOUN
*She put her coat on a peg.*
▶ hook, pin, spike, knob

**peg** VERB
**1** *Make sure you peg the tent to the ground.*
▶ fasten, fix, secure, attach
**2** *Prices will be pegged for six months.*
▶ fix, hold, hold down, keep down, freeze, control

**pelt** VERB
**1** *The men were pelting each other with snowballs.*
▶ bombard, shower, attack, assail, batter
**2** *It was pelting down outside.*
▶ pour, teem, rain cats and dogs
**3** *The players pelted back to the dressing room.*
▶ rush, dash, run, hurry, sprint, charge, streak

**pen** NOUN
**1** *sheep in a pen*
▶ enclosure, compound, paddock, stockade
**2** *He wrote it down with a pen.*
▶ ballpoint, biro, felt-tipped pen, fountain pen

**penalize** VERB
*The authorities can penalize parents of children who miss school.*
▶ punish, impose a penalty on, fine, discipline
AN OPPOSITE IS reward

**penalty** NOUN
*a fixed penalty for illegal parking*
▶ punishment, fine, forfeit
AN OPPOSITE IS reward

**pending** ADJECTIVE
*A decision is pending.*
▶ imminent, impending, forthcoming, in the offing, about to happen

**penetrate** VERB
1 *Make sure the screws do not penetrate the top surface of the shelf.*
▶ pierce, puncture, perforate, bore through, make a hole in
2 *An advance force penetrated the city's outer defences.*
▶ infiltrate, enter, get through, slip through, probe
3 *Damp had penetrated the stone-work.*
▶ impregnate, permeate, pervade, seep into

**penetrating** ADJECTIVE
1 *She looked away from his penetrating dark eyes.*
▶ piercing, probing, staring, sharp, keen
2 *The students asked some penetrating questions.*
▶ perceptive, sharp, acute, intelligent, incisive, profound, searching
3 *The silence was interrupted by a penetrating scream.*
▶ shrill, piercing, strident, ear-splitting, deafening

**penniless** ADJECTIVE
*Epstein was a penniless student in Paris.*
▶ poor, impoverished, destitute, poverty-stricken, moneyless, (*more informal*) skint

**pensive** ADJECTIVE
*He sipped his coffee with a pensive expression on his face.*
▶ thoughtful, reflective, contemplative, absorbed, meditative, ruminative, preoccupied, wistful, serious

**people** NOUN
1 *By mid-afternoon many people were hungry People like to read books like these.*
▶ persons, individuals, human beings, humans, folk, mortals, humanity, humankind, mankind
**USAGE** Note that *humanity, humankind,* and *mankind* are all singular nouns and you use a singular verb with them, e.g. *Humankind likes to read books like these.*
2 *The government will appeal to the people in a general election.*
▶ nation, electorate, voters, electors, community
3 *a shopping centre that serves the people of the area a proud and brave people*
▶ populace, population, citizens, inhabitants, public, society, common people, community, electorate, nation
RELATED ADJECTIVES ethnic, national
4 *Her people live in Ireland.*
▶ family, relatives, relations, parents, clan, kith and kin
**USAGE** Note that *family* and *clan* are singular nouns but you can use a singular or plural

verb with them, e.g. *Her family lives in Scotland* or *Her family live in Scotland.*

**people** VERB
*the inhabitants who once peopled this fine island*
▶ populate, inhabit, occupy, live in, settle, colonize

**pep** NOUN
(*informal*) *The project needed a lot more pep.*
▶ energy, vigour, vitality, spirit, verve, exuberance, fizz

**pep** VERB
**pep up** *He added some herbs to pep up the flavour.*
▶ liven up, vitalize, enhance, intensify

**peppery** ADJECTIVE
*Dried chillies add a peppery touch.*
▶ hot, spicy, pungent, peppered, sharp

**perceive** VERB
1 *Those in the room perceived voices outside.*
▶ hear, discern, distinguish, make out, notice, recognize, become aware of
2 *Some animals cannot perceive colour.*
▶ see, discern, distinguish, recognize, observe, identify
3 *I began to perceive her meaning.*
▶ understand, comprehend, apprehend, grasp, realize, sense, deduce, gather, know
4 *We all perceive the world in different ways. an enemy perceived as a major threat*
▶ regard, consider, view, judge, deem, think of, look on

**perceptible** ADJECTIVE
1 *There followed a perceptible pause in the conversation.*
▶ noticeable, perceivable, distinct, evident, marked, palpable, detectable, appreciable, obvious, audible
AN OPPOSITE IS imperceptible
2 *The coast was perceptible from the aircraft windows.*
▶ visible, discernible, observable, recognizable

**perception** NOUN
1 *The public's perception of the government's honesty has changed.*
▶ impression, consciousness, apprehension, sense, view, awareness, cognition, comprehension, understanding, recognition, sensation
2 *She speaks with great perception on these problems.*
▶ insight, perceptiveness, discernment, understanding, perspicacity, astuteness, shrewdness, intelligence, observation

**perceptive** ADJECTIVE
*A few perceptive questions can liven up the interview.*
▶ discerning, astute, shrewd, intelligent, insightful, perspicacious
OPPOSITES ARE obtuse, inept

**perch** VERB
*A monkey came in and perched on a table.*
▶ sit, settle, rest, balance, alight

**perfect** ADJECTIVE (with the stress on *per-*)
 **1** *It was the start to a perfect day.*
 ▶ superb, excellent, superlative, wonderful, marvellous, idyllic, blissful
 **2** *a second-hand book in perfect condition*
 ▶ impeccable, flawless, immaculate, spotless, pristine
 OPPOSITES ARE imperfect, flawed
 **3** *a copy so perfect you can't tell it from the original*
 ▶ exact, precise, faithful, accurate, true, close
 AN OPPOSITE IS inaccurate
 **4** *A digital radio will make a perfect birthday present.*
 ▶ ideal, suitable, fitting, apt, appropriate
 OPPOSITES ARE unsuitable, inappropriate
 **5** *He felt a perfect fool. They had never met; they were perfect strangers.*
 ▶ complete, absolute, utter, total, entire, thoroughgoing

**perfect** VERB (with the stress on *-fect*)
 *He is spending some time perfecting his speech.*
 ▶ improve, make perfect, refine, complete, finish, fulfil, realize

**perfection** NOUN
 **1** *the perfection of her complexion*
 ▶ faultlessness, flawlessness, excellence, beauty, completeness, ideal, wholeness
 AN OPPOSITE IS imperfection
 **2** *the perfection of their plans*
 ▶ completion, consummation, fulfilment, realization, accomplishment, fruition, achievement

**perfectionist** NOUN
 *He was such a perfectionist he wouldn't allow any mistakes.*
 ▶ idealist, purist, precisionist, (*more informal*) stickler

**perfectly** ADVERB
 **1** *He brought in a perfectly baked cake.*
 ▶ superbly, impeccably, faultlessly, flawlessly, beautifully, excellently
 **2** *I'm perfectly happy to let them use the house. He can be perfectly horrid at times.*
 ▶ absolutely, completely, entirely, totally, utterly
 **3** *You know perfectly well what I mean.*
 ▶ very, quite, full, (*more informal*) jolly

**perforate** VERB
 *a teabag perforated with tiny holes*
 ▶ pierce, prick, puncture, penetrate, bore through, drill

**perform** VERB
 **1** *The two devices perform the same function. She has her duties to perform.*
 ▶ fulfil, exercise, carry out, execute, discharge, accomplish, achieve
 **2** *The company performed the new play in London.*
 ▶ present, stage, put on, produce, mount
 **3** *The speakers perform best at a fairly high volume.*
 ▶ work, function, operate, behave

**performance** NOUN
 **1** *the performance of their duties*
 ▶ carrying out, execution, discharge, accomplishment, fulfilment, completion, implementation
 **2** *The music received a fine performance.*
 ▶ rendition, interpretation, rendering, account
 **3** *The review praised the new range of cars for their performance*
 ▶ operation, running, functioning, behaviour
 **4** *He made a huge performance of thanking them.*
 ▶ fuss, exhibition, act, scene, parade

**performer** NOUN
 *The song was sung by the original performers.*
 ▶ singer, entertainer, artist, artiste, musician, player, star, actor, actress

**perfume** NOUN
 **1** *With a final spray of exotic perfume she left the room.*
 ▶ scent, toilet water, eau de cologne
 **2** *the fresh, sweet perfume of roses*
 ▶ smell , scent, fragrance, aroma, odour, whiff

**perfunctory** ADJECTIVE
 *They greeted each other with perfunctory grunts.*
 ▶ cursory, desultory, fleeting, casual, hurried, offhand, half-hearted, unthinking, mechanical, automatic
 OPPOSITES ARE enthusiastic, careful

**perhaps** ADVERB
 *Perhaps they took the train to Glasgow.*
 ▶ maybe, possibly, conceivably, feasibly

**peril** NOUN
 **1** *the perils of the sea*
 ▶ danger, hazard, risk, menace, uncertainty
 OPPOSITES ARE security, safety
 **in peril** *The climbers found themselves in great peril.*
 ▶ in danger, at risk, in jeopardy

**perilous** ADJECTIVE
 *a perilous journey through tropical swamps*
 ▶ dangerous, hazardous, fraught, unsafe, risky
 AN OPPOSITE IS safe

**perimeter** NOUN
 **1** *The airport perimeter is closely guarded.*
 ▶ boundary, periphery, confines, edge, fringe, border, margin, borderline, bounds, circumference
 **2** *The perimeter is about twelve miles.*
 ▶ circumference, outer edge

**period** NOUN
 **1** *They suffered from several long periods of separation.*
 ▶ spell, interval, stretch, term, bout, run, span, phase, session
 **2** *the Hanoverian period of English history*
 ▶ age, era, years, epoch, time
 **3** *There was a double period of maths on Monday.*
 ▶ lesson, class, session

**periodic** ADJECTIVE
 *He suffered periodic lapses of memory.*
 ▶ occasional, regular, intermittent, recurrent, repeated, spasmodic

a
b
c
d
e
f
g
h
i
j
k
l
m
n
o
**p**
q
r
s
t
u
v
w
x
y
z

**periodical** NOUN

*The library has a special catalogue of periodicals.*
▶ journal, magazine, review, monthly, quarterly, weekly

**peripheral** ADJECTIVE

1 *migrants travelling from peripheral parts of Europe*
▶ distant, outermost, outlying, outer
AN OPPOSITE IS central

2 *These issues are peripheral to the main question.*
▶ secondary, subsidiary, inessential, non-essential, incidental, marginal, borderline, minor, irrelevant, unimportant
OPPOSITES ARE essential, crucial

**perish** VERB

1 *Many people perished in the floods.*
▶ die, be killed, lose your life, pass away

2 *The tyres had started to perish.*
▶ decay, decompose, disintegrate, crumble away, rot

**perk** NOUN

*(informal) company cars and other perks*
▶ benefit, extra, bonus, (more formal) perquisite, (more informal) plus

**perk up** VERB

*He perked up when he saw Susan coming.*
▶ cheer up, liven up, brighten, take heart, pick up, bounce back

**perky** ADJECTIVE

*Margaret was in one of her perky moods.*
▶ lively, cheerful, vivacious, animated, bubbly, bouncy, buoyant, sparkly

**permanent** ADJECTIVE

1 *We are looking for a permanent solution to the problem.*
▶ lasting, continuing, durable, fixed, long-term, unchangeable, irreversible, everlasting, perpetual, eternal

2 *Leslie has got his first permanent job.*
▶ stable, fixed, established, secure, firm

**permeate** VERB

*A delicious smell permeated the whole house.*
▶ pervade, pass through, spread through, filter through, flow through, penetrate, percolate through, saturate

**permissible** ADJECTIVE

*Pollution exceeds permissible levels.*
▶ permitted, allowable, allowed, legal, lawful, legitimate, acceptable, admissible, authorized
OPPOSITES ARE forbidden, unacceptable

**permission** NOUN

*We will need permission to miss the afternoon classes.*
▶ authorization, authority, leave, consent, approval, agreement, licence, assent, clearance, dispensation, (more informal) the go-ahead, (informal) the green light

**permissive** ADJECTIVE

*the permissive society of the sixties and seventies*
▶ liberal, broad-minded, open-minded, tolerant, free-and-easy, indulgent, lenient

**permit** VERB

1 *The authorities would not permit release of the documents.*
▶ allow, authorize, endorse, agree to, consent to, approve of, give permission for, sanction, license, tolerate
OPPOSITES ARE prohibit, prevent, ban

2 *His club will permit him to play in the national side.*
▶ allow, authorize, give an opportunity, make it possible
OPPOSITES ARE forbid, prohibit (from)

**permit** NOUN

*The warden asked to see his permit.*
▶ authorization, licence, pass, warrant, certification, passport, visa, charter

**perpetual** ADJECTIVE

1 *The Arctic is in almost perpetual daylight.*
▶ continuous, constant, uninterrupted, permanent, ceaseless, everlasting, eternal, non-stop
AN OPPOSITE IS temporary

2 *Their perpetual rows upset the children.*
▶ continual, interminable, incessant, constant, eternal, endless, ceaseless
OPPOSITES ARE occasional, intermittent

**perplex** VERB

*a helpline that answers any questions that perplex you*
▶ baffle, bewilder, puzzle, mystify, confuse, bemuse, disconcert, confound, fox, (more informal) flummox, (more informal) floor

**persecute** VERB

1 *In Rome, Christians were being persecuted by the Emperor Nero.*
▶ oppress, victimize, martyr, discriminate against, maltreat, ill-treat, tyrannize

2 *He thought everyone was persecuting him.*
▶ harass, hound, pester, pursue, bother, plague, torment, intimidate, bully, terrorize

**persecution** NOUN

*victims of political persecution*
▶ oppression, victimization, discrimination, harassment, maltreatment, martyrdom, tyranny, abuse

**perseverance** NOUN

*The job required perseverance and patience.*
▶ persistence, tenacity, determination, resolve, doggedness, diligence, dedication, application, commitment, endurance, stamina

**persevere** VERB

*He decided to persevere, in spite of some early failures.*
▶ continue, persist, keep going, carry on, press on, endure, (more informal) soldier on, (more informal) hang on, (more informal) keep at it, (informal) stick at it, (more informal) plug away
OPPOSITES ARE give up, stop

# persist VERB

**1** *The officer persisted with his questions.*
▶ continue, persevere, keep going, carry on, press on, endure, (*more informal*) soldier on, (*more informal*) hang on, (*more informal*) keep at it, (*informal*) stick at it, (*more informal*) plug away
OPPOSITES ARE desist, give up, stop

**2** *If the pain persists, you should see a doctor.*
▶ continue, carry on, keep on, go on, linger, last, remain
AN OPPOSITE IS cease

**3** *persist in He would persist in interrupting her*
▶ keep on, insist on

# persistent ADJECTIVE

**1** *The company should respond to its more persistent critics.*
▶ determined, tenacious, persevering, resolute, single-minded

**2** *They were interrupted by a persistent knocking at the door.*
▶ continuing, constant, steady, incessant, endless, non-stop

# person NOUN

*We must find the person responsible. She was the first person to arrive. There was not a person to be seen.*
▶ individual, man or woman, being, human being, soul, body

# personal ADJECTIVE

**1** *a story based on the author's personal experiences*
▶ own, individual, particular, special, exclusive
OPPOSITES ARE general, public

**2** *The letter was marked 'personal'.*
▶ private, confidential, secret

# personality NOUN

**1** *He has a warmth of personality and a generous nature.*
▶ character, nature, disposition, temperament, identity, individuality, (*more informal*) make-up

**2** *a television personality*
▶ celebrity, star, superstar, name

# personify VERB

*The dancers are meant to personify Spring.*
▶ represent, symbolize, personalize, epitomize, allegorize, embody, give a human shape to, incarnate

# personnel NOUN

*An alert has been sent out to security personnel.*
▶ staff, workers, employees, manpower, workforce, force, crew, people

# perspective NOUN

*Since the war we see history from a different perspective.*
▶ outlook, viewpoint, point of view, slant, view, angle

**in perspective** *To put this in perspective, ten percent of buyers admitted to being dissatisfied with what they had bought.*
▶ in context, in proportion

# perspire VERB

*Women glow and men perspire.*
▶ sweat, break out in a sweat, exude, drip

# persuade VERB

*Will you be able to persuade Susie to go back to England?*
▶ convince, tempt, prevail on or upon, induce, coax, talk into, make, entice, influence, pressure, pressurize, urge, bring round, cajole, inveigle
AN OPPOSITE IS dissuade

# persuasion NOUN

**1** *I shall need a lot of persuasion to change my mind.*
▶ persuading, coaxing, coercion, convincing, inducement, exhortation, cajolery, enticement, argument

**2** *people with a wide range of political persuasions*
▶ belief, conviction, view, opinion, faith

# persuasive ADJECTIVE

*There's a lot of persuasive talk but not much action.*
▶ convincing, compelling, cogent, sound, valid, plausible, reasonable, forceful, strong, telling, credible, effective, eloquent, influential, logical, watertight
OPPOSITES ARE unconvincing, unpersuasive

# pert ADJECTIVE

*The barmaid was a pert, slightly plump girl called Rose.*
▶ cheeky, impudent, impertinent, insolent, impolite, disrespectful, brazen, audacious, forward

# pertinent ADJECTIVE

*The questions he asked me were very pertinent.*
▶ relevant, apposite, suitable, fitting, apt, material, to the point

# perturb VERB

*Her arrival did not perturb him in the slightest.*
▶ alarm, disturb, upset, dismay, distress, unnerve, agitate, shock, fluster, daunt, (*more informal*) put the wind up
AN OPPOSITE IS reassure

# peruse VERB

*Visitors can relax in the reading room, perusing books or using the online facilities.*
▶ read, study, browse through, inspect, glance at, look through, skim through, thumb through, scrutinize

# pervade VERB

*A pleasant smell of cooking pervaded the room.*
▶ permeate, pass through, spread through, filter through, flow through, penetrate, affect, imbue, percolate through, saturate

# pervasive ADJECTIVE

*Their jaunty behaviour masked a pervasive sense of anxiety.*
▶ prevalent, pervading, widespread, inescapable, insidious, permeating, general, ubiquitous, universal, rife

**USAGE** Note that *rife* is only used after a verb, e.g. *A sense of anxiety was rife.*

a b c d e f g h i j k l m n o **p** q r s t u v w x y z

**perverse** ADJECTIVE
*He has the perverse habit of calling all young girls 'madam' and all older women girls.*
▶ contrary, wayward, awkward, unreasonable, tiresome, capricious, wilful, obstinate, stubborn, unhelpful, rebellious
OPPOSITES ARE reasonable, obliging

**perversion** NOUN
1 *The evidence was a perversion of the truth.*
▶ distortion, misrepresentation, falsification, travesty, debasement, corruption, aberration, twisting
2 *new attitudes to sexual perversion*
▶ deviation, abnormality, deviance, unnaturalness, (more informal) kinkiness

**pervert** NOUN (with the stress on per-)
*They called him a sexual pervert.*
▶ deviant, degenerate, (more informal) perv, (more informal) weirdo, (more informal) sicko

**pervert** VERB (with the stress on -vert)
1 *He was charged with perverting the course of justice.*
▶ distort, subvert, twist, bend, abuse, falsify, undermine
2 *a dictator perverted by years of power*
▶ corrupt, deprave, lead astray, debase, degrade

**perverted** ADJECTIVE
*Just put it down to my perverted sense of humour.*
▶ unnatural, deviant, twisted, warped, distorted, depraved, debased, abnormal, degenerate, (more informal) sick, (more informal) kinky
OPPOSITES ARE natural, normal

**pessimism** NOUN
*His pessimism prevented him from taking any risks.*
▶ despondency, fatalism, negativeness, hopelessness, gloom, despair, resignation, unhappiness, cynicism
AN OPPOSITE IS optimism

**pessimistic** ADJECTIVE
*Manufacturers are pessimistic about the economic future.*
▶ negative, fatalistic, gloomy, downbeat, downhearted, unhopeful, defeatist, despairing, despondent, resigned, unhappy, cynical
AN OPPOSITE IS optimistic

**pest** NOUN
1 *Vincent's demands for attention were becoming a pest.*
▶ nuisance, bother, annoyance, irritation, curse, trial, bore, bane, vexation, (more informal) pain, (more informal) pain in the neck
2 *the rise in crop pests*
▶ insect, bug, parasite, (more informal) creepy-crawly

**pester** NOUN
*Claire was nice and didn't pester him with silly questions.*
▶ annoy, bother, irritate, badger, harass, nag, harry,

chivvy, hound, trouble, besiege, (more informal) hassle, (more informal) bug, (more informal) keep on at, (more informal) go on at

**pet** NOUN
(informal) *They teased him and called him teacher's pet.*
▶ favourite, darling, treasure, blue-eyed boy or girl

**pet** ADJECTIVE
1 *Whoever heard of a pet rattlesnake?*
▶ tame, domestic
2 *The shop was very much his own pet scheme.*
▶ favourite, cherished, prized, precious, special, personal

**pet** VERB
*Kim sat holding the kitten and petting it.*
▶ pat, stroke, pamper, caress, cuddle, fondle, kiss, touch

**peter out** VERB
*The traffic began to peter out.*
▶ dwindle, diminish, decrease, subside, disappear, fall off, die out, wane, shrink

**petite** ADJECTIVE
*She had a slender petite figure and a lovely complexion.*
▶ small, slight, delicate, elfin, gamine

**petition** NOUN
*a petition protesting at the new building plans*
▶ appeal, list of signatures, application, supplication, entreaty, plea

**petition** VERB
*After his death his widow petitioned the governor for justice.*
▶ appeal to, call upon, make a plea to, plead with, supplicate, beseech, apply to, solicit

**petrified** ADJECTIVE
*The child stood petrified with fright.*
▶ terrified, paralysed, terror-struck, horrified, frozen

**petty** ADJECTIVE
1 *The meeting was called for petty reasons.*
▶ trivial, minor, trifling, unimportant, insignificant, slight, secondary, paltry
2 *The criticisms were unfair and petty.*
▶ spiteful, small-minded, vindictive, mean, ungenerous, grudging

**petulant** ADJECTIVE
*He sounded as petulant as an obstinate child.*
▶ bad-tempered, peevish, irritable, fractious, irascible, fretful, touchy, sullen, snappy, crotchety
OPPOSITES ARE good-humoured, agreeable

**phantom** NOUN
1 *a phantom that appeared at night*
▶ ghost, spectre, spirit, apparition, wraith, (more informal) spook
2 *He realized that what he had seen had been a phantom of his own mind.*
▶ hallucination, figment, illusion, delusion, vision
3 *a phantom pregnancy*
▶ imaginary, imagined, false, unreal

## phase NOUN

1 *the final phase of the war*
▶ stage, part, period, step, chapter
2 *The marriage was going through a difficult phase.*
▶ period, stage, spell, time, state

## phase out VERB

*The old version of the software has been phased out.*
▶ withdraw, remove, close, eliminate, terminate

## phenomenal ADJECTIVE

*Lutyens had a phenomenal memory for detail.*
▶ remarkable, extraordinary, outstanding, amazing, astonishing, astounding, staggering, sensational, breathtaking
OPPOSITES ARE ordinary, run-of-the-mill

## phenomenon NOUN

1 *Retirement was a largely twentieth-century phenomenon*
▶ occurrence, circumstance, feature, experience, event, situation, thing
2 *The band became a cult phenomenon.*
▶ sensation, wonder, marvel, spectacle, prodigy

## philanthropic ADJECTIVE

*He donated the money for genuinely philanthropic motives.*
▶ charitable, altruistic, beneficent, benevolent, humanitarian, public-spirited, generous, bountiful, munificent, caring, humane, kind
AN OPPOSITE IS misanthropic

## philanthropist NOUN

*a cricket-loving Edwardian philanthropist*
▶ benefactor, patron, donor, contributor, sponsor, backer

## philanthropy NOUN

*Nineteenth-century philanthropy seeking to protect the elderly*
▶ benevolence, generosity, beneficence, humanitarianism, public-spiritedness, patronage, liberality, altruism, munificence

## philosopher NOUN

*Thales, the first Greek philosopher*
▶ thinker, sage, student of philosophy, theorizer

## philosophical ADJECTIVE

1 *a new approach to old philosophical ideas*
▶ theoretical, analytical, rational, reasoned, abstract, academic, metaphysical, ideological, intellectual, learned, logical, wise, erudite
2 *He felt in a philosophical mood.*
▶ thoughtful, reflective, contemplative, meditative, introspective, studious, ruminative
3 *Jane was philosophical about life's problems.*
▶ calm, composed, collected, resigned, unemotional, unruffled, stoical, self-possessed, patient
AN OPPOSITE IS emotional

## philosophy NOUN

1 *a student of philosophy*
▶ thinking, reasoning, metaphysics, wisdom, knowledge, logic
2 *Taylor spent his life promoting his philosophy.*
▶ convictions, beliefs, ideology, principles, theories, credo, attitudes, viewpoint

## phlegmatic ADJECTIVE

*Ronnie, in his own phlegmatic way, could live with the problem better than most.*
▶ calm, cool, composed, placid, impassive, unemotional, unexcitable, cool-headed, serene
OPPOSITES ARE excitable, passionate

---

## phobia NOUN

*He has a phobia about noise.*
▶ aversion (to), dread (of), fear (of), anxiety, obsession, neurosis, revulsion, dislike (of), hatred (of), horror, (*more informal*) hang-up, (*more informal*) thing

**TYPES OF PHOBIA**
The three most common **phobia** words are
**agoraphobia**: fear of open spaces.
**claustrophobia**: fear of enclosed spaces.
**xenophobia**: hostility to foreigners.

**OTHER TYPES OF FEAR ARE:**
**aerophobia**: aeroplanes.
**zoophobia**: animals.
**homophobia**: homosexuals.
**haemophobia**: blood.
**ailurophobia**: cats.
**cryophobia**: cold.
**cyberphobia**: computers.
**ochlophobia**: crowds.
**scotophobia**: darkness.
**thanatophobia**: death .
**cynophobia**: dogs.
**panphobia**: everything.
**phasmophobia**: ghosts.
**acrophobia**: heights.
**photophobia**: light.
**androphobia**: men.
**hypnophobia**: sleep.
**triskaidekaphobia**: the number thirteen.
**brontophobia**: thunder.
**hydrophobia**: water.
**gynophobia**: women.
**ergophobia**: work.

---

## phone VERB

*She tried to phone home on her mobile.*
▶ call, ring, telephone, reach, dial

## phoney ADJECTIVE

*He gave a phoney name.*
▶ false, bogus, sham, fake, made-up, invented, fictitious, assumed, spurious
OPPOSITES ARE genuine, authentic

## phoney NOUN
*The lawyer was a phoney.*
▶ impostor, sham, fraud, fake, charlatan, swindler

## photograph NOUN
*She published her best photographs in a magazine.*
▶ photo, picture, snapshot, snap, image, print, slide, transparency

## photograph VERB
*I photographed them as people first and models second.*
▶ shoot, snap, take a picture of

## phrase NOUN
*He searched in his mind for the right phrase to describe his feelings.*
▶ expression, wording, group of words, form of words, construction, idiom

## phrase VERB
*She thought about how to phrase the question.*
▶ express, word, put in words, formulate, couch, frame, present

## physical ADJECTIVE
**1** *It is hard to describe his physical appearance*
▶ bodily, corporal, corporeal, carnal
AN OPPOSITE IS mental
**2** *our physical existence*
▶ earthly, material, mortal, terrestrial, tangible, fleshly, substantial
AN OPPOSITE IS spiritual

## physique NOUN
*He had the physique of a rugby forward.*
▶ body, build, figure, frame, physical condition, proportions, form, muscles, shape

## pick VERB
**1** *We spent the afternoon picking fruit.*
▶ gather, collect, pluck, harvest, garner
**2** *He picked a card and held it to his chest.*   *Pick a time and place that suit you.*
▶ choose, select, take, decide on, opt for, settle on, fix on, single out
**pick on** *They are always picking on Freddie.*
▶ victimize, bully, persecute, tease, (more informal) get at
**pick out** *It was difficult to pick anything out in the fog.*
▶ see, discern, spot, distinguish, make out, recognize, identify
**pick up**
**1** *It was too heavy to pick up.*
▶ lift, raise, take up, hoist
**2** *You can pick up a bargain at the car-boot sales.*
▶ find, discover, obtain, acquire, get hold of, buy, purchase
**3** *Lisa picked up some Spanish during her stay abroad.*
▶ learn, acquire, absorb, get to know, master
**4** *He offered to pick up the children from school.*
▶ collect, fetch, go to get, call for
**5** *The weather began to pick up.*
▶ improve, recover, get better, brighten
**6** *Be careful you don't pick up an infection.*
▶ catch, contract, get, come down with

## pick NOUN
**1** *Take your pick.*
▶ choice, preference, selection, option
**2** *the pick of the bunch*
▶ best, finest, prime, top, cream, choicest, élite

## picket VERB
*Over a hundred workers picketed the depot.*
▶ blockade, cordon off, surround, enclose, demonstrate at, protest at

## pickle VERB
*Mary likes to pickle most of her fruit.*
▶ preserve, conserve, bottle, marinade, souse

## pictorial ADJECTIVE
*a mosaic with pictorial designs*
▶ illustrated, graphic, diagrammatic, representational, illustrative

---

## picture NOUN
**1** *the famous picture of Bubbles*
▶ painting, portrait, likeness, portrayal, representation, depiction, profile, image
**2** *Kevin wanted to take a picture of them.*
▶ photograph, snapshot, snap, shot
**NAMES FOR TYPES OF PICTURE**
**paintings:** oil painting, watercolour, pastel; landscape, portrait, still-life, abstract; frieze (along the top of a wall), mural (large painting on a wall), fresco (watercolour painted on plaster when still wet), impasto (using thick layers of paint); transfer; reproduction (copy of a painting); collage (made from small pieces of paper and fabric);
**drawings:** drawing, sketch, doodle, engraving, etching, print, tracing; silhouette (outline of subject coloured in black).
**photographs:** photograph ((*informal*)photo, pic), snapshot, portrait, enlargement ((*informal*) blow-up), vignette (subject fading into background); print, positive, negative, transparency or slide; Polaroid; still (taken from a cinema film); digital.

---

## picturesque ADJECTIVE
**1** *He had spent the morning painting picturesque views of his master.*
▶ attractive, pretty, beautiful, charming, pleasant, scenic
AN OPPOSITE IS ugly
**2** *She was trying to find a more picturesque way to describe it.*
▶ colourful, graphic, descriptive, expressive, vivid, imaginative, poetic
AN OPPOSITE IS prosaic

## piece NOUN
**1** *a piece of cheese*   *a piece of stone*
▶ bit, chunk, lump, hunk, portion, fragment, morsel, particle
**2** *a piece of furniture*
▶ item, article

**piece**

**3** *She wrote a piece for the local newspaper.*
► article, story, feature, essay, account

**piece** VERB

**piece together** *It is difficult to piece the evidence together into a convincing case.*
► assemble, compose, fit together, join together

**piecemeal** ADJECTIVE

*a few piecemeal changes*
► intermittent, gradual, disjointed

**pied** ADJECTIVE

*a breed of pied cattle*
► dappled, flecked, mottled, particoloured, piebald, spotted, variegated

**pier** NOUN

**1** *Boats were tied up at the pier.*
► jetty, quay, wharf, dock , landing stage, breakwater

**2** *Immense piers supported a high vault.*
► column, pillar, support, buttress, upright, pile

**pierce** VERB

*a spear that could pierce the thickest armour*
► penetrate, puncture, perforate, make a hole in, probe, enter, transfix, impale

**piercing** ADJECTIVE

**1** *From the wood comes a piercing screech.*
► shrill, sharp, penetrating, shattering, ear-splitting, high-pitched, strident, deafening, loud

**2** *a piercing wind*
► freezing, bitter, biting, wintry, stinging

**3** *a piercing pain*
► stabbing, intense, excruciating, agonizing, stinging

**piety** NOUN

*a priest respected for his piety*
► devoutness, devotion, piousness, holiness, godliness, saintliness, sanctity, religion, faith
AN OPPOSITE IS impiety

**pig** NOUN

**1** *(informal) He was always a bit of a pig when it came to food.*
► glutton, guzzler, gourmand, (informal) greedy guts

**2** *Her husband can be a real pig at times.*
► brute, monster, beast, fiend, animal, demon

**pile** NOUN

**1** *a pile of stones*
► heap, stack, mass, mound, mountain, collection, hoard

**2** *We have piles of work to do.*
► plenty, a lot, a great deal, (more informal) lots, (more informal) masses, (more informal) heaps

**pile** VERB

*They piled everything into a corner.*
► heap, stack, pack, jam, accumulate, amass, load, mass, store, collect, gather, hoard

**pile up** *Problems were beginning to pile up*
► build up, mount up, increase, grow, accumulate

**pilfer** VERB

*People were pilfering bricks from building sites.*
► steal, take, snatch, pinch, filch, (more informal) swipe, (more informal) nick, (more informal) knock off

**pillar** NOUN

*A row of pillars supports the roof.*
► column, pier, support, buttress, upright, pile

**pillow** NOUN

*She rested her head on a pillow.*
► cushion, bolster, headrest, pad

**pilot** NOUN

**1** *the pilot of an aircraft*
► airman or airwoman, (old-fashioned) aviator

**2** *a harbour pilot*
► navigator, helmsman, steersman, coxswain, guide

**pilot** ADJECTIVE

*a pilot scheme*
► experimental, trial, test, sample, model

**pilot** VERB

*He piloted the little plane to the island.*
► fly, guide, lead, navigate, steer, direct, drive

**pimple** NOUN

*a face covered in pimples*
► spot, blackhead, swelling, (more informal) zit

**pin** NOUN

*The notice was attached by a pin.*
► tack, nail, spike, brad, skewer

**pin** VERB

*She pinned a badge on him*
► fasten, attach, fix, stick

**pinch** VERB

**1** *She pinched his arm.*
► nip, squeeze, crush, tweak

**2** *Someone has pinched my pen.*
► steal, take, pilfer, snatch, filch, (more informal) swipe, (more informal) nick, (more informal) knock off

**pine** VERB

*He thinks you were pining from love.*
► languish, wither, fade, droop, sicken

**pine for** *The Smiths were pining for their home.*
► long for, yearn for, hanker after, miss, crave

**pinnacle** NOUN

**1** *This win marked the pinnacle of her career in athletics.*
► peak, climax, height, highest point, summit, zenith, acme, apex, top
OPPOSITES ARE nadir, trough

**2** *tall pinnacles of rock*
► peak, spire, steeple, turret, crest

**pinpoint** VERB

*Black boxes in trains can pinpoint the cause of accidents.*
► identify, determine, discover, distinguish, locate, detect, track down

**pioneer** NOUN

1 *pioneers of the American West*
► settler, colonist, colonizer, discoverer, explorer

2 *a pioneer of birth control*
► developer, innovator, originator, pathfinder, groundbreaker

**pioneer** VERB

*a scientist who pioneered genetic fingerprinting*
► develop, introduce, evolve, create, discover, invent, originate, initiate, spearhead

**pious** ADJECTIVE

1 *His second wife was a remarkably pious woman.*
► religious, devout, devoted, spiritual, dutiful
OPPOSITES ARE impious, irreligious

2 *The remark was no more than a pious platitude.*
► sanctimonious, insincere, self-righteous
AN OPPOSITE IS sincere

**pipe** NOUN

*a water pipe*
► duct, channel, tube, conduit, hose, pipeline

**pipe** VERB

*The liquid is piped into containers.*
► channel, funnel, siphon, carry, run

**pipe down** (*informal*) *He got annoyed and told them to pipe down.*
► be quiet, be silent, quieten down, stop talking, hush

**pique** NOUN

*He walked out in a fit of pique*
► irritation, annoyance, anger, displeasure, petulance, exasperation

**pirate** NOUN

*Pirates attacked the ship.*
► marauder, privateer, (*historical*) buccaneer, (*old-fashioned*) corsair

**pirate** VERB

*A large number of CDs are pirated.*
► plagiarize, copy illegally, poach

**pit** NOUN

1 *A deep pit had been dug in the ground.*
► hole, ditch, trench, shaft, hollow, depression, trough, cavity, chasm, abyss

2 *increasing pit closures*
► mine, coal mine, colliery, quarry, shaft, working

**pitch** NOUN

1 *Their voices rose in pitch with the excitement.*
► tone, timbre, key, modulation

2 *His anger reached such a pitch that he became almost violent.*
► level, point, height, degree, intensity

3 *the pitch of the roof*
► steepness, angle, gradient, incline, slope, slant, tilt

4 *The referee ordered the players off the pitch.*
► playing field, field, park, ground

**pitch** VERB

1 *This is where we pitch our tents for the night.*
► put up, raise, fix, erect, set up

2 *She picked up the ball and pitched it into the neighbouring garden.*
► throw, fling, toss, hurl, lob, sling, bowl, heave, cast, (*more informal*) bung, (*more informal*) chuck

3 *Several lads pitched into the water.*
► plunge, dive, plummet, drop, topple

4 *The boat was pitching in the storm.*
► lurch, toss, wallow, rock, roll, reel, flounder, dip up and down

**pitch in** *Everyone needs to pitch in to get the work done.*
► help out, lend a hand, do your bit

**piteous** ADJECTIVE

*She gave a long piteous cry.*
► plaintive, mournful, pathetic, pitiful, pitiable, sad, sorrowful, wretched, touching, affecting, distressing, heartbreaking, heartrending

**pitfall** NOUN

*Drama producers no longer need to fear the pitfalls of live television.*
► hazard, snag, trap, danger, peril, snare, difficulty, drawback, catch

**pitiful** ADJECTIVE

1 *She was a pitiful sight, still lying where she had fallen.*
► sad, pathetic, pitiable, sorrowful, wretched, touching, affecting, distressing, heartbreaking, heartrending

2 *He trudged off with the pitiful few pounds he had made that day.*
► meagre, negligible, paltry, miserable, modest, scanty, scant, sparse, (*more informal*) mingy, (*more informal*) measly
OPPOSITES ARE generous, extravagant

**pitiless** ADJECTIVE

*Dinah did not break under the pitiless criticism.*
► merciless, relentless, ruthless, unrelenting, callous, cruel, hard, heartless, inexorable, unfeeling
OPPOSITES ARE merciful, compassionate

**pittance** NOUN

*She cleaned people's houses for a pittance.*
► crumb, tiny sum, (*more informal*) peanuts

**pitted** ADJECTIVE

*a pitted surface*
► scarred, uneven, marked, pockmarked, blemished, rough
AN OPPOSITE IS smooth

**pity** NOUN

**1** *He had never felt pity for anyone in his life.*
▶ compassion, sympathy, commiseration, tenderness, understanding, feeling, forbearance, mercy, forgiveness, humanity, kindness
OPPOSITES ARE indifference, animosity

**2 a pity** *It's a pity it was dark and we couldn't see the garden.*
▶ a shame, unfortunate, a piece of bad luck, a cause for regret

**pity** VERB

*He always pitied people who had to ask for money.*
▶ feel sorry for, feel pity for, feel for, sympathize with, commiserate with, take pity on

**pivot** NOUN

*The weight turns on a pivot.*
▶ axis, axle, fulcrum, spindle, linchpin, centre, swivel, hub

**pivot** VERB

*She watched as Leo pivoted on one foot.*
▶ swivel, rotate, turn, swing, spin, twirl, whirl, revolve

**placate** VERB

*He was placated by a glass of beer that was put before him.*
▶ pacify, calm, appease, mollify, soothe, win over, conciliate, assuage

**place** NOUN

**1** *She rose quietly from her place at the table.*
▶ seat, chair, position, space

**2** *They would choose a foreign place for their next holiday.*
▶ locality, region, resort, city, town, village

**3** *'Seaview' is the ideal place to write and work quietly.*
▶ spot, locale, location, venue, point

**4** *They badly wanted a place of their own.*
▶ home, house, residence, dwelling, property, flat, apartments, establishment, accommodation

**5** *She was offered a place on the company's board.*
▶ position, post, appointment, situation

**6** *I know my place and won't interfere.*
▶ status, position, station, standing, rank

**in place of** *The bed was supported by a pile of books in place of a missing leg.*
▶ instead of, in lieu of, as a replacement for, as a substitute for

**out of place** *a remark that seemed out of place*
▶ inappropriate, unsuitable, improper, unseemly, unbecoming

**take place** *The competition will take place next month.*
▶ happen, occur, be held, come about

**place** VERB

**1** *He placed the shopping on the table.*
▶ put, set, lay, deposit, leave, (*more informal*) stick, (*more informal*) dump, (*more informal*) plonk

**2** *The judges placed her second overall.*
▶ rank, grade, position

**3** *The face was familiar but I couldn't quite place it.*
▶ recognize, identify, remember

**placid** ADJECTIVE

**1** *My normally placid father became a raging bull.*
▶ even-tempered, calm, equable, tranquil, collected, composed, level-headed, self-possessed, imperturbable, unruffled, gentle, mild, cool, unexcitable, phlegmatic
AN OPPOSITE IS excitable

**2** *a four-mile stretch of placid water*
▶ calm, quiet, tranquil, peaceful, unruffled, undisturbed, motionless
OPPOSITES ARE stormy, rough

**plagiarize** VERB

*She accused him of plagiarizing the results of her research.*
▶ copy, pirate, steal, poach, reproduce, (*more informal*) lift, (*more informal*) crib

**plague** NOUN

**1** *a study of the effects of the plague on two major cities*
▶ pestilence, blight, epidemic, contagion, infestation, outbreak

**2** *a plague of flies*
▶ infestation, invasion, nuisance, scourge, swarm

**3** *the plague of street crime in the area*
▶ curse, blight, bane, scourge, affliction, cancer

**plague** VERB

**1** *The fears which had menaced her before returned to plague her.*
▶ afflict, bedevil, beset, torment, hound, torture, persecute

**2** *He was being plagued with questions.*
▶ pester, badger, harass, trouble, annoy, bother, disturb, irritate, molest, vex, worry, (*more informal*) nag

**plain** ADJECTIVE

**1** *The forms are written in plain English.*
▶ clear, simple, straightforward, understandable, intelligible, direct
OPPOSITES ARE obscure, unclear

**2** *It was plain that someone had been in the house before them.*
▶ obvious, clear, evident, apparent, manifest

**3** *They thought some plain speaking was needed.*
▶ frank, candid, outspoken, blunt, direct, explicit, unequivocal

**4** *The house had a rather plain appearance.*
▶ unattractive, ordinary, unprepossessing, ugly
AN OPPOSITE IS attractive

**5** *The room was decorated in a plain style.*
▶ simple, basic, restrained, unadorned, unembellished, unelaborate, unpretentious
OPPOSITES ARE elaborate, fancy

**plain** NOUN

*the movement of wildebeest across the plains of Africa*
▶ grassland, flatland, prairie, savannah, steppe, prairie

**plain** ADVERB

*Many people are just plain scared of making the change.*
▶ downright, completely, totally, utterly, really, thoroughly, absolutely, simply

**plaintive** ADJECTIVE

*the faint, plaintive wail of her two-month-old baby*
▶ sad, mournful, sorrowful, piteous, pitiful, doleful, melancholy, wistful

**plan** NOUN

**1** *(informal) a plan of the building*
▶ chart, diagram, map, layout, blueprint, representation

**2** *a clever plan for raising money*
▶ scheme, idea, proposal, project, programme, strategy, suggestion, proposition

**plan** VERB

**1** *She began planning tomorrow's journey.*
▶ organize, arrange, work out, think out, prepare

**2** *some tips for anyone planning a new garden*
▶ design, devise, contrive, sketch out

**3** *We plan to go abroad this year.*
▶ intend, propose, aim, mean, envisage, contemplate, be thinking of

**USAGE** If you use any of the last three synonyms, you need to say *going* instead of *to go*, e.g. *We envisage going abroad this year.*

**plane** NOUN

**1** *The plane rose gently in the air.*
▶ aeroplane, aircraft, jet, airliner, craft

**2** *The thought that came to her now was on a more creative plane.*
▶ level, stage, degree, position

**planet** NOUN

*the population of the planet*
▶ globe, world, orb

**PLANETS OF THE SOLAR SYSTEM (SHOWN WITH INCREASING DISTANCE FROM THE SUN)**
Mercury, Venus, Earth, Mars, Jupiter, Saturn, Uranus, Neptune, Pluto.

**plank** NOUN

*a plank of wood*
▶ board, floorboard, beam, timber

**plant** NOUN

**1** *plants*
▶ greenery, growth, flora, undergrowth, vegetation

**2** *industrial plant*
▶ machinery, machines, equipment, apparatus

**3** *a plant of British intelligence*
▶ informer, informant, spy, agent, infiltrator, mole

    ▶▶

**USAGE** Many plants produce flowers or cones in which seeds form. Some of the simpler ones do not have seeds; instead they reproduce with tiny objects called spores. There are several large groups of plants, examples of which are given below.

**NAMES FOR TYPES OF PLANTS**

**flowering plants** (having flowers and seeds; fruit and vegetables come from these):
apple, ash, bluebell, buttercup, carnation, chrysanthemum, cornflower, cowslip, crocus, daffodil, daisy, dandelion, forget-me-not, foxglove, geranium, hollyhock, hyacinth, iris, lilac, lupin, marigold, oak, orchid, pansy, pear, peony, plum, poppy, primrose, rose, strawberry, sunflower, tulip, vegetables, violet, wallflower, water-lily.

**coniferous** (cone-bearing) plants: fir, juniper, larch, monkey puzzle, pine, redwood, spruce, yew.

**flowerless plants** (reproducing with spores) :
algae (seaweeds and other simple water plants); mosses, liverworts; ferns, horsetails.

**plant** VERB

**1** *Plant the seeds in September.*
▶ sow, bury, set out, put in the ground

**2** *Someone had planted the idea in her mind.*
▶ put, establish, introduce, fix, lodge, impress, instil, imprint

**plaster** NOUN

**1** *He stripped the wall down to the plaster.*
▶ plasterwork, mortar, stucco

**2** *A nurse put a plaster on the cut.*
▶ dressing, sticking plaster, bandage

**plaster** VERB

*The floor was plastered with mud.*
▶ cover, daub, coat, smother, smear, spread

**plastic** ADJECTIVE

*They were drinking warm beer from plastic tumblers.*
▶ PVC, polystyrene, polyurethane, celluloids

**plate** NOUN

**1** *She helped herself to a plate of food.*
▶ dish, platter, dinner plate, plateful, helping, serving, portion, bowl

**2** *Someone had removed the plates from the end of the book.*
▶ illustration, picture, print, photograph, lithograph

**3** *There was a brass plate by the front door.*
▶ plaque, nameplate, sign

**platform** NOUN

**1** *A speaker addressed the audience from the platform.*
▶ dais, rostrum, podium, stand, stage

**2** *the Liberal Democrats' election platform*
▶ policy, programme, manifesto, plan, party line

**platitude** NOUN

*She ignored the somewhat patronizing platitude.*
▶ commonplace, banality, truism, cliché, chestnut

**plausible** ADJECTIVE

1 *He knew he had presented a plausible explanation.*
▶ credible, reasonable, believable, convincing, persuasive, tenable, likely, feasible, probable, possible, acceptable, conceivable
AN OPPOSITE IS implausible

2 *He had the sort of plausible charm that Georgina was wary of.*
▶ smooth, smooth-talking, glib, specious

**play** NOUN

1 *a balance between work and play*
▶ amusement, entertainment, relaxation, recreation, enjoyment, leisure, pleasure, diversion, fun

2 *a play by Shakespeare*
▶ drama, theatrical work, stage play, tragedy, comedy, production, performance, show

3 *There was some play in the mechanism.*
▶ movement, freedom of movement, looseness, flexibility, latitude, leeway

**play** VERB

1 *The children were playing in the garden.*
▶ amuse yourself, have fun, enjoy yourself, play games, romp, frolic, caper

2 *I enjoy playing indoor sports.*
▶ take part in, engage in, participate in, join in, compete in

3 *The two sides play each other next week.*
▶ compete against, take on, challenge, oppose, vie with

4 *We need someone to play Hamlet.*
▶ act, perform, portray, act the part of, play the part of, take the role of

5 *He regretted not being able to play a musical instrument.*
▶ perform on, make music on

**play down** *The Government played down the effect of the tax increases.*
▶ minimize, make light of, gloss over, underplay
OPPOSITES ARE exaggerate, play up

**play on** *advertising that plays on people's anxieties*
▶ exploit, take advantage of, make use of, capitalize on, trade on

**play up** *Some of the children began to play up.*
▶ misbehave, behave badly, be naughty, cause trouble

**playboy** NOUN

*Maria realized that she had married an unreliable playboy.*
▶ womanizer, philanderer, ladies' man, libertine, rake

**player** NOUN

1 *The team has bought some new players.*
▶ team member, sportsman or sportswoman, competitor, contestant

2 *players on stage*
▶ actor or actress, performer, artist, entertainer

3 *players in an orchestra*
▶ musician, performer, instrumentalist, soloist, artist

**playful** ADJECTIVE

1 *She came back from the party in a playful mood.*
▶ frisky, lively, jolly, spirited

2 *a few playful remarks*
▶ light-hearted, joking, teasing, jocular, frivolous

**playground** NOUN

*a playground behind the school*
▶ play area, recreation ground, amusement park

**playing field** NOUN

*The train passed a playing field where a game was going on.*
▶ sports ground, ground, pitch, recreation ground

**playwright** NOUN

*an Elizabethan playwright*
▶ dramatist, writer, tragedian

**plea** NOUN

1 *a plea for mercy*
▶ appeal, petition, request, entreaty, supplication, invocation, prayer

2 *His plea was that he had been ill.*
▶ claim, excuse, defence, justification, pretext

**plead** VERB

*The prisoners pleaded for their lives.*
▶ beg, implore, entreat, petition, request, solicit, appeal, ask, importune

**pleasant** ADJECTIVE

1 *It was a pleasant afternoon.*
▶ enjoyable, pleasing, agreeable, satisfying, delightful, lovely, nice
AN OPPOSITE IS unpleasant

2 *The assistants are all very pleasant.*
▶ friendly, agreeable, congenial, likeable, personable, good-humoured, nice
OPPOSITES ARE unpleasant, disagreeable

**please** VERB

1 *She did her best to please them.*
▶ make happy, satisfy, give pleasure to, gladden, gratify, amuse, content, delight, entertain

2 *Do what you please*
▶ want, like, wish, desire, feel like

**pleased** ADJECTIVE

*We were so pleased to see you.*
▶ happy, glad, delighted, satisfied, overjoyed, thrilled
OPPOSITES ARE displeased, annoyed

**pleasing** ADJECTIVES

*a very pleasing result*
▶ pleasant, agreeable, gratifying, satisfying, welcome, acceptable

**pleasure** NOUN

1 *She found great pleasure in fashionable clothes.*
▶ enjoyment, gratification, happiness, satisfaction, amusement, contentment, fulfilment, delight, comfort, entertainment, gladness, joy, solace

2 *the pleasures that children bring*
▶ joy, delight, enjoyment

a b c d e f g h i j k l m n o **p** q r s t u v w x y z

## pledge NOUN

**1** *Labour's pledge to spend billions on education*
▶ promise, undertaking, assurance, commitment, guarantee

**2** *She gave her rings as a pledge.*
▶ surety, security, bond, deposit, bail

## pledge VERB

*They all pledged their loyalty to the Queen.*
▶ promise, swear, vow, guarantee, undertake

## plentiful ADJECTIVE

*a plentiful supply of fruit*
▶ abundant, copious, ample, liberal, profuse, generous, lavish, rich, bountiful, prolific, inexhaustible
OPPOSITES ARE sparse, scarce

## plenty NOUN

**1** *a time of plenty*
▶ prosperity, wealth, affluence, opulence, luxury, well-being, comfort

**2** *plenty of There is plenty of time before they arrive.*
▶ a lot of, a great deal of, much, enough, (more informal) lots of, (more informal) heaps of, (more informal) loads of, (more informal) masses of

## pliable ADJECTIVE

**1** *a pliable material*
▶ flexible, bendable, pliant, supple, plastic, springy, (more informal) bendy
AN OPPOSITE IS stiff

**2** *a pliable mind*
▶ adaptable, impressionable, responsive, suggestible, compliant, flexible, tractable, biddable, accommodating
AN OPPOSITE IS rigid

## plight NOUN

*the plight of the homeless*
▶ difficulty, predicament, danger, trouble, extremity, quandary, straits

## plod VERB

**1** *Mary plodded up the path.*
▶ trudge, tramp, lumber, stomp

**2** *It will take hours to plod through the whole book.*
▶ plough, wade, trawl, labour, persevere, grind on

## plot NOUN

**1** *He grew vegetables in a plot behind the house.*
▶ piece of ground, patch, allotment, smallholding, lot

**2** *The novel has a complicated plot.*
▶ storyline, story, outline, action, thread, scenario, narrative

**3** *A plot was revealed against the government.*
▶ conspiracy, intrigue, plan, scheme, cabal, machination

## plot VERB

**1** *The president's brother was plotting his downfall.*
▶ plan, scheme, concoct, devise, hatch

**2** *He was accused of plotting against the government.*
▶ conspire, scheme, intrigue

**3** *They plotted their course on the map.*
▶ chart, mark, map

## plough VERB

**1** *Farmers ploughed the fields.*
▶ cultivate, till, work, turn over

**2** *A van had ploughed into a shop window.*
▶ plunge, crash, career, smash, bulldoze

## ploy NOUN

*It was just a ploy to get rid of Doreen.*
▶ trick, ruse, move, device, stratagem, manoeuvre

## pluck NOUN

*It must have taken a lot of pluck to walk along a path marked 'danger'.*
▶ courage, daring, nerve, audacity, boldness, heroism, (more informal) bottle, (more informal) grit, (more informal) guts

## pluck VERB

**1** *She began to pluck hairs off her skirt.*
▶ pick, pull, take off, snatch

**2** *He sang and plucked a guitar.*
▶ pick, twang, strum, finger

**3** *The girls stood plucking fruit from the trees.*
▶ pick, gather, collect, harvest, garner

## plucky ADJECTIVE

*a plucky young woman's tale of escape*
▶ brave, courageous, bold, daring, intrepid, valiant, resolute
OPPOSITES ARE timid, cowardly

## plug NOUN

**1** *He put a plug in the top of the bottle.*
▶ stopper, cork, bung

**2** *(informal) They put in a plug for their new song.*
▶ advertisement, piece of publicity, mention, (informal) puff, (informal) boost

## plumb ADVERB

*The arrow hit the target plumb in the middle.*
▶ exactly, precisely, dead, (more informal) slap

## plumb VERB

*They seem to have plumbed the depths of despair.*
▶ penetrate, probe, sound, explore, measure

## plummet VERB

*A stone came loose and plummeted to the ground.*
▶ plunge, fall, hurtle, drop, crash, dive

## plump ADJECTIVE

*a plump little boy*
▶ chubby, podgy, tubby, fat, dumpy, rotund, round, overweight, stout, portly, pudgy
OPPOSITES ARE thin, slim, skinny

## plump VERB

*Jill plumped down on the sofa and fell asleep.*
▶ sink, drop, flop, fall, collapse

**plump for** *I'm going to plump for the vegetarian meal.*
▶ choose, opt for, go for, pick, decide on

## plunder VERB

*Pirates plundered towns and villages near the coast.*
▶ loot, pillage, raid, ransack, ravage, despoil, rifle, rob, sack, steal from

**plunder** NOUN

*The army was bent on plunder and murder.*
▶ looting, robbery, pillage, pillaging, marauding

**plunge** VERB

**1** *The plane plunged to the ground.*
▶ dive, plummet, fall, hurtle, drop, crash, swoop, nosedive

**2** *I plunged into the lake.*
▶ dive, leap, jump, throw yourself, hurl yourself

**3** *He plunged the knife into the man's back.*
▶ thrust, force, stab, shove, stick, push

**4** *She plunged a hand in the water.*
▶ dip, immerse, submerge, sink

**poach** VERB

*The new company was poaching staff from its rivals.*
▶ steal, purloin, filch, (*more informal*) pinch, (*more informal*) nick

**pocket** NOUN

*There were some pockets of resistance to the new regime.*
▶ area, patch, centre, cluster

**pocket** VERB

*The management was accused of pocketing all the profits.*
▶ take, steal, appropriate, help yourself to, take for yourself

**podgy** ADJECTIVE

*She looked a bit podgy.*
▶ plump, chubby, tubby, fat , dumpy, rotund, round, overweight, pudgy
OPPOSITES ARE thin, slim, skinny

---

**poem** NOUN

*He read her some of his poems.*
▶ verse, rhyme, poetry

**NAMES FOR TYPES OF POEM**

**longer narrative poems:** epic, ballad, lay, chanson.

**poems for singing:** chanson, madrigal, lay, dithyramb (ancient choral hymn), ballad.

**laments:** elegy.

**short pastoral and romantic poems:** eclogue, pastoral, georgic, idyll.

**short poems and rhymes:** lyric, ode, sonnet (of fourteen lines), nursery rhyme, epigram, limerick, clerihew, nonsense verse, lay.

**Japanese poems:** haiku, tanka.

**NAMES FOR POETIC FEATURES**

verse, stanza; rhyme, enjambement, free verse, rhythm, couplet, imagery, metre, alliteration (use of similar sounds at the beginning of a sequence of words), assonance (similarity of syllables in words, e.g. *stone* and *cold*), simile, metaphor, blank verse (without end-of-line rhymes), concrete poetry (with the meaning echoed by visual patterns in the words).

---

**poet** NOUN

*She wrote stories and was a poet.*
▶ writer of verse, rhymester, rhymer, lyricist, versifier, bard

**poetic** ADJECTIVE

*poetic language*
▶ expressive, lyrical, poetical, emotive, metrical, imaginative
AN OPPOSITE IS prosaic

**poetry** NOUN

*a book of poetry*
▶ poems, verses, rhymes

**poignant** ADJECTIVE

*a poignant moment of farewell*
▶ touching, moving, affecting, sad, tender, emotional, pitiful, pathetic, sorrowful

**point** NOUN

**1** *the point of the needle*
▶ tip, end, sharp end, spike, extremity

**2** *points of light*
▶ spot, speck, dot, fleck

**3** *At this point, the door opened.*
▶ moment, instant, time, stage

**4** *I wish they would get to the point.*
▶ essence, crux, meaning, thrust

**5** *a few points of detail*
▶ detail, item, issue, factor, consideration, particular, facet, feature

**6** *She admitted he had some good points*
▶ characteristic, feature, attribute, aspect, peculiarity, side

**7** *There didn't seem much point in staying.*
▶ purpose, reason, object, aim, goal, advantage, benefit

**8** *They could get on the train at a point further up the line.*
▶ place, position, location, spot, site, locality

**point** VERB

**1** **point** or **point to** *An official pointed the way. He pointed to a picture on the stairs.*
▶ indicate, point out, draw attention to, show, signal

**2** *She saw the man was pointing a gun at her.*
▶ aim, direct, level, train

**3** *I'll point you in the right direction.*
▶ direct, guide, lead, steer

**point-blank** ADJECTIVE

**1** *The gun was fired at point-blank range.*
▶ close

**2** *Their request met with a point-blank refusal.*
▶ blunt, direct, straight, plain, frank, open, explicit, forthright

**point-blank** ADVERB

*She told him point-blank that it was over.*
▶ bluntly, directly, straight, straight out, frankly, openly, plainly, clearly, forthrightly

**pointed** ADJECTIVE

**1** *He used the pointed end of a stick.*
▶ sharp, tapered, spiky

2 *Kathleen greeted this pointed remark with a smile.*
▶ cutting, biting, trenchant, caustic, acerbic, scathing, barbed, sharp, insinuating, hurtful
AN OPPOSITE IS bland

**pointer** NOUN
*The pointer moved into 'danger'.*
▶ needle, indicator, hand, arrow

**pointless** ADJECTIVE
*The country was being dragged into a pointless military conflict. It was pointless to try to catch them now.*
▶ futile, senseless, fruitless, useless, needless, vain, aimless, meaningless, unprofitable
OPPOSITES ARE useful, valuable

**poise** NOUN
*Claudia admired her poise.*
▶ calmness, composure, equanimity, aplomb, assurance, self-confidence, self-control, coolness, dignity, elegance, equilibrium

**poised** ADJECTIVE
1 *Both forces were poised to take the city.*
▶ prepared, ready, set, waiting, keyed up
2 *She gave a poised performance.*
▶ assured, self-assured, self-confident, dignified, composed, graceful, elegant

**poison** NOUN
1 *A gram of the poison is enough to kill a man.*
▶ toxin, venom
2 *a poison in society*
▶ blight, contamination, contagion, cancer

**poison** VERB
1 *The murderer had poisoned his victim.*
▶ kill
2 *Chemicals are poisoning the country's rivers.*
▶ pollute, contaminate, infect, foul, taint
3 *The media were accused of trying to poison people's minds.*
▶ prejudice, subvert, corrupt, embitter, colour, warp, affect, pervert

**poisonous** ADJECTIVE
1 *a poisonous insect*
▶ venomous, deadly, virulent
2 *a cloud of poisonous gases*
▶ toxic, lethal, noxious, fatal, mortal
3 *a poisonous remark*
▶ malicious, malevolent, hostile, vicious, spiteful, vitriolic

**poke** VERB
*They poked burning sticks at him. He poked her with his elbow.*
▶ prod, dig, jab, nudge, thrust, stab, shove, stick
**poke about** or **around** *Someone was poking about in the cupboard.*
▶ search, rummage, root around
**poke fun at** *They laughed and poked fun at him.*
▶ ridicule, mock, make fun of, jeer at
**poke out** *A hand was poking out of the back window.*
▶ protrude, stick out, jut out, peek, project

**poke** NOUN
*Amy gave him a poke.*
▶ prod, dig, jab, nudge, shove

**poky** ADJECTIVE
*a poky room with one chair*
▶ tiny, small, confined, cramped, uncomfortable, restrictive
AN OPPOSITE IS spacious

**pole** NOUN
1 *The fence was held up by a series of poles.*
▶ post, pillar, stake, stick, upright, support, shaft, spar
2 *Their opinions are at opposite poles.*
▶ extreme, extremity, limit
**poles apart** *Our political views are poles apart.*
▶ completely different, worlds apart, like chalk and cheese, irreconcilable, incompatible

**police** NOUN
*The police soon arrived at the scene.*
▶ police force, constabulary, (more informal) the Law, (more informal) the Fuzz, (more informal) the Bill

**police** VERB
*It would be difficult to police such a large area*
▶ control, supervise, watch over, monitor, patrol, keep in order, keep the peace at, provide a police presence at

**policeman, policewoman** NOUN
*A policeman stood at the gate.*
▶ police officer, officer, constable, (more informal) bobby, (more informal) cop, (more informal) copper

**policy** NOUN
1 *the school's policy on truancy*
▶ strategy, code of practice, code of conduct, approach (to), procedure
2 *It's always a good policy to read the instructions carefully.*
▶ practice, habit, custom, rule

**polish** VERB
*I must polish my shoes.*
▶ shine, brush up, clean, buff up, burnish, brighten, rub down, rub up, wax
**polish off** *The boys polished off a plate of burgers.*
▶ finish, eat up
**polish up** *She sat down to polish up her essay.*
▶ improve, refine, enhance, brush up

**polish** NOUN
1 *The table had a lovely bright polish.*
▶ shine, sheen, gloss, lustre, patina, finish
2 *His years abroad had given him polish.*
▶ refinement, sophistication, suavity, urbanity, class, finesse, grace, style, elegance

**polished** ADJECTIVE
1 *a polished table*
▶ shiny, shining, bright, glossy, gleaming, lustrous, burnished, glassy
OPPOSITES ARE dull, tarnished

**2** *polished manners*
▶ refined, sophisticated, suave, urbane, polite, cultured, elegant, gracious, perfected, (*more informal*) posh
OPPOSITES ARE rough, crude

**3** *a polished performance*
▶ accomplished, skilful, masterly, expert, flawless, faultless

**polite** ADJECTIVE
*They were too polite to complain.*
▶ well-mannered, courteous, respectful, civil, well behaved, considerate, cultivated
AN OPPOSITE IS rude

**politics** NOUN
*Fiona took an interest in local politics.*
▶ political affairs, government, political science, public affairs

**poll** NOUN
**1** *There would have to be a second poll to decide the winner.*
▶ ballot, vote, election
**2** *The store organized a poll to determine views on smoking.*
▶ survey, opinion poll, sampling, census, plebiscite, referendum

**pollute** VERB
*Industrial waste has polluted the lake.*
▶ contaminate, poison, taint, foul, defile, infect

**pollution** NOUN
*pollution caused by city traffic*
▶ contamination, impurity, poisoning, defilement, dirtiness, adulteration

**pomp** NOUN
*He gave up the pomp of courtly life.*
▶ splendour, magnificence, grandeur, ostentation, pageantry, ritual, solemnity, spectacle, ceremonial, ceremony, display, formality, show

**pompous** ADJECTIVE
*He sounded so pompous I couldn't help giggling.*
▶ self-important, grandiose, overbearing, haughty, arrogant, conceited, pretentious, puffed up, condescending, domineering
AN OPPOSITE IS modest

**ponder** VERB
**ponder** or **ponder about** *It was a good time to ponder the events of the last week.*
▶ consider, think about, contemplate, reflect on, meditate on, review, mull over

**ponderous** ADJECTIVE
*He spoke in a slow ponderous way.*
▶ clumsy, awkward, lumbering, cumbersome, ungainly
OPPOSITES ARE elegant, graceful

**pool** NOUN
**1** *a pool of water*
▶ pond, puddle, lake, mere, tarn
**2** *a pool of hire cars*
▶ supply, stock, reserve

**pool** VERB
*They could buy more if they pooled their money.*
▶ combine, amalgamate, put together, merge, share

**poor** ADJECTIVE
**1** *The scheme was intended to rehouse poor families.*
▶ impoverished, poverty-stricken, badly off, impecunious, hard-up, destitute, penniless
OPPOSITES ARE rich, wealthy
**2** *The workmanship was of poor quality.*
▶ inferior, substandard, deficient, defective, unsatisfactory, mediocre, second-rate, shoddy
OPPOSITES ARE superior, fine
**3** *The poor man had to wait ten hours for a train.*
▶ unfortunate, unlucky, luckless, wretched, pitiful, unhappy
OPPOSITES ARE fortunate, lucky

**poorly** ADJECTIVE
*She began to feel poorly in the taxi home.*
▶ ill, unwell, sick, out of sorts, off colour, indisposed, ailing, peaky, queasy, nauseous

**pop** VERB
*Corks were popping everywhere.*
▶ crack, go bang, explode, go off, burst, snap

**pop** NOUN
*the pop of an air rifle*
▶ crack, bang, explosion, burst, snap

**popular** ADJECTIVE
**1** *a popular student*
▶ well-liked, favoured, favourite, liked, admired, accepted
**2** *a popular line in women's clothing*
▶ fashionable, modish, sought-after, well-known, current, (*more informal*) trendy

**popularize** VERB
**1** *a campaign to popularize their new products*
▶ make popular, bring into vogue or fashion, promote, spread
**2** *There are several good books that popularize the subject.*
▶ simplify, make accessible, make easy, present in a popular way, universalize

**populate** VERB
*The island is populated mainly by visitors.*
▶ inhabit, occupy, people, live in

**population** NOUN
*the population of the country*
▶ inhabitants, people, populace, residents, citizens, occupants, community

**populous** ADJECTIVE
*the most populous city in the north*
▶ densely or heavily populated, heavily settled, crowded, congested, populated

**porch** NOUN
*He sat all day in a rocking chair in the porch.*
▶ vestibule, entrance, entrance hall, lobby, portico, doorway

## pore VERB

**pore over** *She was poring over a map of Greece.*
▶ study, peruse, scan, scrutinize, be absorbed in, be engrossed in

## pornographic ADJECTIVE

*a pornographic film*
▶ obscene, indecent, lewd, erotic, titillating

## porous ADJECTIVE

*a porous substance*
▶ permeable, pervious, absorbent, spongy, cellular, holey
AN OPPOSITE IS impermeable

## port NOUN

*A large liner had entered the port.*
▶ harbour, seaport, marina, anchorage, dock, dockyard, haven

## portable ADJECTIVE

*a portable computer*
▶ transportable, mobile, movable, lightweight, compact, easy to carry, handy, light, manageable, small

## porter NOUN

1 *The apartment block had its own porter.*
▶ caretaker, doorkeeper, doorman, janitor, commissionaire, concierge
2 *A porter helped her with her luggage.*
▶ baggage-carrier, baggage-handler, baggage-attendant, bearer, carrier

## portion NOUN

1 *a large portion of rice*
▶ helping, serving, plateful, bowlful, share, amount, ration, (more informal) dollop
2 *Use the rear portion of the train.*
▶ section, part, segment
3 *Her portion of the inheritance came to several millions.*
▶ share, allocation, quota, division, ration, percentage

## portly ADJECTIVE

*a portly figure in a dark suit*
▶ stout, plump, podgy, tubby, fat, chubby, dumpy, rotund, round, overweight, pudgy
OPPOSITES ARE thin, slim, skinny

## portrait NOUN

*a portrait of the Prince Regent*
▶ painting, picture, drawing, portrayal, depiction, representation, image, likeness

## portray VERB

1 *The artist portrayed her in profile.*
▶ paint, draw, sketch, depict, show
2 *The novel portrays London life in Victorian England.*
▶ describe, depict, picture, characterize, represent, illustrate, show, delineate, evoke

## pose VERB

1 *River levels pose a threat at this time of year.*
▶ present, constitute, create, produce

2 *The article poses a number of important questions.*
▶ raise, put forward, advance, offer, posit, broach, suggest
3 *She posed for a local artist on Saturday afternoons.*
▶ sit, model, be a model
4 *From his manner it was clear he was only posing.*
▶ pretend, put on an act, strike a pose, put on airs, feign, masquerade
5 **pose as** *He decided to pose as a police officer.*
▶ impersonate, pretend to be, masquerade as, pass yourself off as

## pose NOUN

1 *a model in a suggestive pose*
▶ attitude, position
2 *His behaviour was only a pose.*
▶ pretence, act, affectation, façade, show, front, masquerade, posture

## poser NOUN

1 (*informal*) *How to get home in time was a bit of a poser.*
▶ problem, difficulty, dilemma, puzzle
2 (*informal*) *The bar was full of posers showing off to the girls.*
▶ exhibitionist, poseur, (*informal*) phoney, (*informal*) pseud, (*informal*) show-off

## posh ADJECTIVE

(*informal*) *The car was parked outside a posh hotel.*
▶ smart, stylish, high-class, luxury, luxurious, fashionable, elegant, plush, showy, (*informal*) classy, (*informal*) swanky, (*informal*) snazzy, (*informal*) swish

## position NOUN

1 *The map shows the position of the house.*
▶ location, situation, setting, locality, site, point
2 *She rose to a standing position.*
▶ posture, pose, stance, attitude
3 *His lack of money left him in an awkward position.*
▶ situation, circumstances, predicament, plight
4 *They well knew their position in society.*
▶ status, standing, level, role, rank, grade
5 *advertisements for positions in banking*
▶ job, post, situation, appointment, vacancy
6 *the opposition's position on the war*
▶ point of view, viewpoint, attitude, policy, stand, standpoint, stance, outlook

## position VERB

*Chairs had been positioned along the walls.*
▶ put, arrange, deploy, dispose, locate, place, settle, situate, stand, station

## positive ADJECTIVE

1 *I was positive they would come back.*
▶ certain, sure, convinced, confident, satisfied, assured
OPPOSITES ARE uncertain, unsure
2 *The case lacked positive proof.*
▶ definite, conclusive, categorical, unequivocal, incontrovertible, irrefutable, indisputable, clear, explicit
OPPOSITES ARE doubtful, unclear

a b c d e f g h i j k l m n o p q r s t u v w x y z

**possess**

3 *The criticism was positive.*
▶ helpful, constructive, practical, useful
AN OPPOSITE IS negative

4 *a positive advantage*
▶ definite, conclusive, clear, unmistakable, emphatic, unequivocal, undeniable
AN OPPOSITE IS vague

5 *a positive attitude*
▶ optimistic, confident, hopeful, assured
AN OPPOSITE IS pessimistic

6 *The journey was a positive nightmare.*
▶ absolute, utter, complete, sheer, perfect

**possess** VERB

1 *The family possessed a house in France.*
▶ own, have, be in possession of

2 *Foreign armies possessed the country*
▶ seize, occupy, take over, acquire, control, dominate, govern, rule

3 *A strange feeling possessed him.*
▶ preoccupy, obsess, dominate, haunt, consume

**possession** NOUN

1 *She came into possession of the fortune.*
▶ ownership, control, title, tenure, custody

2 **possessions** *She put her few possessions in the van.*
▶ belongings, things, property, chattels, effects, assets, goods, bits and pieces

**possessive** ADJECTIVE

*He was very possessive and grew angry when she wanted to leave.*
▶ jealous, overprotective, proprietorial, clinging, domineering, selfish

**possibility** NOUN

1 *There was still a possibility they might come.*
▶ chance, likelihood, probability, prospect, hope, fear

2 *the possibility of starting their own business*
▶ feasibility, practicality, capability, potentiality

3 *They even considered the possibility of going to war.*
▶ option, alternative, choice

**possible** ADJECTIVE

1 *An improvement next year might be possible.*
▶ feasible, practicable, achievable, attainable, viable, workable
AN OPPOSITE IS impossible

2 *There is another possible explanation.*
▶ conceivable, imaginable, plausible, likely, believable, tenable, credible
OPPOSITES ARE unlikely, inconceivable

3 *He is regarded as a possible party leader.*
▶ potential, prospective, probable, promising, likely
OPPOSITES ARE unlikely, improbable

**possibly** ADVERB

1 *Possibly Jane will be there too.*
▶ maybe, perhaps, conceivably

2 *Could you possibly bring some food?*
▶ by any chance, conceivably, at all

**post** NOUN

1 *a flat roof supported by wooden posts*
▶ pole, pillar, stake, stick, upright, support, shaft, spar

2 *The post hasn't come yet.*
▶ mail, letters, delivery

3 *The post will be advertised in the local newspaper.*
▶ job, position, situation, appointment, vacancy

**post** VERB

1 *An announcement had been posted on all notice boards.*
▶ display, pin up, put up, stick up, advertise, announce

2 *I must go and post a letter.*
▶ mail, send, dispatch, put in the post, send off, get off

**poster** NOUN

*He collects old film posters.*
▶ notice, placard, display, sign, bill, sticker, advertisement, announcement, playbill

**posterity** NOUN

*Everything that happened has been recorded for posterity.*
▶ future generations, the future, descendants, heirs, offspring, successors

**postpone** VERB

*The game was postponed for a fortnight.*
▶ put off, defer, delay, put back, adjourn, hold over, suspend, put on ice

**posture** NOUN

*He bent his head forward in a posture of respect.*
▶ position, stance, pose, attitude, bearing, deportment

**posy** NOUN

*a posy of violets and freesias*
▶ bouquet, bunch, spray, nosegay, buttonhole, corsage

**pot** NOUN

*a pot of stew*
▶ pan, saucepan, vessel, casserole, cauldron, stewpot, stockpot, crock, urn

**potent** ADJECTIVE

1 *a potent drug*
▶ strong, powerful, pungent, intoxicating

2 *a potent influence*
▶ strong, powerful, vigorous, compelling, impressive, dominant, overpowering, weighty

**potential** ADJECTIVE

*a potential cause of trouble*
▶ probable, likely, imminent, impending, prospective, latent, dormant, possible, promising, budding, embryonic, future

**potential** NOUN

*The area has great potential for industrial expansion.*
▶ possibilities, capacity, capability, scope, prospects, promise

## potion NOUN
*a love potion*
► mixture, concoction, draught, elixir, brew, dose, drug, philtre, tonic

## potter VERB
**potter about** or **around** *I love pottering around the house.*
► mess about or around, amuse yourself, pass time

## pottery NOUN
*a sale of local pottery*
► ceramics, earthenware, porcelain, stoneware, china, crockery

## potty ADJECTIVE
1 (*informal*) *Maybe I'm going potty.*
► mad, insane, crazy, (*informal*) round the bend, (*informal*) bonkers
2 **potty about** *She's potty about her two sons.*
► devoted to, infatuated with, smitten with, mad about, crazy about

## pounce VERB
**pounce on** *The animal pounced on its prey.*
► jump on, spring on, leap on, swoop on, bound at, lunge at, attack, ambush

## pound VERB
1 *Hans pounded his huge fists on the desk and glared.*
► beat, strike, thump, thud, batter, bang, bash
2 **pound on** *He pounded on the gates, shouting wildly.*
► batter, beat, thump, pummel, bang on, strike, hit
3 *Her heart was pounding.*
► throb, pulsate, thump, thud, race
4 *Pound the garlic with a little salt.*
► crush, grind, powder, mash, pulverize

## pour VERB
1 *Blood poured from his wound.*
► spill, issue, stream, run, discharge, flow, gush, spout
2 *She poured milk from the jug.*
► serve, tip, decant

## pout VERB
*Carrie pouted, complaining that she had been left out.*
► sulk, pull a face, look petulant, scowl, mope

## poverty NOUN
*The region suffered from years of poverty.*
► want, penury, privation, destitution, hardship, shortage, need, necessity
AN OPPOSITE IS wealth

## powdery ADJECTIVE
*a white powdery deposit*
► dusty, sandy, grainy, chalky, crumbly, fine, granular, loose, pulverized

## power NOUN
1 *His father had a stroke and lost the power of speech.*
► faculty, property, capability, capacity, ability, competence
2 *Who knows where the real power lies.*
► control, authority, influence, dominance, mastery, domination

3 *The governor has the power to impose a curfew.*
► right, prerogative, authorization, authority
4 *a speech of great power*
► force, strength, potency, vigour, intensity, energy
AN OPPOSITE IS weakness

## powerful ADJECTIVE
1 *a powerful blow*
► violent, hard, strong, forceful
AN OPPOSITE IS weak
2 *a powerful ruler*
► strong, dominant, commanding, forceful, vigorous, effective
OPPOSITES ARE weak, ineffective
3 *a powerful physique*
► strong, muscular, sturdy, hefty, mighty, solid, burly
OPPOSITES ARE weak, puny
4 *a powerful argument*
► strong, convincing, compelling, cogent, overwhelming
OPPOSITES ARE weak, unconvincing

## powerless ADJECTIVE
1 *We felt powerless in the face of such determination.*
► helpless, impotent, ineffectual, ineffective, incapable, defenceless, feeble, weak
OPPOSITES ARE powerful, strong
2 *The police were powerless to act.*
► unable, incapable (of acting), without power

## practicable ADJECTIVE
*Such a detailed plan would not be practicable.*
► realistic, feasible, viable, workable, achievable, attainable, possible, sensible, practical
OPPOSITES ARE impracticable, impractical

## practical ADJECTIVE
1 *You need practical experience of the work before you apply for the job.*
► real, actual, hands-on, empirical, relevant
AN OPPOSITE IS theoretical
2 *We can't think of any practical alternatives.*
► workable, feasible, realistic, viable, reasonable, sensible, possible, achievable
AN OPPOSITE IS impractical
3 *Let's be practical and not try far-fetched ideas.*
► sensible, realistic, pragmatic, down-to-earth, commonsensical, hard-headed
AN OPPOSITE IS impractical
4 *a cute little gadget that is also practical*
► handy, functional, useful, serviceable, utilitarian
OPPOSITES ARE impractical, useless

## practically ADVERB
*The place was practically deserted.*
► almost, nearly, virtually, just about, more or less, close to

## practice NOUN
1 *It has become a common practice to use robots to disarm devices.*
► custom, procedure, convention, policy, routine, method, system
2 *It takes a lot of practice to play that well.*
► training, rehearsal, preparation, exercise, drill

**3** *He was better at the theory than the practice of medicine.*
▶ use, application, exercise, execution, implementation

**4 in practice** *The idea is good but probably won't work in practice.*
▶ in real life, for real, in reality, in actuality, in effect, in operation

**practise** VERB

**1** *They practised these pieces for weeks.*
▷ do exercises, drill, exercise, prepare, rehearse, train, warm up

**2** *These customs are still practised in some parts of the world.*
▶ follow, carry out, perform, put into practice, observe, apply, engage in

**pragmatic** ADJECTIVE

*a pragmatic approach to the problem*
▶ practical, sensible, realistic, down-to-earth, commonsensical, hard-headed
AN OPPOSITE IS impractical

**praise** VERB

**1** *The judge praised her for her bravery.*
▶ commend, applaud, pay tribute to, express approval of, compliment, congratulate, admire, acclaim, acknowledge, eulogize

**2** *They praised God for the good harvest.*
▶ worship, glorify, honour, exalt, adore

**praise** NOUN

**1** *The rescue services deserve all our praise.*
▶ approval, acclaim, admiration, commendation, applause, adulation, recognition, tribute

**2** *Give praise to God.*
▶ homage, honour, worship, thanks, thanksgiving, glory, adoration

**praiseworthy** ADJECTIVE

*a praiseworthy attempt to put things right*
▶ commendable, laudable, admirable, creditable, worthy, estimable, exemplary, deserving, honourable, meritorious
OPPOSITES ARE deplorable, blameworthy

**prance** VERB

*James was prancing about wrapped in a towel.*
▶ dance, cavort, romp, jump, leap, skip, hop, frolic, gambol

**prank** NOUN

*It had been a prank that had gone tragically wrong.*
▶ trick, practical joke, escapade, game, hoax, stunt, (*more informal*) lark

**pray** VERB

**pray to** *The village prayed to God for a good harvest.*
▶ ask, beg, call upon, entreat, beseech, invoke, supplicate, say prayers to

**prayer** NOUN

*The priest murmured some prayers.*
▶ invocation, devotion, supplication, entreaty

**preach** VERB

**1** *The bishop will preach in the cathedral.*
▶ give or deliver a sermon, speak

**2** *We try to preach tolerance.*
▶ teach, advocate, urge, recommend, champion

**3 preach to** *You are in no position to preach to us about honesty.*
▶ moralize to, pontificate to, lecture, harangue

**precarious** ADJECTIVE

*The cliff walk looked more and more precarious.*
▶ dangerous, risky, insecure, shaky, unstable, unsteady, vulnerable, wobbly, uncertain, perilous, rocky, unsafe
OPPOSITES ARE secure, safe

**precaution** NOUN

*As an extra precaution, tell a neighbour when you are going to be away.*
▶ safeguard, safety measure, insurance, protection, defence, provision

**precede** VERB

**1** *Three months of advertising preceded the launch of the new models.*
▶ come before, go before, lead up to, pave the way for, usher in

**2** *He preceded his speech with an announcement.*
▶ preface, open, prefix, start, lead into
AN OPPOSITE IS follow

**precedent** NOUN

*They were reluctant to give way because it might create a precedent.*
▶ pattern, model, standard, example, previous instance

**precinct** NOUN

*These streets now form a pedestrian precinct.*
▶ area, zone, sector, quarter, region

**precious** ADJECTIVE

**1** *a collection of precious paintings*
▶ valuable, priceless, choice, costly, inestimable, rare

**2** *The ring was her most precious possession.*
▶ treasured, cherished, valued, prized, favourite, dearest, beloved

**3** *This action gained them a few precious minutes.*
▶ valuable, priceless, vital

**precipitate** VERB

*The police action precipitated a riot.*
▶ cause, spark off, trigger off, induce, occasion, bring on, encourage

**précis** NOUN

*a précis of the story*
▶ summary, synopsis, resumé, outline, abstract, abridgement, short version

**precise** ADJECTIVE

**1** *I don't know the precise time. Here are the precise measurements of the room.*
▶ exact, accurate, correct, detailed, definite
OPPOSITES ARE imprecise, approximate, rough

A B C D E F G H I J K L M N O **P** Q R S T U V W X Y Z

2 *The train stopped at that precise moment.*
► exact, particular, specific, actual
3 *The workmanship is very precise.*
► careful, meticulous, exact, detailed, finicky, punctilious, scrupulous
AN OPPOSITE IS careless

**precisely** ADVERB
1 *The plane took off at three o'clock precisely.*
► exactly, on the dot, promptly
2 *The house is precisely what we are looking for.*
► exactly, absolutely, entirely, altogether, in every way

**precocious** ADJECTIVE
*From an early age he showed a precocious talent for computing.*
► advanced, clever, gifted, talented, forward, mature, quick
OPPOSITES ARE backward, slow

**predecessor** NOUN
1 *a programme about our Victorian predecessors*
► ancestor, forerunner, forefather, forebear
AN OPPOSITE IS descendant
2 *The Prime Minister learned from his predecessor's mistakes.*
► precursor, forerunner, antecedent
AN OPPOSITE IS successor

**predicament** NOUN
*Can't you see the predicament I'm in?*
► difficulty, dilemma, mess, crisis, plight, quandary, jam, embarrassment, emergency, (*more informal*) pickle, (*more informal*) spot, (*more informal*) hole, (*more informal*) corner

**predict** VERB
*The polls predicted a landslide victory.*
► forecast, prophesy, foretell, foresee, divine, forewarn, anticipate, envisage

**predictable** ADJECTIVE
*David's reaction was entirely predictable.*
► foreseeable, to be expected, likely, probable, certain
AN OPPOSITE IS unpredictable

**prediction** NOUN
*A little later, the prediction came true.*
► prophecy, forecast, conjecture, prognosis

**predominant** ADJECTIVE
*The predominant feeling was one of relief.*
► chief, main, principal, overriding, primary, prime

**predominantly** ADVERB
*The guests in the hotel were predominantly American.*
► chiefly, mainly, primarily, principally, mostly, especially, essentially

**predominate** VERB
*Bright colours predominate in these designs.*
► dominate, prevail, preponderate, be in the majority, be most common, outnumber

**pre-eminent** ADJECTIVE
*Spain was then the pre-eminent power in Europe.*
► leading, foremost, greatest, chief, principal, major

**prefer** VERB
1 *I prefer tea thanks.*
► like better, would rather have, favour, go for, opt for, plump for
2 *prefer to We'd prefer to travel by car.*
► would rather, would sooner, would like better

**preferable** ADJECTIVE
*Many people find self-catering preferable.*
► better, more suitable, advantageous, more desirable, superior, nicer, advisable, preferred
OPPOSITES ARE disadvantageous, undesirable

**preference** NOUN
1 *Our preference is for winter holidays.*
► liking, choice, inclination, option, partiality, predilection, leaning, wish, fancy
2 *Preference will be given to applicants with a foreign language.*
► precedence, priority, favour, advantage

**preferential** ADJECTIVE
*I'm not asking for preferential treatment, only what I deserve.*
► special, better, favoured, privileged, advantageous

**pregnant** ADJECTIVE
*It is probably best to cut out alcohol altogether when pregnant.*
► expecting a baby, carrying a child, expectant, (*more informal*) expecting

**prehistoric** ADJECTIVE
*Stonehenge is a unique and powerful prehistoric monument.*
► ancient, early, primitive
**USAGE** Note that *prehistoric* strictly refers to ancient times before there were written records. It is best to avoid using *primitive* because it also has an unfavourable meaning.

**prejudice** NOUN
*They were the victims of widespread prejudice.*
► discrimination, bigotry, bias, partisanship, chauvinism, favouritism, intolerance, racialism, racism, sexism
AN OPPOSITE IS tolerance

**prejudice** VERB
1 *He feared the accused's attitude might prejudice the jury.*
► influence, bias, sway, predispose, colour
2 *The reports might prejudice his election chances.*
► damage, harm, injure, be detrimental to, adversely affect, undermine

**prejudiced** ADJECTIVE
1 *Racially prejudiced attitudes are thought to be widespread.*
► biased, discriminatory, chauvinistic, intolerant, partial
2 *The staff seemed prejudiced against the poor.*
► biased, intolerant (of), partial, conditioned

## prejudicial ADJECTIVE

*a procedure that is prejudicial to public health*
▶ harmful, detrimental, injurious, damaging, unfavourable
OPPOSITES ARE beneficial, advantageous

## preliminary ADJECTIVE

1 *I should like to make a few preliminary remarks.*
▶ opening, introductory, initial
2 *A preliminary report will be issued next month.*
▶ provisional, initial, first, preparatory

## prelude NOUN

*The trade agreement is seen as a prelude to full membership of the EU.*
▶ introduction, preliminary stage, preparation, precursor, curtain raiser
AN OPPOSITE IS epilogue

## premature ADVERB

1 *His career was cut short by his premature death.*
▶ early, untimely, unseasonable
2 *Congratulations at this stage might be premature.*
▶ hasty, overhasty, rash, precipitate, too soon

## premeditated ADJECTIVE

*The attack was clearly premeditated.*
▶ planned, intentional, pre-planned, calculated, deliberate, intended, pre-arranged, predetermined, wilful, conscious, considered
OPPOSITES ARE unpremeditated, spontaneous

## premise NOUN

*The argument is based on a false premise.*
▶ proposition, assumption, thesis, hypothesis, postulate, presupposition

## premises PLURAL NOUN

*The premises are locked every evening.*
▶ building or buildings, property, establishment, site, office

## premonition NOUN

*The situation was like a bad dream, with premonitions of the events to come.*
▶ foreboding, presentiment, intuition, suspicion, inkling, portent, warning, forewarning, misgiving, omen

## preoccupied ADJECTIVE

1 *He looked anxious and preoccupied.*
▶ pensive, thoughtful, lost in thought, absent-minded, rapt
2 *preoccupied with Sarah became more and more preoccupied with her child.*
▶ engrossed in, absorbed in, obsessed with, involved with, taken up with, concerned with, wrapped up in, engaged in, immersed in

## preparation NOUN

1 *They devoted the next week to the preparation of plans.*
▶ devising, drawing up, putting together, development, formulation

2 *More staff were taken on to help with the preparations for the hotel's opening.*
▶ arrangements, plans, provisions, preliminaries, groundwork

## preparatory ADJECTIVE

*Preparatory negotiations were going on in the Austrian capital.*
▶ preliminary, provisional, initial, first

## prepare VERB

1 *Students have to prepare their presentations well in advance.*
▶ draw up, write, compose, construct, put together, get ready, make ready
2 *The cooks have to start preparing the food early each morning.*
▶ make ready, get ready, make, assemble, cook
3 *We should begin to prepare for the future.*
▶ plan, make arrangements, make provision or provisions, get ready
**prepare yourself** *We prepared ourselves for the worst.*
▶ brace yourself, gird yourself, steel yourself, fortify yourself

## prepared ADJECTIVE

1 *We are prepared to wait for the right person to be found.*
▶ willing, ready, disposed, predisposed, inclined, able, set
AN OPPOSITE IS unwilling
2 *His solicitor read out a prepared statement.*
▶ pre-arranged, arranged, agreed, organized

## preposterous ADJECTIVE

*Anyone who maintained such a preposterous theory would be considered mad.*
▶ absurd, ridiculous, ludicrous, laughable, incredible, farcical, risible, foolish, idiotic, (more informal) crazy, (more informal) daft, (more informal) barmy, (more informal) zany
OPPOSITES ARE reasonable, sensible

## prerequisite NOUN

*A knowledge of computing would be helpful but is not a prerequisite of the course.*
▶ requirement, precondition, condition, stipulation, essential, qualification

## prerogative NOUN

*The government has the exclusive prerogative to allow an amnesty.*
▶ right, entitlement, privilege, authority, sanction

## prescribe NOUN

1 *The doctor decided to prescribe penicillin.*
▶ write a prescription for, authorize, advise, recommend
2 *The teachers would prescribe the topics to be dealt with.*
▶ specify, stipulate, lay down, assign, fix, impose, ordain, dictate

**prescription** NOUN
1 *Some of these medicines can be bought without a prescription.*
▶ authorization, order, instruction, direction
2 *She ran to the chemist to fetch her prescription before closing time.*
▶ medicine, medication, mixture, pills, tablets, drug

**presence** NOUN
1 *She could not explain the presence of Richard's car outside her flat.*
▶ existence, being there
2 *He requested the presence of a solicitor.*
▶ attendance, company, appearance, support
3 *She had a strong presence which gave her added authority.*
▶ aura, air, demeanour, bearing, manner, appearance, charisma
4 *the presence of her family in the area*
▶ proximity, nearness, closeness, vicinity
5 *They felt some sort of presence in the room*
▶ spirit, ghost, spectre, phantom

**present** ADJECTIVE (with the stress on *pres-*)
1 *A police officer should be present whenever possible.*
▶ in attendance, at hand, nearby, attending, available, there or here
AN OPPOSITE IS absent
2 *The shares are not expected to maintain their present high value.*
▶ current, present-day, existing, prevailing, contemporary
**at present** or **at the present time** *We have no plans to increase taxes at present.*
▶ just now, right now, at the moment, at this time, currently

**present** NOUN (with the stress on *pres-*)
1 *a history of the family from the sixteenth century to the present*
▶ present day, modern times, today
2 *She let him keep the pen as a present.*
▶ gift, donation, gratuity, contribution, offering

**present** VERB (with the stress on *-sent*)
1 *She presented a prize to the winners.*
▶ hand out, give out, hand over, award, grant, bestow (on)
2 *The committee has presented its report.*
▶ submit, tender, hand in, offer, proffer, publish
3 *The situation presents some novel features.*
▶ show, demonstrate, display, exhibit
4 *A compère presented each act.*
▶ introduce, announce

**presentable** ADJECTIVE
*He wanted to go and buy some presentable clothes.*
▶ respectable, smart, neat, tidy, elegant, decent, suitable, satisfactory
OPPOSITES ARE untidy, shabby

**presentation** NOUN
1 *They will give a presentation, with slides, on their recent trip to Kenya.*
▶ talk, lecture, address, lecture, display, demonstration

2 *the presentation of the evidence*
▶ submission, advancing, offering, propounding

**present-day** ADJECTIVE
*the archaeology of Persia, present-day Iran*
▶ modern, contemporary, present

**presently** ADVERB
1 *We'll be there presently.*
▶ shortly, soon, directly, in a while, (*more informal*) in a bit
2 *The family is presently abroad.*
▶ currently, at present, at the moment, now

**preserve** VERB
1 *Local action can also preserve wildlife.*
▶ protect, safeguard, secure, conserve, maintain, sustain, uphold, defend, guard
OPPOSITES ARE endanger, neglect
2 *She wanted to preserve him from harm.*
▶ protect, defend, guard, safeguard, shield
3 *special containers for preserving fruit*
▶ conserve, bottle, store, keep, save

**preside** VERB
1 *We elect a chairman to preside at the meeting.*
▶ be in charge, take charge, officiate, take the chair
2 **preside over** *The finance director presides over the annual budget review.*
▶ be in charge of, direct, have responsibility for, manage, be in control of

**president** NOUN
*The society has a new president.*
▶ head, director, chief, leader

**press** VERB
1 *She pressed his hand.*
▶ squeeze, grip, clutch, clinch
2 *He pressed some clothes into a suitcase.*
▶ squash, stuff, cram, push, squeeze, force
3 *Donna needed time to press her clothes.*
▶ iron, smooth, smooth out, flatten
4 *The next process is to press the grapes.*
▶ crush, squeeze, compress, mash, pulp
5 *People pressed round to see what was going on.*
▶ gather, cluster, crowd, swarm, throng
6 *You must press them to give you an answer.*
▶ urge, persuade, pressure, compel, plead with, force, insist on
**USAGE** If you use *insist on* you say *You must insist on them giving* (or *their giving*) *you an answer.*

**press** NOUN
1 *There was quite a press round the entrance.*
▶ crowd, throng, crush, mob
2 **the press** *The press would pay huge sums for an interview.*
▶ the newspapers, the papers, the media, journalists, reporters

**pressing** ADJECTIVE
*a pressing need for changes*
▶ urgent, acute, critical, crucial, vital, essential, serious, drastic
OPPOSITES ARE non- urgent, inessential

## pressure NOUN

1 *The pressure on the foundations caused them to crack.*
▶ force, load, weight, burden, strain, stress
2 *The team is working under severe pressure.*
▶ stress, strain, difficulty, (*more informal*) hassle
3 *She was under a lot of pressure to accept the offer.*
▶ constraint, coercion, duress, harassment, compulsion, intimidation

## pressurize VERB

*He didn't want to pressurize them into agreeing if they were still uncertain.*
▶ force, coerce, pressure, press, influence, goad, harass, badger, pester, bully, browbeat, bulldoze

## prestige NOUN

*Achieving an agreement would bring the president added prestige.*
▶ status, reputation, standing, credit, kudos, renown, esteem, fame, glory, honour, importance

## prestigious ADJECTIVE

*She won a prestigious award for her contributions to medical science.*
▶ distinguished, reputable, highly regarded, honourable, esteemed, acclaimed, respected, celebrated, illustrious

## presumably ADVERB

*Presumably you won't be coming with us.*
▶ I assume, I presume, I suppose, I expect, doubtless, probably

## presume VERB

1 *We presume there will be a call-out charge.*
▶ assume, expect, suppose, imagine, take it, dare say, guess, conjecture, surmise, believe
2 *Don't presume to take charge yourself.*
▶ dare, venture, have the nerve, have the temerity, have the audacity, be so bold as, go so far as

## presumptuous ADJECTIVE

*It was presumptuous to make a decision without consulting us.*
▶ arrogant, audacious, forward, bold, impudent, insolent, bumptious, unwarranted, conceited, impertinent, overconfident, shameless, (*more informal*) pushy, (*more informal*) cheeky

## pretence NOUN

*Their self-confidence turned out to be just a pretence.*
▶ make-believe, act, show, display, front, affectation, deception, posturing, façade, masquerade, charade, subterfuge, falsehood, sham, pose, ruse, bluff, cover, faking, dissembling

## pretend VERB

1 *She pretended to understand, but we were all confused*
▶ affect, profess, claim, purport
2 *Let's pretend we're ghosts.*
▶ imagine, make believe, suppose, play being

## pretend ADJECTIVE

(*informal*) *He made his room into a pretend cave.*
▶ imaginary, make-believe, fantasy, fanciful, mythical, pretended

## pretentious ADJECTIVE

*The best food can often be found in smaller, less pretentious restaurants.*
▶ ostentatious, showy, affected, conspicuous, flashy, grandiose, extravagant
OPPOSITES ARE modest, unassuming

## pretext NOUN

*He called on the pretext of leaving some plants for Diane.*
▶ excuse, grounds, ploy, pretence, ruse, guise

## pretty ADJECTIVE

*a pretty little garden*
▶ attractive, lovely, good-looking, beautiful, charming, appealing, pleasing, (*more informal*) cute
OPPOSITES ARE plain, ugly, hideous

## pretty ADVERB

(*informal*) *It was a pretty daft thing to do.*
▶ rather, quite, somewhat, fairly, moderately, (*more informal*) kind of

## prevail VERB

1 *attitudes that prevailed in the 1960s*
▶ exist, hold, be prevalent, be current
2 *Common sense prevailed in the end.*
▶ win, win through, triumph, reign, rule, predominate
3 *The Greek army prevailed against all the odds.*
▶ be victorious, triumph, win
4 **prevail on** or **upon** *Can you prevail on her to change her mind?*
▶ persuade, induce, urge, pressure, pressurize, tempt

## prevailing ADJECTIVE

*The prevailing view was that war could be avoided.*
▶ current, general, established, popular, widespread, prevalent, predominant, dominant, principal, fashionable

## prevaricate VERB

*He prevaricated when they asked him personal questions.*
▶ equivocate, be evasive, hedge, cavil, beat about the bush, (*more informal*) shilly-shally, (*more informal*) pussy-foot

## prevent VERB

1 *It was too late to prevent the accident.*
▶ stop, avert, avoid, head off, forestall, frustrate, hinder
2 *I'll try to prevent them from coming in before you're ready.*
▶ stop, restrain, check, inhibit, block, bar

## previous ADJECTIVE

*a review of the previous three years*
▶ preceding, foregoing, antecedent, last, earlier, former, prior
AN OPPOSITE IS following

## previously ADVERB

*Previously she had worked in a nightclub.*
▶ earlier, formerly, in the past, at one time, before this or that, hitherto

**prey** NOUN
*Lions are often slower than their prey.*
▶ quarry, victim, game, kill

**prey** VERB
**prey on**
1 *Wild dogs will also prey on cattle.*
▶ hunt, catch, kill, eat, feed on
2 *The thought kept preying on his mind.*
▶ trouble, oppress, disturb, distress, haunt, beset, burden, weigh down, worry

**price** NOUN
1 *The price of your holiday is fully guaranteed.*
▶ cost, terms, rate, amount, charge (for), outlay (on)
2 *What price should you charge?*
▶ amount, figure, sum, fee, rate, charge, levy
3 *Isolation was one price of their peaceful existence.*
▶ consequence, result, penalty, sacrifice, downside

**priceless** ADJECTIVE
1 *a priceless collection of watercolours  a priceless away goal*
▶ precious, valuable, irreplaceable, inestimable, treasured, prized, costly
2 (*informal*) *a priceless remark that made them all laugh*
▶ hilarious, riotous, uproarious, funny, (*more informal*) hysterical

**prick** VERB
1 *He pricked the lid and put it in the microwave.*
▶ pierce, puncture, perforate, make a hole in, stab, jab, punch
2 *The smoke made my eyes start to prick.*
▶ sting, smart, prickle, hurt
3 *His conscience was pricking him.*
▶ trouble, worry, disturb, distress, oppress, torment, afflict

**prickle** NOUN
1 *The bush was covered with prickles.*
▶ thorn, spike, needle, spine, quill, barb
2 *The shuffling sound outside sent a prickle down my spine.*
▶ tingle, tingling, prickling, chill, thrill

**prickle** VERB
*The grass prickled their legs.*
▶ sting, prick, tickle

**prickly** ADJECTIVE
1 *a prickly bush*
▶ spiky, spiny, thorny, bristly, scratchy, sharp
2 (*informal*) *He's quite a prickly character.*
▶ irritable, irascible, peevish, testy, edgy, touchy, grumpy, short-tempered, fractious

**pride** NOUN
1 *Pride prevented him from accepting the offer.*
▶ conceit, vanity, arrogance, snobbery
2 *She took great pride in her work.*
▶ satisfaction, pleasure, delight, joy, comfort, sense of achievement
3 *Their victory was a source of great pride to them.*
▶ self-esteem, self-respect, gratification, honour, dignity

**priest** NOUN
*They looked for a priest to marry them.*
▶ clergyman or clergywoman, minister, pastor, vicar, padre
RELATED ADJECTIVE sacerdotal

**NAMES FOR PRIESTS AND RELIGIOUS OFFICIALS**
**ancient:** (Roman) augur, flamen, haruspex, pontifex; (Celtic) druid, ovate.
**Christian:** abbess, abbot, archimandrite, archbishop, archdeacon, bishop, brother, canon, chaplain, clergyman, clergywoman, curate, deacon, deaconess, father, friar, mendicant, minister, monk, mother superior, nun, parson, prior, prioress, rector, sister, vicar.
**Buddhist:** Dalai Lama, lama, Panchen Lama, pongyi, talapoin.
**Hindu:** Brahman, guru, mahant, panda, pandit, pujari, rishi.
**Jewish:** cantor, chief rabbi, hazzan, kohen, Levite, rabbi, rebbe, rebbetzin.
**Muslim:** ayatollah, caliph, fakir, imam, muezzin, mullah, sheikh.
**Sikh:** guru.

**prig** NOUN
*She regarded him as an arrogant stand-offish prig.*
▶ prude, puritan, hypocrite, killjoy

**priggish** ADJECTIVE
*She too was in danger of seeming priggish and opinionated.*
▶ self-righteous, smug, sanctimonious, sententious, prudish, prim, strait-laced, stuffy, starchy

**prim** ADJECTIVE
*She sat behind her desk looking prim.*
▶ demure, proper, formal, strait-laced, prissy, prudish, starchy, fastidious
AN OPPOSITE IS broad-minded

**primarily** ADVERB
*The work is primarily funded by a grant from the Lottery Fund.*
▶ chiefly, principally, mainly, mostly, predominantly, basically, in the main

**primary** ADJECTIVE
1 *Their primary aim was to make money.*
▶ main, chief, principal, key, prime, paramount, overriding, ultimate, supreme
2 *the primary cause of the infection*
▶ original, initial, first

**prime** ADJECTIVE
1 *The prime reason for his decision was a wish for change.*
▶ main, chief, principal, key, primary, paramount, overriding, ultimate, supreme
2 *a hundred acres of prime agricultural land*
▶ best, choice, select, superior, first-class, high-grade, top-quality

**primitive** ADJECTIVE

**1** *primitive peoples*
► ancient, early, earliest, prehistoric
AN OPPOSITE IS developed

**2** *primitive tools*
► crude, basic, rudimentary, simple, undeveloped, elementary, rough
OPPOSITES ARE sophisticated, advanced

**principal** ADJECTIVE
*Traffic noise is the principal objection to the new road scheme.*
► main, chief, primary, prime, most important, overriding, foremost, fundamental, key, crucial, central, paramount, predominant, basic, essential

**principally** ADVERB
*The place was full of foreigners, principally Americans.*
► mainly, chiefly, primarily, mostly, predominantly, especially, essentially

**principle** NOUN

**1** *a woman of principle*
► honour, integrity, morality, ideals, conscience, scruples, decency, virtue

**2** *a basic principle of physics*
► rule, law, formula, canon, dictum, axiom, tenet
**in principle** *In principle the idea is a good one.*
► in theory, theoretically, in general, in the main, by and large

**principles** PLURAL NOUN

**1** *They were praised for sticking to their principles.*
► morals, values, morality, standards, moral standards, code of behaviour

**2** *the first principles of a subject*
► essentials, fundamentals, basics, elements, laws

**print** VERB

**1** *The company logo is printed at the top of each page.*
► mark, stamp, imprint, impress, engrave, reproduce

**2** *The books are printed in the Far East.*
► set in print, run off, produce, reproduce, manufacture

**3** *The publishers plan to print ten thousand copies of the book.*
► publish, issue, produce

**4** *Print your name at the top of the form.*
► write in capital letters or large letters

**print** NOUN

**1** *The print was difficult to read.*
► type, typeface, printing, lettering, letters, characters

**2** *There were prints of feet in the sand*
► mark, impression, imprint, indentation, stamp

**3** *A print would be less costly than an original painting.*
► reproduction, engraving, lithograph, copy, duplicate, photograph

**prior** ADJECTIVE
*He said he already had a prior engagement that morning.*
► previous, earlier, existing, advance

**priority** NOUN

**1** *Traffic from the right has priority.*
► right of way, precedence

**2** *Education will have priority at this year's conference.*
► precedence, preference, first place, first importance, primacy, predominance

**prise** VERB
*She carefully prised off the lid.*
► lever, wrest, twist, force

**prison** NOUN
*They would spend the next three years in prison.*
► jail, confinement, detention, custody, place of detention, penitentiary

**prisoner** NOUN
*The prisoners staged a demonstration on the prison roof.*
► detainee, convict, captive, hostage, inmate, internee, (*more informal*) jailbird

**prissy** ADJECTIVE
*Asking him to stop swearing might sound prissy.*
► prudish, prim, priggish, stuffy

**pristine** ADJECTIVE
*a book in pristine condition*
► perfect, immaculate, spotless, mint, unspoilt, unblemished, unmarked

**privacy** NOUN
*The little room gave her some privacy.*
► seclusion, solitude, tranquillity, peace and quiet, quietness, secrecy, isolation

**private** ADJECTIVE

**1** *He had amassed a huge private fortune.*
► personal, exclusive, individual, special

**2** *Private talks were held at Chequers.*
► secret, confidential, covert, clandestine
OPPOSITES ARE public, open

**3** *She had her own private thoughts on the matter.*
► personal, secret, hidden, intimate

**4** *They needed somewhere private to talk.*
► quiet, secluded, undisturbed, out of the way, isolated, solitary, peaceful, tranquil
AN OPPOSITE IS busy

**5** *John is a very private sort of person.*
► reserved, withdrawn, intimate, reticent, unsocial

**privilege** NOUN

**1** *Full members enjoy special privileges.*
► benefit, entitlement, advantage, prerogative, concession, right

**2** *It had been a privilege to meet them.*
► honour, pleasure

**privileged** ADJECTIVE
*He enjoyed a privileged social position.*
► advantaged, affluent, prosperous, wealthy, favoured, fortunate, special, superior, élite, powerful
OPPOSITES ARE disadvantaged, underprivileged

**prize** NOUN
*Helen won the prize three years in a row.*
► award, reward, trophy, honour, accolade

A
B
C
D
E
F
G
H
I
J
K
L
M
N
O

**P**

Q
R
S
T
U
V
W
X
Y
Z

## prize VERB

*They prize their freedom above all else.*
▶ value, appreciate, cherish, esteem, treasure, hold dear, regard, rate, approve of, revere, like

## probable ADJECTIVE

*Engine failure was the most probable cause of the crash. It is probable that this road was heavily guarded.*
▶ likely, plausible, credible, feasible, believable, expected, possible, predictable, presumed, (*more informal*) odds-on, (*more informal*) on the cards
OPPOSITES ARE improbable, unlikely

## probation NOUN

*New staff have six months of probation.*
▶ apprenticeship, test, trial period, traineeship

## probe VERB

1 *The inquiry will probe the circumstances of the accident.*
▶ investigate, examine, inquire into, look into, scrutinize, analyse, study, go into
2 *Unmanned underwater vehicles probed the ocean depths.*
▶ sound, plumb, penetrate, explore, feel

## probe NOUN

1 *a space probe*
▶ exploration, expedition
2 *a police probe*
▶ inquiry, investigation, examination, study, research, scrutiny

## problem NOUN

1 *He gave them a page of problems to solve.*
▶ puzzle, question, riddle, conundrum, enigma, mystery, (*more informal*) brainteaser, (*more informal*) poser
2 *Money was becoming a big problem for them.*
▶ difficulty, complication, worry, burden, trouble, predicament, quandary, dilemma, set-back, snag, (*informal*) headache

## problematic ADJECTIVE

*Unravelling this argument can be problematic.*
▶ difficult, complicated, complex, problematical, intractable, tricky, thorny, knotty, taxing, involved, enigmatic, controversial
OPPOSITES ARE straightforward, simple, easy

## procedure NOUN

*There is a special procedure for dealing with complaints.*
▶ course of action, process, routine, system, policy, strategy, approach, proceeding

## proceed VERB

1 *We still don't know how to proceed.*
▶ begin, make a start, act, take action, make a move, progress
2 *They turned off the main road and proceeded as far as the village.*
▶ advance, continue, progress, make your way, carry on, press on

3 *proceed with Despite opposition, they decided to proceed with the changes.*
▶ go ahead with, carry out, implement, put into effect

## proceedings PLURAL NOUN

1 *He began proceedings against the newspaper.*
▶ legal action, action, lawsuit, litigation
2 (*informal*) *The proceedings of the meeting will be published shortly.*
▶ records, report, transactions, minutes
3 *They had enjoyed the day's proceedings more than they expected.*
▶ events, activities, happenings, affairs, (*more informal*) goings-on

## proceeds PLURAL NOUN

*All proceeds from the sale will go to charity.*
▶ profits, receipts, takings, returns, revenue, income, earnings, money

## process NOUN

1 *Sending email attachments is a simple process.*
▶ operation, procedure, activity, exercise, method
2 *a new process for producing colour pictures*
▶ system, method, technique, procedure
3 *The learning process continues for many years.*
▶ progression, course, development, experience, evolution

## process VERB

1 *Officials hope to process asylum claims more quickly.*
▶ deal with, attend to, handle, expedite, treat, see to, sort out
2 *The crude oil is processed at this refinery.*
▶ refine, convert, make usable, prepare, transform, treat

## procession NOUN

*A procession passed through the town.*
▶ parade, march, cavalcade, spectacle, display, pageant, review, show

## proclaim VERB

1 *She proclaimed her love for him.*
▶ declare, announce, profess, make known, affirm, assert, give out, pronounce
2 *The president proclaimed the day a public holiday.*
▶ declare, decree, pronounce

## proclamation NOUN

*The Queen issues a proclamation dissolving Parliament.*
▶ decree, edict, order, command, ruling, announcement, declaration

## procrastinate VERB

*Fear of making a mistake caused him to procrastinate.*
▶ delay, put things off, be indecisive, temporize, defer a decision, stall, dither, (*more informal*) dilly-dally, (*more informal*) shilly-shally, (*more informal*) drag your feet

## procure VERB

*He persuaded a friend to procure him a ticket.*
▶ get, obtain, acquire, secure, find, pick up, get hold of, buy

# prod VERB

**1** *The cook grumbled as he prodded the potatoes. He continued to prod her palms with the needle.*
► jab, poke, stab, dig, nudge, push

**2** *He always needs someone to prod him into action.*
► goad, spur, stir, rouse, prompt, urge, stimulate, egg on, incite, provoke

# prod NOUN

**1** *She gave him a prod that woke him up.*
► jab, poke, stab, dig, nudge, shove, push

**2** *The phone call was a prod to remind him to put the bins out that night.*
► prompt, reminder, stimulus

# prodigy NOUN

*Mozart met Thomas, another musical prodigy, in Florence.*
► genius, marvel, phenomenon, sensation, talent, wonder

# produce VERB (with the stress on -duce)

**1** *The remark produced a wave of sniggers through the room.*
► cause, give rise to, occasion, provoke, bring about, result in, generate, effect

**2** *He had failed to produce an essay for the third week running.*
► present, submit, offer, hand in, supply, provide

**3** *He put his hand in his pocket and produced his passport.*
► show, display, present, bring out, take out

**4** *It would be difficult to produce the required output that year.*
► supply, yield, deliver, provide

**5** *The company produced Hamlet at the Edinburgh Festival.*
► stage, mount, present, put on, show

# produce NOUN (with the stress on prod-)

*an increase in organically grown produce*
► food, crops, harvest, output, products, commodities, yield, fruit, vegetables

# product NOUN

**1** *The company will announce its new product at the trade fair.*
► commodity, output, production, artefact, produce, end-product, goods, merchandise

**2** *The story was the product of a vivid imagination.*
► result, consequence, outcome, effect, fruit, upshot

# productive ADJECTIVE

**1** *He still had years of productive work ahead.*
► useful, valuable, worthwhile, constructive, creative, effective, gainful, profitable, profitmaking, rewarding, beneficial, busy
OPPOSITES ARE unproductive, fruitless

**2** *a productive area of land*
► fertile, fruitful, rich, prolific, lush
OPPOSITES ARE unproductive, barren

# profane ADJECTIVE

**1** *He used coarse, profane language*
► indecent, offensive, obscene, crude, coarse, vulgar, blasphemous
AN OPPOSITE IS respectful

**2** *the sacred and the profane*
► secular, temporal, worldly, irreligious, unholy, sacrilegious
OPPOSITES ARE religious, sacred, holy

# profess VERB

**1** *They professed their faith in a moving ceremony.*
► declare, proclaim, announce, make known, affirm, assert, give out, pronounce

**2** *He professed to hate everything about the place.*
► claim, pretend, purport, allege, make out

# profession NOUN

*She was no longer attracted by the teaching profession.*
► career, occupation, vocation, line of work, business, calling, employment, work

# professional ADJECTIVE

**1** *the study of modern languages as a preparation for professional life*
► working, business, executive

**2** *the use of professional judgement*
► expert, qualified, skilled, trained, competent, efficient, proficient

**3** *The plays were recorded in a studio with professional actors.*
► paid, salaried, full-time
OPPOSITES ARE amateur, voluntary

**4** *He was a thoroughly professional journalist.*
► conscientious, businesslike, proficient, dutiful, responsible
AN OPPOSITE IS unprofessional

# proficiency NOUN

*Applicants should have some proficiency in Japanese.*
► skill, ability, competence, expertise, mastery (of), aptitude

# proficient ADJECTIVE

*She was now a highly proficient pilot.*
► able, capable, skilled, accomplished, skilful, expert, qualified, competent, experienced

# profile NOUN

**1** *a beautiful woman with a perfect profile*
► shape, side view, contour, figure, outline, silhouette

**2** *a profile of John F Kennedy*
► biography, sketch, portrait, study, account

**3** *The company has raised its profile in Eastern Europe.*
► influence, presence, image

# profit NOUN

**1** *The company made a modest profit in the last financial year.*
► return, surplus, yield, excess

**2** *profits Two percent of profits contribute to the social fund.*
► revenue, income, takings, earnings, proceeds

**3** *There would be no profit in continuing.*
▶ advantage, benefit, value, use, gain, point, purpose

**profit** VERB
**1** *It would profit us to wait for a while.*
▶ benefit, advantage, be an advantage to, pay, help
**2 profit by** or **from** *No one profited from these changes.*
▶ benefit from, gain advantage from, do well out of

**profitable** ADJECTIVE
*a profitable undertaking*
▶ moneymaking, profitmaking, remunerative, lucrative, paying, productive, fruitful, gainful, rewarding, advantageous, beneficial, commercial, useful, valuable, worthwhile
AN OPPOSITE IS unprofitable

**profound** ADJECTIVE
**1** *I offered my profound sympathy.*
▶ sincere, deep, heartfelt, intense
AN OPPOSITE IS insincere
**2** *a profound disagreement*
▶ complete, total, utter, absolute, extreme
**3** *a profound argument*
▶ learned, wise, erudite, intelligent, perceptive, penetrating, thoughtful

**profuse** ADJECTIVE
*She left with profuse goodbyes.*
▶ copious, effusive, plentiful, abundant, lavish, extravagant, generous

**programme** NOUN
**1** *a varied programme of events*
▶ schedule, agenda, timetable, calendar, listing, plan, order, scheme, *(more informal)* line-up
**2** *a television programme*
▶ broadcast, transmission, performance, production, show

**progress** NOUN (with the stress on *pro-*)
**1** *major progress in medical research*
▶ advance, development, headway, improvement, movement, progression, breakthrough, *(more informal)* step forward
**2** *The heavy rain made further progress difficult.*
▶ travel, headway, advance, movement

**progress** VERB (with the stress on *-gress*)
*The plans are progressing slowly.*
▶ advance, develop, move forward, make progress, make headway, proceed, prosper, mature, improve, *(more informal)* come on
OPPOSITES ARE regress, deteriorate

**progression** NOUN
*a progression of days and nights*
▶ sequence, series, string, succession, cycle, chain, row

**progressive** ADJECTIVE
**1** *a progressive improvement in health*
▶ continuous, continuing, steady, increasing, ongoing, accelerating, growing, escalating
OPPOSITES ARE faltering, fluctuating, unsteady

**2** *a party leader with progressive ideas*
▶ liberal, advanced, radical, modern, go-ahead, forward-looking, enlightened, avant-garde, contemporary, enterprising, up-to-date
AN OPPOSITE IS conservative

**prohibit** VERB
**1** *a law prohibiting the advertising of tobacco products.*
▶ forbid, ban, disallow, proscribe, outlaw, make illegal
**2** *Her commitments prohibited her from attending the funeral.*
▶ prevent, preclude, rule out, restrict, impede, obstruct

**prohibited** ADJECTIVE
*Dumping waste is prohibited.*
▶ forbidden, illegal, not allowed, not permitted, banned

**project** NOUN (with the stress on *proj-*)
**1** *a project to create more conservation areas*
▶ scheme, undertaking, plan, proposal, venture, enterprise, idea
**2** *They're doing a history project.*
▶ assignment, piece of research, piece of work, activity, task

**project** VERB (with the stress on *-ject*)
**1** *Balconies project from the upstairs windows.*
▶ stick out, extend, protrude, stand out, jut out, overhang, bulge
**2** *The torch projected a strong beam.*
▶ cast, throw, throw out, flash, shine
**3** *You can project the year's income from these monthly figures.*
▶ estimate, reckon, forecast, predict, extrapolate

**proliferate** VERB
*The problems proliferated.*
▶ multiply, increase, escalate, build up, mushroom, intensify, snowball, spread

**prolific** ADJECTIVE
**1** *a prolific crop of vegetables*
▶ plentiful, abundant, copious, profuse, productive, rich, bountiful, fertile, fruitful
AN OPPOSITE IS unproductive
**2** *a prolific writer*
▶ productive, creative, inventive

**prolong** VERB
*She didn't want to prolong the argument.*
▶ lengthen, protract, extend, continue, perpetuate, spin out, draw out, increase, make longer, stretch out
OPPOSITES ARE shorten, curtail

**prolonged** ADJECTIVE
*a prolonged trip abroad*
▶ long, lengthy, extended, protracted
OPPOSITES ARE short, brief

**prominence** NOUN
*The city was captured, but rose again to prominence.*
▶ fame, celebrity, eminence, distinction, renown, importance, greatness

## prominent ADJECTIVE
*a prominent member of the government*
► important, well-known, leading, eminent, distinguished, notable, noteworthy, celebrated

## promiscuous ADJECTIVE
*I went through a promiscuous period after I left Sam.*
► loose, immoral, licentious, dissolute, abandoned, wanton, casual
OPPOSITES ARE moral, chaste

## promise VERB
**1** *He promised to pay for the damage.*
► undertake, guarantee, agree, contract
**2** *He promised she'd be there.*
► give your word, say, pledge, swear
**3** *The bright sky promised a fine day*
► indicate, presage, suggest, signify, augur, predict

## promise NOUN
**1** *You have my promise.*
► word, assurance, word of honour, pledge, undertaking, commitment, guarantee, oath, vow
**2** *a group of pupils showing outstanding promise*
► potential, ability, aptitude, talent, capability

## promising ADJECTIVE
**1** *There are promising signs of an improvement.*
► encouraging, hopeful, favourable, auspicious, propitious, talented
**2** *a promising young talent*
► budding, gifted, up-and-coming, able

## promontory NOUN
*The castle stands on a rocky promontory.*
► headland, projection, prominence, cape, cliff, foreland, ridge, spit, spur

## promote VERB
**1** *She was promoted in the recent cabinet reshuffle.*
► upgrade, move up, give a promotion to, advance, honour
**2** *He will promote his new novel at the Book Fair.*
► advertise, publicize, push, sponsor, boost, (more informal) plug
**3** *an organization promoting equal opportunities*
► champion, further, advance, sponsor, encourage, stimulate, foster, nurture, boost

## promotion NOUN
**1** *He is hoping for a promotion next year.*
► advancement, upgrading, elevation, preferment, rise
**2** *the promotion of her new film*
► marketing, publicity, advertising, backing, selling, pushing, (more informal) plugging

## prompt ADJECTIVE
*We hope for a prompt response.*
► quick, swift, rapid, speedy, early, punctual, immediate, expeditious
OPPOSITES ARE late, slow

## prompt VERB
**1** *We are not sure what prompted such an angry outburst.*
► cause, give rise to, bring about, occasion, lead to, produce, bring on, precipitate, trigger, spark off
OPPOSITES ARE deter, prevent
**2** *A noise prompted her to turn round.*
► cause, lead, induce, stimulate, prod, provoke
AN OPPOSITE IS discourage (from)
**3** *He forgot what to say and his wife had to prompt him.*
► remind, cue, prod, jog the memory

## prone ADJECTIVE
**1** *A man was lying prone on the floor*
► face down, on your front, prostrate
AN OPPOSITE IS upright
**2** *People here are prone to exaggerate.*
► apt, inclined, liable, susceptible, predisposed, disposed, given
OPPOSITES ARE resistant, immune

## prong NOUN
*the prong of a fork*
► point, spike, spur, tine

## pronounce VERB
**1** *The name is difficult to pronounce.*
► say, enunciate, articulate, sound, speak, utter, get your tongue round
**2** *The doctor pronounced me well.*
► declare, proclaim, judge, announce, affirm, assert
USAGE If you use *affirm* or *assert* you say *The doctor affirmed* or *asserted that I was well.*

## pronounced ADJECTIVE
*He walked with a pronounced limp.*
► distinct, marked, noticeable, clear, definite, decided, conspicuous, obvious, prominent, unmistakable, striking, evident

## pronunciation NOUN
*The key to pronunciation of long words is often the stress.*
► enunciation, articulation, intonation, accent, diction, elocution, inflection

## proof NOUN
*If there is a problem, return the goods with proof of purchase.*
► evidence, confirmation, verification, authentication, certification, corroboration, demonstration

## prop NOUN
**1** *The bridge is supported by steel props.*
► post, strut, upright, support, buttress, bolster
**2** *She had become the family's emotional prop.*
► support, mainstay, pillar, anchor, backbone

## prop VERB
*He propped his bike against the wall.*
► lean, rest, stand

**prop up** *The old tree was propped up with posts.*
► support, hold up, brace, strengthen, reinforce, shore up, buttress

**propaganda** NOUN
*a master of political propaganda*
▶ information, misinformation, advertising, publicity, brainwashing, indoctrination, persuasion

**propagate** VERB
1 *The plants are propagated in large greenhouses.*
▶ breed, grow , cultivate, generate
2 *Wild flowers thrive and propagate.*
▶ reproduce, multiply, proliferate, procreate
3 *They were accused of propagating false reports.*
▶ spread, transmit, disseminate, pass on, communicate, put about, circulate, proliferate

**propel** VERB
1 *He propelled the ball high into the air.*
▶ throw, toss, fling, hurl, pitch, launch, shoot, kick, punt
2 *The little craft was propelled by a small outboard motor.*
▶ drive, move, power, impel, set in motion, push

**proper** ADJECTIVE
1 *It was about time he found a proper job.*
▶ real, genuine, bona fide
2 *She doesn't think it proper to share a room with him.*
▶ right, correct, decent, respectable, decorous
3 *You have to apply through the proper channels.*
▶ correct, right, appropriate, official, established, usual
4 *(informal) He felt a proper fool.*
▶ complete, utter, perfect, absolute, positive

**property** NOUN
1 *He left all his property to his nephew.*
▶ possessions, belongings, assets, worldly goods, wealth, valuables, chattels, effects, fortune
2 *Brits looking for property to buy abroad.*
▶ buildings, premises, houses, estate
3 *the medicinal properties of garlic*
▶ quality, attribute, characteristic, power, peculiarity, trait, feature

**prophecy** NOUN
*The prophecy is coming true.*
▶ prediction, forecast, prognostication, divination, augury, prognosis

**prophesy** VERB
*Some pessimistic types had prophesied a bad outcome.*
▶ predict, forecast, foretell, foresee, forewarn of, prognosticate

**prophet** NOUN
*an Old Testament prophet*
▶ seer, soothsayer, clairvoyant, oracle, forecaster, fortune teller

**prophetic** ADJECTIVE
*He wrote a story that proved prophetic of his own future life.*
▶ predictive, prescient, far-seeing, oracular, prophesying, apocalyptic

**proportion** NOUN
1 *the proportion of girls to boys in a class*
▶ ratio, balance, relationship, distribution

2 *A large proportion of the country is forested.*
▶ part, portion, amount, quantity, percentage, section, share, piece, quota
3 **proportions** *a building of huge proportions*
▶ dimensions, measurements, size, magnitude

**proportionate** ADJECTIVE
*Air fares are proportionate to the distance travelled.*
▶ proportional, in proportion, commensurate, relative, comparable, corresponding
AN OPPOSITE IS disproportionate

**USAGE** You can also say *Air fares correspond to (or relate to) the distance travelled.*

**proposal** NOUN
*There is a proposal to build a ring road.*
▶ plan, scheme, proposition, suggestion, project, bid, motion , offer, recommendation

**propose** VERB
1 *Charles proposed Greece for their next holiday.*
▶ suggest, put forward, recommend, offer, come up with, submit, ask for, present
AN OPPOSITE IS withdraw
2 *How do you propose to find the money?*
▶ plan, intend, mean, aim, have in mind
3 *Six candidates have been proposed for election.*
▶ nominate, put up

**proposition** NOUN
1 *They discussed the proposition that war was inevitable.*
▶ theory, hypothesis, premise, notion, idea
2 *a business proposition*
▶ proposal, plan, scheme, suggestion, project

**proprietor** NOUN
*the proprietor of a shop*
▶ owner, manager, boss

**propriety** NOUN
*He always behaves with great propriety.*
▶ decorum, delicacy, correctness, appropriateness, decency, good manners, sensitivity, etiquette, politeness, seemliness, tact
AN OPPOSITE IS impropriety

**prosaic** ADJECTIVE
*a prosaic name for such a beautiful place*
▶ dull, unimaginative, dry, humdrum, pedestrian, lacklustre, insipid
AN OPPOSITE IS poetic

**prosecute** VERB
*The police are going to prosecute him for dangerous driving.*
▶ charge, prefer charges against, institute legal proceedings against, bring to trial, take legal proceedings against, indict

**prospect** NOUN
1 *She went to India with every prospect of a long stay.*
▶ chance, expectation, likelihood, possibility, probability, promise, hope

**2** *There is a magnificent prospect from the penthouse apartment.*
▶ view, vista, outlook, panorama, landscape, perspective, scene, sight, spectacle

**3** **prospects** *His job prospects were looking good.*
▶ future, potential, outlook, possibilities, hopes

**prospective** ADJECTIVE
*A survey is commissioned by the prospective purchaser of the property.*
▶ potential, possible, probable, likely, future, eventual, intended, would-be, aspiring, -to-be (purchaser-to-be)

**prospectus** NOUN
*The prospectus included information on part-time courses.*
▶ brochure, manifesto, programme, syllabus, pamphlet

**prosper** VERB
*The market in mobiles continues to prosper.*
▶ thrive, do well, flourish, boom, blossom, expand, succeed, progress, make progress

**prosperity** NOUN
*The future prosperity of inner cities depends on how safe they are to live in.*
▶ success, welfare, wealth, affluence, growth, plenty, profitability

**prosperous** ADJECTIVE
*She took out a dress she had been given by a prosperous banker.*
▶ well-off, wealthy, affluent, rich, successful, thriving, prospering, flourishing, well-to-do
AN OPPOSITE IS unsuccessful

**protect** VERB
**1** *The men were anxious to protect their women and children. The city fought a war to protect its democracy.*
▶ defend, safeguard, keep safe, preserve, secure, shield, guard, save

**2** *An armed guard protected the convoy.*
▶ escort, guard, accompany, defend, cover, shield

**protection** NOUN
**1** *They looked for some form of protection from the wind and rain.*
▶ shelter, refuge, security, shield

**2** *Military strength would be no protection against terrorist activities of that sort.*
▶ barrier, buffer, screen, bulwark, security, insurance

**protective** ADJECTIVE
**1** *protective clothing*
▶ protecting, insulating, shielding, sheltering, defensive

**2** *Her parents had always been protective towards her.*
▶ caring, solicitous, watchful, vigilant, jealous, defensive, possessive

**protest** NOUN (with the stress on *pro-*)
**1** *The violence shown in the programme caused a wave of protests.*
▶ complaint, objection, outcry, protestation, remonstrance, cry of disapproval

**2** *There will be a large protest in the town square.*
▶ demonstration, rally, march, sit-in, (*more informal*) demo

**protest** VERB (with the stress on -*test*)
**1** *People protested against the export of live animals.*
▶ demonstrate, object, make a protest, remonstrate, express disapproval (of)

**2** *The neighbours protested that the music was too loud.*
▶ complain, object, grumble, expostulate, fulminate, argue, take exception

**3** *He continued to protest his innocence.*
▶ maintain, insist on, claim, profess, proclaim, assert, contend

**protocol** NOUN
*They are real sticklers for protocol.*
▶ procedure, formalities, etiquette, propriety, rules of conduct, rules of behaviour, manners, good form, custom

**protrude** VERB
*A long snout protrudes at the front of the animal.*
▶ stick out, poke out, project, stand out, jut out

**proud** ADJECTIVE
**1** *He's too proud to admit his mistake.*
▶ conceited, arrogant, vain, big-headed, self-important, full of yourself, presumptuous, boastful
OPPOSITES ARE modest, unassuming, humble

**2** *They are a proud people.*
▶ noble, dignified, honourable, self-respecting

**3** **proud of** *Anna was so proud of her garden.*
▶ pleased with, delighted with, thrilled with, satisfied with, happy about, glad about, gratified at, fond of
AN OPPOSITE IS ashamed of

**prove** VERB
**1** *The new evidence proves your innocence.*
▶ confirm, corroborate, demonstrate, establish, substantiate, attest, authenticate, bear out, show to be true, verify
AN OPPOSITE IS disprove

**2** *The story proved to be true.*
▶ turn out, happen, be found

**proven** ADJECTIVE
*an actor of proven ability*
▶ demonstrated, established, tested, tried, certified, confirmed, proved, undoubted, unquestionable
AN OPPOSITE IS doubtful

**proverb** NOUN
*the old proverb about too many cooks*
▶ saying, maxim, adage, dictum, byword, catchphrase

a b c d e f g h i j k l m n o **p** q r s t u v w x y z

**proverbial** ADJECTIVE

*the proverbial ruthlessness of business executives*
▶ well-known, famous, legendary, traditional, conventional, clichéd, customary

**provide** VERB

**1** *The hotel can provide a picnic.*
▶ supply, furnish, serve, produce, present, contribute, lay on, arrange for

**2 provide for** *He now made enough money to provide for his family.*
▶ support, maintain, feed, keep, sustain, provide food for

**3 provide for** *The agreement provides for arbitration in the case of disputes.*
▶ allow for, make provision for, stipulate, specify, require, call for, arrange for

**providence** NOUN

*the workings of providence*
▶ fate, destiny, fortune

**provident** ADJECTIVE

*They are always provident in money matters.*
▶ prudent, judicious, far-sighted, shrewd, thrifty

**province** NOUN

**1** *a province of the Roman Empire*
▶ territory, region, department, district, dependency

**2** *Politics was not my province at that time.*
▶ responsibility, concern, domain, territory, preserve, sphere

**provincial** ADJECTIVE

**1** *the provincial government*
▶ local, regional, district, territorial

**2** *the provincial attitudes of the middle classes*
▶ unsophisticated, insular, parochial, suburban, small-town, narrow-minded, dreary, dull

**provisional** ADJECTIVE

*The provisional total is over a million dollars.*
▶ interim, temporary, tentative, conditional, stopgap
OPPOSITES ARE definite, permanent

**provisions** PLURAL NOUN

*The army was running out of provisions.*
▶ supplies, food and drink, foodstuff, stores, subsistence, rations, groceries, requirements

**proviso** NOUN

*He allowed friends to use his house, with the proviso that they tend to the garden.*
▶ condition, stipulation, provision, requirement, qualification, restriction, understanding

**provocation** NOUN

*(informal) He refused to react despite extreme provocation.*
▶ annoyance, goading, aggravation, irritation, harassment, taunting, incitement, inducement, grounds, justification, motivation

**provoke** VERB

**1** *Plans for a new ring road have provoked a lot of interest.*
▶ arouse, rouse, prompt, cause, kindle, instigate, spark off, stimulate, stir up, *(more informal)* whip up
AN OPPOSITE IS allay

**2** *She was provoked into making comments that she later regretted.*
▶ goad, spur, prick, sting

**3** *Better not to provoke him while he's in a good mood.*
▶ annoy, irritate, anger, incense, offend, tease, taunt

**prowess** NOUN

**1** *the knights' prowess in battle*
▶ bravery, courage, valour, gallantry, heroism, daring, spirit

**2** *her prowess as a dancer*
▶ ability, skill, talent, expertise, accomplishment, aptitude, competence, excellence

**prowl** VERB

*Dogs prowled about at night.*
▶ slink, skulk, sneak, steal, creep, roam, sidle

**proximity** NOUN

**1** *the proximity of the enemy*
▶ closeness, nearness, presence, propinquity

**2** *There are good hotels in the proximity*
▶ vicinity, neighbourhood

**prudent** ADJECTIVE

**1** *It's not always prudent to speak to strangers.*
▶ wise, advisable, sensible, shrewd
AN OPPOSITE IS unwise

**2** *a prudent attitude to money*
▶ cautious, careful, shrewd, far-sighted, thoughtful, wary

**prudish** ADJECTIVE

*Her aunt was a rather prudish woman.*
▶ puritanical, prim, priggish, easily shocked, strait-laced, narrow-minded, old-fashioned, illiberal, intolerant, proper, *(more informal)* prissy
OPPOSITES ARE broad-minded, permissive, liberal

**pry** VERB

*I didn't mean to pry, I was just curious.*
▶ interfere, meddle, delve, poke about, nose about, ferret about, be inquisitive, snoop, *(informal)* stick your nose in

**pseudonym** NOUN

*George Orwell is a pseudonym*
▶ alias, assumed name, *(French)* nom de plume, pen name, sobriquet, false name

**psychic** ADJECTIVE

*She seemed to have psychic powers and knew exactly what would happen.*
▶ clairvoyant, telepathic, extrasensory, supernatural, mystic, occult, psychical

**psychological** ADJECTIVE
*The effects are mostly psychological.*
► mental, subconscious, emotional, subjective, irrational
AN OPPOSITE IS physical

**puberty** NOUN
*the age of puberty*
► adolescence, maturity, pubescence, growing up

**public** ADJECTIVE
1 *public gardens*
► communal, open, free, community, unrestricted
AN OPPOSITE IS private
2 *a public figure*
► well-known, prominent, celebrated, leading, eminent, important, distinguished, notable, famous
OPPOSITES ARE unknown, obscure
3 *This is all public knowledge by now.*
► general, common, recognized, widely known, open

**public** NOUN
*houses open to the public*
► people, the populace, the community, the country, the nation, citizens

**publication** NOUN
1 *Publication of the report will be in July.*
► issuing, appearance, publishing, printing, production, dissemination
2 *a list of the latest publications*
► book, volume, title, work, tome, opus, newspaper, magazine

**publicity** NOUN
1 *The film was launched in a blaze of publicity.*
► attention, media attention, public interest, exposure
2 *Publicity will include television advertising.*
► promotion, marketing, advertising, (*more informal*) hype

**publicize** VERB
*The event is being publicized weeks in advance.*
► advertise, make known, announce, report, (*more informal*) plug
OPPOSITES ARE suppress, conceal

**publish** VERB
1 *A sequel to the story was published last year.*
► issue, bring out, produce, print
2 *The letters should be published as soon as possible.*
► make public, make known, publicize, disseminate, put out, make available

**pucker** VERB
*She felt her lips pucker and her eyes grow moist.*
► wrinkle, screw up, crease, purse, tighten, compress

**pudding** NOUN
*When Steve arrived the others were starting their pudding.*
► dessert, sweet, (*more informal*) afters

**puddle** NOUN
*He woke up to find a puddle of water on his sleeping bag.*
► pool, splash, spill

**puerile** ADJECTIVE
*He was making puerile excuses.*
► childish, infantile, immature, juvenile, silly, inane, fatuous

**puff** NOUN
1 *a puff of wind*
► gust, blast, breath, rush, draught, flurry
2 *a puff of grey smoke*
► cloud, whiff

**puff** VERB
*He was puffing when he reached the top of the stairs.*
► gasp, pant, wheeze, breathe heavily, blow
**puff out** *The curtains puffed out in the draught.*
► swell, distend, become inflated, billow, rise

**puke** VERB
*She had eaten something that upset her and went off to puke.*
► be sick, vomit, retch, heave, (*informal*) throw up

**pull** VERB
1 *She pulled another chair to where she was sitting.*
► drag, draw, tug, heave, (*more informal*) yank
2 *Cars were pulling trailers and caravans.*
► tow, haul, lug, drag, trail
3 *The match will pull huge crowds.*
► attract, draw, bring in, entice, allure, tempt
4 *He had pulled a muscle and was forced to withdraw.*
► strain, sprain, wrench
5 *A dentist might need to pull the tooth.*
► extract, take out, remove, pull out
**pull apart** *Only pull the machine apart if you know how to put it together again.*
► dismantle, take apart, take to pieces, dismember, separate
**pull down** *A row of houses will be pulled down to make space for the new complex.*
► demolish, knock down, tear down, bulldoze, dismantle
**pull someone's leg** *They stopped pulling his leg when they realized he was upset.*
► tease, rag, make fun of, play tricks on
**pull off** *The gang have pulled off another bank robbery.*
► achieve, accomplish, manage, carry out, bring off, succeed in
**pull out** *The army will pull out by the end of the year.*
► withdraw, retreat, leave, depart, quit, move out
**pull through** *She is likely to pull through despite severe injuries.*
► recover, get better, improve, come through, recuperate
**pull together** *Everyone has to pull together if we are going to succeed.*
► cooperate, work together, work as a team, collaborate

**pull** NOUN
1 *He gave the handle a pull.*
► tug, jerk, heave, (*more informal*) yank

a
b
c
d
e
f
g
h
i
j
k
l
m
n
o
p
q
r
s
t
u
v
w
x
y
z

**pulp**

2 *The beauty of the place exerted quite a pull.*
► attraction, lure, draw, influence, enticement

**pulp** NOUN

*a fruit with a juicy pulp*
► flesh, mash, mush, paste, pap

**pulp** VERB

*Pulp the damsons through a sieve.*
► crush, mash, pound, squash, liquidize, pulverize, purée, smash

**pulsate** VERB

*The machine sprang to life and began pulsating.*
► throb, pulse, beat, oscillate, palpitate, quiver, drum, tick, vibrate

**pulse** NOUN

*The music lacked a regular pulse*
► beat, rhythm, throb, oscillation, vibration

**pulverize** VERB

*The seeds are pulverized into a powder.*
► pound, crush, grind, press, powder

**pump** VERB

*The crew rushed to pump the water out of the boat.*
► drain, draw off, empty, force, drive, raise, siphon

**pump up** *We'd better pump up the tyres.*
► inflate, blow up, fill

**pun** NOUN

*a pun on the words 'entrance' and 'entrancing'*
► double meaning, wordplay, play on words

**punch** VERB

1 *Ken punched him in the stomach.*
► hit , strike, bash, thump, box, sock, clout, jab, poke, prod, beat, cuff, slog
2 *He punched a hole in the wall.*
► pierce, puncture, perforate

**punch** NOUN

*a punch on the nose*
► blow, bash, thump, box, poke

**punctual** ADJECTIVE

*We're expected to be punctual.*
► on time, prompt, in good time, (*more informal*) on the dot
OPPOSITES ARE unpunctual, late

**puncture** NOUN

*Her bike had a puncture on the way home.*
► flat tyre, burst tyre, (*more informal*) flat

**puncture** VERB

*Vandals had punctured her tyres.*
► make a hole in, pierce, rupture, let down, deflate

**punish** VERB

*The culprits would be punished.*
► penalize, discipline, correct, chastise, scold, make an example of

**punishment** NOUN

*The punishment has to be reasonable.*
► penalty, discipline, correction, chastisement
RELATED ADJECTIVE penal

**punitive** ADJECTIVE

*The court can impose a punitive fine.*
► harsh, severe, drastic, stringent, exemplary

**puny** ADJECTIVE

*He looked small and puny for his age.*
► weak, feeble, frail, sickly, undersized, undernourished, stunted
OPPOSITES ARE sturdy, strong

**pupil** NOUN

*She is an able pupil.*
► student, scholar, schoolgirl or schoolboy, learner

**purchase** VERB

*The library has purchased new computer hardware.*
► buy, acquire, obtain, invest in, pay for, procure, secure, get
OPPOSITES ARE sell, dispose of, market

**pure** ADJECTIVE

1 *pure gold*
► genuine, unalloyed, unmixed, natural
OPPOSITES ARE impure, adulterated
2 *places where the air is pure*
► clean, fresh, clear, untainted, unpolluted, uncontaminated
OPPOSITES ARE impure, polluted
3 *a pure mind*
► virtuous, moral, chaste, good, innocent, righteous, blameless
OPPOSITES ARE immoral, dirty

**purely** ADVERB

*The lights are purely for show.*
► simply, only, solely, entirely, totally, completely, exclusively

**purify** VERB

*Trees help to purify the air.*
► clean, make pure, refine, sterilize, freshen, disinfect, filter
OPPOSITES ARE pollute, contaminate

**puritanical** ADJECTIVE

*a puritanical attitude to pleasure*
► moralistic, puritan, austere, strict, severe, disapproving, intolerant, narrow-minded, strait-laced
AN OPPOSITE IS permissive

**purity** NOUN

1 *the purity of the water*
► cleanliness, clearness, freshness, naturalness, wholesomeness
2 *the purity of their thoughts*
► goodness, virtue, morality, rightness, uprightness, integrity, honesty

**purpose** NOUN

  **1** *They made their purpose clear.*
  ▶ intention, motive, justification
  **2** *I can't see any purpose in doing that.*
  ▶ point, advantage, benefit, gain
  **3** *Their actions show a lot of purpose.*
  ▶ determination, resolution, resolve, single-mindedness, tenacity, enthusiasm

  **on purpose** *He says it was an accident but I'm sure he did it on purpose.*
  ▶ deliberately, intentionally, purposely, consciously, knowingly

**purposeful** ADJECTIVE

*He cleared his throat in a purposeful manner.*
  ▶ deliberate, determined, resolute, calculated, decided, decisive, single-minded, firm, positive, steadfast, unwavering
AN OPPOSITE IS hesitant

**purposely** ADVERB

*Old trees are left purposely to rot.*
  ▶ on purpose, deliberately, intentionally, consciously, knowingly

**purse** NOUN

  **1** *Keep your foreign money in a separate purse.*
  ▶ pouch, wallet, money bag, bag
  **2** *activities that are paid for out of the public purse*
  ▶ fund or funds, resources, money, kitty, finances, exchequer

**purse** VERB

*He pursed his lips and thought hard.*
  ▶ tighten, close, compress, pucker, contract, screw up

**pursue** VERB

  **1** *I pursued a fox to the end of the lane.*
  ▶ chase, go after, run after, follow, track
  **2** *It was an ambitious objective to pursue.*
  ▶ strive for, work towards, aim at, aspire to
  **3** *She is determined to pursue a career in politics.*
  ▶ follow, undertake, take up, engage in
  **4** *He pursues a number of interests in his spare time.*
  ▶ carry on, maintain, follow, continue, devote yourself to

**pursuit** NOUN

  **1** *Police gave up the pursuit when they lost the trail in London.*
  ▶ chase, hunt, search, tracking
  **2** *The family enjoy their outdoor pursuits.*
  ▶ activity, pastime, diversion, amusement
  **3** *the pursuit of knowledge*
  ▶ search (for), quest (for), striving (for), aim, goal, objective

**push** VERB

  **1** *She pushed a chair against the door.*
  ▶ shove, thrust, press, propel, nudge
AN OPPOSITE IS pull
  **2** *I pushed a few things into a bag.*
  ▶ pack, cram, squash, squeeze, jam, ram, crush, put, insert

  **3** *He tried to push his way through the crowd.*
  ▶ force, thrust, shove, elbow, jostle, shoulder, prod, press
  **4** *Better not to push them to come if they don't want to.*
  ▶ press, pressure, pressurize, put pressure on, urge, persuade, cajole, browbeat, coerce, bully, compel, (*more informal*) lean on
  **5** *Each software company wants to push its own product.*
  ▶ promote, publicize, advertise, popularize, make known, market, (*more informal*) plug

**push around** *He was fed up with being pushed around.*
  ▶ bully, domineer, boss about or around, trample on, mistreat

**push for** *Trade unions are pushing for the repeal of some of these laws.*
  ▶ demand, insist on, press for, urge

**push off** (*informal*) *She was busy and told us to push off.*
  ▶ go away, leave, be off, run along, depart, (*informal*) beat it, (*informal*) scram

**push** NOUN

  **1** *She felt a push in her back.*
  ▶ shove, thrust, prod, nudge, jolt, poke, knock
  **2** *The enemy's push was aimed at reaching the coast.*
  ▶ advance, thrust, drive, offensive, onslaught, assault

**pushy** ADJECTIVE

*He needed to appear in control without seeming too pushy.*
  ▶ assertive, dominating, dominant, aggressive, forceful, officious

---

**put** VERB This word is often overused. Here are some alternatives:

  **1** *He put the case on the table. They put a guard on the door.*
  ▶ place, leave, set, deposit, position, stand, settle, station, post
  **2** *I wanted to say something but I wasn't sure how to put it.*
  ▶ express, word, phrase, formulate, couch
  **3** *The government will put a tax on it.*
  ▶ impose, inflict, levy, apply (to), assign (to)
  **4** *They put the cost at over a million.*
  ▶ estimate, reckon, calculate, assess, evaluate, measure, judge
  **5** *We have some ideas to put to you*
  ▶ submit, present, propose, advance, offer, suggest

**put across** *The government needs to put its message across clearly.*
  ▶ communicate, convey, get across, spell out, make clear, express

**put aside** *We have put aside some money.*
  ▶ save, set aside, put by, keep, keep in reserve, reserve

▶▶

**put back**
1 *The meeting has been put back for a week.*
▶ postpone, defer, delay, hold over
AN OPPOSITE IS bring forward
**put by** *She wanted to put something by each week for emergencies.*
▶ save, set aside, keep, earmark
**put down**
1 *I'd better put down some details.*
▶ write down, record, enter, note down, make a note of
2 *The army quickly put down the rebellion.*
▶ suppress, crush, quell, quash, defeat
3 *He enjoyed putting people down, especially in public.*
▶ criticize, belittle, disparage, humiliate, mortify
4 *You can put it down to laziness.*
▶ attribute, ascribe, blame (on)
**put forward** *Stella put forward a new suggestion.*
▶ advance, offer, propose, suggest, present, submit
AN OPPOSITE IS withdraw
**put in** *You have to put in a new ink cartridge*
▶ insert, install, fit
OPPOSITES ARE remove, take out
**put off**
1 *The noise put her off.*
▶ deter, discourage, disconcert, unnerve, repel, distract, intimidate
AN OPPOSITE IS attract
2 *We'd better put off a decision.*
▶ postpone, defer, delay, hold over, shelve, reschedule
AN OPPOSITE IS bring forward
**put on**
1 *He put on an air of importance.*
▶ assume, affect, simulate, feign, sham
2 *The gallery is putting on a special exhibition.*
▶ mount, organize, stage, produce, present
**put out**
1 *Nina was put out by this criticism.*
▶ offend, annoy, anger, irritate, affront, insult
2 *I hope it won't put you out if I stay a few days.*
▶ inconvenience, bother, trouble, impose on
3 *The BBC put out an appeal.*
▶ announce, publish, broadcast, circulate
**put up**
1 *He put up a shed in the garden*
▶ erect, build, construct, assemble
OPPOSITES ARE take down, demolish
2 *We can put you up for a few days.*
▶ accommodate, house, lodge, take in, give a bed to, shelter
3 *They have put up their prices.*
▶ increase, raise, lift, (more informal) bump up
**put up with** *She is not prepared to put up with such behaviour.*
▶ tolerate, stand for, accept, bear, take, endure, stomach

**puzzle** NOUN
*It is a hard puzzle to solve.*
▶ problem, riddle, question, enigma, paradox

**puzzle** VERB
*Mike's angry response puzzled me.*
▶ confuse, perplex, baffle, mystify, bewilder, disconcert, confound, fox, (more informal) flummox
**puzzle out** *She was trying to puzzle out who the caller might have been.*
▶ work out, figure out, resolve, decide, get to the bottom of, make sense of

**puzzled** ADJECTIVE
*Freda had a puzzled look on her face.*
▶ confused, baffled, perplexed, mystified, bewildered, at a loss, nonplussed, (more informal) stumped

**puzzling** ADJECTIVE
*There was something puzzling about the shape of the house.*
▶ confusing, baffling, bewildering, perplexing, mystifying, mysterious, inexplicable, extraordinary
OPPOSITES ARE straightforward, comprehensible

# Qq

**quagmire** NOUN
*Heavy rain turned the field into a quagmire.*
▶ swamp, morass, marsh, mire, bog

**quail** VERB
*The force of her anger made him quail.*
▶ tremble, cower, cringe, shrink, shudder, wince, quake, recoil, blench, flinch

**quaint** ADJECTIVE
*a quaint little shop that served teas*
▶ charming, picturesque, antiquated, strange, sweet, old-world, (more informal) twee

**quake** VERB
*Passing trains make the walls quake.*
▶ tremble, quiver, shake, shiver, quaver, vibrate, shudder, wobble

**qualification** NOUN
1 *You need a professional qualification in social work.*
▶ certificate, diploma, degree, training, skill, competence, eligibility, fitness
2 *He agreed without any qualification.*
▶ reservation, hesitation, restriction, exception, condition, modification

## qualified ADJECTIVE

**1** *His two sons were both qualified doctors.*
▶ certified, chartered, skilled, trained, professional, graduate, competent
AN OPPOSITE IS unqualified

**2** *She could only give the idea qualified approval.*
▶ limited, modified, conditional, cautious, guarded, reserved, restricted, equivocal, half-hearted
OPPOSITES ARE unqualified, unconditional

## qualify VERB

**1** *The course qualifies you to teach young children.*
▶ authorize, permit, allow, entitle, prepare, equip, fit
AN OPPOSITE IS disqualify (from)

**2** *I may qualify for a discount.*
▶ be eligible, be entitled (to), be allowed

**3** *He qualified his conclusion with a few reservations.*
▶ moderate, modify, restrict, mitigate, limit

## quality NOUN

**1** *work of a high quality*
▶ standard, calibre, class, grade, rank, sort, value, condition, excellence

**2** *He has many good qualities*
▶ characteristic, feature, attribute, point, aspect, peculiarity, property, trait

## qualm NOUN

*She had some qualms about leaving the old man alone.*
▶ concern, anxiety, misgiving, unease, disquiet, apprehension, doubt, worry, reservation, scruple

## quandary NOUN

*James was in a quandary about what to do next.*
▶ predicament, state of confusion, state of uncertainty, state of perplexity, plight, dilemma

## quantify VERB

*The cost will be hard to quantify.*
▶ measure, put a figure on, determine, gauge, assess

## quantity NOUN

*A huge quantity of stolen goods was recovered.*
▶ amount, number, total, volume, lot, portion, proportion, consignment

## quarrel NOUN

*A quarrel developed in which Kemp was struck over the head.*
▶ argument, row, disagreement, altercation, difference of opinion, dispute, squabble, clash, tiff
OPPOSITES ARE agreement, reconciliation

## quarrel VERB

**1** *People quarrel in different ways.*
▶ argue, disagree, row, have a row, squabble, bicker, fall out, tiff, fight
AN OPPOSITE IS agree

**2** *quarrel with I can't quarrel with your version of what happened.*
▶ disagree with, find fault with, criticize, oppose

## quarrelsome ADJECTIVE

*He didn't want to stay with such a quarrelsome family.*
▶ argumentative, contentious, belligerent, disputatious, aggressive, factious, confrontational, ill-tempered
AN OPPOSITE IS peaceable

## quarry NOUN

*The cat came in with its quarry still hanging from its mouth.*
▶ prey, victim, prize, kill

## quarter NOUN

**1** *a house in the poor quarter of the city*
▶ district, locality, neighbourhood, vicinity, area, region, part, sector

**2** *There was help from an unexpected quarter.*
▶ source, direction, point, location

## quarter VERB

*The troops were quartered in a country house.*
▶ accommodate, house, board, lodge, put up, station, billet

## quarters PLURAL NOUN

*Her bedroom had once been part of the servants' quarters.*
▶ accommodation, rooms, lodging, chambers

## quash VERB

**1** *The Court of Appeal may quash the sentence.*
▶ overrule, revoke, rescind, overturn, set aside, cancel, retract, repeal, nullify

**2** *The rebellion was brutally quashed. The statement failed to quash rumours.*
▶ put an end to, stamp out, suppress, crush, quell, subdue, overthrow

## quaver VERB

*She broke off as her voice began to quaver.*
▶ tremble, quiver, waver, shake, flutter, vibrate, pulsate

## quay NOUN

*Overlooking the quay was a small hotel.*
▶ dock, wharf, pier, harbour, jetty, landing-stage, berth

## queasy ADJECTIVE

*He had been feeling tired and queasy for the past few days.*
▶ sick, nauseous, bilious, unwell, poorly, queer, out of sorts

## queen NOUN

*She knew she would be queen one day.*
▶ ruler, monarch, sovereign, crowned head
RELATED ADJECTIVES regal, royal

## queer ADJECTIVE

**1** *There was something queer going on.*
▶ odd, strange, unusual, weird, peculiar, funny, curious, bizarre, puzzling, mysterious, remarkable
OPPOSITES ARE ordinary, normal

**2** *I was feeling a bit queer.*
▶ sick, unwell, poorly, queasy, out of sorts, nauseous, bilious, faint, dizzy

**quell** VERB
*Troops were sent in to quell the rising.*
▶ suppress, put an end to, stamp out, crush, quash, subdue, overthrow

**quench** VERB
1 *The fire brigade was called in to quench the flames.*
▶ extinguish, put out, smother, damp down, douse, snuff out
2 *We stopped at a small village to quench our thirst.*
▶ relieve, satisfy, sate, slake, cool

**query** NOUN
*Please send a stamped addressed envelope with any queries.*
▶ question, enquiry, problem, doubt, uncertainty

**query** VERB
*She had to query the wisdom of such a plan.*
▶ question, doubt, suspect, have doubts about, have reservations about, feel uneasy about, challenge, dispute
AN OPPOSITE IS accept

**quest** NOUN
*a quest to find iron-age remains*
▶ expedition, mission, search, hunt, crusade

**question** NOUN
1 *You haven't answered the question.*
▶ enquiry, query, problem
AN OPPOSITE IS answer
2 *There is the question of all his debts.*
▶ issue, matter, business, point, subject, problem
3 *There's some question about who will be in charge.*
▶ uncertainty, doubt, misgiving, argument, reservation, debate, dispute, controversy, objection
**out of the question** *Sending them more money was out of the question.*
▶ impossible, inconceivable, unthinkable, unrealistic, not feasible, impractical, (*more informal*) not on
OPPOSITES ARE possible, feasible

**question** VERB
1 *A man is being questioned at Gloucester police station.*
▶ interrogate, interview, cross-examine, investigate, (*more informal*) quiz, (*more informal*) grill, (*more informal*) pump
2 *She never questioned his right to be there.*
▶ query, doubt, suspect, have doubts about, have reservations about, feel uneasy about, challenge, dispute

**questionable** ADJECTIVE
*All these arguments are highly questionable.*
▶ debatable, doubtful, dubious, suspect, unreliable, disputable, uncertain, unclear, unprovable, (*more informal*) iffy, (*more informal*) shady
OPPOSITES ARE unquestionable, indisputable, acceptable

**questionnaire** NOUN
*The results of the questionnaire showed that children were enthusiastic about learning science.*
▶ question sheet, survey, opinion poll, quiz, test

**queue** NOUN
1 *To my surprise there was no queue at the Post Office.*
▶ line, line of people
2 *There were traffic queues all down the motorway.*
▶ jam, tailback, file, column, procession

**queue** VERB
*They queued for hours to be sure of tickets.*
▶ line up, form a queue, wait in a queue

**quibble** VERB
*He accepted the offer without quibbling.*
▶ complain, find fault, carp, cavil, object, equivocate, split hairs, nitpick

**quibble** NOUN
*Her only quibble was about the cost.*
▶ complaint, objection, reservation, doubt, query, criticism

**quick** ADJECTIVE
1 *She gave a quick glance at her watch.*
▶ hasty, brief, cursory, furtive, fleeting, rapid
OPPOSITES ARE long, careful
2 *He was always a quick worker.*
▶ fast, swift, rapid, speedy, lively, sprightly, prompt
AN OPPOSITE IS slow
3 *There is no quick solution to the problem.*
▶ instant, instantaneous, ready, sudden
4 *Kevin wasn't as quick as some of the others in the class.*
▶ bright, clever, intelligent, gifted, able, sharp, alert, acute, (*more informal*) on the ball
AN OPPOSITE IS dull

**quicken** VERB
*The pace quickened.*
▶ speed up, accelerate, get or go faster, hasten, hurry
OPPOSITES ARE slow, slow down

**quickly** ADVERB
1 *She began to walk more quickly.*
▶ fast, swiftly, rapidly, speedily
AN OPPOSITE IS slowly
2 *We quickly realized they had gone.*
▶ soon, at once, straight away, right away, rapidly, immediately, instantly, directly, suddenly

**quiet** ADJECTIVE
1 *The house is in a quiet village near the river.*
▶ peaceful, tranquil, secluded, isolated, calm, restful, pleasant
OPPOSITES ARE noisy, busy
2 *He spoke in a quiet voice.*
▶ soft, low, muted, muffled
OPPOSITES ARE loud, raised
3 *Can we have a quiet word together?*
▶ private, confidential, secret
4 *Fiona's a lovely, quiet person.*
▶ shy, reserved, private, subdued, taciturn, withdrawn, calm, placid, serene, composed, untroubled, unruffled
AN OPPOSITE IS outgoing
5 *It's hard to keep rumours like that quiet.*
▶ secret, silent, private, confidential, undisclosed
AN OPPOSITE IS public

## quieten VERB

**1** *The audience quietened when the curtain went up.*
▶ go quiet, fall silent, grow silent, hush, shush, (*more informal*) shut up
**2** *He was so excited it was impossible to quieten him.*
▶ calm, calm down, pacify, mollify, appease, assuage

## quilt NOUN

*He put a quilt on the bed.*
▶ eiderdown, bedcover, bedspread, counterpane, duvet

## quip NOUN

*He finished the speech with a quip.*
▶ joke, witticism, witty remark, jest, (*more informal*) wisecrack

## quirk NOUN

*One of his quirks is that he checks things over and over again.*
▶ peculiarity, oddity, idiosyncrasy, foible, whim, caprice

## quit VERB

**1** *She's much too determined to quit now.*
▶ give up, stop, leave, depart, go, cease
**2** *It's time you quit smoking.*
▶ give up, stop, cease, discontinue, drop, (*more informal*) pack in
**3** *He decided to quit his job and go abroad.*
▶ leave, resign from, retire from, renounce, forsake, abandon

## quite ADVERB

**1** *The two sisters are quite different in appearance.*
▶ completely, totally, wholly, entirely, utterly
**2** *It was quite late by now.*
▶ rather, fairly, a bit, somewhat, comparatively, relatively, (*more informal*) pretty

## quits ADJECTIVE

*After four games we were quits.*
▶ level, even, square, equal

## quiver VERB

*The trees quivered in the wind. I sat quivering with fright.*
▶ shake, tremble, shudder, shiver, quaver, flutter

## quiz NOUN

*The day ended with a quiz between the two teams.*
▶ competition, questionnaire, test, examination, questioning

## quiz VERB

(*informal*) *The police are quizzing a suspect.*
▶ question, interrogate, interview, cross-examine, investigate

## quizzical ADJECTIVE

*She had a quizzical expression.*
▶ puzzled, questioning, enquiring, perplexed, baffled, curious

## quota NOUN

*He wouldn't take his full quota of leave this year.*
▶ allocation, allowance, ration, share, portion

## quotation NOUN

**1** *a quotation from Shakespeare*
▶ citation, quote, reference, excerpt, extract, piece, passage
**2** *First we need a quotation for the work.*
▶ estimate, price, quote, figure, tender

## quote VERB

**1** *She quoted a few lines from a poem.*
▶ cite, recite, recall, repeat, mention, refer to
**2** *The figure the builder quoted was too high.*
▶ estimate, offer, tender, bid, specify

# Rr

## rabble NOUN

*He was met by a rabble of angry, noisy youths.*
▶ crowd, throng, horde, mob, gang, group, herd, swarm

## race NOUN

**1** *people of many different races*
▶ ethnic group, nation, people, clan, tribe
RELATED ADJECTIVES ethnic, racial
**2** *Donald won the race easily.*
▶ contest, competition, chase, heat, event

## race VERB

**1** *The children were racing each other in the garden.*
▶ have a race with, run against, compete with, try to beat
**2** *Herds of waterbuck raced across the swamps. She raced towards the house.*
▶ dash, rush, shoot, sprint, streak, dart, hare, hasten, hurry, run, tear, zoom, career, fly, gallop, move fast
**3** *All kinds of thoughts raced through my mind.*
▶ rush, dart, fly, shoot, zoom

## racial ADJECTIVE

*laws against racial discrimination*
▶ ethnic, national, cultural

## racism NOUN

*the struggle to end racism in all its forms*
▶ discrimination, racialism, racial hatred, intolerance, prejudice, xenophobia, bigotry, chauvinism

## racist ADJECTIVE

*racist attitudes*
▶ discriminatory, racialist, intolerant, prejudiced, xenophobic, biased, bigoted, chauvinist
OPPOSITES ARE tolerant, unbiased

## rack NOUN

*a vegetable rack a luggage rack*
▶ stand, shelf, support, framework, frame

a b c d e f g h i j k l m n o p q r s t u v w x y z

## racket NOUN

**1** (*informal*) *The machines make a frightful racket.*
▶ noise, din, commotion, hubbub, clamour, tumult, rumpus, uproar

**2** (*informal*) *He was involved in a stolen car racket.*
▶ swindle, fraud, dodge, fiddle, deception, (*more informal*) con, (*informal*) scam

## racy ADJECTIVE

*a writer of racy novels*
▶ bawdy, spicy, indecent, naughty, risqué

## radiant ADJECTIVE

**1** *a radiant moon*
▶ bright, shining, brilliant
OPPOSITES ARE dark, dull

**2** *a radiant smile*
▶ beautiful, glowing, dazzling, sparkling, beaming, joyful, elated, happy
OPPOSITES ARE faint, weak

## radiate VERB

**1** *Electric bulbs radiate more heat than light.*
▶ emit, send out, give off, spread, transmit, diffuse, shed

**2** *a face that radiates confidence*
▶ show, display, exhibit, emanate, breathe, transmit, send out

## radical ADJECTIVE

**1** *a radical course of action*
▶ fundamental, drastic, thoroughgoing, thorough, comprehensive, sweeping, rigorous, complete, basic
AN OPPOSITE IS superficial

**2** *a government committed to radical change*
▶ revolutionary, extreme, extremist, militant
OPPOSITES ARE moderate, conservative

## raffle NOUN

*She won a prize in a raffle.*
▶ draw, lottery, tombola, sweepstake

## rage NOUN

**1** *He stormed out of the room in a burst of rage.*
▶ anger, fury, temper, outrage, passion, pique, exasperation

**2** *the rage for portable DVD players*
▶ craze, vogue, trend, fashion, passion

## rage VERB

**1** *He was raging about what had happened.*
▶ fume, storm, seethe, rant, fulminate, be angry

**2** *A fierce blizzard raged for days.*
▶ blow, storm, thunder, rampage

## ragged ADJECTIVE

**1** *She spent the morning mending ragged clothes.*
▶ tattered, torn, frayed, threadbare, ripped, shabby, tatty, unkempt, worn out

**2** *He drilled his ragged collection of men.*
▶ disorganized, disordered, disorderly, erratic, irregular, uneven

## raid NOUN

**1** *Sentries watched out for any air raids.*
▶ attack, assault, strike, swoop, blitz, foray, sortie, onslaught, invasion

**2** *He had killed a guard during a bank raid.*
▶ robbery, burglary, break-in, hold-up, (*more informal*) heist

## raid VERB

**1** *The army raided towns on the border.*
▶ attack, pillage, loot, plunder, ransack, maraud, assault, storm, descend on

**2** *Burglars raided local jewellers for the second time.*
▶ rob, hold up, burgle, break into

**3** *Police raided homes and offices in the area.*
▶ search, swoop on

## railing NOUN

*A notice had been put on the railing.*
▶ fence, paling, barrier

## railway NOUN

*They were warned not to cross the railway*
▶ track, line, rails

## rain NOUN

*The rain had started again.*
▶ rainfall, wet weather, drizzle, shower, downpour, cloudburst, raindrops, rainstorm, squall, deluge, (*more formal*) precipitation

## rain VERB

*It rained all afternoon.*
▶ pour, bucket, teem, pelt, drizzle, spit

## rainy ADJECTIVE

*a rainy day*
▶ wet, showery, drizzly, damp
AN OPPOSITE IS dry

## raise VERB

**1** *Ben raised his hand.*
▶ put up, lift

**2** *A crane will raise the load to the top of the building.*
▶ lift, hoist

**3** *The company was forced to raise its prices.*
▶ increase, put up, push up, lift

**4** *United will need to raise their game for the away match.*
▶ improve, enhance, strengthen, heighten, boost, step up, put more life into

**5** *We need to raise five thousand pounds.*
▶ collect, get, obtain, gather, net, amass, scrape together, yield, assemble

**6** *This good news raised their hopes.*
▶ encourage, increase, improve, arouse, rouse, excite

**7** *She raised three children on her own.*
▶ bring up, provide for, nurture, look after, educate

**8** *Charles raised several objections to the idea.*
▶ bring up, put forward, advance, present, introduce, pose, offer

**9** *The incident raises questions about rail safety.*
▶ give rise to, occasion, cause, bring about, produce, engender

## rally NOUN

*an anti-war rally*
▶ demonstration, meeting, protest, march, (*more informal*) demo

## rally VERB

**1** *The king rallied his troops at the border.* *They tried to rally support for the election.*
▶ muster, assemble, marshal, amass, gather, round up, organize
**2** *Our spirits rallied.*
▶ recover, improve, pick up, get better, look up, perk up

## ram VERB

*The getaway van rammed a police car.*
▶ hit, strike, smash into, be in collision with, slam into, collide with, crash into

## ramble VERB

**1** *We spent a week rambling in the countryside.*
▶ walk, roam, trek, tramp, hike, rove, stroll
**2** *He was rambling on about his schooldays.*
▶ chatter, blather, prattle, drift, run, maunder, (*more informal*) rabbit, (*more informal*) witter

## rambling ADJECTIVE

*a long rambling speech*
▶ long-winded, verbose, diffuse, disjointed, disconnected, incoherent, roundabout, digressive

## ramp NOUN

*There's a ramp for wheelchairs*
▶ slope, incline, gradient, rise, sloping surface

## rampage VERB

*A mob rampaged through the streets.*
▶ run riot, run amok, go on the rampage, riot, go berserk, go wild, race about, rush about, behave violently

## rampant ADJECTIVE

*years of rampant corruption*
▶ unrestrained, unchecked, unbridled, widespread, pervasive, wild

## ramshackle ADJECTIVE

*a ramshackle old house*
▶ dilapidated, tumbledown, derelict, decrepit, rickety, shaky, unsafe, broken down, ruined, tottering, crumbling
AN OPPOSITE IS sturdy

## random ADJECTIVE

*Her house came up in a random sample of houses in the area.*
▶ indiscriminate, arbitrary, chance, haphazard, casual, unplanned, accidental, unconsidered, unpremeditated, fortuitous, irregular
AN OPPOSITE IS systematic

## range NOUN

**1** *a range of mountains*
▶ chain, row, line, series, string, file
**2** *a wide range of food*
▶ variety, assortment, selection, array, scope, choice, spectrum, extent
**3** *an age range between 20 and 30*
▶ span, scope, compass, radius

## range VERB

**1** *Prices range between £100 and £600*
▶ vary, extend, differ, fluctuate, reach
**2** *Sheep ranged over the hills.*
▶ roam, rove, wander, stray, travel
**3** *Pupils are ranged by ability.*
▶ classify, class, categorize, rank, order, group

## rank NOUN

**1** *She was promoted to the rank of assistant manager.*
▶ level, grade, position, status, standing, station, title, class, degree
**2** *a family of rank*
▶ high standing, distinction, importance, nobility, aristocracy
**3** *The front rank began to move forward.*
▶ row, line, file, column

## rank VERB

*He's ranked number two in the world.*
▶ grade, class, categorize, classify, designate, list

## rank ADJECTIVE

**1** *a ditch full of rank water*
▶ foul-smelling, noxious, fetid, smelly
**2** *There was rank disbelief at the numbers.*
▶ utter, sheer, outright, downright, complete, total, wholesale, absolute

## rankle VERB

*rankle with The criticism still rankles with him.*
▶ annoy, upset, anger, offend, irritate, nettle, irk

## ransack VERB

**1** *Thieves had ransacked the buildings.*
▶ plunder, pillage, loot, raid, rob, ravage, wreck
**2** *I ransacked the cupboard for a clean shirt.*
▶ rummage through, hunt through, scour, search, comb, (*more informal*) turn upside down

## ransom NOUN

*The ransom was set at four million dollars.*
▶ pay-off, release money, payment, price

## ransom VERB

*The kidnappers demanded a million pounds to ransom the girl.*
▶ obtain the release of, release, redeem, liberate, free

## rant VERB

*The old man was ranting in German.*
▶ hold forth, shout, yell, roar, bellow, declaim

## rap VERB

*rap on He rapped on the big oak door.*
▶ knock on, strike, tap, hit

## rape NOUN

*a charge of rape*
▶ sexual assault, sexual attack, sexual abuse

## rape VERB

*He raped her at gunpoint.*
▶ sexually assault, violate, force yourself on, sexually abuse

# rapid ADJECTIVE
*They made rapid progress.*
▶ fast, quick, swift, speedy, brisk, lively, smooth, sharp, prompt, headlong
OPPOSITES ARE slow, leisurely

# rapt ADJECTIVE
*a rapt audience*
▶ engrossed, enthralled, absorbed, captivated, enraptured, fascinated, spellbound

# rapture NOUN
*They gazed at each other in rapture.*
▶ ecstasy, bliss, joy, delight, happiness, euphoria, wonderment, exaltation

# rapturous ADJECTIVE
*They got a rapturous reception from the teenage audience.*
▶ ecstatic, joyful, joyous, enthusiastic, euphoric, enraptured, delighted

# rare ADJECTIVE
1 *a rare moment of peace*
▶ uncommon, infrequent, scarce, occasional, sporadic, odd, singular
OPPOSITES ARE frequent, common
2 *a person of rare abilities*
▶ exceptional, remarkable, incomparable, unusual, uncommon, special, abnormal

# raring ADJECTIVE
*They were raring to begin.*
▶ eager, keen, enthusiastic, longing, impatient, (*more informal*) itching, (*more informal*) dying

# rascal NOUN
1 *One of the rascals had stolen money from the till.*
▶ rogue, scoundrel, ne'er-do-well
2 *Dad asked, 'What's the little rascal been up to?'*
▶ scamp, scallywag, monkey, mischief-maker, wretch, monster

# rash ADJECTIVE
*He regretted making such a rash promise.*
▶ reckless, impulsive, impetuous, foolhardy, hasty, precipitate, imprudent, incautious, injudicious, indiscreet, ill-advised, ill-considered, headstrong, unthinking, heedless, hot-headed, hurried
OPPOSITES ARE cautious, considered, prudent

# rash NOUN
1 *Her skin broke out in a rash.*
▶ spots, eruption, hives
2 (*informal*) *a rash of break-ins in the area*
▶ outbreak, spate, series, succession

# rasping ADJECTIVE
*the old man's rasping voice*
▶ hoarse, grating, croaking, jarring, raspy, croaky, rough, harsh, husky, gravelly, gruff

# rate NOUN
1 *They were pedalling at a furious rate.*
▶ speed, pace, tempo, velocity, (*more informal*) lick
2 *You can hire a boat for a reasonable daily rate.*
▶ charge, amount, price, cost, payment, fare, fee, figure

# rate VERB
1 *They do not rate our chances very highly.*
▶ assess, evaluate, appraise, judge, regard, value, count, weigh, estimate, calculate, consider, measure
2 *The suggestion only rated a brief mention.*
▶ merit, deserve, warrant, be worthy of
3 (*informal*) *I don't rate this stuff like you do.*
▶ think much of, think highly of, admire, value, enjoy

# rather ADVERB
1 *It sounds rather difficult.*
▶ fairly, somewhat, quite, slightly, moderately, relatively, (*more informal*) pretty
2 *I'd rather leave it until the weekend.*
▶ sooner, preferably

# ratify VERB
*All member countries have to ratify the agreement simultaneously.*
▶ confirm, approve, endorse, affirm, sign, authorize, validate

# rating NOUN
*The restaurant might lose its five-star rating.*
▶ grade, grading, classification, ranking, category, designation, evaluation, placing, mark

# ratio NOUN
*The ratio of men to women has changed.*
▶ proportion, balance, relationship, correlation, correspondence

# ration NOUN
*They decided not to increase their daily ration of biscuits.*
▶ allowance, allocation, quota, share, measure, helping, portion
**rations** *The expedition might soon run out of rations.*
▶ supplies, provisions, stores, food, necessaries, necessities

# ration VERB
*Fuel is strictly rationed in wartime.*
▶ control, limit, restrict, conserve, allocate, allot, apportion

# rational ADJECTIVE
1 *Feelings are so high it's difficult to have a rational discussion.*
▶ reasoned, logical, sensible, coherent, cogent, reasonable, balanced, sane, intelligent, judicious, lucid, normal
OPPOSITES ARE irrational, illogical
2 *In the last year of his life he was often barely rational.*
▶ lucid, coherent, sane, intelligible, in your right mind

# rationale NOUN
*The government lacks a rationale for reducing taxes.*
▶ reason, reasoning, logical basis, ground or grounds, philosophy, justification

## rationalize VERB

**1** *Martin tried to rationalize his behaviour of the day before.*
► justify, explain, account for, excuse, defend, make allowances for

**2** *a proposal to rationalize the postal services*
► reorganize, streamline, make more efficient, trim, slim down, modernize

## rattle VERB

**1** *He rattled the coins in his purse.*
► jangle, clink, clunk

**2** *A row of trucks rattled along the track.*
► clatter, jolt, shake, bounce

**3** *The wind rattled at the doors and windows*
► shake, batter, beat

**4** *This news had rattled her badly.*
► disconcert, disturb, unnerve, fluster, shake, discomfit, (*more informal*) throw

**rattle off** *He rattled off the words he had learned.*
► recite, run through, reel off, repeat, list

## rattle NOUN

*the rattle of crockery in the kitchen*
► clatter, clattering, clank, clanking

## ratty ADJECTIVE

*Upset neighbours can get very ratty.*
► bad-tempered, irritated, irascible, grumpy, testy, grouchy, touchy, crotchety, cantankerous, peevish, fractious, cross, (*more informal*) stroppy, (*more informal*) shirty

## raucous ADJECTIVE

*the raucous clamour of alarm bells*
► noisy, harsh, shrill, strident, jarring, grating, loud, rough

## ravage VERB

*He let his army ravage the Norman countryside.*
► devastate, lay waste, ruin, destroy, loot, pillage, plunder, raid, damage, despoil, ransack

## rave VERB

**1** *He was raving and swearing at them.*
► rage, rant, shout, roar, bellow, storm

**2** *rave about Everyone raved about Leeds that day.*
► praise, idolize, be ecstatic about, go into raptures over

## rave ADJECTIVE

*The film got a rave review.*
► enthusiastic, rapturous, glowing, ecstatic, wonderful

## ravenous ADJECTIVE

*By evening the walkers were ravenous.*
► hungry, famished, ravening, insatiable

## ravine NOUN

*At this point the river flows in a deep ravine*
► gorge, canyon, defile, gully, chasm, pass

## ravishing ADJECTIVE

*She looked ravishing in a summer dress.*
► beautiful, gorgeous, stunning, enchanting, radiant, dazzling

## raw ADJECTIVE

**1** *She ate a piece of raw onion.*
► uncooked, fresh

**2** *the high cost of raw materials*
► natural, untreated, unprocessed, basic

**3** *His skin had become raw.*
► sore, inflamed, red, tender

**4** *You could sense the raw passion.*
► strong, intense, powerful, fervent, unrestrained

**5** *They walked against the raw wind.*
► cold, bitter, biting, freezing, piercing, chilly

## ray NOUN

**1** *A ray of light shone through the branches.*
► beam, shaft, stream, streak, finger, glint, glimmer

**2** *There was one ray of hope left.*
► glimmer, flicker, gleam, spark, trace, sign, hint, indication

## raze VERB

*Enemy troops razed the buildings to the ground.*
► demolish, tear down, flatten, destroy, bulldoze

## reach VERB

**1** *After a while the walkers reached a village.*
► arrive at, get to, come to, get as far as, (*more informal*) end up at, (*more informal*) make it to

**2** *The Government has not reached any of its major targets yet.*
► achieve, attain, succeed in, (*more informal*) hit, (*more informal*) make

**3** *I can't reach the switch.*
► get hold of, grasp, get your hand to, take, touch

**4** *You can reach me on my mobile.*
► contact, get in touch with, communicate with

**reach out** *She reached out her hand.*
► stretch out, stick out, hold out, put out, extend, raise

## reach NOUN

**1** *The station is within easy reach*
► distance, range, compass, scope

**2** *The fugitives were now beyond the reach of the law.*
► jurisdiction, authority, control, sway, command

**3** *Aim at achievements that are within your reach.*
► capabilities, abilities, capacity

## react VERB

*Zoe wondered how he would react if she told him everything.*
► respond, reply, answer, behave, take it, act

## reaction NOUN

*His reaction had puzzled her.*
► response, manner of response, reply, answer, rejoinder, retort, behaviour

## read VERB

**1** *He sat in the sofa, reading the papers.*
► peruse, study, scan, skim, glance at, pore over, dip into

**2** *She promised to read them a story*
► read out, tell, say aloud, recite

**3** *The writing is not hard to read.*
► make out, decipher, make sense of, understand, decode

a b c d e f g h i j k l m n o p q r s t u v w x y z

**readable** ADJECTIVE

1 *a readable book*
▶ enjoyable, entertaining, interesting, well-written, compulsive, gripping
OPPOSITES ARE boring, unreadable

2 *readable handwriting*
▶ legible, clear, decipherable, understandable, neat, plain
AN OPPOSITE IS illegible

**readily** ADVERB

1 *Janet readily agreed.*
▶ willingly, gladly, happily, unhesitatingly, promptly, eagerly, freely, voluntarily
AN OPPOSITE IS reluctantly

2 *The town is readily reached from the shore.*
▶ easily, quickly, without difficulty

**reading** NOUN

1 *He gave the letters a hurried reading.*
▶ study, perusal, scrutiny, scan, browse, glance, look through

2 *This is our reading of the evidence.*
▶ interpretation, understanding, construal, reconstruction

**ready** ADJECTIVE

1 *We are ready to leave. He wasn't ready for the answer he got.*
▶ prepared, set, primed, (*more informal*) psyched up

2 *They were more than ready to take us to the station.*
▶ willing, prepared, happy, pleased, eager, keen, agreeable, disposed

3 *Everything was ready to start the game.*
▶ prepared, in place

4 **ready to** *By the time she got home she was ready to collapse.*
▶ about to, close to, likely to, on the point of, on the verge of, on the brink of

5 *He has a ready answer to all criticisms.*
▶ prompt, quick, immediate, telling, perceptive, sharp, astute

**real** ADJECTIVE

1 *Is that real cream?*
▶ genuine, natural, authentic, bona fide, (*German*) echt
OPPOSITES ARE false, artificial

2 *Some viewers treat characters in soaps as if they were real people.*
▶ actual, physical, existing, unimaginary
OPPOSITES ARE imaginary, made-up

3 *'Carl' is not his real name.*
▶ true, actual, proper
AN OPPOSITE IS assumed

4 *She began to feel real remorse for what had happened.*
▶ sincere, genuine, honest, heartfelt
AN OPPOSITE IS insincere

5 (*informal*) *I felt a real idiot.*
▶ complete, utter, absolute, total, (*informal*) right, (*informal*) proper

**realistic** ADJECTIVE

1 *The film was meant to be a realistic portrayal of the events.*
▶ authentic, truthful, true to life, faithful, lifelike, natural, genuine, convincing, recognizable, representational, graphic
OPPOSITES ARE fictional, imaginary

2 *To stand any chance the plan has to be realistic.*
▶ practical, sensible, pragmatic, reasonable, common-sensical
OPPOSITES ARE impractical, idealistic

3 *Wage rises have to be realistic.*
▶ reasonable, moderate, acceptable, adequate, fair, justifiable
OPPOSITES ARE unrealistic, excessive

**reality** NOUN

*He sometimes finds it hard to distinguish reality from fantasy.*
▶ truth, fact, actuality, certainty, the real world
AN OPPOSITE IS fantasy

**realize** VERB

1 *I realized it was going to be difficult.*
▶ understand, grasp, register, comprehend, appreciate, recognize, accept, (*more informal*) twig

2 *They will realize their life's ambition at last.*
▶ achieve, accomplish, fulfil, attain, bring about, bring off, complete

3 *The picture could realize thousands at auction.*
▶ fetch, sell for, be sold for, earn, bring in, produce

**realm** NOUN

1 *the defence of the realm*
▶ kingdom, monarchy, state, empire, principality

2 *the realm of scientific research*
▶ sphere, domain, field, area, activity, department

**rear** NOUN

1 *There is a door at the rear of the house.*
▶ back, back part, other end, other side

2 *We went to the rear of the queue.*
▶ end, tail, back

3 *He gave her a slap on the rear.*
▶ bottom, backside, behind, rump, buttocks, (*more informal*) bum

**rear** ADJECTIVE

*The animal had hurt one of its rear legs.*
▶ back, hind, hindmost, rearmost
AN OPPOSITE IS front

**rear** VERB

*I was born and reared in Liverpool.*
▶ bring up, raise, educate, care for, nurture

**rearrange** VERB

1 *Someone had rearranged the furniture.*
▶ reposition, switch round, swap round, reorganize

2 *We'll have to rearrange our plans for the weekend.*
▶ reorganize, alter, adjust, reschedule, rejig

**reason** NOUN

1 *Money was his main reason for changing jobs.*
▶ cause, ground or grounds, justification, excuse, pretext, case, motive, explanation, apology, argument, incentive, rationale

**2** *arguments based on reason rather than emotion*
▶ reasoning, logic, sense, rationality, intellect, judgement, common sense

**3** *She was terrified of losing her reason.*
▶ sanity, mind, mental faculties, senses, wits, (*more informal*) marbles
RELATED ADJECTIVE rational

## reason VERB

**1** *John reasoned that it was too late to reach home in time now.*
▶ calculate, conclude, come to the conclusion, work out, deduce, judge, consider, infer, resolve

**2** *Her husband tried to reason with her.*
▶ persuade, talk round, bring round, prevail on, debate with, argue with, remonstrate with, discuss with

## reasonable ADJECTIVE

**1** *Any reasonable person would have to agree with you.*
▶ sensible, rational, logical, fair-minded
OPPOSITES ARE unreasonable, irrational

**2** *It was a reasonable explanation.*
▶ logical, convincing, credible, compelling, cogent, plausible, sound, viable
OPPOSITES ARE unreasonable, illogical

**3** *They charge a reasonable fee for this service.*
▶ modest, moderate, acceptable, tolerable
OPPOSITES ARE unreasonable, excessive

## reasoning NOUN

*I couldn't follow his reasoning.*
▶ thinking, logic, train of thought, rationality, rationale, argumentation, arguments, hypothesis, interpretation

## reassure VERB

*Danny tried hard to reassure us.*
▶ comfort, calm, hearten, support, encourage, assure, bolster up, inspirit, give confidence to
OPPOSITES ARE unnerve, disconcert

## reassuring ADJECTIVE

*He gave her a reassuring smile.*
▶ sympathetic, understanding, comforting, encouraging, calming, caring, supportive
AN OPPOSITE IS disconcerting

## rebate NOUN

*He was delighted to get a tax rebate.*
▶ refund, repayment, discount, concession

## rebel NOUN (with the stress on *reb-*)

*The rebels took control of the region.*
▶ revolutionary, insurgent, revolutionist, guerrilla, dissenter, malcontent, mutineer, renegade

## rebel ADJECTIVE (with the stress on *reb-*)

*Rebel forces captured the town.*
▶ insurgent, revolutionary, rebellious, mutinous

## rebel VERB (with the stress on -*bel*)

*The people of the south rebelled.*
▶ revolt, mutiny, riot, rise up, mount a rebellion

## rebellion NOUN

*Troops were sent in to crush the rebellion.*
▶ uprising, revolt, rising, insurrection, insurgency, sedition, mutiny, insubordination, resistance, revolution

## rebellious ADJECTIVE

**1** *rebellious troops*
▶ mutinous, insurgent, rebel, rebelling, mutinying, subversive

**2** *rebellious staff*
▶ defiant, insubordinate, unruly, ungovernable, unmanageable, uncontrollable, recalcitrant, obstreperous

## rebound VERB

**1** *The ball rebounded off the wall.*
▶ bounce, bounce back, ricochet, recoil, boomerang

**2** (*informal*) *His devious tactics rebounded on him.*
▶ backfire, misfire, recoil, boomerang, come back

## rebuff VERB

*The offer was rebuffed again. She rebuffed him many times before finally accepting.*
▶ reject, refuse, turn down, decline, spurn, dismiss, snub
OPPOSITES ARE accept, welcome

## rebuff NOUN

*He carried on despite this rebuff.*
▶ rejection, refusal, snub, repulse, (*more informal*) put-down, (*more informal*) slap in the face
OPPOSITES ARE acceptance, welcome

## rebuild VERB

*It will cost a fortune to rebuild the theatre.*
▶ reconstruct, renovate, restore, reassemble
AN OPPOSITE IS demolish

## rebuke VERB

*She didn't want to rebuke him in front of his friends.*
▶ tell off, reprimand, reprove, reproach, admonish, scold, chide
OPPOSITES ARE praise, commend

## rebuke NOUN

*He did not know how to answer this stinging rebuke.*
▶ reprimand, reproach, admonishment, admonition, scolding, telling-off, censure

## rebut VERB

*They were determined to rebut all these charges.*
▶ deny, counter, repudiate, refute, disprove, dispute, reject, prove false

## recall VERB

*She could not recall what he had said.*
▶ remember, recollect, call to mind, think, cast your mind back to
AN OPPOSITE IS forget

## recede VERB

*The flood waters slowly receded.*
▶ subside, ebb, retreat, regress, go back, abate, shrink back, decline, retire, return, slacken

## receipt NOUN

1 *Make sure you keep the receipt.*
▶ sales slip, proof of purchase, bill, ticket, counterfoil, stub

2 *Receipt of your tickets is guaranteed within three working days.*
▶ delivery, arrival, receiving

**receipts** *receipts from the sale of council houses*
▶ income, proceeds, revenue, earnings, profits, takings, gains

## receive VERB

1 *He received an award for gallantry.*
▶ be given, earn, get, accept, collect, obtain, gain, take, acquire, be sent
OPPOSITES ARE give, present

2 *He received some minor injuries in the accident.*
▶ suffer, sustain, experience, undergo, bear
AN OPPOSITE IS inflict

3 *She received the news in complete silence.*
▶ hear, listen to, respond to, react to, take, greet

## recent ADJECTIVE

*Recent events have caused them to change their minds.*
▶ new, current, fresh, latest, present-day, up-to-date, contemporary, modern, novel
OPPOSITES ARE old, earlier

## receptacle NOUN

*a receptacle for umbrellas*
▶ container, holder, vessel, repository, box, canister, pot, basket

## reception NOUN

1 *We got a friendly reception.*
▶ greeting, welcome

2 *A reception will be held at the local hotel.*
▶ party, function, gathering, celebration, get-together, social event, (more informal) do

## receptive ADJECTIVE

*We must be receptive to new ideas.*
▶ responsive, open, open-minded, susceptible, sympathetic, welcoming, amenable, interested (in), kindly disposed

## recess NOUN

1 *The room has two recesses with fitted bookshelves.*
▶ alcove, bay, niche, nook, hollow, cavity, apse, indentation

2 *The chairman announced a twenty-minute recess.*
▶ break, adjournment, respite, rest, interval, intermission, interlude

## recession NOUN

*an economic recession*
▶ decline, downturn, depression, slump, trough

## recipe NOUN

1 *She would try out her new soufflé recipe.*
▶ method, procedure, directions, instructions

2 *The measures might prove to be a recipe for disaster.*
▶ prescription, formula, procedure, likely cause (of)

## recital NOUN

1 *She gave her first piano recital at the age of eight.*
▶ concert, public performance, programme

2 *a recital of poems*
▶ recitation, rendering, saying aloud, delivery, narration

## recite VERB

1 *She announced that she would recite a poem.*
▶ say aloud, read out, deliver, perform, declaim

2 *It would take too long to recite all the events of the week.*
▶ list, enumerate, detail, recount, relate, repeat, run through, reel off, specify

## reckless ADJECTIVE

*For such a mild man he could be amazingly reckless behind the wheel of a car.*
▶ rash, careless, heedless, mindless, thoughtless, negligent, foolhardy, daredevil

## reckon VERB

1 *They reckoned the cost at about three thousand pounds.*
▶ assess, estimate, calculate, work out, figure out, gauge, evaluate, count, add up, compute, total

2 *(informal) I reckon she's keen on him.*
▶ think, believe, suspect, consider, dare say, have an idea, fancy, guess

3 *These animals are reckoned the most dangerous.*
▶ consider, regard as, deem, judge, count

4 **reckon on** *We didn't reckon on such stiff opposition.*
▶ expect, foresee, plan for, bargain for, figure on

## reckoning NOUN

*By my reckoning we should make a small profit.*
▶ calculation, estimation, estimate, judgement, evaluation

## reclaim VERB

1 *You can reclaim your travelling expenses.*
▶ get back, claim back, recover, (more informal) put in for

2 *an area of land reclaimed from the sea*
▶ recover, restore, save, make usable, regenerate

## recline VERB

*His aunt was reclining on a sofa.*
▶ lie, rest, lie down, lie back, lean back, stretch out, lounge, loll, sprawl

## recognize VERB

1 *I didn't recognize him in his smart suit.*
▶ identify, place, know, remember, recall, call to mind, put a name to

2 *They recognize his abilities without liking his work very much.*
▶ acknowledge, admit, accept, concede, grant, allow, appreciate, confess, realize

3 *The qualification is not recognized in Britain.*
▶ accept, approve, acknowledge, accredit, admit, endorse, support

## recoil VERB

*She recoiled instinctively as he put his hand out.*
▶ flinch, draw back, shy away, jerk back, start, wince, shrink back

**recollect** VERB
*I don't recollect any such promise.*
► remember, recall, call to mind, think, cast your mind back to
AN OPPOSITE IS forget

**recollection** NOUN
*She had no recollection of what happened.*
► memory, remembrance, recall, impression

**recommend** VERB
**1** *His doctor recommended surgery.*
► advise, counsel, propose, advocate, suggest, urge, prescribe
**2** *This book is recommended by teachers.*
► approve of, advocate, endorse, commend, suggest, praise, speak well of, vouch for, (*more informal*) plug

**recommendation** NOUN
**1** *The governors accepted the main recommendation of the committee.*
► advice, counsel, guidance, proposal, suggestion
**2** *She supported him with her personal recommendation.*
► commendation, endorsement, advocacy, testimonial, reference, blessing

**reconcile** VERB
**1** *Their shared grief reconciled them after years of being apart.*
► reunite, bring together, conciliate, harmonize, placate
**2** **reconcile yourself to** *We have reconciled ourselves to a long wait.*
► accept, resign yourself to, learn to live with, get used to, submit to, tolerate

**reconnoitre** VERB
(*informal*) *Helicopters reconnoitred the area ahead of ground troops.*
► survey, patrol, scout, spy out, explore, investigate, scan, examine, gather intelligence about, inspect

**reconsider** VERB
*She refused to reconsider her decision.*
► rethink, review, reassess, reappraise, think over, alter, modify

**reconstruct** VERB
**1** *They will have to reconstruct a large part of the building.*
► rebuild, renovate, restore, reassemble
AN OPPOSITE IS demolish
**2** *Police will reconstruct the incident using actors.*
► recreate, re-enact

**record** NOUN (with the stress on *rec-*)
**1** *You should keep a record of everything they say.*
► account, report, note, log
**2** *records There are more historical records for these years.*
► documents, archives, evidence, accounts, documentation, annals
**3** *She stayed in listening to records.*
► CD, disc, compact disc, album, recording, LP

**4** *There is not a single mistake to tarnish his record.*
► background, career, CV
**5** *The new time was a world record.*
► best performance, fastest time

**record** VERB (with the stress on *-cord*)
**1** *He recorded everything he heard in a notebook.*
► note, register, enter, put down, set down, write down, transcribe, log, minute
**2** *They wanted to record the song and send it in.*
► tape, tape-record, make a recording of, video, preserve, keep

**recount** VERB
*Her brother recounted all his adventures.*
► tell, describe, relate, report, retail, detail, depict, narrate, recite

**recover** VERB
**1** *She was recovering from a mild stroke.*
► recuperate, convalesce, get better, improve, heal, mend, rally, revive, pull round or through, (*more informal*) be on the mend
**2** *Police say they have recovered some of the stolen property.*
► trace, find, get back, track down, retrieve, reclaim, recoup, repossess, salvage

**recovery** NOUN
**1** *Her recovery is proving slow.*
► recuperation, convalescence, return to health, improvement, healing, cure
**2** *The economy is showing signs of recovery.*
► improvement, revival, upturn, picking up
**3** *A reward will be paid on recovery of the stolen paintings.*
► retrieval, repossession, restoration, recapture, reclamation, salvaging

**recreation** NOUN
*a study of the use of the countryside for recreation*
► relaxation, amusement, diversion, enjoyment, pleasure, leisure, entertainment, fun, play, games, pastime

**recrimination** NOUN
*If things go wrong there will be questions and recriminations.*
► accusation, quarrelling, squabbling, bickering

**recruit** NOUN
**1** *The Army is trying to attract more recruits.*
► new member, initiate, conscript
**2** *Many recruits to the industry turn out to be unsuitable.*
► new entrant, trainee, apprentice, novice, new member, newcomer

**recruit** VERB
**1** *The services recruit a high proportion of graduates.*
► enlist, enrol, draft, conscript
**2** *The Company provides training for the staff it has recruited.*
► hire, employ, enrol, engage, take on, advertise for
OPPOSITES ARE dismiss, lay off, make redundant

a b c d e f g h i j k l m n o p q r s t u v w x y z

**rectify** VERB
*The engineers put in extra work to rectify the problem.*
► correct, put right, resolve, sort out, deal with, fix, remedy, redress

**recuperate** VERB
*She went to Brighton to recuperate from her illness.*
► recover, get better, get back to normal, regain your health or strength, improve

**recur** VERB
*The problem is certain to recur if we don't do something about it.*
► return, happen again, reappear, come again, be repeated, persist

**recurrent** ADJECTIVE
*recurrent attacks of fever*
► repeated, recurring, continual, persistent, regular, chronic, cyclical, frequent, intermittent, periodic

**recycle** VERB
*The department is advising customers on how to recycle their waste.*
► reuse, reprocess, reclaim, recover, salvage, use again

**red** ADJECTIVE
1 *She wore a red dress.*
► scarlet, vermilion, ruby, crimson, cherry, claret, maroon, flame-coloured
2 *He was red in the face with embarrassment.*
► flushed, blushing, flaming, ruddy, florid, glowing, inflamed, rosy, rubicund
3 *The chemicals in the water made his eyes red.*
► bloodshot, inflamed, swollen, sore

**redden** VERB
*Her face reddened.*
► colour, flush, go red, blush, glow

**redeem** VERB
1 *Freddie had to redeem his oboe from the pawnbroker's.*
► reclaim, retrieve, recover, repossess, buy back
2 **redeem yourself** *He failed the first test but redeemed himself in the second.*
► vindicate, absolve
3 *You can redeem your voucher at any branch of the store.*
► exchange, cash in, exchange for cash, return, trade in

**reduce** VERB
1 *The goal is to reduce carbon emissions by 20 percent.*
► lessen, lower, decrease, bring down, curtail, moderate
OPPOSITES ARE increase, enlarge
2 *The novel has been greatly reduced in the television adaptation.*
► shorten, abridge, condense
AN OPPOSITE IS expand
3 *The father's gambling debts reduced the family to poverty.*
► drive, force, bring to the point of

**reduction** NOUN
1 *a reduction in pollution*
► decrease, drop, fall, lessening, lowering, diminution
AN OPPOSITE IS increase
2 *a series of price reductions*
► cut, discount, (*more informal*) slash
AN OPPOSITE IS increase

**redundant** ADJECTIVE
*There are three redundant churches in the area.*
► unnecessary, unwanted, superfluous, surplus, excessive, too many
AN OPPOSITE IS necessary
**make someone redundant** *They plan to make twenty members of the workforce redundant just before Christmas.*
► lay off, dismiss, sack, discharge

**reel** VERB
1 *A woman reeled towards him clutching a half-eaten burger.*
► stagger, stumble, sway, totter, lurch, swerve
2 **reel from** *When the worst happens you reel from it and the shock is enormous.*
► be shaken by, be shocked by, be stunned by, be staggered by, be aghast at
**reel off** *He reeled off one joke after another.*
► recite, rattle off, fire off, run off

**refer** VERB
1 *His GP referred him to a specialist. The manager referred the matter to head office.*
► pass, send, transfer, direct, entrust, hand on, send on
2 **refer to** *The police officer referred to her notes.*
► consult, look up, turn to, look in, search in
3 **refer to** *The third paragraph of the article refers to new publications.*
► mention, detail, list, touch on, describe, allude to, cite

**referee** NOUN
1 *The referee blew his whistle.*
► umpire, judge, adjudicator, arbitrator, (*more informal*) ref
2 *Your CV must include the names of two referees.*
► supporter, character witness, backer, advocate

**reference** NOUN
1 *The title 'Brave New World' is a reference to a Shakespeare play.*
► allusion, quotation (from), citation (from), example (of), illustration (from), instance (of), mention (of)
2 *His teacher had given him a glowing reference.*
► testimonial, recommendation, endorsement, backing
**with reference to** *She spoke to him with reference to his recent conduct.*
► about, with regard to, in relation to, a propos of, on the subject of ►►

---

**NAMES FOR TYPES OF REFERENCE SOURCES**

**books:** dictionary, thesaurus, encyclopedia, almanac, directory, companion, guidebook; atlas, gazetteer, catalogue; timetable.

**electronic:** database, website, Internet, World Wide Web.

**places of information:** library, archive, museum, gallery; local record office.

---

**refill** VERB
*It was time to refill the tank.*
▶ top up, replenish, refuel, renew

**refine** VERB
**1** *By refining cereals we lose valuable fibre.*
▶ process, purify, clarify, distil, treat
**2** *ways of refining your computing skills*
▶ improve, perfect, sharpen, polish, hone, touch up

**refined** ADJECTIVE
**1** *refined sugar*
▶ purified, pure, processed, clarified, distilled, concentrated
**2** *a refined man*
▶ cultivated, sophisticated, urbane, well-mannered

**refinement** NOUN
**1** *Computer programs usually need refinement to get rid of the bugs.*
▶ improvement, modification, alteration, perfection, fine-tuning, change
**2** *the poise, refinement, and eloquence of his playing*
▶ style, elegance, finesse, polish, sophistication, subtlety, discrimination

**reflect** VERB
**1** *The window reflected their faces staring in.*
▶ mirror, send back, shine back, throw back
**2** *The looks on their faces reflected their feelings.*
▶ show, indicate, reproduce, demonstrate, correspond to, echo, exhibit, match, reveal, bear witness to
**3** **reflect on** *She reflected on the promises she had made to her friends.*
▶ think about, consider, contemplate, meditate on, ponder, brood on, ruminate on, mull over, muse on, reminisce about, (*more informal*) chew over

**reflection** NOUN
**1** *We could see our reflections in the water.*
▶ image, likeness
**2** *The test will provide an accurate reflection of a child's ability.*
▶ indication, demonstration, manifestation, expression, evidence, echo, result
**3** *After some reflection, he decided to accept the offer.*
▶ thought, deliberation, consideration, contemplation, thinking, meditation, rumination, pondering, musing

**reform** VERB
**1** *He realized he would have to reform.*
▶ mend your ways, turn over a new leaf, improve, do better
**2** *Everyone agrees on the need to reform the prison system.*
▶ reorganize, reconstitute, regenerate, purge, remodel, revolutionize

**reform** NOUN
*the need for reform*
▶ improvement, betterment, change, adjustment, reorganization, (*more informal*) shake-up

**refrain** VERB
**refrain from** *Please refrain from shouting comments during the speeches.*
▶ desist from, avoid, do without, forgo, abstain from, eschew, forbear, (*more informal*) quit, (*more informal*) leave off, stop

**refresh** VERB
**1** *A bit of air will refresh us.*
▶ invigorate, cool, freshen, revive, revitalize, restore, enliven, renew
**2** *Revisiting the scene might refresh my memory.*
▶ prompt, jog, stimulate, remind, prod

**refreshing** ADJECTIVE
**1** *a refreshing drink    a refreshing breeze*
▶ invigorating, revitalizing, reviving, enlivening, stimulating, bracing, exhilarating, cool, restorative, thirst-quenching, tingling
**2** *a refreshing change*
▶ welcome, stimulating, different, interesting, fresh, new, original

**refreshment** NOUN
*You can get some refreshment in the interval.*
▶ food and drink, sustenance, snack, (*more informal*) eats, (*more informal*) nibbles

**refuge** NOUN
**1** *The homeless seek refuge in doorways and under bridges.*
▶ shelter, protection, safety, sanctuary, security, cover, hideout, hiding-place, retreat
**2** *The mountains provide a refuge for the freedom fighters.*
▶ sanctuary, shelter, haven, retreat, hideaway, hideout, hiding place, (*more informal*) bolt hole

**refugee** NOUN
*He had come to Britain as a refugee.*
▶ displaced person, asylum seeker, stateless person, exile, fugitive, outcast

**refund** NOUN (with the stress on *re*-)
*Refunds will be given only if you produce a receipt.*
▶ repayment, rebate, reimbursement

**refund** VERB (with the stress on -*fund*)
*We will refund travelling expenses.*
▶ repay, reimburse, pay back, recoup, give back

**refusal** NOUN

**1** (*informal*) *There have been two refusals to the invitation so far.*
▶ rejection, negative reply, non-acceptance, regrets, no
AN OPPOSITE IS acceptance

**2** *Her refusal to see him again caused great distress.*
▶ unwillingness, disinclination, reluctance, aversion

**refuse** VERB (with the stress on -*fuse*)

**1** *He refused several invitations that week.*
▶ turn down, decline, reject, say no to, rebuff, spurn, baulk at, give a negative reply to
AN OPPOSITE IS accept

**2** *The local council refused permission for the building to go ahead.*
▶ withhold, deny, not grant, deprive of
AN OPPOSITE IS grant

**refuse** NOUN (with the stress on *ref*-)

*Flies buzzed round the pile of refuse.*
▶ rubbish, waste, litter, garbage

**refute** VERB

*It is an argument we can refute quite easily.*
▶ disprove, rebut, invalidate, prove wrong, counter, discredit, negate

**regain** VERB

*Government forces regained most of the city.*
▶ recover, get back, win back, repossess, recapture, reclaim, retake, take back

**regal** ADJECTIVE

**1** *A regal feast was spread out in front of them.*
▶ grand, splendid, magnificent, impressive, superb, majestic, kingly, noble, princely, queenly, royal, stately

**2** *the tombs of his regal ancestors*
▶ royal, kingly, sovereign, princely, queenly, noble

**regard** VERB

**1** *She regarded them closely for a while.*
▶ look at, observe, eye, gaze at, stare at, watch, contemplate, scrutinize, view
AN OPPOSITE IS disregard

**2** *We regard these paintings as the best from the 11-14 age group.*
▶ consider, look on, view, judge, rate, deem, reckon, account, esteem, value

**regard** NOUN

**1** *Good planning must have due regard for the costs involved.*
▶ attention, care, concern, consideration, deference, heed, notice, respect, thought

**2** *They have a high regard for your opinions.*
▶ respect, esteem, appreciation (of), approval (of), estimation (of), admiration, affection

**3** *She became nervous of his constant regard.*
▶ gaze, look, stare, scrutiny

**regarding** PREPOSITION

*She got a letter from the bank regarding her overdraft.*
▶ concerning, about, with regard to, with reference to, on the subject of, connected with

**regardless** ADJECTIVE

**1** *The cliff walk was dangerous, but we carried on regardless.*
▶ anyway, anyhow, nonetheless, nevertheless, even so, just the same

**2** *regardless of Dinghy sailing has something to offer everyone, regardless of age or fitness.*
▶ irrespective of, without regard to, disregarding, no matter
OPPOSITES ARE mindful of, taking account of

**regime** NOUN

**1** *members of the former military regime*
▶ government, administration, rule, reign, jurisdiction, command

**2** *It is usually a Monday that slimmers pick for a new health regime.*
▶ programme, plan, system, arrangement, scheme, diet

**region** NOUN

*The family came from the coastal region.*
▶ district, area, territory, neighbourhood, locality, sector, quarter, zone, terrain, land

**in the region of** *It will cost in the region of five million dollars.*
▶ about, approximately, roughly, in the neighbourhood of

**register** NOUN

*The local authority keeps a register of disabled people.*
▶ list, official list, directory, record, index, file

**register** VERB

**1** *We wish to register a protest.   The car is registered in his wife's name.*
▶ record, put on record, file, log, list, enter, submit, report

**2** *You can still register for a place on the course.*
▶ enrol, enlist, put your name down, check in, apply, enter

**3** *Their faces registered relief.*
▶ show, display, express, indicate, exhibit, betray, manifest

**regret** VERB

**1** *You may come to regret your decision.*
▶ be sorry about, repent, rue, deplore

**2** *She said how much she regretted her uncle's death.*
▶ lament, mourn, grieve over, feel sorrow for, be upset about

**regret** NOUN

**1** *Both men expressed regret for their actions.*
▶ remorse, sorrow, shame, contrition, repentance, guilt

**2** *We left our old home with a feeling of regret.*
▶ sadness, sorrow, unhappiness, disappointment

**regretful** ADJECTIVE

*She was regretful about what had happened.*
▶ sorry, remorseful, apologetic, repentant, contrite, penitent, ashamed, sorrowful, disappointed, sad
OPPOSITES ARE unrepentant, happy

**regrettable** ADJECTIVE
*It was a regrettable thing to say but it was too late to change it.*
▶ unfortunate, undesirable, unwelcome, ill-advised, inappropriate, unsuitable, distressing, upsetting, lamentable, shameful
OPPOSITES ARE fortunate, suitable

**regular** ADJECTIVE
**1** *She had a regular route to work each morning.*
▶ routine, habitual, customary, typical, usual, normal, established
**2** *There were regular complaints about the noise.*
▶ frequent, periodic, constant, continual, persistent
OPPOSITES ARE rare, occasional
**3** *a regular procedure for dealing with enquiries*
▶ systematic, methodical, efficient, well organized, established, approved, conventional
AN OPPOSITE IS haphazard

**regulate** VERB
**1** *a body that regulates the railways*
▶ supervise, oversee, monitor, administer, manage, control, *(more informal)* keep an eye on
**2** *The clocks need to be regulated every so often.*
▶ control, manage, adjust, alter, change, moderate

**regulation** NOUN
**1** *A copy of the regulations about working hours is pinned on the notice board.*
▶ rule, ruling, law, order, requirement, procedure, ordnance, statute, decree, edict
**2** *the regulation of traffic in the city centre*
▶ control, management, supervision, direction, monitoring, overseeing, administration

**rehearsal** NOUN
*a rehearsal for the school concert*
▶ practice, trial performance, preparation, exercise, *(more informal)* run-through

**rehearse** VERB
*We need to rehearse the last scene a bit more.*
▶ practise, go over or through, run through, try out, prepare, *(informal)* run over

**reign** VERB
*Victoria reigned for sixty-four years.*
▶ rule, be queen or king, be on the throne, wear the crown, govern, be in power
RELATED ADJECTIVE regnal

**reign** NOUN
*She had a long and successful reign.*
▶ rule, monarchy, sovereignty

**reinforce** VERB
**1** *Two stone supports reinforce the old wall. These events reinforced all our suspicions.*
▶ strengthen, fortify, support, bolster, buttress, underpin, prop up, hold up, stiffen, toughen, back up, give strength to
**2** *Two more legions were sent to reinforce the army on the Rhine.*
▶ strengthen, supplement, increase, augment

**reinforcements** PLURAL NOUN
*The police unit badly needed reinforcements.*
▶ support, back-up, additional help

**reinstate** VERB
*He was reinstated as president the following year.*
▶ restore, re-establish, reinstall, reappoint, take back, recall
AN OPPOSITE IS dismiss

**reject** VERB
**1** *The union rejected the new offer.*
▶ turn down, refuse, decline, say no to, dismiss, veto
AN OPPOSITE IS accept
**2** *Although she loved him, in the end she rejected him.*
▶ rebuff, spurn, jilt, repudiate, cast aside, *(more informal)* dump

**rejection** NOUN
**1** *Their leaders urged rejection of the offer.*
▶ refusal, non-acceptance, dismissal, turning down
AN OPPOSITE IS acceptance
**2** *Her rejection of Clive hurt him deeply.*
▶ spurning, repudiation, rebuff, shunning, *(more informal)* dumping

**rejoice** VERB
*Scientists rejoiced at the new discovery.*
▶ celebrate, delight, exult, revel, be happy
OPPOSITES ARE lament, be sad

**rejoicing** NOUN
*It was a time for rejoicing.*
▶ celebration, festivity, jubilation, euphoria, gladness, happiness
AN OPPOSITE IS mourning

**relapse** NOUN
*The nurses watched her closely in case she suffered a relapse.*
▶ worsening, deterioration, setback, regression, turn for the worse, complications, recurrence

**relapse** VERB
**1** *A few patients relapse in spite of the treatment.*
▶ get worse, become ill again, deteriorate, regress, fall back, have a relapse, slip back, weaken, degenerate
**2** *No one could think of anything to say, and the meeting relapsed into silence.*
▶ sink, lapse, regress

**relate** VERB
**1** *They have many stories to relate about their adventures abroad.*
▶ tell, recount, narrate, report, present, describe, recite
**2** *Police are relating the two crimes.*
▶ link, connect, associate, see a connection between
**3 relate to** *The questions relate to an incident that took place the previous week.*
▶ refer to, concern, have to do with, apply to, bear on, pertain to, involve

**4 relate to** *They wanted a worker who could communicate with the young and relate to them.*
▶ identify with, sympathize with, understand, feel for, have a rapport with

**related** ADJECTIVE
**1** *a set of related ideas*
▶ connected, associated, linked, allied, concomitant, analogous
**2** *It turned out that the two women were related.*
▶ of the same family, kindred, kin

**relations** NOUN
**1** *His relations were coming to visit that weekend.*
▶ relatives, family, (more formal) kinsmen
**2** *He wanted to improve his relations with the eastern bloc.*
▶ dealings, associations, communications, connections

**relationship** NOUN
**1** *the relationship between religion and politics*
▶ connection, relation, link, association, correlation, correspondence, affinity
**2** *Her relationship with her stepmother had deteriorated.*
▶ friendship, rapport, understanding, attachment, closeness

**relative** ADJECTIVE
**1** *Assess the relative importance of each fact.*
▶ comparative, respective, corresponding, respective
**2 relative to** *evidence relative to the incident*
▶ related to, relevant to, pertinent to, connected with, germane to, associated with

**relative** NOUN
*She's a relative of mine.*
▶ relation, member of the same family, (more formal) kinsman or kinswoman

**relax** VERB
**1** *Yoga helps you to relax.*
▶ unwind, unbend, ease up, let up, take it easy
**2** *She relaxed her grip on the handle.*
▶ loosen, slacken, loose, let go, weaken, reduce
**3** *His presence helped to relax her.*
▶ calm, calm down, soothe, pacify

**relaxation** NOUN
*a few hours left for relaxation*
▶ recreation, relaxing, rest, unwinding, enjoyment, loosening up

**relaxed** ADJECTIVE
*a relaxed atmosphere*
▶ informal, casual, easygoing, pleasant, carefree
OPPOSITES ARE tense, formal

**relay** NOUN
*a live television relay*
▶ broadcast, transmission, programme

**relay** VERB
*They did not relay all the information to the passengers.*
▶ pass on, hand on, transmit, communicate, broadcast, send out, spread

**release** VERB
**1** *The guerrillas promised to release one hostage.*
▶ free, liberate, let go
OPPOSITES ARE imprison, detain
**2** *The names of the victims were released when the families had been informed.*
▶ make public, make known, publish, reveal, divulge, disclose, publicize, circulate, communicate
OPPOSITES ARE withhold, keep secret

**release** NOUN
**1** *the release of the prisoners*
▶ freeing, liberation, deliverance, letting go, ransom
**2** *a new release of the software*
▶ issue, version, edition, publication

**relent** VERB
*The woman calmed down and appeared to relent.*
▶ give in, give way, relax, soften, weaken, yield, show pity, become more lenient
OPPOSITES ARE harden, stiffen

**relentless** ADJECTIVE
*The home side faced relentless pressure.*
▶ constant, continuous, unrelenting, remorseless, persistent, unremitting, unflagging, merciless, ruthless
AN OPPOSITE IS intermittent

**relevant** ADJECTIVE
*Take a note of any relevant information.*
▶ pertinent, applicable, significant, apposite, material, suitable
AN OPPOSITE IS irrelevant

**reliable** ADJECTIVE
**1** *The case lacked any reliable evidence.*
▶ dependable, valid, trustworthy, sound, genuine, authentic
AN OPPOSITE IS unreliable
**2** *John was his most reliable friend.*
▶ faithful, trustworthy, dependable, devoted, staunch, constant, true, good

**reliance** NOUN
*She had much reliance on her family's support.*
▶ dependence, confidence (in), faith (in), trust (in)

**relic** NOUN
**1** *The book was a relic of her schooldays.*
▶ survival (from), souvenir, memento, remnant, reminder, token, vestige
**2 relics** *a saint's relics*
▶ remains, sacred objects

**relief** NOUN
**1** *It was a relief to find the village after miles of empty countryside.*
▶ reassurance, consolation, comfort, solace
**2** *The medicine offered some relief from the pain.*
▶ alleviation (of), easing (of), lessening (of), remedy (for), assuagement (of), mitigation (of)
AN OPPOSITE IS intensification
**3** *He needed a little light relief from his work.*
▶ respite, diversion, release, recreation, amusement, entertainment

4 *Aircraft brought relief to the beleaguered inhabitants.*
▶ help, aid, assistance, succour, deliverance

**relieve** VERB
1 *The pills helped to relieve her headache.*
▶ alleviate, ease, lessen, assuage, mitigate, diminish
2 *A video might relieve the boredom of the afternoon.*
▶ reduce, counteract, lighten, dispel
3 *It relieved us to know she was safely home.*
▶ reassure, comfort, console, soothe, please, gladden
4 *The army sent in supplies to relieve the townspeople.*
▶ help, aid, support, assist, sustain
5 *Her spell of duty was nearly over and a colleague would soon relieve her.*
▶ replace, take over from, stand in for

**religion** NOUN
*the country's official religion*
▶ faith, belief, form of worship

**NAMES FOR WORLD RELIGIONS**
Baha'ism, Buddhism, Christianity, Hinduism, Islam, Jainism, Judaism, Shinto, Sikhism, Taoism, Zen, Zoroastrianism.

**religious** ADJECTIVE
1 *religious beliefs religious music*
▶ spiritual, sacred, holy, theological
AN OPPOSITE IS secular
2 *a religious person*
▶ devout, pious, reverent, holy, saintly, God-fearing
AN OPPOSITE IS irreligious
3 *a religious attention to duty*
▶ scrupulous, meticulous, punctilious, zealous, strict, close

**relinquish** VERB
*The dictator relinquished many of his powers.*
▶ give up, surrender, hand over, let go, cede, yield, resign, renounce, repudiate, discard, drop

**relish** NOUN
1 *He ate his meal with relish.*
▶ appetite, delight, enjoyment, enthusiasm, gusto, zest
OPPOSITES ARE disgust, dislike
2 *fish with a spicy relish*
▶ seasoning, condiment, flavouring, dressing, sauce
3 *a spice to add special relish*
▶ piquancy, taste, flavour, tang

**relish** VERB
*He was relishing his moment of triumph.*
▶ enjoy, delight in, revel in, take pleasure in, savour, appreciate, like, love

**reluctant** ADJECTIVE
*I was reluctant to admit where I had been.*
▶ unwilling, disinclined, averse, hesitant (about), resistant, opposed, loath
OPPOSITES ARE willing, ready, eager

**rely** VERB
*We can rely on them to help us.*
▶ depend on, count on, trust, have confidence in, (*more informal*) bank on

**remain** VERB
1 *He remained in hospital for several weeks.*
▶ stay, continue, stop, linger
2 *Even after the revolution the chief of police remained in power.*
▶ continue, survive, persist, prevail, endure
3 *By the end of the evening only a handful of guests remained.*
▶ be left, be present, survive, stay around

**remainder** NOUN
1 *They were excused duties for the remainder of the day.*
▶ rest, residue, balance
2 *Finish what you can and do the remainder tomorrow.*
▶ rest, extra, difference, remnant, residue, what is left

**remaining** ADJECTIVE
1 *She wanted to remove any remaining doubts.*
▶ persisting, surviving, lingering, abiding, continuing, residual
2 *Melt the remaining butter and brush it over the pastry.*
▶ left over, unused, surplus, extra

**remains** NOUN
1 *He ate the remains of his sandwich in one huge mouthful.*
▶ remainder, rest, residue, remnant
2 *The saint's remains are in the crypt.*
▶ body, corpse, ashes, relics

**remark** NOUN
*We had the usual conversational remarks about the weather.*
▶ comment, observation, thought, utterance, reflection, statement, word, opinion

**remark** VERB
1 *He remarked that it was very quiet in the room.*
▶ comment, observe, mention, note, say, state, declare, reflect
2 *We did not remark anything unusual.*
▶ note, mark, notice, observe, heed, see, perceive

**remarkable** ADJECTIVE
1 *They were bubbling with excitement after their remarkable journey.*
▶ extraordinary, amazing, astonishing, memorable, unforgettable, wonderful, marvellous, breathtaking, fantastic, strange, incredible, astounding, startling, staggering, stunning
AN OPPOSITE IS ordinary
2 *It was certainly a remarkable achievement.*
▶ outstanding, striking, impressive, noteworthy, exceptional, memorable, phenomenal, distinguished

**remedy** NOUN
1 *a flu remedy*
▶ cure, treatment, medicine, medication, relief, antidote

a b c d e f g h i j k l m n o p q r s t u v w x y z

**2** *He suggested a day out as a remedy for their boredom.*
▶ answer, solution, cure, relief, corrective, palliative

**remedy** VERB
*The government will pass a bill to remedy the problem.*
▶ put right, correct, rectify, solve, resolve, fix, deal with, sort out, redress, counteract

**remember** VERB
**1** *a lot of facts to remember*
▶ memorize, learn, commit to memory
**2** *Do you remember my cousin Alice? I can't remember where I put my keys.*
▶ recall, recollect, recognize
**3** *Remember that she won't be here for several days yet.*
▶ bear in mind, keep in mind, take into account, not forget
**4** *They sat on the terrace remembering their childhoods.*
▶ reminisce about, recall, recollect, look back on, muse on, be nostalgic about

**remind** VERB
**1** *A note on the fridge reminded me to feed the cat.*
▶ prompt, nudge, hint at, tell
**2** **remind you of** *The music reminded me of my holiday.*
▶ make you think of, take you back to

**reminder** NOUN
**1** *She forgot about him and needed a reminder to phone.*
▶ prompt, nudge, cue, hint, suggestion
**2** *The photo was a reminder of a happy time.*
▶ souvenir, memento

**reminisce** VERB
**reminisce about** *We reminisced about our schooldays.*
▶ recall, remember, hark back to, think back to, review, be nostalgic about

**reminiscences** PLURAL NOUN
*reminiscences of her wartime childhood*
▶ memories, recollections, reflections, remembrances

**reminiscent** ADJECTIVE
**reminiscent of** *a story reminiscent of Dickens*
▶ similar to, comparable with, suggestive of, recalling, evocative of, redolent of

**remnants** PLURAL NOUN
*Remnants of the meal lay on the floor.*
▶ remains, residue, leavings

**remonstrate** VERB
*He had remonstrated furiously with the referee.*
▶ protest (to), complain (to), argue, take issue, expostulate

**remorse** NOUN
*He was filled with remorse for the harm he had done.*
▶ guilt, shame, sorrow, repentance, contrition, penitence, compunction, regret, bad conscience

**remorseful** ADJECTIVE
*You felt remorseful because if you hadn't been so late none of this would have happened.*
▶ sorry, regretful, repentant, contrite, sad, ashamed, self-reproachful

**remorseless** ADJECTIVE
*The remorseless heat was becoming too much for Hugh.*
▶ relentless, unrelenting, persistent, unremitting, constant, continuous, unflagging, merciless, ruthless

**remote** ADJECTIVE
**1** *The works would be sited at a remote place for safety.*
▶ isolated, outlying, secluded, out-of-the-way, distant, faraway, inaccessible, cut-off
AN OPPOSITE IS central
**2** *There was a remote chance the decision would be overruled.*
▶ slight, small, slim, slender, faint, unlikely, doubtful, improbable, negligible
AN OPPOSITE IS strong
**3** *His manner was remote and unfriendly.*
▶ aloof, detached, distant, withdrawn, reserved, stand-offish, uncommunicative
OPPOSITES ARE warm, friendly

**removal** NOUN
**1** *A local company would take care of the removal.*
▶ relocation, transfer, transportation
**2** *The nail took some removal*
▶ extraction, withdrawal, taking out, drawing
**3** *The king insisted on the Prime Minister's removal from office.*
▶ dismissal, expulsion, displacement, elimination, ejection, ousting
OPPOSITES ARE restoration, appointment

**remove** VERB
**1** *It took two hours to remove the tooth.*
▶ pull out, take out, extract, withdraw
**2** *She decided to remove the last sentence from her letter.*
▶ delete, erase, expunge, efface, rub out, strike out
AN OPPOSITE IS restore (to)
**3** *He tidied up the garden and removed some dead branches.*
▶ cut off, pull off, detach, strip off
**4** *Karen went into the bathroom and removed her clothes.*
▶ take off, peel off, slip out of, shed, cast off
AN OPPOSITE IS put on
**5** *The more severe penalties had been removed.*
▶ abolish, get rid of, eliminate, withdraw, do away with, (more informal) axe
OPPOSITES ARE impose, restore

**render** VERB
**1** *The blow rendered him unconscious.*
▶ make, leave, cause to be
**2** *People were eager to render assistance.*
▶ offer, give, provide, tender, furnish, supply
**3** *Scholars rendered the Latin original into modern English.*
▶ translate, transcribe, adapt

## renew VERB

**1** *It was time to renew her interest in the countryside.*
▶ refresh, revive, restore, revitalize, resurrect, awaken

**2** *I'll have to renew my passport next month.*
▶ extend, prolong

**3** *The interior of the building was completely renewed in the eighteenth century.*
▶ renovate, restore, rebuild, modernize, refurbish, revamp, reconstruct, redecorate, make over, recondition, overhaul, transform

## renewal NOUN

**1** *the renewal of their friendship*
▶ revival, resumption, resurgence, resurrection, reawakening, rebirth

**2** *the renewal of the inner cities*
▶ renovation, restoration, regeneration, modernization, reconditioning

**3** *You are allowed one renewal of your passport.*
▶ updating, revalidation, replacement

## renounce VERB

**1** *They refused to renounce violence.*
▶ reject, abandon, repudiate, abjure, forsake, forswear, forsake, spurn, declare your opposition to, discard

**2** *Edward would renounce his claim to the French throne.*
▶ give up, abandon, relinquish, resign, abdicate, surrender

## renovation NOUN

*the renovation of an old building*
▶ improvement, modernization, overhaul, reconditioning, redevelopment, refit, refurbishment, renewal, repair, restoration, transformation, updating

## renovate VERB

*The hotel will be renovated for the Olympics.*
▶ renew, restore, rebuild, modernize, refurbish, revamp, reconstruct, redecorate, make over, recondition, overhaul, transform

## renown NOUN

*Their renown spread far and wide.*
▶ fame, distinction, reputation, celebrity, eminence

## renowned ADJECTIVE

*His father had been a renowned film actor.*
▶ famous, celebrated, distinguished, prominent, acclaimed, esteemed, notable

## rent VERB

**1** *You can rent a car at the airport.*
▶ hire, lease, charter

**2** *They rent out their apartment during the Festival.*
▶ let, lease, sublet

## reorganize VERB

*He helped to reorganize the local youth club.*
▶ restructure, make changes to, change, alter, rearrange, transform, rationalize, (more informal) shake up

## repair VERB

*Public money will be spent to repair the damage.(informal) He longed to get back with Maggie and repair their broken marriage.*
▶ mend, fix, put right, rectify, overhaul, patch up, renew, renovate

## repair NOUN

**1** *The engine is in dire need of repair.*
▶ mending, fixing, overhaul, maintenance, renovation

**2** *The building is in good repair.*
▶ condition, state, shape, fettle

## repay VERB

**1** *The debt has been completely repaid.*
▶ pay off, pay back, settle, expunge, extinguish

**2** *We must repay your train fare.*
▶ refund, reimburse, pay back, recompense, compensate, remunerate, settle

**3** *He was eager to repay their kindness*
▶ return, reciprocate, recompense, requite

## repeal VERB

*Most of the legislation had lapsed or been repealed.*
▶ revoke, rescind, abolish, cancel, quash, set aside, withdraw, retract

## repeat VERB

**1** *Neither of them had any wish to repeat their experience.*
▶ have again, do again, redo, re-experience, reproduce, duplicate

**2** *The tale became more colourful every time someone repeated it.*
▶ say again, restate, reiterate, reproduce, recite, relate

## repeat NOUN

**1** *We are hoping for a repeat of last week's successes.*
▶ repetition, repeating, recurrence, reiteration, rerun, return

**2** *I watched a repeat of the programme.*
▶ replay, rerun, reshowing, rebroadcast, repetition

## repeated ADJECTIVE

*The Russians made repeated attempts to break through the enemy lines.*
▶ frequent, persistent, continual, constant, ceaseless, unremitting, recurrent

## repeatedly ADVERB

*She had repeatedly refused all his proposals of marriage.*
▶ often, frequently, constantly, time after time, again and again, over and over

## repel VERB

**1** *The invaders were repelled at the border.*
▶ drive back, beat back, push back, repulse, ward off, parry, put to flight

**2** *a device for repelling cats*
▶ deter, keep away, scare off
AN OPPOSITE IS attract

**3** *Such selfishness repelled me.*
▶ revolt, disgust, sicken, offend, nauseate
OPPOSITES ARE delight, please

## repellent ADJECTIVE
**1** *Reviewers found the programme repellent.*
▶ revolting, disgusting, sickening, repulsive, offensive, repugnant, nauseating
**2** *The material is repellent to rainwater.*
▶ resistant, impermeable, impervious

## repent VERB
*This miraculous event caused him to repent his past life and become a monk.*
▶ regret, feel remorse for, be sorry for, be ashamed of, lament, rue, atone

## repentance NOUN
*He was given a long sentence because he refused to show repentance for what he had done.*
▶ regret, remorse, sorrow, penitence, contrition

## repentant ADJECTIVE
*He admitted blame and was repentant for his part in the crime.*
▶ sorry, apologetic, regretful, remorseful, ashamed, contrite, penitent
AN OPPOSITE IS unrepentant

## repercussion NOUN
*Changes in the environment are having considerable repercussions for neighbouring regions.*
▶ consequence, implication, effect, result, outcome, backlash

## repetition NOUN
*The authorities do not want to see any repetition of last week's incident.*
▶ repeat, repeating, recurrence, reiteration, rerun, return, reappearance, duplication

## repetitive ADJECTIVE
*To him fixing tiles was repetitive and boring.*
▶ monotonous, tedious, boring, humdrum, mechanical, repetitious, unchanging, unvaried, (more informal) samey
AN OPPOSITE IS varied

## replace VERB
**1** *She replaced the book on the shelf.*
▶ put back, return, reinstate, restore
**2** *He did not need to look far for someone to replace him when he left.*
▶ succeed, follow, take over from, take the place of, supersede, supplant, be a substitute for, come after
**3** *a scheme to replace dying trees*
▶ renew, change, provide a substitute for

## replacement NOUN
*Thomas had lost his mobile and bought a replacement.*
▶ substitute, alternative, successor, surrogate, stand-in

## replenish VERB
*The maid had gone to replenish the jug of milk.*
▶ refill, top up, fill up, recharge

## replica NOUN
*Katie wore a replica of her sister's dress.*
▶ copy, duplicate, imitation, reproduction, likeness, double, clone, facsimile, model, reconstruction

## reply VERB
**1** *She replied that they would just have to wait.*
▶ answer, respond, retort, counter
**2 reply to** *He never replies to letters.*
▶ answer, acknowledge, give a reply to, respond to, react to

## reply NOUN
*My letter called for a reply.*
▶ answer, response, acknowledgement, reaction, rejoinder, retort

## report VERB
**1** *She threatened to report him to the police.*
▶ inform on, make a complaint against
**2** *You must report for duty at 9 o'clock.*
▶ present yourself, arrive, appear, turn up, check in, clock in
**3** *The government has reported an increase in exports.*
▶ announce, proclaim, declare, communicate, notify, relate, recount, note

## report NOUN
**1** *There is a full report of the incident in today's newspaper.*
▶ account, description, review, article, announcement, record, statement, story, (more informal) write-up
**2** *We heard the report of a gun.*
▶ bang, blast, crack, noise, explosion, detonation, pop

## reporter NOUN
*A group of reporters waited outside the house.*
▶ journalist, correspondent, newspaperman or newspaperwoman

## reprehensible ADJECTIVE
*Their conduct was reprehensible.*
▶ deplorable, disgraceful, shameful, despicable, dishonourable, blameworthy, regrettable, culpable, objectionable, remiss, unworthy, bad, wicked

## represent VERB
**1** *The picture represents a winter scene.*
▶ show, depict, describe, portray, illustrate, delineate, draw, paint, picture, exhibit, enact
**2** *Each character in the play represents a particular human quality.*
▶ stand for, embody, symbolize, typify, personify, epitomize, exemplify
**3** *They chose a spokesperson to represent their views.*
▶ speak for, express, present, be an example of

## representation NOUN
*The bust is a representation of a young woman.*
▶ portrayal, depiction, likeness, image, picture, portrait, resemblance, delineation

## representative ADJECTIVE
**1** *a representative sample of British society*
▶ typical, characteristic, average, archetypal, illustrative, normal
AN OPPOSITE IS abnormal
**2** *The Greeks devised forms of representative government.*
▶ democratic, elected, elective, popular, chosen

**representative** NOUN

1 *the queen's representative abroad*
▶ ambassador, delegate, deputy, consul, diplomat, spokesperson, spokesman or spokeswoman, proxy, stand-in

2 *a sales representative*
▶ agent, salesperson, salesman or saleswoman, (informal) rep

**repress** VERB

(informal) *It was hard to repress our feelings.*
▶ control, restrain, suppress, curb, stifle, bottle up, keep down, crush, inhibit, quell
OPPOSITES ARE express, release

**repression** NOUN

1 *an era of political repression*
▶ oppression, subjugation, suppression, domination, despotism, dictatorship, totalitarianism, tyranny, authoritarianism
AN OPPOSITE IS freedom

2 (informal) *the repression of feelings*
▶ suppression, restraint, stifling, bottling up, inhibition, suffocation

**repressive** ADJECTIVE

*a repressive military regime*
▶ authoritarian, autocratic, coercive, cruel, despotic, dictatorial, harsh, illiberal, oppressive, restricting, severe, totalitarian, tyrannical, undemocratic, unenlightened
OPPOSITES ARE liberal, democratic

**reprieve** VERB

*He was sentenced to death but later reprieved.*
▶ pardon, spare, set free, let off, forgive

**reprimand** VERB

*They were reprimanded for their bad behaviour.*
▶ rebuke, admonish, reprove, reproach, upbraid, censure, scold, chide, criticize, reprehend, (more informal) tell off, (more informal) tick off
OPPOSITES ARE praise, commend

**reprimand** NOUN

*The police gave them a formal reprimand.*
▶ telling-off, talking-to, rebuke, admonishment, admonition, reproof, scolding, (more informal) ticking-off

**reprisal** NOUN

*He was afraid of reprisals if he owned up.*
▶ retaliation, retribution, revenge, counter-attack, vengeance

**reproach** VERB

*Mr Smith reproached her for being late.*
▶ reprimand , rebuke, admonish, reprove, upbraid, censure, scold, chide, criticize, reprehend, (more informal) tell off, (more informal) tick off
AN OPPOSITE IS praise

**reproach** NOUN

*a look of reproach*
▶ disapproval, reprimand, scorn, rebuke, admonishment, reproof
AN OPPOSITE IS approval

**reproachful** ADJECTIVE

*She gave him a reproachful frown.*
▶ disapproving, reproving, scornful, accusatory, censorious, critical, withering
AN OPPOSITE IS approving

**reproduce** VERB

1 *The drawings are reproduced in beautiful colour illustrations.*
▶ copy, reprint, duplicate, transcribe, print, simulate, reissue, repeat, photocopy

2 *These animals reproduce in large numbers.*
▶ breed, bear young, produce offspring, multiply, propagate, procreate, spawn, increase

**reproduction** NOUN

1 *methods of reproduction in fish*
▶ breeding, propagation, procreation, multiplying

2 *The portrait is only a reproduction.*
▶ copy, replica, duplicate, facsimile, imitation, fake, forgery, likeness, print
AN OPPOSITE IS original

**reproof** NOUN

*He tutted at her in mild reproof.*
▶ reprimand, rebuke, admonishment, admonition, censure
AN OPPOSITE IS approval

---

**reptile** NOUN

KINDS OF REPTILE INCLUDE

**snakes:** snake, serpent, adder, anaconda, asp, boa constrictor, cobra, grass snake, king cobra, mamba, pit viper, puff adder, python, rattlesnake, sidewinder, viper.

**alligators and lizards:** alligator, basilisk (mythical), blindworm (legless), caiman, chameleon, crocodile, gecko, goanna, gharial, iguana, lizard, monitor lizard, salamander (mythical), skink, slow-worm (legless), tuatara.

**other reptiles:** loggerhead, terrapin, tortoise, turtle.

---

**repudiate** VERB

1 *He repudiated all the charges made against him.*
▶ dispute, rebuff, reject, deny, disagree with, renounce, refute
OPPOSITES ARE accept, acknowledge

2 *She did not want to repudiate their agreement.*
▶ disown, go back on, recant, rescind, retract, reverse, revoke

**repugnant** ADJECTIVE

*Polygamy may seem repugnant to us.*
▶ abhorrent, repulsive, revolting, repellent, offensive, disgusting, loathsome

**repulse** VERB

1 *The rebels attacked and were repulsed.*
▶ drive back, beat back, push back, repel, ward off, parry, put to flight

2 *He showed her affection but was repulsed.*
▶ reject, rebuff, spurn, snub, jilt

**repulsive** ADJECTIVE
*His appearance was repulsive.*
▶ revolting, disgusting, repugnant, repellent, loathsome, obnoxious, hideous
AN OPPOSITE IS attractive

**reputable** ADJECTIVE
*Make sure you get a reputable builder to do the work.*
▶ reliable, dependable, highly regarded, well thought of, tried and trusted, respectable, respected, trustworthy, creditable
AN OPPOSITE IS disreputable

**reputation** NOUN
*His reputation had been damaged by the affair.*
▶ good name, name, standing, stature, character, esteem, honour, repute, image, prestige

**reputed** ADJECTIVE
*They are reputed to be descended from the French nobility.*
▶ thought, believed, rumoured, said, held, considered, supposed, alleged, reckoned

**request** NOUN
*Our request for assistance has been accepted.*
▶ appeal, plea, petition, entreaty, application, call, supplication

**request** VERB
**1** *We requested immediate help.*
▶ ask for, appeal for, call for, seek, plead for, require, solicit
**2** *They requested us to stop.*
▶ ask, call on, require, implore, beseech

**require** VERB
**1** *One of the victims required immediate surgery.*
▶ need, have to have
**2** *The situation required extreme care.*
▶ call for, need, necessitate, involve, entail
**3** *An official required me to show my passport.*
▶ order, instruct, direct, command, oblige, request

**required** ADJECTIVE
*This book is required reading for this age group.*
▶ essential, indispensable, vital, obligatory, necessary, prescribed, requisite, compulsory, mandatory
AN OPPOSITE IS optional

**requirement** NOUN
*One of the requirements for this work is a quiet place to go and do it.*
▶ need, necessity, essential, requisite, prerequisite, stipulation, condition, proviso

**requisite** ADJECTIVE
*She wasn't sure she had the requisite qualifications for the job.*
▶ required, necessary, prescribed, obligatory, indispensable, vital

**requisition** VERB
*The army requisitioned the house for the duration of the war.*
▶ commandeer, appropriate, seize, take possession of, take over, occupy

**rescue** VERB
**1** *In a few hours someone would come and rescue them.*
▶ set free, free, release, save, liberate, deliver, extricate, ransom
**2** *I went back to the house to rescue some of my belongings.*
▶ recover, retrieve, salvage, get back, bring away

**rescue** NOUN
*The news was all about a dramatic sea rescue.*
▶ saving, rescuing, recovery, release, deliverance, liberation

**research** NOUN
*More research is needed into the causes of violent crime.*
▶ investigation, experimentation, testing, exploration, inquiry, analysis, searching, study

**research** VERB
*The disease has been widely researched.*
▶ investigate, study, inquire into, explore, probe, look into

**resemblance** NOUN
*There is a close resemblance between the two accounts.*
▶ similarity, correspondence, conformity, agreement, comparison, equivalence, likeness
OPPOSITES ARE difference, dissimilarity

**resemble** VERB
*The garden resembled a wilderness.*
▶ look like, be like, remind you of, be similar to, mirror
AN OPPOSITE IS differ from

**resent** VERB
*Jack resented his mother's interference.*
▶ begrudge, take exception to, take umbrage at, object to, be annoyed about, be resentful of, dislike

**resentful** ADJECTIVE
*Her parents' constant complaining left her feeling resentful.*
▶ aggrieved, indignant, disgruntled, discontented, offended, bitter, hurt, irritated, antagonistic, sour, jealous, (more informal) put out, (more informal) peeved, (more informal) miffed

**resentment** NOUN
*The appointment of an outsider caused intense resentment among the workforce.*
▶ indignation, discontent, bad feelings, disgruntlement, rancour, antagonism, irritation

**reservation** NOUN
**1** *You will need to make a reservation if you come on a Friday.*
▶ booking, advance booking, prior arrangement
**2** *Some members of the group had reservations about the plan.*
▶ misgiving, doubt, scepticism, unease, scruple, qualification, hesitation, qualm

**reserve** VERB
**1** *Demand will be high so make sure your newsagent reserves you a copy.*
▶ keep, put aside, set aside, hold, retain, earmark

2 (*informal*) *Chuck reserved a room at the local hotel.*
▶ book, secure, arrange for, order

## reserve NOUN
1 *Her reserve of money was running out.*
▶ supply, fund, stock, store, reservoir, hoard, accumulation
2 *a wildlife reserve*
▶ preserve, reservation, sanctuary, park
3 *His reserve prevented him from joining in the fun.*
▶ shyness, reticence, diffidence, timidity, restraint, modesty, aloofness
AN OPPOSITE IS openness

## reserved ADJECTIVE
*As a young man he had been rather reserved.*
▶ shy, reticent, diffident, retiring, unforthcoming, quiet, timid, restrained, distant, aloof
OPPOSITES ARE forthcoming, outgoing

## reside VERB
**reside in** *Most students reside in halls during their first year.*
▶ live in, stay in, have a room in, dwell in, lodge in, settle in, occupy, have as a home, inhabit

## residence NOUN
*They spent the summer in their country residence.*
▶ home, house, dwelling, domicile, abode, address, mansion, quarters, habitation

## resident NOUN
1 *the residents of Boston*
▶ inhabitant, citizen, townsman or townswoman, denizen, native
2 *The hotel's first duty is to ensure the safety of its residents.*
▶ guest, boarder, lodger, client, occupant
AN OPPOSITE IS non-resident

## resident ADJECTIVE
1 *People resident in the EU do not need to complete the form.*
▶ living, residing, dwelling
AN OPPOSITE IS non-resident
2 *The family once had a resident butler.*
▶ live-in, living-in, permanent

## resign VERB
1 *The manager resigned at the end of the season.*
▶ leave, stand down, step down, give in your notice, quit, (*more informal*) call it a day, give up
2 *She resigned all her rights in the matter.*
▶ renounce, relinquish, abandon, surrender, cede, give up, forsake
AN OPPOSITE IS take up
3 **resign yourself to** *We had resigned ourselves to a long wait.*
▶ reconcile yourself to, become resigned to, accept, come to terms with

## resignation NOUN
1 *They faced an uncertain future with resignation.*
▶ patience, forbearance, tolerance, stoicism, endurance, fortitude, sufferance, acceptance, fatalism

2 *There would be many resignations from the right wing of the party.*
▶ departure, notice, standing down, retirement, relinquishment

## resilient ADJECTIVE
1 *Use a resilient material for harder wear.*
▶ flexible, supple, pliable, pliant, durable, tough, elastic, springy
AN OPPOSITE IS inflexible
2 *She was still young and resilient.*
▶ adaptable, buoyant, irrepressible, tough, hardy, strong
OPPOSITES ARE vulnerable, sensitive

## resist VERB
1 *He resisted all our attempts to persuade him.*
▶ oppose, withstand, stand up to, defy, balk at, fend off, confront, fight
OPPOSITES ARE yield to, submit to
2 *a hard varnish that resists wear for years*
▶ withstand, be proof against, combat, weather, endure, keep out
AN OPPOSITE IS be susceptible to
3 *The temptation was so strong he was unable to resist any longer.*
▶ hold out, desist, restrain yourself, forbear
OPPOSITES ARE yield, give in

## resistant ADJECTIVE
1 **resistant to** *a material that is resistant to heat*
▶ impervious to, proof against, repellent to, immune to, unaffected by
AN OPPOSITE IS susceptible
2 **resistant to** *He was always resistant to change.*
▶ opposed to, averse to, hostile to, suspicious of
OPPOSITES ARE receptive to, attracted to

## resolute ADJECTIVE
*The local people put up a resolute resistance.*
▶ determined, purposeful, resolved, firm, steadfast, staunch, tenacious, unflinching, undaunted
OPPOSITES ARE irresolute, half-hearted, feeble

## resolution NOUN
1 *They showed great resolution in the face of danger.*
▶ determination, resolve, spirit, boldness, courage, firmness, fortitude, commitment, perseverance, doggedness, staunchness, steadfastness, tenacity, will power
2 *The committee passed the resolution by a large majority.*
▶ motion, proposal, proposition, declaration, decision, judgement
3 *Let's hope financial aid can be a resolution of the country's difficulties.*
▶ settlement, solution, answer (to)

## resolve VERB
1 *It will take months to resolve the matter completely.*
▶ settle, sort out, work out, solve, put right, straighten out, rectify, deal with
2 *The boys resolved to keep going until dark.*
▶ determine, decide, make up your mind, take a decision

### resolve NOUN

*Opposition to his ideas only strengthened his resolve.*
▶ determination, resolution, firmness of purpose, steadfastness, tenacity
OPPOSITES ARE indecision, hesitancy

### resort NOUN

1 *Going on strike would be a last resort.*
▶ option, choice, alternative, course of action, expedient, recourse, refuge
2 *a seaside resort on the south coast*
▶ holiday town, tourist spot, retreat, spa

### resort VERB

**resort to** *I don't want to have to resort to threats.*
▶ make use of, have recourse to, fall back on, turn to, adopt, utilize, use, sink to, stoop to

### resound VERB

*Thunder resounded in the hills.*
▶ resonate, reverberate, ring, echo, boom, vibrate

### resounding ADJECTIVE

1 *His fist hit the table with a resounding thump.*
▶ loud, echoing, booming, resonant, vibrant, reverberating, clear, ringing
2 *The show had been a resounding success.*
▶ decided, emphatic, decisive, thorough, complete, outstanding, tremendous, great

### resourceful ADJECTIVE

*They were resourceful in using the few materials available.*
▶ imaginative, enterprising, inventive, creative, ingenious, innovative, original, talented, clever
AN OPPOSITE IS unimaginative

### resources PLURAL NOUN

*The business had to survive on limited resources.*
▶ assets, funds, wealth, money, riches, capital, reserves

### respect NOUN

1 *He showed the respect due to such a great writer.*
▶ esteem, regard, honour, deference, homage, admiration, awe, reverence, veneration, consideration
2 *The conclusions were correct in every respect.*
▶ aspect, regard, particular, point, characteristic, detail, facet, feature, way

### respect VERB

1 *We respected them for their honesty.*
▶ admire, esteem, think well of, appreciate, regard, commend
AN OPPOSITE IS despise
2 *She promised to respect her father's wishes.*
▶ comply with, abide by, observe, honour, obey, follow, conform to, adhere to

### respectable ADJECTIVE

1 *He came from a respectable family in New England.*
▶ decent, reputable, honourable, respected, upright, worthy
AN OPPOSITE IS disreputable

2 *She found a job and now earns a respectable income*
▶ decent, reasonable, substantial, considerable, sizeable

### respectful ADJECTIVE

*Two chambermaids were standing at a respectful distance.*
▶ polite, deferential, courteous, dutiful, reverential, gracious, civil
OPPOSITES ARE disrespectful, rude

### respective ADJECTIVE

*We handed the horses back to their respective lads.*
▶ separate, individual, own, various, particular, several

### respite NOUN

*It was good to get a few moments' respite from the noise.*
▶ rest, break, breathing space, pause, (more informal) let-up

### respond VERB

**respond to** *He responded to each question with a shrug.*
▶ answer, react to, reply to, acknowledge, greet, counter

### response NOUN

*The comment brought an angry response.*
▶ answer, reply, retort, reaction, rejoinder, riposte, acknowledgement, counter, (more informal) comeback

### responsible ADJECTIVE

1 *Mr Jones was one of her most responsible tenants.*
▶ trustworthy, reliable, dependable, conscientious, honest, sensible
AN OPPOSITE IS irresponsible
2 *She has a responsible position in a city bank.*
▶ important, powerful, influential, authoritative, executive
3 **responsible for** *He is responsible for the day-to-day running of the computer system.*
▶ in charge of, accountable for, answerable for
4 **responsible for** *Kim was responsible for the damage*
▶ guilty of, culpable of, liable for

### responsive ADJECTIVE

*Educational institutions must become more responsive to the needs of students.*
▶ alert, alive, aware, impressionable, interested, open, perceptive, receptive, sympathetic, warm-hearted, willing
OPPOSITES ARE insensitive, apathetic

### rest NOUN

1 *The rest of the group went to visit a gallery.*
▶ remainder, balance, remains, others
2 *You need a rest, Fran, you look tired.*
▶ break, breathing space, time off, lie-down, nap, snooze, respite, pause, (more informal) breather
3 *alternating periods of rest and exercise*
▶ relaxation, leisure, respite, inactivity, ease, calm, tranquillity

## rest VERB

**1** *She went to rest in her room*
▶ relax, take a rest, lie down, ease up, have a sleep, have a nap, have a snooze
**2** *Her hand rested on his shoulder.*
▶ lie, be laid
**3** *She rested her bike against the wall.*
▶ prop, lean, stand, support, place, put
**4** *The success of the idea rests on the financial support they can bring in.*
▶ depend, rely, hang, hinge

---

### restaurant NOUN

*She wondered if the restaurant had a sushi bar.*
▶ eating place, eating house

**KINDS OF RESTAURANT INCLUDE**

bistro (small), brasserie (French), cafe, cafeteria, canteen (in a school, office, etc.), carvery (serving meat joints), chophouse, coffee shop, crêperie (serving pancakes), diner, drive-in, grill, milk bar, pizzeria (serving pizzas), roadhouse (in the country), rotisserie (serving roast meat), snack bar, steakhouse, sushi bar (Japanese), takeaway, tapas bar (Spanish), taqueria (Mexican), taverna (Greek), tea room, transport cafe, trattoria (Italian), wine bar.

---

## restful ADJECTIVE

*He enjoyed the most restful night he could remember.*
▶ relaxing, soothing, calm, peaceful, placid, tranquil, leisurely, untroubled
OPPOSITES ARE restless, disturbed

## restless ADJECTIVE

**1** *My mother was restless, waiting for the family to return.*
▶ agitated, anxious, edgy, nervous, restive, fidgety, impatient, jittery, jumpy, worried
AN OPPOSITE IS relaxed
**2** *a restless night of tossing and turning*
▶ sleepless, disturbed, troubled, uncomfortable, unsettled, interrupted
AN OPPOSITE IS restful

## restore VERB

**1** *The interim government wished to restore democracy as soon as possible.*
▶ bring back, reinstate, reinstitute, reinstall, give back, put back, replace, return
AN OPPOSITE IS abolish
**2** *We must restore the property to its rightful owners.*
▶ return, give back, hand back, take back, replace
AN OPPOSITE IS retain
**3** *The building has been beautifully restored.*
▶ renovate, repair, rebuild, recondition, reconstruct, refurbish, clean, (more informal) do up, renew
AN OPPOSITE IS neglect
**4** *An operation was needed to restore the girl's sight.*
▶ bring back, re-establish, rehabilitate, reinstate, reintroduce, revive

## restrain VERB

**1** *The dogs were restrained by leads.*
▶ bind, fetter, confine, restrict, tie, shackle

**2** *She found it hard to restrain her laughter.*
▶ control, hold back, suppress, check, curb, prevent
OPPOSITES ARE encourage, stimulate
**3** *He had to restrain himself from jumping up and looking out of the window..*
▶ stop, keep, prevent, hold back
AN OPPOSITE IS force

## restrained ADJECTIVE

*He was unusually restrained and conventional.*
▶ self-controlled, muted, unemotional, undemonstrative, inhibited, quiet, discreet, reserved, reticent, repressed, subdued
AN OPPOSITE IS uninhibited

## restrict VERB

**1** *A busy working life restricted her opportunities to get away.*
▶ limit, constrain, impede, hinder, hamper, restrain, curtail
AN OPPOSITE IS increase
**2** *The prisoners were restricted to their cells*
▶ confine, restrain, enclose, imprison, keep, shut
AN OPPOSITE IS free

## restriction NOUN

**1** *There is a restriction on the number of places available.*
▶ limit, limitation, constraint, control, curb, restraint, check
**2** *a society that imposes restrictions on personal freedom.*
▶ limitation, reduction, diminution, curtailment, cutback

## result NOUN

**1** *The water shortage is a result of the hot weather*
▶ consequence, effect, outcome, sequel, repercussion, upshot, fruit, issue, product, end-product
**2** *the result of a trial*
▶ verdict, decision, judgement
**3** *the result of an exam*
▶ mark, grade, score, assessment, ranking
**4** *the result of a calculation*
▶ answer, solution

## result VERB

**1** *What resulted from your interview?*
▶ arise, come about, culminate, develop, emanate, emerge, ensue, eventuate, follow, happen, issue, occur, proceed, spring, stem, take place, turn out
**2** *result in The accident resulted in serious injuries.*
▶ end in, cause, involve, bring about, lead to, give rise to, achieve, provoke

## resume VERB

*It is essential to resume talks to reach an agreement.*
▶ restart, reopen, recommence, continue, begin again, start again, carry on, proceed with, reconvene

## resumption NOUN

*Failure of the ceasefire led to a resumption of hostilities.*
▶ continuation, renewal, reopening, restarting, recommencement, resurgence

## résumé NOUN
*a brief résumé of the facts*
▶ summary, outline, overview, precis, abstract

## resurgence NOUN
*a resurgence of interest in archaeology*
▶ renewal, revival, recovery, reawakening, re-emergence

## resurrect VERB
*It's just an old idea that someone has resurrected.*
▶ revive, renew, restore, resuscitate, bring back, revitalize

## retain VERB
1 *When he retired he retained his shares in the company.*
▶ keep, hold on to, hang on to, preserve
AN OPPOSITE IS surrender
2 *She retained her composure despite much provocation.*
▶ keep control of, maintain, preserve
AN OPPOSITE IS lose
3 *Some students are good at retaining facts from their reading.*
▶ remember, memorize, keep in mind, learn, recall, recollect
AN OPPOSITE IS forget

## retaliate VERB
*(informal) After the attack the Egyptians were powerless to retaliate.*
▶ fight back, strike back, hit back, respond, reciprocate, take revenge, get even

## retaliation NOUN
*The best safeguard is the power to threaten retaliation.*
▶ reprisal, retribution, revenge, counter-attack, vengeance

## reticent ADJECTIVE
*She remained reticent about the whole episode.*
▶ guarded, reserved, inhibited, unforthcoming, uncommunicative, unresponsive

## retire VERB
1 *She retired two years ago after a long career in teaching.*
▶ stop working, give up work
2 *Jane retired to her room for the evening.*
▶ withdraw, adjourn, retreat, decamp
3 *retire from He intended to retire from Parliament at the next election.*
▶ resign from, withdraw from, give up, leave, quit

## retiring ADJECTIVE
*He has a quiet, retiring nature*
▶ shy, reserved, unassuming, diffident

## retort NOUN
*She intended to make a sharp retort.*
▶ response, answer, reply, riposte, rejoinder, comeback, counter

## retort VERB
*'It's worth a try, surely,' Jenkins retorted.*
▶ reply, answer, respond, counter, react, snap back

## retract VERB
1 *The landing gear is retracted on takeoff.*
▶ pull in, draw in, pull back
2 *She apologized and retracted the accusations.*
▶ withdraw, take back, abandon, rescind, reverse, revoke, recant

## retreat NOUN
1 *Before he could say anything I made a hasty retreat.*
▶ departure, withdrawal, escape, exit, flight
2 *The family had a holiday retreat in the hills.*
▶ refuge, resort, haven, hideaway, hideout, sanctuary, shelter

## retreat VERB
1 *The army retreated in disarray.*
▶ withdraw, retire, draw back, fall back, move back, back away, depart, go away, leave, (more informal) run away, (more informal) turn tail
AN OPPOSITE IS advance
2 *The tide retreated rapidly.*
▶ go out, recede, shrink back, ebb, flow back
AN OPPOSITE IS come in
3 *The management had to retreat over their modernization plan.*
▶ back down, climb down, change your mind, backtrack, do a U-turn, withdraw
AN OPPOSITE IS persevere

## retribution NOUN
*The victims' families demanded retribution.*
▶ revenge, vengeance, justice, recompense, redress, reprisal, punishment, retaliation, compensation
AN OPPOSITE IS forgiveness

## retrieve VERB
1 *She went next door to retrieve her ball.*
▶ get back, fetch back, bring back, recover, regain, rescue, find, reclaim, repossess, track down, salvage, save, trace
2 *It would not be easy to retrieve such an awkward situation.*
▶ put right, set right, rectify, remedy, sort out, straighten out, put to rights

## retrograde ADJECTIVE
*Pulling out of overseas markets is seen as a retrograde step.*
▶ backward, negative, regressive, deteriorating
AN OPPOSITE IS progressive

## retrospect NOUN
*in retrospect In retrospect, they could have made a better job of it.*
▶ with hindsight, looking back, on reflection

## return VERB
1 *They returned to Paris the next day.*
▶ go back, come back, get back, depart (for), set off (for), set out (for)
2 *I'll see you when I return.*
▶ come back, get back, arrive back, come home, get home, reappear

**3** *She had found a stray cat and wanted to return it to its owner.*
► give back, send back, take back, restore, deliver, reunite (with)
**4** *Things will soon return to their normal state*
► go back, be back, revert
**5** *After a while the headaches returned.*
► happen again, recur, reappear
**6** *Neil came to return the money I had lent him.*
► give back, repay, refund, reimburse
**7** *Jenny was eager to return the favour.*
► reciprocate, repay, requite, recompense

**return** NOUN
**1** *Their return was delayed by bad weather.*
► setting off back, departure
**2** *We look forward to your return*
► arrival, homecoming, reappearance
**3** *the country's return to normality after the war*
► reversion, restoration (of), re-establishment (of)
**4** *There is every danger of a return of the problem.*
► recurrence, reappearance, repetition
**5** *We all want a good return on our investments.*
► income, profit, gain, interest
**6** *There was a notice requesting the return of all library books.*
► replacement, bringing back, giving back, restitution

**reveal** VERB
**1** *Kenny revealed the truth at last.*
► admit, confess, impart, divulge, tell, disclose, communicate, expose
OPPOSITES ARE hide, conceal
**2** *The police were unwilling to reveal the man's whereabouts.*
► disclose, divulge, publicize, broadcast, publish, betray
OPPOSITES ARE conceal, keep secret
**3** *He removed the cloth to reveal a beautiful bronze statuette.*
► expose, display, exhibit, show, uncover, unveil
AN OPPOSITE IS cover

**revel** VERB
**1** *When the exams were over we revelled all night.*
► celebrate, have fun, make merry, enjoy yourself, carouse, roister
**2** *revel in She always revelled in the limelight.*
► delight in, enjoy, love, adore, lap up, wallow in, relish, take pleasure in, rejoice in

**revelation** NOUN
*Further revelations appeared in the next day's tabloids.*
► disclosure, exposé, discovery, exposure, bringing to light, announcement, admission, confession, unmasking, news

**revelry** NOUN
*a night of wild revelry*
► celebration or celebrations, festivity, carousing, carousal, partying, enjoyment, conviviality, merrymaking, revelling, revels, roistering, jollity, fun, frolics

**revenge** NOUN
**1** *The family is seeking revenge for Nino's killing.*
► vengeance, retribution, retaliation, reprisal, satisfaction
**2** *They shot Maria's brother out of revenge.*
► vengefulness, vindictiveness, spite, malice, maliciousness, hatred

**revenge** VERB
*He was determined to revenge his brother's ill-treatment.*
► avenge, take revenge for, retaliate for, have satisfaction for, repay, (more informal) get your own back for
**be revenged** *He would be revenged on them before the year was out.*
► take revenge on, have revenge on, retaliate against, get even with

**revenue** NOUN
*The government is looking to increase its revenue from taxes on tobacco.*
► income, proceeds, receipts, return, yield, gain, profits, takings, money

**reverberate** VERB
*His voice reverberated round the room.*
► echo, resound, resonate, re-echo, ring, boom, vibrate

**revere** VERB
*They still revere him as a national hero.*
► respect, honour, esteem, admire, venerate, pay homage to, idolize, exalt, feel reverence for
AN OPPOSITE IS despise

**reverence** NOUN
*a deep reverence for their country's heroic past*
► respect, esteem, veneration, awe, homage, admiration, adoration (of), devotion (to), deference (to)
OPPOSITES ARE disrespect, contempt

**reverent** ADJECTIVE
*A reverent silence fell on the room.*
► respectful, reverential, deferential, awe-struck, awed, solemn, devout, dutiful, pious
OPPOSITES ARE irreverent, disrespectful

**reversal** NOUN
**1** *There would soon be a reversal of their fortunes.*
► turnround, turnaround, change (in), shift
**2** *The two principal actors suggested a reversal of their roles.*
► exchange, swap, interchange, change, transposition, inversion

**reverse** NOUN
*The story turned out to be the reverse of the truth*
► opposite, contrary, converse, inverse, antithesis

**reverse** VERB
**1** *We can reverse the order of events if you like.*
► turn round, swap round, change round, transpose, invert, alter

**2** *He reversed the car into a tree.* *The lorry reversed into the opening.*
► back, go or drive backwards
**3** *The referee refused to reverse his decision.*
► change, rescind, retract, revoke, undo, countermand, negate, overturn, repeal

**review** NOUN
**1** *a review of the year's achievements*
► survey, report, reappraisal, study, analysis, reassessment, look back (at)
**2** *On Saturday the paper has book reviews.*
► criticism, critique, notice, appreciation, (*informal*) write-up
**3** *The research is described in a scientific review.*
► journal, periodical, magazine, publication
**4** *a military review*
► inspection, parade, display, demonstration

**review** VERB
**1** *Let's review the situation and decide what to do.*
► consider, survey, assess, evaluate, appraise, weigh up, go over, study, reconsider, re-examine, scrutinize
**2** *She reviewed the book on a television arts programme.*
► criticize, discuss, assess, evaluate

**revile** VERB
*The people reviled him as a traitor.*
► denounce, condemn, abuse, lambaste, rail against

**revise** VERB
**1** *I am not about to revise my opinion.*
► reconsider, reassess, rethink, change, alter
**2** *She spent the weekend revising for her exam.*
► study, read up, cram, (*more informal*) swot, (*more informal*) bone up
**3** *The text was revised in the second edition.*
► amend, correct, edit, adapt

**revival** NOUN
*a revival of interest in politics*
► resurgence, reawakening, renewal, recovery, restoration, resurrection, upsurge, rebirth, renaissance, return, revitalization
AN OPPOSITE IS decline

**revive** VERB
**1** *The man was unconscious but soon revived.*
► regain consciousness, recover, come round, come to, awake
**2** *Hot drinks soon revived us.*
► reinvigorate, revitalize, resuscitate, refresh, freshen up, renew, restore, bring back to life

**revoke** VERB
*The new regime revoked his passport.*
► cancel, withdraw, rescind, abrogate, invalidate, retract, nullify

**revolt** VERB
**1** *The island revolted against Athenian rule.*
► rebel, rise up, defect, mutiny
**2** *Their cruelty revolted us.*
► disgust, sicken, shock, outrage, offend, repel, nauseate

**revolt** NOUN
*a revolt in the Netherlands*
► rebellion, uprising, revolution, defection, mutiny

**revolting** ADJECTIVE
*There was a revolting mess on the floor.*
► disgusting, repulsive, nauseating, offensive, sickening, loathsome, repugnant, unpleasant

**revolution** NOUN
**1** *A revolution brought the democrats to power again.*
► rebellion, revolt, rising, uprising, coup, coup d'état, mutiny, civil war
**2** *a revolution of the earth*
► rotation, circuit, cycle, orbit, turn
**3** *a revolution in information technology*
► transformation, dramatic change, sea change, shift

**revolutionary** ADJECTIVE
**1** *Revolutionary forces attacked the city.*
► rebel, rebellious, renegade, seditious, subversive, extremist
**2** *a revolutionary idea for traffic control*
► original, innovative, innovatory, radical, novel, new, unconventional, progressive, inventive, advanced, experimental, avant-garde, challenging
AN OPPOSITE IS conservative

**revolutionize** VERB
*a technique that will revolutionize heart surgery*
► transform, change for ever, transfigure, reshape, remould

**revolve** VERB
**1** *The ceiling fan began to revolve.*
► turn, go round, rotate, spin, whirl
**2** *The moon revolves round the earth.*
► circle, orbit, gyrate
**3** *revolve around* *Their lives revolved around their dogs.*
► concentrate on, centre on, focus on or be focused on, be absorbed in, be preoccupied with

**revulsion** NOUN
*a feeling of revulsion against the savagery of these acts*
► disgust, repulsion, abhorrence, repugnance, horror, loathing, nausea, contempt (for)

**reward** NOUN
**1** *a reward for years of loyal service*
► honour, award, remuneration, prize, bonus, return, decoration, medal
**2** *The dog's owners have offered a reward for its safe return.*
► payment, recompense, compensation, inducement, present, bounty
AN OPPOSITE IS punishment

**reward** VERB
**1** *All three soldiers were rewarded for their bravery.*
► decorate, honour, recognize
AN OPPOSITE IS punish
**2** *You will be well rewarded for your work.*
► pay, recompense, remunerate, repay, compensate, give a reward to
AN OPPOSITE IS punish

## rewarding ADJECTIVE

*The trip proved to be a rewarding experience.*
▶ satisfying, worthwhile, pleasing, gratifying, fulfilling, fruitful, valuable
OPPOSITES ARE unrewarding, thankless

## reword VERB

*Do you think you should reword the last sentence?*
▶ rephrase, recast, rewrite, put another way, express differently, revise, redraft, edit

## rhetoric NOUN

1 *a statesman renowned for his rhetoric*
▶ oratory, eloquence, power of speech
2 *Ignore the rhetoric and there are some interesting things in these speeches.*
▶ pomposity, bombast, extravagant language, grandiloquence, verbosity, wordiness, exaggeration, hyperbole

## rhyme NOUN

*She tried to remember the words of the rhyme.*
▶ poem, verse, ditty, ode, song, jingle

## rhythm NOUN

1 *the rhythm of the poem*
▶ metre, measure, accent, flow
2 *the heavy rhythm of the rock music upstairs*
▶ beat, throb, pulse
3 *It was all part of the rhythm of their daily lives.*
▶ pattern, flow, pace, tempo

## rhythmic ADJECTIVE

*the rhythmic beat of the music*
▶ pulsing, rhythmical, metrical, throbbing, steady, regular, lilting
AN OPPOSITE IS irregular

## rich ADJECTIVE

1 *Rich people pay higher rates of tax.*
▶ wealthy, affluent, moneyed, well-off, well-to-do, prosperous, opulent, (*more informal*) flush, (*more informal*) loaded
OPPOSITES ARE poor, impoverished
2 *a room of rich furnishings*
▶ luxurious, sumptuous, opulent, ornate, lavish, costly, fine, gorgeous, elaborate, splendid
3 *acres of rich agricultural land*
▶ fertile, productive, fruitful, lush
OPPOSITES ARE infertile, unproductive
4 *a rich output of music dramas*
▶ plentiful, abundant, copious, prolific, profuse, plenteous, ample, teeming
5 *the rich colours of autumn*
▶ deep, full, strong, intense, vibrant, vivid, warm
AN OPPOSITE IS pale

## riches NOUN

*He spoke dreamily of the riches of America.*
▶ wealth, money, affluence, fortune, treasure, assets, means, property

## rickety ADJECTIVE

*a small wild garden with a rickety greenhouse*
▶ shaky, unsteady, unstable, wobbly, flimsy, decrepit, ramshackle, dilapidated, broken-down

## rid VERB

*The builders should rid the house of asbestos and all dangerous substances.*
▶ clear, free, strip, purge, cleanse

**get rid of** *Scotland had got rid of its usurper.*
▶ dispose of, expel, remove, eject, evict, throw out, dispense with, (*more informal*) dump

## riddle NOUN

*The authorities want to solve the riddle of the man's identity.*
▶ enigma, mystery, puzzle, question, problem, conundrum, (*more informal*) poser

## riddle VERB

1 *The gunman riddled the door with holes.*
▶ puncture, perforate, pepper, pierce
2 *Her body was riddled with arthritis.*
▶ overrun, infest, permeate, pervade, cripple

## ride VERB

1 *I'm learning to ride a horse.*
▶ control, handle, manage, sit on
2 *She rode through the town on a bicycle.*
▶ travel, pedal, drive, steer, progress

## ride NOUN

*The house is a short ride from the city centre.*
▶ journey, trip, drive, run, jaunt, outing, (*more informal*) spin

## ridicule NOUN

*We will be open to ridicule if we get things wrong.*
▶ mockery, derision, scorn, contempt, taunting, jeering, banter, teasing

## ridicule VERB

*I did not ridicule him as the others did.*
▶ mock, make fun of, deride, laugh at, jeer at, sneer at, scoff at, humiliate, taunt

## ridiculous ADJECTIVE

*It was ridiculous to feel so worried.*
▶ absurd, preposterous, ludicrous, senseless, silly, stupid, unreasonable, nonsensical, incredible, irrational, insane, mad

## rife ADJECTIVE

*Terror and torture were rife then.*
▶ widespread, common, prevalent, general, universal, endemic, abundant

## rift NOUN

1 *a rift in the ice*
▶ crack, fault, flaw, fracture, split, break, fissure
2 *a rift between the two leaders*
▶ breach, division, disagreement, difference of opinion, falling-out, estrangement, schism, alienation

## rig NOUN

1 *He was wearing the rig of an army captain.*
▶ uniform, dress, outfit, livery
2 *She was busy setting up the recording rig for the afternoon.*
▶ equipment, apparatus, machinery, gear, system, kit, tackle

a b c d e f g h i j k l m n o p q **r** s t u v w x y z

## rig VERB

*They were accused of rigging the election.*
▶ manipulate, falsify, tamper with, interfere with, gerrymander, influence

## right ADJECTIVE

**1** *What is the right thing to do? Are you sure he's the right person for the job?*
▶ proper, appropriate, suitable, fitting, ideal
OPPOSITES ARE wrong, unsuitable

**2** *She gave the right answer.*
▶ correct, accurate, exact, precise, true, actual, real, apposite, appropriate, apt, factual, genuine, proper
OPPOSITES ARE wrong, incorrect

**3** *It's not right for them to be treated in this way.*
▶ fair, just, equitable, lawful, ethical, honourable, moral
AN OPPOSITE IS unjust

## right NOUN

**1** *Everyone should have the right to say what they believe.*
▶ entitlement, prerogative, freedom, liberty, privilege (of saying), facility

**2** *We believe we have right on our side.*
▶ justice, virtue, fairness, goodness, legality, integrity, morality, honesty

## right VERB

*We will do our best to right the situation.*
▶ remedy, rectify, put right, set right, redress, repair, resolve, correct, sort out, make amends for

## rightful ADJECTIVE

**1** *The car was returned to its rightful owner.*
▶ lawful, legal, legitimate, genuine, approved, authorized, proper, real, true, valid
AN OPPOSITE IS wrongful

**2** *He felt he had been denied his rightful place in the company.*
▶ deserved, due, merited, earned, proper, fitting, just, right

## rigid ADJECTIVE

**1** *It's best to keep your lunch in a rigid container.*
▶ stiff, hard, firm, inflexible

**2** *He had not yet established a rigid routine for his work.*
▶ fixed, set, firm, definite, unvarying, hard-and-fast

**3** *She had a reputation as a rigid disciplinarian.*
▶ strict, stern, severe, harsh, uncompromising, unyielding
AN OPPOSITE IS flexible

## rigorous ADJECTIVE

*a rigorous attention to detail*
▶ meticulous, thorough, careful, scrupulous, painstaking, conscientious, diligent, fastidious, stringent
OPPOSITES ARE lax, careless

## rile VERB

*(informal) His companions seemed determined to rile him.*
▶ irritate, annoy, anger, enrage, exasperate, incense, upset, peeve, vex, (more informal) needle, (more informal) bug, (more informal) rub up the wrong way

## rim NOUN

*They stared over the rim of the crater.*
▶ brim, edge, lip, border, brink, verge, circumference

## rind NOUN

*the rind of a lemon*
▶ peel, skin, husk, crust, outer layer

## ring NOUN

**1** *A ring of fire would protect her.*
▶ circle, loop, round, circuit, halo

**2** *a spy ring*
▶ network, organization, syndicate, association, gang, group, cell, cartel

**3** *a ring of spectators*
▶ circle, band, group, crowd, throng

**4** *a circus ring*
▶ arena, enclosure
RELATED ADJECTIVE annular

## ring VERB

**1** *Riot police ringed the area.*
▶ surround, circle, encircle, confine, enclose, encompass, form a ring round

**2** *Church bells rang all morning.*
▶ peal, chime, toll, clang, resound, jangle, reverberate

**3** *I'll ring you tomorrow evening.*
▶ phone, call, telephone, ring up, (informal) give a buzz

## rinse VERB

*Campers were rinsing their plates in the stream.*
▶ wash, wash out, swill, bathe, clean, sluice

## riot NOUN

*The authorities were reluctant to make arrests for fear of sparking a riot.*
▶ uproar, insurrection, uprising, rising, tumult, commotion, brawl, street fight, fracas

## riot VERB

*The crowd rioted and pulled down the gates.*
▶ rampage, run riot, create a riot, run amok, go berserk, revolt, rise up, mutiny, rebel

## riotous ADJECTIVE

*a riotous party*
▶ wild, lively, boisterous, roisterous, loud, noisy, uproarious, rollicking
OPPOSITES ARE orderly, restrained

## rip VERB

*She read the note and ripped it into little pieces. The travellers ripped a way through the foliage.*
▶ tear, slash, cut, rend, gash
**rip off** *(informal) The shop had ripped them off.*
▶ overcharge, swindle, cheat, defraud, (informal) rob

## ripe ADJECTIVE

**1** *a ripe melon*
▶ mature, ripened, tender, juicy
OPPOSITES ARE unripe, green

**2** *an area ripe for development*
▶ ready, suitable, fit
AN OPPOSITE IS unsuitable

## ripen VERB
*The apples need time to ripen.*
▶ become ripe, mature, develop, mellow

## rip-off NOUN
*(informal) At that price it was a rip-off*
▶ fraud, cheat, overcharge

## rise VERB
**1** *The little plane rose into the air.*
▶ ascend, go up, fly up, climb
OPPOSITES ARE fall, descend

**2** *The castle walls rose above us.*
▶ tower, soar, loom, reach up

**3** *Incomes have risen by an average 3 percent.*
▶ increase, grow, go up, get higher, escalate
OPPOSITES ARE fall, decrease

**4** *She rose from her chair.*
▶ stand up, get up, jump up, leap up

## rise NOUN
**1** *We walked up the rise to the castle.*
▶ slope, incline, elevation, ascent, hill, ramp, bank

**2** *another rise in interest rates*
▶ increase, jump, leap, upturn
OPPOSITES ARE fall, drop, decrease

## risk NOUN
**1** *She faced the risk of being stopped by the police.*
▶ chance, likelihood, possibility, danger

**2** *Travelling at such a high speed involved risk.*
▶ hazard, peril, danger, speculation, uncertainty, gamble

## risk VERB
**1** *He didn't want to risk leaving her alone.*
▶ chance, dare, venture

**2** *She risked everything to meet him again.*
▶ endanger, jeopardize, put at risk, put at peril, chance, imperil, hazard

## risky ADJECTIVE
**1** *Any project involving rockets is always risky.*
▶ dangerous, hazardous, unsafe, perilous, (more informal) dodgy
AN OPPOSITE IS safe

**2** *Farming is a risky business.*
▶ uncertain, chancy, precarious, touch-and-go
AN OPPOSITE IS secure

## ritual NOUN
**1** *a religious ritual*
▶ ceremony, rite, ceremonial, observance, service, liturgy

**2** *The Sunday outing had become something of a ritual.*
▶ custom, tradition, habit, formality

## rival NOUN
*Leo was his main rival for the job.*
▶ competitor, adversary, challenger, opponent, contender, contestant

## rival ADJECTIVE
*A rival supermarket has opened.*
▶ competing, competitive, opposing

## rival VERB
*Few countries rival Greece for its beauty.*
▶ compete with, contend with, compare with, equal, match, be as good as, emulate, vie with

## rivalry NOUN
*There was growing rivalry between the two teams.*
▶ competitiveness, competition, contention, opposition, conflict, antagonism
AN OPPOSITE IS cooperation

## river NOUN
*a trip down the river*
▶ stream, waterway, watercourse, brook, rivulet, creek

---

## road NOUN
*a busy road*
▶ roadway, route, way, highway, motorway, street, avenue, boulevard

KINDS OF ROADS AND PATHWAYS

**main roads**: thoroughfare, trunk road (or arterial road, linking towns and cities), motorway (or (*American*) freeway), clearway (no stopping), dual carriageway (or (*American*) highway), bypass (avoiding a town or city), ring road (round a town or city), slip road (leading to and from a main road).

**roads in towns and cities**: street, avenue (or boulevard, broad with trees) drive, driveway, crescent, cul-de-sac (closed at one end), one-way street, service road (giving access to houses), side road, side street.

**minor and country roads**: byroad, byway, lane, track, trail, cart track, causeway (across wet ground), bridleway (or bridle path, for horse riding)

**paths for walking**: alley, path, pathway, footpath, pavement (or (*American*) sidewalk), beside a road), esplanade (broad open space for walking), walk, walkway, towpath (beside a river or canal, originally for pulling barges).

---

## roadworthy ADJECTIVE
*a roadworthy vehicle*
▶ safe, usable

## roam VERB
*People like to roam over the hills.*
▶ wander, rove, ramble, stroll, amble, walk, meander, travel, stray, range

## roar VERB
**1** *Bill roared at them to stop.*
▶ shout, bellow, yell, clamour, shriek

**2** *A motorbike roared past.*
▶ speed, zoom, whizz, flash

**3** *He had the audience roaring.*
▶ guffaw, howl, hoot, (*more informal*) split your sides, (*more informal*) kill yourself laughing

**roar** NOUN

*the roars of the crowd*
► shout, yell, clamour, bellow, howl

**rob** VERB

**1** *The gang had robbed banks all over the south-east.*
► burgle, hold up, steal from, break into, raid, loot, rifle

**2** *She was attacked and robbed on her way home that evening.*
► mug, steal from, hold up

**3** *They thought they had been robbed of their victory.*
► cheat, deprive, defraud, swindle

**robber** NOUN

*Robbers attacked the travellers on the road north.*
► thief, brigand, bandit, raider, highwayman, marauders

**USAGE** You can also use *burglar* and *housebreaker* for robbers who steal from buildings, and *mugger* for robbers who attack people in the street.

**robbery** NOUN

*a wave of robberies and other crimes*
► burglary, theft, thieving, housebreaking, shoplifting, pilfering, hold-up, mugging, *(more informal)* stick-up

**robot** NOUN

*In a future world robots do much of the work.*
► automaton, computerized machine, automated machine, android

**robust** ADJECTIVE

**1** *a man with a robust physique*
► strong, vigorous, hardy, muscular, powerful, rugged, athletic, brawny, healthy, sound

**2** *The tools will need to be very robust*
► sturdy, durable, strong, tough, serviceable
AN OPPOSITE IS fragile

**rock** NOUN

**1** *a castle high up on a rock*
► cliff, crag, outcrop

**2** *Rocks were strewn across the road*
► boulder, stone

**WORDS FOR TYPES OF ROCK**

**igneous rocks:** andesite, basalt, diorite, granite, kimberlite, obsidian, peridotite, rhyolite.

**sedimentary rocks:** chalk, chert, clay, conglomerate, dolomite, limestone, sandstone.

**metamorphic rocks:** gneiss, hornfels, marble, quartzite, schist, slate.

**minerals:** argentite, barite, beryl, cassiterite, cinnabar, diamond, galena, gold, gypsum, magnetite, mica, topaz, tourmaline.

**rock** VERB

**1** *The woman rocked gently in her chair.*
► sway, swing, move gently

**2** *The ship rocked in the storm*
► toss, lurch, sway, pitch, plunge, roll

**3** *News of the disaster rocked the nation.*
► stun, shake, stagger, astound, astonish, startle, dumbfound

**rocket** VERB

*Prices have rocketed under this government.*
► shoot up, soar, escalate, spiral, increase rapidly, *(more informal)* go through the roof

**rocky** ADJECTIVE

**1** *a rocky hillside*
► stony, rock-strewn, craggy, shingly, pebbly, rugged

**2** *The table is rocky.*
► unsteady, shaky, wobbly, rickety, tottery

**3** *The marriage had become decidedly rocky.*
► difficult, precarious, problematic, unstable

**rod** NOUN

**1** *an iron rod*
► bar, pole, baton, staff, shaft, sceptre

**2** *He was beaten with a rod.*
► cane, switch

**rodent** NOUN

**SOME NAMES OF RODENTS**

agouti, beaver, capybara (largest), cavy, chinchilla, coypu, degu, dormouse, field mouse, gerbil, gopher, guinea pig, hamster, harvest mouse, jerboa, lemming, marmot, mouse, muskrat, paca, porcupine, rat, squirrel, vole, water rat.

**rogue** NOUN

*In the story, everyone is either a fool or a rogue.*
► villain, scoundrel, rascal, good-for-nothing, reprobate, crook

**role** NOUN

**1** *The director took a small role in the film.*
► part, character, portrayal

**2** *He spoke in his role of government adviser.*
► capacity, function, position, office, post, job

**roll** NOUN

**1** *a roll of film*
► reel, spool, cylinder, drum, scroll

**2** *an electoral roll*
► register, list, record, index, catalogue, schedule, inventory

**roll** VERB

**1** *The can rolled into the gutter The huge wheels began to roll.*
► spin, rotate, revolve, turn, whirl, gyrate

**2** *She rolled the paper into a ball.*
► wind, fold, coil, twist, curl, screw

**3** *The ship began to roll.*
► rock, sway, lurch, pitch, toss, reel

**4** *He was in the kitchen, rolling pastry.*
► smooth, flatten, level, even out

**5** *Thunder rolled in the distance.*
► rumble, boom, resound, reverberate, thunder

**roll up** *(informal)* He rolled up with some friends just as we were leaving.

► arrive, appear, come, show your face, (informal) turn up, (informal) show up

## romance NOUN

1 *a historical romance*
► love story, romantic novel, fantasy

2 *the romance of travel*
► glamour, excitement, adventure, fascination, mystique

3 *Romance was in the air.*
► love, passion, ardour

4 *They were having a wild romance.*
► love affair, relationship, attachment

## romantic ADJECTIVE

1 *He was handsome and romantic.*
► amorous, passionate, loving, tender-hearted, affectionate

2 *romantic stories set in the Far East*
► imaginary, fanciful, sentimental, (more informal) soppy

3 *a pretty village in a romantic landscape*
► idyllic, picturesque, fairy-tale

4 *Their notions about life were highly romantic.*
► idealistic, idealized, starry-eyed, unrealistic, visionary, utopian, fanciful, dreamy

## romp VERB

*The children romped in the garden.*
► leap about, cavort, caper, run about, skip about, bound about, frisk, frolic, gambol

---

## room NOUN

1 *There wasn't enough room for a bed.*
► space, capacity, volume

2 *(informal) We need more room to live our own lives.*
► freedom, latitude, leeway, allowance, elbow room

3 *There's always room for improvement.*
► scope, capacity, margin, opportunity

**THE MAIN KINDS OF ROOM ARE**

**rooms in a house or flat**: hall, cloakroom, living room (or drawing room or sitting room or lounge), front room, dining room, study, den, studio (large living room in a flat), breakfast room, conservatory; kitchen, pantry, scullery, utility room; landing, bedroom, boudoir, dressing room, guest room (or spare room), nursery, boxroom, lumber room, playroom (or rumpus room), bathroom, lavatory (or toilet or (informal) loo); attic, loft; basement, cellar.

**rooms in a school**: foyer, lobby, hall, assembly room, cloakroom, office, common room, classroom, library, laboratory (or (informal) lab), workshop, music room, gymnasium (or gym), locker room, changing room, lavatories (or toilets), boiler room, storeroom; sickroom, dormitory (in a boarding school).

**rooms in an office**: foyer, lobby, office, working area (open plan), meeting room, boardroom, lavatories (or toilets), boiler room.

---

## roomy ADJECTIVE

*The apartment was bright and roomy.*
► spacious, capacious, large, sizeable, extensive, commodious, voluminous
OPPOSITES ARE cramped, poky

## root NOUN

1 *The plant had long stringy roots.*
► tuber, rhizome, rootlet, radicle

2 *Money is the root of the problem.*
► source, origin, cause, basis, starting point, seed, germ

## root VERB

**root out** *The magistrates were determined to root out corruption.*
► discover, unearth, dig out, ferret out, remove, eliminate, extirpate

## rope NOUN

*A rope attached the boat to the quayside.*
► cable, cord, line, halyard, hawser, lanyard

## rope VERB

**rope in** *They roped us in to help too.*
► enlist, persuade, talk (into helping), inveigle (into helping), drag

## rot NOUN

1 *The surveyor found traces of rot in the roof timbers.*
► decay, decomposition, mould, mildew, dry rot, wet rot

2 *(informal) You're talking rot*
► nonsense, rubbish, gibberish, drivel, codswallop, claptrap

## rot VERB

*The floorboards had begun to rot.*
► decay, decompose, perish, become rotten, degenerate, deteriorate, crumble, disintegrate

## rota NOUN

*a washing-up rota for the week*
► roster, schedule, list, timetable

## rotary ADJECTIVE

*rotary motion*
► rotating, rotatory, revolving, gyrating, twirling, twisting, spinning, turning, whirling

## rotate VERB

1 *The arms of the windmill were rotating.*
► revolve, turn round, go round, move round, spin, gyrate, twirl, swivel, roll

2 *The role of chairman rotates every year.*
► alternate, take turns, change, switch, swap, move round

## rotation NOUN

1 *the rotation of the earth*
► revolution, turn, orbit, spinning

2 *the rotation of a wheel*
► turning, revolving, spinning, gyration

**rotten** ADJECTIVE

**1** *Some of the wood looked rotten.*
▶ decayed, decaying, decomposed, crumbling, disintegrating

**2** *the stench of rotten meat*
▶ mouldy, mouldering, putrid, decayed, decaying, foul, tainted
AN OPPOSITE IS fresh

**3** *(informal) They had a rotten time.*
▶ unpleasant, disagreeable, terrible, bad
OPPOSITES ARE pleasant, good

**4** *(informal) The builders had done a rotten job. He would make a rotten teacher.*
▶ poor, inferior, inadequate, bad, low-grade, (informal) crummy, (informal) ropy, (informal) lousy
OPPOSITES ARE fine, good

**rough** ADJECTIVE

**1** *She picked her way over the rough ground*
▶ bumpy, rugged, uneven, broken, irregular, rocky, stony, coarse, craggy
AN OPPOSITE IS even

**2** *rough skin*
▶ dry, chapped, coarse, hairy, bristly, shaggy, unshaven
AN OPPOSITE IS smooth

**3** *rough treatment   It was pretty rough on your mother.*
▶ harsh, severe, hard, tough, stern

**4** *a rough sea   the ability to withstand rough weather*
▶ choppy, turbulent, agitated, stormy, tempestuous, violent, wild
AN OPPOSITE IS calm

**5** *a rough voice*
▶ harsh, grating, gruff, rasping, hoarse, husky
AN OPPOSITE IS soft

**6** *She doesn't like rough kids.*
▶ rowdy, boisterous, disorderly, unrestrained
AN OPPOSITE IS polite

**7** *The tower is of rough workmanship.*
▶ amateurish, careless, clumsy, crude, hasty, imperfect, inept, (informal) rough and ready, unfinished, unpolished, unskilful
AN OPPOSITE IS skilful

**8** *This gives you a rough idea of what we mean.*
▶ vague, approximate, imprecise, inexact, estimated, hazy, crude
AN OPPOSITE IS exact

**9** *To begin with I made a rough drawing.*
▶ quick, sketchy, crude, hasty, preliminary, basic, outline

**10** *He went home. He was feeling rough.*
▶ ill, unwell, sick, poorly, out of sorts, queasy, off colour, (more informal) lousy, (more informal) grotty
OPPOSITES ARE well, fit

**roughly** ADVERB

**1** *There were roughly equal numbers of men and women.*
▶ about, around, approximately, nearly, close to

**2** *Geoffrey pulled his arm roughly away.*
▶ violently, forcefully, forcibly, abruptly

**round** ADJECTIVE

**1** *a round window*
▶ spherical, circular, bulbous, curved, cylindrical, globular

**2** *a man with a short round figure*
▶ rounded, plump, chubby, rotund, ample, full, fat

**round** NOUN

**1** *the most exciting tie of the second round*
▶ stage, game, series, sequence, contest

**2** *an endless round of radio and television interviews*
▶ cycle, series, succession, sequence

**round** VERB

*A large van rounded the corner.*
▶ travel round, skirt, turn

**round off** *We rounded the evening off with some drinks.*
▶ end, finish, complete, conclude, cap, top

**round on** *Jo rounded on her. 'You're supposed to be looking after this place.'*
▶ turn on, snap at, attack, weigh into, let fly at

**round up** *His dog, Nell, rounded up 300 sheep.*
▶ herd, drive together, muster, marshal, assemble

**roundabout** ADJECTIVE

*He reached the town square by a roundabout route*
▶ indirect, circuitous, devious, winding, rambling, meandering, tortuous, twisting, long
AN OPPOSITE IS direct

**roundabout** NOUN

**1** *Let's play on the roundabout.*
▶ merry-go-round, carousel

**2** *Turn right at the next roundabout.*
▶ traffic circle, rotary

**rouse** VERB

**1** *Next morning he was roused by the clanging of church bells.*
▶ arouse, awaken, wake up

**2** *His words roused feelings of sympathy in her.*
▶ aroused, provoke, stir up, trigger, spark off, kindle, cause

**3** *He can be violent when he's roused.*
▶ anger, annoy, provoke, incite, inflame, incense, work up

**rousing** ADJECTIVE

*a rousing speech*
▶ stirring, inspiring, moving, stimulating, exciting

**rout** VERB

*They went on to rout the Royalist forces.*
▶ crush, defeat, overwhelm, trounce, thrash, put to flight, drive off, (more informal) hammer

**rout** NOUN

*The defence prevented the game from turning into a rout.*
▶ crushing defeat, trouncing, thrashing, debacle

**route** NOUN

*This route is direct but gets tedious in the later stages.*
▶ way, road, course, direction, path, passage, itinerary, journey

**routine** NOUN

1 *Their evening routine never varied.*
▶ procedure, pattern, way, method, course of action, practice, system, custom, drill, habit
2 *I've been practising a new dance routine.*
▶ act, performance, programme, number, turn

**routine** ADJECTIVE

*It is now a fairly routine operation done under local anaesthetic.*
▶ standard, normal, ordinary, everyday, run-of-the-mill

**row** NOUN (rhymes with *crow*)

*a row of small plants*
▶ line, string, chain, series, sequence, cordon, file

**row** NOUN (rhymes with *cow*)

1 *She and Paul had had a row.*
▶ quarrel, argument, squabble, fight, scrap, altercation, disagreement, dispute, (*more informal*) slanging match
AN OPPOSITE IS reconciliation
2 (*informal*) *The crowd was making a dreadful row.*
▶ noise, racket, rumpus, tumult, din, disturbance, uproar, commotion

**row** VERB (rhymes with *cow*)

*They had been shouting and rowing all evening.*
▶ quarrel, argue, wrangle, bicker, squabble, fight, scrap

**rowdy** ADJECTIVE

*a bunch of rowdy men*
▶ unruly, disorderly, riotous, noisy, badly behaved, rough, wild, disruptive, boisterous
OPPOSITES ARE quiet, peaceful

**royal** ADJECTIVE

1 *the royal family*
▶ regal, imperial, kingly, princely, queenly, majestic, stately
2 *We received a royal welcome*
▶ magnificent, splendid, excellent, fine

**rub** VERB

1 *John rubbed the back of his leg.*
▶ stroke, knead, massage, caress, smooth
2 *She rubbed lotion on the children's backs.*
▶ apply (to), smear, smooth, spread, put on
3 *His new shoes were rubbing dreadfully.*
▶ pinch, chafe, abrade, graze, scrape, hurt
4 *Stella rubbed the table with polish.*
▶ polish, buff, shine, wipe

**rub out** *Someone had rubbed out his name.*
▶ remove, erase, delete, efface, expunge, blot out

**rubbish** NOUN

1 *Household rubbish is collected on Wednesdays.*
▶ refuse, waste, garbage, debris, junk, leavings, litter, trash
2 *They are talking rubbish.*
▶ nonsense, balderdash, gibberish, claptrap, drivel, gobbledegook, (*more informal*) rot, (*more informal*) twaddle

**rubble** NOUN

*Often he had to clear away piles of rubble before he could continue.*
▶ debris, ruins, remains, wreckage, fragments

**ruddy** ADJECTIVE

*a cheerful pipe-smoking man with a ruddy complexion*
▶ reddish, rubicund, flushed, glowing, healthy

**rude** NOUN

1 *He was sometimes rude, but always honest.*
▶ impolite, discourteous, disrespectful, impertinent, impudent, insolent, ill-mannered, ill-bred, uncivil, offensive, abusive
OPPOSITES ARE polite, civil
2 *a rude joke*
▶ vulgar, coarse, dirty, smutty, filthy
AN OPPOSITE IS clean

**rudeness** NOUN

*'You,' she called, with uncharacteristic rudeness.*
▶ impoliteness, bad manners, discourtesy, disrespect, incivility, impertinence, impudence, insolence, churlishness, cheek

**rudimentary** ADJECTIVE

1 *You'll need a rudimentary knowledge of first aid.*
▶ simple, basic, elementary, primitive, fundamental, crude
AN OPPOSITE IS advanced
2 *The pelycosaurs tended to develop rudimentary teeth.*
▶ incomplete, embryonic, vestigial, primitive
3 *a rudimentary language course*
▶ introductory, basic, elementary, preliminary, initial

**ruffian** NOUN

*A group of ruffians assaulted a university student on his way home.*
▶ thug, hoodlum, hooligan, lout, rogue, scoundrel, brute, bully, villain, mugger, (*more informal*) tough, (*more informal*) yob

**ruffle** VERB

1 *A light wind ruffled the leaves of the trees.*
▶ stir, agitate, ripple, disturb
2 *Isobel took off her scarf and ruffled her hair.*
▶ rumple, tousle, run your fingers through, dishevel, mess up
AN OPPOSITE IS smooth
3 *Don't let their stupid remarks ruffle you.*
▶ annoy, upset, unsettle, disconcert, fluster, irritate, vex, worry, (*more informal*) nettle, (*more informal*) rattle
AN OPPOSITE IS calm

**rug** NOUN

**1** *The children sat on a rug on the floor.*
▶ mat, runner, matting

**2** *She was wrapped in a rug to keep out the cold.*
▶ blanket, coverlet, throw

**rugged** ADJECTIVE

**1** *a Spanish village nestling in rugged hills*
▶ rough, uneven, rocky, craggy, stark, bumpy, jagged, irregular
OPPOSITES ARE smooth, gentle

**2** *The only softness about his rugged face was in his lips.*
▶ strong, sturdy, rough, tough, robust, hardy, burly, husky, muscular, weather-beaten

**ruin** NOUN

**1** *They now face financial ruin.*
▶ bankruptcy, insolvency, failure, breakdown, collapse, downfall, ruination, undoing

**2** *It was the ruin of all their hopes.*
▶ destruction, disintegration, devastation, overthrow, failure, undoing, ruination

**3** *Crackpot Hall is a sad ruin in a beautiful location.*
▶ remnant, shell, group of remains

**4** **ruins** *Villagers had discovered three unidentifiable bodies among the ruins of the house.*
▶ remains, rubble, debris, wreckage

**ruin** VERB

**1** *Once again the rain has ruined what promised to be a good contest.*
▶ spoil, wreck, destroy, shatter, blight, wreak havoc on, torpedo, (*more informal*) mess up
OPPOSITES ARE save, rescue

**2** *He would be ruined if he had to pay.*
▶ bankrupt, impoverish, financially cripple

**ruined** ADJECTIVE

*the gateway to a ruined fortress*
▶ derelict, dilapidated, ramshackle, tumbledown, crumbling

**ruinous** ADJECTIVE

**1** *activity that has a ruinous effect on the environment*
▶ disastrous, catastrophic, devastating, calamitous, destructive, cataclysmic, dire, fatal

**2** *They found the building in a ruinous condition*
▶ ruined, dilapidated, derelict

**rule** NOUN

**1** *the rules governing procedures in case of fire*
▶ regulation, law, code, convention, precept, principle, routine, practice, custom

**2** *British rule had ended in 1947.*
▶ control, jurisdiction, administration, sovereignty, mastery, command, domination, dominion, authority, government, supremacy, sway

**3** *The normal rule is to apply for tickets by letter.*
▶ procedure, practice, protocol, form, custom, convention

**rule** VERB

**1** *How could a city-state like Rome rule an empire?*
▶ govern, administer, manage, run, control, direct, command, dominate, lead, reign over

**2** *The king's successor ruled for less than a year.*
▶ reign, be ruler, be in power, be monarch

**3** *The judge ruled that the defendant should be awarded the costs of the case.*
▶ decree, order, direct, pronounce, resolve, decide, determine, adjudicate, find, judge

**rule out** *We cannot rule out suicide as a cause of death.*
▶ exclude, discount, reject, eliminate, dismiss, preclude, disregard

---

**ruler** NOUN

*a much-respected ruler*
▶ leader, sovereign, overlord, governor, dynast, monarch, president (of a republic), head of state

NAMES FOR TYPES OF RULER

**general words in addition to the ones above:** emperor, empress, king, queen, prince, princess, lord, regent (ruling on behalf of someone unable to rule, e.g. a minor), viceroy (representing a monarch in a colony), dictator, tyrant.

**historical and regional rulers:** aga (Turkish), caesar (Roman), caliph (Muslim), emir (Muslim), Führer (German, title of Hitler), kaiser (German or Austrian), khan (Muslim), Khedive (Turkish viceroy in Egypt), maharajah (Indian prince), maharani (wife or widow of a maharajah), mikado (Japanese), nawab (Mogul governor), pharaoh (ancient Egypt), raja (Indian king or prince), rani (Hindu queen), satrap (ancient Persia), shah (Iranian king), sheikh (Arab leader), shogun (Japan), sultan (Muslim), sultana (wife of a sultan), tsar (Russian emperor before 1917), tsarina (Russian empress before 1917).

---

**ruling** NOUN

*A ruling came from the president himself.*
▶ decision, pronouncement, resolution, decree, judgement, adjudication, order, command, instruction

**rumble** VERB

*Thunder rumbled in the distance.*
▶ boom, reverberate, resound, echo

**rummage** VERB

*She started to rummage in her handbag for her keys.*
▶ search, hunt, scrabble, burrow, root

**rumour** NOUN

**1** *A rumour had started that the company would close.*
► report, story, piece of gossip, whisper
**2** *The suggestion was only rumour.*
► gossip, hearsay, talk, tittle-tattle

**rumpus** NOUN

*A terrible rumpus was going on outside.*
► commotion, uproar, racket, tumult, hullabaloo,
hubbub, fracas, furore, upheaval, agitation,
excitement

---

**run** VERB This word is often overused. Here are some
alternatives:
**1** *We ran across the field.*
► sprint, race, jog, tear, dash, rush, hasten, speed,
streak, bolt, scamper, scoot
**2** *The buses don't run on Sundays.*
► operate, function, go, provide a service
**3** *The car has been running erratically.*
► function, perform, work, behave
**4** *His car was stolen because he had left the engine
running.*
► operate, tick over, go
**5** *Water ran down the wall.*
► stream, trickle, flow, flood, pour, spill, gush,
cascade, dribble, leak
**6** *She was running a small business in Leeds.*
► manage, be in charge of, direct, control,
administer, conduct, supervise, govern, look after,
maintain, rule
**7** *He could no longer afford to run a car.*
► maintain, keep, own, use, drive
**8** *She ran me back to my house.*
► drive, take, bring, ferry, give a lift to
**9** *It is important to run exhaustive tests.*
► carry out, perform, complete, do, fulfil
**10** *A sharp pain ran up her arm.*
► pass, move, shoot, travel, go
**11** *The road runs north.*
► extend, reach, stretch, go, continue
**run across** *I ran across your sister in Paris.*
► meet, encounter, come across, run into,
chance on
**run after** *Jill ran after him with his keys.*
► chase, pursue, follow
**run away** *He threw down his shield and ran away.*
► escape, flee, bolt, abscond, (more informal) make
off
**run down**
**1** *A dog ran into the road and he ran it down.*
► run over, knock over, hit, struck
**2** *She didn't want to run him down in public.*
► criticize, denigrate, disparage, belittle, find
fault with
**run into** *Did you run into any of your friends?*
► meet, encounter, come across, run across,
chance on
**run out** *My subscription runs out in December.*
► expire, terminate, end, come to an end, cease,
dry up

---

**run** NOUN
**1** *a run across the park*
► jog, dash, sprint, spurt, trot, gallop, canter,
race
**2** *a run in the car*
► drive, ride, trip, excursion, journey, (more informal)
spin
**3** *a run of bad luck*
► sequence, stretch, series, chain, course
**4** *a chicken run*
► enclosure, compound, coop, pen

**runaway** NOUN
*a safe house for young runaways*
► fugitive, escapee, refugee, absconder

**runner** NOUN
**1** *There are seven runners in the next race.*
► competitor, entrant, participant, athlete
**2** *The commanding officer sent a runner to
headquarters*
► courier, messenger

**running** NOUN
**1** *A private company has taken over the running of the
school.*
► administration, management, direction,
controlling, supervision
**2** *These measures will ensure the smooth running of the
organization.*
► operation, working, functioning

**runny** ADJECTIVE
*a runny mixture of egg and milk*
► watery, thin, fluid, liquid, free-flowing
OPPOSITES ARE solid, viscous

**run-of-the-mill** ADJECTIVE
*The songs are all run-of-the-mill efforts.*
► ordinary, routine, average, mediocre,
unremarkable, unexceptional, unimpressive

**rupture** NOUN
*The rupture in the blood vessel was not caused by the
operation.*
► split, crack, tear, puncture, fracture, burst

**rupture** VERB
*The impact ruptured both fuel tanks.*
► split, puncture, fracture, crack, tear, burst, sever

**rural** ADJECTIVE
*The majority lived in rural communities outside London.*
► country, rustic, pastoral, agricultural, agrarian,
countrified
AN OPPOSITE IS urban

**rush** VERB
*She rushed into the garden.*
► hurry, hasten, dash, run, sprint, race, tear, dash,
hasten, streak, bolt
OPPOSITES ARE dawdle, saunter

**rush** NOUN
**1** *a frantic rush to put out the flames*
► hurry, haste, dash, race, scramble
**2** *It stopped the rush of water for a time.*
► flood, gush, spate, cataract

**3** *There was a sudden rush for the doors*
► charge, stampede, surge (towards)

**rust** VERB
*a special coating to prevent the iron from rusting*
► corrode, become rusty, oxidize, crumble away, decay, rot

**rustic** ADJECTIVE
**1** *a house in rustic surroundings*
► rural, country, pastoral, agricultural, agrarian, countrified
AN OPPOSITE IS urban
**2** *She sat down on a rustic wooden seat.*
► plain, simple, crude, rough, artless, unsophisticated

**rustle** VERB
*The rain rustled in the grass.*
► crackle, swish, whisper, whoosh

**rusty** ADJECTIVE
**1** *Nothing causes more blisters than using a rusty trowel.*
► corroded, rusted, oxidized, rotten, tarnished, discoloured
**2** *My French is a little rusty.*
► unpractised, neglected, below par, deficient, weak, unused, (more informal) creaky

**rut** NOUN
**1** *There were deep ruts in the track.*
► furrow, groove, trough, channel, indentation
**2** *He was in a rut; comfortable, but in a rut all the same.*
► groove, grind, dull routine, treadmill

**ruthless** ADJECTIVE
**1** *a ruthless dictator*
► merciless, pitiless, brutal, cruel, callous, unfeeling, heartless, vicious, violent, ferocious, fierce
AN OPPOSITE IS compassionate
**2** *He carried out his instructions with ruthless efficiency.*
► relentless, unrelenting, inexorable, unremitting, intense, implacable

# Ss

**sabotage** NOUN
*The crash was probably caused by engine failure and not sabotage.*
► wilful damage, deliberate destruction, vandalism, wrecking, disruption, treachery

**sabotage** VERB
**1** *A gang had sabotaged the cash machines in the shopping mall.*
► wreck, deliberately damage, destroy, disable, put out of action, cripple, vandalize

**2** *Are you telling me he deliberately set out to sabotage your work?*
► wreck, ruin, spoil, thwart, undermine, disrupt

**sack** NOUN
**1** *The flour was in an open sack on the floor.*
► bag, pack, pouch
**2** *When she complained she promptly got the sack.*
► notice, dismissal, discharge, your cards, (more informal) the boot

**sack** VERB
**1** *Unbelievably, he sacked his son-in-law and replaced him with Trevor.*
► dismiss, give notice to, get rid of, lay someone off, let someone go, (more informal) fire, (more informal) kick out
**2** *Edward I had sacked the town in 1296.*
► destroy, raid, loot, plunder, pillage, ravage

---

**sacred** ADJECTIVE
**1** *The new pope was enthroned in the most sacred place in the basilica.*
► holy, blessed, consecrated, sanctified, hallowed, dedicated, venerated
OPPOSITES ARE unconsecrated
**2** *The recital mixed operatic arias with traditional sacred melodies.*
► religious, spiritual, devotional, ecclesiastical
OPPOSITES ARE secular

NAMES FOR SACRED TEXTS AND HOLY BOOKS
**Buddhism:** Tripitaka.
**Christianity:** Bible, Old Testament, New Testament, Gospel, Epistle.
**Confucianism:** I Ching.
**Hinduism:** Bhagavadgita, Mahabharata, Ramayana, Veda.
**Islam:** Koran.
**Judaism:** Talmud, Torah.
**Sikhism:** Adi Granth.
**Zoroastrianism:** Zend-Avesta.

---

**sacrifice** NOUN
**1** *The festival involved a sacrifice of a ram and seven lambs.*
► offering, ritual slaughter, votive offering, oblation
**2** *The building was rebuilt with some sacrifice of its earlier features.*
► loss, abandonment, discarding, rejection, surrender, giving up, yielding, renunciation, renouncing

**sacrifice** VERB
**1** *They have sacrificed their principles and lost their good name. a memorial to the bomber crews who sacrificed their lives in the war*
► give up, forfeit, relinquish, surrender, forgo, go without
**2** *The goat had been sacrificed at the shrine.*
► offer up, kill, slaughter, immolate

## sacrilege NOUN

*Wearing armour in a holy place was sacrilege.*
▶ blasphemy, desecration, impiety, profanity, irreverence, disrespect, ungodliness
OPPOSITES ARE piety, respect

---

**sad** ADJECTIVE This word is often overused. Here are some alternatives:
**1** *Everyone was sad to be leaving.  He looked at her sad face.*
▶ unhappy, sorrowful, dejected, downcast, despondent, downhearted, depressed, miserable, glum, in low spirits
**2** *I told my brother and sister the sad news.  The story is sadder than we realized.*
▶ distressing, upsetting, depressing, grave, tragic, unfortunate, regrettable, serious, heart-rending
**3** *This sad state of affairs does not have to continue.*
▶ sorry, wretched, unfortunate, regrettable, shameful, disgraceful
**4** (*informal*) *They live in a sad little house.*
▶ pathetic, pitiful, inadequate

---

## sadden VERB

*That brief reminder of her husband saddened her.*
▶ upset, distress, dispirit, grieve, dishearten
AN OPPOSITE IS cheer up

## saddle VERB

*It seemed a pity to saddle them with so much work.*
▶ burden, encumber, lumber, load, impose
**USAGE** If you use *impose* you have to say It seemed a pity to *impose* so much work on them.

## sadistic ADJECTIVE

*a sadistic killer*
▶ callous, cruel, brutal, brutish, pitiless, cold-blooded, ruthless, merciless, vile

## sadness NOUN

*She could not hide her sadness.*
▶ unhappiness, sorrow, dejection, misery, melancholy, low spirits, depression, regret

## safe ADJECTIVE

**1** *The building was safe from attack.*
▶ secure, protected, guarded, invulnerable, impregnable
**2** *The missing children were all safe.*
▶ unharmed, unhurt, uninjured, out of danger
**3** *She is a safe driver.  Better safe than sorry.*
▶ cautious, prudent, circumspect, attentive
**4** *He's a safe person to be with.*
▶ reliable, trustworthy, responsible, sensible, level-headed, upright
**5** *a medicine that is safe for young children*
▶ harmless, innocuous, proven

## safeguard NOUN

*Burglar alarms are an additional safeguard.*
▶ protection, defence, guard, shield, precaution, security, assurance

## safeguard VERB

*The charter safeguards your human rights.*
▶ protect, preserve, defend, secure, look after, shield, guard

## safety NOUN

**1** *The safety of passengers is paramount.*
▶ security, protection, welfare, well-being
AN OPPOSITE IS danger
**2** *The refugees looked for a place of safety.*
▶ refuge, shelter, sanctuary, protection

## safety belt NOUN

*The bus was fitted with safety belts.*
▶ seat belt, safety harness

## sag VERB

*The ceiling sags in the middle.*
▶ hang down, sink, slump, dip, droop, fall

## saga NOUN

*They longed to tell the saga of their day's adventures.*
▶ tale, story, catalogue, rigmarole

---

**sail** VERB
**1** *John loves sailing his boat.*
▶ pilot, navigate, skipper, steer, captain
**2** *We had a holiday sailing in the Mediterranean.*
▶ cruise, voyage, boat, yacht, go sailing, navigate
**3** *The ferry sails at midday.*
▶ put to sea, set sail, leave harbour, weigh anchor
**SOME TYPES OF SAILING SHIP**
barque, brigantine, caique, caravel, catamaran, clipper, cutter, dhow, felucca, frigate, galleon, junk, ketch, longship, lugger, man-of-war, merchantman, merchant ship, monohull, schooner, skiff, sloop, smack, trimaran, xebec, yacht, yawl.

---

## sailor NOUN

*He did not make a very good sailor.*
▶ seaman, seafarer, mariner, boatman, yachtsman or yachtswoman

## saintly ADJECTIVE

*a saintly priest*
▶ holy, godly, pious, devout, spiritual, God-fearing, blessed, virtuous
AN OPPOSITE IS unholy

## sake NOUN

**for the sake of** *He did it for the sake of his family.*
▶ for the good of, in the interests of, for the benefit of, for the advantage of, on behalf of

## salary NOUN

*She is paid an annual salary of £45,000.*
▶ income, earnings, pay, wages, remuneration, emolument, payment

## sale NOUN

*laws to control the sale of drugs*
▶ selling, marketing, trading (in), dealing (in), traffic (in), disposal
AN OPPOSITE IS purchase

**salesperson** NOUN
*A salesperson must know their products' benefits.*
▶ salesman or saleswoman, sales assistant, shop assistant, shopkeeper

**sallow** ADJECTIVE
*a sallow complexion*
▶ pale, pallid, wan, sickly, yellowish, anaemic, colourless

**salty** ADJECTIVE
*a thick salty paste used for flavouring*
▶ salt, salted, piquant, saline, briny, tangy, spicy
OPPOSITES ARE fresh, bland

**salubrious** ADJECTIVE
*We reached the more salubrious outskirts of the city.*
▶ healthy, health-giving, beneficial, wholesome, sanitary, hygienic, invigorating, refreshing, pleasant
OPPOSITES ARE unhealthy, unpleasant

**salutary** ADJECTIVE
*Their experiences offer some salutary warnings.*
▶ beneficial, helpful, useful, valuable, advantageous, productive, profitable

**salute** VERB
**1** *You call me 'sir' but you don't salute me, OK?*
▶ greet, acknowledge, hail, address, welcome
**2** *I salute them for having the courage to admit their mistakes.*
▶ pay tribute to, acknowledge, celebrate, recognize, honour

**salute** NOUN
*He gave a quick salute.*
▶ greeting, acknowledgement, salutation, wave

**salvage** NOUN
*the search and salvage of aircraft wreckage*
▶ recovery, rescue, retrieval, saving, reclamation

**salvage** VERB
**1** *We might be able to salvage the car before it goes right under.*
▶ recover, rescue, reclaim, retrieve, save
**2** *She strives to salvage her family's battered reputation.*
▶ save, preserve, rescue, recover, regain

**salvation** NOUN
**1** *Faith alone might not be enough to secure salvation.*
▶ redemption, deliverance, saving
AN OPPOSITE IS damnation
**2** *The growing mail-order business proved to be the company's salvation.*
▶ deliverance, lifeline, help, rescue, way out

**salve** NOUN
*a lip salve*
▶ ointment, cream, lotion, balm

**same** ADJECTIVE
**1** *Is that the same person?*
▶ actual, identical, selfsame
**2 the same** *The witnesses' versions were all essentially the same.*
▶ similar, identical, alike, comparable, equivalent, matching, indistinguishable
OPPOSITES ARE different, unalike

**3 the same** *The timetable tends to remain the same from year to year.*
▶ unchanged, constant, unvarying, identical
**4** *Let's celebrate again on the same day next year.*
▶ corresponding

**sample** NOUN
**1** *Finalists will submit samples of their photographic work.*
▶ specimen, example, representative piece, selection, demonstration, illustration, indication, instance, model, pattern
**2** *The survey was based on a sample of a thousand voters.*
▶ cross section, sampling

**sample** VERB
*Guests will sample some of the great wines of the world with their dinner.*
▶ try out, try, test, check out, inspect, taste

**sanctimonious** ADJECTIVE
*What happened to all the sanctimonious talk about putting his family first?*
▶ self-righteous, holier-than-thou, smug, superior, moralizing, priggish, mealy-mouthed, pious, unctuous
AN OPPOSITE IS modest

**sanction** NOUN
*The scheme has official sanction.*
▶ permission, consent, authority, approval

**sanction** VERB
*He decided to sanction the work on his own initiative.*
▶ authorize, allow, permit, approve, consent to, give permission for, endorse

**sanctions** PLURAL NOUN
*The UN will vote on whether to lift the sanctions.*
▶ restrictions, penalties, embargo, boycott, prohibition

**sanctity** ADJECTIVE
**1** *the sanctity of St Francis*
▶ holiness, sacredness, godliness, piety, spirituality, goodness
**2** *It is an issue for anyone who cares about the sanctity of human life*
▶ importance, inviolability

**sanctuary** NOUN
**1** *a sanctuary dedicated to Apollo*
▶ holy place, temple, shrine
**2** *The place was a quiet sanctuary where they could do their work.*
▶ refuge, haven, retreat, shelter

**sand** NOUN
*The children played on the sand for hours.*
▶ beach, sands, shore, seaside, strand

**sane** ADJECTIVE
*Humour was what helped keep them sane.*
▶ rational, lucid, normal, balanced, reasonable, sensible, (*informal*) compos mentis, level-headed, sound, stable
AN OPPOSITE IS mad

## sanitary ADJECTIVE
*The area has cleaner air and more sanitary conditions.*
▶ hygienic, clean, aseptic, antiseptic, sterile, healthy, salubrious, germ-free, pure, uncontaminated
AN OPPOSITE IS insanitary

## sanity NOUN
*He was not sure enough of his own sanity to take these risks.*
▶ reason, senses, rationality, balance of mind, mental health, lucidity

## sap VERB
*a fever that sapped his strength and depressed his mind*
▶ drain, exhaust, deplete, erode, bleed, wear away

## sarcasm NOUN
*She spoke with more than a hint of sarcasm in her voice.*
▶ ridicule, derision, mockery, irony, scorn, scoffing

## sarcastic ADJECTIVE
*If bosses are sarcastic, try not to react.*
▶ mocking, contemptuous, sardonic, ironic, derisive, ironic, scornful, scathing, scoffing, sneering, withering

## sash NOUN
*She wore a girlish blue sash round her waist.*
▶ girdle, belt, band, waistband, cummerbund

## satire NOUN
*a smutty satire about marriage*
▶ parody, lampoon, burlesque, caricature, invective, irony, mockery, (*more informal*) spoof, (*more informal*) send-up, (*more informal*) take-off

## satirical ADJECTIVE
*a satirical cartoon series*
▶ ironical, irreverent, mocking, critical, disparaging, disrespectful, sarcastic

## satirize VERB
*an attempt to satirize films and film-makers*
▶ mock, parody, ridicule, caricature, burlesque, criticize, deride, lampoon, travesty, make fun of, (*more informal*) send up, (*more informal*) take off

## satisfaction NOUN
**1** *This year, she thought with satisfaction, she was well-prepared. Job satisfaction tends to be high.*
▶ contentment, comfort, happiness, pleasure, pride, self-satisfaction, sense of achievement, enjoyment, fulfilment, gratification
AN OPPOSITE IS dissatisfaction
**2** *They may have to turn to the courts for satisfaction.*
▶ settlement, reparation, compensation, recompense, reparation, amends, justice, redress

## satisfactory ADJECTIVE
*There was no satisfactory method of dealing with trivial complaints.*
▶ adequate, acceptable, satisfying, suitable, reasonable, tolerable, fair, passable, sufficient, (*more informal*) all right, (*informal*) up to scratch
AN OPPOSITE IS unsatisfactory

## satisfy VERB
**1** *There are not enough terminals to satisfy demand.*
▶ fulfil, gratify, answer, meet, fill, service, provide for
AN OPPOSITE IS frustrate
**2** *Neither place had fully satisfied him.*
▶ content, make happy
AN OPPOSITE IS dissatisfy

## saturate VERB
*Heavy rainfall had saturated the ground. The Colombian cartel saturated the market with cocaine.*
▶ soak, drench, impregnate, permeate, suffuse, steep, wet

## saturated ADJECTIVE
**1** *Saturated soil lacks air.*
▶ soaked, sodden, waterlogged, steeped (in)
**2** *Her clothes had become saturated in the downpour.*
▶ soaked, soaking wet, sopping, drenched, wringing

## saucy ADJECTIVE
**1** *a saucy child*
▶ cheeky, rude, impudent, insolent, impertinent, disrespectful, pert, brazen, cocky, presumptuous
OPPOSITES ARE polite, respectful
**2** *saucy postcards*
▶ rude, suggestive, titillating, lewd

## saunter VERB
*She sauntered over to the pool.*
▶ stroll, amble, wander, drift, dawdle

## savage ADJECTIVE
**1** *Savage dogs roamed the streets.*
▶ fierce, wild, ferocious, vicious, untamed
AN OPPOSITE IS tame
**2** *a savage assault*
▶ fierce, ferocious, brutal, cruel, sadistic
AN OPPOSITE IS humane
**3** *The speech was a savage attack on cronyism.*
▶ fierce, scathing, vitriolic, harsh, blistering, searing

## save VERB
**1** *They wanted to save money for a holiday.*
▶ put by, set aside, store up, conserve, reserve, retain, scrape together, (*more informal*) stash away
OPPOSITES ARE waste, squander
**2** *Try to save petrol during the fuel crisis.*
▶ economize on, cut back on, be sparing with, use wisely
AN OPPOSITE IS waste
**3** *The crew managed to save all the passengers after an emergency landing.*
▶ rescue, free, release, liberate, recover, retrieve, salvage, set free
**4** *A bit of help would have saved me from exhausting myself.*
▶ prevent, preserve, protect, safeguard, defend, guard, shield

## saving NOUN
**1** *a saving of 20% on the regular price*
▶ reduction, cut, discount

**2 savings** *With all his savings gone he needed to find work again.*
► funds, reserves, nest egg, resources

**saviour** NOUN
*Gorbachev presented himself as the saviour of socialism.*
► rescuer, liberator, champion, protector, defender, redeemer, guardian

**savour** VERB
*It was his first curry for three months and he was going to savour it.*
► enjoy, relish, appreciate, delight in, take pleasure in

**savoury** ADJECTIVE
*Sun-dried tomatoes give a pizza a savoury taste.*
► spicy, piquant, appetizing, mouth-watering, delectable, delicious, luscious

---

**say** VERB This word is often overused. Here are some alternatives:
**1** *She could not say his name.*
► speak, utter, voice, articulate, enunciate
**2** *'It's snowing,' he said*
► observe, remark, declare, state, announce, answer, reply, respond
**3** *Hugh says he didn't do it.*
► maintain, claim, assert, insist, contend
**4** *He lit a candle and said a prayer.*
► recite, utter, speak
**5** *What are you trying to say?*
► express, put into words, communicate, make known
**6** *We cannot say what might happen.*
► guess, foretell, imagine, judge, estimate

---

**saying** NOUN
*You know the saying about too many cooks.*
► proverb, adage, maxim, dictum, aphorism

**scale** NOUN
**1** *people at different ends of the social scale*
► hierarchy, ladder, spectrum, ranking, sequence, progression
**2** *the scale of a map*
► proportion, ratio, measure, relative size
**3** *the scale of the tragedy*
► size, extent, scope, magnitude, degree, range

**scale** VERB
*The intruders had to scale a 10-foot fence.*
► climb, ascend, clamber up, scramble up, shin up, go up, go over, mount

**scamp** NOUN
*He was an idle young scamp in those days.*
► rascal, scallywag, devil, monkey, imp

**scamper** VERB
*Sam scampered off and waited at the gate.*
► scurry, scuttle, dash, dart, scoot, run, rush, hasten, hurry
**scamper about** *Dogs scampered about the churchyard.*
► run about, gambol, frisk, frolic, romp

**scan** VERB
**1** *We scanned the trees and caught sight of a magpie.*
► study, examine, regard, view, watch, gaze at, look at, scrutinize, survey, search, stare at
**2** *Mungo scanned the books to see what Vic might like.*
► skim, glance through, flick through, have a look at

**scandal** NOUN
**1** *The tabloids loved reporting scandal.*
► gossip, rumour, aspersions, notoriety, sensation, slander, calumny, (more informal) tittle-tattle
**2** *The college had been involved in a drugs scandal.*
► wrongdoing, affair, business
**3** *It's a scandal that the hospital has to close.*
► disgrace, outrage, injustice, affront, insult, shame

**scandalize** VERB
*behaviour that scandalized polite society*
► shock, outrage, horrify, disgust, appal, sicken, insult

**scandalous** ADJECTIVE
**1** *This is a scandalous way to treat people who have risked their lives for the sake of their country.*
► shameful, disgraceful, shocking, outrageous, monstrous, appalling, wicked
**2** *This was scandalous behaviour and the Palace gave her a firm warning.*
► improper, shameful, discreditable, disreputable
**3** *The scandalous rumours had been quickly forgotten.*
► shocking, scurrilous, malicious, libellous, slanderous, defamatory

**scanty** ADJECTIVE
**1** *a conclusion based on scanty evidence*
► meagre, sparse, scant, paltry, minimal, negligible, pitiful, miserable, modest, (more informal) mingy, (more informal) measly
AN OPPOSITE IS plentiful
**2** *They looked bored and cold in their scanty dresses.*
► skimpy, revealing, insubstantial, short, thin

**scar** NOUN
*a scar on his left cheek*
► mark, injury, wound , disfigurement, blemish, cicatrix

**scar** VERB
**1** *The wound scarred his face.*
► disfigure, mark, leave a scar on, deface, brand, damage, spoil
**2** *He was scarred for life by his mother's early death.*
► traumatize, disturb, distress, upset, damage

**scarce** ADJECTIVE
*(informal)* *When money became scarce, he tried to go on welfare.*
► sparse, meagre, in short supply, hard to find, hard to come by, scanty, at a premium, rare, lacking, deficient
AN OPPOSITE IS plentiful

**scarcely** ADVERB
*There was scarcely enough to go round.*
► barely, hardly, only just

**scarcity** NOUN

*a scarcity of good job opportunities*
▶ shortage, dearth, deficiency, want, paucity, inadequacy, insufficiency, lack
OPPOSITES ARE abundance, surplus

**scare** VERB

**1** *I didn't mean to scare you. I just wanted to talk.*
▶ alarm, startle, shake, unnerve, dismay, shock
AN OPPOSITE IS calm
**2** *The bogeyman could not scare him any more.*
▶ frighten, intimidate, terrorize, threaten, make afraid, menace, panic, bully, cow
AN OPPOSITE IS reassure

**scare** NOUN

*Finding the door unlocked gave her a scare.*
▶ fright, shock, start, turn, jolt, alarm

**scared** ADJECTIVE

*Many of us are too scared to go out alone.*
▶ frightened, afraid, fearful, anxious, alarmed, terrified, panic-stricken

**scary** ADJECTIVE

*It's not so scary now with all these people around.*
▶ frightening, scaring, alarming, eerie, spooky, creepy, terrifying, chilling, spine-chilling, intimidating

**scathing** ADJECTIVE

*There followed a scathing attack on the government for its lack of action.*
▶ critical, scornful, cutting, withering, caustic, vitriolic, devastating, harsh
AN OPPOSITE IS complimentary

**scatter** VERB

**1** *The crowd quickly scattered.*
▶ disperse, break up, disband, separate, disintegrate, dissolve, go off in all directions
**2** *She scattered breadcrumbs across the path.*
▶ strew, sprinkle, spread, throw, fling, toss, shower
AN OPPOSITE IS gather

**scatterbrained** ADJECTIVE

*She was scatterbrained about such things and left everything to Tod.*
▶ absent-minded, disorganized, forgetful, dreamy, feather-brained, muddled, empty-headed, unsystematic, vague, (*more informal*) scatty

**scavenge** VERB

*Hens scavenged for bits of food.*
▶ search, rummage, forage, look, root about

**scene** NOUN

**1** *Police were called to the scene of the accident.*
▶ location, site, place, position, point, spot, setting, locale, locality, whereabouts
**2** *a beautiful scene by the lake*
▶ view, vista, outlook, prospect, panorama, landscape, picture, tableau, sight, spectacle
**3** *A large picture of the setting sun formed the scene for the farewell.*
▶ backdrop, scenery, set, stage

**4** *The last scene of the novel is set in France.*
▶ part, section, episode, sequence
**5** *He lost his money and there was a scene at the checkout.*
▶ fuss, commotion, disturbance, outburst, row, contretemps, exhibition, argument, quarrel, drama, (*more informal*) to-do, (*more informal*) carry-on

**scenery** NOUN

*They stopped to admire the scenery.*
▶ landscape, terrain, panorama, scene, vista, outlook, surroundings

**scenic** ADJECTIVE

*There is a scenic route through the mountains.*
▶ picturesque, panoramic, pretty, pleasing, attractive, beautiful, lovely, spectacular, striking

**scent** NOUN

**1** *The scent of rose water hung in the air.*
▶ smell , odour, perfume, fragrance, aroma, redolence
**2** *a bottle of scent*
▶ perfume, toilet water, lavender water, cologne
**3** *The dogs picked up the scent.*
▶ trail, track

**scented** ADJECTIVE

*a smell of scented soap*
▶ perfumed, fragrant, aromatic

**sceptic** NOUN

*He is a sceptic about the dangers of global warming.*
▶ doubter, unbeliever, sceptical person, cynic, agnostic
AN OPPOSITE IS believer

**sceptical** ADJECTIVE

*He was initially sceptical about her abilities but soon changed his mind.*
▶ dubious, doubtful, distrustful, mistrustful, disbelieving, incredulous, suspicious, uncertain, unconvinced, unsure, cynical
AN OPPOSITE IS confident

**scepticism** NOUN

*Others expressed scepticism about using this method.*
▶ distrust, mistrust, disbelief, suspicion, doubt, incredulity, lack of confidence, cynicism
AN OPPOSITE IS confidence

**schedule** NOUN

*There was hardly any spare time in her busy schedule. I will organize a schedule of visits.*
▶ timetable, agenda, programme, scheme, calendar, diary, list, plan

**scheme** NOUN

**1** *Pitt proposed a national scheme of cash allowances for children.*
▶ plan, project, proposal, programme, venture, enterprise, strategy, system, blueprint, idea, method, procedure
**2** *a scheme to steal the jewels*
▶ plot, conspiracy, intrigue, secret plan, ruse, ploy, (*more informal*) racket, (*more informal*) scam

scheme 440 scorching

**scheme**

3 *a bright colour scheme*
► design, arrangement, pattern, layout

**scheme** VERB

*The emperor's wife schemed to exercise power through her son.*
► plot, intrigue, connive, conspire, collude, plan

**schism** NOUN

*the widening schism between the king and the church*
► division, split, rift, breach, break, quarrel, disagreement

**scholar** NOUN

*a leading classical scholar*
► academic, authority, expert, savant, intellectual, intellect, man or woman of letters

**scholarly** ADJECTIVE

*a serious, scholarly woman*
► intellectual, learned, erudite, academic, lettered, knowledgeable

**scholarship** NOUN

1 *a music scholarship worth £2,000 a year*
► award, grant, bursary, exhibition
2 *a person of great scholarship*
► learning, erudition, knowledge, wisdom, academic achievement, intellectual attainment

**school** NOUN

*Have you asked them what makes a good school?*
► college, academy, educational institution, centre of learning, institute

**schooling** NOUN

*the last two years of schooling.*
► education, instruction, tuition, teaching, training, coaching

**science** NOUN

*the science of forensic medicine*
► technology, discipline, field, technique, art

BRANCHES OF SCIENCE AND TECHNOLOGY

acoustics, aeronautics, agricultural science, anatomy, anthropology, artificial intelligence, astronomy, astrophysics, behavioural science, biochemistry, biology, biophysics, botany, chemistry, climatology, computer science, cybernetics, dietetics, domestic science, dynamics, earth science, ecology, economics, electronics, engineering, entomology, environmental science, food science, genetics, geographical science, geology, geophysics, hydraulics, information technology, life science, linguistics, materials science, mathematics, mechanics, medicine (medical science), metallurgy, meteorology, microbiology, mineralogy, ornithology, pathology, pharmacology, physics, physiology, political science, psychology, robotics, sociology, space technology, sports science, telecommunications, thermodynamics, toxicology, veterinary science, zoology.

**scientific** ADJECTIVE

1 *scientific research*
► science-based, technical, technological
2 *Our methods are not scientific enough.*
► systematic, methodical, analytical, organized, precise, rigorous, thorough, regulated

**scientist** NOUN

*the accusation that scientists are 'playing God'*
► researcher, scientific expert, technologist, (more informal) boffin

**scintillating** ADJECTIVE

1 *The bright lights looked scintillating reflected in the surface of the water.*
► sparkling, glittering, dazzling, shining, bright
2 *The team gave a scintillating display of skill and stamina.*
► brilliant, exciting, dazzling, exhilarating, stimulating

**scoff** VERB

1 *scoff at Experts are inclined to scoff at such theories.*
► mock, ridicule, sneer at, jeer at, scorn, deride, make fun of, poke fun at
2 *(informal) You feel guilty when you scoff a sherry trifle.*
► eat up, guzzle, gobble up, wolf, wolf down, devour, (more informal) tuck into, (more informal) polish off

**scold** VERB

*Busy young mothers scolded their children.*
► tell off, reprimand, rebuke, admonish, reprove, reproach, upbraid, censure, chide, criticize, reprehend, (more informal) tick off
OPPOSITES ARE praise, commend

**scoop** VERB

**scoop out**
1 *They would scoop out holes in the sand.*
► dig, gouge, scrape, excavate, hollow, cut
2 *Scoop out the flesh of the pineapple halves.*
► remove, take out, scrape out, spoon out, extract
**scoop up** *She scooped up her things and left hurriedly.*
► pick up, gather up, grab, collect

**scope** NOUN

1 *issues that are beyond the scope of the inquiry*
► extent, limit, range, competence, terms of reference, remit, ambit, capacity, compass, sphere, reach
2 *There is plenty of scope for new ideas.*
► opportunity, chance, latitude, leeway, freedom, room, space

**scorch** VERB

*Some of the walls had been scorched by fire.*
► burn, singe, char, blacken

**scorching** ADJECTIVE

*The desert is a place of scorching heat by day and bitter cold by night.*
► blazing, boiling, flaming, baking, roasting, sweltering, burning
OPPOSITES ARE freezing, bitter

# score NOUN

**1** *The final score did not reflect the balance of the game.*
▶ result, tally, total, mark, number of points
**2** *They had a score to settle*
▶ debt, grievance

# score VERB

**1** *a move that scored double points*
▶ earn, win, gain, achieve, make, (*more informal*) chalk up
**2** *A pattern had been scored in the surface.*
▶ cut, engrave, incise, mark, gouge, scratch, scrape, slash

# scorn NOUN

*She treated that remark with the scorn it deserved.*
▶ contempt, disdain, derision, disparagement, ridicule, mockery
AN OPPOSITE IS admiration

# scorn VERB

*Their haircuts are severe and they scorn make-up.*
▶ despise, deride, scoff at, ridicule, mock, spurn, look down on, dismiss
AN OPPOSITE IS admire

# scornful ADJECTIVE

*Richard was prepared to put up with the scornful disapproval of Eve and Ted.*
▶ contemptuous, derisive, disdainful, supercilious, scathing, disparaging, mocking, scoffing, sneering, withering
OPPOSITES ARE admiring, respectful

# scotch VERB

*Hopes of trying a first kiss were scotched when she fell asleep the moment she got into the car.*
▶ end, bring to an end, put paid to, frustrate, shatter, wreck, destroy, scupper

# scot-free ADJECTIVE

*You wouldn't want to see the real villains getting off scot-free.*
▶ unpunished, unscathed, unharmed, unhurt, safe

# scoundrel NOUN

*It wasn't her fault she had a scoundrel for a grandson.*
▶ rascal, rogue, ruffian, ne'er-do-well, good-for-nothing, villain, knave, scallywag, scamp

# scour VERB

**1** *They were made to scrub kitchen floors and scour out pans.*
▶ scrub, clean, scrape, wash, buff up, burnish, polish, rub
**2** *Rita scoured the junk shops for second hand pieces to fill the rooms.*
▶ search, comb, ransack, rummage through, forage through, hunt through

# scourge NOUN

*There is hardly an area where the scourge of unemployment is not biting hard.*
▶ affliction, bane, curse, misfortune, torment

# scout NOUN

*Scouts came back with information about the enemy positions.*
▶ lookout, outrider, advance guard, spy

# scout VERB

**scout about** or **around** *I asked Claire to scout around to find him a place to stay.*
▶ look about, reconnoitre, search, explore, hunt, investigate, cast about, get information

# scowl VERB

*She scowled at him and told him to go away.*
▶ glower, frown, glare, grimace

# scowl NOUN

*There was an unmistakable scowl on his face.*
▶ frown, glower, grimace

# scrabble VERB

*She scrabbled about in her pockets until she found her glasses.*
▶ rummage, grope, root, fumble, claw, dig

# scraggy ADJECTIVE

*She kept out of the way of her sister's scraggy old cat.*
▶ scrawny, skinny, thin, lanky, gaunt, lean, bony, emaciated, underfed
OPPOSITES ARE plump, fat

# scram VERB

(*informal*) *Scram or I'll call the police.*
▶ go away, leave, get going, get moving, (*informal*) beat it, (*informal*) shove off, (*informal*) clear off

# scramble NOUN

*Getting there in time proved quite a scramble.*
▶ struggle, rush, hustle, dash

# scramble VERB

**1** *I scrambled down the slope towards the car. Daniel scrambled to his feet and left the room.*
▶ clamber, climb, crawl, scrabble, move awkwardly
**2** *She saw the two men scramble for the fallen gun.*
▶ scuffle, struggle, tussle, fight, jostle
**3** *They quickly scrambled into the plane.*
▶ dash, hasten, hurry, run, rush

# scrap NOUN

**1** *There were a few scraps of food on the table.*
▶ bit, piece, morsel, particle, crumb, speck, fragment, mouthful
**2** *Not a scrap of evidence could be found.*
▶ shred, speck, iota, jot, ounce, trace
**3** *a lorry loaded with scrap*
▶ junk, refuse, rubbish, salvage, waste, litter, odds and ends
**4** *He wanted to avoid a scrap with Kevin.*
▶ fight, quarrel, disagreement, tussle, brawl

# scrap VERB

**1** *Local residents want the road plan to be scrapped.*
▶ abandon, cancel, discard, (*informal*) ditch, drop, give up, jettison, throw away, write off
**2** *The younger children are always scrapping.*
▶ fight, quarrel, argue, brawl

A B C D E F G H I J K L M N O P Q R S T U V W X Y Z

**scrape** VERB

1 *Elaine had scraped her skin against the wall.*
▶ graze, scratch, scuff, abrade, bark, lacerate
2 *He scraped his boots before going inside.*
▶ scrub, scour, rub, clean

**scrape together** *We scraped enough money together to get home*
▶ collect, amass, rake together, dredge up

**scrape** NOUN

*Try not to get into any scrapes*
▶ difficulty, predicament, tight spot, mischief, trouble

**scrappy** ADJECTIVE

*The game turned out to be a scrappy affair.*
▶ disorganized, disjointed, uneven, slipshod, unsatisfactory
AN OPPOSITE IS well-organized

**scratch** VERB

1 *Be careful not to scratch the table top.*
▶ scrape, mark, score, gash, cut, damage the surface of, gouge
2 *The thorns were scratching his legs.*
▶ graze, chafe, prick, cut, lacerate

**scratch** NOUN

1 *There were scratches in the paintwork.*
▶ gash, groove, line, mark, scoring, scrape
2 *He had a long scratch down one side of his face.*
▶ graze, laceration, wound, cut

**up to scratch** *The work was not up to scratch.*
▶ satisfactory, adequate, acceptable, good enough, passable, all right

**scrawl** VERB

*He scrawled a quick note to his mother.*
▶ scribble, dash off, jot down, write

**scrawny** ADJECTIVE

*A bald scrawny man came in.*
▶ skinny, scraggy, thin, gawky

**scream** VERB

*She screamed at them to stop.*
▶ yell, shriek, shout, bawl, screech, roar, howl, wail

**scream** NOUN

*He let out a scream of pain.*
▶ yell, shriek, shout, screech, roar, howl, wail

**screen** NOUN

1 *a computer with a 17-inch screen*
▶ monitor, display, VDU or visual display unit
2 *A screen divided the room in two.*
▶ partition, divider, curtain, blind

**screen** VERB

1 *A low hedge screened the dustbins.*
▶ hide, conceal, mask, shield, shelter
2 *Staff are regularly screened in the interests of security.*
▶ vet, scrutinize, examine, investigate

**screw** VERB

1 *She screwed the lid on the jar.*
▶ fasten, tighten, twist, turn
2 *James screwed the piece of paper into a tight ball.*
▶ twist, wind, wring

3 *The last thing to do was screw the boards back down.*
▶ fix, fasten, secure
4 *(informal) He was not going to let them screw him for money like that again.*
▶ cheat, swindle, defraud, pressurize, extort, squeeze

**USAGE** If you use *extort* or *squeeze* you have to say (for example) *He was not going to let them extort money from him like that again.*

**scribble** VERB

*He quickly scribbled a shopping list.*
▶ scrawl, dash off, jot down, write

**scribe** NOUN

*He would need to get a scribe to write his letter for him.*
▶ copyist, clerk, transcriber, amanuensis, scrivener, secretary

**script** NOUN

1 *The note had been written in an elegant script.*
▶ handwriting, hand, autograph
2 *The film was spoilt by a poor script.*
▶ screenplay, text, dialogue

**scrounge** VERB

*Street urchins scrounged money from the tourists.*
▶ beg, cadge, sponge

**scrounger** NOUN

*He was neither a scrounger nor a misfit.*
▶ cadger, sponger, parasite

**scrub** VERB

1 *She decided to scrub the bathroom floor.*
▶ wash, clean, rub, brush, scour
2 *(informal) If interest rates went up again they would have to scrub their holiday.*
▶ cancel, scrap, go without, do without, call off, drop, abandon, (informal) ditch

**scruffy** ADJECTIVE

1 *He had worn scruffy jeans and a T-shirt to his Downing Street breakfast.*
▶ shabby, worn, ragged, worn-out, dirty
AN OPPOSITE IS smart
2 *He was standing in a bar, scruffy and long-haired.*
▶ unkempt, untidy, dishevelled, ungroomed, messy, bedraggled
AN OPPOSITE IS tidy

**scruples** NOUN

*He has no scruples about bending the rules.*
▶ qualms, compunction, conscience, misgivings, hesitation, doubts

**scrupulous** ADJECTIVE

1 *The story had been written with a scrupulous attention to historical accuracy.*
▶ conscientious, diligent, fastidious, meticulous, minute, painstaking, precise, punctilious, rigorous, strict, systematic, thorough
2 *The accounts will be reviewed by the most scrupulous auditor.*
▶ honest, honourable, upright, upstanding, principled, right-minded, fair-minded, ethical
AN OPPOSITE IS unscrupulous

**scrutinize** VERB
*Bernard scrutinized the poster.*
▶ examine, inspect, survey, study, peruse, scan, investigate

**scrutiny** NOUN
*She continued her scrutiny of the house.*
▶ examination, inspection, investigation, survey, perusal, study, search

**scuff** VERB
*The toe was scuffed and the shoes would need mending.*
▶ scrape, scratch, rub, graze, brush

**scuffle** NOUN
*There was a scuffle and the sound of people running.*
▶ fight, fracas, brawl, struggle, tussle, scrap, rumpus, commotion, argument

**scuffle** VERB
*Three teenage boys were scuffling and messing around.*
▶ fight, brawl, struggle, tussle, scrap, come to blows

**sculpture** NOUN
*a marble sculpture of Venus*
▶ carving, figure, statue, effigy, image
**USAGE** A small sculpture is called a *statuette*. A *bust* is a sculpture of the top part of a person.

**scum** NOUN
*The water had a thick scum on it.*
▶ froth, foam, film, impurities

**scupper** VERB
1 *The captain decided to scupper the ship.*
▶ scuttle, sink, submerge
2 *Lack of funds might scupper the project.*
▶ ruin, wreck, destroy, put paid to, frustrate, shatter, scotch, end, bring to an end

**scurrilous** ADJECTIVE
*a scurrilous attack on their integrity*
▶ offensive, abusive, insulting, defamatory, scandalous, slanderous, libellous, unfounded, unwarranted

**scurry** VERB
*Officials scurried about.*
▶ scamper, scuttle, dash, dart, rush, hurry

**scuttle** VERB
1 *The fleet was scuttled next day.*
▶ scupper, sink, submerge
2 *A waitress scuttled past carrying a cake.*
▶ scurry, scamper, dash, dart, scoot, run, rush, hasten, hurry

**sea** NOUN
1 *They caught sight of the sea in the distance.*
▶ water, ocean, waves
RELATED ADJECTIVES marine, maritime, nautical, naval
2 *sea creatures*
▶ aquatic, marine, seafaring, ocean, salt
3 *a sea voyage*
▶ ocean-going, oceanic, seagoing
4 *a sea of friendly faces*
▶ mass, host, multitude, profusion

**seal** NOUN
*the queen's seal*
▶ emblem, crest, insignia, symbol, stamp
**seal of approval** *The senior partner gave his seal of approval to the scheme.*
▶ endorsement, blessing, ratification, assent, consent

**seal** VERB
1 *She folded the letter and sealed the envelope.*
▶ stick down, close, fasten, secure
2 *He filled the jar and sealed it.*
▶ stop up, close, plug, stopper
3 *He held out a hand to seal the agreement.*
▶ confirm, clinch, complete, secure, (*more informal*) sew up
**seal off** *Police sealed off the city centre.*
▶ close off, shut off, cordon off, fence off, isolate

**seam** NOUN
1 *Small stitches will ensure a neat seam.*
▶ join, stitching
2 *a seam of coal*
▶ layer, stratum, vein

**seamy** ADJECTIVE
*He had discovered the seamy side of life.*
▶ sordid, seedy, sleazy, squalid, disreputable, unpleasant

**search** VERB
1 *We searched for clues.*
▶ look, hunt, explore, ferret about, nose about, poke about, prospect, pry, seek
2 *Security staff will search passengers and their luggage.*
▶ check, examine, investigate, scrutinize, inspect, (*more informal*) frisk
3 *I searched the house for my keys.*
▶ hunt through, scour, comb, ransack, rummage through, forage through

**search** NOUN
*We began our search for a place to eat.*
▶ hunt, quest, exploration, investigation, look, check

**searching** ADJECTIVE
1 *You have to ask yourself some searching questions.*
▶ penetrating, probing, incisive, sharp, shrewd, deep
AN OPPOSITE IS superficial
2 *He gave her a searching look.*
▶ observant, perceptive, discerning

**seaside** NOUN
*a trip to the seaside*
▶ coast, beach, seashore, shore
RELATED ADJECTIVE littoral

**season** NOUN
*The holiday season lasts until October these days.*
▶ period, time of year, time, phase

a b c d e f g h i j k l m n o p q r s t u v w x y z

**season** VERB

1 *herbs for seasoning fish*
► flavour, spice, salt, add seasoning to
2 *The wood should be well seasoned.*
► mature, age, temper, condition

**seasonable** ADJECTIVE

*seasonable weather*
► usual, normal, appropriate, expected, predictable, suitable

**seasoned** ADJECTIVE

*a seasoned traveller*
► experienced, practised, veteran, well versed

**seasoning** NOUN

*Add the garlic and a little seasoning.*
► flavouring, salt and pepper, spices, herbs

**seat** NOUN

1 *There were not enough seats for everyone to sit on.*
► chair, bench, stool, pew, place
2 *The capital city is not always the seat of government.*
► centre, headquarters, location, site, base, nucleus, heart, hub
3 *a country seat in Scotland*
► residence, ancestral, mansion, abode, stately home

**seat** VERB

1 *She seated her guests round a large oval table.*
► place, position, put, settle
2 *The smaller cinema seats thirty.*
► accommodate, holds, takes, have seats for, sit

**secede** VERB

**secede from** *The southern states seceded from the Union.*
► withdraw from, separate from, break away from, leave, quit, split with

**secluded** ADJECTIVE

*The path leads down to a secluded beach.*
► sheltered, private, concealed, hidden, undisturbed, unfrequented, isolated, remote
OPPOSITES ARE busy, public

**seclusion** NOUN

*a millionaire living in seclusion in Surrey*
► isolation, solitude, privacy, retreat, retirement, solitariness, concealment, secrecy

**second** ADJECTIVE

1 *There won't be a second chance.*
► another, further, additional, repeated, alternative, extra
2 *We keep a second set of data in another building.*
► spare, extra, alternative, backup

**second** NOUN (with the stress on *sec-*)

1 *They were only gone for a second.*
► moment, instant, bit, flash, (*more informal*) jiffy, (*more informal*) tick
2 *Chris was acting as his second.*
► assistant, attendant, supporter, right-hand man or woman, helper

**second** VERB (with the stress on *-cond*)

*She was seconded to another branch of the company for a year.*
► transfer, assign temporarily, move, relocate

**secondary** ADJECTIVE

1 *issues that are regarded as secondary*
► subsidiary, subordinate, minor, lesser, lower, inferior, second-rate
2 *A secondary action was started in support of the main attack.*
► extra, ancillary, auxiliary, supplementary, supportive, reinforcing, second, reserve

**second-class** ADJECTIVE

*They felt as though they were second-class citizens.*
► second-best, second-rate, inferior, lesser, unimportant

**second-hand** ADJECTIVE

1 *a second-hand car*
► used, pre-owned, old
AN OPPOSITE IS new
2 *She was relying on second-hand information.*
► indirect, secondary, derivative
AN OPPOSITE IS personal.

**second-rate** ADJECTIVE

*a second-rate holiday camp entertainer*
► second-class, second-best, substandard, mediocre, middling, ordinary, below par, commonplace, indifferent, inferior, low-grade

**secret** ADJECTIVE

1 *secret information*
► confidential, classified, restricted, (*more informal*) hush-hush
AN OPPOSITE IS public
2 *They met at a secret location.*
► private, secluded, hidden, isolated, remote, unknown, undisclosed
OPPOSITES ARE public, well-known
3 *a secret operation*
► undercover, clandestine, covert, surreptitious
AN OPPOSITE IS overt

**secretary** NOUN

*She called in her secretary to take notes of the meeting.*
► assistant, personal assistant or PA, clerk, typist

**secrete** VERB

1 *He secreted the money in a drawer.*
► hide, conceal, stow away, bury
2 *The bladder is a store for urine secreted by the kidneys.*
► discharge, emit, exude, produce, ooze, leak

**secretion** NOUN

*the secretion of hormones*
► discharge, production, emission, exudation

**secretive** ADJECTIVE

*He was being very secretive about his intentions.*
► uncommunicative, unforthcoming, reticent, tight-lipped, cagey, close, withdrawn
AN OPPOSITE IS communicative

## sect NOUN
*a religious sect*
▶ cult, denomination, faction, group, order

## sectarian ADJECTIVE
*sectarian politics*
▶ factional, schismatic, partisan, parochial, doctrinaire

## section NOUN
**1** *You must complete every section of the application form*
▶ part, division, portion, paragraph
**2** *the reference section of your local library*
▶ department, part, division

## sector NOUN
**1** *the northern sector of the city*
▶ district, region, section, area, part, quarter, zone
**2** *the private sector of industry*
▶ branch, arm, division

## secular ADJECTIVE
*secular music   a secular ceremony*
▶ non-religious, temporal, worldly, earthly, civil, lay
OPPOSITES ARE sacred, religious

## secure ADJECTIVE
**1** *Check that all doors and windows are secure.*
▶ locked, sealed, closed tight, impregnable, invulnerable
OPPOSITES ARE insecure, vulnerable
**2** *We felt secure indoors during the storm.*
▶ safe, protected, unharmed, unhurt, unscathed
OPPOSITES ARE exposed, in danger
**3** *The ladder needs to be made secure.*
▶ stable, steady, firm, fast, fixed, immovable
OPPOSITES ARE insecure, unsteady

## secure VERB
**1** *Secure the front door when you leave.*
▶ fasten, close, lock, shut, seal, bolt
**2** *a charter that secures the rights of the individual*
▶ ensure, assure, guarantee, protect, confirm
**3** *Jenny secured a senior post in the company.*
▶ obtain, acquire, gain, get, be given

## security NOUN
**1** *The first priority is the security of passengers.*
▶ safety, protection, care, guarding, freedom from harm
AN OPPOSITE IS vulnerability
**2** *The president's visit called for unprecedented levels of security.*
▶ safety measures, safeguards, protection, surveillance

## sedate ADJECTIVE
**1** *The procession moved forward at a sedate pace.*
▶ steady, unhurried, deliberate, gentle, easy-going, comfortable, slow
OPPOSITES ARE brisk, lively
**2** *They enjoyed their sedate suburban life and didn't hanker after the bright lights.*
▶ calm, staid, prim, sober, seemly, demure, dignified, serene

## sedate VERB
*The patient had to be sedated.*
▶ tranquillize, treat with sedatives, pacify, drug

## sedative NOUN
*The doctor prescribed him a sedative.*
▶ tranquillizer, sleeping pill, barbiturate, narcotic

## sedentary ADJECTIVE
*People with sedentary lifestyles need to take exercise.*
▶ seated, sitting, desk-bound, immobile, inactive
AN OPPOSITE IS active

## sediment NOUN
*There was a thick layer of sediment at the bottom of the bottle.*
▶ deposit, dregs, lees, residue, sludge

## seduce VERB
*They were seduced into buying by the clever sales talk.*
▶ entice, allure, lure, attract, beguile, mislead, ensnare, entrap, tempt, inveigle

## seduction NOUN
*the seductions of city life*
▶ attraction, temptation, allure, appeal, enticement

## seductive ADJECTIVE
**1** *Lori gave him one of her most seductive smiles.*
▶ sexy, alluring, captivating, ravishing, bewitching, appealing, attractive, enticing, irresistible, provocative, tempting
OPPOSITES ARE repulsive, repellent
**2** *the seductive warmth of a coal fire*
▶ attractive, appealing, enticing, comforting

## see VERB
**1** *She saw Eve waiting for her.   Did you see who got into the car with him?*
▶ perceive, glimpse, discern, make out, pick out, recognize, identify, distinguish
RELATED ADJECTIVE visible
**2** *She could see how difficult it might be..*
▶ understand, follow, know, comprehend, realize, recognize, take in, grasp, appreciate, fathom
**3** *I can see trouble ahead.*
▶ foresee, envisage, picture, visualize, predict, imagine, anticipate, conceive
**4** *We'll see what we can do.*
▶ consider, think about, reflect on, weigh up, decide, investigate
**5** *They are going to see the game on Saturday.*
▶ watch, attend, be a spectator at
**6** *Is she still seeing Stephen?*
▶ go out with, be dating, meet, visit
**7** *Keith offered to see her home.*
▶ take, escort, accompany, conduct
**8** *Stuart went to see the doctor about his leg.*
▶ visit, consult, confer with, talk to, speak to
**9** *I saw an old friend in town.*
▶ meet, encounter, run into, run across, chance on, (more informal) bump into
**10** *I must go and see what the dog is up to.*
▶ find out, discover, ascertain, establish

**11 see to** *Will you see to the repairs?*
► attend to, deal with, take care of, look after, sort out, organize, manage

**seed** NOUN
1 *The male provides the seed to fertilize the female egg.*
► sperm, semen, seminal fluid
2 *The birds feed on insects, seed, and shoots.*
► grains
3 *The fruit was full of seeds.*
► pip, stone
4 *The conflict was the seed for all future troubles.*
► source, origin, cause, basis
RELATED ADJECTIVE seminal

**seedy** ADJECTIVE
*a seedy hotel on the seafront*
► sleazy, squalid, shabby, run-down, sordid, seamy, rough

**seek** VERB
1 *The fleet sailed south to seek the enemy.*
► look for, search for, pursue, follow, try to find, hunt
2 *They will need to seek advice from a lawyer.*
► ask for, call on, get
3 *Spain is seeking the extradition of the suspects.*
► request, solicit, try to obtain
4 *We seek to please our customers.*
► try, attempt, endeavour, strive, aspire

**seem** VERB
*The woman seemed too afraid to speak.*
► appear, look, sound, give the impression of being

**seemly** ADJECTIVE
*It was not seemly to look too closely.*
► proper, decent, fitting, suitable

**seep** VERB
*Smoke seeped into the auditorium.*
► leak, ooze, escape, exude, flow, trickle, dribble

**seething** ADJECTIVE
1 *Rose was seething about what had happened.*
► fuming, furious, angry, livid, infuriated, incensed, outraged
2 *The water in the pan was seething.*
► boil, bubble, foam, froth up

**segment** NOUN
*Segments of orange decorated the top of the cake.*
► section, piece, slice, wedge, chunk

**segregate** VERB
*The school agreed to segregate them for swimming lessons.*
► separate, isolate, keep apart, set apart, put apart, exclude, cut off

**segregation** NOUN
1 *Racial segregation has been outlawed.*
► apartheid, discrimination, separation
2 *the segregation of smokers and non-smokers in public places*
► isolation, separation, keeping apart

**seize** VERB
1 *He seized the remote and turned up the volume.*
► grab, snatch, take hold of
OPPOSITES ARE release, let go of
2 *Rebels have seized an outpost in the jungle.*
► capture, take, take possession of, take over, overrun
OPPOSITES ARE abandon, relinquish
3 *Customs officers seized a large cache of drugs.*
► confiscate, appropriate, impound
OPPOSITES ARE return, give back
4 *Bandits seized his wife and children.*
► kidnap, abduct, take prisoner, capture, (more informal) snatch
OPPOSITES ARE release, let go

**seizure** NOUN
1 *Alexander's seizure of the city.*
► capture, occupation, subjugation, annexation
2 *He suffered a seizure on the journey home.*
► convulsion, attack, fit, stroke, spasm, paroxysm, apoplexy
3 *the unlawful seizure of goods*
► confiscation, impounding, appropriation, sequestration

**seldom** ADVERB
*She was seldom away from home for long.*
► rarely, not often, hardly ever, infrequently
AN OPPOSITE IS often

**select** VERB
*The committee met to select a chairperson.*
► choose, pick, appoint, name, elect, vote for, nominate, decide on

**select** ADJECTIVE
*a select group of former pupils*
► exclusive, élite, privileged, choice, chosen, hand-picked, preferred, special
AN OPPOSITE IS ordinary

**selection** NOUN
1 *There's a wide selection of food to choose from.*
► range, variety, assortment
2 *Mike put a coin in the machine and made his selection.*
► choice, pick, option

**selective** ADJECTIVE
*She's very selective in her reading.*
► discerning, discriminating, particular, careful, (more informal) choosy
AN OPPOSITE IS indiscriminate

**self-centred** ADJECTIVE
*Old people tend to become more self-centred as the years go by.*
► selfish, egocentric, self-absorbed, self-obsessed, inconsiderate

**self-confident** ADJECTIVE
*In self-confident mood, Franco pressed ahead with his plans.*
► self-assured, self-possessed, sure of yourself, confident, positive, assertive, assured, poised
AN OPPOSITE IS diffident

**self-conscious** ADJECTIVE

*He felt self-conscious about having to borrow money from his father.*
▶ embarrassed, bashful, diffident, uneasy, awkward, uncomfortable, unnatural, coy, shy, ill at ease, nervous
OPPOSITES ARE natural, confident

**self-contained** ADJECTIVE

**1** *The house was converted into four self-contained apartments.*
▶ complete, separate
**2** *This self-contained person was not going to admit anything.*
▶ independent, self-reliant, self-sufficient, aloof, unemotional
AN OPPOSITE IS sociable

**self-control** NOUN

*He lost self-control and killed her.*
▶ composure, restraint, self-discipline, calmness, coolness, self-command

**self-denial** NOUN

*a life of self-denial and humility*
▶ self-sacrifice, abstemiousness, selflessness, moderation, austerity
AN OPPOSITE IS self-indulgence

**self-employed** ADJECTIVE

*If you are self-employed you need to protect your livelihood.*
▶ freelance, independent, casual

**self-evident** ADJECTIVES

*The reasons are pretty self-evident.*
▶ obvious, plain, clear, apparent, transparent, evident

**self-important** ADJECTIVE

*A self-important figure in uniform was strutting about.*
▶ conceited, pompous, arrogant, bumptious, overbearing

**self-indulgent** ADJECTIVE

*For many, a second home seems a self-indulgent luxury.*
▶ extravagant, pleasure-seeking, hedonistic, intemperate
OPPOSITES ARE restrained, abstemious

**selfish** ADJECTIVE

*People are seen as being more selfish and less tolerant.*
▶ self-centred, egocentric, inconsiderate, self-absorbed, self-obsessed
OPPOSITES ARE unselfish, considerate, generous, selfless

**selfishness** NOUN

*They were motivated by greed and selfishness.*
▶ egotism, self-obsession, self-interest, thoughtlessness, meanness
OPPOSITES ARE unselfishness, generosity

**selfless** ADJECTIVE

*He made a selfless sacrifice for his country.*
▶ unselfish, generous, magnanimous

**self-respect** NOUN

*Under the new president, the country prospered and recovered its self-respect.*
▶ pride, dignity, self-confidence, self-esteem

**self-righteous** ADJECTIVE

*He called her a stuck-up, self-righteous Miss Perfect.*
▶ sanctimonious, holier-than-thou, priggish, smug, self-satisfied, moralizing, unctuous

**self-sacrifice** NOUN

*Day-to-day living was based on constant toil and self-sacrifice.*
▶ self-denial, selflessness, unselfishness

**self-satisfied** ADJECTIVE

*Hilary relaxed and gave a little self-satisfied smile.*
▶ smug, complacent, self-congratulatory

**self-supporting** ADJECTIVE

*measures that would make more colleges self-supporting*
▶ independent, self-sufficient, self-reliant, self-contained

**sell** VERB

**1** *The corner shop sells basic provisions.*
▶ stock, trade in, deal in, retail, handle, peddle
**2** *They are having problems selling their house.*
▶ put on the market, dispose of, (more formal) vend

**seller** NOUN

*sellers of household goods*
▶ supplier, trader (in), dealer (in), vendor, retailer, stockist, purveyor

**semblance** NOUN

*A semblance of order was restored.*
▶ appearance, show, pretence, air, facade, front

**send** VERB

**1** *I'll send you a letter.*
▶ post, mail, dispatch, convey, forward
**2** *She sent John a message.*
▶ fax, email, wire, transmit
**3** *The space programme will be sending a satellite into orbit.*
▶ launch, propel, shoot, direct, fire
**4** *It's the sort of remark that sends you mad.*
▶ make, drive, cause to be
**send for** *They decided to send for the police.*
▶ call, fetch, summon, ask to come
**send out** *The chimneys send out grey fumes.*
▶ discharge, emit, give off, belch
**send round** *The manager sent round a questionnaire.*
▶ circulate, distribute, publish, issue
**send up** *The sketch sent up story-book heroes.*
▶ satirize, ridicule, parody, make fun of, caricature, lampoon

**send-off** NOUN

*They gave Anthony a magnificent send-off.*
▶ farewell, goodbye, leave-taking

**send-up** NOUN

*a hilarious send-up of a spy movie*
▶ satire, parody, caricature, lampoon, (more informal) spoof

**senile** ADJECTIVE
*Her husband was becoming senile and difficult to cope with.*
► old, aged, doddering, infirm, feeble, decrepit, (*more informal*) past it
AN OPPOSITE IS in his or her prime

**senior** ADJECTIVE
1 *a senior pupil*
► older, elder
2 *a senior official*
► high-ranking, superior, chief
OPPOSITES ARE junior, subordinate

**seniority** NOUN
*The Chief Clerk was next in seniority.*
► rank, standing, precedence, superiority

**sensation** NOUN
1 *She felt a sensation of floating.*
► feeling, sense, awareness, impression
2 *The affair caused a sensation.*
► commotion, excitement, stir, furore, outrage, scandal, surprise, thrill

**sensational** ADJECTIVE
1 *a sensational murder trial*
► shocking, horrifying, lurid, scandalous, thrilling, blood-curdling, breathtaking, exciting, hair-raising
2 *Her singing was sensational.*
► amazing, extraordinary, remarkable, wonderful, fabulous, fantastic, magnificent, great, marvellous, spectacular, superb

**sense** NOUN
1 *She has a strong sense of rhythm.*
► feeling, sensation, perception
2 *He felt a sense of guilt.*
► feeling, awareness, sensation, perception
3 *They had the sense to get out in time.*
► wisdom, common sense, intelligence, wit, shrewdness
4 *I couldn't see the sense of leaving then.*
► point, purpose, advantage, benefit
5 *I didn't grasp the sense of their message.*
► meaning, significance, substance, implication, import, drift, gist, point
**make sense of** *It's hard to make sense of these remarks.*
► understand, grasp, comprehend

**sense** VERB
*We sensed that they didn't trust us.*
► feel, suspect, discern, perceive, realize, get the impression, appreciate, guess, notice, be aware, detect

**senseless** ADJECTIVE
1 *It was a senseless crime.*
► pointless, futile, needless, aimless, absurd, nonsensical, foolish, stupid
2 *They found him in the morning, senseless but alive.*
► unconscious, comatose, stunned, out cold

**sensible** ADJECTIVE
1 *Joanna was sensible enough to listen. Everyone agreed that this was a sensible decision.*
► wise, prudent, thoughtful, far-sighted, shrewd, judicious, intelligent, pragmatic, responsible, realistic, rational, level-headed
OPPOSITES ARE foolish, unwise
2 *She liked to wear sensible clothes.*
► practical, functional, comfortable, useful, (*informal*) no-nonsense
OPPOSITES ARE impractical, fashionable

**sensitive** ADJECTIVE
1 *The human eye is very sensitive to green.*
► responsive, reactive, susceptible, affected (by), conscious (of)
AN OPPOSITE IS insensitive
2 *The problem needs sensitive handling.*
► tactful, thoughtful, considerate, sympathetic, understanding, perceptive
OPPOSITES ARE insensitive, tactless
3 *She's a very sensitive girl, so take care what you say.*
► emotional, easily offended, easily upset, volatile, thin-skinned, touchy
AN OPPOSITE IS thick-skinned
4 *Take care in the sun if you have a fair sensitive skin.*
► delicate, soft, tender, fragile, fine
OPPOSITES ARE tough, resilient
5 *The court ruling comes at a sensitive time for the government.*
► awkward, tricky, controversial, delicate
AN OPPOSITE IS uncontroversial

**sensual** ADJECTIVE
1 *sensual pleasures*
► physical, sexual, erotic, carnal, bodily
2 *a beautiful sensual woman*
► sexually attractive, sexy, voluptuous, seductive, passionate
**USAGE** *Sensual* and *sensuous* are often used in the same way, although there is a formal distinction in that *sensual* has stronger sexual connotations whereas *sensuous* is more neutral.

**sensuous** ADJECTIVE
*sensuous music*
► emotional, lush, rich, affecting, appealing, beautiful, richly embellished
AN OPPOSITE IS simple

**sentence** NOUN
1 *The judge will decide on a sentence next week.*
► judgement, ruling, decision, verdict
2 *Her husband is serving a three-year sentence for robbery.*
► prison term, (*more informal*) stretch

**sentence** VERB
*The men will be sentenced at a later date.*
► pass judgement on, pronounce sentence on, punish

## sentiment NOUN

**1** *I agree with the sentiments expressed in your letter.*
▶ view, opinion, belief, thought, attitude, idea, judgement
**2** *There's not much room for sentiment in this kind of business.*
▶ sentimentality, emotionalism, finer feelings, sensibility, soft-heartedness, mawkishness

## sentimental ADJECTIVE

**1** *The family held a sentimental attachment to their old home.*
▶ emotional, nostalgic, affectionate, tender, romantic, soft-hearted
**2** *a sentimental story about separated twins*
▶ maudlin, mawkish, over-emotional, sickly, saccharine, syrupy, indulgent, gushing, corny, (*more informal*) soppy, (*more informal*) mushy, (*more informal*) treacly
OPPOSITES ARE unsentimental, realistic

## sentry NOUN

*A sentry was on duty at the gate.*
▶ guard, sentinel, lookout, watchman, patrol, picket

## separable ADJECTIVE

*The components are separable and can be replaced individually. Teaching and research are not completely separable activities.*
▶ separate, distinct, detachable, divisible, removable, distinguishable

## separate ADJECTIVE

**1** *The guards took care to keep the two groups separate.*
▶ apart, segregated, cut off, divided, divorced, fenced off, isolated
OPPOSITES ARE together, united
**2** *You may prefer to have the kitchen separate from the dining area. The reports may have been referring to two separate events.*
▶ distinct, detached, different, discrete, unattached (to), unconnected (to)
AN OPPOSITE IS joined

## separate VERB

**1** *They were arguing so fiercely it was difficult to separate them. The war separated us for many years.*
▶ divide, part, break up, split up, segregate
AN OPPOSITE IS unite
**2** *Only a short distance separated them.*
▶ divide, come between
AN OPPOSITE IS unite
**3** *We separated at the station and I went home.*
▶ part company, go different ways, split up
AN OPPOSITE IS meet
**4** *The path separated and went up the hill.*
▶ diverge, fork, branch off
AN OPPOSITE IS merge
**5** *Separate the yolks of the eggs from the whites.*
▶ remove, extract, isolate, abstract, filter out
AN OPPOSITE IS mix
**6** *When his parents separated he lived with his mother.*
▶ split up, break up, divorce, part, become estranged, part company

**7** **separate from** *She separated herself from the company and formed her own business.*
▶ withdraw from, break away from, leave, quit, dissociate yourself from
AN OPPOSITE IS join

## separation NOUN

**1** *the separation of church and state*
▶ division, splitting, dissociation, severance, detachment, disconnection, parting, isolation, removal, segregation, cutting off
OPPOSITES ARE merging, unification
**2** (*informal*) *The separation of the prince and princess has been formally announced.*
▶ break-up, split, parting, rift, estrangement
AN OPPOSITE IS marriage

## septic ADJECTIVE

*One of her toes looked septic.*
▶ infected, poisoned, putrefying, festering, putrid, inflamed, purulent, suppurating

## sequel NOUN

**1** *The immediate sequel was a riot in the capital.*
▶ consequence, result, outcome, upshot
**2** *a sequel to Daphne du Maurier's 'Rebecca'.*
▶ continuation, (*more informal*) follow-up

## sequence NOUN

**1** *A similar sequence of events occurred in the Baltic States.*
▶ succession, order, course, progression, series, chain, cycle
**2** *Here is a short sequence from her new film.*
▶ excerpt, scene, clip, extract, section, episode

## serene ADJECTIVE

*Her eyes lit up, and a serene smile spread across her face.*
▶ calm, composed, contented, untroubled, unruffled, placid, tranquil, peaceful, imperturbable, quiet
AN OPPOSITE IS agitated

## series NOUN

**1** *Guerrillas carried out a series of kidnappings.*
▶ succession, sequence, string, chain, wave, spate, rash, outbreak, run
**2** *Filming has started on a six-part drama series.*
▶ serial, run of programmes

## serious ADJECTIVE

**1** *She wore a serious expression.*
▶ solemn, grave, earnest, thoughtful, pensive, sombre, unsmiling, grim, dour
OPPOSITES ARE jovial, cheerful
**2** *A serious disagreement arose between them.*
▶ important, significant, momentous, critical, urgent, weighty, crucial, grave
OPPOSITES ARE unimportant, frivolous
**3** *She suffered serious injuries when she fell from her horse. robbery, assault, theft, and other serious crimes*
▶ severe, critical, bad, acute, shocking, terrible, appalling, dreadful, grave, grievous
AN OPPOSITE IS trivial

**4** *He said he was only interested in serious literature*
▶ intellectual, scholarly, learned, highbrow, profound, (*more informal*) heavy
**5** *Are you serious about leaving?*
▶ sincere, in earnest, genuine, committed, wholehearted
AN OPPOSITE IS uncommitted

**seriously** ADVERB
**1** *He looked at her seriously, frowning deeply.*
▶ solemnly, earnestly, thoughtfully, sternly, dourly
**2** *The baby was seriously ill in hospital.*
▶ severely, critically, badly, acutely, gravely
**3** *Do you seriously expect me to believe you?*
▶ really, actually, honestly

**sermon** NOUN
*His sermon on patriotism fell completely flat.*
▶ homily, address, lesson, talk

**servant** NOUN
*A servant appeared, carrying a tray.*
▶ attendant, retainer, domestic, valet, butler, maid, menial, helper, (*more informal*) skivvy, (*more informal*) flunkey

**serve** VERB
**1** *They served their masters well.*
▶ attend, assist, look after, minister to, work for
**2** *He claimed to use his business skills to serve the public interest.*
▶ further, advance, benefit, advantage, support
**3** *The book served as a useful guide to the city's attractions. a slogan that would serve for the whole range of products*
▶ function, be adequate, be useful
**4** *a tool that serves a special purpose*
▶ fulfil, answer, perform, satisfy, complete, discharge
**5** *At that point he went in to serve the food.*
▶ give out, dish up, distribute, provide
**6** *Molly spent the summer serving in a local shop.*
▶ assist, be an assistant, sell
**7** *serve on He had served on the committee for ten years.*
▶ work on, be a member of, sit on, contribute to

**service** NOUN
**1** *The contract lists the terms of service.*
▶ employment, work, business, labour, duty
**2** *They have done us quite a service.*
▶ favour, benefit, assistance, kindness, good turn
**3** *products that will give years of service*
▶ use, usage, utility
**4** *She took the car in for a service.*
▶ overhaul, maintenance check
**5** *a church service*
▶ ceremony, worship, ritual, rite, observance

**service** VERB
*A local garage services their car.*
▶ maintain, repair, check, mend, overhaul

**serviceable** ADJECTIVE
**1** *He was conscious of his own serviceable but dowdy clothes.*
▶ functional, practical, dependable, hard-wearing, durable, tough, robust, lasting, strong, sensible
AN OPPOSITE IS impractical
**2** *The door of the cottage had stout and serviceable bolts.*
▶ working, usable, functioning, operational, workable

**servile** ADJECTIVE
*Parents have no right to expect servile obedience from their children.*
▶ obsequious, subservient, submissive, unctuous, abject, craven, cringing, fawning, sycophantic, grovelling, menial, slavish, humble, ingratiating, (*more informal*) bootlicking
AN OPPOSITE IS domineering

**serving** NOUN
*a large serving of pasta*
▶ portion, helping, plateful, plate, share, amount, ration, (*more informal*) dollop

**session** NOUN
**1** *The council held its first session in October.*
▶ meeting, sitting, assembly, conference, discussion, hearing
**2** *More practice sessions were needed.*
▶ period, time, spell, bout

**set** NOUN
**1** *There was a set of keys on the table. The government will announce a set of new proposals on human rights.*
▶ collection, group, series, batch, bunch, assortment, array
**2** *She belonged to a fashionable London set.*
▶ circle, clique, group, crowd, coterie, company
**3** *a television set*
▶ apparatus, receiver
**4** *a chemistry set*
▶ kit, outfit, apparatus
**5** *The production boasted a spectacular set and lavish costumes.*
▶ staging, setting, scenery, stage furniture

**set** VERB
**1** *She set the bags on a bench in the porch.*
▶ put, place, deposit, position, stand, leave, settle, station, post
**2** *We should set a date for the next meeting.*
▶ fix, decide on, agree on, establish, choose, select, name, arrange, schedule
**3** *She set the alarm for five the next morning.*
▶ adjust, regulate, programme, synchronize
**4** *The sun was setting.*
▶ go down, sink, subside, vanish, disappear

**5** *Leave the jelly in the fridge to set.*
▶ harden, solidify, thicken, stiffen, gel

**set about**
**1** *He set about the task with gusto.*
▶ begin, start, make a start on, get down to, embark on, tackle
**2** *A gang set about them in a dark alley.*
▶ attack, assault, assail, fall on, lay into

**set aside**
**1** *Daphne set aside money each month towards her holiday.*
▶ save, put by, keep, earmark
**2** *The decision was set aside in the Appeal Court.*
▶ overrule, overturn, reverse, revoke, quash, annul

**set off** *We set off early for the airport.*
▶ start out, leave, depart

**set out** *He set out his collection of coins.*
▶ lay out, arrange, display, exhibit, present

**set up**
**1** *A statue will be set up in the main square.*
▶ erect, put up, raise, construct
**2** *The company plans to set up a branch in New York.*
▶ open, establish, found, start, institute
**3** *Her secretary set up a meeting for the following week.*
▶ organize, arrange, fix, schedule

**setback** NOUN
*He had survived a whole series of setbacks.*
▶ difficulty, problem, hitch, delay, hold-up, obstacle, reverse, snag, blow, upset, disappointment, complication, misfortune, *(more informal)* glitch, *(more informal)* hiccup
OPPOSITES ARE advance, breakthrough

**setting** NOUN
**1** *a relaxing holiday in a quiet setting*
▶ surroundings, location, position, site, background, environment, locale
**2** *diamonds in a silver setting*
▶ mounting, mount, fixture, surround
**3** *a drama in a historical setting*
▶ backdrop, context, *(French)* mise en scène, scene, set

**settle** VERB
**1** *Further talks will be held today in an attempt to settle the dispute.*
▶ resolve, conclude, clear up, put an end to, find a solution to, reach an agreement about
**2** *The solicitors will settle their affairs.*
▶ arrange, organize, sort out, put in order, order, complete
**3** *After the war the family settled in Liverpool.*
▶ move (to), set up home, make your home, establish yourself
**4** *We can settle the bill in the morning.*
▶ pay, square, clear
**5** *Jack settled into an armchair by the fire.*
▶ sink, fall, drop, subside
**6** *A bird settled on a branch.*
▶ land, alight, descend

**7** *He needed something to settle his nerves.*
▶ calm, soothe, compose, pacify, quell
AN OPPOSITE IS agitate

**settle down** *Why can't you settle down?*
▶ calm down, quieten down, be quiet, be still, relax
**settle down to** *Rachel wanted her to settle down to something.*
▶ get down to, apply yourself to, concentrate on, focus on
**settle for** *Shelby wasn't a man to settle for a dull life.*
▶ agree to, accept, acquiesce in, compromise on
**settle on** *It was high time they settled on a date for the wedding.*
▶ decide, choose, fix, agree on, name, arrange, organize, schedule

**settlement** NOUN
**1** *a legal settlement*
▶ agreement, deal, arrangement, treaty, contract
**2** *The dispute is no nearer settlement.*
▶ resolution, solution, sorting out, settling
**3** *an Iron-Age settlement near the modern trunk road*
▶ community, colony, encampment, commune, town, village

**settler** NOUN
*Settlers had established a town there.*
▶ colonist, immigrant, pioneer, newcomer

**set-up** NOUN
*a modern communications set-up   a new constitutional set-up for the EU*
▶ system, arrangement, framework, organization, business, operation

**sever** VERB
**1** *The arm had been severed at the shoulder.*
▶ cut off, cut, chop off, hack off, shear off, slice off, separate, amputate, disconnect, remove
**2** *Henry VIII severed his relationship with the Church of Rome.*
▶ break off, cut off, terminate, disconnect, cease

**several** ADJECTIVE
**1** *The cable is split into several strands.   He had admitted the murder several times.*
▶ a number of, many, some, a few
**2** *There are several ways of looking at the problem.*
▶ various, miscellaneous, a number of, sundry, assorted

**severe** ADJECTIVE
**1** *The region faced a severe threat of mass starvation. Wreckage covered the road, causing severe traffic disruption.*
▶ serious, acute, grave, extreme, critical, dire, grievous
AN OPPOSITE IS minor
**2** *Many birds were found injured or dead after the severe weather.*
▶ harsh, hard, extreme, turbulent, stormy
AN OPPOSITE IS mild
**3** *Oliver developed a severe stomach ulcer.   The pains could be severe and disruptive.*
▶ acute, intense, painful, excruciating
AN OPPOSITE IS slight

**sew** VERB

4 *The expedition will be a severe test of their stamina.*
► demanding, hard, formidable, difficult, onerous, burdensome
OPPOSITES ARE simple, easy

5 *She did not expect the criticism to be so severe.*
► fierce, harsh, sharp, scathing, caustic
AN OPPOSITE IS mild

6 *More severe penalties were needed for hit-and-run drivers. They deplored the imposition of such severe censorship.*
► strict, harsh, draconian, ruthless
AN OPPOSITE IS mild

7 *It was described as neoclassical architecture in a severe style.*
► plain, simple, spare, stark, unadorned
OPPOSITES ARE ornate, elaborate

**sew** VERB
*His aunt sewed the badge on his sleeve.*
► stitch, tack, attach, fasten
OPPOSITES ARE unpick, remove
**sew up** *You need to sew up the hole in your sleeve.*
► darn, stitch, mend, patch, repair

**sewing** NOUN
*She always had a piece of sewing tucked in her belt.*
► embroidery, mending, needlepoint, needlework

**sex** NOUN
1 *The disease affects children of both sexes.*
► gender
2 *There is nothing wrong in asking questions about sex.*
► the facts of life, sexual activity, reproduction, sexual reproduction
3 *Unsafe sex in this age group was increasing.*
► sexual intercourse, intercourse, making love, lovemaking, sexual relations
**have sex** *Derek said they'd been having sex.*
► have sexual intercourse, make love, go to bed together, (more informal) go all the way

**sexual** ADJECTIVE
1 *A bit of petting had been the only sexual activity.*
► erotic, physical, sensual, carnal, sexy
2 *A diagram of the sexual organs might help.*
► reproductive, procreative, genital

**sexy** ADJECTIVE
1 *'You're young,' he said coolly, 'beautiful, sexy, and intelligent.'*
► sexually attractive, desirable, seductive, sensual
2 *Louise stripped to her sexy lace underwear.*
► titillating, erotic, suggestive, salacious, lewd, racy, sexually explicit, pornographic, (more informal) steamy

**shabby** ADJECTIVE
1 *Florrie straightened the lapel of her shabby coat.*
► worn, scruffy, ragged, tattered
2 *She went into a shabby coffee bar in the centre of town.*
► run-down, scruffy, dilapidated, seedy, dingy, dirty, poky, tatty
3 *He hated resorting to such shabby lying.*
► shameful, mean, cheap, contemptible, despicable, rotten

**shack** NOUN
*a shack in the woods*
► hut, cabin, shanty, shed, hovel

**shade** NOUN
1 *They spend most of the day lying in the shade.*
► shadow, shelter, cover
2 *The shades of evening drew on.*
► darkness, twilight, gloominess, dimness, obscurity, shadow
3 *She pulled the shade down over the window.*
► blind, screen, curtain, awning, canopy
4 *a mass-produced shirt in a harsh shade of blue*
► hue, tinge, tint, tone, colour
5 *All shades of opinion were represented.*
► variety, variation, form, nuance, subtlety
6 *a shade* *Silvio laughed a shade too heartily.*
► a little, a bit, a touch, rather, (more informal) a tad

**shade** VERB
1 *A tall fence shaded most of the garden.*
► overshadow, cast a shadow over, screen, shield, shroud, veil, conceal, obscure, mask, protect
2 *You can shade the background with a dark pencil.*
► colour in, darken, block in

**shadow** NOUN
1 *He lingered in the shadow of the corridor outside the room.*
► shade, darkness, dimness, semi-darkness, gloom
2 *She saw a shadow on the wall.*
► silhouette, outline, shape, profile, contour
3 *There's not a shadow of doubt that they were there at the time of the crime.*
► trace, slightest bit, scrap, shred, crumb, ounce, particle, iota, jot
4 *There was a shadow of a smile across her face.*
► hint, flicker, suspicion, trace, suggestion, sign

**shadow** VERB
*He continued to shadow the van until forced to return.*
► follow, trail, track, stalk, pursue

**shadowy** ADJECTIVE
1 *They made out a shadowy form in front of them.*
► indistinct, hazy, vague, blurred, blurry, nebulous, unsubstantial, indeterminate, indistinguishable, unrecognizable
2 *She let herself out into the shadowy hall.*
► dark, shady, shaded

**shady** ADJECTIVE
1 *Mrs Halliday took Dot down a shady footpath.*
► shaded, shadowy, sheltered, dark, shrouded, sunless
OPPOSITES ARE sunny, bright
2 *Blake had been authorized to do shady deals with Russian intelligence.*
► dubious, suspect, suspicious, disreputable, unethical, dishonest, untrustworthy, (more informal) fishy, (more informal) dodgy, (more informal) shifty
AN OPPOSITE IS honest

## shaft NOUN

**1** *a wooden shaft*
▶ pole, rod, stick, staff, shank, post

**2** *The shaft of a pickaxe lay on the ground.*
▶ handle, stem, stock

**3** *The first shaft of light broke through the window.*
▶ ray, beam, gleam, bar, finger

**4** *a shaft in a mine*
▶ passage, mineshaft, tunnel, duct

## shaggy ADJECTIVE

*He had a shaggy coat you could lose a hairdryer in. The big shaggy head turned to look at me.*
▶ hairy, bushy, thick, woolly, fleecy, unkempt, dishevelled, unshorn, hirsute
OPPOSITES ARE smooth, sleek

## shake VERB

**1** *The whole building seemed to shake. We were shaking with fear.*
▶ tremble, quiver, shudder, shiver, convulse, judder, heave, wobble

**2** *The wind shook the window frame.*
▶ rattle, vibrate

**3** *She shook her umbrella at an approaching taxi.*
▶ wave, waggle, wag, brandish, flourish, jiggle, joggle

**4** *The news shook them.*
▶ shock, startle, unnerve, unsettle, upset, alarm, distress, disturb, frighten, perturb

**shake something off** *Bobby finally shook off his flu and was able to play again.*
▶ get over, recover from, get rid of, (more informal) see the back of

**shake someone off** *He looked round to see if he had shaken off his pursuer.*
▶ escape, elude, get away from, leave behind, give someone the slip

## shaky ADJECTIVE

**1** *They sat at a shaky table.*
▶ unsteady, flimsy, wobbly, rickety, rocky, weak, frail, ramshackle

**2** *She let out a deep, shaky breath.*
▶ trembling, shaking, faltering, quivering

**3** *His voice was shaky with emotion.*
▶ quavering, unsteady, faltering, nervous, tremulous
AN OPPOSITE IS steady

**4** *He had to admit it was a shaky alibi, but he got away with it.*
▶ precarious, uncertain, unpromising, doubtful, unsound

## shallow ADJECTIVE

*I do not agree with that shallow view of the situation.*
▶ superficial, facile, oversimplified, simplistic, narrow, flimsy, lightweight, surface
OPPOSITES ARE profound, deep

## sham NOUN

*The lad's appearance and manner could be a sham.*
▶ pretence, act, fake, fraud, fiction, lie
AN OPPOSITE IS real thing

## sham ADJECTIVE

*She felt trapped in a sham marriage.*
▶ false, fake, bogus, pretended, simulated, imitation
AN OPPOSITE IS genuine

## sham VERB

*He wasn't shamming, he was obviously injured.*
▶ pretend, fake, dissemble

## shambles NOUN

*(informal) The room was a shambles. The loans scheme had degenerated into a shambles.*
▶ mess, muddle, chaos, confusion, disorder

## shame NOUN

**1** *He couldn't face the shame of being found out.*
▶ humiliation, opprobrium, dishonour, disgrace, stigma, remorse, guilt, embarrassment, ignominy, mortification, degradation, discredit
OPPOSITES ARE honour, pride

**2** **a shame** *It's a shame he didn't stick to chess instead of cards.*
▶ a pity, unfortunate, a piece of bad luck, a cause for regret
OPPOSITES ARE fortunate, lucky

## shame VERB

**1** *He had been shamed in public.*
▶ humiliate, mortify, humble, chasten, embarrass, (more informal) show up

**2** *You have shamed your family name. He would have shamed an angel with his table manners.*
▶ disgrace, dishonour, discredit, degrade, taint, tarnish
OPPOSITES ARE honour, do credit to

## shamefaced ADJECTIVE

*'I'm sorry,' said Anthony, looking shamefaced.*
▶ ashamed, embarrassed, abashed, penitent, repentant, self-conscious, sheepish, hangdog, mortified, sorry
OPPOSITES ARE proud, unrepentant

## shameful ADJECTIVE

*The scheme had been a shameful waste of money.*
▶ disgraceful, deplorable, contemptible, outrageous, reprehensible, scandalous, unworthy, wicked, vile
AN OPPOSITE IS honourable

## shameless ADJECTIVE

**1** *People said he was a shameless sponger.*
▶ brazen, bold, audacious, forward, incorrigible, abandoned
OPPOSITES ARE reticent, bashful

**2** *They knew it was a shameless lie.*
▶ blatant, flagrant, barefaced, unashamed, overt

**shape** NOUN
1 *The shape of their bodies changes with astonishing speed.*
▶ form, figure, configuration, physique, outline, profile, silhouette, pattern
2 *For his age he was in pretty good shape.*
▶ condition, health, state, trim, fettle, (*more informal*) nick

**TWO-DIMENSIONAL GEOMETRICAL SHAPES**

**shapes with straight sides**: decagon (10 sides), diamond, dodecagon (12 sides), hendecagon (11 sides), heptagon (7 sides), hexagon (6 sides), lozenge (diamond shape), nonagon (9 sides), oblong (4 sides with right angles and opposite sides equal in length), octagon (8 sides), parallelogram (4 sides with opposite sides parallel), pentagon (5 sides), polygon (5 or more sides), quadrangle (4 sides), quadrilateral (4 sides), rectangle (4 sides with right angles and opposite sides equal in length), rhombus (4 equal sides), square (4 equal sides with right angles), trapezium (4 sides with 2 opposite sides parallel), triangle (3 sides: an isosceles triangle has two sides equal in length and an equilateral triangle has three sides equal in length).

**shapes with curved sides**: circle, ellipse, ovoid, semicircle.

**THREE-DIMENSIONAL SHAPES**

cone, cube, cuboid, cylinder, prism, pyramid, sphere.

**shape** VERB
*She shaped the clay into a tall pot. A number of factors have shaped their ideas.*
▶ form, fashion, mould, cast, make, sculpt

**shapeless** ADJECTIVE
1 *This shapeless mass was my dinner.*
▶ formless, amorphous, indeterminate, irregular, nebulous, undefined, unformed, vague
AN OPPOSITE IS defined.
2 *Gladys removed a shapeless cardigan and hung it over the chair.*
▶ baggy, saggy, sagging, unshapely, formless, dumpy
AN OPPOSITE IS shapely

**shapely** ADJECTIVE
*advertisements full of shapely hips and pretty faces*
▶ well-proportioned, elegant, graceful, attractive, trim
AN OPPOSITE IS shapeless

**share** NOUN
*We will get a share of the profits.*
▶ portion, part, division, quota, allocation, allowance

**share** VERB
1 *Member countries will have to share the costs.*
▶ divide, split, deal out, distribute, ration out, share out, apportion, allocate, allot, go halves with

2 *She had to share a room with two other people.*
▶ use jointly, live in
3 **share in** *It is important for everyone to share in the decision-making process.*
▶ be involved in, take part in, participate in, join in, cooperate in

**sharp** ADJECTIVE
1 *A sharp knife is essential.*
▶ keen-edged, keen, pointed, spiky
AN OPPOSITE IS blunt
2 *Kittens can strike out with their sharp claws.*
▶ pointed, jagged, cutting
3 *She felt a sharp pain in her arm.*
▶ acute, piercing, intense, fierce, stabbing, severe
OPPOSITES ARE gentle, mild
4 *a cheese with a sharp flavour*
▶ strong, piquant, pungent, bitter
OPPOSITES ARE mild, mellow
5 *There was a sharp cry from outside. There was a series of sharp raps on the door.*
▶ loud, piercing, shrill, high-pitched
AN OPPOSITE IS soft
6 *A sharp wind blew outside.*
▶ cold, chilly, bitter, keen, brisk, biting, cutting
OPPOSITES ARE gentle, warm
7 *If he disapproves there will be frowns and sharp words.*
▶ harsh, bitter, cutting, scathing, caustic, acerbic, tart
8 *She adjusted the focus to make the image sharper.*
▶ distinct, clear, crisp
OPPOSITES ARE blurred, indistinct
9 *There could be a sharp drop in prices.*
▶ rapid, steep, sudden, abrupt
AN OPPOSITE IS gradual
10 *His sharp eyes spotted something moving.*
▶ keen, perceptive, observant, keen-sighted, acute
AN OPPOSITE IS weak
11 *He had a quick wit and a sharp mind.*
▶ perceptive, incisive, discerning, percipient
OPPOSITES ARE dull, slow

**sharpen** VERB
*You will need to sharpen the knife.*
▶ make sharp, whet, hone, grind, strop, file
AN OPPOSITE IS blunt

**shatter** VERB
1 *The blast was loud enough to shatter windows. The glass shattered like an eggshell.*
▶ break, smash, blow out, splinter, crack
2 *The silence was shattered by a warning shout from the alley.*
▶ destroy, wreck, ruin, dash, overturn, upset

**shattered** ADJECTIVE
1 *She seemed shattered by the refusal.*
▶ upset, devastated, stunned, shocked, staggered, distraught

**shave**

2 *By the time he reached home he felt shattered.*
▶ exhausted, tired out, worn out, weary, fatigued, (*more informal*) dead tired, (*more informal*) played out, (*more informal*) washed out

**shave** VERB
*His shot shaved the near post.*
▶ brush, graze, touch, glance off
**shave off** *Michael shaved off his moustache.*
▶ cut off, snip off, crop

**sheath** NOUN
*He had the knife half out of its sheath.*
▶ case, casing, covering, sleeve, scabbard

**shed** NOUN
*Marion kept her rabbits in a garden shed.*
▶ hut, shack, shelter, storehouse, lean-to, outhouse, potting shed

**shed** VERB
*A lorry had shed its load on the inside lane.*
▶ spill, throw off, drop, scatter, cast off, discard, let fall, shower

**sheen** NOUN
*Using the right polish will give the surface a delicate sheen.*
▶ shine, gloss, lustre, brightness, gleam, patina, burnish, polish

**sheepish** ADJECTIVE
*His smile turned into a sheepish grin..*
▶ embarrassed, shamefaced, abashed, ashamed, bashful, coy, guilty, mortified, self-conscious, shy, timid
AN OPPOSITE IS unabashed

**sheer** ADJECTIVE
1 *It was sheer chance that Beverley had been to the same hotel. The offence was an act of sheer desperation.*
▶ utter, complete, absolute, total, pure, unmitigated, unqualified, out-and-out
2 *A few yards ahead was a sheer drop.*
▶ vertical, abrupt, precipitous, perpendicular
3 *Sheer fabrics look great in a bathroom setting.*
▶ fine, gauzy, flimsy, see-through, diaphanous, transparent, thin

**sheet** NOUN
1 *a sheet of paper*
▶ piece, leaf, page, folio
2 *a sheet of ice*
▶ layer, film, covering, strip, expanse, surface
3 *a sheet of glass*
▶ pane, panel, plate

**shelf** NOUN
*She put the vase back on the shelf.*
▶ ledge, mantelpiece, sill, rack

**shell** NOUN
1 *an insect that has no hard shell to protect it*
▶ case, casing, crust, husk, hull, pod
2 *All that was left of the building was its shell.*
▶ frame, framework, skeleton, hull

**shelter** NOUN
1 *Their house provided shelter for countless escapees.*
▶ protection, refuge, sanctuary, safety, cover, haven, lee, asylum
2 *We set up a shelter against the wind.*
▶ shield, screen, barrier, cover
3 *She ran a shelter for the homeless*
▶ sanctuary, refuge, haven, safe haven, retreat

**shelter** VERB
1 *The hut sheltered us from the storm.*
▶ protect, keep safe, shield, cover, safeguard, screen, guard
2 *The walkers sheltered in doorways.*
▶ take shelter, take refuge, seek protection, take cover
3 *His family took it in turns to shelter him.*
▶ harbour, accommodate, give shelter to, hide

**sheltered** ADJECTIVE
1 *a sheltered spot behind the sand dunes*
▶ protected, enclosed, screened, shielded, covered, calm, quiet, windless
AN OPPOSITE IS exposed
2 *She had led a sheltered life.*
▶ secluded, withdrawn, cloistered, reclusive, isolated, unadventurous, unexciting
AN OPPOSITE IS adventurous

**shelve** VERB
*The plans had to be shelved for the time being.*
▶ postpone, defer, put off, put to one side, suspend, abandon, mothball, (*more informal*) put on ice, (*more informal*) put on the back burner
OPPOSITES ARE implement, revive

**shield** NOUN
*One coating will afford the metal a shield against corrosion.*
▶ protection, safeguard, guard, screen, shelter, barrier, defence, bulwark

**shield** VERB
*She tried to shield her eyes from the glare of the sun.*
▶ protect, shade, screen, cover, defend, guard, keep safe, safeguard, shelter

**shift** VERB
1 *Les shifted the furniture to make more space.*
▶ move, rearrange, reposition, relocate, adjust, transfer, switch round, haul, lug
2 *It wouldn't be easy to shift all that dirt.*
▶ remove, dislodge, budge
3 *Their opinions had shifted somewhat.*
▶ change, alter, modify, vary, fluctuate

**shift** NOUN
1 *constant shifts in public opinion*
▶ change, alteration, variation, fluctuation
2 *His mum was working on the night shift.*
▶ period, stint, stretch

**shifty** ADJECTIVE
*She had seen that shifty look before.*
▶ dishonest, untrustworthy, deceitful, furtive, underhand, shady, wily, scheming, dubious
AN OPPOSITE IS straightforward

## shimmer VERB

*The lights shimmered on the surface of the water.*
▶ glimmer, glint, gleam, glow, glisten, glitter, sparkle, shine, flash

## shine VERB

**1** *The sun shone through the windows.*
▶ beam, gleam, glow, glisten, glint, sparkle, flash

**2** *He had forgotten to shine his shoes.*
▶ polish, brush, buff, brighten

**3** *There was one thing they all shone at.*
▶ excel, stand out, be outstanding

## shine NOUN

*a shine on the furniture*
▶ polish, sheen, lustre, patina, burnish, gleam

## shining ADJECTIVE

**1** *a knight in shining armour*
▶ gleaming, brilliant, radiant, glittering, glowing, luminous, shiny, sparkling

**2** *a shining example*
▶ outstanding, conspicuous, splendid, eminent, glorious, praiseworthy, resplendent

## shiny ADJECTIVE

*He liked her shiny black boots.*
▶ bright, glossy, gleaming, shining, glistening, polished, burnished, lustrous
OPPOSITES ARE dull, matt

## ship NOUN

*Another very big wave hit the ship.*
▶ vessel, craft, boat, liner, steamer

## ship VERB

*Twenty flamingoes were shipped from Tanzania to London.*
▶ send, consign, transport, post, mail

## shipment NOUN

*There's a grain shipment due out tomorrow.*
▶ load, cargo, consignment, freight, vanload, lorryload, truckload, (more formal) lading

## shirk VERB

*We've got responsibilities, and we can't shirk them.*
▶ dodge, duck, evade, avoid, shun, get out of, shrink from, neglect

## shiver VERB

*Maria stood at the door shivering.*
▶ tremble, quiver, shake, shudder, palpitate, flutter

## shock NOUN

**1** *the shock of an explosion*
▶ impact, blow, vibration, collision, concussion, jolt

**2** *The news came as a shock.*
▶ blow, upset, surprise, bombshell, bolt from the blue

**3** *The state of the room always gave her a shock.*
▶ surprise, fright, scare, jolt, start, (more informal) turn

**4** *She was in a state of shock for several days.*
▶ trauma, distress

## shock VERB

*The brutal attack shocked the whole community.*
▶ horrify, appal, stun, stagger, alarm, outrage, dismay, scandalize, repel, offend, disgust, sicken, revolt

## shocking ADJECTIVE

**1** *Next day they heard the whole shocking story.*
▶ horrifying, horrific, appalling, alarming, distressing, terrible, dreadful, awful, frightening, upsetting

**2** *Their language was quite shocking.*
▶ offensive, disgusting, outrageous

## shoddy ADJECTIVE

**1** *the shoddy state of our national services*
▶ inferior, poor-quality, second-rate, cheap, trashy, rubbishy, (more informal) tacky
AN OPPOSITE IS well-made

**2** *The workmanship was noticeably shoddy.*
▶ careless, slapdash, slipshod, sloppy
OPPOSITES ARE painstaking, careful

## shoot VERB

**1** *The gunman had been daring the police to shoot him.*
▶ hit, kill, gun down, snipe at, pick off

**2** *A motor cycle shot past.*
▶ race, dash, zoom, career, fly, rush, streak, hare

**3** *They plan to shoot the outdoor scenes on location in Africa.*
▶ film, make, capture

---

## shop NOUN

*His father opened a shop in the town.*
▶ store, retail store, outlet, emporium

TYPES OF SHOP

**large general shops**: department store, multiple; hypermarket, supermarket, megastore.

**small general shops**: convenience store, corner shop; confectioner, grocery, newsagent, tobacconist, paper shop.

**shops selling food and drink**: bakery (bread and cakes), butcher (meat), charcuterie (cold cooked meats), confectioner (sweets), creamery (dairy products), dairy, delicatessen (special meats, cheeses, spices, etc) fish and chip shop, fishmonger, florist (flowers), greengrocer or greengrocery (fruit and vegetables), grocer or grocery, patisserie (cakes and pastries), takeaway (cooked food to take away), tuck shop (sweets); off licence (alcoholic drinks), vintner (wine), winery.

**shops selling clothes**: boutique, clothes shop, clothier (old-fashioned), couturier (smart fashionable clothes), dressmaker, haberdasher or haberdashery (dressmaking materials), menswear shop, outfitter (men's clothes), shoe shop or shoemaker, tailor (men's clothes).

**shops selling medicines and drugs**: chemist, drugstore, pharmacy.
▶▶

**other shops**: antique shop, barber, bookshop, bookstall (kiosk), chandler (old-fashioned: general supplies), cleaner (for cleaning clothes), DIY shop, draper (old-fashioned: fabrics), electrician, furniture store, garden centre, hairdresser, hardware store, health-food shop, heel bar (for repairing shoes), herbalist (herbs and medicinal plants), ironmonger, jeweller, launderette, perfumery, post office, stationer (paper and writing materials), toyshop, video shop, watchmaker (selling and repairing clocks and watches).

**shopping** NOUN
*She put her shopping in the back of the car.*
▶ goods, purchases

**shore** NOUN
*They stopped for a picnic near the shore.*
▶ seashore, beach, sands, coast, foreshore, seaboard, shingle, bank, strand
RELATED ADJECTIVE littoral

**short** ADJECTIVE This word is often overused. Here are some alternatives:
**1** *a short piece of string*
▶ small, little
AN OPPOSITE IS long
**2** *a short person*
▶ small, little, petite, squat, stocky, diminutive
AN OPPOSITE IS tall
**3** *a short account of the voyage*
▶ brief, concise, succinct, pithy
OPPOSITES ARE long, elaborate, lengthy
**4** *Take a short look at this.*
▶ brief, cursory, fleeting, momentary
OPPOSITES ARE prolonged, lengthy
**5** *Supplies were short.*
▶ low, meagre, scant, deficient, inadequate, insufficient
OPPOSITES ARE plentiful, abundant
**6** *She was rather short with me.*
▶ curt, abrupt, sharp, blunt, brusque, snappy, impatient
OPPOSITES ARE courteous, patient

**shortage** NOUN
*a shortage of water*
▶ scarcity, sparseness, dearth, deficiency, insufficiency, lack, want, paucity, shortfall
AN OPPOSITE IS abundance

**shortcoming** NOUN
*He was well aware of his own shortcomings.*
▶ defect, failing, fault, imperfection, weakness, drawback, foible, vice
AN OPPOSITE IS strength

**shorten** VERB
*The composer shortened the work for concert performance.*
▶ cut down, reduce, condense, compress, cut, trim, abridge
OPPOSITES ARE lengthen, expand

**shortly** ADVERB
*A note arrived shortly afterwards.*
▶ soon, presently, directly, before long, by and by

**short-sighted** ADJECTIVE
*The media tend to be short-sighted when dealing with the arts.*
▶ narrow-minded, narrow, improvident, intolerant, conservative, illiberal, insular, parochial, small-minded

**shot** NOUN
**1** *A shot rang out.*
▶ bang, blast, report, explosion
**2** *This is a shot of us on the beach.*
▶ photo, photograph, snap, snapshot
**3** *He managed a winning shot.*
▶ stroke, hit, strike, throw
**4** (informal) *He wanted a shot at driving the car.*
▶ attempt, try, go, (informal) bash

**shoulder** VERB
**1** *The Minister shouldered the main responsibility for the new policy.*
▶ bear, carry, accept, sustain, take on, undertake
**2** *He shouldered his way through the crowd.*
▶ shove, push, thrust, elbow, force

**shout** VERB
*'Come on,' she shouted.*
▶ cry, call, yell, exclaim, shriek, scream, bawl

**shove** VERB
**1** *She shoved the boy into the back of the van.*
▶ push, thrust, drive, propel, force
**2** *Several large men shoved past them.*
▶ push, barge, elbow, jostle, hustle, shoulder, crowd

**shovel** VERB
*Supporters helped to shovel snow off the pitch.*
▶ dig, scoop, shift, clear, move

**show** NOUN
**1** *Thousands came to watch the show.*
▶ entertainment, performance, production, presentation, spectacle, pageant
**2** *They had to put on a show of strength.*
▶ display, exhibition, demonstration, appearance, impression, facade, pretence, illusion, affectation

**show** VERB
**1** *Shall I show you how to do it?*
▶ demonstrate, explain, point out, clarify
**2** *There's a hole in the sleeve but it won't show.*
▶ be visible, be seen, be obvious, appear
**3** *This shows you what you can achieve with limited resources.*
▶ demonstrate, reveal, illustrate, prove, exemplify
**4** *They are showing his watercolours at the local gallery.*
▶ exhibit, display
**5** *Finn began to show her impatience.*
▶ reveal, manifest, convey, indicate, communicate, expose
**6** *A girl showed them to their seats.*
▶ take, escort, accompany, conduct, walk

a
b
c
d
e
f
g
h
i
j
k
l
m
n
o
p
q
r
s
t
u
v
w
x
y
z

**showdown** NOUN
*The government expected a showdown with the unions over pay.*
▶ confrontation, crisis, clash

**shower** NOUN
1 *a shower of rain*
▶ fall, drizzle, downpour
2 *a shower of compliments*
▶ spate, wave, flood, rush, volley, barrage, torrent, flurry

**shower** VERB
1 *A passing lorry showered mud over the pavement.*
▶ spray, spatter, splash, sprinkle, rain
2 *The awards committee showered praise on the winners.*
▶ lavish, pour, heap, load

**show-off** NOUN
*a show-off with a big flashy car*
▶ exhibitionist, boaster, poser, bragger, egotist

**showy** ADJECTIVE
*showy fake jewellery*
▶ gaudy, flashy, ostentatious, pretentious, flamboyant, conspicuous, garish, tawdry, (*more informal*) tacky
OPPOSITES ARE sober, restrained

**shred** NOUN
1 *Not a shred of evidence could be found.*
▶ scrap, speck, iota, jot, ounce, trace
2 **shreds** *The dress had been torn to shreds.*
▶ tatters, ribbons, rags, strips

**shred** VERB
*Shred the vegetables and add them to the blender.*
▶ grate, chop finely, tear, mince

**shrewd** ADJECTIVE
*a shrewd politician   a shrewd sense of timing*
▶ clever, astute, sharp, acute, canny, prudent, intelligent, quick-witted, perceptive, discerning, crafty, wily
AN OPPOSITE IS stupid

**shriek** VERB
*The audience shrieked with laughter.  'Come and see, quick!' Mary shrieked.*
▶ scream, screech, squeal, roar, howl, bellow, yell

**shrill** ADJECTIVE
*'That's not true!' she protested in a shrill voice.*
▶ piercing, penetrating, high-pitched, screaming, sharp, strident, screechy
OPPOSITES ARE soft, gentle

**shrink** VERB
1 *Your sweater has shrunk in the wash.*
▶ become smaller, contract, dwindle, shrivel, wither
AN OPPOSITE IS expand
2 *The woman shrank in alarm.*
▶ draw back, cower, cringe, flinch, hang back, back off, recoil

**shrivel** VERB
*The plants were shrivelling in the heat.*
▶ wilt, wither, droop, become parched, dehydrate, dry up, wrinkle, shrink

**shroud** NOUN
*a shroud of mist over the sea   The outfit operates behind a shroud of secrecy.*
▶ covering, blanket, mantle, pall, veil

**shroud** VERB
*A mist shrouded the seafront.*
▶ cover, envelop, wrap, blanket, cloak, enshroud, hide, mask, conceal, screen, swathe, veil

**shrug** VERB
**shrug off** *She shrugged off suggestions that she had been unfair.*
▶ dismiss, disregard, ignore, take no notice of, pay no heed to, set aside

**shudder** VERB
*She still shuddered at the thought of what had happened.*
▶ shake, quiver, shiver, tremble, be horrified, convulse, quake, squirm

**shudder** NOUN
*Another mighty shudder passed through the ship.*
▶ tremor, spasm, convulsion, trembling, tremble, quiver

**shuffle** VERB
1 *He shuffled over to the fireplace.*
▶ shamble, hobble, scuffle, stumble, teeter, totter
2 *She shuffled the cards and began dealing.*
▶ mix, mix up, jumble, rearrange, reorganize

**shun** VERB
*The group shunned all forms of publicity.*
▶ avoid, shy away from, stay clear of, evade, steer clear of, keep away from

**shut** VERB
*I'll shut the window.*
▶ close, fasten, latch, lock, push to, bolt, seal, secure
**shut down** *They will have to shut down the operation in South Africa.*
▶ close down, discontinue, terminate, cease, suspend
OPPOSITES ARE open up, activate
**shut in** or **up** *She closed the door to shut the dogs in.*
▶ keep in, confine, detain, enclose, imprison, incarcerate
**shut off** *They had been shut off without food for two days.*
▶ cut off, isolate, separate, segregate
**shut out**
1 *He shut them out of the house by mistake.*
▶ lock out, keep out, exclude
AN OPPOSITE IS let in
2 *She tried to shut out those bad memories.*
▶ exclude, keep out, suppress, forget
AN OPPOSITE IS recall
**shut up** *He told them to say something sensible or shut up.*

► be quiet, be silent, stop talking, say nothing, hold your tongue

**shy** ADJECTIVE

*He was too shy to say his name.*
► embarrassed, coy, reserved, diffident, bashful, sheepish, inhibited, modest, self-conscious, hesitant, timid, retiring
OPPOSITES ARE assertive, forward, bold, confident

**shy** VERB

**shy away from** *They shied away from any sign of danger.*
► avoid, flinch from, recoil from, hang back from, be chary of

**sick** ADJECTIVE

**1** *He had been sick and had to stay at home.*
► ill, unwell, poorly, out of sorts, off colour, indisposed, ailing, peaky, queasy, nauseous
**2 be sick of** *We are all sick of having to wait so long.*
► be fed up with, be tired of, be weary of, have had enough of

**sicken** VERB

*It sickened us to see so much waste.*
► make someone sick, disgust, revolt, nauseate, repel, put off

**sickening** ADJECTIVE

*The stench of burnt fuel oil is sickening. There was a sickening sound of tearing metal.*
► revolting, disgusting, nauseating, offensive, repulsive, repellent, appalling

**sickly** ADJECTIVE

**1** *He was a sickly child with a bad chest.*
► unhealthy, poorly, sick, ill, infirm, frail, feeble, weak
**2** *She had a sickly complexion.*
► pale, wan, pasty, sallow, pallid, ashen
**3** *The walls were painted a sickly green.*
► insipid, pale, wan

**sickness** NOUN

**1** *She was away because of sickness.*
► illness, disease, ailment, disorder
**2** *The spells of sickness lasted four or five days.*
► nausea, biliousness, queasiness, vomiting

**side** NOUN

**1** *The box has an address label on one side.*
► surface, face, facet, elevation, flank
**2** *A hut stood by the side of the lake.*
► edge, border, verge, boundary, margin, fringe, brink, limit, perimeter, rim
**3** *He was driving over the limit on the wrong side of the road.*
► half, part, carriageway
**4** *I could see both sides in the argument.*
► point of view, aspect, perspective, standpoint, opinion, stance, angle, view, viewpoint, slant
**5** *The family had backed the winning side in the civil war.*
► faction, camp, army, team

**6** *The home side was one player short.*
► team, squad, lineup
RELATED ADJECTIVE lateral

**side** VERB

**side with** *They didn't know who to side with.*
► support, favour, prefer, take the side of, agree with

**side effect** NOUN

*The drug can have alarming side effects.*
► consequence, repercussion, result, by-product

**sideline** NOUN

*He does magic shows as a sideline.*
► diversion, second job, secondary activity, additional activity, extra

**sidestep** VERB

*She managed to sidestep the most awkward questions.*
► avoid, evade, dodge, circumvent, skirt round, steer clear of, bypass

**sidetrack** VERB

*He was too easily sidetracked by minor difficulties.*
► distract, deflect, put off, divert

**sideways** ADVERB

*He fell sideways and hurt his arm.*
► to the side, laterally, obliquely

**sideways** ADJECTIVE

**1** *There should be no sideways movement in the shaft.*
► lateral, oblique, indirect
**2** *He gave us a sideways glance as he left.*
► oblique, furtive, covert, sidelong, sly

**sidle** VERB

*He sidled into the room hoping not to be seen.*
► creep, sneak, slink, slip, steal, slide

**siege** NOUN

*The city was under siege for a year.*
► blockade, encirclement, investment

**sieve** NOUN

*Use a sieve to strain the fruit.*
► strainer, sifter, colander, filter, riddle, screen

**sieve** VERB

*Sieve the mixture into a bowl.*
► strain, sift, filter, riddle, screen

**sift** VERB

**1** *Sift the flour over the eggs and milk.*
► sieve, strain, filter, riddle, screen
**2 sift through** *Police have been sifting through piles of evidence.*
► examine, inspect, sort out, analyse, scrutinize, investigate, review

**sigh** VERB

**1** *She sighed with relief.*
► breathe out, exhale
**2** *'Not again,' he sighed.*
► moan, complain, lament, grumble

A B C D E F G H I J K L M N O P Q R S T U V W X Y Z

## sight NOUN

**1** *His sight was failing.*
▶ eyesight, vision, seeing, visual perception
RELATED ADJECTIVES visual, optic or optical

**2** *The enemy was almost in sight.*
▶ range, view, field of vision

**3** *In the early afternoon they had their first sight of land.*
▶ view, glimpse, appearance, look (at), glance (at)

**4** *Thousands of visitors enjoy the sights every year.*
▶ place of interest, landmark

**5** *The fireworks were an impressive sight.*
▶ spectacle, display, show, exhibition, showpiece, scene

## sight VERB

*A spotter plane sighted the survivors.*
▶ spot, discern, make out, glimpse, notice, observe, perceive, distinguish, recognize, see, behold

## sign NOUN

**1** *There are no signs yet of a change in the weather.*
▶ indication, intimation, hint, warning, forewarning, promise, threat, omen, pointer, portent, presage, augury

**2** *He gave the sign to begin.*
▶ signal, cue, gesture , nod

**3** *There were signs of a much earlier occupation at the site.*
▶ trace, vestige, clue, proof, reminder

**4** *Cards are sent as a sign of affection.*
▶ token, marker, manifestation, symptom

**5** *We'll have to put a sign in the window.*
▶ notice, placard, poster, publicity, signboard, advertisement

**6** *The walls were daubed with signs and pictures.*
▶ symbol, mark, device, emblem, insignia, badge, logo, cipher, trademark

## sign VERB

*She signed her name at the bottom of the page.*
▶ write, autograph, inscribe, initial, endorse

## sign up

**1** *The brothers all signed up in the army.*
▶ enlist, enrol, register, join

**2** *The company has signed up many more clerical staff.*
▶ enrol, enlist, recruit, engage, take on, hire

## signal NOUN

**1** *The captain gave the signal to move forward.*
▶ sign, gesture, wave, prompt, cue, nod, (more informal) go-ahead

**2** *The city mob took Edward's flight as the signal for an orgy of destruction.*
▶ cue, prompt, occasion, excuse, stimulus

## signal VERB

**1** *A police officer signalled to him to stop.*
▶ gesture, indicate, motion, sign, wave, beckon, communicate, flag, gesticulate, give a signal

**2** *The pointed gun signalled his intentions very clearly.*
▶ indicate, express, reveal, announce, proclaim, declare, show

## signature NOUN

*He couldn't read his own signature.*
▶ autograph, initials, mark, name, endorsement

## significance NOUN

*He thought hard about the significance of her remarks.*
▶ importance, import, force, purport, implication, meaning, relevance, sense, point, signification, message
AN OPPOSITE IS insignificance

## significant ADJECTIVE

**1** *The tests produced some significant results.*
▶ important, meaningful, revealing, informative, indicative, (more informal) tell-tale

**2** *The measures would have a significant effect on prices*
▶ considerable, important, noteworthy, serious, sizeable, remarkable, influential, big
AN OPPOSITE IS insignificant

## signify VERB

*Red signifies danger.*
▶ mean, denote, symbolize, represent, indicate, stand for, imply

## silence NOUN

**1** *There was silence for a time, while they thought.*
▶ quiet, quietness, stillness, tranquillity, peace, peacefulness, calm, hush
AN OPPOSITE IS noise

**2** *The criticism reduced him to silence.*
▶ speechlessness, dumbness, muteness, reticence, taciturnity, uncommunicativeness
OPPOSITES ARE speech, verbosity

## silence VERB

**1** *The menace in his voice silenced them.*
▶ quieten, keep quiet, make silent, suppress, muzzle, shut up, gag

**2** *A special muffler helps to silence exhaust noise*
▶ deaden, muffle, quieten, mute

## silent ADJECTIVE

**1** *George was silent until they reached the car park.*
▶ quiet, speechless, unspeaking, voiceless, dumb, mute, taciturn, reticent

**2** *It was totally silent in the kitchen.*
▶ quiet, hushed, peaceful, tranquil, noiseless, soundless

## silhouette NOUN

*I made out the long silhouette of a tall man.*
▶ outline, profile, contour, shape, figure, form, features

## silky ADJECTIVE

*She ran her fingers through her dark silky hair.*
▶ smooth, soft, sleek, velvety, glossy, fine, satiny

**silly** ADJECTIVE

*People often do silly things. 'I'm not quite as silly as you think,' she said.*
▶ foolish, unwise, stupid, imprudent, rash, reckless, foolhardy, senseless, idiotic, crazy, mad, (*more informal*) daft

**similar** ADJECTIVE

1 *The boys are similar in appearance.*
▶ alike, identical, indistinguishable, close, like, the same
OPPOSITES ARE dissimilar, different

2 *hills and similar features*
▶ comparable, analogous, equivalent

3 *similar to Her views are similar to my own.*
▶ like, comparable to, close to
OPPOSITES ARE unlike, dissimilar to, different from

**similarity** NOUN

*There is a startling similarity between them.*
▶ resemblance, likeness, affinity, closeness, correspondence, congruity, similitude, sameness, uniformity
AN OPPOSITE IS difference

**simmer** VERB

1 *Vegetables were simmering on the hob.*
▶ boil gently, bubble, stew

2 *She simmered with suppressed anger.*
▶ fume, seethe, rage, be incensed

**simple** ADJECTIVE

1 *a simple method of fixing up shelving*
▶ straightforward, easy, uncomplicated, elementary, undemanding
OPPOSITES ARE complicated, difficult

2 *The forms are written in simple language.*
▶ clear, plain, straightforward, unambiguous, direct

3 *They led simple, honest lives. He is a simple sort of guy.*
▶ ordinary, unpretentious, unsophisticated, unassuming, innocent, artless

**simplicity** NOUN

1 *The solution was amazing for its simplicity.*
▶ straightforwardness, simpleness, ease
AN OPPOSITE IS difficulty

2 *The house appealed because of the simplicity of its style.*
▶ plainness, unpretentiousness, restraint, purity, austerity
AN OPPOSITE IS ornateness

**simplify** VERB

*The rules are difficult to apply and need to be simplified.*
▶ make simple, clarify, disentangle, streamline
AN OPPOSITE IS complicate

**simplistic** ADJECTIVE

*The solution is appealing but far too simplistic.*
▶ facile, superficial, oversimple, inadequate, naive, pat
AN OPPOSITE IS sophisticated

**simply** ADVERB

1 *It was simply impossible to tell the difference.*
▶ wholly, absolutely, completely, utterly

2 *She did it simply because we asked her to.*
▶ merely, just, purely, solely, only

3 *It is important to dress simply and avoid flamboyance.*
▶ plainly, soberly, without fuss, without frills, with restraint

4 *He writes simply and effectively.*
▶ clearly, plainly, straightforwardly, intelligibly

5 *They lived simply.*
▶ modestly, unpretentiously, naturally, quietly

**simulate** VERB

1 *The capsule simulates the actual conditions of space travel.*
▶ imitate, reproduce, replicate, mimic, duplicate, parallel

2 *She did her best to simulate a smile.*
▶ put on, feign, fake, sham, pretend

**simultaneous** ADJECTIVE

*There were three simultaneous bomb attacks in the city.*
▶ concurrent, coinciding, synchronized, synchronous, contemporaneous, parallel

**sin** NOUN

1 *It was a sin against their gods*
▶ offence, wrong, transgression, evil, iniquity

2 *a powerful sermon on the dangers of sin*
▶ wickedness, wrongdoing, sinfulness, immorality, evil
AN OPPOSITE IS virtue

**sin** VERB

*He confessed he had sinned and incurred the wrath of his God.*
▶ do wrong, be guilty of sin, transgress, err, go astray, offend

**sincere** ADJECTIVE

1 *Their praise was completely sincere.*
▶ heartfelt, honest, candid, genuine, truthful, wholehearted, open
AN OPPOSITE IS insincere

2 *Jane is a very sincere person.*
▶ honest, genuine, truthful, straightforward, ingenuous, artless

**sincerity** NOUN

*I trust the sincerity of their intentions.*
▶ honesty, genuineness, integrity, openness, straightforwardness, trustworthiness, truthfulness

**sinful** ADJECTIVE

*Such behaviour was sinful.*
▶ wicked, wrong, evil, iniquitous, unrighteous, ungodly
AN OPPOSITE IS virtuous

**sing** VERB

*To cheer herself up she began to sing.*
▶ chant, croon, hum, intone, trill

a b c d e f g h i j k l m n o p q r s t u v w x y z

## singer NOUN
*an arrangement for a singer with small orchestra*
▶ vocalist, soloist, songster

**TYPES OF SINGER**

**general words:** chorister, folk singer, opera singer, pop singer or pop star, soloist.

**female singers:** alto, coloratura soprano (singing high elaborate music), contralto, mezzo-soprano, soprano; choirgirl, diva (famous opera singer), prima donna (chief singer of an opera company).

**male singers:** baritone, bass, basso profundo (lowest bass), countertenor (higher than tenor), falsetto (singing unusually high notes), tenor, treble; castrato (historical: castrated and higher than tenor), choirboy, crooner, folk singer, minstrel (medieval singer), troubadour (medieval French poet and singer).

## single ADJECTIVE
**1** *All the chocolates were gone apart from a single orange cream.*
▶ solitary, lone, sole, isolated
**2** *He had remained single all his life.*
▶ unattached, unmarried, a bachelor, unwedded
AN OPPOSITE IS married
**3** *She listened to every single word.*
▶ individual, particular

## single VERB
single out *It would be invidious to single out any individual for praise.*
▶ pick out, choose, select, fix on, separate out

## single-handed ADJECTIVE
*She ran the guest house single-handed.*
▶ alone, by yourself, unaided, without help, independently

## single-minded ADJECTIVE
*She seemed ambitious and single-minded.*
▶ determined, resolute, persevering, unwavering, steadfast, dedicated

## singular ADJECTIVE
*They acted with singular determination.*
▶ extraordinary, remarkable, exceptional, uncommon, unusual, conspicuous, notable

## sinister ADJECTIVE
*His words had a sinister undertone.*
▶ menacing, threatening, ominous, disturbing, alarming, disquieting, malevolent, baleful, (*more informal*) scary, (*more informal*) creepy

## sink VERB
**1** *The sun sank below the horizon.*
▶ descend, dip, fall, drop, disappear, vanish
AN OPPOSITE IS rise
**2** *Their hopes began to sink.*
▶ dwindle, fade, flag, fail, weaken, lessen, subside, collapse
AN OPPOSITE IS revive

**3** *The ship sank with the loss of many lives.*
▶ founder, go under, submerge, capsize
OPPOSITES ARE rise, float

## sinner NOUN
*a sermon about how we are all sinners of one kind or another*
▶ wrongdoer, offender, transgressor, reprobate

## sip VERB
*She sat sipping tea.*
▶ drink slowly, taste, sample, (*more informal*) slurp

## sip NOUN
*He took another sip of his beer.*
▶ mouthful, drink, drop, taste, (*more informal*) slurp

## sister NOUN
*He had a younger sister in Liverpool.*
▶ sibling
RELATED ADJECTIVE sororal

## sit VERB
**1** *Julian sat in an armchair.*
▶ settle, perch, flop, ensconce yourself
**2** *The hall sat about a hundred people.*
▶ seat, accommodate, have seats for, holds, takes, has room for
**3** *Parliament sits again in a week's time.*
▶ meet, assemble, convene, gather, be in session
**4** *She sits her exams this year.*
▶ take, go in for, be a candidate in

## site NOUN
*the site for the new hospital*
▶ location, situation, setting, spot, plot, locality, ground

## site VERB
*Bus stops are sited at intervals of no more than half a mile.*
▶ position, place, situate, locate, erect, station, install

## sitting NOUN
*a sitting of Parliament*
▶ session, assembly, meeting, period

## sitting room NOUN
*a long sitting room with an open fireplace*
▶ living room, drawing room, lounge, front room, reception room

## situated ADJECTIVE
*a hypermarket situated near the bypass*
▶ located, positioned, sited, built, placed, established

## situation NOUN
**1** *new houses in a pleasant situation*
▶ locality, location, position, setting, site, spot, place
**2** *Their financial situation had improved significantly.*
▶ circumstances, position, state, state of affairs, condition, plight, predicament
**USAGE** You use plight and predicament about bad situations.
**3** *She applied for a situation with an estate agent.*
▶ job, position, post, employment

**size** NOUN
1 *the vast size of the main bedroom*
▶ dimensions, proportions, scale, magnitude, area, volume
2 *the size of the job*
▶ scale, extent, scope, range, immensity

**sizeable** ADJECTIVE
*A sizeable reward is being offered.*
▶ large, substantial, considerable, significant, decent, generous, worthwhile, (*more informal*) tidy

**sizzle** VERB
*Food sizzled in the pan.*
▶ crackle, frizzle, hiss, sputter

**skeleton** NOUN
1 *the skeleton of a building*
▶ framework, frame, bones, structure
2 *a skeleton of the plan*
▶ outline, draft, abstract, blueprint, sketch

**sketch** NOUN
1 *She drew a sketch of the scene.*
▶ drawing, outline, picture, diagram, plan
2 *a biographical sketch*
▶ description, portrait, profile, cameo
3 *a brief sketch of the main events*
▶ outline, summary, synopsis, rundown
4 *a comic sketch from the television series*
▶ scene, skit, turn, routine, number

**sketch** VERB
*He decided to sketch the garden instead of taking a photograph.*
▶ draw, make a drawing of, portray, depict, rough out, represent
**sketch out** *We will sketch out our plan.*
▶ outline, describe, summarize, rough out, draft, give the gist of

**sketchy** ADJECTIVE
*The information was too sketchy to act on.*
▶ incomplete, imperfect, perfunctory, bitty, scrappy, skimpy, meagre, rough, vague, imprecise, scanty
OPPOSITES ARE detailed, comprehensive

**skilful** ADJECTIVE
*a skilful negotiator   a skilful use of the materials*
▶ expert, skilled, able, capable, accomplished, proficient, adroit, deft, talented, clever, masterly, consummate
AN OPPOSITE IS incompetent

**skill** NOUN
*work that needs a lot of skill*
▶ expertise, ability, skillfulness, aptitude, adeptness, dexterity, competence, talent
AN OPPOSITE IS incompetence

**skilled** ADJECTIVE
*a skilled engineer*
▶ experienced, trained, qualified, skilful, proficient, accomplished, expert, practised, versed
OPPOSITES ARE unskilled, inexperienced

**skim** VERB
1 *The boat skimmed across the water.*
▶ glide, skate, plane, slide, float, coast
2 *skim through He skimmed through a picture book.*
▶ scan, skip through, flick through, look through, riffle through, read quickly

**skimp** VERB
*Despite the low price you won't skimp on comfort here.*
▶ stint on, be frugal with, economize on, cut corners on

**skimpy** ADJECTIVE
*I'd rather have my clothes too long than looking skimpy.*
▶ scanty, short, flimsy, low-cut

**skin** NOUN
1 *The animal has a tough skin.*
▶ hide, pelt
2 *the skin of an apple*
▶ peel, rind, outside

**skin** VERB
*She skinned three tomatoes.*
▶ peel, pare, strip

**skinflint** NOUN
(*informal*) *He's such a skinflint considering how much he must be earning.*
▶ miser, pinchpenny, penny-pincher, niggard, (*informal*) meanie

**skinny** ADJECTIVE
*We have to find skinny people to try our designs on.*
▶ thin, scrawny, scraggy, lean, lanky, spindly, emaciated

**skip** VERB
1 *Cathy skipped along the path.*
▶ dance, prance, trip, frisk
2 *We can skip these details.*
▶ pass over, ignore, omit, leave out, miss out, dispense with, forget
3 *We skipped school to go on the demo.*
▶ miss, be absent from, play truant from, absent yourself from, cut

**skirmish** NOUN
*Other border skirmishes have gone unreported.*
▶ encounter, fight, tussle, scrap, conflict, engagement, confrontation, battle

**skirt** VERB
**skirt round**
1 *If you stop here we can skirt round the fence.*
▶ go round, pass round, border, encircle, circle, surround
2 **skirt round** *Fran skirted round the answers, aware of who was listening.*
▶ avoid, evade, steer clear of, sidestep, ignore, gloss over

**skit** NOUN
*She plays a pram-pushing mother in a skit on daytime magazine programmes.*
▶ parody, satire, caricature, spoof, sketch

a b c d e f g h i j k l m n o p q r s t u v w x y z

**skulk** VERB

*He passed the day skulking around cafés.*
▶ loiter, prowl, lurk, slink, sneak

**sky** NOUN

*Suddenly the whole sky around them was filled with birds.*
▶ heavens, atmosphere, blue yonder
RELATED ADJECTIVE celestial

**slab** NOUN

*slabs of rock cut from the quarries*
▶ block, piece, tablet, chunk, hunk, lump, slice

**slack** ADJECTIVE

1 *The rope suddenly went slack.*
▶ limp, loose
AN OPPOSITE IS tight

2 *A slack defence let in several goals.*
▶ disorganized, negligent, careless, undisciplined, inattentive, lax, lazy, listless, easygoing
OPPOSITES ARE alert, diligent.

3 *Business tends to be slack just after Christmas.*
▶ sluggish, slow, quiet, inactive, slow-moving, depressed
OPPOSITES ARE brisk, busy

**slack** VERB

*This was no time for slacking.*
▶ idle, shirk, be lazy, (*more informal*) skive

**slacken** VERB

1 *The boat lurched as he slackened his grip on the wheel.*
▶ loosen, relax, release, ease off
AN OPPOSITE IS tighten

2 *The rain might just have slackened by now.*
▶ decrease, ease, lessen, abate, lower, moderate, reduce, slow down

**slacker** NOUN

*There was no room for slackers.*
▶ layabout, idler, shirker, loafer, malingerer, sluggard

**slam** VERB

*He stormed out and slammed the door.*
▶ bang, shut, fling shut, crash

**slander** NOUN

*He'd sue me for slander if I made the accusations publicly.*
▶ defamation, misrepresentation, calumny, libel, slur, aspersion, malicious gossip, scandalmongering
OPPOSITES ARE compliment, praise

**slander** VERB

*She discovered that her friend had been slandering her behind her back.*
▶ defame, libel, smear, vilify, besmirch

**slanderous** ADJECTIVE

*The truth can often be slanderous if you put it in a certain way.*
▶ defamatory, libellous, disparaging, pejorative, scurrilous, malicious, abusive

**slant** NOUN

1 *The floor seemed to be on a slant.*
▶ slope, angle, incline, diagonal, gradient, list, rake, ramp, pitch, tilt

2 *The Youth Theatre brings a new slant to Christmas shows.*
▶ point of view, viewpoint, standpoint, angle, perspective, emphasis, bias

**slant** VERB

1 *The handwriting slants to the right. Joe slanted his gaze towards her.*
▶ tilt, lean, slope, incline, be at an angle, be skewed

2 *He slanted his version of the story to avoid awkward admissions.*
▶ bias, distort, twist, warp, weight, colour, prejudice

**slanting** ADJECTIVE

*The slanting sunlight cast long shadows.*
▶ sloping, oblique, angled, inclined, diagonal, listing, raked, askew, skewed, slantwise, tilted
OPPOSITES ARE straight, level

**slap** VERB

1 *Anne was at the end of her patience and wanted to slap him.*
▶ smack, strike, hit, clout, whack, spank

2 *She had slapped a parking ticket on his Mercedes.*
▶ fling, throw, toss, hurl

3 *Slap some varnish on to seal the surface.*
▶ spread, daub, plaster, apply

**slap** NOUN

*He heard the sound of a slap from the next room.*
▶ smack, clout, whack, blow, thump

**slapdash** ADJECTIVE

*The book is full of phoney, slapdash arguments.*
▶ careless, slipshod, slovenly, untidy, thoughtless

**slash** VERB

1 *Someone had slashed the tyres.*
▶ cut, slit, gash, rip, tear, knife

2 *Prices will be slashed out of the high season.*
▶ reduce, cut, drop

**slash** NOUN

*He had a deep slash across his arm.*
▶ cut, gash, laceration, wound, injury

**slate** VERB

(*informal*) *The critics all slated the production, though they like the music.*
▶ criticize, pillory, lambaste, revile, (*informal*) pan

**slaughter** NOUN

*The senseless slaughter of dolphins takes place merely to catch a few extra tuna.*
▶ massacre, carnage, killing, butchery, murder, bloodshed

**slaughter** VERB

*A whole legion was ambushed and slaughtered.*
▶ massacre, butcher, kill, annihilate, eliminate, murder, slay

**slave** NOUN

*Most of the work was done by slaves at that time.*
▶ serf, thrall, vassal, drudge, servant
RELATED ADJECTIVE servile

**slave** VERB

*That's all the thanks you get for slaving over a hot stove all morning.*
▶ toil, labour, grind, sweat, work , drudge, exert yourself, work your fingers to the bone, (*more informal*) work your socks off
OPPOSITES ARE relax, skive

**slavery** NOUN

*They were being sent back to torture, slavery, and death.*
▶ bondage, enslavement, servitude, captivity, serfdom
AN OPPOSITE IS freedom

**slavish** ADJECTIVE

**1** *He was no slavish follower of a party.*
▶ servile, submissive, abject, cringing, fawning, grovelling, humiliating, menial, obsequious
AN OPPOSITE IS assertive
**2** *It was a slavish copying of older ideas.*
▶ unoriginal, unimaginative, close, imitative, literal, uninspired
AN OPPOSITE IS independent

**slay** VERB

*Thousands of men and women were slain in the reprisals.*
▶ kill, slaughter, massacre, butcher, murder, put to death, exterminate, annihilate, cut down, (*informal*) finish off

**sleazy** ADJECTIVE

*a sleazy little café on the edge of town*
▶ dirty, squalid, shabby, run-down, sordid, seamy, rough

**sleek** ADJECTIVE

**1** *She combed her sleek dark hair.*
▶ silky, glossy, shiny, smooth, brushed, soft, velvety, well-groomed
AN OPPOSITE IS dull
**2** *a sleek sports car*
▶ streamlined, graceful, elegant, aerodynamic
**3** *a group of sleek young men in smart suits*
▶ stylish, well-groomed, prosperous
AN OPPOSITE IS unkempt

**sleep** NOUN

*She often had a sleep in the afternoon.*
▶ snooze, nap, rest, doze, catnap, siesta, (*more informal*) kip, (*more informal*) forty winks

**sleep** VERB

*He had slept for about an hour.*
▶ snooze, doze, rest, slumber, (*more informal*) kip, (*more informal*) drop off, (*more informal*) nod off, (*more informal*) doss down

**sleepless** ADJECTIVE

*The shock caused him sleepless nights for a week.*
▶ wakeful, restless, disturbed

**sleepy** ADJECTIVE

**1** *I wasn't sleepy, so I decided to walk round for a bit.*
▶ tired, drowsy, somnolent, lethargic, weary, torpid, sluggish, soporific, heavy-eyed, (*informal*) dopey, ready to sleep
AN OPPOSITE IS awake
**2** *a sleepy little town near the border*
▶ quiet, peaceful, tranquil, inactive, dull, unexciting
OPPOSITES ARE lively, busy

**slender** ADJECTIVE

**1** *a slender youth with dark hair*
▶ slim, lean, slight, thin, graceful, svelte
AN OPPOSITE IS fat
**2** *a slender thread*
▶ fine, fragile, tenuous, feeble
AN OPPOSITE IS strong
**3** *slender hopes*
▶ faint, slim, remote, flimsy
**4** *a verdict based on slender evidence*
▶ meagre, scanty, flimsy, tenuous, inadequate
AN OPPOSITE IS adequate

**slice** NOUN

*a slice of bread*
▶ piece, sliver (=thin slice), chunk (= thick slice), hunk (= thick slice), tranche, slab

**slice** VERB

*She sliced the cheese into thin pieces.*
▶ cut, cut up, chop, carve, divide

**slick** ADJECTIVE

*a slick marketing campaign*
▶ smooth, efficient, smart, polished, streamlined, skilful, professional
AN OPPOSITE IS inept

**slide** VERB

*The spoon slid across the table.*
▶ glide, slither, skim, skid, slip

**slight** ADJECTIVE

**1** *There was a slight problem with this plan.*
▶ small, modest, tiny, imperceptible, insignificant, negligible, slim, minor, trivial
**2** *her slight figure*
▶ slim, slender, delicate, dainty, graceful, petite, svelte
AN OPPOSITE IS big

**slight** NOUN

*He was seething at the slight to his authority.*
▶ insult, affront, slur, snub, rebuff

**slightly** ADVERB

*The new models are slightly bigger.*   *He was slightly taken aback by this.*
▶ a little, a bit, rather, somewhat, a shade, moderately
AN OPPOSITE IS very

**slim** ADJECTIVE

**1** *She is tall, slim, and dignified.*
▶ slender, lean, slight, thin, graceful, svelte
**2** *a slim chance of winning*
▶ faint, slender, remote, flimsy

## slim VERB
*a diet to help you slim*
► lose weight, reduce weight, become slimmer, shape up

## slime NOUN
*The path was covered in a green slime.*
► sludge, muck, mucus, mud, ooze

## slimy ADJECTIVE
*He slid helplessly down the slimy walls.*
► slithery, slippery, sticky, oozy, greasy

## sling VERB
*He slung his coat on a chair.*
► throw, hurl, toss, fling, cast, pitch, heave

## slink VERB
*He slunk round to the back of the house.*
► creep, sneak, slip, steal, edge, sidle

## slinky ADJECTIVE
*(informal) a slinky long dress*
► sleek, close-fitting, clinging, tight, sexy

## slip VERB
1 *People were slipping on the icy ground.*
► slide, slither, fall, trip, stumble
2 *He got up and slipped quietly out of the door.*
► creep, sneak, slink, steal, edge, sidle
3 *He slipped some money into his pocket.*
► put, tuck, stick, shove, stuff

## slip NOUN
1 *a slip of paper*
► piece, scrap, chit, sheet
2 *Did you mean to write 'yes' or was that a slip?*
► mistake, error, gaffe, lapse, blunder

## slippery ADJECTIVE
1 *The floor was wet and slippery.*
► slithery, greasy, slimy, slippy
2 *a slippery character*
► devious, unreliable, dishonest, crafty, cunning

## slipshod ADJECTIVE
*a slipshod performance*
► careless, slapdash, slovenly, untidy, thoughtless

## slit NOUN
1 *He peeped through a slit in a fence*
► opening, chink, gap, crack, aperture, slot
2 *She made a slit in the side of the box.*
► cut, incision, gash, tear, slash

## slit VERB
*Henry looked for a knife to slit open his letter.*
► cut, tear, rip, slice

## slither VERB
*A snake slithered through the grass.*
► slide, slink, slip, creep, glide, snake, worm

## slobber VERB
*The dog slobbered on the carpet.*
► drool, dribble, salivate, slaver

## slog NOUN
*(informal) The work was a year's hard slog.*
► toil, labour, struggle, work, (informal) grind

## slogan NOUN
*a well-known advertising slogan*
► jingle, motto, catchphrase, catchword, watchword, saying

## slope NOUN
1 *A flat roof must have a slope for drainage.*
► incline, gradient, slant, angle, pitch
2 *They had their picnic on a grassy slope.*
► hillock, hill, bank, rise

## slope VERB
*The garden slopes gently away from the house.*
► slant, fall or rise, fall away, shelve, bank, incline

## sloppy ADJECTIVE
1 *The cement mixture was much too sloppy.*
► liquid, runny, slushy, watery, messy, wet
AN OPPOSITE IS solid
2 *sloppy work*
► careless, slovenly, slapdash, slipshod
AN OPPOSITE IS careful

## slosh VERB
1 *Water was sloshing about*
► splash, slop, spill, splatter
2 *Michael threatened to slosh anyone else who said anything.*
► hit, thump, bash, clout

## slot NOUN
1 *She put another coin in the slot and waited.*
► slit, chink, aperture, opening
2 *a weekly radio slot for listeners' comments*
► spot, time, place, space

## slouch VERB
*Martin was slouching in a low chair.*
► slump, droop, loaf, lounge, flop, hunch, stoop

## slovenly ADJECTIVE
1 *He was criticized for his slovenly appearance.*
► untidy, scruffy, messy, dishevelled
AN OPPOSITE IS careful
2 *The work is slovenly and needs to be redone.*
► careless, slapdash, slipshod, untidy, thoughtless

## slow ADJECTIVE
1 *They walked on at a slow pace.*
► leisurely, unhurried, measured, moderate, steady, deliberate, plodding
OPPOSITES ARE fast, quick, rapid
2 *It was slow work.*
► lengthy, prolonged, protracted, tedious
OPPOSITES ARE rapid, speedy
3 *He could be extremely slow at times.*
► stupid, slow-witted, dim, obtuse, (more informal) dense
OPPOSITES ARE bright, quick, astute

## slow VERB
*The huge vehicle slowed to a halt.*
► decelerate, go slower, slow down, reduce speed, brake
OPPOSITES ARE accelerate, speed up

**sluggish** ADJECTIVE
*He woke up feeling sluggish after a sleepless night.*
▶ lethargic, lifeless, listless, torpid, unresponsive, dull, idle, lazy, slothful
OPPOSITES ARE lively, vigorous

**slump** NOUN
*a financial crisis and a slump in world trade*
▶ decline, depression, downturn, collapse, drop, fall, tumble, crash, trough
AN OPPOSITE IS boom

**slump** VERB
1 *House values have slumped in the last few months.*
▶ decline, drop, fall off, collapse, plummet, plunge, sink, worsen
OPPOSITES ARE soar, rise
2 *Joanna slumped into a chair.*
▶ flop, loll, droop, sag, slouch, collapse
3 *He slumped to the ground, clutching his leg.*
▶ fall, sink, collapse, drop

**slur** NOUN
*This is a slur on one of our great national heroes.*
▶ insult, slight, slander, libel, defamation

**sly** ADJECTIVE
*The master was a devious, sly man.*
▶ cunning, crafty, clever, wily, foxy, canny, knowing, shifty, sneaky, furtive, scheming, conniving

**smack** VERB
*She lost control and smacked him.*
▶ slap, strike, hit, clout, whack, spank

**smack** NOUN
*He frowned and gave her a smack.*
▶ slap, clout, whack, blow, thump

**small** ADJECTIVE This word is often overused. Here are some alternatives:
1 *A small packet lay on the mat.*
▶ little, tiny, minute, compact, baby, diminutive, minuscule
AN OPPOSITE IS large
2 *His mother was a small woman.*
▶ short, little, slight, petite
OPPOSITES ARE big, large, tall
3 *We will need to make some small changes.*
▶ minor, trivial, trifling, insignificant, unimportant, negligible
OPPOSITES ARE major, substantial
4 *They wanted to complain about the small portions.*
▶ meagre, inadequate, paltry, insufficient
OPPOSITES ARE large, generous, ample

**small-minded** ADJECTIVE
*a lot of small-minded chauvinists*
▶ narrow-minded, intolerant, narrow, bigoted, conservative, illiberal, insular, parochial, short-sighted, hidebound
OPPOSITES ARE broad-minded, open-minded, tolerant

**smarmy** ADJECTIVE
*His manner was over-polite and smarmy.*
▶ smooth, oily, unctuous, obsequious, fawning

**smart** ADJECTIVE
1 *He looked smart in his new suit.*
▶ elegant, well dressed, stylish, spruce, trim, chic, fashionable
AN OPPOSITE IS scruffy
2 *Jenny had always been the smart member of the family.*
▶ clever, bright, intelligent, sharp, shrewd, astute
AN OPPOSITE IS stupid
3 *They would stay in a smart hotel and eat out every night.*
▶ fashionable, high-class, exclusive, fancy, (more informal) posh
AN OPPOSITE IS low-class
4 *They set off at a smart pace.*
▶ brisk, fast, quick, lively, spirited
AN OPPOSITE IS slow

**smart** VERB
*The smoke made her eyes smart.*
▶ sting, tingle, prickle, prick, hurt

**smarten** VERB
1 **smarten up** *The house had been smartened up before it was put on the market.*
▶ do up, refurbish, redecorate, renovate, improve
2 **smarten yourself up** *Eleanor went to smarten herself up for dinner.*
▶ dress, spruce yourself up, freshen yourself up, make yourself smart

**smash** VERB
1 *He dropped the glass and smashed it.*
▶ break, shatter, crack
2 **smash into** *A car had smashed into the lamppost.*
▶ crash into, collide with, smack into, bash into, thump into, hit

**smashing** ADJECTIVE
*They had a smashing time.*
▶ marvellous, excellent, wonderful, splendid, lovely, delightful, (more informal) terrific

**smattering** NOUN
*She is fluent in French and has a smattering of German.*
▶ bit, modicum, small amount, dash, rudiments, basics

**smear** VERB
1 *He smeared grease on the bearings.*
▶ daub, spread, wipe, plaster, rub, dab, smudge
2 *The canvas was smeared with paint*
▶ cover, coat, rub, streak
3 *The newspapers tried to smear his reputation*
▶ sully, besmirch, tarnish, blacken, defame, malign, vilify

**smear** NOUN
1 *a smear of paint*
▶ streak, smudge, daub, mark
2 *smears about them in the press*
▶ slander, libel, defamation, imputation, false report

## smell NOUN

**1** *the fresh smells of spring*
▶ fragrance, scent, perfume, aroma

**2** *a smell of cooking*
▶ aroma, odour

**3** *a bad smell*
▶ odour, stench, stink, reek, (*more informal*) pong, (*more informal*) niff
RELATED ADJECTIVE olfactory

## smell VERB

**1** *Smell the flowers.*
▶ scent, sniff

**2** (*informal*) *The milk was starting to smell.*
▶ stink, whiff, pong, reek

## smelly ADJECTIVE

*The room was damp and smelly.*
▶ smelling, stinking, malodorous, reeking, foul, putrid, (*more informal*) pongy

## smile VERB

*Jo smiled at her.*
▶ beam, grin, simper, smirk, leer
**USAGE** Note that *smirk* and *leer* are unpleasant expressions.

## smoke VERB

**1** *The fire was smoking.*
▶ smoulder, emit smoke, fume, reek

**2** *He was smoking a cigar.*
▶ puff on, draw on, inhale

## smooth ADJECTIVE

**1** *a smooth road*
▶ even, level, flat, horizontal
OPPOSITES ARE uneven, rough

**2** *a smooth surface*
▶ shiny, polished, glossy, silky
AN OPPOSITE IS dull

**3** *a smooth sea*
▶ calm, still, tranquil, placid, serene, glassy
AN OPPOSITE IS rough

**4** *a smooth talker*
▶ suave, articulate, glib, slick, smarmy, plausible, persuasive
AN OPPOSITE IS awkward

**5** *the smooth running of the engine*
▶ regular, steady, rhythmic, flowing, fluent
OPPOSITES ARE irregular, jerky

**6** *a smooth operation*
▶ straightforward, efficient, well-run, trouble-free, untroubled
OPPOSITES ARE troubled, fraught

## smooth VERB

**1** *He took his clothes out of the bag and smoothed them before putting them away.*
▶ flatten, press, iron

**2** *Use sandpaper to smooth the surface.*
▶ plane, sand, polish, level

**3** *Extra support would smooth their progress.*
▶ ease, facilitate, help, assist, expedite

## smother VERB

**1** *He tried to smother the flames with his coat.*
▶ put out, extinguish, snuff out, damp down, dampen, douse

**2** *A young mother was accused of smothering her baby.*
▶ suffocate, stifle, asphyxiate, strangle, choke

## smoulder VERB

**1** *The fire was still smouldering a week later.*
▶ smoke, glow, burn slowly

**2** *He was smouldering with rage.*
▶ fume, seethe, burn, boil

## smudge NOUN

*His thumb left a smudge on the paper.*
▶ smear, mark, stain, blot, streak

## smudge VERB

**1** *Her hand slipped and she smudged the writing.*
▶ blur, smear, streak

**2** *The wall was smudged with heavy drops of rain.*
▶ mark, stain, blot, dirty

## smug ADJECTIVE

*He tried not to look smug when the results were announced.*
▶ self-satisfied, conceited, superior, self-righteous, complacent, priggish
AN OPPOSITE IS humble

## smutty ADJECTIVE

*They had been telling each other smutty jokes.*
▶ dirty, rude, filthy, crude, indecent, coarse, obscene

## snack NOUN

*They had a quick snack before leaving.*
▶ bite, bite to eat, light meal, refreshments, (*more informal*) nibble

## snag NOUN

*The snag was that nobody wanted to make the first move.*
▶ problem, disadvantage, catch, hitch, obstacle, setback, complication, hindrance, difficulty, (*informal*) stumbling-block

---

## snake NOUN

**TYPES OF SNAKE**

**poisonous snakes:** adder, asp (small viper), boomslang, cobra, copperhead, coral snake, flying snake, grass snake, king cobra (or hamadryad), mamba, pit viper, puff adder, rattlesnake, sea snake, sidewinder (type of rattlesnake), tree snake, viper.

**snakes that crush their prey:** anaconda, boa constrictor, python.

**harmless snakes:** grass snake, green snake, racer.

---

## snap VERB

**1** *The rope snapped and the trailer slipped backwards.*
▶ break, split, separate

**2** *The dogs were snapping at them.*
▶ snarl, growl, bark, bite

# snap

3 *'I wasn't there,' Ginny snapped.*
▶ bark, retort, snarl, say angrily, rejoin
4 *After years of suffering she finally snapped.*
▶ crack, lose control, go to pieces, (*more informal*) lose your cool, (*more informal*) freak out

## snap NOUN

1 *He closed the case with a snap.*
▶ click, crack
2 *There is often a cold snap just after Christmas.*
▶ spell, period, interval, stretch
3 *She showed us her holiday snaps.*
▶ photo, photograph, picture, image

## snap ADJECTIVE

*a snap decision*
▶ instant, on-the-spot, off-the-cuff, abrupt

## snappy ADJECTIVE

1 *We need a snappy answer*
▶ quick, prompt, brisk
2 *a snappy dresser*
▶ smart, stylish, fashionable, chic, (*more informal*) trendy
3 *The campaign needs a slogan that's snappy.*
▶ pithy, crisp, memorable

## snare NOUN

1 *A rabbit was caught in a snare.*
▶ trap, noose, (*old-fashioned*) gin
2 *Try to avoid the snare of overspending in the sales.*
▶ pitfall, trap, danger, hazard, catch

## snare VERB

*The smaller traps can snare dogs out for walks.*
▶ ensnare, trap, net, catch

## snarl VERB

*'Leave me alone,' he snarled.*
▶ growl, snap, bark, say angrily

## snatch VERB

*Thieves had snatched her handbag near the station.*
▶ steal, seize, grab, take, grasp, pluck, wrench away, wrest away

## sneak VERB

1 *The boys sneaked in when nobody was about.*
▶ creep, steal, slink, slip, sidle
2 *sneak on* (*informal*) *Someone must have sneaked on me.*
▶ inform on or against, report, tell tales about, (*informal*) grass on

## sneaking ADJECTIVE

1 *She has a sneaking fondness for Turkish delight.*
▶ secret, private, hidden, concealed, inward, unexpressed
2 *Claudia had a sneaking feeling that Myra could be right.*
▶ nagging, niggling, lingering, lurking

## sneaky ADJECTIVE

(*informal*) *a sneaky trick*
▶ sly, cunning, crafty, clever, wily, foxy, canny, knowing, shifty, sneaky, furtive, scheming, conniving
OPPOSITES ARE honest, open

## sneer VERB

*sneer at It is easy to sneer at their first efforts.*
▶ scoff at, mock, scorn, ridicule, deride, jeer at, laugh at, look down on

## snide ADJECTIVE

*His snide remarks became irritating.*
▶ disparaging, deprecating, sarcastic, scornful, sneering, spiteful, sneering, mocking, nasty
AN OPPOSITE IS complimentary

## snigger VERB

*They might snigger at him behind his back.*
▶ laugh, snicker, giggle, titter, chuckle, sneer

## snip VERB

1 *She snipped the ends off the stalks.*
▶ cut, clip, trim, crop, chop, dock
2 *The inspector snipped our tickets.*
▶ clip, nick, notch, snick

## snippet NOUN

*snippets of information*
▶ piece, scrap, bit, morsel, fragment, particle, shred, snatch

## snivel VERB

*If you get caught, don't snivel about the consequences.*
▶ complain, grizzle, moan, grouse, whine, make a fuss, (*more informal*) whinge

## snobbery NOUN

*Forget the snobbery and mystique that is associated with choosing wine.*
▶ snobbishness, snootiness, arrogance, affectation, pretension, superciliousness

## snobbish ADJECTIVE

*She dislikes the snobbish and materialistic attitudes of many people.*
▶ snooty, snobby, pretentious, superior, condescending, (*more informal*) stuck up, (*more informal*) toffee-nosed
AN OPPOSITE IS unpretentious

## snoop VERB

*You shouldn't snoop into our affairs.*
▶ pry, meddle (in or with), nose, sneak, (*informal*) stick your nose (in or into)

## snooze VERB

(*informal*) *There he was snoozing by the fire.*
▶ sleep, doze, rest, nap, take a nap, catnap

## snub VERB

*They snubbed the hosts by leaving the party early.*
▶ insult, affront, offend, rebuff, reject, scorn, (*more informal*) put down

## snug ADJECTIVE

1 *The cottage was warm and snug.*
▶ cosy, comfortable, homely, cheerful, welcome, reassuring, (*more informal*) comfy
OPPOSITES ARE forbidding, unwelcoming
2 *She wore a snug long dress.*
▶ close-fitting, tight, figure-hugging

a b c d e f g h i j k l m n o p q r s t u v w x y z

## soak VERB

**1** *You need to soak the beans overnight in liquid.*
▶ immerse, steep, wet, submerge
**2** *Days of rain had soaked the ground.*
▶ drench, saturate, swamp, inundate
**soak into** *Ink had soaked into the paper*
▶ permeate, penetrate, saturate
**soak up** *A sponge soaks up water*
▶ absorb, take up, draw up, suck up

## soaking ADJECTIVES

*By the time they returned their clothes were soaking.*
▶ drenched, soaked, wet through, dripping, wringing, sodden, sopping
AN OPPOSITE IS dry

## soar VERB

**1** *Birds soared overhead.*
▶ climb, ascend, wing, glide, drift
**2** *Prices have continued to soar.*
▶ rise, escalate, rocket

## sob VERB

*He turned his face to the wall and began to sob.*
▶ cry, weep, shed tears, blubber, snivel

## sober ADJECTIVE

**1** *Matt craved a drink but knew he had to stay sober.*
▶ temperate, abstemious, not drunk
AN OPPOSITE IS drunk
**2** *After sober reflection I decided to stay the way I was.*
▶ serious, thoughtful, calm, level-headed, sensible, sombre, grave, earnest, down-to-earth, commonsensical
AN OPPOSITE IS light-hearted
**3** *She dressed in a sober style.*
▶ subdued, sombre, austere, severe, staid
AN OPPOSITE IS flamboyant

## sociable ADJECTIVE

*She had been a lively, bright, and sociable girl before the accident.*
▶ friendly, outgoing, companionable, convivial, gregarious, clubbable, cordial, affable, amicable
OPPOSITES ARE unsociable, unfriendly

## social ADJECTIVE

**1** *Ants are social creatures.*
▶ gregarious, organized, civilized, collaborative
AN OPPOSITE IS solitary
**2** *a range of cultural and social interests*
▶ communal, community, public, group
AN OPPOSITE IS individual

## social NOUN

*The club has a social every month.*
▶ party, gathering, function

## socialize VERB

*Students tend to socialize in the evenings.*
▶ associate, be sociable, entertain, fraternize, get together, join in, mix, relate

## society NOUN

**1** *In our society, men historically have occupied the positions of power.*
▶ civilization, nation, culture, community

**2** *We must remember our position in society.*
▶ the community, the population, the public
**3** *They enjoy the society of their friends*
▶ company, fellowship, friendship, companionship, camaraderie
**4** *He joined a local history society.*
▶ association, club, group, organization, circle, fraternity

## soft ADJECTIVE

**1** *a soft pillow*
▶ supple, pliable, springy, yielding, flexible, malleable, squashy
AN OPPOSITE IS hard
**2** *soft ground*
▶ squelchy, swampy, marshy, boggy, heavy
AN OPPOSITE IS firm
**3** *soft music*
▶ gentle, soothing, melodious
AN OPPOSITE IS harsh
**4** *a soft voice*
▶ quiet, low, faint, muted, subdued
AN OPPOSITE IS loud
**5** *soft colours*
▶ pale, pastel, muted, subtle
OPPOSITES ARE bright, lurid
**6** *a soft fabric*
▶ velvety, silky, smooth, downy, fleecy
**7** *Some teachers are too soft with their pupils.*
▶ lenient, easygoing, indulgent, permissive, forbearing
OPPOSITES ARE strict, severe

## soften VERB

**1** *Lower interest rates might soften the effect of the tax increases.*
▶ moderate, temper, alleviate, ease, relieve, assuage
AN OPPOSITE IS intensify
**2** *The butter softened in the warmth of the kitchen.*
▶ melt, liquefy, go soft
AN OPPOSITE IS harden

## soft-hearted ADJECTIVE

*You were always too soft-hearted to tell them what you thought.*
▶ kind, kind-hearted, gentle, easygoing, generous, charitable

## soggy ADJECTIVE

*a pile of soggy clothes*
▶ sodden, sopping, saturated, soaked, drenched, wet through
AN OPPOSITE IS dry

## soil NOUN

**1** *The tiny eggs can also be picked up in garden soil.*
▶ earth, loam, ground, humus, topsoil
**2** *English troops withdrew from Scottish soil.*
▶ territory, land, space, jurisdiction

## soil VERB

*Try not to soil your clothes.*
▶ dirty, make dirty, stain, tarnish, contaminate, defile, pollute

**soiled** ADJECTIVE
*Lightly soiled surfaces can be cleaned with a good detergent.*
▶ dirty, stained, grubby

**soldier** NOUN
*The town was surrounded by enemy soldiers.*
▶ serviceman or servicewoman, fighting man or woman, trooper
RELATED ADJECTIVE military

**sole** ADJECTIVE
*The sole intention is to raise money.*
▶ one, only, single, solitary, exclusive, singular, individual, unique

**solemn** ADJECTIVE
1 *He was tall with a thin, solemn face.*
▶ serious, earnest, sombre, staid, sober, thoughtful, reverential, glum, grave, grim
AN OPPOSITE IS cheerful
2 *The ceremony was a solemn occasion.*
▶ dignified, formal, grand, stately, majestic, impressive, pompous, awe-inspiring, ceremonious, imposing
AN OPPOSITE IS frivolous

**solid** ADJECTIVE
1 *The floor was of solid concrete. The metal below him was quite solid.*
▶ hard, firm, dense, rigid, fixed, unyielding
OPPOSITES ARE liquid, gaseous, hollow
2 *a solid sort of person*
▶ reliable, dependable, trustworthy, honest, upright, level-headed
OPPOSITES ARE unreliable, dishonest
3 *The police needed solid evidence.*
▶ real, genuine, substantial
4 *a ring of solid gold*
▶ pure, genuine, unalloyed
AN OPPOSITE IS alloyed
5 *He can expect solid support from a third of the delegates.*
▶ firm, united, unanimous
AN OPPOSITE IS divided

**solidarity** NOUN
*feelings of solidarity in the workforce*
▶ unity, harmony, unanimity, agreement, cohesion, concord, like-mindedness
AN OPPOSITE IS disunity

**solidify** VERB
*As the liquid cools it rapidly solidifies.*
▶ harden, set, thicken, stiffen, congeal, clot, coagulate
AN OPPOSITE IS liquefy

**solitary** ADJECTIVE
1 *He leads a solitary existence.*
▶ lonely, unsociable, friendless, isolated, cloistered, companionless
AN OPPOSITE IS sociable
2 *a solitary survivor*
▶ single, sole, one, only

3 *a few solitary villages dotted on the landscape*
▶ isolated, out-of-the-way, remote, secluded, hidden, sequestered, unfrequented, desolate

**solitude** NOUN
*She craved a few hours of peace and solitude.*
▶ privacy, seclusion, isolation, loneliness, remoteness, retirement
AN OPPOSITE IS companionship

**solo** ADJECTIVE
*a solo performance*
▶ unaccompanied, unattended
AN OPPOSITE IS accompanied

**solution** NOUN
1 *There is no easy solution to the problem.*
▶ answer, resolution, key, solving (of), explanation (of)
2 *a solution of ammonia in water*
▶ mixture, mix, blend, compound

**solve** VERB
*This will solve our immediate problem.*
▶ resolve, answer, settle, sort out, put right, deal with

**sombre** ADJECTIVE
1 *sombre colours*
▶ dark, dull, sober, drab, dreary, gloomy
AN OPPOSITE IS cheerful
2 *His face bore a sombre expression*
▶ serious, solemn, thoughtful, reverential, glum, grave

**sometimes** ADVERB
*He sometimes seems preoccupied.*
▶ occasionally, from time to time, at times, now and then, now and again

---

**song** NOUN
*She sung an old song.*
▶ tune, melody, air, strain, number

NAMES FOR TYPES OF SONG

**songs telling a story**: ballad, lay, calypso (West Indian).

**popular songs**: folk song, love song, pop song, golden oldie (old song still popular).

**religious songs**: hymn, psalm, spiritual, carol (associated with Christmas), bhajan, qawwali.

**childrens' songs**: lullaby, nursery rhyme, ditty (short simple song).

**special songs**: shanty (sea song), barcarolle (sung by gondoliers), chanson (French song), Lied (German song); dirge (mournful song), lament (sad song), paean (song of praise).

**songs for several singers**: chorus, round, duet, trio, quartet, madrigal (early song for several voices), part song.

---

**soon** ADVERB
*We'll be there soon.*
▶ shortly, presently, quickly, before long, in a while, in a moment or minute

**sooner** ADVERB

**1** *I wish you'd said something sooner.*
► earlier, before, already

**2** *I'd sooner stay and wait for them.*
► rather, preferably

**soothe** VERB

*She patted him gently to soothe him.*
► calm, comfort, console, pacify, mollify, settle, subdue, quiet, still
OPPOSITES ARE agitate, disturb

**soothing** ADJECTIVE

**1** *a soothing ointment*
► healing, palliative, comforting, emollient, balmy, mild

**2** *soothing words*
► calming, relaxing, restful, gentle, peaceful, pleasant

**sophisticated** ADJECTIVE

**1** *sophisticated techniques for crime detection*
► advanced, developed, complex, elaborate

**2** *a sophisticated person*
► worldly, experienced, cultivated, refined, urbane

**soporific** ADJECTIVE

*soporific drugs   soporific music*
► sedative, sleep-inducing, calmative, tranquillizing, hypnotic
OPPOSITES ARE stimulating, invigorating

**soppy** ADJECTIVE

*(informal)*

**1** *a soppy story*
► sentimental, mawkish, maudlin, sugary, corny

**2** *a soppy child*
► silly, daft, feeble, soft, foolish

**sorcerer, sorceress** NOUN

*Come and see the sorcerer's workshop.*
► wizard or witch, magician, conjuror, enchanter or enchantress, warlock, witch doctor

**sorcery** NOUN

*She was charged with sorcery by his successor, Richard III, and made to do public penance.*
► magic or black magic, charms, witchcraft, wizardry, conjuring, magic, voodoo

**sordid** ADJECTIVE

**1** *He had a series of sordid affairs with older women.*
► sleazy, seamy, seedy, tawdry, cheap

**2** *a sordid little eating-place off the motorway*
► dirty, squalid, shabby, run-down, rough

**sore** ADJECTIVE

**1** *a sore arm*
► painful, hurting, aching, smarting, tender, stinging, burning, injured, wounded

**2** *(informal) They were sore at us for leaving them like that.*
► annoyed, angry, upset, aggrieved, peeved (with), *(more informal)* miffed (with)

**sore** NOUN

*There were sores all down his leg.*
► swelling, inflammation, abscess, laceration, contusion, lesion, boil, carbuncle, ulcer

**sorrow** NOUN

**1** *The loss caused him great sorrow.*
► sadness, unhappiness, regret, misery, grief, distress, anguish, heartbreak, tribulation
AN OPPOSITE IS joy

**2** *He related all the sorrows of his life.*
► trouble, difficulty, affliction, problem

**sorrowful** ADJECTIVE

*She gave a sorrowful smile.*
► sad, unhappy, dejected, miserable, despondent, disconsolate
OPPOSITES ARE happy, cheerful

**sorry** ADJECTIVE

**1** *He called his parents to say he was sorry for what he had done.*
► apologetic, ashamed (of), penitent, regretful, remorseful, repentant, conscience-stricken, contrite

**2** *He felt rather sorry for his father.*
► sympathetic, compassionate, full of pity, pitying, understanding

**3** *The house was in a sorry state.*
► pitiful, pitiable, wretched, unfortunate, pathetic, dismal

**sort** NOUN

*What sort of films do you like to see?*
► type, kind, variety, category, class, genre, style, nature

**sort** VERB

*The eggs are sorted by size and colour.*
► class, grade, group, categorize, classify, divide
**sort out** *It took a long time to sort out the difficulties.*
► settle, resolve, put right, deal with

**soul** NOUN

**1** *the immortality of the soul*
► psyche, spirit, inner being

**2** *(informal) The poor soul had to wait for hours to be seen.*
► person, individual, creature

**soulful** ADJECTIVE

*She gave him a soulful look.*
► emotional, expressive, heartfelt, deeply felt, passionate
AN OPPOSITE IS soulless

---

**sound** NOUN

*They could hear the sound of traffic in the street.*
► noise, din, hubbub, racket, tone
RELATED ADJECTIVES aural, acoustic, sonic

**NAMES FOR TYPES OF SOUND**

**crying and shouting sounds:** bawl, bellow, boo, cry, groan, howl, moan, scream, screech, shout, shriek, sigh, snarl, sniff, snore, snort, sob, splutter, squawk, squeak, squeal, wail, whimper, whine, whoop, yell, yelp.  ►►

**animal sounds**: bark, bay, bleat, bray, buzz, cackle, caw, chirp, chirrup, cluck, coo, croak, grate, grizzle, growl, grunt, gurgle, low, miaow, moo, neigh, purr, quack, roar, snort, tweet, twitter, warble, whinny, woof, yap, yowl.

**heavy sounds**: bang, boom, chug, crunch, drone, plop, rumble, throb, thud.

**sharp sounds**: bleep, chime, chink, clack, clap, clash, clatter, click, clink, crack, crackle, creak, fizz, hiss, jangle, jingle, ping, pop, rattle, ring, snap, squelch, tick, ting, tinkle, toot, twang, whistle.

**loud sounds**: blare, clamour, clang, clank, crash, honk, hoot, peal (of bells), roar, slam, smash, thunder, trumpet.

**gentle sounds**: hum, murmur, patter, rustle, sizzle, swish, whir.

## sound VERB

**1** *A signal sounded.*
▶ be heard, become audible, resound, resonate, reverberate, make a noise

**2** *Opening a door or window will sound the alarm.*
▶ set off, operate, blast

**3** *He sounded angry.*
▶ seem, appear, give the impression of being

**4** *You can sound the depth of a river with a pole.*
▶ measure, gauge, plumb, determine, probe, test, try

**sound out** *The survey will sound out public opinion.*
▶ measure, gauge, canvass, test, investigate

## sound ADJECTIVE

**1** *sound advice*
▶ good, sensible, valid, well-founded, reasonable, dependable
AN OPPOSITE IS unsound

**2** *The foundations seem sound.*
▶ firm, sturdy, solid, well built, substantial, stable
AN OPPOSITE IS unsafe

**3** *a sound investment*
▶ wise, judicious, well chosen
AN OPPOSITE IS unwise

**4** *She fell into a sound sleep.*
▶ deep, prolonged, unbroken, uninterrupted
OPPOSITES ARE light, shallow

## sour ADJECTIVE

**1** *a sour taste*
▶ sharp, acid, tart, bitter

**2** *a sour look*
▶ embittered, resentful, peevish, acrimonious, disagreeable

## source NOUN

**1** *the source of the problem*
▶ cause, origin, originator, initiator, author, fount, root, derivation, starting point

**2** *the source of the river*
▶ start, beginning, spring, origin, head

## souvenir NOUN

*They issued a recording of the concert as a souvenir.*
▶ memento, keepsake, reminder, token

## sovereign NOUN

*The Act reduced the powers of the sovereign.*
▶ ruler, monarch, king or queen, emperor or empress
RELATED ADJECTIVES regal, royal

## sovereign ADJECTIVE

**1** *Sovereign power should belong to the people.*
▶ supreme, absolute, principal, dominant

**2** *a sovereign state*
▶ autonomous, independent, self-governing

## sow VERB

*Sow the seeds in parallel rows.*
▶ plant, scatter, spread, distribute, put in the ground

## space NOUN

**1** *A minibus would have space for ten people.*
▶ room, capacity, accommodation, seating, seats, volume

**2** *The city has very few green spaces left.*
▶ area, stretch, expanse

**3** *There are spaces between the houses.*
▶ gap, interval, opening, aperture

## spacious ADJECTIVE

*A spacious hallway leads to the living rooms.*
▶ roomy, sizeable, ample, capacious, commodious, extensive, generous, large, big
OPPOSITES ARE cramped, poky

## span NOUN

**1** *It can be achieved within the span of a week.*
▶ space, period, course, duration, extent

**2** *a large bird with a six-foot wing span*
▶ width, length, reach, stretch, spread

## span VERB

*An old iron bridge spans the river.*
▶ cross, straddle, bridge, pass over, reach over, stretch over, extend across, traverse, arch over

## spank VERB

*She warned him that next time she would spank him.*
▶ smack, slap, chastise, give someone a spanking

## spare ADJECTIVE

**1** *Our neighbours have a spare set of our house keys.*
▶ extra, additional, supplementary, alternative, backup

**2** *Do you have any spare paper?*
▶ leftover, surplus, odd, unwanted, superfluous, unused, unnecessary

**3** *a spare figure*
▶ slender, slim, lean, slight, thin
AN OPPOSITE IS fat

**go spare** (*informal*) *They'll go spare if they find out.*
▶ lose your temper, be or become angry, go wild, (*informal*) hit the roof, (*informal*) go bananas, (*informal*) go ballistic

**spare** VERB
1 *We can't spare all that money.*
► afford, manage, part with, do without
2 *The captors would not spare any of the hostages.*
► pardon, show mercy to, let off, be lenient with, leave unharmed or unhurt

**sparing** ADJECTIVE
*He was always sparing with his praise.*
► careful, economical, frugal, mean, miserly, niggardly, prudent, stingy, thrifty, close
OPPOSITES ARE lavish, generous

**spark** NOUN
*a spark of light*
► flash, gleam, glint, flicker, sparkle, twinkle

**spark** VERB
*The comments sparked a furious row.*
► cause, give rise to, bring about, occasion, set off, stir up, provoke, stimulate, precipitate

**sparkle** VERB
*Lights sparkled in the distance.*
► glitter, glint, glisten, glimmer, twinkle, gleam, shimmer

**sparkle** NOUN
1 *a sparkle of light*
► flash, gleam, glint, flicker, spark, twinkle
2 *Life had lost its sparkle.*
► excitement, vitality, vivacity, verve, exuberance

**sparkling** ADJECTIVE
1 *sparkling jewellery*
► glittering, glinting, glistening, twinkling, flashing, scintillating, brilliant, shining, shiny
AN OPPOSITE IS dull
2 *a sparkling drink*
► fizzy, effervescent, bubbly, bubbling, aerated, carbonated, foaming
OPPOSITES ARE still, flat

**sparse** ADJECTIVE
*an area of sparse vegetation*
► meagre, sparse, scarce, scant, paltry, minimal, negligible
AN OPPOSITE IS dense

**spartan** ADJECTIVE
*They led a spartan life.*
► harsh, austere, frugal, ascetic, arduous, stringent, strict, stern
OPPOSITES ARE luxurious, opulent

**spasm** NOUN
1 *a spasm of coughing*
► fit, attack, outbreak, eruption, seizure
2 *a muscular spasm*
► convulsion, contraction, twitch

**spasmodic** ADJECTIVE
*The night was interrupted by spasmodic gunfire.*
► intermittent, fitful, sporadic, occasional, irregular, erratic
OPPOSITES ARE regular, continuous

**spate** NOUN
*a spate of burglaries*
► series, succession, run, string, outbreak, wave
AN OPPOSITE IS trickle

**spatter** VERB
*He spattered water all over the bathroom.*
► splash, splatter, spray, sprinkle

**speak** VERB
1 *She left before anyone could speak. He refused to speak about the incident.*
► talk, say anything, converse, communicate
2 *We must speak the truth.*
► tell, utter, express, declare, voice
3 *The chairman spoke for an hour.*
► lecture, give a speech, hold forth, declaim
4 **speak to** *She promised to speak to them soon. He did not speak to her for six months after that.*
► communicate with, say something or anything, converse with, contact

**special** ADJECTIVE
1 *a special occasion*
► important, exceptional, significant, particular, remarkable, extraordinary
2 *a perfume with a special smell*
► distinct, distinctive, characteristic, peculiar, unique, exclusive

**specialist** NOUN
*a specialist in gynaecology*
► expert, authority (on), consultant, connoisseur (of)

**speciality** NOUN
*Her speciality is interior design.*
► expertise, forte, strong point, special interest, strength, line

**specific** ADJECTIVE
*There is no specific evidence to support the allegations.*
► definite, particular, explicit, precise, special, clear-cut, detailed, exact
AN OPPOSITE IS general

**specify** VERB
*He would not specify the source of his information.*
► name, identify, state, mention, spell out, indicate, designate, detail, be specific about

**specimen** NOUN
*They asked for a specimen of his handwriting.*
► sample, illustration, example, demonstration, instance, model, pattern, copy

**speck** NOUN
*a speck of dust*
► particle, bit, fleck, grain, speckle, spot, trace, dot

**speckled** ADJECTIVE
*a speckled brown egg*
► flecked, speckly, spotted, freckly, freckled, mottled

**spectacle** NOUN
1 *The parade proved quite a spectacle*
► display, show, performance, pageant, extravaganza, exhibition

## spectacular

**2** *The group did look quite an odd spectacle*
▶ sight, scene, vision, picture

**3** *I think we're making a spectacle of ourselves.*
▶ exhibition, laughing stock, fool

## spectacular ADJECTIVE

*a spectacular display*
▶ magnificent, splendid, impressive, sensational, dazzling, showy, stunning, outstanding

## spectator NOUN

*Spectators lined the streets.*
▶ onlooker, watcher, viewer, observer, bystander, looker-on

## speculate VERB

**1** *His colleagues tended to speculate about his private life.*
▶ conjecture, theorize, wonder, hypothesize, make guesses, meditate, reflect, muse

**2** *People have been speculating on the stock exchange.*
▶ gamble, venture, hazard

## speculative ADJECTIVE

**1** *Their conclusions are merely speculative.*
▶ conjectural, theoretical, hypothetical, notional, tentative

**2** *a series of speculative investments*
▶ risky, hazardous, unpredictable, unsafe, unsound

## speech NOUN

**1** *the power of speech*
▶ speaking, talking, verbal communication
RELATED ADJECTIVES oral, phonetic

**2** *His speech was slurred.*
▶ diction, articulation, enunciation, utterance, elocution, delivery

**3** *an after-dinner speech*
▶ talk, address, lecture, oration, discourse

## speechless ADJECTIVE

*She was speechless with rage.*
▶ dumbfounded, dumbstruck, thunderstruck, aghast, tongue-tied
OPPOSITES ARE talkative, verbose

## speed NOUN

**1** *It's important to check your speed on this piece of road.*
▶ velocity, pace, rate, tempo

**2** *They completed the work with amazing speed.*
▶ rapidity, swiftness, alacrity, celerity, quickness, expeditiousness, promptness, fleetness, dispatch

## speed VERB

**1** *We sped back home*
▶ hurry, hasten, rush, dash, chase, hurtle, hustle, move quickly, (more informal) belt
OPPOSITES ARE go slowly, amble

**2** *He was over the limit and speeding.*
▶ break the speed limit, go or drive too fast

**speed up** *He called to them to speed up.*
▶ hurry up, go faster, increase speed, get a move on, quicken, accelerate

## speedy ADJECTIVE

*We got a speedy response.*
▶ quick, rapid, swift, fast, prompt, immediate, brisk

## spell NOUN

**1** *a magic spell*
▶ charm, incantation, magic formula, bewitchment, sorcery, witchcraft, conjuration, conjuring, enchantment

**2** *She cast her spell on all around her.*
▶ magic, allure, charm, fascination, influence, glamour

**3** *a spell of dry weather*
▶ period, interval, stretch, run, patch, turn, stint

## spell VERB

*Lack of rain has spelt disaster for the natural life of the region.*
▶ mean, lead to, result in, signal, signify, presage, herald, foretell, indicate, suggest

**spell out** *Let me spell out what I plan to do.*
▶ explain, elucidate, clarify, make plain, set out, specify, detail

## spellbound ADJECTIVE

*The audience was spellbound by the performance.*
▶ enthralled, entranced, captivated, enchanted, transfixed, mesmerized, gripped, bewitched, charmed, fascinated, hypnotized, transported

## spend VERB

**1** *You needn't spend more than £50 on it.*
▶ pay, pay out, expend, disburse, fritter, squander, (more informal) fork out, (more informal) shell out

**2** *They spent all their time arguing.*
▶ pass, occupy, fill, while away

## spendthrift NOUN

*He was a spendthrift and lived luxuriously.*
▶ big spender, profligate, prodigal, wastrel, squanderer
OPPOSITES ARE miser, scrooge, skinflint

## sphere NOUN

**1** *A glass sphere hung from the ceiling.*
▶ ball, globe, orb, spheroid, globule

**2** *She has a lot of experience in this sphere*
▶ field, area, domain, milieu, department, scope, subject, province, range, territory

## spherical ADJECTIVE

*a spherical paper lantern*
▶ round, globular, ball-shaped, rotund, spheroidal

## spice NOUN

**1** *Add some spices to liven up your dish.*
▶ herb, seasoning, flavouring

**2** *The risk of getting caught added spice to the adventure.*
▶ excitement, interest, zest, colour

## spicy ADJECTIVE

*a spicy casserole*
▶ highly flavoured, hot, piquant, tangy, pungent, seasoned

a b c d e f g h i j k l m n o p q r s t u v w x y z

**spiel** NOUN
(informal) He gave the usual spiel about raising standards.
▸ speech, monologue, rigmarole, patter, line

**spike** NOUN
She tore her dress on a spike.
▸ prong, point, barb, stake, skewer, spit

**spike** VERB
He spiked another pea with his fork.
▸ pierce, spear, skewer, impale

**spill** VERB
1 Keith slipped and spilled his drink.
▸ knock over, tip over, upset, slop, overturn, splash about
2 Water spilled over the top of the bath.
▸ overflow, flow, brim, run, pour
3 A lorry had spilled its load.
▸ shed, tip, scatter, discharge, drop
4 People spilled into the streets.
▸ stream, pour, surge, swarm, throng

**spin** VERB
1 A wheel spins on an axle
▸ turn, rotate, revolve, gyrate, whirl, twirl
2 My head was spinning.
▸ reel, swim, whirl, go round

**spindle** NOUN
The yarn is spun on a spindle.
▸ axle, rod, shaft

**spine** NOUN
1 The posture puts an unnecessary stress on the spine.
▸ backbone, spinal column, vertebrae
2 the spines of a hedgehog
▸ needle, quill, spike, bristle, point

**spine-chilling** ADJECTIVE
Head for the roller-coasters for a spine-chilling ride.
▸ frightening, terrifying, hair-raising, scaring, chilling, (more informal) scary

**spineless** ADJECTIVE
He is depicted as sly, drunken, and spineless.
▸ weak, feeble, ineffective, ineffectual, cowardly, faint-hearted, timid, irresolute, helpless
AN OPPOSITE IS brave

**spin-off** NOUN
The project is a spin-off from the work done last year.
▸ by-product, consequence, result, complement, corollary

**spiral** ADJECTIVE
a spiral column of smoke
▸ coiled, curling, winging, corkscrew, turning

**spiral** NOUN
a spiral of smoke
▸ coil, twist, whorl, corkscrew, screw

**spiral** VERB
1 Costs continued to spiral.
▸ soar, rise, mount, escalate, shoot up
OPPOSITES ARE tumble, fall

2 Feelings of anger and jealousy can spiral violently out of control.
▸ deteriorate, decline, degenerate, worsen, nosedive

**spire** NOUN
The spire of a church was just visible.
▸ steeple, spike, pinnacle, point

**spirit** NOUN
1 a philosophy of reconciling the body and the spirit
▸ soul, psyche, inner self, inner being
2 They went about their task with a good deal of spirit.
▸ enthusiasm, vigour, energy, vivacity, ardour, zest, keenness, eagerness, liveliness, animation, resolution
3 There is a legend of spirits haunting the place.
▸ ghost, spectre, phantom, apparition, wraith, shadow
4 We need to approach this challenge with a positive spirit.
▸ attitude, frame of mind, outlook
5 My spirit was dampened by these setbacks.
▸ mood, morale, temperament, disposition, humour
6 an action that breaks the spirit of the law if not the letter
▸ substance, essence, true meaning

**spirited** ADJECTIVE
The team gave a spirited performance an attractive and spirited young person
▸ lively, vivacious, vibrant, animated, energetic, high-spirited, vigorous, dynamic, sparkling, vital
OPPOSITES ARE timid, lifeless

**spiritual** ADJECTIVE
1 a spiritual existence
▸ non-material, incorporeal, unworldly, other-worldly, metaphysical
OPPOSITES ARE physical, material
2 spiritual music
▸ religious, sacred, holy, divine, devotional

**spit** VERB
Don't spit in public.
▸ expectorate, hawk
**spit out** He spat out a lemon pip.
▸ eject, spew

**spit** NOUN
He wiped the spit from his face.
▸ spittle, saliva, dribble, sputum

**spite** NOUN
He publicly criticized her out of spite.
▸ malice, maliciousness, spitefulness, animosity, vindictiveness, rancour, ill will, ill feeling, resentment, malevolence

**spiteful** ADJECTIVE
The speech contained many spiteful remarks.
▸ malicious, malevolent, ill-natured, hostile, hurtful, vicious, venomous, wounding, unkind, snide, cruel, nasty

## splash VERB

**1** *A passing van splashed water over us.*
► splatter, spray, shower, spatter, slosh, slop, sprinkle, squirt, wash

**2** *Children splashed about in the water.*
► paddle, wade, dabble, wallow, slosh

**3** *The newspapers splashed the story across their front pages.*
► blazon, plaster, display, spread, flaunt, trumpet, publicize

**splash out** (*informal*) *He was tempted to splash out on a Porsche.*
► spend money, splurge, be extravagant

## splash NOUN

**1** *a splash of colour*
► spot, patch, splodge, speck, burst, touch, dash

**2** *The scandal made quite a splash.*
► effect, impact, display

## splendid ADJECTIVE

**1** *The roses can be enjoyed in a splendid park setting.*
► magnificent, impressive, imposing, noble, glorious, spectacular, gorgeous, sumptuous

**2** *He is a splendid police officer.*
► distinguished, outstanding, remarkable, exceptional, celebrated, acclaimed

**3** *He had clearly had a splendid day out.*
► wonderful, marvellous, excellent, lovely, delightful

## splendour NOUN

*the classical splendour of the viceroy's palace*
► magnificence, grandeur, sumptuousness, brilliance, resplendence, majesty, richness, pomp, spectacle, stateliness

## splice VERB

*The cables were spliced in mid-ocean.*
► join, unite, connect, interweave, mesh, entwine

## splinter NOUN

*a splinter of wood  small splinters of glass*
► sliver, chip, flake, shard, fragment, shaving, shiver

## splinter VERB

*She had a voice that could splinter a glass.*
► shatter, shiver, crack, fracture, chip, smash, split

## split NOUN

**1** *There was a large split in the rock.*
► crack, fissure, crevice, breach, break, cleft

**2** *Her dress was stained and has a split in the side.*
► tear, rip, cut, slash, slit

**3** *The policy might produce a split in the party.*
► division, schism, rift, breach
AN OPPOSITE IS union

**4** *After the split with her partner she moved to London.*
► break-up, separation (from), parting, estrangement (from)

## split VERB

**1** *The child had pulled the curtain and split it.*
► tear, rip, slash, slit

**2** *He split the log with an axe.*
► chop, cut, hew, break, cleave

**3** *They worked out a system for splitting the proceeds.*
► divide, share, distribute, allocate, apportion

**4** *Further on the paths split.*
► fork, divide, diverge, branch
AN OPPOSITE IS merge

**5** *The proposal would split the Party.*
► divide, disunite

**split up** *Her parents had split up when she was small.*
► separate, break up, part, divorce

## spoil VERB

**1** *She stayed off the beach because she didn't want to spoil her shoes.*
► damage, harm, mar, hurt, blemish, disfigure, deface
OPPOSITES ARE improve, enhance

**2** *An emergency at a time like this could spoil everything.*
► ruin, wreck, upset, mess up, destroy, undo, scupper, sabotage, scotch
AN OPPOSITE IS further

**3** *She decided to spoil herself with a vintage champagne.*
► indulge, pamper, cosset
AN OPPOSITE IS neglect

## spoils NOUN

*Looters were filmed carrying off their spoils.*
► booty, loot, plunder, stolen goods, pickings

## sponge VERB

**1** *He asked his nephew to sponge the windows.*
► wash, clean, swab, mop, rinse, wipe

**2** **sponge on** *He didn't want to be sponging on his parents any longer.*
► live off, impose on, cadge from, scrounge from

## spongy ADJECTIVE

*The material was light and spongy.*
► soft, springy, squashy, cushioned, absorbent, porous
OPPOSITES ARE solid, hard

## sponsor NOUN

*To raise enough funds they would need more than one sponsor.*
► backer, patron, benefactor, promoter, donor

## sponsor VERB

*A local firm agreed to sponsor the championship.*
► back, promote, subsidize, support, be a sponsor of, finance, fund, help

## sponsorship NOUN

*Private sponsorship generated an additional ten million.*
► backing, promotion, support, benefaction, patronage, subsidy

## spontaneous ADJECTIVE

**1** *The March Revolution was a spontaneous uprising.*
► unplanned, unpremeditated, unprepared, unrehearsed, voluntary, impromptu, impulsive, unconstrained, unforced
AN OPPOSITE IS premeditated

**2** *The verdict was announced to cheers and spontaneous applause.*
► involuntary, automatic, natural, reflex, instinctive

a b c d e f g h i j k l m n o p q r s t u v w x y z

**3** *She always seems so friendly and spontaneous.*
▶ natural, uninhibited, unaffected, open, genuine
AN OPPOSITE IS inhibited

**spoof** NOUN
*The movie was a spoof of his own career.*
▶ parody, skit, take-off, burlesque, satire

**spooky** ADJECTIVE
*I bet this place is really spooky late at night.*
▶ eerie, sinister, creepy, frightening, ghostly, weird, (*more informal*) scary

**spool** NOUN
*a spool of cotton*
▶ reel, bobbin

**spoon-feed** VERB
*She was surprised at how much she had to spoon-feed them.*
▶ indulge, spoil, cosset, mollycoddle, pamper, help

**sporadic** ADJECTIVE
*There had been sporadic outbreaks of heavy rain*
▶ occasional, intermittent, periodic, infrequent, irregular

---

**sport** NOUN
*They showed a lot of interest in sport.*
▶ games, competitive games, physical recreation, physical exercise

**NAMES FOR TYPES OF SPORT**

**team sports**: football, soccer (Association football), rugby, American football, hockey; baseball, basketball, volleyball, lacrosse, netball, rounders, cricket, bowls, croquet; polo (on horseback).

**individual sports**: tennis, badminton, squash; gymnastics, trampolining; boxing, wrestling; billiards, snooker, pool, table tennis; darts; roller skating, rollerblading, skateboarding, cycling, free running.

**athletic sports**: track events, field events; running, sprint, long-distance race, marathon, cross-country; hurdles; relay race; pentathlon (five events), decathlon (ten events), discus, javelin, shot put, long jump, high jump, triple jump, pole vault.

**cross-country sports**: cross-country running, orienteering, mountaineering, climbing, potholing, rock-climbing, skydiving.

**sports with animals and machines**: horse racing, show jumping, dog racing; motor racing; gliding.

**water sports**: swimming, diving, rowing, surfing, windsurfing, sailing, yachting, canoeing, waterskiing, water polo, kayaking.

**winter sports**: bobsleigh, ice hockey, skating, skiing, tobogganing, snowboarding.

**blood sports**: hunting, beagling (hunting hares with beagles), shooting, fishing.

---

**sporting** ADJECTIVE
*It was sporting of them to pay the bill.*
▶ generous, considerate, decent, sportsmanlike
AN OPPOSITE IS unsporting

**sporty** ADJECTIVE
*They look sporty in their jogging suits.*
▶ athletic, fit, healthy, energetic

**spot** NOUN
**1** *There was a dirty spot in the middle of the carpet.*
▶ stain, mark, smudge, blotch, smear
**2** *He had a small spot on the side of his nose.*
▶ pimple, freckle, mole, blemish
**3** *a bright fabric with small spots*
▶ dot, speck, fleck
**4** *We stopped at a quiet spot near the sea.*
▶ place, position, location, locality, setting, site
**5** *Money problems left them in a bit of a spot.*
▶ predicament, difficulty, plight, mess, corner, trouble, awkward situation, quandary, dilemma, (*more informal*) jam, (*more informal*) fix

**spot** VERB
**1** *My apron was spotted with splashes of grease.*
▶ stain, mark, smudge, spatter, speckle, streak, blot, discolour, fleck, mottle
**2** *She spotted Jack weeding in the garden.*
▶ notice, observe, glimpse, spy, see, make out, discern, detect

**spotless** ADJECTIVE
**1** *He could wear a white shirt if it was spotless.*
▶ unmarked, perfectly clean, immaculate, gleaming
**2** *They had a spotless reputation for fair dealing.*
▶ unblemished, unsullied, untarnished, blameless, faultless, pure, immaculate, irreproachable, pure, (*more informal*) whiter than white

**spotty** ADJECTIVE
*a spotty face*
▶ pimply, pimpled, potmarked, spotted, blotchy, freckled

**spouse** NOUN
*Spouses were also invited to the office party.*
▶ husband or wife, partner

**spout** NOUN
*Water poured from the spout.*
▶ nozzle, outlet, jet, sprinkler

**spout** VERB
**1** *Molten lava was spouting from the crater.*
▶ spurt, gush, spew, pour, stream, shoot, surge, discharge, issue
**2** *He spouted endlessly about how much better life used to be.*
▶ hold forth, sound off, go on, pontificate, declaim, (*more informal*) mouth off, (*more informal*) rabbit on

# sprawl

**sprawl** VERB
1 *He sprawled on a huge armchair.*
▶ stretch out, lounge, recline, slump, slouch, flop
2 *The woods sprawled across the hillside.*
▶ spread, stretch, straggle, be scattered

**spray** NOUN
1 *a fine spray of water*
▶ shower, sprinkling, fountain, splash, mist
2 *a spray of flowers*
▶ bouquet, bunch, posy, nosegay, garland
3 *a paint spray*
▶ aerosol, atomizer, spray gun, sprinkler

**spray** VERB
1 *A sprinkler was spraying water over the grass.*
▶ sprinkle, spread, shower, disperse, diffuse
2 *Water sprayed into the air.*
▶ spout, gush, spurt, shoot

**spread** NOUN
1 *the spread of civilization*
▶ expansion, extension, growth, proliferation, diffusion, advance
2 *a vast spread of open country*
▶ stretch, expanse, extent, sweep, span
3 *(informal) There was a good spread on the table.*
▶ meal, feast

**spread** VERB
1 *He sat back and spread his arms.*
▶ extend, stretch
2 *I found a map and spread it on the table.*
▶ open out, unfurl, unroll, display
3 *She spread seeds along the edge of the flower bed.*
▶ scatter, strew, diffuse
4 *new ways of spreading information*
▶ communicate, diffuse, propagate, broadcast, transmit, circulate, advertise
5 *These feelings of resentment were beginning to spread.*
▶ grow, increase, proliferate, escalate, develop, broaden

**spree** NOUN
*a shopping spree*
▶ bout, fling, orgy, revel, (more informal) binge

**sprightly** ADJECTIVE
*He's very sprightly for his age.*
▶ lively, active, spry, agile, nimble, spirited, vivacious, vigorous
OPPOSITES ARE doddering, lethargic

**spring** NOUN
1 *With a sudden spring he was out of the door.*
▶ leap, jump, bound, vault
2 *The cushion had lost its spring.*
▶ bounce, springiness, resilience, elasticity, flexibility

**spring** VERB
1 *Steve sprang to his feet.*
▶ leap, jump, bound, bounce
2 *Some of these ideas spring from earlier research.*
▶ originate, derive, arise, develop, come
**spring up** *New hotels are springing up all along the coast.*
▶ appear, develop, emerge, shoot up

**springy** ADJECTIVE
1 *The floor felt springy under their feet.*
▶ elastic, stretchy, pliable, resilient, spongy, supple, bendy, flexible
AN OPPOSITE IS rigid
2 *He walked on with a springy step.*
▶ jaunty, bouncy, buoyant, lively, light

**sprinkle** VERB
1 *He sprinkled sugar over his cereal.*
▶ scatter, strew, shower
2 *Sprinkle the grass with seed.*
▶ dust, powder, pepper

**sprint** VERB
*She sprinted up the road.*
▶ run, dash, tear, shoot, dart, (more informal) belt

**sprout** VERB
*The seeds began to sprout.*
▶ grow, germinate, shoot up, spring up, bud, develop, emerge

**spruce** ADJECTIVE
*He looked spruce in his new uniform.*
▶ smart, neat, well-groomed, well-dressed, dapper, elegant, (more informal) natty
OPPOSITES ARE scruffy, dishevelled

**spruce** VERB
**spruce up** *They would have to spruce up the house for the visit.*
▶ smarten up, tidy up, clean up, put in order, (more informal) do up

**spry** ADJECTIVE
*She looks spry despite her age.*
▶ lively, active, sprightly, agile, nimble, spirited, vivacious, vigorous
OPPOSITES ARE doddering, lethargic

**spur** NOUN
*Music can become a spur to our imaginations.*
▶ stimulus, incentive, impetus, encouragement, enticement, filip
**on the spur of the moment** *He decided to go with her on the spur of the moment.*
▶ on impulse, impulsively, impetuously, spontaneously, all of a sudden

**spur** VERB
*The boy's frantic calls spurred her to action.*
▶ stimulate, encourage, drive, prompt, goad, incite

**spurious** ADJECTIVE
*The hotel may well bump up the bill with all sorts of spurious charges.*
▶ false, bogus, fake, specious, fraudulent, trumped up

**spurn** VERB
*Many visitors spurn the use of public transport.*
▶ reject, refuse, decline, scorn, turn down, disdain, disregard
OPPOSITES ARE welcome, accept

**spurt** VERB
*Blood spurted from his finger and he swore.*
▶ squirt, gush, shoot, stream, pour, spew, erupt, surge

**spy** NOUN
*He had never thought of himself as a traitor, or a spy.*
▶ secret agent, undercover agent, double agent, (*more informal*) plant, (*more informal*) mole

**spy** VERB
**1 spy on** *She sent you to spy on me.*
▶ snoop on, keep a watch on, watch, shadow, trail
**2** *We heard a rustle and spied a baby adder slithering away.*
▶ notice, observe, glimpse, spot, see, make out, discern, detect

**squabble** VERB
*Every evening a crowd gathered to squabble over politics.*
▶ argue, quarrel, bicker, wrangle, dispute, clash, fight

**squalid** ADJECTIVE
**1** *a depressing mixture of cheap housing and squalid surroundings*
▶ dirty, filthy, grimy, grubby, sordid, seedy, dingy
AN OPPOSITE IS clean
**2** *squalid attempts to rig the election*
▶ improper, shameful, sordid, dishonest, corrupt
AN OPPOSITE IS honourable

**squander** VERB
*The servant girl he married squandered every penny of his.*
▶ waste, misspend, fritter away, dissipate, (*more informal*) blow
AN OPPOSITE IS save

**square** ADJECTIVE
**1** *They sat at a square table.*
▶ rectangular, right-angled, quadrilateral
**2** *The sides were still square at full time.*
▶ level, even, neck and neck
**3** *All they wanted was a square deal.*
▶ fair, honest, just, equitable, genuine, above-board, (*more informal*) on-the-level

**square** NOUN
**1** *They arranged to meet in the town square.*
▶ piazza, plaza

**2** (*informal*) *He must have seemed such a square to them.*
▶ old fogy, conservative, traditionalist, conformist, conventional person, (*informal*) stick-in-the-mud

**square** VERB
**1** *He went in to square his bill.*
▶ settle, pay, clear, discharge
**2** *He needed to square a few things with his dad.*
▶ resolve, settle, sort out, clear up, put right, remedy, reconcile
**3** *These facts don't quite square with the accepted version of what happened.*
▶ agree, tally, accord, harmonize

**squash** VERB
**1** *Someone had squashed the flowers in the garden.*
▶ crush, flatten, press, mangle, trample on, compress
**2** *He squashed a few things into his case.*
▶ stuff, force, cram, ram, pack
**3** *The uprising was ruthlessly squashed.*
▶ suppress, quash, quell, put down
**4** *He meanly squashed them in front of everyone.*
▶ humiliate, humble, show up, put down, mortify, snub

**squashy** ADJECTIVE
*a squashy pudding*
▶ spongy, squelchy, mushy, pulpy, soft, yielding
AN OPPOSITE IS firm

**squat** ADJECTIVE
*a cathedral with two squat towers*
▶ short, dumpy, stocky, chunky, stubby, stunted, low
AN OPPOSITE IS tall

**squat** VERB
*The children squatted on the floor to listen.*
▶ crouch, stoop, sit

**squawk** VERB
*A bird squawked overhead.*
▶ screech, shriek, squeal, cry, call

**squeak** VERB
**1** *The door squeaked.*
▶ creak, grate, rasp
**2** *The bird squeaked in its cage.*
▶ chirp, peep, cheep

**squeal** VERB
*She squealed with pain.*
▶ cry, yell, yelp, screech, scream, shriek

**squeamish** ADJECTIVE
*Her father had always been squeamish about changing nappies.*
▶ queasy, nauseated, fastidious, finicky, fussy, choosy, particular, prim, prissy

**squeeze** VERB
**1** *Katherine squeezed her daughter's hand affectionately.*
▶ press, clasp, grip, hug, squash, wring, compress, crush, embrace, enfold

**2** *She put her arm round him and squeezed him.*
▶ hug, embrace, cuddle, hold, clasp
**3** *They squeezed the audience into a room that was obviously too small. She squeezed herself into a bright red minidress.*
▶ cram, push, ram, shove, stuff, thrust, crowd, wedge
**4** *Two elderly Americans squeezed past her chair.*
▶ push, force your way
**5** *The government seems determined to squeeze as much money out of the motorist as it can.*
▶ wring, wrest, extort, extract, force, milk

**squeeze** NOUN
**1** *He gave her hand a squeeze.*
▶ press, pinch, grip, grasp, clasp
**2** *Three of us in the back of the car was quite a squeeze.*
▶ crush, jam, huddle, crowd

**squint** VERB
*I saw him squint across at her.*
▶ peer, peek, peep, glance, glimpse, look

**squint** NOUN
*(informal)* *Kate had time for a bacon sandwich and a squint at the papers.*
▶ look, glance, peek, peep

**squirm** VERB
*Some scenes in the film make you squirm in your seat.*
▶ wriggle, writhe, twist, fidget, twitch

**squirt** VERB
**1** *The first bite made jam squirt down my chin.*
▶ spurt, shoot, gush, spout, spray, erupt, surge
**2** *She squirted me with water.*
▶ splash, spray, shower, spatter, splatter, sprinkle

**stab** NOUN
**1** *He got a stab in the leg.*
▶ wound, wounding, blow, jab, cut, prick, thrust
**2** *She felt a brief stab of pain.*
▶ twinge, pang, sting, throb, spasm
**3** *(informal)* *I'll have a stab at it.*
▶ try, go, attempt, *(informal)* bash, *(informal)* shot

**stab** VERB
**1** *One of the gang stabbed him in the arm.*
▶ knife, spear, pierce, jab, stick, thrust, wound
**2** *She stabbed at the ground with a spade.*
▶ thrust, jab, prod, lunge, poke

**stability** NOUN
**1** *It is important to check the stability of the equipment.*
▶ firmness, solidity, steadiness, security, safety
**2** *The refugee problem was affecting the stability of the region.*
▶ equilibrium, balance, permanence, soundness, strength
AN OPPOSITE IS instability

**stabilize** VERB
*An increase in interest rates would stabilize the currency.*
▶ settle, balance, strengthen, support, make secure
OPPOSITES ARE destabilize, upset

**stable** ADJECTIVE
**1** *Make sure the equipment is stable.*
▶ steady, firm, secure, balanced, fixed, solid
OPPOSITES ARE unstable, flimsy
**2** *Their power and authority depend on a stable regime.*
▶ well-founded, well-established, secure, firm, enduring, durable, lasting, sound, strong
OPPOSITES ARE unstable, changeable

**stack** NOUN
**1** *The publisher had a stack of unsold copies on his hands.*
▶ heap, pile, mound, mass, load, accumulation, stockpile, mountain
**2** *a stack of hay*
▶ rick, stook, haycock

**stack** VERB
*The boxes were stacked on desks and tables.*
▶ pile, heap, load, mass, assemble, collect, accumulate, build up, gather

**stadium** NOUN
*a sports stadium*
▶ arena, ground, field, pitch

**staff** NOUN
**1** *We have extra staff on duty over the busy period.*
▶ personnel, assistants, employees, workers, workforce, crew, officers, team
**2** *Magistrates carried a staff as a sign of their authority.*
▶ cane, crosier, pole, rod, sceptre, stave, stick

**staff** VERB
*The shop is staffed by volunteers.*
▶ man, people, crew, operate, run

**stage** NOUN
**1** *They faced the long last stage of their journey.*
▶ part, section, phase, portion, stretch, lap
**2** *The treaty marks a new stage in relations between the two countries.*
▶ point, phase, step, juncture

**stage** VERB
**1** *They even staged an opera.*
▶ mount, put on, present, perform, arrange
**2** *Workers staged a two-hour strike on 5 November.*
▶ organize, mount, set up, go through with

**stagger** VERB
**1** *He staggered up the stairs to bed.*
▶ totter, stumble, lurch, reel, sway, falter, walk unsteadily, waver, wobble
**2** *Rory was staggered by his answer.*
▶ astonish, amaze, astound, surprise, dumbfound, flabbergast, shock, startle, stun, stupefy

**stagnant** ADJECTIVE
*a mass of marshy grass and stagnant water*
▶ still, motionless, standing, stale, brackish, static, foul, putrid
OPPOSITES ARE flowing, fresh

a
b
c
d
e
f
g
h
i
j
k
l
m
n
o
p
q
r
s
t
u
v
w
x
y
z

**stagnate** VERB

*While revenues stagnate, expenditure has soared.*
▶ stand still, stay still, languish, achieve nothing, vegetate, become stale, deteriorate, idle
OPPOSITES ARE rise, boom

**staid** ADJECTIVE

*Surely she's too flamboyant for marriage to such a staid man.*
▶ sedate, respectable, conventional, serious, demure, solemn

**stain** NOUN

1 *Her eyes alighted on a milk stain on the tablecloth.*
▶ mark, spot, smear, blemish, smudge, blot, blotch, discoloration
2 *It was not seen as a stain on their character.*
▶ blemish, taint, blot, slur, disgrace, discredit

**stain** VERB

1 *Sweat had stained his shirt.*
▶ discolour, mark, blemish, dirty, sully, spoil, blacken
2 *There is a product that will stain and varnish in one go.*
▶ dye, colour, tinge, tint, paint

**stake** NOUN

1 *The soldier had been speared with a wooden stake.*
▶ pole, post, spike, stave, stick, paling, pile
2 *The multinational has bought a 40% stake in the company.*
▶ share, interest, involvement
3 *If you win, you get your stake back plus ten times its value*
▶ bet, pledge, wager

**stale** ADJECTIVE

1 *You can make the pudding with stale bread and milk.*
▶ dry, hard, old, musty, mouldy
2 *The war had already become stale news.*
▶ worn out, jaded, hackneyed, out-of-date, uninteresting, unoriginal, overused
AN OPPOSITE IS fresh

**stalemate** NOUN

*The negotiations ended in a stalemate.*
▶ deadlock, impasse, standstill

**stalk** NOUN

*the stalk of a plant*
▶ stem, shoot, branch, trunk, twig

**stalk** VERB

1 *The cat began to stalk her through the long grass.*
▶ track, trail, hunt, pursue, shadow, tail, follow
2 *He rose and stalked out of the door.*
▶ stride, strut, march, flounce, sweep

**stall** NOUN

*The school will have a stall at Fun in the Parks.*
▶ stand, booth, kiosk

**stall** VERB

*He clearly believed she was only stalling.*
▶ play for time, delay, procrastinate, prevaricate, temporize, hang back

**stalwart** ADJECTIVE

*a stalwart supporter of the new democracy*
▶ staunch, faithful, loyal, devoted, reliable, resolute, robust, strong, dependable, sturdy, trustworthy, tough, valiant
AN OPPOSITE IS weak

**stamina** NOUN

*The soft ground will make the event a real test of stamina.*
▶ endurance, resilience, staying-power, energy

**stammer** VERB

*He always began to stammer when he was under pressure.*
▶ stutter, falter, splutter, stumble, hesitate

**stamp** NOUN

1 *The licence needs an official stamp to be valid.*
▶ mark, seal, brand, imprint
2 *She left her stamp on history as an inspired visionary.*
▶ mark, impression
3 *The new head was of a different stamp from her predecessor.*
▶ type, kind, sort, brand, character

**stamp** VERB

1 *'Bad girl,' she said and stamped her foot.*
▶ strike, bring down, thump
2 *Sir George had stamped his authority firmly on the subject.*
▶ imprint, mark, print, brand, engrave, impress
**stamp on** *Ellie moved forward and stamped on the creature.*
▶ tread on, crush, trample
**stamp out** *The police are trying to stamp out racism.*
▶ eliminate, eradicate, extinguish, end, put an end to, suppress

**stampede** NOUN

*In the stampede that follows, the young elephants can easily get trampled.*
▶ charge, rush, dash, rout, panic

**stampede** VERB

*The audience panicked and stampeded for the exit.*
▶ dash, bolt, charge, rush, flee

**stance** NOUN

*The country has moved away from the neutral stance it previously took.*
▶ attitude, stand, viewpoint, position, policy, posture

**stand** VERB

1 *The choir stood for the final chorus.*
▶ rise, get to your feet, get up
2 *A house once stood on this spot.*
▶ be situated, be located, be sited, exist, sit, be
3 *She stood the packet on the table.*
▶ put, place, set, deposit, position, situate, station, locate, *(more informal)* plonk
4 *The offer still stands*
▶ remain in force, remain valid, be unchanged, stay, continue
5 *Her heart could not stand the strain.*
▶ withstand, endure, handle, cope with

**6** *I can't stand noise.*
▶ bear, abide, endure, tolerate, put up with, suffer, (more informal) stick, (more informal) stomach, (more informal) wear

**stand by** *He was determined to stand by his friends.*
▶ support, defend, stand or stick up for, be faithful to, be loyal to, adhere to, stay with, stick to
OPPOSITES ARE betray, let down

**stand down** *He would have to accept responsibility and stand down.*
▶ resign, step down, retire, (more informal) quit

**stand for** *What do the initials stand for?*
▶ mean, represent, signify, denote, indicate, symbolize, be a sign for

**stand in for** *She stood in for the lead singer who was unwell.*
▶ replace, substitute for, take over from, be a substitute for, deputize for, cover for, understudy

**stand out** *He stands out in that suit.*
▶ be prominent, be obvious, catch the eye, show, stick out

**stand up for** *It is important to stand up for our principles.*
▶ support, defend, champion, stand or stick by, be faithful to, be loyal to, adhere to, stay with, stick to
AN OPPOSITE IS betray

**stand up to** *The little band stood up bravely to the attack.*
▶ resist, withstand, confront, face up to, defy, oppose
OPPOSITES ARE give in to, succumb to

**stand** NOUN
**1** *a large vase on a stand*
▶ base, pedestal, support, tripod, trivet, rack
**2** *a newspaper stand*
▶ stall, booth, kiosk
**3** *They are taking a bold stand.*
▶ attitude, stance, viewpoint, position, policy, posture

**standard** ADJECTIVE
*The fee is subject to VAT at the standard rate. The council said the letter was part of their standard procedure.*
▶ normal, usual, typical, customary, conventional

**standard** NOUN
**1** *The standard of music-making can be very high indeed.*
▶ quality, level, calibre, grade, excellence
**2** *a standard of behaviour*
▶ norm, principle, yardstick, criterion, benchmark, example
**3** *Next day at dawn they raised the regimental standard for the last time.*
▶ flag, banner, pennant, colours, ensign

**standardize** VERB
*Some attempt has been made to standardize the menus.*
▶ average out, conform to a standard, equalize, normalize, regiment, stereotype

**stand-in** NOUN
*They needed a stand-in for the injured goalkeeper.*
▶ substitute, replacement, reserve

**standing** NOUN
*The superintendent has to be a medical practitioner of high standing.*
▶ reputation, distinction, status, repute, rank, stature, seniority, eminence

**standoffish** ADJECTIVE
*I kept telling myself to relax and not be so standoffish.*
▶ aloof, detached, reserved, uncommunicative

**standpoint** NOUN
*From the consumer standpoint there are two main hazards.*
▶ point of view, viewpoint, perspective, position, outlook, slant, view, angle

**standstill** NOUN
*Traffic is forced to a standstill until visibility improves.*
▶ stop, halt, dead stop

**staple** ADJECTIVE
*a staple diet*
▶ basic, standard , fundamental, principal, chief, main

**star** NOUN
**1** *a sky full of stars*
▶ celestial body, heavenly body
RELATED ADJECTIVES astral, stellar
**2** *She was an international star by the age of nineteen.*
▶ celebrity, famous person, public figure, big name, idol

**stare** VERB
**1** *She seemed stunned and sat staring in front of her.*
▶ gaze, gape, glare, goggle, look fixedly, peer
**2** *stare at Simon was staring at him.*
▶ gaze at, eye, scrutinize, study, watch, contemplate, examine

**stark** ADJECTIVE
**1** *Those who survived had the stark choice of submitting or fleeing into exile.*
▶ grim, blunt, harsh, plain, bald
**2** *Their barracks are a stark contrast to the brightness elsewhere.*
▶ absolute, complete, utter, total, sheer

**start** VERB
**1** *The film starts at 8.*
▶ begin, (more formal) commence
**2** *She wants to start a reading group.*
▶ set up, establish, found, launch, begin, institute, originate, activate, create, embark on, inaugurate, initiate, instigate, introduce, open
AN OPPOSITE IS finish
**3** *The bus was ready to start*
▶ depart, leave, move off, set off, set out, (more informal) get going
AN OPPOSITE IS stop
**4** *We'd better start if we are going to finish in time.*
▶ make a start, begin, (more informal) get going, (more informal) get cracking

**5** *A crash in the kitchen made us start.*
▶ jump, recoil, flinch, spring up, blench, jerk, twitch, wince

**start out** *They would have to start out before breakfast.*
▶ set off, set out, set forth, make a start, depart, leave, (*more informal*) get going, (*more informal*) hit the road

**start** NOUN

**1** *It was the start of a long process.*
▶ beginning, outset, inception, birth, dawn, initiation, inauguration
OPPOSITES ARE end, conclusion

**2** *A good education gives you a start in life.*
▶ advantage, opportunity, encouragement, helping hand

**3** *This was the start of all our problems.*
▶ origin, cause, source, starting point
OPPOSITES ARE end, culmination

**4** *The doorbell rang, giving me a start*
▶ shock, jump, surprise

**startle** VERB

*Some caterpillars manage to startle their attackers by raising themselves up like small snakes.*
▶ alarm, frighten, scare, surprise, give you a start, take by surprise, catch unawares, make you start, shake, shock
AN OPPOSITE IS calm

**startling** ADJECTIVE

*It was startling to see hundreds of people toiling up and down the hill. The letter contained some startling news.*
▶ surprising, astonishing, amazing, staggering, disconcerting, unsettling

**starvation** NOUN

*The civil war left most of the population facing starvation.*
▶ hunger, malnutrition, undernourishment, malnourishment, deprivation, famine

**starve** VERB

*Many starved in the famine.*
▶ die of starvation, go hungry, go without, perish

**starving** ADJECTIVE

**1** *She devoted her energies to helping the starving children of the world.*
▶ starved, underfed, undernourished, emaciated

**2** *Let's go and eat, I'm starving.*
▶ very hungry, famished, ravenous

**state** NOUN

**1** *The closure reflects the state of the town's economy.*
▶ condition, situation, shape, circumstances, predicament, position, health

**2** *a sovereign state*
▶ country, nation, land, (*more formal*) polity

**in a state** *Try not to get in a state.*
▶ agitated, flustered, anxious, panicky, frenzied, (*more informal*) uptight

**state** VERB

*In the speech she stated her company's objectives.*
▶ declare, express, communicate, voice, utter, tell, say, affirm, make known, reveal, disclose, divulge

**stately** ADJECTIVE

*a stately procession through the town*
▶ dignified, majestic, ceremonious, grand, splendid, imposing, noble

**statement** NOUN

*The minister issued a brief statement.*
▶ announcement, declaration, account, report, communication, utterance

**statesman** NOUN

*a distinguished banker and statesman who amassed a huge art collection*
▶ senior politician, politician

**static** ADJECTIVE

**1** *a static display of work and photographs*
▶ stationary, immobile, motionless, fixed, still, unmoving
AN OPPOSITE IS mobile

**2** *Prices have remained static for several years.*
▶ unchanged, steady, stable, constant, invariable, stagnant
AN OPPOSITE IS variable

**station** NOUN

**1** *a nuclear power station in Armenia a research station funded by the EU*
▶ establishment, facility, base, depot, post, plant, headquarters, office

**2** *a radio station*
▶ channel, transmitter, wavelength, company

**3** *It's one of the busiest railway stations in the world*
▶ stopping place, terminus, halt, platform

**4** *a grand station in life*
▶ standing, status, position, rank, situation, calling

**station** VERB

*She used to date John when he was stationed in Berlin.*
▶ post, base, assign (to), deploy, locate, establish

**stationary** ADJECTIVE

*One moment we were stationary, the next moving forward smoothly.*
▶ still, at a standstill, motionless, standing, immobile, at rest, halted, static
AN OPPOSITE IS moving

**stationery** NOUN

*a shop selling cards and stationery*
▶ paper, writing materials

**statistics** NOUN

*a comprehensive volume of facts, records, and statistics*
▶ data, figures, information, numbers

**statue** NOUN

*a bronze statue of a Roman emperor*
▶ figure, sculpture, effigy, carving, bronze

**stature** NOUN

**1** *a family who were all of small stature*
▶ build, size, height, tallness

**2** *His stature as a war-chief grew.*
▶ reputation, status, standing, esteem, distinction, importance, prominence, recognition, greatness, significance

**status** NOUN
**1** *people who enjoy money and status*
▶ prestige, standing, position or social position, stature, rank
**2** *The money is paid to every individual regardless of marital status.*
▶ position, standing

**staunch** ADJECTIVE
*My grandfather was a miner and a staunch socialist.*
▶ faithful, firm, loyal, steadfast, strong, reliable, dependable, constant, stalwart, unswerving, true, trustworthy
OPPOSITES ARE disloyal, unreliable

**stave** VERB
**stave off** *The government is anxious to stave off a back-bench rebellion.*
▶ prevent, avert, avoid, forestall, nip in the bud

**stay** VERB
**1** *The officer told him to stay where he was.*
▶ wait, remain, continue, (*more informal*) hang on
OPPOSITES ARE leave, depart
**2** *It was vital to stay calm.*
▶ remain, keep, continue, carry on being
**3** *He said it would be better to stay in a hotel.*
▶ live, lodge, reside, settle, board, dwell, be accommodated, be a guest, be housed, sojourn, stop, visit

**stay** NOUN
*I had several suitcases, in preparation for a long stay.*
▶ visit, stop, stopover, break, holiday, sojourn

**steadfast** ADJECTIVE
*She is among the most steadfast opponents of electoral reform.*
▶ faithful, firm, loyal, staunch, strong, reliable, dependable, constant, stalwart, unswerving, true, trustworthy
OPPOSITES ARE disloyal, unreliable

**steady** ADJECTIVE
**1** *The ladder doesn't look steady.*
▶ secure, stable, settled, fixed, balanced, fast, firm, solid, safe
AN OPPOSITE IS unsteady.
**2** *The Middle East has provided Wimpey with a steady stream of work.*
▶ continuous, regular, constant, even, reliable, uninterrupted, consistent, dependable, ceaseless, non-stop
AN OPPOSITE IS intermittent
**3** *Talk in a firm steady voice without shouting.*
▶ regular, even, invariable, rhythmic, smooth, uniform
**4** *He didn't then have a steady girlfriend.*
▶ regular, habitual, settled, established, devoted, faithful, loyal, serious, steadfast

**steady** VERB
**1** *Alec steadied himself as the ground shook again.*
▶ stabilize, balance, brace, make steady, secure
**2** *I needed something to steady my nerves.*
▶ calm, soothe, settle, quieten, quell, control

**steal** VERB
**1** *He rushed in to help when a mugger tried to steal a fan's camera. He had been caught stealing from a friend.*
▶ thieve, pilfer, purloin, appropriate, rob, run off with, (*more informal*) filch, (*more informal*) pinch, (*more informal*) nick, (*more informal*) swipe, (*more informal*) snaffle
**2** *I stole quietly out of the room.*
▶ creep, slink, sneak, move stealthily, tiptoe
**3** *Carson stole sideways glances at his passenger.*
▶ snatch, sneak, take

**stealing** NOUN
*They were convicted of stealing.*
▶ theft, thieving, robbery, burglary, pilfering, shoplifting

**stealthy** ADJECTIVE
*a lot of stealthy movement from one room to another*
▶ furtive, secretive, covert, secret, surreptitious, sneaking, sly, slinky, clandestine
AN OPPOSITE IS blatant

**steam** NOUN
*The kitchen was full of steam.*
▶ vapour, condensation, moisture, haze, mist

**steamy** ADJECTIVE
**1** *The windows were steamy.*
▶ misty, cloudy, hazy
**2** *the hot steamy jungle*
▶ humid, muggy, sticky, close, sultry, sweaty, damp, moist

**steel** VERB
*She steeled herself for bad news.*
▶ brace, stiffen, harden, prepare, nerve

**steep** ADJECTIVE
**1** *steep cliffs overlooking the sea*
▶ sheer, precipitous, abrupt, perpendicular, vertical, sudden, sharp
AN OPPOSITE IS gentle
**2** *The costs seem rather steep.*
▶ expensive, dear, costly, exorbitant, extortionate, (*more informal*) pricey, (*more informal*) stiff
OPPOSITES ARE reasonable, moderate

**steer** VERB
*She steered the huge vehicle into the garage.*
▶ drive, direct, guide, navigate, control, pilot
**steer clear of** *The rickety old barn was a place to steer clear of.*
▶ avoid, keep away from, give a wide berth to

**stem** NOUN
*The plants are nourished by water drawn up the stem.*
► trunk, stalk, stock

**stem** VERB
*The important thing is to stem the spread of the disease. She could no longer stem the flow of tears.*
► stop, check, restrain, restrict, hold back, control, curb

**stench** NOUN
*The stench of rotting flesh is enough to make you vomit.*
► stink, reek, foul smell, bad smell

**step** NOUN
1 *She took a step backwards*
► pace, stride, footstep
2 *Anyone seeking political asylum is taking a major step.*
► decision, move, action, course, measure
3 *This was a good first step towards retaining her title.*
► phase, stage, action, measure, manœuvre
4 *an important step towards achieving peace*
► advance, movement, progress, progression
5 *steps I climbed the steps and knocked on the door.*
► stairs, staircase

**step** VERB
*I stepped over several mounds of brick and rubble.*
► tread, put your foot, walk, stamp, trample
**step down** *The minister would step down at the next election.*
► resign, stand down, retire, (*informal*) quit
**step up** *The army stepped up the attack.*
► increase, intensify, escalate, augment, boost

**stereotype** NOUN
*man's stereotype of how a woman should look*
► conventional image, cliché, received idea, pattern, model, formula

**sterile** ADJECTIVE
1 *sterile soil*
► infertile, barren, unproductive, arid, dry, lifeless
AN OPPOSITE IS fertile
2 *a sterile bandage*
► sterilized, antiseptic, aseptic, clean, disinfected, germ-free, hygienic, uninfected
AN OPPOSITE IS unsterilized
3 *a sterile discussion*
► useless, fruitless, unfruitful, pointless, unprofitable, abortive, hopeless
AN OPPOSITE IS fruitful

**sterilize** VERB
1 *The room should be clean but you don't have to sterilize everything.*
► disinfect, fumigate, decontaminate, make sterile, pasteurize, purify, clean, cleanse
OPPOSITES ARE contaminate, infect
2 *In the poorest families both husband and wife have been sterilized.*
► make infertile, give a hysterectomy or vasectomy to

**stern** ADJECTIVE
1 *Their father looked stern for a while, but soon went to them.*
► strict, severe, harsh, grim, grave, serious, austere, authoritarian, dour
OPPOSITES ARE genial, kindly
2 *Stern measures were needed.*
► strict, severe, stringent, rigorous, harsh, drastic, tough
OPPOSITES ARE lenient, lax

**stew** NOUN
*stew for dinner*
► casserole, hot-pot, ragout, goulash, hash

**stew** VERB
*The meat should be stewed slowly.*
► braise, casserole, boil, simmer

**stick** NOUN
1 *a pile of dry sticks*
► twig, branch, stalk
2 *She threatened him with a stick.*
► rod, cane

**stick** VERB
1 *Iris stuck her fork in the earth.*
► poke, prod, dig, jab, stab, thrust
2 *He stuck a message on her computer screen.*
► attach, affix, fasten, fix, glue, paste, pin
3 *The plastic seats stuck to her skin.*
► cling, adhere, bond, fuse
4 (*informal*) *I've got some stewed fruit I stuck in the freezer.*
► put, place, leave, deposit, drop, (*informal*) bung, (*informal*) dump
5 *The wheels stuck in the soft mud.*
► become trapped, jam
6 *A particular memory stuck in his mind.*
► remain, linger, persist, stay
7 (*informal*) *I couldn't stick it any longer.*
► tolerate, put up with
**stick at** (*informal*) *If you want to learn a language, you'll have to stick at it.*
► persevere with, persist with, keep at, work hard at
**stick out** *He had his hands on his hips and his chin stuck out.*
► jut out, protrude, project
**stick to** *She advises her staff to stick to six basic safety guidelines.*
► abide by, adhere to, keep, hold to, fulfil
**stick up** *The monument sticks up above the trees.*
► rise, stand out, loom, tower
**stick up for** *I was born here and I try to stick up for Britain.*
► support, defend, stand up for

**sticky** ADJECTIVE
1 *She tied up the package with sticky tape.*
► adhesive, gummed, self-adhesive, glued
2 *There was a patch of sticky fluid on the carpet.*
► gluey, tacky, gummy, treacly, (*more informal*) gooey
AN OPPOSITE IS dry

# stiff

**3** *It was a hot sticky afternoon.*
► humid, muggy, sultry, clammy, close
OPPOSITES ARE fresh, cool

## stiff ADJECTIVE

**1** *You'll need a sheet of stiff cardboard.*
► rigid, firm, hard
OPPOSITES ARE limp, flexible

**2** *Make a stiff paste.*
► thick, firm, semi-solid, viscous

**3** *Her muscles were stiff. I was so stiff it was difficult to climb upstairs.*
► achy, aching, arthritic, painful, immovable, rheumatic, taut, tight
AN OPPOSITE IS supple

**4** *a long stiff climb up the hillside*
► difficult, arduous, strenuous, tough, exacting, hard, tiring
AN OPPOSITE IS easy

**5** *We will face some stiff competition later this year.*
► strong, powerful, severe

**6** *His manner was stiff and aloof.*
► formal, reserved, unfriendly, cool, awkward
AN OPPOSITE IS relaxed

**7** *The judge handed out stiff sentences.*
► harsh, severe, punitive, strict, hard, swingeing
AN OPPOSITE IS lenient

**8** *A stiff breeze made it hard going.*
► fresh, strong, brisk
AN OPPOSITE IS gentle

**9** *They all needed a stiff drink.*
► strong, potent, alcoholic
AN OPPOSITE IS weak

## stiffen VERB

*Stir until the mixture stiffens.*
► become stiff, harden, set, solidify, thicken

## stifle VERB

**1** *The heat can stifle you.*
► suffocate, choke, smother

**2** *Margaret stifled a cough. The policy has stifled realistic thinking.*
► suppress, check, smother, restrain, muffle, curb

## stifling ADJECTIVE

*a stifling June afternoon*
► stuffy, sweltering, oppressive

## stigma NOUN

*the stigma of being branded a cheat*
► disgrace, shame, taint, dishonour, reproach, slur, stain, blot

## still ADJECTIVE

**1** *Paul stood still and looked around.*
► motionless, immobile, stationary, unmoving, static, inert, lifeless
AN OPPOSITE IS moving

**2** *The evening was warm and still.*
► quiet, calm, silent, soundless, noiseless, wind-free
OPPOSITES ARE windy, stormy

## still VERB

*The wind had stilled.*
► die down, abate, weaken, slacken

## stimulate VERB

**1** *The literature course stimulated their interest in modern fiction.*
► trigger, activate, kindle, rouse, arouse, stir, increase, enhance
AN OPPOSITE IS discourage

**2** *The right words from you might stimulate them to keep trying.*
► encourage, prompt, motivate, inspire, provoke

## stimulating ADJECTIVE

*a stimulating lecture by Professor Smithers*
► interesting, thought-provoking, entertaining, challenging, exciting, rousing, stirring, exhilarating, inspiring, invigorating, provoking
OPPOSITES ARE boring, dull

## stimulus NOUN

*Cash is the best stimulus to economic development in the region.*
► spur, stimulant, encouragement, incentive, inducement, impetus, fillip
AN OPPOSITE IS deterrent

## sting NOUN

**1** *an ointment to soothe a wasp sting*
► bite, prick, wound

**2** *He felt the sting of the wound still.*
► smarting, stinging, pain, burn, pricking

## sting VERB

**1** *an insect that stings*
► bite, nip, prick

**2** *The salt water began to sting*
► smart, tingle, hurt, burn

## stingy ADJECTIVE

*Derek was notoriously stingy.*
► mean, miserly, niggardly, penny-pinching, parsimonious, (more informal) tight-fisted
AN OPPOSITE IS generous

## stink VERB

**1** *The room stank of smoke.*
► reek, smell, (more informal) pong

**2** *The whole idea stinks.*
► be unpleasant, be abhorrent, be repellent

## stink NOUN

*The stink hits you as soon as you open the door.*
► stench, reek, foul smell, odour, (more informal) pong, (more informal) niff

## stint NOUN

*a three-month stint on night duty*
► spell, stretch, period, term, turn, shift, run, session

a b c d e f g h i j k l m n o p q r s t u v w x y z

**stipulate** VERB
*The will stipulated certain conditions.*
▶ specify, lay down, set down, demand, require, insist on

**stipulation** NOUN
*The only stipulation was that the house should not be sold.*
▶ condition, proviso, provision, demand, requirement, qualification

**stir** NOUN
*The arrival of the royal car caused quite a stir.*
▶ commotion, fuss, excitement, disturbance, sensation, to-do

**stir** VERB
1 *Use a wooden spoon to stir the mixture.*
▶ mix, blend, beat, agitate, whisk, fold in
2 *Mary stirred in her sleep.*
▶ move slightly, quiver, tremble, twitch
3 *A gentle breeze stirred.*
▶ rustle, shake, flutter
4 *a thought to stir our imaginations*
▶ kindle, rouse, arouse, stimulate, excite, inspire, trigger, activate
**stir up** *These remarks stirred up considerable anger.*
▶ whip up, work up, rouse, arouse, trigger, spark off, provoke

**stirring** ADJECTIVE
*a stirring piece of music*
▶ exciting, rousing, stimulating, thrilling, gripping, riveting, dramatic
AN OPPOSITE IS boring

**stitch** VERB
*He stitched a patch on his jeans.*
▶ sew, tack, darn, mend, repair

**stock** ADJECTIVE
*a stock response to an old question*
▶ standard, routine, customary, conventional, familiar
AN OPPOSITE IS unexpected

**stock** NOUN
1 *a stock of fuel   a stock of jokes*
▶ supply, store, hoard, reserve, quantity, cache, fund
2 *During winter the stock is kept in sheds*
▶ livestock, farm animals, cattle, beasts
3 *The shop will be closed for a day to review its stock.*
▶ goods, merchandise, wares, commodities
4 *He is descended from Italian stock.*
▶ descent, ancestry, origins, parentage, pedigree, heritage

**stock** VERB
*The corner shop stocks cat food.*
▶ sell, supply, keep, keep in stock, have, market, handle, provide

**stocky** ADJECTIVE
*a short stocky man*
▶ sturdy, thickset, heavily built, solid, squat, dumpy
AN OPPOSITE IS skinny

**stodgy** ADJECTIVE
1 *a rich stodgy pudding*
▶ starchy, indigestible, heavy, lumpy, soggy, solid, filling
AN OPPOSITE IS light
2 *a stodgy story about his childhood*
▶ boring, dull, tedious, turgid, unexciting, unimaginative, uninteresting, stuffy
OPPOSITES ARE lively, exciting

**stoical** ADJECTIVE
*Her mother had been stoical all through these troubled years.*
▶ patient, long-suffering, uncomplaining, philosophical, resigned, calm, dispassionate
OPPOSITES ARE excitable, anxious

**stolid** ADJECTIVE
*a stolid, red-faced clergyman*
▶ impassive, unemotional, calm, placid, dull, tedious
OPPOSITES ARE lively, emotional

**stomach** NOUN
*I was hungry and my stomach started to rumble.*
▶ gut, belly, abdomen, (more informal) tummy
RELATED ADJECTIVE gastric

**stomach** VERB
*He had taken all the criticism he could stomach for one day.*
▶ stand, bear, take, tolerate, endure

**stone** NOUN
1 *A gang threw stones.*
▶ rock, pebble, boulder
2 *a ring with a bright red stone*
▶ gem, gemstone, jewel
3 *A memorial stone stood by the grave.*
▶ gravestone, headstone, tombstone, tablet

**stony** ADJECTIVE
1 *a stony path*
▶ rocky, pebbly, rough, shingly
2 *a stony silence*
▶ unfriendly, cold, chilly, frosty, icy, hostile, stern, severe, unfeeling, heartless
AN OPPOSITE IS friendly

**stoop** VERB
1 *Fred stooped to pick up the dog.*
▶ crouch, bend, kneel, lean, squat, bow, duck
2 *I would never stoop to accepting such an idea.*
▶ lower yourself, sink, descend, condescend, deign

**stop** VERB

1 *measures taken to stop tax fraud*
► check, prevent, thwart, frustrate, reduce, put and end to, put a stop to
OPPOSITES ARE start, encourage

2 *He wanted to stop smoking.*
► give up, discontinue, cease, desist from, refrain from, quit
OPPOSITES ARE begin, start, resume

3 *The bus stopped near the corner.*
► halt, come to a stop, come to a halt, pull up, draw up, pull in, come to rest

4 *He tried to stop her leaving the house.*
► prevent, intercept, hinder, obstruct, bar

5 *a special dressing to stop the escape of blood*
► stem, staunch, check, restrict, block, arrest

**stop** NOUN

1 *Business came to a stop for the day.*
► halt, end, finish, standstill, conclusion, stoppage, cessation

2 *They had a short stop at the motorway services.*
► break, pause, stopover, rest

**stoppage** NOUN

1 *the stoppage of livestock exports*
► stopping, halting, cessation, termination, discontinuation, interruption

2 *a three-day stoppage by baggage handlers*
► strike, shutdown, walkout, closure

**stopper** NOUN

*a bottle with a stopper*
► cork, plug, bung

**store** NOUN

1 *a store of food*
► supply, stock, hoard, reserve, quantity, cache, fund

2 *the coal store*
► storeroom, storehouse, repository, depository

3 *a DIY store*
► shop, outlet, retail business, retailers, supermarket, mart

**store** VERB

*a place to store food for the winter*
► stow, keep, save, put aside, hoard, accumulate, amass, lay by, deposit, (*more informal*) stash

**storey** NOUN

*an apartment on the third storey*
► floor, level, stage, tier

**storm** NOUN

1 *A storm blew up out at sea.*
► tempest, gale, squall, hurricane, typhoon, deluge

2 *a storm of protest*
► outburst, outcry, uproar, clamour, commotion, furore

**storm** VERB

1 *Police decided to storm the building.*
► attack, assault, rush, charge

2 *He stormed out in a rage.*
► march, stomp, stalk, flounce

**stormy** ADJECTIVE

1 *The weather was wet and stormy.*
► blustery, squally, tempestuous, turbulent, gusty, wild
AN OPPOSITE IS calm

2 *a stormy relationship*
► volatile, passionate, violent, intense

**story** NOUN

1 *the dramatic story of a rescue at sea   What happened that night turned out to be a long story.*
► tale, account, narrative, history, yarn, (*more informal*) spiel

2 *a novel with a gripping story*
► plot, storyline, scenario

3 *She read the newspaper stories.*
► news item, report, article, feature, piece

**NAMES FOR TYPES OF STORY**

adventure story, bedtime story, children's story, cliffhanger (exciting end to each part), crime story, detective story, epic, fable, fairy story or fairy tale, fantasy, folk story or folk tale, ghost story, gothic novel (with horror and mystery), historical novel (set in the past), legend, mystery, myth, novel, parable, romance, saga, science fiction, short story, thriller, (*informal*) whodunnit.

**stout** ADJECTIVE

1 *You'll need a stout pair of boots.*
► strong, sturdy, substantial, robust, solid, thick, tough, reliable, sound
AN OPPOSITE IS flimsy

2 *The small stout man marched on ahead.*
► fat, plump, stocky, portly, beefy, bulky, burly, chubby, heavy, tubby, well-built
OPPOSITES ARE thin, slender

3 *The defenders put up a stout resistance.*
► brave, courageous, determined, spirited, valiant, strong, forceful, staunch, resolute, firm
AN OPPOSITE IS feeble

**stow** VERB

*He left her to stow the shopping in the fridge.*
► store, load, put, stack, (*more informal*) stuff, (*more informal*) stash

**straight** ADJECTIVE

1 *They were driving along a straight stretch of road*
► direct, smooth, undeviating, unswerving
OPPOSITES ARE winding, crooked

2 *I'll make the room straight for our visitors.*
► tidy, neat, orderly, shipshape, organized, right
AN OPPOSITE IS untidy

3 *They have staged something of a comeback with three straight victories.*
► consecutive, continuous, unbroken, uninterrupted, non-stop

4 *John is a straight character and very much his own man. I'll give you a straight answer if I can.*
► honest, direct, frank, straightforward
AN OPPOSITE IS evasive

**straight** ADVERB

*We would be walking straight into a trap,   She looked straight into his face.*
▶ directly, squarely, plumb, (*more informal*) slap bang

**straight away** *He went to see her straight away when he got the news.*
▶ at once, directly, immediately, instantly, now, without delay

**straighten** VERB

*Rick straightened his tie.*
▶ adjust, arrange, put straight, neaten, order

**straighten out** *It will take a while to straighten out all the confusion.*
▶ sort out, put right, settle, disentangle, make straight, clear up, tidy, unbend, untwist

**straightforward** ADJECTIVE

**1** *It is hard to resist one straightforward conclusion.*
▶ plain, simple, direct, easy, intelligible, lucid, open, straight, uncomplicated

**2** *These people seem straightforward enough.*
▶ honest, genuine, sincere, forthright, truthful, frank, candid
AN OPPOSITE IS devious

**strain** VERB

**1** *The dog strained at its leash.*
▶ tug, pull, stretch, haul, tighten

**2** *Martha strained to hear but heard only faint sounds.*
▶ struggle, strive, make an effort, endeavour, exert yourself, attempt, try

**3** *Try not to strain yourself.*
▶ weaken, wear out, exhaust, tire out, weary

**4** *She had strained a muscle in the last race.*
▶ pull, sprain, twist, wrench, rick, damage, hurt, injure

**5** *Strain the liquid to remove impurities.*
▶ sieve, sift, filter, separate

**strain** NOUN

*the strain of doing jobs for which they are unsuited*
▶ stress, pressure, tension, worry, anxiety, burden, difficulty, effort

**strained** ADJECTIVE

*the strained relations between Russia and Japan,   Her strained face.*
▶ tense, awkward, uneasy, fraught, uncomfortable, troubled
AN OPPOSITE IS relaxed

**strand** NOUN

*Sibyl frowned, absent-mindedly twirling a strand of hair round her fingers.*
▶ fibre, filament, string, thread, wire

**stranded** ADJECTIVE

**1** *marks left by jellyfish stranded on the beach*
▶ grounded, run aground, marooned, beached

**2** *The waiting rooms were filled with stranded passengers.*
▶ helpless, abandoned, deserted, forsaken, lost

**strange** ADJECTIVE

**1** *I heard a strange noise outside.*
▶ funny, odd, unusual, weird, peculiar, curious, extraordinary, unexplained
AN OPPOSITE IS ordinary

**2** *They wear strange clothes.*
▶ weird, eccentric, bizarre, unconventional, idiosyncratic, (*more informal*) oddball, (*more informal*) wacky
AN OPPOSITE IS normal

**3** *He found it hard to get to sleep in a strange house.*
▶ unfamiliar, unknown, new, alien
AN OPPOSITE IS familiar

**4** *She began to feel a little strange and went to the bathroom.*
▶ unwell, ill, sick, poorly, indisposed, (*more informal*) funny
AN OPPOSITE IS well

**stranger** NOUN

*They were strangers in the town.*
▶ newcomer, outsider, visitor, alien, foreigner, guest

**strangle** VERB

**1** *The victim had been strangled and left in a ditch.*
▶ throttle, asphyxiate, choke, suffocate, strangulate

**2** *She strangled a cry of alarm.*
▶ suppress, smother, stifle, restrain, choke back

**strap** NOUN

*The package was tied with straps.*
▶ thong, tie, belt, cord

**strap** VERB

*He strapped the bag to his bicycle.*
▶ fasten, secure, tie, bind, lash

**strapping** ADJECTIVE

*Three strapping men arrived to help.*
▶ strong, sturdy, big, brawny, well-built, muscular

**strategy** NOUN

*a highly effective political strategy*
▶ plan, policy, scheme, approach, programme, procedure, design

**stray** VERB

**1** *The aircraft had strayed into unauthorized airspace*
▶ wander, drift, roam, meander

**2** *We are rather straying from the main point.*
▶ digress, diverge, drift, wander, deviate, be sidetracked

**stray** ADJECTIVE

**1** *A stray cat came into the kitchen.*
▶ lost, strayed, homeless, abandoned

**2** *Stray images wandered into her mind.*
▶ random, chance, haphazard, casual, odd, freak

**streak** NOUN

**1** *His hair had several streaks of white.*
▶ strip, stripe, vein, band, line, smear, stain

**2** *She admits to having a competitive streak in her.*
▶ element, trace, component

## streak VERB

1 *Their dirty faces were streaked with tears.*
▶ stain, smear, smudge, daub
2 *Huge lorries streaked past him.*
▶ rush, speed, tear, hurtle, flash, zoom, whistle

## streaky ADJECTIVE

*The windows were streaky from the rain*
▶ smeary, smudged, streaked, lined, stripy, veined

## stream NOUN

1 *a mountain stream*
▶ brook, burn, beck, rill, river, rivulet, watercourse, channel
2 *a stream of water*
▶ jet, flow, rush, gush, surge, spurt, spout
3 *a steady stream of visitors*
▶ series, succession, string, flood, torrent

## stream VERB

*Rain streamed through the hole*
▶ flow, pour, gush, surge, spurt, flood

## streamer NOUN

*Streamers hung from the buildings.*
▶ pennant, pennon, ribbon, banner, flag

## streamlined ADJECTIVE

1 *a streamlined car*
▶ aerodynamic, sleek, smooth, graceful
AN OPPOSITE IS air-resistant
2 *the streamlined image of the organization*
▶ smooth-running, efficient, slick, well-organized

## street NOUN

*The streets are deserted at this time of night.*
▶ road, avenue, boulevard, thoroughfare

## strength NOUN

1 *Physical strength is important.*
▶ power, brawn, muscle, toughness, sturdiness, robustness, vigour, might
AN OPPOSITE IS weakness
2 *She has enormous strength of character.*
▶ courage, firmness, resolution, spirit, commitment
AN OPPOSITE IS feebleness

## strengthen VERB

1 *The exercises will help strengthen your back.*
▶ build up, fortify, toughen, make stronger, harden, tone up
AN OPPOSITE IS weaken
2 *Stone columns strengthen the massive walls.*
▶ support, reinforce, bolster, brace, buttress, prop up
3 *The police want to strengthen their links with the local communities.*
▶ reinforce, consolidate, substantiate, bolster, fortify, enhance, back up, increase, invigorate
AN OPPOSITE IS undermine

## strenuous ADJECTIVE

1 *Success was the result of three years' strenuous work.*
▶ hard, tough, demanding, arduous, taxing, gruelling, exhausting
2 *He has made strenuous efforts to get to know the area.*
▶ determined, vigorous, resolute, energetic, active, forceful

## stress NOUN

1 *She was obviously under a lot of stress.*
▶ anxiety, difficulty, hardship, pressure, strain, tension, trauma, worry
2 *We need to lay greater stress on accuracy.*
▶ emphasis, accent, beat, importance, weight

## stress VERB

*I stressed the importance of a balanced diet.*
▶ emphasize, accentuate, assert, insist on, lay stress on, put the stress on, repeat, underline

## stressful ADJECTIVE

*She'd had an extremely stressful day.*
▶ anxious, difficult, tense, traumatic, worrying
AN OPPOSITE IS easy

## stretch NOUN

1 *a five-hour stretch on duty*
▶ spell, stint, period, run, term, time
2 *a fine stretch of moorland*
▶ expanse, sweep, spread, tract, area

## stretch VERB

1 *He stretched the rubber until it snapped.*
▶ pull, strain, tighten, extend, lengthen
AN OPPOSITE IS compress
2 *The road stretched into the distance*
▶ extend, continue, spread
3 *stretch to My money won't stretch to a two-week holiday.*
▶ be enough for, cover, reach to
**stretch out** *She stretched out on a couch.*
▶ recline, lean back, lie down, sprawl, relax

## strict ADJECTIVE

1 *Their parents could be too strict at times.*
▶ severe, stern, harsh, authoritarian, rigid, austere
AN OPPOSITE IS lenient
2 *strict controls on public spending*
▶ tough, stringent, rigorous, severe, extreme
AN OPPOSITE IS liberal
3 *a strict interpretation of the rule*
▶ exact, precise, scrupulous, rigid, rigorous
AN OPPOSITE IS loose

## strident ADJECTIVE

*a strident voice*
▶ harsh, shrill, jarring, grating, raucous, rasping, screeching, loud
OPPOSITES ARE soft, quiet

a b c d e f g h i j k l m n o p q r s t u v w x y z

**strife** NOUN

*years of strife in the manufacturing industries*
▶ conflict, discord, friction, dissension, wrangling, controversy

**strike** NOUN

*The dispute ended in a prolonged strike.*
▶ stoppage, withdrawal of labour, industrial action, work-to-rule, walkout

**strike** VERB

1 *I struck my head on the low ceiling.*
▶ hit, knock, bump, smack, thump
2 *The commandos struck without warning*
▶ attack, raid, pounce
3 *The two sides struck a deal at the last moment.*
▶ agree, agree on, reach, endorse, settle on, sign
4 *(informal) The workforce threatened to strike.*
▶ down tools, stop work, come out, take industrial action, withdraw your labour

**striking** ADJECTIVE

*She has a striking resemblance to her sister.*
▶ noticeable, conspicuous, outstanding, prominent, distinctive, impressive, memorable, obvious, stunning, telling, unmistakable
AN OPPOSITE IS inconspicuous

**string** NOUN

1 *a piece of string*
▶ twine, cord, line, rope
2 *a string of vehicles*
▶ row, file, line, series, succession, procession, queue
3 *a string of misfortunes*
▶ series, sequence, chain, progression

**string** VERB

*Lights had been strung across the road.*
▶ hang, link, thread, connect, join, line up

**stringent** ADJECTIVE

*stringent rules*
▶ strict, firm, severe, harsh, rigorous, binding
AN OPPOSITE IS lenient

**strip** NOUN

1 *a strip of paper   a narrow strip of land*
▶ slip, band, ribbon, belt, sliver, narrow piece, stripe, swathe, lath, line, shred, slat
2 *The team were sporting a new strip.*
▶ outfit, kit

**strip** VERB

1 *He stripped and climbed into the shower.*
▶ undress, take off your clothes, remove your clothes, (more informal) peel off
2 *Thieves had completely stripped the house.*
▶ empty, clear out, ransack, loot, pillage, burgle
**strip down** *Mechanics were busy stripping down the engine*
▶ dismantle, take to pieces, take apart, disassemble
**strip off** *First you must strip off the old paint.*
▶ peel off, remove, take off, scrape off, flake off

**stripe** NOUN

*tracksuit bottoms with a stripe down the side*
▶ line, strip, band, bar, flash

**striped** ADJECTIVE

*a striped blue and white shirt*
▶ lined, banded, stripy, barred, streaky

**strive** VERB

*We strive to please.*
▶ try, attempt, endeavour, aim, aspire, struggle, strain

**stroke** NOUN

1 *a swift stroke of the axe*
▶ blow, swipe, hit, knock
2 *a stroke of genius*
▶ feat, accomplishment, achievement, attainment
3 *She gave the cat a gentle stroke.*
▶ pat, rub, caress

**stroke** VERB

*You can stroke the dog if you like.*
▶ pat, caress, fondle, touch, brush, pass your hand over, pet

**stroll** VERB

*They strolled together round the grounds.*
▶ wander, saunter, amble, meander, ramble, dawdle

**stroll** NOUN

*There was time for a stroll in the woods.*
▶ walk, saunter, amble, ramble, turn

**strong** ADJECTIVE This word is often overused. Here are some alternatives:

1 *a strong lad of nineteen*
▶ tough, muscular, powerful, brawny, well built, strapping, burly
OPPOSITES ARE weak, puny
2 *The door needs a strong lock*
▶ robust, sturdy, firm, durable, sound, secure
AN OPPOSITE IS weak
3 *She had a strong interest in what they were doing.*
▶ keen, eager, deep, dedicated, passionate, fervent, zealous
AN OPPOSITE IS feeble
4 *a cup of strong coffee*
▶ highly flavoured, pungent, piquant
AN OPPOSITE IS weak
5 *We have a strong case to make.*
▶ convincing, forceful, persuasive, cogent, effective
OPPOSITES ARE weak, unconvincing

**stronghold** NOUN

*The army advanced on the enemy stronghold.*
▶ fortress, fort, castle, citadel, keep, bastion

**stroppy** ADJECTIVE

*(informal) I hope he doesn't get stroppy with us.*
▶ bad-tempered, irritable, grumpy, cross, peevish, truculent, sulky

## structure NOUN

*a tall structure of five storeys*
► construction, edifice, building, erection, pile

## structure VERB

*The classes are carefully structured to cater for all levels of ability.*
► organize, arrange, design, shape, construct, put together

## struggle VERB

1 *We struggled to get free.*
► work hard, strive, strain, toil, try, endeavour, exert yourself, labour, wrestle, make an effort, move violently, wriggle about, writhe about
2 *They had to struggle with a determined enemy.*
► fight, contend, battle, grapple, wrestle, vie
3 *She struggled over the wet rocks.*
► scramble, flounder, stumble, labour

## struggle NOUN

1 *It was a struggle to finish the work in time.*
► effort, challenge, difficulty, endeavour, exertion, labour, problem
2 *The police arrested the gang without a struggle*
► fight, scuffle, brawl, fracas, affray

## stub NOUN

1 *a cigarette stub*
► butt, end, (more informal) dog-end
2 *the stub of a ticket*
► counterfoil, slip

## stubborn ADJECTIVE

*He was too stubborn to admit he was wrong.*
► obstinate, obdurate, strong-willed, headstrong, wilful, pig-headed
OPPOSITES ARE compliant, yielding

## stuck ADJECTIVE

1 *The door was stuck and wouldn't open.*
► jammed, fixed, fast, immovable
2 *He admitted he was stuck and needed help.*
► baffled, beaten, at a loss, bewildered, (more informal) stumped

## stuck-up ADJECTIVE

*a bunch of stuck-up businessmen*
► arrogant, conceited, snobbish, snobby, haughty, supercilious, overweening, (more informal) snooty, (more informal) uppish, (more informal) toffee-nosed

## student NOUN

1 *a student at the university*
► undergraduate, postgraduate, scholar
2 *a student at the local school*
► pupil, schoolboy or schoolgirl, schoolchild, scholar
3 *a nursing student*
► learner, novice, trainee

## studio NOUN

*the artist's studio*
► workroom, workshop, atelier

## studious ADJECTIVE

*a studious young pupil*
► scholarly, serious-minded, hard-working, diligent, industrious, thoughtful, intellectual, academic, bookish, brainy, earnest

## study NOUN

1 *two years of study in the sixth form*
► learning, education, schooling, reading, academic work, (informal) cramming
2 *a study of the causes of conflict*
► investigation (into), inquiry (into), survey, examination, research (into)
3 *The study deals with all aspects of the subject.*
► essay, article, report, review

## study VERB

1 *She studied the information carefully.*
► examine, analyse, survey, consider, investigate, inspect, scrutinize, look into, peruse
2 *They both wanted to study languages.*
► learn, work at, be taught, read
3 *Alan had studied hard at school.*
► work, apply yourself

## stuff NOUN

1 *There was some wet stuff on the floor.*
► matter, substance
2 *The skirt was made of a tough lightweight stuff.*
► material, fabric, cloth, textile
3 *I'll put all my stuff in a suitcase.*
► belongings, effects, possessions, things, (more informal) gear

## stuff VERB

1 *I stuffed everything in a drawer.*
► pack, push, cram, ram, shove, squeeze, force, jam
2 *Use foam to stuff the cushions.*
► fill, pad, pack
**stuff yourself** *They had been stuffing themselves all day and were no longer hungry.*
► gorge, guzzle, cram, overindulge, eat

## stuffing NOUN

*The stuffing was coming out of the chair.*
► padding, filling, wadding, quilting

## stuffy ADJECTIVE

1 *a stuffy atmosphere*
► airless, close, muggy, sultry, musty, stifling, oppressive, unventilated
AN OPPOSITE IS airy
2 *a stuffy lecture on citizenship*
► dull, boring, staid, prim, strait-laced, pompous, conventional, stodgy
AN OPPOSITE IS informal

**stumble** VERB

1 *She stumbled on a loose paving stone.*
▶ trip, totter, tumble, lose your balance

2 *He stumbled back to his house.*
▶ stagger, totter, lumber, lurch, blunder, bumble, hobble

3 *The speaker stumbled through the rest of the speech.*
▶ stammer, stutter, falter, flounder, hesitate

**stump** VERB

*One of the questions stumped us.*
▶ baffle, puzzle, perplex, mystify, bewilder, outwit, confound, confuse, defeat, (*more informal*) flummox

**stun** VERB

1 *A hard blow had stunned him.*
▶ daze, knock out, knock senseless, make unconscious

2 *The election results stunned everyone.*
▶ amaze, astonish, astound, stagger, stupefy, shock, dumbfound, flabbergast, bewilder, confound

**stunning** ADJECTIVE

1 *a stunning victory*
▶ remarkable, sensational, spectacular, extraordinary, staggering, incredible

2 *She looked stunning in a red dress.*
▶ beautiful, dazzling, gorgeous, ravishing, sensational, lovely
AN OPPOSITE IS unattractive

**stunt** NOUN

*a circus stunt*
▶ trick, exploit, feat, turn, performance

**stunt** VERB

*a disease that can stunt growth*
▶ inhibit, hamper, impede, retard, restrict

**stupendous** ADJECTIVE

*a stupendous achievement*
▶ amazing, astounding, astonishing, extraordinary, remarkable, wonderful, staggering, breathtaking, (*more informal*) mind-boggling
AN OPPOSITE IS ordinary

**stupid** ADJECTIVE

1 *They are not as stupid as they seem.*
▶ foolish, silly, foolhardy, unintelligent, dim-witted, half-witted, empty-headed, vacuous, dim, dumb, thick
OPPOSITES ARE intelligent, wise

2 *It was a stupid thing to do.*
▶ foolish, silly, unwise, senseless, mindless, idiotic, crass, absurd, ridiculous, ludicrous
AN OPPOSITE IS sensible

**stupidity** NOUN

*Their stupidity had been breathtaking.*
▶ foolishness, folly, silliness, irresponsibility, ineptitude, idiocy
OPPOSITES ARE wisdom, intelligence

**stupor** NOUN

*He lay slumped in a drunken stupor*
▶ daze, lethargy, coma, trance, state of insensibility, torpor, shock, oblivion

**sturdy** ADJECTIVE

1 *a sturdy and handsome young man*
▶ strong, strapping, big, brawny, well-built, muscular
AN OPPOSITE IS weak

2 *He packed a sturdy pair of shoes for the walk.*
▶ stout, strong, substantial, robust, solid, thick, tough, reliable, sound
AN OPPOSITE IS flimsy

**stutter** VERB

*He stuttered over the next word.*
▶ stammer, stumble, falter, hesitate

**style** NOUN

1 *an old-fashioned style of writing*
▶ manner, technique, mode, method, fashion, tone, way

2 *the latest styles in the fashion magazines*
▶ design, pattern, fashion, mode, vogue, cut, taste

3 *She always dresses with style.*
▶ elegance, refinement, flair, panache, stylishness, smartness, sophistication, refinement, taste

**stylish** ADJECTIVE

*stylish clothes*
▶ fashionable, elegant, chic, modish, trendy, snappy, smart, (*more informal*) snazzy
OPPOSITES ARE unfashionable, dowdy

**suave** ADJECTIVE

*a suave man of about forty*
▶ charming, sophisticated, urbane, debonair, refined, polished, civilized
OPPOSITES ARE unsophisticated, crude

**subconscious** ADJECTIVE

*Dreams reflect a person's subconscious desires*
▶ subliminal, unacknowledged, unconscious, inner, hidden, intuitive, repressed
AN OPPOSITE IS conscious

**subdue** VERB

1 *The army quickly subdued all opposition.*
▶ overcome, defeat, quell, suppress, crush, overpower

2 *It was difficult to subdue their excitement.*
▶ restrain, suppress, check, curb, repress, hold back, keep under, quieten

**subdued** ADJECTIVE

1 *Sylvie was in a subdued mood.*
▶ serious, sombre, downcast, restrained, silent, sober, solemn, depressed, grave, reflective, thoughtful
AN OPPOSITE IS lively

2 *They spoke in subdued tones.*
▶ hushed, muted, quiet, soft, low, faint, calm
AN OPPOSITE IS loud

## subject NOUN

**1** *a British subject*
▶ citizen, national, passport-holder

**2** *a subject for discussion*
▶ theme, topic, affair, business, issue, matter, point, question

**3** *a subject of study*
▶ discipline, field, branch, course, area

## subject ADJECTIVE

**1** *subject nations*
▶ dependent, subjugated, subservient, tributary
AN OPPOSITE IS independent

**2** *The trains are subject to constant delays.*
▶ liable, prone, disposed, vulnerable

**3** **subject to** *The decision is subject to approval by the board.*
▶ dependent on, contingent on, conditional on

## subject VERB

**subject to** *Thye have been subjected to a lot of verbal abuse.*
▶ expose to, lay open, put through

## subjective ADJECTIVE

*It is difficult to build a theory on such subjective criteria.*
▶ biased, prejudiced, personal, individual, intuitive, idiosyncratic
OPPOSITES ARE objective, unbiased

## sublime ADJECTIVE

*Mozart's sublime masterpiece*
▶ exalted, elevated, noble, awesome, majestic, supreme, lofty, spiritual, transcendent
OPPOSITES ARE ordinary, lowly

## submerge VERB

**1** *The utter darkness submerged them.*
▶ inundate, overwhelm, immerse, engulf, flood, swamp, cover, drown

**2** *Submerge the vegetables in cold water.*
▶ dip, plunge, immerse, dunk

**3** *The submarine had no time to submerge*
▶ dive, go down

## submission NOUN

**1** *Complete submission was the key point of women in the eighteen-forties.*
▶ compliance, submissiveness, acquiescence, passivity, docility, meekness

**2** *The enemy's submission was only a matter of time.*
▶ surrender, capitulation, defeat

**3** *There was an alternative submission that the money had been paid under duress.*
▶ claim, contention, proposal, argument, suggestion, theory

## submissive ADJECTIVE

*Be polite, but not submissive.*
▶ meek, passive, acquiescent, compliant, servile, deferential, ingratiating, subservient, docile, uncomplaining, humble
OPPOSITES ARE domineering, assertive

## submit VERB

**1** *She had only submitted under duress.*
▶ give in, yield, accede, back down, surrender, capitulate, relent, succumb, comply, (*more informal*) knuckle under

**2** *They submitted a revised version of their plan. The union agreed to submit their disagreement to arbitration.*
▶ present, offer, tender, put forward, suggest, propose

**3** **submit to** *We refuse to submit to political pressure. Applicants have to submit to a full medical examination.*
▶ accept, agree to, succumb to, undergo, tolerate, endure, comply with, conform to, defer to, bow to, keep to, obey

## subordinate ADJECTIVE

*It would not be easy to accept a subordinate role.*
▶ inferior, lower, lesser, secondary, subservient, subsidiary, minor, junior

## subordinate NOUN

*There stood the manager with her three subord inates.*
▶ assistant, junior, inferior, dependant, employee, (*more informal*) underling
AN OPPOSITE IS superior

## subscribe VERB

**1** **subscribe to** *There are so many good causes to subscribe to.*
▶ contribute to, support, donate to, give to

**2** **subscribe to** *How many magazines do they subscribe to?*
▶ buy regularly, pay a subscription to, take, read

**3** **subscribe to** *I don't subscribe to that view at all.*
▶ agree with, accept, endorse, support, approve of, believe in, advocate, give your blessing to

## subsequent ADJECTIVE

*She needed a lot of help during the subsequent months.*
▶ following, ensuing, succeeding, later, next
AN OPPOSITE IS previous

## subside VERB

**1** *We'd better wait for the storm to subside.*
▶ die down, abate, diminish, moderate, slacken, quieten, ease up, let up
AN OPPOSITE IS intensify

**2** *The flood waters had begun to subside.*
▶ recede, fall back, ebb

**3** *Paul subsided into a chair.*
▶ collapse, sink, settle, drop
AN OPPOSITE IS rise

## subsidiary ADJECTIVE

*Money should be of subsidiary importance.*
▶ secondary, subordinate, lesser, minor, ancillary, supplementary

A
B
C
D
E
F
G
H
I
J
K
L
M
N
O
P
Q
R
**S**
T
U
V
W
X
Y
Z

**subsidize** VERB
*We do not believe that we should subsidize international rail services.*
▶ finance, fund, sponsor, support, back, promote, underwrite

**subsidy** NOUN
*The corporation needed an even bigger subsidy from public funds.*
▶ grant, backing, financial help, sponsorship, support

**subsistence** NOUN
1 *people living on the margins of subsistence*
▶ survival, existence, livelihood, sustenance, nourishment
2 *The grant was to cover travel and subsistence*
▶ maintenance, upkeep, livelihood

**substance** NOUN
1 *a strange sticky substance*
▶ material, matter, stuff, chemical
2 *The substance of the story is not hard to follow.*
▶ essence, gist, theme, meaning, content, subject-matter
3 *We may wonder how much substance there was in many of the accusations.*
▶ meaning, force, weight, significance

**substandard** ADJECTIVE
*low income, substandard housing, and high crime rates*
▶ inferior, poor, inadequate, shoddy, below par, disappointing, unworthy
AN OPPOSITE IS superior

**substantial** ADJECTIVE
1 *a substantial building*
▶ strong, sturdy, hefty, solid, well-made, durable, sound
AN OPPOSITE IS flimsy
2 *If you make substantial improvements to your home they might increase its value.*
▶ significant, sizeable, worthwhile, big, considerable, generous, large
AN OPPOSITE IS trivial

**substitute** ADJECTIVE
*a substitute teacher*
▶ acting, replacement, deputy, relief, reserve, standby, surrogate, temporary

**substitute** NOUN
1 *There is no substitute for practical experience.*
▶ replacement, alternative (to)
2 *Nurses can often be effective substitutes for doctors.*
▶ alternative, replacement, stand-in, proxy, surrogate

**substitute** VERB
1 *You can substitute yoghurt for cream cheese in this recipe.*
▶ change, exchange, interchange, swop, switch, replace
**USAGE** If you use *replace*, you have to say *You can replace cream cheese with yoghurt.*

2 *Maggie agreed to substitute for her boss for a few days.*
▶ deputize, stand in, act as a substitute

**subterfuge** NOUN
*Journalists should not use subterfuge to gain admission to hospitals.*
▶ trickery, deception, deviousness, duplicity, evasion, dishonesty

**subtle** ADJECTIVE
1 *Add a subtle yet striking change to your hair*
▶ mild, slight, faint, delicate, elusive, unobtrusive
2 *a subtle hint*
▶ gentle, tactful, indirect, understated
AN OPPOSITE IS tactless
3 *subtle colours*
▶ muted, subdued, delicate, faint, pale
AN OPPOSITE IS lurid
4 *a subtle distinction*
▶ fine, nice, precise, tenuous
AN OPPOSITE IS crude

**subtract** VERB
*Half a pint of skimmed milk supplies 100 calories, which must be subtracted from your daily total.*
▶ deduct, take away, remove, debit
AN OPPOSITE IS add

**suburban** ADJECTIVE
*The couple disappeared from their suburban house about two weeks ago.*
▶ residential, outlying, provincial, outer

**suburbs** NOUN
*an apartment in the southern suburbs of Rome*
▶ residential area, outskirts, fringes, outer areas, suburbia

**subversive** ADJECTIVE
*Why isn't she in prison for her subversive activities?*
▶ revolutionary, seditious, disruptive, treacherous, inflammatory, traitorous, undermining, unsettling
AN OPPOSITE IS loyal

**subvert** VERB
*The country saw him as a liberal subverting the president's conservative instincts.*
▶ undermine, destabilize, disrupt, corrupt, destroy, overthrow, challenge, pervert

**succeed** VERB
1 *For some people, happiness is to compete and succeed no matter how.*
▶ be successful, do well, prosper, thrive, flourish, triumph, be victorious, accomplish your objective, (*more informal*) get on, (*more informal*) make it
2 *The scheme might still succeed.*
▶ be effective, produce results, work, (*more informal*) catch on
AN OPPOSITE IS fail
3 *Kim's ambition to succeed Roh as President*
▶ replace, take the place of, take over from, supersede, come after, follow
AN OPPOSITE IS precede

# succeeding ADJECTIVE

*This trend continued in succeeding years.*
▶ subsequent, successive, following, ensuing, later, future, coming, next

# success NOUN

1 *The criteria for judging success would not be the same for all pupils.*
▶ achievement, accomplishment, attainment, fame, prosperity
AN OPPOSITE IS failure

2 *Links with industry are essential for the success of the programme.*
▶ effectiveness, successful outcome, completion
OPPOSITES ARE failure, collapse

3 (*informal*) *Her first novel was an instant success.*
▶ triumph, hit, sensation, victory, (*more informal*) winner
OPPOSITES ARE failure, disaster

4 *This performance alone might well have made him a success.*
▶ celebrity, star, big name, household name, sensation

# successful ADJECTIVE

1 *Blazer, the successful menswear chain*
▶ thriving, flourishing, prosperous, effective, profitable, fruitful, lucrative, productive, profit-making
OPPOSITES ARE unsuccessful, unprofitable

2 *He had been a successful prize fighter at the time. This wooden aeroplane was one of the most successful aircraft of all time.*
▶ victorious, triumphant, winning, effective
OPPOSITES ARE unsuccessful, ineffective

# succession NOUN

*He drifted into a succession of menial jobs.*
▶ series, sequence, string, chain, run, line, cycle, course, progression

# successive ADJECTIVE

*Thousands were forced into exile by successive military governments.*
▶ consecutive, succeeding, following

# succinct ADJECTIVE

*He gave a succinct judgement about what had happened.*
▶ concise, short, brief, compact, condensed, terse, pithy

# succulent ADJECTIVE

*a vine that produces succulent black grapes*
▶ juicy, fleshy, luscious, moist, mouth-watering, rich

# succumb VERB

*We may succumb to flattery because it makes us feel good.*
▶ yield, surrender, capitulate, submit, give way, give in
OPPOSITES ARE resist, overcome

# suck VERB

1 *The boys sat sucking their drinks.*
▶ sip, sup, slurp, drink

2 *Extra roads can suck people away from buses and trains.*
▶ draw, entice, attract, pull

**suck up** *He fetched a cloth to suck up the water.*
▶ soak up, absorb, draw up, pull up

**suck up to** (*informal*) *They suck up to him, hanging on his every word.*
▶ flatter, grovel to, kowtow to, behave obsequiously towards

# sudden ADJECTIVE

*Lydia emitted a sudden giggle. a sudden increase in student numbers*
▶ unexpected, startling, abrupt, sharp, unforeseen, unlooked for, impulsive, quick, rash
OPPOSITES ARE expected, gradual

# suds NOUN

*The basin was full of suds.*
▶ lather, foam, froth, bubbles, soapsuds

# sue VERB

*He could sue the railway company for negligence.*
▶ take to court, take legal action against, persecute

# suffer VERB

1 *She loved him too much to see him suffer.*
▶ feel pain, hurt, be in pain, be in distress

2 *England suffered a humiliating defeat.*
▶ experience, undergo, meet with, receive, be subjected to, sustain, encounter

3 *Dustin's relationship with Anne did suffer.*
▶ deteriorate, decline, be damaged, be impaired

# suffering NOUN

*Damage and suffering are inflicted on the population.*
▶ hardship, distress, misery, anguish, pain, unhappiness, sorrow, grief

# suffice VERB

*Whatever you have in the freezer will suffice.*
▶ be enough, be sufficient, be adequate, do, serve, satisfy

# sufficient ADJECTIVE

*There should be sufficient staff day and night.*
▶ enough, adequate, satisfactory
OPPOSITES ARE insufficient, inadequate

# suffocate VERB

*She reacted violently, as if he was trying to suffocate her.*
▶ asphyxiate, strangle, throttle, smother, stifle, choke

# suggest VERB

1 *Connie suggested an outing to the lake.*
▶ propose, recommend, advise, propound, put forward, raise, advocate, moot, move

2 *The evidence suggests we could be right.*
▶ imply, indicate, hint, intimate, mean, signal

A
B
C
D
E
F
G
H
I
J
K
L
M
N
O
P
Q
R
**S**
T
U
V
W
X
Y
Z

**suggestion** NOUN

1 *We have a few suggestions to consider.*
▶ recommendation, proposal, proposition, idea, plan

2 *There has been no suggestion of dishonesty.*
▶ hint, trace, suspicion, sign, implication, insinuation

**suggestive** ADJECTIVE

1 *a view suggestive of Tuscany*
▶ evocative, reminiscent, characteristic, expressive, typical

2 *suggestive remarks*
▶ indecent, improper, indelicate, immodest, unseemly, risqué

**suit** NOUN

*He wore a dark suit with a cream shirt.*
▶ outfit, set of clothes, ensemble, clothing

**suit** VERB

1 *credit terms to suit all pockets*
▶ satisfy, accommodate, be suitable for, please, gratify, fit

2 *Black doesn't really suit me.*
▶ look attractive on, look right on, become, flatter

**suitable** ADJECTIVE

1 *Would tomorrow afternoon be a suitable time?*
▶ convenient, appropriate, fitting, acceptable, satisfactory, apposite
AN OPPOSITE IS unsuitable

2 *a film that is considered suitable for all age groups*
▶ appropriate (to), suited (to), right, relevant (to)

**sulk** VERB

*Dave was sulking in his room.*
▶ mope, brood, be sullen, pout

**sulky** ADJECTIVE

*A row of sulky faces greeted him.*
▶ moody, sullen, surly, morose, glum, moping, pouting, disgruntled
AN OPPOSITE IS cheerful

**sullen** ADJECTIVE

1 *a sullen expression*
▶ sulky, moody, morose, glum, gloomy, surly, sour
AN OPPOSITE IS cheerful

2 *a sullen sky*
▶ dark, dull, gloomy, leaden, dismal, grey, sombre
OPPOSITES ARE bright, fine

**sully** VERB

*He would not sully the family name with such behaviour.*
▶ taint, defile, dirty, soil, tarnish, blemish, dishonour, disgrace

**sultry** ADJECTIVE

*a hot sultry day in July*
▶ humid, close, airless, muggy, stifling, stuffy, sticky, sweltering, oppressive
AN OPPOSITE IS cool

**sum** NOUN

1 *a large sum of money*
▶ amount, quantity

2 *a sum you can do in your head*
▶ calculation, problem

3 *These books were the sum of her life's work.*
▶ total, entirety, totality, sum total, whole, aggregate

**sum up** VERB

*It took two days to present the case and ten minutes to sum it up.*
▶ summarize, review, recapitulate, outline

**summarize** VERB

*The ideas can be summarized very easily.*
▶ sum up, outline, review, precis

**summary** NOUN

1 *There is a summary of the main arguments at the end of the article.*
▶ resumé, review, summing-up, summation, outline, recapitulation, abstract, digest

2 *a summary of a story*
▶ synopsis, precis, abridgement

**summit** NOUN

1 *This year thirty-two people reached the summit of Everest.*
▶ top, peak, crest, crown, apex, pinnacle
OPPOSITES ARE foot, bottom

2 *the summit of their success*
▶ high point, acme, culmination, apogee, zenith
AN OPPOSITE IS nadir

**summon** VERB

1 *Coleman was summoned to Washington for a final briefing.*
▶ send for, call, order, command, demand, invite

2 *The lawyers then summon a meeting.*
▶ call, convene, assemble, convoke, gather together, announce

**sumptuous** ADJECTIVE

*Emily thought ruefully of the sumptuous meals she used to eat.*
▶ lavish, luxurious, extravagant, splendid, magnificent, grand, gorgeous
AN OPPOSITE IS humble

**sun** NOUN

*Enjoy the sun while you can.*
▶ sunlight, sunshine
RELATED ADJECTIVE solar

**sunbathe** VERB

*Jill was sunbathing on the beach.*
▶ sun yourself, bask, get a tan

**sunburnt** ADJECTIVE

*His neck and shoulders were sunburnt.*
▶ burnt, inflamed, peeling, red, blistered
AN OPPOSITE IS pale

**sundry** ADJECTIVE

*In London yesterday he addressed sundry gatherings.*
▶ various, varied, assorted, miscellaneous, mixed, diverse, motley

**sunken** ADJECTIVE

1 *The Palace has a sunken garden and an orangery.*
▶ submerged, recessed

**2** *He was tall and gaunt, with sunken eyes.*
▶ hollowed, haggard

**sunny** ADJECTIVE

**1** *It will be a day of sunny spells and showers.*
▶ bright, clear, fine, cloudless, summery, sunlit
AN OPPOSITE IS dull

**2** *There was rage beneath the sunny smile.*
▶ cheerful, happy, joyful, joyous, smiling, beaming, bright, jolly
OPPOSITES ARE miserable, gloomy

**sunrise** NOUN

*A farmer's day begins at sunrise.*
▶ dawn, daybreak, daylight, crack of dawn

**sunset** NOUN

*Walk along the beach at sunset.*
▶ dusk, twilight, sundown, evening, close of day, half-light, (*literary*) gloaming

**super** ADJECTIVE

*There is a super kitchen with a traditional tiled stove.*
▶ excellent, superb, superlative, first-class, first-rate, marvellous, magnificent, wonderful, splendid, fine, remarkable, (*more informal*) brilliant, (*more informal*) fantastic, (*more informal*) terrific, (*more informal*) awesome

**superb** ADJECTIVE

*The large bay has a superb backdrop of mountains.*
▶ excellent, superlative, marvellous, magnificent, wonderful, splendid, fine, remarkable, (*more informal*) fantastic, (*more informal*) awesome

**supercilious** ADJECTIVE

*His manner was supercilious and he had a way of making you feel silly.*
▶ arrogant, superior, condescending, patronizing, overbearing, haughty, pretentious, (*more informal*) snooty, (*more informal*) hoity-toity

**superficial** ADJECTIVE

**1** *He sustained superficial injuries which soon disappeared. Time spent on repairing superficial damage is well worthwhile.*
▶ surface, exterior, external, slight, moderate
OPPOSITES ARE severe, deep

**2** *These similarities are purely superficial.*
▶ apparent, cosmetic, slight, shallow, specious
OPPOSITES ARE significant, meaningful

**3** *At a superficial level these categories appear to be the same.*
▶ shallow, surface
AN OPPOSITE IS deep

**4** *It was no more than a superficial examination of the subject.*
▶ cursory, casual, perfunctory, desultory, hurried, lightweight
OPPOSITES ARE thorough, rigorous

**superfluous** ADJECTIVE

**1** *Superfluous material can be trimmed from around the edges.*
▶ excess, surplus, spare, redundant, unwanted

**2** *This is so obvious that at first sight it might seem superfluous to state it.*
▶ unnecessary, needless, pointless, gratuitous, redundant

**superhuman** ADJECTIVE

**1** *Their madness gives them superhuman strength.*
▶ extraordinary, phenomenal, exceptional, immense, prodigious, herculean, heroic
AN OPPOSITE IS average

**2** *The myths describe encounters with superhuman beings of all kinds.*
▶ divine, higher, metaphysical, supernatural
OPPOSITES ARE earthly, mundane

**superior** ADJECTIVE

**1** *Lewis watched, aware of his superior status.*
▶ senior, higher, higher-level, higher-ranking, greater, more important
OPPOSITES ARE inferior, lower

**2** *Superior rooms are all recently renovated. The Americans have superior technology.*
▶ first-class, first-rate, high-quality, top-quality, better, exclusive, choice, fine, select, surpassing
OPPOSITES ARE inferior, low-quality

**3** *He found her cold and superior.*
▶ haughty, arrogant, disdainful, condescending, patronizing, supercilious, self-important, stuck-up, (*informal*) snooty, (*informal*) hoity-toity
OPPOSITES ARE modest, approachable

**superiority** NOUN

*The professional troops soon proved their technical superiority over the poorly trained local forces.*
▶ advantage, supremacy, dominance, predominance, ascendancy, pre-eminence, edge, lead
AN OPPOSITE IS inferiority

**superlative** ADJECTIVE

*The mountains offer superlative climbing and trekking.*
▶ excellent, magnificent, wonderful, marvellous, unsurpassed, unbeatable, unrivalled
OPPOSITES ARE poor, average

**supernatural** ADJECTIVE

*Certain animals were thought to have supernatural powers*
▶ paranormal, preternatural, unearthly, unnatural, abnormal, inexplicable, magical, metaphysical, miraculous, mysterious, mystic, occult, psychic
OPPOSITES ARE natural, normal

**supersede** VERB

*Steel began to supersede iron in the 1880s.*
▶ replace, supplant, take the place of, displace, oust, succeed

**superstition** NOUN

*the old superstition that seagulls were the souls of dead sailors*
▶ myth, superstitious belief, delusion, illusion, old wives' tale

## superstitious ADJECTIVE

*a haze of superstitious beliefs and practices*
▶ irrational, mythical, traditional, unfounded, unprovable, groundless, illusory
OPPOSITES ARE rational, factual, scientific

## supervise VERB

*People are needed during the summer to supervise children and organize activities.*
▶ oversee, watch over, superintend, be in charge of, be responsible for, direct, manage

## supervision NOUN

*These tasks should be carried out under the supervision of a senior member of staff.*
▶ control, direction, oversight, surveillance, care, charge, oversight, management

## supervisor NOUN

*The housewife is her own supervisor.*
▶ manager, director, overseer, superintendent, controller, boss

## supplant VERB

*the society which Marx believed would eventually supplant capitalism*
▶ replace, supersede, take the place of, displace, oust, succeed

## supple ADJECTIVE

**1** *Regular exercise keeps the body supple.*
▶ lithe, nimble, agile, graceful, limber, lissom
OPPOSITES ARE stiff, unfit
**2** *a strip of supple leather*
▶ flexible, pliable, pliant, soft
AN OPPOSITE IS rigid

## supplement NOUN

**1** *A supplement is payable for rooms with a sea view.*
▶ surcharge, additional payment, excess
**2** *the newspaper's new travel supplement*
▶ insert, pull-out, addendum, addition

## supplement VERB

*the need to supplement the family income*
▶ add to, top up, augment, increase, boost, enlarge, swell, complement, reinforce

## supplementary ADJECTIVE

*The answers may be followed up by supplementary questions.*
▶ extra, additional, complementary, auxiliary, accompanying

## supplier NOUN

*This kit can be ordered from your usual supplier.*
▶ dealer, retailer, seller, shopkeeper, vendor, wholesaler, provider

## supply NOUN

**1** *As a breeder, I give one week's supply of food with each puppy.*
▶ stock, store, quantity, amount, stockpile, reserve
**2 supplies** *Many people use their cars to buy a whole week's supplies.*
▶ provisions, stores, rations, materials, shopping, food, necessities

## supply VERB

**1** *studios set up to supply cheaply-made films*
▶ provide, produce, purvey, sell, contribute
**2** *The reservoir supplies water to an area of about five hundred square miles.*
▶ serve, provide, furnish
**3** *They were unable to supply us with what we needed.*
▶ equip, provide, furnish
**4** *A supermarket that supplies all your needs.*
▶ provide, fulfil, fill

## support NOUN

**1** *The group offers emotional support to members in times of stress.*
▶ encouragement, solace, comfort, succour, relief, strength, friendship, protection
**2** *The Arts Council eventually withdrew all financial support.*
▶ backing, funding, funds, aid, subsidy, donations, money
**3** *The shelf was resting on three supports.*
▶ prop, brace, bracket, pillar, foundation

## support VERB

**1** *The walls were too weak to support the weight of the roof. He supported the old man over to his bed.*
▶ carry, bear, sustain, hold up, prop up, provide a support for, underpin
**2** *She was determined to support Alice during these difficult weeks.*
▶ comfort, be a support to, sustain, encourage, hearten, console, fortify, reassure, succour
AN OPPOSITE IS abandon
**3** *His land was not fertile enough to support his family.*
▶ maintain, nourish, provide for, sustain, feed, keep
AN OPPOSITE IS neglect
**4** *The company supports research into the causes of back pain.*
▶ sponsor, subsidize, fund, patronize, contribute to, encourage
AN OPPOSITE IS discourage
**5** *They both support some sort of fees. The Socialist Party agreed to support the bill. There is no evidence to support such a notion.*
▶ agree with, argue for, advocate, endorse, promote, substantiate, uphold, confirm, corroborate, defend, justify
AN OPPOSITE IS oppose

## supporter NOUN

**1** *The perpetrators were unlikely to be genuine rugby supporters.*
▶ enthusiast, follower, devotee, fan
**2** *The United States became an important supporter of the project.*
▶ champion, advocate, adherent, defender, seconder, upholder, apologist (for)
**3** *Labour's supporters in business*
▶ backer, adherent, ally, sponsor, henchman

## supportive ADJECTIVE

*Alan and Ian were the most supportive friends in her life.*
▶ encouraging, helpful, caring, concerned,

reassuring, sympathetic, understanding, protective, interested, kind, loyal, positive
OPPOSITES ARE unhelpful, discouraging

## suppose VERB

**1** *I suppose it would be nice for you to earn a little pin money.*
▶ assume, expect, guess, infer, dare say, presume, imagine, fancy, surmise, suspect, think, conclude, conjecture, judge

**2** *Just suppose I saw her again.*
▶ imagine, pretend, hypothesize, fancy, assume

## supposed ADJECTIVE

*Where is this supposed cousin of yours?*
▶ alleged, assumed, presumed, rumoured, reputed, imagined, conjectural, hypothetical, reported, putative

**be supposed to** *You are supposed to read the whole book.*
▶ be meant to, be expected to, be required to, be obliged to, have to, need to, ought to

## supposition NOUN

*Terry had gone to bed happy in the supposition that he would get revenge.*
▶ belief, assumption, presumption, notion, suspicion, expectation, conjecture, idea, hunch, feeling

## suppress VERB

**1** *The National Guard was established to suppress anti-government demonstrations.*
▶ quash, quell, crush, subdue, overcome, overthrow, conquer, put an end to, put down, stamp out, stop

**2** *She had been advised to suppress all critical remarks. McGuire made a conscious effort to suppress his emotions.*
▶ hide , conceal, restrain, stifle, repress, control, contain, hold back, smother, silence, cover up, bottle up, choke back

## supremacy NOUN

*the doctrine of the supremacy of parliament*
▶ dominance, predominance, sovereignty, ascendancy, primacy, pre-eminence, domination, lead

## supreme ADJECTIVE

**1** *He was on course to carry off skiing's supreme prize*
▶ greatest, highest, top, foremost, principal, chief
OPPOSITES ARE lowest, least

**2** *the supreme achievement of God's creation*
▶ greatest, superlative, crowning, ultimate, pre-eminent, unsurpassed, matchless, incomparable, extraordinary, remarkable
OPPOSITES ARE unremarkable, insignificant

## sure ADJECTIVE

**1** *I'm sure Dan will be perfectly safe.*
▶ certain, convinced, confident, positive, assured, definite, persuaded, satisfied, decided, resolute
OPPOSITES ARE doubtful, uncertain

**2** *He's sure to ask us what we were doing.*
▶ bound, certain, likely, destined, compelled, obliged, required
AN OPPOSITE IS unlikely

**3** *He left in the sure knowledge that he would be returning. He was pacing the floor, a sure sign of anxiety.*
▶ clear, undoubted, indisputable, inescapable, undeniable, undisputed, guaranteed, convincing, precise, proven, inevitable, accurate, true
OPPOSITES ARE uncertain, doubtful, unsure

**4** *James was always a sure friend.*
▶ reliable, faithful, dependable, steadfast, steady, firm, solid, trusty, trustworthy, effective, loyal, safe, secure, unfailing, unswerving
OPPOSITES ARE fickle, unreliable.

## surf VERB

*surfing the Internet*
▶ browse, explore, search, probe, research, survey, scrutinize

## surface NOUN

**1** *The surface of the door had become rotten.*
▶ outside, exterior, facade, veneer, covering, face
AN OPPOSITE IS inside

**2** *A cube has six surfaces.*
▶ face, side, facet, plane

## surface VERB

*A submarine surfaced in the loch. A new idea has surfaced*
▶ come up, rise, appear, emerge, materialize, come to light, (*informal*) pop up
AN OPPOSITE IS dive

## surge NOUN

**1** *a surge of water*
▶ gush, rush, sweep, flow, wave

**2** *a surge of excitement*
▶ outburst, upsurge, outpouring, rush, gush, increase, onrush

## surge VERB

**1** *Water surged into people's houses.*
▶ gush, rush, stream, flow, swirl, roll

**2** *The crowd surged forward*
▶ rush, sweep, push, stampede

## surly ADJECTIVE

*A surly parking attendant had spoken to him.*
▶ bad-tempered, unfriendly, churlish, ungracious, morose, sullen, sulky
AN OPPOSITE IS friendly

## surpass VERB

*The television adaptation far surpassed the film version.*
▶ outclass, outdo, eclipse, excel over, outshine, outstrip, better, do better than, beat, exceed, overshadow

## surplus NOUN

*a fruit surplus*
▶ excess, surfeit, glut, superfluity, oversupply, oversufficiency, superabundance, profusion

**surplus** ADJECTIVE

*Wipe off any surplus paint.*
► excess, superfluous, spare, redundant, unwanted

**surprise** NOUN

1 *Alice looked at him in surprise.*
► amazement, astonishment, incredulity, wonder, alarm, consternation, bewilderment, dismay
2 *This might come as a surprise to you.*
► shock, revelation, bolt from the blue, (*more informal*) bombshell, (*more informal*) eye-opener

**surprise** VERB

1 *Here's a piece of information that will surprise you.*
► astonish, amaze, astound, shock, stupefy, dumbfound, stagger, disconcert, flabbergast, nonplus, take your breath away, take aback, (*more informal*) bowl over, (*more informal*) gobsmack
2 *He surprised an intruder, who ran off.*
► discover, take unawares, take by surprise, come upon, catch out, catch in the act, catch red-handed, detect

**surprised** ADJECTIVE

*I was surprised to see Lisa sitting up in bed reading.*
► astonished, amazed, astounded, dumbfounded, flabbergasted, nonplussed, shocked, speechless, staggered, disconcerted, incredulous, startled, stunned, taken aback, taken by surprise, thunderstruck, (*more informal*) gobsmacked

**surprising** ADJECTIVE

*They completed the task with surprising speed.*
► astonishing, amazing, astounding, unexpected, extraordinary, remarkable, incredible, staggering, startling, stunning
OPPOSITES ARE predictable, unsurprising

**surrender** VERB

1 *The rebels surrendered after months of fierce fighting.*
► give up, capitulate, submit, yield, succumb, resign, (*more informal*) throw in the towel
2 *We are being asked to surrender personal freedoms in the national interest.*
► give up, forgo, relinquish, cede, abandon, renounce, waive

**surreptitious** ADJECTIVE

*Stacey sneaked a surreptitious look at her watch.*
► secret, furtive, discreet, stealthy, clandestine, sneaky, sly, covert
AN OPPOSITE IS blatant

**surround** VERB

1 *The garden surrounds the ruins of a fourteenth-century castle.*
► encircle, ring, skirt, encompass
2 *Anabelle found herself surrounded by angry faces.*
► besiege, beset, engulf, girdle, hedge in, hem in

**surroundings** NOUN

*The hotel is set in the beautiful surroundings of a country park.*
► environment, location, setting, vicinity, neighbourhood, background, ambience, milieu

**surveillance** NOUN

*Police surveillance prevented us from contacting your sister-in-law.*
► check, observation, scrutiny, supervision, vigilance, watch

**survey** NOUN

1 *In our main survey, people were asked where they would go for a loan.*
► poll, investigation, appraisal, inquiry, census, count, evaluation, study, assessment, examination
2 *a survey of recent work on the subject*
► review, overview, synopsis, summary
3 *Be sure to get a survey of the house before making an offer.*
► inspection, assessment, appraisal, examination, valuation

**survey** VERB

1 *Those who wish can survey the scene from a panoramic tower.*
► observe, view, look at, look over
2 *The artist stood back to survey his work.*
► examine, inspect, study, scrutinize, consider, review
3 *Engineers arrived to survey the area.*
► do a survey of, reconnoitre, plot, map out, plan out, measure, (*technical*) triangulate

**survival** NOUN

*longer-term threats to the survival of capitalism*
► continuance, continued existence

**survive** VERB

1 *They had enough water to survive until help came.*
► remain alive, live, last, carry on, keep going, sustain yourself, continue, endure
AN OPPOSITE IS perish
2 *Some of the workers' cottages still survive.*
► remain, exist
3 *Six people survived the crash.*
► live through, withstand, come through, weather
AN OPPOSITE IS succumb to
4 *She is survived by her husband and three sons.*
► outlast, outlive

**susceptible** ADJECTIVE

*Network cables are susceptible to electrical interference.*
► liable, vulnerable, prone, subject, sensitive, inclined, predisposed
OPPOSITES ARE resistant, immune

**suspect** ADJECTIVE

*Two suspect packages stood by the door.*
► suspicious, doubtful, dubious, questionable, (*more informal*) fishy, (*more informal*) dodgy

**suspect** VERB

1 *The plan's only going to be successful if they don't suspect anything.*
► distrust, mistrust, call into question, have doubts about, doubt
2 *I suspect another visit may not be possible.*
► expect, surmise, presume, assume, imagine, dare say, think, fancy, guess, infer, conclude, conjecture, judge

# suspend VERB

**1** *Long sacks were suspended from hooks on the wall.*
▶ hang, sling, swing, dangle, drape
**2** *The Stock Exchange decided to suspend trading.*
▶ interrupt, break off, adjourn, discontinue, postpone, put off, defer, delay
**3** *Two directors were suspended for a year.*
▶ exclude, debar, remove, dismiss, expel

# suspense NOUN

*There is an art to building up suspense.*
▶ tension, uncertainty, doubt, anticipation, expectation, expectancy, excitement, apprehension, drama

# suspicion NOUN

**1** *The KGB did not need proof; suspicion was more than enough.*
▶ intuition, conjecture, speculation, supposition, belief, caution, wariness
**2** *As we drank our coffee I outlined my suspicions about Martinez.*
▶ doubt, misgiving, qualm, uncertainty, reservation
**3** *A suspicion of a grin appeared on her face.*
▶ trace, hint, glimmer, shadow, suggestion, tinge, touch

# suspicious ADJECTIVE

**1** *It was clear that he was increasingly suspicious of his visitor.*
▶ doubtful, distrustful, mistrustful, unsure, sceptical, apprehensive, wary, chary, disbelieving, incredulous, unconvinced (about), uneasy (about)
OPPOSITES ARE trusting, credulous
**2** *He's a highly suspicious character and we haven't spoken for years. At first the police treated the case as a suspicious death.*
▶ questionable, suspect, dubious, disreputable, unreliable, untrustworthy, peculiar, irregular, (more informal) fishy, (more informal) shady
OPPOSITES ARE straightforward, innocent

# sustain VERB

**1** *The country would have to sustain a large population.*
▶ maintain, keep, continue, preserve, provide for, nurture
**2** *She had some bread and cheese to sustain her.*
▶ nourish, feed
**3** *They were sustained by these happy memories.*
▶ comfort, support, encourage, succour, hearten, (more informal) buck up
**4** *It was doubtful whether the structure could sustain the increased weight.*
▶ support, bear, carry

# sustained ADJECTIVE

*They might succeed with a sustained effort.*
▶ continuous, prolonged, protracted, determined, unremitting, steady
OPPOSITES ARE intermittent, sporadic

# sustenance NOUN

*Without sustenance the animals will die.*
▶ nourishment, food, nutriment, nutrition, provisions

# swagger VERB

*He swaggered into the room, looking for Susan.*
▶ strut, prance, parade

# swagger NOUN

**1** *She walked with a slight swagger.*
▶ strut, prance
**2** *His behaviour was full of swagger now.*
▶ boasting, bluster, ostentation, brashness

# swallow VERB

**1** *He was finding it hard to swallow food*
▶ eat, drink, consume, devour, gulp down, guzzle
**2** *I was a little surprised when they swallowed my story.*
▶ accept, believe, (more informal) buy
**swallow up** *The darkness swallowed them up.*
▶ engulf, enfold, envelop, absorb, enclose

# swamp NOUN

*The rains had turned the fields into a huge swamp.*
▶ marsh, bog, quagmire, mire, fen, marshland, morass, wetland, slough

# swamp VERB

**1** *A tidal wave swamped the coastal regions.*
▶ flood, inundate, overwhelm, engulf, drench, saturate, submerge, waterlog
**2** *Journalists had swamped the unfortunate village.*
▶ overrun, overwhelm, besiege, beset

# swampy ADJECTIVE

*swampy ground*
▶ marshy, boggy, soggy, waterlogged, miry, muddy, soft
AN OPPOSITE IS firm

# swap VERB

*Helen swapped her Spanish stamps for some Belgian ones she didn't have.*
▶ exchange, barter, bargain, switch

# swap NOUN

*They had arranged a house swap for July.*
▶ exchange, switch, interchange

# swarm NOUN

*There were swarms of police everywhere.*
▶ crowd, horde, mass, throng, multitude, host

# swarm VERB

*Reporters were swarming all over the place.*
▶ crowd, throng, flock, mass, cluster, congregate
**be swarming with** *The beaches were swarming with tourists.*
▶ be overrun with, be crawling with, be teeming, be full of, be infested with, be invaded by, abound in

# swarthy ADJECTIVE

*a swarthy complexion*
▶ dark, dark-skinned, dusky, tanned, brown

# sway VERB

**1** *The branches swayed in the breeze.*
▶ swing, bend, rock, wave, lurch, lean from side to side, move to and fro, oscillate
**2** *Many people are swayed by what they read in the newspapers.*
▶ influence, persuade, affect, govern

a b c d e f g h i j k l m n o p q r s t u v w x y z

## swear VERB

**1** *He swore he had told the truth.*
► promise, give your word, pledge, vow, affirm, attest, declare, state on oath, take an oath, testify
**2** *She spilled her drink and swore.*
► blaspheme, curse, use bad language

## swear word NOUN

**1** *In those days you never heard a swear word on television.*
► expletive, obscenity, profanity, curse, oath, four-letter word
**2** *swear words*
► bad language, foul language, profanity, swearing

## sweat VERB

*He had begun to sweat in the heat.*
► perspire, swelter, exude

## sweat NOUN

**1** *By now he was drenched in sweat.*
► perspiration, moisture, dampness
**2** *(informal)* *We were in a sweat to get away.*
► panic, fluster, state of agitation, state of anxiety

## sweaty ADJECTIVE

*He shook Karl's sweaty hand.*
► sweating, perspiring, sticky, clammy, damp, moist

## sweep VERB

**1** *It was time to sweep the kitchen floor.*
► brush, clean, scrub, wipe, hoover
**2** *Another bus swept past them.*
► sail, glide, streak, tear, hurtle, whizz

## sweeping ADJECTIVE

**1** *We are expecting sweeping changes.*
► far-reaching, wide-ranging, extensive, comprehensive, wholesale, thoroughgoing, radical, indiscriminate
AN OPPOSITE IS limited
**2** *Avoid sweeping statements.*
► broad, general, over-general, oversimplified, unqualified, simplistic
OPPOSITES ARE precise, specific

## sweet ADJECTIVE

**1** *The tea was too sweet.*
► sweetened, sugary, saccharine, honeyed, cloying
**2** *the sweet perfume of roses*
► fragrant, aromatic, sweet-smelling, balmy, scented
**3** *She sang a sweet song.*
► melodious, lyrical, mellifluous, sweet-toned
**4** *Life can be sweet.*
► pleasant, pleasing, enjoyable, satisfying, delightful, agreeable
**5** *the sweet air of the mountains*
► fresh, pure, wholesome, clear, clean
**6** *a sweet little baby*
► cute, pretty, delightful
**7** *Dora has a sweet nature.*
► loving, appealing, affectionate, adorable, lovely, charming

## sweeten VERB

**1** *You may need to sweeten the juice a little.*
► make sweeter, sugar
**2** *She was furious and he had no idea how to sweeten her.*
► pacify, calm, mollify, soothe, appease, mellow

## sweetheart NOUN

*Maureen was my school sweetheart.*
► girlfriend or boyfriend, darling, admirer, lover

## swell VERB

**1** *He could almost feel his stomach swelling.*
► expand, dilate, distend, enlarge, bloat, bulge, balloon, inflate, puff up, billow
OPPOSITES ARE contract, shrink
**2** *The droning in her head swelled and faded.*
► increase, intensify, heighten, surge
AN OPPOSITE IS subside
**3** *The population swelled with immigration after the war.*
► increase, enlarge, expand, grow or get bigger, build up, extend
OPPOSITES ARE decrease, decline

## swell NOUN

*a heavy swell in the Channel*
► surge, roll, billow, undulation

## swelling NOUN

*There was redness and a swelling in his throat.*
► inflammation, protuberance, puffiness, lump, bump, excrescence, tumour

## sweltering ADJECTIVE

*a sweltering day in July*
► stifling, baking, scorching, sultry, oppressive, hot, sticky, humid

## swerve VERB

*The car swerved to avoid a squirrel.*
► turn aside, deviate, swing, weave, change direction, veer, take avoiding action

## swift ADJECTIVE

**1** *Her letter brought a swift reply.*
► quick, rapid, prompt, immediate, instant, speedy, fast, instantaneous, punctual
AN OPPOSITE IS slow
**2** *They all made swift progress.*
► rapid, quick, speedy, fast, brisk, lively

## swindle VERB

*The company had been swindled out of a large sum of money.*
► cheat, defraud, trick, fleece, dupe, deceive, *(informal)* con, *(more informal)* diddle, *(more informal)* do, *(more informal)* bamboozle

## swindle NOUN

*an insurance swindle*
► fraud, fiddle, racket, deception, sham, *(more informal)* con

## swindler NOUN

*Thousands of pensioners had fallen victim to the swindlers.*
▶ fraudster, confidence trickster, confidence man, trickster, imposter, cheat, charlatan, (*more informal*) con man

## swing VERB

1 *The inn sign swung in the wind.*
▶ sway, flap, dangle, hang loose, rock, swivel, oscillate, turn, wave about
2 *The van swung across the carriageway.*
▶ swerve, veer, turn aside, deviate, weave
3 *Public opinion was swinging in favour of the war.*
▶ shift, change, fluctuate, waver, move, alter, oscillate

## swing NOUN

1 *a huge swing in public opinion*
▶ shift, change, fluctuation, movement, oscillation, variation
2 *a swing of the pendulum*
▶ oscillation

## swingeing ADJECTIVE

*a swingeing increase in taxes*
▶ drastic, severe, extreme, harsh, draconian, exorbitant

## swipe VERB

1 *He threatened to swipe at her with the bottle.*
▶ hit, strike
2 (*informal*) *Someone swiped my pen.*
▶ steal, take, filch, snatch, (*informal*) nick, (*informal*) pinch

## swipe NOUN

*She took a playful swipe at his face.*
▶ blow, strike, swing, slap, smack, clout, hit

## swirl VERB

*The water swirled round their feet.*
▶ surge, whirl, churn, eddy, spin, twirl, twist

## switch NOUN

*Whitlock activated the switch on the dashboard.*
▶ button, control, key, lever, handle

## switch VERB

*She managed to switch places so she was sitting next to Neil.*
▶ change, swap, exchange, replace, shift, substitute
**switch on** or **off** *The user must not switch off the computer before this option is chosen.*
▶ turn on or off, put on or off, activate or deactivate, power up or down

## swivel VERB

*I had to swivel round to see her.*
▶ turn, swing, spin, twirl, gyrate, pivot, revolve, rotate, wheel

## swollen ADJECTIVE

*I climbed the ladder despite my swollen foot.*
▶ inflamed, distended, bloated, enlarged, puffed up, puffy, tumescent
OPPOSITES ARE **shrunken**, **shrivelled**

## swoop VERB

1 *Wagtails swooped across my path.*
▶ dive, sweep, plunge, plummet, drop, descend, fly down, lunge
2 **swoop on** *Fifty police officers swooped on a group of farm buildings.*
▶ descend on, pounce on, raid, besiege, search

## sword NOUN

*James had armed himself with the sword of Robert the Bruce.*
▶ blade, foil, rapier, sabre, broadsword, cutlass, scimitar

## swot VERB

**swot up on** (*informal*) *Choose a topical issue each week and swot up on it from newspapers and magazines.*
▶ study, work on, research, (*informal*) mug up, (*informal*) bone up on

## syllabus NOUN

*They must begin teaching the syllabus this September.*
▶ curriculum, course, course of study, programme of study, schedule

## symbol NOUN

1 *Snakes were seen as symbols of sexuality.*
▶ emblem, token, sign, image, figure, representation, mark
2 *Too many symbols make the timetable difficult to use if you are in a hurry.*
▶ sign, character, hieroglyph
3 *The Red Cross symbol was painted on the roof of the vehicle.*
▶ logo, badge, mark, crest, insignia

## symbolic ADJECTIVE

1 *John Wayne was held up as being symbolic of everything that was good and right about America.*
▶ representative, suggestive, typical, characteristic, emblematic, figurative, meaningful, significant
2 *The treaty is more than a symbolic milestone.*
▶ allegorical, metaphorical, representative, token

## symbolize VERB

*The beaver was chosen to symbolize the school because it was an industrious as well as a social animal.*
▶ represent, epitomize, encapsulate, stand for, be a sign of, be a symbol of, embody, signify, exemplify, betoken, denote

## symmetrical ADJECTIVE

*Note the symmetrical design of the building.*
▶ balanced, regular, uniform, harmonious, even
AN OPPOSITE IS **asymmetrical**

## sympathetic ADJECTIVE

1 *She managed a sympathetic smile.*
▶ commiserating, comforting, supportive, understanding, appreciative, consoling, caring, compassionate, considerate, tender
OPPOSITES ARE **unsympathetic**, **unfeeling**

a
b
c
d
e
f
g
h
i
j
k
l
m
n
o
p
q
r
s
t
u
v
w
x
y
z

**2 sympathetic to** *All the parents felt very sympathetic to what their daughters were going through.*
▶ understanding of, appreciative of, concerned about, well-disposed towards

**3 sympathetic to** *Some of the republics seem to have been sympathetic to this idea.*
▶ in favour of, in sympathy with, in agreement with, supportive of, receptive to

**sympathize** VERB

**1 sympathize with** *We sympathize with the views of the people living in the area.*
▶ understand, agree with, approve of, support, commend, appreciate

**2 sympathize with** *Many trade unionists instinctively sympathized with the plight of the miners.*
▶ commiserate with, show sympathy for, be sympathetic towards, be sorry for, identify with, empathize with, feel for, side with, pity

**sympathy** NOUN
*Friends expressed sympathy for those who died or were injured. Don't waste your sympathy on them.*
▶ commiseration, pity, compassion, condolences, feeling, fellow-feeling, tenderness, understanding, consideration, empathy

**symptom** NOUN

**1** *Several patients suffered from symptoms such as nausea and vomiting.*
▶ manifestation, indicator, indication, feature

**2** *The first symptom of a frozen waste pipe is that the water won't flow out.*
▶ sign, evidence, indication, warning, testimony

**symptomatic** ADJECTIVE
*The town's poverty is symptomatic of chronic unemployment.*
▶ indicative, characteristic, suggestive, typical, representative

**synopsis** NOUN
*a short synopsis of last week's episode*
▶ resumé, summary, precis, outline

**synthetic** ADJECTIVE
*The whole pitch has been replaced by a synthetic surface*
▶ artificial, imitation, manufactured, simulated, substitute, man-made, unnatural, concocted, mock, ersatz, fabricated, fake
OPPOSITES ARE natural, real, genuine

**system** NOUN

**1** *a reform of the criminal justice system*
▶ organization, structure, framework, network, institution, (*informal*) set-up

**2** *a system for recording accidents at work*
▶ procedure, process, routine, scheme, arrangement, means (of), method, methodology, plan, structure, set of rules

**3** *a system of government that commands the confidence of all the people*
▶ regime, philosophy, science, constitution, principles

**systematic** ADJECTIVE
*Citizenship should be taught in every school in a systematic way.*
▶ methodical, ordered, orderly, organized, structured, planned, systematized, coherent, scientific, logical
AN OPPOSITE IS unsystematic

# Tt

**table** NOUN

**1** *He put the glasses on the table.*
▶ dining table, kitchen table, worktop, working surface, coffee table

**2** *The table on page three shows monthly rainfall in the region.*
▶ chart, diagram, graph, list

**tablet** NOUN

**1** *There is a stone tablet over the doorway.*
▶ plaque, slab, plate, sign

**2** *She rang reception and asked for another tablet of soap.*
▶ bar, piece, block, chunk, slab

**3** *He went to his room and took a headache tablet.*
▶ pill, capsule, caplet

**taboo** NOUN
*There is a taboo against doing business on the sabbath.*
▶ ban, prohibition, proscription, veto, restriction, anathema

**taboo** ADJECTIVE
*Politics were a taboo subject at the dinner table.*
▶ forbidden, prohibited, banned, proscribed, unacceptable, disapproved of, unmentionable

**tacit** ADJECTIVE
*The deal continued with their tacit agreement.*
▶ implicit, unspoken, silent, implied, understood, unvoiced

**tack** NOUN

**1** *The carpet was held down with a row of tacks.*
▶ pin, drawing-pin, nail, tin tack

**2** *We ought to change tack and speak out more.*
▶ approach, policy, tactic, method, technique, direction

**tack** VERB

**1** *He tacked a photo to the notice board.*
▶ pin, nail, fix

**2** *She tacked the hem and tried it on for length.*
▶ stitch, sew

**tack on** *A few maps and plans are tacked on at the back of the book.*
▶ attach, add, append

**tackle** NOUN
  1 *He wanted to buy new fishing tackle.*
  ▶ gear, equipment, apparatus, implements, kit, outfit, paraphernalia, rig, tools
  2 *The referee penalized him for a late tackle.*
  ▶ challenge, interception, attack, block

**tackle** VERB
  1 *The Government is determined to tackle the issue of tax avoidance.*
  ▶ deal with, grapple with, address yourself to, confront, cope with, face up to, sort out, handle, manage, attend to, combat, set about, undertake
  2 *An opposing player tackled him near the touchline.*
  ▶ challenge, intercept, stop, confront, attack, take on
  3 *Lettie decided to tackle him directly about her pay.*
  ▶ confront, approach, challenge, address

**tacky** ADJECTIVE
  1 *The paint was still tacky.*
  ▶ sticky, wet, gluey
  AN OPPOSITE IS dry
  2 *tacky quizzes and game shows*
  ▶ vulgar, coarse, crude, tawdry, garish, trashy
  AN OPPOSITE IS tasteful

**tact** NOUN
  *A police officer told her the news with great tact.*
  ▶ discretion, consideration, sensitivity, tactfulness, delicacy, diplomacy, thoughtfulness, understanding
  OPPOSITES ARE indiscretion, tactlessness

**tactful** ADJECTIVE
  *Molly gave them a tactful reminder about the rent*
  ▶ discreet, judicious, considerate, polite, delicate, diplomatic, sensitive, thoughtful
  OPPOSITES ARE tactless, indiscreet

**tactical** ADJECTIVE
  *a tactical move to force the authorities to act*
  ▶ calculated, planned, deliberate, strategic, politic

**tactics** NOUN
  *The enemy drove them back by superior tactics.*
  ▶ planning, battle plans, logistics, moves, manoeuvres, strategy
  **USAGE** There is a difference between *tactics* and *strategy*: a *strategy* is an overall plan, whereas *tactics* are the way in which you carry out the plan.

**tactless** ADJECTIVE
  *She was plainly upset by his tactless remark.*
  ▶ indiscreet, insensitive, thoughtless, unthinking, indelicate, clumsy
  OPPOSITES ARE tactful, discreet

**tag** NOUN
  *His jacket still had a price tag on it.*
  ▶ label, ticket, tab, sticker

**tag** VERB
  *Each bottle was tagged with a different coloured label.*
  ▶ label, mark, identify, ticket
  **tag along** *Sometimes he let me tag along.*
  ▶ follow, go along, accompany

**tag on** *A note was tagged on at the end of the letter.*
  ▶ add, attach, append, tack on

**tail** NOUN
  *They waited at the tail of the queue.*
  ▶ back, end, rear, extremity, tail end

**tail** VERB
  *A squad of reporters had tailed him for five years.*
  ▶ follow, shadow, stalk, pursue, track, trail
  **tail off** *Her words tailed off at the expression in his eyes.*
  ▶ fade, wane, ebb, peter out, drop away, subside, dwindle, decline, decrease, lessen, reduce, slacken

**taint** NOUN
  *free from the taint of corruption*
  ▶ stain, smear, hint, trace, blight, contamination

**taint** VERB
  1 *an area tainted by pollution*
  ▶ contaminate, pollute, poison, soil, adulterate, dirty, infect
  2 *These unhappy events tainted their reputation for ever.*
  ▶ tarnish, stain, sully, besmirch, blacken, dishonour, smear, ruin, slander

**take** VERB
  1 *Many prisoners were taken.*
  ▶ catch, seize, capture, take captive, arrest
  2 *He took her hand gently.*
  ▶ clasp, clutch, grasp, grab, grip, take hold of, lay hold of
  3 *Someone had taken his car.*
  ▶ steal, remove, make off with, appropriate, (more informal) pinch, (more informal) nick, (more informal) filch, (more informal) swipe
  4 *Take ten percent from the total.*
  ▶ subtract, deduct, knock off, discount
  5 *It takes a long time to recover from an illness like this.*
  ▶ need, require, call for, necessitate
  6 *The pain was more than he could take.*
  ▶ bear, put up with, endure, tolerate, suffer, stomach
  7 *I'll take you home.*
  ▶ accompany, drive, bring, convey, conduct, escort, guide, transport, carry
  **be taken with** *Tanya was rather taken with the idea.*
  ▶ be interested in, be attracted to, be captivated by, be fascinated by, be delighted by, be enchanted by
  **take aback** *This suggestion took us aback.*
  ▶ surprise, astonish, astound
  **take apart** *a cot that can be easily taken apart*
  ▶ dismantle, take to pieces, disassemble
  **take back** *I took back everything I had said.*
  ▶ withdraw, retract, disown, recant, repudiate, deny
  **take down** *A police officer took down the details.*
  ▶ write down, note, jot down, record
  **take in**
  1 *a confidence trick that took everyone in*
  ▶ fool, deceive, mislead, dupe, trick, hoodwink, cheat

**2** *It was too much information to take in at once.*
► understand, comprehend, grasp, absorb, assimilate, digest
**3** *a cruise that takes in the main Greek islands*
► include, incorporate, encompass, comprise, cover

**take it** *I take it you want to stay.*
► assume, infer, deduce

**take off**
**1** *I took off my shoes before going in.*
► remove, shed, throw off, discard
**2** *a plan that might never take off*
► succeed, do well, catch on
**3** *The man took off at a run.*
► run off, run away, leave, escape, depart, disappear

**take on** *She took on more responsibilities that year.*
► accept, assume, undertake, acquire, shoulder

**take up**
**1** *She took up painting in her forties.*
► engage in, practise, become interested in
**2** *a cupboard that takes up a lot of space*
► occupy, absorb, use up, fill

**take-off** NOUN
**1** *The flight was bumpy for a while after take-off.*
► lift-off, departure, ascent
**2** *The sketch is a take-off of the American President.*
► parody, imitation, pastiche, satire, lampoon

**takeover** NOUN
*a plan for the takeover of a British bank*
► acquisition, purchase, buyout, gaining of control

**takings** NOUN
*She took the day's takings to the bank*
► proceeds, returns, receipts, earnings, income, profits, revenue, gains

**tale** NOUN
*a tale about dragons and heroes*
► story, narrative, narration, history, account, yarn

**talent** NOUN
*a talent for playing the violin*
► gift, aptitude, ability, accomplishment, flair, genius, skill, capacity, expertise, knack, prowess

**talented** ADJECTIVE
*a talented young player*
► gifted, able, accomplished, skilful, skilled, artistic, brilliant, clever, distinguished, expert
OPPOSITES ARE inept, unskilful

**talk** VERB
**1** *I was talking to a friend.*
► speak, chat, converse (with)
**2** *They were talking complete rubbish.*
► speak, utter, express, articulate, communicate
**3** *They looked for a quiet spot to talk.*
► have a talk, have a chat, converse, confer, speak to one another, communicate with one another
**4** *He refused to talk.*
► give information, confess, admit anything
**5** *People were beginning to talk.*
► gossip, spread rumours, make remarks, pass comments

**6** *talk of She talked of leaving and settling abroad.*
► speak about, mention, refer to
**7** *talk to He talked to an eager audience.*
► speak to, address, lecture

**talk** NOUN
**1** *too much talk and not enough action*
► conversation, speaking, chatter, discussion, dialogue, *(more informal)* yakking
**2** *There was talk of an affair.*
► rumour, gossip (about), *(more informal)* tittle-tattle
**3** *a talk in the village hall*
► lecture, address, speech, presentation, discourse
**4** *talks Peace talks will resume next week.*
► negotiations, discussions, consultations

**talkative** ADJECTIVE
*He had chanced on an unusually talkative taxi driver*
► chatty, loquacious, garrulous, voluble, effusive, vocal, communicative, forthcoming, articulate
OPPOSITES ARE taciturn, unforthcoming

**talking-to** NOUN
*(Informal) He was given a severe talking-to and told not to come back.*
► reprimand, lecture, scolding, *(informal)* telling-off, *(informal)* dressing-down

**tall** ADJECTIVE
**1** *a tall man*
► large, big
**2** *a tall building*
► high, lofty, towering, soaring, elevated

**tally** NOUN
*a final tally of twenty goals scored during the season*
► total, count, reckoning, account

**tally** VERB
*Her explanation did not tally with the evidence before their eyes.*
► agree, accord, correspond (with or to), concur, fit

**tame** ADJECTIVE
**1** *The animal was so tame that it shinned up his leg and dived into a deep pocket.*
► domesticated, gentle, manageable, disciplined, trained, meek, obedient, safe, subdued, submissive, tractable
AN OPPOSITE IS wild
**2** *Aren't you Joe's tame reporter?*
► cooperative, willing, amenable, biddable
AN OPPOSITE IS uncooperative
**3** *It turned out to be a tame evening after all.*
► dull, tedious, boring, unexciting, uninteresting, humdrum, bland, feeble, flat, lifeless, uninspiring, unadventurous
AN OPPOSITE IS exciting

**tame** VERB
**1** *Wild rabbits can be tamed in captivity.*
► domesticate, break in, train, discipline, house-train, master
**2** *She made strenuous efforts to tame her behaviour.*
► control, subdue, curb, conquer, master, moderate, mitigate, quell, repress, subjugate, suppress, temper

## tamper VERB

**tamper with** *A student was able to enter the cockpit of an empty aircraft and tamper with the controls.*
► interfere with, meddle with, tinker with, alter, change, adjust, play about with, fiddle about with, make adjustments to

## tan ADJECTIVE

*a tan overcoat*
► light brown, pale brown, tawny

## tan VERB

*Be careful not to overdo it when tanning in the sun.*
► get a tan, bronze, brown

## tang NOUN

1 *Olives will add a special tang to your stews.*
► flavour, taste, zest, savour, piquancy, spice
2 *We could already smell the tang of the sea.*
► smell, odour, fragrance

## tangible ADJECTIVE

*The experiment brought no tangible results.*
► definite, solid, substantial, concrete, actual, real, material, positive, discernible
AN OPPOSITE IS intangible

## tangle NOUN

*a tangle of wires and cables*
► mass, muddle, jumble, confusion, maze, jungle, knot, twist

## tangle VERB

1 *She had managed to tangle her hair.*
► entangle, knot, twist, ravel
OPPOSITES ARE untangle, disentangle
2 *A dolphin had become tangled in the net.*
► trap, ensnare, entrap, catch, enmesh
3 *Better not to tangle with people like that.*
► become involved with, come into conflict with, confront, quarrel with, cross swords with

## tangled ADJECTIVE

1 *Later they emigrated, but could never escape their tangled past.*
► complicated, complex, confused, convoluted, involved, entangled, intricate
AN OPPOSITE IS straightforward
2 *an undergrowth of tangled bushes and trees*
► knotted, matted, convoluted, dishevelled, tousled, unkempt, untidy
AN OPPOSITE IS tidy

## tangy ADJECTIVE

*Citrus adds a tangy taste to all sorts of savoury dishes.*
► sharp, pungent, piquant, appetizing, spicy, strong, tart, fresh, refreshing
OPPOSITES ARE insipid, bland

## tank NOUN

1 *a hot water tank*
► container, cistern, reservoir, basin
2 *a tank of fish*
► aquarium, bowl

## tantalize VERB

*Selina's cool aloofness has tantalized her audience for years.*
► tease, frustrate, titillate, intrigue, fascinate, provoke

## tantamount ADJECTIVE

**tantamount to** *Killing a dolphin was tantamount to killing a person.*
► equivalent to, comparable to, commensurate with, the same as

## tantrum NOUN

*He threw a tantrum and rolled on the floor, kicking and screaming.*
► fit of rage, fit of temper, scene, outburst, (*more informal*) paddy, (*more informal*) wobbly

## tap NOUN

1 *a water tap*
► faucet, stopcock, valve
2 *There was a tap at the window.*
► knock, rap, knocking, touch

## tap VERB

1 *She tapped on the door.*
► knock, rap, strike
2 *I leaned forward to tap her shoulder.*
► pat, touch, poke, nudge

## tape NOUN

1 *The parcel was bound with tape.*
► band, binding, strip, braid, ribbon
2 *They listened to music on tapes.*
► cassette, tape recording

## tape VERB

*I'll tape up the parcel.*
► bind, tie, seal

## taper VERB

1 *The leaves taper to a point.*
► narrow, thin, become narrower
2 *Their enthusiasm soon tapered off.*
► decrease, lessen, dwindle, wane, diminish, die down, peter out

## target NOUN

1 *a target of £100,000*
► goal, objective, aim, ambition, end, intention
2 *the target of attacks*
► victim, butt, object, quarry, prey

## tariff NOUN

1 *the hotel's high-season tariff*
► price list, list of charges, schedule
2 *the reduction of import tariffs*
► tax, duty, toll, excise, levy

## tarnish VERB

1 *Constant use of abrasives has tarnished the metal.*
► dull, discolour, stain, blacken, corrode
2 *The accusations will tarnish his reputation.*
► taint, stain, sully, besmirch, blacken, dishonour, smear

**tart** ADJECTIVE

**1** *the tart taste of cooked apples*
► sharp, sour, acid, tangy, piquant, pungent
OPPOSITES ARE sweet, bland

**2** *He regretted his rather tart response.*
► acerbic, sharp, biting, cutting, caustic, scathing

**tart** NOUN

*a jam tart*
► pastry, flan, tartlet, pie, quiche

**task** NOUN

*Finishing the book in time proved a daunting task.*
► job, undertaking, enterprise, exercise, chore, duty, charge, burden, labour, work, mission, requirement

**take to task** *He took his advisers to task for misleading him.*
► criticize, rebuke, reproach, reprove, upbraid, censure, admonish

**taste** NOUN

**1** *I don't much like the taste of raisins.*
► flavour, savour, character

**2** *Would you like a taste of my pudding?*
► mouthful, bite, morsel, nibble, bit, piece, sample

**3** *a millionaire with a taste for travel*
► liking, appreciation, fondness, desire, inclination, preference

**4** *Hilary is a person of taste. The decoration was done with taste.*
► judgement, discernment, discretion, discrimination, perception, refinement, sensitivity, style

**taste** VERB

*Anna tasted her drink and smiled.*
► sample, test, try, sip, check

**tasteful** ADJECTIVE

*a plain and tasteful decor*
► discriminating, refined, restrained, sensitive, smart, stylish, well-judged, elegant, fashionable, in good taste, judicious, fastidious, proper
AN OPPOSITE IS tasteless

**tasteless** ADJECTIVE

**1** *The vegetables were overcooked and tasteless.*
► flavourless, bland, insipid, weak, watery, characterless, mild, uninteresting
AN OPPOSITE IS tasty

**2** *a tasteless remark*
► crude, indelicate, uncouth, vulgar, tactless, crass, injudicious, unseemly
OPPOSITES ARE tasteful, delicate

**tasty** ADJECTIVE

*a tasty meal*
► delicious, appetizing, luscious, mouth-watering, (more informal) yummy, (more informal) scrumptious

**tattered** ADJECTIVE

*When he arrived his clothes were tattered.*
► ragged, ripped, frayed, tatty, shabby, threadbare, torn
AN OPPOSITE IS smart

**tatters** PLURAL NOUN

*The paintwork had peeled and the curtains were in tatters.*
► shreds, rags, ribbons, pieces

**taunt** VERB

*People taunted him about his marriage.*
► tease, torment, jeer at, mock, ridicule, bait

**taut** ADJECTIVE

*The rope should be taut.*
► tight, tense, firm, rigid, stretched
AN OPPOSITE IS slack

**tawdry** ADJECTIVE

*She wore tawdry ornaments on her arms.*
► cheap, vulgar, tasteless, gaudy, showy, fancy, flashy, garish, inferior, worthless, (more informal) tatty, (more informal) tacky
AN OPPOSITE IS superior

**tax** NOUN

*The new government immediately imposed a tax on imports.*
► duty, tariff, charge, imposition, levy
RELATED ADJECTIVE fiscal

**tax** VERB

**1** *It seems unfair to many people to tax pensions.*
► impose a tax on, levy a tax on

**2** *The long walk taxed them severely.*
► tire, strain, exhaust, burden, make heavy demands on

**teach** VERB

**1** *He taught me to swim in the holidays.*
► instruct, train, coach

**2** *She teaches children with special needs.*
► educate, tutor, instruct, coach

**teacher** NOUN

*He had been a teacher all his working life.*
► educator, tutor, instructor, schoolteacher, schoolmaster or schoolmistress, pedagogue, academic
RELATED ADJECTIVE pedagogic or pedagogical

**teaching** NOUN

**1** *Languages need experience in the country as well as rigorous teaching.*
► instruction, tuition, schooling, grounding, coaching

**2** *the Church's teaching on marriage*
► doctrine, dogma, tenet

**team** NOUN

**1** *the local cricket team*
► squad, side, line-up

**2** *the BBC's production team*
► group, crew, company, body, gang

## team VERB

**team up** *She teamed up with her fellow artists for a joint exhibition.*
▶ join forces, collaborate, cooperate, get together, band together, work together, combine, unite

**SOME TEAM SPORTS**

American football, Association football or soccer, Australian Rules football, baseball (chiefly American and Canadian), basketball, beach ball, cricket, curling (played on ice, chiefly Scottish and Canadian), football, goalball (for visually handicapped players), hurling, ice hockey, lacrosse, netball, polo (played with on horseback with long-handled mallets), punchball (American), rounders, Rugby League, Rugby Union, shinty (Scottish), stoolball (simple form of cricket with a stool or board for a wicket), volleyball, water polo.

## tear NOUN (rhymes with *fear*)

1 *There was a tear in his eyes.*
▶ teardrop, droplet
2 *tears She was so upset she was close to tears.*
▶ crying, weeping, sobbing, blubbering

## tear VERB (rhymes with *bear*)

1 *Take care you don't tear your clothes.*
▶ rip, slit, snag, split
2 *She tore the packet open.*
▶ rip, pull
3 *He tore the book from my hands.*
▶ snatch, grab, seize, wrench, wrest
4 (*informal*) *James tore round to the shop.*
▶ rush, hurry, race, speed, sprint, shoot, bolt
AN OPPOSITE IS stroll

## tear NOUN (rhymes with *bear*)

*There's a tear in my jeans.*
▶ rip, hole, split, slit, rent, gash

## tearaway NOUN

*a young tearaway*
▶ hooligan, hoodlum, ruffian, roughneck, (*more informal*) yob

## tearful ADJECTIVE

1 *Glenda was tearful.*
▶ in tears, crying, weeping, close to tears, upset
OPPOSITES ARE cheerful, happy
2 *a tearful farewell*
▶ emotional, distressing, upsetting, sorrowful, sad, heartbreaking

## tease VERB

*His friends teased him about his hair.*
▶ make fun of, poke fun at, laugh at, mock, taunt, provoke, torment

## technical ADJECTIVE

1 *The information is fairly technical.*
▶ specialized, specialist, esoteric, professional
2 *an important technical advance*
▶ scientific, practical

## technique NOUN

1 *There are various techniques for dealing with this problem.*
▶ method, procedure, approach, system
2 *She played the cello with a brilliant technique.*
▶ skill, ability, expertise, proficiency, facility

## tedious ADJECTIVE

*The work is tedious and time-consuming.*
▶ dull, boring, monotonous, uninteresting, dreary, humdrum, laborious, irksome, tiresome, unexciting, wearisome
OPPOSITES ARE interesting, exciting

## tedium NOUN

*We played cards to relieve the tedium of the evening.*
▶ monotony, boredom, tediousness, dreariness, dullness

## teem VERB

**teem with** *The pond teemed with fish.*
▶ be full of, abound in, seethe with, swarm with, be infested with, be crawling with

## teenager NOUN

*a club for teenagers*
▶ adolescent, youth, young person, juvenile, boy or girl, minor

## tell VERB

1 *Tell me what happened.*
▶ inform, advise, notify (of), let know, acquaint (with)
2 *She told us there would be another train in an hour.*
▶ assure, promise, advise, inform
3 *I'll tell you a secret.*
▶ disclose, reveal, confess, admit
4 *He became more and more excited as he told his story.*
▶ recount, narrate, relate, describe, communicate, speak
5 *Colin told us to leave.*
▶ order, instruct, command, direct, call on
6 *It's not easy to tell them apart.*
▶ distinguish, differentiate, identify, recognize, discern

**tell off** (*informal*) *He told them off for being late.*
▶ reprimand, scold, rebuke, upbraid, censure, berate, (*informal*) tick off

## telling ADJECTIVE

*The argument is expressed in a few telling phrases.*
▶ revealing, forceful, striking, persuasive, potent, compelling, effective
AN OPPOSITE IS insignificant

## telling-off NOUN

(*informal*) *They were lucky to escape with a mild telling-off.*
▶ reprimand, scolding, rebuke, caution, admonishment, (*informal*) ticking-off

a b c d e f g h i j k l m n o p q r s **t** u v w x y z

**temerity** NOUN
*(usually disapproving) You have the temerity to refuse me, do you?*
▶ cheek, nerve, audacity, effrontery, boldness, impertinence, impudence, insolence, presumptuousness, shamelessness, *(more informal)* sauce

**temper** NOUN
**1** *He walked out in a temper.*
▶ rage, fury, fit of rage, passion, tantrum
**2** *Jenny's temper flared.*
▶ anger, fury, rage, annoyance, irritation, irritability, petulance
**3** *Both children had a calm temper*
▶ temperament, disposition, nature, character, personality
**lose your temper** *Diana was capable of losing her temper.*
▶ become angry, fly into a rage, lose control, blow up, go berserk, *(more informal)* go mad, *(more informal)* go crazy, *(more informal)* go bananas, *(more informal)* fly off the handle, *(more informal)* go through the roof, *(more informal)* have a fit, *(more informal)* see red

**temper** VERB
*William was a man who tempered sentiment with business sense.*
▶ moderate, modify, modulate, mitigate, qualify, tone down

**temperament** NOUN
*His main problem was an anxious temperament.*
▶ disposition, nature, temper, character, personality

**temperamental** ADJECTIVE
**1** *The new king proved to be a temperamental despot.*
▶ moody, excitable, emotional, volatile, unpredictable, highly-strung, sensitive, capricious, mercurial, touchy, neurotic
OPPOSITES ARE placid, phlegmatic
**2** *He had a strong temperamental dislike of all conflict.*
▶ natural, inherent, innate, inborn, characteristic, congenital, constitutional

**temperate** ADJECTIVE
**1** *Lizards and snakes bask in the sun in temperate climates.*
▶ mild, clement, warm, pleasant, balanced
AN OPPOSITE IS extreme
**2** *He was patient and temperate in his habits.*
▶ moderate, restrained, self-restrained, self-controlled, disciplined, abstemious
AN OPPOSITE IS intemperate

**tempestuous** ADJECTIVE
**1** *Not long after there arose a tempestuous wind.*
▶ stormy, blustery, squally, turbulent, wild, gusty, raging
AN OPPOSITE IS calm
**2** *It was the first of many tempestuous scenes he was to be involved in.*
▶ passionate, emotional, temperamental
OPPOSITES ARE placid, phlegmatic

**temporal** ADJECTIVE
*The bishops enjoyed considerable temporal authority.*
▶ secular, earthly, terrestrial, worldly, mundane
AN OPPOSITE IS spiritual

**temporary** ADJECTIVE
*The restrictions on imports were a temporary measure only.*
▶ short-term, interim, provisional, stop-gap, short-lived, transitory, momentary, transient, ephemeral
AN OPPOSITE IS permanent

**tempt** VERB
*Window displays tempt shoppers into their stores.*
▶ entice, lure, allure, attract, persuade, coax, woo, inveigle, seduce
OPPOSITES ARE deter, repel, discourage

**temptation** NOUN
**1** *She had to resist the temptation to call him from her mobile.*
▶ urge, desire, impulse, inclination
**2** *I could see the dangers in the temptations of life in London.*
▶ attraction, appeal, lure, pull, fascination, seduction, allurement, draw, enticement

**tempting** ADJECTIVE
*It was a tempting package, and I bought the whole deal.*
▶ attractive, enticing, appealing, beguiling, tantalizing, irresistible

**tenable** ADJECTIVE
*This theory is disproved by modern science and is no longer tenable.*
▶ credible, defensible, plausible, reasonable, sensible, viable, sound, feasible, justifiable, arguable, legitimate, logical, rational
OPPOSITES ARE untenable, indefensible

**tenacious** ADJECTIVE
*Nick was our tenacious, skilful, and hard-running midfield man.*
▶ persevering, persistent, determined, resolute, dogged, pertinacious, strong-willed, single-minded, unwavering, unyielding
OPPOSITES ARE weak, feeble

**tenant** NOUN
*The top floor was occupied by tenants.*
▶ lodger, leaseholder, lessee, occupant, resident

**tend** VERB
**1** *She spends many hours in the garden tending her flowers.*
▶ look after, attend to, manage, take care of, care for, cultivate, mind
**2** *Nurses tend the sick and wounded in the field hospitals.*
▶ look after, attend to, care for, minister to, treat, nurse
**3 tend to** *At this time of year, our appetites tend to favour rich, stodgy puddings.*
▶ be inclined to, be apt to, be liable to, have a tendency to, be disposed to

**tendency** NOUN

*John has a tendency to put his foot in it.*
▶ propensity, proclivity, readiness, susceptibility, predilection, predisposition, disposition, inclination, liability, partiality, penchant, trend

**tender** ADJECTIVE

1 *She liked him tender, gentle like this.*
▶ kind, caring, compassionate, considerate, humane, affectionate, sensitive, warm-hearted
OPPOSITES ARE hard-hearted, callous, uncaring

2 *He pressed a tender loving kiss on her fingertips.*
▶ fond, loving, affectionate

3 *In my tender pre-teen years, I hadn't yet learned to be critical.*
▶ young, youthful, early, callow, immature, green, inexperienced, impressionable
OPPOSITES ARE advanced, mature

4 *Alan's voice cut into the tender little scene coldly. This is one of the author's most tender passages.*
▶ romantic, touching, moving, poignant

5 *Cook the rice in boiling salted water until tender.*
▶ soft, succulent, juicy, fleshy
OPPOSITES ARE hard, tough

6 *He lifted her up with tender care, holding her head to his cheek.*
▶ gentle, fond, loving

7 *Her ankle felt tender.*
▶ sore, painful, sensitive, inflamed, raw

**tense** ADJECTIVE

1 *The muscles in his neck were tense.*
▶ taut, tight, strained, stretched
AN OPPOSITE IS slack

2 *Angela was feeling tense and nervy.*
▶ anxious, nervous, edgy, on edge, strained, stressed, agitated, apprehensive, jittery, fidgety, ill at ease, jumpy, (more informal) uptight
OPPOSITES ARE calm, relaxed

3 *There was a tense atmosphere in the room.*
▶ fraught, uncomfortable, strained, charged
AN OPPOSITE IS relaxed

**tension** NOUN

1 *the tension of the ropes*
▶ tightness, tautness, strain, stretching
AN OPPOSITE IS slackness

2 *The tension was unbearable.*
▶ stress, strain, anxiety, suspense, apprehension, excitement, nervousness, unease, worry
AN OPPOSITE IS relaxation.

**tentative** ADJECTIVE

1 *This conclusion can only be tentative.*
▶ provisional, unconfirmed, cautious, diffident, doubtful, halfhearted

2 *a few tentative steps*
▶ hesitant, indecisive, indefinite, nervous, timid, uncertain
AN OPPOSITE IS decisive

**tenuous** ADJECTIVE

*a tenuous argument*
▶ slight, insubstantial, flimsy, thin, weak, unconvincing
AN OPPOSITE IS strong

**tepid** ADJECTIVE

1 *tepid water*
▶ warm, lukewarm

2 *The offer got a tepid response.*
▶ unenthusiastic, lukewarm, half-hearted, apathetic
AN OPPOSITE IS enthusiastic

**term** NOUN

1 *a technical term*
▶ word, expression, name, designation

2 *a five-year term of office*
▶ period, duration, interval, spell, session

**terminal** ADJECTIVE

*a terminal illness*
▶ incurable, untreatable, inoperable, fatal, mortal, lethal, deadly

**terminate** VERB

*Doctors decided to terminate the treatment.*
▶ end, cease, bring to an end, break off, cut short, abort, conclude, finish

**terminology** NOUN

*scientific terminology*
▶ language, phraseology, vocabulary, technical language, nomenclature, jargon

**terms** PLURAL NOUN

1 *She was on good terms with all her staff.*
▶ relations, standing, footing

2 *The two kings came to terms.*
▶ agreement, understanding, deal

3 *The terms of the contract prevented this.*
▶ conditions, provisos, stipulations, specifications

4 *The hotel offers good terms out of season.*
▶ rates, prices, tariff, charges

**terrain** NOUN

*They were back on familiar terrain in the foothills.*
▶ country, territory, ground, land, landscape, topography

**terrestrial** ADJECTIVE

*one of the factors that give rise to intelligent terrestrial life*
▶ earthly, worldly, mundane, earthbound, ordinary
OPPOSITES ARE heavenly, extraterrestrial

USAGE *Mundane* has the special meaning 'ordinary'. Also, be careful how you use the opposite word *heavenly*, which has a common second meaning 'wonderful'.

**terrible** ADJECTIVE

1 *I had a terrible fall which left me with two broken legs.*
▶ dreadful, frightful, horrible, awful, fearful, ghastly, hideous, shocking, frightening, terrifying

2 *There was a terrible smell in the kitchen.*
▶ disgusting, nasty, unpleasant, dreadful, horrible

A
B
C
D
E
F
G
H
I
J
K
L
M
N
O
P
Q
R
S
**T**
U
V
W
X
Y
Z

**terribly** ADVERB

1 *This is terribly important.*
▶ very, extremely, exceptionally, exceedingly, dreadfully, awfully

2 *In the next game they played terribly.*
▶ badly, dreadfully, atrociously, awfully, appallingly, dismally

**terrific** ADJECTIVE

1 *We heard a terrific thud.*
▶ tremendous, huge, mighty, massive, colossal, enormous, gigantic

2 *The novel provides the basis for a terrific movie.*
▶ excellent, wonderful, marvellous, outstanding, magnificent, superb, splendid, first-class, first-rate

**terrified** ADJECTIVE

*She gave them a terrified glance, and then bolted.*
▶ petrified, frightened, scared, alarmed, terror-stricken, horror-stricken, panic-stricken

**terrify** VERB

*The prospect of all that responsibility terrified him.*
▶ frighten, petrify, scare, horrify, appal, dismay, shock, unnerve

**terrifying** ADJECTIVE

*Water was pouring in with terrifying speed.*
▶ frightening, horrifying, petrifying, dreadful, hair-raising, blood-curdling, spine-chilling, appalling, unnerving, (more informal) scary

**territory** NOUN

1 *France sought to locate the launching site on French territory.*
▶ land, country, terrain, ground

2 *a Dutch territory in the East*
▶ domain, state, dependency, dominion, colony, possession

**terror** NOUN

*Men were driven to do these things by hunger and terror.*
▶ fear, extreme fear, alarm, fright, horror, panic, shock, trepidation

**terrorist** NOUN

*Security loopholes allowed the terrorists to plant the bomb.*
▶ bomber, assassin, gunman, hijacker

**terrorize** VERB

*In the 1820s, Romney Marsh was openly terrorized by armed gangs of smugglers.*
▶ threaten, intimidate, torment, tyrannize, menace, persecute, victimize, oppress, terrify, frighten

**terse** ADJECTIVE

*'Good,' came the terse reply.*
▶ brief, curt, brusque, succinct, concise, abrupt, laconic
AN OPPOSITE IS verbose

**test** NOUN

1 *They will have to pass a test to continue to be paid for the work.*
▶ exam, examination, appraisal, assessment, evaluation

2 *We'll be conducting a series of scientific tests.*
▶ trial, experiment, study, evaluation, investigation, analysis, probe

**test** VERB

1 *Psychologists have developed experiments to test their ideas.*
▶ check, appraise, evaluate, validate, examine, analyse, assess, study, screen, try out

2 *Here's a chance to test your DIY skills.*
▶ try out, put to the test, explore, trial

3 *These demands tested his patience to breaking point.*
▶ strain, tax, put a strain on, stretch, make demands on, sap, drain

**testify** VERB

1 *I may be called on to testify in court.*
▶ give evidence, be a witness, go into the dock

2 *He testified that he had not been present at the time of the incident.*
▶ swear, state on oath, attest, declare, affirm, give evidence

3 *testify to The latest finds testify to the great wealth of the city in antiquity.*
▶ confirm, attest to, demonstrate, substantiate

**testimonial** NOUN

*Jim received a glowing and thoroughly deserved testimonial.*
▶ commendation, recommendation, reference, character reference

**testimony** NOUN

1 *The girls would not be subjected to the trauma of giving testimony in court.*
▶ evidence, statement, submission

2 *testimony to His survival was a testimony to his courage and spirit after horrific injuries.*
▶ evidence of, proof of, witness to, testament to, confirmation of

**testy** ADJECTIVE

*I would get very testy if things weren't exactly right.*
▶ irritable, bad-tempered, irascible, grumpy, grouchy, touchy, tetchy, crotchety, cantankerous, peevish, fractious, cross, (more informal) stroppy, (more informal) shirty
AN OPPOSITE IS good-humoured

**tether** NOUN

*A goat was tangled up in its tether.*
▶ rope, lead, leash, chain, cord

**tether** VERB

*When they want to shoot a tiger, Sophie told him, they tether a goat near a tree.*
▶ tie, tie up, chain, rope, secure, fasten

## text NOUN

**1** *Supplying material on disk saves having to retype the text.*
▶ words, wording, content
**2** *a literary text*
▶ piece of writing, work, book, textbook
**3** *a text from the Bible*
▶ passage, extract, reading, quotation

## texture NOUN

*The dough should have a soft spongy texture.*
▶ consistency, composition, quality, feel, constitution, structure, touch

## thank VERB

**1** *I want to thank all those people who have supported us over the years.*
▶ acknowledge, express thanks to, show or express gratitude to, express appreciation of, recognize
**2** *He only had himself to thank for the mess he was in.*
▶ blame, hold responsible

## thankful ADJECTIVE

*She was thankful for the moonlight, without which she would never have found her way.*
▶ grateful, appreciative (of), pleased (about), relieved (about), happy (about)
OPPOSITES ARE disappointed, ungrateful
**USAGE** Note that *thankful* and *thankless* are not opposites: *thankful* is normally used about a person, whereas *thankless* is used about a person, whereas *thankless* is used about an activity.

## thankless ADJECTIVE

*America inherited Britain's thankless task of maintaining stability in the region.*
▶ unenviable, unappreciated, unrecognized, unrewarding, fruitless
OPPOSITES ARE worthwhile, rewarding
**USAGE** See the note at *thankful*.

## thanks NOUN

*Julia smiled her thanks and then turned to accept David's invitation.*
▶ gratitude, appreciation, acknowledgement, recognition, thanksgiving

## thaw VERB

*The snow was beginning to thaw.*
▶ melt, unfreeze, soften, liquefy, defrost
AN OPPOSITE IS freeze

## theatre NOUN

**1** *This is a work that needs to be heard in a theatre.*
▶ playhouse, auditorium
**2** *What made you take up the theatre?*
▶ acting, drama, theatricals, performing
**PARTS OF A THEATRE**
**entrance area**: box office, foyer, front of house.
**audience area**: auditorium, aisles; stalls, circle, dress circle, gallery, balcony, box, upper circle; house lights.
▶▶

**stage area**: stage, set (collection of scenery, stage furniture, and props), scenery, props (small portable items used on the set), apron or proscenium (part of stage in front of curtain), trap (on floor of stage, through which actors can come up); curtain, fire curtain, drop curtain (lowered on stage, forming part of the set); flies (space over the stage), wings (at side of the stage, from which actors come on stage); footlights, orchestra pit.

**backstage area**: backstage, dressing room, green room, stage door.

## theatrical ADJECTIVE

**1** *She wanted a theatrical career.*
▶ dramatic, acting, stage, thespian
**2** *'My dear,' cried Ruby making a theatrical gesture.*
▶ affected, exaggerated, ostentatious, melodramatic, showy, stagy, stilted, unnatural
AN OPPOSITE IS natural
**USAGE** In the first meaning, be careful how you use *dramatic*, which has a common second meaning 'sudden and exciting'.

## theft NOUN

*a report of the theft of jewels from a hotel room*
▶ robbery, stealing, thieving, pilfering, burglary

## theme NOUN

**1** *Public services have become the dominant theme of domestic politics.*
▶ topic, issue, subject, concern, question, matter
**2** *The theme is played by the orchestra and then picked up by the soloist.*
▶ melody, motif, subject, tune, air

## theoretical ADJECTIVE

**1** *theoretical physics*
▶ conceptual, pure, abstract, academic
OPPOSITES ARE practical, applied
**2** *a theoretical possibility*
▶ hypothetical, notional, conjectural, suppositional, speculative, postulated
OPPOSITES ARE concrete, actual, real

## theorize VERB

*We cannot theorize without data.*
▶ form a theory, hypothesize, conjecture, postulate, speculate

## theory NOUN

**1** *His theories are based on observations and experiments.*
▶ argument, assumption, belief, conjecture, explanation, guess, hypothesis, idea, notion, speculation, supposition, surmise, thesis, view
**2** *the theory of quantum physics*
▶ laws, principles, rules, science
AN OPPOSITE IS practice

## therapeutic ADJECTIVE

*the therapeutic effect of gardening*
▶ beneficial, corrective, curative, healing, helpful, restorative
AN OPPOSITE IS harmful

## therapy NOUN

*They are still undergoing therapy following the accident.*
► treatment, remedial treatment, healing, cure, remedy

## therefore ADVERB

*This is only a story and therefore you shouldn't believe a word of it.*
► consequently, accordingly, for this or that reason, as a result, as a consequence, so, thus, hence

## thesis NOUN

1 *The facts do not bear out his thesis.*
► theory, hypothesis, argument, premise or premiss, proposition, idea
2 *Her research was presented in her PhD thesis.*
► dissertation, monograph, paper, treatise

## thick ADJECTIVE

1 *He was stuffing a thick wad of notes into his jacket pocket. The thick felt curtains were closely fastened.*
► fat, chunky, broad, wide, hefty, bulky, solid, stout, sturdy, substantial
AN OPPOSITE IS thin

2 *The lava deposit was no more than a few metres thick. He was a good-looking man with a head of thick black hair.*
► deep, heavy

3 *The collision occurred in thick fog. The path wound through thick oak and pine forests.*
► dense, solid, impenetrable
OPPOSITES ARE sparse, clear, open

4 *The shallow water was thick with paddling children.*
► crowded, filled, packed, swarming, teeming, covered

5 *Beat the mixture into a thick smooth paste.*
► stiff, heavy, concentrated, condensed, clotted, coagulated, viscous
OPPOSITES ARE thin, watery

6 (*informal*) *'Some of these councillors are so thick,' said the woman.*
► stupid, foolish, dull, slow, dim-witted, brainless
OPPOSITES ARE clever, bright

## thicken VERB

*Put a little flour in to thicken the sauce.*
► stiffen, concentrate, condense, reduce, set
AN OPPOSITE IS thin out

## thickness NOUN

1 *You can use paper of similar thickness.*
► breadth, width, bulk
2 *The thickness of the smoke made it impossible to see.*
► density, denseness, murkiness
3 *Great thicknesses of pumice and ash had piled up on the slopes of Vesuvius.*
► layer, coating, stratum, seam

## thick-skinned ADJECTIVE

*He was too thick-skinned to notice the insult.*
► insensitive, unfeeling, hardened, tough, (*informal*) hard-boiled
OPPOSITES ARE sensitive, thin-skinned

## thief NOUN

*The 28-year-old thief was arrested when he returned to collect his dog.*
► robber, burglar, housebreaker, shoplifter, pilferer, bandit

## thieving NOUN

*a life of thieving*
► theft, robbery, stealing, pilfering, burglary

---

**thin** ADJECTIVE This word is often overused. Here are some alternatives:

1 *Frankie was small and thin for his age. He wore a silk shirt with a cravat tucked in round his thin neck.*
► slim, slender, lean, slight, skinny
AN OPPOSITE IS fat

2 *She was clad only in a thin nightgown. Thermal underwear keeps you warm by trapping a thin layer of air in its fibres.*
► fine, delicate, light, filmy, flimsy, diaphanous, insubstantial, wispy
OPPOSITES ARE thick, heavy

3 *When the paint is nearly dry, apply another thin coat.*
► light, runny, watery, dilute, flowing, fluid
OPPOSITES ARE thick, heavy

4 *a thin spread of butter*
► sparse, meagre, scanty, scarce
AN OPPOSITE IS thick

5 *The soft thin mist gave a mysterious air to the scene.*
► light, rarefied
AN OPPOSITE IS dense

6 *'Get on with it,' said a thin, peevish voice.*
► weak, faint, feeble
OPPOSITES ARE strong, loud

7 *a thin excuse*
► feeble, tenuous, unconvincing, implausible
AN OPPOSITE IS convincing

---

## thin VERB

*Thin the paint with water before use.*
► dilute, water down, weaken

**thin out** *The crowds began to thin out.*
► decrease, diminish, dwindle, disperse, scatter

## thing NOUN

1 *The cupboard was full of weird things.*
► object, item, artefact, article, body, device, entity, implement

2 *A strange thing happened today.*
► event, occurrence, incident, eventuality, happening, phenomenon, affair, circumstance, deed

3 *He didn't have a single thing to add.*
► idea, point, statement, thought, concept, detail, fact, factor

4 *There's a thing we have to do.*
► job, task, deed, act, action

5 (*informal*) *He's got this thing about wasps.*
► obsession, preoccupation, phobia, fear (of), terror (of), dislike (of), (*informal*) hang-up

**6 things** *Susan put her things in the back of the car*
▶ belongings, possessions, baggage, clothing, luggage, equipment, (*more informal*) gear, (*more informal*) stuff

**7 things** *Things improved once I had a job.*
▶ circumstances, conditions, life

## think VERB

**1** *Do you think Molly will come? We thought Rose must have gone home.*
▶ believe, expect, imagine, consider, surmise, conclude

**2** *Jennifer thought hard for a few moments.*
▶ concentrate, ponder, contemplate, deliberate, cogitate, reflect, muse

**think about** *It was time to start thinking about the future.*
▶ consider, contemplate, weigh up, deliberate about

**think of** *He thought of all the good times they had had together.*
▶ recall, remember, recollect, call to mind

**think over** *Think over what we have said.*
▶ consider, reflect on, muse on, ponder, mull over, (*more informal*) chew over

**think to be** *She was thought to be worthy of high office.*
▶ consider, deem, judge, hold, reckon

**think up** *We tried to think up a convincing excuse.*
▶ concoct, invent, contrive, devise

## thinker NOUN

*Russell was one of the great thinkers of recent times.*
▶ philosopher, intellect, scholar, theorist, ideologist, brain, innovator

## thinking ADJECTIVE

*He seems to be a thinking man.*
▶ intelligent, sensible, rational, reasonable, thoughtful, educated
OPPOSITES ARE stupid, irrational

**USAGE** Note that *unthinking* is not a true opposite, as it normally means 'without proper consideration', as in *an unthinking remark*.

## thinking NOUN

*Their thinking on the matter has changed.*
▶ opinion, view, reasoning, rationale, philosophy, outlook, judgement, policy

## thin-skinned ADJECTIVE

*He is thin-skinned and hates criticism.*
▶ sensitive, touchy, defensive, paranoid
AN OPPOSITE IS insensitive

## third-rate ADJECTIVE

*a third-rate piece of work*
▶ inferior, poor, poor-quality, substandard, inadequate, deplorable, dismal, atrocious

## thirst NOUN

**1** *We needed a drink to quench our raging thirst.*
▶ dehydration, thirstiness, dryness

**2** *their thirst for knowledge*
▶ appetite, hunger, longing, love (of), yearning, craving, hankering, desire, eagerness, passion

## thirst VERB

**thirst for** *They thirsted for power.*
▶ be thirsty for, crave, strive after, long for, have a thirst for, hunger after, yearn for

## thirsty ADJECTIVE

**1** *The boys were hot and thirsty after their run.*
▶ dehydrated, dry, parched, (*more informal*) gasping (for a drink), (*more informal*) panting

**2** *They were thirsty for adventure.*
▶ eager, hungry, yearning, greedy, itching, longing, avid

## thorny ADJECTIVE

**1** *They had to scramble through thorny undergrowth.*
▶ prickly, bristly, sharp, spiky, spiny, scratchy, barbed

**2** *the thorny question of who would pay*
▶ tricky, difficult, problematic, awkward, delicate

## thorough ADJECTIVE

**1** *a thorough inquiry*
▶ rigorous, exhaustive, thoroughgoing, detailed, in-depth
AN OPPOSITE IS superficial.

**2** *He was slow but very thorough.*
▶ meticulous, scrupulous, conscientious, assiduous, methodical, diligent

**3** *He's being a thorough nuisance.*
▶ utter, complete, downright, absolute, perfect, thoroughgoing, total

## thought NOUN

**1** *She appeared to be lost in thought. It only needs a moment's thought.*
▶ thinking, contemplation, deliberation, meditation, reflection, pondering, regard, consideration, introspection

**2** *I had a sudden thought.*
▶ idea, notion, belief, concept, conception, perception, conjecture, conviction, opinion

**3** *We've given up all thought of extending the project.*
▶ hope, expectation, intention, aspiration, aim, plan, purpose, design, objective

**4** *They seem to have no thought for others.*
▶ consideration, sympathy, regard, concern, caring, understanding, compassion

## thoughtful ADJECTIVE

**1** *The thoughtful look on his face did not change.*
▶ pensive, reflective, contemplative, introspective, absorbed, preoccupied
OPPOSITES ARE blank, vacant

**2** *Members of the audience added thoughtful comments after the lecture.*
▶ profound, studious, intelligent, scrupulous, thorough, diligent, meticulous
AN OPPOSITE IS superficial

**3** *It was thoughtful of you to visit.*
▶ considerate, kind, caring, attentive, helpful, concerned, friendly, good-natured, unselfish
AN OPPOSITE IS thoughtless

## thoughtless ADJECTIVE

**1** *She realized it was thoughtless of her to rush off like that.*
▶ inconsiderate, insensitive, unthinking, unkind, unfeeling, uncaring
AN OPPOSITE IS considerate

**2** *One thoughtless remark can prompt a feeling of depression.*
▶ unthinking, careless, unmindful, injudicious, ill-considered, unwise, rash
AN OPPOSITE IS thoughtful

## thrash VERB

**1** *The boy was thrashed by his exasperated mother.*
▶ punish, beat, whip, flog, spank, cane, strap, birch

**2** *She thrashed her arms, attempting to swim towards him.*
▶ jerk, toss, flail

**3** (*informal*) *They were thrashed by six wickets in the final.*
▶ defeat, beat, trounce, overwhelm

**thrash out** *I must thrash things out with him over the next few months.*
▶ resolve, settle, sort out, clarify

## thread NOUN

**1** *He sewed it up with a needle and thread in his girlfriend's flat.*
▶ cotton, yarn, fibre, strand, twine

**2** *I lost the thread of the argument.*
▶ train of thought, line of thought, drift, tenor, continuity, course, direction, theme

## threadbare ADJECTIVE

*He inched his way along the threadbare strip of carpet.*
▶ worn, frayed, ragged, shabby, tattered, tatty

## threat NOUN

**1** *We got bomb threats against our building.*
▶ warning, ultimatum, menace

**2** *It is a brutal regime that poses a threat to world peace.*
▶ danger, risk, hazard, menace

## threaten VERB

**1** *When they came in they threatened us.*
▶ intimidate, menace, make threats against, browbeat, bully, terrorize, frighten, pressurize

**2** *The freedom fighters threatened reprisals. A mass of rain clouds threatened a dramatic change in the weather.*
▶ warn of, forebode, foreshadow, forewarn of, give warning of, portend, presage, indicate

**3** *Dumping waste here will threaten the safety and well-being of the region.*
▶ endanger, imperil, jeopardize, put at risk

## threatening ADJECTIVE

*The dog was baring its teeth in threatening snarls.*
▶ ominous, menacing, sinister, forbidding, grim, minatory, stern, unfriendly
AN OPPOSITE IS comforting

## threshold NOUN

**1** *They stood on the threshold of the main entrance.*
▶ doorstep, doorway, entrance, sill

**2** *These events marked the threshold of a new era.*
▶ brink, verge, dawn, beginning, start, outset, opening

## thrift NOUN

*He succeeded through thrift and business acumen.*
▶ prudence, providence, economy, thriftiness, good management

## thrifty ADJECTIVE

*Students were expected to be hard-working and thrifty.*
▶ careful, economical, frugal, prudent, provident, parsimonious, sparing
AN OPPOSITE IS extravagant

## thrill NOUN

*Just to work with him was a thrill.*
▶ adventure, excitement, sensation, pleasure, tingle, tremor, (*more informal*) buzz, (*more informal*) kick

## thrill VERB

*She knew he was hers and it thrilled her.*
▶ excite, delight, rouse, stimulate, exhilarate, stir, electrify, titillate
AN OPPOSITE IS bore

## thrilling ADJECTIVE

*a thrilling boat ride to the base of Niagara falls*
▶ exciting, electrifying, riveting, gripping, stirring, rousing, sensational, spectacular, stimulating, (*more informal*) hair-raising
OPPOSITES ARE unexciting, boring

## thrive VERB

*Plants often thrive when the same species are massed together. Two-year-olds thrive on attention.*
▶ flourish, burgeon, grow, prosper, succeed, be vigorous, develop strongly, do well
OPPOSITES ARE decline, wither

## thriving ADJECTIVE

*By Tudor times distilling was a thriving industry in Scotland.*
▶ flourishing, growing, prosperous, booming, burgeoning, vigorous, developing, expanding, successful, healthy, affluent, lively, profitable
OPPOSITES ARE failing, dying

## throaty ADJECTIVE

*Lucinda's smile gave way to a throaty laugh.*
▶ gruff, guttural, deep, hoarse, husky, croaky, gravelly, rasping, rough, thick

## throb NOUN

*the annoying dull throb of a neighbour's stereo*
▶ beat, rhythm, pulsation, pounding, thud, thump, thrum, vibration

## throb VERB

*A vein started to throb in his forehead.*
▶ pound, pulsate, pulse, beat, thump, palpitate

## throng NOUN

*Vehicles mingled with the throng of foot passengers.*
▶ crowd, mass, horde, mob, crush

**throng** VERB
*Tourists thronged the streets and canals.*
▶ pack, cram, fill, press into, squeeze into

**throttle** VERB
*You're lucky Lewis didn't throttle you.*
▶ strangle, choke, stifle, smother, suffocate, asphyxiate

**throw** VERB
1 *They asked her to throw their ball back.*
▶ toss, fling, hurl, pitch, lob, cast, (*more informal*) chuck, (*more informal*) sling
2 *He threw a quick glance at them.*
▶ direct, cast, send, shoot, dart
3 *The horse threw its rider.*
▶ unseat, dislodge, upset, bring down
4 *The torch threw a beam of light across the passage.*
▶ cast, project, send, emit, radiate
**throw away** *He cleared out his room and threw lots of stuff away.*
▶ discard, throw out, dispose of, get rid of, (*more informal*) ditch
**throw off** *He hoped he had thrown off his pursuers.*
▶ shake off, escape, elude, give the slip to, get away from
**throw out** *He tried to get in the house but was thrown out. The government might be thrown out at the next election.*
▶ eject, expel, remove, force out, oust, get rid of
**throw up** *He was tempted to throw up his job and go abroad.*
▶ abandon, relinquish, give up, (*more informal*) quit, (*more informal*) chuck in

**throw** NOUN
*With one mighty throw the ball went over the fence.*
▶ heave, fling, toss, lob, pitch

**throwaway** ADJECTIVE
*a throwaway remark*
▶ casual, offhand, passing, unthinking, unimportant

**thrust** VERB
1 *He thrust a mug of tea into my hands.*
▶ push, shove, force, press, stick, poke
2 *His attacker thrust at him with a knife.*
▶ lunge, jab, prod, stab, plunge, poke, stick

**thrust** NOUN
1 *He gave the door a firm thrust.*
▶ shove, push, prod, poke
2 *I strongly support the thrust of your argument.*
▶ gist, substance, drift, burden, force

**thud** VERB
*Heavy footsteps thudded across the front porch.*
▶ thump, clump, stomp, crash

**thud** NOUN
*He was hammering on the door, thud after thud.*
▶ thump, bang, rap, clunk, clonk, crash

**thug** NOUN
(*informal*) *A fight broke out between two armies of thugs.*
▶ ruffian, hoodlum, tough, bully

**thumb** VERB
*She thumbed through her notes.*
▶ browse, flick, flip, leaf, riffle, scan

**thump** NOUN
1 *He sat down with a painful thump on the floor.*
▶ thud, bang, clunk, clonk, crash
2 *The heavy thump of acid house music was everywhere.*
▶ beat, rhythm, pulsation, pounding, throb, thud, thrum, vibration

**thump** VERB
*The woman thumped the table with her fist.*
▶ bang, hit, strike, pound, beat, rap, batter, wallop, knock

**thunder** NOUN
*Her musings were interrupted by the thunder of hooves.*
▶ rumble, rumbling, boom, booming, roar, roaring, thud, thump, ringing

**thunder** VERB
*Fighter aircraft thundered overhead.*
▶ roar, boom, rumble, blast

**thunderous** ADJECTIVE
*The speech was greeted by thunderous applause and standing ovations.*
▶ deafening, tumultuous, resounding, loud, booming

**thwart** VERB
*He stayed in power as long as he could, just to thwart his main rival.*
▶ frustrate, hinder, impede, foil, obstruct, prevent, stand in the way of, stop
OPPOSITES ARE help, further

**tick** NOUN
1 *Put a tick in the box marked 'no'.*
▶ mark, stroke, dash, line
2 *They heard the tick of a clock.*
▶ ticking, clicking
**in a tick** (*informal*) *I'll be back in a tick.*
▶ in a moment, in a minute, in a second, in a trice, very soon, very shortly, (*informal*) in a jiffy

**tick** VERB
1 *It was so quiet I could hear my watch ticking.*
▶ click, make a tick, beat
2 *Tick the box against your preferred method of payment.*
▶ mark, check off, indicate
**tick off** (*informal*) *She ticked off the children for making a noise.*
▶ tell off, scold, reprimand, admonish, rebuke

**ticket** NOUN
1 *a ticket to the game*
▶ pass, permit, token, voucher, coupon
2 *a price ticket*
▶ label, tag, sticker, marker, slip, tab

**tickle** VERB
1 *He tickled her toes until she gurgled happily.*
▶ touch, stroke, pet
2 *The little story tickled us.*
▶ amuse, entertain, delight, cheer

**ticklish** ADJECTIVE

**1** *'It's lucky I'm not ticklish,' she squealed.*
▶ giggly, wriggly, sensitive

**2** *He had the ticklish problem of explaining where he had been all night.*
▶ tricky, awkward, delicate, thorny, difficult, hazardous, risky, touchy, (*more informal*) dodgy

**tide** NOUN

*The tide of opinion was turning against the government.*
▶ trend, tendency, current, course, drift, movement

**tidy** ADJECTIVE

**1** *Each desk should be tidy and have a place card.*
▶ neat, orderly, uncluttered, shipshape, smart, spick and span
OPPOSITES ARE untidy, messy

**2** *He tried to be tidy in his new apartment.*
▶ methodical, meticulous, organized, systematic, house-proud
OPPOSITES ARE untidy, disorganized

**3** (*informal*) *All those books will cost a tidy sum.*
▶ sizeable, considerable, substantial, appreciable, large, (*informal*) hefty

**tidy** VERB

*The girls started to wash up and tidy.*
▶ clean up, put in order, set straight, arrange, smarten, spruce up, neaten, straighten
OPPOSITES ARE untidy, muddle

**tie** VERB

**1** *The dog was tied to a lamppost.*
▶ fasten, secure, attach, tether, bind, hitch
AN OPPOSITE IS untie

**2** *Her new job tied her to the office.*
▶ restrict, limit, confine, restrain

**3** *The home side tied its next game.*
▶ draw, finish level

**tie up**

**1** *He tied up the boat at the jetty.*
▶ moor, tether, fasten, attach

**2** *We were keen to tie up the deal.*
▶ complete, finalize, conclude, settle

**3 be tied up** *The manager is still tied up I'm afraid.*
▶ be busy, be occupied, be engaged

**tie** NOUN

*Family ties are important.*
▶ bond, connection, link, attachment, relationship, association

**tier** NOUN

*The seats are arranged in three tiers*
▶ row, rank, line, level, stage, storey, terrace

**tight** ADJECTIVE

**1** *The rope was pulled tight.*
▶ taut, stretched, rigid, stiff, tense
OPPOSITES ARE slack, loose

**2** *Her grip was tight.*
▶ firm, fast, secure, clenched
AN OPPOSITE IS relaxed

**3** *The joint was completely tight.*
▶ sealed, airtight, impervious
AN OPPOSITE IS leaking

**4** *The bed had to fit into a tight space.*
▶ small, compact, constricted, snug, poky

**5** *He can be very tight with his money.*
▶ mean, stingy, niggardly, miserly, parsimonious, (*more informal*) tight-fisted, (*more informal*) penny-pinching
AN OPPOSITE IS generous

**6** *There is tight security at the airport.*
▶ strict, stringent, rigorous, severe, tough, scrupulous
AN OPPOSITE IS lax

**tighten** VERB

**1** *Jane tightened her grip on the rail.*
▶ strengthen, squeeze, tense, stiffen, increase
OPPOSITES ARE loosen, relax

**2** *You need to tighten your shoelaces.*
▶ make tight, pull tighter, tauten, stretch
AN OPPOSITE IS slacken

**3** *Tighten all screws when the chair is assembled.*
▶ make tighter, screw up, give another turn to
AN OPPOSITE IS loosen

**tighten up** *Security will be tightened up during the peak season.*
▶ increase, heighten, strengthen, intensify, escalate

**tight-fisted** ADJECTIVE

*We were too tight-fisted to pay a motorway toll.*
▶ mean, stingy, niggardly, miserly, parsimonious, (*more informal*) penny-pinching

**till** VERB

*country people who till the land*
▶ cultivate, work, farm, plough, dig

**tilt** VERB

*He tilted his hat to one side The wall tilted alarmingly.*
▶ lean, slant, slope, tip, angle

**tilt** NOUN

*The tray was on a tilt.*
▶ slant, slope, incline, angle

**at full tilt** *They ran at full tilt down the bank.*
▶ headlong, pell-mell, at full speed, at full pelt, at a gallop, fast

**timber** NOUN

*Houses built of timber and mud would be very damp.*
▶ wood, planks, planking, beams, laths, boarding, boards, logs, lumber, trees

**time** NOUN

**1** *in the time of Queen Mary*
▶ age, era, period, generation

**2** *He lived here for a time.*
▶ while, period, spell

**3** *It took a long time to fix the problem.*
▶ while, interval, duration

**4** *When is the best time to come? I didn't know what to do at that time.*
▶ moment, point, juncture, stage, date, occasion
RELATED ADJECTIVES temporal, chronic, chronological

## time VERB

**1** *She had timed her arrival for half an hour after the party was due to start.*
▶ regulate, choose, fix, set, schedule

**2** *The nurse timed ten minutes.*
▶ measure, count

## timeless ADJECTIVE

*the instant, timeless attraction of a good tune*
▶ immortal, ageless, enduring, lasting, perennial, abiding

## timely ADJECTIVE

*The incident was a timely reminder of how dangerous these waters had become.*
▶ opportune, fitting, suitable, appropriate, apt, prompt

## timetable NOUN

*They established a timetable for elections and political reform.*
▶ schedule, agenda, programme, calendar, diary, roster, rota

## timid ADJECTIVE

*Elaine handed him her bag with a timid smile.*
▶ shy, diffident, bashful, modest, timorous, faint-hearted, weak, fearful
OPPOSITES ARE bold, brazen

## tinge NOUN

**1** *The light took on a green tinge.*
▶ tint, shade, hue, colour

**2** *There was a tinge of amusement on his face.*
▶ trace, touch, note, suggestion, flavour, streak

## tingle NOUN

**1** *There was a strange tingle in her fingers.*
▶ prickling, stinging, tickle, tickling, itch, itching, pins and needles

**2** *Melissa felt a tingle of excitement.*
▶ quiver, tremor, thrill, sensation, shiver

## tingle VERB

*His shoes were so tight they made his feet tingle.*
▶ itch, prickle, sting, tickle

## tinker VERB

*He watched Nathan tinkering with his bike.*
▶ fiddle, play, meddle, tamper, dabble, trifle, interfere, (more informal) mess about, (more informal) play about

## tinny ADJECTIVE

**1** *She pressed a button and a tinny voice rang out.*
▶ jangling, jingly, metallic
OPPOSITES ARE full, deep

**2** *He drove his tinny little car west out of Oxford.*
▶ cheap, inferior, poor-quality
AN OPPOSITE IS solid

## tint NOUN

*smooth glossy paper with a yellowish tint*
▶ tinge, shade, hue, colour

## tiny ADJECTIVE

**1** *We've got a tiny pond in the front garden.*
▶ minute, miniature, diminutive, midget, mini, very small, (more informal) teeny, (more informal) titchy
AN OPPOSITE IS huge

**2** *These man-made gases are present in the atmosphere only in tiny amounts.*
▶ minute, insignificant, negligible, paltry, meagre

## tip NOUN

**1** *He ran the tip of his finger along the handlebar. The tip of the arrow couldn't be far into the tree.*
▶ end, point, extremity, sharp end, nib

**2** *The tip of a mountain was visible above the clouds.*
▶ summit, peak, pinnacle, top, apex, cap, crown, head

**3** *He paid his bill, left a good tip, and walked home.*
▶ gratuity, gift

**4** *My tip is to go for really good-quality ski pants.*
▶ hint, suggestion, advice, clue, information, warning

**5** *To most people the rubbish tip is an eyesore.*
▶ dump, heap, pit

## tip VERB

**1** *He tipped his head back to look. The van was tipping to one side.*
▶ lean, incline, list, slant, slope, tilt, keel over

**2** *She tipped the fish into the sink and began to clean them.*
▶ empty, dump, pour out, spill, unload

**3** *He decided to tip the driver after all.*
▶ give a tip to, remunerate, reward

**tip over** *A whale is capable of tipping over a small boat.*
▶ overturn, capsize, topple, turn over, upset, knock over

## tip-off NOUN

*(informal) The police received a tip-off about a shipment of cocaine.*
▶ alert, clue, prompt, piece of information

## tire VERB

*The long walk tired us.*
▶ exhaust, fatigue, weary, tire out, wear out, drain
OPPOSITES ARE refresh, invigorate

## tired ADJECTIVE

**1** *He was tired from his hectic battle with the goblins.*
▶ exhausted, fatigued, wearied, worn out
OPPOSITES ARE energetic, refreshed

**2** *tired old debates about nature and nurture*
▶ stale, hackneyed, overworked, banal
OPPOSITES ARE fresh, new

**tired of** *They grew tired of waiting.*
▶ bored with, fed up with, sick of, impatient with

## tiredness NOUN

*He felt good despite his tiredness.*
▶ exhaustion, fatigue, weariness, lethargy, listlessness, sleepiness, drowsiness, inertia, lassitude
OPPOSITES ARE vigour, energy

**tireless** ADJECTIVE

*a tireless campaigner on behalf of chimpanzees in the wild*

▶ vigorous, energetic, determined, unflagging, untiring, indefatigable, persistent, zealous, diligent, sedulous, unceasing

AN OPPOSITE IS lazy

**USAGE** Note that *tireless* and *tiresome* are not opposites.

**tiresome** ADJECTIVE

*Richard was back from work after a tiresome day.*

▶ irritating, annoying, wearisome, troublesome, trying, irksome, bothersome, vexing, distracting, exasperating

OPPOSITES ARE stimulating, exciting

**USAGE** See the note at *tireless*.

**tiring** ADJECTIVE

*Infant care can be tiring.*

▶ exhausting, exacting, taxing, wearying, fatiguing, demanding, difficult, hard

AN OPPOSITE IS refreshing

**tissue** NOUN

1 *body tissue*

▶ substance, material, matter, structure, stuff

2 *a box of tissues*

▶ paper handkerchief, paper napkin

3 *a tissue of lies*

▶ web, network, tangle, maze, series

**titbit** NOUN

1 *She fed the dogs titbits.*

▶ scrap, bit, morsel, delicacy

2 *a titbit of information*

▶ piece, morsel, scrap

**titillate** VERB

*sensational news articles to titillate readers*

▶ stimulate, excite, thrill, intrigue, fascinate, stir, arouse

**title** NOUN

1 *The title of the picture was printed underneath.*

▶ caption, heading, name

2 *Specify the title you want to be known by.*

▶ form of address, designation, appellation, rank, status, office, position

3 *He sought to prove his title to the land.*

▶ right, entitlement, claim, ownership (of), tenure (of)

**titter** NOUN

*The remark caused a few titters.*

▶ giggle, snigger, chuckle, laugh

**titter** VERB

*Some of the audience began to titter.*

▶ giggle, snigger, chuckle, laugh

**toast** VERB

1 *They toasted bread by the fire.*

▶ grill, brown, heat, warm

2 *The guests then toasted their host.*

▶ drink a toast to, drink the health of, raise your glass to, salute, honour

**together** ADVERB

1 *They were all speaking together.*

▶ simultaneously, at the same time, at once, collectively, concurrently, in chorus, in unison, jointly

OPPOSITES ARE independently, separately

2 *Naim and I work together.*

▶ jointly, with each other, in concert, side by side

OPPOSITES ARE separately, alone

3 *Nothing happened for days together.*

▶ in a row, in succession, continuously, consecutively

**toil** NOUN

*years of hardship and toil*

▶ work , labour, donkey work, slaving, drudgery, effort, exertion, industry

**toil** VERB

*The team needed to toil all day.*

▶ work, labour, slave, sweat, struggle, (*more informal*) slog, (*more informal*) grind away

**toilet** NOUN

1 *There is a toilet on the first floor.*

▶ lavatory, WC, convenience, facilities, privy, (*more informal*) loo

2 *She was taking ages over her toilet.*

▶ washing, bathing

**token** NOUN

1 *Saladin's ring was sent as a token of good faith.*

▶ symbol, sign, mark, expression, testimony, evidence, indication, proof, reminder

2 *He had a cross tattooed on his chest as a token of this religious experience.*

▶ memento, souvenir, record, keepsake

3 *a book token*

▶ voucher, coupon, counter

**token** ADJECTIVE

1 *She did the work for a token fee.*

▶ nominal, minimal, trivial, slight

AN OPPOSITE IS substantial

2 *The garrison offered only token resistance.*

▶ perfunctory, insignificant, superficial, symbolic

AN OPPOSITE IS considerable

**tolerable** ADJECTIVE

1 *The pain was barely tolerable.*

▶ bearable, acceptable, endurable, sufferable, supportable

AN OPPOSITE IS intolerable

2 *He was fond of music and had a tolerable voice.*

▶ adequate, passable, middling, ordinary, satisfactory, fair, mediocre, indifferent

**tolerance** NOUN

1 *He has always preached tolerance for people of whatever religion.*

▶ toleration, forbearance, sufferance, acceptance, open-mindedness, broad-mindedness, liberalism, understanding, permissiveness

2 *Allow a slight tolerance in measurement.*

▶ variation, fluctuation, deviation, leeway

**tolerant** ADJECTIVE

*He's a tolerant chap who didn't seem to mind if I got it wrong.*
▶ understanding, open-minded, long-suffering, forbearing, sympathetic, fair, magnanimous, charitable
OPPOSITES ARE intolerant, unsympathetic

**tolerate** VERB

1 *At work she will not tolerate interference.*
▶ put up with, bear, endure, stand, abide, stomach, suffer, take, (*more informal*) stick
2 *This sort of behaviour is difficult to tolerate.*
▶ accept, condone, countenance, admit, brook, make allowances for, permit, sanction

**toll** NOUN

1 *a road toll*
▶ charge, fee, levy, tariff, payment, duty, tax
2 *the death toll from the accident*
▶ count, tally, total, reckoning

**toll** VERB

*We heard a bell toll.*
▶ ring, peal, chime, sound

**tomb** NOUN

*the tomb of Ramesses II*
▶ burial chamber, burial place, sepulchre, grave, catacomb, crypt, mausoleum
RELATED ADJECTIVE sepulchral

**tone** NOUN

1 *He objected to the arrogant tone of the letter.*
▶ manner, mood, spirit, attitude, tenor, quality
2 *She called out in an angry tone of voice.*
▶ expression, timbre, quality, sound, modulation, intonation
3 *emulsion paint with a rosy tone*
▶ tint, tinge, hue, shade, blush, colour

**tone** VERB

**tone with** *The pastel shades of the wallpaper tone beautifully with the light wood of the furniture.*
▶ harmonize with, coordinate with, match, go well with, suit

**tone down** *He was unwilling to tone down his criticisms of the management.*
▶ moderate, modify, temper, mitigate, soften, restrain, dampen, subdue, play down
AN OPPOSITE IS intensify

**tongue** NOUN

*He spoke in a foreign tongue.*
▶ language, vernacular, idiom, talk, speech, utterance

**tongue-tied** ADJECTIVE

*He is often tongue-tied in company.*
▶ lost for words, inarticulate, dumbstruck, speechless, mute, silent

**tonic** NOUN

*A tonic will do you good.*
▶ stimulant, restorative, refresher, cordial, (*more informal*) pick-me-up

**tool** NOUN

1 *a set of garden tools*
▶ implement, utensil, device, gadget, appliance, contraption
2 *The tabloid press became a tool of the government.*
▶ dupe, pawn, puppet, creature, stooge, minion, (*more informal*) poodle

**VARIOUS TOOLS**

**tools for cutting and chopping**: knife; saw, hacksaw; axe, chopper, cleaver, hatchet, mattock, pickaxe.

**tools for drilling**: brace and bit, bradawl, drill, gimlet.

**tools for nails and screws**: hammer, mallet, punch; screwdriver.

**tools for gripping and forcing**: clamp, vice, jack; crowbar; spanner; pincers, pliers, tweezers, wrench.

**tools for shaping**: chisel, plane, spokeshave, file, sander, sandpaper.

**gardening and agricultural tools**: fork, spade, shovel; dibble or dibber, hoe; rake, pitchfork; scythe, secateurs, shears, sickle.

**top** NOUN

1 *The top of the mountain was still covered in snow*
▶ summit, peak, pinnacle, tip, apex, cap, crown, head
AN OPPOSITE IS foot

2 *The top of the jar was stuck.*
▶ lid, cap, cover, covering
AN OPPOSITE IS bottom

**top** ADJECTIVE

1 *an office on the top floor*
▶ highest, topmost, uppermost, upper
OPPOSITES ARE bottom, lowest

2 *some of the world's top golf professionals*
▶ leading, finest, foremost, principal, chief, pre-eminent, prime

3 *the top Paris restaurants*
▶ best, prime, superior, leading, foremost, finest
AN OPPOSITE IS inferior

**top** VERB

1 *The cake can be topped with chopped nuts.*
▶ cover, cap, decorate, finish off, garnish, crown
2 *Sales are expected to top the million mark.*
▶ exceed, beat, be higher than, outdo, surpass, better, cap, excel

**topic** NOUN

*An article on this topic appeared last month.*
▶ subject, theme, issue, matter, question, talking-point

**topical** ADJECTIVE

*Choose a news item of topical interest each week.*
▶ current, contemporary, recent, up-to-date, up-to-the-minute, newsworthy

## topple VERB

1 *The heavy winds toppled several pylons, causing power cuts.*
▶ knock down, overturn, tip over, throw down, upset

2 *She saw a man topple sideways into the gutter. If kangaroos had no tails, they would topple over.*
▶ fall, overbalance, tumble

3 *A party revolt had toppled the conservative leadership.*
▶ bring down, overthrow, oust, unseat, depose

## topsy-turvy ADJECTIVE

*The carts lay in a topsy-turvy heap at the bottom of the hill. My emotions are all topsy-turvy.*
▶ disordered, confused, mixed up, muddled, jumbled, untidy, higgledy-piggledy
OPPOSITES ARE ordered, neat

## torment NOUN

*Jason never escaped the torment of self-doubt.*
▶ agony, affliction, anguish, pain, ordeal, distress, misery, suffering, torture

## torment VERB

1 *The urge to express her feelings tormented her. Sometimes, he was tormented by jealousy.*
▶ afflict, torture, distress, persecute, plague, bedevil, bother, be a torment to, pain, vex

2 *Marjory loved tormenting her younger brother.*
▶ tease, bait, pester, harass, annoy, bully, victimize

## torrent NOUN

1 *The sky opened and a heavy torrent fell down.*
▶ downpour, deluge, flood, shower, flow
AN OPPOSITE IS trickle

2 *These points are lost to the reader in a torrent of words.*
▶ cascade, gush, rush, outburst, spate, stream, tide

## torrential ADJECTIVE

*They landed safely in torrential rain.*
▶ heavy, violent, teeming, relentless, soaking

## tortuous ADJECTIVE

*They took a tortuous route through Dijon and Lyons. Acquiring skills can be a tortuous process.*
▶ twisted, twisting, winding, circuitous, devious, meandering, roundabout, indirect
OPPOSITES ARE straight, direct

## torture NOUN

1 *Human rights groups claimed that torture of prisoners had taken place.*
▶ maltreatment, persecution, cruelty, torment, humiliation, degradation, inquisition

2 *The rest of the journey was torture.*
▶ agony, torment, misery, affliction

## torture VERB

1 *They were out to torture their victims.*
▶ persecute, inflict pain on, inflict suffering on, be cruel to, degrade, humiliate, hurt, torment

2 *I was having thoughts that tortured me.*
▶ afflict, torment, distress, persecute, plague, bedevil, bother, be a torment to, pain, vex

## toss VERB

1 *He tossed a ball high in the air.*
▶ throw, fling, hurl, cast, pitch, heave

2 *The boat was tossing about in shallow water.*
▶ lurch, pitch, reel, rock, roll, bob, shake, wallow, welter, writhe

3 *Marion tossed restlessly in bed.*
▶ twist and turn, move restlessly, flail, thrash about, wriggle, fidget

## toss NOUN

*a toss of a coin*
▶ flip, fling, throw, jerk, heave

## tot VERB

*tot up He was totting up some figures.*
▶ add up, calculate, count, total, find the total of, reckon up, totalize, work out

## total ADJECTIVE

1 *The total volume of sales reached five million.*
▶ complete, comprehensive, entire, full, gross, overall, whole

2 *A senior fire officer said it was total carnage.*
▶ sheer, utter, absolute, downright, thorough, unmitigated, unqualified, perfect, out-and-out

## total NOUN

*The airport will handle a total of a million passengers in the week before Christmas.*
▶ sum, totality, aggregate, amount, whole

## total VERB

1 *The cash bag totalled £1,200.*
▶ amount to, come to, add up to, make, reach
**total up** *Total up your scores.*
▶ add up, calculate, count, tot up, find the total of, reckon up, totalize, work out

## totalitarian ADJECTIVE

*In totalitarian societies, newspapers are wholly controlled by the state.*
▶ authoritarian, autocratic, dictatorial, one-party, oppressive, repressive, tyrannical, undemocratic, unrepresentative
OPPOSITES ARE democratic, liberal

## totter VERB

*Lizzy held out her arms and the child tottered towards her.*
▶ stagger, teeter, dodder, stumble, shuffle, waddle, shamble, stagger, falter, reel

## touch NOUN

1 *Animals communicate by touch.*
▶ feeling, touching, contact

2 *She jumped under his touch.*
▶ pat, stroke, tap, caress, contact, dab

3 *Funny speeches need a bubbly, light touch.*
▶ manner, style, technique, flair, knack, feel, sensitivity

4 *There was a touch of genius in the way he talked that night.*
▶ hint, suggestion, suspicion, tinge, trace

5 *A gift of flowers can be a nice touch.*
▶ feature, detail, extra

**6** *He and Carol kept in touch.*
▶ contact, communication, correspondence
RELATED ADJECTIVE tactile

## touch VERB

**1** *She touched his arm and he turned.*
▶ pat, brush, contact, feel, rub, stroke, tap, caress, dab

**2** *Their sorrow touched him.*
▶ move, affect, concern, disturb, influence, inspire, stir, upset

**3** *Their speed touched 100 m.p.h.*
▶ reach, rise to, attain

**4** *(informal) Nothing could touch them for good value.*
▶ equal, match, compare with, rival, come up to, parallel

**touch on** *The programme touched on recent concerns.*
▶ refer to, deal with, mention, treat, raise, cover

**touch up** *The room had been touched up and given a new carpet.*
▶ improve, repaint, renovate, refurbish, redecorate

## touched ADJECTIVE

**1** *I was touched by their generosity.*
▶ moved, affected, impressed, stirred, responsive (to)

**2** *(informal) You have to be a bit touched to do something like that.*
▶ mad, crazy, deranged, disturbed, insane, unbalanced, (more informal) barmy

## touching ADJECTIVE

*She was beautiful, her face crossed by a touching sadness.*
▶ moving, affecting, poignant, emotional, tender

## touchy ADJECTIVE

*Like most tired children she was touchy and uncooperative.*
▶ irritable, bad-tempered, irascible, grumpy, grouchy, testy, tetchy, crotchety, cantankerous, peevish, fractious, cross, (more informal) stroppy, (more informal) shirty
AN OPPOSITE IS good-humoured

## tough ADJECTIVE

**1** *It was my first outing in my tough new boots.*
▶ strong, stout, durable, hard-wearing, indestructible, lasting, unbreakable, well-made
OPPOSITES ARE flimsy, delicate

**2** *(informal) He is tall with a tough physique.*
▶ sturdy, muscular, strong, beefy, brawny, burly, hardy, robust, stalwart
AN OPPOSITE IS weak

**3** *They proved to be tough rivals. She's a tough, single-minded woman.*
▶ determined, tenacious, unyielding, resilient, resolute, resistant, stiff, stubborn
AN OPPOSITE IS weak

**4** *The meat was overcooked and tough.*
▶ chewy, leathery, gristly, rubbery, hard, uneatable
AN OPPOSITE IS tender

**5** *There was a tough climb ahead.*
▶ difficult, arduous, strenuous, exacting, exhausting, gruelling, stiff, hard, laborious
AN OPPOSITE IS easy

**6** *They had some tough questions to answer.*
▶ difficult, baffling, intractable, puzzling, perplexing, (more informal) thorny, (more informal) knotty
AN OPPOSITE IS easy

## toughen VERB

*ways of toughening wood*
▶ harden, strengthen, make tougher, reinforce
AN OPPOSITE IS weaken

## tour NOUN

*a tour round the castles of southern Bavaria*
▶ journey, expedition, trip, ride, drive, outing, excursion

## tour VERB

*The town is well situated for touring the area.*
▶ travel round, visit, explore, sightsee, go round, make a tour of

## tourist NOUN

*Tribal dances are performed for the tourists.*
▶ sightseer, holidaymaker, visitor, tripper, traveller

## tournament NOUN

*He was due to take part in a celebrity golf tournament.*
▶ competition, contest, championship, match, meeting, series

## tow VERB

*The rope seemed too slender to tow the forty-foot barge.*
▶ pull, drag, tug, draw, haul, transport, trail

## tower NOUN

*We passed two abbeys, one with a tower and one without.*
▶ steeple, turret, column, pillar, belfry

## tower VERB

*Clouds towered on every side. He stood up, and he towered above her.*
▶ loom, rear, rise, dominate, stand out, stick up, ascend

## towering ADJECTIVE

*towering crags and cliffs*
▶ tall, high, lofty, soaring, mighty, colossal, gigantic, imposing

## town NOUN

*The family moved to an industrial town.*
▶ conurbation, urban area, borough, city, municipality, settlement
RELATED ADJECTIVE urban, civic, municipal

## toxic ADJECTIVE

*You have two minutes to get out before the heat and toxic fumes overcome you.*
▶ poisonous, noxious, lethal, deadly, dangerous, harmful
OPPOSITES ARE harmless, safe

A B C D E F G H I J K L M N O P Q R S **T** U V W X Y Z

**toy** ADJECTIVE
*giant toy animals*
► model, imitation, make-believe, simulation, (*more informal*) pretend

**toy** NOUN
*The children can bring their favourite toy.*
► plaything, game, doll

**toy** VERB
**toy with**
1 *She picked up her fork and toyed with her food.*
► play with, fiddle with, fidget with, tinker with, peck at, pick at
2 *He toyed with the idea of walking to the station to meet her.*
► think about, play with, consider

**trace** NOUN
1 *'No,' he said with a trace of irritation.*
► hint, touch, suggestion, suspicion
2 *The animal had left no trace.*
► trail, track, mark, sign, spoor, indication
3 *The investigators could find no trace of blood.*
► sign, remnant, remains, vestige

**trace** VERB
1 *Police are trying to trace the owner of the car.*
► track down, find, discover, uncover, unearth, detect
2 *It would be best to trace the map from an atlas.*
► copy, draw, outline, mark out, sketch, make a copy of

**track** NOUN
1 *An animal had left clear tracks.*
► trace, trail, mark, scent, spoor, footmark, footprint
2 *a track across the fields*
► path, way, pathway, footpath, route, lane, trail
3 *a racing track*
► course, circuit, dirt-track, race-track
4 *Passengers were seen walking along the tracks.*
► rail, line

**track** VERB
*He tracked a bear all day.*
► follow, trail, pursue, stalk, chase, hunt, dog, shadow, trace
**track down** *It took years to track everyone down.*
► discover, trace, find, detect, recover, retrieve

**tract** NOUN
*large tracts of land*
► area, expanse, region, stretch, extent, sweep, span, parcel

**trade** NOUN
1 *international trade*
► commerce, buying and selling, dealing, trading, traffic, transactions, barter, business, marketing
RELATED ADJECTIVE mercantile
2 *He wanted to be trained in a trade.*
► craft, occupation, job, career, profession, calling, pursuit, line of work

**trade** VERB
1 *The family traded in diamonds.*
► deal, traffic, buy and sell, do business
2 *She traded her old car for a new model.*
► exchange, part-exchange, barter, swap, switch

**trader** NOUNS
*local high-street traders*
► dealer, merchant, retailer, tradesman, shopkeeper, stockist, supplier, vendor

**tradition** NOUN
*the old tradition of first-footing*
► custom, practice, convention, institution, observance, habit, routine

**traditional** ADJECTIVE
1 *a traditional white wedding*
► conventional, customary, established, accustomed, familiar, time-honoured, typical, orthodox, regular, usual
AN OPPOSITE IS unconventional
2 *traditional beliefs*
► popular, folk, oral, unwritten, historical
OPPOSITES ARE modern, contemporary

**traffic** NOUN
1 *Road traffic is not allowed in the park.*
► vehicles, cars, transport
2 *goods traffic*
► transport, transportation, movement
3 *illegal traffic in antiquities*
► trade, trading, dealing, commerce, peddling

**traffic** VERB
*He was arrested on suspicion of trafficking in illegal exports.*
► trade, deal, buy and sell

**tragedy** NOUN
*the tragedy of their son's death*
► disaster, calamity, catastrophe, affliction, blow, misfortune, misadventure

**tragic** ADJECTIVE
1 *a tragic accident*
► disastrous, catastrophic, calamitous, dreadful, fatal, appalling, terrible, unfortunate
AN OPPOSITE IS fortunate
2 *a tragic expression on her face*
► sad, sorrowful, woeful, wretched, distressed, grief-stricken, hurt, pathetic, piteous, pitiful
AN OPPOSITE IS comic

**trail** NOUN
1 *The fox followed the trail of its prey.*
► track, footprints, mark, scent, signs, spoor, traces
2 *a nature trail*
► path, pathway, route, track, road
3 *They left a trail of clues.*
► series, string, stream, chain, line

# trail VERB

**1** *The car was trailing a large caravan.*
▸ draw, haul, drag, pull, tow
**2** *His feet were trailing in the water.*
▸ dangle, hang
**3** *She suspected someone was trailing her.*
▸ follow, pursue, shadow, stalk, track, trace, tail, chase
**4** *The smaller children were trailing behind.*
▸ straggle, linger, lag, fall behind, dawdle, dally

# train NOUN

**1** *a strange train of events*
▸ chain, series, sequence, succession
**2** *The minister had a train of attendants.*
▸ entourage, retinue, cortège, following, suite

# train VERB

**1** *Now she had three assistants to train.*
▸ teach, instruct, tutor, coach, educate, prepare
**2** *The team was training hard.*
▸ practise, exercise, prepare yourself, get fit, (*more informal*) work out
**3** *The guns were trained on a position in the hills.*
▸ aim (at), point (at), direct (at), level (at)

# trainee NOUN

*For half price you can have your hair done by a trainee.*
▸ beginner, apprentice, novice, pupil, starter, cadet, student, tiro

# trainer NOUN

*a fitness trainer*
▸ instructor, coach, teacher, tutor, mentor

# training NOUN

*Next week he would report for training.*
▸ exercise, exercises, physical exercise, fitness routine, (*more informal*) working out

# traipse VERB

*She didn't want to traipse round town all afternoon.*
▸ trudge, trek, tramp, trail, plod

# trait NOUN

*This was an unfortunate trait for a prime minister.*
▸ characteristic, quality, attribute, peculiarity, idiosyncrasy, quirk

# traitor NOUN

*Thousands of students denounced Kim as a traitor.*
▸ betrayer, defector, deserter, double-crosser, apostate, blackleg, turncoat, collaborator, informer, quisling, renegade

# tramp NOUN

**1** *the ritual tramp across Ilkley Moor*
▸ trek, trudge, march, walk, (*more informal*) slog
**2** *He remembered an old tramp he used to see by the tube station.*
▸ beggar, vagrant, homeless person, destitute person, (*more informal*) dosser, (*more informal*) down and out

# tramp VERB

*We tramped across the wet grass and bracken.*
▸ trudge, trek, traipse, hike, march, plod, stride, toil

# trample VERB

**trample on** *Her dog had trampled on his tulips.*
▸ tread on, stamp on, walk over, crush, flatten, squash

# trance NOUN

*She was lost in a trance.*
▸ daze, dream, hypnotic state, reverie, daydream, ecstasy, spell

# tranquil ADJECTIVE

**1** *the tranquil and pretty hamlet of Blore*
▸ peaceful, quiet, calm, restful, placid, serene, still, undisturbed, unruffled
OPPOSITES ARE noisy, busy
**2** *He felt relaxed and tranquil.*
▸ calm, placid, sedate, sober, unemotional, unexcited, untroubled, collected, composed, dispassionate, (*more informal*) laid-back
AN OPPOSITE IS excited

# transaction NOUN

*The assets can be purchased or sold in a single transaction.*
▸ deal, agreement, settlement, arrangement, proceeding, undertaking, deed

# transcend VERB

*events that transcended their worst fears*
▸ exceed, surpass, outdo, go beyond, eclipse, outstrip

# transcribe VERB

*The recording had to be transcribed for circulation.*
▸ copy out, write out, take down, put in writing, reproduce

# transcript NOUN

*a transcript of the tapes*
▸ written version, printed version, record, text, reproduction

# transfer VERB (with the stress on -*fer*)

*The books will be transferred to the central library.*
▸ move, remove, shift, relocate, take over, take across, convey, transmit

# transfer NOUN (with the stress on *trans*-)

*the transfer of rights to the new owner*
▸ change, changeover, shift, shifting, handover, transferral, transmission

# transform VERB

*The new owners transformed the property into a lovely family house.*
▸ convert, change, alter, develop, renovate, reorganize, (*more formal*) metamorphose

a
b
c
d
e
f
g
h
i
j
k
l
m
n
o
p
q
r
s
**t**
u
v
w
x
y
z

## transformation NOUN

*There was a transformation in her attitude.*
► change, conversion, alteration, improvement, revolution, transfiguration, transition, (*more formal*) metamorphosis, (*more informal*) turn-about

## transient ADJECTIVE

*a transient change in public opinion*
► transitory, temporary, passing, brief, momentary, fleeting, impermanent, short-term
AN OPPOSITE IS permanent

## transit NOUN

*Some of the goods had been lost in transit.*
► shipment, transportation, passage, conveyance, movement, shipment, travel

## transition NOUN

*the transition from childhood to adulthood*
► change , alteration, changeover, evolution, progress, progression, shift, transformation

## translate VERB

*a poem by Goethe translated into English*
► render, convert, interpret, express, paraphrase, transcribe

## translation NOUN

*an English translation of the Iliad*
► version, rendering, transcription, interpretation, gloss, paraphrase

## transmission NOUN

*The programme was scheduled for transmission after 9 o'clock.*
► broadcast, relaying, diffusion, dissemination, sending out

## transmit VERB

**1** *The broadcast will be transmitted next Saturday.*
► broadcast, relay, send out
**2** *Short-wave radios are used to transmit messages.*
► communicate, convey, dispatch, disseminate, emit, pass on
AN OPPOSITE IS receive

## transparent ADJECTIVE

*a transparent fabric*
► see-through, translucent, diaphanous, clear, sheer, filmy, gauzy, limpid, pellucid

## transpire VERB

**1** *The witnesses explained what had transpired.*
► happen, occur, take place, come about, ensue
**2** *It transpired that Martha had been at home all the time.*
► become known, become evident, become apparent, be discovered, be revealed, be divulged

## transplant VERB

*Transplant the seedlings when they need spreading out.*
► transfer, move, relocate, reposition, shift, uproot

## transport VERB (with the stress on -*port*)

*The larger components will be transported by rail.*
► take, carry, convey, ship, transfer, bring, fetch, haul, move, shift

## transport NOUN (with the stress on *trans-*)

*The village has limited access to public transport.*
► conveyance, haulage, shipping, transportation

**NAMES FOR TYPES OF TRANSPORT**

**road transport:** car, bus, minibus, coach, tram, taxi, lorry, van, bicycle or cycle.

**rail transport:** train, diesel, electric train, express, high-speed train, intercity train, sleeper, freight train or goods train; locomotive, rolling stock, coach, buffet car, dining car, goods van, guard's van, wagon; sleeping car; monorail; main line; branch line; metro, underground or (*informal*) tube; shuttle.

**transport by water:** boat, ship, liner, ferry; tanker, supertanker; barge, narrow boat, gondola; cabin cruiser; motor boat, launch, yacht; catamaran, hovercraft, hydrofoil, raft, dinghy, kayak, canoe, punt.

**air transport:** aircraft, aeroplane or plane, airliner, passenger aircraft, jump jet, jumbo jet, supersonic aircraft; biplane; STOL (short take-off and landing), shuttle (making short journeys back and forth); helicopter; airship; balloon.

## transpose VERB

*Two of the images had been transposed.*
► interchange, switch, reverse, swap, change, exchange, move round, rearrange, substitute, transfer

## transverse ADJECTIVE

*a transverse bar*
► crosswise, horizontal, oblique, diagonal

## trap NOUN

**1** *Some kinds of animal traps are illegal.*
► snare, noose, net, gin
**2** *The cavalry rode straight into a trap.*
► ambush, lure, decoy, ambuscade
**3** *The last question might be a trap.*
► trick, ploy, deception, artifice

## trap VERB

**1** *They had to find a way of trapping the fox before it did any more damage.*
► snare, capture, catch, ensnare, entrap, corner
**2** *The question was designed to trap them.*
► trick, deceive, fool, dupe

## trappings NOUN

*Although a top executive, he spurns the visible trappings of success.*
► finery, accoutrements, adornments, accessories, trimmings, accompaniments, decorations, equipment, fittings, ornaments, paraphernalia

## trash NOUN

**1** *The cleaners shake out your carpets and empty your trash.*
► rubbish, waste, refuse, garbage, litter
**2** *He despised himself for having to write such trash.*
► rubbish, nonsense, drivel, gibberish, junk

## trash VERB

*He went to a phone box but it had been trashed.*
▶ vandalize, wreck, ruin, destroy

## trashy ADJECTIVE

*(informal) a trashy horror movie from the sixties*
▶ inferior, poor-quality, second-rate, rubbishy, worthless

## trauma NOUN

*the trauma of being snatched from her mother*
▶ shock, distress, ordeal, suffering, stress, upset, anguish, upheaval, pain, grief

## traumatic ADJECTIVE

*She talked about her traumatic divorce from Ronnie.*
▶ distressing, stressful, disturbing, shocking, upsetting, hurtful, painful
AN OPPOSITE IS soothing

## travel NOUN

*When he retired he had much more time for travel.*
▶ travelling, touring, tourism, journeying, sightseeing, excursions, globetrotting

## travel VERB

*With this ticket you can travel as many miles as you wish.*
▶ journey, go, ramble, wander, rove, tour, move, proceed, progress

## traveller NOUN

1 *refreshments for the weary traveller*
▶ voyager, passenger, tourist, tripper, holidaymaker, sightseer
2 *ground set aside for travellers' camps*
▶ gypsy, itinerant, nomad

## travelling ADJECTIVE

*travelling tribes*
▶ wandering, itinerant, migrant, vagrant, migratory, nomadic, roaming, roving

## travesty NOUN

*Their claim was a travesty of the facts.*
▶ distortion, misrepresentation, perversion, corruption, parody, mockery, caricature

## treacherous ADJECTIVE

1 *She did not believe him capable of such treacherous behaviour.*
▶ traitorous, disloyal, deceitful, faithless, false, unfaithful, perfidious, double-dealing, duplicitous
AN OPPOSITE IS loyal
2 *There was a mile of deep treacherous water separating him from the mainland.*
▶ dangerous, hazardous, perilous, unsafe, unreliable, deceptive, misleading, risky, shifting, unpredictable, unstable
OPPOSITES ARE safe, reliable

## treachery NOUN

*His resignation from the party would be seen as an act of treachery.*
▶ betrayal, disloyalty, infidelity, perfidy, treason, dishonesty, double-dealing, duplicity, faithlessness, untrustworthiness
AN OPPOSITE IS loyalty

## tread VERB

1 *There is erosion along the route and walkers should tread carefully.*
▶ step, walk, proceed, pace, stride
2 *tread on His father accidentally trod on a model boat he'd been making.*
▶ step on, walk on, trample, crush, squash, stamp on

## tread NOUN

*I heard the familiar tread of Dad's boots on the cobbles.*
▶ footstep, footfall, step, tramp, trudge, plod, stomp

## treason NOUN

*In July 1540 he was beheaded for treason.*
▶ treachery, betrayal, sedition, rebellion, mutiny
OPPOSITES ARE loyalty, allegiance

## treasure NOUN

1 *The treasure sank to the bottom of the sea, along with the ship that held it.*
▶ hoard, cache, jewels, riches, fortune, gold, treasure trove, valuables, wealth
2 *Rosie was a treasure who had brought happiness to the house.*
▶ gem, paragon, angel, prize, star

## treasure VERB

*It's a very special photo and we'll treasure it for ever.*
▶ prize, value, cherish, esteem, guard, keep safe, adore, appreciate, love

## treat NOUN

1 *Add some prawns to the dish for a special treat.*
▶ indulgence, extravagance
2 *She would give the children a birthday treat next year.*
▶ celebration, surprise, entertainment, outing
3 *The ballet is a treat to the eye.*
▶ pleasure, delight, joy, thrill

## treat VERB

1 *They didn't treat her badly, but she was made to feel a nuisance.*
▶ behave towards, deal with, look after, care for, use, serve, attend to
2 *The lectures treat all broad aspects of the subject.*
▶ deal with, discuss, cover, consider, tackle
3 *attempts to treat illness by radiation*
▶ cure, heal, medicate, dress, tend
4 *People tend to treat the videos as entertainment rather than information.*
▶ regard, consider, view
5 *If you like, I'll treat you to a film.*
▶ give, pay for, provide for, entertain

## treatment NOUN

1 *She found it difficult to accept his treatment of her.*
▶ care, handling, management, behaviour (towards), conduct (towards), dealing (with), use
2 *He was responding well to the treatment.*
▶ therapy, medical care, medication, nursing, healing

**3** *The book's treatment of this topic is extremely thorough.*
► coverage, handling, explanation, analysis, discussion

**treaty** NOUN
*The two countries signed a treaty of mutual support.*
► agreement, settlement, pact, deal, entente, alliance, compact, concordat, convention, protocol, understanding

**trek** NOUN
*a long trek through the hills*
► journey, trip, expedition, march, hike, slog, tramp, trudge, walk

**trek** VERB
*They've trekked all over the Greek mainland.*
► hike, tramp, march, journey, walk, slog

**tremble** VERB
**1** *His hands were trembling.*
► shake, shiver, quake, quaver, quiver
**2** *Heavy traffic outside makes the ornaments tremble.*
► vibrate, shake, wobble, shudder, waver

**tremendous** ADJECTIVE
**1** *It had been a tremendous achievement.*
► great, wonderful, marvellous, sensational, stupendous, extraordinary, considerable, significant, immense
OPPOSITES ARE insignificant, trivial
**2** *There was a tremendous crash.*
► terrible, terrific, frightful, awful, fearful, fearsome, alarming, appalling, frightening, horrifying, shocking
OPPOSITES ARE faint, slight

**tremor** NOUN
**1** *There was a tremor in Susan's voice.*
► trembling, quiver, agitation, shaking, hesitation, quavering, vibration
**2** *Tremors were recorded all afternoon.*
► shock, earthquake
RELATED ADJECTIVE seismic

**trend** NOUN
**1** *a downward trend in unemployment*
► tendency, movement, shift, bias, leaning, direction, inclination
**2** *the latest trend in rock music*
► fashion, vogue, craze, rage, mode, style, fad, way

**trendy** ADJECTIVE
*(informal) trendy clothes*
► fashionable, stylish, up-to-date, contemporary, latest, modern, (more informal) cool, (more informal) in
AN OPPOSITE IS unfashionable

**trespasser** NOUN
*The high wall discouraged trespassers.*
► intruder, interloper, poacher

**trial** NOUN
**1** *The trial will last about a month.*
► lawsuit, court case, hearing, tribunal, proceedings, examination
**2** *The latest model is undergoing trials.*
► test, testing, experiment, pilot, try-out
**3** *Such a long meeting was a real trial.*
► ordeal, problem, tribulation, difficulty, trouble, burden, worry, affliction, hardship
**4** *Joan can be a trial at times.*
► nuisance, pest, bother, (more informal) pain

**tribe** NOUN
*nomadic tribes*
► people, race, nation, group, horde, stock, clan

**tribute** NOUN
**1** *Tributes came in from friends and colleagues.*
► praise, accolade, eulogy, testimonial, appreciation, commendation, recognition, compliment, panegyric
**2** *Their eventual success was a tribute to their courage and determination.*
► testimony, evidence (of), proof (of)
**3** *The city had to pay an annual tribute to the king.*
► tax, payment, levy, duty, contribution
**pay tribute to** *She paid tribute to her staff for their hard work.*
► praise, commend, applaud, celebrate, honour, pay homage to, respect

**trick** NOUN
**1** *He entertained the children with conjuring tricks.*
► feat, stunt, illusion, magic
**2** *He saw through every trick she used.*
► ruse, scheme, stratagem, deceit, deception, subterfuge, manœuvre, ploy, pretence, fraud, wile, cheat, (more informal) con
**3** *My favourite trick was to hide above everyone and jump on them. Who else would play a trick like that on me?*
► joke, practical joke, prank, stunt, (informal) leg-pull
**4** *The essential trick is to think backwards and write forwards.*
► knack, secret, skill, device, dodge, technique, art, craft, expertise, gimmick, (informal) know-how

**trick** VERB
*He was furious with himself for being tricked so easily.*
► fool, deceive, cheat, dupe, hoodwink, swindle, trap, outwit, hoax, bluff, mislead, catch out, defraud, (informal) con, (informal) bamboozle

**trickery** NOUN
*The excuses he makes sound like the old trickery.*
► deception, pretence, cheating, chicanery, deceit, mischief, dishonesty, bluffing, fraud, (informal) monkey business, (informal) jiggery-pokery, (informal) shenanigans

**trickle** VERB

*Sweat trickled down his sides despite the cold.*
► drip, dribble, seep, ooze, leak, flow slowly, percolate, run
OPPOSITES ARE pour, gush

**trickle** NOUN

*She saw a trickle of blood flow over her fingers.*
► dribble, seepage, thin stream
OPPOSITES ARE flood, gush

**trickster** NOUN

*I shall reveal you for the sly trickster that you are.*
► cheat, swindler, fraud, fraudster, impostor, charlatan, deceiver, dissembler

**tricky** ADJECTIVE

1 *Tony was a tricky individual.*
► cunning, crafty, wily, artful
2 *Tricky negotiations were taking place.*
► difficult, complicated, awkward, delicate, sensitive

**trifle** NOUN

1 *It cost a mere trifle.*
► small amount, next to nothing, pittance, (*more informal*) peanuts
2 **a trifle** *He looked a trifle embarrassed.*
► a little, a bit, somewhat, a touch, a spot

**trifle** VERB

**trifle with** *You should not trifle with people's feelings.*
► treat lightly, toy with, dally with, fool about with, play about with, behave frivolously towards

**trifling** ADJECTIVE

*We shouldn't bother them with such a trifling matter.*
► trivial, unimportant, insignificant, inconsequential, minor, petty

**trigger** VERB

*The spending cuts triggered many protests.*
► cause, provoke, stimulate, give rise to, lead to, spark off, set off

**trim** VERB

1 *He had trimmed his hair and beard.*
► cut, crop, clip, tidy, shape, shear
2 *The Chancellor will have either to increase taxes or trim his budget.*
► reduce, cut, prune, scale down
3 *The silk curtains were trimmed with gold.*
► decorate, embellish

**trim** ADJECTIVE

1 *a housing estate with trim gardens*
► neat, tidy, orderly, smart, spruce, well-groomed, well-kept
AN OPPOSITE IS untidy
2 *Trousers help to accentuate a trim figure.*
► slim, slender, lean

**trip** NOUN

*He met the czar during a trip to Russia in 1908.*
► journey, visit, voyage, excursion, expedition, holiday, jaunt, outing, tour

**trip** VERB

1 *Angela tripped along in her red mac and hood.*
► run, skip, walk
2 *She tripped over and gashed her knee.*
► stumble, totter, tumble, catch your foot, fall, stagger

**trite** ADJECTIVE

*However trite it may sound, there is joy to be found in a spring day.*
► banal, commonplace, ordinary, hackneyed, clichéd, stale

**triumph** NOUN

1 *He was a key figure in the party's election triumph.*
► victory, win, conquest, (*informal*) walkover
AN OPPOSITE IS defeat
2 *She smiled in triumph.*
► celebration, joy, exultation, jubilation, elation
3 *The visit to Wales had been a triumph.*
► success, accomplishment, achievement, master stroke, (*more informal*) hit

**triumph** VERB

**triumph over** *He had triumphed over disease and misfortune.*
► overcome, defeat, conquer, prevail over, succeed against, be victorious over, win over

**triumphant** ADJECTIVE

1 *The communists emerged triumphant from the revolution.*
► successful, victorious, dominant, conquering, winning
AN OPPOSITE IS unsuccessful
2 *He gave her a knowing, triumphant look.*
► exultant, jubilant, boastful, joyful, elated, gleeful, gloating, immodest, proud
OPPOSITES ARE modest, humble

**trivial** ADJECTIVE

*The offence was regarded as trivial.*
► insignificant, unimportant, inconsequential, minor, trifling, incidental
OPPOSITES ARE important, significant

**troop** NOUN

*A troop of tourists crossed the square.*
► group, party, band, body, company

**troop** VERB

*Rod looked up as Sara and the others trooped in.*
► march, file, flock, parade, straggle

**trophy** NOUN

1 *trophies of war*
► souvenir, memento, reward, spoils, booty, loot
2 *a sports trophy*
► award, cup, medal, prize

**tropical** ADJECTIVE

*tropical areas such as East Africa*
► equatorial, hot, humid, sultry, torrid

**trot** VERB

*Danny trotted into the house.*
► run, scurry, scamper, scuttle, hurry

## trouble NOUN

1 *See what trouble you've caused.*
▶ difficulty, bother, problems, inconvenience, distress, anxiety

2 *He recounted his troubles and asked for advice.*
▶ problem, misfortune, difficulty, tribulation, trial, affliction, suffering, hardship

3 *We took some trouble to help them.*
▶ care, effort, bother, exertion, pains

4 *I hope I wasn't a trouble to you.*
▶ nuisance, bother, irritation

5 *The trouble with these machines is the lack of spare parts.*
▶ problem, difficulty, disadvantage, weakness, failing
OPPOSITES ARE advantage, benefit

6 *There was crowd trouble after the match.*
▶ disturbance, disorder, unrest, conflict, fighting, violence
OPPOSITES ARE order, peace

7 *She suffered from back trouble.*
▶ ailment, disorder, complaint, illness, disability

## trouble VERB

1 *Something was troubling him.*
▶ bother, worry, distress, concern, pain, vex, torment, upset

2 *I'm very sorry to trouble you.*
▶ disturb, interrupt, bother, inconvenience

## troubled ADJECTIVE

1 *Tara looked troubled.*
▶ anxious, worried, bothered, concerned, disturbed, perturbed, uneasy, unhappy, vexed, restless
OPPOSITES ARE untroubled, peaceful

2 *We live in troubled times.*
▶ difficult, unsettled, uncertain

## troublemaker NOUN

*She was branded a troublemaker for complaining about a colleague who harassed her.*
▶ mischief-maker, agitator, rabble-rouser, ringleader, wrongdoer

## troublesome ADJECTIVE

1 *Craig was recovering from a troublesome knee injury.*
▶ annoying, irritating, irksome, tiresome, trying, bothersome, vexing, distressing, inconvenient, upsetting
OPPOSITES ARE trouble-free, harmless

2 *The younger boy was being particularly troublesome.*
▶ badly behaved, naughty, unruly, disobedient, disorderly, uncooperative, rowdy

## trounce VERB

*Essex trounced Cambridgeshire in the final.*
▶ defeat, beat, crush, rout, overwhelm, annihilate

## trousers NOUN

*He was wearing a pair of pale trousers.*
▶ pants, slacks

## truancy NOUN

*We are determined to crack down on truancy.*
▶ absenteeism, malingering, shirking, (more informal) skiving
AN OPPOSITE IS attendance

## truant NOUN

*I was a truant from a Youth Custody Centre.*
▶ absentee, non-attender, runaway, malingerer, shirker, (more informal) skiver
**play truant** *52 percent admitted to playing truant for the odd lesson now and then.*
▶ be absent, stay away, desert, malinger, (more informal) skive off

## truce NOUN

*The enemy broke the truce and resumed the war.*
▶ ceasefire, armistice, moratorium, pact, peace, suspension of hostilities, treaty

## truck NOUN

*The truck was skidding all over the motorway.*
▶ lorry, heavy goods vehicle, juggernaut

## trudge VERB

*Tony and I were trudging through deep snow.*
▶ plod, slog, tramp, clump

## true ADJECTIVE

1 *The story turned out to be true.*
▶ correct, right, accurate, factual, authentic, confirmed, proper, veracious, veritable
OPPOSITES ARE untrue, false

2 *The document was certified as a true copy.*
▶ exact, faithful, genuine, real, actual
AN OPPOSITE IS false

3 *Anne, true friend though she was, would never give in to him.*
▶ loyal, faithful, devoted, firm, constant, sincere, steady, trustworthy, dependable, honest, honourable
OPPOSITES ARE false, unfaithful

4 *He was acting under the authority of the property's true owner.*
▶ legal, legitimate, rightful, authorized, valid

5 *Such studies do not give a true reflection of people's needs.*
▶ accurate, precise, exact, perfect, unerring
AN OPPOSITE IS inaccurate

## truly ADVERB

1 *a truly remarkable woman*
▶ really, absolutely, extremely, very

2 *I'm truly glad for you.*
▶ sincerely, genuinely, honestly

3 *Tell us truly what you think.*
▶ truthfully, frankly, candidly, honestly

## trumpet NOUN

*a part for solo trumpet*
▶ bugle, clarion, cornet
**blow your own trumpet** *He was blowing his own trumpet and promoting his new show.*
▶ boast, brag, sing your own praises, congratulate yourself, show off, swank

## trunk NOUN

1 *A squirrel leapt on a branch and ran up the trunk.*
▶ stem, bole, stock
2 *A slit in his shirt revealed his powerful trunk.*
▶ torso, frame, body
3 *He locked the trunk and stored it in a shed.*
▶ chest, case, coffer, box, crate, suitcase

## trust NOUN

1 *I am grateful to you for your trust.*
▶ confidence, faith, belief, reliance, certainty, credence
2 *She enjoyed a position of trust in the City.*
▶ responsibility, obligation

## trust VERB

1 *He doesn't trust me not to do it again.*
▶ believe in, have confidence in, have faith in, rely on, be sure of, bank on, count on, depend on
2 *We trust they will be here soon.*
▶ hope, expect, presume, suppose, assume, imagine, surmise
AN OPPOSITE IS doubt

## trusting ADJECTIVE

*The trouble with me is I'm too trusting.*
▶ trustful, credulous, gullible, unquestioning, unsuspecting, ingenuous, innocent
OPPOSITES ARE suspicious, cynical

## trustworthy ADJECTIVE

*Harriet was always trustworthy and hard-working.*
▶ reliable, dependable, responsible, honest, upright, steadfast
OPPOSITES ARE untrustworthy, deceitful

## truth NOUN

1 *He doubted the truth of some of these statements.*
▶ veracity, accuracy, validity, truthfulness, correctness, candour, honesty, authenticity, reliability
AN OPPOSITE IS falseness
2 *Elizabeth was telling the truth.*
▶ fact or facts, reality, actuality
3 *an acknowledged truth*
▶ fact, axiom, maxim, certitude, truism
AN OPPOSITE IS lie

## truthful ADJECTIVE

1 *Clive had been less than truthful.*
▶ honest, sincere, candid, frank, reliable, straight, forthright, credible, straightforward, trustworthy, veracious
2 *The truthful answer has to be 'no'.*
▶ proper, right, accurate, correct, true, valid
AN OPPOSITE IS dishonest

## try VERB

1 *Always try to respond positively.*
▶ aim, attempt, endeavour, essay, exert yourself, make an effort, strain, strive, struggle, venture
2 *(informal) Why not try another school?*
▶ check out, evaluate, examine, experiment with, investigate, test, try out, undertake

## try NOUN

*I'll have another try.*
▶ attempt, endeavour, effort, experiment, test, trial, *(more informal)* bash, *(more informal)* go, *(more informal)* shot

## trying ADJECTIVE

1 *This could be quite a trying evening.*
▶ difficult, stressful, taxing, frustrating, troublesome, vexatious
2 *Clare can be very trying.*
▶ annoying, irritating, tiresome, exasperating, infuriating

## tub NOUN

1 *Corbett bathed in the guest house's one and only tub.*
▶ bath, bathtub
2 *a plastic tub of sandwiches*
▶ pot, barrel, drum, cask, keg, vat

## tubby ADJECTIVE

*(informal) A short tubby man was waiting at the front door.*
▶ chubby, podgy, plump, fat, dumpy, rotund, round, overweight, stout, portly, pudgy
OPPOSITES ARE thin, slim, skinny

## tuck VERB

1 *He tucked his shirt into his jeans.*
▶ push, ease, insert, stuff, shove, cram, *(more informal)* pop
2 *tuck into We tucked into plates of fish and chips.*
▶ eat up, consume, devour, gobble up, wolf down

## tuft NOUN

*tufts of grass and weeds*
▶ clump, cluster, bunch, knot, tuffet, tussock

## tug VERB

1 *Lee tugged the rope.*
▶ pull, heave, drag, draw, haul, lug, tow
2 *tug at A little boy tugged at her skirt.*
▶ jerk, pluck, twitch, wrench, yank

## tumble VERB

1 *He let out a yell as he tumbled into the water.*
▶ topple, collapse, pitch, stumble, plummet, drop, fall, flop, trip up
2 *Most of the audience then tumbled out of the room.*
▶ hurry, rush, pile, scramble
3 *Interest rates were set to tumble.*
▶ plunge, fall, drop, dive, slump
OPPOSITES ARE soar, rise
4 *Her long dark hair tumbled down her back.*
▶ flow, fall, cascade

## tumbledown ADJECTIVE

*I demolished a tumbledown shed at the bottom of the garden.*
► ramshackle, dilapidated, rickety, crumbling, decrepit, derelict, ruined

## tumult NOUN

*His voice could not be heard above the tumult.*
► noise, din, commotion, hubbub, clamour, racket, rumpus, uproar

## tumultuous ADJECTIVE

*John Knox returned to a tumultuous welcome.*
► loud, excited, uproarious, boisterous, unrestrained, deafening, passionate, tempestuous, hectic, turbulent, wild
AN OPPOSITE IS restrained

## tune NOUN

*She sang a tune to the baby.*
► melody, song, air, strain, theme

## tune VERB

*A mechanic tuned the engine.*
► adjust, regulate, set, temper

## tuneful ADJECTIVE

*She spoke in a quiet, tuneful voice.*
► musical, melodious, mellifluous, pleasant, sweet, rhythmical, catchy
OPPOSITES ARE tuneless, discordant

## tunnel NOUN

*a tunnel under the Thames*
► underpass, passage, passageway, subway, shaft, gallery

## tunnel VERB

*A dog had tunnelled under the fence.*
► burrow, dig, excavate, mine, penetrate

## turbulent ADJECTIVE

**1** *Her turbulent feelings got the better of her.*
► passionate, excited, violent, volatile, seething, unrestrained

**2** *an increasingly turbulent part of the world*
► unstable, unsettled, troubled, restless, explosive, anarchic
AN OPPOSITE IS peaceful

**3** *The ship was in turbulent waters.*
► rough, stormy, tempestuous, choppy, violent, wild
AN OPPOSITE IS calm

## turgid ADJECTIVE

*A violent episode livened up this otherwise turgid prose.*
► pompous, pretentious, stilted, wordy, affected, bombastic, flowery, fulsome, grandiose, high-flown, overblown
OPPOSITES ARE clear, simple

## turmoil NOUN

*(informal) Her mind was in a state of turmoil.*
► confusion, chaos, disorder, upheaval, turbulence, agitation, disruption, disturbance, mayhem, unrest, upset
OPPOSITES ARE calm, peace

## turn VERB

**1** *The big wheel started to turn.*
► go round, revolve, rotate, whirl, roll

**2** *The gates turned on a set of massive hinges.*
► swivel, hinge

**3** *She turned to return home.*
► change direction, change course, turn round

**4** *The van turned the corner and disappeared.*
► go round, negotiate, take

**5** *The path turned to the right.*
► bend, curve, twist, loop, snake

**6** *Ellie turned pale.*
► become, go, grow

**7** *The house will be turned into luxury apartments.*
► convert, adapt, transform, modify, change, rebuild

**8** *The milk had turned.*
► go off, go sour, curdle

**9** **turn to** *She turned to her neighbour for help.*
► resort to, appeal to, approach, have recourse to, apply to

**turn away** *Reporters were turned away from the house.*
► send away, dismiss, rebuff, reject
AN OPPOSITE IS admit (to)

**turn down** *The panel turned down her application.*
► reject, refuse, decline, dismiss, spurn
AN OPPOSITE IS approve

**turn in**

**1** *I decided to turn in early.*
► go to bed, retire

**2** *He was ordered to turn in his passport.*
► hand in, hand over, surrender, submit

**turn off**

**1** *They had to turn off the motorway.*
► leave, branch off, deviate from
AN OPPOSITE IS join

**2** *She turned off the lights and left the building.*
► switch off, turn out, put out, extinguish
OPPOSITES ARE turn on, switch on

**3** *The violence in the film turned many people off.*
► deter, put off, discourage, disconcert, unnerve, repel, distract
OPPOSITES ARE appeal to, attract

**turn on**

**1** *She turned on the radio.*
► switch on, put on
AN OPPOSITE IS turn off

**2** *Rick always turned her on.*
► excite, arouse, stimulate, titillate
AN OPPOSITE IS turn off

**turn out**

**1** *Her father might well turn her out of the house.*
► throw out, expel, evict, eject, drive out
OPPOSITES ARE admit (to), welcome (to)

**2** *It was a relief that things turned out so well.*
► occur, happen, evolve, develop, end up, come out, work out

3 *Don't forget to turn out the light.*
▶ switch off, turn off, put out, extinguish
OPPOSITES ARE turn on, switch on

**turn over**
1 *The car skidded and turned over.*
▶ overturn, roll over, keel over, capsize
2 *I've been turning it over in my mind.*
▶ consider, ponder, deliberate, think about, weigh up, mull over, chew over

**turn up**
1 *Several guests failed to turn up.*
▶ arrive, appear, put in an appearance
2 *A gardener in Oxfordshire has turned up a hoard of ancient coins.*
▶ discover, unearth, uncover, bring to light, dig up, find
3 *The voices are inaudible unless you turn the sound up.*
▶ increase, raise, amplify

**turn** NOUN
1 *hot water at the turn of a tap*
▶ twist, spin, twirl, whirl, rotation, revolution, circle, cycle
2 *The car came to a turn in the road*
▶ bend, corner, curve, angle, deviation, hairpin bend, junction, loop, twist
3 *an unexpected turn of events*
▶ reversal, shift, change of direction, turning point
4 *It's your turn to speak.*
▶ chance, opportunity, occasion, time, stint, spell
5 *She was trying to do James a good turn.*
▶ favour, support
6 *a comic turn in a concert*
▶ act, performance, show
7 *His sudden appearance gave her quite a turn.*
▶ shock, start, surprise, fright, scare, jolt
**in turn** *The Eastern capital in turn influenced the culture of Venice.*
▶ in succession, successively

**turning** NOUN
*Take the second turning on the right.*
▶ turn-off, turn, exit

**turning point** NOUN
*Their meeting was a turning point in his life.*
▶ watershed, critical moment, landmark, crisis, crossroads, new direction

**turnout** NOUN
*The game attracted a good turnout.*
▶ crowd, attendance, audience, assembly, gate

**turnover** NOUN
*a company with a turnover of over three million*
▶ revenue, throughput, income

**tussle** NOUN
*His glasses were broken in the tussle.*
▶ fight, scuffle, fracas, brawl, struggle, scrap, rumpus, commotion, argument

**tussle** NOUN
*Some of the crowd tussled with police.*
▶ fight, scuffle, brawl, struggle, scrap, come to blows

**tutor** NOUN
*Mr Groves was looking for a tutor for his children.*
▶ teacher, instructor, mentor, coach, educator

**tutor** VERB
*Until two years ago, he had been tutored at home.*
▶ teach, instruct, educate, coach

**tweak** VERB
1 *She tweaked Peter's ear.*
▶ twist, pinch, nip, pull, squeeze
2 *They know how to tweak gadgets.*
▶ adjust, modify, alter, adapt, refine, improve

**tweak** NOUN
*The controls needed a few gentle tweaks.*
▶ adjustment, alteration, modification, refinement

**twee** ADJECTIVE
*(informal) twee little harbours with neat fishing boats*
▶ quaint, sweet, cute, (informal) cutesy

**twiddle** VERB
*Link your fingers in your lap so you're not tempted to twiddle them.*
▶ fiddle with, fidget with, twirl, twist

**twig** VERB
*(informal) I finally twigged where they had come from.*
▶ realize, understand, grasp, comprehend

**twin** ADJECTIVE
*twin towers on the French pattern*
▶ identical, matching, balancing, corresponding, duplicate, paired, similar, symmetrical, indistinguishable

**twin** NOUN
*Fiona drove her own car, the twin of Harry's.*
▶ double, duplicate, clone, match, (more informal) lookalike

**twine** NOUN
*He slowly unrolled the ball of twine.*
▶ string, cord, thread, yarn

**twine** VERB
*All she could do was twine her arms round him.*
▶ wind, wrap, twist, coil

**twinge** NOUN
1 *I was getting sharp twinges in one knee.*
▶ pain, stab, spasm
2 *She felt a twinge of sadness.*
▶ pang, prick, qualm

**twinkle** VERB
*I could see Beverly Hills twinkling in the distance.*
▶ glimmer, glitter, glint, glow, shine, flash, glisten, gleam, sparkle, shimmer

**twinkle** NOUN
*the twinkle of a thousand lights*
▶ sparkle, glimmer, glitter, glint, glow, shimmer

**twirl** VERB
1 *They twirled round the room arm in arm.*
▶ spin, turn, twist, whirl, wheel, gyrate, pirouette, revolve, rotate
2 *He twirled his empty glass in his hands.*
▶ twiddle, twist, play with

## twist VERB

**1** *Huge girders had been twisted in the explosion.*
► crush, buckle, mangle, misshape, deform
**2** *He twisted a strand of her hair round his fingers.*
► coil, curl, wind, entwine, twine
**3** *Twist the cork slowly as you pull it.*
► turn, screw, revolve
**4** *She fell off her bike and twisted her ankle.*
► sprain, wrench, rick
**5** *He accused the newspaper of twisting his words.*
► distort, change, alter, misrepresent, garble, contort, pervert

## twist NOUN

**1** *Give the lid a firm twist.*
► turn, screw, jerk, spin
**2** *a twist in the rope*
► coil, curl, loop, kink, tangle, knot
**3** *a twist in the road*
► bend, turn, zigzag
**4** *There was an unexpected twist to the story.*
► development, surprise, quirk, oddity

## twisted ADJECTIVE

**1** *A mass of twisted metal barred the way.*
► crumpled, buckled, crushed, mangled, distorted, misshapen, deformed, warped
**2** *It seemed to be the product of a twisted mind*
► perverted, depraved, warped, deviant, corrupt

## twit NOUN

*(informal)* *You're an ignorant little twit.*
► fool, idiot, clot, ass, halfwit, dimwit, blockhead, dunderhead, nincompoop

## twitch NOUN

*She suppressed an involuntary twitch of her lip.*
► spasm, jerk, tremor, tic, blink, convulsion, flutter, jump

## twitch VERB

*The bushes twitched again.*
► start, tremble, jerk, jump, fidget, flutter

## two-faced ADJECTIVE

*I consider you have been a two-faced liar.*
► deceitful, insincere, double-dealing, dishonest, duplicitous, hypocritical
OPPOSITES ARE sincere, honest

## tycoon NOUN

*a newspaper advertisement sponsored by an oil tycoon*
► magnate, mogul, industrialist, baron, supremo, big businessman

## type NOUN

**1** *This type of injury could happen to any player at any time.*
► kind, sort, category, class, form, variety, classification, description, designation, genre, group, species
**2** *Footnotes are printed in small type.*
► print, characters, typeface, font, letters

## typhoon NOUN

*aid for victims of the typhoon*
► cyclone, tornado, hurricane, whirlwind

## typical ADJECTIVE

**1** *Decorative carving is a typical feature of late Gothic architecture.*
► characteristic, distinctive, particular, representative, special
OPPOSITES ARE untypical, uncharacteristic
**2** *It had been a fairly typical week.*
► average, ordinary, normal, usual, conventional, orthodox, predictable, standard, unsurprising
OPPOSITES ARE untypical, unusual

**USAGE** There is a slight difference in meaning between *untypical* and *atypical*: *untypical* means 'not typical, unusual', whereas *atypical* means 'not belonging to this type'.

## typify VERB

*The village typifies the beauty of the Lake District.*
► epitomize, exemplify, characterize, embody, represent

## tyrannical ADJECTIVE

*His father is portrayed as a stern, tyrannical disciplinarian.*
► authoritarian, autocratic, despotic, dictatorial, domineering, oppressive, overbearing, cruel, brutal, harsh, imperious, ruthless, severe, tyrannous, unjust
OPPOSITES ARE liberal, tolerant, easygoing

## tyrannize VERB

*He tyrannized his family.*
► dominate, domineer over, oppress, bully, intimidate

## tyranny NOUN

*the injustice, cruelty, and tyranny in the world*
► despotism, autocracy, dictatorship, oppression

## tyrant NOUN

*She was a tyrant to the girls.*
► despot, autocrat, dictator, oppressor, slave-driver

# Uu

## ubiquitous ADJECTIVE

*You can store them in a shoebox or the ubiquitous plastic bag.*
► ever-present, universal, pervasive, widespread
OPPOSITES ARE scarce, rare

## ugly ADJECTIVE

**1** *He may be ugly, but at least he writes good songs.*
► unattractive, unsightly, deformed, repulsive, hideous, plain, grisly, unpleasant, monstrous
AN OPPOSITE IS attractive
**2** *an ugly iron bedstead*
► unsightly, hideous, inelegant, tasteless, unattractive, unpleasant, displeasing, inartistic, plain
AN OPPOSITE IS beautiful

**3** *There were a number of ugly scenes behind the goalposts.*
▶ angry, dangerous, threatening, ominous, unpleasant, sinister, unfriendly, forbidding, hostile, menacing
AN OPPOSITE IS pleasant

**ulterior** ADJECTIVE
*They assumed she had some ulterior motive in coming here.*
▶ hidden, personal, private, covert, concealed, secondary, secret, undeclared, undisclosed
AN OPPOSITE IS overt

**ultimate** ADJECTIVE
*the decline and ultimate disappearance of the city-state*
▶ eventual, final, consequent

**ultimately** ADVERB
*Perhaps these problems will ultimately prove too great.*
▶ eventually, finally, in the end, in the long run, in time

**ultimatum** NOUN
*The ultimatum contained the threat of military force.*
▶ final demand

**umbrage** NOUN
**take umbrage** *He amused them without taking umbrage when they laughed at him.*
▶ take offence, take exception, be offended, be annoyed, be aggrieved, be insulted, bridle

**umpire** NOUN
*They all abided by the umpire's decision.*
▶ referee, adjudicator, arbiter, judge, linesman, arbitrator, moderator, (more informal) ref

**umpteen** ADJECTIVE
(informal) *He had to tell the story umpteen times.*
▶ many, numerous, plenty of, countless, innumerable

**unacceptable** ADJECTIVE
*Public opinion has rejected this strategy as shortsighted and unacceptable.*
▶ intolerable, unsatisfactory, inadmissible, inappropriate, unsuitable, inadequate
OPPOSITES ARE acceptable, satisfactory

**unaccountable** ADJECTIVE
*He could hear an unaccountable noise in front of him.*
▶ inexplicable, unexplainable, incomprehensible, bewildering, puzzling, mystifying
AN OPPOSITE IS explicable

**unaided** ADJECTIVE
*by your own unaided efforts*
▶ single-handed, alone, by yourself, without help, independently

**unambiguous** ADJECTIVE
*an unambiguous response*
▶ definite, categorical, unequivocal, explicit, clear
OPPOSITES ARE ambiguous, unclear

**unanimous** ADJECTIVE
*The resulting decision was unanimous.*
▶ united, harmonious, of one mind

**unarmed** ADJECTIVE
*Troops shot at unarmed civilians.*
▶ defenceless, undefended, weaponless, unprotected, exposed, vulnerable
AN OPPOSITE IS armed

**unassuming** ADJECTIVE
*Sparks was an unassuming and kindly man.*
▶ modest, retiring, humble, self-effacing, unobtrusive

**unattractive** ADJECTIVE
*The existing unattractive shop front would be replaced by a timber one.*
▶ ugly, unsightly, plain, unappealing, uninviting, repulsive, unprepossessing
OPPOSITES ARE attractive, beautiful

**unauthorized** ADJECTIVE
*The train made an unauthorized stop.*
▶ unofficial, irregular, unapproved, abnormal, unsanctioned, illegal, unlawful, unusual
AN OPPOSITE IS authorized

**unavoidable** ADJECTIVE
*Job losses are unavoidable.*
▶ inevitable, inescapable, certain, necessary, obligatory, mandatory
OPPOSITES ARE avoidable, unnecessary

**unaware** ADJECTIVE
*They seemed to be unaware of everything that had happened.*
▶ ignorant, oblivious, unconscious, unmindful, heedless
OPPOSITES ARE aware, conscious

**unbalanced** ADJECTIVE
**1** *We must not give an unbalanced picture.*
▶ unfair, unjust, biased, one-sided, partial, partisan, prejudiced
OPPOSITES ARE balanced, fair

**2** *She said her husband had become unbalanced and capable of doing nasty things.*
▶ unstable, disturbed, deranged, demented, crazy, insane

**3** *The wallpaper pattern looked unbalanced.*
▶ asymmetrical, irregular, uneven, lopsided, off-centre
OPPOSITES ARE balanced, symmetrical

**unbearable** ADJECTIVE
*The pain was unbearable.*
▶ unendurable, intolerable, excruciating, agonizing, insufferable, unmanageable
OPPOSITES ARE bearable, tolerable

**unbeatable** ADJECTIVE
**1** *When in good form the side is unbeatable.*
▶ invincible, unassailable, indestructible, indomitable, unconquerable, matchless, supreme

**2** *As a flavour enhancer, lemon is unbeatable.*
▶ incomparable, unrivalled, unsurpassed, matchless, supreme

**unbelievable** ADJECTIVE

1 *You may find the story bizarre, even unbelievable.*
▶ incredible, improbable, implausible, far-fetched, unconvincing, preposterous
2 *He acted with unbelievable recklessness.*
▶ incredible, unimaginable, inconceivable, unthinkable

**unbend** VERB

1 *Michael tried to unbend the damaged rail.*
▶ straighten, uncurl, untwist
AN OPPOSITE IS bend
2 *We have a few days to unbend and enjoy ourselves.*
▶ relax, rest, unwind, loosen up, (*more informal*) let your hair down

**unbiased** ADJECTIVE

*Every effort is made to obtain an unbiased opinion.*
▶ impartial, objective, dispassionate, neutral, independent
OPPOSITES ARE biased, partial

**unbreakable** ADJECTIVE

*a sheet of unbreakable glass*
▶ toughened, shatter-proof, indestructible, non-breakable, resistant

**unbroken** ADJECTIVE

1 *an unbroken night's sleep*
▶ continuous, uninterrupted, constant
2 *a world record that remains unbroken*
▶ unbeaten, unsurpassed, unequalled, unrivalled

**uncalled-for** ADJECTIVE

*Such strict rules are totally uncalled-for.*
▶ unnecessary, gratuitous, needless, inappropriate, unwarranted, unjustified, unreasonable, unwelcome
OPPOSITES ARE opportune, appropriate

**uncanny** ADJECTIVE

1 *The silence was uncanny.*
▶ eerie, unnatural, weird, creepy, unreal, ghostly, unaccountable
AN OPPOSITE IS normal
2 *He has an uncanny eye for spotting talent.*
▶ unusual, extraordinary, remarkable, exceptional, striking
AN OPPOSITE IS unremarkable

**uncertain** ADJECTIVE

1 *The side effects of the treatment are uncertain.*
▶ unknown, unclear, indefinite, undetermined, unforeseeable, unresolved, undecided, inconclusive, ambiguous, imprecise, indeterminate, speculative
OPPOSITES ARE known, definite
2 *I was uncertain what to say.*
▶ unsure, undecided, doubtful, unconvinced (about), ambivalent (about), dubious (about), hazy (about), wavering (about), in two minds (about)
3 *Workers in the industry face an uncertain future.*
▶ changeable, variable, erratic, unpredictable, unreliable, precarious
AN OPPOSITE IS certain

**uncertainty** NOUN

1 *He tried to disguise his uncertainty.*
▶ doubt, misgiving, apprehension, qualm, hesitation, scruple
OPPOSITES ARE certainty, positiveness
2 *Some degree of uncertainty is bound to ensue.*
▶ unpredictability, unreliability, changeability, risk, danger
OPPOSITES ARE certainty, assurance

**uncivilized** ADJECTIVE

*I am sorry to see such uncivilized behaviour.*
▶ uncouth, primitive, barbaric, rough, boorish, antisocial, barbarous, uncultured, uneducated, unenlightened, unsophisticated, wild
OPPOSITES ARE civilized, respectable

**unclear** ADJECTIVE

1 *The answers are all very unclear.*
▶ vague, obscure, ambiguous, equivocal, puzzling, opaque, cryptic, hazy, imprecise
OPPOSITES ARE clear, straightforward, unambiguous
2 *It was unclear whether the move was backed by the government.*
▶ uncertain, debatable, unsure, unsettled, doubtful, dubious
OPPOSITES ARE clear , obvious

**uncomfortable** ADJECTIVE

1 *The lecture room had uncomfortable plastic chairs.*
▶ hard, cramped, restrictive, stiff, tight, ill-fitting, tight-fitting, lumpy
AN OPPOSITE IS comfortable
2 *Carrying the bike over your shoulder is uncomfortable in the extreme.*
▶ painful, disagreeable, excruciating, inconvenient
3 *British workers felt uncomfortable about the slogans common in Japanese factories.*
▶ uneasy, embarrassed, awkward, troubled, worried, distressed, nervous, restless

**uncommon** ADJECTIVE

*Two or three nights without sleep were not uncommon.*
▶ unusual, infrequent, rare, exceptional, abnormal
OPPOSITES ARE common, usual

**uncomplimentary** ADJECTIVE

*some very uncomplimentary remarks*
▶ disapproving, disparaging, unfavourable, unflattering, depreciatory, censorious, critical, derogatory, pejorative, scathing
AN OPPOSITE IS complimentary

**unconcerned** ADJECTIVE

1 *They seemed unconcerned by our presence.*
▶ unaffected, unmoved, unruffled, indifferent (about), relaxed (about)
2 *She didn't want to appear unconcerned.*
▶ uninterested, indifferent, apathetic, complacent, uncaring

**unconditional** ADJECTIVE

*All four offered their unconditional support.*
▶ unqualified, unrestricted, unlimited, unreserved, unquestioning, total, outright, absolute, complete
AN OPPOSITE IS conditional

**unconnected** ADJECTIVE
*The two events were unconnected. She has since died from causes unconnected with the incident.*
▶ unrelated (to), distinct (from), irrelevant (to), independent, discrete, disparate

**unconscious** ADJECTIVE
**1** *My mother was still unconscious in hospital.*
▶ concussed, knocked out, insensible, senseless, comatose
**2 unconscious of** *He ranted on, unconscious of the danger.*
▶ unaware of, heedless, ignorant of, disregardful of, disregarding, ignoring, impervious to
**3** *He carries with him an unconscious guilt for his little sister's death.*
▶ subconscious, repressed, suppressed, involuntary, latent, subliminal, instinctive

**unconventional** ADJECTIVE
*A wide range of colours can be used to create unconventional patterns.*
▶ unusual, unorthodox, unfamiliar, innovative, original, experimental, individual
OPPOSITES ARE conventional, orthodox

**unconvincing** ADJECTIVE
*They found that an unconvincing explanation. She put on a smile, but it was unconvincing.*
▶ dubious, doubtful, implausible, incredible, strained, forced, feeble, weak

**uncooperative** ADJECTIVE
*The lawyers were proving to be uncooperative.*
▶ unhelpful, disobliging, awkward, obstructive, unaccommodating, inflexible, unwilling
AN OPPOSITE IS cooperative

**uncoordinated** ADJECTIVE
*If the body is used in an uncoordinated fashion, some of the reflexes are not triggered.*
▶ clumsy, awkward, disjointed, lumbering, ungainly
OPPOSITES ARE coordinated, dextrous

**uncouth** ADJECTIVE
*They were rough uncouth men with the air of outcasts.*
◀ coarse, rude, ill-mannered, uncivilized, unrefined
AN OPPOSITE IS refined

**uncover** VERB
**1** *The earth had to be scraped away to uncover a trap door.*
▶ reveal, disclose, expose, lay bare, exhibit, show, strip, unmask, unveil, unwrap
OPPOSITES ARE cover, conceal
**2** *The intention was to uncover the causes of human social behaviour.*
▶ detect, discover, locate, unearth, expose, make known, come across, make public, dig up
OPPOSITES ARE conceal, cover up

**undaunted** ADJECTIVE
*They were undaunted, despite the huge amount of work needed to restore the house.*
▶ undeterred, unbowed, unafraid, resolute, steadfast, intrepid, determined, positive

**undecided** ADJECTIVE
**1** *The question of where to hold the trial remained undecided.*
▶ uncertain, unresolved, undetermined, unsettled, unclear, indefinite
OPPOSITES ARE decided, settled
**2** *She stood undecided in the rain, wanting to find Simon but not daring to step inside.*
▶ hesitant, wavering, indecisive, unsure, uncertain, dithering, in two minds
AN OPPOSITE IS certain

**undeniable** ADJECTIVE
*The undeniable fact is that chlorine is building up in the atmosphere.*
▶ indisputable, irrefutable, unquestionable, incontrovertible, undoubted, proven, certain
OPPOSITES ARE questionable, debatable

**undercover** ADJECTIVE
*Undercover agents are suspected of the assassination.*
▶ secret, covert, clandestine, underground, surreptitious, hidden, furtive

**undercurrent** NOUN
*There was an undercurrent of curiosity surrounding the visit.*
▶ undertone, overtone, suggestion, atmosphere, sense, feeling, trace, hint

**underestimate** VERB
**1** *Radiation fallout was underestimated by 40 times.*
▶ misjudge, miscalculate, set too low
OPPOSITES ARE overestimate, exaggerate
**2** *Sara puzzled him; he had underestimated her.*
▶ underrate, undervalue, misjudge, belittle, disparage, minimize, dismiss
OPPOSITES ARE overestimate, overrate

**undergo** VERB
*He may have to undergo more surgery.*
▶ experience, endure, go through, submit to, be subjected to, put up with, face, bear, suffer, withstand

**underground** ADJECTIVE
**1** *the waters of an underground river*
▶ subterranean, buried, sunken
AN OPPOSITE IS surface
**2** *The two main underground opposition groups have decided to unite.*
▶ secret, clandestine, covert, surreptitious, undercover, unofficial

**undergrowth** NOUN
*There were rustling noises in the undergrowth.*
▶ brush, shrubbery, vegetation, scrub, bushes

**underhand** ADJECTIVE
*He had behaved in a thoroughly sneaky, underhand way.*
▶ deceitful, dishonest, dishonourable, unethical, improper, sly
OPPOSITES ARE honest, open

**underline** VERB
*The killings underlined the need for political talks to resume.*
▶ emphasize, highlight, stress, accentuate, point up
OPPOSITES ARE minimize, play down

**underling** NOUN
*They reckoned the underlings could be trusted to deal with the pudding and dessert.*
▶ subordinate, inferior, junior, minion, menial, flunkey

**underlying** ADJECTIVE
*He took issue with their underlying aims.*
▶ basic, fundamental, essential, intrinsic, principal

**undermine** VERB
*He denied that the change would undermine local democracy.*
▶ weaken, subvert, threaten, compromise, enfeeble, sap, wear away, destroy, ruin
OPPOSITES ARE support, enhance, boost

**underprivileged** ADJECTIVE
*Many children from underprivileged families have been able to join youth clubs.*
▶ needy, deprived, disadvantaged, impoverished, destitute, poor
OPPOSITES ARE privileged, wealthy

**underrate** VERB
*Most of us have a tendency to underrate our own skills.*
▶ underestimate, undervalue, belittle, disparage, minimize, dismiss, misjudge
OPPOSITES ARE overrate, exaggerate

**understand** VERB
**1** *They were unusually quiet, and I could not understand why. He began to understand the story in its full horror.*
▶ comprehend, grasp, perceive, discern, apprehend, fathom, follow, take in
**2** *Do they not understand how much people like me love Morrissey?*
▶ appreciate, realize, recognize, acknowledge
**3** *We understand that the university doesn't have a science park.*
▶ believe, think, suppose, conclude, surmise, fancy

**understanding** NOUN
**1** *Coins can contribute to our understanding of the past.*
▶ knowledge, comprehension, perception, grasp
AN OPPOSITE IS ignorance
**2** *We should look on them with deep understanding.*
▶ compassion, sympathy, feeling, consideration
AN OPPOSITE IS indifference
**3** *My understanding was that there is a three-year guarantee.*
▶ belief, perception, conviction, notion, idea, conclusion
**4** *She is a woman of acute understanding.*
▶ intelligence, intellect, intuition, discernment, judgement
**5** *The various groups had come to an understanding.*
▶ agreement, arrangement, deal, settlement, pact, treaty, entente

**understate** VERB
*The level of complaints received may well understate the scale of the problem.*
▶ play down, underplay, minimize, belittle, make light of, soft-pedal
OPPOSITES ARE overstate, exaggerate

**undertake** VERB
**1** *He undertook to guarantee her son's safety.*
▶ agree, promise, guarantee, pledge, consent
**2** *Some students undertake an industrial placement in their third year.*
▶ begin, commence, embark on, take on, take up, engage in, take responsibility for, manage, handle

**undertaking** NOUN
**1** *Finding a suitable site is a difficult undertaking.*
▶ enterprise, venture, project, operation, endeavour, business, task, affair, scheme
**2** *Booksellers agreed to sign an undertaking not to sell the book.*
▶ agreement, commitment, pledge, assurance

**undertone** NOUN
*Meredith caught a sinister undertone in his words.*
▶ undercurrent, overtone, connotation, association, implication, reverberation, suggestion

**undervalue** VERB
*He seemed to undervalue his own work.*
▶ underestimate, underrate, misjudge, belittle, disparage, minimize, dismiss
OPPOSITES ARE overestimate, overrate

**underwater** ADJECTIVE
*Underwater sonar equipment was used to test for the presence of Nessie.*
▶ undersea, subaquatic, submarine, submerged, immersed

**undesirable** ADJECTIVE
**1** *These undesirable side effects cannot be disregarded.*
▶ unpleasant, unwelcome, unwanted, disagreeable
OPPOSITES ARE desirable, pleasant
**2** *Adam had allowed some undesirable people access to the place.*
▶ nasty, repellent, objectionable, disagreeable, distasteful
OPPOSITES ARE pleasant, agreeable

**undignified** ADJECTIVE
*Getting off the boats was often an undignified scramble.*
▶ unseemly, indecorous, ungainly, inelegant, unbecoming, ignominious
AN OPPOSITE IS dignified

**undisciplined** ADJECTIVE
*An undisciplined cheer went up from the crew members. The Byzantine Greeks were regarded as a brilliant but undisciplined people.*
▶ disorganized, disorderly, chaotic, unruly, intractable, rebellious, uncontrolled, wild, wilful, anarchic, disobedient, unsystematic, untrained
OPPOSITES ARE disciplined, controlled

## undisputed ADJECTIVE
*A few years earlier he had been the undisputed master of the empire.*
▶ undoubted, unchallenged, unquestioned, indubitable, indisputable, incontrovertible
OPPOSITES ARE disputed, doubtful

## undivided ADJECTIVE
*Be prepared to give your undivided attention and listen carefully.*
▶ complete, unqualified, unreserved, unbroken, full, total, whole, absolute
OPPOSITES ARE divided, partial

## undo VERB
1 *She hardly had time to undo her safety belt and get out of the car.*
▶ unfasten, release, untie, unbutton, unlock, unhitch, loosen
OPPOSITES ARE fasten, tie up
2 *Human error undid years of endeavour in a few seconds.*
▶ undermine, subvert, overturn, nullify, scupper, sabotage
3 *A higher court might undo this decision.*
▶ reverse, overturn, revoke, overrule, disallow, rescind, annul

## undoing NOUN
*At this point fear was his undoing.*
▶ ruin, downfall, ruination, destruction, overthrow, weakness, failing

## undoubted ADJECTIVE
*The one undoubted gain has been improved health.*
▶ indisputable, unquestionable, indubitable, incontrovertible, unchallenged

## undoubtedly ADVERB
*There will undoubtedly be things you do well already.*
▶ definitely, doubtless, indubitably, certainly, of course, surely, undeniably, unquestionably
AN OPPOSITE IS possibly

## undress VERB
*The patient has to undress slowly and carefully.*
▶ take off your clothes, strip, disrobe, *(more informal)* peel off
AN OPPOSITE IS dress

## undressed ADJECTIVE
*She was half undressed when the doorbell rang.*
▶ naked, unclothed, disrobed, nude, stripped, bare

## undue ADJECTIVE
*If people are under undue stress, they make mistakes.*
▶ excessive, extreme, unwarranted, unreasonable, disproportionate, unnecessary
OPPOSITES ARE due, appropriate

## unduly ADVERB
*Perhaps you think me unduly harsh to express these things so openly.*
▶ excessively, unreasonably, inordinately, immoderately, unnecessarily

## unearth VERB
*They have done all they can to unearth the truth.*
▶ uncover, detect, discover, expose, make known, make public, dig up
OPPOSITES ARE conceal, cover up

## unearthly ADJECTIVE
1 *She was a lady of unearthly beauty.*
▶ eerie, uncanny, strange, supernatural, otherworldly, weird
OPPOSITES ARE ordinary, mundane
2 *(informal) I had a job that involved getting up at an unearthly hour.*
▶ unreasonable, abnormal, unusual, *(informal)* ungodly
OPPOSITES ARE reasonable, comfortable

## uneasy ADJECTIVE
1 *The uneasy peace lasted a few months.*
▶ precarious, insecure, unsettled
AN OPPOSITE IS comfortable
2 *Moore was uneasy about the coat.*
▶ anxious, nervous, apprehensive, troubled, worried, concerned, fearful, jittery
AN OPPOSITE IS confident
3 *There was an uneasy atmosphere in the room.*
▶ tense, awkward, fraught, strained, edgy, uncomfortable

## uneducated ADJECTIVE
*The superstition was by no means confined to uneducated people.*
▶ ill-educated, untaught, ignorant, ill-informed, uninformed, uncultured, unsophisticated
OPPOSITES ARE educated, learned

## unemployed ADJECTIVE
*I don't know what his job is; is he unemployed at the moment?*
▶ out of work, jobless, on the dole, not working, redundant
OPPOSITES ARE employed, working, in work

## unending ADJECTIVE
*Her work seemed to be unending.*
▶ endless, interminable, never-ending, everlasting, unceasing, incessant

## unenthusiastic ADJECTIVE
*He was distinctly unenthusiastic about the idea.*
▶ indifferent, apathetic, half-hearted, lukewarm

## unenviable ADJECTIVE
*The job of being a project leader is an unenviable one.*
▶ unpleasant, disagreeable, undesirable, unwelcome, thankless

## unequal ADJECTIVE
1 *The chair had four legs of unequal length.*
▶ different, differing, varying, uneven, dissimilar, disparate
AN OPPOSITE IS equal
2 *the unequal distribution of power and resources in society*
▶ unfair, unjust, inequitable, disproportionate
OPPOSITES ARE fair, equitable

**3** *Should I give up the unequal struggle?*
▶ unbalanced, uneven, unfair, ill-matched, one-sided
OPPOSITES ARE equal, well-balanced

**4 unequal to** *Melanie felt unequal to the task she had been given.*
▶ inadequate for, incapable of, unqualified for, not up to, (*more informal*) not cut out for

**unequalled** ADJECTIVE
*Gregory of Tours provides evidence of unequalled richness.*
▶ incomparable, unmatched, unparalleled, unrivalled, unsurpassed, inimitable, supreme, matchless, peerless

**unequivocal** ADJECTIVE
*His answer was a swift and unequivocal 'no'.*
▶ definite, clear, unambiguous, categorical, explicit
OPPOSITES ARE ambiguous, unclear

**uneven** ADJECTIVE
**1** *Be careful when wheeling a trolley over uneven ground.*
▶ bumpy, rough, rutted, undulating, bent, broken, crooked, irregular, jagged, jerky, pitted, wavy
AN OPPOSITE IS smooth
**2** *The demand for electricity is uneven throughout the day.*
▶ inconsistent, variable, spasmodic, unpredictable, varying, erratic, fitful, fluctuating
AN OPPOSITE IS consistent.
**3** *Uneven steps led down to a rocky cove.*
▶ irregular, unsteady, lopsided, unbalanced
**4** *He soon gave up the uneven contest.*
▶ unequal, unfair, ill-matched, one-sided, unbalanced
AN OPPOSITE IS balanced

**uneventful** ADJECTIVE
*Annie led a quiet, uneventful life.*
▶ dull, monotonous, unexciting, uninteresting, tedious, humdrum
OPPOSITES ARE eventful, exciting

**unexceptional** ADJECTIVE
*Most of the music is functional and unexceptional.*
▶ ordinary, routine, average, typical, undistinguished, unremarkable, uninteresting
OPPOSITES ARE exceptional, remarkable

**unexpected** ADJECTIVE
*An unexpected error had occurred.*
▶ unforeseen, accidental, unpredictable, chance, fortuitous, sudden, surprising, unhoped for, unlooked for, unplanned, unusual
OPPOSITES ARE expected, predictable

**unfair** ADJECTIVE
**1** *It was so unfair that she could never see him.*
▶ unjust, unreasonable, inequitable
OPPOSITES ARE fair, just

**2** *It seemed to Watson a cruel, unfair remark. He claims I have unfair advantages.*
▶ undeserved, unwarranted, uncalled-for, unreasonable, unjustified
OPPOSITES ARE fair, justified

**3** *The law was placing an unfair burden on small businesses.*
▶ unreasonable, discriminatory
OPPOSITES ARE reasonable, legitimate

**4** *The rules relating to unfair play need to be tightened up.*
▶ illegal, unsporting, dishonourable, illegitimate
OPPOSITES ARE fair, honourable

**unfaithful** ADJECTIVE
*He could not deny that he had been an unfaithful husband.*
▶ adulterous, disloyal, untrustworthy, deceitful, duplicitous, faithless
OPPOSITES ARE faithful, loyal

**unfamiliar** ADJECTIVE
*An unfamiliar smell was drifting from the flat.*
▶ strange, unusual, curious, novel, different

**unfashionable** ADJECTIVE
*Now they were unfashionable, maybe it would be OK to get a personal organizer.*
▶ old-fashioned, outmoded, out of date, passé, obsolete
OPPOSITES ARE fashionable, trendy

**unfavourable** ADJECTIVE
**1** *A new head would face unfavourable comparison with his predecessor.*
▶ critical, hostile, unfriendly, adverse, negative, uncomplimentary, unsympathetic
OPPOSITES ARE favourable, positive
**2** *A high cost of living and unfavourable exchange rates ate into their holiday funds.*
▶ bad, adverse, unsatisfactory, undesirable, unenviable
OPPOSITES ARE favourable, advantageous

**unfeeling** ADJECTIVE
*He smiled, but it was a cool, unfeeling smile.*
▶ insensitive, heartless, hard-hearted, callous, uncaring
OPPOSITES ARE sensitive, sympathetic

**unfinished** ADJECTIVE
*The work remained unfinished on his death.*
▶ incomplete, uncompleted, imperfect, rough, sketchy, unpolished
AN OPPOSITE IS complete

**unfit** ADJECTIVE
**1** *The house was rapidly becoming unfit for habitation. They were unfit to pass judgement on modern architecture.*
▶ unsuited, ill-equipped, inadequate, unsatisfactory, useless, incapable (of)
**2** *Kevin was also unfit, leaving the defence weakened.*
▶ out of condition, out of shape, unhealthy, feeble
OPPOSITES ARE fit, healthy

## unfold VERB

**1** *Mick unfolded the space blanket.*
▶ open out, spread out, straighten out, unfurl
AN OPPOSITE IS fold up

**2** *Come and see history unfold before your eyes.*
▶ happen, evolve, develop, take place, progress, emerge

## unforeseen ADJECTIVE

*Many of the long-term results were unforeseen.*
▶ unexpected, unpredicted, unthought of, surprising, unanticipated
OPPOSITES ARE foreseen, predictable

## unforgettable ADJECTIVE

*The recreation park will provide hours of fun and an unforgettable experience.*
▶ memorable, striking, noteworthy, remarkable, impressive, distinctive
OPPOSITES ARE forgettable, unexceptional

## unforgivable ADJECTIVE

*Losing your temper with him was unforgivable.*
▶ inexcusable, reprehensible, shameful, unjustifiable, unpardonable, unwarrantable
AN OPPOSITE IS forgivable

## unfortunate ADJECTIVE

**1** *Some of these unfortunate prisoners were later found to be innocent.*
▶ unlucky, hapless, wretched, poor, unhappy, ill-fated, luckless

**2** *The incident led to the most unfortunate disagreement between the Allies.*
▶ disastrous, disadvantageous, unwelcome, inopportune, harmful, regrettable, lamentable, deplorable

**3** *He said it would be most unfortunate if one year's results were regarded as typical.*
▶ regrettable, inappropriate, unsuitable

## unfounded ADJECTIVE

*We now realize that these claims are totally unfounded.*
▶ groundless, baseless, unsupported, unsubstantiated, unjustified, spurious

## unfriendly ADJECTIVE

*He glowered back in an unfriendly manner.*
▶ hostile, aggressive, disagreeable, unpleasant, antagonistic, unsociable, standoffish, aloof
OPPOSITES ARE friendly, amiable

## ungainly ADJECTIVE

*A kangaroo must use a lot of energy in its lopsided and ungainly walk.*
▶ awkward, clumsy, ungraceful, graceless, inelegant
OPPOSITES ARE elegant, graceful

## ungrateful ADJECTIVE

*I'm going to seem so ungrateful if I refuse the offer.*
▶ unappreciative, unthankful, ungracious, ill-mannered, selfish
OPPOSITES ARE grateful, thankful

## unhappy ADJECTIVE

**1** *Her absence made Thomas unhappy.*
▶ sad, sorrowful, melancholy, miserable, dejected, despondent, dispirited, depressed
OPPOSITES ARE happy, pleased

**2** *One person at least had benefited from these unhappy events.*
▶ unlucky, unfortunate, luckless, ill-fated
AN OPPOSITE IS fortunate

**3** *Clearly it has been an unhappy compromise.*
▶ inappropriate, unsuitable, inapt, unsatisfactory, unfortunate
OPPOSITES ARE happy, satisfactory

**4** *Graham was very unhappy with his performance.*
▶ dissatisfied, disappointed, displeased, discontented

## unharmed ADJECTIVE

*Almost all the population seem to have escaped unharmed.*
▶ safe, safe and sound, uninjured, unhurt, unscathed, intact
OPPOSITES ARE harmed, injured

## unhealthy ADJECTIVE

**1** *He was looking tired and unhealthy.*
▶ sickly, ill-looking, ailing, unwell, poorly, frail, weak
OPPOSITES ARE healthy, well

**2** *They lived in an unhealthy environment.*
▶ insalubrious, dirty, insanitary, polluted, unhygienic, unwholesome
OPPOSITES ARE healthy, salubrious

**3** *As a nurse I knew it was unhealthy to be so overweight.*
▶ harmful, unnatural, deleterious
AN OPPOSITE IS healthy

## unheard of ADJECTIVE

*It was unheard of in those days for anyone to get so much money.*
▶ unprecedented, inconceivable, unimaginable, exceptional, extraordinary, unusual, uncommon
AN OPPOSITE IS common

## unhelpful ADJECTIVE

*The bank cashier had been unhelpful.*
▶ uncooperative, disobliging, inconsiderate, uncivil, unwilling, negative, slow
OPPOSITES ARE helpful, obliging

## unidentified ADJECTIVE

*An unidentified vandal drew a Hitler moustache on the portrait.*
▶ unknown, unnamed, nameless, unrecognized, unspecified, anonymous, incognito, unfamiliar
OPPOSITES ARE identified, known, named

## uniform ADJECTIVE

*A thermostat will maintain a uniform temperature.*
▶ regular, consistent, unvarying, homogeneous, identical, indistinguishable, similar, single
OPPOSITES ARE varying, inconsistent

## uniform NOUN

*He had never worn a uniform in his life.*
▶ outfit, livery, regalia, costume

## unify VERB

*He was concerned to unify the country.*
▶ unite, integrate, harmonize, bring together, combine, consolidate, amalgamate, bind, fuse, join, merge, weld together
OPPOSITES ARE divide, separate, split

## unimaginable ADJECTIVE

*He was motivated by the promise of unimaginable rewards.*
▶ inconceivable, unbelievable, incredible, unthinkable, unheard of, untold, mind-boggling

## unimaginative ADJECTIVE

*The drawings were flat and unimaginative.*
▶ boring, dull, uninspired, uncreative, uninventive, uninteresting, unexciting, unoriginal, pedestrian, prosaic, stale, trite, banal, derivative, ordinary
OPPOSITES ARE imaginative, creative

## unimportant ADJECTIVE

*The size of the power supply is unimportant.*
▶ insignificant, inconsequential, immaterial, irrelevant, trivial, trifling, minor, of no account, of no consequence, of no moment
AN OPPOSITE IS important

## uninhabited ADJECTIVE

*The centre of the island is vast and uninhabited.*
▶ empty, unoccupied, unpeopled, unsettled, deserted, depopulated, uncolonized, vacant
AN OPPOSITE IS inhabited

## uninhibited ADJECTIVE

1 *He shared her uninhibited sense of humour and fun.*
▶ unrestrained, unconstrained, spontaneous, unrepressed, abandoned, impetuous, carefree, reckless
AN OPPOSITE IS inhibited

2 *She's a lively and uninhibited girl.*
▶ unselfconscious, unreserved, unrestrained, liberated, relaxed, informal

## unintelligible ADJECTIVE

*The conversation was unintelligible to Gina.*
▶ incomprehensible, incoherent, unfathomable, baffling, perplexing, obscure, cryptic, opaque, mysterious, confusing, inscrutable, enigmatic
OPPOSITES ARE intelligible, comprehensible

## unintentional ADJECTIVE

*Sometimes the harassment may be unintentional.*
▶ unintended, inadvertent, accidental, involuntary, unconscious, unplanned, unwitting, fortuitous
AN OPPOSITE IS intentional

## uninterested ADJECTIVE

**uninterested in** *He was uninterested in politics.*
▶ indifferent to, unconcerned about, uninvolved in, incurious about, apathetic about, bored by, unenthusiastic about, unresponsive to
AN OPPOSITE IS interested

## uninteresting ADJECTIVE

*She was struggling through an uninteresting article on cosmetics.*
▶ dull, boring, unexciting, tedious, dreary, monotonous, humdrum, uninspiring, vapid, wearisome
AN OPPOSITE IS interesting

## uninterrupted ADJECTIVE

*A few extra hours of uninterrupted sleep can remedy the situation.*
▶ continuous, unbroken, undisturbed, constant, sustained, consecutive
OPPOSITES ARE interrupted, intermittent, broken

## union NOUN

1 *A union was formed to fight the war with Persia.*
▶ alliance, coalition, league, federation, confederation, confederacy

2 *The company was formed from the union of three smaller firms.*
▶ merger, merging, amalgamation, fusion, combination, unification, uniting, joining

## unique ADJECTIVE

1 *Each file has got a unique name.*
▶ distinctive, special, individual, peculiar, single, singular, (*more informal*) one-off
AN OPPOSITE IS common

2 *The production was a unique opportunity to hear the music in its original form.*
▶ remarkable, outstanding, incomparable, extraordinary, unparalleled, unprecedented, unusual
AN OPPOSITE IS unremarkable

## unit NOUN

*The family is a fundamental unit of society.*
▶ component, constituent, element, entity, item, portion, section, segment

## unite VERB

1 *They tried to unite the population in a common war effort against the English.*
▶ unify, integrate, combine, bring together, bind, join
AN OPPOSITE IS divide

2 *Police and publicans united to solve the problem.*
▶ combine, join forces, cooperate, collaborate

3 *Mother and son were united after the war.*
▶ bring together, join

## united ADJECTIVE

*the potential power of a united Germany*
▶ unified, integrated, merged, amalgamated, combined
AN OPPOSITE IS disunited

**be united** *They were united on this one issue.*
▶ agree, be in agreement, be in accord, be unanimous, be of the same mind, have the same opinion
OPPOSITES ARE be disunited, disagree

## unity NOUN

**1** *Creating national unity is a fundamental task for our people.*
▶ agreement, harmony, accord, consensus, concord
OPPOSITES ARE discord, disagreement

**2** *the issue of European unity*
▶ union, unification, federation
OPPOSITES ARE division, disunity

## universal ADJECTIVE

*A sudden fall in house prices is a universal fear.*
▶ common, general, ubiquitous, widespread, worldwide, global, all-embracing, all-round
OPPOSITES ARE restricted, local

## unjust ADJECTIVE

**1** *She was still smarting from her unjust dismissal.*
▶ unfair, unjustified, undeserved, unmerited, unreasonable, unwarranted, unlawful, wrong, wrongful, indefensible, inequitable
OPPOSITES ARE just, justified

**2** *The report was widely criticized for being unjust.*
▶ unfair, biased, one-sided, partial, partisan, prejudiced, bigoted
OPPOSITES ARE just, fair, balanced

## unjustifiable ADJECTIVE

*Some might consider it an unjustifiable expense.*
▶ unreasonable, unwarrantable, indefensible, inexcusable, unacceptable, unforgivable, excessive, immoderate
OPPOSITES ARE justifiable, acceptable

## unkempt ADJECTIVE

*He had long unkempt hair and several missing teeth.*
▶ untidy, messy, scruffy, dishevelled, disordered, rumpled, bedraggled
OPPOSITES ARE tidy, neat, well-groomed

## unkind ADJECTIVE

*He says unkind things that cause her pain.*
▶ cruel, thoughtless, unfeeling, callous, uncharitable, unpleasant, inconsiderate, unfriendly, malicious, malevolent, spiteful, harsh
OPPOSITES ARE kind, considerate

## unknown ADJECTIVE

**1** *Some of the civilians were transferred to unknown destinations. For some unknown reason, the blinds were always drawn. The date of their marriage is unknown.*
▶ unspecified, unidentified, unnamed, undisclosed, mysterious, strange, unrecognized, anonymous, nameless
AN OPPOSITE IS named

**2** *Lowell began a search for this unknown planet.*
▶ undiscovered, unfamiliar, unexplored, unmapped, uncharted, alien, foreign
AN OPPOSITE IS familiar

**3** *The part was taken by the then unknown Maria.*
▶ unheard-of, obscure, little known, undistinguished, lowly, inconsequential, insignificant, unimportant
AN OPPOSITE IS famous

## unlawful ADJECTIVE

*It was unlawful for any foreigner to enter the temple.*
▶ forbidden, prohibited, unauthorized, illegal, banned, outlawed
OPPOSITES ARE lawful, allowed

## unlikely ADJECTIVE

**1** *It is unlikely that they will attend, being so busy.*
▶ doubtful, improbable, dubious
AN OPPOSITE IS likely

**2** *They would hardly believe such an unlikely explanation.*
▶ implausible, improbable, far-fetched, incredible, suspect, suspicious, dubious, questionable, unbelievable, unconvincing
AN OPPOSITE IS likely

## unlimited ADJECTIVE

**1** *The President emphasized that the USA did not have unlimited funds.*
▶ limitless, inexhaustible, infinite, unbounded, boundless, bottomless
OPPOSITES ARE limited, finite

**2** *All parts carry a 12-month unlimited mileage warranty.*
▶ unrestricted, unqualified, unconditional, open, unhindered, clear
OPPOSITES ARE limited, restricted

## unload VERB

**1** *Unload the box of essential items first.*
▶ remove, take off, offload, drop off, unpack, discharge
AN OPPOSITE IS load

**2** *About thirty men would be needed to unload the ship.*
▶ unpack, empty, unburden

## unlock VERB

*He took the keys from his pocket and unlocked the boot.*
▶ open, release, unfasten, undo
OPPOSITES ARE lock, fasten

## unloved ADJECTIVE

*As a child I felt very unloved.*
▶ uncared-for, unwanted, neglected, rejected, spurned, friendless, forsaken, unpopular, uncherished, unvalued
AN OPPOSITE IS loved

## unlucky ADJECTIVE

**1** *You could be ruined as a result of some unlucky accident.*
▶ chance, untimely, unfortunate, unintended, disastrous, ominous, dreadful, tragic, calamitous, unwelcome
OPPOSITES ARE lucky, timely, fortunate

**2** *Miss Hill was unlucky not to get a medal. Phil was again unlucky with injuries.*
▶ unfortunate, hapless, luckless, unhappy, unsuccessful, wretched
OPPOSITES ARE lucky, fortunate

**3** *The 13th proved to be unlucky for one American skier.*
▶ inauspicious, ominous, unfavourable, jinxed, cursed, ill-fated, ill-omened, ill-starred
OPPOSITES ARE lucky, auspicious

A
B
C
D
E
F
G
H
I
J
K
L
M
N
O
P
Q
R
S
T
**U**
V
W
X
Y
Z

**unmistakable** ADJECTIVE
*Then came the unmistakable sound of a shot.*
▶ distinct, distinctive, clear, plain, obvious, unambiguous, telltale
OPPOSITES ARE uncertain, unclear

**unmitigated** ADJECTIVE
*an unmitigated disaster*
▶ absolute, complete, total, utter, unqualified, outright
OPPOSITES ARE qualified, partial

**unnatural** ADJECTIVE
**1** *It was an unnatural crime: was the man mad? He was uneasy in this unnatural silence.*
▶ abnormal, unusual, uncanny, weird, bizarre, strange, odd, unaccountable, inexplicable, extraordinary
AN OPPOSITE IS normal

**2** *Her voice sounded unnatural.*
▶ affected, self-conscious, mannered, stilted, theatrical, unspontaneous, feigned, (more informal) put on
OPPOSITES ARE natural, normal

**3** *The white fur looked unnatural.*
▶ artificial, fabricated, imitation, man-made, manufactured, simulated, synthetic
OPPOSITES ARE natural, genuine

**unnecessary** ADJECTIVE
**1** *Don't let's take any unnecessary risks.*
▶ inessential, non-essential, needless, uncalled-for, unjustified, unneeded, unwanted, excessive, extra
OPPOSITES ARE necessary, essential

**2** *A deposit is unnecessary with this order.*
▶ superfluous, dispensable, redundant
OPPOSITES ARE necessary, obligatory

**unofficial** ADJECTIVE
**1** *She acted as an unofficial bank, cashing cheques for customers.*
▶ informal, casual, private, personal, unauthorized
OPPOSITES ARE official, formal

**2** *Unofficial figures put the dead and wounded at over 300.*
▶ unconfirmed, unauthenticated, unsubstantiated
OPPOSITES ARE official, confirmed

**unorthodox** ADJECTIVE
*A former pupil remembers his unorthodox teaching methods.*
▶ unconventional, unusual, radical, irregular, novel, idiosyncratic, bizarre
OPPOSITES ARE orthodox, conventional

**unpaid** ADJECTIVE
**1** *There were unpaid bills spread all over the table.*
▶ outstanding, overdue, unsettled, owing, due
OPPOSITES ARE paid, settled

**2** *Some staff also did unpaid charity work.*
▶ voluntary, unremunerative
OPPOSITES ARE paid, professional

**unpleasant** ADJECTIVE
**1** *It reminded him of an earlier unpleasant experience.*
▶ disagreeable, distressing, distasteful, nasty, horrible, horrid, uncomfortable
OPPOSITES ARE pleasant, agreeable

**2** *They were the most unpleasant people I had ever met.*
▶ unlikable, disagreeable, objectionable, unattractive, unfriendly, obnoxious, repugnant, repulsive, revolting, repellent, ill-natured
OPPOSITES ARE friendly, agreeable

**3** *substances that give rise to unpleasant odours*
▶ repulsive, revolting, unappealing
OPPOSITES ARE pleasant, appealing

**unpopular** ADJECTIVE
**1** *The tax proved deeply unpopular and was later abolished.*
▶ hated, disliked, detested, unwelcome, unwanted, rejected, despised
AN OPPOSITE IS popular

**2** *He was unpopular at school.*
▶ disliked, friendless, unliked, shunned
AN OPPOSITE IS popular

**unprecedented** ADJECTIVE
*an unprecedented growth in small businesses*
▶ exceptional, extraordinary, abnormal, unequalled, unrivalled, extreme, unusual
AN OPPOSITE IS normal

**unpredictable** ADJECTIVE
**1** *The weather is unpredictable in the hills.*
▶ changeable, variable, erratic, uncertain, unreliable, unforeseeable, unexpected
AN OPPOSITE IS predictable

**2** *She was unpredictable and likely to say anything.*
▶ unreliable, fickle, erratic, volatile, capricious, moody, unstable
AN OPPOSITE IS predictable

**unprepared** ADJECTIVE
*unprepared for They were often inexperienced and unprepared for the demands of the work.*
▶ ill-equipped for, unqualified for, unready for, surprised by, caught out by

**unpretentious** ADJECTIVE
**1** *The exterior of the house is very simple and unpretentious.*
▶ plain, simple, ordinary, unostentatious, straightforward
OPPOSITES ARE pretentious, elaborate

**2** *He was a friendly and unpretentious man.*
▶ modest, unassuming, unaffected, humble
OPPOSITES ARE pretentious, vain

**unproductive** ADJECTIVE
**1** *His lands were not encumbered by a costly and unproductive bureaucracy.*
▶ ineffective, worthless, unprofitable, useless, fruitless, futile, pointless, unrewarding, valueless
AN OPPOSITE IS productive

**2** *The land is unproductive for much of the year. The rest of the week was equally unproductive.*
▶ unfruitful, barren, infertile, sterile, arid
AN OPPOSITE IS productive

## unprofessional ADJECTIVE

1 *The work was sloppy and unprofessional.*
▶ amateurish, inexpert, unskilled, incompetent, inefficient, irresponsible
OPPOSITES ARE professional, skilful

2 *We wouldn't like to be accused of unprofessional conduct.*
▶ improper, unethical, unprincipled, unscrupulous, lax, incompetent, unworthy
AN OPPOSITE IS professional

## unprofitable ADJECTIVE

*Airlines will start pulling out of unprofitable routes.*
▶ unproductive, uneconomic, loss-making, uncommercial, unremunerative, unrewarding
AN OPPOSITE IS profitable

## unqualified ADJECTIVE

1 *Too many nursing lectures are given by unqualified lecturers.*
▶ untrained, inexperienced, incapable, incompetent, unsuitable, ineligible
OPPOSITES ARE qualified, competent

2 *The experiment was an unqualified success.*
▶ absolute, unreserved, complete, outright, total, utter, unmitigated
OPPOSITES ARE qualified, partial

## unravel VERB

1 *He cut the climbing rope and started to unravel its strands.*
▶ disentangle, untangle, unwind, untwist, undo, separate
AN OPPOSITE IS entangle

2 *the sequence of events that archaeologists attempt to unravel*
▶ resolve, sort out, solve, puzzle out, interpret, explain, elucidate, clarify

## unreal ADJECTIVE

*It is a curiously unreal state of affairs.*
▶ false, artificial, fake, sham, illusory, imaginary
OPPOSITES ARE real, genuine

## unrealistic ADJECTIVE

*It would be unrealistic to think of removing road congestion entirely.*
▶ impractical, unreasonable, unworkable, fanciful, impracticable, over-ambitious, idealistic, impossible
OPPOSITES ARE realistic, practical, pragmatic

## unreasonable ADJECTIVE

1 *I knew I was being unreasonable.*
▶ unfair, unjust, unhelpful, uncooperative, obstructive
OPPOSITES ARE reasonable, helpful, fair

2 *It was unreasonable of him to expect her to know the answer.*
▶ irrational, illogical, perverse, unwarranted, absurd
OPPOSITES ARE reasonable, sensible

3 *They were making unreasonable demands.*
▶ excessive, immoderate, exorbitant, extortionate
OPPOSITES ARE reasonable, moderate

## unrecognizable ADJECTIVE

*He's unrecognizable as the boy we once knew.*
▶ unidentifiable, unknowable, changed (from), altered (from)
AN OPPOSITE IS recognizable

## unrelated ADJECTIVE

1 *Two men had been charged after the match in unrelated incidents.*
▶ separate, distinct, unconnected

2 *He was assigned to a menial post unrelated to his abilities.*
▶ irrelevant, unconnected (with), dissimilar

## unrelenting ADJECTIVE

*Success came through unrelenting hard work.*
▶ constant, continuous, relentless, remorseless, persistent, unremitting, unflagging, merciless, ruthless
AN OPPOSITE IS intermittent

## unreliable ADJECTIVE

1 *The official figures are unreliable for gauging levels of unemployment.*
▶ inaccurate, misleading, deceptive, suspect, false, implausible, unconvincing
OPPOSITES ARE reliable, accurate

2 *The more he defended himself, the more unreliable he sounded.*
▶ untrustworthy, irresponsible, undependable, changeable, inconsistent, unpredictable, unsound, unstable, fallible, fickle
OPPOSITES ARE reliable, dependable

## unrepentant ADJECTIVE

*He remains unrepentant about his comments last week.*
▶ unapologetic, unashamed, impenitent, unrepenting, unabashed, shameless, hardened
AN OPPOSITE IS repentant

## unreserved ADJECTIVE

*Clara admired the results with unreserved satisfaction.*
▶ absolute, unqualified, complete, wholehearted, outright, total, utter, unmitigated
OPPOSITES ARE qualified, partial

## unrest NOUN

*There was Jacobite unrest throughout much of England.*
▶ rebellion, disorder, agitation, disturbance, disruption, upheaval, tumult, insurrection
OPPOSITES ARE order, peace

## unrestricted ADJECTIVE

*The public has unrestricted access to the gardens during daylight hours.*
▶ unlimited, open, unhindered, clear, unqualified, unconditional
OPPOSITES ARE limited, restricted

## unrivalled ADJECTIVE

*From the hotel you look out on unrivalled views of Venice.*
▶ incomparable, unequalled, unmatched, unparalleled, unsurpassed, inimitable, supreme, matchless, peerless

**unruffled** ADJECTIVE

*Matthew's unruffled manner had evidently soothed them.*
▶ calm, composed, collected, self-possessed, cool, poised, unperturbed, unflustered, unbothered, untroubled, (*more informal*) unflappable, (*more informal*) laid-back
OPPOSITES ARE excited, anxious, upset

**unruly** ADJECTIVE

*A military unit had been stoned by a hungry and unruly mob.*
▶ disorderly, rowdy, wild, rebellious, disruptive, undisciplined, disobedient, boisterous, rough
OPPOSITES ARE orderly, disciplined

**unsafe** ADJECTIVE

**1** *They agreed it would be unsafe to try to get a message to London.*
▶ dangerous, risky, hazardous, precarious, insecure
OPPOSITES ARE safe, harmless

**2** *The verdicts were unsafe because they were based entirely on confessions.*
▶ unreliable, unsound, insecure, doubtful, unstable
OPPOSITES ARE safe, reliable, secure

**unsatisfactory** ADJECTIVE

*It was an unsatisfactory conclusion to an otherwise useful visit.*
▶ disappointing, dissatisfying, unacceptable, unhappy, displeasing, inadequate, unworthy, poor, unsatisfying
AN OPPOSITE IS satisfactory

**unsavoury** ADJECTIVE

*There were too many unsavoury characters lurking about.*
▶ unpleasant, disreputable, objectionable, unwholesome, obnoxious, repellent
AN OPPOSITE IS reputable

**unscathed** ADJECTIVE

*Richard walked away unscathed from the wreckage of his car.*
▶ unharmed, unhurt, uninjured, safe, intact
OPPOSITES ARE injured, hurt

**unscrupulous** ADJECTIVE

*He showed himself to be a cunning and unscrupulous politician.*
▶ dishonest, dishonourable, unprincipled, unethical, immoral, improper, self-interested, shameless
OPPOSITES ARE honest, principled

**unseemly** ADJECTIVE

*There was another unseemly row that evening.*
▶ undignified, unbecoming, embarrassing, indecorous, indelicate, discreditable, unsuitable
OPPOSITES ARE seemly, dignified

**unseen** ADJECTIVE

*The practice was activated by some unseen hands.*
▶ hidden, concealed, invisible, unnoticed, obscured, imperceptible
OPPOSITES ARE visible, seen

**unselfish** ADJECTIVE

*They were motivated by entirely unselfish motives.*
▶ kind, selfless, thoughtful, altruistic, disinterested, magnanimous, charitable, considerate, caring, generous, humanitarian, philanthropic
AN OPPOSITE IS selfish

**unsettled** ADJECTIVE

**1** *Unsettled weather makes a long painting session impossible.*
▶ changeable, variable, changing, unreliable, unpredictable, unsteady
OPPOSITES ARE settled, calm

**2** *He looked anxious and unsettled.*
▶ disturbed, upset, troubled, agitated, restless, uneasy, flustered
OPPOSITES ARE settled, composed

**unsightly** ADJECTIVE

*There is already an unsightly quarry there.*
▶ ugly, unattractive, hideous, inelegant, tasteless, unpleasant, displeasing
AN OPPOSITE IS beautiful

**unskilled** ADJECTIVE

*For unskilled workers the death rate was 40% above average.*
▶ unqualified, untrained, inexperienced, unskilful
AN OPPOSITE IS skilled

**unsociable** ADJECTIVE

*He was grumpy and unsociable.*
▶ unfriendly, aloof, distant, taciturn, reclusive, uncommunicative, uncongenial
OPPOSITES ARE sociable, friendly

**unsolicited** ADJECTIVE

*You might get unsolicited mail every so often.*
▶ unrequested, unsought, unwanted, uninvited, unasked-for
AN OPPOSITE IS requested

**unsophisticated** ADJECTIVE

*She was unsophisticated and shy.*
▶ innocent, naive, unworldly, artless, ingenuous, unpretentious, childlike
AN OPPOSITE IS sophisticated

**unsound** ADJECTIVE

**1** *Many of the older buildings were structurally unsound.*
▶ unsafe, unstable, unsteady, flimsy, weak
OPPOSITES ARE sound, strong

**2** *These arguments are obviously unsound.*
▶ untenable, flawed, erroneous, defective, ill-founded, fallacious
OPPOSITES ARE sound, cogent

**unspeakable** ADJECTIVE

*The gang was guilty of the most unspeakable acts.*
▶ indescribable, awful, dreadful, appalling, repellent, frightful, unutterable, inexpressible, monstrous

## unstable ADJECTIVE

1 *The buildings are highly unstable.*
▶ unsteady, shaky, rickety, wobbly, flimsy, insecure, unsafe, precarious

2 *an emotionally unstable young student named Karl*
▶ unbalanced, disturbed, insecure, deranged, demented

*The country has a history of unstable government.*
▶ unreliable, changeable, erratic, unsettled, volatile

## unsteady ADJECTIVE

1 *She balanced her cup on an unsteady iron table. He smelled of alcohol and was unsteady on his feet.*
▶ shaky, rickety, unstable, wobbly, insecure, unsafe, precarious
OPPOSITES ARE steady, firm

2 *She took a deep unsteady breath.*
▶ irregular, uneven, changeable, erratic, inconstant, intermittent, variable
OPPOSITES ARE steady, regular

3 *He read by the unsteady light of a candle*
▶ flickering, fluctuating, wavering, quavering, quivering, trembling, tremulous
AN OPPOSITE IS steady

## unsuccessful ADJECTIVE

*He was the leader of an unsuccessful military coup against the previous government.*
▶ failed, abortive, fruitless, futile, ill-fated, vain, ineffective, ineffectual, unproductive, unsatisfactory, useless
OPPOSITES ARE successful, effective

## unsuitable ADJECTIVE

*I think the proposed new site is unsuitable.*
▶ inappropriate, unsuited, ill-suited, inapt, unsatisfactory, unfitting, unfit, out of keeping, ill-chosen, ill-judged, mistaken, inapposite
OPPOSITES ARE suitable, appropriate

## unsure ADJECTIVE

*I was unsure of my welcome when I visited the cottage the next afternoon.*
▶ uncertain, doubtful, dubious, sceptical, suspicious, mistrustful, distrustful
AN OPPOSITE IS confident

**unsure of yourself** *She was still a little unsure of herself in formal society.*
▶ unconfident, hesitant, diffident, timid, timorous
OPPOSITES ARE sure of yourself, self-confident

## unsympathetic ADJECTIVE

1 *The planning authority showed an unsympathetic attitude to applications for new homes*
▶ uncaring, unconcerned, unresponsive, indifferent, insensitive, unfeeling, hostile, antagonistic
AN OPPOSITE IS sympathetic

2 **unsympathetic to** *The new assembly was quite unsympathetic to these views.*
▶ opposed to, hostile to, unconcerned about, antagonistic towards, ill-disposed towards
OPPOSITES ARE sympathetic to, understanding of

## unsystematic ADJECTIVE

*Their use of data was unsystematic.*
▶ disorganized, unmethodical, disorderly, haphazard, muddled, jumbled, unstructured, indiscriminate, inconsistent
AN OPPOSITE IS systematic

## unthinkable ADJECTIVE

*In a free society such a ban would be unthinkable*
▶ inconceivable, unimaginable, unbelievable, undreamed of, incredible, absurd, preposterous, implausible
OPPOSITES ARE conceivable, plausible

## untidy ADJECTIVE

1 *He staggered out of his untidy bedroom. The handwriting was untidy.*
▶ disorganized, messy, cluttered, muddled, disordered, chaotic
OPPOSITES ARE tidy, orderly

2 *Her hair looked untidy.*
▶ dishevelled, scruffy, bedraggled, uncombed, ungroomed, unkempt, rumpled, shabby, tangled, tousled, uncared for
OPPOSITES ARE tidy, neat

## untie VERB

*She began to untie the string around the box.*
▶ undo, loosen, unfasten, unknot, release, unbind, disentangle, free, untether
AN OPPOSITE IS tie up

## untimely ADJECTIVE

*Accounts vary as to how William met his untimely death.*
▶ premature, unseasonable, unfortunate, inopportune, inauspicious
OPPOSITES ARE timely, opportune

## untold ADJECTIVE

*Vandals caused untold damage.*
▶ incalculable, boundless, infinite, unlimited, countless
AN OPPOSITE IS limited

## untrue ADJECTIVE

*The claims were completely untrue.*
▶ wrong, false, inaccurate, erroneous, incorrect, mistaken, unfounded, fallacious
OPPOSITES ARE true, correct

## unusual ADJECTIVE

1 *The town had electric lighting, unusual in those days.*
▶ uncommon, rare, unfamiliar
OPPOSITES ARE usual, common

2 *It was an unusual story.*
▶ strange, odd, curious, weird, queer, bizarre, peculiar, exceptional, unconventional
OPPOSITES ARE normal, conventional

3 *Vera was a woman of unusual quality.*
▶ remarkable, exceptional, extraordinary, untypical
AN OPPOSITE IS typical

# unwanted ADJECTIVE

**1** *Lila kept guard dogs to ward off unwanted visitors.*
▶ unwelcome, undesirable, undesired, unsolicited, uninvited, rejected
OPPOSITES ARE welcome, wanted, desirable

**2** *The ants will bring dead ants and unwanted rubbish from their nests.*
▶ superfluous, discarded, redundant, unused
OPPOSITES ARE needed, useful, wanted

# unwary ADJECTIVE

*Deep potholes can bring down an unwary rider and his horse.*
▶ careless, unthinking, inattentive, absent-minded, thoughtless, unguarded, incautious
OPPOSITES ARE wary, attentive

# unwelcome ADJECTIVE

**1** *As she went downstairs, an unwelcome voice reached her ears.*
▶ disagreeable, unacceptable, undesirable, unwanted
AN OPPOSITE IS welcome

**2** *He had been made to feel unwelcome.*
▶ unwanted, unpopular, excluded, spurned, uninvited

# unwell ADJECTIVE

*She told the ambulance service she was feeling unwell.*
▶ ill, sick, poorly, indisposed, out of sorts, under the weather
OPPOSITES ARE well, in good health

# unwieldy ADJECTIVE

*He would also need to transport some unwieldy equipment.*
▶ awkward, cumbersome, clumsy, bulky, unmanageable, ungainly, heavy, massive
OPPOSITES ARE manageable, handy

# unwilling ADJECTIVE

**1** *He called together his group of unwilling helpers.*
▶ unenthusiastic, grudging, reluctant, uncooperative, half-hearted, hesitant
OPPOSITES ARE willing, keen

**2** *A spokesman was unwilling to give a precise date.*
▶ reluctant, disinclined, averse, loath
OPPOSITES ARE willing, ready

# unwind VERB

**1** *Kittie unwound balls of pink and blue wool.*
▶ unroll, unreel, unravel, untwist, undo, uncoil, untwine

**2** *He found the farm a place to unwind and let himself go.*
▶ relax, ease up, loosen up

# unwise ADJECTIVE

*You would be unwise to ignore the warning signs.*
▶ foolish, stupid, silly, ill-advised, crazy, mad, insane, (*more informal*) daft
OPPOSITES ARE wise, sensible

# unworthy ADJECTIVE

**1** *His was an unworthy remark.*
▶ shameful, discreditable, dishonourable, undeserving, unsuitable, despicable, disreputable, ignoble, inappropriate
AN OPPOSITE IS worthy

**2** *Such claims are unworthy of consideration.*
▶ undeserving, unfit (for), ineligible (for)
OPPOSITES ARE worthy, deserving

# upbringing NOUN

*They knew all about his birth, upbringing, and police record.*
▶ education, breeding, raising, rearing, teaching, training, bringing up, upkeep, care, instruction, nurture

# update VERB

*You should continually update your information.*
▶ review, amend, upgrade, bring up to date, correct, revise, modernize

# upgrade VERB

*You can upgrade our system free of charge.*
▶ improve, enhance, update, make better, renovate, expand

# upheaval NOUN

*Further changes could be made without major upheaval.*
▶ disruption, commotion, disturbance, confusion, disorder, turmoil

# uphill ADJECTIVE

*We are all facing an uphill struggle.*
▶ hard, arduous, strenuous, taxing, tough, difficult, exhausting, gruelling, laborious, stiff
AN OPPOSITE IS easy

# uphold VERB

*The courts robustly upheld the right of freedom of speech.*
▶ support, endorse, confirm, defend, sustain, back, vindicate
AN OPPOSITE IS oppose

# upkeep NOUN

*Each owner is liable to contribute to the upkeep of the building as a whole.*
▶ maintenance, running, repair, care, keep, conservation, preservation
AN OPPOSITE IS neglect

# uplifting ADJECTIVE

*It's an uplifting story about an English girl in India.*
▶ inspiring, moving, touching, warming, cheering, enlightening, encouraging, edifying, enriching, humanizing, improving
AN OPPOSITE IS dispiriting

# upper ADJECTIVE

*There are lifts to the upper floors of the building.*
▶ higher, upstairs, raised, elevated, superior

## upright ADJECTIVE

1 *Crude figures are incised on upright stones.*
▶ perpendicular, vertical, erect

2 *upright Victorians with a strong sense of family pride*
▶ honourable, honest, respectable, reputable, righteous, upstanding, moral, principled, righteous, virtuous, trustworthy
OPPOSITES ARE dishonourable, corrupt

## uprising NOUN

*The uprising was soon suppressed by the army.*
▶ rebellion, revolt, rising, insurrection, insurgence, revolution, mutiny

**USAGE** You use *mutiny* about members of the armed forces.

## uproar NOUN

1 *There was an uproar when the council refused to hear the delegation.*
▶ outcry, clamour, protest, furore, rumpus

2 *They found the place in uproar.*
▶ turmoil, confusion, disorder, pandemonium, mayhem, commotion

## uproot VERB

1 *He always imagined himself as some great monster uprooting trees.*
▶ pull up, tear up, rip out, root out, weed out, remove, destroy, (*more formal*) extirpate
AN OPPOSITE IS plant

2 *Building a dam would uproot over a million people.*
▶ displace, disrupt, remove

## upset VERB

1 *I would never want to upset anyone.*
▶ distress, trouble, agitate, disturb, unsettle, disquiet, disconcert, unnerve, dismay, grieve, perturb, fluster, confuse
OPPOSITES ARE reassure, put at ease

2 *Grazing sheep is prohibited so as not to upset the natural balance.*
▶ disrupt, disturb, interfere with, affect, throw out, ruin
OPPOSITES ARE maintain, restore

3 *He upset a pot of soup.*
▶ tip over, knock over, spill, overturn

## upset NOUN

*The youngsters put the upset behind them.*
▶ distress, worry, trouble, upheaval, bother, anxiety

## upset ADJECTIVE

1 *She was upset about missing all the excitement.*
▶ distressed, dismayed, disturbed, troubled, unsettled, disconcerted, worried, anxious, grieved

2 *He rang in to say he had an upset stomach.*
▶ queasy, disordered, (*more informal*) gippy

## upshot NOUN

*The upshot was that George received a written apology.*
▶ result, consequence, outcome, conclusion, effect, sequel

## upside-down ADJECTIVE

1 *I could read the writing upside-down on his desk.*
▶ the wrong way up, inverted, topsy-turvy, upturned
OPPOSITES ARE upright, the right way up

2 *Somebody broke in and turned the place upside-down. It is traumatic having one's life turned upside-down like this.*
▶ into disarray, into chaos, into a muddle, untidy, chaotic
AN OPPOSITE IS tidy

## uptight ADJECTIVE

(*informal*) *When Ian gets uptight it can affect his game.*
▶ tense, anxious, nervous, edgy, on edge, strained, stressed, agitated, apprehensive, jittery, fidgety, ill at ease, jumpy
OPPOSITES ARE calm, relaxed

## up-to-date ADJECTIVE

1 *None of the disks contained up-to-date programs.*
▶ current, latest, recent, new, modern, present-day, advanced
AN OPPOSITE IS out-of-date

2 *Use the Internet to keep yourself up to date on this topic.*
▶ informed (about), in touch (with), conversant (with), (*more informal*) up to speed
AN OPPOSITE IS uninformed

## upward ADJECTIVE

*Take the upward path. an upward trend in prices*
▶ rising, ascending, uphill

## urban ADJECTIVE

*greenfield sites on the edge of urban areas*
▶ built-up, town, city, densely populated, metropolitan, suburban, municipal

## urge VERB

1 *We would urge people to be aware and alert with fireworks.*
▶ encourage, entreat, exhort, advise, counsel, appeal to, entreat, beg, press, plead with, beseech, implore, recommend
OPPOSITES ARE deter, discourage

2 *The working group urged caution in implementing any changes.*
▶ advise, recommend, counsel, advocate, suggest

3 *He urged his crew on through the mountainous waves.*
▶ drive, spur, press, force, compel, impel, propel, push

## urge NOUN

*The urge to give him a hug was almost impossible to resist.*
▶ desire, wish, need, impulse, inclination, eagerness, compulsion, craving, fancy, instinct, longing, yearning, (*more informal*) itch, (*more informal*) yen

## urgent ADJECTIVE

1 *The buildings are in urgent need of renovation.*
▶ immediate, pressing, acute, grave, dire, desperate, critical, serious, essential, drastic, extreme, instant, top-priority

2 *He was roused from sleep by the urgent calls of his mother.*
▶ insistent, persistent, earnest, determined, eager, pleading
AN OPPOSITE IS casual

**usable** ADJECTIVE
1 *a thousand square metres of usable floor space*
▶ functional, working, available, practical, serviceable, fit for use, functioning, operating, operational
AN OPPOSITE IS unusable.
2 *The ticket is usable at all the country's museums and galleries.*
▶ valid, acceptable, current
AN OPPOSITE IS invalid

**use** NOUN
1 *What's the use of arguing?*
▶ point, advantage, purpose, benefit, value, sense, usefulness, reason (for)
2 *There isn't much use for mechanical calculators any more.*
▶ need, call, demand, necessity, reason, justification
3 *There was trial and error in the use of video equipment.*
▶ utilization, employment, operation, application, usage
4 *People have to make the best use of their time.*
▶ application, utilization, employment, exercise

**use** VERB
1 *They use the garden like an extra room.*
▶ utilize, make use of, employ, avail yourself of, put to use
2 *He learned to use a word processor.*
▶ work, operate, utilize, handle, manage, make use of
3 *You will need to use all your judgement.*
▶ exercise, apply, employ, draw on, make use of, implement
4 *How much milk did you use?*
▶ use up, consume, exhaust, waste
**use up** *By now Billy had used up all his money.*
▶ spend, get through, exhaust, deplete, squander, consume
**USAGE** You use *squander* when you are talking about wasting something or using it extravagantly. You use *consume* when you are talking about food.

**used** ADJECTIVE
1 *They always bought used cars.*
▶ second-hand, pre-owned, nearly new, old
OPPOSITES ARE unused, new
2 **used to** *He was used to being woken up in the middle of the night.*
▶ accustomed to, familiar with, in the habit of, no stranger to

**useful** ADJECTIVE
1 *These specialists can offer useful advice and practical support.*
▶ helpful, beneficial, worthwhile, valuable, profitable, advantageous, positive, constructive, good, invaluable
OPPOSITES ARE useless, unhelpful
2 *This is a useful tool for working in tight spaces.*
▶ handy, practical, convenient, effective, efficient, powerful, productive, utilitarian
OPPOSITES ARE useless, awkward
3 *They had some useful players.*
▶ skilful, talented, competent, capable, proficient, effective, successful
OPPOSITES ARE useless, incompetent

**useless** ADJECTIVE
1 *I'm full of useless bits of knowledge like that. Further inquiries would be useless.*
▶ worthless, pointless, futile, fruitless, vain, hopeless, unavailing, unprofitable, unsuccessful
OPPOSITES ARE useful, helpful, practical
2 *It was a useless suggestion.*
▶ impractical, unusable, unworkable, ineffective, hopeless, (more informal) dud
OPPOSITES ARE useful, positive
3 *She's useless at spelling.*
▶ bad, inept, no good, incompetent, ineffective, untalented, incapable (of)
OPPOSITES ARE useful, competent

**usual** ADJECTIVE
*Today he didn't take his usual route home.*
▶ normal, customary, habitual, regular, routine, typical, familiar, accustomed, conventional, traditional, standard, orthodox
OPPOSITES ARE unusual, exceptional

**usually** ADVERB
*Usually he lingered by the stream to throw in stones.*
▶ normally, generally, habitually, as a rule, customarily, routinely, regularly, often
OPPOSITES ARE exceptionally, seldom, rarely

**usurp** VERB
*The military had usurped the functions of the civil government.*
▶ seize, appropriate, take over, assume, commandeer, steal

**utensil** NOUN
*During the recession people were not buying kitchen utensils.*
▶ implement, appliance, device, gadget, instrument, machine, tool

**utility** NOUN
*The utility of teaching a foreign language should not be underestimated.*
▶ usefulness, use, advantage, benefit, value, helpfulness, efficacy

**utilize** VERB
*All combatants utilize armour and weapons of the period.*
▶ use, make use of, employ, avail yourself of, deploy

**utmost** ADJECTIVE

1 *I was able to breathe only with the utmost difficulty.*
▶ greatest, maximum, enormous, extreme, supreme
OPPOSITES ARE minimum, least

2 *The house was at the utmost tip of the island.*
▶ furthest or farthest, extreme, outermost, ultimate

**utter** ADJECTIVE
*Amy stared at him in utter disbelief.*
▶ absolute, complete, total, sheer, positive, thorough, outright, downright, out-and-out, unmitigated

**utter** VERB
*They were all too stunned to utter a word.*
▶ say, speak, express, voice, articulate, enunciate

**utterly** ADVERB
*The whole exercise seems utterly pointless.*
▶ absolutely, completely, totally, perfectly, quite, unquestionably, unreservedly

**U-turn** NOUN
*It had been the most dramatic U-turn of her political career.*
▶ change of mind, reversal of policy, volte-face, about-face, about-turn, shift

# Vv

**vacancy** NOUN
*There was a vacancy for part-time work.*
▶ opening, post, place, opportunity, position, situation

**vacant** ADJECTIVE

1 *There is a plan to build offices on a vacant site in the city centre.*
▶ unused, unoccupied, unfilled, empty, bare, blank, clear, free, available
AN OPPOSITE IS occupied

2 *Guns and ammunition were found in a planned search of a vacant house.*
▶ empty, unoccupied, deserted
AN OPPOSITE IS occupied

3 *She maintained a vacant expression.*
▶ blank, expressionless, deadpan, absent-minded, vacuous, abstracted, inattentive, dreamy, far away
OPPOSITES ARE attentive, alert

**vacate** VERB
*They must vacate the premises by the end of the month.*
▶ leave, evacuate, quit, withdraw from, abandon, depart from, give up
AN OPPOSITE IS occupy

**vacation** NOUN
*Although I'm officially on vacation, I'm actually working.*
▶ holiday, leave, time off

**vacuous** ADJECTIVE
*He still wore his vacuous expression.*
▶ blank, expressionless, deadpan, absent-minded, vacant, abstracted, inattentive, dreamy, far away
OPPOSITES ARE attentive, alert

**vacuum** NOUN
*The fall of the president resulted in a brief power vacuum.*
▶ gap, space, void, emptiness

**vagrant** NOUN
*He lived as a vagrant for several months.*
▶ tramp, beggar, drifter, destitute person, homeless person, itinerant, vagabond, (more informal) down-and-out

**vague** ADJECTIVE

1 *He was full of vague promises.*
▶ indefinite, imprecise, inexact, unspecific, ill-defined, generalized
OPPOSITES ARE specific, definite

2 *Vague shapes could be made out in the distance.*
▶ hazy, unclear, indistinct, indefinite, blurred
OPPOSITES ARE distinct, clear

3 *He always seemed vague about money.*
▶ uncertain, unclear, unsure, confused, indecisive, uninformed
OPPOSITES ARE certain, informed

4 *Our plans are fairly vague at this stage.*
▶ unsettled, uncertain, inexact, open, unsure, indefinite
OPPOSITES ARE firm, definite

**vain** ADJECTIVE

1 *They are vain and ostentatious by nature.*
▶ conceited, arrogant, self-satisfied, self-important, boastful, egotistical
AN OPPOSITE IS modest

2 *Dr Neil made vain attempts to stop the bleeding.*
▶ unsuccessful, ineffective, futile, abortive, fruitless, unavailing
OPPOSITES ARE successful, effective

**valiant** ADJECTIVE
*Valiant efforts have been made to collect the backlog of refuse.*
▶ brave, determined, resolute, courageous, gallant, bold, intrepid
OPPOSITES ARE weak, irresolute

**valid** ADJECTIVE

1 *This may be a valid conclusion.*
▶ legitimate, reasonable, rational, sound, cogent, convincing, acceptable
OPPOSITES ARE invalid, spurious

2 *Make sure you have a valid passport and a visa if necessary.*
▶ current, up-to-date, legal, certified, approved, authorized, official, suitable, bona fide, genuine
AN OPPOSITE IS invalid

## validate VERB

**1** *There is no independent control that can validate the data.*
▶ support, substantiate, endorse, uphold, back up, vindicate, justify, prove
OPPOSITES ARE invalidate, disprove

**2** *A witness is needed to validate the signature on the contract.*
▶ authenticate, authorize, certify, legitimize, make valid, ratify, legalize
AN OPPOSITE IS invalidate

## valley NOUN

*Pupils will be taught in the school across the valley.*
▶ dale, glen, dell, vale, hollow, gorge, gulch

## valour NOUN

*The medals are awarded for acts of valour.*
▶ bravery, courage, daring, gallantry, heroism
AN OPPOSITE IS cowardice

## valuable ADJECTIVE

**1** *You need separate insurance cover for the more valuable jewellery.*
▶ costly, high-priced, expensive, precious, priceless, dear
OPPOSITES ARE valueless, worthless

**2** *The work provided them with valuable experience.*
▶ helpful, beneficial, advantageous, constructive, invaluable, positive, profitable, useful, valued, worthwhile, good
AN OPPOSITE IS worthless

**USAGE** Note that *invaluable* is not an opposite of *valuable*, but means 'too great to be valued', i.e. 'extremely valuable', as in *an invaluable member of the team.*

## value NOUN

**1** *Houses in the area have practically doubled in value.*
▶ price, cost, worth, market value

**2** *The value of regular exercise cannot be overestimated.*
▶ importance, merit, benefit, advantage, significance, usefulness, use

## value VERB

**1** *The vineyard is valued at £160 million.*
▶ assess, evaluate, price, cost, estimate the value of, (more informal) put a figure on

**2** *His honesty endeared him to many who valued his wise advice.*
▶ appreciate, prize, rate highly, esteem, hold in high regard, have a high opinion of, set store by
OPPOSITES ARE neglect, disregard

## valueless ADJECTIVE

*The shares had become completely valueless.*
▶ worthless, of no value, trifling
AN OPPOSITE IS valuable

## values PLURAL NOUN

*Each generation has its special values.*
▶ principles, standards, morality, morals, moral code, code of behaviour

## vanish VERB

**1** *Maria had vanished into the garden.*
▶ disappear, leave, withdraw, clear off
OPPOSITES ARE appear, reappear

**2** *All thoughts of her vanished in the excitement.*
▶ evaporate, melt away, dissolve, end, come to an end, dwindle, fade, go away, disperse, pass
OPPOSITES ARE materialize, endure

## vanity NOUN

*A divorce would hit her vanity and her pocket.*
▶ pride, self-regard, self-admiration, conceit, arrogance, egoism
AN OPPOSITE IS modesty

## vapour NOUN

*His breath formed a vapour on the air.*
▶ mist, haze, fog, smoke, steam, fumes, gas, miasma

## variable ADJECTIVE

*The photos are of variable quality.*
▶ changing, varying, changeable, fluctuating, irregular, inconsistent, unpredictable, vacillating, unstable, unsteady, temperamental
OPPOSITES ARE constant, uniform

## variation NOUN

**1** *There was considerable regional variation in these findings.*
▶ diversity, deviation, diversification, disparity, inequality, difference, discrepancy

**2** *Prices are subject to variation.*
▶ change, alteration, adjustment, modification

## varied ADJECTIVE

*There is a varied choice of restaurants and tavernas.*
▶ diverse, assorted, wide-ranging, miscellaneous, mixed, sundry, motley, (more formal) heterogeneous

## variety NOUN

**1** *It is hard work, but the variety makes it stimulating.*
▶ diversity, variation, diversification, change, many-sidedness, unpredictability

**2** *one-day courses on a variety of cookery themes*
▶ assortment, array, miscellany, mixture, multiplicity, range, collection, medley

**3** *The list offers sixteen varieties of drinking chocolate.*
▶ kind, sort, type, form, brand, category, class, strain, make, species, breed

## various ADJECTIVE

**1** *The job can be done in various ways.*
▶ different, differing, diverse, distinct, varying, varied, assorted, dissimilar, miscellaneous
AN OPPOSITE IS similar

**2** *An uneasy truce existed between the various political parties.*
▶ numerous, many, several, innumerable, countless, multifarious, sundry

## vary VERB

**1** *Prices vary enormously for group holidays.*
▶ differ, fluctuate, range, change, shift, go up and down, (more formal) oscillate
OPPOSITES ARE be static, be fixed

**2** *The routine never varies.*
▶ change, alter, differ, deviate, diverge, fluctuate
**3** *You can vary the size of your pictures.*
▶ alter, adapt, adjust, modify, diversify
AN OPPOSITE IS fix

**vast** ADJECTIVE
**1** *The birds fly over vast distances.*
▶ huge, great, extensive, enormous, immense, colossal, tremendous
OPPOSITES ARE small, short
**2** *The vast majority of patients are elderly.*
▶ great, huge, large

**vat** NOUN
*a vat of wine*
▶ tank, tub, vessel, cask

**vault** NOUN
*The treasures are locked in a vault.*
▶ strongroom, repository, depository, basement, cellar, crypt

**vault** VERB
*'That rock,' she pointed. 'Vault over it.'*
▶ jump, leap, leapfrog, spring, bound, clear, hurdle
**USAGE** You can say either *vault over it* or *vault it*, and you can use *jump*, *leap*, and *leapfrog* in the same ways. If you use *spring* or *bound* you have to use *over* ( e.g. *spring over it*); if you use *clear* or *hurdle* you do not use *over* (e.g. *clear it*).

**veer** VERB
*She was about to veer in a different direction.*
▶ turn, swerve, swing, shift, tack, change course, skew, dodge, wheel

---

**vegetable** NOUN
**VARIOUS VEGETABLES**
**beans and peas:** bean, broad bean, butter bean, pea, runner bean, sweetcorn.
**root vegetables:** beet, beetroot, carrot, onion, parsnip, potato, shallot (= small onion), swede, turnip.
**leaf vegetables:** broccoli, Brussels sprout, cabbage, calabrese, cauliflower, celeriac (type of celery), celery, chicory, fennel, kale (variety of cabbage), kohlrabi (variety of cabbage), spinach.
**flesh vegetables (some are also regarded as fruits):** asparagus, artichoke, aubergine, chicory, courgette (small variety of marrow), cucumber, eggplant (= aubergine), fennel, marrow, leek, okra, pepper, pumpkin, tomato, zucchini (= courgette).

---

**vegetation** NOUN
*Here on the island there is lush vegetation.*
▶ foliage, plant life, plants, growth, undergrowth, greenery

**vehemence** NOUN
*We were surprised by the vehemence of their opposition.*
▶ force, passion, intensity, ardour, vigour, violence, strength, urgency
OPPOSITES ARE mildness, apathy

**vehement** ADJECTIVE
*We are quite vehement in our pursuit of safety procedures. Opposition to the whale hunt drew vehement criticism from the islanders.*
▶ fierce, passionate, forceful, impassioned, intense, ardent, eager, fervent, vigorous, violent, enthusiastic, animated, excited, heated, strong, powerful, urgent
OPPOSITES ARE mild, apathetic

**vehicle** NOUN
*Vehicles are not allowed in the town centre.*
▶ motor vehicle, car, automobile, wheeled transport

**veil** NOUN
**1** *The veil came from her head to her feet.*
▶ covering, cloak, mask
**2** *The city lay under a veil of darkness.*
▶ cover, screen, layer, blanket, film, curtain

**veil** VERB
*The mountain was veiled in mist.*
▶ hide, cover, shroud, envelop, conceal, screen
AN OPPOSITE IS expose

**vein** NOUN
*Sebastian went on in the same vein for several minutes.*
▶ mood, tenor, tone, manner

**vendetta** NOUN
*He was the victim of a personal vendetta.*
▶ feud, quarrel, blood-feud, rivalry

**veneer** NOUN
**1** *chipboard with a mahogany veneer*
▶ surface, finish, coating, covering, layer
**2** *His veneer of good humour vanished instantly.*
▶ show, display, pretence, facade, front, appearance, guise

**venerable** ADJECTIVE
*He was interviewed by three venerable gentlemen.*
▶ respected, venerated, revered, esteemed, honoured, august, dignified
AN OPPOSITE IS disreputable

**vengeance** NOUN
*He swore vengeance when he was banished four years ago.*
▶ revenge, retribution, retaliation, reprisal

**vengeful** ADJECTIVE
*He felt vengeful towards his attackers.*
▶ revengeful, unforgiving, spiteful, bitter, avenging, vindictive, rancorous
AN OPPOSITE IS forgiving

a b c d e f g h i j k l m n o p q r s t u v w x y z

## venom NOUN

1 *Snake venom is usually clear yellow.*
▶ poison, toxin

2 *She was told to leave with such venom she recoiled.*
▶ malice, malevolence, rancour, ill-will, acrimony, animosity, bitterness, vitriol, virulence, hatred

## venomous ADJECTIVE

1 *The only mammals with venomous bites are certain moles and shrews.*
▶ poisonous, toxic, noxious, deadly
AN OPPOSITE IS harmless

2 *He wrote a venomous criticism of their work.*
▶ vicious, spiteful, malicious, malevolent, vindictive, baleful, vitriolic, rancorous
AN OPPOSITE IS friendly

## vent NOUN

*Open the air vent to increase the rate of flow.*
▶ opening, outlet, duct, aperture, hole, passage, slit

## vent VERB

*The crowd vented their fury on the police rather than one another.*
▶ express, release, emit, pour out, give vent to

## venture NOUN

*This new venture holds great promise for the future.*
▶ enterprise, undertaking, project, scheme, endeavour, operation, adventure

## venture VERB

1 *Harry ventured an opinion.*
▶ put forward, suggest, offer, dare, risk, chance

2 *We venture to ask you for your permission.*
▶ dare, presume, be so bold as to

3 *When darkness came he ventured out.*
▶ journey, set forth, proceed, dare to go, risk going

## verbal ADJECTIVE

*A verbal exchange was recorded between two people.*
▶ spoken, oral, word-of-mouth, unwritten
AN OPPOSITE IS written

## verbatim ADJECTIVE

*The article includes several verbatim quotations.*
▶ word-for-word, exact, precise, direct, literal, close
AN OPPOSITE IS loose

## verbatim ADVERB

*He passed on the complaint verbatim.*
▶ word for word, exactly, precisely, faithfully
AN OPPOSITE IS loosely

## verbose ADJECTIVE

*Parts of the speech were repetitive and verbose.*
▶ wordy, loquacious, diffuse, effusive, garrulous, talkative, long-winded, rambling
AN OPPOSITE IS succinct

## verdict NOUN

*The verdict was suicide, but many people thought he was murdered.*
▶ judgement, decision, finding, ruling, adjudication, assessment, conclusion, opinion

## verge NOUN

1 *Cars were parked on the grass verge.*
▶ edge, bank, kerb, margin, border, roadside, shoulder, side, wayside

2 *The country was on the verge of bankruptcy.*
▶ brink, point, threshold

## verge VERB

**verge on** *By this time the urgency verged on desperation.*
▶ border on, tend towards, approach, come close to

## verifiable ADJECTIVE

*The theory may be verifiable by means of experiments.*
▶ demonstrable, provable
AN OPPOSITE IS unverifiable

## verify VERB

*There was no one around to verify what happened.*
▶ prove, support, confirm, substantiate, establish, uphold, show the truth of, validate, authenticate, corroborate, check out, ascertain
AN OPPOSITE IS refute

## versatile ADJECTIVE

1 *She was a gifted and versatile teacher.*
▶ adaptable, many-sided, all-round, flexible, resourceful, talented, skilful

2 *The property offers spacious and versatile accommodation.*
▶ flexible, adaptable, modifiable, all-purpose
AN OPPOSITE IS restricted

## verse NOUN

*a story written in verse*
▶ rhyme, lines, lyrics, metre, stanza

## version NOUN

1 *Would you like to tell us your version of the story?*
▶ account, record, explanation, interpretation, rendering

2 *a new version of the machine*
▶ form, type, model, design

## vertical ADJECTIVE

1 *Pull the lever back to its vertical position.*
▶ upright, perpendicular, standing, erect
AN OPPOSITE IS horizontal

2 *The passageway ended with a vertical drop into darkness.*
▶ sheer, steep, precipitous

## vertigo NOUN

*A feeling of vertigo kept him from the edge.*
▶ dizziness, giddiness, fear of heights, light-headedness

## verve NOUN

*He played the piano with great verve.*
▶ enthusiasm, vigour, liveliness, spirit, energy, vitality, vivacity, gusto, relish

**very** ADVERB This word is often overused. Here are some alternatives:
*He felt very ashamed.*
► extremely, highly, deeply, exceedingly, acutely, truly, (*more formal*) terribly
AN OPPOSITE IS slightly

**very** ADJECTIVE
1 *The key on the floor was the very one he had lost the week before.  Those were her very words.*
► actual, same, selfsame, identical, exact, precise
2 *The very thought of it made him tremble.*
► mere, sheer, simple

**vessel** NOUN
1 *Pour the liquid into a sterile vessel.*
► container, receptacle, flask, bottle, jar, jug, holder
2 *Small vessels were bobbing about in the harbour.*
► craft, boat, ship
**USAGE** Note that *craft* can be singular or plural (e.g. *a small craft was bobbing about* or *small craft were bobbing about*).

**vet** VERB
*Peter vetted all the outfits and knew exactly what would suit Tara.*
► inspect, examine, screen, assess, evaluate, appraise, scrutinize, investigate, check out

**veteran** ADJECTIVE
*He handled it all like a veteran superstar.*
► established, seasoned, mature, hardened, master, expert

**veto** NOUN
*He in effect acquired a right of veto over all sales of land.*
► rejection, refusal, embargo, prohibition, ban, (*more informal*) thumbs down
AN OPPOSITE IS approval

**veto** VERB
*The government had vetoed the proposal in late July.*
► reject, turn down, overrule, rule out, throw out, disallow, refuse, dismiss, ban, bar, blackball, forbid, prohibit, say no to, vote against
AN OPPOSITE IS approve

**vex** VERB
*His remarks had vexed her deeply.*
► annoy, irritate, displease, anger, infuriate, enrage, exasperate, incense, madden, aggravate, nettle, antagonize, inflame, make angry, (*more informal*) needle, (*more informal*) rile, (*more informal*) bug, (*more informal*) rub up the wrong way
OPPOSITES ARE please, gratify

**vexed** ADJECTIVE
1 *She was still vexed with me for bringing Frankie.*
► annoyed, irritated, angry, cross, displeased, peeved, infuriated, incensed, enraged, (*more informal*) miffed, (*more informal*) put out
AN OPPOSITE IS pleased
2 *The note was about the vexed question of sexism.*
► controversial, difficult, contentious, disputed, thorny, knotty

**viable** ADJECTIVE
*Pirate TV might become a viable possibility.   It was not viable to work on a computer of that age.*
► practical, realistic, feasible, workable, practicable, usable, achievable, operable, sustainable, possible
OPPOSITES ARE impractical, unworkable

**vibrant** ADJECTIVE
1 *Green plants provide splashes of vibrant colour.*
► bright, vivid, brilliant, intense, striking
OPPOSITES ARE dull, pale
2 *She made the most of her cheerful and vibrant personality.*
► vivacious, spirited, alert, alive, energetic, electric
OPPOSITES ARE restrained, reserved

**vibrate** VERB
1 *The room was vibrating from the sounds of rock music.*
► reverberate, throb, pulsate, resonate, resound, thud, ring, boom
2 *The machinery began to vibrate alarmingly.*
► tremble, shake, shudder, judder, quiver, oscillate, rattle, shiver, wobble, quake

**vibration** NOUN
*The special smoke detector produces a vibration as well as a flashing light.*
► reverberation, oscillation, pulsation, throbbing, trembling, juddering, quivering, rattling, shaking, shivering, shuddering, tremor, wobbling

**vice** NOUN
1 *They are determined to put an end to vice and prostitution.*
► immorality, depravity, corruption, wickedness, wrongdoing, degeneracy, evil-doing, evil, sin, (*more formal*) venality, (*more formal*) iniquity
AN OPPOSITE IS virtue
2 *Cowardice isn't the worst vice.*
► failing, fault, weakness, shortcoming, bad habit, blemish, defect, deficiency, imperfection
OPPOSITES ARE virtue, strength

**vicinity** NOUN
*There are several castles and abbeys in the vicinity.*
► neighbourhood, area, district, locality, region, locale, environs, outskirts, proximity

**vicious** ADJECTIVE
1 *He was finally captured in the vicious street fighting in Berlin in 1945.*
► brutal, savage, fierce, ferocious, wild, barbaric
OPPOSITES ARE gentle, humane
2 *He hadn't the vicious streak that showed in his brother.*
► cruel, malicious, spiteful, malevolent, vindictive, sadistic, brutish, callous, heartless, cold-blooded, aggressive, pitiless, ruthless, merciless, inhuman, vile
OPPOSITES ARE kind, benevolent

## victim NOUN

**1** *It's thought she was the victim of a random attack by a thief.* *He is the third victim of this tough new policy.*
▶ target, casualty, sufferer, injury, fatality, scapegoat

**USAGE** You use *fatality* about someone who has died as a result of an incident.

**2** *At their feet, a white-clad sacrificial victim, was the body.*
▶ offering, martyr, prey, sacrifice

## victimize VERB

*The company had been victimizing workers for reporting safety concerns.*
▶ discriminate against, persecute, intimidate, oppress, mistreat, harass, treat unfairly, bully, terrorize, torment, (*more informal*) pick on

## victor NOUN

*The victors pressed on and captured the city.*
▶ winner, conqueror, hero, champion
AN OPPOSITE IS loser

## victorious ADJECTIVE

*He emerged victorious in the second round of voting.*
▶ triumphant, successful, first, top, winning, leading, prevailing, undefeated, unbeaten
OPPOSITES ARE defeated, unsuccessful

## victory NOUN

*Her well-deserved victory in this year's Olympics was a boost for the British team.*
▶ win, success, triumph, conquest, knockout, mastery, superiority, achievement, (*more informal*) walkover
AN OPPOSITE IS defeat

## vie VERB

*A dozen teams vie for honours in a novelty sand-building competition.*
▶ compete, contend, contest, struggle, grapple, jostle, strive, fight, cross swords, lock horns

## view NOUN

**1** *From the top floor you get a magnificent view across the city.*
▶ outlook, prospect, panorama, perspective, vista, scene, aspect, picture, landscape, scenery, spectacle
**2** *She caught a brief view of her top half in the mirror.*
▶ look, sight, glance, peek, vision
**3** *Luke came into view.*
▶ sight, vision, range of vision, perspective
**4** *He declined to give any official view of the situation.*
▶ opinion, viewpoint, point of view, belief, judgement, notion, perception, idea, thought, attitude, conviction

**in view of** *In view of the length of time since the incident, no action was taken.*
▶ because of, on account of, considering, as a result of, as a consequence of, owing to, due to

## view VERB

**1** *He set out at ten and viewed as many houses as possible.* *A drop from a pond, viewed through a microscope, swarms with tiny organisms.*
▶ look at, inspect, survey, examine, observe, behold, eye, scan, gaze at, stare at
**2** *She viewed him with dislike.*
▶ regard, contemplate, consider, perceive, behold
**3** *Some of the guests were viewing a television programme.*
▶ watch, look at, see

## viewer NOUN

*The presenter has been asking viewers to write in.*
▶ spectator, watcher, audience, observer

## viewpoint NOUN

*Parents are not altogether good from a child's viewpoint.*
▶ point of view, standpoint, outlook, perspective, way of thinking, angle, position, stance, slant

## vigilant ADJECTIVE

*Everyone should be vigilant and report anything of a suspicious nature.*
▶ watchful, observant, alert, attentive, awake, on the lookout, on your guard, on the watch, sharp-eyed, eagle-eyed, careful, wide-awake, (*more informal*) on your toes
AN OPPOSITE IS negligent

## vigorous ADJECTIVE

**1** *Regular vigorous exercise can help to reduce blood pressure.*
▶ strenuous, energetic, animated, brisk, full-blooded
AN OPPOSITE IS feeble
**2** *The child is strong and vigorous.*
▶ healthy, in good health, energetic, vivacious, active, lively, lusty, virile, vital
**3** *He made a vigorous case for controlling the money supply.*
▶ strong, spirited, forceful, effective, robust, energetic, dynamic, active

## vigour NOUN

**1** *Geoffrey supported his wife's cause with vigour.*
▶ energy, force, forcefulness, spirit, vitality, gusto, verve, animation, dynamism
**2** *He recovered from the illness with renewed vigour.*
▶ energy, fitness, vitality, stamina, robustness, life, strength, health, resilience, potency

## vile ADJECTIVE

**1** *It's ironic that such a fine building should house so vile an organization.*
▶ wicked, evil, foul, contemptible, despicable, obnoxious, shameful, abhorrent, repellent, loathsome
AN OPPOSITE IS pleasant
**2** *I drank three cups of vile, greyish coffee.*
▶ nasty, horrible, foul, unpleasant, disgusting, revolting, repulsive, repellent, dreadful, terrible
AN OPPOSITE IS pleasant

3 *The vile weather had emptied the streets.*
▶ unpleasant, bad, foul, disagreeable, inclement
AN OPPOSITE IS fine

**villain** NOUN

*Did not two of history's greatest villains come from beautiful surroundings?*
▶ wrongdoer, evil-doer, rogue, scoundrel, criminal, reprobate, (*more formal*) malefactor, (*more formal*) miscreant

**vindicate** VERB

1 *He left claiming that history would vindicate him.*
▶ clear, exonerate, absolve, acquit, excuse, endorse, support, rehabilitate
OPPOSITES ARE blame, censure

2 *She was desperate to vindicate her decision to be an artist.*
▶ justify, uphold, defend, sustain, maintain, assert
AN OPPOSITE IS compromise

**vindictive** ADJECTIVE

*His eyes flashed vindictive rage.*
▶ malicious, spiteful, malevolent, hostile, baleful, malign, malignant, pernicious, hurtful, offensive, venomous
AN OPPOSITE IS forgiving

**vintage** NOUN

*They needed four aircraft of 1940s vintage.*
▶ period, era, epoch, time, date, origin

**vintage** ADJECTIVE

*He gave his usual vintage performance.*
▶ high-quality, fine, classic, choice, good, mature

**violate** VERB

1 *Uses of these weapons against civilian targets violate international law.*
▶ breach, break, contravene, infringe, transgress, flout, defy, disobey, disregard, ignore
AN OPPOSITE IS comply with

2 *Several of the royal tombs had been violated.*
▶ desecrate, defile, vandalize, deface

3 *I did not like having my privacy violated.*
▶ invade, disturb, encroach on, interfere with, abuse
AN OPPOSITE IS respect

4 *He set out to trap and violate women.*
▶ rape, abuse, indecently assault, sexually assault, molest, interfere with

**violation** NOUN

*the violation of human rights throughout the world*
▶ contravention, breach, infringement, flouting, defiance, transgression, offence (against)

**violence** NOUN

1 *A whole generation had been brought up in violence.*
▶ brutality, brute force, savagery, cruelty, barbarity, destructiveness

2 *The violence of the blow made him reel.*
▶ force, forcefulness, strength, power, might, ferocity

**violent** ADJECTIVE

1 *There were violent clashes between police and demonstrators.*
▶ brutal, vicious, rough, aggressive, forceful
AN OPPOSITE IS mild

2 *Too often violent criminals do not get sent to prison as they should.*
▶ rough, brutal, wild, fierce, vicious, aggressive, bloodthirsty, headstrong
AN OPPOSITE IS gentle

3 *He felt a rush of violent jealousy.*
▶ intense, extreme, acute, forceful, devastating
AN OPPOSITE IS weak

**VIP** NOUN

*Only visitors and VIPs get that special treatment.*
▶ celebrity, dignitary, luminary, grandee, important person

**virile** ADJECTIVE

*It pleases them to have a virile young man about the place.*
▶ masculine, vigorous, manly, potent, (*more informal*) macho

**virtual** ADJECTIVE

*The traffic was at a virtual standstill.*
▶ effective, near, almost, practical, potential

**virtually** ADVERB

*Once on, paint is virtually impossible to remove.*
▶ effectively, in effect, practically, as good as, almost

**virtue** NOUN

1 *the virtue of a simple life*
▶ goodness, righteousness, virtuousness, rectitude, integrity, honesty, dignity, uprightness, worthiness, decency, morality, honour, nobility, principle, rectitude
AN OPPOSITE IS iniquity

2 *I can see no virtue in such an arrangement.*
▶ merit, advantage, benefit, point
AN OPPOSITE IS disadvantage

3 *Punctuality is not one of her virtues.*
▶ strength, quality, good point, redeeming feature
OPPOSITES ARE failing, weakness

**virtuous** ADJECTIVE

*Sam's virtuous and superior tone was beginning to irritate him.*
▶ moral, righteous, upright, worthy, honourable, exemplary, high-minded, right-minded, high-principled
OPPOSITES ARE wicked, sinful

**visible** ADJECTIVE

*There is no visible pattern in the paper. Kim received the news without any visible signs of emotion.*
▶ noticeable, perceptible, discernible, obvious, apparent, conspicuous, recognizable, evident, manifest, clear, detectable, distinct
AN OPPOSITE IS invisible

## vision NOUN

1 *Symptoms include blurred vision and sensitivity to bright lights.*
► eyesight, sight, seeing

2 *The Great Society remained more a vision than a reality.*
► ideal, fantasy, apparition, illusion, mirage, phantasm, daydream, delusion, ghost, hallucination, phantom, spectre

3 *The plan made sense but lacked vision.*
► foresight, farsightedness, insight, imagination

## visionary ADJECTIVE

*It was one of the most powerful and visionary speeches I had heard.*
► imaginative, farsighted, creative, inventive, idealistic, prophetic, speculative

## visit NOUN

1 *Mrs Curdle paid her final visit to the place.*
► call, stay

2 *It was their first visit to Rome.*
► trip, outing, excursion, day out

## visit VERB

1 *He was ten years old when he first started visiting the old woman.*
► call on, come to see, make a visit to, pay a call on, stay with, descend on, (more informal) drop in on, go to see, (more informal) look up

2 *The chairman of the airline recently visited Moscow.*
► travel to, make a trip to, spend time in, stay in

## visitor NOUN

1 *Edward was a frequent and welcome visitor.*
► guest, caller

2 *The site will attract visitors during the festival.*
► tourist, holidaymaker, sightseer, tripper, globetrotter

## visualize VERB

*I like to visualize the mood of the song and take it from there.*
► picture, imagine, envisage, conceive, dream up

## vital ADJECTIVE

1 *It's vital to keep momentum going. The college is expected to play a vital role in promoting these languages.*
► essential, crucial, fundamental, imperative, important, necessary, indispensable
OPPOSITES ARE unimportant, inessential

2 *He was a vital force in British music.*
► dynamic, lively, energetic, vibrant, vigorous, vivacious, life-giving, invigorating, exuberant, sparkling, spirited, animated, sprightly, zestful
AN OPPOSITE IS lifeless

## vitality NOUN

*For all her vitality, Faye was only five feet four inches tall.*
► energy, vivacity, vigour, spirit, gusto, verve, dynamism, exuberance, zest, (more informal) go
AN OPPOSITE IS lethargy

## vivacious ADJECTIVE

*She must once have been quite a vivacious woman.*
► lively, high-spirited, exuberant, animated, alert, active, spirited, exciting, cheerful
OPPOSITES ARE lifeless, dull

## vivid ADJECTIVE

1 *a bouquet with four vivid blue flowers*
► bright, brilliant, colourful, vibrant, showy, striking, gaudy
AN OPPOSITE IS dull

2 *Wilson's autobiography gives a vivid account of his experiences.*
► clear, graphic, dramatic, lively, powerful, evocative, lucid, memorable, imaginative, lifelike, realistic
AN OPPOSITE IS lifeless

## vocabulary NOUN

1 *He was learning English and had a limited vocabulary.*
► word stock, lexicon, lexis

2 *There is a vocabulary at the back of the book.*
► glossary, word list, dictionary, lexicon

## vocal ADJECTIVE

1 *animals capable of vocal sounds*
► voiced, spoken, oral, said, articulated

2 *The students were becoming the most vocal critics of reform.*
► outspoken, vociferous, forthright, plain-spoken, candid

## vogue NOUN

*Small-scale farming is enjoying a new vogue.*
► fashion, mode, trend, style, craze, rage, taste

**in vogue** *Suddenly it was in vogue to have an all-over tan.*
► fashionable, in fashion, stylish, modish, smart, chic, (more informal) trendy, (more informal) all the rage, (more informal) cool, (more informal) hip

---

## voice NOUN

1 *There was no emotion in his voice.*
► speaking, speech, utterance, tone, inflection

2 *They were able to have a voice in choosing the chairman.*
► opinion, view, say, input, vote

**TYPES OF SINGING VOICE**

**male voices**: basso profundo, bass, baritone, tenor, castrato, countertenor, falsetto, treble.

**female voices**: alto, contralto, mezzo or mezzo-soprano, soprano.

---

## voice VERB

*Right-thinking people have voiced their disgust.*
► express, speak, utter, convey, communicate, articulate, give voice to, give vent to

## void ADJECTIVE

*The contract was declared void.*
► invalid, null, cancelled, inoperative, worthless
AN OPPOSITE IS valid

## volatile ADJECTIVE

She was headstrong and volatile.
▶ temperamental, unpredictable, variable, changeable, erratic, vacillating, inconstant, unsteady
OPPOSITES ARE stable, constant

## volley NOUN

They maintained their composure under a volley of missiles
▶ barrage, bombardment, battery, blast, salvo, hail, storm, shower, deluge

## volume NOUN

1 I bought his Travels and read through all five volumes.
▶ book, tome
2 They expect an increased volume of traffic over the bridge this year.
▶ amount, quantity, size, body, mass, capacity

## voluntary ADJECTIVE

1 Voluntary work tends to carry higher prestige than paid work.
▶ optional, unpaid, willing
AN OPPOSITE IS paid
2 The pay cuts will be voluntary.
▶ optional, discretionary, unforced
OPPOSITES ARE obligatory, compulsory
3 Her decision had been a voluntary act.
▶ deliberate, conscious, intentional, intended, wilful
AN OPPOSITE IS involuntary

**USAGE** Note that involuntary is an opposite of voluntary only in the third meaning.

## volunteer VERB

Having promised his help, he had better volunteer at least.
▶ offer your services, present yourself, step forward, make an offer, propose yourself, show willing

## vomit VERB

He rushed towards the drain before the urge to vomit overcame him.
▶ be sick, regurgitate, retch, heave, bring up, spew up, (more informal) throw up, (more informal) puke

## voracious ADJECTIVE

There is a voracious demand for holiday homes and weekend cottages.
▶ insatiable, unquenchable, unsatisfiable, uncontrollable, ravenous, immoderate, prodigious

## vote NOUN

People suspected the vote of being rigged.
▶ ballot, poll, election, plebiscite, referendum, show of hands

## vote VERB

1 Less than a third of the electorate voted in the last election.
▶ cast a vote, go to the polls, ballot
2 I vote we play another round.
▶ suggest, propose, recommend, move
3 vote for You may vote for one candidate only.
▶ choose, pick, select, opt for, nominate

## vouch VERB

**vouch for** I can vouch for the accuracy of these figures.
▶ guarantee, verify, affirm, attest to, testify to, corroborate, endorse, confirm, support, speak for

## voucher NOUN

You get a wallet of vouchers to pay for the various parts of your holiday.
▶ coupon, ticket, token, certificate

## vow NOUN

The monks take a vow of silence.
▶ pledge, oath, promise, commitment, avowal, assurance, guarantee, undertaking, word of honour

## vow VERB

She vowed to do better.
▶ promise, pledge, swear, take an oath, give an assurance, give your word, guarantee

## voyage NOUN

The voyage lasted two weeks.
▶ journey, passage, crossing, trip, expedition, excursion

## vulgar ADJECTIVE

1 She sent him a postcard with a vulgar picture on the back.
▶ rude, indecent, lewd, suggestive, racy, risqué
2 The decor was new and vulgar.
▶ tasteless, gaudy, garish, tawdry, flashy, (more informal) tacky
3 He was a bit too vulgar for her taste. It was considered vulgar to smoke in public.
▶ ill-mannered, unrefined, unseemly, impolite, indecorous, coarse, ill-bred

## vulnerable ADJECTIVE

1 We are most vulnerable when we are asleep.
▶ defenceless, exposed, unguarded, unprotected, at risk, weak, wide open
AN OPPOSITE IS invulnerable
2 **vulnerable to** More people are vulnerable to age discrimination.
▶ in danger of, at risk of, exposed to, open to, liable to, prone to, susceptible to
AN OPPOSITE IS immune to

# Ww

## wad NOUN

1 He took a wad of notes from his pocket and began to count them.
▶ bundle, roll, pad, (more informal) wodge
2 I needed a wad of cotton wool.
▶ lump, mass, chunk, hunk

**wadding** NOUN

*sleeping bags insulated with wadding*
▶ padding, lining, packing, filling, stuffing

**waddle** VERB

*He waddled across the garden to join Sylvia.*
▶ totter, toddle, teeter, dodder, stumble, shuffle

**waffle** NOUN

*(informal) My panic reduced the interview to waffle.*
▶ blather, prattle, nonsense, verbosity, wordiness, evasiveness, padding, prevarication

**waffle** VERB

*(informal) She waffled on for a while about things that didn't matter.*
▶ blather, prattle, ramble, babble, chatter on, gibber, gabble

**wag** VERB

1 *The dog's tail began to wag frantically.*
▶ shake, swing, wave, waggle

2 *'You see what I mean,' Eleanor said, wagging her finger.*
▶ wave, shake, waggle, brandish

**wage** VERB

*The country lacks any means to wage war.*
▶ carry on, conduct, engage in, fight, undertake

**wages** PLURAL NOUN

*He was pleased to be earning regular wages at last.*
▶ earnings, income, pay, recompense

**wail** VERB

*He was tearing at his hair and wailing 'Why me?'*
▶ howl, bawl, weep, moan, sob, shriek, whimper, snivel, cry, lament, yowl

**wail** NOUN

*Tom let out a wail.*
▶ howl, bawl, moan, sob, shriek, cry, whimper, yowl

**wait** NOUN

*The photos were ready after a short wait.*
▶ interval, pause, delay, hold-up, break, hiatus, halt, hesitation, rest, stay

**wait** VERB

*She left the room and waited outside. I can't wait for you any longer.*
▶ remain, rest, linger, stay, stop, halt, delay, mark time, stand by, hold back, pause, hesitate, *(old-fashioned)* tarry, *(more informal)* hang about
AN OPPOSITE IS proceed

**waive** VERB

*Some agencies might waive their fee if you register with them.*
▶ give up, forgo, relinquish, renounce, cede, resign, disclaim, dispense with, surrender, abandon
AN OPPOSITE IS enforce

**wake** VERB

1 *Be careful not to wake the baby.*
▶ waken, rouse, disturb, stir, awaken, arouse

2 *Sara woke to find Rodney's arm round her. When I woke up I was in the back of a car.*
▶ awake, awaken, waken, become conscious, come round, stir, get up, rise

**wake up to** *Parliament finally woke up to the electronic age.*
▶ become aware of, appreciate, comprehend, realize

USAGE See the note at *awake* (verb).

**wakeful** ADJECTIVE

*He had been wakeful all night.*
▶ sleepless, restless, disturbed
OPPOSITES ARE sleepy, asleep

**walk** NOUN

1 *Go for short walks near your home.*
▶ stroll, ramble, saunter, march, hike, tramp, trek

2 *There is a pretty walk round the cathedral.*
▶ path, pathway, walkway, lane, alley, footway, promenade

3 *He observed her elegant walk.*
▶ gait, tread, carriage, stride

**walk of life** *There are cheats in every walk of life.*
▶ sphere, class, field, calling, profession, activity

---

**walk** VERB This word is often overused. Here are some alternatives:

1 *She decided to save her bus fare and walk to work.*
▶ go on foot, travel on foot, be a pedestrian

2 *They walked together along the sands, and talked.*
▶ stroll, amble, saunter, stride, pace, trudge, proceed, promenade

3 *I'll walk the children home.*
▶ accompany, escort, take, see, show

**walk all over** *(informal) You don't want to let the cops walk all over you.*
▶ take advantage of, make use of, exploit, impose on, manipulate

**walk away** or **off with** *(informal) Someone had walked off with his wallet.*
▶ steal, pilfer, purloin, filch, take

**walk out on** *(informal) He had just walked out on his girlfriend.*
▶ leave, abandon, desert, run out on, *(informal)* jilt

---

**walker** NOUN

*Keen walkers will be spoilt for choice.*
▶ rambler, hiker, wayfarer, pedestrian

**walkout** NOUN

*The workers staged a walkout.*
▶ strike, stoppage, withdrawal of labour, go-slow

**walkover** NOUN

*The election will be no walkover.*
▶ easy victory, rout, landslide, triumph, *(more informal)* piece of cake

## **wall** NOUN

**1** *There was a noticeboard on the wall.*
► partition, screen, room divider

**2** *The east wall of the castle had been breached.*
► fortification, rampart, barricade, palisade, barrier, bulwark, stockade

RELATED ADJECTIVE mural

## **wallet** NOUN

*The wallet contained some money in euros.*
► purse, notecase, pouch, pocketbook

## **wallop** VERB

*She walloped his back with her hand.*
► thump, hit, strike, pound, beat, bang, rap, batter, knock

## **wallow** VERB

**1** *I was wallowing in a hot bath.*
► luxuriate, loll about, splash about, lie

**2** *Jack loves to wallow in praise.*
► revel, glory, take delight, indulge yourself

## **wand** NOUN

*No magic wand can solve these problems.*
► baton, stick, rod, staff, sceptre

## **wander** VERB

**1** *We spent the day wandering about the old town.*
► ramble, roam, meander, range, rove, stray, walk, wind

**2** *She had wandered away from the main group.*
► stray, deviate, digress, drift, veer

**3 wander off** *I've told you not to wander off like that.*
► go away, drift off, leave, get lost

## **wane** VERB

*Support for their action was waning.*
► diminish, decrease, subside, be reduced, dwindle, ebb, lessen, go down, drop away

AN OPPOSITE IS strengthen

## **want** NOUN

**1** *The client always has wants and feelings.*
► demand, desire, need, requirement, wish

**2** *The bridge is decaying for want of repair.*
► absence, lack, need

## **want** VERB

**1** *A clever alien wants to steal the spaceship.*
► wish, desire, hope, long

**2** *That is exactly what he wanted.*
► wish for, desire, long for, yearn for, hanker after, crave, covet, fancy, hunger for, thirst for

**3 want to** (*informal*) *You want to keep an eye on them.*
► need to, ought to, should

## **wanton** ADJECTIVE

*There are stories of wanton violence against civilians.*
► wilful, malicious, malevolent, spiteful, vicious, shameless, unprovoked, needless, unnecessary, unrestrained

## **war** NOUN

**1** *During the war he joined the police force. They had been badly affected by the chaos of war.*
► conflict, fighting, hostilities, struggle, warfare, action, military action, strife

RELATED ADJECTIVES martial, belligerent

**2** *a war against drugs*
► campaign, crusade, battle, fight, struggle

## **ward** VERB

### **ward off**

**1** *Garlands of garlic are worn to ward off evil spirits.*
► fend off, drive away, beat off, repel, avert, stave off, thwart, turn aside, repulse

**2** *He brought up his arm to ward off the blow.*
► deflect, parry, block, check

## **warden** NOUN

*The resident warden let us look over the apartments.*
► caretaker, custodian, guardian, supervisor, superintendent, janitor

## **warder** NOUN

*Her husband was a warder at the local prison.*
► prison officer, prison warden, guard, jailer, keeper

## **wardrobe** NOUN

**1** *Large areas of wardrobe doors can look plain.*
► cupboard, clothes cupboard, closet, cabinet

**2** *Her mother organized her wedding and her wardrobe.*
► clothes, outfit, attire

## **warehouse** NOUN

*The goods were stored in a heated warehouse.*
► store, storehouse, storeroom, depot, depository, repository

## **wares** PLURAL NOUN

*Luxury firms can sell their wares at high prices by keeping them 'exclusive'.*
► merchandise, goods, products, commodities, stock, produce

## **warfare** NOUN

*thirty years of continuous warfare*
► fighting, hostilities, war, conflict, combat, bloodshed, action, battle, arms

RELATED ADJECTIVES martial, belligerent

## **warlike** ADJECTIVE

*Tethlis was another warlike ruler.*
► belligerent, aggressive, warmongering, warring, combative, pugnacious

AN OPPOSITE IS peaceable

## **warm** ADJECTIVE

**1** *She strolled in warm winter sunshine towards San Marco. The sun was already warm on their backs.*
► hot, balmy, summery, sultry, sunny, temperate, tropical, warmish

AN OPPOSITE IS cold

**2** *the warm waters of the western Mediterranean*
► heated, lukewarm, tepid

**3** *She was dressed in warm clothes.*
► thick, cosy, woolly, thermal, winter

**4** *He gave them a warm welcome.*
▶ friendly, cordial, amiable, enthusiastic, affable, genial, affectionate, loving, sympathetic, warm-hearted, pleasant
OPPOSITES ARE cool, unfriendly

**warm** VERB
**1** *She was in the kitchen warming some soup.*
▶ heat (up), reheat, thaw
OPPOSITES ARE cool, chill
**2** *warm to Anne was by now warming to her theme.*
▶ take to, become enthusiastic about, get on with, feel attracted by

**warm-hearted** ADJECTIVE
*She is a generous, warm-hearted person.*
▶ kind, caring, good, kind-hearted, kindly, considerate, sympathetic, thoughtful, obliging, tender-hearted, benevolent
OPPOSITES ARE unkind, unfriendly

**warmth** NOUN
**1** *Despite the warmth of the fire, Isabel began to shiver.*
▶ heat, warmness, comfort
AN OPPOSITE IS coldness
**2** *The warmth of their welcome took them by surprise.*
▶ friendliness, cordiality, geniality, enthusiasm
AN OPPOSITE IS hostility

**warn** VERB
*The manufacturers had failed to warn doctors of the possible side effects.*
▶ advise, alert, notify, inform, caution, remind, forewarn, give a warning about, (*more informal*) tip off

**warning** NOUN
**1** *The changes were announced without warning.*
▶ notice, advance notice, forewarning, hint, indication, omen, premonition, presage, sign, signal, threat, augury, (*informal*) tip-off
**2** *The remarks were a warning of what might be in store.*
▶ omen, sign, signal, presage, portent, premonition, foreboding, prediction, token
**3** *The warning in his voice was clear.*
▶ caution, reservation, caveat, doubt
**4** *England received their third and final warning.*
▶ caution, reprimand, admonition

**warp** VERB
*A steel door won't rot, split, or warp.*
▶ twist, bend, buckle, distort, deform, kink, contort, become deformed, curve

**warrant** NOUN
**1** *They now had a warrant to search the building.*
▶ authorization, authority, permit, commission, document
**2** *On leaving prison he was given a travel warrant.*
▶ voucher, permit, pass, licence

**warrant** VERB
*This is another area that warrants attention.*
▶ need, deserve, call for, justify, necessitate

**warrior** NOUN
*a mighty warrior*
▶ fighter, soldier, fighting man, combatant

**wary** ADJECTIVE
*She had been wary of making known her name.*
▶ cautious, chary, careful, circumspect, suspicious, apprehensive, vigilant (about), watchful (about), alert (to), distrustful, heedful
OPPOSITES ARE unwary, heedless

**wash** NOUN
**1** *I said I needed to go for a wash.*
▶ bath, shower, rinse, shampoo
**2** *They give all the cars a wash each morning.*
▶ clean, shampoo, hosing-down

**wash** VERB
**1** *She took a couple of minutes to wash her face and comb her hair. Wash all fruit and vegetables thoroughly before use.*
▶ clean, cleanse, rinse, scrub, shampoo, mop, sluice, swill, wipe
OPPOSITES ARE dirty, soil
**2** *It was time to wash the dog.*
▶ soap down, sponge down, swab down, hose down
**3** *He found the soap and began to wash.*
▶ bath, bathe, shower
**4** *She washed, dried, and ironed the clothes.*
▶ launder, clean, scrub, rinse, sponge
**wash your hands of** *They cannot wash their hands of social problems.*
▶ disown, renounce, have nothing to do with, disclaim, reject, abandon
AN OPPOSITE IS embrace

**washing** NOUN
*Even the washing hanging from the windows seemed to be fluttering a welcome.*
▶ laundry, clothes, wash

**washout** NOUN
(*informal*) *The summer had been a total washout.*
▶ flop, failure, disappointment, fiasco, disaster, debacle

**waste** ADJECTIVE
**1** *Energy savings are achieved by recycling waste materials.*
▶ unwanted, discarded, superfluous, unused, extra
**2** *There was a patch of waste ground for them to play on.*
▶ bare, wild, empty, overgrown, barren, derelict, undeveloped, run-down, uncared for, uncultivated

**waste** NOUN
**1** *Sewage and industrial waste still enter the North Sea.*
▶ refuse, rubbish, debris, effluent, garbage, dross, detritus, trash, junk, litter, scraps
**2** *The trip had been a waste of time and money.*
▶ squandering, misuse, frittering away, misspending, dissipation

**waste** VERB

*He didn't want to waste money on a taxi fare.*
► squander, fritter away, misspend, misuse, throw away, lavish, consume, exhaust, dissipate, use wastefully, use up
AN OPPOSITE IS conserve

**waste away** *Many people wasted away from disease and malnutrition.*
► wither, become emaciated, become weaker, decline, pine, weaken
AN OPPOSITE IS thrive

**wasteful** ADJECTIVE

*a wasteful use of resources*
► extravagant, prodigal, profligate, spendthrift, lavish, reckless, thriftless, excessive, improvident, imprudent, uneconomical, needless
AN OPPOSITE IS economical

**watch** NOUN

1 *David checked the time by his new watch.*
► wristwatch, pocket watch, timepiece, chronometer, clock, timer

2 *One of us should keep watch at the back of the house.*
► guard, vigil, lookout, surveillance, heed
**on the watch** *Be on the watch for jellyfish.*
► alert, vigilant, attentive

**watch** VERB

1 *She watched him as he cleaned the room.*
► look at, observe, keep your eyes on, contemplate, eye, gaze at, survey, heed, regard, see, stare at, take notice of, view, pay attention to, concentrate on, attend to, mark, note

2 *We need someone to watch the children for a few hours.*
► look after, mind, supervise, keep an eye on, keep watch on, care for, tend, guard, protect, safeguard, shield

**watch out** *Watch out for snakes.*
► look out for, be alert, be vigilant, be attentive, (*more informal*) keep an eye open for

**watcher** NOUN

*There was a little group of watchers on the touchline.*
► onlooker, spectator, viewer, observer, witness, looker-on

**watchful** ADJECTIVE

*Their father kept a watchful eye on them.*
► observant, alert, vigilant, careful, sharp, attentive, heedful, perceptive
AN OPPOSITE IS inattentive

**water** NOUN

1 *a glass of water*
► drinking water, tap water, mineral water

2 *a picnic by the water*
► river, lake, sea, ocean, loch, pond, pool
RELATED ADJECTIVES aquatic, hydraulic

**water** VERB

*She went out to water the plants.*
► sprinkle, wet, moisten, dampen, hose, soak, douse, drench, flood, irrigate, souse

**water down**

1 *He asked her to water down his drink.*
► dilute, add water to, weaken, thin

2 *The proposals had to be watered down to stand any chance of success.*
► moderate, tone down, soften, mitigate, temper, mellow, weaken

**waterfall** NOUN

*They looked down from the top of the waterfall.*
► cascade, cataract, shower, torrent, falls, rapids, chute

**waterproof** ADJECTIVE

*a waterproof jacket*
► water-repellent, water-resistant, weatherproof, watertight, damp-proof, impermeable, impervious

**watertight** ADJECTIVE

1 *Use a watertight container.*
► sealed, hermetic, sound, waterproof
AN OPPOSITE IS leaky

2 *a watertight excuse*
► foolproof, unassailable, flawless, conclusive, perfect
AN OPPOSITE IS flawed

**watery** ADJECTIVE

1 *a bowl of watery porridge*
► runny, sloppy, thin, watered down, weak, insipid, liquid, tasteless, (*more informal*) wishy-washy

2 *His eyes looked watery.*
► damp, moist, tear-filled, tearful, wet

**wave** NOUN

1 *Surfers were riding the waves.*
► breaker, roller, billow, crest, ridge, surf, white horse

2 *A wave of panic seemed to grip the crowd.*
► surge, upsurge, outbreak, current, flood, rash, sweep, stream, swell

3 *She gave a wave of her hand as he sped past.*
► gesture, shake, signal, flourish, gesticulation

4 *Her hair flowed in long waves.*
► curl, twist, kink

**wave** VERB

1 *Jill waved at us to go over.*
► beckon, gesture, signal, motion, indicate

2 *He waved his umbrella at them.*
► shake, brandish, flourish, waggle, wiggle, wag

3 *A flag waved in the breeze.*
► flap, flutter, ripple, quiver, move to and fro

**wave aside** *All these objections were waved aside.*
► dismiss, reject, disregard, ignore, discount, brush aside, shrug off

## wavelength NOUN

*Tune your radio to the right wavelength*
► channel, station, waveband

## waver VERB

1 *Her voice began to waver and she looked faint.*
► tremble, falter, quaver, quiver, become unsteady, change, quake, shake, shiver, shudder, sway, teeter, totter, wobble

2 *He could see I was wavering.*
► hesitate, be undecided, be indecisive, dither, equivocate, vacillate

3 *the wavering light from the candle*
► flicker, quiver, tremble, glimmer

## wavy ADJECTIVE

*She ran her hand through her wavy hair.*
► curly, curling, curving, rippling, sinuous, undulating, winding, zigzag
AN OPPOSITE IS straight

## way NOUN

1 *His engine overheated on the way home.*
► road, route, journey, direction

2 *There was a long way to go.*
► distance, length, measurement

3 *It was the best way of dealing with the problem.*
► method, means, manner, approach, mode, procedure, process, avenue, course, system, technique, mechanism

4 *He knew he had to change his ways.*
► habit, practice, routine, custom, fashion, style, tradition

5 *The arts benefit society in several ways.*
► respect, particular, aspect, circumstances, detail, feature

## waylay VERB

1 *They were waylaid by bandits on the road to the coast.*
► ambush, hold up, attack, accost

2 *She waylaid me to chat as I was leaving.*
► catch, accost, intercept, buttonhole, detain, (more informal) get hold of, (more informal) nab

## way-out ADJECTIVE

*(informal) He introduced some way-out visual ideas that no one had tried before.*
► unconventional, offbeat, eccentric, quirky, bizarre, weird, odd, (informal) wacky

## wayward ADJECTIVE

*Her husband treated her like a wayward child.*
► disobedient, naughty, wilful, stubborn, headstrong, self-willed, perverse, obstinate, contrary, badly behaved, uncontrollable, uncooperative
OPPOSITES ARE cooperative, well-behaved

## weak ADJECTIVE

1 *The bridge was weak as a result of metal fatigue.*
► unsafe, unsound, fragile, unsteady, rickety, shaky, flimsy, decrepit, substandard
AN OPPOSITE IS strong

2 *He was still too weak to get up by himself.*
► frail, feeble, poorly, ill, infirm, sickly, debilitated, helpless, delicate, enervated, exhausted, listless, puny
AN OPPOSITE IS strong

3 *A weak man, when provoked, is often more dangerous than a violent one.*
► timid, timorous, irresolute, spineless, ineffectual, pusillanimous, cowardly, fearful, impotent, indecisive, ineffective
OPPOSITES ARE strong, brave

4 *His mistakes had put him in a weak position.*
► vulnerable, exposed, defenceless, unguarded, unprotected
OPPOSITES ARE strong, powerful

5 *The weak joke fell hollowly.*
► feeble, lame, unconvincing, unsatisfactory

6 *She sipped the sweet, weak tea and began to feel better.*
► watery, diluted, watered down, insipid, bland, thin, tasteless
AN OPPOSITE IS strong

7 *The light was becoming weak.*
► dim, pale, faint, feeble
OPPOSITES ARE strong, bright

## weaken VERB

1 *Their purpose was to weaken the unions' power.*
► reduce, sap, enfeeble, erode, impair, lessen, diminish, lower, debilitate, destroy, emasculate, enervate, make weaker, ruin, soften, undermine
OPPOSITES ARE strengthen, boost

2 *Our resolve had weakened.*
► dwindle, ebb, fade, flag, wane, abate, become weaker, decline, decrease, give way
OPPOSITES ARE strengthen, increase, intensify

## weakness NOUN

1 *There is an obvious weakness in your argument.*
► fault, flaw, defect, imperfection, weak point, blemish, error, failing, mistake, shortcoming
OPPOSITES ARE strength, strong point

2 *The economy is showing signs of weakness.*
► fragility, frailty, flimsiness, inadequacy, softness

3 *Her illness left her with a permanent physical weakness.*
► infirmity, debility, feebleness, illness, impotence, lassitude, vulnerability
OPPOSITES ARE strength, vigour

4 *He has a weakness for chocolate cake.*
► liking, fondness, inclination, penchant, predilection, (more informal) soft spot

## wealth NOUN

1 *We want to see wealth passed down from generation to generation.*
► affluence, assets, opulence, property, prosperity, capital, fortune, money, possessions, riches
AN OPPOSITE IS poverty

2 *You realize the wealth of information inside the government.*
► abundance, profusion, plethora, store, plenty

**wealthy** ADJECTIVE

*Her mother was a very wealthy woman.*
▶ rich, affluent, prosperous, well-off, well-to-do, moneyed, comfortable, (more informal) flush, (more informal) loaded
OPPOSITES ARE poor, impoverished

**wear** VERB

1 *Did you have to wear any special kind of clothing? Ruth wore a pale lavender cotton dress. He often wore dark glasses to hide the bags under his eyes.*
▶ dress in, be dressed in, clothe yourself in, put on, have on, present yourself in, wrap up in, don
2 *He wore his usual benign expression.*
▶ show, assume, present, exhibit
3 *Years of passing footsteps had badly worn the carpet.*
▶ damage, fray, scuff, mark, weaken
4 *The tyres have worn well.*
▶ last, endure, survive, hold up, (more informal) stand the test of time

**wear away** *Most of the grass had been worn away by the spectators.*
▶ rub away, erode, grind down, abrade, corrode, eat away

**wear off** *The effect of the tranquillizers was wearing off.*
▶ fade, subside, dwindle, reduce, lessen, diminish, peter out, disappear

**wear out**
1 *His shoes wear out twice as fast when he's working.*
▶ become worn, deteriorate, become damaged, become scuffed
2 *They cheered until their lungs were worn out.*
▶ exhaust, fatigue, tire out

**wear** NOUN

1 *Repairs were made necessary by heavy wear.*
▶ use, service, utility, wearing
2 *The brakes showed signs of wear.*
▶ damage, deterioration, friction, erosion, wear and tear
3 *The guests were dressed in formal wear.*
▶ dress, clothes, clothing, costume, outfit

**wearing** ADJECTIVE

*The care of others can be a wearing business.*
▶ tiring, exhausting, tiresome, fatiguing, wearying, wearisome, trying, taxing
AN OPPOSITE IS refreshing

**wearisome** ADJECTIVE

*Waiting is the most wearisome of all activities.*
▶ tedious, monotonous, boring, dreary, tiring, troublesome, exhausting
AN OPPOSITE IS stimulating

**weary** ADJECTIVE

*I have been too sad and too weary to write anything.*
▶ tired, exhausted, fatigued, wearied, worn out, sapped, drained, spent, (more informal) knackered

**weary** VERB

*Gemma had not the heart to say how much they wearied her.*
▶ tire, exhaust, fatigue, bore

**wearying** ADJECTIVE

*The wearying journey lasted for three days.*
▶ tiring, exhausting, tiresome, fatiguing, wearing, wearisome, trying, taxing
AN OPPOSITE IS refreshing

---

**weather** NOUN

*She was tempted to use the weather as an excuse to postpone her visit. All farmers are exposed to the vagaries of the weather.*
▶ climate, the elements, meteorological conditions, atmospheric conditions
**under the weather** *She felt under the weather and went to rest.*
▶ unwell, poorly, indisposed, out of sorts, ill, sick
OPPOSITES ARE well, in good health
RELATED ADJECTIVE meteorological

**WORDS TO DO WITH WEATHER**

**general words to do with weather:** climate, forecast, foul, lightning, meteorology, meteorologist, outlook, rough, thunder.

**meteorological instruments:** barometer, barograph; thermometer; anemometer (measuring the force of the wind); weathercock, weathervane.

**words to do with air pressure:** high, low; anticyclone, cyclone, depression.

**words to do with rain and other precipitation:** rain, sleet, slush, hail; snow; blizzard, deluge, downpour, drizzle, drought, flood, ice storm, shower, torrent; dew.

**words to do with sky and clouds:** cirrus, clear, cumulus, cumulo-nimbus, haze, mist, stratus, sunless, sunny, sunshine, thundercloud; thunder, lightning; blue, bright, brilliant; fair, fine, cloudless, cloudy; misty, overcast, dull, fog, foggy, grey, hazy.

**words to do with temperature:** cold, hot, freezing, frost, frosty, hoar-frost, ice, icy; oppressive, sultry, sweltering, wintry; heatwave.

**words to do with wind:** blustery, breeze, cyclone, gale, hurricane, monsoon, squall, storm, tempest, tornado, dust devil; typhoon, waterspout, whirlwind, willy-willy, wind-vane.

---

**weather** VERB

*Many small businesses had managed to weather the recession.*
▶ survive, endure, withstand, ride out, come through, live through, overcome

**weave** VERB

1 *The design had been woven into the carpet.*
▶ intertwine, interweave, knit, plait, sew, entwine, interlace

2 *Victorian novelists weave romances round great houses. She wove a spell over him, so that he slept for ever and never grew old.*
▶ create, compose, make, plot, put together

**3** *He dragged himself out of bed and weaved his way to the bathroom.*
▶ thread, wind, work, dodge, zigzag

**web** NOUN
**1** *The webs are built to a definite pattern.*
▶ mesh, net, netting, network, crisscross, lattice
**2** *Their lives were caught up in a web of deception.*
▶ network, nexus, maze, complex

**wedding** NOUN
*The wedding went ahead with two hundred guests.*
▶ marriage, marriage ceremony, nuptials, union
RELATED ADJECTIVE nuptial, bridal

**wedge** NOUN
**1** *He put a huge wedge of gleaming white pudding on her plate.*
▶ slice, segment, triangle, chunk, lump
**2** *The window was held open with a wedge.*
▶ chock, block, door stop

**wedge** VERB
*She wedged the string bag between her feet and took out a book. The children were wedged so tightly that it was difficult to move.*
▶ squeeze, jam, cram, push, force, thrust, stick, push, fasten, (more informal) shove

**weedy** ADJECTIVE
**1** *I walked up through the weedy garden.*
▶ untidy, unweeded, overgrown, unkempt, wild, rank
**2** (informal) *He was short and physically weedy.*
▶ weak, puny, feeble, frail

**weep** VERB
*I began to weep, burying my face in my hands.*
▶ cry, sob, shed tears, whimper, blubber, snivel, wail

**weepy** ADJECTIVE
*She was weepy and nervy, anxious about her baby.*
▶ tearful, in tears, crying, weeping, sobbing, upset, emotional

**weigh** VERB
**1** *The man weighed some vegetables and put them in a bag.*
▶ measure the weight of, measure out, put on the scales
**2** *I weigh the same now as when I married.*
▶ have a weight of, tip the scales at
**3** **weigh** or **weigh up** *These were considerations that she weighed carefully. I weighed up my chances and decided to go.*
▶ consider, evaluate, assess, examine, think about, give thought to, ponder, study, mull over, meditate on
**4** *Two other matters weigh in their favour.*
▶ be important, count, have weight

**weigh down**
**1** *No one wants to be weighed down with heavy gear.*
▶ burden, weight, saddle, load, overload
**2** *She walked to her room, mentally weighed down by her thoughts.*
▶ depress, oppress, trouble, bother, beset, afflict, prey on

**weight** NOUN
**1** *The supports could no longer sustain the weight of the bridge, and it collapsed.*
▶ heaviness, load, burden, mass, pressure, strain
**2** *The Prime Minister has attached a lot of weight to the scheme.*
▶ importance, seriousness, significance, authority, emphasis, gravity, substance

**weight** VERB
**1** *Driftwood can be sealed and weighted in the same way.*
▶ weigh down, make heavy, ballast, hold down, keep down, load
**2** *The odds were weighted against them.*
▶ bias, load, slant, balance

**weighty** ADJECTIVE
**1** *A pile of books can be very weighty.*
▶ heavy, bulky, cumbersome, massive, clumsy
**2** *The weighty question, what is happiness?*
▶ serious, important, significant, momentous, far-reaching, consequential
**3** *It is a weighty responsibility to be given.*
▶ demanding, onerous, exacting, taxing, troublesome

**weird** ADJECTIVE
**1** *Some pretty weird things seemed to be happening.*
▶ uncanny, eerie, unearthly, unnatural, ghostly, mysterious, scary, supernatural, unaccountable, (more informal) spooky, (more informal) creepy
OPPOSITES ARE normal, ordinary
**2** *They wouldn't make those weird garden ornaments if they'd ever seen a real gnome. The fridge made some really weird noises yesterday.*
▶ strange, peculiar, bizarre, grotesque, odd, curious, eccentric, outlandish, queer, unusual, abnormal, quirky, unconventional, (more informal) wacky, (more informal) freaky, (more informal) way-out
AN OPPOSITE IS conventional

**welcome** ADJECTIVE
*We've received some welcome news.*
▶ pleasant, pleasing, gratifying, encouraging, good, nice
OPPOSITES ARE unwelcome, disappointing

**welcome** NOUN
*Make for the Visitors' Centre, where you can be sure of a warm welcome.*
▶ reception, greeting, hospitality

**welcome** VERB
**1** *Sophie welcomed her warmly and pulled out a chair.*
▶ greet, receive, hail, meet
**2** *His colleagues welcomed his cheerfulness.*
▶ appreciate, approve of, delight in, like, want, accept

**weld** VERB
*Steel spikes were welded on to the toecaps.*
▶ fuse, join, attach, fasten, solder, bond, cement, unite

**welfare** NOUN

*the safety and welfare of people at work*
▶ well-being, good, security, prosperity, comfort, benefit, happiness, health, interests

**well** ADJECTIVE

*Mary was looking well.*
▶ healthy, in good health, fit, fine, sound, strong, thriving, flourishing, hearty, lively, robust, vigorous

**well** ADVERB

**1** *They behaved well.*
▶ satisfactorily, correctly, nicely, properly
AN OPPOSITE IS badly
**2** *She sings well.*
▶ ably, skilfully, expertly
OPPOSITES ARE badly, poorly
**3** *Mix the ingredients well.*
▶ thoroughly, fully, completely, rigorously
AN OPPOSITE IS lightly
**4** *You have been working well.*
▶ carefully, diligently, conscientiously, attentively
OPPOSITES ARE badly, poorly
**5** *He has made enough money to live well.*
▶ comfortably, in comfort, prosperously

**well** VERB

*The tears welled in her eyes.*
▶ flow, stream, spring, course, surge, flood, gush, rise, run, trickle

**well-behaved** ADJECTIVE

*You will have to be quiet and well-behaved.*
▶ well-mannered, polite, obedient, respectful, courteous, cooperative, good, dutiful, nice
AN OPPOSITE IS naughty

**well-being** NOUN

*The medical staff are responsible for the well-being of the patients.*
▶ welfare, good, security, prosperity, comfort, benefit, happiness, health, interests

**well-dressed** ADJECTIVE

*A well-dressed young woman came in.*
▶ smart, stylish, elegant, fashionable, well-groomed, chic, trim

**well-known** ADJECTIVE

**1** *They played well-known types such as the domineering wife and the henpecked husband.*
▶ familiar, widely known, popular, common, typical
**2** *She came from a well-known North London family.*
▶ famous, notable, prominent, leading, distinguished, eminent

**well-off** ADJECTIVE

*dream gardens of well-off homeowners*
▶ rich, wealthy, well-to-do, affluent, moneyed, prosperous, opulent
AN OPPOSITE IS poor

**wet** ADJECTIVE

**1** *Her jacket was soaking and clung to her like a wet tea towel.*
▶ damp, soaked, saturated, drenched, moistened, sopping, dripping
AN OPPOSITE IS dry
**2** *The mowers could not be used because the ground was too wet.*
▶ waterlogged, sodden, boggy, soggy, spongy, swampy, squelchy
OPPOSITES ARE dry, firm
**3** *They were unlucky enough to meet wet weather at harvest time.*
▶ rainy, raining, drizzly, showery, pouring, humid, misty
OPPOSITES ARE dry, fine
**4** *The paint was still wet.*
▶ runny, sticky, tacky
OPPOSITES ARE dry, set
**5** *(informal) Some of the trainees seemed a bit wet.*
▶ feeble, weak, silly, soft, (informal) weedy, (informal) wimpish
OPPOSITES ARE tough, strong

**wet** NOUN

*The front wheels were prone to locking in the wet.*
▶ rain, dampness, wet weather, damp weather, drizzle

**wet** VERB

*There is no need to wet your hair first.*
▶ dampen, damp, douse, drench, soak, spray, sprinkle, water, steep, irrigate, moisten, saturate
AN OPPOSITE IS dry

**whack** VERB

*I saw him take a stick and whack his dog.*
▶ hit, strike, smack, slap, thump, (more informal) slug

**whack** NOUN

*She gave him a hefty whack across his shoulders.*
▶ blow, hit, slap, punch, thump, knock, smack

**wheel** VERB

**1** *He grabbed a trolley and began to wheel the luggage away.*
▶ push, trundle, roll
**2** *A flock of birds wheeled above them.*
▶ circle, gyrate, turn, orbit
**wheel round** *Elinor wheeled round, a look of horror on her face.*
▶ turn, swing round, change direction, swerve, veer

**wheeze** VERB

*He was wheezing now, as if in the grip of an asthma attack.*
▶ gasp, breathe noisily, cough, pant, puff

**whereabouts** NOUN

*Despite inquiries, his whereabouts remain unknown.*
▶ location, position, situation, vicinity, address, site

**whet** VERB

**1** *He whetted his knife on a stone.*
▶ sharpen, hone, put an edge on
**2** *There are many new brews to whet the appetite.*
▶ stimulate, excite, arouse, rouse, kindle, awaken

**whiff** NOUN

**1** *He caught a whiff of expensive perfume.*
▶ scent, aroma, smell , breath, puff, odour
**USAGE** You normally use *odour* when you
mean an unpleasant smell.
**2** *At the slightest whiff of trouble he takes to his bed.*
▶ hint, trace, suggestion, suspicion, intimation

**whim** NOUN

*It was silly to waste a whole morning on a foolish whim.*
▶ impulse, notion, urge, fancy, caprice, desire, quirk

**whimper** VERB

*He began to whimper with fear.*
▶ snivel, wail, moan, cry, groan, weep, (*more
informal*) grizzle

**whimper** NOUN

*The dog made off with a whimper.*
▶ whine, cry, snivel

**whine** NOUN

*There was a whine from the engines.*
▶ drone, whimper, hum

**whine** VERB

**1** *Mosquitos whined in my ears.*
▶ drone, hum
**2** (*informal*) *I'm sick of him whining to me about you.*
▶ grumble, complain, carp, grouch, moan, beef,
(*informal*) whinge

**whip** NOUN

*He threatened to use a whip on any intruders.*
▶ lash, scourge, cat, cat-o'-nine-tails, horsewhip,
riding-crop, switch

**whip** VERB

**1** *He whipped the boys and sent them away.*
▶ thrash, beat, flog, lash, scourge
**2** *Why can you whip cream but not milk?*
▶ whisk, beat, stir vigorously
**3** (*informal*) *She whipped a piece of paper out of her
pocket.*
▶ pull, whisk, pluck, tug, take
**4** (*informal*) *I can always whip round to the corner shop.*
▶ dash, hurry, shoot, run, sprint, rush, race, tear

**whirl** NOUN

**1** *His mind was in a whirl and he was worried.*
▶ daze, spin, muddle, stupor, state of confusion
**2** (*informal*) *The only way to find out was to give it a
whirl.*
▶ try, test, (*informal*) shot, (*informal*) bash

**whirl** VERB

*The dancers appear to whirl round with their hands on
their hips.*
▶ circle, gyrate, twirl, spin, rotate, pirouette, reel,
revolve, swivel, turn, twist, wheel

**whisk** VERB

**1** *Whisk the sugar and eggs together.*
▶ beat, mix, stir, whip
**2** *You will be whisked off to a studio for a photo session.*
▶ rush, speed, hurry, sweep, shoot, hurtle
**3** *He whisked a blanket off the nearest trolley.*
▶ pull, pluck, tug, take, (*more informal*) whip

**whisper** VERB

*Anne whispered something in his ear.*
▶ murmur, breathe, mutter, mumble
AN OPPOSITE IS shout

**whisper** NOUN

**1** *He spoke in a whisper.*
▶ murmur, mutter, undertone, hushed voice
**2** *I heard a whisper that he's left the country.*
▶ rumour, report, piece of gossip, piece of hearsay

**white** ADJECTIVE

**1** *He rested his fingers on the white keys.*
▶ ivory, snowy, chalky, pale , snow-white, cream
**2** *Her face was white with fear.*
▶ pale, pallid, ashen, colourless, bloodless

**whittle** VERB

**whittle away** *The monarch's powers were gradually
whittled away.*
▶ erode, wear away, reduce, undermine
**whittle down** *The original hundred contestants have
been whittled down to six.*
▶ reduce, cut down, cut back, trim, scale down, pare
down

**whole** ADJECTIVE

**1** *I don't have time to read the whole book.*
▶ entire, complete, full, total, full-length,
unabridged, uncut, unexpurgated
OPPOSITES ARE incomplete, partial
**2** *The archaeologists uncovered a Greek vase that
turned out to be whole.*
▶ intact, in one piece, unbroken, undamaged,
unharmed, unscathed, perfect
OPPOSITES ARE broken, fragmentary

**wholehearted** ADJECTIVE

*You have our wholehearted support.*
▶ total, complete, unreserved, unqualified,
committed, absolute, outright, utter
OPPOSITES ARE half- hearted, partial

**wholesale** ADJECTIVE

*the wholesale destruction of sacred images*
▶ total, comprehensive, extensive, large-scale,
indiscriminate, widespread, mass, universal

**wholesome** ADJECTIVE

**1** *wholesome food*
▶ nourishing, nutritious, healthy, good,
health-giving, hygienic
AN OPPOSITE IS unhealthy
**2** *a good wholesome story*
▶ decent, innocent, moral, edifying, improving
AN OPPOSITE IS unwholesome

**wholly** ADVERB

*The money collected was wholly inadequate.*
▶ completely, totally, utterly, absolutely,
altogether, downright

**whopping** ADJECTIVE

*The bill came to a whopping £500.*
▶ huge, enormous, gigantic, mammoth, immense, massive, colossal

**wicked** ADJECTIVE

**1** *a wicked person   a wicked act*
▶ evil, bad, sinful, base, immoral, corrupt, depraved, heinous, iniquitous
OPPOSITES ARE moral, good, upright

**2** *It was wicked of you to say such things.*
▶ naughty, wrong, nasty, mischievous, unkind
OPPOSITES ARE good, kind

**3** *There was a wicked gleam in his eye.*
▶ mischievous, playful, rascally, impish, devilish, cheeky

**4** (*informal*) *He makes a wicked fruit salad.*
▶ excellent, marvellous, wonderful, superb
AN OPPOSITE IS lousy

**wickedness** NOUN

*the sheer wickedness of their plan*
▶ evil, enormity, iniquity, vileness, baseness, foulness, heinousness, immorality, infamy, sinfulness, villainy, turpitude, wrong, wrongdoing
AN OPPOSITE IS goodness

**wide** ADJECTIVE

**1** *The river was fast and wide.   Players are spread over a wide area*
▶ broad, expansive, extensive, vast, large, spacious, spread out, outspread
AN OPPOSITE IS narrow

**2** *There is a wide choice of dinner menu.   The programmes reach a wide audience.*
▶ extensive, comprehensive, wide-ranging, inclusive, all-embracing, broad, ample, universal
OPPOSITES ARE narrow, limited

**3** *Wide trousers became fashionable again.*
▶ baggy, loose, full, flared
OPPOSITES ARE narrow, tight

**4** *The shot went wide*
▶ off course, off target, off the mark
AN OPPOSITE IS on target

**wide** ADVERB

*Her eyes opened wide.*
▶ fully, completely

**widen** VERB

**1** *There are plans to widen parts of the motorway.*
▶ broaden, make wider, expand, enlarge, extend, open out, spread, stretch
AN OPPOSITE IS narrow

**2** *Her smile widened.*
▶ broaden, become wider, spread
AN OPPOSITE IS narrow

**3** *They must widen the scope of the inquiry.*
▶ expand, extend, broaden, enlarge, increase
OPPOSITES ARE narrow, restrict, limit

**widespread** ADJECTIVE

**1** *These incidents provoked widespread protest.*
▶ general, extensive, universal, wholesale, far-reaching, global
AN OPPOSITE IS uncommon

**2** *Death and disease were widespread in these years.*
▶ rife, prevalent, endemic, pervasive, common

**width** NOUN

*Two white lines should be drawn across the width of the pitch.*
▶ breadth, span, girth, diameter

**wield** VERB

**1** *He was wielding a piece of wood outside a pub.*
▶ brandish, flourish, wave, swing, ply, flaunt

**2** *He did not wield the same influence as his father.*
▶ have, exercise, exert, command, possess

**wife** NOUN

*His new wife is a Parisian.*
▶ spouse, partner, (*more formal*) consort, (*more informal*) woman, (*more informal*) mate, (*more informal*) better half

**wiggle** VERB

*He removed his shoes and wiggled his toes.*
▶ wriggle, waggle, jiggle

**wild** ADJECTIVE

**1** *He began attacking me like a wild animal.*
▶ fierce, feral, ferocious, untamed, undomesticated
AN OPPOSITE IS tame

**2** *There are many wild flowers that can be legally picked.*
▶ natural, uncultivated, indigenous
AN OPPOSITE IS cultivated

**3** *Even seemingly wild ideas may be aired at this point.*
▶ crazy, ridiculous, madcap, absurd, foolish, silly, outrageous, extravagant, impractical, rash, foolhardy
OPPOSITES ARE sensible, practical

**4** *A wild urge rose up inside her to tell everything.*
▶ reckless, rash, intense, extreme
OPPOSITES ARE gentle, mild

**5** *My father liked these wild people.*
▶ primitive, savage, barbarous, uncivilized, uncultured
AN OPPOSITE IS civilized

**6** *She said she was sorry for her wild behaviour.*
▶ unruly, rowdy, violent, disorderly, uncontrolled, unrestrained, undisciplined, unconstrained, unbridled
OPPOSITES ARE calm, restrained

**7** *The parties involve loud music and wild dancing.*
▶ lively, flamboyant, boisterous, exuberant, animated
AN OPPOSITE IS restrained

**8** *Don't plan to go out in really wild weather.*
▶ rough, stormy, tempestuous, blustery, foul, inclement
AN OPPOSITE IS calm

**9** *the beautiful wild scenery of the Highlands*
▶ rugged, rough, desolate, uncultivated, unpopulated, barren

10 *His team mates were wild with joy.*
▶ excited, ecstatic, delirious, frantic, frenzied
11 *Without knowing the answer I decided to risk a wild guess.*
▶ arbitrary, random, haphazard, hit-or-miss
AN OPPOSITE IS considered
12 (*informal*) *Being disturbed at this time made him wild.*
▶ furious, angry, enraged, irate, cross, livid, (*more informal*) hopping mad
AN OPPOSITE IS pleased
13 **wild about** (*informal*) *I'm not wild about the music.*
▶ keen on, enthusiastic about, (*informal*) mad about, (*informal*) crazy about

**wilful** ADJECTIVE
1 *He was charged with wilful damage and assault.*
▶ deliberate, intentional, premeditated, intended, planned, calculated, conscious, voluntary
AN OPPOSITE IS accidental
2 *She checked her wilful and impulsive self.*
▶ headstrong, self-willed, strong-willed, obstinate, stubborn, perverse, determined, dogged, intransigent, obdurate
AN OPPOSITE IS amenable

**will** NOUN
1 *Corruption exists when politicians have lost the will to enforce the law.*
▶ determination, resolve, resolution, intention, purpose, aim, desire, inclination, volition, will-power, wish
2 *I don't think it's the will of the people.*
▶ desire, wish, choice, preference
3 *She had died without making a will.*
▶ testament, last wishes

**will** VERB
1 *He willed them not to panic.*
▶ encourage, inspire, influence, wish
2 *She willed her money equally to all her nephews and nieces.*
▶ bequeath, leave, pass on

**willing** ADJECTIVE
1 *Let us know if you are willing to make cakes or prepare sandwiches.*
▶ prepared, ready, disposed, agreeable, eager, inclined, content, pleased, (*more informal*) game
OPPOSITES ARE unwilling, reluctant, disinclined
2 *You'd be surprised what can be achieved by willing hands eager to do good turns.*
▶ enthusiastic, helpful, obliging, cooperative, amenable, compliant, consenting
OPPOSITES ARE unwilling, unhelpful

**wilt** VERB
1 *The flowers had begun to wilt.*
▶ droop, fade, shrivel, wither, become limp, flop, languish, sag
OPPOSITES ARE thrive, revive, perk up
2 *Their joy soon wilted.*
▶ fail, flag, wane, dwindle, evaporate, weaken, diminish, sink
AN OPPOSITE IS grow

**wily** ADJECTIVE
*He was constantly in danger of being outwitted by his wily opponents.*
▶ clever, crafty, shrewd, artful, astute, cunning, devious, guileful, knowing, scheming, shifty, foxy, sly, underhand
AN OPPOSITE IS naïve

**win** VERB
1 *She had a good chance of winning.*
▶ be victorious, be the winner, succeed, triumph, come first, finish first, prevail, conquer, overcome
AN OPPOSITE IS lose
2 *Next year they would win first prize.*
▶ achieve, receive, acquire, (*more informal*) carry off, (*more informal*) come away with, (*more informal*) pick up, (*more informal*) walk away with
3 *Charles II managed to win the support of the Scots.*
▶ gain, secure, obtain, earn, deserve, get

**win** NOUN
*His win ended eleven years of American domination of the championship.*
▶ victory, triumph, success, conquest
AN OPPOSITE IS defeat

**wind** NOUN (rhymes with *pinned*)
*She shivered in the chill wind.*
▶ breeze, air current, gust, blast, puff, breath, draught, gale, squall

**wind** VERB (rhymes with *mind*)
1 *He wound the cord tightly.*
▶ coil, loop, twist, twine, curl, curve, furl, turn, roll
2 *The Saigon River begins to wind like a serpent.*
▶ twist, snake, bend, curve, meander, ramble, twist and turn, zigzag
**wind up** (*informal*) *We could wind up paying the whole lot.*
▶ end up, finish up, land up, find yourself
**wind someone up** (*informal*) *I'm sure he's just doing it to wind me up.*
▶ tease, annoy, disconcert, trick

**winding** ADJECTIVE
*A winding road leads down to the village.*
▶ bending, sinuous, snaking, meandering, tortuous, rambling, roundabout, serpentine, circuitous, (*more informal*) windy, (*more informal*) twisty, (*more informal*) bendy
AN OPPOSITE IS straight

**windy** ADJECTIVE
*It was too cold and windy to sit and wait.*
▶ blowy, breezy, blustery, gusty, squally, boisterous, draughty, stormy
AN OPPOSITE IS calm

**wing** NOUN
1 *The maternity department is in the north wing of the hospital.*
▶ section, annexe, end, extension
2 *the military wing of the organization*
▶ section, faction, branch, group

**wink** VERB

*The red light winked.*
► flash, gleam, flicker, sparkle, twinkle

**wink** NOUN

*Then, in a wink, it all turned to dust.*
► instant, moment, second, flash

**winner** NOUN

*The points system produces an overall winner.*
► victor, champion, conqueror, first, prizewinner
AN OPPOSITE IS loser

**winning** ADJECTIVE

**1** *For the fourth time he was on the winning side.*
► victorious, successful, triumphant, champion, conquering, prevailing, leading, top-scoring
AN OPPOSITE IS losing

**2** *The show lacks a really winning song.*
► appealing, attractive, fetching, charming, engaging

**winnings** PLURAL NOUN

*She used part of her winnings to buy a new house.*
► prize money, gains
AN OPPOSITE IS losses

**wintry** ADJECTIVE

*He opened a window, letting in damp wintry air.*
► chilly, frosty, cold, bleak, freezing, icy, biting, snowy

**wipe** VERB

*She wiped the table with a damp cloth. Nathan wiped the crumbs from his mouth.*
► rub, brush, clean, mop, sponge, swab, wash
**wipe out** *Two hurricanes almost wiped out the flourishing egg industry.*
► destroy, obliterate, annihilate, eradicate, exterminate, demolish

**wisdom** NOUN

*He would persuade them of the wisdom of adopting this course.*
► sense, prudence, common sense, good sense, intelligence, judgement, astuteness, sagacity, discernment, insight, reason

**wise** ADJECTIVE

**1** *Wise parents are able to give support and advice.*
► sensible, prudent, shrewd, perceptive, intelligent, sagacious, sage, clever, astute, informed, judicious, discerning, enlightened
OPPOSITES ARE unwise, foolish

**2** *The action they took seemed wise and reasonable.*
► sensible, prudent, advisable, appropriate, proper, fair, just, right, sound
OPPOSITES ARE unwise, foolish, ill-advised

**wish** NOUN

**1** *It was her parents' dearest wish that she should be happy.*
► desire, ambition, objective, want, longing, inclination, aim, aspiration, craving, fancy, hankering, hope, yearning

**2** *He had no wish to appear impolite.*
► desire, inclination

**3** *We will respect your wishes.*
► request, bidding, direction, will, order

**wish** VERB

**1** *If guests wish to eat out, there are several pubs in the village.*
► want, hope

**2** **wish for** *I wish for a really good night's sleep.*
► desire, want, long for, yearn for, crave, fancy, hanker after

**wisp** NOUN

*She brushed aside a wisp of hair.*
► strand, lock, shred, streak

**wispy** ADJECTIVE

*The sky was streaked with wispy white clouds.*
► streaky, feathery, light, thin, flimsy, fragile, gossamer, insubstantial

**wistful** ADJECTIVE

*His anger passed, and a wistful smile crossed his face.*
► sad, melancholy, thoughtful, pensive, nostalgic, forlorn

**wit** NOUN

**1** *The speech was improved by moments of great wit.*
► humour, wittiness, banter, repartee, drollery, badinage, facetiousness, ingenuity, comedy, jokes

**2** *Jack was regarded as the club wit.*
► joker, comedian, wag, comic, humorist, jester

**3** *She was a woman of great wit and wisdom.*
► intelligence, shrewdness, cleverness, sense, understanding

**witch** NOUN

**1** *She must look for the witch's hat.*
► sorceress, enchantress

**2** *What are you talking about, you stupid witch?*
► hag, crone, harpy

**withdraw** VERB

**1** *She withdrew the photo abruptly and returned it to the folder.*
► take back, remove, snatch

**2** *All the objections were eventually withdrawn.*
► retract, rescind, revoke, take back, cancel, remove, disclaim, renounce, take away
AN OPPOSITE IS introduce

**3** *The rebels were forced to withdraw into the hills.*
► retreat, retire, draw back, move back, fall back
AN OPPOSITE IS advance

**4** *One of the representatives decided to withdraw from future discussions.*
► pull out, back out, drop out, secede, (more informal) cry off
AN OPPOSITE IS enter

**withdrawn** ADJECTIVE

*Frank appeared even more withdrawn than usual.*
► reserved, shy, retiring, introverted, uncommunicative, unsociable, unforthcoming
AN OPPOSITE IS outgoing

a
b
c
d
e
f
g
h
i
j
k
l
m
n
o
p
q
r
s
t
u
v
**w**
x
y
z

**wither** VERB

*The flowers had withered in the strong sun.*
▶ wilt, droop, become limp, dehydrate, dry up, sag, shrivel, waste away, flag, flop
AN OPPOSITE IS thrive

**withhold** VERB

*He had deliberately withheld the fact that he couldn't sail.*
▶ suppress, repress, conceal, hide, hold back, keep back, keep secret, retain

**withstand** VERB

*The boat must be strong enough to withstand the roughest weather.*
▶ resist, endure, hold out against, last out against, bear up against, stand up to, survive, tolerate, brave, cope with
AN OPPOSITE IS succumb to

**witness** NOUN

*The only witness was the office cleaner.*
▶ observer, bystander, onlooker, spectator, eyewitness, looker-on, watcher

**witness** VERB

*He said he has witnessed several instances of police brutality.*
▶ see, observe, be present at, be a witness to, notice, view, watch, attend, behold, look on

**witty** ADJECTIVE

*Dolly is witty and entertaining.*
▶ humorous, amusing, funny, quick-witted, sharp-witted, waggish, droll, comic, facetious, sparkling
AN OPPOSITE IS dull

**wizard** NOUN

1 *We were still under the wizard's spell.*
▶ magician, sorcerer, enchanter, warlock
2 *He's an absolute wizard with engines.*
▶ expert, genius, adept, master, (*more informal*) star

**wobble** VERB

1 *She reached out and caught it without so much as wobbling.*
▶ shake, sway, teeter, totter, be unsteady, oscillate, quake
2 *Once more the glass wobbled.*
▶ tremble, shake, quiver, vibrate, rock

**wobbly** ADJECTIVE

1 *The table had a wobbly leg.*
▶ unsteady, loose, rickety, rocky, unstable, shaky, insecure, unbalanced, unsafe
AN OPPOSITE IS steady
2 *He felt wobbly and had to sit down.*
▶ giddy, dizzy, faint, groggy, unsteady

**woman** NOUN

*The car pulled up and a woman got out.*
▶ female, lady, girl
RELATED ADJECTIVES female, feminine

**wonder** NOUN

1 *We were speechless with wonder.*
▶ awe, admiration, amazement, wonderment, astonishment, fascination, respect, reverence, surprise
2 *a wonder of nature*
▶ marvel, miracle, sensation, spectacle, prodigy
3 *It's a wonder there were no casualties.*
▶ marvel, miracle, extraordinary thing

**wonder** VERB

1 *I was beginning to wonder if they would ever come.*
▶ ponder, speculate, ask yourself, be curious about, reflect on
2 *wonder at We wondered at such bravery.*
▶ marvel at, admire, be amazed by, feel wonder at, stand in awe of

**wonderful** ADJECTIVE

*We had a wonderful time.*
▶ excellent, marvellous, fantastic, splendid, lovely, delightful, smashing, (*more informal*) terrific
OPPOSITES ARE awful, dreadful

**wood** NOUN

1 *There is a nature trail through the wood.*
▶ forest, woodland, woods, trees, coppice, copse, thicket, grove, spinney
RELATED ADJECTIVE sylvan
2 *a little cabin made from wood*
▶ timber, planks, planking, lumber
RELATED ADJECTIVE ligneous

**KINDS OF WOOD USED IN BUILDING AND CARPENTRY**

ash (hard pale wood), balsa (lightweight wood used for making models), beech (hard pale wood with fine grain), cedar (fragrant durable wood), chestnut, deal (fir or pine used as a building material), ebony (hard very dark wood), elm, mahogany (hard reddish-brown wood used for furniture), oak (hard durable wood), pine (soft wood), rosewood (used for furniture and musical instruments), sandalwood (fragrant wood), sapele (African hardwood like mahogany), teak (hard durable wood), walnut.

**wooded** ADJECTIVE

*a wooded valley*
▶ tree-covered, forested or afforested, woody, timbered, (*poetic*) sylvan

**wooden** ADJECTIVE

1 *wooden furniture*
▶ timber, wood
2 *The acting and production were wooden.*
▶ stiff, unnatural, stilted, lifeless, leaden, deadpan, emotionless, unemotional, expressionless, awkward, clumsy, graceless
AN OPPOSITE IS lively

**woody** ADJECTIVE

**1** *a woody plant*
► tough, hard, fibrous, ligneous, wooden

**2** *a woody hillside*
► wooded, tree-covered, forested or afforested, timbered, (*poetic*) sylvan

**woolly** ADJECTIVE

**1** *a woolly hat*
► woollen, wool, fleecy

**2** *a sheep's woolly coat*
► fleecy, furry, downy, fuzzy, hairy, shaggy, soft

**3** *woolly thinking*
► vague, ill-defined, unfocused, unclear, imprecise, confused, muddled, blurry, hazy, foggy

**word** NOUN

**1** *She wanted to find another word for 'chuckle'.*
► expression, term, locution
RELATED ADJECTIVES verbal, lexical

**2** *Have you had any word from the hospital?*
► news, information, communication, report, comment, advice

**3** *I'll have a word with them in private.*
► talk, conversation, chat, discussion, consultation, exchange of views, tête-à-tête
**USAGE** Note that tête-à-tête is normally used about a personal conversation between two people.

**4** *I gave her my word.*
► promise, guarantee, pledge, assurance, word of honour, oath

**word for word** *He had copied it word for word from the Internet.*
► verbatim, exactly, precisely, faithfully
AN OPPOSITE IS loosely

**word** VERB

*The book has advice on how to word your CV.*
► phrase, express, construct, formulate, frame, couch, write, say, put

**wording** NOUN

*The wording of the contract was unclear.*
► phrasing, phraseology, language, choice of words, mode of expression, terminology, style, diction

**wordy** ADJECTIVE

*a wordy essay a wordy speaker*
► long-winded, verbose, diffuse, rambling, repetitious, protracted, prolix, garrulous, loquacious, talkative
OPPOSITES ARE brief , succinct
**USAGE** You would normally use the last three synonyms about a person.

**work** NOUN

**1** *The plastering will be several days' work.*
► labour, effort, exertion, toil, industry, (*more informal*) slog

**2** *Stella's looking for work abroad.*
► employment, a job, an occupation, a career, business

**3** *He had finished all his work by lunchtime.*
► tasks, jobs, assignments, projects, commissions

**4** *He has written a new work for mixed choir.*
► composition, piece, opus, oeuvre, production

**5** *It is a fine literary work.*
► creation, achievement, accomplishment

**work** VERB

**1** *Some staff were still working at nine in the evening.*
► labour, toil, exert yourself, be at your desk, slave, (*more informal*) keep at it
AN OPPOSITE IS rest

**2** *Margaret works in a bank.*
► have a job, be employed, earn a living

**3** *The dishwasher was working again, thank goodness.*
► function, operate, perform, run, in working order, (*more informal*) behave
AN OPPOSITE IS break down

**4** *He showed me how to work the coffee machine.*
► operate, use, manipulate

**5** *The plan had worked.*
► succeed, be successful, work out, take effect, (*more informal*) pay off, (*more informal*) do the trick
AN OPPOSITE IS fail

**6** *farmers who work the land*
► cultivate, till, dig, farm

**7** *You can work miracles with the right ingredients.*
► achieve, accomplish, produce, perform, bring about, cause, (*more informal*) pull off

**8** *Work the mixture into a thick dough.*
► knead, form, mould, mix, blend, stir, shape

**work out**

**1** *The idea should work out.*
► succeed, be successful, work, (*more informal*) pay off, (*more informal*) do the trick
AN OPPOSITE IS fail

**2** *Things didn't quite work out as expected.*
► turn out, occur, happen, evolve, develop, end up, come out

**work out at** *The cost worked out at over a million dollars.*
► amount to, add up to, come to, total, reach

**work something out**

**1** *Let's work out a plan.*
► devise, draw up, formulate, prepare, put together

**2** *I can't work out the answer.*
► calculate, determine, reckon up, resolve, solve

**3** *We're trying to work out what all this means.*
► understand, comprehend, make sense of, puzzle out, figure out, clear up

**work up** *It's hard to work up any enthusiasm.*
► raise, rouse, generate, stimulate, stir up

**workable** ADJECTIVE

*A law on such matters could be workable.*
► practical, practicable, feasible, realistic, possible, sensible, practical
OPPOSITES ARE unworkable, impractical

**worker** NOUN

**1** *A strike by clerical workers brought the system to a standstill.*
► employee, member of staff, operative, working person

**2** *She was a tireless worker for the party.*
► labourer, campaigner, supporter

# workforce NOUN
*The company will lay off 15% of its workforce.*
▶ employees, workers, staff, labour force, personnel

# working ADJECTIVE
**1** *extra support for working mothers*
▶ employed, in work, salaried, waged
AN OPPOSITE IS unemployed
**2** *a working model of a steam engine*
▶ functioning, operational, operating, running, usable, going, in use, in working order
AN OPPOSITE IS non-functioning

# workmanship NOUN
*The quality of workmanship is of a high standard.*
▶ craftsmanship, artistry, handiwork, technique, expertise, skill

# works PLURAL NOUN
**1** *Visitors can explore the glass works and blacksmith's shop.*
▶ factory, workshop, foundry, plant, unit
**2** *The works of the clock needed cleaning.*
▶ mechanism, movement, action, parts, machinery, insides

# workshop NOUN
**1** *Her husband had a workshop at the end of the garden.*
▶ workroom, studio
**2** *The company organized a workshop on teleconferences.*
▶ seminar, discussion group, meeting, class

# world NOUN
**1** *The university has links with academic institutions around the world.*
▶ earth, globe, planet
**2** *Representatives came from the world of high finance*
▶ sphere, domain, field, area, realm, circle, milieu
**3** *The world knows that these people need help.*
▶ everyone, everybody, people, humankind, humanity

# worldly ADJECTIVE
**1** *He had no ambitions for worldly power.*
▶ earthly, terrestrial, temporal, physical, material, materialistic, mundane, avaricious, greedy, selfish
AN OPPOSITE IS spiritual
**2** *She was worldly enough to understand what was going on.*
▶ sophisticated, experienced, worldly-wise, knowing
AN OPPOSITE IS naive

# worn ADJECTIVE
*His coat was old and worn.*
▶ shabby, threadbare, tattered, frayed, worn out, moth-eaten, ragged, scruffy, (more informal) tatty
AN OPPOSITE IS smart

**worn out** *By the time they got home they were all worn out.*
▶ exhausted, tired out, weary, fatigued, shattered, (more informal) dead tired, (more informal) played out, (more informal) washed out

# worried ADJECTIVE
**1** *She had a worried look on her face. You seem worried about something.*
▶ anxious, troubled, disturbed, uneasy, distraught, apprehensive, bothered, tense, strained, nervous
**2** *I was worried that our money would run out.*
▶ afraid, fearful, concerned, frightened, scared

# worry VERB
**1** *Try not to worry Dad while he's working.*
▶ bother, pester, disturb, annoy
**2** *A dog had been worrying the sheep.*
▶ attack, torment, savage
**3** *I was trying not to worry.*
▶ be anxious, be troubled, be disturbed, fret, panic
AN OPPOSITE IS be unconcerned
**4** *Something was worrying her.*
▶ trouble, bother, disturb, distress, upset, concern

# worry NOUN
**1** *I was too affected by worry to concentrate on the work.*
▶ anxiety, agitation, apprehension, unease, distress, fear, misgiving, tension
**2** *Each day seems to bring another worry.*
▶ problem, difficulty, trouble, concern, care, burden, misgiving

# worrying ADJECTIVE
*There was a worrying smell of gas.*
▶ alarming, disturbing, worrisome, disquieting, distressing, perturbing, troublesome
AN OPPOSITE IS reassuring

# worsen VERB
**1** *Development of the site would worsen traffic problems.*
▶ aggravate, exacerbate, make worse, intensify, magnify, increase
AN OPPOSITE IS improve
**2** *The economic situation was beginning to worsen.*
▶ get or become worse, deteriorate, decline, degenerate, weaken, slide
OPPOSITES ARE improve, recover

---

# worship NOUN
*Temples are places of worship.*
▶ adoration, veneration, reverence (for), adulation, exaltation, devotion (to), idolatry

**PLACES OF WORSHIP**
abbey, church, cathedral, chapel, gurdwara, mandir, meeting house (for Quakers), minster, mosque, synagogue, tabernacle, temple, vihara.

---

# worship VERB
**1** *They worshipped the sun as the giver of life.*
▶ revere, reverence, venerate, glorify, exalt, laud, pray to
**2** *a materialistic society that worships consumer goods*
▶ idolize, revere, adore, dote on, be devoted to, look up to, love
AN OPPOSITE IS despise

## worth NOUN

**1** *She knows her own worth.*
▶ value, merit, excellence, worthiness, quality, calibre, talents, strengths
**2** *He was forced to sell the car for a fraction of its true worth.*
▶ value, cost, selling price

## worthless ADJECTIVE

**1** *The certificate turned out to be worthless.*
▶ valueless, of no value
AN OPPOSITE IS valuable
**2** *Their advice proved worthless.*
▶ useless, futile, ineffective, ineffectual, pointless
OPPOSITES ARE useful, worthwhile
*She regarded him as a worthless slob.*
▶ good-for-nothing, useless, contemptible, despicable, miserable, wretched, vile, (*more informal*) no-good
AN OPPOSITE IS worthy

## worthwhile ADJECTIVE

**1** *I've never done anything worthwhile like writing a book.*
▶ useful, valuable, worthy, meaningful, significant, positive, productive, important, invaluable
OPPOSITES ARE worthless, useless
**2** *It might be worthwhile to join a local archaeology society.*
▶ advantageous, beneficial, helpful, useful, profitable, rewarding
OPPOSITES ARE pointless, useless

## worthy ADJECTIVE

**1** *Our support extends to worthy causes around the country.*
▶ worthwhile, praiseworthy, deserving, creditable, honourable, reputable, commendable, respectable, admirable
OPPOSITES ARE unworthy, disreputable
**2** *a worthy member of society*
▶ virtuous, honourable, honest, upright, moral, decent
OPPOSITES ARE unworthy, disreputable
**3** **worthy of** *The site yielded pottery worthy of study and publication.*
▶ deserving, meriting, warranting, good enough for

## would-be ADJECTIVE

*Are we asking too much of would-be adoptive parents?*
▶ aspiring, budding, intending, hopeful, prospective

## wound NOUN

**1** *There was a deep wound in the animal's forehead.*
▶ injury, scar, gash, cut, abrasion, disfigurement, hurt
**2** *She survived these wounds inflicted by fate.*
▶ blow, insult, trauma, slight, affront, hurt

## wound VERB

*He was trying to rescue a colleague who had been wounded.*
▶ injure, hurt, harm, maim, disable, damage, disfigure

## wrangle VERB

*I did not come here to wrangle with you.*
▶ quarrel, argue, row, fight, squabble

## wrangle NOUN

*The courts rejected the appeal after a long legal wrangle.*
▶ dispute, argument, disagreement, quarrel, row, fight, squabble

## wrap VERB

**1** *She wrapped a rug round her legs.*
▶ fold, swathe, wind, pack, place
**2** *Harry wrapped himself in a towel.*
▶ cover, swathe, envelop, sheathe, enfold
**3** *I'll wrap the sandwiches in foil.*
▶ cover, pack, fold, enclose

## wrapper NOUN

*The chocolate bar had 'extra value' printed on its wrapper.*
▶ wrapping, cover, packaging

## wreath NOUN

*A wreath of artificial poppies was held down by a brick.*
▶ garland, circlet, coronet, crown, ring

## wreck NOUN

**1** *The wreck of an ancient galley was discovered off Sicily.*
▶ wreckage, shipwreck, remains, hulk, skeleton
**2** *It was the wreck of all their hopes.*
▶ ruin, destruction, undoing, demolition, devastation, overthrow, termination

## wreck VERB

**1** *The ship had been wrecked in a storm.*
▶ shipwreck, sink, destroy, break up
**2** *He had wrecked his car when it skidded off the road.*
▶ crash, smash, demolish, shatter, crumple, crush, (*more informal*) write off
**3** *A freak virus wrecked their holiday plans.*
▶ ruin, spoil, disrupt, undo, dash, put an end to

## wreckage NOUN

**1** *One person had to be cut from the wreckage by firemen.*
▶ wreck, debris, rubble, remains, ruin
**2** *Wreckage from the aircraft was scattered for miles.*
▶ debris, fragments, remains, detritus, pieces, relics

## wrench NOUN

**1** *With a wrench he tore himself free.*
▶ jerk, jolt, pull, tug, twist, (*informal*) yank
**2** *It was a wrench leaving the children behind with Polly.*
▶ trauma, painful experience

## wrench VERB

*Charlotte heard her wrench the door open.*
▶ pull, jerk, tug, force, prise, lever, wrest, (*informal*) yank

a b c d e f g h i j k l m n o p q r s t u v **w** x y z

## wretch NOUN

**1** *He was a lonely, miserable wretch.*
▶ poor creature, down and out, beggar, pauper
**2** *He had been mugged by some wretches in the park.*
▶ ruffian, scoundrel, rogue, villain, rascal, delinquent

## wretched ADJECTIVE

**1** *She had seldom felt so tired or so wretched.*
▶ miserable, unhappy, sad, despondent, melancholy, cast down, unwell, poorly
**2** *The weather was wretched all week. The family had to endure wretched living conditions.*
▶ atrocious, appalling, dreadful, dismal, bleak

## wriggle VERB

*He wriggled further back on the bed till he was leaning up against the wall.*
▶ twist, writhe, squirm, waggle, wiggle, worm
**wriggle out of** *He tried to wriggle out of work, as usual.*
▶ avoid, shirk, dodge, evade, escape from

## wring VERB

**1** *He went to the sink to wring out the socks.*
▶ squeeze, twist, compress, crush, press
**2** *They managed to wring more money out of the government.*
▶ extract, coerce, force, wrest, exact, extort
**3** *The look on his face wrung her heart.*
▶ stab, tear, pierce, rend, distress, pain, hurt

## wrinkle NOUN

*Despite being carefully ironed the shirt was full of wrinkles. The wrinkles on her neck moved when she swallowed.*
▶ crease, fold, pucker, crinkle, ridge, furrow, dimple, gather, line, pleat

## wrinkle VERB

*You have to wrinkle your nose to break the spell.*
▶ crease, crinkle, pucker up, crumple, fold, furrow, ridge, ruck up, rumple
AN OPPOSITE IS smooth

## wrinkled ADJECTIVE

*His hands were white and very wrinkled.*
▶ creased, wrinkly, crinkly, crumpled, furrowed, shrivelled, lined, pleated, ridged, rumpled, wavy, wizened

## write VERB

**1** *He wrote the details in a notebook.*
▶ write down, jot down, take down, put down, record, transcribe, make a note of, note down, scribble, register
**2** *After a while she stopped writing to him.*
▶ communicate (with), send letters, keep in touch

**3** *The music was written one summer at the lakeside retreat.*
▶ compose, create, set down, compile, pen, draft
**write off** *He wrote off for a free voucher.*
▶ apply, send off, send away
**write something off**
**1** *The Inland Revenue wrote off millions of pounds in unpaid taxes.*
▶ disregard, cancel, delete, annul
**2** (*informal*) *He wrote off his car on a Belgian motorway.*
▶ crash, smash, wreck

---

**writer** NOUN
one of the great writers of the 20th century
▶ author, novelist, poet, dramatist, essayist, wordsmith

**NAMES FOR WRITERS**

**books:** author, novelist, biographer, essayist, ghostwriter (writes for another person named as author), fabulist (writer of fables).
**newspapers:** journalist, reporter, columnist, copywriter, correspondent, leader-writer, diarist, reviewer.
**poetry and drama:** poet; dramatist, playwright, comedian, tragedian; librettist (texts of operas), scriptwriter.

---

## writhe VERB

*I tossed and writhed on the hard bed.*
▶ wriggle, squirm, thrash about, toss, flail, struggle, twist, contort

## writing NOUN

**1** *Her writing is neater than mine.*
▶ handwriting, penmanship, calligraphy, script, letters, longhand, scribble, scrawl
**2** *She took up writing in old age.*
▶ composition, literature, letters
**3 writings** *His political views are clearly reflected in his writings.*
▶ literary texts, literature, texts, works

## wrong ADJECTIVE

**1** *It was wrong to take the books without asking.*
▶ bad, dishonest, blameworthy, reprehensible, sinful, wicked
AN OPPOSITE IS right
**2** *The law lays down limits and it is wrong to exceed them.*
▶ unlawful, illegal, criminal, delinquent
OPPOSITES ARE lawful, legal
**3** *She knew she had given a wrong answer. The visitor pressed the wrong buzzer.*
▶ incorrect, erroneous, inaccurate, mistaken
OPPOSITES ARE correct, right
**4** *I must have said something wrong.*
▶ inappropriate, unsuitable, inapt, ill-advised, ill-judged, unfitting
AN OPPOSITE IS appropriate

**5** *There's something wrong with the equipment.*
▶ faulty, defective, amiss, broken down, out of order, unusable
AN OPPOSITE IS right

**wrong** NOUN

**1** *He had done many wrongs that needed putting right.*
▶ misdeed, bad deed, offence, crime, injury, injustice
AN OPPOSITE IS good deed

**2** *We know the difference between right and wrong.*
▶ immorality, badness, sinfulness, wickedness, evil
OPPOSITES ARE goodness, virtue

**wrong** VERB

*She was determined to forget the man who had wronged her.*
▶ mistreat, abuse, be unfair to, maltreat, ill-treat, treat unfairly, cheat, do an injustice to, harm, hurt, misrepresent, traduce

**wrongdoer** NOUN

*Wrongdoers will be punished.*
▶ offender, transgressor, miscreant, lawbreaker, culprit, delinquent, malefactor, criminal, crook, evildoer, sinner

**wrongdoing** NOUN

*The law prevents criminals profiting from their wrongdoings.*
▶ lawbreaking, criminality, misbehaviour, delinquency, offence, crime, sinfulness, wickedness, immorality

**wrongful** ADJECTIVE

*She is claiming damages for wrongful dismissal.*
▶ unjust, unfair, unlawful, unjustified, unwarranted, undeserved, unreasonable, uncalled-for
OPPOSITES ARE rightful, fair

**wry** ADJECTIVE

**1** *Robbie sipped his drink and pulled a wry face.*
▶ twisted, distorted, contorted, crooked, uneven, bent

**2** *Lawrence allowed himself a wry smile.*
▶ mocking, sardonic, derisive, dry, ironic, droll

**xenophobia** NOUN

*Feelings of xenophobia can so easily be whipped up.*
▶ nationalism, jingoism, racism

**xenophobic** ADJECTIVE

*the triumphs of xenophobic right-wing parties*
▶ nationalistic, jingoistic, racist

**yank** VERB

*(informal) He yanked the door open and stumbled inside.*
▶ pull, force, jerk, tug, wrench, prise, wrest

**yap** VERB

*A dog yapped frantically somewhere inside.*
▶ yelp, bark, woof

**yard** NOUN

*A pony stood in the middle of the yard.*
▶ court, courtyard, enclosure, quadrangle, (more informal) quad

**yardstick** NOUN

*They regard the family as the yardstick to measure values by.*
▶ standard, criterion, benchmark, gauge, guideline, measure

**yarn** NOUN

**1** *This is a lovely soft yarn.*
▶ thread, wool, fibre, strand, twine

**2** *(informal) He rang with a yarn about problems at his hotel.*
▶ story, tale, rigmarole, anecdote, narrative

**yearn** VERB

*They yearned to be home.*
▶ long, crave, pine, desire, hanker, wish

**yearning** NOUN

*She had always had a yearning to play the piano.*
▶ longing, desire, craving, hankering, wish, (more informal) yen

**yell** VERB

*He yelled at them to stop.*
▶ shout, cry out, call, shriek, scream, bawl, exclaim

**yell** NOUN

*She gave a yell of pain.*
▶ cry, shriek, scream, screech

**yelp** VERB

*He yelped with delight.*
▶ squeal, squawk, shriek, scream, howl, yell

**yelp** NOUN

*The dog let out a yelp.*
▶ yap, bark, woof

**yen** NOUN

*(informal) a yen for travel*
▶ yearning, longing, desire, craving, hankering, wish

**yield** NOUN

**1** *The farm has produced a good yield.*
▶ crop, harvest, produce, product

**2** *I'm looking for a savings bond with a high yield.*
▶ return, interest, earnings, income, profit

a
b
c
d
e
f
g
h
i
j
k
l
m
n
o
p
q
r
s
t
u
v
w
x
y
z

# yield VERB

**1** *The contest continues until one side yields.*
▶ surrender, succumb, capitulate, submit, give in, give way, concede defeat, (*more informal*) cave in, (*informal*) throw in the towel, (*informal*) throw up the sponge

**2** *The allotment yields a fine crop of root vegetables.*
▶ produce, grow, bear, supply

**3** *an investment yielding a high interest*
▶ earn, generate, provide, return, pay, attract

# yob NOUN

*A gang of yobs were making a nuisance of themselves.*
▶ hooligan, hoodlum, lout, ruffian, troublemaker, vandal, thug, bully, delinquent, tough, rough, tearaway

# young ADJECTIVE

**1** *She enjoyed working with young people.*
▶ youthful, juvenile, teenage, adolescent
OPPOSITES ARE old, elderly

**2** *They seem young for their age.*
▶ immature, childish, babyish
AN OPPOSITE IS mature

---

**young NOUN**
**1** *Parents have an instinct to protect their young.*
▶ offspring, family, progeny, brood, issue, litter
**2 the young** *They enjoyed talking to the young.*
▶ young people, youths, youngsters, juveniles, minors
RELATED ADJECTIVE juvenile

**SOME NAMES FOR YOUNG ANIMALS**

calf (cattle, elephant, seal, and other large animals), chick (chicken, hawk, pheasant), colt (horse), cub (badger, bear, fox, leopard, lion, tiger, walrus, wolf), cygnet (swan), duckling (duck), eaglet (eagle), elver (eel), fawn (deer), filly (horse), foal (horse, zebra), gosling (goose), joey (kangaroo, wallaby, possum), kid (antelope, goat), kitten (cat), lamb (sheep), leveret (hare), owlet (owl), parr (salmon), piglet (pig), pup (dog, wolf, seal), puppy (dog), smolt (salmon), tadpole (frog, toad), whelp (dog, wolf).

---

# youth NOUN

**1** *She had spent most of her youth abroad.*
▶ early life, early years, teenage years, adolescence, boyhood or girlhood, childhood, infancy, (*informal*) teens

**2** *a group of youths*
▶ young person, teenager, youngster, adolescent, boy or girl, juvenile, (*more informal*) kid, (*more informal*) lad

# youthful ADJECTIVE

**1** *They sang before a youthful audience.*
▶ young

**2** *He had a youthful appearance.*
▶ young-looking, fresh, lively, sprightly, vigorous, well-preserved

---

# Zz

# zany ADJECTIVE

*a zany thriller about ecological disaster*
▶ crazy, weird, bizarre, eccentric
OPPOSITES ARE serious, sensible

# zeal NOUN

*a zeal to improve society*
▶ enthusiasm, fervour, ardour, zest, passion, devotion, keenness, eagerness, dedication

# zealous ADJECTIVE

*Bran was a zealous patriot and served his country well.*
▶ keen, fervent, enthusiastic, fanatical, passionate, conscientious, committed, diligent, eager, earnest
AN OPPOSITE IS apathetic

# zenith NOUN

*The country was then at the zenith of its power.*
▶ peak, pinnacle, height, top, acme, apex, climax
AN OPPOSITE IS nadir

# zero NOUN

*Opportunities for further education might be reduced to zero.*
▶ nothing, nought, nil

# zero VERB

**zero in on** *We need to zero in on being accurate and careful.*
▶ focus on, concentrate on, fix on, centre on, home in on

# zest NOUN

*After his recovery he had a renewed zest for life.*
▶ eagerness, energy, enjoyment, enthusiasm, zeal, liveliness, pleasure

# zigzag ADJECTIVE

*Some escaping animals take a zigzag course.*
▶ winding, meandering, serpentine, twisting, weaving, bendy, crooked

# zigzag VERB

*A narrow path zigzagged steeply down to the shore.*
▶ wind, meander, snake, twist, weave, curve, bend

# zone NOUN

*He decided to leave the war zone and get back to his family.*
▶ area, sector, section, region, sphere, district, vicinity, locality, neighbourhood, territory, tract

# zoom VERB

(*informal*) *A motorbike zoomed across their path.*
▶ race, rush, speed, dash, hurry, hurtle, (*informal*) whiz, (*informal*) zip

A B C D E F G H I J K L M N O P Q R S T U V W X Y Z